PRELUDE TO CIVIL WAR

SOUTHERN ECONOMIC NECESSITY

 VS.

NORTHERN ANTI-BLACK RACISM

www.roadtothecivilwar.org

Publisher's Cataloging-In-Publication Data
Drane, Robert
   Prelude to Civil War

ISBN: 979-8-9866188-8-3

Editor/Publisher: Joy E. Stocke
Front Cover Design: Mark Kuehn
Publication Design: Tim Ogline / Ogline Design

Published in the United States by Tree of Life Books.
102 Sandy Ridge-Mt. Airy Road
Stockton, New Jersey 08559
www.treeoflifetreeofjoy.com

PRELUDE TO CIVIL WAR

SOUTHERN ECONOMIC NECESSITY
 VS.
NORTHERN ANTI-BLACK RACISM

BY ROBERT DRANE

JBY
STUDIOS

Tree
of Life
Books

TABLE OF CONTENTS

INTRODUCTION

HOW THIS BOOK CAME ABOUT

It began with the photo collection.

Almost all people collect something, and it usually starts off casually, on a small scale, then picks up momentum, and eventually becomes something of an obsession.

Interest in the Civil War period flows from an early childhood set of lead Civil War soldiers, carefully painted, imported from Britain, and played with on an indoor sand table, with miniature infantrymen and cavalry in Blue and Gray, locked imaginatively in mortal combat.

It graduates into hours spent with history books, two in particular. *The American Heritage Picture History of the Civil War*, with narrative by noted historian, Bruce Catton (1960), and the monumental 10 volume *Photographic History of the Civil War*, edited by Francis Trevalyan Miller (1911). Here were literally thousands of images of the war, taken by Brady, Gardner, O'Sullivan and other pioneer cameramen, with maps and text breathing actual life and valor into the lead warriors on the sand table.

It weaves a circuitous route into adulthood, marriage, a corporate career, children, and family vacations, not in wished for flights to Disneyworld, rather packed together in a car, off to this or that small rural town to trek in the footsteps of long forgotten heroes. "Oh no, please not another civil war trip."

Major General George Meade

It finally finds its destination in 1986 with a birthday gift from the ever inquisitive great gramma Shirley (GGS) in the form of an original carte d'visite photograph of Major General George Meade.

There he is, brought back to life in sharp focus, a proud Pennsylvanian, "Old Snapping Turtle" to laggards in his army, who leads the defense of his state at the pivotal Battle of Gettysburg.

From that moment on, the collector is all in, hook, line and sinker.

What follows initially is attendance at occasional week-end shows, where Civil War dealers display and sell their wares, from weapons to uniforms, autographs to images, in daguerreotype to tintype to paper formats. From these shows comes a network of sellers, often with catalogues arriving by snailmail off and on throughout the year.

The collection grows, as does the intellectual curiosity about the war itself.

It is fed by Michael Shaara's 1974 Pulitzer Prize winning work, *Killer Angels*, which rewinds Pickett's Charge into a behind the scenes struggle: Lee versus Longstreet on whether or not to run across 1800 yards of open ground on July 3, 1863, toward cannons ringing the copse of trees.

The scope broadens to the entire war. The journalist historian Douglas Southall Freeman's four volume work *R.E. Lee: A Biography* (1934-35) leads into Shelby Foote's three volume masterpiece *The Civil War: A Narrative* (1954-74).

Period photographs take center stage in William Frassanito's 1975 book *Gettysburg: A Journey in Time* and its 1978 companion *Antietam*. Here are the photos taken at the time of the battles, and here are the precise camera locations on the modern landscape. Good reason to re-visit the sites.

And why not try to buy original CDV photos of all the generals who fought at Gettysburg and Antietam, frame them, and display them on a den wall according to the positions they fought over on the days of battle?

Something of a home museum begins to take shape, and collecting remains a quite affordable pastime until the "market takes off" in response to the 125th anniversary of the war's end, in 1990. That's when an amazing documentarian, Ken Burns, launches his monumental TV series, *The Civil War*, which weaves the period photographs, movie-like, into a riveting historical narrative. Suddenly some 40 million Americans catch the civil war bug, many for the first time.

Other blockbusters follow Burns. The Shaara book is transformed into a screenplay, Gettysburg, which appears in theaters across the nation in 1993. Princeton's famed professor, James McPherson, publishes his one volume *Battle Cry of Freedom* in 1994. Novelists join in, including Charles Frazier, whose 1997 book, *Cold Mountain*, is converted in 2003 into a popular movie of the same name. The 200th anniversary of Abraham Lincoln's birth in 1809 is circumscribed by Doris Kearns Goodwin's *Lincoln: A Team of Rivals* in 2005 and by the much acclaimed screenplay which follows in 2012.

For the collector of Civil War photographs, two things follow from all this publicity: competitive interest drives up the ante to buy the CDV's and whole new marketing channels expand their availability. Auction houses find and offer many seldom seen images, and eBay introduces its daily online service for those addicted to the search.

What comes along with eBay is a much more diverse set of photographs, extending beyond the military men to the American population at large, "we the people," our homes and occupations, our politics and institutions, our fashions and our entertainment, our triumphs as a nation and our fatal flaws, including our slavery.

And also a new line of inquiry: how could these Americans, who struggled to create a free and prosperous and unified country for so long, possibly have descended into a civil war that broke the bonds of brotherhood and almost ended the idealistic drive for democratic government?

Why were "the better angels of our nature" silenced in 1861? Why indeed did the apparently civilized people in the photographs kill and maim and devastate each other for four solid years?

In the beginning were the photographs, and the photographs became the book. Of course the war was fought over slavery, but what exactly does that simple explanation imply, especially for those in the North? Were they the white knights in the battle, the enlightened side, fighting to save the Union by freeing the abused Africans and welcoming them into their society? Or were there true motives far darker than that? Were they, in fact, driven more by self-interest then by putting an end to slavery?

Amazingly, after four decades of reading about the Civil War, saying that "it was fought over slavery" was no longer a sufficient explanation.

So began another quest: to walk along with "we the people" from Jamestown in 1607 to Ft. Sumer in 1861 and try to discover how the war actually came about.

This has been a fascinating journey—with much reading and research, many twists and turns, all leading to a much deeper understanding of how the moral stains of slavery and racism combined with the age-old furies of greed and power to nearly destroy America.

Of course these furies, these divisions within "we the people," all occurred over 150 years ago, and could not be repeated today.

Or could they?

## 1

THE EARLIEST SETTLERS APPEAR

TIME: 16,000BC–1,500AD

THE NORTH AMERICAN CONTINENT

From the mountains, to the prairies, to the oceans white with foam... the land awaited its first settlers.

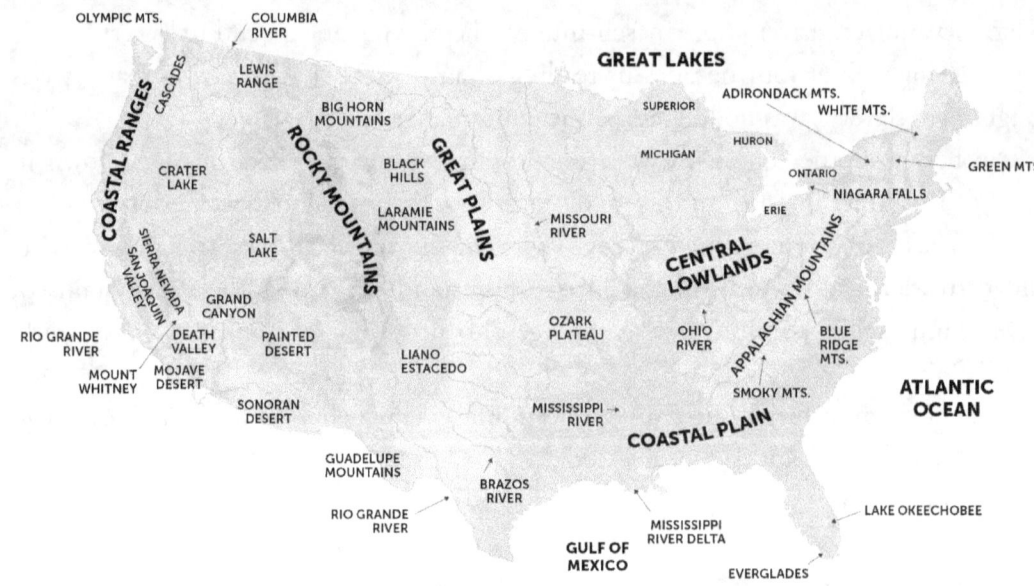

NATIVE AMERICAN TRIBES ARRIVE

Historians believe that around 16,000 BC, America's first settlers wend their way from Central Asia and what is now Russia across a 1,000 mile "land bridge," formed by a sea level drop in the Bering Straits, which once linked the eastern edges of Siberia to western-most Alaska.

They operate in tribes and become adept at hunting and gathering. They are the first farmers of the land, sustained by a wide range of indigenous crops, including corn, potatoes, peanuts, chocolate, cotton and tobacco.

Thus, the New World is born.

Over time the settlers fan out across the northern continent, east to the Atlantic coast and south through Mexico to the southern hemisphere. Along the way they build enduring civilizations.

The Tlingit people of the Pacific Northwest master the arts of fishing and record their history on totem poles. The Hohokam tribes of Arizona introduce irrigation systems to facilitate desert farming. The Puebloans build roads connecting some 2500 communities from New Mexico to Utah. The Siouans roam the Great Plains over to the upper Mississippi, while the Natchez people, living in adobe huts with thatched roofs and led by their Sun King, dominate the lower valley.

Lakota Chief Rain-In-The-Face

The Hopewell nation flourishes in the Midwest from Missouri to Wisconsin and east through Illinois and Indiana, their past evident in huge burial mounds throughout the region.

The Algonquians extend across Canada from the Rockies to New England, chasing seasonal food supplies with their portable wigwams. They eventually collide with the Iroquoians, who flourish in New York and the upper Atlantic states. Meanwhile the Southeast is home to what will later become known as the "five civilized tribes" – the Cherokee, Choctaws, Creeks, Chickasaw and Seminoles.

By 1500 AD, Native American civilizations, speaking upwards of 250 unique languages, dot the landscape from coast to coast.

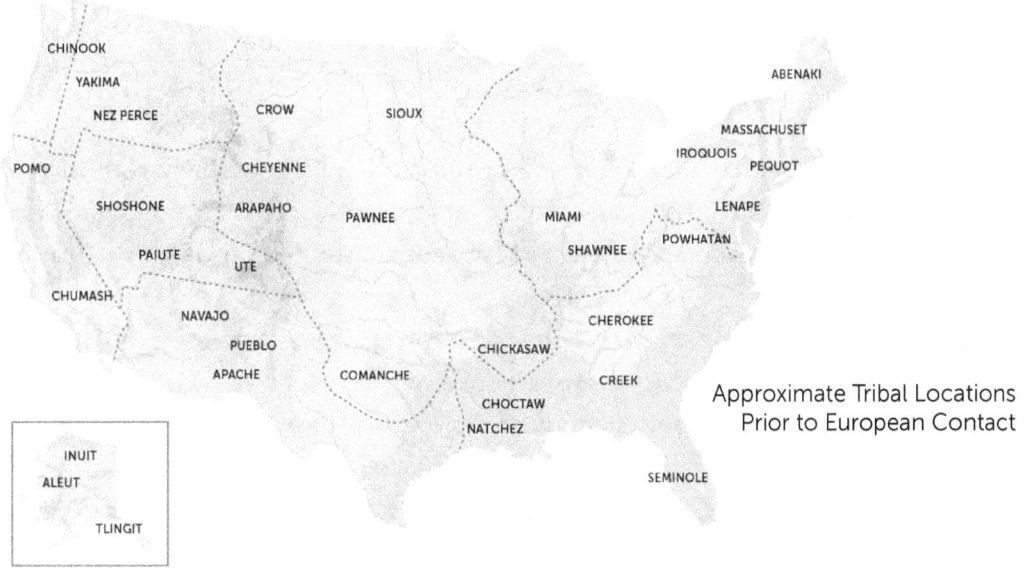

Approximate Tribal Locations
Prior to European Contact

There are no reliable population statistics for this timeframe, but estimates tend to range upwards of 10 million people at the time European explorers enter their homeland.

TIME: 1492–1673

CHRISTOPHER COLUMBUS REACHES THE NEW WORLD

The Europeans arrive in the New World by accident.

Since Roman times, Europe is attracted to the spices of Asia – cinnamon, cardamom, ginger, pepper, turmeric, not to mention opium. But the overland trade routes to the East are precarious. Instead, perhaps by sailing west, a shorter and more commercially favorable route could be found.

This is what Christopher Columbus has in mind on October 12, 1492, when he begins his voyage with three ships in service to the Spanish crown. After 70 days at sea, he encounters land, most likely the tiny island of San Salvador. From there he spends the next three months navigating his way south to Cuba, then

Christopher Columbus (1451-1506)

east to Hispaniola (later Haiti and the Dominican Republic). Along the way, he encounters natives with gold earrings, whom he describes as "docile in nature, lacking in weaponry, and easily capable of being conquered, converted to Christianity, and placed into servitude."

Still believing he has found his way to India, Columbus refers to the islands as the East Indies and the natives as "Indios" or Indians. He kidnaps many along the way, and some 7-8 who survive the journey home are put on display as proof of his success.

On March 4, 1493 Columbus is back in Portugal. Despite losing his lead ship, Santa Maria, and failing to locate any spice treasures, his encounter with the Caribbean islands sets off an exploration frenzy that lasts over the next two centuries.

Within a decade of the 1492 voyage, Europe recognizes that Columbus has reached a whole New World, rather than Asia. The Italian explorer, Amerigo Vespucci, argues this fact after his 1502 voyage, and in 1507 a German mapmaker, Martin Waldseemueller, officially christens the continent "America" in his honor.

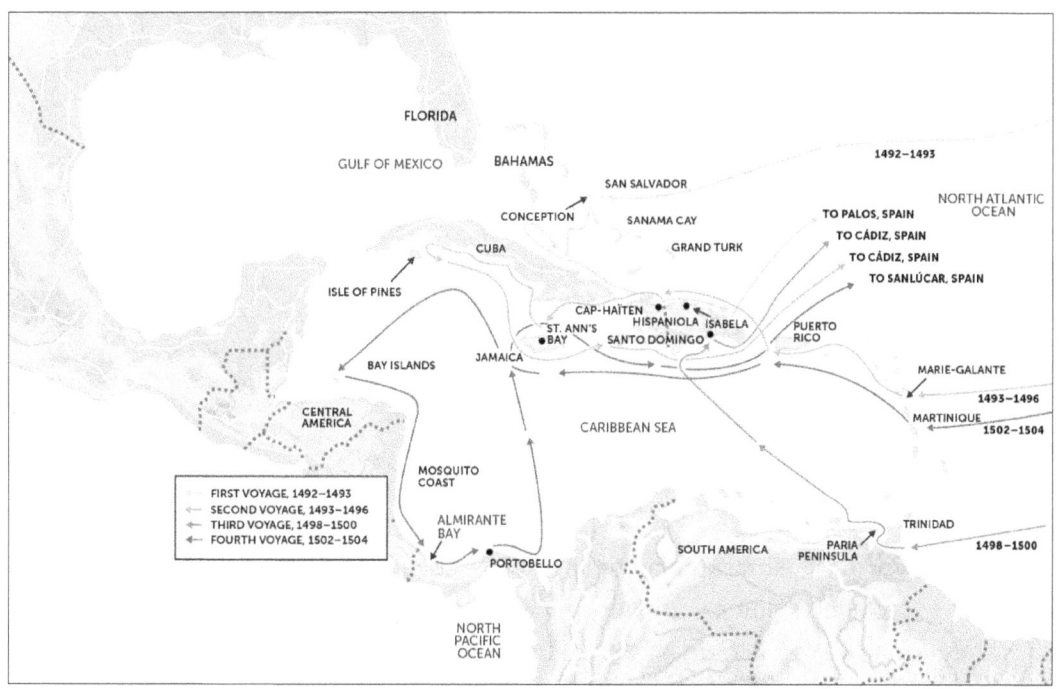

FLORIDA

GULF OF MEXICO   BAHAMAS   1492–1493

SAN SALVADOR

NORTH ATLANTIC
OCEAN

CONCEPTION   SANAMA CAY   TO PALOS, SPAIN

TO CÁDIZ, SPAIN

CUBA   GRAND TURK   TO CÁDIZ, SPAIN

TO SANLÚCAR, SPAIN

ISLE OF PINES

CAP-HAÏTEN   HISPANIOLA ISABELA
ST. ANN'S   PUERTO
BAY   SANTO DOMINGO   RICO

BAY ISLANDS   JAMAICA

MARIE-GALANTE

CENTRAL
AMERICA   CARIBBEAN SEA   MARTINIQUE   1493–1496
1502–1504

MOSQUITO
COAST

FIRST VOYAGE, 1492–1493
SECOND VOYAGE, 1493–1496   ALMIRANTE
THIRD VOYAGE, 1498–1500   BAY   TRINIDAD
FOURTH VOYAGE, 1502–1504
PORTOBELLO   SOUTH AMERICA   PARIA   1498–1500
PENINSULA

NORTH
PACIFIC
OCEAN

Voyages by Columbus to the New World

TIME: 1492–1602

SPAIN LEADS THE EUROPEAN INVASION OF THE AMERICAS

In turn America becomes a sought-after chip in the game played by the monarchs of Spain, France, and England for control over Europe and for global hegemony.

Spain takes the lead as the dominant power in Europe after the 1469 marriage of two Catholic monarchs, Isabelle of Castille and Ferdinand of Aragon, who unify the nation. Dynastic matches of their children extend their power into Portugal and the Hapsburg dynasty.

From 1516 to 1558, their grandson, Charles I, reigns supreme over much of Europe, including Spain, Italy and the sprawling remnants of the Holy Roman Empire, from the Netherlands in the north to Austria-Hungary in the south.

Catholic Monarch, Charles, battles against the Protestant Reformation, sparked by Martin Luther in 1517, and against France in various European wars. He also sent his conquistadors, Hernan Cortez and Francisco Pizarro, across the Atlantic after gold and territory in the Americas.

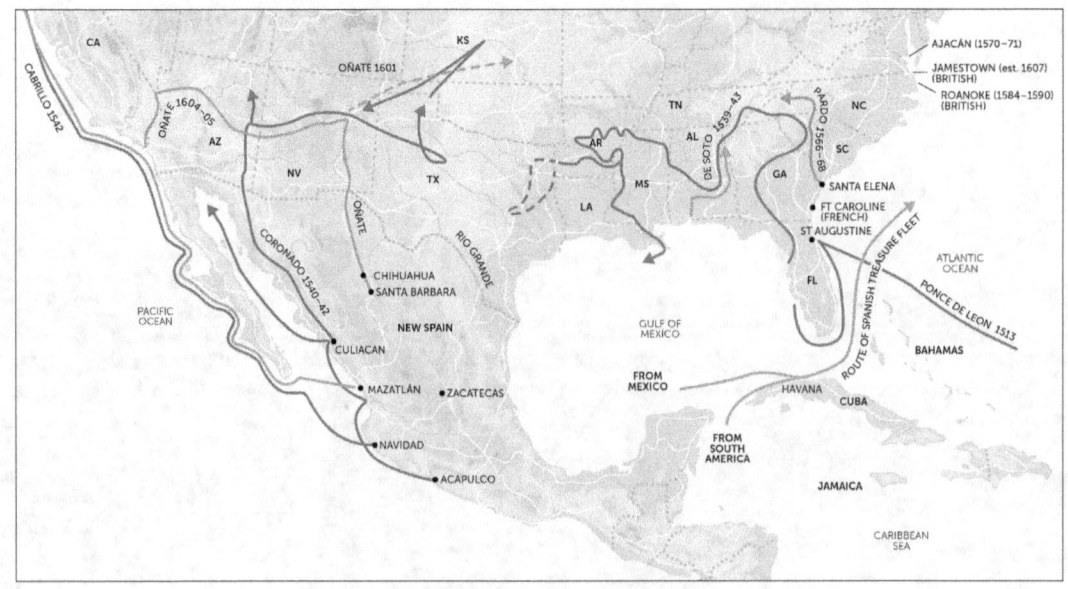

Spanish Exploration of North America

Two remarkable civilizations fall to Spain's swords and cannons in short order, as Hernan Cortez conquers Montezuma and the Aztec empire in1521 and Francisco Pizarro ends the Incas rule over Peru in 1541.

Hernando De Soto and his men storm through Central America and the Caribbean, then north to Florida and west to Louisiana. Alvar Cabeza and Francisco Coronado extend De Soto's tracks in America, driving through Texas to Arizona and up through Oklahoma to Kansas. Fifty years later, in 1596, Sebastien Vizcaino explores the west coast, from San Diego to Oregon.

Spain becomes first to assert its "rights" throughout the New World.

By 1600, it controls much of the Caribbean Islands, Peru, Central America, Mexico, and over half of the North American continent from Florida across the deep South to San Diego, then north to Oregon.

THE EUROPEAN EXPLORATION OF AMERICA: EARLY SPANISH EXPEDITIONS

YEARS	EXPLORER	FROM	LAND COVERED
1492-1504	Columbus, Christopher	Spain	San Salvador, Cuba, Haiti, Trinidad, Jamaica, Venezuela, Mexico, Honduras, Panama
1493-1521	De Leon, Ponce	Spain	Santo Domingo (DR), Puerto Rico, Florida
1497-98	Cabot, John	England	Newfoundland
1497-1538	Da Gama, Vasco	Portugal	Opens trade route with India ("the Indies")

YEARS	EXPLORER	FROM	LAND COVERED
1499-1502	Vespucci, Amerigo	Italy	S. America, recognizes that new world is not Asia
1519-21	Cortez, Hernan	Spain	Mexico, conquers Montezuma and Aztecs
1524-42	De Soto, Hernando	Spain	Nicaragua, Peru, Cuba, Florida, Louisiana
1524-28	Verrazzano, Giovani	Italy	Cape Fear, NC, New York, Maine, Newfoundland
1528-37	Cabeza, Alvar	Spain	Cuba, Florida, Louisiana, Texas, Mexico City
1532-41	Pizarro, Francisco	Spain	Conquers Incas in Peru, into Panama
1534-41	Cartier, Jacques	France	1000 miles up St Lawrence seaway
1540-42	Coronado, Francisco	Spain	Arizona, NM, Texas, Oklahoma, Kansas
1577-80	Drake, Sir Francis	England	2nd after Magellan around the world, California
1584-87	Raleigh, Sir Walter	England	Roanoke colony (NC) in 1584-87, Florida
1596-1602	Vizcaino, Sebastian	Spain	Pacific coast, San Diego to Oregon

But Spain comes to the New World more as plunderers than as settlers. In North America, their main attempts at establishing deep roots occur in the Florida's, notably at St. Augustine in 1565, in Santa Fe around 1598 and Texas in San Antonio by 1717.

The failure of Spain to populate and formally colonize in North America will come back to haunt them when their land claims are later threatened by France and the United States.

EARLY SPANISH SETTLEMENTS IN AMERICA

YEAR	LOCATION
1585	St. Augustine, Fla
1696	Pensacola, Fla
1718	San Antonio
1772	St. Luis Obispo, Ca
1780	Yuma, Az
1786	Santa Barbara, Ca
1828	San Francisco Solano, Ca

TIME: 1497–1611

BRITAIN BEGINS TO COLONIZE AMERICA

Aside from John Cabot's 1497 voyage to Newfoundland, the English show little early interest in the New World.

This changes, however, during the reigns of Queen Elizabeth, from 1533–1603, and King James I from 1603–1625.

Once they turn their attention toward America, England's strategy differs sharply from the Spanish. Instead of in and out probes for gold and silver, the English set their sights on establishing permanent colonies on the continent to work the land and carry on profitable trade over time.

The development of Britain's Royal Navy during Elizabeth's reign assures Britain's control over the sea lanes required for safe import and export of goods.

Queen Elizabeth I of England (1533-1603)

British merchants and the crown begin to formulate a "business arrangement" that will create incentives to build permanent colonies across the ocean. The solution is the "joint stock corporation," a model that will become a permanent feature of the future economic landscape in America.

"Corporations" begin as a legal agreement between the monarch and a set of private investors ("stock owners") based on a mutually agreeable "exchange." In this case, the crown grants ownership of sizable chunks of land in America to investors in return for sponsoring settlements that create and sustain trade.

The principal corporation during Elizabeth's reign, The London Company, is granted Atlantic coast territory extending from the 34th (Cape Fear, North Carolina) to the 41st parallel (Long Island Sound). This results in England's first American settlement, the Roanoke Colony, set up by Sir Walter Raleigh in 1584 on lands he calls Virginia, in honor of the Virgin Queen. But when long-delayed supply ships from England revisit the colony in 1590, all signs of the 110 settlers have vanished without a trace.

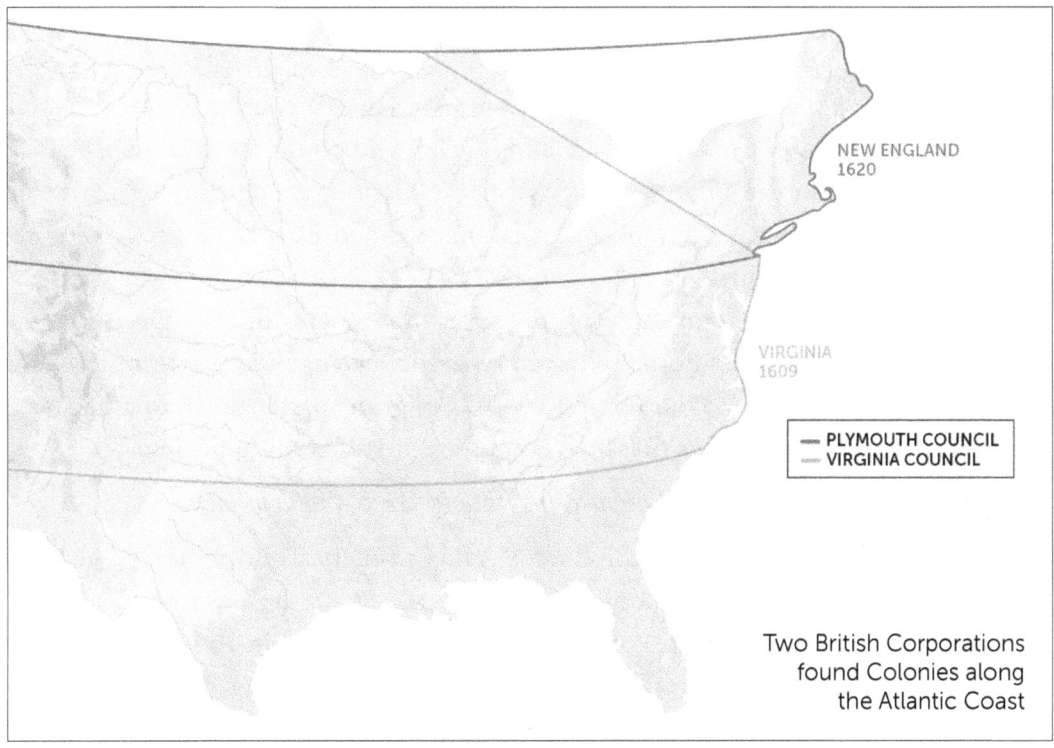

NEW ENGLAND
1620

VIRGINIA
1609

— PLYMOUTH COUNCIL
— VIRGINIA COUNCIL

Two British Corporations
found Colonies along
the Atlantic Coast

The "Lost Colony of Roanoke" halts English colonization until King James I grants two pivotal and somewhat overlapping charters in 1606:

JOINT STOCK CORPORATIONS CHARTERED BY JAMES I IN 1606

COMPANY NAME	GRANT LONGITUDE	PRIMARY DEVELOPMENT AREAS
Virginia Company of London	34th to 41st parallel	Virginia, North Carolina
Virginia Company of Plymouth	38th to 45th parallel	New England

On May 13, 1607, 105 men led by Captain John Smith land at Jamestown, Virginia, with their London Company charter ordering them to accomplish three things:

- Find precious metals;
- Establish a Protestant presence on the continent; and
- Expand English naval power.

But like Roanoke, Jamestown is almost another failure. There is no gold to be found, malaria strikes, and in June, 1610 the 38 survivors re-board their ship to head home. Destiny shifts, however, when sailing out on James River, they encounter a second wave of London Company settlers and return, 1700 strong, to search again for a path to prosperity. After experimenting with a series of possible exports, from timber to iron to sassafras, the colonists finally settle on tobacco, which becomes an overnight sensation in Britain, and triggers the formation of other southern colonies: Carolina in 1629 and Maryland in 1632.

On August 13, 1607, the Plymouth Company lands a contingent of 120 souls under the command of George Popham and Raleigh Gilbert on the southwest coast of Maine, near the mouth of the Kennebec River. While they are able to construct Fort St. George, hard living conditions and a falling out between the leaders causes the colony to close after its first year.

A second Plymouth Company venture proves more successful. On December 21, 1620, Captain William Bradford, a Puritan separatist fleeing the Church of England, navigates the aging ship Mayflower and its 102 "pilgrim" passengers into a harbor at Plymouth, Massachusetts. His first impressions are anything but uplifting:

It is a hideous and desolate wilderness, full of wild beasts and wild men.

Surviving the winter, they establish a toe-hold in America, and are joined in 1628, by settlers associated with another corporation—The Massachusetts's Bay Company.

The British then consolidate control over the Atlantic coast in 1664 by forcing the Dutch to surrender their claim to the New Netherlands territory, in and around the island of Manhattan. This claim originates with Henry Hudson's 1609 voyage on behalf of the Dutch East Indies Company. By 1626, its Director-General, Peter Minuit, has "purchased" the island from the Delaware tribe and constructed Ft. Amsterdam to defend the harbor.

But the Dutch defenses are no match for the four British frigates that appear on August 27, 1664, and demand surrender. By 1665 New Netherlands has officially become New York colony, and the Manhattan settlement, New Amsterdam, is rechristened New York. A final treaty to this effect is signed in 1674 after conclusion of the 3rd Anglo-Dutch War.

EARLY EXPLORATION OF AMERICA: ENGLISH EXPEDITIONS

YEARS	EXPLORER	FROM	LAND COVERED
1497–98	Cabot, John	England	Newfoundland
1577–80	Drake, Sir Francis	England	2nd after Magellan around the world, California
1578–83	Gilbert, Sir Humphrey	England	Newfoundland and Nova Scotia
1584–87	Raleigh, Sir Walter	England	Roanoke colony (NC) in 1584-87, Florida
1596–1602	Vizcaino, Sebastian	Spain	Pacific coast, San Diego to Oregon
1603–09	Champlain, Samuel	France	Settles Quebec

EARLY EXPLORATION OF AMERICA: ENGLISH EXPEDITIONS

YEARS	EXPLORER	FROM	LAND COVERED
1606–14	Smith, John	England	Jamestown in 1607, Richmond, Baltimore
1607–08	Popham, George	England	Maine
1609–11	Hudson, Henry	England	New York (for Dutch East Indies Co.), Hudson River

TIME: 1664-1732

A TOTAL OF THIRTEEN BRITISH COLONIES ARE ESTABLISHED

By the end of the 17ᵗʰ century Britain's holdings in America comprise thirteen colonies along the Atlantic coast.

APPROXIMATE DATES AND CHARTERS FOR THE THIRTEEN CROWN COLONIES

DATE	NAME	FOUNDED BY	ANNOUNCED PURPOSE
1607	Virginia	The London Co.	To find gold
1620	Plymouth (Mass)	Separatist Puritans	To separate from the Church of England

**APPROXIMATE DATES AND CHARTERS FOR THE
THIRTEEN CROWN COLONIES**

DATE	NAME	FOUNDED BY	ANNOUNCED PURPOSE
1630	Massachusetts Bay	Reform Puritans	To reform the Church of England
1635	Connecticut	Thomas Hooker	For Puritan gentlemen
1636	Rhode Island	Roger Williams	For total religious freedom (and Baptists)
1664	New York	The Dutch	To secure and trade furs
1664	New Jersey	The Dutch	For farming
1692	New Hampshire	John Mason	For farming
1632	Maryland	Lord Baltimore	To secure religious freedom for Catholics
1681	Pennsylvania	William Penn	To secure religious freedom for Quakers
1703	Delaware	New Sweden Co	For farming
1719	Carolinas	Virginians	For farming and trade
1732	Georgia	James Oglethorpe	To provide relief for the English in poverty

They are a diverse lot to say the least. All favor the English language and share some form of allegiance to the crown; but their make-up and missions often have little in common.

The three New England colonies (Massachusetts, Connecticut and Rhode Island) probably come closest to a shared purpose—that being a wish to practice the Puritan religion without interference from the Church of England hierarchy back home. The Puritans are committed to driving all residual traces of Catholicism out of their worship and living lives of "Christian charity" according to the principles of the French theologian, John Calvin (1509-64):

- Total Depravity: All men are born as sinners.
- Unconditional election: God selects which will be saved and which damned.
- Limited atonement: Christ died only for those who are to be saved.
- Pre-destination: Man cannot affect his own salvation through deeds or prayer.
- Anti-Catholicism: Purify church practices and rely on congregations to run them.

But even within this umbrella of Puritanism, there are fissures. Those clustered in Massachusetts Bay wish to stay within the Church of England, while reforming it as they see fit. The Puritan "pilgrims" of Plymouth, Massachusetts, opt for creating a separate church entirely. The Rhode Islanders, under the break-away Puritan preacher Roger

Williams, are eager to explore other new religious approaches, notably the Baptist movement.

Two other colonies are also predicated on offering citizens the right to practice their own form of religion. In Maryland, Cecil Calvert, 2nd Baron Baltimore, establishes a haven for Roman Catholic settlers in the New World. In Pennsylvania, the English real estate magnate, William Penn, provides a home for Quakers.

Georgia is also focused on a higher calling, in this case secular in nature and aimed at providing a better life for settlers caught in the misery of poverty back home in England.

The other seven colonies are more concerned with everyday matters related to homesteading and commerce.

By 1700, the population has grown to roughly 250,000 settlers. For most, the early days of struggle against the elements to simply stay alive have passed, and their attention has turned to farming and other forms of making a living. Their tenacity in reaching and settling the new land seems to be paying fine rewards.

TIME: 1534 – 1682

FRANCE OPENS CANADA AND THE MISSISSIPPI VALLEY

France's interest in America picks up during the 72-year reign (1643-1715) of Louis XIV, the Sun King, who is arguably the dominant force in Europe in his time.

In search of fur trading outposts, the French locate and explore the great waterways into and across America.

They arrive from the north in 1534, with Jacque Cartier's 1000-mile voyage down the St. Lawrence seaway. In 1541 Cartier sets up the first European settlement in North America, 400 strong, at Cap Rouge (Quebec City). But a year later it is abandoned, owing to an unforgiving winter climate and conflicts with local tribes.

Like the British, the French learn that it is one thing to reach the New World and quite another to survive there.

After a hiatus lasting six decades, Samuel

The Sun King, Louis IV of France
(1638-1715)

Champlain retraces Cartier's route and successfully opens a French outpost at Quebec in 1608.

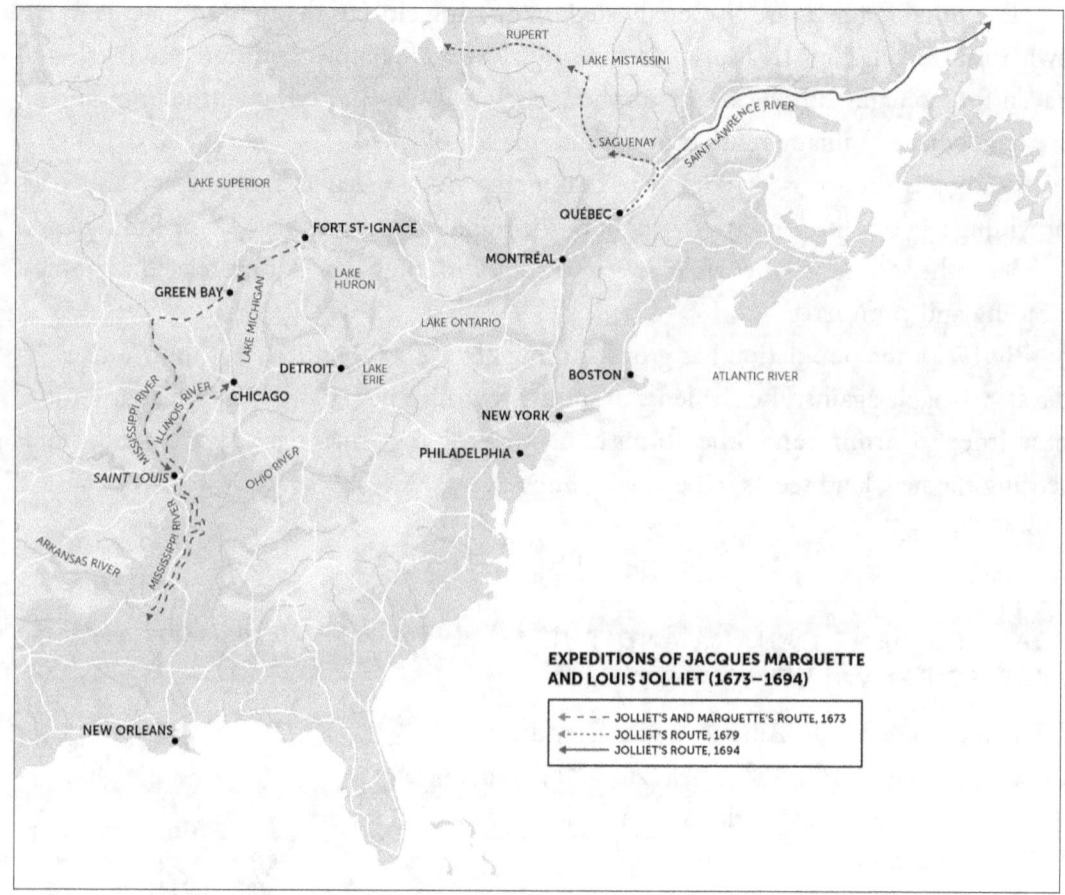

French Exploration of the Mississippi River

From there, the French drive west proceeds across Canada and the Great Lakes to the mighty Mississippi, led by Jean Nicollet, Louis Joliet and Father Jacques Marquette.

EARLY EXPLORATION OF AMERICA: FRENCH EXPEDITIONS

YEARS	EXPLORER	FROM	LAND COVERED
1534–41	Cartier, Jacques	France	1000 miles up St Lawrence seaway
1540-42	Coronado, Francisco	Spain	Arizona, NM, Texas, Oklahoma, Kansas
1577–80	Drake, Sir Francis	England	2nd after Magellan around the world, California
1584–87	Raleigh, Sir Walter	England	Roanoke colony (NC) in 1584-87, Florida
1596–1602	Vizcaino, Sebastian	Spain	Pacific coast, San Diego to Oregon
1603–09	Champlain, Samuel	France	Settles Quebec
1606–14	Smith, John	England	Jamestown in 1607, Richmond, Baltimore

EARLY EXPLORATION OF AMERICA: FRENCH EXPEDITIONS

YEARS	EXPLORER	FROM	LAND COVERED
1609–11	Hudson, Henry	England	New York (for Dutch East Indies Co.), Hudson River
1618–42	Nicollet, Jean	France	Canada, Great Lakes, Wisconsin, Illinois
1626–38	Minuit, Peter	Dutch	Bought Manhattan Island in 1826 for the Dutch East Co
1645–72	Stuyvesant, Peter	Dutch	Governor of New Amsterdam (NYC), West Indies
1673	Joliet, Louis	Canada	Mississippi R (Green Bay to Arkansas)
1673	Marquette, Jacques	France	Mississippi R along with Joliet
1679–82	De La Salle, Robert	France	Great Lakes and length of Mississippi
1774–1830	DuSable, Jean	France	Chicago, Michigan, Missouri

Along the way, French forts and outposts translate into many of the enduring cities of the Midwest.

EARLY FRENCH SETTLEMENTS IN AMERICA

YEAR	LOCATION
1608	Quebec City
1642	Montreal
1669	Ft. La Baye (Green Bay)
1679	Ft. Niagra
1680	Ft. Crevecoeur (Peoria,IL)
1698	Caho Kia (Cahokia, IL)
1699	Biloxi
1701	Ft. Ponchetrain (Detroit)
1716	Ft Rosalie (Natchez)
1718	La Nouvelle Orleans
1720	Baton Rouge
1780s	Chicago

In honor of King Louis XIV, the New France territories along the Mississippi are christened "Louisiana."

## 2

COMES THE SCOURGE: SLAVERY ARRIVES IN THE COLONIES

TIME: 1600–1860

THE INTERNATIONAL SLAVE TRADE FLOURISHES

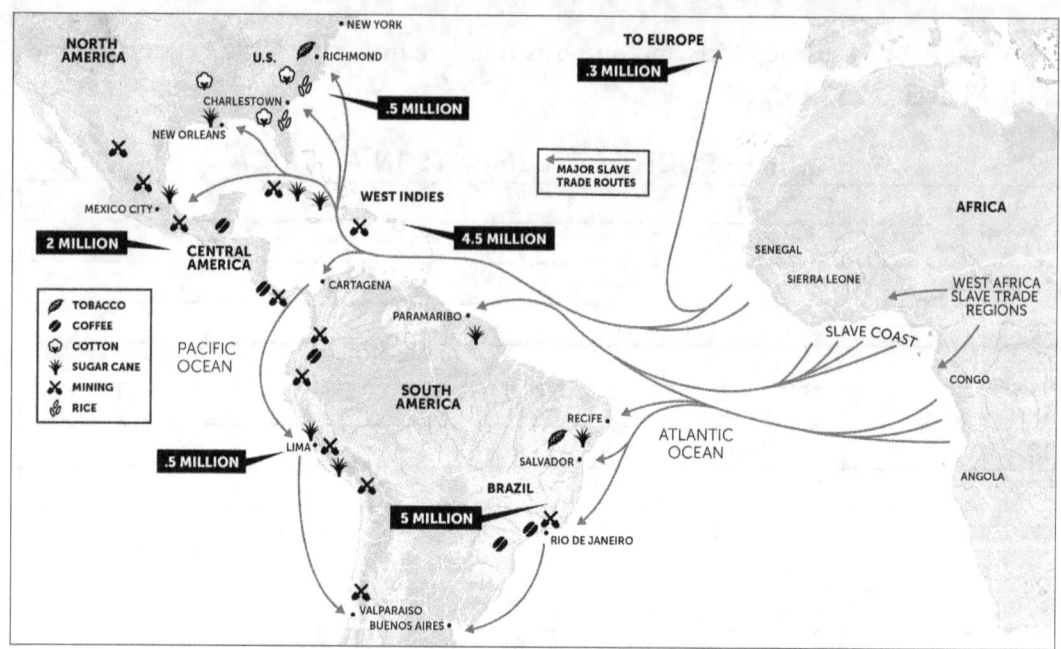

Slave Trade Routes to the Americas from Africa, 1650–1860
Approximately 10 to 15 million enslaved people were transported from western Africa to the Americas. Most were shipped to the West Indies, Central America, and South America.

The practice of slavery arrives in the new World with white explorers, a common scourge across the world in the 17th and 18th centuries.

Between 1600 and 1800, roughly 11 million blacks are transported from their homes along the west coast of Africa (from Senegal to Angola) to the Americas.

Two nations dominate this market for slaves: the Portuguese, who import 5 million Africans for their mining operations and sugar cane fields in Brazil; and the Dutch, who claim another 4.5 million for sugar cane production in the West Indies.

African Tribesmen in Front of Thatched Hut

About 500,000 Africans eventually arrive in North America.

Slave trafficking originates with deals between European agents ("factors/middlemen") and tribal chiefs, who raid rival villages, round up families, rope them together in "coffles," and drive them to collection centers, known as "barracoons."

Chained Africans being Readied for Transport

From there they are packed, 100 at a time, into the holds of ships for the 6-8 week "middle passage" across the Atlantic, where about 15 out of every 100 die in transit.

The survivors are stored in pens, "graded and priced," and then auctioned off to the highest bidders. Strong male field hands one way; their wives and children another.

At that point the slaves became the "personal property" of their owner to do with them as they choose.

TIME: 1619–1750

SLAVERY BEGINS IN AMERICA WITH RHODE ISLAND AS THE TRADING HUB

The first slaves in America appear at Jamestown colony in 1619, working as field hands on farms, raising tobacco and rice.

In 1644, an association of Boston traders sends a ship to Africa in search of slaves; and by 1678, the first sales are recorded in Virginia. But it is not until 1700, when the British begin to dominate the Dutch that New England merchants see the opportunity to set up a profitable business around the slave trade.

Many of the prominent New England families in colonial America trace their early wealth to the slave trade:

- The Faneuils, Royalls and Cabots of Massachusetts;
- The Whipples of New Hampshire and the Eastons of Connecticut;
- The Willing and Morris families of Philadelphia;
- The Wantons, Browns, and Champlains of Rhode Island.

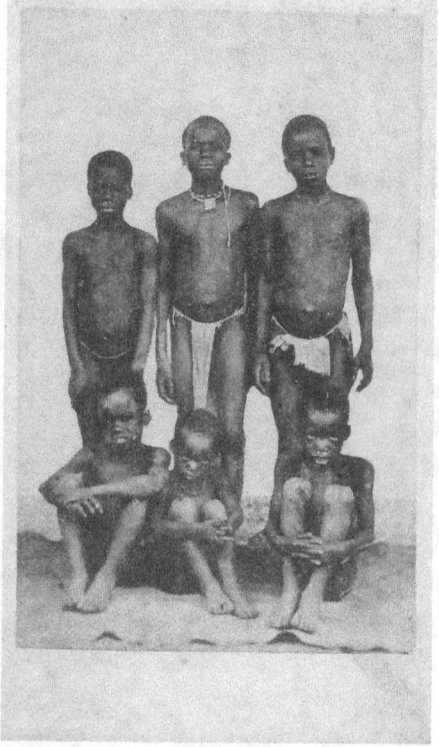

Six Enslaved Boys

Rhode Island, however, controls roughly 75% of the business. In 1740, the port city of Newport is home to some 150 slave ships—many run by the four Brown brothers, who found a university bearing their name after making a fortune selling lumber, salt, meat, and African slaves.

The British, too, are heavily invested in the "triangular commerce" between Africa, their American colonies, and Europe. So much so that their permanent "slave stations" dot Africa's west coast ports.

By 1750, slavery is a widely accepted and well entrenched institution in America.

Slaves are owned in all thirteen British colonies and they play a critical role in America's economic growth.

In the South, slaves are used to grow and harvest labor-intensive crops, initially tobacco, rice and indigo. They are also systematically "bred" to produce offspring for sale in the open market.

The early New England economy profits from slaves in several ways:

- Distilleries across the region rely on sugar and molasses imports from slave plantations in the West Indies to make rum. In turn, rum is distributed across the colonies and exported to Europe and Africa.
- The New England shipping industry—from boat builders and sail-makers through sailors and long-shore men and accountants—hinges on cargo that is in

global demand, including slaves sent from Africa to Newport, Rhode Island; and from there to Southern ports like Savannah and New Orleans.

- Northern textile mills spin raw cotton picked by Southern slaves into yarn and thread, which is then shipped to Britain and France to make clothing and other finished goods.

But these sectional patterns are about to change as America enters the second half of the 18th century.

In the South, the institution of slavery becomes firmly entrenched. In the North it gradually withers away.

TIME: 1775 FORWARD

SLAVERY WITHERS AWAY IN THE NORTH

Meanwhile, in the North, by 1775, slavery is disappearing, an outcome welcomed by many of the region's founding fathers.

One of them is the Quaker, Ben Franklin, who calls slavery:

An atrocious debasement of human nature.

Another is Dr. Benjamin Rush, the renowned Philadelphia physician, who assails the institution in his 1773 pamphlet *An Address to the inhabitants of the British Settlements in America upon Slave-Keeping.* As a scientist, Rush argues against the widely accepted belief that blacks are inherently inferior intellectually. He is also a life-long supporter of abolition, calling the practice of slavery:

Aunt Fannie of the Lott Household

So foreign to the human mind that the moral faculties… are rendered torpid by it.

Franklin and Rush are joined by John Jay, who, in 1785, serves as Secretary of Foreign Affairs, when he founds the New York Manumission Society, which endures over the next six decades. The Society first battles to end the slave trade, then supports abolition, and finally the education of black children. In 1794, the society opens the first African Free School in the city, a one-room facility that teaches forty students. Over time, these Free Schools proliferate widely and prepare many next generation blacks for assimilation into white society.

Moral concerns fail to explain the decline in northern slavery.

Instead, the reason boils down to economics: By 1775, the slave trade is no longer profitable. After two centuries of abduction, purchase and sale of healthy young blacks for the salve trade, tribes living along the west coast of Africa have literally become de-populated.

This alters the profit margins for the New England merchants. Sending a ship across the Atlantic is both costly and risky, and returning late or without a full cargo of slaves becomes the unattractive norm.

While importation of African slaves drags on until it is banned in 1808, the boom profits of the 1750 period are long gone.

The Northern colonies look away from the slave trade and toward other industries to sustain their drive for wealth. Fortunately, new options are right before their eyes. The "triangular trade" between America, Africa, and Europe has taught the North that it can manufacture goods like rum and cotton yarn and use its ships to distribute them across the Atlantic. The making and selling of goods begins to replace the slave trade in the Northern economy.

By 1775, it's clear that for economic reasons, the North is no longer committed to slavery, and instead begins to question "what to do about both slaves and free blacks" in the future.

TIME: 1750–1775

THE SOUTH'S DEPENDENCY ON SLAVERY DEEPENS

The Southern commitment to slavery is evident in population data from 1775.

In 1775, there are roughly 500,000 blacks in America—with 90% of them are living in the South.

They comprise 41% of the South's total population, and in some places, like South Carolina, blacks outnumber whites.

ESTIMATED POPULATION COUNTS BY RACE IN 1775

SECTION	STATES	WHITES	BLACKS	TOTAL	% BLACK
Lower South	Ga, NC, SC	247,000	171,000	418,000	41%
Upper South	Va, Md, Del	481,000	282,000	763,000	37%
Mid-Atlantic	Pa, NY, NJ	462,000	30,000	492,000	6%
New England	Con, RI, NH, Ma	621,000	19,000	640,000	3%
GRAND TOTAL		1,811,000	502,000	2,313,000	22%

Slaves Harvesting Southern Cotton

Their role in the economy of the South is crucial.

While the North is already diversifying and modernizing its economy, Southern wealth is concentrated almost entirely in two areas.

The first is agriculture, where its favorable climate and coastal access make the South uniquely equipped to succeed.

In the upper South, tobacco is the dominant crop. The coastal Carolinas are ideally suited to rice and indigo (used for dyeing). Cotton is grown throughout the region, but is not yet the "king" it will become. All of these crops are in popular demand both domestically and internationally, and all are labor intensive to produce.

Profits are maximized through economies of scale—the more one produces, the lower the unit cost and the higher the margin. This in turn leads to the creation of vast plantations across the South, the early precursors of modern agri-business operations.

The labor required to plant, grow, harvest and ship these crops is physically demanding, and it falls on the backs of Southern slaves—especially field hands working from dawn to dusk during peak seasons.

As these plantations yield ever greater profits to their owners, the intrinsic "value" of the slaves themselves increases dramatically, opening up a second vital revenue stream.

This second driver of Southern wealth—its "second crucial crop"—lies in the "breeding and sale" of offspring slaves to growers aspiring to ascend to the planter class.

In effect, "producing" more slaves becomes an end unto itself.

More slaves translate to more profits, either from greater crop yields to be sold, or from auctioning off one's excessive inventory—black men, women and children—to other growers.

By 1775, the men of the South—unlike those up North—have their economic futures inextricably bound to the presence and expansion of slavery across the colonies.

Indeed, many Southerners think of it, with varying degrees of discomfort, as the "peculiar institution."

But it is their institution, and they mean to defend it with all their wits and might.

3

THE REFORMATION AND ENLIGHTENMENT THREATEN BOTH CHURCH & CROWN

TIME: 1517 FORWARD

LUTHER PROTESTS CATHOLIC CHURCH DOCTRINES

The period leading up to the settlement of the British colonies in America is marked by a series of challenges to the unquestioned authority of both the Church and the Crown.

In 1517, Martin Luther, a German monk nails his 95 Theses on the door of the All Saints Church in Wittenberg, Saxony, protesting the notion that paying indulgences to the clergy can insure one's eternal salvation.

What follows Luther's act is the great religious schism known as the Protestant Reformation.

It takes hold, and in 1527 intersects with affairs of state when Pope Clement VI refuses to grant a marriage annulment to King Henry VIII.

Martin Luther (1483-1546)

Exercising his "divine right" as monarch, Henry responds by banishing the existing Catholic Church and replacing it with his own Church of England.

This ends the monolithic dominance of Catholicism in Britain and across much of Europe.

TIME: 1642–1660

THE ENGLISH CIVIL WARS CHALLENGE THE MONARCHY

The 17th century also ushers in early resistance to the despotic rule of hereditary Monarchies.

A principal figure here is King Charles I of England xercises the "divine right of kings" to tax the people at will and marry a queen who is both French and Catholic.

In 1642, after almost 25 years of King Charles I's affronts, a Parliamentarian movement rises up under the Puritan leader, Oliver Cromwell leading to the First English Civil War. Cromwell's "Roundheads" (for their bowl-cut hairdos) defeat the Royalists on May 5, 1646. After a series of failed attempts to rally his forces and regain the throne, Charles is captured and tried for treason.

TIME: 1689–1789

ENLIGHTENMENT PHILOSOPHERS EXPLORE NEW FORMS OF GOVERNANCE

The Enlightenment or the Age of Reason follows on the heels of the English Civil Wars. Its focus is again on the Monarchy and challenges the notion that Kings have the divine right to absolute power over the lives of the citizenry.

Four leading philosophers of The Enlightenment argue the time has come for new forms of government that respond to the will of the people.

The English philosopher and physician, John Locke (1632-1704), lives through the turmoil after Cromwell's death in 1658 and the restoration of Charles II, whose reign includes the Black Plague, the Great Fire of London, and a deathbed conversion to Catholicism. When his son James II marries a Catholic, another popular rebellion places the Protestant William III of Orange and his wife Mary on the throne. As part of the deal, the pair agree to a "Declaration of Rights" which limits the power of the crown over its subjects.

Grave of Jean Jacques Rousseau (1712-1778)

In 1689, as William and Mary ascend, Locke publishes his "Second Treatise of Government" in which he argues on behalf of "classical liberalism"—that the size and power of government should be limited in order to preserve and enlarge the freedom of the individual:

- The end of law... is to preserve and enlarge freedom.
- The state of nature has a law of nature to govern it, which obliges every one: and reason is that law.
- The natural liberty of man is to be free from any superior power on earth.
- All mankind, being equal and independent, no one ought to harm another in his life, health, liberty or possessions.
- Men being by nature, all free, equal, and independent, no one can be subjected to the political power of another, without his own consent.

Locke's preferred form of government is a monarchy, but he demands that it be "constitutional" in nature, with all property owners given the right to vote.

The Swiss writer and musician, Jean Jacques Rousseau (1712–1778), grows up in a middleclass family in Geneva, leads a bohemian lifestyle, and records his observations about the nature of man and society in a series of tracts that challenge conventional thought. He asserts that men are born free, equal and happy and then surrender these joys by entering into a destructive social contract based on property rights:

> The first person who, having enclosed a plot of land, took it into his head to say this is mine and found people simple enough to believe him was the true founder of civil society. What crimes, wars, murders, what miseries and horrors would the human race have been spared, had someone pulled up the stakes or cried out to his fellow men: "Do not listen to this imposter. You are lost if you forget that the fruits of the earth belong to all and the earth to no one!"

According to Rousseau, governments, especially monarchies, are typically dedicated to protecting the property rights of the haves at the expense of the have nots, who are left in chains. The only way around this are laws that balance out the score:

> In truth, laws are always useful to those with possessions and harmful to those who have nothing; from which it follows that the social state is advantageous to men only when all possess something and none has too much.

The path to just laws lies in forming a government based on "pure Democracy" where decisions are arrived at in open debate, with full participation on all sides, and a final vote based on "majority rules." In this regard, the English system—a "Republic," where lawmakers are elected to represent their constituencies—falls short of Rousseau's ideal:

> The people of England regard itself as free; but it is grossly mistaken; it is free only during the election of members of parliament. As soon as they are elected, slavery overtakes it, and it is nothing.

Rousseau is seen as a dangerous radical by the establishment, and his works are banned in the Calvinistic canton of Geneva. Still, his populist views will fuel reformers on behalf of Democracy.

Two other Enlightenment thinkers also weigh heavily in the search for options to the absolute monarchies.

The Scottish essayist, David Hume (1711-1778), focuses on two essential ingre-dients—unfettered free speech and a written, formally approved Constitution. The French Baron and lawyer, Charles Montesquieu (1689-1775), calls for dividing gov-ernment into separate branches to insure "checks and bal-ances" on major decisions and to prevent concentrations of power.

But unlike Rousseau, both Hume and Montesquieu fear that "direct Democracy" will trample on the rights of minority interests. Protecting these interests, they feel, re-quires a "Republican" government, with elected statement using personal judgment and wisdom to guard against un-bridled "majority rules."

In the end, all four of the Enlightenment thinkers and writers will play a significant role in shaping the beliefs of the American colonists about the full range of institutions they choose to create.

Baron Charles-Louis
Montesquieu (1689-1775)

4

AMERICA'S FOUNDATIONAL CHURCHES TAKE HOLD IN THE COLONIES

TIME: 1607 FORWARD

THE COLONISTS ARE DEDICATED CHURCH-GOERS

One thing that bonds the early American colonists is their church-going traditions and their focus on securing eternal salvation.

For the majority of those who arrive in Virginia in 1607 and Massachusetts in 1620, this means a commitment to the Protestant religion.

Some are conservative Anglicans, who will assume an American identity as the Episcopalian Church. Their doctrines remain consistent with King Henry VIII's patchwork amalgamation of Catholicism and Protestant reform, and their governance is clearly top-down with authority over all church matters resting with a clerical hierarchy. The Anglican liturgy mimics the old-world Mass, and its tonality is formal. Followers are heavily skewed toward the Southern colonies.

Baptist Roger Williams (1603–1683)

Others reject what they regard as corrupt practices within the Church of England and intend to go their own way in the new world. Included here are the Puritans and Lutherans who tend to evolve into the Congregational Church. It eliminates the clerical hierarchy and, consistent with democratic impulses, places authority for religious practices in the hands of the membership. Its influence is centered in New England.

Like the Congregationalists, Baptists embrace basic Calvinist tenets: salvation through faith alone, predestination, the Bible as the word of God dictating the right path, authority in the hands of the congregation rather than a clergy. What distinguishes them, however, is a belief that the act of baptism should be reserved for adults, not newborns, as a symbol of their studied commitment to entering the church. After its founding by Roger Williams in 1632, the Baptist Church spreads beyond Rhode Island, especially into the South.

In 1656, another sect, the Society of Friends, or Quakers (who "tremble" at the name of God) and take up residence in the Massachusetts Bay Colony. They believe every man can attain salvation by listening to and obeying an "Inner Light", which guides their path toward moral perfection. They have no formal clergy and their church services are "spontaneous" and marked by individual testimonials. In 1681, William Penn founds the Pennsylvania Colony as a "home for persecuted Quakers." From then on, the Quakers play a central role in opposing slavery.

The Presbyterian Church is founded by the Scottish preacher, John Knox (1505-1572) and its theological roots are linked to John Calvin (1509-1564). But church governance falls to a body of "elders" rather than to the members of the congregation as a whole. Hence its name, derived from the Greek word for elders—"presbyteros." The Presbyterian Church appears in America around 1706, accompanying immigrants from Scotland. It takes hold mainly in North Carolina, Pennsylvania and the western territories. During the 1830's "new school and old school" Presbyterians will divide, with the former evolving into Unitarians.

These four important sects—Episcopalians, Congregationalists, Baptist and Quakers—will be joined by Methodists and a host of other Protestant off-shoots, which emerge around the "Second Great Awakening" of the 1830's.

The Catholic Church also finds a home within the colonies. It originates in the Spanish "mis-

Quaker William Penn (1644–1718)

sions" scattered from Florida west to New Orleans and up the Mississippi River. In 1632, England's Catholic King Charles I cedes the Colony of Maryland to his former Secretary of State, Lord Baltimore. Despite this, the religious ill-will evident in Europe carries over to the colonies, with Catholics accused of being loyal to the Pope in Rome instead of the American government.

By 1730, each religious denomination is settling into place in the colonies, some holding on to traditional church hierarchies and liturgy, others breaking away toward new options.

At this point the Enlightenment spirit strikes the American church scene.

TIME: 1730's

THE "FIRST GREAT AWAKENING" SPARKS EVANGELICAL CHRISTIANITY

Along with the Enlightenment comes a growing sense that by relying on their own capacity to reason, individuals can shape their personal destinies, their societies and their government.

This is a transformative idea, and its impact is felt throughout colonial America in the 18th century.

Within the religious realm, the enlightenment spirit is reflected in what be-

Germantown Church

comes known as the "First Great Awakening" which begins in the 1730s. The embodiment of this movement is an otherwise conservative Puritan minister, Reverend Jonathan Edwards, preaching in Northampton, Massachusetts.

Edwards is born in 1703 in East Windsor, Connecticut, a single son surrounded by ten sibling sisters. The family survives on modest means, a minister father eking out spare income by tutoring boys prior to entering college. One such boy is the son, Jonathan, a precocious student who enters Yale at age 13 and graduates as valedictorian of his class in 1720. Young Edwards is intensely disciplined throughout his life, studying and writing every day for up to 13 hours, taking time out only when other duties demand his attention. He is naturally drawn to the sciences, but sees in them a framework for man that is divinely inspired. His life will be devoted to faith not Deism.

He serves briefly as a novice pastor in 1722 before returning to Yale as a theological tutor, affirming his strict adherence to traditional Calvinist principles. His personal life is ascetic, marked by self-imposed control over his time, his diet, his study and contemplation, his search for the moral perfection expected of those committed to the Puritan theology.

The way to Heaven is ascending; we must be content to travel uphill, though it be hard and tiresome and contrary to the natural bias of our flesh.

Edwards is formally ordained as a Congregationalist minister in 1727, and marries the daughter of the clergyman James Pierpont, founder of Yale.

By 1732 his spiritual journey comes up against the Arminian movement, named after the Dutch Reformed Church theologian, Jacob Arminius (1560-1609). It posits a profoundly different view about eternal salvation, and one that will be adopted by many American sects over time:

FOUNDER	BELIEF ABOUT ETERNAL SALVATION
Calvin	"Pre-destination." Only those who are chosen by God's grace alone to be among "the elect" are saved.
Arminius	"Free will." All persons are capable of being saved if they choose to lead their lives in accordance with Christian principles and practices.

As the pure Calvinist, Edwards comes down on the side of God as sole arbiter of salvation. In his most famous sermon, "Sinners In The Hands Of An Angry God," delivered in 1741, he exhibits his "fire and brimstone" fervor:

O sinner! Consider the fearful danger you are in: it is a great furnace of wrath, a wide and bottomless pit, full of the fire of wrath, that you are held over in the hand of that God, whose wrath is provoked and incensed as much against you, as against many of the damned in hell.

But what distinguished Edwards as the "father of the First Great Awakening" is not his theology but rather the manner of preaching he adopts at his "revival meetings" in Northampton.

These center on "conversion experiences" whereby members of the congregation publicly pledge their lives to Christ. Edwards describes one such event in 1741:

In the month of May, 1741, a sermon was preached to a company, at a private house. One or two persons were so greatly affected with a sense of the glory of divine things and the infinite importance of the things of eternity that... it had a visible effect upon their bodies... The affection was quickly propagated throughout the room (with) many of the young people overcome... with admiration, love, joy and praise and compassion (while) others were overcome with distress about their sinful and miserable state and condition. The whole room was full of nothing but outcries, faintings and the like. The meeting continued for some hours, the time being spent in prayer, singing, counseling, and conferring. There seemed to be a consequent happy effect on many people and on the state of religion in the town.

Suddenly, with Edwards, the preacher is no longer held above and apart from his flock, but instead comes down from the pulpit to spontaneously share and explore religious feelings and experiences.

Thus "Evangelical Christianity"—the belief that all men can be "re-born" by openly embracing the literal word of God in the Bible—begins to assert itself in America.

Needless to say, Edward's traditional colleagues are shocked and dismayed by the "revival meetings," which may draw up to 500 people, extend over several days, and dominate a town's entire life while they last. On rare occasions they are also followed by suicides, as some attendees leave convinced they are among the doomed.

The effect is that by 1751, Jonathan Edwards falls out of favor with the forces around him, and is driven out of his Northampton Church. He lives eight more years, dying one month after being named President of the College of New Jersey (Princeton).

TIME: 1730s

METHODISTS EXPAND THE EVANGELICAL SPIRIT

This Evangelical spirit also manifests itself in the Methodist Church, which comes to America in 1736.

The sect is founded by the English cleric, John Wesley, who insists throughout his life that its roots are firmly in the Anglican tradition— hence its followers are often called Methodist Episcopalians.

The church tenets are worked out at Oxford University around 1730 by Wesley, his younger brother William, and one George Whitefield. Together they start a prayer group on campus, the "Holy Club," which is so disciplined in its practice of piety that fellow students cast them as "The Oxford Methodists." And the nickname sticks.

Unlike his brother and Whitefield—both staunch Calvinists—John Wesley is drawn toward Arminianism, with its promise that all men can be saved by trying to live a life of "moral perfection."

John Wesley (1703-1791)

For Wesley a signal of "perfection" lies not only in worshipping Christ, but also engaging in "reform missions" aimed at correcting injustices and supporting those in need.

To rally people toward these ends, Wesley embraces the "Evangelical revival meetings" currently popularized by Edwards.

In February 1736, John Wesley sails to America, eager to hold his revivals in the Georgia colony, especially among poor whites and various Native American tribes. His stay, however, lasts just under a year, and he regards it as a total failure.

After Wesley returns to London, his 23-year-old colleague, George Whitefield follows him to Georgia in 1737.

Whitefield proves to be much more adept than the reserved Wesley with the open-air context—probably a reflection of his love for theater and for acting out Bible stories as a youth. He travels broadly in America, even preaching in 1739 alongside Edwards in Northampton. The colonial editor and inventor, Benjamin Franklin befriends him in Philadelphia and publishes several of his sermons in his newspaper. He also notes the positive effects of his ministry on the local community:

Wonderful...change soon made in the manners of our inhabitants. From being thoughtless or indifferent about religion, it seem'd as if all the world were growing religious, so that one could not walk thro' the town in an evening without hearing psalms sung in different families of every street.

The Reverend George Whitefield will make thirteen Atlantic crossings back and forth to England before dying in 1770 in Newburyport, Massachusetts.

John Wesley survives Whitefield by two more decades. During that time he faces many challenges from the Anglican Church hierarchy. But he forever moves forward to establish his Methodist Church.

His beliefs will have great impact on mainstream religious development in America, especially the conviction that all men can achieve salvation, and that the proper path lies in studying God's words in the Bible and in completing soul-saving "missions."

Over time, Methodists will outnumber all other sects in terms of membership.

It will also play a pivotal role within the black community after a bishop named James Varick opens the first African Methodist Episcopal Zion Church in 1721, located in New York City. From there, the "AME Church" provides a safe harbor and much needed support for blacks trying to survive and become assimilated.

TIME: 1688 FORWARD

EARLY CHURCH OPPOSITION TO SLAVERY IS MUTED

Despite the professed interest in salvation, America's churches are generally silent when it comes to addressing chattel slavery in the land.

The one institutional exception is the Society of Friends in Pennsylvania. In 1688, a settler named Francis Pastorious submits the "Germantown Quaker Petition Against

Slavery" at his local meeting, basing his argument simply on the Bible's Golden Rule admonition:

> *Therefore, all things whatsoever ye would that men should do to you, do ye even so to them: for this is the law.*

In 1743, John Woolman, a New Jersey Quaker, picks up the cause and resolves to "purify himself from the sin of slavery." He publishes an anti-slavery pamphlet, *Some Considerations on the Keeping of Slaves*, and completes over thirty missionary tours from New England to the Carolinas, preaching in support of abolition.

Years later, Woolman's personal crusade will make at least one key convert, Benjamin Lundy, an Ohio Quaker who, in the 1830's, will pass the torch on to the towering champion of abolition, William Lloyd Garrison.

Quakers also lead the way in establishing a formal organization to oppose slavery. The Pennsylvania Society for the Relief of Negroes Unlawfully Held In Bondage is founded in 1775, with support over time from two "natural law" Deists, Thomas Paine and Benjamin Franklin.

In 1747, Jonathan Mayhew, minister of the West Church in Boston, preaches against a host of moral injustices and sets the stage for the creation in the 1820's of the Unitarian Church, and its on-going crusade against slavery.

In 1774 the First Baptist Church of Petersburg, Va, opens its doors to a black congregation and ministers—to be followed in 1777 by the First African Baptist Church of Savannah, founded by a former slave, and in 1801 by the First Baptist Church of Columbia, SC. At first, some church's missionaries also call for the end of slavery and equality of all men, while encouraging blacks to become both members and preachers. But this aggressive stance becomes muted over time, as Baptists try to extend their membership with Southern whites, many of whom are slave owners.

Within the emerging Methodist Church, John Wesley takes aim at slavery in his quest to achieve "Christian Perfection" through missionary work. His fervor here is evident in his 1774 tract, Thoughts Upon Slavery, as he rhetorically questions a slave trader's humanity:

> *Are you a man? Than you should have a human heart. But have you indeed? What is your heart made of? Is there no such principle as Compassion there? Do you never feel another's pain? Have you no Sympathy? No sense of human woe? No pity for the miserable?*
>
> *When you saw the flowing eyes, the heaving breasts, or the bleeding sides and tortured limbs of your fellow-creatures, were you a stone, or a brute? Did you look upon them with the eyes of the tiger?*

When you squeezed the agonizing creatures down in the ships, or when you threw their poor mangled remains into the sea, had you no relenting? Did not one tear drop from your eye, one sigh escape from your breast?

Do you feel no relenting now?

If you do not, you must go on, till the measure of your iniquities is full. Then will the Great God deal with You, as you have dealt with them, and require all their blood at your hands.

The Presbyterians are largely content to stay away from the issue early on, although synods in New York and Pennsylvania do file anti-slavery petitions.

Within the Anglican and Catholic churches, the record on colonial slavery suggests the same kind of institutional indifference evident across the mainstream Protestant sects.

5

BRITAIN AND FRANCE BEGIN THEIR BATTLES FOR GLOBAL HEGEMONY

TIME: 1701–1714

THE WAR OF SPANISH SUCCESSION SPILLS OVER TO NORTH AMERICA

Beginning with the 1066 AD invasion of England by William the Conqueror of Normandy, Britain and France have struggled for land and power.

On November 1, 1700, the Spanish throne is left vacant by the death of the mentally and physically handicapped King Charles II, "the Bewitched", whose 40-year rule incapacitates the country. In his will, Charles names Philip of Anjou, grandson of Louis XIV, as his successor, which threatens to unite Spain, the Hapsburg empire and France under one crown.

Monument to General Wolfe at Quebec

The British, ruled by the Protestant Queen Anne, decide to go to war to prevent France from expanding its power in Europe. The War of Spanish Succession lasts from 1701 to 1714, and ends with a major victory for the English over Louis XIV.

One phase of this conflict is fought in North America, known as Queen Anne's War, it leaves the Spanish missions in Florida weakened and costs the French its territory in Newfoundland, Acadia, and Hudson Bay.

TIME: 1756-1763

THE FRENCH & INDIAN WARS END WITH RULE BRITANNIA

But the battle over succession in Spain proves only a warm-up for the Seven Year's War, waged 1756 to 1763.

It becomes the world's "first true global war" eventually pitting France, Austria, Spain, Sweden and Saxony against an alliance of England, Prussia, Portugal and Russia. It is fought on land and sea, with human casualties estimated at well over one million men, and fearful financial losses on all sides.

The American theater is christened the French & Indian War, with most of the action centered on control over trade-route forts along the Canadian border.

As the war begins, the French have 75,000 settlers living in North America vs. 1.5 million British colonists. Their military consist of roughly 10,000 regular army forces, complemented by their tribal partners, the Algonquins and the Mohawks. The British muster roughly 40,000 men between their regulars and militia volunteers from their colonies, including one George Washington of Virginia. Their Indian allies are the Iroquois, historical foes of the Algonquin.

Despite these odds, the war begins badly for England. General Braddock is defeated at Ft. Duquense (Pittsburgh), and overall commander of the French troops, General Montcalm, scores victories in upstate New York over Ft. Oswego and Ft. William Henry. Both of these battles are marred by atrocities against British prisoners.

In 1758, the tide turns in favor of Britain, culminating in the fall of the French garrison at Quebec City. This follows a vicious ten-week siege of the city, ending September 13, 1759, with both General Wolfe and General Montcalm killed in action. From there, the British navy cuts off re-supply efforts by France along the St. Lawrence, and the last stronghold at Montreal falls in 1760.

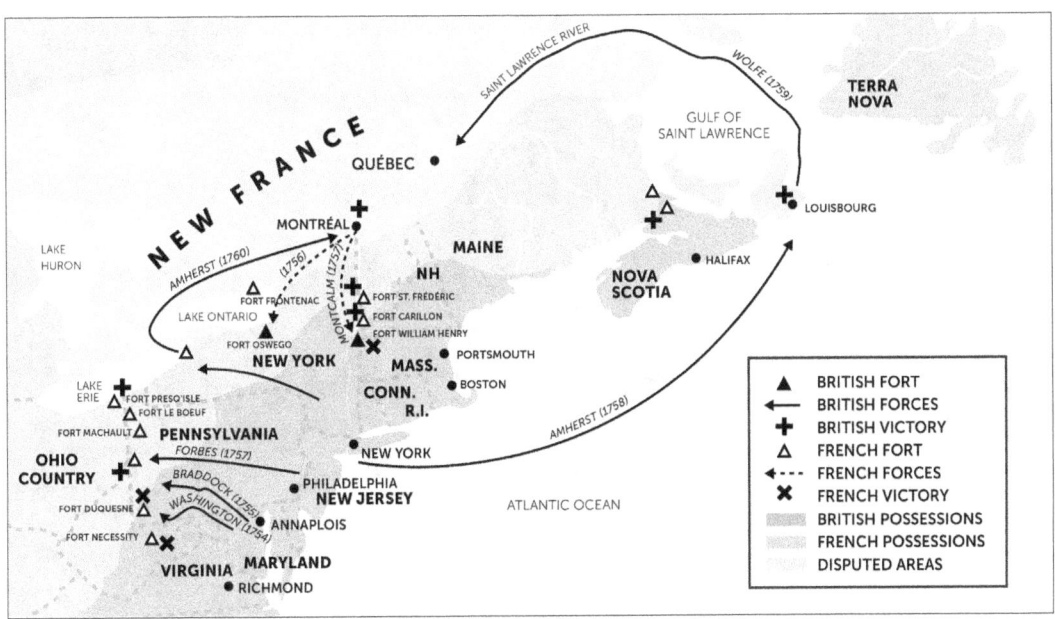

Britain Drives France out of America in the French and Indian Wars of 1750

During the full course of the Seven Year's War, British naval and army power has sweep across the globe. In the east, the Spanish colony at Manilla has fallen along with the French trading posts in India. Spain has lost control over much of the Caribbean, including its Havana colony in Cuba. Canada is wrested from France.

The war ends with the 1763 Treaty of Paris and sets the stage for creation of the British Empire.

After several rounds of post-war territorial horse-trading, the face of North America changes profoundly:

- The French have vacated the continent. Britain picks up France's holdings in Canada, along with their claims to land east of the Mississippi. By 1764, it is also revealed that they have transferred their vast "Louisiana" territory west of the Mississippi to Spain. For the sake of on-going peace, the English promise to allow Catholicism to continue in the former French territories and to return the sugar-rich, Caribbean island of Guadalupe to France.
- Spain hands both west and wast Florida over to Britain, in exchange for retaining Cuba and securing control over the port of New Orleans.

As of 1763, Britain controls 39% of the 3.1 million square miles that will eventually comprise the nation.

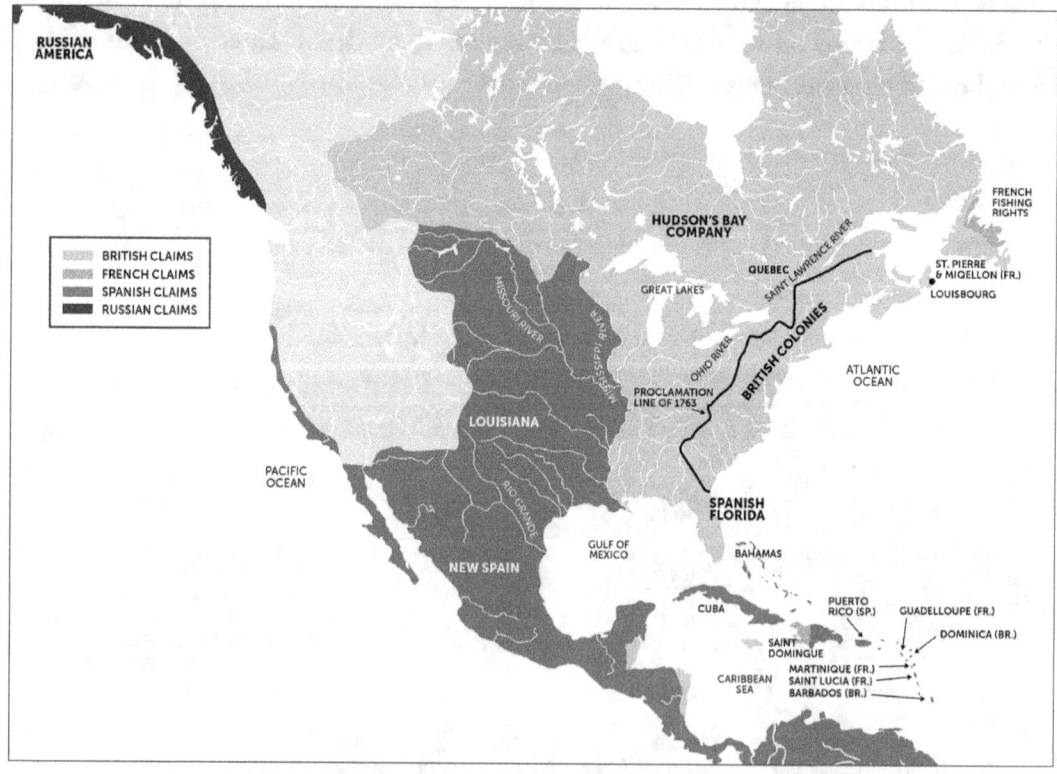

Ownership of North America in 1763

THE AMERICAN LANDSCAPE IN 1760

To better understand the historical events as they occur, we will pause the narrative on occasion to describe what it was like to be living in America at the time. While contemporary records are sketchy, these ethnographical interludes will variously touch on: the size and make-up of the population; how people dressed; their homes and evolving cities; their education and religion; gender roles; modes of transportation; their daily work, money supply, income and expenses; the national economy and industrialization; their commonly shared values and aspirations.

AMERICA'S GROWING POPULATION

Amidst the swirl of global events, the population of English settlers in America has grown dramatically, reaching roughly 1.6 million by 1760 when the French & Indian War comes to an end.

COLONIAL POPULATION GROWTH

YEAR	ESTIMATED # SETTLERS
1620	2,300
1650	50,000
1680	150,000
1710	330,000
1740	905,000
1750	1,170,000
1760	1,590,000

Just over 60% of the population is white with two-thirds of them coming from the British Isles. African slaves are already established across the country.

POPULATION PROFILE AROUND 1760

COUNTRY OF ORIGIN	% OF POPULATION
British Isles	44%
Germany	11%
Other Europe	7%
African Slaves	38%
TOTAL	100%

The majority of people continue to reside east of the 1,000 mile long Appalachian Mountain range, which runs 15 degrees off vertical, from Newfoundland to central Alabama. This puts most settlers within 100 to 250 miles of the Atlantic Ocean.

Across the entire region villages and cities dot the landscape.

EARLY BRITISH SETTLEMENTS IN AMERICA

YEAR	LOCATION
1607	Jamestown, Virginia
1620	Plymouth, Massachussetts
1630	Boston, Massachusetts
1661	Schenectady, NY
1664	New York, NY
1680	Charleston, SC
1682	Philadelphia, Pa
1683	Williamsburg, Va
1694	Annapolis, Md
1703	Ft. Saratoga, NY
1710	New Bern, NC
1713	Fort St. John, NY
1729	Baltimore, Md
1733	Richmond, Va
1733	Savannah, Ga
1736	Ft. Frederica, Ga
1740	Wilmington, NC

THE SEARCH FOR A BETTER LIFE

From the beginning, overtones of religious idealism resonate across the colonies.

Many settlers have been touched by the Catholic-Protestant schism across Europe, and many are left dissatisfied by the "compromises" they see in the Church of England. This is particularly true in the New England colonies, where various Puritan factions hope to live in closer accord to the teaching of the French theologian, John Calvin, an early 16th century contemporary of Martin Luther.

Having surrendered their former lives by sailing across the Atlantic, they wonder if a "better life" for themselves and their families might be possible in the New World.

One voice that captures this wish belongs to the Puritan minister, John Winthrop. In a 1603 sermon, "A Model of Christian Charity," he announces his vision of this "better life" and argues that it is America's duty and destiny to live up to its ideals.

Our posterity will be to do justly, to love mercy, to walk humbly with our God…For this end, we must be knit together…as one man, we must entertain each other in brotherly affection…make others conditions our own always having before our eyes our community as members of the same body… so the Lord will delight to dwell among us as his own people and will command a blessing upon us in all our ways.

We shall than be as a City upon a Hill, with the eyes of all people upon us.

Herein lays the image of America as a shining beacon of light rising

Homilies from the Bible

above the historical failings of Europe, an image that will become a lasting part of the national heritage.

BUILDING A VIABLE ECONOMY

Along with Winthrop's religious idealism, the settlers share a very practical and self-centered wish—to maximize their own economic prosperity by acquiring and working their own land.

This intense motivation to acquire land is recognized in the so-called "headright system" written into the crown's early corporate charters. Any single man who intends to "inhabit" Virginia for at least three years is granted 50 acres of free land. If he actually follows through and cultivates the land, he receives a bonus of 50 more acres. If he is accompanied by a wife and four children the ante climbs to 300 acres of free land.

Devoting the long hours of labor required to prosper on the land seems built into the American character from the beginning. For many this "work ethic" falls out of their

Protestant religious convictions. It is regarded as the dignified duty each man owes to God, according to the Puritans, and the prosperity that follows for some may signal their improved odds of "election" into eternal salvation.

And so, the colonists work their land and take from it what is given.

But much to the dismay of their English joint-stock investors this fails to include either gold or silver.

Instead, each of the colonies takes advantage of the natural resources it finds, first to sustain their immediate families, then to live up to the "export requirements" in their corporate charters.

Harsh winters and stony soil require the North to look elsewhere for desirable exports. They find it first in lumber, for ship-building, and then in the world's richest supply of what Bostonians call the "sacred cod," the catch that spawns the fishing industry in America. Europe also proves eager for New England rum and for fur pelts used in top hats and winter clothing.

PRIMARY COMMODITIES PRODUCED AS OF 1763

COLONY	GOODS
Massachussets	Cod, herring, timber, iron
New Hampshire	Fish
Rhode Island	Rum
Connecticut	Corn, horses
New York	Furs
Pennsylvania	Flax, wheat, iron
New Jersey	Sheep, apples, copper
Maryland	Peaches
Virginia	Tobacco, furs, cattle, iron
North Carolina	Tobacco, pigs, cattle, furs
South Carolina	Rice, indigo, cattle
Georgia	Rice, indigo, silk, hides

A vigorous export/import trade cycle evolves with the colonists shipping their raw commodities to England and receiving a variety of "finished goods" turned out in British manufacturing facilities. These range from shirts, trousers, dresses, shoes, furniture, tableware, linen, glass, paper, and tea.

As goods flow in and out, British officials collect tariffs (i.e. taxes) on them to add to corporate and crown profits.

The Royal Navy plays an important role in guaranteeing this trade. It guards the sea lanes to Britain and battles two main threats – smugglers seeking to avoid payment of tariffs, and pirates intent on stealing shipments for themselves.

TIME: 1655–1718

SIDEBAR: THREE 17TH CENTURY PIRATES OF THE CARIBBEAN

While the Royal Navy is mostly successful in controlling piracy, three brigands are immortalized for their high seas raiding exploits.

A Two-Masted Schooner

The first is Henry Morgan (1635-88), a Welshman, who is said to have boarded some 400 British ships in the Caribbean before finally being captured. On his way back home to the gallows, King Charles II of Spain is able to intercept, free him and name him Governor of Jamaica, in honor of his good works. Like a cat with nine lives, Morgan lives out his life on the island, dying there in peace after decades of crime.

The pirate William Kidd (1645-1701) is not as lucky as Morgan. He is a Scotsman who actually takes up residence for a time in New York City before settling on a life devoted to attacking ships of the British East Indies company along the coast. He is eventually arrested in Boson and hanged back in England.

Perhaps the most famous of all pirates is the Englishman, Edward Teach (1680-1718), whose moniker becomes "Blackbeard." Teach roams the Caribbean for years at will until finally, as a warning to any future pirates, the British display his head on a pike in the harbor at Hampton, Virginia.

TIME: 1607–1775

GOVERNING THE COLONIES

From the 1607 settlement of Jamestown onward, the thirteen colonies are governed according to the "charters" worked out between the monarchy and the mercantile investors.

All policy decisions affecting the colonist fall under the purview of the King.

Local administration resides with the Governor of each colony, who is appointed by the crown. In turn, the Governor receives "advice" on local affairs from two "administrative bodies."

One is a "Council," typically consisting of twenty or so representatives of the joint-stock Corporation who are focused mainly on maximizing the profit flow from the colony.

The other becomes known as the "House of Burgesses," officials elected by property-owning male colonists, and charged with communicating issues and wishes to the Governor.

Each colony is eventually broken into shires, or counties, as the population becomes distributed across villages. Again, the officials in each county are appointed by the Governor.

Surveying the land and settling on boundaries is an important and on-going administrative task.

Border conflicts, at times violent, persist in some regions. Massachusetts sprawls all the way to future day Maine, interrupted by New Hampshire, which also contends with New York for territory. The delayed seizure of New Netherlands from the Dutch in 1664 leads to disputes between New York and New Jersey. Meanwhile, the east coast colony of Connecticut lays claim to "western reserve" land across the Appalachians, in what becomes the state of Ohio.

A Typical English Magistrate

By 1763, however, the shape of all thirteen colonies is pretty well determined.

Relations with England are generally harmonious. The colonists have acquired their land, developed a viable economy, and enjoy the free pursuit of the religious practices many have sought. The joint-stock corporations have established a profitable system of import/export trade. The local militias have fought side by side along with the British regulars to defeat France and Spain.

By and large then, 150 years after the 1607 landing at Jamestown, the colonists' risky voyages to the New World and their ongoing allegiance to the British crown have paid off handsomely.

6

THE DECLARATION OF INDEPENDENCE

TIME: 1763–66

BRITAIN BEGINS "TAXATION WITHOUT REPRESENTATION"

Meanwhile, in Britain, the 25-year-old King George III and Charles Townshend, his Chancellor of the Exchequer, turn their attention to conditions in their American colonies.

Money

What they find is that while Britain has triumphed in the field during the French & Indian Wars (1754–63), the battle for North America has been financially costly for the crown. To help pay off the debts, the king decides to extract more revenue from the colonists in a series of heavy-handed acts that cumulatively end the harmony that existed between Britain and the colonies, and leaves the Americans feeling bullied and angered, then outright rebellious.

The initial indignity is the Proclamation of 1763, which demands that any colonial families who have settled west of the Appalachians abandon their homes and return east. Presumably so the crown can sell back this land, won in the war, for a profit.

The Sugar Act of 1764 adds taxes on sugar, coffee, and wine, while prohibiting imports of rum and French spirits.

Another 1764 command, the Currency Act, prohibits the colonies from issuing its own paper money, a move that tightens British control over all economic transactions in the colonies.

In March 1765, the crown further ups the drive for revenue with the Stamp Act, which requires that a paid-for seal be affixed to all printed material—from legal documents and licenses to everyday items like newspapers, pamphlets, almanacs, and even playing cards. Attempts to justify this move center on the "*need to defend the colonies from future invaders.*"

Colonial resistance to the Stamp Act is immediate and widespread, especially among the more influential segments of the population: land owners, merchants, ship-builders, lawyers, and printers. Britain has imposed another tax absent any input or debate from the elected burgesses with their local councils and governors. Where will this end? And, besides, which enemies are left? And hasn't the performance of the local troops during the recent war demonstrated that the colonists are now capable of defending themselves?

Resistance from abroad shocks the English. For show, Parliament passes the Declaratory Act, stating that the crown has the absolute right to impose whatever demands it deems appropriate on its colonies. But then it repeals the Stamp Act in 1766, a first "flinch" that signals at least a token American victory.

For the moment, both sides back off from the building tension.

TIME: DECEMBER 16, 1773

THE BOSTON TEA PARTY SIGNALS OPEN RESISTANCE

Commercial ships in port

The period of calm, however, is brief.

In 1767, Townshend imposes a series of taxes on staples such as lead, paint, glass, paper, and tea.

Organized resistance materializes around Boston. Members of a "revolutionary body" known as the "Sons of Liberty" vow to oppose collection of the new duties by boycotting the imports. Shortages are offset by increases in local production and smuggling.

In 1768, Britain responds with a show of force by sending troops into Boston to ensure tax collection, and handing the bill for housing them to the colonists through the Quartering Act.

The result is a growing sense of betrayal among the colonists. Only five years earlier, they fought and died on behalf of the king in the war against France. In return comes the imposition of onerous taxes and armed enforcers.

Almost inevitably, anger turns into violence. On March 5, 1770, a mob of protesters at the custom house begin pelting British guards with stones. The redcoats fire into the crowd, killing five civilians and wounding seven. One victim, some say the first, is Crispus Attucks, a "mixed race mulatto," who is either a freedman or a run-away slave at the time of his death.

This event is christened "the Boston Massacre" and word of it spreads rapidly across the colonies.

Again, the British back off with Prime Minister Lord Frederick North rescinding the Townshend taxes on everything but tea.

This stand-off lasts until 1773 when a new Tea Act imposes restrictions on free trade—demanding that all sales of the commodity be funneled through British agents of the East India Company rather than local merchants.

Reaction comes quickly. On December 16, 1773, a Sons of Liberty band, poorly disguised as Mohawk Indians, climbs aboard British ships in the Boston Harbor and dumps 342 crates of tea into the water.

A British Redcoat

Britain reacts quickly to this "Boston Tea Party."

A series of punitive measures known as the "Coercive or Intolerable Acts" are mandated. The most severe measure closes the port of Boston, which effectively shuts down the economy in the city and threatens to starve the population. The order is to remain in place until the locals pay 15,000 pounds to cover the cost of the lost tea.

TIME: SEPTEMBER 5, 1774

THE FIRST CONTINENTAL CONGRESS CONVENES

Carpenters' Hall in Philadelphia, scene of the First Continental Congress

These "Intolerable Acts" further inflame colonial passions.

Sons of Liberty chapters begin to spread beyond New York, Massachusetts, Connecticut, and Pennsylvania, eventually reaching into all thirteen colonies. Meetings are held at "Liberty Trees" in town centers or local taverns, often led by local merchants like Sam Adams and John Hancock, those hit hardest by new taxes.

Newspapers and broadsides capture the growing antagonism toward Britain. In July 1774, Thomas Jefferson, a 34-year-old Virginia planter and burgess, publishes a pamphlet, *A Summary View of the Rights of British America*, laying his grievances against the crown and asserting that men have the right to govern themselves.

This is quickly followed by a First Continental Congress—a watershed moment for the colonists, and a precursor to the formation of a future independent national government.

It is held at the two-story Carpenters' Hall guild house in Philadelphia over a seven-week period beginning on September 5, 1774. Twelve of the thirteen colonies are present, with only Georgia missing.

Peyton Randolph, speaker of the House of Burgesses in Virginia, presides over the Congress, which comprises a total of 56 delegates, all elected by their local legislatures to speak for their colony's interest. Among those present are many of the men who will shape America's future.

SOME DELEGATES AT THE FIRST CONTINENTAL CONGRESS

REPRESENTING	TOTAL #	SOME MEMBERS
New York	9	John Jay Robert Livingston
Pennsylvania	8	Thomas Mifflin Joseph Galloway Thomas McKean Robert Morris
Virginia	7	George Washington Peyton Randolph Richard Henry Lee Patrick Henry
South Carolina	5	John Rutledge Christopher Gadsden
Maryland	5	Matthew Tilghman
New Jersey	5	William Livingston
Massachusetts	4	John Adams Samuel Adams
Connecticut	3	Roger Sherman
Delaware	3	George Read
North Carolina	3	Richard Caswell
Rhode Island	2	Stephen Hopkins
New Hampshire	2	John Sullivan

The central debate occurs between those like the Virginian, Patrick Henry, who favor a clean break with England, and opponents, such Joseph Galloway, a Loyalist from Pennsylvania, who will ultimately join the British army.

In the end, the majority agree to send a sharp message to the crown by imposing a boycott on all British imports to begin on December 1, 1774. This will not only reduce revenue flowing to Britain, but also signal the growing capacity of the colonies to manufacture the finished goods on their own.

On the question of actual independence, the Congress decides to take a wait-and-see stance for the moment, and then reconvene a second Congress on May 10, 1775 to revisit conditions at that time.

The Americans now look to Boston to see what happens next.

TIME: APRIL 19, 1775

THE SHOT HEARD ROUND THE WORLD

A new figure is now on the scene in Boston, Major General Thomas Gage—named on May 13, 1774, Governor of the Province of Massachusetts Bay—ready to impose martial law if need be.

Gage has been in America for almost twenty years, arriving to fight in the French & Indian Wars, rising to become commander in chief of all British forces, settling down with his family in New York City. He misses the Boston Tea Party while on leave in England, and returns with orders to quell the rebellion.

Over the next year, Gage tries to harness what he regards as the potentially dangerous impulse toward "democracy." Rather than resort directly to force, he makes several attempts to stabilize the situation by forming local councils to resolve conflicts. But these fail, and he becomes increasingly concerned about rumors that the Sons of Liberty are threatening violence against the crown.

Indeed, talk of open rebellion is now sweeping across the colonies.

Four weeks later, the inflammatory rhetoric turns into bloodshed.

On April 14, 1775, Gage orders his troops to march sixteen miles west to the town of Concord, arrest two rabble-rousers, John Hancock and Samuel Adams, and seize all weapons that might be used against the crown. Around 10 p.m. on the night of April 18, some 700 Infantry Regulars under Lt. Colonel Francis Smith depart Boston to carry out Gage's directive.

However, their plan to take the Americans by surprise is foiled by one Paul Revere, a Boston silversmith who doubles as an intelligence agent for the "Committee on Public Safety." Revere learns of the planned British route—by boat across to the Charleston peninsula—and signals advance warning by having two lanterns ("*one if by land and two if by sea*") hung in the bell tower of the Old North Episcopal Church. He then completes a midnight ride across the countryside to Lexington, awakening the minuteman militias along the way, before meeting up with Adams and Hancock to plan a defense.

Upon hearing Revere's news, they decide to make a stand against the British troops when they arrive.

The American forces gather at the village of Lexington, roughly ten miles west of Boston on the road to Concord. There, around 5 a.m., some 80 colonists exchange fire with British Regulars. After suffering eight men killed and ten others wounded, they are driven away.

The redcoats reassemble and march another six miles to the town square in Concord, which the local militia has abandoned in favor of higher ground to the west. When a unit of roughly 90 British Regulars cross over the Concord River at the North Bridge, they are attacked and overwhelmed by 400 militiamen storming down from the hills.

The colonists have won their first organized battle with the mighty British army!

> *By the rude bridge that arched the flood*
> *Their flag to April's breeze unfurled*
> *Here once the embattled farmers stood*
> *And fired the shot heard round the world.*

– "Concord Hymn" (1837),

Ralph Waldo Emerson

John Burns of Gettysburg (1793–1872)

The shocked and alarmed Lt. Colonel Smith decides to retreat from Concord around noon—but his movement is vexed by continuous harassment from the colonists, whose forces reach over 2,000 strong as the day wears on.

All that saves the redcoats is a rescue contingent of 1,000 men under Earl Percy that meets them around 2:30 p.m. in Lexington and opens cannon fire to momentarily stem the militia attacks. Still, the skirmishing continues back to Boston with the infuriated redcoats ransacking homes and stores along the way as retribution for their losses.

By nightfall, they are securely entrenched within the city, despite the remarkable assembly of some 15,000 armed militiamen who surround it by daybreak.

The battles at Lexington and Concord are no more than minor skirmishes when it comes to real warfare.

But April 19 casts yet another die against any hope for reconciliation with Britain.

TIME: MAY 2, 1775

AMERICANS SEIZE THE GOVERNOR'S PALACE IN VIRGINIA

The Colony of Virginia rivals Massachusetts as a center of discontent.

Since 1771, the Governor of the "Province" has been the Right Honorable John Murray, a Scotsman whose formal title is Lord Dunmore.

Dunmore's approach to governing Virginia lies in ignoring the local council, the House of Burgesses, and acting on his own agenda, which focuses on warfare against the

Shawnee Tribe for control over inland territory. His efforts deplete the Virginia militia and the financial coffers.

When Dunmore turns to the burgesses in 1773 for more men and money, it responds with a list of complaints about increased taxes in general and his administrative abuses in particular. After that, Dunmore dissolves the House of Burgesses in 1774.

This infuriates the Virginians, especially Patrick Henry, already known as the "Son of Thunder" for his fiery oratory. On March 23, 1775, Henry's speech to the Virginia Convention, a de facto House backup, ends with this stirring plea:

Is life so dear, or peace so sweet, as to be purchased at the price of chains and slavery?

Forbid it, Almighty God! I know not what course others may take; but as for me, give me liberty, or give me death!

Like General Gage in Boston, Dunmore also chooses to deprive rebel access to military supplies in April 1775. His focus is on gunpowder stored in the armory at Williamsburg. On April 20, he orders a small band of Royal Navy marines to transfer the gunpowder to their ship docked on James River. But when the fifteen barrels arrive, they are met by a contingent of local militia ordering they be returned, as property of the colony and not the king.

The stand-off boils over shortly. The rebels threaten to storm the Governor's Palace in Williamsburg. Dunmore announces his intent to impose martial law, free all slaves held by the rebels, and "reduce the city to ashes." As word of the April 19 battle at Concord spreads, more Virginia militiamen appear, eager to drive Dunmore and the British out of Williamsburg.

Two prominent Virginians, Peyton Randolph and George Washington, lobby for a peaceful resolution. But, on May 2, the 150-man Hanover County Militia, serving under Patrick Henry, march on the capital. They drive Dunmore and his family out of the palace and extract a £330 payment for the gunpowder from a wealthy Loyalist in town. This temporarily ends the conflict. Henry attends the Continental Congress and Dunmore boards the HMS Fowey, from which he will direct future attacks against the rebels before returning to England in 1776.

TIME: MAY 10, 1775

THE SECOND CONTINENTAL CONGRESS CONVENES

As the conflict mounts, the colonists must now figure out what to do next.

On May 10, 1775, they convene the Second Continental Congress in Philadelphia at the Pennsylvania State House, subsequently known as Independence Hall.

While many delegates are holdovers from the prior meeting eight months earlier,

some important new faces include John
Hancock from Massachusetts, who succeeds an ailing Peyton Randolph as President of the Congress. Ben Franklin, the
69-year-old writer, inventor, publisher,
and political operative from Pennsylvania
joins them, as does the youthful Thomas
Jefferson of the Virginia House of Burgesses.

The Loyalists in the chamber muster
enough support to block the "radical faction," who continue to call for an immediate
declaration of independence from Britain.

Still, after the April 19 bloodshed at Concord and the surrounding of Boston by
angry militiamen, all delegates recognize the importance of united decisions and actions.

The first priority is national defense, in case violence intensifies. The delegates agree
to form the Continental Army, funded by domestic and foreign borrowing, with each
state expected to contribute a fair share of money, men, and materials.

The Loyalists balance the military initiatives with what becomes known as the "Olive
Branch Petition," written by the intensely principled Quaker pacifist, John Dickinson of
Pennsylvania, whose 1768 plea calls for a unified front among the colonists:

Then join hand in hand, brave Americans all! By uniting we stand, by dividing we fall.

The petition criticizes Parliament (not King George) for onerous taxing policies, but
expresses hope for a peaceful resolution with America remaining in the British Empire.
This will be one of many back and forth entreaties on both sides of the dispute over time,
none of them healing the breach.

Once this Second Congress opens, it will function continuously until March 1, 1781,
an almost six-year period that sees 343 delegates cycling in and out of the meetings and
thirteen different men serving as president.

Despite the lack of formal legal authority to govern, the Second Continental Congress will muddle its way to the policies and procedures that determine the destiny of the
fragile new nation.

TIME: MAY 10, 1775

THE GREEN MOUNTAIN BOYS CAPTURE FT. TICONDEROGA

On the same day the Second Continental Congress convenes to map out a unified strategy, an independent band of New Hampshire militiamen known as the "Green

Mountain Boys" capture Ft. Ticonderoga, at the southern tip of Lake
Champlain, some 300 miles northwest of Boston.

The raid is led by two firebrands,
Ethan Allen, leader of the Boys, and
Benedict Arnold of Massachusetts,
who joins the initiative at the last
second.

The main goal is to prevent the

RUINS OF FORT TICONDEROGA.

A typical fortress guarding a river

British from using Ticonderoga as a staging area to mount an attack from behind against the American militiamen surrounding Boston. They also hope to capture the fort's weapons, and to encourage Canada to ally with the colonies in rebellion against the crown.

A force of 200 raiders approach the fort at daybreak on May 10, ready for action. The outcome, however, is comical rather than heroic.

Ft. Ticonderoga, so pivotal in the French & Indian Wars, has been left essentially unprotected by the British.

The raiders finally corral a sentry who announces the American's presence to the fort's commander who, in turn, surrenders his sword.

Unlike Concord, the rebels never fire a single shot to record their victory, one with strategic importance.

The colonists now control a critical stepping stone into Canada and the long-range French cannon and mortars they will use later on.

TIME: JUNE 17, 1775

THE BATTLE OF BUNKER HILL

Back in Boston, the battered redcoats have retreated from Concord to their city enclave where General Gage is tardily plotting his strategy. He has 6,500 troops at the moment, and a Royal Navy which controls sea lanes that almost totally envelop Boston. He faces more than twice that number of militiamen arrayed across the various land approaches to the city from the east and south.

When word of the Concord defeat reaches England, King George III ships off three top field generals to support, then replace Gage: the conspicuously courageous, but sometimes tardy Lord William Howe; Howe's second in command and personal adversary, Henry Clinton, who grew up in New York City; and finally, "Gentleman John" Burgoyne, aristocrat, playwright, rake, and military man, ambitious for glory.

On June 14, the Continental Congress counters by naming George Washington

Commander in Chief of the Continental Army. They give Washington 2 million continental dollars to fund an army, and order him to consult closely with Congress on all major operations. The new commander has served in the British army for seven years, demonstrating remarkable courage and leadership during the French & Indian Wars before resigning in 1759 at age twenty-seven. His life since then has been that of an English aristocrat, running a vast plantation in Virginia and mastering politics as a local burgess.

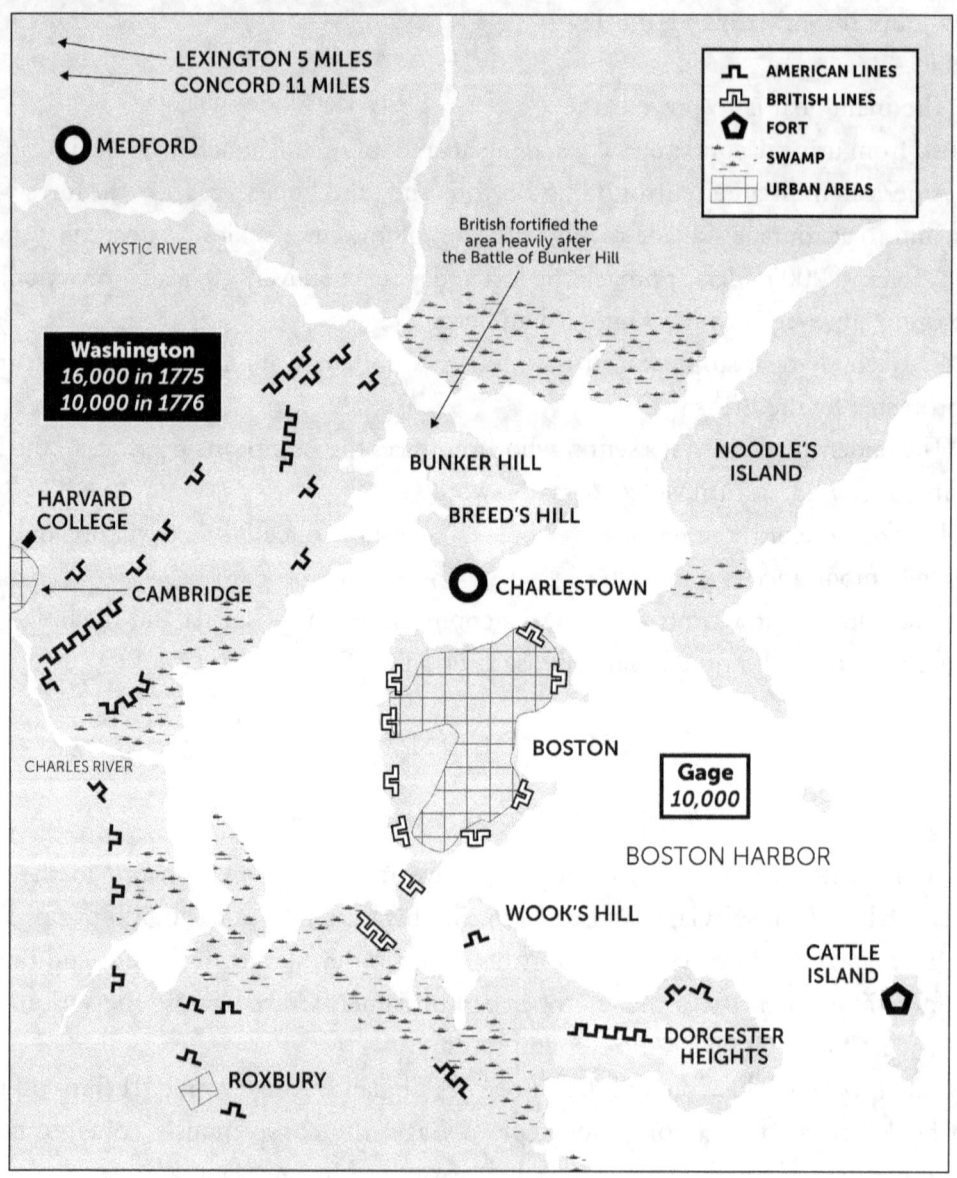

Gage's forces surrounded the city of Boston

His Continental Army is a motley crew, short on weapons, gunpowder, training, even uniforms—with its officers distinguished by colored ribbons pinned to their vests—

pink for brigadiers, purple for major generals, and blue for the commander in chief. In the beginning they enlist simply to "stand up for their basic rights as Englishmen." But soon enough, in response to the king's declaration that they are "traitors," they swing to the "Glorious Cause of America" and independence from the crown.

General George Washington
(1732–1799)

Washington arrives with two initiatives in mind: drive the British out of Boston by siege and out of Canada by striking at Quebec City. The key to the siege will lie in controlling the high ground encircling the city—Bunker and Breed's Hills to the north on the Charleston peninsula and the Dorchester Heights east of the "Boston neck."

On June 17, 1775, Washington moves in the north at the Battle of Bunker Hill that ends with the British controlling the field, but at a cost of over 1,000 casualties. Henceforth there will be no doubt in Howe's mind about the determination of the rebels.

TIME: AUGUST 23, 1775

GEORGE III VOWS TO QUASH THE REBELLION

The initial American move into Canada and the siege of Boston provoke a sharp response from Britain.

On August 23, 1775, King George declares that an *"open and avowed"* rebellion is under way in America and refuses to receive the so-called "Olive Branch Petition" offered by the Second Continental Congress.

In early October, Admiral Samuel Graves, overall commander of the British fleet in North America, orders Lt. Henry Mowat to conduct reprisal raids on colonial seaports associated with the rebellion.

Mowat assembles a five-ship fleet, heads out of Boston Harbor, and drops anchor about 115 miles up the coast at Falmouth Harbor. On October 18, he informs the townspeople that he intends to mete out punishment for their defiance of the crown, to commence in two hours. When the locals refuse to pledge allegiance to the king,

General Washington (1732–1799)

Mowat begins an eight-hour bombardment of the now abandoned city, followed by a landing party of marines instructed to burn everything left standing. In the end some 400 buildings and homes are destroyed.

The king then takes another signal step against the colonists on October 27, 1775 in a hardline speech delivered to the opening of Parliament. He states that the rebels have broken their vows of allegiance to the crown—in effect calling them traitors—and that he intends to use his own forces, as well as foreign alliances, to suppress the conspirators.

So much hope of some for an "Olive Branch" solution.

TIME: DECEMBER 30, 1775

AMERICANS RETREAT AFTER DEFEAT AT QUEBEC CITY

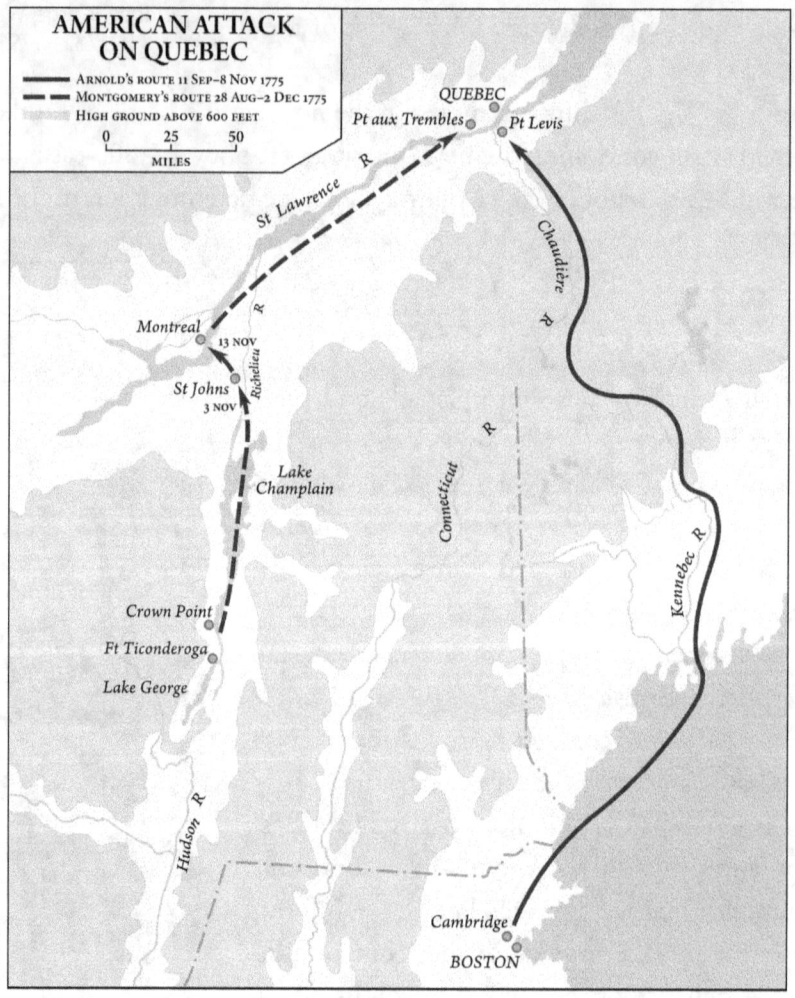

Soon after the June 1775 battle at Bunker Hill, Washington decides to go on the offensive and invade Canada.

The prize is the British citadel at Quebec City, scene of their famous victory over the French in 1759. The additional hope, which will prove futile, being that once the fighting begins the British settlers in Canada will join the rebel cause.

Overall command of the invasion is given to Major General Philip Schuyler, a member of the Second Continental Congress from New York, who previously fought for England in the French & Indian Wars.

Field command falls to General Richard Montgomery, who moves northeast up the St. Lawrence River, taking Ft. Ticonderoga on May 10, 1775 and Montreal on November 14.

He is joined there by a precocious nineteen-year-old, Aaron Burr, who interrupts his study of law to engage in frontline combat against Britain over the next four years. Montgomery immediately promotes Burr to the rank of captain, and selects him as his aide-de-camp.

On December 2, these two join up below Quebec with Benedict Arnold, who has slogged his way overland from the southeast. Between them, they have 900 men to throw against the 1,000 British troops under Major General Guy Carleton, recently appointed to defend the stronghold.

On the snowy night of December 30, 1775, the Americans begin to move against Quebec City, with Arnold's 600 men advancing on the right toward the Palace Gate and Montgomery's 300 men coming up on the left, across the Plains of Abraham.

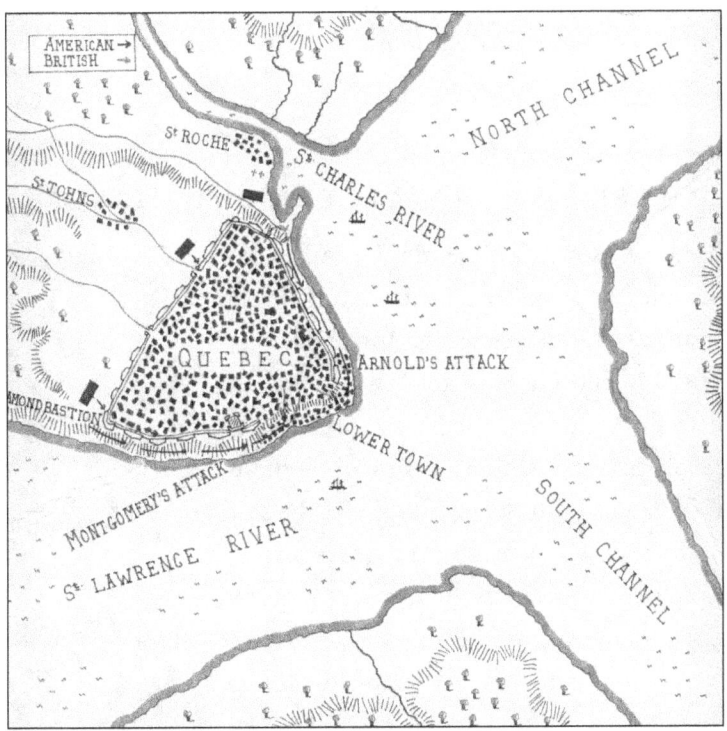

Montgomery and Arnold attack Quebec City

But the American assault fails. Arnold is shot in the ankle and turns command over to Brigadier Daniel Morgan. Montgomery is killed by the first English volley, and Burr, along with his disheartened troops, turns back. By dawn on New Year's Eve, Carleton retains control of the city, with casualties of only eighteen men against 60 killed or wounded Americans and 426 others captured.

A lackluster siege of the city follows, but the American momentum has run its course—and the British soon begin their roll-back of America's incursion into Canada.

Naval control around Quebec brings Carleton reinforcements—7,000 Regulars and 3,000 German mercenaries—bringing his muster up to 11,000 men. Over the next ten months he throws them against an expanded force of 6,000 retreating Americans under Schuyler and General Horatio Gates, who succeeds the dead Montgomery.

Back come the rebels, exiting Montreal in June 1776, with even the belligerent Arnold voicing his dismay.

> *The junction (with) Canada is now at an end. Let us quit (here) and secure our*
> *own country before it is too late.*

But the English chase him, sailing another 75 miles down Lake Champlain to a victory on October 11, at Valcour Island, over a ramshackle "fleet" of mostly flat-bottomed, single-masted, three-gun boats scrounged up by Arnold.

Both sides now pause for the winter, with Carleton back north at St. John's Island and Schuyler, Gates, and Arnold returning south to their final stronghold at Ft. Ticonderoga.

TIME: MARCH 17, 1776

THE BRITISH ARE FORCED OUT OF BOSTON

After the Battle of Bunker Hill, a nine-month period of essential stalemate sets in around Boston. Washington lacks the long-range cannon needed to threaten Gage's troops in the city—while Gage is able to resupply his force from British ships entering the harbor unmolested.

Washington's focus now shifts south, to Dorchester Heights, which threatens both the city itself and the shipping lanes. But to succeed, Washington needs artillery with two-mile range, and obtaining them will require a minor miracle.

The miracle is performed by 25-year-old Colonel Henry Knox.

His feat lies in transporting 54 heavyweight mortars

Bunker Hill Monument, Boston

and cannon from the captured Ft. Ticonderoga 300 miles down Lake George and overland across the Berkshire Mountains to Boston. The task is one of brute force, made doubly difficult by severe snow, ice, and bitter cold. On January 27, after a seven-week trek, Knox and his guns reach Boston.

Once they arrive, Washington throws all his resources into constructing a surprise redoubt and battery on Dorchester Heights. His engineers work secretly and silently throughout the night of March 4. When the British in Boston wake the next day, they see the guns of Ft. Ticonderoga pointed their way.

Washington now hopes that Howe will come out to attack him, but with Howe's fleet vulnerable to the shore batteries, evacuation becomes the only option. On March 8, Howe signals Washington that he will not burn Boston if he is allowed to leave unmolested. Washington accedes, and on March 17, 120 craft carry 8,900 troops and just over 2,000 women, children, and Loyalists out to sea, headed for Halifax, Nova Scotia.

Boston is now back in the hands of the rebels.

TIME: JULY 4, 1776

THE SECOND CONTINENTAL CONGRESS DECLARES AMERICAN INDEPENDENCE

Signing the Declaration of Independence

The summer of 1776 marks fifteen months since the outbreak of fighting at Concord—fifteen months in which the colonies have governed themselves and roughly held their own in battle against the British Regulars.

Driven by these tailwinds, the "radicals" at the Second Continental Congress in Philadelphia are ready to force the issue of a final break with the crown.

The move is reinforced by a widely circulated pamphlet titled *Common Sense*, written by Thomas Paine, formerly a disgruntled tax collector in Britain.

Paine emigrates to Philadelphia in 1774 on the advice of Ben Franklin, with whom he shares a penchant for science, invention, and journalism. He becomes editor of the *Pennsylvania Magazine* and soon takes up the cause of the American rebellion. Paine is a visionary, and his stirring rhetoric touches the colonists.

We have it in our power to begin the world over again.

On June 7, 1776, Virginian Richard Henry Lee, who works hand in glove over time with John Adams of Massachusetts, offers a resolution to that effect.

Resolved: That these United Colonies are, and of right ought to be, free and independent States, that they are absolved from all allegiance to the British Crown, and that all political connection between them and the State of Great Britain is, and ought to be, totally dissolved.

Seven states immediately support Lee's resolution, but six others waver, which leads to a three-week hiatus as delegates return home for further local debate.

Thomas Paine
(1737–1809)

In the interim, the remaining delegates set up a series of "writing committees" to draft documents directed at gaining credibility and worldwide acceptance for a new nation.

First and foremost is a Declaration of Independence, assigned to a Committee of Five, including John Adams, Roger Sherman, Robert Livingston, Ben Franklin, and Thomas Jefferson, who pens a first draft.

The tone is restrained and appropriately respectful for an audience including the world's hereditary monarchs—George III in England, Louis XVI in France, Charles III in Spain, and Frederick II in Prussia—all of whom will be threatened by the content.

It begins with a statement of overall purpose—to explain why America is breaking away from the crown.

When in the course of human events, it becomes

Thomas Jefferson (1743–1826)

necessary for one people to dissolve the political bonds which have connected them with another, and to assume...the separate station to which the laws of nature entitle them, a decent respect to the opinions of mankind requires that they should declare the causes...of the separation.

From there, it sets out a series of beliefs about the nature of man and of government. These beliefs ring out with bold Enlightenment assertions. That all men are born free, and that natural law endows each with an equal right to seek happiness. That the role of government is to support this quest. That the form of government is up to the will of the people and that they may change it any time it fails to meet their needs.

We hold these truths to be self-evident, that all men are created equal, that they are endowed by their Creator with certain unalienable Rights, that among these are Life, Liberty, and the pursuit of Happiness.

That to secure these rights, governments are instituted among men, deriving their just powers from the consent of the governed. That whenever any form of government becomes destructive of these ends, it is the right of the people to alter and abolish it, and to institute new government laying its foundation on principles...most likely to effect their safety and happiness.

The declaration then moves into a bill of particulars, in effect a formal indictment of the ways in which the king and the British government in the colonies have jeopardized the well-being of the citizenry. The list includes 27 separate counts, among them refusal to pass necessary statutes, obstruction of justice, imposition of taxes without consent, maintaining a standing army in times of peace, arbitrarily suspending local legislatures, cutting off trade with countries abroad, abolishing charters, imposing martial law, and "plundering our seas, ravaging our coasts, burning our towns, and destroying the lives of our people."

All attempts at redress have failed, leading on to a conclusion:

A Prince whose character is thus marked by every act which may define a tyrant is unfit to be the ruler of a free people... We, therefore, the representatives of the united States of America...declare that...these United Colonies...are free and independent States...absolved from all allegiances to the British Crown.

And for the support of this Declaration, with a firm reliance on the protection of divine Providence, we mutually pledge to each other our lives, our fortunes and our sacred honor.

The document runs to only 1,337 words, and Jefferson's original draft has been heavily edited by delegates, including the memorable opening sentence.

JEFFERSON'S ORIGINAL	FINAL RESOLUTION
We hold these truths to be sacred and undeniable that all men are created equal & independent, that from that equal creation they derive rights, inherent & unalienable, that among which are the preservation of life & liberty and the pursuit of happiness.	We hold these truths to be self-evident that all men are created equal, that they are endowed by their creator with certain unalienable rights, that among these are life, liberty and the pursuit of happiness.

With a final declaration in hand, on July 2, a second vote is taken on the Lee resolution with Pennsylvania and New York still hanging in the balance. When both vote "aye," the motion passes, and the break with Britain becomes official.

Two days later, on July 4, delegates sign the formal Declaration of Independence and the new nation is born.

Once this declaration is made public, Franklin tells his colleagues, *"...now we must, indeed, all hang together, or most assuredly we shall all hang separately."*

SIDEBAR: A GLARING DELETION REGARDING SLAVERY

Headquarters of Price & Birch, slave dealers of Alexandria, VA

Amidst the back and forth editing that goes into the final declaration, one other change in Jefferson's original draft will come back to haunt the conscience of the new nation through the ages.

It occurs in the original list of "indictments" against King George—the charge being that he has been responsible for introducing and sustaining slavery in the colonies.

> *He has waged cruel war against human nature itself, violating its most sacred rights of life and liberty in the persons of a distant people who never offended him, captivating and carrying them into* **slavery** *in another hemisphere, or to incur miserable death in their transportation thither.*

> *This piratical warfare, the opprobrium of infidel powers, is the warfare of the Christian King, determined to keep open a market where men should be bought & sold.*

> *He has…suppressed every legislative attempt to prohibit or restrain this execrable commerce.*

> *He is now exciting those very people to rise in arms among us, and to purchase the liberty of which he has deprived them by murdering the people upon whom he also obtruded them; thus paying former crimes committed against the liberties of one people, with crimes which he urges them to commit against the lives of another.*

Jefferson's language here is unequivocal.

Slavery is a "crime" committed upon "men" which "violates their sacred rights to life and liberty"—it is an "execrable commerce" which the colonists have tried to "prohibit or restrain."

The irony is not lost that Jefferson himself is a lifetime slave owner, as are very many of the leaders of the Second Continental Congress.

One can never know what internal debates took place in Jefferson's mind as he wrote these words—nor in the minds of the delegates who had to consider them.

But the fact remains that the final declaration deleted this paragraph on slavery in its entirety.

Perhaps in seeking to indict the king over slavery, too many attendees felt they were indicting themselves.

TIME: JULY 12, 1776

WORK BEGINS ON THE ARTICLES OF CONFEDERATION

Along with the declaration, a separate group of delegates, the Committee of Thirteen, begins work on how a "government of and for the people" will operate in practice. This committee is chaired by John Dickinson, who authored the Olive Branch Petition a year earlier.

From the beginning the committee and the delegates as a whole are divided over one central issue: the proper size and power of the central government. The two sides become known as Federalists and Anti-Federalists, and each is well represented in the Congress.

James Madison (1751–1836)

PROMINENT DIVISIONS OVER FEDERALISM

"FEDERALISTS"	"ANTI-FEDERALISTS"
John Adams	Sam Adams
Alexander Hamilton	George Clinton
John Jay	Christopher Gadsden
Thomas McKean	Eldridge Gerry
James Madison	John Hancock
Robert Morris	Benjamin Harrison
George Read	Patrick Henry
John Rutledge	Thomas Jefferson
Roger Sherman	Richard Henry Lee
George Washington	George Mason

The "Federalist" faction argues that a strong central government is needed to create a sense of unity throughout the country, and to act with one purpose in foreign affairs—especially during the current war with Britain.

The "Anti-Federalists" feel that a powerful center compromises the essence of what the rebellion is all about—enabling the common men to decide what government actions best suit their needs at the local level. In turn they argue that a strong center will end up like a monarchy—with a distant aristocracy of elites, focused on their own agenda, spending and taxing at will, overruling the wishes of individual states and local citizens.

This debate, however, is far too complex and potentially divisive to resolve in the middle of a war for survival, so the delegates put it off for the moment. Instead, the committee comes forward on July 12 with thirteen Articles of Confederation, summed up as follows:

1. *The new nation will be referred to as The United States of America.*

2. *Each state will retain control of governing itself, except where specific powers are ceded to the federal level.*

3. *The whole will act together to insure their common defense, secure liberties, support general welfare.*

4. *Citizens will be free to cross state lines and enjoy fair treatment; criminals will be extradited back home.*

5. *Each state will have one vote in a Congress of the Confederation, and 2-7 delegates chosen by the legislature.*

6. *The central government alone conducts foreign policy, declares war, and establishes commercial treaties.*

7. *State militias will be maintained with officers named by the legislature and called out for common defense.*

8. *Central government funding will come from the states, apportioned on assessed real property values.*

9. *Congress declares war, approves treaties, names diplomats, resolves interstate disputes, defines coinage.*

10. *A quorum of nine of the thirteen states is required for Congress to take action.*

11. *If Canada decides to join the Confederation, it will be admitted.*

12. *The Confederation is accountable for paying war debts accumulated before its existence.*

13. *The above articles are perpetual and can be changed only if Congress approves and the states then ratify.*

Aside from failing to resolve the broad philosophical issue of federalism, a host of other shortcomings related to the articles will become apparent over time. Rules affecting international commerce have not been spelled out. Plans to set and collect taxes remain iffy, and the government is perpetually underfunded. Perhaps most critical in the short run, the center is given little control over individual states when it comes to supplying troops, funds and materials to prosecute the war.

The entire document defining the thirteen articles runs to only five pages, and begs for greater detail on every point. Final ratification will drag on. Ten states ratify the articles within two years; the last state to approve, Maryland, doesn't do so until February 1781, almost five years later.

Still the articles, while not "official," will provide the framework for governing the new nation forward from July, 1776.

They must do for now. Time for talking is up; time for intensified fighting is on the way

## 7

THE REVOLUTIONARY WAR

TIME: AUGUST TO NOVEMBER 1776

WASHINGTON ALMOST LOSES HIS ARMY ON MANHATTAN ISLAND

Washington and his Revolutionary War generals

In June of 1776, while Benedict Arnold flees Montreal, the British signal their absolute determination to put down the colonies' rebellion by off-loading some 32,000 imported troops on Staten Island, eight miles below the southern tip of Manhattan.

From this moment on, Washington's garrison of 28,000 men around Ft. George is in dire jeopardy, absent a naval force to protect either flank of his island salient. His second-in-command, Major General Charles Lee, a professional soldier, sees this immediately:

Whoever commands the sea, must command the town.

But Washington rejects Lee's assessment, with encouragement from a Congress that just declared independence and is loath to have it commence with the loss of New York.

Howe recognizes that the fortifications on Long Island are crucial to the American defense, since they dominate both the Hudson and East Rivers surrounding Manhattan. If he can take Brooklyn Heights, he'll transport troops up both rivers, send them inland to link up in a defensive chain, and defeat Washington's entire army before it can escape to the north.

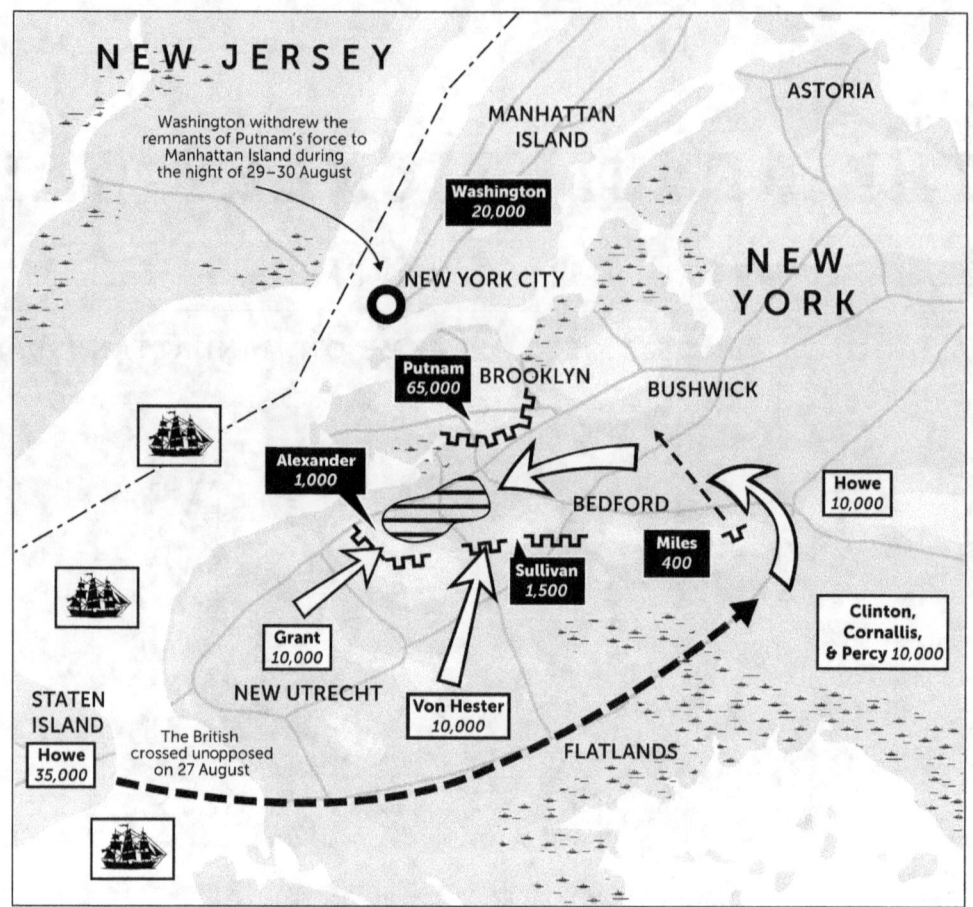

Howe takes Brooklyn Heights and moves on Manhattan

On August 22, the British land on Long Island and move toward Brooklyn. The astute general Clinton leads a flanking movement which routs the American right flank on August 27, in the first truly sizable battle of the war. But Howe pauses just long enough to allow Washington to execute a risky nighttime evacuation, ferrying 9,500 troops across the East River from Brooklyn to Ft. George. Despite this success, the Long Island battle has cost him 1,012 casualties.

But Washington moves from one trap to another in New York City. Once again, it is only Howe's slow pursuit that allows the Continental Army to survive. Much to Clinton's chagrin, Howe waits until September 15 to move across the river and force Washington to abandon the city.

Captain Aaron Burr engineers the escape plan, which saves both Washington and his aide, Alexander Hamilton. But when he fails to receive a promotion for this action, Burr never quite forgives these two superiors.

Howe gives chase, but on September 16, Washington survives a crucial stand-up battle nine miles north at Harlem Heights, which provides another momentary respite.

Still Congress refuses to entirely surrender New York, and Washington makes another tactical mistake to try to save it. He divides his army in two, with his main body of 16,000 troops scurrying north another ten miles to White Plains, and the rest staying behind to hold two Hudson River forts. Colonel Robert Magaw and his 2,800 men are left to defend Ft. Washington on the east bank of the Hudson and 3,500 men under General Nathanael Greene are assigned to hold Ft. Lee on the west bank, in New Jersey.

One other man left behind is 21-year-old Captain Nathan Hale, assigned to spy on Howe's army.

The British quickly apprehend Hale, accuse him of planning to torch the city, and hang him on September 21. His last words from the gallows, however, endure.

The Hanging of Nathan Hale (1755–1776)

I only regret that I have but one life to give for my country.

On October 28, Howe catches up with Washington at White Plains and a pitched battle along the Bronx River ends with the Americans holding their own, but then abandoning the field for another retreat fifteen more miles north to Peekskill.

Instead of chasing Washington's main army further, Howe turns back south to make him pay for dividing his army by destroying it in detail.

On November 16, Howe attacks the two undermanned Hudson River forts. Magaw and his 2,800 men capitulate, and Greene just manages to escape west to Hackensack. The battle for New York is over, with 4,000 Americans lost along the way. From start to finish it has been an unmitigated disaster for the Americans.

TIME: DECEMBER 25, 1776

WASHINGTON CROSSES THE DELAWARE FOR A MUCH-NEEDED VICTORY AT TRENTON

With the winter of 1776 approaching, Washington senses that the morale of his army and his nation are rapidly dwindling after the loss of New York. The time has come for bold strokes. Two upcoming battles—at Trenton, New Jersey and Saratoga, New York—will begin to swing the war's momentum.

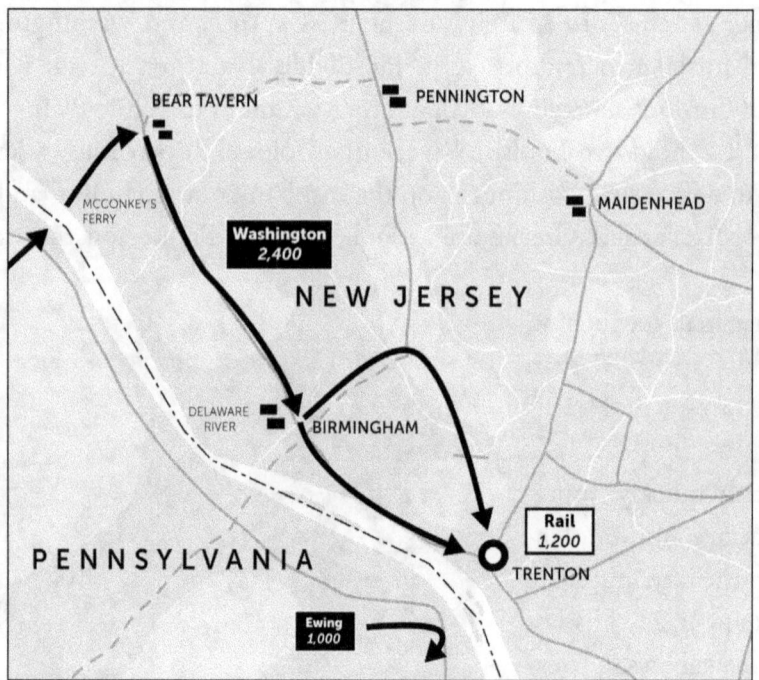

Washington crosses the Delaware and wins at Trenton

Once Washington realizes that Howe is no longer chasing him toward Peekskill, he swings his 5,000 troops west across the Hudson and then all the way south through Hackensack, Newark, Princeton, and over the Delaware River, just below Trenton. By December 8 his weary forces are camped there, facing a superior British army of 10,000 troops under Major General Charles Cornwallis across the river. The outlook here is ominous, until Howe decides to end the campaign for the winter. Instead of attacking Washington, Cornwallis decamps Trenton, leaving behind a small force of Hessians.

At this moment, Washington does the totally unexpected.

On Christmas Day, he decides to hurl his entire army across the Delaware against the Hessian rearguard. Washington's plan to make two feints downstream is foiled by icy river conditions, but he himself leads some 2,400 men to an upriver ferry and follows up with a devastating surprise attack on the Hessian's right flank. The result is a rout. The Hessian commander, Colonel Johann Rall, is killed, and 918 troops are forced to surrender.

Washington continues with another victory at Princeton on January 2, 1777, then decides to rest his fought-out troops and prepare for the spring.

TIME: OCTOBER 10, 1777

AMERICA'S VICTORY OVER BURGOYNE AT SARATOGA
STUNS THE WORLD

As both sides pause, it's clear the British have become frustrated by the failure to end the rebellion in 1776 and the mounting costs associated with their efforts. General Carleton's efforts in Canada are questioned by the crown, and his northern army command is handed over to Major General John Burgoyne—who lays out a bold plan to sail down Lake Champlain, take Ft. Ticonderoga, and then move over-land to assault Albany—thus cutting off New England from the other colonies.

On June 13, 1777, Burgoyne moves from Montreal to Lake Champlain, and sets sail with a force of 4,000 Regulars, 3,000 Hessians, and 1,000 tribesmen. On July 5, he wins a major victory by forcing General Arthur St. Clair and his 2,500 troops to abandon Ft. Ticonderoga. Ten weeks of hard overland marching and skirmishing follow, bringing him to the town of Saratoga, 35 miles north of his objective, Albany.

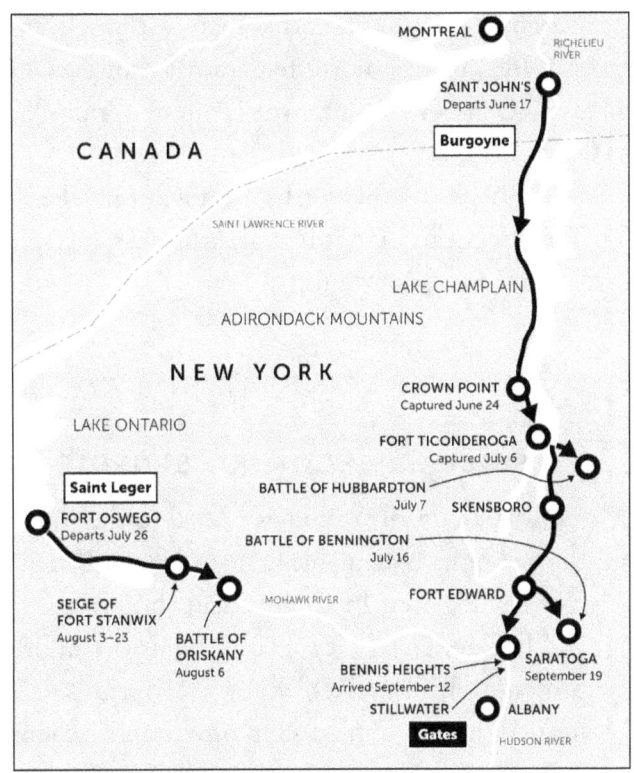

Burgoyne's roadmap to taking Albany

Waiting for him there is General Horatio Gates, named on August 19 to replace Schuyler, who has arrayed his 7,000 troops in a strong defensive position at Bemis Heights, south of town, along the west bank of the Hudson River.

Burgoyne decides to attack the American's left flank, and finally moves out on September 19. But his path west takes him into a series of dense woods that first confuse and hinder the British and by mid-morning they enter a pitched battle at Freeman's Farm, an outpost commanded by Benedict Arnold, well north of Gates' main position. After inflicting 600 casualties, Arnold signals Gates that he will bag the entire British force if given reinforcements. The more cautious Gates declines the request, and Burgoyne's demoralized troops retreat to lick their wounds for the day.

At this point, Burgoyne is growing desperate for a victory. He constructs two redoubts around the Freeman Farm ground and on October 7 attempts to move south from there toward Gates. But again, General Arnold turns him back, before falling with a grievous wound to his leg.

Burgoyne loses another 600 men, without even approaching the Bemis Heights position. When he flees north to Saratoga, however, Gates comes after him with his entire force. By October 10, Burgoyne is out of options, and he surrenders his remaining army to Gates.

This British capitulation at Saratoga stuns the world!

The Americans' Continental Army has just proven that it can go toe to toe with Britain and come out on top

TIME: 1776–1781

SIDEBAR: BECOMING BENEDICT ARNOLD (1741–1801)

One of the great ironies related to the American victory at Saratoga involves the fate of its undeniable hero—General Benedict Arnold.

Arnold, born in Connecticut, builds a successful business as a pharmacist and book seller in New Haven, joins the militia, and later the Sons of Liberty, protesting British taxes. When the war begins, Arnold is a captain in the Connecticut militia. But he soon proves an excellent military strategist and leader of men in the field, famous on both counts for his aggressiveness.

His two most famous battles—at Quebec City in December 1776 and Saratoga in October 1777—end with crippling gunshot wounds to his left leg. Medical attempts at reconstruction leave it two inches shorter than his right leg, resulting in a permanent limp.

Had this second wound at Saratoga been fatal, Benedict Arnold would be regarded today as a military legend. But that was not to be his destiny.

Instead, his path leads on to bitterness and betrayal.

In June 1778, Washington appoints him military commander of Philadelphia, the nation's capital city. But Arnold becomes gradually dismayed by America's prospects in the war. He marries into a family with Loyalist sympathies and makes a series of investments in the city that are seen by some as taking advantage of his position for personal gains. Arnold is outraged by the criticism:

Having become a cripple in the service of my country,
I little expected to meet ungrateful returns.

As his disillusionment grows, he opens a secret channel of communication with Sir Henry Clinton, overall commander of British forces in America from 1778–82. His efforts are supported by his wife and by William Franklin, illegitimate son of Ben Franklin, who is a lifelong supporter of the crown.

Further inquiries into his personal conduct lead to a rebuke from his long-time supporter, George Washington, and a monetary fine for mishandling finances. This tips Arnold over to the British side and marks the beginning of treasonous disclosures about American military operations.

After resigning his post in Philadelphia, he is given command over West Point, a bastion on the Hudson that Clinton plans to attack. On August 15, 1778, Clinton offers Arnold 20,000 pounds to weaken the defenses at West Point and support a British attempt to capture it. Arnold accepts the offer on August 30, and the two begin plotting through coded messages delivered by couriers.

On September 23, one of these couriers is arrested by militiamen and the Arnold-Clinton plot is revealed to Washington. However, Arnold manages to escape, joining British forces in Virginia as a brigadier general, and later leading successful attacks on Richmond and around New York.

In December 1781, Arnold and his wife, granted safe passage despite her role in the plots, leave America for London—and another decade of life as a British military advisor, politician, businessman, and adventurer, before dying at the age of 60.

But the name Benedict Arnold will ring down through the ages in American lore not as the hero of Saratoga as he was, but as the turncoat and traitor he became.

TIME: SEPTEMBER 26, 1777

THE BRITISH TAKE THE AMERICAN CAPITAL OF PHILADELPHIA

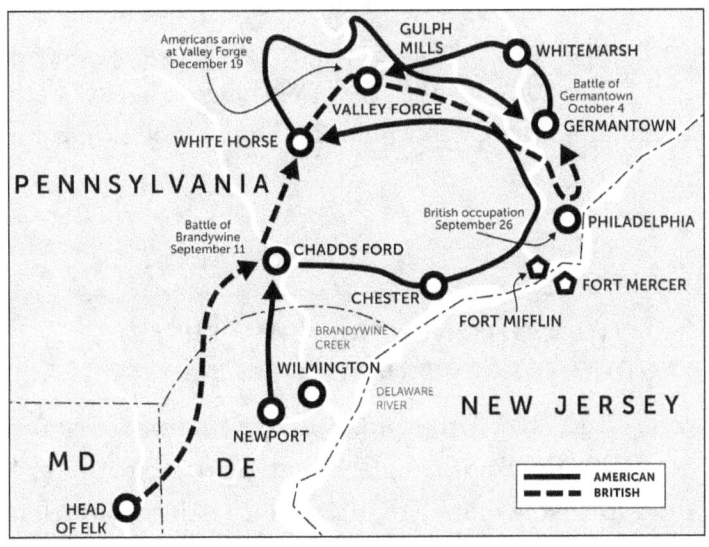

Howe takes Philadelphia and Washington retreats to Valley Forge

While Burgoyne moves south in Canada, on July 13, General William Howe loads 13,000 troops onto 260 ships and exits New York, intent on capturing the American capital of Philadelphia.

He plans to embark in Delaware Bay, but is warned off and diverts to Chesapeake Bay, where he finally lands on August 25. From there, he begins to march north through Newark and toward Philadelphia.

Washington decides to cut him off along Brandywine Creek 25 miles southwest of the city, along Brandywine Creek where he entrenches.

The two armies, both numbering around 11,000 men, meet on September 11 in a battle that is a mirror image of the British win on Long Island.

Once again Howe outmaneuvers Washington, feinting at his center and executing a flanking movement which leaves the right wing of the American army vulnerable to a crushing blow.

Then Howe characteristically pauses, this time just long enough to allow Major General John Sullivan to realign his men to face the assault head on rather than from their flank. This shift doesn't prevent a victory for Howe at Brandywine, but it does allow Washington to escape east once again, after suffering roughly 1,000 casualties.

Hearing of the defeat, the Continental Congress decides to vacate the capital on September 19 in favor of greater safety at York.

This move proves wise when Howe overruns American forces under "Mad" Anthony Wayne at Paoli on September 20, then crosses the Schuylkill River near Valley Forge, putting his army between Washington and Philadelphia.

On September 26, Howe marches triumphantly into the American capital.

Fighting around Philadelphia continues into the winter as Washington tries to siege the British from two forts that command the Delaware river. But Howe eventually weakens both in mid-November.

Between August 1776 and September 1777, Washington has lost both New York and Philadelphia to Howe. It is indeed a low point for him as he goes into winter quarters at Valley Forge.

TIME: WINTER 1777

THE CONTINENTAL ARMY SUFFERS
AND IS TRANSFORMED AT VALLEY FORGE

The winter of 1777 at Valley Forge proves to be a test of America's willingness and ability to fight on against the British, and of Washington's capacity to lead. As overall commander of the army, he is roundly criticized for "losing Philadelphia," and he responds with defiance.

Whenever the public gets dissatisfied with my service...I shall quit the helm and retire to a private life.

His sense of despair, however, continues to mount. He wonders how men can survive, much less fight, when upwards of two-thirds face a winter without shoes for their feet?

Unless some great and capital change suddenly takes place...this Army must inevitably starve, dissolve, or disperse, in order to obtain subsistence in the best manner they can.

This is almost the case, as 2,500 men perish from malnutrition, poor sanitation, and disease over the next five months.

But Washington and his men at Valley Forge are eventually saved by two things: renewed financial support from Congress and the arrival of one Baron Friedrich von Steuben on the scene.

Washington and his key generals, among them are Henry Knox, Charles Lee, and Nathanael Greene.

Von Steuben is 48 years old and out of work as a staff officer in the Prussian Army under Frederick the Great when he encounters Benjamin Franklin in Paris and inquiries about service in the American army. He is hired and sent to Valley Forge, arriving late in the winter.

Once there, he introduces the military training and iron-willed discipline characteristic of the Prussian forces.

He begins by selecting the best 100 soldiers he finds to form a "model company," then runs them over and over through basic drills:

- The eight steps/fifteen motions required to fire the standard 5'6" long flintlock musket with accuracy and with maximum speed.
- Marching formations and adjustments to maintain line integrity, respond to enemy maneuvers, and foster courage.
- The basics of camp sanitation and diet to sharply reduce illness such as dysentery and cholera.

All of this is accomplished to bursts of profanity in German aimed at slow learners. Once this "model company" takes shape, von Steuben then distributes his "graduates" among other units to clone the progress.

By late spring his results are self-evident. Washington's rag-tag force now takes on a professional look and feel, and von Steuben is named Inspector-General for the Continental Army.

TIME: FEBRUARY 6, 1778

FRANCE JOINS THE WAR ON THE SIDE OF AMERICA

While Washington struggles at Valley Forge, word of the major American victory at Saratoga reaches Europe in December, and prompts the French government under Louis XVI to re-think its stance on allying with the colonists.

France is still smarting in 1776 from its losses to Britain in the Seven Years War (1756–63), including the bitter defeats driving them out of Canada. So, they are inclined to seek revenge.

America recognizes this historical animosity and tries to leverage it from the start of the war. John Adams drafts a series of possible treaties with the French, and Benjamin Franklin tries repeatedly to sell them in Paris.

Benjamin Franklin (1706–1790)

But the French balk. They do not wish to align with a losing partner and that is exactly what the Americans look like after Washington barely escapes from Howe in New York in August 1776.

This leads to a wait-and-see attitude that prevails in France all the way to December 1777 when Gates and Burr rout Burgoyne at Saratoga.

From that moment on, diplomatic action moves along quickly, the culmination coming on February 6, 1778 at Hotel De Crillon in Paris, where two agreements are signed:

- A Treaty of Alliance, in effect a mutual defense pact, whereby the two sides agreed to take military action in response to any future attacks on either by Britain.
- A Treaty of Amity and Commerce, which confers "most favored nation" status on the two countries, for the purpose of carrying on trade. Included here is promised protection by the French navy of American ships on the high sea.

This recognition by France immediately confers global legitimacy on the Americans, in addition to materially strengthening their military resources, especially in confronting the Royal Navy.

It also greatly ups the financial ante on the British to continue the fight.

When the French ambassador informs England of the two treaties, the response is predictable and fast. On March 17, 1778, Britain declares war on France.

TIME: JUNE 28, 1778

DRAWN BATTLE OF MONMOUTH ENDS
INFANTRY COMBAT IN THE NORTH

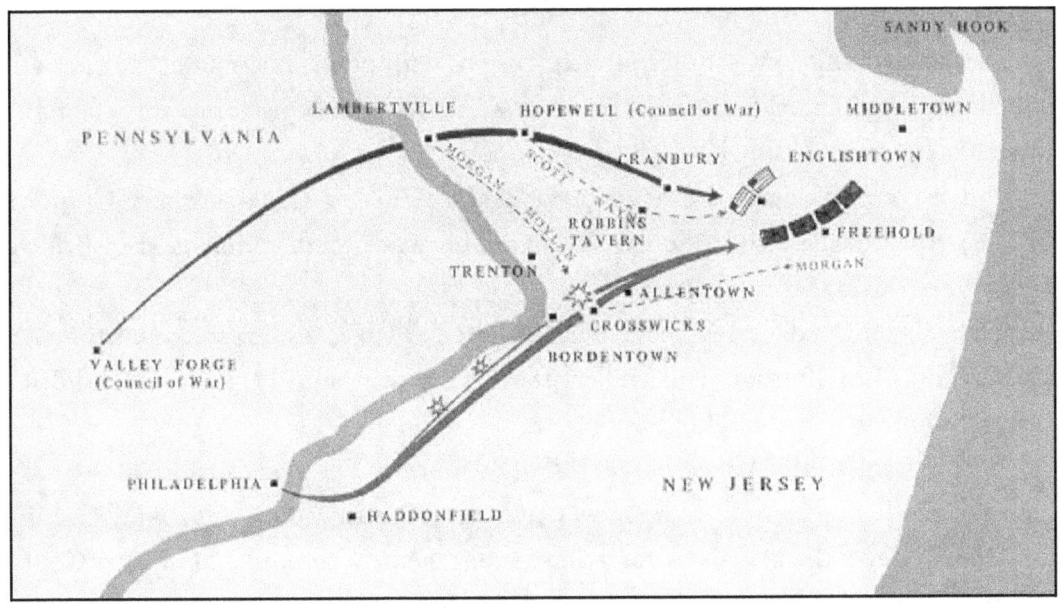

Clinton Heads from Philadelphia toward Manhattan and Washington follows

The French are not the only ones impressed by the American victory at Saratoga.

Three years have now passed since the April 1775 skirmish at Lexington, and British Prime Minister Lord Frederick North comes under increasing pressure from the Opposition Party in Parliament.

The Opposition has three complaints. The first is North's failure to put down the American rebellion. The second is the alarming cost of the war (some 12 million pounds per year) and the tax increases required to pursue it further. And the third is the new global threats associated with France's intervention, especially to the lucrative sugar producing islands in the British West Indies (Jamaica, Barbados, and Grenada).

In response, Britain begins to back off from its determination to crush the colonists.

The first signal of this occurs in June 1778, when King George III sends a delegation to America headed by Frederick Howard, the Earl of Carlisle, to offer terms by which the colonies would remain under British rule but with representation in Parliament and much greater control over their own affairs. The Continental Congress rejects the Carlisle Commission proposals, demanding full independence instead.

The second signal involves changes in military strategy.

Instead of concentrating its forces against the more openly rebellious northern colonies, the decision is made to focus on the South—where public support for the crown is thought to be more widespread and intense.

If Britain can convince Loyalists in the region to fight on their behalf, a faster and cheaper end to the rebellion might materialize.

Execution of this new southern strategy begins with publicity announcing the Carlisle Commission and Britain's willingness to welcome the colonists back into the fold, with greater self-autonomy.

This is coupled with the evacuation of Philadelphia by General Henry Clinton, who has replaced the retired General William Howe as overall commander of British forces.

General Clinton departs Philadelphia on June 18, 1778, hoping for an untroubled transfer of his 11,000 troops and artillery trains northeast toward Manhattan and Britain's last impregnable stronghold in the North.

Washington, still at Valley Forge, responds quickly. He sends small bands of local militia to harass Clinton as he moves across the Pennsylvania countryside and up into New Jersey—then prepares for a general engagement around Monmouth Court House, about 40 miles below the southern tip of Staten Island, New York.

One of Washington's generals, Charles Lee, balks at the notion of risking another major battle, when it appears the British may be in the process of giving up. But Washington will have none of that. His confidence in the Continental Army is high and a win over Clinton before he reaches the safe haven of New York City could prove decisive.

On the morning of June 28, the reluctant Lee and his 5,000 troops approach the British rearguard under the able Cornwallis, just north of Monmouth. Lee fights for several hours, but his battle plan lacks cogency and he is eventually forced to retreat.

Washington is apoplectic when he learns of Lee's defeat and subsequently sacks him. But the battle resumes in the afternoon, another stand-up affair, with Washington in a superior defensive position able to beat back multiple assaults by the British Regulars.

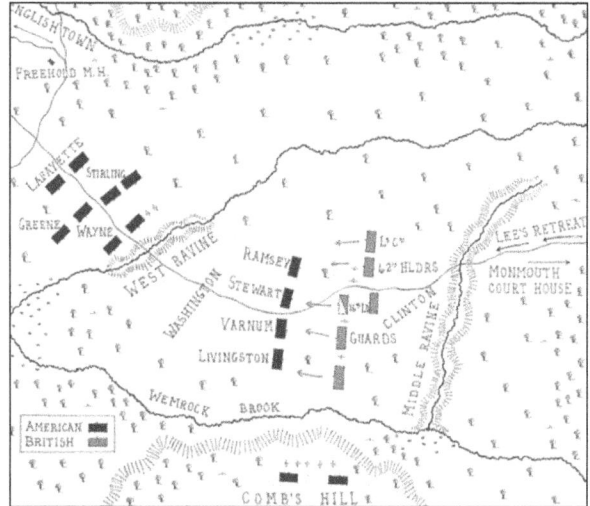

The final clash in the North is fought at Monmouth, NJ

In the end, the battle is a draw.

Washington is unable to stop Clinton's move to New York, but he does demonstrate the newly gained proficiency of his army.

The Battle of Monmouth represents another turning point in the war. It is the last sizable infantry clash that will take place in the North, despite the fact that the conflict drags on for another three years and the final resolution treaty is five years hence.

TIME: 1779–1781

BRITAIN'S "SOUTHERN STRATEGY" SUCCEEDS THEN STALLS

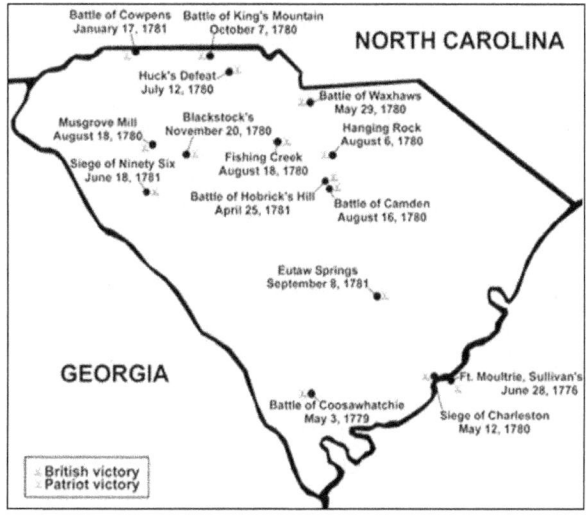

Revolutionary War battles rage across South and North Carolina in 1779–81

To succeed with their new efforts in the South, the British need a strong supply base similar to their position in New York City. They already hold Savannah, Georgia, after a failed American siege in the autumn of 1779. But they want a more central location, and they decide that the port city of Charleston, South Carolina is their best bet.

On December 26, 1779, Clinton and Cornwallis leave New York harbor with 8,500 men, weaponry, and supplies, for what proves to be a six-week stop and start voyage through winter storms, ending on February 11, 1780, just to the south of their objective.

What follows is a siege of Charleston, lasting through the spring, and finally forcing the surrender on May 12 of General Benjamin Lincoln's entire 5,500-man army trapped in the city.

At this stage, Clinton turns command of his southern forces over to Cornwallis and his second in command, Lt. Colonel Banastre Tarleton, who quickly earns a "no quarters" reputation on the battlefield.

After Charleston, the Americans are left with only local militia to fend off the British.

For the next two and a half years, the Revolutionary War will be fought across the South, often pitting local Loyalists against their Secessionist neighbors.

Many of the encounters take place in the interior of South Carolina. On August 16, 1780, General Horatio Gates, chosen by Congress to revitalize American troops after Charleston, blunders into a solid trouncing at Camden, South Carolina. At King's Mountain on October 7, Cornwallis's move toward North Carolina is turned back by frontiersmen under Colonel John Sevier.

American resistance stiffens further when Washington sends 39-year-old Major General Nathanael Greene to replace Gates. On January 17, 1781, Greene's men thrash Tarleton's Loyalist cavalry at Cowpens, South Carolina. Tarleton loses 1,000 men, along with his image for invincibility. Cornwallis remains undaunted, and again pushes into North Carolina, encountering Greene on March 15, 1781 at Guilford Court House (later the town of Greensboro). At day's end, Britain owns the field but at a disproportionately high cost of 500 casualties.

After one more draw with Greene at Hobkirk's Hill near Camden, South Carolina, Cornwallis decides it's time to fight the war in Virginia, the linchpin between Washington's northern army and Greene in the South.

The broad "Loyalist uprising" across the Carolinas and Georgia that British Prime Minister Lord North hoped for has failed to materialize, and the Americans have now proven they can stand toe to toe with the redcoats in land battles. All that England has left to show for its move south are Savannah and Charleston, both secured by their superior fleet.

But the Royal Navy is about to be tested in Virginia by America's new ally, the French.

TIME: AUGUST TO SEPTEMBER 1791

THE THREE-YEAR-OLD AMERICAN-FRENCH ALLIANCE TAKES HOLD IN 1781

By the time Cornwallis completes his 240-mile trek from Wilmington, North Carolina to Petersburg, Virginia, units under turncoat British General Benedict Arnold and William Phillips have burned and pillaged towns along James River and taken control of the new capital city of Richmond.

Gilbert du Motier, Marquis de Lafayette (1757–1834)

This incursion into his home state alarms Washington and he sends 5,000 troops under command of the French General Marquis de Lafayette to defend Virginia and capture the traitor, Arnold.

Given that Cornwallis has 7,000 troops at his disposal, Lafayette decides to avoid a major battle, instead maneuvering his army along the Rapidan River toward Williamsburg. They fight a sharp skirmish there on July 6, 1781.

At this point, General Clinton, resting comfortably in Manhattan, senses that the combined 9,000-man force of Washington and the Frenchman, comte de Rochambeau, may be readying a move against him. In response, he first orders Cornwallis to detach 3,000 men back to New York City, then changes his mind and tells him to occupy the deep-water port at Yorktown, which he does.

At first, this move to Yorktown looks safe. But then two crucial factors shift the equation.

On May 22, Washington learns that French Admiral François Joseph Paul, comte de Grasse, plans to move his fleet from the Caribbean to America in autumn to support the alliance. For the first time during the war, Britain's absolute dominance of all sea lanes will be challenged.

Then Washington settles on a major gamble, reminiscent of his desperate move across the Delaware to Trenton some five years earlier.

He leaves a shadow army of 3,000 to contain Clinton in New York, and secretly marches with Rochambeau and 6,000 men on August 21 to join Lafayette. Fortunately, Clinton does not learn of the move until September 2, when Washington's army meets Admiral de Grasse's fleet in Chesapeake Bay, north of Baltimore.

Lafayette and Washington

In addition to his navy, the admiral brings another pleasant surprise—2,500 French troops, who disembark to bolster the American-French infantry.

Suddenly, a joint land and sea attack on Cornwallis at Yorktown becomes possible.

TIME: OCTOBER 19, 1781

THE WORLD TURNED UPSIDE DOWN AT YORKTOWN

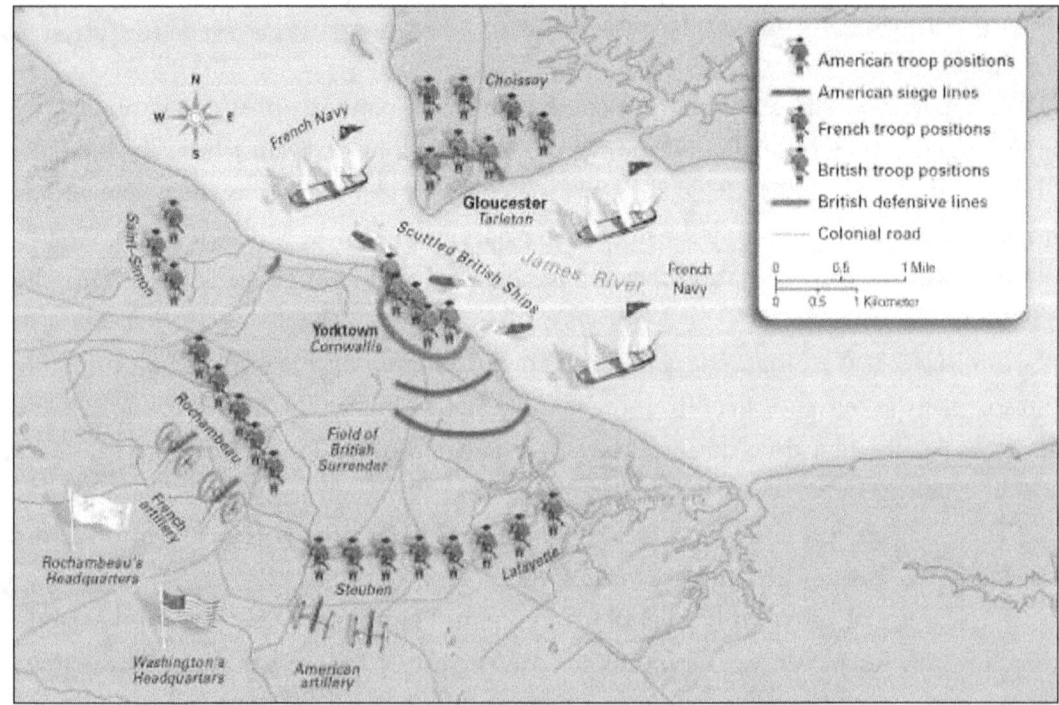

Cornwallis is trapped by Washington and the French at Yorktown

After settling on a plan of attack, Washington and Rochambeau move overland for twelve days to join up with Lafayette in Williamsburg on September 14.

In the interim, Admiral de Grasse fights a crucial sea battle with British Admirals Sir Thomas Graves and Sir Samuel Hood, that will seal the fate for Cornwallis at Yorktown.

When de Grasse moves north from Haiti on August 15, Graves and Hood follow him, but with only a part of the fleet, leaving the rest behind to defend the West Indies. This decision proves fateful on September 5 in the Battle of the Capes, fought for control of the entrance to James River and the Yorktown harbor.

In the early afternoon de Grasse brings his 24 warships out past Cape Henry, heading southeast and signaling the classical order "form line of battle." The awaiting British fleet of nineteen ships tacks with him, foregoes a thrust at his center, and instead opts for a broadside exchange of fire. But Hood's rear guard never quite catches up to the French, and only eight of the Royal Navy actually close within range of de Grasse's main body of fifteen. This nearly two to one advantage in firepower results in a French victory after two hours of intense fighting.

The two fleets continue to maneuver out of range off the capes until September 10 when de Grasse moves back into the shelter of Chesapeake Bay. There, he is greeted by another French squadron under Admiral de Barras, which brings his strength up to 35 ships and guarantees control of the waters surrounding Yorktown.

At this point, Cornwallis's 7,200-man army is trapped—between the French fleet on the York River and Washington's predominantly French force of 16,500 infantry who have surrounded him by September 28 from the east and south.

When Clinton sends word promising a relief force from New York, Cornwallis abandons his outer defenses and pulls back to a more tightly controlled perimeter. In turn, Washington and Lafayette are able to construct close-in siege operations, with cannon fire taking its daily toll on the British defenders. By October 10, Cornwallis signals Clinton that his only remaining hope is a rescue by the Royal Navy. Four days later, two critical British redoubts (#9 and #10) are stormed, closing the gap between the redcoats and their assailants to only 250 yards.

TIME: SEPTEMBER 3, 1783

THE TREATY OF PARIS OFFICIALLY ENDS THE REVOLUTIONARY WAR

The success of the American-French alliance at Yorktown effectively signals the end of British rule over the thirteen colonies, although it takes almost two more years of sporadic warfare to drive the point home in London.

King George is willing to continue the fight, but his Parliament is not. The wartime Prime Minister, Lord North, is forced out of office in March of 1782.

In the spring, Ben Franklin opens unilateral talks with British counterparts, fearing that the French commitment to an ongoing alliance may be softening. He is joined over time by two other American diplomats, John Adams and John Jay.

By November 1782 a draft treaty is signed with the opening declaration reading:

> *His Britannic Majesty*
> *acknowledges the*
> *said United States…*
> *to be free, sovereign and*
> *independent.*

John Adams (1735–1826)

Still another ten months pass before a final agreement is concluded in Paris on September 3, 1783.

Franklin wants Britain to cede eastern Canada to reduce the odds of a future invasion, but the crown balks at the idea. Instead, the British transfer the land west of the Appalachians to the Mississippi River, to the dismay of their tribal allies.

Other articles grant fishing rights to the United States in Canadian waters and access by Britain to the Mississippi River, finalize payment of outstanding debts, arrange for exchange of prisoners, and protect the rights of any residual Loyalists.

The end comes on the morning of October 19, 1781, to the beat of the long roll followed by a white flag of surrender from Cornwallis. Formal papers are signed and in the early afternoon the British army marches out of their fortifications to surrender, accompanied appropriately by a popular London tune, "The World Turned Upside Down."

The World Turned Upside Down

The Treaty of Paris closes the first war between mostly British brethren in America.

The victory of the upstart rebels is an improbable one, and much of the credit falls to one man, General George Washington, whose leadership and sheer determination span over six years of often desperate warfare.

Before long, the new nation he secured will ask him to forego private life for another call of duty.

8

DEBT PLAGUES THE NEW CONGRESS OF THE CONFEDERATION

TIME: 1781–1787

THE CONGRESS OF THE CONFEDERATION IS BORN

In March 1781, the Second Continental Congress gives way to what becomes known as the "Congress of the Confederation" or "the United States in Congress Assembled," operating under the Thirteen Articles framed in 1777.

At that time, the war with Britain remains very much in doubt. Cornwallis's army is still rampaging across Virginia and the French fleet has not yet committed to supporting Washington and Lafayette. So, managing the conflict gives purpose and focus to the body.

However, by the end of October 1781, the victory at Yorktown makes it quite clear that America will soon emerge victorious—and the standing army shrinks from 29,000 soldiers in 1781 to 13,000 by 1783.

Once the Treaty of Paris is finalized in September 1783, many see the relevance of the federal government as receding since its powers—limited to declaring war, making peace, signing treaties, and printing money—seem already accomplished.

"We the People"

The President of the "Congress Assembled" at the time is Samuel Huntington of Connecticut, who previously signed both the Declaration of Independence and the Articles of Confederation. He serves until July 1781, when Thomas McKean of Delaware succeeds him.

But the position of president is largely ceremonial, and the consensus is that government decisions should reside with the individual states—in accord with the wishes of the Anti-Federalist politicians.

Each state is headed by a governor—among them men like Thomas Jefferson of

Virginia, Rutledge of South Carolina, Hancock of Massachusetts, Clinton of New York, and Reed of Pennsylvania—who will continue to shape America's destiny.

STATE GOVERNORS AS THE CONFEDERATION PHASE BEGINS

STATE	NAME	SERVED
Connecticut	Jonathan Trumbull	1769–84
Delaware	John Dickinson	1781–83
Georgia	Myrick Davies	1780–81
Maryland	Thomas Sim Lee	1779–82
Massachusetts	John Hancock	1780–85
New Jersey	William Livingston	1776–90
New York	George Clinton	1777–95
North Carolina	Abner Nash	1780–81
Pennsylvania	Joseph Reed	1778–81
Rhode Island	William Greene, Jr.	1778–86
South Carolina	John Rutledge	1779–82
Vermont	Thomas Chittenden	1778–89
Virginia	Thomas Jefferson	1779–81

One issue, however, will prevent the total withering away of central government. That issue is financial debt.

TIME: 1783–1787

THE WAR DEBT BECOMES A MAJOR CHALLENGE

Fighting the Revolutionary War has proven immensely costly to both sides.

For Britain the estimate is £250 million, more than enough to antagonize its taxpayers, sack the prime minister, and eventually lead to capitulation. For the American Congress the tab is pegged around $150 million—in a nation whose treasury probably

Printed money, often not "backed" by gold or silver, suffers from inflation

has no more than $12 million in "hard money" (gold and silver) in 1775, as the first shots are fired.

To pay for wars and other spending, advanced eighteenth-century governments typically rely on three sources of revenue—collecting taxes, selling assets, and floating interest bearing bonds.

But Anti-Federalist sentiment dominates the 1777 Articles of Confederation, and it has no interest in granting the central government authority to lay and collect taxes. British abuse of this "taxing power" is what prompted the war in the first place, and the colonists do not intend to repeat this outcome on their own.

So, under the Articles, any tax collection will be left up to each individual state, with the expectation that a portion of the revenues will be shared with the Continental Congress to support the war effort. In effect then, the states are asked to "donate" some of their tax revenue to Congress—a path that, in practice, fails miserably over time.

A second revenue source, selling assets, involves auctioning off leftover federal land, but state rivalries over ownership make this a contentious affair

Congress does enjoy some success with the third option, selling bonds—collecting money now in exchange for a promised return of both principal and interest at a future date. The risk for lenders is that the Americans might lose the war and be unable to pay. Despite this, some bonds are sold domestically—often to wealthy patriots (e.g., Washington and George Clinton) investing in the nation's survival—and abroad, to nations like France, Spain, and the Netherlands, which all had an interest in seeing Britain lose the war.

One American plays a particularly noteworthy role in this kind of fundraising. He is Haym Salomon, a Polish-born Jewish businessman. He emigrates to New York City in 1775, becomes a wealthy international trader, and joins a Sons of Liberty chapter in protest against the crown. Then, he is sentenced to death by the British but escapes to safety in Philadelphia. Once there, he is instrumental in securing French loans, as well as rallying domestic support. George Washington himself calls repeatedly for Salomon's help whenever his army is desperate for supplies. Sadly, Salomon never recoups his loans after the war, and dies in poverty at age 44 in 1785.

After failing to cover the cost of the war with these three conventional paths, Congress turns to an alternative option as a last resort.

The federal government begins to print its own money.

TIME: 1783–1787

SIMPLY PRINTING MONEY FAILS TO SOLVE THE PROBLEM

During the colonial period, America's economy has utilized three forms of "money:"

- Commodities acting as money, such as plugs of tobacco or beaver pelts, used in bartering.
- Minted coins called "specie," most often Spanish dollars, comprising 24 grams of pure silver.

- Paper notes, issued by banks in each state, denominated in pounds, shillings, or pence, and redeemable upon demand for a fixed quantity of specie, coined silver, or gold.

Benjamin Franklin (1706–1790)

The war, however, forces the desperate Congress to come up with a fourth form—printed "bills of credit" that will become known as "continentals."

Between 1776 and 1783, continentals with a face value totaling some $240 million will be put into circulation by order of Congress. Denominations run from 1/6 of a dollar up to $80, with variations in-between.

The government will use this new money to pay for all things needed to fight the war: gunpowder, armaments, supplies, and soldiers. As such, they keep the army and the nation afloat from year to year.

But these continentals will turn out to be a sham form of money. The reason being that, unlike prior soft money, holders of the new bills are not guaranteed the right to redeem them for hard assets, silver, or gold coins.

Without this backing in specie, suspicions build about the actual worth of the continentals—and as more flood into the market, inflation effects drive their purchasing power well below their asserted face value.

What was a $1.00 bill of credit in 1776 drops in worth to around $0.58 by 1778 and to about $0.11 in 1780. Thereafter the bills become the butt end of jokes, such as, "shoddy goods, not worth a continental."

Of course, astute financial men in Congress, like Ben Franklin, recognize the inflated continentals for what they are—a devious way around the "direct tax" prohibited in the Thirteen Articles.

Thus, when the federal government buys a barrel of gunpowder with a $10.00 face value continental actually worth $8.00, it is in effect "directly taxing" the seller $2.00.

Like many financial charades, the funny money Congress prints allows the nation to get through the war.

Still, no such sleight of hand can overcome the stark reality that America is bankrupt by 1780.

TIME: 1782

A CONTROVERSIAL "CENTRAL BANK" PROVES HELPFUL

The perils of this bankruptcy are best known to the soldiers fighting the war, especially George Washington and his principal aide-de-camp, Alexander Hamilton. Both men are Federalists, and together they push congress to name a "Superintendent of Finance" to restore the American economy.

Alexander Hamilton (1755–1804)

Their pick for the job is Robert Morris, and Congress approves him in 1781.

Morris is born in 1734 in Liverpool and emigrates to Maryland at age thirteen to work with his father as a "factor" (middleman) in the international tobacco trade. He masters his craft and moves to Philadelphia where he apprentices with Charles Willing, a wealthy financier who serves as mayor of the city before an early death.

In 1757 Morris and Thomas Willing (Charles Willing's son) create the firm of Willing, Morris & Co., which becomes wildly successful in everything from marine insurance to real estate to shipping ventures, including the slave trade.

By 1776 their stature around Philadelphia leads both men to be named delegates to the Second Continental Congress. Although they both oppose the Declaration of Independence, they play a crucial role in financing the war once it begins.

Morris recognizes right away that funding the Congress will depend upon linking public men who understand government with private men who operate in the world of finance.

With this goal in mind, Morris proposes that a "central bank" be chartered to effectively manage the assets and debts of the federal government, as well as establish credible backing in specie for the money supply.

He titles this "The Bank of North America" and seeks approval from Congress to form a private corporation to run it. Startup funds will come from investors who will receive 1,000 "shares" in the company in return for every $400 they put in. In effect, this central bank will operate like any other joint-stock corporation.

Resistance to this idea comes immediately from the Anti-Federalists. They fear that a federal bank will erode the power and policies of Congress by putting too much financial influence into the hands of an elite class of private investors. Besides, men like James Madison argue that the Articles of Confederation actually prohibit Congress from chartering any corporations, that being the province of the states.

Despite this opposition, the desperate circumstances surrounding the debt are such that Congress backs the central bank, and it opens on January 4, 1782. Its first president is none other than Morris's long-time partner, Thomas Willing.

While Willing's son-in-law purchases 9.5% of the bank's shares at the first offering,

63% of the shares come from foreign investors in France and the Netherlands brought in by Morris. Over time, this heavy stake in America held abroad will also become a sore point with the Anti-Federalists.

Once up and running, The Bank of North America will become a major success. It attracts investors and builds a sizable war-chest of money to help deal with the debt. It helps stabilize the true value of the money supply, by assuring that new bills of debt are backed by reserves of silver and gold. It reassures other nations that America's finances are sound enough to warrant renewed international commerce.

GROWTH OF STATE BANKS CHARTERED TO PRINT "BACKED" US DOLLARS

1783	1790	1800	1810	1820	1830	1840	1850	1860
0	1	15	49	131	163	353	190	494

source: Warren Weber, Federal Reserve Bank of Minneapolis, 2006

TIME: 1785

THE LAND ORDINANCE OF 1785 ALSO HELPS FINANCE THE GOVERNMENT

One other development—the Land Ordinance of 1785—will also help the federal government finance itself in the long-run.

In winning the war, America acquires all of the British land from west of the Appalachians to the Mississippi River. This land represents a very attractive asset, capable of generating needed government revenue if Congress can figure out who actually owns the acreage and how to sell it off.

OWNERSHIP OF EVENTUAL US LAND IN 1783

TOTAL SQ. MI.	US	SPAIN	BRITAIN
3.09 million	29%	61%	10%
	East of Mississippi River	West of MS and FL	OR

The issue of ownership is immediately contentious, and heated debates on this point begin way back in 1776, when the Second Continental Congress is drafting the Declaration of Independence and the Thirteen Articles of Confederation.

Seven states claim ownership of the new land, based largely on historical "sea to sea" border grants made between the British crown and the joint-stock corporations who founded their colony.

ORIGINAL STATE CLAIMS ON BRITISH LAND WEST OF APPALACHIA

AREA	BOUNDARY	CLAIMED BY
Northwest Territory	Above the Ohio River	Massachusetts, Connecticut, and New York
Southwest Territory	Below the Ohio River	Virginia, North and South Carolina, and Georgia

Predictably the other six "left out" states balk at this arrangement and announce that they will refuse to ratify the Thirteen Articles of Confederation unless they share access to this land. This threat leads to a compromise whereby the states agree the land is "public domain property" belonging to the federal government, and to be sold to help cover war debts owed by both the Congress and the states.

In 1784, the Confederation Congress goes to work on a structured plan for surveying and selling land in the new territories, and eventually creating new states. The challenge goes to a Committee of Five: Thomas Jefferson of Virginia, Elbridge Gerry of Massachusetts, Jacob Reed of South Carolina, David Howell of Rhode Island, and Hugh Williamson of North Carolina.

Together, they accomplish the first part of the task in the Land Ordinance of 1785.

It calls for certified surveyors to map out all of the new land, and then divide it into 6 square mile plots called townships. From there each township is broken into 36 equal sections of 640 acres. Each section is then numbered according to a set schematic, from 1 to 36.

36	30	24	18	12	6
35	29	23	17	11	5
34	28	22	16	10	4
33	27	21	15	9	3
32	26	20	14	8	2
31	25	19	13	7	1

Each section is put up for sale on a first come, first served basis, at an initial price of $1 per acre, bumped up to $2 in 1796. Buyers could be either settlers or speculators, and anyone owning a section was free to sub-divide it for re-sale. The Ordinance also requires that one section—number 16—be set aside for a township school to encourage the spread of public education.

The Ordinance passes Congress on May 20, 1785.

It fails, however, to resolve several important issues related to governance in the new territories—among them the qualifications for becoming a new state and, ominously, whether or not slavery will be permitted or banned.

The slave owner Jefferson attacks the practice once again, as he did in one of the deleted sections of the Declaration of Independence. But his efforts to outlaw it in the new territories after 1800 are turned back.

TIME: 1830

SIDEBAR: A TYPICAL FEDERAL LAND GRANT DOCUMENT

A land register document selling 80 acres in Vincennes, Indiana to Demas Deming on December 3, 1830, signed by President Andrew Jackson

TIME: MID-1780S

DEBATES ON THE NEED FOR A STRONGER CENTRAL GOVERNMENT RE-EMERGE

The Revolutionary War has proven a sobering experience for the new nation—not only for George Washington and his generals, but also for leaders in the Confederation Congress.

It has tested—and found wanting—the theory in the Thirteen Articles that the independent states will act together effectively around big challenges like war. Neither the men nor the money needed from the states arrives when it is needed.

While the war is eventually won, it is the French who make a difference at Yorktown.

America enters the war as a remarkably prosperous country and exits it with severe financial and economic problems. Best estimates available from scholars of the Confederation period show that annual per capita income drops by 22% across the entire nation—from $86 per person in 1775 to $67 in 1800.

The South is hit particularly hard by the war, and its agriculture-based economy will never regain the regional edge it enjoys in 1775, despite the fabulous wealth concentrated in the "planter class."

ESTIMATES OF REAL PER CAPITA INCOME DURING THE CONFEDERATION ERA

YEAR	NEW ENGLAND	MID-ATLANTIC	SOUTH ATLANTIC	TOTAL AMERICA
1774	$57	$76	$108	$86
1800	56	68	71	67
Change	(2%)	(11%)	(34%)	(22%)

source: Professors Peter Lindert (UC-Davis) and Jeffrey Williamson (Harvard)

The crushing financial debt experienced by both federal and state governments reverberates across the entire population. Ex-soldiers are often hardest hit by the economic downturn, having left their farms to chance, and returned with worthless continentals. Many have only broken promises of future pay to show for their sacrifices and Washington fears the result will be domestic unrest.

But the veterans are not alone. Debt is widespread across the land and many families are unprepared when the state shows up at their doors to collect taxes.

Under the Thirteen Articles, state governments are allowed to levy direct taxes, and they do so in a variety of ways. New Englanders often pay excise taxes on specified goods, taxes on their real estate, and occupational taxes. Mid-Atlantic residents pay property taxes and a "head or poll tax" charged to each adult male. In the South, taxes tend to focus more on import and export levies.

Those unable to pay their taxes with "bills of credit" issued by state banks or with minted coins end up in debtors' prison until they sell off their farms or otherwise pay what they owe.

By the mid-1780s, those in debt have reached alarming proportions and revolts begin to break out against tax collectors—American this time, not British.

The most famous revolt occurs in January 1787 in Massachusetts, where local farmers plead with the legislature to provide tax relief and to release those held in debtors' prisons. After being turned down, some 1,500 protesters band together under former Continental Army Captain Daniel Shays and disrupt court hearings and efforts to collect taxes. George Washington hears of this revolt and urges the governor to act.

Commotions of this sort, like snow-balls, gather strength as they roll, if there is no opposition in the way to divide and crumble them.

On January 27, 1787, the crisis comes to a head. Shays' men attempt to storm the Springfield federal armory and are met by the 1,200 militia troops called out by Massachusetts. General Benjamin Lincoln, a close associate of Washington's, leads them. The ensuing battle is brief but bloody, with Shays' routed men suffering 24 casualties.

While this ends Shays' Rebellion, the protest has gathered widespread public sympathy, which alarms members of the Confederation Congress as well as George Washington, retired at his Mount Vernon plantation. Something must be done to rally and unify the states to escape from its economic woes.

It is Washington's observation—"we have errors to correct"—that prompts a series of conferences at Mount Vernon and Annapolis, where a consensus is reached around the call for another "grand convention."

This convention will become the first chance for the new nation to exercise its "right to institute a new government," exactly as promised in the Declaration of 1776!

## 9

A NEW CONSTITUTION IS APPROVED FOR THE UNITED STATES

TIME: MAY 14, 1787

THE CONSTITUTIONAL CONVENTION CONVENES

INDEPENDENCE HALL, Philadelphia.

The Constitutional Convention at Independence Hall in Philadelphia is in session for four months, from May 14 to September 17, 1787—with spotty attendance throughout. Rhode Island boycotts the entire event, infuriating Washington. Delegates from New Hampshire appear nine weeks late. Only two states, Virginia and Pennsylvania, are present on the first day, and a quorum of seven isn't achieved until May 25. Of the 74 men chosen to attend, only 55 ever show up, and less than 30 stay from start to finish.

The 55 delegates who do attend are consistently white males, well-educated, wealthy, and have been active in politics. All have participated in the Revolution—41 having attended the Continental Congress and 29 having served in the Continental Army. Their careers are diverse: 35 are lawyers (but not all practicing), fourteen oversee plantations and slaves, thirteen are merchants, eleven are financiers, seven are land speculators, four are doctors, two are small farmers, another two are scientists, and one is a college president. Just over half are slave owners.

At the state level, attendance is well balanced. Six states are smaller (populations under 300,000) and six are larger. Six are from the North and six are from the mid- to deep- South. Six have very sizable slave populations and six do not.

COMPOSITION OF DELEGATES WHO ATTEND

NORTH (25)	# DELEGATES	1790 POP. (THOUSANDS)	HIGH % SLAVE OWNERS
PA	8	434	No
MA	4	379	No
NY	3	340	No
CT	3	238	No
NJ	5	184	No
NH	2	142	No
RI	0	69	No
BORDER (10)			
MD	5	320	Yes
DE	5	59	Yes
SOUTH (20)			
VA	7	748	Yes
NC	5	394	Yes
SC	4	249	Yes
GA	4	82	Yes

Several prominent figures from prior meetings are missing from this one. Thomas Jefferson and John Adams are serving as ambassadors to Paris and London respectively, and leading Anti-Federalists such as Sam Adams, John Hancock, Richard Henry Lee, and Patrick Henry are also absent.

The work of the convention is thus done by a relatively small number of men with, fair to say, a tilt toward strengthening the hand of the federal government vis a vis the individual states. The work is hard and it is contentious. So much so that the delegates agree to operate entirely in closed session—for fear that the acrimony involved in the debates will tear the country apart rather than strengthen its unity.

The record of each session is compiled by the unofficial secretary, James Madison, whose "Notes of Debates in the Federal Convention of 1787" will not be made public until 1840.

Decisions reached by the body are often very close calls, based on horse-trading compromises. Some issues are so divisive they are simply set aside for future generations to resolve. Then comes the need for each state to vote on the agreements. This process drags on for over three years, with Rhode Island's approval in May 1790 and Vermont, as the fourteenth state, agreeing in January 1791.

In hindsight the fact that the convention successfully institutes a new government is remarkable.

The lion's share of the credit for this outcome belongs to George Washington, who comes out of retirement to attend, who only speaks out on issues once during the session, but whose reputation for placing the needs of the nation above his own personal preferences sets the standard for the delegates.

Benjamin Franklin, now 81 years old, supports Washington throughout the process. Franklin is instrumental in defining the vision and values of the new nation, negotiating disputes among the delegates at the convention, and codifying the agreements in plain-spoken language. Of all the founding fathers, Franklin alone signs all four documents integral to the Revolution: the Declaration of Independence, the Treaty of Alliance with France, the Treaty of Paris ending the war, and the US Constitution.

In a room full of 55 strong-willed, often self-interested and hot-tempered delegates, Washington and Franklin act as the two wise men who eventually steer the ship of state into safe harbor.

TIME: MAY 14 – SEPTEMBER 17, 1787

A HOST OF COMPLICATED ISSUES FACES THE ASSEMBLED DELEGATES

Procedural matters mark the start of the convention. The superintendent of finance, Robert Morris of Pennsylvania, nominates Washington to serve as presiding officer. After John Rutledge, the powerful leader of the South Carolina delegation, seconds the nomination, Washington is affirmed unanimously. He sits at the front of the hall on a raised dais, in an armchair backed with an elaborate carving of a rising sun. He wears his old military uniform, and is addressed throughout as "General Washington."

Next comes the gentlemen's pledge to conduct the proceedings in secrecy, doors and windows shut despite the stifling summer heat—with some 600 pages of notes captured by Madison as record keeper.

From there the business of the convention gets underway quickly.

Most of the delegates share Washington's observation that the Articles of Confederation need to be reworked, given the hard lessons learned from conducting the war and the financial and economic crises that follow.

But having a shared problem is not the same as arriving at a shared solution.

This will prove especially true for the Anti-Federalists who are present. One is Patrick

Henry, who declares "I smell a rat" upon learning of the secrecy pledge. His fear, and that of his faction, is that a rewrite of the Articles will result in a victory for those who favor an all-powerful centralized government that behaves like the British monarchy—distant from the people, dictatorial in power, taxing and spending at will, and totally eroding the sovereign prerogatives of the individual states.

These concerns will set the stage for the vigorous debates that occur over the next four months. A host of diverse and important issues will take center stage at various times:

1. How will authority for governing be split between the federal vs. state levels?
2. Does the federal government need more than just a legislative branch?
3. How will representation within the legislature be apportioned across the states?
4. How will the interests of small states vs. larger states be protected in legislative voting?
5. How will the interests of states with large vs. small slave populations be balanced?
6. How will the rights of any minority groups be protected against the will of the majority?
7. What range of powers will be granted to the legislative branch?
8. How will the government be sufficiently funded?
9. Can an executive branch be created with enough, but not too much, power?
10. How should the executive be chosen and for how long a term?
11. What should the executive's role be in relation to the military?
12. What checks and balances will exist between the executive and the legislature?
13. How will state compliance with federal laws be monitored and assured?
14. Should there be a judicial branch created to oversee the legal system?
15. How might such a judiciary be structured and what powers would it have?

SIDEBAR: A SHORT PROFILE OF SEVERAL LESS FAMOUS FOUNDING FATHERS AT PHILADELPHIA

NAME AND AGE	STATE	IMPACT
John Dickinson, 54	Delaware	His "two solar systems" speech clarifies roles of the national government vis a vis the states
Oliver Ellsworth, 42	Connecticut	Gave input on the Connecticut Plan, member of the Committee on Detail
Elbridge Gerry, 43	Massachusetts	Challenges South on "counting slaves," leads Anti-Federalist drive for state legislatures to ratify, refuses to sign the Constitution

NAME AND AGE	STATE	IMPACT
William Johnson, 59	Connecticut	Chair of the Committee of Style & Arrangement, gave input on the Connecticut Plan, calming influence start to finish
Rufus King, 32	Massachusetts	Serves on Committee of Style & Arrangement
Luther Martin, 39	Maryland	Opposes slave trade, voice for Anti-Federalist faction
George Mason, 62	Virginia	Anti-Federalist who still pushes for supremacy of the people, demands Bill of Rights and second convention, refuses to sign
Gouverneur Morris, 35	Pennsylvania	Aristocratic by birth, a witty debater, makes most motions at convention. Lead author of final Constitution, proposes a strong, singular president, openly attacks slavery
William Patterson, 41	New Jersey	Authors New Jersey Plan and opens several key issues
Charles Pinckney, 29	South Carolina	Only delegate to openly defend the practice of slavery
Charles C. Pinckney, 41	South Carolina	A lead spokesman for the Southern states, later runs for president as a Federalist.
Edmund Randolph, 34	Virginia	Authors the pivotal Virginia Plan and Committee on Detail report, calls for a flexible Constitution changing with the times, also amendments, critical role throughout, refuses to sign
John Rutledge, 48	South Carolina	The "Dictator," a famed general during the war, and a planter. Another key spokesperson for the South, Chairman of the Committee on Detail, defends need for slavery, supports a strong executive
Roger Sherman, 66	Connecticut	Once a shoemaker, he authors the Enumeration Clause (3/5 slave count) in support of the Great Compromise, gave input on the Connecticut Plan, strong role in ratification
James Wilson, 45	Pennsylvania	Leads Connecticut Plan with two senators per state enabling the Great Compromise, member of the Committee on Detail, a voice for closure, supports equality of new western states

Note: Hamilton is 30, Madison 36, Washington 55, Franklin 81. Average life expectancy for white males is 38 in 1787.

TIME: MAY 30, 1787

GOVERNOR EDMUND RANDOLPH OFFERS THE VIRGINIA PLAN

On May 30, Governor Edmund Randolph of Virginia gets things underway by proposing a series of nineteen "Resolves" to create a new central government, fundamentally different in scope and procedures from the Thirteen Articles of Confederation.

The primary author of the plan is James Madison. The First Resolve argues that:

MADISON.

James Madison (1751–1836)

1. A national government ought to be established consisting of a supreme legislative, executive, and judiciary.

This sentence alone strikes the Anti-Federalists in the hall like a thunderbolt, turning their most fundamental beliefs upside down. The Thirteen Articles guaranteed the sovereignty of the states, and now the national government claims the supremacy of its laws over individual state laws.

Later comes another blow to state sovereignty in the Seventh Resolve. Under the Thirteen Articles, each state enjoys equal power—one vote apiece—in deciding on new legislation. The tiniest state of Delaware has as much say in the outcomes as the largest state, Virginia. But under Randolph's proposal, the number of votes would vary according to the size of its population. Virginia might now have thirteen votes against one for Delaware.

7. The national legislature ought to accord to some equitable ratio of representation—namely in proportion to the whole number of white and other free citizens…and 3/5ths of all other persons, except Indians…

The Second Resolve divides the national legislature into two chambers, a clever move that will eventually result in a House of Representatives and a Senate, yielding crucial compromises with the Anti-Federalists and small state factions.

2. That the national legislature ought to consist of two branches.

The Third Resolve ensures that legislators in the first chamber be chosen directly by the people—rather than being "named" by those already serving in the state's legislature.

3. That the members of the first branch of the national Legislature ought to be elected by the People of the several States for the term of three years.

A fourth defines the second legislative chamber, with presumably more senior figures serving seven-year terms, chosen by state officials.

4. That the members of the second Branch of the national Legislature ought to be chosen by the individual Legislatures. to be of the age of thirty years at least. to hold their offices for a term sufficient to ensure their independency, namely seven years.

The Sixth Resolve lays out a broad scope for the new national legislature, covering issues "beyond the competence" of the individual states or where the "harmony" across all states is in play. It also grants the national body power to "negative" (i.e., overrule) state laws which violate the common interests of the nation.

> 6. To legislate in all cases to which the separate States are incompetent: or in which the harmony of the United States may be interrupted by the exercise of individual legislation. to negative all laws passed by the several States contravening, in the opinion of the national Legislature

The executive branch of the new government is profiled in the Ninth Resolve. Randolph calls for one person=to be chosen by the national legislature. They will serve seven years, charged with seeing that the laws are carried out and at risk of being impeached for violations.

> 9. That a national Executive be instituted to consist of a single person. to be chosen by the National Legislature for the term of seven years with power to carry into execution the national Laws…and to be removable on impeachment and conviction of malpractice or neglect of duty.

The Tenth Resolve gives the executive power to veto any legislative act, unless overturned by a 2/3 vote.

> 10. That the national executive shall have a right to negative any legislative act: which shall not be afterwards passed unless by two third parts of each branch of the national Legislature

Resolves Eleven to Thirteen establish the judicial branch of government, along with various operating rules.

> 11. That a national Judiciary be established to consist of One Supreme Tribunal. The Judges of which to be appointed by the second Branch of the National Legislature to hold their offices during good behavior

The remaining eight Resolves fill in other considerations for the new government. Among them are the admission of new states to the union and future passage of amendments to the Constitution.

The "Virginia Plan" offered by Randolph on May 30 proves critical to the life of the convention.

It serves as the starting point for the debates that follow. Despite the appearance of other plans, delegates always cycle back to the Virginia Plan's basic framework when decisions are required. Ironically, the man who proposes the plan, Randolph, will be one of only three men who refuse to sign the final document he has done so much to advance.

TIME: JUNE 15, 1787

NEW JERSEY PROPOSES A "SMALL STATE" ALTERNATIVE

Once the Virginia Plan is on the table, two things become immediately clear: a House of Representatives dealing with the nation's important issues enjoys overwhelming support, while the proposed composition of this House is intensely divisive.

The sticking point lies with the smaller states, who have no intention of surrendering their power in the new legislature to the larger states. If Virginia is to end up with thirteen votes and Delaware with just one, then Delaware will never support the new Constitution.

After fifteen days of paralysis over this apportionment barrier, the Attorney General of New Jersey, William Patterson, offers the convention his "small state alternative."

What Patterson proposes on the legislative branch is that the unicameral approach existing under the Thirteen Articles be kept in place, with each state retaining its equal voting power.

PROPOSED PLANS FOR THE NEW LEGISLATURE

	VIRGINIA PLAN	NEW JERSEY PLAN
# OF CHAMBERS	2 - bicameral	1 - unicameral
APPORTIONMENT	Based on state population	Every state has one vote
POWER DERIVED FROM	Popular voting in House	States legislators

When this is put to a vote, the New Jersey alternative goes down, with only three states favoring it against seven for the Virginia Plan and two states divided.

While this loss is decisive, it fails to resolve the matter—with several small states threatening to go home rather than surrender their sovereignty.

Despite this fundamental failure, the New Jersey Plan announces several other ideas that will become relevant as the sessions continue.

- Congress can raise funds by tariffs and taxes collected from the states.
- A federal treasury will be set up to handle revenue and expenses and quality assure the money supply.
- Congress will regulate interstate and foreign commerce.
- The executive branch will include several people, elected by congress, for one term only.
- A supreme tribunal appointed by the executive will resolve legal disputes (borders, treaties, and impeachment).
- A standing army will be created, with states contributing troops in proportion to their population size.
- Military officers will be approved jointly by states and the congress.

TIME: JUNE 18, 1787

HAMILTON ANNOUNCES HIS REVOLUTIONARY OPTION

The next move belongs to Alexander Hamilton of New York, who has lobbied to hold this convention over seven long years. On June 18 he addresses it in an impassioned six-hour speech.

The 32-year-old Hamilton is already a renowned Federalist, whose standing traces to his father-in-law, Major General Philip Schuyler of Revolutionary War fame, and to none other than George Washington, for whom he has served as chief of staff during four years on the battlefield.

Despite these credentials, many view the British West Indies-born Hamilton as a foreigner who, as Jefferson later writes, has been "bewitched and perverted by the British example."

Indeed, Hamilton's speech is a paean to the British government, which he calls "the best in the world."

Alexander Hamilton (1755–1804)

He advises the convention to adopt the core British principles, especially that of an all-powerful executive. He proposes that this be a single person, titled "governor," with power comparable to a monarch and holding office for life.

> He ought to be hereditary, and to have so much power, that it will not be in his interest to risk much to acquire more. The advantage of a monarch is this—he is above corruption—he must always intend, in respect to foreign nations, the true interest and glory of the people.

Like many others, Hamilton is very suspicious of a "pure democracy," fearing its tendency toward momentary passions and mob-like swings in governance.

> The voice of the people has been said to be the voice of God...but it is not true in fact.

Neither does he trust the states, who "will prefer their particular concerns to the general welfare."

Now is the time, Hamilton argues, for the United States to act as one nation, unified and powerful, capable of taking its place alongside Britain, France, and Spain on the world stage. This will only be possible if power is placed in the hands of responsible statesmen who will devote their lives to advancing the welfare of the nation.

Hamilton's views are those of the Federalist faction writ large.

They are immediately rejected by his two fellow delegates from New York, Robert

Yates and John Lansing, both pledged to the virulently Anti-Federalist governor George Clinton, now serving his fourth term in office.

Others in the room signal their displeasure toward Hamilton's plan in their silence.

Two days later, disheartened, Hamilton heads home for a two-month hiatus from the convention.

His fierce commitment to a powerful union is appreciated by all, but his vision for an executive is far too reminiscent of King George III for his audience.

TIME: JULY 5, 1787

ROGER SHERMAN SHARES THE CONNECTICUT PLAN IN COMMITTEE

Another two weeks pass with progress stalled over the apportionment of seats in the new legislature.

A committee is set up to deal with the matter, chaired by Elbridge Gerry of Massachusetts and including Roger Sherman of Connecticut—"a man who never said a foolish thing" according to Jefferson.

On July 5 Sherman presents a compromise to Gerry's committee intended to break the logjam.

- The legislative branch will have two chambers (House and Senate), according to the Virginia Plan.
- The number of House seats a state enjoys will be based on its population count in a census.
- The number of Senate seats for each state will be set equally, at two.
- State legislatures will elect its two senators.
- To pass congress, all bills must gain majorities in both chambers.

PROPOSED PLANS FOR THE NEW LEGISLATURE

	VIRGINIA PLAN	NEW JERSEY PLAN	CONNECTICUT PLAN
# of Chambers	2 - bicameral	1 - unicameral	2 - bicameral
# seats in House	Based on state population	Every state has one	Based on state population
# seats in Senate	Based on state population	---	Every state has two

Sherman's proposal leaves the Virginia Plan untouched when it comes to having two chambers in the legislature and having apportionment in the House based on each state's population.

But in the Senate, he restores the equality of the Thirteen Articles by allocating two seats to each state, regardless of their size.

This proposal becomes known as the Connecticut Plan, in honor of the three state delegates who have crafted it: Sherman, Dr. William Johnson, and Oliver Ellsworth.

Gerry supports the plan and promises to take it to the full assembly.

As the Connecticut Plan is taking shape in committee, the atmosphere in the hall is rapidly deteriorating.

It reaches a low point on July 10 when the two remaining New York delegates, Lansing and Yates, announce they are giving up and going home, the first open defections so far. As he leaves, Lansing offers his summary of the various plans:

Utterly unattainable, too novel and complex.

Hearing of these departures, Washington writes that same day:

I almost despair of seeing a favorable issue to the proceedings of the Convention.

Everywhere he looks, Washington sees the "monster of state sovereignty" blocking the path to progress.

On one hand, the smaller states balk at a possible loss of power to the larger states. On the other, the larger states feel like they are forfeiting their authority to a new "national" power. As James Wilson of Pennsylvania puts it…

If no state will part with any of its sovereignty, it is in vain to talk of a national government.

TIME: JULY 9–13, 1787

SHARP CONFLICTS OVER SLAVERY ALMOST DERAIL THE CONVENTION

And now another issue emerges—one that is capable of blowing up the entire convention. That issue is slavery.

Its presence has been reptilian all along, and now it strikes over "apportionment"—the process by which states will be allocated seats in the House.

The question becomes: Will the Northern states allow the South to include its slaves in their population counts—or not?

In his records, James Madison picks up on the crucial nature of this issue.

The most important question regarding the make-up of the legislature was whether or not to count slaves.

The mathematics associated with "if and how" the slaves are counted register immediately with the politically savvy men present, both Southern and Northern.

Father Abraham,
a formerly enslaved man

A 1775 estimate says that some 450,000 slaves live in the South, roughly 40% of its entire population—while in the North, Black people number around 50,000 or 5% of the total.

THE IMPORTANCE OF ENSLAVED PEOPLE TO VARIOUS STATES' POPULATION COUNTS IN 1775

SECTION	STATES	WHITE	ENSLAVED	TOTAL	% BLACK
Lower South	GA, NC, SC	247,000	171,000	418,000	41%
Upper South	VA, MD, DE	481,000	282,000	763,000	37%
Mid-Atlantic	PA, NY, NJ	462,000	30,000	492,000	6%
New England	CT, RI, NH, MA	621,000	19,000	640,000	3%
		1,811,000	502,000	2,313,000	22%

Nothing short of "regional power" in the legislature therefore rests on the counting outcome.

Assuming that slaves are counted fully in each state's official population, and one seat is allocated for every 40,000 residents, the legislature would be divided 30–28 in favor of the South.

On the other hand, if the slaves do not count at all, the North ends up with a commanding 27–18 majority.

NUMBER OF VOTES IN HOUSE DEPENDING ON HOW ENSLAVED PEOPLE ARE COUNTED

SECTION	STATES	ENSLAVED = 1	ENSLAVED = 0	DIFFERENCE
Lower South	GA, NC, SC	11	6	+5
Upper South	VA, MD, DE	19	12	+7
All South		30	18	+12
Mid-Atlantic	PA, NY, NJ	12	12	+0
New England	CT, RI, NH, MA	16	15	+1
All North		28	27	+1
Grand Total		58	45	+13

Note: Assumes 1 House member for every 40,000 people and a total population of 2.3 million, 22% Black.

As the debate here unfolds, the depth of the dilemma facing the new nation around slavery becomes apparent.

What began as an economic initiative benefitting both the South and the North is now the source of deep division between the two regions.

The North wishes to rid itself of the entire "African problem." Meanwhile, the South is dependent on slavery to prosper.

Jefferson's words capture the dilemma best.

Slavery is like holding a wolf by the ears—one can neither safely hold him, nor safely let him go.

Conflicting motives spill over into personal distrust.

If the North gains dominance in the new "national" legislature, will it try to force the South to follow its lead and "let go" of slavery?

This is what's on the minds of the Southern delegates as the slave counting debate opens up.

Southerners quickly begin to make their case. The Anti-Federalist Virginian, George Mason, first claims personal disdain for slavery, then blames the British for forcing it upon his region. Given this historical context, Mason argues that the Africans should be viewed as a "national burden," shared equally by the South and North.

This infernal traffic originated in the avarice of British merchants, and they checked the attempts of Virginia to put a stop to it.

Slavery discourages arts and manufactures. The poor despise labor when performed by slaves. They prevent the immigration of whites, who enrich and strengthen a country. They produce the most pernicious effect on manners.

Charles Cotesworth Pinckney of Charleston is next to weigh in, admitting openly that after slavery took hold in the South, several states, including his own, have become economically dependent on it.

South Carolina and Georgia cannot do without slaves.

His fellow South Carolina delegate, Rawlins Lowndes, reinforces this theme—then openly lashes out against the North, accusing them of trying to rob his region of its wealth.

Without negroes, this state is one of the most contemptible in the Union. Negroes are our wealth, our only natural resource.

Yet behold how our kind friends in the North are determined soon to tie up our hands, and drain us of what we have.

Pinckney's cousin, also named Charles, becomes the only member arguing not only that slaves are good for the South, but that the institution lifts the slaves from savagery to civilization.

To drive these views home, both the South Carolina and Georgia delegations threaten to leave Philadelphia unless the slaves are included in their population counts.

Two Northerners will have none of this and stand nose to nose against their Southern counterparts.

The first is the merchant Elbridge Gerry of Massachusetts, who asks how the South can assert that slaves are "property"—the moral equivalent of cattle—and simultaneously argue they are "persons," the same as white men, when it comes to the population count?

Blacks are property and are used by the South as horses and cattle in the North, so why should their representation be increased on account of the number of slaves?

Gerry's views are seconded by the pugnacious peg-legged Federalist from New York, Gouverneur Morris, who leads all of his colleagues in speaking time and motions offered over the entire convention.

Morris is one of the few delegates unrestrained in his opposition to slavery, and his wish to have it end.

His attack on the Southern position is devastating, and will ring down the decades to come.

Like Gerry, he asks whether enslaved people are property or persons. Surely the South cannot have it both ways.

On what principle shall slaves be computed in the representation? Are they men? Then make them Citizens and let them vote. Are they property? Why then is no other property included (in calculating votes)?

The inhabitant of Georgia and SC who goes to the coast of Africa and in defiance of the most sacred laws of Humanity tears away his fellow creatures from their dearest connections and damns them to the most cruel bondages, shall have more votes in a Government instituted to protect the rights of mankind than the citizen of Pennsylvania or New Jersey who views this practice with laudable horror.

At this point the debate has become personal and threatens to turn into a firestorm. To save the day, a delegate from Pennsylvania, James Wilson, offers up a possible compromise.

TIME: JULY 13, 1787

THE "ENUMERATION CLAUSE" COUNTS ENSLAVED PEOPLE AS 3/5 OF A PERSON

Wilson is born in Scotland, mingles with leading Enlightenment thinkers such as David Hume and Adam Smith, emigrates to America in 1776, and becomes a successful lawyer in Philadelphia. As a pamphleteer, he argues that Britain has no right to raise taxes on the colonies because they have no representation in Parliament. When the war breaks out, he serves as a brigadier general in the Pennsylvania militia. He plays a large role in shaping the Connecticut Plan, and is considered by many to be the most learned man at the 1787 convention.

When confronted with the dispute over whether or not to include Black people in a state's population count, his solution is positively Solomon-like. He proposes to split the difference between the two sides.

Relying on simple math, he calls for weighting slaves as 3/5 of a person for the sake of determining each state's official population count. When applied to estimated head counts from 1775, the result projects to 28 seats in the House for the North and 25 for the South.

This gives the North prospects for a slight majority, albeit not the commanding lead if slaves were excluded entirely from the calculations.

On the other hand, the South gets partial credit for enslaved people without needing to accede to the notion that they are "full persons" rather than "property." Besides, Southerners firmly believe that future census figures will show much greater population growth in their region given its favorable climate—an outcome that fails to materialize in the long run.

Wilson's "solution" will eventually be captured in the infamous "Enumeration Clause" of the Constitution, favoring white people over both Black people and Native people.

COMPROMISE UNDER ENUMERATION CLAUSE

SECTION	STATES	ENSLAVED = 3/5
Lower South	GA, NC, SC	9
Upper South	VA, MD, DE	16
All South		25
Mid-Atlantic	PA, NY, NJ	12
New England	CT, RI, NH, MA	16
All North		28
Grand Total		53

Note: Assumes 1 House member for every 40,000 in official population count

Redeemed in Virginia

By Catharine S. Lawrence. Baptized in Brooklyn, at Plymouth Church, by Henry Ward Beecher, May, 1863, Fannie Virginia Casseopia Lawrence, a Redeemed SLAVE CHILD, 5 years of age.
Entered according to Art of Congress, in the year 1863, by C. S. Lawrence, in the Clerk's Office of the District Court of the United States, for the Southern District of New York.
Photograph by Renowden, 65 Fulton Av. Brooklyn.

Fannie Casseopia, a freed child

Article I, Section 2. *Representation and direct taxes shall be apportioned among the several states which may be included within this Union, according to their respective Numbers, which shall be determined by adding the whole Number of free Persons, including those bound to Service for a Term of Years, and excluding Indians not taxed, and three fifths of all other Persons.*

"All other Persons" is the euphemism chosen to avoid the indelicate word "slaves."

To allow the convention to move forward, they are to count as 3/5 of a white man—somewhere between cattle and human beings.

The importance of Wilson's compromise cannot be overstated, and in later years many will regard him as the "unsung hero of the convention."

Madison's convention notes, withheld until 1840, state flat-out that the North-South divide over slavery was the biggest threat to finalizing a new government.

I was always convinced that the difference of interest in the US lay not between the large and small but the northern and southern states…and it was pretty well understood that the institution of slavery and its consequences formed the line of discrimination.

With the Enumeration Clause in place, the Connecticut Plan is almost ready to move from the Gerry Committee to the full floor.

TIME: JULY 16, 1787

THE NORTHWEST ORDINANCE PROVIDES A FIRM TRUCE ON SLAVERY IN THE NEW TERRITORY

On July 16, another piece in the new government puzzle falls into place. It is called the Northwest Ordinance, often regarded as the third most important document (behind the Declaration of Independence and the Constitution itself) in the formation of the United States.

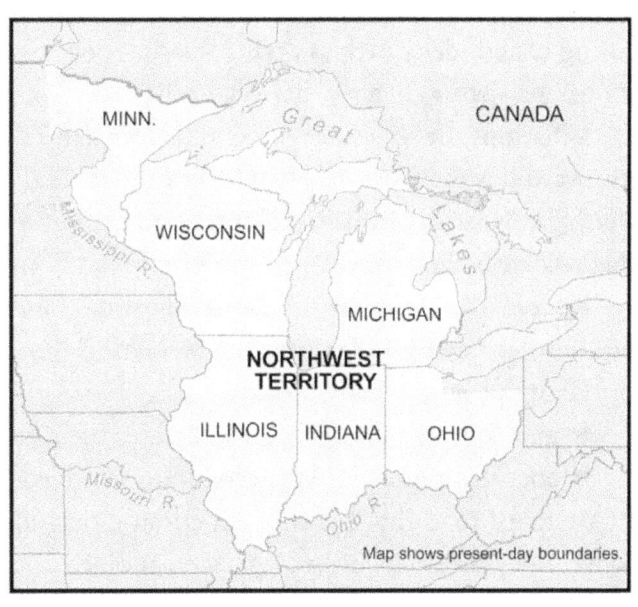

It deals with a topic on the mind of all delegates from the first day of the convention: what to do with the new territories west of the Appalachians, won from Britain and then ceded to the federal government in the Land Act of 1785. Surveys are already under way to divide this land into plots, but many questions remain. How will it be settled and governed? Will it involve the creation of new states and, if so, how will they be tied into the union?

Finally, will slavery be allowed in this new land—or not?

As a practical matter, some 100,000 settlers have already put down stakes in "the West" by 1787. They have also christened their territories with a host of new names—some lasting (Ohio, Kentucky, and Tennessee) and some that will fade away (Transylvania, Westsylvania, and Franklin).

The Northwest Ordinance agreed to on July 16 says that the land will be divided into 3 to 5 new territories, with exact borders to be laid out when the time comes to do so. Once the population in a new territory reaches a threshold of 5,000 settlers, the federal congress will appoint a governor, a secretary, and three judges to provide administrative oversight. The territory may also elect a representative to attend the House of Representatives as a non-voting member.

When a territory achieves a threshold population of 60,000, it can then write and pass a local constitution, identify its boundaries, and apply for formal admittance to the union as a new state.

These same governance principles are to apply across the South, as soon as documents are signed to cede certain lands still in dispute. When this is completed in 1789, a Southwest Ordinance is signed into law.

A vigorous debate follows on whether new states will enjoy "equal treatment" vis a vis the original thirteen. The answer is eventually "yes" by a 5–4 floor vote, despite a lasting eastern delegate bias against sharing power with "backwards westerners sporting coonskin caps and twangy dialects."

What tips the scales here is genuine fear that the Appalachian Mountains—and the westward flowing rivers it feeds—will forever tie the new states to Spanish settlements along the Mississippi River, rather than to the new American union. This is an outcome that few are willing to risk.

All told, the Northwest Ordinance provides for orderly movement of settlers into the new territory in a way that also binds them to the union—albeit ignoring the rights of the Native peoples already present.

Remarkably, the Ordinance also defuses the rising tensions over slavery!

It does this through a last second article added by Nathan Dane of Massachusetts, later referred to as the "father of American jurisprudence." Dane is not a delegate to the convention, but is a renowned legal scholar called upon to draft the Ordinance. The article he includes is simple but profound, and, to Dane's surprise, readily approved by the body.

> **Art. 6.** *There shall be neither slavery nor involuntary servitude in the said territory, otherwise than in the punishment of crimes whereof the party shall have been duly convicted: Provided, always, that any person escaping into the same, from whom labor or service is lawfully claimed in any one of the original States, such fugitive may be lawfully reclaimed and conveyed to the person claiming his or her labor or service as aforesaid.*

Article 6 lays out a geographical line—in this case the course of the Ohio River—and openly declares that the institution of slavery will be prohibited to its north and permitted to its south.

In agreeing to this line of demarcation, the South acknowledges that the North wishes to ban the spread of slavery in "its region" of the country.

The North, meanwhile, agrees to respect continuation of slavery in the South, and to facilitate it by supporting the return of any runaway slaves who cross the Ohio River.

This definitive Ohio River line will quell some of the acrimony left over the subject of slavery, both in the hall and over the next three decades.

It also opens the door for a deal on slave trading, agreed to a month later, on September 6. The practice will be allowed to continue for twenty more years, but then cease in 1808. During that period the Congress will collect a tax of $10 on every imported slave.

While at first glance, this 1808 ban on importing more slaves may appear detrimental to the South, that is not the case at all. The reason being that, in twenty years, domestic owners expect to "breed" a sufficient inventory of "excess slaves" for sale, thus keeping the profits for themselves rather than handing them over to the importers. This "breeding scheme" is particularly important to the state of Virginia, which is already seeing that selling slaves can be more lucrative than selling tobacco.

TIME: JULY 16, 1787

A "GREAT COMPROMISE" DEFINES THE LEGISLATIVE BRANCH STRUCTURE

One final roadblock needs resolution before the legislative branch plan is finalized. It involves fear among the larger states that money bills (taxing and spending) coming out of the equalized Senate might be tilted unfairly against them by the smaller states.

Ben Franklin steps forward with a solution that becomes known as the "Origination Clause"—stating that all money bills are to originate in the House and cannot be unilaterally changed by the Senate. In exchange for losing some financial powers, the Senate will be given several important "advise and consent" assignments— approving certain judges and ambassadors, ratifying treaties, and trying impeachment cases.

The convention is well in need of good news, and on July 16 it arrives in

The Senate chamber, in later years

the form of "The Great Compromise," Mr. Sherman's plan to structure the nation's new bicameral congress aided by the Northwest Ordinance.

Henceforth the "will of the American people" is to be expressed through a House of

Representatives, with members chosen state by state in direct elections and apportioned according to a population count which factors in slaves.

A second body, the Senate, will also weigh in, with large and small states each having two members to be elected by local legislatures.

All new laws must pass in both chambers for approval.

Members in the House will be elected by the people to two-year terms of office. To qualify they must be citizens for a minimum of seven years, residents of the state, and at least 25 years old.

Senators will be named by state legislatures for six-year terms. To qualify they must be citizens for a minimum of nine years, a state resident, and at least 30 years old.

The legislature must meet at least once a year, for sure on the first Monday in December. All members who participate will be paid out of the National Treasury with amounts ascertained by law.

FINAL PLAN FOR THE NEW LEGISLATURE

# OF CHAMBERS	2 - BICAMERAL
# seats in House	Based on state population
# seats in Senate	Every state has two

On July 16 then, the logjam is broken—and agreement is reached on the structure of the legislative branch.

TIME: JULY 16, 1787

AMERICA WILL BE A REPUBLIC, NOT A PURE DEMOCRACY

The "Great Compromise" reflects the tensions felt by many delegates around "how far to trust" the will of the masses, and of the majority.

The new government intends to respond to the people's will. Both James Madison and George Mason are crystal clear about this.

The people are the fountain of all power... We must resort to the people...so this doctrine with supreme authority over the government. Be cherished as the basis of free government.

"Majority rules" will also be the norm, as Alexander Hamilton points out.

The fundamental maxim of government...requires the sense James Madison (1751-1836)
that the majority should prevail.

From these observations one might expect the convention to have arrived at a "pure democracy"—with every future decision resolved through a direct poll of the people, on a winner-take-all basis.

But this is not what the delegates decide. Instead of a pure democracy, their solution is to create a republic.

I pledge allegiance to the Flag of the United States of America, and to the Republic for which it stands.

Between the people and the law stand "representatives" charged with adding their own wisdom and experience to the mix.

The explanation for this goes beyond the geographical impracticality of direct polling, to underlying suspicions that "the people" can easily transform into a mob, inflamed by short-term passions, liable to act out of rashness rather than reason.

There is also fear that, left to their own devices, "the people" may be inclined to trample on the rights of various minorities within the population—for example, the landed gentry, as none other than Madison points out.

In England, at this day, if elections were open to all classes of people, the property of landed proprietors would be insecure... Landholders ought to have a share in the government, to support these invaluable interests, and to balance and check the other. They ought to be so constituted as to protect the minority of the opulent against the majority. The Senate, therefore, ought to be this body; and to answer these purposes, they ought to have permanency and stability.

For every Ben Franklin or George Mason in the hall expressing unequivocal faith in the intrinsic wisdom of the masses, there are others, like Alexander Hamilton and John Sherman, who are much less confident.

The committed democrat Thomas Jefferson is another. As he writes, the odds of "mischief" are high whenever men and motives are joined.

In questions of power then, let no more be heard of confidence in man, but bind him down from mischief by the chains of the constitution.

John Adams, simultaneously like and unlike Jefferson, sees it the same way—any group of men given too much power will become "ravenous beasts of prey."

The message then from the worldly founders in Philadelphia is that governments are delicate in nature and prone to going off-course, either through the masses as mobs, or individual men as dictators.

In turn, the path to preserving the values of self-government lies in a series of "checks and balances," Jefferson's "binding chains of the Constitution."

Representatives in the House will "check" the masses and the Senate will "check" the House. Together they will "balance" the wishes of the majority against the proper concerns of the minority.

With that much settled, the delegates turn their attention to the executive branch.

LATE JULY 1787

A PRESIDENT OF THE UNITED STATES WILL HEAD THE EXECUTIVE BRANCH

Once again, the Virginia Plan of May 30 becomes the starting place for discussions, this time on structuring the executive branch. It calls for a council of several men selected by Congress, charged with insuring that the laws of the land are being properly carried out.

Then comes Hamilton on June 18 with his radically different approach—insisting that the executive be one man, titled Governor, serving for life, with powers approaching those of a monarch.

Neither plan feels right to the full body. Somewhere there must be a middle ground between the executive as fairly minor pawn or mighty king.

A month passes before the ubiquitous Gouverneur Morris of Pennsylvania rises with an alternative on July 19.

Morris argues that a strong executive, one man for sure, is needed as a "check" on the legislative branch, a final "guardian of the people."

- The executive will be titled the president of the United States and called "His Excellency."
- His term will be four years, but he is allowed to continue in office for as long as he is re-elected.

This approach sits well with the majority, although several concerns are voiced.

George Washington (1732–1799)

The Anti-Federalists warn that it will become the "fetus of monarchy."

James Wilson and James Madison worry that a president directly elected by the people might be too prone to short-sighted populist urgings rather than what is best in the long-term.

On top of this, a direct election raises the same questions about state sovereignty that arose with the legislature. Wouldn't the states with larger populations and therefore more votes dominate the will of their smaller neighbors?

What falls out here is the creation of an "electoral college" charged with actually choosing the president.

- He will be chosen by electors from each state, who will be named by the state's legislature.
- Each state will have a number of electors that match their total seats in Congress.
- Each elector will nominate two men for the position, including one not from their home state.
- The man with the most votes will become president; second most will be vice president.
- In case of a tie, House members will be called upon to break it.

This approach again involves a balancing act.

The bigger states do end up with more voting power—but this seems less threatening in the executive branch than in the legislature, where new laws are originating.

The will of the masses is to be harnessed by electors chosen by state officials, exhibiting statesmanship and wisdom in casting their two ballots.

Over 60 separate votes are taken at the convention before the process for electing a president is resolved.

The outcome also leads to the office of the vice president—to be filled by the runner-up in the Electoral College voting. The exact duties of the vice president are vague all along. Most feel he would act as a "stand-in" in case the president died, until the Electoral College had time to gather and pick a true replacement. Other than that, he is given the mostly ceremonial job of ex-officio president of the Senate, with the power to break tie votes.

It is abundantly clear that the new president is to be more than a figurehead and less than a monarch. So, what exactly are his powers?

JULY 26, 1787

PRESIDENTIAL POWERS ARE DEFINED

Resolving the executive's role requires another wrestling match between Federalists and Anti-Federalists.

In the end, the convention retains the two powers identified in the Virginia Plan—to "take care that the laws are faithfully executed" and to make a host of "appointments," such as ambassadors and federal judges, with the Senate's consent.

Layered on top of these are a broad range of add-ons. Some are very specific: vetoing bills, writing government checks, granting pardons, making treaties, receiving foreign dignitaries, and commissioning officers.

One other power is also on the delegates' minds: the role of the president in any future warfare, especially involving a sudden invasion. At the time, this prospect is by no means far-fetched, with the British in Canada and Spain still controlling Florida and all land west of the Mississippi River.

The Revolutionary War has proven the futility of hoping for congressmen from thirteen states to agree on military strategy in timely fashion. Organizing a standing army to speed up action is suggested but rejected by some who are committed to state militias and fear a military coup. As Madison writes:

> *Oppressors can tyrannize only when they achieve a standing army, an enslaved press, and a disarmed populace.*

Of course, the solution to these concerns is before their very eyes, sitting at the front of the hall, in the person of George Washington—one man with mastery over both military and political affairs. Some, like his aide Hamilton, might wish to make him king. Others simply wish that his persona can be cloned over time in future presidents. But for now, it's clear the delegates intend to look to the executive to oversee military affairs, if and when war arises.

> *The President shall be Commander-in-Chief of the Army and Navy of the United States and of the Militia of the several States when called into the actual service of the United States.*

A final addition to presidential powers is remarkably open-ended: to do whatever is required "to preserve, protect and defend the Constitution." They expect a wise statesman-like president who nudges Congress toward actions in the national interest and vetoes harmful legislation when he senses it.

In the long arc of history to follow, America will occasionally swear in a president who lives up to these wishes.

THE ENUMERATED POWERS OF THE PRESIDENT CIRCA 1787

ARTICLE I	POWER TO
Section 7, clauses 2-3	Approve or veto bills and resolutions passed by Congress
Section 9, Article II	Write checks (via Treasury) pursuant to appropriations made by Congress
Section 1, last clause	Preserve, protect and defend the Constitution
Section 2, clause 2	Serve as commander-in-chief when Congress calls the army to service
	Require executive department officers to write up their assigned duties
	Grant reprieves and pardons for offenses against the United States
Section 2, clause 3	Advise the Congress periodically on the state of the union

ARTICLE I	POWER TO
Section 3	Recommend to Congress such measures as he deems wise
	Convene one or both chambers of Congress on extraordinary occasions
	Receive ambassadors and other public ministers
	Take care that the laws are faithfully executed
	Commission all the officers of the United States

TIME: AUGUST 6, 1787

AN ENUMERATED LIST OF POWERS IS APPROVED
FOR THE CONGRESS

By the end of July, the delegates begin to sense that what they set out to do back in May might actually be within their reach. A whole new government, respectful of each state's sovereignty but bound together by a central authority dedicated to the common good for all.

The time has come for the many lawyers in the room to worry about the fine print—especially codifying the exact powers of the new Congress they intend to create. The Virginia Plan simply assigns it "any tasks the States are incompetent to do."

This "leftovers" definition is far too vague for the delegates, and on July 26 they create a "Committee of Detail" to enumerate the powers one by one.

This very powerful group is chaired by John Rutledge of South Carolina, known to colleagues as "the Dictator" for his dual role during the war as governor of his state and commander-in-chief of its military forces. He is joined by Edmund Randolph of Virginia, Oliver Ellsworth of Connecticut, James Wilson of Pennsylvania, and Nathaniel Gorham of Massachusetts.

A colonial magistrate

After a two-week adjournment, the committee reports on August 6, including a list of about thirty specific recommendations. Edmund Randolph, who authored the Virginia Plan, also crafts this document. In a preamble, he expresses his hope that each power is clear as written and yet flexible enough to accommodate external change. His stated goals:

1. To insert essential principles only; lest the operations of government should be clogged by rendering those provisions permanent and unalterable, which ought to be accommodated to times and events, and
2. To use simple and precise language, and general propositions, according to the example of the constitutions of the several states.

At the top of the list is the "power of the purse" bestowed to the new Congress. Instead of the futile reliance on "voluntary state donations" under the Thirteen Articles, the House is authorized:

To lay and collect Taxes, Duties, Imposts and Excises, to pay the Debts and provide for the common Defense and general Welfare; but all Duties, Imposts and Excises shall be uniform throughout the US.

Delegates, however, remain very aware of America's visceral opposition to burdensome taxes, tracing from the Boston Tea Party to Shays' rebellion.

Thus "direct" taxes on a given person's income or wealth are ruled out in favor of "indirect" taxes—duties or imposts (later called tariffs) on imported or exported goods, and excises aimed mainly at taxing the manufacture, sale, or consumption of certain goods (e.g., spirits).

Another important financial change gives Congress the power:

To coin Money, regulate the Value thereof, and of foreign Coin, and fix the Standard of Weights and Measures.

This takes control of the money supply out of the hands of state banks (with their often grossly inflated "bills of credit" printed locally) and places it at the federal level.

A third proposal relates to war powers:

To declare War, grant Letters of Marque and Reprisal, and make Rules concerning Captures on Land and Water;

The enumeration goes on, granting Congress the authority to raise armies, call forth the militia, build a navy, suppress insurrections, negotiate and enforce treaties, regulate commerce, establish post offices and postal routes, promote science and the arts, issue patents, set up appeals courts, punish counterfeiters and high seas pirates, and oversee the naturalization process.

Finally, the Federalists slip in one last catch-all clause, authorizing Congress to:

Make all laws which shall be necessary and proper for carrying into Execution the foregoing Powers, and all other Powers vested by the Constitution in the Government of the United States.

This "necessary and proper" clause will boomerang after the original Constitution is signed and the convention adjourns. It will result in a set of ten amendments known as The Bill of Rights, not approved until December 1791, wherein the Anti-Federalists succeed in reining in the scope and power of the federal government.

TIME: MID-AUGUST 1787

NAGGING DIVISIONS OVER SLAVERY PERSIST

While the Enumeration Clause has enabled the convention to move forward, issues surrounding slavery continue to touch a raw nerve every time they surface.

Southerners are already becoming wary of Northern intentions, and they press hard for three guarantees in the final Constitution:

1. Continuation of the slave trade with Africa until 1808.
2. A promise that Northern states will return fugitive enslaved people to the South.
3. Ironclad assurance that slavery shall continue over time in America.

Pushback materializes on all counts. Gouverneur Morris assails the entire practice of slavery.

I would never concur in upholding domestic slavery.

Maryland's Luther Martin resists the further importation of slaves.

It is inconsistent with the principles of the Revolution and dishonorable to the American character to legitimize the importation of slaves in the Constitution.

LEARNING IS WEALTH.

WILSON, CHARLEY, REBECCA & ROSA.

Slaves from New Orleans.

"Learning is wealth"

Even the Virginia plantation owner, James Madison, expresses discomfort over the high moral aims of the new government and the suspect ethics of human bondage.

I think it wrong to admit in the Constitution the idea that there could be property in men.

Given these sentiments, it is not by accident that the final Constitution, largely drafted by Madison himself, never once references the word "slavery" in its text.

But the debates prove that dismissing slavery in writing is far easier than resolving it in practice. Just below the outward mask of diplomacy, the two sides remain far apart on the issue.

- The North wishes it could wash its hands of the "African problem," especially since their presence is no longer important to economic progress in the region. Perhaps the new nation, in service to white men, would be best served by turning back the clock and shipping the enslaved people off to Africa?

- The South rejects this thinking entirely. For better or for worse, the economic well-being of its entire region now relies on slavery. The North must recognize this fact as well as its original complicity in supporting slave trading in the first place. If true comity is to prevail within the new government, the North needs to support the continuation of slavery, not try to erase its presence.

As John Rutledge of South Carolina puts it:

I would never agree to give a power by which the articles relating to slaves might be altered by the States not interested in that property and prejudiced against it.

Recognizing fundamental impasses here, the exhausted delegates simply end with a temporary truce on slavery based on compromises already reached.

TIME: LATE AUGUST 1787

A VAGUELY DEFINED SUPREME COURT SYSTEM IS APPROVED

As time begins to run out on the Convention, delegates return to the third branch of government identified in the Virginia Plan, the Eleventh Resolve:

> 11. That a national Judiciary be established to consist of One Supreme Tribunal. The Judges of which to be appointed by the second Branch of the National Legislature, to hold their offices during good behavior.

The idea for a judicial branch at the federal level springs from the conviction that legislatures—locally or nationally—must be prohibited from passing laws that violate the principles laid out in the Constitution. As Alexander Hamilton says:

No legislative act contrary to the Constitution can be valid…It therefore is the duty of the courts of justice…to declare all acts contrary to the Constitution void.

But who would be responsible for policing the violations?

The Virginia Plan posits a "Council of Revision," composed of the executive and several members of a national judiciary, who would review new laws before they are finalized and then nullify any deemed to be contradictory to the intent of the Constitution.

Resistance to this council is widespread and varied.

- A review of every new law before it takes effect will paralyze the entire system.
- It would signal distrust and disrespect for the good intentions of the legislative branch.
- Power over the law would be transferred to a handful of judges, none of whom are elected by the people.
- Including an executive who may have no legal training makes little sense.

Eventually a proposal to review laws only after they have taken effect, and only if they are challenged for non-compliance with the Constitution, wins support, as does dropping the executive from the council in favor of trained lawyers only.

As time runs out on the convention, the assembly settles for Article III of the Constitution:

> *The judicial Power of the United States, shall be vested in one Supreme Court, and in such inferior Courts as the Congress may from time to time ordain and establish.*

The effect of this is to signal the wish for a Supreme Court, with details to be worked out later by the Congress.

Two years will pass before the Judiciary Act of 1789 provides some definition. The Supreme Court will consist of a chief justice and five associates who will be nominated by the president and approved by the Senate. Their duties will include "riding the circuit"—traveling twice a year to each of thirteen "judicial districts" across the country to identify laws that may be violating the Constitution. This Act also creates the office of attorney general, the chief federal lawyer, whose role is to prosecute all suits that come before the Supreme Court, and to provide general legal advice the president and other government officials.

Over time the Supreme Court will define its own scope and authority, often to the dismay of future presidents, legislators, and various segments of the public.

TIME: EARLY SEPTEMBER 1787

RATIFICATION PROCEDURES ARE DEBATED

The delegates know now that they will soon be asked to sign their names to a final document, a prospect that prompts last minute soul searching.

Two topics assume center stage: procedures for ratifying and amending the contract.

Friction materializes around the question of "who will be asked to approve the new Constitution, and by what margin must it pass?"

Two of the most vocal Anti-Federalists, Elbridge Gerry of Massachusetts and Maryland's Luther Martin, insist that approval must rest with the state legislatures. But their pleas are beaten back after another strong Anti-Federalist, Virginia's George Mason, speaks up.

> *Whither must we resort? To the people…It is of great moment that this doctrine be cherished as the basis of free government.*

With Mason's support, the assembly returns to the Virginia Plan, which proposes that special conventions be held in each state involving representatives, elected by the people for the express purpose of debating and voting on the Constitution. As Madison writes, it must be backed…

> *By the supreme authority of the people themselves…the fountain of all power.*

George Washington (1732–1799)

The focus now shifts to whether or not all thirteen states must ratify the new contract before it becomes the law of the land. While the rules of the Confederation require unanimity, many fear this will be impossible—especially since one state, Rhode Island, has refused to even show up in Philadelphia.

After some give and take, the requirement is set at nine states needed for approval.

This further inflames resistance from Gerry and Martin.

Gerry broadens his attack, insisting that, as it stands, the document is full of flaws, and that amendments are needed. He adds his doubts that Maryland will ever agree. This time George Mason takes his side, announcing his wish that…

> *Some points not yet decided should (be) brought to a decision before being compelled to give a final opinion on the Article. Should these points be improperly settled, (we need) another general convention.*

Alexander Hamilton weighs in, supporting Gerry's demand that the document be approved unanimously.

Edmund Randolph, author of the Virginia Plan, also supports Gerry's call for amendments—as does Ben Franklin, who surprisingly offers a motion in favor of state conventions developing amendments to be brought back for approval to a second Convention.

For Madison and Washington, the notion of any lengthy delay in the startup of a new functioning government is tantamount to failure. James Wilson shares their frustration in his admonition to the hall:

After spending four or five months…on the arduous task of forming a government for our country, we are ourselves at the close throwing insuperable obstacles in the way of its success.

Wilson's sentiment prevails, and Franklin's motion is tabled for the moment.

TIME: SEPTEMBER 5–12, 1787

THE CONVENTION MOVES TOWARD SUMMING UP

On September 5 the body names a "Committee of Style and Arrangement" to assemble all of the decisions reached so far and draft a final Constitution, with a one-week deadline.

The committee is headed by Dr. William Johnson of Connecticut, graduate of Yale and Harvard, an honorary doctorate from Oxford, accomplished lawyer, and president of Kings (Columbia) College in New York. He is joined by James Madison, Alexander Hamilton, Gouverneur Morris, and Rufus King, the latter generally regarded as the finest orator in the nation.

As they labor on, several other issues are wrapped up.

A national capitol comprising ten square miles of land is to be established at a site to be determined. It will not be a sovereign state, but rather administered by the federal congress.

SHIFTING LOCATIONS OF THE NATION'S CAPITAL

GOVERNING PERIODS	TIMEFRAME	LOCATIONS
First Continental Congress	9/5–10/24 1775	Philadelphia
Second Continental Congress	5/10/75–3/1/81	Philadelphia, Baltimore, Lancaster, York, Philadelphia
Articles of Confederation	3/1/81–Fall 1788	Philadelphia, Princeton, Annapolis, Trenton, New York City
US Constitution	3/4/89–11/17/1800	New York City, Philadelphia, Washington

Foreigners may serve in Congress after living in America for either seven years (for the House) or nine years (for the Senate)—but the president must be native born.

The executive, along with members of Congress and the judiciary will swear an oath to uphold the Constitution.

A small standing army will be allowed, even in peacetime—while state militias will continue to be relied on in case of war.

The definition of treason is resolved: engaging directly in war against the United States or giving aid and comfort to the enemy. Two witnesses to treasonous acts are required for conviction. Punishment for the crime will be determined by Congress and confined to the traitor himself and not carried over to his offspring.

On September 12, Dr. Johnson's committee arrives in the hall with a final draft of the new Constitution.

James Madison acknowledges that authorship belongs mainly with Gouverneur Morris of Pennsylvania.

The finish given to the style and arrangement belongs to the pen of Mr. Morris.

The opening words of the document ring true to the spirit of the entire endeavor.

We the People *of the United States, in Order to form a more perfect Union, establish Justice, insure domestic Tranquility, provide for the common defense, promote the general Welfare, and secure the Blessings of Liberty to ourselves and our Posterity, do ordain and establish this Constitution for the United States of America.*

It is the people acting as one unified body who are declaring the form and substance by which they expect to be governed. It is the people who will decide, not the states acting like corporate entities.

The individual states will retain their sovereignty, but within specified boundaries. As Gouverneur Morris says:

When the powers of the national government clash with the states, then must the states concede.

Out of the countless resolves presented to the convention, Morris arrives at a final set of seven articles, each with subsections, codifying the three branches of government and declaring how the Constitution is to be ratified by the states and amended over time if need be.

TIME: SEPTEMBER 15, 1787

THE CONSTITUTION IS APPROVED WITHOUT A "BILL OF RIGHTS"

Once again, the persistent George Mason of Virginia is on his feet, this time asking that a Bill of Rights be added to the final document. He points out that eight state constitutions identify these rights, and that a committee could draft them in a few hours.

If prefaced with a bill of rights…it would give great quiet to the people.

The legal scholar, Wilson, rejects Mason's plea on the grounds that the Constitution deals with municipal laws, not "natural laws."

Other opponents are less diplomatic in their criticisms.

Hearing about Mason's call, the lexicographer and political observer, Noah Webster, cites the folly of trying to codify the rights of man. His sarcastic call goes out for a clause that…

> *Everybody shall, in good weather, hunt on his own land…that Congress shall never restrain any American from eating and drinking…or prevent him from lying on his left side…when fatigued by lying on his right.*

Charles Cotesworth Pinckney of South Carolina offers another sound regional reason to skip a bill of rights.

> *These generally begin that all men are by nature born free. We should make that declaration with very bad grace when a large part of our property consists in men who are actually born slaves.*

Others insist that the document itself, from start to finish, guarantees personal values and rights.

When a vote is taken, Mason's call for a Bill of Rights is voted down by a 10–0 margin.

The delegates want closure at the moment—and a full year will elapse before Mason's wish is realized in ten amendments that finally codify many of America's most cherished freedoms.

A vote is now taken on adopting the Constitution as written, with all states voting "aye."

E pluribus unum. Out of many, one.

The thirteen sovereign states have become a new national Union.

TIME: SEPTEMBER 17, 1787

THE DELEGATES SIGN THE CONSTITUTION

After approving the draft, a calligrapher named Jacob Shallus is given the task of "engrossing" the text. He does so on four large pages (28 in. by 23 in.) of parchment, comprising some 4,000 words in total. A fifth page is left for signatures.

The document is ready for signing on Monday, September 17, as summer turns into autumn in Philadelphia.

Thirty-eight of the original 55 delegates are present.

After the new Constitution is read aloud, Benjamin Franklin is recognized for a speech delivered for him by his Pennsylvanian colleague, James Wilson.

> *I confess there are several parts of this Constitution which I do not at present approve,*

but the older I grow, the more apt I am to doubt my own judgment. But I consent, sir,
to this Constitution because I expect no better and because I am not sure it is not the
best. I cannot help expressing a wish that every member…[vote] with me…to make
manifest our unanimity.

With hope for unanimity in mind, Franklin offers a motion, written by Gouverneur
Morris, that would allow any individual dissenters to sign the document under the banner of majority support by their state delegation.

Next comes a last-second plea from Nathaniel Gorham of Massachusetts on behalf of
expanding the size of the House by allocating one representative for every 30,000 rather
than 40,000 state residents.

This suggestion prompts George Washington to speak for the first and only time
during the convention. His remarks are couched within his usual tone of humility. Madison records them as follows:

Although his situation had hitherto restrained him from offering his sentiments on
questions depending in the House, and it might be thought ought now to impose silence
on him, yet he could not forbear expressing his wish that the alteration proposed (by
Gorham) might take place…since the smallness of the proportion of representatives
had been considered by many members…an insufficient security for the rights and
interests of the people.

With Washington's backing, the change is approved, the result being a sizable jump
from 51 to 68 total seats in the House when it finally convenes in 1789.

At this point, members are given a final chance to say what they will.

It is with great sadness that Edmund Randolph announces he cannot sign the final document. His role all along has been critical, from presenting the Virginia Plan to authoring
the Committee on Detail report. But now he declares that his duty as a Virginian is to refrain from endorsing the Constitution until he can hear directly from the people of his state.

Not surprisingly Randolph is joined by George Mason, whose opposition has been
clear all along. Mason doesn't speak on this day, but writes up three pages of objections,
which he later shares with Washington. These focus on the erosion he senses in state
sovereignty, and the absence of a bill of rights.

After Gouverneur Morris voices his support for the document and urges others,
including Randolph, to follow. The third and final dissenter left in the room, Elbridge
Gerry, has his say. The Massachusetts delegate finds the outcome still too divisive, and
likely to lead on to civil war between factions in his own state.

Four others who oppose the Constitution have already departed: the two New Yorkers (Lansing and Yates) and two Marylanders (Luther Martin and John Mercer).

But September 17 belongs not to the dissenters, rather to the 35 other men present who have labored on behalf of a grand vision of government of the people, by the people and for the people.

Each in turn steps forward to sign, beginning with New Hampshire and working sequentially south to Georgia.

THE THIRTY-NINE EVENTUAL SIGNERS OF THE CONSTITUTION

STATES	DELEGATES
New Hampshire	Gilman, Langdon
Massachusetts	Gorham, King
Rhode Island	No delegates
Connecticut	Johnson, Sherman
New York	Hamilton
Pennsylvania	Clymer, Fitzsimons, Franklin, Ingersoll, Mifflin, G. Morris, R. Morris, Wilson
New Jersey	Brearly, Dayton, Livingston, Patterson
Delaware	Bassett, Bedford, Broom, Dickinson, Read
Maryland	Carroll, Jenifer, McHenry
Virginia	Blair, Madison, Washington
North Carolina	Blount, Spaight, Williamson
South Carolina	Butler, C.C. Pinckney, C. Pinckney, Rutledge
Georgia	Baldwin, Few

The grand convention then closes, with delegates off for a celebratory dinner together at the City Tavern. Afterwards, several reflect on the outcome.

Washington expresses amazement: "much to be wondered at…little short of a miracle."

So does the South Carolinian Charles Cotesworth Pinckney: "astonishingly pleased (that a government) so perfect could have been formed from such discordant and unpromising material."

The delegate from New Hampshire, Nicholas Gilman, explains how it happened:

It was done by bargain and compromise…[testing] whether or no we shall become a respectable nation, or a people torn to pieces by intestine commotions, and rendered contemptible for ages.

From abroad, staunch Federalist John Adams and Anti-Federalist Thomas Jefferson both applaud, the latter wishing only for a bill of rights and term limits on the executive.

Almost all agree that something amazing has just taken place in Philadelphia.

TIME: 1787–1788

FIVE STATES RATIFY WITHIN THE FIRST YEAR

On October 27, 1787, Congress submits the Constitution to the States for ratification.

The bar for acceptance has been set at nine states, but no one is particularly comfortable about imposing the contract on holdouts. The unanimity Franklin lobbied for is deemed essential.

Proponents are well aware of the states most likely to balk at ratification, including a big three—Massachusetts, Virginia, and New York—whose populations combined comprise 40% of the nation's total.

Massachusetts state house

To promote acceptance, the strategy lies in front-loading the process in states more likely to vote "yes," thereby putting pressure on the others to follow suit.

At the same time, a publicity campaign is mounted in the popular press. Philadelphia alone boasts over 100 newspapers in 1787, and scholars have pegged literacy at 90% in New England, a level surpassed at the time only in Scotland.

The campaign comes in the form of a series of 85 articles, titled *The Federalist Papers*. These are the work of three men: Alexander Hamilton, who authors 51 of the 85, James Madison with 26, John Jay with 5, and the rest are collaborations.

They are all published under the pseudonym of Publius, "friend of the people," a Roman aristocrat who helped overthrow a corrupt monarchy in 509BC. Their content is intended to inform the public about the ideas within the new Constitution and reasons why it should be supported.

By January 9, 1788 these strategies are working, with five states voting approval by wide margins, mostly after less than a week of debate.

FIRST FIVE STATES TO RATIFY THE CONSTITUTION

STATES	# DAYS	DATE	PRE- VOTE	FINAL VOTE	KEY DELEGATES
Delaware	3	Dec 7, 1787	30–0	30–0	Bedford
Pennsylvania	23	Dec 12, 1787	46–23	46–23	Wilson

STATES	# DAYS	DATE	PRE-VOTE	FINAL VOTE	KEY DELEGATES
New Jersey	7	Dec 18, 1787	38–0	38–0	Brearly
Georgia	6	Dec 31, 1787	29–0	26–0	Few
Connecticut	6	Jan 9, 1788	128–40	128–40	Sherman, Ellsworth, Johnson

TIME: BY JULY 26, 1788

MASSACHUSETTS, VIRGINIA, AND NEW YORK ASSURE PASSAGE

The first real test is in Massachusetts, where the 355 convention delegates are evenly divided with 177 for and 178 against ratification as they assemble. The debates extend over four weeks, with Rufus King and Nathaniel Gorham pitted against Anti-Federalists led by Sam Adams and Elbridge Gerry behind the scenes. The wildcard here turns out to be Governor John Hancock, who is accused of tipping toward the "pro" side in exchange for promises of higher office in the new government. Ten votes switch sides and the Constitution is ratified by 187–168 with an accompanying call for amendments.

Despite Luther Martin's dire predictions, Maryland votes "aye" by a comfortable 63–11 margin. South Carolina follows, and when New Hampshire agrees on June 25, 1788, the nine-state target is achieved. Still, all eyes remain focused on Virginia and New York.

Both Madison and Washington have been disappointed by the fact that only three of Virginia's seven delegates signed their names to the Constitution. The venerable George Mason has refused, as has the sitting governor, Edmund Randolph. The state also boasts two famous patriots—Patrick Henry and Richard Henry Lee—both outspoken critics of the new contract and Washington himself. The delegates go into the state convention with 84 tentatively pledging to vote "aye" and 84 pledging "nay." After three weeks, five votes change hands, and the Constitution is ratified. Ironically, Edmund Randolph decides to lend his support, and plays an important role along the way.

New York is next. Going into the convention, the pledges are stacked against approval. Governor George Clinton, a fierce Anti-Federalist, is chosen to chair the assembly. Other opponents include Robert Yates and John Lansing, the two delegates who left Philadelphia in a huff back in July. The battle is joined by an impressive array on the other side: Alexander Hamilton, the diplomat John Jay, as well as many of the state's old Dutch patroon families (Roosevelt, DeWitt, Ten Eyck). New York's convention will last the longest (39 days) and prove the most contentious. Opponents insist on a bill of rights, along with 32 amendments. However, they cannot make the case for being a lone holdout in the grand scheme of things, and a tight 30–27 "aye" vote prevails.

EIGHT REMAINING STATES TO RATIFY THE CONSTITUTION

STATES	# DAYS	DATE	PRE- VOTE	FINAL VOTE	KEY DELEGATES
Massachusetts	28	Feb 6, 1788	177–178	187–168	King, S. Adams, Hancock
Maryland	5	April 26, 1788	64–12	63–11	Martin
South Carolina	11	May 23, 1788	149–73	149–73	Rutledge, C.C. Pinckney, C. Pinckney
New Hampshire	3	June 21, 1788	52–52	57–47	Gilman
Virginia	23	June 25, 1788	84–84	89–79	Madison, Mason, Randolph, Henry
New York	39	July 26, 1788	19–46	30–27	Hamilton, Clinton, Yates, Lansing, Jay
North Carolina	5	Nov 21, 1789	194–77	194–77	Iredell
Rhode Island	3	May 29, 1790	34–32	34–32	---

While two other states—North Carolina and Rhode Island—are still more than a year away from officially signing on, the victories in Massachusetts, Virginia, and New York assure the creation of the new Union, known henceforth as the United States.

The time has now arrived to elect those who will convert theory into practice.

A national government ought to be established consisting of a supreme legislative, executive and judiciary.

TIME: MAY 14, 1787 TO MARCH 1, 1792

SIDEBAR: TIMELINE OF KEY EVENTS RELATED TO THE 1787 CONSTITUTION

DATE	CONVENTION EVENTS
May 14, 1787	Open, no quorum
May 25	Quorum
May 30	Virginia Plan
June 15	New Jersey Plan
June 18	Hamilton's plan
July 5	Connecticut Compromise
July 13	Northwest Ordinance
July 16	Great Compromise
July 26	The presidency is born
August 6	Committee of Detail report
August 23	Slave trade debate
September 15	Committee on Style and Arrangement draft

DATE	CONVENTION EVENTS
September 17	Signing day
	Post-Convention
September 19	Constitution is published
September 28	Constitution submitted to states for ratification
October 27	Federalist Papers appear
December 7	Delaware is first to ratify the Constitution
March 24, 1788	Rhode Island rejects Constitution
June 21, 1788	New Hampshire becomes ninth state to ratify
Sept 13, 1789	New York chosen as site of capitol
March 4	New government goes into effect
April 1	Quorum met in House of Representatives
April 6	Washington elected as first president
April 30	Washington and Adams inaugurated
September 25	Congress passes twelve amendments for ratification
December 15	Three-fourths of states ratify Bill of Rights
January 1, 1790	North Carolina ratifies constitution and amendments
February 2	Supreme Court meets
May 29	Rhode Island ratifies constitution and amendments
March 1, 1792	Bill of Rights go into effect

10

THE PLIGHT OF
THOSE ENSLAVED

TIME: 1790

SLAVERY CONTINUES TO WITHER AWAY IN THE NORTH

As of 1790, there are some 698,000 enslaved people living in America alongside another 57,000 who are freed men and women.

BLACK POPULATION IN AMERICA IN 1790

TOTAL	ENSLAVED	FREED
755,000	698,000	57,000

But by that time, six of the eight Northern states have already banned slavery.

DATES OF NORTHERN STATES' BANS ON SLAVERY

YEAR	STATE	TERMS
1777	VT	Constitution bans immediately
1780	PA	Current slaves kept for life, but their children are free
1783	NH	Current gradually freed; children born free
1783	MA	All freed immediately
1784	CT	All 25+ years old and newborns freed immediately
1784	RI	All freed immediately
1799	NY	Current freed in 1827; children born free
1804	NJ	Current slaves kept for life, but their children are free

The result being that only 40,000 enslaved people remain up North, with the majority of them in New York and New Jersey.

THE BLACK POPULATION IN THE EIGHT NORTHEASTERN STATES IN 1790

	NY	PA	NJ	CT	MA	RI	VT	NH	TOTAL
Enslaved	21,193	3,707	11,423	2,648	0	958	0	157	40,086
Free	4,785	6,567	2,762	2,924	5,463	3,397	271	631	26,800
Total	25,978	10,274	14,185	5,572	5,463	4,355	271	788	66,886
Total Pop.	340,120	434,373	184,139	237,846	378,787	68,825	85,425	141,885	1,871,400

The end of slavery in the region is reflected by the journey of the roughly 2,700 slaves still remaining in Connecticut. By 1774, some 6,500 slaves remain, with the Puritans justifying the practice based on various Bible verses and on the notion that captivity had enabled the enslaved people to learn about Christianity.

To control these slaves, Connecticut passes "Black Codes" in 1730 that outline a series of "whipping offenses:" being outside after 9 p.m. without a signed pass, drinking liquor or selling goods without written permission, and disturbing the peace or threatening a white person.

The Puritans tend to treat their slaves in a paternalistic fashion. Many act as household servants rather than field hands, and they are allowed to attend church services with their owners, albeit sitting in segregated pews. Some black children are also allowed to attend local schools.

While voluntary "manumission" occurs from time to time, the formal movement away from slavery begins in Connecticut in 1774 with a ban on the importation of Africans, in response to complaints from white laborers looking for work. When the war with England breaks out in 1776, some Black people join the Continental Army, fight in integrated units, and gain their freedom as a result of their service. Others find ways to accumulate the money needed to purchase freedom from their owners.

Then, in 1784, a Connecticut state law grants freedom at age 25 to all future newborn slaves, and by the 1820 census, only 97 enslaved people remain.

Meanwhile, in 1790, the picture across the South is radically different. The region accounts for 94% of all those in bondage, and in four of them, enslaved people make up over one-third of the state's total population.

THE BLACK POPULATION IN THE SIX SOUTHERN STATES IN 1790

	TOTAL	VA	SC	MD	NC	GA	DE
Total	658,000	293,000	115,000	108,000	104,000	29,000	9,000
% of State Pop.	18%	39%	43%	32%	26%	35%	15%

TIME: 1790

JEFFERSON'S STEREOTYPICAL VIEWS OF ENSLAVED PEOPLE

By 1790 native Africans have lived among white Americans for well over 150 years. The practice of slavery has gradually withered away in the North and the total Black population there has leveled off at around 67,000, with some 27,000 living as "manumitted" or free men. Not so in the South, where upwards of 650,000 slaves are critical to the economic prosperity of the region.

Despite these different outcomes, what is common among white men both Northern and Southern is a stereotypical view of all Black people as an inferior "sub-species" to be contained, controlled, and feared.

Thomas Jefferson, plantation owner (1743–1826)

No one articulates these prejudices more clearly than Thomas Jefferson, the squire of the Monticello Plantation. They are best captured in his 1785 book, *Notes on the State of Virginia* where, in clinical fashion, he discusses the differences between Black people and white people, and why these will never be reconciled.

In memory they are equal to the whites; in reason much inferior, as I think one could scarcely be found capable of tracing and comprehending the investigations of Euclid;

They are more ardent after their female: but love seems with them to be more an eager desire, than a tender delicate mixture of sentiment and sensation.

Black men prefer white women over their own, just as orangutans prefer black women over their own.

They secrete less by the kidnies, and more by the glands of the skin, which gives them a very strong and disagreeable odour.

Those numberless afflictions, which render it doubtful whether heaven has given life to us in mercy or in wrath, are less felt, and sooner forgotten with them.

Whether they will be equal to the composition of a more extensive run of melody, or of complicated harmony, is yet to be proved.

In imagination they are dull, tasteless, and anomalous.

Apart from their lack of respect for property laws, which is understandable, there are…numerous instances of the most rigid integrity, of benevolence, gratitude, and unshaken fidelity.

Jefferson goes on to wonder what could explain the differences between himself and the over 100 African slaves who surround him on a daily basis.

In the end, all he can conclude is that perhaps Black people represent a different species from white people.

I advance it therefore as a suspicion only, that the blacks, whether originally a distinct race, or made distinct by time and circumstances, are inferior to the whites in the endowments both of body and mind…

This unfortunate difference of colour, and perhaps of faculty, is a powerful obstacle to the emancipation of these people.

Herein lies the basis for much of the anti-Black racism that infects the white population, both South and North. It argues that the Africans are "a distinct race" and "inferior in both body and mind." In other words, they are sub-human beings by no means created equal, and incapable of ever rising beyond their present station.

The "American Dream" is for white men, not for Black people. So saith the man who will serve as America's third president.

TIME: 1619 AND ONWARD

THE DAILY SUFFERING OF THOSE ENSLAVED IN THE SOUTH

Four enslaved boys

While white Americans are striving to get ahead in 1790, enslaved people are left simply trying to survive.

Standing all day in bug- and worm-infested dirt, mud, or ankle-deep water to cultivate rice, tobacco, or cotton becomes their lot. It is punishing labor and intensely monotonous. It is marked by fear at any moment of the lash, delivered by a displeased or arbitrarily sadistic overseer. It is also endless. The only way out is death, and death is all around, in the faces of the young and the old, all accelerated by meager rations, run-down living quarters, and flimsy attire.

Their later recorded testimonials tell of hard lives marked by back-breaking labor, gnawing hunger, physical punishment, and constant fear of being uprooted from the solace offered by their families and fellow captives.

In 1790, one in every four North Carolinians is a slave. Here are their stories;

MOSES GRANDY OF CAMDEN, NC:

Daily life for a slave in North Carolina was incredibly difficult. Slaves, especially those in the field, worked from sunrise until sunset. Even small children and the elderly were not exempt from these long work hours. Slaves were generally allowed a day off on Sunday, and on infrequent holidays such as Christmas or the Fourth of July.

I was next with Mr. Enoch Sawyer of Camden county: my business was to keep ferry, and do other odd work. It was cruel living; we had not near enough of either victuals or clothes; I was half-starved for half my time. I have often ground the husks of Indian corn over again in a hand-mill, for the chance of getting something to eat out of it, which the former grinding had left. In severe frosts, I was compelled to go into the fields and woods to work, with my naked feet cracked and bleeding from extreme cold: to warm them, I used to rouse an ox or hog, and stand on the place where it had lain. I was at that place three years, and very long years they seemed to me.

MOSES ROPER OF CASWELL, NC:

At this time I was quite a small boy, and was sold to Mr. Hodge, a negro trader. Here I began to enter into hardships. After travelling several hundred miles, Mr. Hodge sold me to Mr. Gooch, the cotton planter, Cashaw county, South Carolina; he purchased me at a town called Liberty Hill, about three miles from his home. As soon as he got home, he immediately put me on his cotton plantation to work, and put me under overseers, gave me allowance of meat and bread with the other slaves, which was not half enough for me to live upon, and very laborious work. Here my heart was almost broke with grief at leaving my fellow slaves. Mr. Gooch did not mind my grief, for he flogged me nearly every day, and very severely.

HARRIET JACOBS OF EDENTON, NC:

Why does the slave ever love? Why allow the tendrils of the heart to twine around objects which may at any moment be wrenched away by the hand of violence? ...I did not reason thus when I was a young girl. Youth will be youth. I loved, and I indulged the hope that the dark clouds around me would turn out a bright lining. I forgot that in the land of my birth the shadows are too dense for light to penetrate.

There was in the neighborhood a young colored carpenter; a free born man. We had been well acquainted in childhood, and frequently met together afterwards. We became mutually attached, and he proposed to marry me. I loved him with all the ardor of a young girl's first love. But when I reflected that I was a slave, and that the laws gave no sanction to the marriage of such, my heart sank within me. My lover wanted to buy me; but I knew that Dr. Flint was too willful and arbitrary a man to consent to that arrangement.

JAMES CURRY OF PERSON COUNTY, NC:

During their few hours of free time, most slaves performed their own personal work. The diet supplied by slaveholders was generally poor, and slaves often supplemented it by tending small plots of land or fishing. Many slave owners did not provide adequate clothing, and slave mothers often worked to clothe their families at night after long days of labor. One visitor to colonial North Carolina wrote that slaveholders rarely gave their slaves meat or fish, and that he witnessed many slaves wearing only rags. Although there were exceptions, the prevailing attitude among slave owners was to allot their slaves the bare minimum of food and clothing; anything beyond that was up to the slaves to acquire during their very limited time away from work.

In the following spring, my master bought about one hundred yards of coarse tow and cotton, which he distributed among the slaves. After this, he provided no clothing for any of his slaves, except that I have known him in a few instances to give a pair of thoroughly worn-out pantaloons to one. They worked in the night upon their little patches of ground, raising tobacco and food for hogs, which they were allowed to keep, and thus obtained clothes for themselves. These patches of ground were little spots, they were allowed to clear in the woods, or cultivate upon the barrens, and after they got them nicely cleared, and under good cultivation, the master took them away, and the next year they must take other uncultivated spots for themselves.

11

BLACK PEOPLE BEGIN
THEIR UPHILL STRUGGLE
TOWARD JUSTICE

TIME: 1700 AND ONWARD

RELIGION OFFERS AN EARLY BEACON OF HOPE

The kidnapped Africans soon search for ways to sustain themselves in captivity.

One opportunity lies in Sabbath gatherings that some white masters hold to introduce Christian beliefs and the promise of salvation—a practice they cite as proof that, in saving heathen souls, "slavery is a positive good."

Wherever possible, the Africans co-opt these moments with storytelling and rituals that recall their own cultural and religious roots.

Ancestor worship is a common thread, as is the belief that the dead remain among the living along with supernatural beings who govern the earth. This is evident in West African Vodun, which involves the divine creator Mawu and her youngest son Lêgba, the chief deity, who is sometimes characterized as a wise and boldly priapic old man. Other lesser gods oversee everything from love and childbirth to agriculture and war.

Vodun also teaches that a spiritual essence exists not only in living creatures, but also in all of nature and all of man's handiworks, including crafts, medicines, and even languages. Deities are believed to inhabit Vodun fetishes such as carvings and dried animal remains, and these can be invoked to cast curses on enemies and to protect one's personal well-being.

Unlike the staid liturgy and hierarchy of the Puritans, the African religious expressions are spontaneous and kinetic. Many a white master who attends the Sabbath events to deliver a Bible sermon is shaken by the optics:

After the sermon they formed a ring, and with coats off sung, clapped their hands and stomped their feet in a most ridiculous and heathenish way. I requested the pastor to go and stop their dancing. At his request, they stopped their dancing and clapping of hands, but remained singing and rocking their bodies to and fro. This they did for about fifteen minutes.

Songs known as "Negro spirituals" are born in these Sabbath gatherings. They give voice to the suffering endured by the enslaved people, along with their hope for a better future, to be reunited with lost kin, and to be transported to a better place.

That place is most typically a metaphorical "home."

Oh yes, I want to go home…where dere's no whips a crackin…I want to go home.

Swing low, sweet chariot, coming for to carry me home…to carry me home.

These spirituals begin with a slow and mournful pace only to shift into rapid fire repetitions, signaling a movement from despair to the strength needed to carry on.

When the Sabbath ends and their back-breaking labor resumes, the lyrics are reinforced in shouts which ring across the fields.

They call upon God to witness their fate and to help them find a way through it. First to survive another day, then to persevere in their remarkable journey toward freedom and equality.

SIDEBAR: A SAMPLING OF "NEGRO SPIRITUALS"

I WANT TO GO HOME.

"Dere's no rain to wet you,
O, yes, I want to go home.
Dere's no sun to burn you,
O, yes, I want to go home ;
O, push along, believers,
O, yes, &c.
Dere's no hard trials,
O, yes, &c.
Dere's no whips a-crackin',
O, yes, &c.
My brudder on de wayside,
O, yes, &c.
O, push along, my brudder,
O, yes, &c.
Where dere's no stormy weather,
O, yes, &c.
Dere's no tribulation,
O, yes, &c."

HAIL MARY.

"One more valiant soldier here,
One more valiant soldier here,
One more valiant soldier here,
To help me bear de cross.
O hail, Mary, hail!
Hail!, Mary, hail!
Hail!, Mary, hail!
To help me bear de cross

SWING LOW, SWEET CHARIOT

Swing low, sweet chariot
Coming for to carry me home,
Swing low, sweet chariot,
Coming for to carry me home.

I looked over Jordan, and what did I see
Coming for to carry me home?
A band of angels coming after me,
Coming for to carry me home.

TIME: 1700 AND ONWARD

FREE BLACK PEOPLE SEEKING ASSIMILATION ARE SHUNNED BY WHITE SOCIETY

While the nearly 700,000 enslaved people struggle daily for survival, another 57,000 "freedmen" are scattered across the land. Just under half live in the North; the rest are in the border states and the deep South.

THE FREE BLACK POPULATION IN 1790

	TOTAL	% OF FB	% ALL BLACK PEOPLE
NORTH	26,800	47%	40%
BORDER	12,056	21%	23%
SOUTH	18,327	32%	3%
TOTAL	57,183	100%	8%

These Black men, women, and children are now left on their own to make their way in America. Their heritage is one of chains and whips and degradations, and most wish now to simply fit in to the white dominated society around them.

But this is no simple task, since the vast majority of white people regard them as an inferior race, prone to antisocial behaviors and possibly bent on violent retaliation against their prior masters.

Rather than trying to assimilate free Black people, white people in both the North and the South are mainly interested in containing and eliminating the "threats" they represent.

Containment comes in the form of efforts to trap the free Black population in segregated ghettos, and to use local government statutes or codes to restrict their rights.

Across the North and South, free Black people huddle together in downtrodden neighborhoods

A no-nonsense free Black woman

designated locally as "darktowns" or "shantytowns," and their daily lives remain shaped by the color of their skin.

Relatively few are able to read or write—skills forbidden to their enslaved ancestors and now limited by a shortage of Black schools. Those lucky enough to find work are typically confined to the lowest rungs of the economic ladder. Men are cast as common laborers, women as servants. All try to survive on minimal wages with little chance of advancement.

Their inferior status is reinforced in subtle sleights and direct prohibitions. Deference to white people is expected in personal interactions, be it stepping aside on the street or speaking only when spoken to. Segregation is also sharply enforced in some locales— where free Black people are unable to own property or are required to carry passes when traveling in certain areas or after dark.

The legal system is rigged against them. Taking disputes with white people to court is discouraged; no Black lawyers exist to represent them, and they are not allowed to serve on juries. Punishment of free Black people is harsh and uneven. They are put back into servitude for offenses ranging from "laziness" to harboring runaway enslaved people or receiving stolen goods. Sexual relations with white women, even consensual, is punished by being sold into slavery, castration, or hanging.

This is the plight of free Black people in 1790. In seeking ways to fit in to the dominant white society, they are met with outright rejection.

While allowed to mingle in public, the color of their skin brands them. For some white people, this branding evokes outright fear. Others react with humiliating disdain or pity.

But, almost always, the lesson is that blackness is something to be looked down upon. A stain of inferiority.

And the darker the color of their skin, the deeper the stain in the eyes of most white people.

In fact, an entire taxonomy develops around "blackness and bloodlines," derived from Spanish and French traditions. Those who are half Black and half white are labeled "mulattos." The offspring of mulattos and whites are "quadroons"—followed in turn by "octoroons" and even "quintoons."

Some free Black people, having escaped from slavery, now attempt to flee to freedom and equality by escaping from their very skins. Hence the concept of light-toned Black people "passing as white."

But this path is a rarity, and the vast majority are left in a kind of limbo—much better off than enslaved people picking cotton in the South, but much worse off than their white counterparts.

While the toll taken by this white racial antipathy is great, it prompts free Black people to band together and form their own society, eager to battle for true freedom, citizenship, and equality.

Their efforts are led by America's first "abolitionists"—free Black men and women whose efforts will prove to be nothing short of heroic.

TIME: 1775–1807

PRINCE HALL FOUNDS BLACK FREEMASONS LODGES

King's Chapel, Boston: site of first Freemasons meeting in America

One of the earliest Black abolitionists in America is Prince Hall, who devotes his life to bridging the racial gap through his involvement with the Order of Freemasons.

The Freemasons are a fraternal group, probably originating is Scotland in 1599, and officially chartered with London's First Grand Lodge in 1717. The order's stated mission is to support mankind's search for truth, charity and brotherly love—a search which progresses for inductees through three phrases or "degrees," from apprenticeship to basic achievement to mastery.

For Freemasons the symbol of this mastery on earth lies in the aesthetic perfection they find in ancient architecture, especially medieval churches. The Freemason's crest offers up two tools of the mason's trade as essential to man's moral quest—the square, encouraging actions that "square with virtue," and the compass, asking that members "circumscribe their own selfish desires" in favor of that which supports society as a whole.

Freemasonry takes hold in Europe and gradually migrates across the Atlantic to America, where the first officially recorded Lodge meeting occurs in 1733 at King's Chapel, Boston.

Several founding fathers are dedicated Freemasons, including George Washington, Ben Franklin, John Hancock, and Paul Revere. President James Monroe also joins the order, as does the sitting president in 1828, Andrew Jackson.

Freemasonry comes to the free Black community in Boston through the lifelong dedication of one man, Prince Hall.

Hall is thought to have been born in 1735 and purchased at age 11 by William Hall, a Boston tanner, who decides to teach him to read and write before freeing him in 1765.

Prince Hall quickly rises up within the free Black community, speaking and writing in favor of abolishing slavery, educating Black children, and allowing Black people to serve in the military.

However, he recognizes that his voice on behalf of these causes will be amplified by association with an institution respected by white people, such as the Freemasons. He first tries to join the Boston St. John's Lodge but is denied admission because he is Black. His next attempt—directed at Irish soldiers stationed in Boston in 1775—pays off, first with the formation of African Grand Lodge #1, comprising 14 free Black members and Hall as Grand Master, and then after the war in 1784 with recognition of Grand Lodge #459.

Within the Freemasons' charter, each Lodge sets its own rules, elects its own officers, and pursues its own agenda on behalf of improving the life and moral growth of its members. For Prince Hall, the Lodge becomes a vehicle for teaching Black people about the American political process, petitioning the Massachusetts state legislature to end slavery (which it does by 1781), and providing the education Black people need to become equal members of society. After being rebuffed here, he begins to school children from his home.

Hall organizes other Freemason Lodges in Philadelphia and Providence and is recognized as "Provincial Grand Master" in 1791.

On several occasions, he tries to unite his Lodge with white Lodges in Boston in the spirit of "brotherly love," but in every attempt is turned away. Frustrated by ongoing white rejection, he also dabbles for many years in a "back to Africa" colonization program.

Although he dies in 1807, the Black Freemason movement will live on in the form of "Prince Hall Lodges," projecting the voice of free Black people beyond the safer confines of the church and into the white political realm.

TIME: 1790s

REVERENDS RICHARD ALLEN AND ABSALOM JONES FOUND THE FREE AFRICAN SOCIETY

While Prince Hall founds his Lodges in Boston, a grassroots movement on behalf of advancing the cause of free blacks is also under way in Philadelphia. It is led by two Black ministers with similar backgrounds.

One is Reverend Absalom Jones, born in 1746 and enslaved in Delaware until manumitted by his master in 1784. After moving to Philadelphia, he takes up the ministry within the Methodist Church. However, he is frustrated by the segregation and racism he encounters and moves on to create the African Episcopal Church of St. Thomas. Its charter rings out its purpose as follows:

To arise out of the dust and shake ourselves, and throw off that servile fear, that the habit of oppression and bondage trained us up in.

The other is the Reverend Richard Allen, born in 1760, and, like Jones, a formerly enslaved man from Delaware. Allen is able to purchase his freedom in 1780, becomes a preacher, and creates the first independently run African Methodist Episcopal Church.

Together, these two men and churches form the rallying point for free Black people in Philadelphia.

Even before their churches open in 1794, Jones and Allen have worked together to set up the Free African Society, aimed at providing aid to Black people in need. Its preamble proposes that men of the African race join together in a society, cutting across religious sects, aimed at helping those in need.

Absalom Jones and Richard Allen, two men of the African race, who…often communed together…(decided) that a society should be formed, without regard to religious tenets, provided, the persons lived an orderly and sober life, in order to support one another in sickness, and for the benefit of their widows and fatherless children.

Members will pay dues of one shilling a month to create a fund which will subsequently be distributed to worthy persons in need.

We, the free Africans...do unanimously agree, for the benefit of each other, to advance one shilling in silver Pennsylvania currency a month; and after one year's subscription from the date hereof, then to hand forth to the needy of this Society, if any should require, the sum of three shillings and nine pence per week of the said money: provided, this necessity is not brought on them by their own imprudence.

Those who join the Society must live up to a series of requirements.

And it is further agreed, that no drunkard nor disorderly person be admitted as a member, and if any should prove disorderly after having been received, the said disorderly person shall be disjointed from us if there is not an amendment...without having any of his subscription money returned.

If any should neglect paying his monthly subscription for three months, and after having been informed of the same by two of the members, and no sufficient reason appearing for such neglect, if he do not pay the whole the next ensuing meeting, he shall be disjointed from us...

If any person neglect meeting every month, for every omission he shall pay three pence, except in case or sickness or any other complaint that should require the assistance of the Society, then, and in such a case, he shall be exempt from the fines and subscription during the said sickness.

We apprehend it to be just and reasonable, that the surviving widow of a deceased member should enjoy the benefit of this Society so long as she remains his widow, complying with the rules thereof, excepting the subscriptions.

We apprehend it to be necessary, that the children of our deceased members be under the care of the Society, so far as to pay for the education of their children, if they cannot attend the free school; also to put them out apprentices to suitable trades or places, if required.

We unanimously agree to choose Joseph Clarke to be our Clerk and Treasurer; and whenever another should succeed him, it is always understood, that one of the people called Quakers, belonging to one of the three monthly meetings in Philadelphia, is to be chosen to act as Clerk and Treasurer of this useful Institution.

The following persons met, viz., Absalom Jones, Richard Allen, Samuel Baston, Joseph Johnson, Cato Freeman, Caesar Cranchell, and James Potter, also William White… This evening the articles were read, and after some beneficial remarks were made, they were agreed unto.

In addition to helping those in financial need, the Free African Society will play an important role in opening schools to educate Black children, as well as providing funds to enslaved people to purchase their freedom.

Reverend Absalom Jones is also remembered for his groundbreaking petitions to the US Congress protesting abuses associated with the 1793 Fugitive Slave Act. This law becomes a daily nightmare for free Black people everywhere—allowing bounty hunting agents to seize Black people off the streets, haul them in front of a judge, use flimsy evidence to label them runaways, and then return them to slavery. He fails to get the act changed, but his petitions set the stage for future political actions by Black people to seek redress from Congress.

Absalom Jones dies in 1818, and Richard Allen lives on until 1831, long enough to see his African Methodist Episcopal Church take hold in early Black communities across the nation. In his later years he also pioneers the Free Produce Society, an economic movement that boycotts the sale of goods made by slave labor.

TIME: 1804–1831

REVEREND THOMAS PAUL OPENS A CHURCH AND MEETING HALL FOR BLACK PEOPLE IN BOSTON

Another pioneer Black minister is the Reverend Thomas Paul who is intent on opening an African Baptist Church in Boston.

Paul is born in 1773 to free parents living in Exeter, New Hampshire. He is educated at the Free Will Society Academy, run by the Free Will Baptist Church. Like two of his brothers, he sets out to become a preacher. He is ordained in 1804 and marries before moving to Boston at age 31.

Once there he takes up residence among some 1,000 other free Black people living just west of City Hall in a segregated area which becomes known as "the Hill."

As an aspiring minister, he finds that the only re-

A free Black man standing tall

ligious services open to Black people occur in white churches, where they are forced to sit in segregated and out-of-sight pews. He recalls this humiliation as follows:

> *I raised my head up (from prayer) and saw one of the trustees having hold of the Reverend Absalom Jones pulling him up off his knees and saying "you must get up, you must not kneel here." Mr. Jones replied, "wait until prayer is over and I will trouble you no more." With that he beckoned to one of the other trustee…and went to William White to pick him up.*

Henceforth Paul is determined to establish an independent Black church in his neighborhood.

At that time, only two such Black-run churches exist in America: one in Savannah, Georgia, and the other in Petersburg, Virginia. Both are Baptist and both are less than two years old.

But Paul is undeterred by the odds, and together with twenty other free Black people, he charters the African Baptist Church and Meeting House in August 1805. His group buys land, builds the church itself, and holds its first service on December 6, 1806. Membership is open to Black people and to all others who are "benevolently disposed to Africans."

Paul's Church of Boston quickly becomes the model for "mutual aid societies" across free Black enclaves.

Children are given their first exposure to education at the church, initially through tutoring by adults who can read and write, then through a more formal school run by Prince Hall's son, Primus.

For free Black adults on the Hill, the Meeting House annex proves as impactful as the church itself. It becomes their social hub, a safe harbor where they can be themselves, away from the humiliations imposed by white society. It is also a place where they can gather freely, locate shelter, engage in commerce from banking to buying groceries and clothing to hairstyling and barbering, advance their own education, and learn trades.

Administering the affairs of the Church provides members with a chance to experience the governmental and political challenges integral to white social structures. In his wisdom, the Reverend Paul charges them with selecting their own leaders and rules, funding their operations, learning from each other, supporting each other, and building self-confidence.

As a clergyman, Thomas Paul is recognized both for his oratory skills, including impassioned sermons to white audiences, and for his theological arguments linking biblical scripture to the cause of abolishing slavery.

Like Prince Hall, his legacy extends beyond his initial work in Boston. In 1808 he helps found the Abyssinian Baptist Church in New York. His work as a Freemason takes him to England, where he meets with William Wilberforce, the evangelical white prime minister instrumental in eventually abolishing slavery in the United Kingdom. He also travels to Haiti as a missionary in 1823.

Reverend Paul dies in 1831 at 58 years old, but his African Baptist Church and Meeting Hall continues to serve the free Black people of Boston.

In 1832, the white abolitionist William Lloyd Garrison convenes the first gathering of the New England Anti-Slavery Society at the church. In 1834 a school building is erected on Joy Street, adjacent to the church, from funds willed by the white philanthropist Abiel Smith for the education of Black children.

Paul's children also advance their father's cause. His son, Thomas Paul, Jr., becomes the first Black graduate of Dartmouth College in 1841, and joins his two siblings in lifelong support of Black advancement, especially through access to schooling.

TIME: 1775–1808

THE ROLL CALL OF BLACK ABOLITIONISTS IS FORMED EARLY ON

Even as the nation prepares to embark on its new form of government under the aegis of "all men created equal," nearly one-fifth of the population is enslaved, the "chattel" of their white masters.

They are regarded as an inferior species, incapable of ever being assimilated into mainstream society.

In the South their presence has become essential to economic prosperity—to pick cotton and to be bought and sold at auctions for profit.

In the North, their economic utility is gone, and they are mostly considered a nuisance—to be feared, constrained, and shunned.

Amidst this daily despair come the voices of America's earliest Black Abolitionists, determined to make a new home for themselves against all odds.

BLACK ABOLITIONISTS: EARLY MILESTONES

YEAR	MILESTONE	WHERE	LEADERS
1775	African Grand Lodge #1	Boston	Prince Hall
1787	The Free African Society	Philadelphia	Jones and Allen
1794	African Methodist Episcopal Church	Philadelphia	Richard Allen
1794	African Episcopal Church of St. Thomas	Philadelphia	Absalom Jones
1805	First African Baptist Church & Meeting Hall	Boston	Thomas Paul
1808	The Abyssinian Baptist Church	New York	Thomas Paul

TIME: 1753–1784

SIDEBAR: PHYLLIS WHEATLEY:
YOUNG, GIFTED, AND BLACK

Despite the declaration in the 1787 Constitution that Black people are only "three-fifths of a person," young prodigy Phyllis Wheatley makes a liar of the inferiority claim.

Phyllis is purchased in 1760 off a slave ship anchored in Boston harbor. The seller gives her up "for a trifle," fearing that his only option is to get nothing for the frail seven-year-old. The buyer is a local tailor named John Wheatley, who gives the girl her last name and turns her over to his wife, Susanna, to make her into a domestic helper.

But it quickly becomes apparent to all that the child is blessed with extraordinary talent, especially when it comes to reading, writing, and lan-

FANNIE VIRGINIA CASSEOPIA LAWRENCE,
A Redeemed SLAVE CHILD, 5 years of age. Redeemed in Virginia by Catharine S. Lawrence; Baptized in Brooklyn, at Plymouth Church, by Henry Ward Beecher, May, 1863.
Entered according to Act of Congress, in the year 1863, by C. S. Lawrence, in the Clerk's Office of the District Court of the United States, for the Southern District of New York.

Fannie Casseopia

guages. She is tutored by the Wheatley's son and daughter, and, at age twelve, has learned both Greek and Latin. She soon turns her attention to poetry, including the works of John Milton and Alexander Pope, and at fourteen, begins to try her own hand at the art form.

Those who read her early poems are won over by their authenticity and emotional impact and encourage her to publish them to reach a wider audience. But neither American printers nor their white audiences are ready to accept the notion of Black authorship—a bias that will persist all the way up to and beyond the narratives of David Walker and Frederick Douglass.

So, in 1773 the Wheatleys send Phyllis and their son off to London to explore the possibility of having her poems published there. She soon finds patrons, and her first collection of poetry is distributed that same year.

It is then that the rest of the world recognizes Phyllis Wheatley.

Celebrity follows, including correspondence with a host of dignitaries and a personal visit with George Washington in 1776, soon after the Revolutionary War is underway.

In 1778 John Wheatley dies and emancipates her in his will. That same year she marries a free Black grocer, John Peters, and begins to make her own way in the segregated enclave of Boston—which will prove to be a difficult journey to the end of her life.

Her husband is thrown into debtor's prison, two of their babies die in infancy, and she is left working as a scullery maid to try to support herself and her one remaining son. Her strength runs out in 1784 and she dies in Boston at age 31, followed shortly by her child.

Phyllis Wheatley is soon forgotten, but not her poetry. It lives on beyond her time, graceful and haunting, telling her story and moving those who hear it.

She writes to her English patron of the trauma surrounding her enslavement in a poem titled *To The Right Honourable William, Earl Of Dartmouth*:

Should you, my lord, while you peruse my song,
Wonder from whence my love of Freedom *sprung,*
Whence flow these wishes for the common good,
By feeling hearts alone best understood,
I, young in life, by seeming cruel fate
Was snatch'd from Afric's *fancy'd happy seat:*
What pangs excruciating must molest,
What sorrows labour in my parent's breast?
Steel'd was that soul and by no misery mov'd
That from a father seiz'd his babe belov'd:
Such, such my case. And can I then but pray
Others may never feel tyrannic sway?

In another poem, On Being Brought From Africa To America, she acknowledges and laments the racial prejudice she has encountered and asserts that "Negroes…may be refin'd and join th' angelic train."

Twas mercy brought me from my Pagan land,
Taught my benighted soul to understand
That there's a God, that there's a Saviour too:
Once I redemption neither sought nor knew.
Some view our sable race with scornful eye,
"Their colour is a diabolic die."
Remember, Christians, Negros, black as Cain,
May be refin'd and join th'angelic train.

In a third poem, To A Clergyman On The Death Of His Lady, she echoes the solace found in many Negro Spirituals about the "perfect bliss" to come in God's hereafter.

WHERE contemplation finds her sacred spring,
Where heav'nly music makes the arches ring,
Where virtue reigns unsully'd and divine,
Where wisdom thron'd, and all the graces shine,
here sits thy spouse amidst the radiant throng,
While praise eternal warbles from her tongue;
There choirs angelic shout her welcome round,
With perfect bliss, and peerless glory crown'd.

In her poetry, her letters, and her manner, Phyllis Wheatley signals the world that Black people are not to be denied freedom and respect.

## 12

GEORGE WASHINGTON BECOMES THE FIRST PRESIDENT

TIME: DECEMBER 1788 TO JANUARY 1789

THE ELECTION OF 1788

In December 1788, the United States is ready to hold its first elections under the new Constitution. Since each state sets its own time, the actual voting runs from December 15 to January 10, 1779.

All states select members of Congress, but three (New York, North Carolina, and Rhode Island) do not participate in the presidential race. Of the ten that do, popular voting occurs in only six: Massachusetts, Pennsylvania, Virginia, Delaware, Maryland, and New Jersey.

The right to vote for president is limited to men with property, with rules varying by state. The resulting popular vote count across the six states is only 43,782, or 1.3% of the nation's total population.

Despite pleas to avoid partisan politics from the Independent candidate, George Washington, divisions between Federalist and Anti-Federalist are evident immediately.

George Washington (1732–1799)

SOME PARTISAN TENDENCIES IN THE 1788 ELECTION

ANTI-FEDERALISTS	FEDERALISTS
Fear federal intrusion on states	Favor a strong central authority
Agricultural economy	Economy is diversifying
Protective of slavery	Not dependent on slavery
Minimize federal costs and taxes	Active funding and support of business
More prevalent in South	More prevalent in North

As expected, Washington is easily elected as the nation's first president. He receives almost 90% of all the popular votes cast and is listed on all 69 of the elector ballots.

According to the Constitution, all "electors" name two choices for president, including one not from their own state—with whomever receives the second most votes becoming vice president. This honor goes to John Adams by a wide margin.

RESULTS OF THE 1788 PRESIDENTIAL ELECTION

CANDIDATES	STATE	PARTY	POP. VOTE	TOTAL EV	SOUTH	BORDER	NORTH
George Washington	Virginia	Independent	39,624	69	22	9	38
John Adams	Mass	Federalist		34			
John Jay	New York	Federalist		9			
Robert Harrison	Maryland	Federalist		6			
John Rutledge	S Carolina	Federalist		6			
John Hancock	Mass	Federalist		4			
George Clinton	New York	Anti-Federalist		3			
All-Others (5)			4,158	7			
Total			43,782	138			
Needed to Win				35			

Note: South (VA, NC, SC, GA), Border (DE, MD), North (NH, MA, NY, NJ, PA, RI, CT)

"Pro-Administration" candidates win the majority of seats in the first House of Representatives by a margin of 37 to 28, with sizable wins in the North offsetting losses in the Southern and Border states.

HOUSE OF REPRESENTATIVES ELECTION OF 1788

SOUTH	# SEATS	PRO-ADMIN	ANTI-ADMIN
Virginia	10	3	7
North Carolina	5	2	3
South Carolina	5	2	3
Georgia	3	0	3
South	23	7	16
Delaware	1	1	0
Maryland	6	2	4
Border	7	3	4
New Hampshire	3	2	1
Massachusetts	8	6	2
Rhode Island	1	1	0
Connecticut	5	5	0

SOUTH	# SEATS	PRO-ADMIN	ANTI-ADMIN
New York	6	3	3
New Jersey	4	4	0
Pennsylvania	8	6	2
North	35	27	8
Total	65	37	28

State legislators are charged with picking their two Senators, and the outcome favors the Pro-Administration forces by 19–7.

SENATE ELECTIONS IN 1788

SOUTH	PRO-ADMIN	ANTI-ADMIN
Virginia		2
North Carolina	2	
South Carolina	2	
Georgia		2
South	4	4
Delaware	1	1
Maryland	2	
Border	3	1
New Hampshire	1	1
Massachusetts	2	
Rhode Island	2	
Connecticut	2	
New York	2	
New Jersey	2	
Pennsylvania	1	1
North	12	2
Total	19	7

Of the 26 men selected to this upper chamber, eleven had been delegates to the 1787 Constitutional Convention.

SENATORS WHO ALSO SERVED AT THE 1787 CONVENTION

SOUTH	CONVENTION MEMBERS
Virginia	None
North Carolina	None
South Carolina	Pierce Butler
Georgia	William Few
Delaware	Richard Bassett, George Read
Maryland	None

SOUTH	CONVENTION MEMBERS
New Hampshire	John Langdon
Massachusetts	Caleb Strong
Rhode Island	None
Connecticut	Oliver Ellsworth, William Johnson
New York	Rufus King
New Jersey	William Patterson
Pennsylvania	Robert Morris

TIME: FEBRUARY 22, 1732 TO DECEMBER 14, 1799

PRESIDENT GEORGE WASHINGTON: PERSONAL PROFILE

America's first president is born on February 22, 1732 at his parents' Pope's Creek Estate, situated in northeast Virginia along the Potomac River.

Washington's father, a plantation owner, dies when he is only eleven. He is raised by his mother and his devoted half-brother, Lawrence, fourteen years his senior.

Lawrence, a military man for years, has married into the prominent Fairfax family, owners of vast tracts of land throughout Virginia. Along with his father-in-law, he is also a partner in the Ohio Company, which is dedicated to acquiring acreage west of the Appalachians and opening new British settlements there.

In many ways, Washington will follow in his brother's footsteps as he matures.

His formal education is sparse, but through Lawrence he is surrounded by "the best fami-

President George Washington (1732–1799)

lies" and quickly masters social graces. He is also a very physical man, drawn to horseback riding and hard work on the farm.

Through Lawrence's connections, Washington is appointed Surveyor for Culpepper County at age seventeen, in 1749. His earnings are substantial, and they go into buying land in the Shenandoah Valley, the first of many such purchases.

In July 1752, Lawrence dies after a long battle with tuberculosis at Mt. Vernon.

At age twenty, Washington comes fully into his own—inheriting Lawrence's estate and also succeeding him in the Virginia militia, where he is assigned the rank of major, by Governor Robert Dinwiddie.

His active military service begins in 1753, just as Britain and France are about to fight the Seven Year's War (1756–63) for worldwide dominion. The North American theater of this war opens in the "Ohio Country" around Pittsburgh, a strategic linchpin connecting French settlements in Quebec with those on the Mississippi—and also the target of the Ohio Company's planned expansion to the west.

When Governor Dinwiddie, also a partner in the Ohio Company, sends Washington to clear out the intruders, it sparks the French and Indian War (1754–63).

Ironically, Washington will then learn about warfare while serving in the British Army.

As colonel of the Virginia Regiment, his experience consists mainly of minor battles fought against assorted Indian tribes. But along the way he masters military organization, recruiting, training, tactics, discipline and logistics.

When the war ends, the crown promises him 20,000 acres of land in Ohio in reward for his service, but then reneges after King George III decides against opening new settlements. While the deal is eventually completed, Washington will never forget the British sleight. (He will die owning just over 41,000 acres, or 64 square miles, of frontier land.)

In 1759 he weds the widow Mary Custis, whose inheritance makes him one of the richest men in the colonies. Washington doubles the size of his Mt. Vernon estate, buys more enslaved people, switches his main crop from tobacco to wheat, and settles into the roles of businessman and social host to all the leading families in Virginia and beyond.

This is a pleasing life for Washington, and he lives it outside of the growing unrest that is forming toward the crown.

While he has been a member of the Virginia House of Burgesses since 1758, it is not until 1769 that he speaks up in opposition to Britain's bullying tactics—in this case the Townshend Act imposing duties on "necessities" such as glass, paper, lead, and tea, that were available only through English shipping.

His proposal is incendiary in character, calling for Virginia to boycott British goods until the act is repealed.

When Parliament responds to the December 1773 Boston Tea Party with the "Intolerable Acts" of April 1774 (closing the port of Boston, banning free assembly, etc.), Washington chairs the session calling for the First Continental Congress to meet in Philadelphia.

As the Revolution plays out, he emerges as the calm and steady presence holding the colonists together, converting the ragtag militias into a real army, and eventually winning America's freedom from Britain.

After his role in calling for and chairing the 1787 Constitutional Convention, it is clear to all that his destiny lies in serving as the new nation's first executive leader.

Washington's "bearing" is noted by all in his presence. An English observer writes: "there is a remarkable air of dignity about him." A Frenchman: "he carries himself freely and with a sort of military grace." The patriot, Benjamin Rush, says that his deportment is such "that you would distinguish him to be a general and a soldier from among 10,000 people; there is not a king in Europe that would not look like a valet by his side." Even the sharp-tongued Abigail Adams, wife of the new vice president, is drawn to his graceful demeanor and confidence.

TIME: 1674 AND ONWARD

SIDEBAR: WASHINGTON'S MOUNT VERNON PLANTATION

George Washington's Mt. Vernon plantation—slave quarters left of house

Washington inherits Mt. Vernon in 1752, at age twenty and expands it from 2,000 acres to over 8,000 acres after he weds the very wealthy widow Martha Custis, in 1759.

The hub of the plantation is a two-and-a-half story mansion with twenty rooms, and twelve outbuildings. This includes slave quarters which, at their peak, house about 317 enslaved people who work in the fields, serve in the residence, or handle duties such as carpentry, shoemaking, weaving, milling, and gardening.

Washington treats Mt. Vernon like a business, dividing the property into five separate farms, each run by an overseer, and each using the latest methods of mulching and annual crop rotation to maximize their output. Over time he experiments with 60 different crops and also runs a sizable fishing operation, with a catch taken from the Potomac, then cleaned, salted, and shipped across the colonies and abroad.

Mt. Vernon is not a cotton plantation.

Its main crop is tobacco up until about 1765, when Washington decides to concentrate on wheat, a move that eliminates his dependence on English "factors" to complete his sales transactions.

But like other plantation barons, Washington discovers that in addition to the tobacco or wheat or cotton in his fields, he has a second "crop" that is incredibly valuable—the crop of enslaved people to be "bred" and sold in the open market.

Like Jefferson, Washington is expanding his inventory of enslaved people all the way up until his death in 1799, when the count tops out at 317.

NUMBER OF SLAVES OWNED BY WASHINGTON

1743	1760	1770	1774	1799
10	49	87	135	317

And he is also selling enslaved people along the way, as in this 1766 request to a sea-going trader:

> *With this letter comes a Negro (Tom) which I beg the favor of you to sell…for whatever he will fetch. This fellow is a rogue…but exceedingly healthy, strong and good at the Hoe…keep him handcuffed till you get to sea.*

Washington is not known to be harsh with the enslaved people and is fairly unique among his class by writing a detailed will guaranteeing that each is to be freed and educated upon his death. Still, while alive, his overall attitudes are typical of plantation owners of his era—Black people are his property and a major source of his total wealth.

As the economist Robert Ransom points out, the presence of even 15–25 slaves on a plantation signals a 60-fold increase in wealth vis a vis the average small farm in the region.

RELATIVE WEALTH OF SOUTHERN PLANTATIONS

SLAVE LABOR	%	VALUE THEN	VALUE IN 2010
No enslaved people	67%	$2,362	$58,000
A few enslaved people	31%	$9,634	$237,000
Plantations	2%	$154,785	$3,808,000

Note: Ransom p. 63 (for 1860)

This puts plantation owners like Washington among the economic elites of America, the Southern version of industrial tycoons emerging in New England.

TIME: 1789–1793

OVERVIEW OF WASHINGTON'S FIRST TERM

Washington's inauguration takes place in the capital, New York City, at Federal Hall, which will serve as the initial home of the US Congress. The oath of office is administered on the balcony in front of a cheering crowd, and he then delivers a brief address in the Senate chamber. Like all presidents over the next 75 years, Washington's annual pay is set at $25,000.

Several critical challenges face the new president as he assumes power:

- On the domestic front, he needs to create from scratch a strong federal government structure capable of fixing the many shortcomings that have plagued the Confederation years.
- In foreign affairs, his number one priority lies in assuring the nation's security against the potential military threats on each of its borders.

Washington in Masonic garb
(1732–1799)

- Above all else, he must ensure that the "sovereign states" he governs begin to behave as one unified entity, avoiding divisive factions, moving America toward the destiny he sees for it.

He begins by setting up the infrastructure needed to run a federal government, including the "cabinet system" that places senior officials at the head of various departments. Washington's cabinet is limited to five men.

WASHINGTON'S FIRST CABINET: 1789

POSITION	NAME	HOME STATE
Vice-President	John Adams	Massachusetts
Secretary of State	Thomas Jefferson	Virginia
Secretary of Treasury	Alexander Hamilton	New York

POSITION	NAME	HOME STATE
Secretary of War	Henry Knox	Massachusetts
Attorney General	Edmund Randolph	Virginia

As secretary of state, Thomas Jefferson's brief is to play the European powers against each other in order to keep America out of further wars. Jefferson has just returned from four years as ambassador to France and is a renowned Francophile all his life. He supports the "people's revolution" already underway there and is forever suspicious of British intentions.

Alexander Hamilton's job is to create a vibrant and forward-looking economy, get the nation out of debt, and set up a stable banking system that protects the value of the currency, both domestically and in foreign markets.

Henry Knox, famed for transporting the cannon of Ft. Ticonderoga to Dorchester Heights in 1776, is charged with building a capable army, should it be needed.

Finally, Edmund Randolph, author of the Virginia Plan, who refused to sign the Constitution in Philadelphia and then worked hard to ratify it in Virginia, is asked to oversee the federal judicial system, as attorney general.

But Washington's focus during this first term is on domestic policy, especially around creating the foundations for economic growth and for running the government.

The burden for setting up the required policies and mechanisms falls on the president's right-hand man, Alexander Hamilton, the first secretary of the treasury.

WASHINGTON'S FIRST TERM: KEY EVENTS

1789	MILESTONES
January 10	Voting ends in first general election
March 4	New York City chosen as site of capital
April 1	New government goes into effect
April 6	Quorum met in House of Representatives
April 30	Washington and Adams are inaugurated
July 4	First Protective Tariff (5–15%) passed by Congress
July 14	Bastille Day: French Revolution begins
1790	
March 26	Naturalization Law (for citizenship) is passed
May 29	Rhode Island is last to ratify the 1787 Constitution
July 16	The District of Columbia chosen as the permanent capital
August 4	Federal government assumes all debts from war with Britain
September 25	Congress passes twelve amendments for ratification
December 6	Capital moves from New York City to Philadelphia
December 13	Hamilton calls for a federal bank of the United States (BUS)

1791	
February 2	North Carolina ratifies Constitution + amendments
February 15	Jefferson protests BUS on the basis of the tenth amendment
February 25	Washington signs bill to create the BUS
March 3	First Internal Revenue Bill (including tax on spirits) is passed
March 4	Vermont admitted to the Union (#14)
May 29	The Supreme Court meets for the first time
November 4	Miami Indians defeat US force of 1,400 in Ohio
1792	
January 12	Thomas Pinckney named first ambassador to England
March 1	Rhode Island ratifies Constitution + amendments
May 8	The Militia Act requires all white males 18–45 to sign up
May 17	The Buttonwood Agreement initiates the NY Stock Exchange
June 1	Kentucky admitted to the Union (#15)
August 21	First protests against the Whiskey Tax in Pittsburg
October 2	Washington tries to end the Jefferson-Hamilton feud
October 13	Cornerstone laid at site of the future White House
December 5	Second presidential election ends with Washington the winner
1793	
January 21	Louis XVI is guillotined during the Reign of Terror in France
February 1	France declares war on Britain, Spain, and the Netherlands
February 12	Congress passes a Fugitive Slave Act mandating return of run-aways
February 18	*Chisolm v Georgia* decided by the Supreme Court; later overturned

Estimates of economic activity during Washington's first term signal the start of rapid expansion for America.

KEY ECONOMIC OVERVIEW: WASHINGTON'S FIRST TERM

	1790	1791	1792	1793
Total GDP	$189,000	$206,000	$225,000	$251,000
% Change	---	9%	9%	12%
Per Capita GDP	$48,000	$51,000	$54,000	$58,000

## 13

A "BILL OF RIGHTS" IS ADDED TO THE CONSTITUTION

TIME: 1787

ANTI-FEDERALISTS ARE STILL NOT SATISFIED WITH THE 1787 CONSTITUTION

Even as Washington takes office, it remains clear that Anti-Federalist factions in many states will not be fully behind the Union unless a Bill of Rights is added to the 1787 Constitution.

To do so will require the development and passage of formal amendments, first in the Congress and then through ratification by at least three-quarters of the states. This promises to be a long and contentious process, and one which neither Washington and Madison, nor their more hardcore Federalist allies, wish to entertain. They point out that the vote was 10–0 against adding a Bill of Rights just before the Philadelphia Convention adjourned, so why reopen the debates again?

The answer lies in the fact that nine states have submitted proposed amendments to Congress coming out of their local ratification meetings—far too many to simply ignore.

CONSTITUTIONAL AMENDMENTS PROPOSED

STATE	#
North Carolina	46
Virginia	40
New York	32
Rhode Island	21
Pennsylvania	15
Maryland	13
New Hampshire	12
Massachusetts	9
South Carolina	4
Total	192

Seven of the states have begun their own constitutions by asserting the "rights of individual citizens" within their borders, mostly modeled after the liberties guaranteed to their English forbears.

Ominously, however, one amendment appearing on all the state submissions relates to federal taxation. If passed, it would prohibit the national government from collecting any "direct taxes" on citizens (e.g., based on their income or total wealth) without first asking state legislatures to donate the funds sought.

Since "direct taxes" are already ruled out by the Constitution, this prohibition is hypothetical in nature. But it still rankles the Federalists, who have fought so hard to guarantee that the new government is properly funded. Washington in particular says he will oppose any amendment that "goes to the prevention of direct taxation."

The task of dealing with the proposed amendments falls to James Madison, whose election to the House of Representatives from Virginia is threatened by his vocal opposition to a Bill of Rights. After switching his position, he wins his seat and is left with the duty of fulfilling on his new promise. His wish, as he says on the floor, is that...

Something should be done, that those who have been friendly to the adoption of this constitution, may have the opportunity of proving to those who were opposed to it, that they were as sincerely devoted to liberty and a republican government, as those who charged them with wishing the adoption of this constitution in order to lay the foundation of an aristocracy or despotism.

TIME: JUNE–OCTOBER 1789

MADISON TAKES THE LEAD IN CRAFTING A "BILL OF RIGHTS"

Madison begins by reading through the nearly 200 amendments developed by the states. They tend to fall into two categories: those focused on personal rights of citizens versus others wishing to alter the setup or functions of the government.

It is the latter group that Madison intends to avoid, since they reopen many old and divisive issues—calls for a larger number of House seats, restrictions on a standing army, term limits for the president and senators, a prohibition on government-sponsored monopolies, rejecting federal accountability for state debts, annual pay for congressmen, and so on.

James Madison (1751–1836) authors the Bill of Rights

Instead, he concentrates on the amendments that spell out the rights of American citizens.

This leads to drafting an initial list of nineteen amendments, which Washington approves, albeit with little enthusiasm.

Madison brings this list to the House on June 8, 1789, where it is soundly rejected by the Federalist majority. Six weeks pass before he tries again on July 21, this time securing an eleven-member committee to study the proposals and report back. This group arrives at seventeen amendments, including one that is crucial to the Anti-Federalists.

In the end it will become the Tenth Amendment—reassuring the states of their authority over all local matters not overtly delegated to the federal government in the Constitution. Included here will be matters related to slavery.

The powers not delegated to the United States by the Constitution, nor prohibited by it to the States, are reserved to the States respectively, or to the people.

The House also agrees to bundle the amendments together as an appendix to the original Constitution, rather than intersperse them throughout the articles as Madison had proposed. After an eleven-day debate, these are passed on August 24, 1789.

The Senate adds its own changes, consolidating from seventeen to twelve Amendments, and passing these on September 9.

The final version is approved by Washington on September 25, 1789 and sent to the states for ratification on October 2.

TIME: NOVEMBER 1789 TO DECEMBER 1791

THE BILL OF RIGHTS BECOME LAW

Another 811 days will elapse before the nation has its Bill of Rights—with Virginia becoming the tenth of the original thirteen states to ratify, on December 15, 1791.

Vermont, admitted on March 4, 1791, approves on November 3, 1791. The remaining three states reject the amendments. Georgia says they aren't needed, Connecticut feels they undercut the original agreement, while Massachusetts simply fails to reach consensus.

FIRST TEN ORIGINAL STATES TO RATIFY THE BILL OF RIGHTS

1789	APPROVED BY	1790	APPROVED BY
November 20	New Jersey	January 28	Delaware
December 19	Maryland	February 24	New York
December 22	North Carolina	March 10	Pennsylvania
1790		June 7	Rhode Island
January 19	South Carolina	**1791**	
January 25	New Hampshire	December 15	Virginia

The first two amendments deal with functional matters—House membership and congressional pay—and fail to gain enough state support for ratification.

The other proposed amendments spell out individual rights possessed by all Americans and not to be infringed upon by the government. The great freedoms—of speech, assembly, religion, and the press. Trial by a jury of one's peers. The right to bear arms. Protection from unlawful search or seizure. Many of these rights respond to violations suffered by the colonists at the hands of the king. In spirit they reflect the motto of the first corps of Marines, assembled during the Revolutionary War: "Don't tread on me!"

CONSTITUTIONAL AMENDMENTS PROPOSED

#	DESCRIPTION
x	Proposes a formula for boosting the # of seats in the House of Representatives.
x	No law increasing congressional pay can take effect until after a new election.
1	Freedom of religion, speech, the press, and right to assemble and petition the government.
2	Right to keep and bear arms and maintain a militia.
3	Protection from being forced to quarter troops on one's property.
4	Protection from unreasonable search and seizure.
5	Right to due process, to avoid self-incrimination, double jeopardy, and unlawful seizure of property.
6	In criminal cases, right to speedy, public trial by impartial jury where crime committed, confront accusers, and have legal adviser.
7	The right to trial by jury also extends to civil (i.e. non-criminal) cases, involving $20 or more.
8	Prohibits excessive bail charges for accused, and cruel and unusual punishment for the guilty.
9	The enumeration in the Constitution of certain rights shall not be construed to deny or disparage others retained by the people.
10	The powers not delegated to the United States by the Constitution, nor prohibited by it to the states, are reserved to the states respectively, or to the people.

Passage of the Bill of Rights ends the Anti-Federalists' call to hold a second Constitutional Convention and enables the country to move forward on matters of foreign and domestic policy.

## 14

THE SUPREME COURT CONVENES FOR THE FIRST TIME

TIME: SEPTEMBER 24, 1789

THE 1789 JUDICIARY ACT STRUCTURES THE COURT

The branch of the federal government set up to oversee compliance with the Constitution and Bill of Rights is finally defined more fully in the 1789 Judiciary Act, passed some two years after the Philadelphia Convention.

It will be called the Supreme Court and will consist of a chief justice and five associates, nominated by the president and confirmed by the Senate. Their duties will include "riding the circuit"—traveling twice a year to "federal courts" in each of thirteen "judicial districts" across the country to identify laws and decisions that may be violating the Constitution.

The Judiciary Act also creates the office of attorney general, the chief federal lawyer, who will prosecute all suits that come before the Supreme Court and provide general legal advice the president and other government officials. Edmund Randolph of Virginia is the nation's first attorney general, and a member of Washington's cabinet.

An early judge, wig and all

All the justices are lawyers and known Federalists. After Jay resigns to serve as Governor of New York, John Rutledge will serve as Chief Justice in 1795 on a "recess appointment" by Washington. The Senate, however, fails to confirm him, and he exits after only four months in office.

THE FIRST US SUPREME COURT

CHIEF JUSTICE	HOME STATE	POSITION WHEN NAMED	YEARS ON COURT
John Jay	New York	US Secretary of Foreign Affairs	1789–1795
ASSOCIATES			
John Blair	Virginia	Judge, Virginia General Court	1790–1796
William Cushing	Massachusetts	Chief Justice, Massachusetts Court	1789–1810
James Iredell	North Carolina	North Carolina State Commissioner of Laws	1790–1799
John Rutledge	South Carolina	South Carolina Court of Chancery	1789–1791, 1795
James Wilson	Pennsylvania	Professor of Law, College of Philadelphia	1789–1798

TIME: 1790–1793

THE COURT'S EARLY CASELOAD AND IMPACT IS MINIMAL

The number of cases coming before the full court averages less than five per year during Jay's tenure, and only two have particular significance.

One, known as "Hayburn's Case," is never actually decided by the court, but represents the first attempt by the judicial branch to overturn an act of Congress, rather than simply clarifying its intent.

In a 1792 bill, Congress charges federal judges with the duty of making recommendations to the secretary of war regarding the eligibility of Revolutionary War veterans to receive pensions. The judges challenge the act on two counts: the legitimacy of Congress assigning them non-judicial duties and then also giving a cabinet member authority to overrule judicial calls. Before this battle is fully joined, however, Congress backs off. Still Hayburn's Case is the first close call around "judicial review" of laws passed by Congress, something that will take center stage with supreme courts in the future.

In the second case—*Chisholm v. Georgia*—the court rules in 1793 that one state can be sued in federal court by a citizen of another state. Anti-Federalists view this decision as another attack on "state sovereignty," and go so far as to pass the Eleventh Amendment in 1795, outlawing this interpretation.

The Judicial power of the United States shall not be construed to extend to any suit in law or equity, commenced or prosecuted against one of the United States by Citizens of another State, or by Citizens or Subjects of any Foreign State.

15

HAMILTON'S CAPITALISM SETS THE ECONOMY IN MOTION

TIME: 1755–1804

PRESIDENT ALEXANDER HAMILTON: PERSONAL PROFILE

Once in office, President Washington's most immediate task lies in setting the US economy in motion. And to do so, he turns to Alexander Hamilton, the first secretary of the US Treasury.

While Hamilton is only 32 years old at the time, he is already a well-known figure on the political stage.

His background is unique among the founding fathers.

Born to an unmarried mother on the island of Nevis in the British West Indies, he grows up in poverty and goes to work at age eleven for a trading firm in St. Croix. His success here is remarkable and the New York owners bring him to Manhattan in 1772 to attend King's (Columbia) College.

When war breaks out, Hamilton distinguishes himself as a soldier, serving over four years as Washington's aide-de-camp and leading a battalion at the decisive battle of Yorktown. Along the way, he learns that a nation unable to finance a war will be hard pressed to fight one successfully. Under the Articles of Confederation, the government is perpetually unable to secure enough revenue to buy needed arms and to pay its soldiers.

After the war, Hamilton returns to civilian life, mastering the law, marrying into the prominent Schuyler family, and in 1784 founding the Bank of New York, the first in the city.

His fame leads to attendance at the 1787 Constitutional Convention, where he breaks with his Anti-Federalist colleagues from New York and joins his mentor, Washington, in calling for a strong central government.

He signs the final document and goes on to author many of the *Federalist Papers* articles that enable it to be ratified by the states.

After Washington is elected president, he calls upon Hamilton to be his Treasury secretary. His task is to establish policies that create sustained growth in the nation's

economy while properly funding the revenue needs of the central government-and guaranteeing a sound and stable money supply.

Hamilton serves in this job for five years, during which time he sets America on the
road to capitalism. Along the way he exhibits his penchant for gathering and analyzing
information prior to reaching policy decisions. In the first two years of his tenure, he
provides seminal reports to Congress on progress.

FIVE KEY REPORTS TO CONGRESS BY HAMILTON ON THE ECONOMY

DATE	TOPIC
January 14, 1790	First Report on Public Credit
April 23, 1790	Operations of the Act Laying Duties on Imports
December 14, 1790	Second Report on Public Credit
January 28, 1791	Report on the Establishment of a Mint
December 5, 1791	Report on Manufactures

Hamilton resigns in 1795 after details appear in the press about his extramarital affair with Maria Reynolds. The two fall in love in 1791 after Hamilton helps her escape
from an abusive husband. But James Reynolds learns of the affair and forces Hamilton to
make blackmail payments to avoid public embarrassment. When a Philadelphia tabloid
publishes the story in 1795, Hamilton is convinced that his political rivals, James Monroe and Aaron Burr, are behind it.

Hamilton challenges Monroe to a duel, which is subsequently avoided. But the damage has been done. Hamilton acknowledges the affair, resigns from his post, and returns
to his law practice in New York, with political scores left to be settled in the future.

Despite his departure, Hamilton continues to lead the Federalist Party and shape
government policy for another decade. He will essentially bend John Adams' cabinet
to his will and hurt Adams' chances for re-election—then go on to ensure that Burr is
denied the presidency.

His political conflicts with Aaron Burr will, however, end in tragedy on July 12,
1804, when the sitting vice president slays him in a duel.

TIME: 1789–1793

HAMILTON AND JEFFERSON HAVE DIFFERENT VISIONS
FOR THE AMERICAN ECONOMY

Within Washington's cabinet there is immediate friction over the future direction of
the economy, which will have much to say about America's upcoming influence worldwide.

One side of the debate rests with Thomas Jefferson, secretary of state and Virginia planter, who envisions a nation of "yeoman farmers." On the other side is the Treasury secretary, Alexander Hamilton, who favors what will become "industrial capitalism."

Jefferson's plan simply involves expansion of the existing agricultural economy. He sees it built around 50-acre farms, operated by an independent and self-sufficient owner, motivated to care for the needs of his family. Each farm would produce food, along with various crops and handmade wares to be exchanged for other goods and services at local markets. Simple bartering is the basis for economic exchange in Jefferson's model. My bale of cotton for your milled wheat and a leather belt.

This plan, according to Jefferson, would leverage America's greatest natural strength: its abundance of prime agricultural land, already equal to that of France and one-and-a-half times that of Britain in 1790. And that is even before casting an eye across the Mississippi River to further westward expansion. All

Bust of Alexander Hamilton. Jefferson kept one in his home in Monticello, saying: "Opposed in death as in life."

good things will follow if the new national government focuses on acquiring more land and transferring it at modest prices to migrating settlers. He says this to Madison in a 1787 letter:

> *I think our governments will remain virtuous for many centuries; as long as they are chiefly agricultural; and this will be as long as there shall be vacant lands in any part of America. when they get piled upon one another in large cities, as in Europe, they will become corrupt as in Europe.*

When it comes to optimizing the local economy, Jefferson argues that the individual states are in the best position to tax and spend efficiently against their unique conditions. If a given state wishes to build new roads or open more schools, the ways and means should be left up to them—likewise on all economic policies related to slavery. The federal government is too far removed from local realities and must be restrained from interfering with "sovereign state" decisions. So says Jefferson.

Hamilton's response is outright rejection across the board.

He argues that Jefferson is stuck looking backward to the eighteenth century, when he should be looking ahead to the nineteenth.

Instead of a landscape filled with small farmers bartering crops to sustain their own families, Hamilton imagines the growth of central cities, along with businesses run by owners who employ wage earners and provide the public with the full range of goods and services they seek.

Hamilton's economic vision is influenced by Adam Smith's 1790 treatise titled *An Inquiry into the Nature and Causes of the Wealth of Nations*. Smith attacks the old-world system called mercantilism, in which enterprise is tightly controlled by the state and fueled by a very limited money supply of gold and silver coins kept largely in the hands of the aristocracy.

To accelerate national wealth, Smith argues that the common man needs to be able to participate in starting his own business. This, he asserts, will benefit society as a whole in two ways:

- To succeed, the businessman will be guided, almost by an "invisible hand," to provide only those things that society needs in order to progress; and
- To maximize personal wealth, he will rely on "specialization," inventing the most clever and efficient ways to provide these things at the lowest possible cost.

As these future businesses prosper, so too will all citizens, according to Hamilton— along with the economy as a whole, and America's standing in Europe.

Hamilton also fundamentally disagrees with Jefferson when it comes to the role of the national government in guiding and supporting economic growth. Instead of a "hands-off" approach, Hamilton argues that the central government must be actively involved in policies that will enable capitalism to succeed. Four of these policies in particular will gall Jefferson and his fellow Anti-Federalists:

- Expanding the supply of capital available by printing soft money to supplement scarce minted coins.
- Creating a central US bank to handle government funds and regulate state banks and the money supply.
- Setting high enough tariffs on imported goods to "protect" the development of American manufacturers.
- Investing national tax dollars in local infrastructure projects that support domestic business growth.

Hamilton's vision of capitalism is both baffling and threatening to Jefferson.

Small farming and personal bartering are transparent and understandable to the common man. But not so this capitalism model with its owners and wage earners, banks and soft money, credit and debt, tariffs, and federal government involvement. Won't these new banks and businesses concentrate great wealth and great power in the hands of a new elite, another form of aristocracy, which would diminish the common man, along with the tenets of freedom and democracy? Won't they further erode state sovereignty and perhaps even threaten the South's commitment to slavery?

Jefferson's nation of yeoman farmers versus Hamilton's call for new cities, capitalism and industrial commerce.

These two views will increasingly come into conflict in the first half of the nineteenth century. At first, they will simply divide a few early industrialists in the northeast from the vast bulk of farmers in the rest of the country.

But as time passed, one region of the country—the South—will become frozen in the old agrarian economy built around slave labor, while the other—the North—will transition to the new industrial capitalism and wage labor.

TIME: 1792

ELI WHITNEY'S "GIN" CEMENTS SOUTHERN COMMITMENT TO COTTON

The Southern commitment to agriculture throughout the colonial period centers around its cash crops of tobacco, rice, wheat, and indigo.

Meanwhile cotton production remains minimal and is concentrated along the coastal islands of South Carolina. In 1790, American exports of cotton total only 140,000 pounds, valued at just over $2 million, with almost all of this in the "long-staple" (2-inch fiber) variety.

Its cousin, "short-staple" (1-inch fiber) cotton, is much heartier when it comes to surviving in lower temperature regions, but it has many more sticky seeds per "boll," and separating these seeds from the fiber by hand is so labor intensive as to be cost prohibitive.

This drawback, however, is about to change.

All because of one Eli Whitney, a Westbor-

Eli Whitney (1765–1825)

ough, Massachusetts man who tinkers with nail manufacturing as a youth, graduates from Yale University and, after visiting a plantation in Georgia in 1792, invents and patents his "cotton gin."

Whitney's "gin" (short for "engine") is ingenious. It removes seeds from cotton lint at 50 times the speed of human hands, and in turn it enables the profitable planting of short staple cotton across the South from Virginia westward.

Almost immediately the production and sale of cotton skyrockets. As it takes off, it also dawns on plantation owners that they have a "second crop" capable of very high demand and very high prices.

That "second crop" lies in breeding and selling excess enslaved Black people to new masters.

TIME: 1789–1793

HAMILTON AGREES TO COVER ALL FEDERAL AND STATE DEBT

In 1790 Washington has turned to Hamilton, not Jefferson, to fix the nation's broken economy and get the new government out of debt.

On September 11, 1789, the Senate confirms Hamilton's appointment as secretary of the Treasury, which consists of 40 staffers (tenfold the four employees approved for Jefferson).

Hamilton faces enormous opening challenges.

The first is the huge debt from the six-year war with Britain.

According to "The First Report on Public Credit" published on January 14, 1790, the United States owes a total of $54 million—$13 million to foreign interests and another $41 million to domestic investors. Individual states owe an additional $14 million in total.

These debts are owed to wealthy men—Americans and many foreigners—who have bet their money on an eventual American victory over Britain in the Revolutionary War.

Their bets are made in the form of bonds or IOUs, typically constructed as follows:

- In exchange for my loan today of $900…
- The government promises to pay me back $1,000 dollars on this later date.

While the above bond would be said to have a par value of $1,000, the holder might decide to sell it to another investor either above or below its face/par value—depending on the outlook for the American cause at any point in the war. In 1790, many of these bonds are owned by secondary investors who purchase them at amounts well below their par value.

Hamilton knows that the United States cannot immediately pay off this entire $68 million debt, given a total economy (GDP) valued at only $190 million. But bold action is integral to Hamilton's persona.

So, he quickly assures bondholders that the Treasury will pay all of them back at full par value. He makes this pledge in spite of resistance from Anti-Federalist factions within

Congress and others who argue the debt should be substantially reduced, since secondary speculators had purchased many of the bonds at prices well below their par value.

But Hamilton beats them back, on the grounds that recalculating bond values would be detrimental to securing future loans.

Many of these same critics also oppose his plan to assume the states' $14 million debt, for fear that this would further concentrate power with the central government. They concede after Jefferson, Madison, and Hamilton work out the so-called "dinner party compromise," whereby they reach an agreement on moving the capital from Philadelphia to Washington City by 1801.

At this point, Hamilton has assumed all US debt under the Treasury. Now all he needs to figure out is how to pay it off.

TIME: 1789–1793

THE FIRST TAXES ARE LEVIED ON FOREIGN IMPORTS AND DOMESTIC SPIRITS

Since the 1787 Constitution expressly forbids anything like an income or property tax on individual citizens, Hamilton begins his quest for funding with a tariff to be imposed on goods entering American ports.

Once he has settled on the idea of the tariff, the challenge then becomes one of deciding which items to tax and at what rates. The debates here produce an immediate firestorm in Congress, with each industry and state attempting to lobby on behalf of its own economic interest.

The most intense conflicts center on tariffs that appear to favor one section of the nation at the expense of another. Goods made from iron are one example—with the North wanting a high tariff to protect their new smelting operations and the South seeking a low tariff on imported necessities such as nails, horseshoes, and the like.

In the end, the Tariff and Tonnage Act of 1789 lays out a simple, compromise formula:

- American ships entering US ports shall be taxed at 6 cents per ton of cargo; and
- Foreign ships shall be taxed at 50 cents per ton.

This tariff provides 85% of the total revenue Hamilton is able to collect to fund the new federal government. The other 15% comes from excise taxes (mostly on whiskey and tobacco) and from the sale of public lands.

The tariff gives Hamilton and the country the revenue stream it needs to begin to pay its debts and to cover its expenses. At the same time, however, it also produces the first threat to secede from the Union, in this case issued by a founding father, Senator Pierce Butler of South Carolina.

Butler is particularly critical because he views the tariff as damaging to the profitability of what is becoming the South's key industry: the production of raw cotton.

High tariffs on finished goods from the UK increase their retail prices and therefore reduce sales demand in the US In turn this reduces UK demand for our cotton. So a win for the new northeastern mills comes at the expense of southern cotton farmers.

This complaint about tariff rates on cotton imports will rage off and on for the next three decades, culminating in the Nullification Crisis of 1830.

TIME: 1789–1793

HAMILTON FLOATS US TREASURY BONDS TO ADD MORE REVENUE

Interior of the New York Stock Exchange, started in May 1792

Hamilton's second source of government funding comes in the form of IOU bonds, similar to those used by the colonialists to finance the war. These are now cast as US Treasury bonds.

He offers these to investors along with a promise to redeem them at a future date, paying the face value plus a rate of interest to be established on a daily basis, depending on economic conditions.

"You lend the government $100 today and it will pay you back $104 in a year."

Hamilton puts these Treasury bonds up for auction to investors six times every week, and because they are backed "by the full faith and credit of the US government," they quickly become popular.

Investors christen these US Treasury notes as "the Stock."

And they begin to meet informally in New York at the Merchant's Coffee House on Wall Street to buy and sell "the Stock," with help from brokers, or "stockjobbers," who manage the transactions.

By 1792 a formal New York Stock Exchange is established to quote prices on five different securities, all bank bonds.

Over time, shares in corporations are added to the menu and the New York Stock Exchange becomes a weathervane on the health of the American economy.

The Anti-Federalists attack both the tariff and Hamilton's Treasury bonds, which they see as a spend-now-pay-later scheme that will run the country into long-term debt and insolvency.

TIME: 1789–1793

HAMILTON TURNS HIS ATTENTION TO THE MONEY SUPPLY

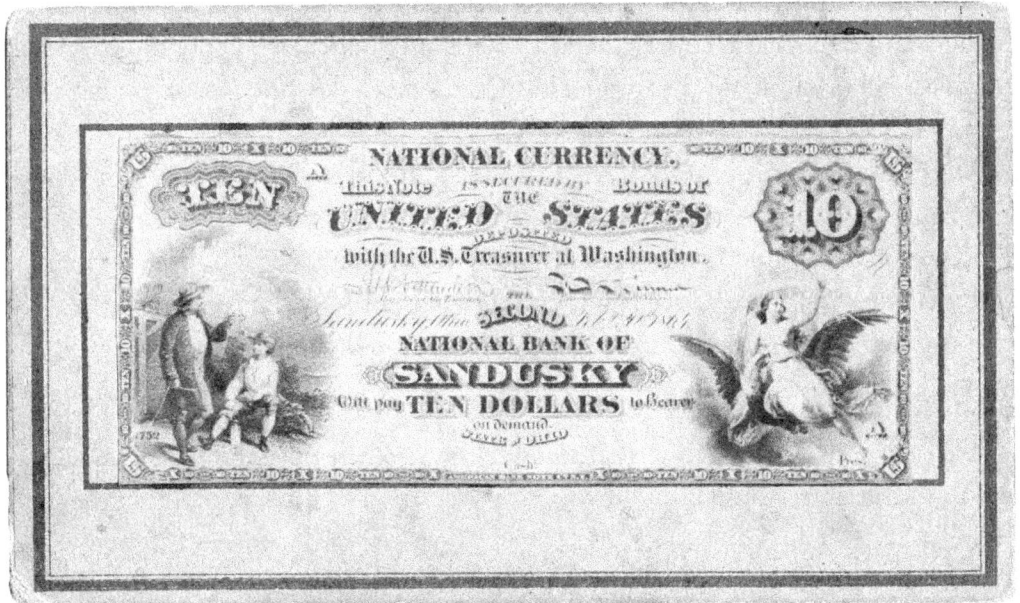

A $10 bill of credit issued by the Bank of Sandusky, Ohio

With his plan in place to secure sufficient funding to run the federal government, Hamilton turns to jumpstarting the nation's economic growth.

He believes the key to this lies in getting sufficient capital (money) into the hands of clever men who are intent on starting up their own businesses—to mill grain, make rum, transport goods over roads or waterways, or open storefronts in small towns or big cities.

The money itself must be simultaneously in abundant supply and viewed as trustworthy in terms of value, so that enough entrepreneurs can access what they need, and transactions can be easily facilitated. This poses a problem for Hamilton:

- The public has great faith in the value of minted gold and silver coins, but there is not enough supply to cover the needs of prospective businesses.

- Conversely, the alternative to coins are "bills of credit" or "continentals," issued by state banks during the war, which are in such out-of-control inflationary quantities that no one trusts them.

Since America is still some 60 years away from discovering large gold and silver deposits in the West, Hamilton will have to make do with "soft money" for the time being.

His challenge then lies in restoring confidence among a skeptical public toward banknotes. As he says:

> *There is scarcely any point in the economy of national affairs of greater moment than the uniform preservation of the intrinsic value of the money unit. On this, the security and steady value of property essentially depend.*

To restore trust, Hamilton will try to ensure that those entities handling "bills of credit"—largely unchartered state banks—maintain a sufficient supply of gold or silver coins on hand to "back up" their value. He decides that a ratio of 3:1 (soft money to hard money) will work.

For every $3 worth of bank notes in circulation the bank must maintain $1 worth of coins.

To enforce this ratio, he promises to bring fraud charges against anyone refusing a customer's demand to exchange banknotes for gold or silver coins on a dollar-for-dollar basis. As time passes this exchange pledge will appear on many banknotes:

> *"Ten Dollars In Gold Coin Payable To Bearer Upon Demand"*

He then adds to his "enforcement power" by another move the Anti-Federalists regard as further intrusion on state sovereignty—creation of the First Bank of the United States.

TIME: ONGOING

SIDEBAR: HOW BANKS WORK AND HOW THEY FAIL

As a banker himself, Hamilton intimately understands how banks are supposed to function.

Their primary role is to distribute capital/money to people who need it to start up or sustain their businesses. Bankers think of these as investments.

The most common form of investment is a loan made by a bank to someone who needs money (e.g., a farmer requiring $20 to purchase seed) in exchange for a promise to pay it back one year later with interest (e.g., after his crop of grain sells, the farmer pays $22 to the bank).

Another form of investment might involve a direct purchase by the bank of an asset that appears likely to appreciate (increase) in value. For example, a bank might decide to buy up land out west at $1 per acre, believing it can later be sold for $2 per acre—delivering a handsome profit.

Bankers are also always interested in expanding the amount of money or coins they have available to make these investments.

They can accomplish this by convincing individuals or businesses to make deposits in exchange for interest paid over time. For example, an individual or merchant with a spare $20 may deposit it today in a bank in exchange for a promise to get $21 back in principal and interest one year hence. To pay this interest, banks expect to invest this $20 in businesses or asset purchases that return more than the $21 they will owe their depositors.

In the vast majority of cases, this banking system works out to the benefit of all sides. Individuals and businesses get access to the money they need and pay back their loans. Banks invest wisely, make a profit, and pay back the principal and interest they owe to depositors.

But this is not always the case. Capitalism involves risks and, as Hamilton knows, banks are perpetually subject to these. They typically involve an unexpected outcome affecting a given investment.

A drought strikes, and the farmer, losing his crop, is unable to pay his loan back to the bank as planned. Perhaps the bank forecloses (seizes) his land instead. The value of the land bought by the banker drops sharply, creating a loss and making it impossible to pay back depositors when they come to collect. Perhaps the bank closes as a result, with all depositors losing their principal and interest.

Or the spread between the interest being paid out to depositors versus collected from borrowers suddenly turns against the bank. For example, the bank finds that it has made too many loans charging only 2% interest, while simultaneously promising too many depositors 3% interest—the spread has turned against them. Or, suddenly, inflation causes new people to demand 4% interest to make deposits, causing sudden withdrawals of cash.

All these banking risks are real and, when they occur, the entire economy can be adversely affected. What's even worse is that the profit motive in banking, as in any form of capitalism, can easily get out of hand.

Defalcation—misuse of funds by bank personnel—occurs from time to time, often in the form of embezzlement. But the effects here are local and limited.

The banking risks that really impact the nation's economy typically involve wild speculation in supposedly surefire investments. In the antebellum US, this speculation will often center on the purchase of new land in the West, where expected jumps in per acre prices fail to materialize and bankruptcy follows, along with panic runs on banks by depositors hoping to retrieve their deposits in time.

America's first Treasury secretary tries, like his successors, to steer between the rewards and risks associated with the banking industry.

TIME: 1791

THE CONTROVERSIAL FIRST BANK OF THE UNITED STATES IS CHARTERED

Hamilton's First Bank of the United States, or BUS, is chartered by Congress on February 25, 1791. It is a private corporation owned not by the government but by individual stockholders expecting to make a profit on their investments.

This charter calls for it to begin with $10 million in capital, allocated across 250,000 shares of stock, offered at $400 apiece. The federal government owns $2 million of this stock, with the remaining $8 million owned by outside stockholders, each required to make 25% of their buy-in payments in gold or silver specie.

Hamilton sees his BUS as having two main public sector functions:
- First, to handle the government's monetary needs—taking in federal revenue and paying bills to cover federal spending—while operating at arm's length to avoid conflicts of interest.
- Second, to help regulate the banking system and money supply across the states.

Bank regulation under Hamilton will take several forms. Formal chartering of state banks will accelerate—from a total of three in 1790 to over 300 three decades hence. The US Mint will take control over setting and insuring weight standards and values for gold and silver coinage. The BUS will also flex its muscles with state banks who appeal to it for cash loans. Those local banks in compliance with the 3:1 soft to hard money target will get loans at lower interest rates; those out of compliance will suffer higher interest charges or be turned down entirely.

Needless to say, these attempts at regulation are viewed as unfavorable intrusions on state sovereignty by the Anti-Federalists, who express a host of concerns:
- Isn't the "fractional formula" a fraud, designed to print imaginary money?
- Won't this system of phony money and usury lead to wild speculation by banks?

- Who are the people profiting from these banks and how can corruption be avoided?
- What happen if everyone wanted their money at the same time, in a panic?

To rein in the power of the BUS, they add a series of constraints to the 1791 charter:
- The charter will last only twenty years, expiring in 1811.
- The BUS must be run as a private company, not another branch of government.
- The directors of the company must be rotated after fixed terms.
- No foreigners will be allowed to own stock in the bank.
- The BUS cannot purchase any government bonds.
- The Treasury secretary may audit the BUS books at any time.
- While it would be the only federal bank, states could open as many banks as desired.

Jefferson's distrust of the BUS—and of Hamilton—is unwavering. He writes:

Hamilton's financial system… had two objects; 1st, as a puzzle, to exclude popular understanding and inquiry; 2nd, as a machine for the corruption of the legislature; for he avowed the opinion, that man could be governed by one of two motives only, force or interest; force, he observed, in this country was out of the question, and the interests, therefore, of the members must be laid hold of, to keep the legislative in unison with the executive.

The BUS also ruptures James Madison's commitment to the Federalist cause. Henceforth he will align himself with Jefferson in what will become the Democratic-Republican Party.

When political power eventually shifts to Jefferson, he will de-charter the BUS and do away with many of the banking controls initiated by Hamilton.

These moves, however, will backfire over time, as banks veer out of control every two decades or so, driven by wild speculation in search of windfall profits accompanied by public panic and often prolonged economic downturns for the nation.

TIME: 1755–1804

ASSESSING HAMILTON'S INFLUENCE

Alexander Hamilton's effect on the US economy will prove profound.

In the short run, the combination of tariffs and excise taxes, along with the issuance of the first US Treasury bonds, moves the nation out of debt despite his bold agreement to assume the state's red ink and to pay full par value to war investors.

By the time he resigns in 1795, America enjoys the highest credit rating in Europe, with its bonds often selling well above par value.

He makes remarkable progress toward his goal of ensuring the intrinsic value of the money unit.

The US Mint standardizes and controls the weight of gold and silver in America's coinage.

He begins to rebuild confidence in soft money banknotes by assuring the public that on-demand conversion into equivalent value coinage is the law of the land.

His efforts to tighten regulations on the banking industry also pay off. The number of officially chartered state banks grows. His 3:1 soft-to-hard money ratio multiplies the capital in circulation without letting the number of banknotes expand to levels where they are devalued. He is also able to enforce the 3:1 ratio by varying the interest rates his BUS charges state banks on loans.

The BUS itself functions as Hamilton hopes. Federal government revenues flow in and bills are paid out in orderly fashion—signals of a stable and confident nation.

But above all else, Hamilton ushers in the system of capitalism that will enable America to build a modern economy which eventually become the envy of the world.

While his career is brief, he goes down in history as the father of American banking and capitalism.

16

THE FRENCH REVOLUTION OVERTHROWS LOUIS XVI

TIME: JANUARY 21, 1793

KING LOUIS XVI IS GUILLOTINED AND ROBESPIERRE TAKES POWER

From the moment George Washington begins his presidency, global events are about to be dictated by the revolution underway in France.

King Louis XVI's authority vanishes on July 14, 1789, when the Paris commoners assault Bastille Prison in search of gunpowder to resist local military intervention. The expectation is for a new government styled after England's combination of Parliament and a constitutional monarchy.

Despite this prospect, other European monarchs remain deeply shaken by events in Paris.

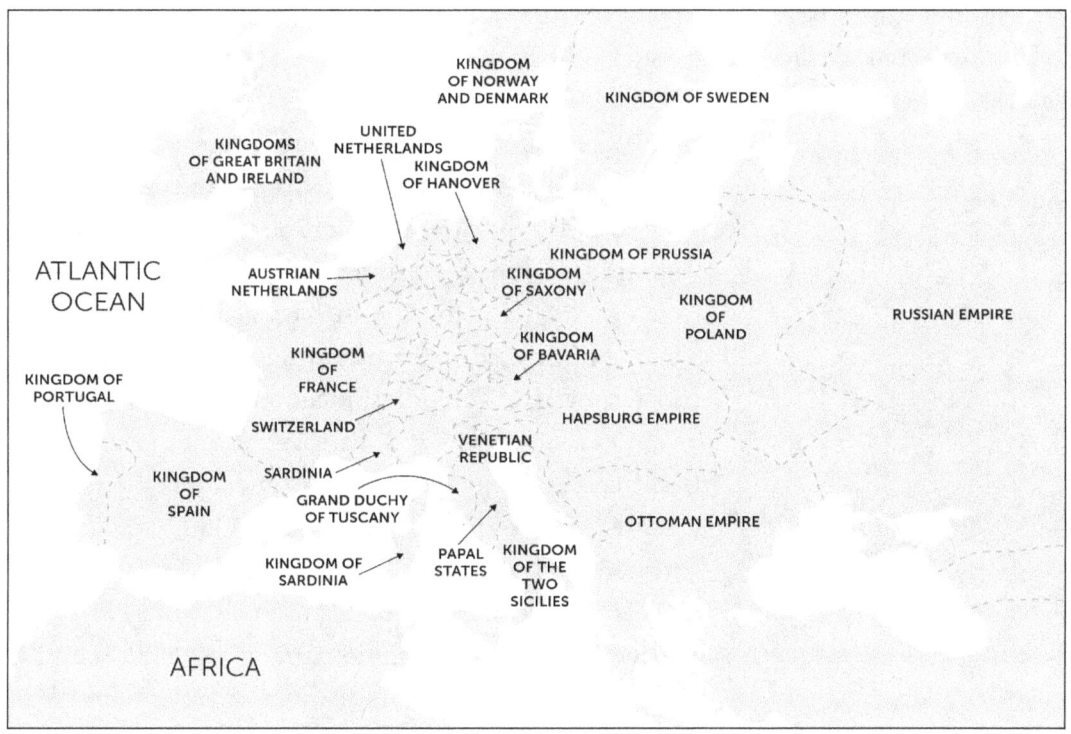

Map of Europe as the French Revolution begins

To the west, the Kingdom of Spain is ruled by Charles IV.

To the east of France lies the Habsburg/ Holy Roman/Austrian Empire, ruled by Leopold II (brother of Louis' wife, Queen Marie Antoinette) and comprised of Holland, Belgium, over 300 middle states of Germany, Austria, Hungary, and Croatia/Bosnia.

To the northeast is the Kingdom of Prussia, which stretches from the capital in Berlin along the Baltic Sea and is ruled by the hawkish monarch Frederick II.

On August 27, 1791, Leopold II and Frederick I decide to warn the French revolutionaries to not harm the royal family. At first these threats simply exacerbate popular contempt for Louis.

But then the threats grow more dire. On April 20, 1792, the French National Assembly declares war on Leopold and the Habsburgs and begins an invasion which quickly draws Prussia into the conflict.

J. DEPLANQUE, Phot.   à Paris.

King Louis XVI

When early battles go against France, a second revolution—called the "Reign of Terror"—sweeps the nation.

It is led by Maximilien Robespierre and far left groups (Jacobins and sansculottes) who envision a "utopian society" run by the direct voice of the common man and marked by increased wages for all, an end to food shortages, and punishment meted out to nobility.

On August 10, 1792, Parisian's attack the king's palace and place him and his family under house arrest. He is tried before the National Convention, convicted of treason, and sentenced to death. On January 21, 1793, Louis XVI is driven through Paris in his carriage, arriving at the Place de la Revolution around 10 a.m. The final act is described by High Executioner Charles-Henri Sanson, who oversees some 3,000 executions in his day and becomes known as "Monsieur de Paris" for his exploits.

Maximilien de Robespierre
(1758–1794)

Arriving at the foot of the guillotine, Louis XVI looked for a moment at the instruments of his execution and asked Sanson why the drums had stopped beating. He came forward to speak, but there were shouts to the executioners to get on with their work. As he was strapped down, he exclaimed "My people, I die innocent!" Then, turning towards his executioners, Louis XVI declared "Gentlemen, I am innocent of everything of which I am accused. I hope that my blood may cement the good fortune of the French." The blade fell. It was 10:22 a.m. One of the assistants of Sanson showed the head of Louis XVI to the people, whereupon a huge cry of "Vive la Nation! Vive la République!" arose and an artillery salute rang out which reached the ears of the imprisoned Royal family.

With the king dead and war in progress, pressure rises on the National Convention to take charge of the nation's destiny. This will involve a new battle between the bourgeoisie (middle class) and the proletariat (lower classes).

Robespierre steps up to the challenge as head of the Committee of Public Safety. He calls on France to create a "republic of virtue," run by the common man and based on concepts laid out by Rousseau.

Included here was the "cult of the supreme being."

Is it not He who decreed for all peoples liberty, good faith and justice? He did not give us priests to harness us to the chariots of kings and to give us examples of baseness, pride, perfidy, avarice, debauchery and falsehood. He created men to help each other, to love each other, to attain happiness by way of virtue.

Anyone standing in the way of Robespierre's vision needs be dealt with quickly and harshly—roughly 16,000 "aristos" or other enemies are publicly guillotined to purify the nation.

Included here, on October 16, 1793 is Louis' wife, Marie Antoinette.

THE FRENCH REVOLUTION: KEY EVENTS OF 1789–1793

1789	Financial crisis over cost of American war triggers increased taxation
	Troops put down riots over low wages and food shortages
	Citizens storm Bastille (July 14), symbol of monarchy
	Great Fear begins, peasants revolt against feudalism and aristos
	Assembly adopts Lafayette's Declaration of the Rights of Man
1790	Nobility abolished by National Assembly
1791	Lafayette orders arrest of 400 aristocrats
	Massive revolt of enslaved people in French colony of Haiti
1792	France declares war on Leopold II's Habsburg monarchy (April 20)
	Frederick II and the Kingdom of Prussia joins Leopold's side
	Tuileries Palace stormed and Louis XVI imprisoned

1793	Louis Capet XVI is guillotined (Jan 21)
	Jacobin Party and Robespierre take control of the government
	France declares war on Britain and Holland (Feb 1)
	France declares war on Spain (March 7)
	Girondist (moderate) faction expelled from National Assembly
	Robespierre's Reign of Terror begins (September 5)
	Marie Antoinette guillotined (Oct 16)

TIME: 1789 AND ONWARD

SIDEBAR: MADAME MARIE TUSSAUD'S DEATH MASKS OF THE KING AND QUEEN

Having just killed their king and queen, the French decide to immortalize both through the ancient practice of creating death masks. This involves molding a wet plaster cast over the head of the deceased, allowing it to dry, and then removing and reassembling the front and back into a lifelike representation. The famed "golden death mask" of the 18-year-old King Tutankhamen dates the art as far back as the Egyptians.

The National Convention calls upon one Marie Tussaud (1760–1851) to create the death masks.

Queen Marie Antoinette (1755–1793)

Madame Tussaud is thirty years old when King Louis is guillotined. She has learned wax sculpture from Dr. Philippe Curtius, a medical man who uses the art mainly to study and teach anatomy. In 1765, Curtius opens a "portrait museum" in Paris featuring wax figures of famous people.

By the 1789 Revolution, Marie Tussaud had already created waxwork representations of the French philosopher Voltaire and the American diplomat and inventor Ben Franklin. Her work is also embraced by the royal family and exhibited at the Palais-Royal.

This connection to nobility almost leads to her own death, as the Reign of Terror sweeps up its victims. Her head is shaved and she awaits transfer to the scaffold before a friend of Curtius gains her release.

Once free, she is called upon to make death masks from the severed heads of the king and queen. Her memoirs are emotionally circumspect about this task, and her work, in this case, is never put on public display.

In the years ahead, Madame Tussaud continues to "capture" many famous personalities of her era. She assists Curtius in creating tableaux, using lifelike wax sculptures to memorialize events and displaying these in pay-to-visit galleries.

In effect, these figures and tableaux serve as precursors to a coming age of photography and film.

When Curtius dies in 1794 she inherits his collection, and in 1804 she moves to London, where she remains until her death at 88 years of age. While there, she and her son establish "Madame Tussaud's Waxworks Museum," a popular attraction located on Baker Street. The establishment stays in her family's hands over many generations and remains open to the present day.

17

AMERICA'S WESTWARD EXPANSION PICKS UP MOMENTUM

TIME: 1775 AND ONWARD

A NEW "COLONY OF TRANSYLVANIA" IS FOUNDED

Throughout the colonial era, the vast majority of Americans live within 125 miles of the Atlantic coast, east of the Appalachian Mountains "barrier," which runs 1,500 miles from Newfoundland and Massachusetts, southwest across seventeen states into Georgia and Alabama.

However, some turn their gaze westward, across the mountains, to land occupied by Indigenous tribes and claimed by the British crown.

Many of these are wealthy speculators, aware of the profits to be had in buying and selling land. Their vision lies in founding corporations similar to those associated with the original colonies—the Virginia Companies of London and Plymouth, the Massachusetts Bay Company, the Dutch East Indies—and then reaping the profits that follow.

One such venture materializes in 1774, when James Henderson, a wealthy judge from North Carolina, founds the Transylvania Company. His vision lies in a new "fourteenth colony" of some twenty million acres lying in the southwestern half of what becomes Kentucky.

On March 14, 1775, Henderson signs the "Treaty of Sycamore Shoals," buying this land from the Cherokees. He thinks his purchase will be declared legal—which won't be the case—and proceeds to generate profits by selling plots to prospective settlers. He then sends his hired explorer, Daniel Boone, to facilitate their movement west.

TIME: 1775 AND ONWARD

DANIEL BOONE ESTABLISHES THE STATE OF KENTUCKY

Boone is a Quaker by birth, who grows up in western Pennsylvania in close contact with the Lenape (Delaware) tribe, and then moves with his family to North Carolina where he earns his reputation as a "back-woodsman." He makes his living as a hunter and trapper, and in 1797 begins to explore Kentucky. James Henderson learns of Boone's prowess and signs him on with the Transylvania Company.

The main challenge Boone faces in this trek is the Appalachian range. It is a formidable natural boundary, rising over two miles above sea level in places, and sprouting dense woods throughout most of its ridges and valleys.

But Boone is already familiar with a depression known as the Cumberland Gap, and a path through it that will become known as the Wilderness Road—a well-traveled route the tribes have used for generations. In early 1775 he guides some 30 pioneers over this path to the Kentucky River, where he founds the settlement of Boonesborough (near Lexington).

Daniel Boone (1734–1820)

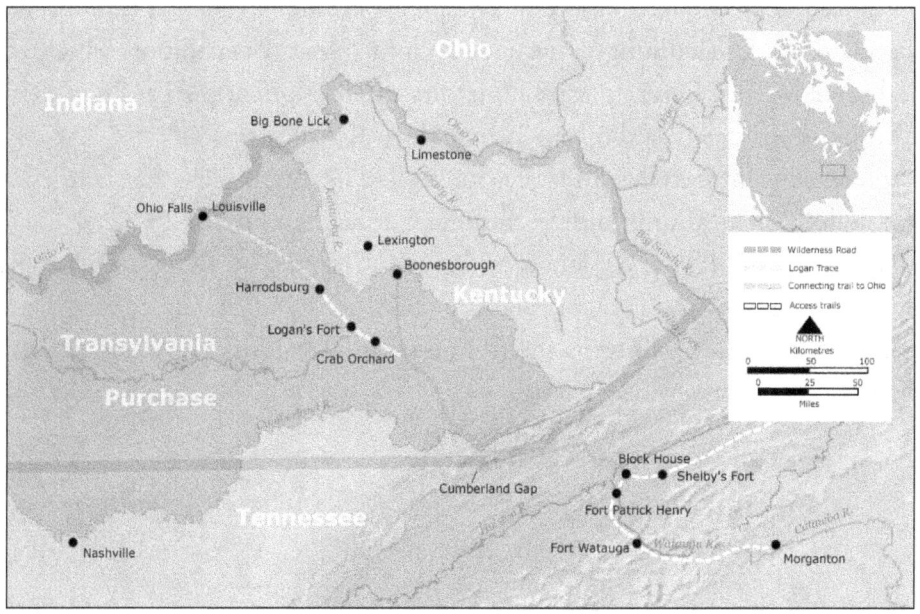

The Transylvania Purchase and the Cumberland Gap

In May 1775 Henderson gathers roughly 100 settlers there for a three day convention aimed at writing a formal constitution for the colony. The result of this is the Transylvania Compact, a document which Henderson tries repeatedly to get approved by the assemblies of both Virginia and North Carolina.

In December 1778, with the Revolutionary War underway, Virginia denies Henderson's claim, while awarding him a twelve square mile parcel of land along the Ohio River. This ends his plan for the fourteenth colony, Transylvania.

However, the die has already been cast for settlers to flow west across the Wilderness Road.

Other homesteaders follow behind, and by 1800, the census reports a total of 387,000 Americans living in new territories west of the Appalachian Mountains. Roughly one in five are enslaved Africans.

AMERICAN POPULATION LIVING WEST OF THE APPALACHIANS IN 1800

ALL TERRITORIES	KENTUCKY	TENNESSEE	OHIO	INDIANA	MISSISSIPPI
387,000	221,000	106,000	45,000	6,000	9,000

Boone himself continues to live in the town bearing his name between 1775 and 1779, and then in other homes across Kentucky, North Carolina, Virginia, Louisiana, and Missouri over the rest of his life. During the Revolutionary War, he serves as Lt. Colonel of the Fairfield Militia, seeing action in Ohio and Kentucky. His second son, Israel, is killed on the battlefield.

After the war, he is elected to the Virginia Assembly, representing the land it will claim until Kentucky becomes a state in 1792. He becomes a vigorous but unsuccessful land speculator, and, according to legend, accompanies an expedition which reaches west to the Yellowstone River at age 82. He dies in 1820 of natural causes in Defiance, Missouri, and is ultimately laid to rest in Frankfort, Kentucky.

His presence is immortalized in tree carvings—"D. Boon kilt a bar here"—and in American folklore. The author James Fenimore Cooper bases his 1826 novel *The Last of the Mohicans* on two of Boone's daughters being kidnapped by Indigenous people and Lord Byron references him in an epic poem.

But his lasting legacy will be as the frontiersman who initiated America's westward expansion.

## 18

WASHINGTON'S SECOND TERM

TIME: 1790

PRO-ADMINISTRATION FORCES WIN THE FIRST MIDTERM ELECTIONS

According to the 1787 Constitution, elections for membership in the House of Representatives are to be held every two years—or "mid-term" in the sitting president's time in office.

America's first such election begins on March 4, 1791 in Vermont and ends on June 1, 1792 in Kentucky—two states which have been recently admitted to the Union. Each has been allocated a pair of seats based on their populations, and this raises the total number in the chamber from 65 to 69.

The results again demonstrate that, despite George Washington's overwhelming personal popularity, the pro-administration forces enjoy only a narrow 39–30 majority in the House.

HOUSE OF REPRESENTATIVES MIDTERM ELECTION OF 1790

	TOTAL # SEATS	PRO-ADMIN	ANTI-ADMIN
1788	65	37	28
1790	69	39	30
Change	+4	+2	+2

Opposition to the administration centers mainly across the South, where many voters regard Washington as tilting toward the Federalists and Hamilton and away from Jefferson.

HOUSE OF REPRESENTATIVES ELECTION OF 1790

1788 ELECTION	TOTAL	SOUTH	BORDER	NORTH
Pro-Administration	37	7	3	27
Anti-Administration	28	16	4	8
1790 ELECTION				
Pro -Administration	39	7	4	28
Anti-Administration	30	16	5	9

Note: South (VA, NC, SC, GA), Border (DE, MD, KY), North (NH, MA, NY, NJ, PA, RI, CT, VT)

Anti-administration sentiment is strongest in Virginia, while support for the president's policies is greatest in Massachusetts, Connecticut, and New Jersey.

HOUSE OF REPRESENTATIVES ELECTION OF 1790

STATE	# SEATS	PRO-ADMIN	ANTI-ADMIN
Virginia	10	2	8 +1
North Carolina	5	2	3
South Carolina	5	3 +1	2
Georgia	3	0	3
SOUTH	23	7	16
Delaware	1	1	0
Maryland	6	3 +1	3
Kentucky	2	0	2 +2
BORDER	9	4	5
New Hampshire	3	3 +1	0
Massachusetts	8	7 +1	1
Rhode Island	1	1	0
Connecticut	5	5	0
New York	6	4 +1	2
New Jersey	4	4	0
Pennsylvania	8	4	4
Vermont	2	0	2 +2
NORTH	37	28	9
TOTAL	69	39	30

Control in the Senate remains with the pro-administration camp by a margin of 18–11.

TIME: NOVEMBER 2 TO DECEMBER 5, 1792

THE PRESIDENTIAL ELECTION OF 1792

The revolutionary events in France are on Americans' minds as they go to the polls in 1792.

The Federalist leaders—especially Hamilton and Adams—applaud the move away from absolute monarchy, but are distressed by the Reign of Terror. They view the riots in Paris and violence against the nobility as what happens when democracy turns into mob rule. They are also very alarmed by France's declaration of war on its European neighbors, and fear that it might spill over to America.

Meanwhile, Jefferson and the Anti-Federalists—now referred to as Democratic-Republicans—are much more comfortable with the will of the people being carried out on the streets of France and in mass assemblies. They are forever suspicious of British intentions toward America and regard the French as more certain allies.

Still, the election of 1792 focuses much more on domestic policies than on foreign affairs. Hamilton's economic initiatives—the assumption of state debts, the tariff and excise taxes, capitalism, and the US Bank—have exacerbated the ongoing rift between the Federalists and their opponents. So the election of 1792 is the first to be openly fought over by "political parties."

Madison in particular senses threats here to national unity and he persuades Washington to accept a second term rather than retire to Mt. Vernon, which is his stated preference. Some worry that this will lead to monarchy, but the fact that Washington is without children quells this fear.

Since all sides share confidence in Washington, the political battle is about who will be the next vice president. The Federalists prefer John Adams of Massachusetts while the Democratic-Republicans offer Governor George Clinton of New York, one who lobbied aggressively against ratifying the 1787 Constitution.

The voting process itself is unchanged from 1788. Each state has a number of presidential electors equal to their representation in the House. Roughly half of the states choose electors by popular voting; the other half relies on votes by state legislators. Each elector names his top two choices for president. The candidate with the most votes will become president as long as he surpasses half of the total ballots cast; the runner-up will become vice president.

Fifteen states participate, but only 28,579 citizens—less than 1% of the roughly 4 million population—cast their own votes for the executive in 1792. Over time this turnout will grow substantially, as suffrage rules become more inclusive and political party divisions intensify public interest in the presidential outcomes.

In 1792 George Washington is again named on every elector's ballot and wins a second term in office.

The race for vice president is fairly close, with John Adams getting 77 votes to Clinton's 50 votes.

RESULTS OF THE 1792 PRESIDENTIAL ELECTION

CANDIDATES	STATE	PARTY	POP. VOTE	TOTAL EV	SOUTH	BORDER	NORTH
George Washington	VA	Independent	28,579	132	45	15	72
John Adams	MA	Federalist		77			
George Clinton	NY	Dem-Rep		50			
Thomas Jefferson	VA	Dem-Rep		4			
Aaron Burr	NY	Dem-Rep		1			
Total			28,579	264			
Needed to Win				67			

Note: South (VA, NC, SC, GA), Border (DE, MD, KY), North (NH, MA, NY, NJ, PA, RI, CT, VT)

TIME: 1792

THE DEMOCRATIC-REPUBLICANS GAIN SEATS IN CONGRESS

The nation's first reapportionment of congressional seats occurs after the national Census of 1790. Based on the results, the House of Representatives adds 36 new seats in 1792, with twenty of these coming from the Northern states.

HOUSE OF REPRESENTATIVES – POST-1790 CENSUS SEAT ADJUSTMENTS

	TOTAL	SOUTH	BORDER	NORTH
1790	69	23	9	37
1792	105	37	11	57
Change	+36	+14	+2	+20

When the votes are in, the majority in the House has shifted from a 39–30 margin for the pro-administration Federalist faction to a 55–50 edge for the Democratic-Republicans.

HOUSE OF REPRESENTATIVES ELECTION TRENDS

	# SEATS	PRO-ADMIN	ANTI-ADMIN
1789	65	37	28
1791	69	39	30
1793	105	50	55

The Democratic-Republicans pick up ground in Pennsylvania and Vermont and expand their control of the South—while the Federalists' stronghold continues to lie in the Northern states.

HOUSE TRENDS BY REGION

PRO-ADMINISTRATION	TOTAL	SOUTH	BORDER	NORTH
1789	37	7	3	27
1791	39	7	4	28
1793	50	6	4	40
ANTI-ADMINISTRATION				
1789	28	16	4	8
1791	30	16	5	9
1793	55	31	7	17

In the Senate, the "staggered cycles" approach has a total of ten seats up for election in 1792. The same patterns seen in the House are evident in the upper chamber; the Anti-Federalist opposition strengthens year after year, particularly in the South.

SENATE TRENDS BY REGION

PRO-ADMINISTRATION	TOTAL	SOUTH	BORDER	NORTH
1789	19	4	3	12
1791	17	3	4	10
1793	16	1	4	11
ANTI-ADMINISTRATION				
1789	7	4	1	2
1791	12	5	2	5
1793	14	7	2	5

TIME: MARCH 4, 1793 TO MARCH 4, 1797

OVERVIEW OF WASHINGTON'S SECOND TERM

When the time comes for Washington's second inauguration on March 4, 1793, the US capital has moved from New York City to Philadelphia, where it remains until "Washington City" is completed in 1800.

Stability is a key virtue for Washington, and his cabinet remains intact as his new term begins. This will not last long, as Jefferson will resign in 1793 over a foreign policy dispute and Hamilton will exit in 1795 after his enemies expose an extramarital affair.

WASHINGTON'S CABINET AS SECOND TERM BEGINS

POSITION	NAME	HOME STATE
Vice President	John Adams	Massachusetts
Secretary of State	Thomas Jefferson	Virginia
Secretary of Treasury	Alexander Hamilton	New York
Secretary of War	Henry Knox	Massachusetts
Attorney General	Edmund Randolph	Virginia

The challenges facing Washington in 1793 are fundamentally different from 1789. The basic structure and daily functions of the federal government are now fairly well established, so the focus shifts to executing the domestic programs set by the Federalists and participating in foreign affairs.

In foreign policy, his second term will be marked by the Amity Treaty and other efforts to remain neutral in the face of renewed warfare involving Britain and France. In October 1795 the Pinckney Treaty with Spain settles US boundary lines—west to the Mississippi River and south to the 31st parallel, the northern line of Spanish Florida.

Domestically, he will sign the Fugitive Slave Act of 1793, and use force to help settlers combat Indigenous tribes west of the Appalachians and to put down a tax revolt in Pennsylvania known as the Whiskey Rebellion. His 1795 Naturalization Act requires that future immigrants reside for five years in America before achieving citizenship.

In regard to the economy, recent estimates of activity during Washington's tenure suggest that America's prosperity—derailed during the Revolutionary War—has been restored by 1793 or so, under Hamilton's leadership.

ECONOMIC GROWTH DURING WASHINGTON'S TERMS

	1790	1791	1792	1793	1794	1795	1796
Total GDP ($ Million)	$189	$206	$225	$251	$315	$383	$417
Per Capita GDP	$48	$51	$54	$58	$71	$84	$89
% Change		6%	6%	7%	22%	18%	6%

While his many supporters urge him to continue with a third term, Washington demurs.

The new nation he helped to found is up and running, at peace, and with the strong central government he wanted in place.

As Washington exits, he will pen a memorable farewell to America, summarizing what he learned as president and his advice to his successors.

WASHINGTON'S SECOND TERM: KEY EVENTS

1793	
March 4	Washington and Adams are sworn in
April 8	"Citizen Genêt" arrives in Charleston and begins to foment anti-British feelings
April 22	Washington issues proclamation of neutrality in France vs. Britain war
May 9	French declare they will seize ships bearing cargo to Britain
June 5	Jefferson warns Genêt against further mischief; Genêt ignores the message.
November 6	Britain begins to seize neutral ships and impress sailors to fight the war
December 31	Jefferson resigns as secretary of state over belief that US is tilting toward Britain

1794	
March 22	Congress bans slave trading with foreign nations
March 27	Congress authorizes establishment of the US Navy
April 19	Chief Justice John Jay appointed ambassador to Britain
May 1	America's first labor union (cordwainers/shoemakers) is created
May 27	James Monroe appointed minister to France
June 5	Congress passes the Neutrality Act
August 7	Washington assembles 13,000-man militia to suppress the Whiskey Rebellion
August 20	Rebellious Miami tribe defeated near Toledo by "Mad" Anthony Wayne
November 19	John Jay concludes an Amity Treaty with Britain
December	The 61-mile Lancaster Turnpike is completed
1795	
January 29	Naturalization Act requires a five year residency prior to citizenship
January 31	Hamilton resigns as treasury secretary amidst marital scandal
June 24	Jay's Amity Treaty is finally approved by the Senate
July 19	The Connecticut Land Company buys the large Western Reserve tract in Ohio
August 3	The Treaty of Greenville cedes large Ohio tribe land tracts to the US
October 27	Treaty of Lorenzo with Spain defines land boundaries in the US southeast
December 15	The Senate rejects John Rutledge, Washington's choice as chief justice
1796	
February 29	The Amity Treat with Britain is announced publicly and France is outraged
March 4	The Senate confirms Oliver Ellsworth is as chief justice of the Supreme Court
March 8	In *Hylton v. United States* the Supreme Court rules its first law unconstitutional
April 30	Democratic-Republicans criticize funding of Amity Act provisions, which pass.
May 18	Land Act opens up more NW Territory Land at $2 per acre, 640 acre minimum.
June 1	Tennessee is admitted to the Union (#16)
July	France announces it will board all ships bound for Britain, even neutrals
August 22	French refuse to accept Thomas Pinckney as new ambassador, given grievances
September 19	Washington's Farewell Address to the nation is published; signals no third term
October 29	First US ship reaches California at Monterrey Bay
November 4	US signs treaty with Tripoli to end pirating raids on commercial ships
November	Andrew Jackson becomes Tennessee's first member of the US House
December 7	John Adams is elected as the second US president, with Jefferson as VP
1797	
February 27	Secretary of State Pickering reports losses from France's prohibitions of trade

TIME: MARCH 4, 1793

SIDEBAR: WASHINGTON'S SECOND INAUGURAL ADDRESS

The president lives up to his reputation for brevity on March 4, 1793, with the shortest inaugural address in American history—135 words delivered in under two minutes.

I am again called upon by the voice of my country to execute the functions of its Chief Magistrate. When the occasion proper for it shall arrive, I shall endeavor to express the high sense I entertain of this distinguished honor, and of the confidence which has been reposed in me by the people of united America.

Previous to the execution of any official act of the President the Constitution requires an oath of office. This oath I am now about to take, and in your presence: That if it shall be found during my administration the Government I have in any instance violated willingly or knowingly the injunctions thereof, I may (besides incurring constitutional punishment) be subject to the upbraidings of all who are now witnesses of the present solemn ceremony.

TIME: SUMMER 1794

A SHOW OF FEDERAL FORCE PUTS DOWN
THE WHISKEY TAX REBELLION

As Washington is busy navigating foreign policy, he faces a domestic revolt over taxes.

The first levy imposed by the new congress on American products targets whiskey and goes into effect on March 3, 1791. It is met by stiff resistance from grain farmers, whose backyard "stills" provide a lucrative source of secondary income.

The economics here are simple. Earn $6 in profit by loading 24 bushels of milled rye on three pack mules and sending them east over the Alleghenies, or earn $16 by shipping two eight gallon kegs of whiskey on one mule.

For many small farmers this income means the difference between surviving the lingering post-war recession or going under and losing their land to banks or wealthy speculators.

Given these realities, they ask why the government has decided to penalize whiskey production in the first place, and why the burden falls disproportionately on small farms, which run their stills below the rated maximum output level which determines the tax.

Western Pennsylvania, which houses a quarter of all the stills in the country, quickly becomes a rallying point for open rebellion against local tax collectors.

The first victim is one Robert Johnson, who is tarred and feathered in September 1791 by a band of anti-tax men while making his rounds. More attacks follow, and in August 1792 the Mingo Creek Association is formed to consolidate resistance in south-western Pennsylvania and beyond. Some 500 men sign on to the cause.

The threat continues to escalate over the next two years, with more violence against tax collectors, talk of seizing and redistributing land from wealthy property owners, and even the possibility of turning to Spain for help.

Two Anti-Federalist congressmen from Pennsylvania, Albert Gallatin and William Findlay, petition Hamilton to change the law. Gallatin, later secretary of the treasury under Jefferson, writes:

We have punctually and cheerfully paid former taxes on our estates...because they were proportioned to our wealth...we believe this (tax) to be founded on no such equitable principles...we respectfully apply for a total repeal of the law.

Hamilton, who needs the money for his budget, will have none of this.

On July 16, 1794, the protests turn into the "Whiskey Rebellion" as a 500 man mob assaults the home of Revolutionary War general John Neville, a wealthy farmer and dis-tiller also serving as the local inspector of revenue. Neville fights off the attack with the help of enslaved people and ten regular army soldiers from the federal fort in Pittsburgh. Two rebels and one soldier are killed in the battle.

In August, a rebel named David Bradford speaks before a gathering of 7,000 near Pittsburg, calling for a redistribution of wealth and independence from the oppressive union.

President Washington knows treason when he sees it and nationalizes state militias from Pennsylvania, Virginia, New Jersey, and Maryland. A total of 13,000 troops, more than participated at Yorktown, march off to suppress the rebels. The old general himself leads the troops into Pennsylvania before turning the lead over to Hamilton and Henry "Light-Horse Harry" Lee.

This overwhelming show of force is enough to shatter the rebellion. The leaders disperse into the mountains, although twenty of them are captured and sent back to Philadelphia for trial. They prove to be a woeful band, and only two are convicted—then pardoned.

In 1802 the hated Whiskey Tax bill is repealed by the staunch Anti-Federalist Jef-ferson.

TIME: JUNE 24, 1795

JOHN JAY'S AMITY TREATY WITH BRITAIN SPARKS CONTROVERSY

Washington is at Mt. Vernon in February 1793 when he learns that Robespierre's France has declared war on Britain. He quickly returns to Philadelphia and calls an emergency meeting where he poses thirteen questions to his cabinet members. These range from the tactical (whether to receive a new French ambassador) to the strategic (whether to issue a proclamation of neutrality).

All agree that America must avoid direct involvement in a British-French conflict, but a rift develops around how quickly and aggressively to signal this policy. Secretary of State Jefferson, forever siding with France, argues for withholding any official proclamation for the time being. Treasury Secretary Hamilton, perpetually pro-British, disagrees vehemently.

John Jay (1745–1829)

This leaves the final call up to Washington, who supports Hamilton and issues a Proclamation of Neutrality on April 22, 1793.

> *Whereas it appears that a state of war exists between Austria, Prussia, Sardinia, Great Britain, and the Netherlands of the one part and France on the other, and the duty and interest of the United States require that they should with sincerity and good faith adopt and pursue a conduct friendly and impartial toward the belligerent powers.*

The president soon learns that two weeks before the neutrality decree, the new ambassador from France, "Citizen" Edmond-Charles Genêt, has landed at Charleston, South Carolina. Genêt has begun to recruit a local militia to attack Spanish Florida. When asked by Washington to desist, Genêt responds by sending his privateer navy to raid British transports along the Atlantic coast. Genêt's stunts undermine Jefferson's pro-French arguments and embarrass him personally. On December 31, 1793 he resigns from the cabinet.

Jefferson has threatened this action before on several occasions, only to be convinced to back down by Washington. But this time the president lets him go. Jefferson expresses relief at the prospect of a return to Monticello.

Liberated from the hated occupations of politics and into the bosom of my family, my farm, and my books.

Federalist critics are suspicious of his real motives. As John Adams writes:

Jefferson thinks by this step to get the reputation as a humble, modest, meek man, wholly without ambition or vanity…But if the prospect opens, the world will see and he will feel that he is as ambitious as Oliver Cromwell.

Washington names Attorney General Edmund Randolph to the secretary of state post, and moves to reassure the British by sending John Jay, the sitting chief justice of the Supreme Court, to London for bilateral talks.

This is just one more critical role for Jay in America's path to independence. He serves as a delegate to both the First and Second Continental Congresses, minister to Spain (1779–1782), and minister of foreign affairs (1784–1790) before joining the high court. He is also comfortable in politics, later becoming governor of New York.

Jay arrives in London on June 8, 1794 and negotiates over the next five months with Foreign Secretary Grenville. Washington feels the results are fairly lackluster, but at least they dampen some ongoing tensions.

- Both sides agree to cease raiding the other's ships and pay compensations for prior damages.
- The British will finally withdraw from border forts along the Detroit to Sandusky line, while any further border disputes will be resolved by a joint commission.
- Free trade will resume across America and the British Indies—including relief of restrictions on American exports and a continuation of England's involvement in the fur industry.
- America will cover debts owed to British interests back to 1776.

Jay signs the treaty on November 21, 1794 and from there resistance to ratifying it increases.

Washington's minister to France, James Monroe, is left in the dark about the terms, and when he learns of them his hostility toward Jay and the treaty boils over. Instead of acting the role of diplomat, Monroe sympathizes with the French, who argue that Jay's treaty violates their 1788 treaty with America. Monroe becomes so publicly outspoken on the matter that Washington fires him.

Many citizens are still smarting from the war with Britain, and recall that it was the alliance with France that led to victory. Both Jefferson and James Madison remain outraged. Still, the Federalists muster enough support in Congress to approve it on June 24, 1795. It squeaks by the two-thirds rule in the Senate on a 20–10 count, and barely secures funding in the House by a 51–48 margin.

The result is that America now has Amity Treaties with both France (the crucial 1778 accord) and Britain—although neither is particularly amicable at the moment.

However, that suits Washington's policy. If the two European powers wish to battle each other, so be it. America intends to remain neutral while also trading freely with both partners.

TIME: AUGUST 3, 1795

AMERICAN FORCES WREST OHIO FROM THE WESTERN INDIAN CONFEDERACY

During his second term, Washington is also forced to come to grips with failing US policies toward the Indian tribes, especially regarding territorial disputes.

From the beginning, the white European settlers have treated the Native Americans in a much more cordial fashion than the enslaved Africans. In addition to their "aboriginal status" on the land, this better treatment is in large part because of the potential they offer as military allies in the international wars to control the continent. Their reputation as warriors is well established, their numbers are sizable, and their tactical knowledge of the geography and potential fields of battle and supply are unmatched. So they are courted.

The Hunkpapa warrior Crow King (died 1884)

In the French & Indian War of 1754–1763, the dominant Algonquin tribes side with France while the Iroquois back Britain. In the Revolutionary War of 1776–1781, almost all northern tribes fight alongside the British while the five main southern tribes (Cherokee, Chickasaw, Creeks, Choctaw, and Seminoles) remain neutral.

It seems likely that this alignment with the redcoats in 1776—and later in 1812—contributes to growing ill will among America toward the Indians. But the stated policy toward them announced by the early presidents is nothing but conciliatory. Unlike the Africans, Indians are officially regarded as somehow akin to white men in their potential—"noble savages" to be "civilized" rather than subjugated.

Washington's initial six-point plan to support this civilizing process includes a call for "impartial justice" toward the tribes, "regulated buying" of their land, punishment of those who violate their rights, and promotion of all efforts to support their commerce and their social advances. The stated hope here being that at least rudimentary assimilation into the American culture would come along with settled villages, property rights, English schooling, farming, and exposure to Christianity.

But this rosy vision soon collapses as the tribes refuse to passively relinquish their historical homelands to white settlers crossing the Appalachian range onto their territory.

Open warfare over the land soon breaks out in the North and, on November 4, 1791, it is marked by a humiliating American loss at the Battle of the Wabash, fought at Fort Recovery on the western edge of Ohio. The Shawnee and Miami tribes—led by Blue Jacket and Little Turtle respectively—are pitted against a militia led by Arthur St. Clair, who was a major-general during the Revolutionary War.

The outcome is a rout, with some 600 soldiers killed, the worst defeat ever suffered by America's military at the hands of tribal forces. Equally alarming is the rumor that Britain played a role in the defeat by sending supplies to the Indians and encouraging them to fight.

When this tribal resistance continues into 1794, Washington finally calls upon one of his most trusted generals from the Revolutionary War to come out of retirement and suppress the Indians.

General "Mad" Anthony Wayne is a Pennsylvania native, first a practicing surveyor and then a legislator in his home state before forming a militia unit in 1775. Fame finds him quickly. He joins Aaron Burr in the failed attack on Quebec City in 1776. He is with Washington at Valley Forge in the winter of 1777 and is a hero in the crucial victory at Monmouth in 1778. Promotions follow and he ends the war at Yorktown in 1781, afterwards being named a major-general. He then negotiates peace treaties with the Creek and Cherokee tribes in Georgia, for which he is rewarded with a rice plantation, where he is living when Washington requests his help in Ohio.

"Mad" Anthony earns his nickname from his fiery temperament and his bold approach to combat. He quickly assembles and trains up 3,000 soldiers at a camp in far western Pennsylvania. He calls them the "Legion of the United States."

Once they are ready, Wayne marches them some 200 miles north and west toward Maumee, Ohio, attacking various Indian outposts as he goes. On June 30, 1794, his troops engage upwards of 2,000 tribesmen, but find safety at Fort Recovery, where St. Clair was beaten in 1791. General Wayne recovers from this setback and advances, meeting the Indians on August 20, 1794 in the pivotal Battle of Fallen Timbers near Toledo. With a two to one edge in manpower, Wayne defeats Blue Jacket and Little Turtle, thus stomping out tribal resistance in Ohio.

Wayne proceeds further west, occupying British forts along the way and finishing up in Indiana, near what will become Ft. Wayne—named in his honor. "Mad" Anthony has once again served Washington well, and the one-sided Treaty of Greenville, signed on August 3, 1795, officially ends the war in the North. It will not, however, be the last time that the native peoples of America are forced to forfeit their land to white settlers in rigged treaties.

TIME: SEPTEMBER 19, 1796

WASHINGTON'S FAREWELL ADDRESS

Washington's time of service to his nation now appears to be ending.

Before leaving for Mt. Vernon, he wants to share parting thoughts on securing the new nation he did so much to create. His farewell address is first published on September 19, 1796, six weeks in advance of the third presidential election.

The president begins by declaring that he will not run again, then goes on to thank the nation for the many honors he has received while in office. At this point he pauses:

> *Here, perhaps, I ought to stop. But solicitude for your welfare... urges me...to offer...some sentiments... which appear to me all-important to the permanency of your felicity as a people. These will be offered to you...as the disinterested warnings of a parting friend...who can have no personal motive to bias his counsel.*

George Washington (1732–1799)

He then charges forward with his advice to all citizens:

The unity of government which constitutes you one people is…now dear to you.

It is of infinite moment that you should properly estimate the immense value of your national union to your collective and individual happiness.

Think and speak of (your union) as of the palladium of your political safety and prosperity;

Discountenance…even a suspicion that it can in any event be abandoned…frown upon…every attempt to alienate any portion of our country from the rest, or to enfeeble the sacred ties which now link together the various parts.

The name of American, which belongs to you…must always exalt the just pride of patriotism.

With slight shades of difference, you have the same religion, manners, habits and political principles. You have in a Common cause fought and triumphed together; the independence and liberty you possess are the work of joint counsels…common sufferings and successes.

The most commanding motives (exist) for carefully guarding and preserving the union of the whole… Protected by the equal laws of a common government…the North…the South…the East…the West…secure enjoyment of…outlets for their own production…across agriculture and manufacturing.

All the parts combined cannot fail to find in the united mass of means and efforts greater strength, greater resource, proportionably greater security from external danger—(along with) an exemption from…wars between themselves, which so frequently afflict countries not tied together by the same government.

(Union will) likewise…avoid the necessity of those overgrown military establishments which under any form of government, are inauspicious to liberty.

To the efficacy and permanency of your Union, a government for the whole is indispensable. The basis of our political systems is the right of the people to make and to alter their constitutions of government…

(It is) the duty of every individual to obey the established government. All obstructions to the execution of the laws…are destructive of this fundamental principle, and of fatal tendency.

(Beware) of cunning, ambitious, and unprincipled men…subverting the power of the people and usurping for themselves the reins of government.

(Beware) of the danger of Parties in the State, with particular reference to the founding of them on geographical discriminations... The alternate domination of one faction over another, shaped by the spirit of revenge, natural to party dissension...is itself a frightful despotism....But it inclines the minds of men to seek security and repose in the absolute power of an individual...and sooner or later the chief of some prevailing faction...turns this disposition to his own elevation, on the ruins of public liberty.

A wise people (will) discourage and restrain...the spirit of party. It agitates the community with Ill founded jealousies and false alarms, kindles the animosity of one part against another, foments occasionally riot and insurrection. It opens the door... to corruption.

(Preserve) the necessity of reciprocal checks in the exercise of political power, by dividing and distributing it into different depositories and constituting each the guardian of the public weal against invasions by others.

Of all the dispositions and habits which lead to political prosperity, religion and morality are indispensable supports.

Promote institutions for the general diffusion of knowledge... (since) it is essential that public opinion should be enlightened.

As a very important source of strength and security, cherish public credit. One method of preserving it is to use it as sparingly as possible.

Observe good faith and justice towards all nations; cultivate peace and harmony with all. In relation to the still subsisting war in Europe, my proclamation of the twenty-second of April, 1793, is the index of my plan.

He then closes.

I fervently beseech the Almighty that, after forty five years of my life dedicated to its service with an upright zeal, the faults of incompetent abilities will be consigned to oblivion, as myself must soon be to the mansions of rest.

Washington's sentiments will ring down the corridors of time, as the nation he helped to found hurtles toward prosperity and then toward dissolution:
- Preserving the Union is sacrosanct to liberty, safety and prosperity.
- Frown upon any attempt to alienate any portion from the rest.
- It is the duty of all men to obey the laws they have created.
- Rely on distributed power and checks and balances to preserve liberty.
- Avoid an overgrown military establishment.

- Religion and morality are essential supports to good government.
- An informed and knowledgeable public is also essential.
- Public credit must be cherished and debt avoided to maintain strength.
- Cultivate peace and harmony towards all nations.
- Beware of political parties who seek domination and revenge.

In addition to Washington's closing advice to his fellow countrymen, his farewell address also signals that he does not intend to run for a third term. This puts an end to early fears that the president would be transformed into a European-style monarch once in office.

It foretells an orderly transition to a successor—even in the midst of threatening events abroad and no small degree of political tension at home.

The fate of the nation will rest on the laws and institutions that have been established between the 1787 Constitution and the first eight years of government of the people.

The United States of America will survive without George Washington, the one man who has done more than any other to set it in motion.

In 1797 the time has come for the still vigorous 65-year-old general and president to lay down the burdens of public office and retire to his beloved Mt. Vernon estate. However, fate has more in store for Washington.

TIME: 1797-1799

WASHINGTON'S "RETIREMENT" AND DEATH AT MT. VERNON

When Washington arrives back home on March 15, 1797, he finds that the time and devotion he has put into the presidency has left Mt. Vernon in need of fundamental repairs, top to bottom. What follows is a daily influx of carpenters, painters, and groundskeepers, all working long days to meet the master's commands. But soon enough, his step-granddaughter, Nelly Custis, reports that:

Grampa is very well and much pleased with being once more Farmer Washington.

In retirement, Washington pursues his art collection, oversees his plantation and

George Washington (1732–1799)

begins to worry about mortality and about the fact that he finds himself land rich, but cash poor. To cover his sizable living expenses he begins to sell off his large land holdings in the West.

A Front View of Washington's Beloved Mt. Vernon

He also finds himself being drawn back into the controversy surrounding what the Democratic-Republicans argue was his favoritism for Britain over France. This has long been a cause célèbre for men like Jefferson and Monroe, and Washington now encounters various pamphlets and messages he finds dismaying. He is particularly upset once again with Monroe, saying in a letter that he has exhibited a:

Mischievous and dangerous tendency, exposing to the public his private instructions and correspondence with his own government.

His dismay soon converts into a level of open hostility toward the Anti-Federalists and the French that he had eschewed over his many years on the political stage. By December 1797 he is intent on stepping back into the arena to ward off the threat he sees from France.

I cannot remain an unconcerned spectator of the attempt of another power to accomplish (our downfall).

As France increases its hostile actions against the US, Adams decides to send a clear warning their way. On July 2, 1798, he nominates Washington to return as lieutenant general and commander-in-chief of all US military forces. Washington accepts the post two days later and devotes the next seventeen months to preparing an army to defend against a French invasion. Along the way, he bickers with Adams over strategy and over his staff, especially his wish to name Hamilton, Adams' nemesis, his top-ranked general.

Washington is still serving his country when he dies suddenly at Mt. Vernon on December 14, 1799.

Two days earlier he records the following in his diary:

Morning cloudy. Winds to northeast and mercury 33. A large circle round the moon last night. At about ten o'clock it began to snow, soon after to hail, and then to a settled cold rain. Mercury 28 at night.

The storm he mentions starts soon after he rides out to inspect the far reaches of his farm. He returns home after five straight hours, soaking wet from the weather. He eats dinner and acknowledges that his throat is sore.

On December 13 he stays close to home and reads the daily newspaper with Martha and his aide before retiring. By 3 a.m. he awakens, feeling very ill, breathing heavily, and barely able to speak. He senses that his life is in danger and physicians are called. Before they arrive, he tries but is unable to swallow a concoction of molasses, butter, and vinegar. He then demands that bleeding should commence immediately, a common practice thought to rid the body of disease.

Three doctors finally arrive on December 14. More blood is drawn directly from Washington's throat and from his arm. He remains unable to swallow liquids. The diagnosis they settle on is "quinsy," a virulent form of tonsillitis, which calls for more bleeding and the application of blisters and purges. When nothing works, a tracheotomy is debated to assist easier breathing, but it is rejected as too dangerous. One doctor finally insists that the bleeding stop, given the patient's age and growing weakness—but the others disagree, and Washington is bled again, for a fourth time.

By afternoon, Washington knows he is about to die, and calls on Martha and his aide to make final arrangements. He burns one of two final wills and finally sends the doctors away when they try to continue the treatment. As night comes on, his mind turns to fear of being buried alive. He says to his aide:

I die hard, but I am not afraid to go....My breath cannot last long...Have me decently buried and do not let my body be put into the vault in less than three days after I am dead. Do you understand me?

With those words, Washington passes. Elaborate memorials honoring his death will follow across the nation, but on December 19 a simple ceremony, organized by his local Masonic Lodge, carries him to a final resting place on his farm.

Washington's burial site at Mt. Vernon

Of all the founding fathers, only Washington is unequivocal in his determination to eventually free all of his slaves. Fearing that a future executor might waver, he issues a military-like command:

> *I do hereby forbid the sale of any slave I may die possessed of, under any pretence whatsoever. See that this clause, respecting slaves, and every part thereof, be religiously fulfilled…without evasion, neglect or delay.*

One year after Washington's death in 1799, Martha declares their freedom and sets aside a fund to educate the formerly-enslaved children in preparation for their new life.

## 19

NAPOLEON BECOMES FIRST CONSUL IN FRANCE

TIME: JULY 28, 1794

ROBESPIERRE IS GUILLOTINED AS THE REIGN OF TERROR ENDS

By March 1793 Robespierre has declared war on most of France's European neighbors and Britain, driven the moderate Girondist faction out of the government and begun what will be known as the proletariat Reign of Terror. In the Place de la Concorde, aristocrats are beheaded daily to the sounds of cheering crowds.

But soon enough this domestic chaos spins out of control and Robespierre's rivals arrest him. They then decapitate him face-up on the guillotine on July 8, 1794.

At this point, the Revolution enters its second stage, lasting from 1794 to 1799.

TIME: NOVEMBER 10, 1799

NAPOLEON ASCENDS TO POWER

The Constitution of 1795 is approved, and establishes a government consisting of 750 legislators led by a rotating Executive Directory of five senior men, one retiring each year.

Not all factions support this outcome, especially the pro-Catholic forces who resent the Revolution's virulent attacks on the church. They band together with Royalist forces and march on Paris with a force of 30,000 men, including 2,000 troops from Britain.

The Directory is ill-prepared to counter this threat.

Napoleon Bonaparte (1769–1821)

In desperate straits, they turn to a 26-year-old artillerist, recently promoted to brigadier general for his daring campaign in December 1793 that drove the Royalists and British out of the Mediterranean port city of Toulon.

The soldier's name is Napoleon Bonaparte.

On October 5, 1795, Napoleon assembles 40 cannons, places them strategically throughout Paris, and fires grapeshot into the Royalist troops, routing them despite being outnumbered by six to one in manpower.

For this feat, Napoleon immediately becomes a national hero. He has calmed the internal struggle for power within the French capital, and now turns his attention to the foreign wars currently underway. He is named Commander of the Armée d'Italie, and heads off to win four years' worth of victories abroad.

On November 10, 1799 he will return to Paris, stage a coup that ends the "Revolutionary period," and makes himself first consul and head of the French Republic.

THE FRENCH REVOLUTION "SECOND STAGE": 1793–1795

1792	France declares war on Leopold II's Habsburg monarchy (April 20)
	Frederick II and the Kingdom of Prussia joins Leopold's side
	Tuileries Palace stormed and Louis XVI imprisoned
1793	Louis Capet XVI is guillotined (Jan 21)
	Jacobin Party and Robespierre take control of the government
	France declares war on Britain and Holland (Feb 1)
	France declares war on Spain (March 7)
	Girondist (moderate) faction expelled from National Assembly
	Robespierre's Reign of Terror begins (September 5)
	Marie Antoinette guillotined (Oct 16)
	Napoleon wins fame at Siege of Toulon (Dec 18)
1794	Robespierre arrested and guillotined (July 28)
	The Executive Directory (5 men) takes control of government
1795	Napoleon Bonaparte quells Paris insurrection (October 5)
1796	Directory names him Commander of the Armée d'Italie (Mar 2)
1797	Napoleon defeats the Austrians (Oct 17)
1798	He clashes with Admiral Nelson's fleet in Egypt
1799	He overthrows the Directorate and leads France as first consul

Between 1799 and 1815 Napoleon's France will largely dictate the fate of nations across the globe.

## 20

JOHN ADAMS' PRESIDENCY

TIME: NOVEMBER – DECEMBER, 1796

THE PRESIDENTIAL ELECTION OF 1796

With Washington retiring, the United States experiences its first genuine "race" for the presidency in 1796.

The contest pits the Federalist Party against the Democratic-Republican Party, each promoting its own distinct philosophies about how the government should operate.

Both parties hold caucuses to select their tickets for president and vice president, even though the actual electoral process as yet fails to distinguish votes for one position versus the other.

When Washington endorses his sitting vice president, John Adams of Massachusetts, he becomes the Federalist nominee for the presidency. To provide geographical balance, Thomas Pinckney of South Carolina is nominated for vice president.

Pinckney is educated abroad, a veteran of many Revolutionary War battles, a member of his state legislature, and the successor to Adams as minister

John Adams (1755–1835)

to Great Britain. He is even favored over Adams by Alexander Hamilton, whose power among the Federalists is undiminished since his departure from the Treasury.

The opposition candidates are Thomas Jefferson of Virginia and Aaron Burr of New York. With Washington gone, they see the 1796 election as an opportunity to turn the country away from the Federalist vision for America—and they almost succeed.

The tone of the election becomes quite contentious. Foreign policy plays a large role during the campaign period, with Adams arguing that Jefferson's philosophy will lead to the kind of "mob rule" chaos being played out in France. In response, Jefferson accuses Adams of favoring an English-style monarchy for America, citing his proposal in 1787 to refer to the president as "His Highness."

Voting takes place between November 4 and December 7, 1796. While the popular turn-out more than doubles to 66,841, this is still only 1.5% of the total population of 4.6 million. When it comes to choosing electors, a total of nine of the sixteen states now rely, at least in part, on the public results.

ROLE OF POPULAR VOTING IN CHOOSING PRESIDENTIAL ELECTORS

HOW ELECTORS ARE CHOSEN	STATES
Exclusively by state legislators	Connecticut, Delaware, New Jersey, New York, Rhode Island, South Carolina, Vermont
Exclusively by popular voting	Georgia, Kentucky, Maryland, North Carolina, Pennsylvania, Virginia
Mix of popular and legislator voting	Massachusetts, New Hampshire, Tennessee

As president of the Senate, Adams himself has the duty of tallying the elector's ballots and announcing the winner. Much to his relief, he finds that he has won by a 71–68 margin in the Electoral College and by a slim margin in the popular voting.

RESULTS OF THE 1796 PRESIDENTIAL ELECTION

CANDIDATES	STATE	PARTY	POP. VOTE	TOTAL EV	SOUTH	BORDER	NORTH
John Adams	MA	Federalist	35,726	71	2	10	59
Thomas Jefferson	VA	Dem-Rep	31,115	68	46	8	15
Thomas Pinckney	SC	Federalist		59			
Aaron Burr	NY	Dem-Rep		30			
Samuel Adams	MA	Dem-Rep		15			
Oliver Ellsworth	CT	Federalist		11			
Other Federalists				13			
Other Dem-Republicans				9			
Total			66,841	276*			
Needed to Win				70			

Note: South (VA, NS, SC, GA), Border (DE, MD, KY), North (NH, MA, NY, NJ, PA, RI, CT, VT)

Note: Total # electors = 138, each casting 2 votes = 276 total votes; must get more than half of 138 voters = 70.

The results reveal a sectional pattern that will persist over time, with large electoral majorities for the Federalists in the North and for the Democratic-Republicans in the South. Ironically Adams' victory rides on support from two southern electors, one in Virginia and the other in North Carolina.

Jefferson congratulates his adversary and friend in a gracious letter:

May your administration be filled with glory and happiness to yourself and advantages to us… (I say this) as one who though, in the course of our voyage through life, various little incidents have happened or been contrived to separate us, retains for you the solid esteem of the moments when we were working for our independence, and sentiments of respect and affectionate attachment.

The Federalists also make a strong comeback in the House, adding twelve new seats and stopping the long-run gains by their opponents. And, they win back control of the Senate.

CONGRESSIONAL ELECTION TRENDS

HOUSE	1789	1791	1793	1795	1797
Democratic-Republicans	28	30	55	61	49
Federalist	37	39	50	45	57
SENATE					
Democratic-Republicans	7	12	14	16	12
Federalist	19	17	16	14	20
	Washington	Washington	Washington	Washington	Adams
Congress #	1st	2nd	3rd	4th	5th

The pick-ups by the Federalists extend across all sections, including the southern and border states.

HOUSE TRENDS BY REGION

DEMOCRATIC-REPUBLICANS	TOTAL	SOUTH	BORDER	NORTH
1795	61	33	7	21
1797	49	30	4	15
Change	(12)	(3)	(3)	(6)
FEDERALISTS				
1795	45	5	4	36
1797	57	8	7	42
	+12	+3	+3	+6

So Adams will go into office with apparently solid backing from the Fifth Congress.

TIME: 1735-1826

PRESIDENT JOHN ADAMS: PERSONAL PROFILE

As Jefferson points out, John Adams has come to the presidency after many years of struggle and personal sacrifices on behalf of the United States.

His roots are humble—the first-born son of a modest farmer and shoemaker in Braintree, Massachusetts.

He is a good student and earns a scholarship to attend Harvard College. His father wishes him to become a minister, but he is uncomfortable with the "pretended sanctity" of the clergy, and eventually switches from being a traditional New England Congregationalist to a much less conventional Unitarian.

After a short stint in teaching, Adams settles on a legal career, earning a master's degree at Harvard and reading law as an apprentice. In 1758, aged 23, he opens an office in Boston. Three years pass before he wins his first case. But from there, his practice flourishes. His distinct personal traits are evident from early on. His logic is pristine and he retains remarkable objectivity about issues that come his way. Once his mind is made up, he is unshakeable in getting others to follow him. He is intensely loyal, ambitious, hardworking, and frugal. His spirits vary from upbeat and humorous to melancholy and bitter. While capable of great warmth, his tendency to speak bluntly and honestly limits his close friendships.

But he is blessed with one unwavering friendship in his wife, Abigail, whom he marries in 1764 and remains by her side for the next 54 years. She is a remarkable figure in her own right; intelligent, witty, an astute judge of political matters, and the one who holds farm and family together when duty calls her husband away.

Adams is first drawn into politics by the British Stamp Act of 1765. He sees the act as a violation of his rights as an Englishman, a principle captured best by another Boston lawyer, James Otis Jr.: "taxation without representation is tyranny."

As the conflict grows around Boston, Adams the lawyer is compelled to stand up for another principle, this time involving "due process." His clients are eight British soldiers, charged with killing five civilians and wounding seven others on March 5, 1770, during the "Boston Massacre." He puts forth a compelling defense, arguing that the soldiers were forced to defend themselves against a mob action threatening their lives. He wins the case and is widely vilified. But to Adams, the law is the law.

Facts are stubborn things, and whatever may be our wishes, our inclinations, or the dictums of our passions, they cannot alter the state of facts and evidence.

After the trial, he is soon back into the political struggle with Britain.

He is elected to the Massachusetts Assembly in 1770, and serves as a delegate to both the First and Second Continental Congresses. When the 1775 fighting breaks out, he nominates George Washington to act as commander-in-chief of the army. He is selected by the Convention to serve on the Committee of Five and draft a Declaration of Independence. He calls upon Jefferson to lead the group, who asks why Adams would ask this of him. In characteristically direct fashion, Adams responds:

Reason first: you are a Virginian and a Virginian ought to appear at the head of this business. Reason second: I am obnoxious, suspected and unpopular. You are very much otherwise. Reason third: You can write ten times better than I can.

During the Revolutionary War, Adams serves on some 70 different committees, most notably as head of the Board of War and Ordinance, charged with trying to provide the troops with adequate supplies. His younger brother, Elihu, dies of dysentery while serving.

In 1778 he begins a ten year tour of duty as roving ambassador in Europe, which will result in five straight years without seeing Abigail. He suffers greatly during this period, racked by frequent loneliness, despair, and illness. But on February 6, 1778 his efforts are rewarded when he joins Franklin in signing the Amity Treaty with France that brings the French into the Revolutionary War on the Americans' side, which leads to the 1781 victory at Yorktown.

In 1782 Adams negotiates a critical loan from the Netherlands to avoid American bankruptcy. A year later, he, Franklin, and John Jay meet with a British delegation from King George III to sign the Treaty of Paris, officially ending the Revolutionary War.

Ben Franklin captures two sides of his long-term colleague:

He means well for his country, is always an honest man, often a wise one, but sometimes, and in some things, absolutely out of his senses.

His experiences abroad have left him with firm convictions about government and the presidency.

The greatest dangers to any polity comes from unbridled democracy and an unrestrained aristocracy capable of becoming an oligarchy. The antidote to these dangers is a strong executive.

He regards the executive as the "father and protector" of the nation and of all its citizens, the one man able to act in an independent and disinterested manner on all issues.

His views are those of the Federalists writ large, and Washington selects him to run on the 1788 ticket. He is chosen by 34 of the 69 electors, far ahead of all other contenders for the second slot.

While the president largely relies on Alexander Hamilton rather than Adams for advice, Adams serves faithfully as vice president from 1789 to 1797 and casts 31 tie-break-ing votes as head of the Senate in favor of Washington's policies over that period.

When the 1796 election rolls around, Adams feels like he is next in line, but also underappreciated within the political arena. The spotlight in Paris has fallen on Franklin rather than him. Washington seems to favor Hamilton, although the treasury secretary has resigned due to his marital scandal. Adams also knows that his basic temperament is not well suited for politics. He is outspoken and often prickly. Those who like him, such as Jefferson, often do so grudgingly.

In light of all this, he is delighted when the president endorses him to lead the coun-try and also openly praises his son, John Quincy, who has served as minister to Holland, Portugal, and Prussia since 1793.

In 1797 John Adams begins his time in office. It will be a challenging time and he will forever rank it as less valuable to America than his efforts to win independence.

TIME: MARCH 4, 1797 TO MARCH 4, 1801

OVERVIEW OF ADAMS' TERM

John Adams arrives at his inauguration as the short, somewhat portly, modestly dressed man walking between two tall and elegantly attired Virginian planters, Washing-ton and Jefferson. But his opening address is forceful and it lays out the central issue that will occupy his entire time in office—navigating toward neutrality and peaceful relations with both France and Britain as they again battle for worldwide supremacy.

This task involves political intrigue not only abroad but also at home. The Federalist Party, especially Alexander Hamilton, is strongly aligned with the British cause, while the Democratic-Republicans, and notably Vice President Jefferson, favor France.

Adams' first decision in office will come back to haunt him. He chooses to retain Washington's entire cabinet, most of whom will prove more loyal to Hamilton than to him. His rationale goes as follows:

Washington had appointed them, and I knew it would turn the world upside down if I removed any of them.

Secretary of State Pickering is a military man who fought alongside Washington and has previously served as postmaster general and secretary of war. He is a particular-ly strong personality, and thoroughly on the side of England—"the world's last hope: Britain's fast anchored isle"—against the French. His views on this are shared by both Treasury Secretary Wolcott and the secretary of war, ex-surgeon James McHenry, a signer of the 1787 Constitution.

Adams finds only one true supporter for his policy of strict neutrality, and that is

Benjamin Stoddert, who joins the cabinet in 1798, after Adams acts to create a formidable US Navy. Unlike the others, Stoddert will actually try to convert the president's policies into their intended outcomes.

JOHN ADAMS' CABINET

POSITION	NAME	HOME STATE
Vice President	Thomas Jefferson	Virginia
Secretary of State	Timothy Pickering	Massachusetts
Secretary of Treasury	Oliver Wolcott, Jr.	Connecticut
Secretary of War	James McHenry	Maryland
Secretary of the Navy	Benjamin Stoddert	Maryland
Attorney General	Charles Lee	Virginia

John Adams' entire presidency will be dominated by the effort to avoid war with America's former ally, France. To do so, he must deal internationally with the likes of the devious and corrupt foreign minister Prince de Talleyrand and his master, Napoleon Bonaparte, who is positioning himself to conquer the world.

As punishment for the 1794 Amity Treaty with Britain, the French begin to intercept American merchant ships on the high seas, seize their cargo, and "impress" captured sailors. Over time some 300 vessels fall victim to this form of piracy.

Adams responds by sending peace commissioners to Paris where they are rebuffed, and by upgrading his military strength at home, which is viewed as needlessly provocative to his Democratic-Republican critics.

When homeland criticism mounts, the president responds with a series of highly divisive "law and order" measures (the Alien and Sedition Acts) that clearly bend, if not break, several guarantees in the five year old Bill of Rights.

The drums of war intensify into 1798, with Adams actually luring George Washington out of retirement to create a standing army capable of combatting a French invasion.

In 1799 Napoleon suddenly turns his focus away from the American conflict for the time being, and toward an invasion of Britain. This shift leads to the Treaty of Mortefontaine which ends the Quasi-War with France.

In response, the American economy, which has dipped in 1797–98, begins a slow rebound as greater safety is restored to international trade.

ECONOMIC GROWTH DURING ADAMS' TERM

	1796	1797	1798	1799	1800
Total GDP ($Million)	$417	$409	$413	$442	$480
Per Capita GDP	$89	$84	$83	$86	$91
% Change	6%	6%	1%	4%	6%

Adams has achieved the neutrality he sought, albeit paying a high price in domestic politics along the way.

JOHN ADAMS' PRESIDENCY: KEY EVENTS

1797	French attack US ships; congress funds 10,000 militia in case of war
March 4	Adams and Jefferson are sworn in
May 10	The first ship in the new US Navy, the *United States,* launches
May 31	With relations eroding, Adams names three emissaries to visit France
June 1	Secretary of State Pickering reports that 300 US ships have been seized by France
June 24	Congress approves an 80,000-man militia in case of war with France
September 7	The *USS Constellation* joins the Navy fleet
October 18	In the XYZ Affair, Talleyrand demands a bribe to negotiate with the US envoys
October 21	The *USS Constitution* ("Old Ironsides") is launched
1798	
January 8	The Eleventh Amendment becomes law
January 17	John Marshall formally rejects the proposed French bribes in the XYZ Affair
April 3	Adams releases the XYZ correspondence to Congress for its scrutiny
April 7	The Mississippi Territory is created by Congress (Alabama and Mississippi area)
May 3	The Department of the Navy is officially created; Stoddert to head it.
May 28	Congress authorizes naval action against French ships interfering with commerce
June 18	Congress passes the first Alien and Sedition Act, silencing criticism of government
June 25	The Alien Act authorizes deportation of any non-citizen deemed dangerous
July 2	Adams appoints George Washington to head an army versus a French invasion
July 11	A fourth Sedition Act prohibits "any false and malicious writing" about government
July 11	The US Marine Corps is founded
September 12	Ben Franklin's grandson, Ben Bache, is imprisoned for Anti-Federalist editorials
November 16	Jefferson's "Kentucky Resolutions" oppose violations of Bill of Rights guarantees
November 20	The French seize the American schooner *Retaliation* in the Caribbean
December 24	Madison's "Virginia Resolution" also oppose the Alien and Sedition crackdown
1799	
February 9	The *USS Constellation* captures the French frigate *l'Insurgente* in the Caribbean
February 18	To the dismay of Hamilton and the hardliners, Adams signals wish to talk with France
March 29	New York passes a "gradual emancipation" statute
November 10	In a coup against the Directory, Napoleon rules France as first consul
December 14	George Washington dies suddenly at Mt. Vernon
1800	
January 2	Free Black people in Philadelphia petition Congress to rescind the Fugitive Slave Act
February 1	The *USS Constellation* battles *LaVengeance* in the Caribbean

March 8	Napoleon officially receives the US envoys seeking negotiations to restore peace
April 24	The Library of Congress is founded
May 10	Congress passes the Harrison Land Act, allowing smaller 320 acre parcels for sale
May 12	Adams sacks Secretary of State Thomas Pickering for colluding against him with Hamilton
June	The government officially transfers from Philadelphia to Washington, DC
June 14	Napoleon scores a major victory over Austria at the Battle of Marengo
August 31	A slave rebellion plot planned by Gabriel Prosser, is foiled near Richmond, VA
September 30	The Treaty of Mortefontaine ends the Quasi-War with France
October 1	Napoleon signs the secret Treaty of Ildefonso whereby Spain returns Louisiana to France
December 3	Voting takes place in the presidential election of 1800
1801	
January 27	Adams' choice for chief justice, John Marshall, is approved by the lame-duck Senate
February 11	Electoral college votes show that Jefferson and Aaron Burr are tied for the presidency
February 17	Hamilton breaks the deadlock in favor of Jefferson, whom he calls "the lesser evil"
February 27	The Judiciary Act defines the structure of the Supreme Court and other federal courts
March 3	Adams attempts to pack the court with Federalist judges, leading to the *Marbury* case

TIME: SUMMER 1797

TENSIONS RISE BETWEEN THE UNITED STATES AND FRANCE

France is very upset by John Jay's 1794 Amity Treaty with Britain. They regard it as a direct betrayal of the 1778 Treaty that Adams and Franklin signed in Paris—which led to the crucial French role in the Battle of Yorktown and America's independence. Adams had promised that America would provide military support to France in case of a future war with Britain and now he is backing out.

To signal displeasure, France threatens the United States militarily and economically by seizing its merchant ships on their way to and from Europe.

As these violations of international trade accelerate, President Adams responds with "a carrot and a stick."

He announces these in a carefully worded speech to Congress on May 16, 1797. The "carrot" to France will be a ministerial commission seeking peace; the "stick" will lie in a build-up of America's military might.

While we are endeavoring to adjust all our differences with France by amicable negotiation, with the progress of the war in Europe, the depredations on our commerce, the personal injuries to our citizens, and the general complexion of our affairs, render it my duty to recommend your consideration of effectual measures of defense.

The pro-British Federalists, including Washington and Hamilton, are delighted by Adams' response. Both men are alarmed by the chaotic Reign of Terror and intent on suppressing any similar breakdown at home.

On the other hand, Jefferson and the Democratic-Republicans roundly criticize Adams, claiming that the buildup of America's military will only boost the odds of French belligerence

Adams is undeterred by the opposition and turns his attention to naming the negotiators he will send to Paris. His first choice is James Madison, and he asks Vice President Jefferson to convince Madison to accept his request. When Madison refuses, Adams holds it against Jefferson for what he regards as allowing party politics to get in the way of the national interest. Adams distances himself from Jefferson, who reacts with a bitter letter to a political friend in France.

> *Mr. Adams is vain, irritable, stubborn, endowed with excessive self-love, and still suffers pique at the preference accorded Franklin over him in Paris.*

With Madison out of the picture, Adams selects a three-man delegation to meet with the French. One is the current minister to France, Charles Cotesworth Pinckney, named to his post by Washington in 1796. Another is Elbridge Gerry, like Pinckney a former delegate to the 1787 Constitutional Convention. John Marshall is the last; a lawyer, Revolutionary War veteran, and a lifelong antagonist of Jefferson, who is his cousin.

The commission completes the ten-week voyage across the Atlantic and arrives in Paris in October 1797.

TIME: OCTOBER 1797 TO JULY 1798

THE "XYZ AFFAIR" PROVOKES OPEN CONFLICT WITH FRANCE

Between October 1797 and July 1798 the American delegation is subjected to a series of humiliations at the hands of the French foreign minister, Charles Maurice de Talleyrand-Périgord.

Talleyrand is the very definition of the scheming political survivor, having served the guillotined King Louis XVI, shifting allegiances to the Robespierre-led rebels, then ingratiating himself to Napoleon Bonaparte before finally backing and serving the restored monarchies of Louis XVIII and Louis Philippe. He will consistently use his power to extract personal bribes during diplomatic negotiations, achieve great wealth, and die peacefully on his estate at age 84, in 1838.

He commences his manipulations of the American ministers as soon as talks begin. He tells them nothing official can occur unless and until President Adams makes a public apology for his threatening policies and France receives a $12 million "loan" from America. For good measure he demands a payment of $250,000 to his personal account to continue the negotiations.

When Charles Pinckney responds with "no, not a sixpence," Talleyrand goes into a prolonged stalling phase that drags on into 1798. As the Americans announce their intention to depart, he threatens that France will declare war on the United States if they do so.

President Adams is informed of all this via dispatches that filter home over time. In March 1798 he learns of the treatment of his ministers and the bullying demands from Talleyrand. He shares the news with his cabinet, but decides to with-

French Minister de Talleyrand (1754–1838)

hold public disclosure of the dispatches in which the exploits of Talleyrand's three go-betweens—codenamed X, Y, and Z—are detailed. He fears that these revelations will fan the American flames of war at a time when he still hopes to prevent it.

Secretary of State Pickering and Attorney General Lee insist that Adams should declare war. Washington and Hamilton also signal their support for aggressive action.

In Congress, the Democratic-Republicans demand that all the dispatches related to the negotiations be released to the public and their bill to this effect wins by a 65–27 margin in the House. On April 3, 1798, Adams complies.

The documents expose what becomes known as the "XYZ Affair," including the

French arrogance toward the American delegation and Talleyrand's bribe. The pro-France Republicans are shocked by the disclosures, which blunt much of their criticism of Adams.

Later in April of 1798, Pinckney and Marshall abandon the talks and sail home. Elbridge Gerry stays in Paris, hoping to break through with Talleyrand on his own and secure peace.

The growing fear of war prompts Congress to finally authorize the funds needed to convert the objectives of the 1794 Naval Act into an actual United States Navy, capable of contending with European adversaries.

Adams is delighted by the congressional support, and on May 3, 1798, he names Benjamin Stoddert as the first secretary of the navy. He considers this move one of the high points of his presidency. The heavy frigates *USS Constitution* ("Old Ironsides"), *United States,* and *Constellation* are about to be joined by the *USS Chesapeake, Congress,* and *President* on the high seas.

Two months later, on July 7, 1798, Congress annuls the landmark 1778 Treaty of Alliance binding America militarily to France in case of war involving Britain and authorizes attacks on French ships at sea. Thus begins what will become known as the Quasi-War with France.

TIME: JULY 1798

ADAMS UNLEASHES FEDERAL POWER TO PREVENT A FEARED BREAKDOWN IN LAW AND ORDER

The collapse of the peace negotiations, together with Napoleon's stunning victories in Austria and Italy, amplify Federalist concerns about national security. With war on the horizon, America's survival may hinge on its ability to prevent the collapse of law and order they associate with the French version of democracy.

They settle on two tactics often employed in the future course of American history to quell internal dissent.

The first is directed against "foreign immigrants," especially those from France and Ireland, whose heritage or religion places them outside the dominant American class: white, Anglo-Saxon, and Protestant.

On June 18 Congress passes a Naturalization Act which sounds this nativist theme. It boosts the waiting period for immigrants to become citizens from five to fourteen years.

This is followed one week later by the Alien Enemies Act—allowing citizens of an enemy nation to be arrested and deported should war break out—and the Alien Friends Act, enabling deportation of any non-US citizen deemed a threat to national safety.

However, the Sedition Act of July 14 is the one that immediately draws criticism.

This Act, in four sections, is aimed at stifling political opposition until March 3, 1801, which encompasses the remainder of Adam's term.

Section 1. That if any persons shall unlawfully combine or conspire together, with intent to oppose any measure or measures of the government of the United States... or attempt to procure any insurrection, riot, unlawful assembly...he or they shall be deemed guilty of a high misdemeanor, and on conviction...shall be punished by a fine not exceeding five thousand dollars, and by imprisonment during a term not less than six months nor exceeding five years...

Section 2. That if any person shall write, print, utter or publish, or...willingly assist or aid in writing, printing, uttering or publishing any false, scandalous and malicious writing or writings against the government of the United States, or the Congress or the President, with intent to defame (them) or bring them...into contempt or disrepute...or to stir up sedition within the United States...or to resist, oppose, or defeat any... law or act, or to aid, encourage or abet any hostile designs of any foreign nation... then such person...shall be punished by a fine not exceeding two thousand dollars, and by imprisonment not exceeding two years.

Section 3. That if any person shall be prosecuted under this act...it shall be lawful for the defendant, upon the trial of the cause, to give in evidence in his defence, the truth of the matter...charged as a libel. And the jury who shall try the cause, shall have a right to determine the law and the fact, under the direction of the court, as in other cases.

Section 4. That this act shall continue and be in force until the third day of March, one thousand eight hundred and one, and no longer:

The Democratic-Republicans oppose the Act, on grounds that it violates the First Amendment right to free speech.

First Amendment. Congress shall make no law respecting an establishment of religion, or prohibiting the free exercise thereof; or abridging the freedom of speech, or of the press; or the right of the people peaceably to assemble, and to petition the government for a redress of grievances.

Federalists respond in line with British law, arguing that free speech is indeed protected "in advance" of its commission, but that any speech is fair game for prosecution if it proves to be factually wrong and damaging to those attacked.

In October 1798, Matthew Lyon, a Democratic-Republican congressman from Vermont, becomes the first citizen convicted under the Sedition Act for asserting that Adams is power hungry and belongs in a madhouse. Lyon serves a four month jail sentence, pays a $1,000 fine, and emerges as a hero in his state for speaking out freely against the president.

Other indictments under the Sedition Act, some thirteen in total, will mainly target Democratic-Republican newspaper editors—such as Benjamin Bache of Philadelphia, Franklin's grandson—who criticize the Federalist administration.

Opponents of the law regard it as one more attempt by the federal government to trample on the rights of the people, and search for a legal basis to overturn it.

TIME: NOVEMBER 10, 1798

THE "KENTUCKY RESOLUTIONS" ASSERT LIMITS ON FEDERAL POWERS

Jefferson ponders a call to the states to nullify the law but instead joins with Madison to criticize it for violating the Tenth Amendment to the Constitution:

> *The powers not delegated to the United States by the Constitution, nor prohibited by it to the States, are reserved to the States respectively, or to the people.*

According to the Virginians, the federal government lacks the power to impose the Alien and Sedition Acts on its citizens. To be legal, any such laws must originate with the people acting through their state legislatures.

Jefferson is the first to act in opposition to the Alien and Sedition Acts by authoring what becomes known as the "Kentucky Resolutions."

He writes these secretly and conveys them to his friend John Breckinridge, who is serving in the Kentucky House of Representatives, to propose their adoption. Jefferson deflects all public inquiries as to his role all the way up to 1821, when one of Breckinridge's sons probes him about the history of the document.

Jefferson's document reaffirms the state's sovereign authority over the kinds of issues raised in the Sedition Act.

> *Kentucky Resolution 1: Be it resolved that the States...are NOT united on the principle of unlimited submission to their general government...but that, under a Constitution, they delegated to that government certain definite powers reserving...to each State the residuary mass of rights to their own self-government*

It then goes on—in its original form—to propose that state nullification is the proper remedy for cases of overreach by the central government.

> *The several states who formed [the Constitution], being sovereign and independent, have the unquestionable right to judge of its infraction; and, that a <u>nullification</u>, by*

those sovereignties, of all unauthorized acts done under color of that instrument, is the rightful remedy.

But the idea of state nullification is softened before the bill passes on November 16, 1798.

And that, whenever the general government assumes undelegated powers, its acts are unauthoritative, void, and of no force and that each party has an equal right to judge for itself the extent of the powers delegated to itself.

It is not until one year later, in a further attempt to rally support, that the nullification remedy is restored in a second Kentucky Resolution of 1799.

After Jefferson, it is Madison's turn to attack Adams and the Sedition Act. He does so in a "Virginia Resolution" passed by the state legislature on December 24, 1798.

RESOLVED, That the General Assembly of Virginia, doth unequivocally express a firm resolution to maintain and defend the Constitution…declares a warm attachment to the Union of the States..views the powers of the federal government…to which the states are parties as limited.. and that in case of a deliberate, palpable, and dangerous exercise of other powers…is duty bound, to maintain…their respective limits…

That the General Assembly doth also express its deep regret, that a spirit has in sundry instances, been manifested the federal government, to enlarge its powers by forced constructions of the constitutional charter which defines them…so as to consolidate the states by degrees, into one sovereignty, the obvious tendency and inevitable consequence of which would be, to transform the present republican system of the United States, into an absolute, or at best a mixed monarchy.

That the General Assembly doth particularly protest against the palpable and alarming infractions of the Constitution, in the two late cases of the "Alien and Sedition Acts"… which exercises… a power not delegated by the constitution, but on the contrary, expressly and positively forbidden by one of the amendments that this state having by its Convention…expressly declared, that among other essential rights, "the Liberty of Conscience and of the Press cannot be cancelled, abridged, restrained, or modified by any authority of the United States,"…it would mark a reproachable inconsistency. If…indifference were now shewn, to the most palpable violation of… the Rights, thus declared…

The two Democratic-Republican resolutions are eventually voted on more broadly, but to no effect. Ten states reject the proposals and another four decide to take no action.

With a possible war looming and the Federalists enjoying political control, debates over state sovereignty win only limited support in 1798. Over the decades ahead, however, this issue will return with a vengeance, first over taxes and then over slavery.

TIME: 1798–1799

ADAMS TRIES AGAIN TO SETTLE THE QUASI-WAR WITH FRANCE

USS Constitution, commissioned in 1797

As 1798 closes, Adams' efforts to hold out for peace are being offset by Hamilton and even Washington, both apparently eager to fight the French. Secretary of War McHenry conspires in the effort, sharing secret documents with Hamilton while cautioning him to act surreptitiously.

> *Do not, I pray you, in writing or otherwise, betray the confidence which has induced me to deal thus with you.*

Plans are underway to raise a standing army. Adams names Washington commander-in-chief, and the old general demands that Hamilton, the president's nemesis, be appointed second in command. Jefferson imagines an upcoming Federalist coup with a crackdown on individual and state's rights, enforced by Hamilton at the head of a federal army.

Suddenly, on October 4, 1798, the tide turns in favor of John Adams.

The lone surviving member of his Paris delegation, Elbridge Gerry, tells him that the French now want peace!

Adams holds this news close to his vest, needing to make sure of its veracity. He continues to publicly back all military preparations under way, while staunchly refusing to ask Congress to declare war. As a result, he is whipsawed between the pro-French Democratic-Republican doves and his own pro-British Federalist hawks.

But Adams is undeterred. In January 1799, his ambassador son in Europe, John Quincy, reassures him that France wants to negotiate, and on February 9, 1799, his naval buildup begins to pay out. The *USS Constellation* defeats the frigate, *La Insurgente*, with its 36 guns and reputation as the fastest boat in the French navy, off the coast of Nevis Island in the Caribbean Sea.

On February 16, the president sends a message to Congress announcing the choice of his Dutch ambassador, William Vans Murray, to lead a second negotiating party to France. This stuns Adams' critics in both political parties. His sanity is questioned by some, including Secretary of State Pickering; others push for older and more experienced replacements for Murray. Adams responds by adding Democratic-Republican Patrick Henry and sitting Chief Justice Oliver Ellsworth to the delegation.

Despite word in August that Talleyrand will officially receive the ministers, departure is delayed. On October 15, 1799, Adams asks his cabinet for support. Pickering, McHenry, and Wolcott refuse, leaving only Lee and the ever loyal Stoddert on Adams' side. After also hearing opposition from Washington and Hamilton, Adams decides to send the delegation anyway. They depart on November 15, 1799.

While they are en route, America suffers an emotional shock: George Washington dies suddenly on December 14, at age 67. Two full days of supervising Mt. Vernon farm work on horseback in snow, hail, and rain lead to a quinsy infection that kills him within 48 hours.

The burden of leading the nation now falls even more heavily on John Adams as the new century dawns.

Naval battles with the French persist across the Caribbean, cleverly countered by Secretary Stoddert. On the night of February 1, 1800, the *USS Constellation* exchanges roughly 1,500 rounds with *La Vengeance*, before scoring another victory off the island of St. Kitts, over 600 miles west of Haiti.

By mid-May, Adams finally concedes that retaining Washington's cabinet was a mistake. On May 5, he asks his scheming war secretary, McHenry, to step aside. On the 15th he sacks Secretary of State Pickering, who refuses to submit his resignation when asked. He then names John Marshall to succeed Pickering—before later ensuring that Marshall is installed as Chief Justice of the Supreme Court instead, in a host of last-second efforts to shape the judicial system along Federalist lines.

Still, peace negotiations with France drag on without resolution into the presidential election season—with Adams attacked by Hamilton and the "hard Federalists," and by the Democratic-Republicans, who decide to run Vice President Jefferson against him in the 1800 election.

The fate of Adams' bid for a second term is sealed by the time the French talks reach resolution.

TIME: SEPTEMBER 30, 1800

THE TREATY OF MORTEFONTAINE ENDS THE CONFLICT (FOR NOW)

By June of 1800, Napoleon Bonaparte is essentially dictator of France. He has overthrown the Directory and replaced it with the Consulate, naming himself first consul. He has also won another landmark victory at the Battle of Marengo in June, driving the Austrians out of Italy. Talleyrand is now his foreign minister, and they are plotting a campaign to invade Britain—the one country that stands in his way of reasserting the global dominance France enjoyed in the seventeenth century.

To do so, he wants to ease all secondary military pressures, first from Spain and then from America.

On October 1, 1800, he concludes the secret Treaty of San Ildefonso with Spain, trading land won in the Tuscan region of Italy for a return of the vast Louisiana Territory that France had ceded to Spain in 1762, after losing the Seven Years' War.

Napoleon turns next to freeing up his naval forces from the Caribbean engagements with the United States.

With ownership of the middle third of North America—along the Mississippi—in his hands, he can assuage the Americans now and return to possible battles there at a later date, after Britain is defeated.

So he tells Talleyrand to conclude a treaty with the US.

The fact that France again owns Louisiana would prove very alarming to the American negotiators, but this fact is kept secret for another year, until November 1801.

A deal ending the Quasi-War is finally concluded on November 30, 1800, the Treaty of Mortefontaine. Article One captures the overall spirit:

> *There shall be a firm, inviolable, and universal peace, and a true and sincere Friendship between the French Republic and the United States of America, and between their respective countries territories, cities, towns, and people without exception of persons, or places.*

The other details are straightforward and standard: captured vessels will be returned, claims dropped, cargo ships shall not be attacked, and favorable commercial terms will be granted to both sides.

After all his years devoted to winning America's freedom as a patriot, John Adams can finally say that he further kept it secure as a president.

As he says later in life:

I desire no other inscription over my gravestone than: 'Here lies John Adams, who took upon himself the responsibility of peace with France in the year 1800.'

TIME: FEBRUARY 20 TO MARCH 3, 1801

ADAMS "PACKS THE COURTS" AND PICKS JOHN MARSHALL AS CHIEF JUSTICE

In the final days of his presidency John Adams attempts to preserve the legal principles he believes in by "packing the judiciary" with newly named federal judges.

Prior to the 1787 Constitution, legal statutes and courtroom disputes are in the hands of the state judiciaries—and this form of local control is favored by Jefferson and his Democratic-Republican supporters.

However, once the new Constitution is ratified, it creates a body of federal laws that apply to all states and the need for a judicial structure to ensure local compliance. The Judiciary Act of 1789 lays out the basic frameworks.

Legal disputes will continue to be adjudicated in the thirteen state courts, by state or district judges.

- Any cases or decisions that may call constitutional laws into question are to be reviewed by the federal Supreme Court, consisting of six justices.
- To conduct these reviews, the Supreme Court justices will travel to each of the states twice a year, in order to hear appeals and either support or overturn the local decisions.
- This travel is referred to as "riding the circuit"—in the beginning there are six circuits in total to cover all thirteen states/districts.

This system remains in place for twelve years, until the lame duck Federalist-dominated Congress changes it in a move referred to by opponents as the "Midnight Judges Act." This Act is passed on February 13, 1801, within two weeks of the end of John Adams' presidency. It makes three significant changes:

- After increasing the number of "districts" from thirteen to sixteen (recognizing the new states of Vermont, Kentucky, and Tennessee), it assigns a new "judicial layer" to each, in the form of sixteen federal Circuit Court judges.
- The burdensome task of "riding the six circuits" is handed to these sixteen new federal Circuit Court judges and removed from the Supreme Court justices, who would now operate solely from Washington, DC.
- It reduces the number of Supreme Court justices from an even number of six to an odd number of five, in case of split decisions.

THE SHAPE OF THE COURT SYSTEMS AFTER THE 1801 JUDICIARY ACT

FEDERAL LEVEL	DETAILS
Focus	Cases involving federal crimes, cases brought against the federal government, and cases involving citizens living across state lines
Supreme Court Judges	One chief justice and four associates, freed from riding the circuit
Circuit Court Judges	Sixteen judges in total, one for each of the sixteen states, riding the circuit, reviewing controversial cases/appeals
District Court Judges	Original jurisdiction/trial court judges on federal cases
STATE LEVEL	DETAILS
Focus	Cases involving state laws, both criminal and civil
General Court Judges	Three judges per state, court of last resort, meet twice a year
Appeals Court Judges	In some states, three judges, meet in each county in October
District Court Judges	Original jurisdiction/trial court, quarter sessions (criminal case), common pleas (civil cases).
Justice of the Peace	Tends to handle misdemeanors or small claims (<$5) disputes.

Between February 20 and March 3, 1801, Adams takes advantage of the new law to name Federalists to all sixteen of the new Circuit Court slots, along with four State District Courts positions and 42 local justices of the peace.

In response, Jefferson's supporters mock the new law as the "Midnight Judges Act" and commit to repealing it once the new Congress is sworn in.

Still, Adams has one more trick up his sleeve. On December 15, 1800, Oliver Ellsworth resigns as chief justice of the Supreme Court, leaving Adams to nominate his successor. After a momentary hesitation, Adams selects his sitting secretary of state, John Marshall of Virginia. And from there, Marshall goes on to become the longest-serving (34.5 years) and most influential chief justice in the history of the Supreme Court. During his early tenure, he will also prove to be a fairly consistent thorn in the side of his second cousin by marriage, Thomas Jefferson.

## 21

THOMAS JEFFERSON'S FIRST TERM

TIME: FEBRUARY 17, 1801

THE ELECTION OF 1800 DECIDED IN THE HOUSE OF REPRESENTATIVES

State voting in the election of 1800—extending from October 31 to December 3, 1800—finds Adams and the Federalist Party in a state of disarray.

The president has sacked disloyal cabinet members in May; his peace commissioners to France won't conclude a treaty until November 30, after most votes are cast; and Hamilton, the de facto head of the party, comes out in favor of Charles C. Pinckney of South Carolina over Adams.

Hamilton's opposition to Adams is long-standing and intense. In October 1800 he attacks the president in a 54-page pamphlet, *Concerning the Public Conduct and Character of John Adams*. In this diatribe, Hamilton says that his choice is Pinckney:

> *Resulted from the disgusting egotism, the distempered jealousy, and the ungovernable indiscretion of Mr. Adams' temper, joined to some doubts of the correctness of his maxims of administration.*

B. M BRADY,   WASHINGTON, D. C.

Thomas Jefferson (1743–1826)

The Democratic-Republicans are delighted by the split within the Federalists and add their own attacks against Adams, especially around the Sedition Act—which they cast as another attempt by the federal government to override individual freedoms guaranteed in the Bill of Rights. Their intended ticket calls for Thomas Jefferson to become president with Aaron Burr as his vice president.

When the electors gather to vote on February 11, 1801, John Adams is able to make a race of it, despite all of his vulnerabilities. In a contest requiring at least 70 of the 138 ballots to win, he is chosen by 65 electors, only six less than his 1796 total.

But what follows next shocks the entire election system set up in the 1787 Constitution. Two men—Jefferson and Burr—end up in a tie for the top spot, with 73 votes apiece.

RESULTS OF THE 1800 PRESIDENTIAL ELECTION

CANDIDATES	STATE	PARTY	POP. VOTE	TOTAL EV	SOUTH	BORDER	NORTH
Thomas Jefferson	VA	Democratic-Republican	41,330	73	44	9	20
Aaron Burr	NY	Democratic-Republican		73	44	9	20
John Adams	MA	Federalist	25,952	65	4	8	53
Charles C. Pinckney	SC	Federalist		64	4	8	52
John Jay	NY	Federalist		1			1
Total			67,282	276	96	34	146
Needed to win				70			

Note: South (VA, NC, SC, GA), Border (DE, MD, KY), North (NH, MA, NY, NJ, PA, RI, CT, VT)
Note: Total # electors = 138, each casting 2 votes = 276 total votes; must get more than half of 138 voters = 70.

This outcome throws the election into the House of Representatives, where each of the sixteen states is asked to caucus and cast one vote for either Jefferson or Burr. The winner must achieve an absolute majority of at least nine votes.

Ironically, the existing House, elected in 1798, is dominated by Federalists who enjoy a 60–46 margin. It is clear to them that the intent of the Democratic-Republicans is to choose Jefferson, but many actually favor Burr, who is a New Yorker, rather than another Virginian.

For eleven days in a row, across 35 ballots, the House voting is frozen, with eight states favoring Jefferson, six favoring Burr, and two deadlocked. Neither man is able to achieve the nine vote majority required by law.

HOUSE VOTING FOR PRESIDENT: BALLOTS 1–35

VOTING FOR:	SOUTH	BORDER	NORTH	TOTAL
Jefferson	VA, NC, GA, TN	KY	NY, NJ, PA	8
Burr	SC	DE	MA, CT, NH, RI	6
Tie		MD	VT	2

On February 17, 1801, just two weeks before the new president is to assume his office, none other than Alexander Hamilton steps in to push for resolution. His very public feuds with both men are legendary at this point. He has clashed with Jefferson repeatedly during his tenure as Treasury secretary, and he holds Burr, along with James Monroe, accountable for publicizing his extramarital affair with Maria Reynolds.

But after weighing the two in the balance, he chooses Jefferson as the lesser of two evils.

Mr. Jefferson, though too revolutionary in his notions, is yet a lover of liberty and will be desirous of something like an orderly government. Mr. Burr loves nothing but himself, thinks of nothing but his own aggrandizement. In the choice of evils, let them take the least. Jefferson is in my view less dangerous than Burr.

Though out of office, Hamilton has retained enough power to derail Adam's reelection bid, and now he does the same against Burr. On the 36th and final ballot, his behind-the-scenes voice helps move Maryland and Vermont into Jefferson's column, while also removing South Carolina and Delaware from the Burr side.

HOUSE VOTING FOR PRESIDENT: BALLOT 36

VOTING FOR:	SOUTH	BORDER	NORTH	TOTAL
Jefferson	VA, NC, GA, TN	KY, MD	NY, NJ, PA, VT	10
Burr			MA, CT, NH, RI	4
Tie	SC	DE		2

Jefferson ends up with ten votes and is named president. Congress ends up convinced that the election process must change to avoid future chaos. This leads to passage of the Twelfth Amendment, ratified on June 15, 1804. It ends the practice of having electors vote for their two top choices for president and forces them to cast one ballot for president and a separate one for vice president.

Ties, of course, will still be resolved by voting in the House of Representatives, as will be seen again as early as the controversial election of 1824.

TIME: 1800

THE DEMOCRATIC-REPUBLICANS GAIN CONTROL OVER BOTH HOUSES OF CONGRESS

In addition to Adams' loss, the Federalists suffer a devastating reversal of fortune in the 1800 races for Congress.

This is particularly true in the House, where the upward momentum they exhibited in the prior two elections comes to a screeching halt. What was a commanding 60–46 majority going into the vote, becomes a 38–68 deficit coming out.

CONGRESSIONAL ELECTION TRENDS

HOUSE	1789	1791	1793	1795	1797	1799	1801
Democratic-Republicans	28	30	55	61	49	46	68
Federalist	37	39	50	45	57	60	38
Congress	1st	2nd	3rd	4th	5th	6th	7th
President	GW	GW	GW	GW	JA	JA	TJ

Furthermore the 22 seats lost by the Federalists are spread across all regions of the country, including their historically strong home base in the North.

HOUSE TRENDS BY REGION

DEMOCRATIC-REPUBLICAN	TOTAL	SOUTH	BORDER	NORTH
1795	61	33	7	21
1797	49	30	4	15
1799	46	21	5	20
1801	68	30	7	31
Change	+22	+9	+2	+11
FEDERALISTS				
1795	45	5	4	36
1797	57	8	7	42
1799	60	17	6	37
1801	38	8	4	26
Change	(22)	(9)	(2)	(11)

This same pattern is repeated in the Senate, where the Federalists' comfortable 22–10 majority swings over to a 15–17 minority position with the losses evident in all regions.

SENATE TRENDS BY REGION

DEMOCRATIC-REPUBLICAN	TOTAL	SOUTH	BORDER	NORTH
1795	16	7	4	5
1797	12	8	1	3
1799	10	8	1	1
1801	17	10	3	4
Change	+7	+2	+2	+3
FEDERALISTS				
1795	14	1	2	11
1797	20	2	5	13
1799	22	2	5	15
1801	15	0	3	12
Change	(7)	(2)	(2)	(3)

History will show that the Federalist Party will never fully recover from the repudiation it suffers in 1800.

The nation now seems intent on tinkering with the form of government it wants—ready to move away from Hamilton's tight federal control in the hands of a few powerful men and toward Jefferson's more decentralized and broadly-shared option.

TIME: 1743 – 1826

PRESIDENT THOMAS JEFFERSON: PERSONAL PROFILE

Thomas Jefferson's life is noted for remarkable personal and public achievements, offset at times by intense self-indulgences and a wavering moral compass.

His father, Peter, starts from modest means, enters public service as a county surveyor and sheriff in Virginia, and along the way befriends William Randolph II and Isham Randolph, two sons of the aristocratic planter William senior. In 1736 Peter buys 200 acres of land at Shadwell from William II, and in 1739 he marries Isham's oldest daughter, Jane.

Thomas Jefferson is born on April 13, 1743, at Shadwell, the oldest son in a family of ten children. He will benefit from the practical know-how of his father and the elite intellectual lifestyles and worldly connections of the Randolphs. The bond between Peter Jefferson and the two Randolph sons is such that both entrust him with guardianship over their younger children when they pass. In turn, Peter's wealth grows dramatically and by 1757 he has extensive land and slave holdings at two estates, Shadwell and Snowden, both in Virginia.

But Peter Jefferson dies suddenly in 1757 and Thomas, age fourteen, inherits his Shadwell Plantation (which includes Monticello), while his younger brother Randolph inherits Snowden.

Two years later, Jefferson enrolls at William & Mary College, where he graduates with high honors in two years, learning six languages and studying philosophy and science. He then masters the law under the renowned George Wythe, and goes on to pass the bar in 1767. As a lawyer he will handle over 900 cases, mostly involving disputes over land claims.

In 1768 he begins a lifelong preoccupation with building his own land at Monticello. The effort will tap into many of his polymorphic capacities. On one day he is an architectural designer, the next an agronomist, then an inventor, a gourmet, an aesthete, a librarian, a manufacturer, a financier, and finally, a very astute capitalist. Over time, Jefferson will raise tobacco here, then switch to wheat, corn, and clover. He will build a 1,200 foot canal and a grain mill for his own use and as a sideline business. He will set up a nail-making operation operated by enslaved children too small to work in the fields.

Other enslaved people will also play a crucial role in the development of Monticello and in Jefferson's accumulation of wealth. In 1757 he begins with 52 enslaved people inherited from his father. In 1769 he marries a widow, Martha Wayles Skelton, whose father, John, dies the following year, leaving her another 135 enslaved Africans. Included here are Betty Hemings and her ten mixed-race children, all fathered by John Wayles. Over the years at Monticello, Jefferson will own roughly 650 enslaved people, and will keep detailed written observations on their "characteristics and capacities" in his *Notes on the State of Virginia*.

Jefferson's lifestyle is lavish, and he is forever in financial difficulties—including a staggering $107,000 debt left upon his death. When in need of short-term cash, he turns to selling off his "slave property"—and some 110 such transactions are recorded in contemporary documents.

With his operations at Monticello moving along, Jefferson steps into the political arena in 1769, representing Albamarle County from then until 1775, when he joins the Virginia House of Burgesses. In 1770 he is appointed colonel in command of his local militia.

Jefferson joins the rebellion against the crown in 1774 after the British impose the Coercive Acts on the colonies in response to the Boston Tea Party. In 1776 he is chosen as a delegate to the Second Continental Congress, where he becomes a friend of John Adams of Massachusetts. Adams uses his influence to get Jefferson to join him on the Committee of Five that writes the Declaration of Independence. His role here in expressing America's values and vision secures his place as a future political leader.

Jefferson is not involved in actual fighting during the Revolutionary War but does continue to oversee activities of the militia, first at the local level and then the state level after he is elected governor of Virginia in 1779.

On September 6, 1782, tragedy strikes with the death of his 33-year-old wife, Martha, soon after delivering the couple's sixth child. Jefferson is shattered by the loss, suffering from depression and "many a violent burst of grief." Months will pass before he records his "emerg(ence) from that stupor of mind which had rendered me as dead to the world as was she whose loss occasioned it."

Jefferson returns to public service as a Virginia delegate to the Confederation Congress in 1783–1784 before heading off on a four-year assignment as minister to France. This experience will mark him forever as an unwavering Francophile.

A fourteen-year-old enslaved girl owned by Jefferson named Sally Hemings will join him in Paris in 1787. Sally is one of Betty Hemings' and John Wayles' ten mixed-race children. John Wayles was also the father of Jefferson's dead wife, Martha. Thus, Martha Jefferson and Sally Hemings are half-sisters by blood.

From this time in Paris until the end of his life, Sally will be Jefferson's mistress, bearing six children and overseeing his domestic life at Monticello. She will be one of only five enslaved people he frees in his will.

This interracial affair will be revealed in 1802 by James Thomson Callender, the same tabloid publisher who Jefferson had supported in his attacks on Adams during the 1800 presidential campaign. The Irish poet Thomas Moore follows with a witty thrust at the hypocrisy inherent in the liaison.

> *The weary statesman for repose hath fled*
> *From halls of council to his negro's shed,*
> *Where blest he woos some black Aspasia's grace,*
> *And dreams of freedom in his slave's embrace!*

Like John Adams, Jefferson is still in Europe throughout the 1787 Constitutional Convention, where his powerful voice is missed on many occasions by his Anti-Federalist cohorts. But he generally approves the outcome, with two exceptions—a wish to add a Bill of Rights and to limit the president to one term in office.

Upon returning home, Jefferson prepares to become president. He serves from 1790–1793 as Washington's secretary of state, then spends the next seven years organizing the Democratic-Republican Party and, by a quirk of Electoral College fate, serves as John Adams' vice president.

On March 3, 1801, his time comes to lead the nation he helped to shape twenty-five years ago.

Despite his eight years in office, the epitaph he subsequently writes for his tombstone will ignore his presidency in favor of other "testimonials I have lived, (which) I wish most to be remembered:"

Here was buried Thomas Jefferson
Author of the Declaration of American Independence
of the Statute of Virginia for religious freedom
& Father of the University of Virginia

THE REMARKABLE LIFETIME ACCOMPLISHMENTS OF THOMAS JEFFERSON

AGE	
9	Studies Latin, French, and Greek
16	Enrolls at William & Mary College
23	Starts his law practice
25	Elected to Virginia House of Burgesses
31	Authors "Summary View of the Rights of British America"
32	Delegate to Second Continental Congress
33	Writes the Declaration of Independence, a revised Virginia legal code, and the Statute of Virginia for Religious Freedom
36	Governor of Virginia
40	Member of Confederation Congress
41	Minister to France
46	Secretary of State
51	Invents "wheel cipher" encryption machine for secret documents
52	Invents the "Jefferson agricultural plow"
53	US vice president and president of American Philosophical Society
55	Writes "Kentucky Resolutions" and organizes his national party
57	President of the United States—first term
61	Second term as president
64	Invents a "polygraph," a letter copying machine
68	Invents "revolving bookstand"

AGE	
76	Completes the "Jefferson Bible," capturing his views on Christianity
80	Helps shape the "Monroe Doctrine"
81	Founds the University of Virginia and serves as first president

TIME: 1801–1805

OVERVIEW OF JEFFERSON'S FIRST TERM

Thomas Jefferson is the first president inaugurated in the new capital city of Washington, DC—still a primitive setting as described by John Adams' wife, Abigail:

The President's House is in a beautiful situation...but the country around is...a wilderness at present. George Town is the very dirtiest hole I ever saw for a place of any trade, or respectability of inhabitants. It is only one mile from me but a quagmire after every rain.

Standing in front of the incomplete Senate wing of the capitol, Jefferson is sworn in by his cousin and frequent opponent, Chief Justice John Marshall. His inaugural address is brief, reflecting his penchant for concise insights delivered in the written word. After a bruising election, he opens with a conciliatory tone.

Every difference of opinion is not a difference of principle. We have called by different names brethren of the same principle. We are all Republicans, we are all Federalists.

He then proceeds to articulate, with great precision, his core beliefs about good government.

It is proper you should understand what I deem the essential principles of our Government, I will compress them within the narrowest compass they will bear.

Equal and exact justice to all men, of whatever state or persuasion, religious or political; peace, commerce, and honest friendship with all nations, entangling alliances with none; the support of the State governments in all their rights, as the most competent administrations for our domestic concerns and the surest bulwarks against anti-republican tendencies; the preservation of the General Government in its whole constitutional vigor, as the sheet anchor of our peace at home and safety abroad; a jealous care of the right of election by the people...; absolute acquiescence in the decisions of the majority, the vital principle of republics a well-disciplined militia, our best reliance in peace and for the first moments of war till regulars may relieve them; the supremacy of the civil over the military authority; economy in the public expense, that labor may be lightly burthened; the honest payment of our debts and sacred preservation of the public faith; encouragement of agriculture, and of commerce as

its handmaid; the diffusion of information and arraignment of all abuses at the bar
of the public reason; freedom of religion; freedom of the press, and freedom of person
under the protection of the habeas corpus, and trial by juries impartially selected.

These principles form the bright constellation which has gone before us and guided
our steps through an age of revolution and reformation. The wisdom of our sages and
blood of our heroes have been devoted to their attainment. They should be the creed
of our political faith, the text of civic instruction, the touchstone by which to try the
services of those we trust; and should we wander from them in moments of error or of
alarm, let us hasten to retrace our steps and to regain the road which alone leads to
peace, liberty, and safety.

Relying, then, on the patronage of your good will, I advance with obedience to the
work, ready to retire from it whenever you become sensible how much better choice it
is in your power to make. And may that Infinite Power which rules the destinies of
the universe lead our councils to what is best, and give them a favorable issue for your
peace and prosperity.

Jefferson assembles a strong cabinet, led by his close confidant, James Madison, as
Secretary of State.

The Treasury will be run for the next thirteen years by Albert Gallatin, whose
wide-ranging accomplishments mirror Jefferson in many ways. Gallatin is born and
schooled in Switzerland, an intellectual who is drawn to the Enlightenment philosophers, before coming to Boston in 1780. He teaches French at Harvard, buys land in
Pennsylvania, tries his hand at farming and glassworks manufacturing, enters politics
and serves in the Senate and House from 1793 to 1801. Along the way he becomes recognized for his mastery of public finance and budgeting, which leads to his selection by
the president. Gallatin is a Democratic-Republican who focuses intently on eliminating
the national debt. But he also supports Hamilton's Bank of the United States and selects
internal improvement projects aimed at strengthening economic growth.

With the possibility of international conflict still looming, Jefferson picks General
Henry Dearborn as secretary of war. Dearborn is a physician and a veteran of Revolutionary War battles fought from Quebec to Yorktown.

THOMAS JEFFERSON'S CABINET IN 1801

POSITION	NAME	HOME STATE
Vice President	Aaron Burr	New York
Secretary of State	James Madison	Virginia
Secretary of Treasury	Albert Gallatin	Pennsylvania
Secretary of War	Henry Dearborn	Massachusetts

POSITION	NAME	HOME STATE
Secretary of the Navy	Robert Smith	Maryland
Attorney General	Levi Lincoln	Massachusetts

The president enters office intending to shift the philosophy and focus of the national government.

The Federalist Adams has concentrated on unifying the original Atlantic coast states behind a strong central authority. Jefferson's sights are set on expanding west to the Mississippi River and contracting federal power in favor of restored sovereignty for state and local legislatures.

His early domestic moves are modest. He allows the Sedition Act to sunset on his first day in office, and pardons all eleven men who have been convicted since its inception. He does away with the unpopular Whiskey Tax and attempts to cover the loss of revenue by downsizing the navy program begun by Adams. He pushes through another judiciary bill, undoing Adams' attempt to limit his impact on the Supreme Court.

During the term he also sets the wheels in motion to support statehood for Ohio and other territories in the Northwest, and convinces Georgia to cede its claims in the Southwest over to the public domain. He also sponsors a series of expeditions to explore the "unknown land" beyond the Mississippi River.

But as with all presidents, his actions are dictated by unpredictable events—in Jefferson's case, like Adams, these are threats of warfare.

This begins on an insignificant scale in May 1801, when Jefferson refuses to pay the Kingdom of Tripoli a bribe of $225,000 to forestall its asserted "right and duty as faithful Muslims to plunder and enslave non-believers." The kingdom responds by declaring war on the US, followed by four years of repeated piracy and sea battles in the Mediterranean Sea. It ends in 1805, when the president sends naval vessels along with a small contingent of marines backed by local mercenaries to the region. They cross the desert from Egypt and win a decisive victory at the port city of Derna, forcing the kingdom to sign a peace treaty. Henceforth, victory on the "shores of Tripoli" will become part of the marines' heritage.

The so-called Barbary War in north Africa is only a minor event relative to threats from both France and Britain that will occupy Jefferson across his entire time in office.

Along with the rest of the world, the new commander-in-chief has his eyes fixed on the predatory figure of Napoleon Bonaparte. Only two years will pass between Adams' treaty ending the "Quasi-War" with France and Napoleon's incursion into the Caribbean to suppress a slave rebellion and take back control over the sugar plantations on Saint Domingue (Haiti). When Jefferson also learns that Spain has ceded its Louisiana lands along the Mississippi to France, he fears that Napoleon will turn on America next.

Instead of waiting, he acts and is rewarded with the pivotal achievement of his administration, the Louisiana Purchase of 1803. In one fell swoop, it doubles the nation's land mass and promises to fulfill the economic vision of his inaugural speech—a nation of independent yeoman farmers with…

Room enough for our descendants to the thousandth generation.

Assuming, of course, that renewed belligerence from Britain—growing during his first term—can be kept under control.

JEFFERSON'S FIRST TERM: KEY EVENTS

1801	
March 4	Jefferson and Burr are sworn in
May 14	The Pasha of Tripoli declares war on the United States
December 7	The 7th Congress convenes after big gains by Democratic-Republicans
1802	
January 8	$2.6 million in war reparations paid by US to British Loyalists and merchants (Jay's Treaty)
January	Napoleon sends 20,000 troops put down the slave rebellion in Saint Dominigue
February	Treasury Secretary Gallatin secures support for road building projects in Ohio
March 8	Congress repeals the 1798 Judiciary Act
March 27	A treaty momentarily pauses the warfare raging in Europe
April 6	Congress repeals all excise taxes, including on whiskey
April 14	Congress repeals the 1798 Naturalization Act; restore a five-year wait period, not fourteen years
April 29	A new Judiciary Act restores the number of justices to six, not five
April 30	An Enabling Act defines how NW territories may organize for statehood
April	Jefferson learns that France now owns Louisiana and starts acquisition plans
June	Toussaint Louverture, who led the Black takeover of Saint Dominque, is captured
July 4	The US Military Academy at West Point opens
October 16	Napoleon has Spain close the port of New Orleans to US commerce
November 29	An Ohio territorial convention passes a state constitution and applies for admission
December 6	Jefferson addresses Congress stressing the need for economy in government spending
1803	
February 24	In *Marbury v. Madison* the Supreme Court asserts its authority over what is lawful
March 1	Ohio is admitted to the Union (#17)
April 19	Spain reopens the port of New Orleans to US commerce
May 2	Ambassador James Monroe signs Louisiana Purchase Treaty with the French for $15 million
June 7	Tribes in Indiana cede more land to Governor William Henry Harrison
August 31	Lewis and Clark set out on their three-year expedition down the Ohio and to the West
October 20	The Senate ratifies the Louisiana Purchase Treaty

October 29	The House appropriates the funding needed to buy the Louisiana land from France
November	France's war versus Britain, Prussia, Austria, Russia, and Sweden begins anew
November 18	France loses a key battle against Black forces on Saint Domingue
December 9	Congress approves the Twelfth Amendment to separate balloting for president and vice president
December 20	The US officially takes possession of the Louisiana Territory from France
1804	
February 15	New Jersey passes law to grant gradual emancipation to enslaved people
February 16	Hamilton calls vice president Burr "a dangerous man" not to be trusted in government
March 26	The Land Grant of 1804 lowers the price to $1.64 per acre and sets 160 acre minimum
April 25	Vice President Burr loses race for NY governor in large part due to Hamilton's opposition
May 18	Napoleon crowns himself emperor of France in Paris
July 11	Burr kills Hamilton in a duel at Weehawken, NJ
August 27	The Treaty of Vincennes cedes more Indian land in the west to the US
September 25	The Twelfth Amendment is approved to separate ballots cast for president and vice president
October 1	The port city of New Orleans is officially in US hands
October 27	Lewis and Clark make their winter camp near present day Bismarck, North Dakota
December 5	Jefferson is reelected with George Clinton as vice president
December	Napoleon withdraws his troops from Saint Domingue and focuses on invading Britain
1805	
January 11	A Michigan Territory is formed out of the western part of the old Indiana Territory
January	Both Britain and France pass laws barring neutral ships to enter enemy harbors

22

JOHN MARSHALL'S SUPREME COURT ASSERTS ITS AUTHORITY IN MARBURY V. MADISON

TIME: FEBRUARY 20 TO MARCH 3, 1801

JEFFERSON UNPACKS ADAMS' COURT

Once in power, Jefferson and the Democratic-Republicans begin to unwind the "Midnight Judges Act" of 1801 and do away with the Federalist appointments made by John Adams.

Their task is complicated by the fact that sitting judges may be removed only by impeachment involving violations of their public trust. To get around this constraint, Jefferson opts to restructure the judiciary once again. He does so in the Judiciary Act (or Repeal Act) of 1802:

The number of Supreme Court justices returns to its original quota of six.

- The jobs of the sixteen new Federal Circuit Court judges added by Adams are eliminated, hence avoiding the impeachment rules.
- Each Supreme Court justice is responsible for riding one of the six national "circuits."

The notion of a handful of Supreme Court justices appointed for life and sitting in the capital imposing federal guidelines over state laws and court decisions is anathema to the Democratic-Republicans. As Jefferson says:

To consider the judges as the ultimate arbiters of all constitutional questions [is] a very dangerous doctrine indeed, and one which would place us under the despotism of an oligarchy. Our judges are as honest as other men and not more so. They have with others the same passions for party, for power, and the privilege of their corps.

By revoking Adams' changes, Jefferson feels he has once again=prevented too much power from being in too few Federalist hands.

TIME: FEBRUARY 11–24, 1803

THE SUPREME COURT ASSERTS ITS CONSTITUTIONAL AUTHORITY

But the aftermath of the "Midnight Judges Act" is not yet fully settled by the 1802 repeal, and now it comes back to stifle Jefferson's efforts to limit Supreme Court power.

The roadblock is a suit filed by one William Marbury, a Maryland resident who is an accomplished businessman, a powerful political figure in the Federalist Party, and an active campaigner against Jefferson in the 1800 election.

He comes before the Supreme Court seeking to assume a prestigious position he has been promised, as justice of the peace in the District of Columbia. He backs his claim with a document signed by President John Adams and "sealed" (notarized) by Secretary of State John Marshall on Adams' last day in office.

John Marshall (1755–1835)

The problem is that Jefferson refuses to honor the commission, arguing that it was not actually delivered to Marbury before Adams' term expired.

Marbury petitions the Supreme Court to support his claim. The case is presented on February 11, 1803 and a decision is handed down quickly on February 24. John Marshall, who was personally involved as the notary before becoming chief justice, concludes three things:

- Marbury does indeed have the right to the commission, since Adams signed it and it is notarized.
- Marbury also has the right to legal protection by a court, even in a case involving the president of the United States—a not so subtle jab at Jefferson for acting like he is above the law.
- But no, the Supreme Court cannot grant Marbury's wish because the Constitution limits its authority to conduct "judicial reviews only to cases involving ambassadors, other public ministers and consuls…and where the state shall be a party."

After being advised to refile his suit within state court and then return to the Supreme Court if he is denied, Marbury drops the protest.

However, the decision itself establishes the crucial precedent Marshall is after—the Supreme Court's authority to overturn state and federal laws on the basis of a failure to comply with the 1787 Constitution.

This power has always been implicit in the formation of the Supreme Court and in the "checks and balances" spirit favored by the founders. But with Marbury, enforcement of the principle is made apparent to all.

In effect then, Jefferson wins the battle against Adams' appointments but loses the war against the concentration of power he now sees vested in the Supreme Court.

He sees no evidence in the Constitution that grants six judges with lifetime appointments the power to override laws written by legislators.

The question whether the judges are invested with exclusive authority to decide on the constitutionality of a law has been heretofore a subject of consideration with me in the exercise of official duties. Certainly there is not a word in the Constitution which has given that power to them more than to the Executive or Legislative branches.

And, while Marshall draws boundaries around the types of cases the Supreme Court will hear, the Democratic-Republicans fear that it will ultimately extend its reach.

In this regard they are reminded that none other than James Wilson, the leading legal scholar at the Constitutional Convention and former associate justice under Washington, called for a Supreme Court capable of striking down any and all federal or state legislation it deemed unjust.

Jefferson records his concern that the Constitution may become...

A mere thing of wax in the hands of the judiciary, which they may twist and shape into any form they please.

Southerners in particular wonder if the Marbury decision might eventually open the door for the court to "twist" the laws affecting the rights of slave owners.

From 1803 forward, the third branch of the federal government becomes a political force to be reckoned with, especially in the hands of Chief Justice John C. Marshall.

TIME: 1801–1809

JOHN MARSHALL AND HIS ONGOING CONFLICTS WITH THOMAS JEFFERSON

Marshall's reprimand of Jefferson in the Marbury decision is characteristic of the personal antipathy that develops between these two intellectual giants over time.

Ironically they are distant cousins, with Jefferson's mother being Jane Randolph, a relative of Marshall's mother, Mary Randolph. Their fathers are both surveyors and they are both Virginians and lawyers, similarly tutored by the legendary George Wythe. The similarities end there.

Jefferson is aristocratic in his dress and bearing; distant from the common man he swears to protect. He is committed to agricultural commerce and his home state; forever suspicious that a powerful central government will evolve into an oligarchy, destructive of personal liberty and prosperity.

Marshall is forever slovenly attired and comfortable around people. He is supportive of Hamilton's brand of capitalism and industrialization. His focus is on national rather than state affairs and he believes that a strong national government is necessary to unify, defend, and build the republic.

John Marshall's roots are considerably more humble than Jefferson's. He has to scrape for an early education and is drawn into the Revolutionary War at age twenty. Both Marshall and his father have distinguished military records. The son enters the war as a lieutenant in 1775 and exits as a captain in 1779 after fighting at Brandywine, Monmouth, and in Virginia during Benedict Arnold's invasion.

Some historians believe that Marshall's disdain for Jefferson traces in part to an episode during this Virginia campaign that finds Governor Jefferson evidently more focused on securing his Monticello estate rather than joining in combat against the British. The question "where is Jefferson?" is asked throughout the ranks at the time.

Marshall's war experiences also influence his political views. Camped at Valley Forge alongside his hero, George Washington, he watches the failure of the disorganized, undisciplined, and self-centered "confederated states" to supply the basic support systems needed to win the war. This marks him forever as a Federalist.

After leaving the army, Marshall enrolls in a three-month course at William & Mary taught by George Wythe which features "combin[ed] theory and practice, readings and lectures, supplemented with moot courts and mock legislative sessions." From there he apprentices under Wythe until his petition to join the Virginia bar is signed in 1780, ironically by Jefferson himself, who is 12 years his senior.

He opens a private practice specializing in suits related to disputes over debts and real estate titles. His style is that of the savvy litigator focused less on legal theory and more on practical arguments. When his efforts in court flourish, he is drawn into politics, serving in the Virginia House of Delegates off and on between 1782 and 1796. He is not yet well enough known in 1787 to attend the Constitutional Convention, but he supports its ratification in 1788, citing Federalist principles against stiff Democratic-Republican opposition.

After that, he is thrust onto the national stage by John Adams, who names him minister to France in 1797, and then chief justice of the Supreme Court on January 31, 1801.

In the final year of Adams' life, Adams—who previously picked George Washington to head the Continental Army—cites Marshall as his proudest act.

> *My gift of John Marshall to the people of the United States was the proudest act of my life. There is no act of my life on which I reflect with more pleasure.*

## 23

TOUSSAINT'S REBELLION IN HAITI ENDS WITH BLACK PEOPLE IN POWER

TIME: 1791–1801

TOUSSAINT LOUVERTURE OVERTHROWS FRENCH RULE

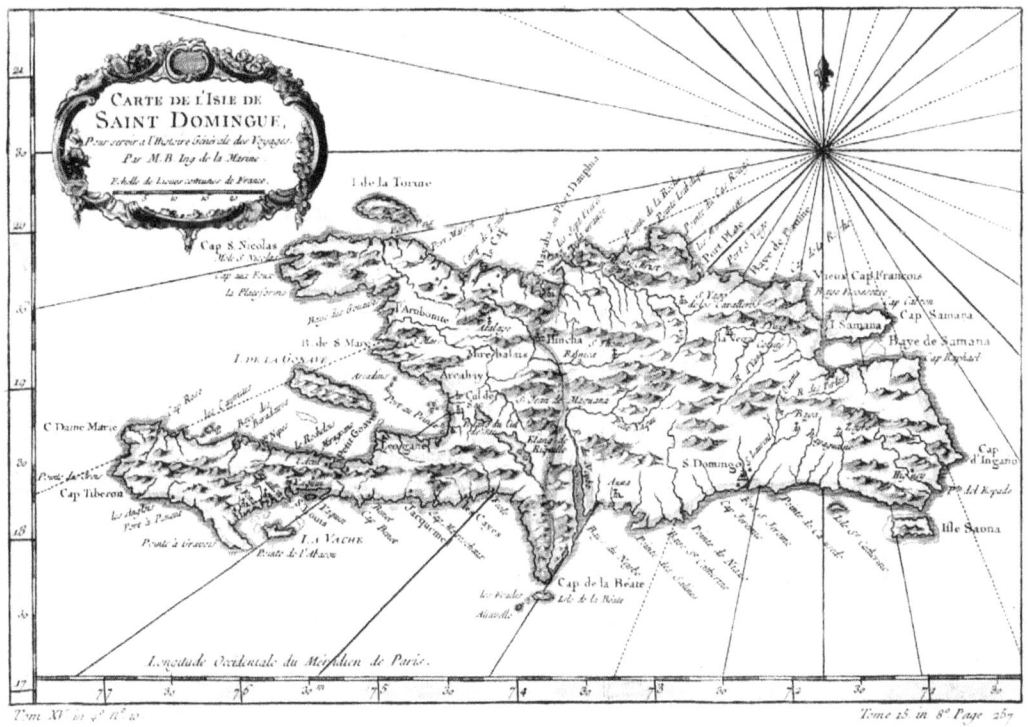

French colony of St. Domingue (in red)—site of Louverture Rebellion Hispaniola Island, with the western third Saint-Domingue (later Haiti)

Thomas Jefferson's dealings with Napoleon will be shaped in part by the results of a rebellion that takes place in the French colony of Saint-Domingue, or Haiti. Starting in August 1791 a remarkable revolution is carried out there by enslaved Black people under the leadership of one Toussaint Louverture.

The rise of Saint-Domingue as an important possession for France follows many years of disappointment with its explorations in the Americas.

The Jesuit priest Jacques Marquette and the fur trader Louis Jolliet have opened up out-posts along the Mississippi in the 1670s–1680s, but these fail to return the gold and silver once sought. By 1762 the French are so dismayed by their economic prospects in North America that they cede their entire Louisiana territory to Spain—an ally who has been forced to surrender both Cuba and the Philippines in the Seven Years' War against Britain.

But an entirely different story plays out south of America's borders for France, in the colony of Saint-Domingue.

The colony lies on the island of Hispaniola, first claimed for Spain by Columbus and divided in 1697, with the French owning the western third (Saint-Domingue) and the Spanish owning the eastern two thirds (later the Dominican Republic).

Saint-Domingue soon becomes the economic jewel in the crown of French holdings in the "New World."

It does so on the backs of some 800,000 enslaved Africans who are abducted by their French masters to raise sugar and coffee crops on vast plantations, later to be replicated in cotton fields across the American South. Various witnesses attest to the gruesome tortures inflicted on the enslaved people by the overseers:

> *Have they not hung up men with heads downward, drowned them in sacks, crucified them on planks, buried them alive, crushed them in mortars? Have they not forced them to consume faeces? And, having flayed them with the lash, have they not cast them alive to be devoured by worms, or onto anthills, or lashed them to stakes in the swamp to be devoured by mosquitoes? Have they not thrown them into boiling cauldrons of cane syrup? Have they not put men and women inside barrels studded with spikes and rolled them down mountainsides into the abyss? Have they not consigned these miserable blacks to man eating-dogs until the latter, sated by human flesh, left the mangled victims to be finished off with bayonet and poniard?*

By 1780 these enslaved people are producing 40% of the sugar and 60% of the coffee consumed across Europe. In turn Saint-Domingue becomes the focal point for all French commerce in the Americas, and wins its nickname as the "pearl of the Antilles."

But all of this comes to a sharp halt in August 1791 due to a rebellion that lasts over three months and eventually pits up to 100,000 Black people against the plantation masters. During this period, an estimated 4,000 white people are killed and hundreds of sugar, coffee, and indigo plantations are overthrown.

Reports on the savagery of the reprisals—marked by rapes, torture, and mutilations—are circulated widely and strike terror in the minds of plantation owners, including in America, for decades to come.

The rebellion is led by two Black men, Toussaint Louverture and his lieutenant (and later successor), Jean-Jacques Dessalines.

Relatively little is known for sure about Toussaint's background beyond the fact that he is born on Saint-Domingue around 1740, and is presumably an enslaved house servant on a plantation until 1776, when he becomes a free man. Along the way he picks up some education (perhaps from Jesuit missionaries) and learns to speak and write French. According to his own account, he also accumulates enough wealth to rent a small coffee plantation and becomes a Freemason.

Toussaint is apparently moved by the spirit of the French Revolution and offers his services behind a rebellion initiated by a Voodoo priest, which has broken out against the plantation owners in August 1791. He announces his intent late in that month:

Brothers and friends, I am Toussaint Louverture; perhaps my name has made itself known to you. I have undertaken vengeance. I want Liberty and Equality to reign in St Domingue. I am working to make that happen. Unite yourselves to us, brothers, and fight with us for the same cause.

Your obedient servant, Toussaint Louverture, General of the armies of the king, for the public good.

He quickly exhibits the skills of a natural-born military commander and civilian leader, and maneuvers through a host of challenges to emerge as head of a functioning government that controls Saint-Domingue for a decade.

On July 7, 1801, he promulgates a new Constitution for the colony. It does not declare outright independence from France, but bans slavery ("all men are born, live and die, free and French") and announces that he will retain the title of governor-general for life.

TIME: MAY 6, 1802

NAPOLEON CAPTURES TOUSSAINT BUT FAILS TO REGAIN CONTROL OVER SAINT-DOMINGUE

When Napoleon learns of Toussaint's bold Constitution, he decides the time has come to restore French control over Saint-Domingue—and, perhaps, to also venture back into America.

As always, Napoleon is exceedingly devious in his approach.

His first step toward America lies in the secret Treaty of San Ildefonso on October 1, 1800, whereby Spain returns Louisiana to France. This is followed by the November 30 Mortefontaine Treaty with Adams, ending the Quasi-War and hopefully lulling the Americans into dropping their guard.

In January 1802, he makes his move against Saint-Domingue.

He sends his brother-in-law, General Charles Leclerc, and a force of 20,000 troops to the island along with an assurance to Toussaint that his intentions are entirely peaceful. But hostilities quickly break out and Toussaint's forces fight back ferociously.

The battles continue until May 6, 1802, when Toussaint meets with Leclerc and works out an apparent ceasefire agreement. But Toussaint's subordinate, Dessalines, turns on him, and he is put under arrest by Leclerc. His response includes this warning to France:

> *In overthrowing me you have cut down in Saint-Domingue only the trunk of the tree of liberty; it will spring up again from the roots, for they are numerous and they are deep.*

Toussaint—known by now as "the Black Napoleon"—is put on a ship back to France and imprisoned there. He is subjected to harsh treatment and dies on April 7, 1803.

But the Black nation he has created on Saint-Domingue lives on after him.

Resistance to the French now falls on Dessalines' shoulders. Its intensity is flamed by the dual threats of white revenge and a return to slavery for the Black citizens. Dessalines is also aided by an outbreak of yellow fever that kills Leclerc and decimates the French ranks.

After a significant loss at the Battle of Vertières on November 18, 1803, the French decide to put their remaining 7,000 soldiers on ships heading home.

Napoleon has had enough for the moment in the Americas, and refocuses all of his energy and resources into a planned invasion of Britain.

Meanwhile Dessalines names himself emperor of Saint-Domingue and oversees a bloodbath that wipes out all white plantation owners who do not swear allegiance to his rule. However, his reign is fleeting, and rival Black factions assassinate him in 1806, breaking the country into the Kingdom of Haiti to the north and a republic to the south—both headed by Black people.

Given these unsettled conditions, along with fears expressed by American slave owners, Jefferson refuses to grant formal recognition to Saint-Domingue. The former French colony does manage to retain its independence over time, and makes Haiti the oldest republic run by Black people in the western hemisphere.

## 24

THE LOUISIANA PURCHASE DOUBLES AMERICA'S LANDMASS

TIME: MAY 2, 1803

NAPOLEON OFFERS TO SELL THE LOUISIANA TERRITORY TO THE US

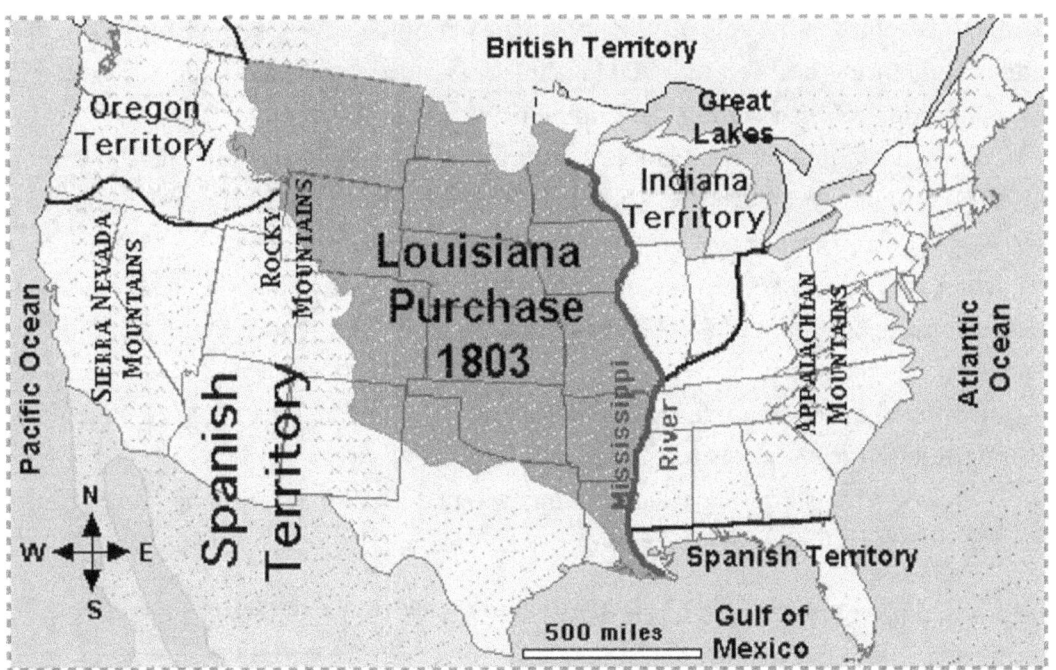

Territory gained by the Louisiana Purchase of 1803

With Leclerc's 1802 efforts against Saint-Domingue in motion, Napoleon looks toward America and begins to test its will. He begins by ordering his Spanish surrogate administrator to shut down the port of New Orleans to US shipping on October 16, 1802. He also assembles an army in Holland intended for a probe into America.

Jefferson and his advisors are fully alarmed at this point. Especially since the American minister to France, Robert Livingston, informs Jefferson of a rumor that Napoleon has reacquired Louisiana.

Jefferson can easily imagine how his aspirations to expand westward would be impacted by hostile French forces lining up along his new western border, the Mississippi River, and closing the port of New Orleans, the emerging hub of all commerce on the frontier. His reaction is telling:

> *There is on the globe one single spot, the possessor of which is our natural and habitual enemy. It is New Orleans.*

Unlike Toussaint, he acts swiftly to deter Napoleon. He vigorously protests the shipping restraints and then, in March 1803, sends his trusted friend James Monroe to France with approval to spend up to $9 million to try to buy the crucial port of New Orleans, along with West Florida.

But by the time Monroe arrives, the situation has changed for Napoleon. The Saint-Domingue intervention, which started so well, has begun to fall apart.

This setback, along with the complexities of planning for the invasion of Britain, dampens Napoleon's interest in any immediate action against America. Instead he decides that France is best served by taking America's money and encouraging it to join in the fight against British with its developing naval power.

So, when Monroe arrives, Napoleon's surrogates Talleyrand and Marbois signal their willingness to discuss a purchase—not only of New Orleans, but of the entire Louisiana Territory.

Jefferson, ever the western expansionist, jumps at the opportunity. On May 2, 1803, Livingston agrees to buy 827,000 square miles of land from France for $15 million, or roughly 3 cents per acre.

The president sees the Louisiana Purchase as "land for the next twenty generations" of American farmers, the key to the agrarian ideal in his vision.

Napoleon shrugs off the deal as a momentary setback. He will use the money to defeat the British and then revisit America at a later date, if he decides to take it.

JEFFERSON'S LOUISIANA PURCHASE: KEY EVENTS

1697	Spain cedes Saint-Domingue to France
1756	The Seven Years' War pits Britain versus France and Spain
1762	France "unloads" Louisiana on Spain
1763	Treaty of Paris ends the Seven Years' War, with Britain victorious
1781	America wins its war with Britain
1794	Jay's Treaty with Britain: abandon forts for fur-trading rights
1780	Saint-Domingue plantations dominate sugar and coffee production
1791	Revolution leaves Toussaint Louverture in control of St. Domingue
1799	Napoleon assumes power in France as first counsel

1800	Spain gives Louisiana back to France in secret Treaty of San Ildefonso
1801	America learns that France owns Louisiana again
	Ambassador Robert Livingston begins negotiations with Talleyrand
1802	In January Leclerc lands in San Domingue with 20,000 troops
	Toussaint is captured and sent back to a French prison to die
	Yellow fever decimates the French troops and kills Leclerc
1803	Monroe arrives with $9 million to try to buy New Orleans
	Napoleon begins to plan invasion of Britain
	The US acquires the entire Louisiana territory for $15 million
	Jefferson sends Lewis and Clark off to explore the new land
1804	Dessalines drives the French out and names himself emperor
1805	Horatio Lord Nelson defeats a French invasion fleet at Trafalgar

TIME: OCTOBER 29, 1803

AFTER FIERY DEBATE CONGRESS APPROVES THE PURCHASE

Ironically, in agreeing to buy Louisiana, Jefferson oversteps the limitations on executive power he has tried so hard to impose in his Tenth Amendment and in the "Kentucky Resolutions" of 1798 where he calls for nullification of Adams' Sedition Acts.

The result is a firestorm of opposition in Congress.

While the Senate is upset by Jefferson's unilateral activities, it does ratify the Louisiana Treaty on October 20, 1803, some five months after the deal was agreed to in Paris.

The House is a different matter. It controls the nation's purse strings, and is determined to demonstrate its prerogatives in this regard. It hurls a series of challenges Jefferson's way.

Some question whether France even owns Louisiana or if it still belongs to Spain.

Others ask about the boundaries of the territory and the number of new states it might generate—only to find that precise answers are lacking.

Easterners are immediately concerned that opening this much new land will eventually erode their power in the Congress and go so far as to suggest that such a deal actually violates the Constitution of 1787.

The debate also touches on the issue of slavery. The 1787 Northwest Ordinance and the 1790 Southwest Ordinance have assigned the Ohio River as the demarcation line for slavery, out to the Mississippi River. But what about the new land to the west of the Mississippi River—will it allow slavery or not?

Jefferson is surprised by the opposition to an acquisition that seems so obviously right to him. In response he ponders the need for a constitutional amendment to justify the deal, but soon dismisses the idea.

Finally a House resolution to reject the Louisiana Purchase fails to pass by a slim majority of 59–57.

On October 29, 1803, the House passes an appropriations resolution giving Jefferson the go-ahead he wants.

Upon completion of the purchase, America now owns 56% of its eventual east to west coast landmass. The remainder is in the hands of Spain.

AMERICA'S ACQUISITION OF LAND

YEAR	LAND GAINED	FROM	VIA	SQUARE MILES	% US
1784	Thirteen colonies to Mississippi River	Britain	War	888,811	29%
1803	Louisiana Territory	France	Purchase	827,192	27%

## 25

THE LEWIS AND CLARK EXPEDITION MAPS A ROUTE TO THE WEST COAST

TIME: JANUARY 18, 1803 TO MAY 14, 1804

JEFFERSON'S SEARCH FOR A NORTHWEST PASSAGE GETS UNDERWAY

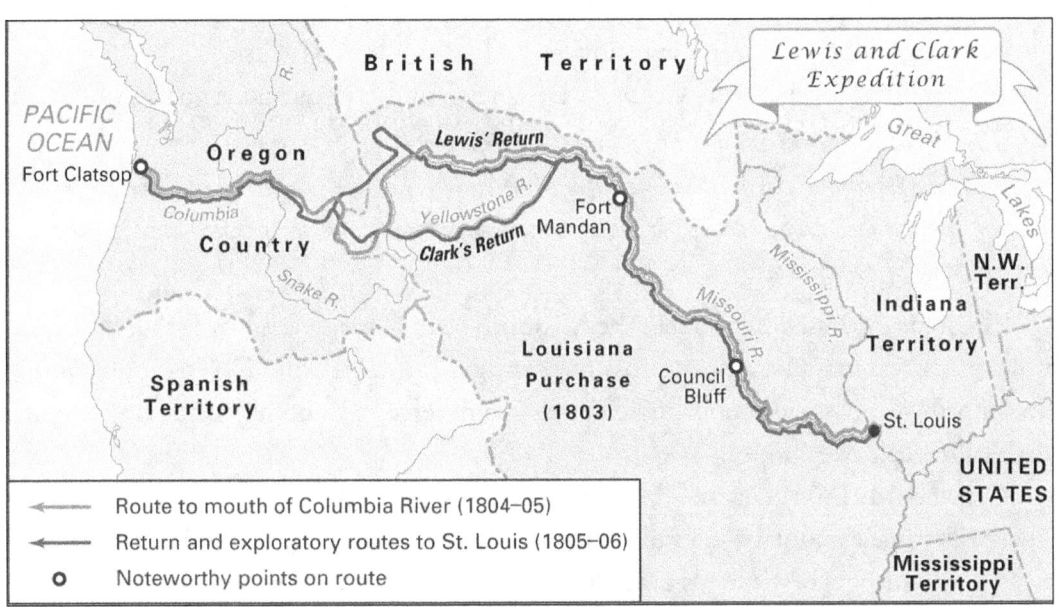

The route followed by Lewis and Clark to reach the west coast

From the moment he enters office, the visionary Jefferson is already imagining an America that stretches from ocean to ocean—with this vast territory bound together by the unifying ideals of freedom, equality, and self-governance.

To begin to realize this vision, he must first focus on exploring the west. Some ten months before the Louisiana Purchase, on January 18, 1803, he gains congressional approval to spend $2,500 on a one-year expedition to complete the task. The actual effort will take 26 months and cost $38,722.

While he himself is a consummate easterner, his interest in mapping the west traces back at least to 1796, when he encourages colleagues at the American Philosophical Society to send expeditions across the Mississippi.

With the opportunity now his, he turns to Meriwether Lewis to lead the effort. Lewis is only 27 years old at the time, but Jefferson has known and respected his parents in the Meriwether and Lewis families for years. He is born only ten miles from Monticello and proves to be a natural backwoodsman. He moves to Georgia for a while, mingling with the Cherokee, then back to Virginia where he graduates from Liberty Hall College before serving as a captain in the state militia.

On April 1, 1801, Jefferson hires him as his personal secretary, at a salary of $500 a year. Lewis lives in the White House, works in the East Room, and dines regularly with the president and his top advisors over the next two years. When Jefferson asks him to head back into the wilderness, he jumps at the opportunity.

Lewis assembles a band of 33 explorers in total, including William Clark, who he knows from his militia days and makes his unofficial co-commander on the trip. Together they assemble their supplies for the journey, including a 55-foot keelboat, two 40-foot-long canoes, food, trading trinkets, and 120 gallons of whiskey.

Jefferson names them the Corps of Discovery, and lays out their goals as follows:

The object of your mission is to explore the Missouri River & such principal stream of it, as, by its course & communication with the waters of the Pacific Ocean, may offer the most direct and practicable water communication across this continent, for the purposes of commerce.

The hope expressed here is that the Missouri River, flowing westward from St. Louis, will actually extend all the way across the continent to the Pacific Ocean—one continuous northwest passage supporting east-west commerce as smoothly as the north-south traffic along the Mississippi.

On May 14, 1804, Lewis and Clark set out west from St. Louis, along the Missouri. They will average about 10–15 miles a day, using sails, oars, and, at times, ropes to head against the current. Lewis tends to explore the shoreline, while Clark guides the boat and handles the critical map-making duties.

TIME: MAY 14, 1804 TO AUGUST 17, 1805

THE EXPEDITION REACHES THE HEADWATERS
OF THE MISSOURI RIVER

In late August, 1804, in South Dakota, they encounter their first tribe of plains Indians, the Sioux. They also begin to spot animals not seen before in the east—antelope, mule deer, buffalo, and coyotes.

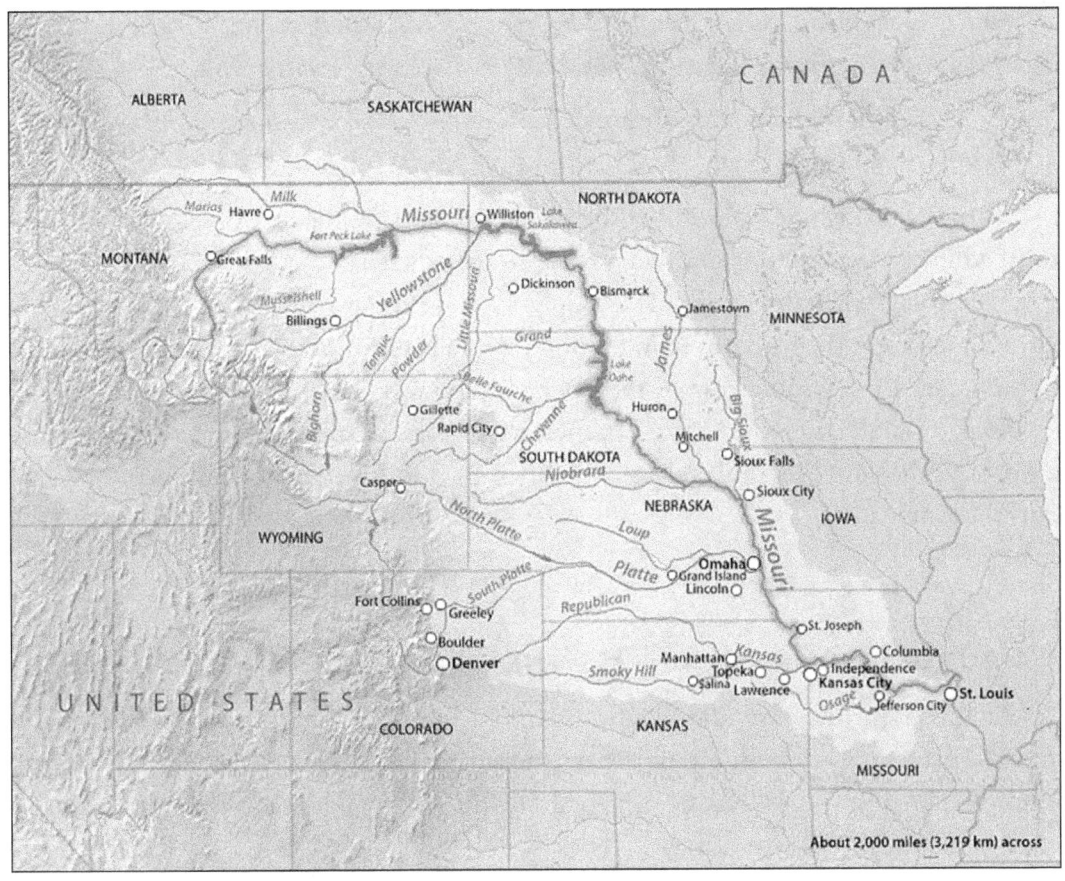

The mighty Missouri River stretching 2,341 miles from St. Louis to Three Forks

By November 1804 they have reached North Dakota, where they bold their winter camp among the Mandan tribe, and hire a guide—Toussaint Charbonneau, a French-Canadian fur trader who is accompanied by his Shoshone wife, Sacagawea. The pair will prove invaluable as the journey unfolds, acting as interpreters and emissaries with future Indian contacts.

Before breaking camp in April 1805, Lewis ships a packet of finds—including elk horns, Indian corn, a magpie, and a prairie dog—back east. Jefferson receives them in the late summer and plants the corn at Monticello. By then he assumes that the Corps has probably reached their destination on the west coast.

In fact, they are only halfway along as they resume their voyage further north on the Missouri and then west into Montana. On June 13, they encounter an amazing sight, a series of volatile rapids leading to five "great falls" over a 21 mile stretch. Lewis records the moment in his diary.

Hearing a tremendious roaring above me I continued my rout across the point of a hill a few hundred yards further and was again presented by one of the most beatifull

objects in nature, a cascade of about fifty feet perpendicular stretching at right angles across the river from side to side to the distance of at least a quarter mile.

I now thought that if a skillfull painter had been asked to make a beautifull cascade that he would most probably have presented the precise image of this one.

As breathtaking and beautiful as these falls are, they are the first signal that the Missouri will not offer a simple unbroken route to the west coast.

The party celebrates the Fourth of July by consuming what's left of their whiskey ration, then totes their gear overland around the falls until July 15, when they are back in the water drifting south toward the Rocky Mountains.

Only a month later, on August 17, their hopes for a northwest passage to the Pacific are over, as they discover the "end point" of the Missouri River at the headwaters at Three Forks, Montana.

TIME: AUGUST 1804 TO OCTOBER 1805

A RUGGED JOURNEY ACROSS THE ROCKIES LEADS TO SUCCESS

At this point they are fifteen months into a journey that was supposed to take a year. Undaunted, they push on to perhaps their most formidable challenge, crossing the Rocky Mountains—the Great Continental Divide, where America's waterways (and river currents) begin to flow advantageously west toward the Pacific. Lewis and Clark will be the first white Americans to cross this divide.

Fortunately the expedition now comes upon the Shoshones, who happen to be Sacagawea's tribe. They know the best routes through the mountains and guide the way—first across the Lehmi Pass, some 7,400 feet above sea level, and then along the Lolo Trail and the rugged Bitterroot Range. Lewis regards this 200 mile slog as the most challenging of the entire trip, with all members suffering from frostbite and a lack of food.

The Great Continental Divide of North America

I have been wet and as cold in every part as I ever was in my life, indeed I was at one time fearful my feet would freeze in the thin Mocki(N) sons which I wore.

After five weeks in the mountains, new canoes have been built and on October 7, 1805 they are moving downstream on the Clearwater River. This flows into the Snake River and then the Columbia River; a known landmark they had previously hoped was linked directly to the Missouri.

On October 18, 1805, they are elated to spot Mount Hood in the dis-

The Columbia River running inland from the Pacific

tance, another identified marker on their original map. Roughly a month later they have reached the Pacific Ocean at Astoria, where they set up winter quarters known as Fort Clatsop. Using his "dead reckoning" skills, Clark estimates they have come 4,162 miles, a figure that proves to be only 40 miles off the true mark. The elapsed time is 18 months, one way.

TIME: MARCH 23, 1806 TO SEPTEMBER 23, 1806

THE EXPEDITION RETURNS HOME

On March 23, 1806, the expedition begins to retrace its path back home. They are now confident enough in their knowledge to break into four separate parties to further map the Louisiana lands. They record various "incidents" along the way. Clark carves his name into a sandstone outcropping near Billings, Montana, which endures. Lewis survives the only hostile encounter with Indians, leaving two Blackfeet dead after they try to steal his horses and rifles. Sacagawea and Charbonneau return to their Mandan village in August. They visit the grave of Charles Floyd, the one casualty of the trip, who died of a burst appendix on the way out.

On September 23, 1806, they are greeted as national heroes back in St. Louis. Both commanders receive land grants of 1,600 acres for their efforts. Jefferson names Lewis the governor of Louisiana, and Clark a brigadier general in the Louisiana militia and Indian agent to the West.

From there the fates of the two explorers will diverge sharply. Meriwether Lewis proves ill-equipped for a life in politics. His land speculation activities go bust, his debts mount along with his alcohol intake, and he either commits suicide or is murdered by gunshot wounds in 1809, at age 35. Clark lives almost 30 years beyond Lewis and becomes a successful businessman, serving seven years as governor of Missouri. He dies in 1838 at the home of his oldest son, Meriwether Lewis Clark.

But the exploits and the learning of these two explorers will fulfill Jefferson's highest hope for the Corps of Discovery expedition.

From 1809 onward, Americans will be intrigued by the land across the Mississippi and Jefferson's vision of one unified nation, from sea to shining sea.

26

VIOLENCE REMAINS THE NORM FOR RESOLVING PUBLIC CONFLICTS

TIME: 1621 AND ONWARD

AMERICA ADOPTS EUROPEAN-STYLE DUELING

While America seeks to become a nation of laws, it continues to embrace violence as a means of resolving disputes throughout the nineteenth century.

Thus a perceived wrongdoing leads to "calling a man out" and engaging in some direct form of battle, from simple fisticuffs to use of deadly weapons.

In less sophisticated circles this is referred to as "frontier justice," while among the more refined it is elevated to the art of dueling.

Dueling is inherited from traditions of the European aristocracy and practiced throughout the colonial period.

The first recorded duel in America takes place in 1621 in the Massachusetts colony between Edward Doty and Edward Lester. It is fought with longswords and ends with minor wounds to both parties. But dueling will also lurk in the biographies of many of the nation's most famous political figures, and will threaten to invade the halls of Congress in several notorious instances.

Taken to the extreme, dueling glorifies the notion of "better to die with honor than live in shame."

The rituals surrounding the combat are carefully codified in a manual published in Ireland in 1777 called the *Code Duello*. This details some 25 rules required to execute a fair duel, including:

- The proper issuance of a challenge from the offended party
- Selection of "seconds" to accompany the combatants and see to their needs
- The choice of weapons, left open to the recipient of the challenge
- Declaration of a time and place for the event
- Exact rules of engagement (e.g. shots fired, blows struck, other "allowances")
- How final "satisfaction" will be expressed and delivered
- Proper care for those who are wounded or killed

- Notification of kin in case of death
- Procedures for calling the duel off short of actual conflict

The vast majority of challenges are resolved "off the field"—using one's "seconds" to talk through the underlying grievances and arrive at "gentlemanly resolutions."

Intemperate men, such as future president Andrew Jackson, will never walk away from a challenge, and will both give and receive grievous wounds in the course of several duels. The more controlled future president Abraham Lincoln will find a peaceful way out when he is challenged.

Only 20% of duels end with shots fired, and the majority of these yield treatable wounds to the legs. "Deloping," or firing one's shot into the ground, is considered a gentlemanly way to conclude a confrontation.

But at times, duels can have lethal outcomes. Such is the case in 1804, the third year of Jefferson's presidency.

JULY 11, 1804

AARON BURR KILLS ALEXANDER HAMILTON

Alexander Hamilton (1757–1804)   Aaron Burr (1756–1836)

On July 11, 1804, Americans learn that Alexander Hamilton, the head of the Federalist Party and former Treasury secretary, has been shot dead in a duel with the current vice president, Aaron Burr.

The bad blood between the two is long-standing.

Both men serve nobly under Washington in the Revolutionary War, but the general always seems to favor Hamilton, a source of some early animosity. Burr fails to get the field promotion he feels he deserves for saving the army on Manhattan. He also fails to get Washington's support for a ministerial post to France. It becomes clear that the general regards him as overly ambitious and prone to intrigues. Burr senses Hamilton's hand at work in these reversals.

The two are also on opposite sides in the political arena—Hamilton a staunch Federalist and Burr a loyal Democratic-Republican. As such, they are forever sniping at each other, especially around New York state elections.

The stakes go way up in 1791, when Burr runs for Senate against Hamilton's father-in-law, General Phillip Schuyler. Burr's tactics and victory seem to represent a final breach with Hamilton.

In 1795, Burr and fellow Democratic-Republican James Monroe apparently conspire to pull Hamilton down from his lofty perch as Washington's secretary of the Treasury by leaking the story of his affair with Maria Reynolds. This forces Hamilton to make an embarrassing public confession and resign from office.

Henceforth Hamilton will search for any and all opportunities to destroy Burr.

His first chance materializes in the election of 1800, when Burr and Jefferson end up tied on electoral votes for the presidency—and the final decision ends up in the Federalist controlled House of Representatives. Hamilton, of course, is unhappy with both options. But, on a 36th ballot, he uses his influence to elect Jefferson, who he claims is "less dangerous than Burr…who loves nothing but himself."

Jefferson's convictions about Burr also sour during his first term, and he plans to seek a new vice president as the 1804 election approaches. Knowing this, Burr decides to run for governor of New York against another Democratic-Republican, former attorney general Morgan Lewis. With no entry of their own in the running, some Federalists come out for Burr, until Hamilton steps in and quashes this movement.

Tensions between the two mount on April 24, when *The Albany Register* publishes a letter where a third party quotes Hamilton as calling Burr "a dangerous man…who ought not be trusted with the reins of government" and referencing "a still more despicable opinion which Mr. Hamilton has expressed of Mr. Burr."

Burr then loses the race for governor by a decisive 58%–42% margin, effectively ending his hopes for high political office. Again he places much of the blame on Hamilton.

After the election, a series of increasingly tense exchanges occur between the two men in written notes. This animosity leads to a challenge from Burr, which Hamilton accepts.

Both men have been "called out" before on numerous occasions, all so far resolved without any shots being fired. But this time, the long-term hostility runs deep, and the duel unfolds.

It is set for July 11, 1804, at the heights of Weehawken, New Jersey—a popular site for dueling, despite the fact that it is officially outlawed both there and in New York. The ground holds special meaning for Hamilton. On November 23, 1801, his 19 year old son, Philip, is shot dead here in a duel he has initiated in defense of his father's name.

Be it premonition or not, the elder Hamilton writes out a will on July 10, the day before the duel. He states that he intends to "withhold his first fire," and then addresses his wife:

Adieu best of wives and best of Women. Embrace all my darling Children for me. Ever yours, AH.

Around 7 a.m., Burr and Hamilton arrive by separate boats, rowed from mid-town Manhattan some three miles across the Hudson. Both men greet each other formally, Colonel Burr and General Hamilton, according to the code.

An area extending some ten paces is cleared, with Hamilton standing at one end, facing the Hudson, and Burr at the other, looking inland. Each man holds a .56 caliber pistol, provided by Hamilton, the same pair his deceased son used. The pistols are loaded by seconds in plain sight. The two combatants assume the classical positions—right foot forward, with bodies tucked sideways to present the smallest possible silhouette for targeting. Hamilton dons his glasses at the last second. The rules are then read aloud, as follows:

The parties being placed at their stations, the second who gives the word shall ask them whether they are ready; being answered in the affirmative, he shall say- present! After this the parties shall present and fire when they please. If one fires before the other, the opposite second shall say one, two, three, fire, and he shall then fire or lose his fire.

Hamilton's second is chosen by lot to say the word *present*, which he does. Exactly what happens next is the subject of some debate. All accounts agree that both men fired, but who shot first is open to question. Some argue that Hamilton fired into the air, throwing away his attempt. A subsequent search for the ball finds it in a tree limb, some seven feet above and four feet wide of Burr's position.

But Burr's ball catches Hamilton above the right hip, fracturing a rib, slicing through his liver, and ending up lodged in a lower vertebrae. Burr advances toward his fallen foe, but is quickly diverted by his seconds and leaves the scene.

Hamilton is in the arms of his second, Nathaniel Pendleton, when his medical man, Dr. Hosack, examines the wound and recognizes that it is mortal. Together the two men carry Hamilton, who remains conscious, to his boat, and row him back to Manhattan. He is put to bed and given heavy dose of laudanum for pain. He lives through the night and dies around 2 p.m. the next day.

The nation is shocked by Hamilton's death, and cries mount to put an end to dueling. Burr is indicted for murder and flees to South Carolina. But the case for retribution against duelists is not intense, and he returns to Washington, DC to serve the remainder of his term as vice president.

He will live in and out of the public spotlight for another 34 years after the events at

Weehawken, forced to flee to Europe for four years after being acquitted in a sensational 1807 trial for treason.

27

JEFFERSON'S SECOND TERM

TIME: 1804

THE PRESIDENTIAL ELECTION OF 1804

As the 1804 election approaches, Jefferson and the Democratic-Republicans discard Aaron Burr as their vice presidential candidate in favor of former general George Clinton, now sitting governor of New York.

With Washington and Hamilton dead and Adams out of the picture, the Federalists begin what will be an ongoing struggle to find a candidate capable of winning widespread popular support. In 1804 they choose Charles C. Pinckney, an aristocratic planter from Charleston, Revolutionary War general, influential pro-slavery delegate to the 1787 Constitutional Convention, minister to France under Washington, and running mate of Adams in 1800.

In advance of the election of 1804, the states have ratified the Twelfth Amendment to the Constitution in order to distinguish between party candidates running for president versus vice president. This is accomplished by a simple change: having the Electoral College shift from one combined vote for the offices to two separate votes, one for president and the other for vice president. Any ties will still be broken in Congress, with the House voting on president and the Senate on vice president. The possibility of having a president from one party and a vice president from the other remains.

CHANGE TO VOTING PROCEDURES BEGINNING IN THE 1804 PRESIDENTIAL ELECTION

| Prior voting process | One ballot, with top vote getter becoming president and the runner-up as vice president |
| After Twelfth Amendment | Two ballots, one for president and the other for vice president |

The election takes place between November 2 and December 5, 1804.

A total of 143,110 "popular votes" are cast, double the level recorded in 1800. Eligibility continues to be limited to white men who own various threshold levels of property—and only eleven of the seventeen states factor popular votes into their process for choosing presidential electors. (In the other six they are chosen exclusively by state legislators.)

Still, the 1804 election is the first where mainstream Americans begin to feel that their direct votes have a great deal to do with who will be president. This trend will grow over time, much to the chagrin of the 1787 convention delegates who felt that selection of the executive was much too important to be left up to "popular passions."

GROWTH IN POPULAR VOTING FOR PRESIDENTIAL ELECTORS

	1788	1792	1796	1800	1804
Popular Votes	43,782	28,579	66,841	67,282	143,110
# States w/ popular votes for electors	7 of 12	6 of 15	9 of 16	6 of 16	11 of 17

When the ballots are all in, Jefferson is reelected by an overwhelming majority. He beats Charles C. Pinckney by a 73% to 27% margin in the popular vote, and by 162–14 in the electoral college. He carries fifteen of the seventeen states (losing only in Connecticut and Delaware), including prior Federalist strongholds across the North.

RESULTS OF THE 1804 PRESIDENTIAL ELECTION

CANDIDATES	STATE	PARTY	POP. VOTE	TOTAL EV	SOUTH	BORDER	NORTH	WEST
Thomas Jefferson	VA	Democratic-Republican	104,110	162	59	17	83	3
Charles C. Pinckney	SC	Federalist	38,919	14	0	5	9	0
Total			143,110	176	59	22	92	3
Needed to win				89				

Note: South (VA, NC, SC, GA), Border (DE, MD, KY), North (NH, MA, NY, NJ, PA, RI, CT, VT), West (OH)

Note: Total # electors = 176; must get more than half of 176 voters = 89.

The same story holds true in the race for vice president, where Governor Clinton easily outdistances Rufus King, the New York Federalist and former ambassador to Britain under Washington.

1804 ELECTORAL COLLEGE VOTE FOR VP

CANDIDATE	PARTY	VOTES
George Clinton	Dem-Rep	162
Rufus King	Federalist	14
Total		176

Jefferson's victory reflects approval for his Louisiana Purchase and an uptick in the economy in 1803–1804 after a lessening of tensions with France.

TIME: 1804

DEMOCRATIC-REPUBLICANS WIN BY A LANDSLIDE IN 1804

The Democratic-Republicans also dominate the Federalists in the 1804 congressional races.

In the House, the total number of seats up for grabs has expanded from 106 to 142 based on the new population counts from the 1800 Census. The largest gains in apportionment are in the Northern states, a fact that is already troubling to politicians in the South.

APPORTIONMENT OF HOUSE SEATS AFTER THE 1800 CENSUS

	TOTAL	SOUTH	BORDER	NORTH	WEST
1790	65	23	7	35	0
1800	106	38	11	57	0
1802	142	49	16	76	1
Change from 1790	+77	+26	+9	+41	+1

The margin of victory for the Democratic-Republicans in the lower chamber is remarkable. Only six years earlier, in 1799, the Federalists held the House by fourteen seats (60–46). After the 1804 votes are in, they trail their opponents by 86 seats (28–114).

ELECTION TRENDS: HOUSE OF REPRESENTATIVES

PARTY	1789	1791	1793	1795	1797	1799	1801	1803	1805
Democratic-Republicans	28	30	55	61	49	46	68	102	114
Federalists	37	39	50	45	57	60	38	40	28
Congress #	1st	2nd	3rd	4th	5th	6th	7th	8th	9th
President	GW	GW	GW	GW	JA	JA	TJ	TJ	TJ

In addition to continuing their dominance across the South, the Democratic-Republicans have now won solid majorities in the North in both 1802 and 1804.

HOUSE TRENDS BY REGION

DEMOCRATIC-REPUBLICAN	TOTAL	SOUTH	BORDER	NORTH	WEST
1789	28	16	4	8	
1791	30	16	5	9	
1793	55	31	7	17	
1795	61	33	7	21	
1797	49	30	4	15	
1799	46	21	5	20	
1801	68	30	7	31	
1803	102	42	13	46	1
1805	114	48	13	52	1
Change from 1803	+12	+6	N/A	+6	N/A

FEDERALISTS					
1789	37	7	3	27	
1791	39	7	4	28	
1793	50	6	4	40	
1795	45	5	4	36	
1797	57	8	7	42	
1799	60	17	6	37	
1801	38	8	4	26	
1803	40	7	3	30	
1805	28	1	3	24	
Change from 1803	(12)	(6)	N/A	(6)	N/A

In the Senate, the Democratic-Republicans now enjoy a 27–7 margin over the Federalists, after picking up two more seats. Recent additions in the upper chamber include the Federalist John Quincy Adams of Massachusetts in 1802 and Henry Clay of Kentucky in 1804, who begins his career as a Democratic-Republican.

ELECTION TRENDS: SENATE

PARTY	1789	1791	1793	1795	1797	1799	1801	1803	1805
Democratic-Republicans	7	12	14	16	12	10	17	25	27
Federalists	19	17	16	14	20	22	15	9	7
Congress #	1st	2nd	3rd	4th	5th	6th	7th	8th	9th
President	GW	GW	GW	GW	JA	JA	TJ	TJ	TJ

Regional results in the Senate mirror those in the House, with a steady erosion for the Federalists in the North.

SENATE TRENDS BY REGION

DEMOCRATIC-REPUBLICAN	TOTAL	SOUTH	BORDER	NORTH	WEST
1789	7	4	1	2	
1791	12	5	2	5	
1793	14	7	2	5	
1795	16	7	4	5	
1797	12	8	1	3	
1799	10	8	1	1	
1801	17	10	3	4	
1803	25	10	4	9	2
1805	27	10	4	11	2
Change from 1803	2	N/A	N/A	2	N/A

FEDERALISTS	TOTAL	SOUTH	BORDER	NORTH	SOUTH
1789	19	4	3	12	
1791	17	3	4	10	
1793	16	1	4	11	
1795	14	1	2	11	
1797	20	2	5	13	
1799	22	2	5	15	
1801	15	0	3	12	
1803	9	0	2	7	
1805	7	0	2	5	
Change from 1803	(2)	N/A	N/A	N/A	

Overall, the Democratic-Republicans emerge from the 1804 election in firm control of the presidency and both chambers of Congress while the Federalists are left reeling.

TIME: MARCH 4, 1805

JEFFERSON'S SECOND INAUGURAL ADDRESS

On March 4, 1805, Jefferson delivers his second inaugural address in the Senate chamber. Unlike the soaring rhetoric achieved four years ago, his tone is defensive, aimed at justifying his policies and programs against what he regards as ongoing slanders by the press, especially surrounding his mistress, Sally Hemings.

He seeks peace with the major foreign powers…

In the transaction of your foreign affairs, we have endeavored to cultivate the friendship of all nations, and especially of those with which we have the most important relations.

Restraint on taxes and federal spending to help fund targeted infrastructure improvements…

The suppression of unnecessary offices, of useless establishments and expenses, enabled us to discontinue our internal taxes. The remaining revenue on the consumption of foreign articles, is paid cheerfully by those who can afford to add foreign luxuries to domestic comforts…it may be the pleasure and pride of an American to ask, what farmer, what mechanic, what laborer, ever sees a tax-gatherer of the United States?

These contributions enable us to give support… in time of peace, to rivers, canals, roads, arts, manufactures, education and other great objects within each state. In time of war… by other resources reserved for that crisis… War will then be but a suspension of useful works, and a return to a state of peace, a return to the progress of improvement.

Support for his controversial Louisiana Purchase…

I know that the acquisition of Louisiana has been disapproved by some, from a candid apprehension that the enlargement of our territory would endanger its union…. and in any view, is it not better that the opposite bank of the Mississippi should be settled by our own brethren and children, than by strangers of another family?

Favorable treatment of the Native American tribes…

Humanity enjoins us to teach (our aboriginal inhabitants) agriculture and the domestic arts; to encourage to that industry which alone can enable them to maintain their place in existence…. But the endeavors to enlighten them… have powerful obstacles to encounter.

An end of the personal attacks he has suffered in the press…

During this course of administration, and in order to disturb it, the artillery of the press has been levelled against us, charged with whatsoever its licentiousness could devise or dare. These abuses of an institution so important to freedom and science, are deeply to be regretted.

Our fellow citizens have looked on, cool and collected… they gathered around their public functionaries, and when the constitution called them to the decision by suffrage, they pronounced their verdict, honorable to those who had served them, and consolatory to the friend of man, who believes he may be intrusted with his own affairs…our wish, as well as theirs, is, that the public efforts may be directed honestly to the public good.

And guidance from that "Being in whose hands we are."

I shall now enter on the duties to which my fellow citizens have again called me, and shall proceed in the spirit of those principles which they have approved. I fear not that any motives of interest may lead me astray; I shall need, too, the favor of that Being in whose hands we are secure to you the peace, friendship, and approbation of all nations.

TIME: MARCH 4, 1805 – MARCH 4, 1809

OVERVIEW OF JEFFERSON'S SECOND TERM

Jefferson's wish to concentrate on domestic policy in his second term will be frustrated by America's inevitable entanglement in the warfare between Napoleon's France and Great Britain.

As the term begins, the president's cabinet is largely unchanged from before, except for Clinton as vice president and John Breckinridge the Virginian as attorney general.

THOMAS JEFFERSON'S CABINET IN 1805

POSITION	NAME	HOME STATE
Vice President	George Clinton	New York
Secretary of State	James Madison	Virginia
Secretary of Treasury	Albert Gallatin	Pennsylvania
Secretary of War	Henry Dearborn	Massachusetts
Secretary of the Navy	Robert Smith	Maryland
Attorney General	John Breckinridge	Virginia

James Monroe continues as ambassador to France, with former New York senator John Armstrong remaining in London at the Court of St. James.

Jefferson's financial priority lies in ridding the nation of debt by reducing the size of the standing army and trimming other federal expenses.

I place economy among the first and most important virtues and public debt as the greatest of dangers to be feared. To preserve our independence, we must not let our rulers load us with public debt.

His commitment to an agrarian economy and way of life is undiminished.

Those who labour in the earth are the chosen people of God, if ever he had a chosen people, whose breasts he has made his peculiar deposit for substantial and genuine virtue. It is the focus in which he keeps alive that sacred fire, which otherwise might escape from the face of the earth.

Achieving this idyllic vision rests on geographic expansion opening more available land for farming. With the Louisiana Territory already in hand, he now tries, unsuccessfully, to buy Florida and Cuba from Spain.

He also has William Henry Harrison, territorial governor of Indiana, negotiate two sizable land cessions with Native tribes to the west. Unlike his successors, Jefferson claims to be favorably impressed by the Indians' capacities. He hopes to teach them agricultural skills and assimilate them, rather than banish them. However, his actions will often belie his words in this regard.

1804 CESSIONS OF TRIBAL LANDS TO THE WEST

TREATY OF:	MAIN TRIBES	LAND CEDED TO US
Vincennes	Miami and Shawnee	1.6 million acres in central Indiana
St. Louis	Fox and Sauk	5.0 million acres in Wisconsin

His far westward explorations continue, with news flowing in from Lewis and Clark about the Missouri River and a pathway to the west coast, and with another expedition setting out under Zebulon Pike.

Pike—later an army general killed in the War of 1812—heads into the Louisiana Territory. First he explores up north to Minnesota, then he moves across the southwest to find the headwaters of the Red River and the Arkansas River. This takes him into Arizona, New Mexico, and Colorado, as well as the famous Rocky Mountain peak that bears his name.

As he drives westward, Jefferson is intent on weaving the new lands into the fabric of the Union.

To link the old east with the new west commercially, he initiates and funds two major road-building projects—despite his philosophical aversion to federal spending and debt.

JEFFERSON'S MAJOR ROAD INITIATIVES

NAME	APPROVED	MILES	LINKING
Cumberland Road	1806	620	Cumberland, MD to Vandalia, IL
Natchez Road	1806	500	Nashville, TN to Natchez, MS.

While Jefferson is pleased with this progress on the domestic front, he soon finds that threats to national security are occupying more of his time and energy.

One threat is particularly grating. Just as he is trying to glue new states onto the Union, he learns that his former vice president, Aaron Burr, is plotting with James Wilkinson, the territorial governor in Louisiana, to mount a "filibustering" campaign to create an independent confederation of states extending through New Orleans and into Mexico. He will go after Burr with a vengeance for this transgression.

But the Burr affair is nothing compared to the repeated acts of war being committed against the United States by Britain and France on the high seas throughout Jefferson's second term, as Napoleon attempts to achieve worldwide hegemony between 1805 and 1815.

The United States' role in the grand scheme is largely that of a pawn, with the two superpowers intent on blocking all shipping traffic between America and ports controlled by the enemy. To do so means breaking commercial laws, interfering with American ships at sea, turning them back or attacking them outright, seizing their cargoes, and impressing their sailors into foreign duty.

After negotiating efforts in Paris and London fail, Jefferson makes a fatal error in attempting to stay out of the war.

To demonstrate neutrality toward both sides, he secures passage of the 1807 Embargo Act, which bans U.S. ships from sailing to all foreign ports. But this move not only fails to improve diplomatic relations, it also crushes the east coast shipping industry. In 1808 the value of U.S. exports fall by almost 80% and talk of "nullification" forces the president to repeal the Act just prior to leaving office.

VALUE OF U.S. EXPORTS: BEFORE AND AFTER EMBARGO ACT

	1805	1806	1807	1808
$ Value	95,566,000	101,537,000	108,343,000	22,431,000
% Change		6%	7%	(79%)

Across his entire time in office, the overall economy drifts up and down, with per capita GDP ending in 1808 about where it was in 1801.

ECONOMIC GROWTH DURING JEFFERSON'S TWO TERMS

	1801	1802	1803	1804	1805	1806	1807	1808
Total GDP ($ Million)	514	451	487	533	561	617	589	646
Per Capita GDP	94	80	84	89	91	97	89	95
% Change		(15%)	5%	6%	2%	6%	(8%)	7%

Milestones during Jefferson's second term are as follows:

JEFFERSON'S SECOND TERM: KEY EVENTS

1805	
March 4	Jefferson and Clinton are inaugurated
April 29	Marines take the port of Derna, a turning point in the Tripolitan War
May 25	A labor strike by the Cordwainer's Union in Philadelphia is suppressed
June 4	War with Tripoli ends with peace treaty
July 23	Britain invokes Rule of 1756 further constraining U.S. shipping to France
August 9	Zebulon Pike begins first expedition, north into the Louisiana Territory
October 18	Lewis and Clark sight Mt. Hood
October 21	Nelson defeats the French fleet at Trafalgar, foiling invasion of England
November 7	Louis and Clark sight the Pacific
December 2	Napoleon annihilates Austrian and Russian armies at the Battle of Austerlitz
1806	
January	Noah Webster publishes his dictionary of the English language
February 12	A Senate resolution condemns British aggression against U.S. shipping
March 29	Congress approves bill to construct the Cumberland Road
May 30	Future president Andrew Jackson kills Charles Dickinson in a duel
July 15	Pike begins second expedition, this time into future New Mexico and Colorado
July 20	Aaron Burr and conspirators meet to plan filibustering invasion of southwest

1806	
September 23	Lewis and Clark arrive back home at St. Louis
October 14	Napoleon destroys the Prussian army at Auerstedt
November 21	Napoleon's Berlin Decree initiates a shipping blockade of the British Isles
November 27	Jefferson learns of Burr's annexation plot in southwest
1807	
January 7	British Order in Council blockades shipping to French ports
February 19	Aaron Burr is arrested and charged with treason
March 2	Congress passes bill banning importation of slaves, starting in 1808
March 4	Jefferson pockets disappointing Monroe-Pinckney Treaty with Britain
June 14	Napoleon defeats Russia at Friedland
June 22	British commit act of war as *HMS Leopold* attacks *USS Chesapeake* off Norfolk, VA
July 2	Jefferson proclamation bans British warships from American territorial waters
September 1	Aaron Burr acquitted of treason by John Marshall on a technicality, then flees to Europe
October 26	Tenth Congress convenes, with large Democratic-Republican majority
December 22	Jefferson's ruinous Embargo Act prohibits all US ships from entering foreign ports
1808	
January 1	Ban on importation of slaves takes effect
April 6	John Jacob Astor incorporates the American Fur Company
April 17	Napoleon's Bayonne Decree says France will seize U.S. ships abroad, per Embargo Act
June 6	Joseph Bonaparte named King of Spain
November 10	Osage Treaty cedes tribal lands in Missouri and Arkansas
December 7	Madison is elected president
1809	
January 9	The Enforcement Act tries to halt smuggling linked to the embargo
February 1	New Englanders debate nullifying the Embargo Act which destroys shipping industry
February 20	In *US v. Peters*, the Marshall court asserts the primacy of federal over state laws
March 1	Pressure on Jefferson finally leads to the repeal of the Embargo Act

## 28

BURR'S FILIBUSTERING CAMPAIGN SIGNALS U.S. COLONIAL INTENTIONS

TIME: 1805–1806

BURR PLANS TO CREATE AN EMPIRE IN THE SOUTHWEST

Aaron Burr is one of those famous figures in American history who climb to the pinnacle of national fame only to fall back into the ranks of the notorious.

He is born on February 6, 1756, in Newark, New Jersey, to parents steeped in religious ties. His mother, Esther, is the daughter of Jonathan Edwards, the famous Puritan minister whose Calvinist-oriented tract, "Sinners in the Hands of an Angry God," helped fuel the First Great Awakening in 1741. His father, Aaron Sr., is a Presbyterian minister and second president of the College of New Jersey (later Princeton).

But both parents die before Aaron reaches the age of three, and he and his sister are left in the care of their uncle, Timothy Edwards, who raises them within the stern traditions of Calvinism. This fails to sit well with young Aaron, who is

The look of a filibusterer

simultaneously precocious and rebellious. After trying to run away from home, he applies for admission to the College of New Jersey at age eleven. Two years later, he is allowed in, and graduates in 1772 at sixteen years old. Despite being pushed toward a career in the ministry, his inclinations are far removed from the Calvinistic austerity he experienced as a youth. Instead he takes up the law, and is three years into his studies when the Revolutionary War breaks out.

Burr immediately enlists in the Continental army, where his affection for combat over a four year period earns him both glory and recognition. He fights with Montgomery in 1775 at Quebec, helps Washington and Hamilton escape from their 1776 trap in Manhattan, rises to lieutenant colonel status in 1777, survives Valley Forge, and takes part in the pivotal 1778 battle at Monmouth. By 1779 the war has taken a sufficient toll on his health that he resigns his commission and returns to his legal pursuits.

He opens a law office in Albany in 1782 and that same year marries Theodosia Prevost, a widow with five children and ten years his senior. Despite dalliances, Burr stays with his wife until her death in 1794 and forever dotes on their daughter, also named Theodosia.

In 1784, Burr enters the rough-and-tumble world of New York politics as an Anti-Federalist. He begins as a state assemblyman, then is chosen as attorney general under Governor George Clinton. He serves as US senator from 1791 to 1797 after defeating General Phillip Schuyler, Alexander Hamilton's father-in-law, in his race.

His ambition leaps ahead and he expects to be elected vice president in 1796, but his electoral votes fall behind Adams, Jefferson, and Pinckney. He tries again in 1800, ties Jefferson in electoral votes, but then loses out in the House runoff engineered by Hamilton.

After the election of 1800, Burr loses Jefferson's trust and is dropped from the ticket in 1804. This leads to his decision to run for governor of New York, but he is soundly defeated.

He blames the loss on political smears coming from his longtime adversary, Hamilton. The result is a series of letters between the two men, a challenge issued by Burr, and the fatal duel at Weehawken that leaves Hamilton dead and Burr's reputation forever tarnished.

With his political days over, Burr joins his old Revolutionary War friend, Major General James Wilkinson, in a plot that will lead to his arrest for treason.

Burr has convinced Jefferson to name Wilkinson governor of the Louisiana territory. But Wilkinson returns the favor first by trying to break off Kentucky and Tennessee from the Union, then by conspiring with Spain to hamper American access to the port of New Orleans, and finally by initiating a "filibustering" scheme with Burr in 1805 to set up an independent confederation of states across the South under his rule as dictator.

Burr's role in the filibustering plan involves raising a small army and heading to New Orleans to foment rebellion. He contacts British officials in an attempt to secure financial backing but is rebuffed. He then meets with one Harman Blennerhassett, who owns an island on the Ohio River where Burr will store weapons and train troops. Next comes a visit to New Orleans, supposedly to visit land he owns in the Tejas Province, but actually intended to recruit locals who support an invasion into Mexico.

TIME: FEBRUARY 19, 1807

THE FORMER VP IS BETRAYED AND ARRESTED FOR TREASON

By 1806 the plan begins to unravel. The Ohio state militia raids Blennerhassett Island and Burr fails in his efforts to gather troops.

The scurrilous Wilkinson, fearing for his own reputation, informs Jefferson that Burr is plotting an insurrection. Jefferson is livid and a warrant is issued for Burr's arrest.

He is taken into custody in Mississippi, escapes briefly, and is then recaptured on February 19, 1807. He is shipped back to Washington to stand trial for treason.

TIME: SEPTEMBER 1, 1807

THE TRIAL ENDS WITH ACQUITTAL AND SHAME

The trial itself captures the nation's attention. It is held over seven months beginning in the summer of 1807 at the Federal Circuit Court in Richmond, Virginia. The judge is none other than Chief Justice John Marshall, who is frequently at odds with Jefferson. Those defending Burr include Edmund Randolph, former attorney general and secretary of state under Washington. An equally stellar lineup of prosecutors—micromanaged from the start by the president—aim to take Burr's life for treason.

Subpoenas are issued to a host of possible witnesses. Included here is Andrew Jackson, ex-senator from Tennessee who had met with Burr and is suspected of encouraging his move into Mexico. President Jefferson himself is also called to testify, and his plea to avoid the subpoena is rejected by Marshall, again asserting that not even the president is above the law. (In the end, neither will actually testify.)

On June 15, 1807, the grand jury hears Wilkinson testify against Burr, but the defense pokes numerous holes in his account and he barely escapes the just indictment he deserves. Nine days later, they enter charges against Burr for treason—"levying war on the United States" in actions on Blennerhassett Island—and for "high misdemeanors" related to organizing a military action against Spain in violation of the 1794 Neutrality Act.

As the trial itself closes, however, Marshall instructs the jury that the 1787 Constitution sets the bar very high for proving treason.

To establish the crime of treason the prosecution must prove that an overt act of treason had been committed by the defendant in a war and that, under the Constitution, the overt act must be testified to by two witnesses and must have occurred in the district of the trial.

After deliberations, the jury concludes the prosecution has failed to show enough evidence to sustain either charge.

Burr walks out of the courtroom as a free man, despite the ongoing certainty expressed by Jefferson and others that he is guilty on all counts.

Henceforth his name will be synonymous across America for slaying Hamilton and plotting treason. In response, Burr flees to England, hoping that time and distance will eventually allow his return to the States. And this proves to be the case. In 1813 he is back home, living momentarily under an assumed name. His star, which shined so brightly up to 1804, is now dimmed. He is left with his notoriety as he roams the streets of his beloved New York before dying in 1836, at age 80, on Staten Island.

## 29

LE JOUR DE GLOIRE ARRIVES FOR NAPOLEON AND FRANCE

TIME: DECEMBER 4, 1804

NAPOLEON CROWNS HIMSELF EMPEROR AND RESUMES WAR WITH BRITAIN

On December 2, 1804, Napoleon Bonaparte establishes hereditary power over France for his family, as he crowns himself emperor at Notre Dame Cathedral.

The service is designed to mimic the standards set for royal successions across Europe.

To insure that Napoleon will reign "in the eyes of God," Pope Pius VII attends the ceremony in person. The 62-year-old pontiff has been in office for four years, and is intent on restoring the church's standing in France after seeing papal authority stripped away during the revolution. His first step here is the Concordat of 1801, negotiated with Napoleon as first counsel, which recognizes Catholicism as the "religion of the great majority" in France, while dropping claims to church lands seized during the overthrow of the old order.

Napoleon enters Notre Dame

Napoleon Bonaparte (1769–1821)

after Pius VII is already seated. He arrives with his wife, Josephine, in a carriage drawn by eight horses. He is gowned up in an eighty-pound coronation mantle, supported by four manservants, and embroidered with golden bees, which he favors over the traditional fleur-de-lis symbol for France.

When the moment comes for the pope to crown him, Napoleon intercedes by placing the laurel wreath on his own head and repeating the act for Josephine as queen. Pius VII then intones his blessing:

May God confirm you on this throne and may Christ give you to rule with him in his eternal kingdom.

The action is completed with Napoleon placing his hands on the Bible and declaring his civil oath of office.

I swear to maintain the integrity of the territory of the Republic, to respect and enforce respect for the Concordat and freedom of religion, equality of rights, political and civil liberty, the irrevocability of the sale of national lands; not to raise any tax except in virtue of the law; to maintain the institution of Legion of Honor and to govern in the sole interest, happiness and glory of the French people.

As absolute monarch he is now eager to turn his energy against fulfilling the "glory of the French people."

His sights, as always, are on the British, and reversing the losses suffered four decades ago in the Seven Years' War. He will attack them on land and sea, along with any confederates who join them.

The days of French ascendance have arrived.

LA MARSEILLAISE (1792)

FRENCH LYRICS	ENGLISH TRANSLATION
Allons enfants de la Patrie,	Arise, children of the Fatherland,
Le jour de gloire est arrivé!	The day of glory has arrived!
Contre nous de la tyrannie,	Against us tyranny's
L'étendard sanglant est levé, (bis)	Bloody banner is raised, (repeat)
Entendez-vous dans les campagnes	Do you hear, in the countryside,
Mugir ces féroces soldats?	The roar of those ferocious soldiers?
Ils viennent jusque dans nos bras	They're coming right into our arms
Égorger nos fils, nos compagnes!	To cut the throats of our sons, our women!
Aux armes, citoyens,	To arms, citizens,
Formez vos bataillons,	Form your battalions,
Marchons, marchons!	Let's march, let's march!
Qu'un sang impur	Let an impure blood
Abreuve nos sillons! (bis)	Water our furrows! (repeat)

TIME: 1715–1855

SIDEBAR: ROLL CALL OF KEY 18ᵀᴴ–19ᵀᴴ CENTURY MONARCHS

FRANCE	BEGINS REIGN	ENDS REIGN
Louis XV	Sept 1, 1715	May 10, 1774
Louis XVI	May 10, 1774	Sept 21, 1792
First Republic	1792	1804
Napoleon I	May 18, 1804	April 11, 1814
Louis XVIII	April 11, 1814	March 20, 1815
Napoleon I	March 20, 1815	June 22, 1815
Napoleon II	June 22, 1815	July 7, 1815
Louis XVIII	July 7, 1815	Sept 16, 1824
Charles X	Sept 16, 1824	Aug 2, 1830
Louis Philippe I	August 9, 1830	Feb 24, 1848
Second Republic	1848	1852
Napoleon III	Dec 2, 1852	Sept 4, 1870
ENGLAND		
George II	June 11, 1727	Oct 25, 1760
George III	Oct 25, 1760	Jan 29, 1820
George IV	Jan 29, 1820	June 26, 1830
William IV	June 26, 1830	June 20, 1837
Victoria	June 20, 1837	Jan 22, 1901
SPAIN		
Charles III	Aug 10, 1759	Dec 14, 1788
Charles IV	Dec 14, 1788	March 19, 1808
Ferdinand VII	March 19, 1808	May 6, 1808
Joseph I	May 6, 1808	Dec 11, 1813
Ferdinand VII	Dec 11, 1813	Sept 29, 1833
Isabella II	Sept 29, 1833	Sept 30, 1868
PRUSSIA		
Frederick I	January 18, 1701	February 25, 1713
Frederick William I	February 25, 1713	May 31, 1740
Frederick II (the Great)	May 31, 1740	Aug 17, 1786
Frederick William II	Aug 17, 1786	Nov. 16, 1797
Frederick William III	Nov. 16, 1797	June 7, 1840
Frederick William IV	June 7, 1840	Jan 2, 1861
RUSSIA		
Catherine the Great	July 9, 1762	Nov 17, 1796
Paul I	Nov 17, 1796	Mar 23, 1801
Alexander I	Mar 23, 1801	Dec 1, 1825
Nicholas I	Dec 1, 1825	Mar 2, 1855
Alexander II	Mar 2, 1855	Mar 13, 1881

TIME: OCTOBER 21, 1805

NAPOLEON'S MOMENTUM IS HINDERED BY LORD NELSON AT TRAFALGAR

By the late summer of 1805, Napoleon has completed his plan to invade the British Isles, and has assembled an armada of French and Spanish ships to support the attack. But the invasion is delayed after Austria and Russia enter the war. Still, Napoleon is displeased by the lack of aggression he sees in the commanding officer of his fleet, Admiral Pierre-Charles de Villeneuve, who learns that he is about to be relieved.

On October 20, 1805, before his replacement can arrive, Villeneuve departs the port of Cádiz on the southwest coast of Spain, intending to sail south past Cape Trafalgar and the Straits of Gibraltar, into the Mediterranean and the French port of Toulon.

Viscount Horatio Nelson (1758–1805)

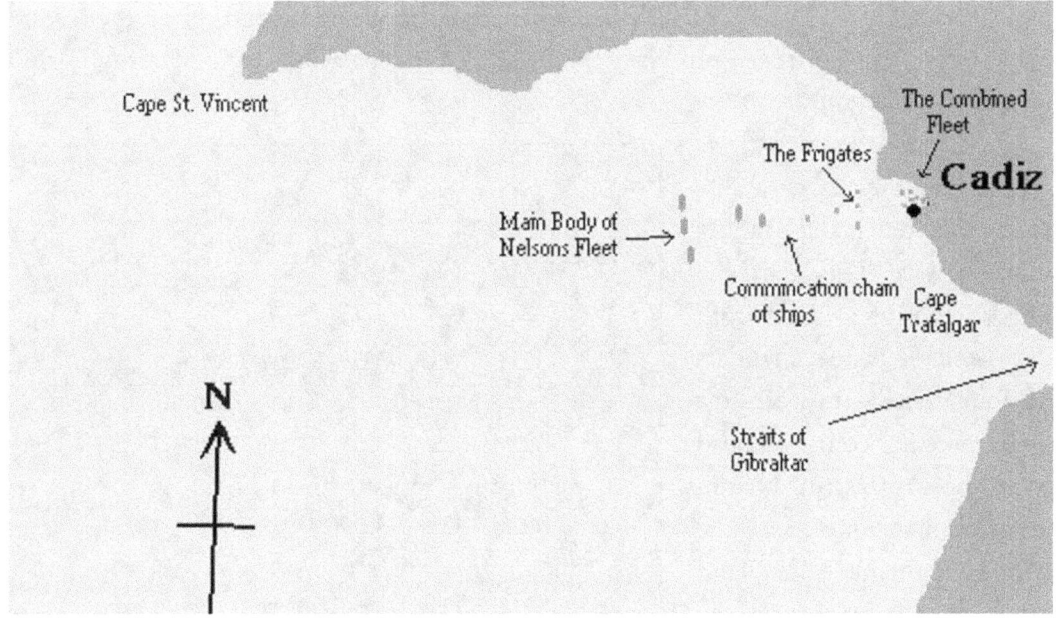

Cape Trafalgar off the coast of Cádiz above Gibraltar

H M S VICTORY IN PORTSMOUTH HARBOUR

HMS *Victory*

Villeneuve's fleet is formidable, comprising 33 heavy-duty warships with some 30,000 sailors and 2,568 guns.

At 11 a.m. on October 21, they encounter the British navy under the command of Captain Horatio Nelson, aboard HMS *Victory*.

Nelson is already a legend within the Royal Navy. He enlists as an ordinary seaman at age twelve, serving under his uncle, Captain Maurice Suckling, who turns him into a first-rate sailor despite his lifelong bouts of seasickness. By December 1778, at age twenty, he is master and commander of the sloop *Badger*. He is engaged briefly around Boston and New York during America's Revolutionary War, then becomes a national hero in February 1797, after capturing two Spanish warships at the Battle of St. Vincent.

He is almost killed on multiple occasions. In 1794, an enemy shot leaves him blinded in his right eye. On July 24, 1797, his left arm is shattered by a musket ball while leading a failed landing party assault on the Canary Island city of Santa Cruz de Tenerife. Amputation follows. In 1798 Nelson is knocked unconscious by shrapnel during the victorious Battle of the Nile. Afterwards he is awarded the honorary titles of baron and viscount.

On October 21, 1805, Nelson has been battling the French off and on for some twelve years. He is 47 years old and Vice Admiral of the White (ensign) Fleet, the second highest command in the Royal Navy. He has 27 warships at his disposal, with 17,000 men and 2,148 guns.

At 8 a.m. the two fleets spot each other from a distance, the French still heading south toward Gibraltar, the English coming at them from the west. Villeneuve orders his four-masters "to wear" (or jibe), reversing course to head back to Cádiz. But Nelson keeps coming=onto him. The famous command—"England expects that every man will do his duty"—is flagged up.

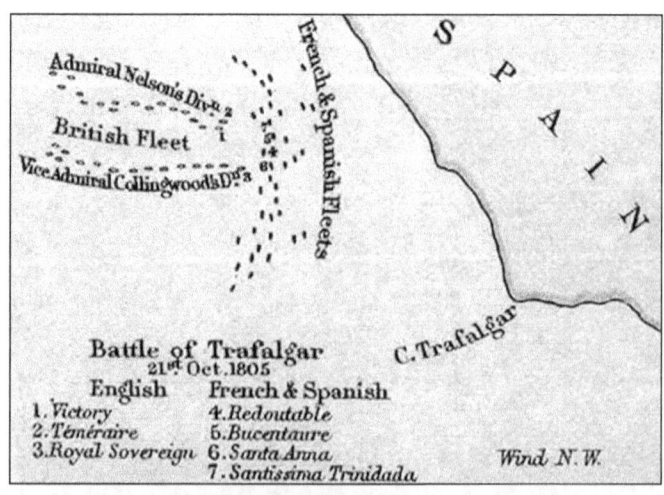

Nelson's very unconventional maneuver against the French fleet at Trafalgar

Around noon, the ships close on one another, with traditional naval strategy calling for Nelson to turn and "form lines of battle" stations parallel to the enemy. Instead, he plows straight ahead, striking the French in perpendicular fashion, and bringing on a pell-mell series of ship-against-ship action favorable to his more skilled seamen. This move, executed at no small risk of receiving initial broadside fire, also allows him to shoot

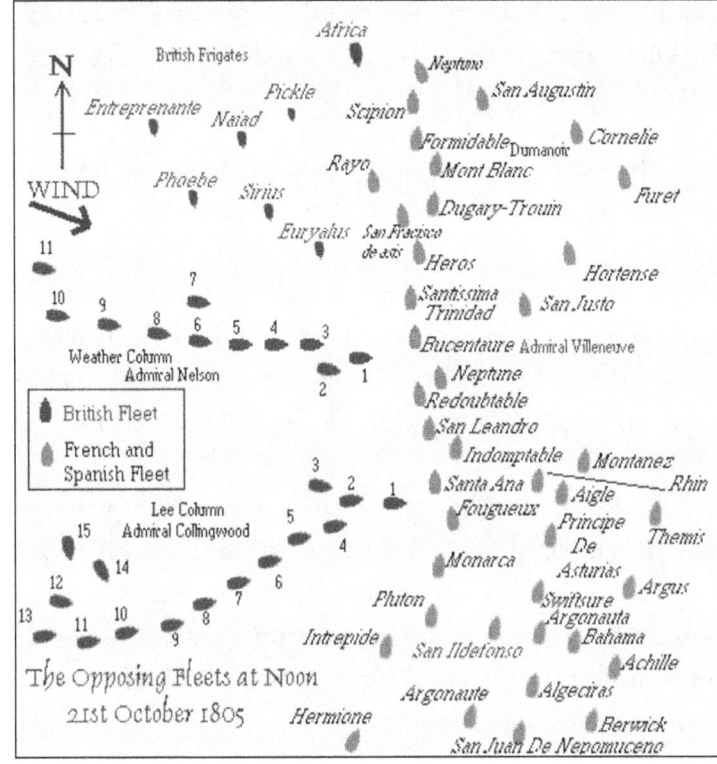

Greater detail on Nelson's straight-on line of attack

into the sterns of many French ships, with the fire traveling through the entire length of the ship to the bow.

Nelson himself commands the lead ship, HMS *Victory*, into the fray.

BRITISH LINE OF BATTLE

WEATHER COLUMN	LEE COLUMN
1. *Victory*	1. *Royal Sovereign*
2. *Temeraire*	2. *Bellisle*
3. *Neptune*	3. *Colossus*
4. *Leviathan*	4. *Mars*
5. *Conqueror*	5. *Tonnant*
6. *Agamemnon*	6. *Bellerophon*
7. *Britannia*	7. *Achille*
8. *Ajax*	8. *Polyphemus*
9. *Orion*	9. *Revenge*
10. *Minotaur*	10. *Swiftsure*
11. *Spartiate*	11. *Defence*
	12. *Thunderer*
	13. *Defiance*
	14. *Prince*
	15. *Dreadnought*

As *Victory* locks with the French *Redoubtable*, a musket ball takes Nelson in the left shoulder, slices through his seventh cervical vertebrae and lodges in his right shoulder. He knows immediately that the wound is fatal, and says so to his surgeon.

You can do nothing for me. I have but a short time to live. My back is shot through.

He lingers below decks for another three and a half hours, still issuing orders, before succumbing to his wound. His last words are recorded as "Thank God I have done my duty."

And his victory at Trafalgar is striking. Villeneuve's fleet has suffered one ship sunk, seventeen ships captured, another eleven partially damaged, and only four escaping unscathed. Some 4,500 of their seamen are killed, with another 2,400 wounded, and 7,000 taken prisoner. On the British side, no ships are lost for good and the dead and wounded total 1,450.

The Royal Navy has again demonstrated its supremacy on the high seas, and Napoleon casts aside all thoughts of an invasion of the English Isles.

Despite this, Britain mourns the loss of its most famous admiral. His body is packed inside a cask of brandy and other agents for preservation. This is towed home alone with his wounded ship, *Victory*. On January 9, 1806, England's most famous naval figure is interred at St. Paul's Cathedral.

DECEMBER 2, 1805 – OCTOBER 14, 1806

ON LAND, THE FRENCH WIN ONE MAJOR BATTLE AFTER ANOTHER

Napoleon is characteristically undaunted by the loss at Trafalgar.

On December 2, 1805, in the nine hour Battle of the Three Emperors near Austerlitz (now in the Czech Republic), his undermanned force (73,000 versus 86,000) pulls a stunning victory against Alexander I of Russia and the Holy Roman Emperor Francis

QUARTER DECK OF H.M.S. "VICTORY," Shewing the spot where Nelson fell.

II. Casualties for the day total a staggering 36,000 men. In response to the loss, Francis gives up his Holy Roman title and becomes simply King of Austria.

Less than a year later, on October 14, 1806, Napoleon soundly defeats the 110,000-man Prussian army in the two-part Battle of Jena-Auerstedt, winning control over territory in what is now central Germany and Poland. Casualties here are even greater than at Austerlitz, totaling 50,000 soldiers.

French soldiers on the march

France extends its borders as Napoleon emerges victorious

With these two pivotal triumphs, Napoleon now effectively controls all of Europe, except for Portugal. He then issues the Berlin Decree on November 21, 1806, which imposes the Continental Blockade on England. It halts all trade between England and any European countries allied with or dependent on France.

NAPOLEON'S EARLY CAMPAIGNS

1792	War of the First Coalition vs. Austria and Prussia (end: 1797)
1793	Siege of Toulon (southern France)—Napoleon wins first fame
1795	Napoleon quells pro-monarchy insurrection in Paris
1797	First Italian campaign (victories at Lodi and Arcola)
1798	Expedition to Egypt and Syria
1799	Napoleon seizes power in Paris as first counsel of the republic
	War of the Second Coalition vs. Russia, Britain, Austria, Naples, Vatican, etc. (end: 1802)
1800	Second Italian campaign (victory at Marengo over Austria)
	Spain trades Louisiana Territory back to France for Tuscan land
	France ends its Quasi-War with the U.S.
1802	Treaty of Amiens ends war with Britain (for one year)
	Napoleon expanding his power over France
1803	Britain declares war on France
1804	War of the Third Coalition vs. Britain, Austria, Prussia (end: 1806)
1805	Napoleon crowns himself emperor of France
1805	British defeat French invasion fleet at Trafalgar
	Battle of the Three Emperors at Austerlitz—Napoleon beats Austria and Russia
1806	War of the Fourth Coalition vs. Prussia and Russia (end: 1807)
	Battle of Jena-Auerstedt—Napoleon beats Prussia

## 30

BRITISH ACTS OF WAR LEAD TO THE RUINOUS "EMBARGO ACT"

TIME: 1805–1806

BRITAIN "IMPRESSES" US SAILORS TO FIGHT FRANCE

Napoleon's rampage across Europe and his war with Britain inevitably brings Jefferson into the middle of a conflict he would rather avoid.

The conflict is triggered by British "impressment" of American sailors.

Unlike the French with its dominant land army, the British rely on their Royal Navy to defend the homeland and their possessions around the globe. By 1805, as Napoleon notches one victory after another, they rush to build up their corps of able-bodied seamen from a peacetime force of 10,000 to the

Ships at sea off Gibraltar

140,000 they feel is needed for war. Their search turns to British sailors who have deserted the harsh conditions and disciplines imposed by their ship captains. Nelson pegs this figure at around 40,000 men, with many of them taking refuge on board more lenient American ships.

Britain's plan is to "retrieve" these nationals and return them to the Royal Navy. King George III, still smarting from the French-backed defeat at Yorktown and assuming that Jefferson favors his former allies, supports the notion of snatching American sailors as a justifiable form of payback.

Before proceeding, Britain looks for a legal rationale to stop and board American ships. Here they cite their own high court decision, rendered on May 22, 1805 against the American merchant ship *Essex*, accused of violating the Rule of 1756 by transporting cargo banned during times of war. They now use the Rule of 1756 as a legal excuse for stopping US ships to examine their cargo and seize American sailors at the same time.

"Press gangs" are formed to carry out this new policy, and by 1806 it's estimated that some 10,000 seamen have been taken, some British deserters, but also many American citizens. A major diplomatic controversy follows.

On February 12, 1806, the Senate passes a resolution condemning Britain's seizure of American ships and seamen. Actual sanctions follow on April 18 in the Non-Importation Act which bans all British hemp, brass, nails, wool, glass, clothing, leather, hats, and beer from entering American ports.

Further commercial interruptions come later. Napoleon adds to the controversy on November 11, 1806 with his Berlin Decree which intends to cut Britain off from all foreign imports, including those from the United States. When the British follow suit, all shipping activities between America and the two combatants are curtailed.

Jefferson continually tries to defuse the tensions with Britain. In August 1806, Secretary of State James Monroe and his aide, William Pinkney, open talks with representatives of the Whig Prime Minister Lord Grenville. These lead nowhere, and end with the December 1 Monroe-Pinkney Treaty, which disappoints Jefferson to the extent that he refuses to send it to the Senate for approval.

TIME: JUNE 22, 1807

HMS *LEOPARD* ATTACKS US SHIP OFF NORFOLK, VIRGINIA

Six months later, on June 22, 1807, the conflict ratchets up sharply as the 50-gun HMS *Leopard* attacks the USS *Chesapeake* off the coast of Norfolk, Virginia. After falsely informing the *Leopard* that it has no British deserters in its 340-man crew and that it will not submit to a boarding party search, the *Chesapeake* turns to sail away. As it does so, it is struck by a full broadside bombardment. The surprised Americans are able to get off only one round of return fire before they strike their colors and surrender. Three US sailors are killed and another eighteen are wounded in the brief action.

A press gang from the *Leopard* boards and searches the *Chesapeake* and arrests four men claimed to be British nationals and deserters. Three turn out to be Americans, released after their sentence of 500 lashes is commuted.

An American sailor

The fourth man, Jenkin Ratford, is in fact a British deserter. He is soon tried and hanged from the yardarm of HMS *Halifax*.

The American public is outraged by the incident, and Jefferson feels the pressure to retaliate.

Never since the Battle of Lexington have I seen this country in such a state of exasperation as at present, and even that did not produce such unanimity.

However, his response is measured and restrained. Secretary of State James Madison issues a protest which demands that the British government condemn the *Leopard*'s actions, return the captured Americans, remove its warships from American waters, and end the practice of impressment.

On October 17, Britain responds publicly, declaring its intent to ignore the American demands and step up its impressment activities.

Jefferson is now caught between the open belligerence of the British and the growing public demand for further action to defend the nation's honor.

He refuses to call Congress into a special session for fear of an immediate war resolution, but he does order all US warships abroad to head home in case they are needed.

He then ponders what to do about America's fleet of merchant ships.

TIME: DECEMBER 22, 1807

THE EMBARGO ACT OF 1807 BOOMERANGS ON THE ADMINISTRATION

Secretary Madison proposes a solution: the safest way to avoid war and to protect the nation's ships lies in restricting all commercial traffic between America and all foreign ports.

Ships that stay in American waters and move only between one domestic port and another cannot be accused of interfering in the European conflict, and will be more readily protected by the US naval fleet.

Jefferson announces this idea in his seventh annual message to Congress on December 18, 1807.

To the Senate and House of Representatives of the United States: The communications now made, showing the great and increasing dangers with which our vessels, our seamen, and merchandise are threatened on the high seas and elsewhere, from the belligerent powers of Europe, and it being of great importance to keep in safety these essential resources, I deem it my duty to recommend the subject to the consideration of Congress, who will doubtless perceive all the advantages which may be expected from an inhibition of the departure of our vessels from the ports of the United States. Their wisdom will also see the necessity of making every preparation for whatever events may grow out of the present crisis.

The Embargo Act of 1807 passes in the Senate on December 18 by a margin of 22–6. Of the six nays, three are Federalists (Pickering of Massachusetts, Hilhouse of Maryland, and White of Delaware) and three are Democratic-Republicans (Crawford of Georgia, Maclay of Pennsylvania, and Goodrich of Connecticut). The House follows suit by an 82–44 margin, and the bill becomes law on December 22.

Details of the Embargo Act are as follows:

- American merchant ships are banned from setting sail to any and all foreign ports.
- Ships engaged in domestic traffic must post a "good will" bond before departing.
- US Navy warships will enforce these rules.
- Any exceptions must be authorized directly by the president.

If effect, Jefferson and Madison intend to pull America back into a defensive posture while Britain and France fight it out for European hegemony.

But instead of the public support they expect for the Embargo Act, the result is open hostility.

States that depend on international trade experience sharp economic downturns. Traders turn to smuggling to earn a living. Prices increase on "necessities of life" in short supply and decrease on embargoed exports. Fear spreads that, if the ban goes on long enough, European customers for American exports will find alternative sources of supply.

On February 1, 1808, former secretary of state Thomas Pickering calls for a convention of states who wish to nullify the Act. Connecticut Governor John Trumbull follows on February 22 by telling his legislature that the Act is unconstitutional, and that he will refuse to have the state militia enforce it.

Treasury Secretary Albert Gallatin also shares his concerns with Jefferson.

As to the hope that it may...induce England to treat us better, I think is entirely groundless...government prohibitions do always more mischief than had been calculated; and it is not without much hesitation that a statesman should hazard to regulate the concerns of individuals as if he could do it better than themselves.

But neither Jefferson nor Madison is ready to back off in the face of the internal pressure. Rather than reversing course, they embark on an almost Adams-like crackdown on those who resist the ban.

The most egregious violations appear in the Northeast, with overland and river route smuggling to and from Canada becoming commonplace. To suppress this,

Jefferson invokes the Insurrection Act of March 3, 1807, which gives him the power to call in the standing federal army to suppress those obstructing the law.

> *[I]n all cases of insurrection, or obstruction to the laws, either of the United States, or of any individual state or territory, where it is lawful for the President of the United States to call forth the militia for the purpose of suppressing such insurrection, or of causing the laws to be duly executed, it shall be lawful for him to employ, for the same purposes, such part of the land or naval force of the United States, as shall be judged necessary, having first observed all the pre-requisites of the law in that respect.*

TIME: MARCH 1, 1809

THE ACT IS REPEALED AS JEFFERSON'S SECOND TERM ENDS

On March 12, 1808, further strictures are added to the Embargo Act. Stiff $10,000 fines for those violating the ban become law, and port authorities are granted the power to search suspect ships and seize cargoes without securing advance warrants. Madison remains convinced that the embargo will succeed if only it is properly enforced.

Jefferson's most devoted backers are surprised by his readiness to use central government weapons—even the standing army—against the clear wishes of a host of individual states and citizens. Hamilton might resort to this tactic, but to watch Jefferson and Madison engage this way is shocking to many Democratic-Republicans.

In the end, the embargo survives over fifteen months before the president gives in. The Act has had little effect on the European war while producing widespread public resistance at home, including a resurgence of the Federalist Party. Its only benefit has been to encourage the growth of domestic manufacturers to fill the void in foreign imports.

Despite opposition from Madison, Jefferson repeals the Embargo Act during his last week in office.

On March 1, 1809, the so-called Non-Intercourse Act goes into effect. It allows shipping to resume with all nations except Britain and France. It also dangles a carrot in front of the two belligerents, offering a resumption of trade in exchange for a commitment to end future interference with American ships and sailors.

As with many presidents, the toll taken by second term reversals weighs heavily on Jefferson. His last six months in office reflect near-paralysis, and as typical he captures his feelings in a succinct metaphor:

> *Never did a prisoner, released from his chains, feel such relief as I shall on shaking off the shackles of power.*

Of course neither his short-term influence on the future course of American politics, nor his long-term legacy, ends in 1809 as he departs for Monticello.

SIDEBAR: THOMAS JEFFERSON'S LASTING LEGACIES

JEFFERSON'S PRINCIPLES OF GOVERNMENT

Thomas Jefferson's political philosophy will dominate the American scene over the next four decades.

The Democratic Party he founds turns the country away from the Federalist principles espoused by Washington, Hamilton, and Adams, and relegates their followers to minority status in Congress.

Jefferson also works the political process in such a way that he hands the presidency over to his two Virginian protégés—Madison and Monroe—thereby extending his behind-the-scenes power another sixteen years, almost to his death (and Adams') on July 4, 1826.

The central themes of Jefferson's presidency will ring down the generations to follow:

THOMAS JEFFERSON.

- The shift in focus from the original thirteen colonies to the acquisition and development of the vast lands west of the Appalachians and the Mississippi River, which sets America's "manifest destiny" in motion and provides the Democratic Party with a long-run lock on western voters.
- Commitment to firmly integrating the new states into the Union based on the ideals in the Constitution.
- The libertarian drive to ensure that power remains in the hands of individual citizens distributed across the states and away from centralized

power blocks, be they in the form of government, churches, or economic
entities.

- A wish to sharply limit the size of a central government and concentrate
  its role on foreign policy rather than domestic policy which, according to
  "his" Tenth Amendment, involves "rights belonging to the states."
- Belief that common local men will prove superior to distant politicians
  in debating and resolving social needs or problems arising in their own
  communities.
- Abhorrence of public debt and strict limits on taxation and spending in
  order to minimize the government's impact on the lives of citizens.
- A deep and abiding distrust of bankers, soft money, and the banking system in general, especially Hamilton's central Bank of the United States.
- A similar fear of capitalism and corporations, where money trumps labor
  and white men run the risk of being reduced to wage slaves.
- A conviction that all white Americans should have access to free public
  education and to the development of outstanding colleges, such as the
  University of Virginia, which he founded in 1785.
- Undying faith in the power of the Union and a commitment to preserve
  it against all threats, foreign or domestic.

While also having faith in the basically good intentions of common men,
Jefferson firmly believes that leadership belongs with a "natural aristocracy." As
he says in a note to Adams in 1813:

> *For I agree with you that there a natural aristocracy among men. The grounds
> of this are virtue and talents. There is an artificial aristocracy founded on
> wealth and birth, without either virtue or talents. The natural aristocracy I
> consider the most precious gift of nature for the instruction, the trusts, and
> government of society.*

Interwoven with all these principles is Jefferson's commitment to the southern, agrarian way of life he has known since childhood—including slavery.

So the final part of his legacy comes to an examination of his words and
deeds relative to that institution.

JEFFERSON'S RATIONALIZATIONS ON SLAVERY

Thomas Jefferson lives among enslaved people all his life. They provide the
hard labor required to build his mountaintop home and miniature town; to grow
and harvest his farm crops; operate his mill, brewery, spindles, and nailery; cook

and serve his fine French cuisine; pay off his debts; and, in the case of Sally Hemings, act as his surrogate wife after Martha dies in 1782.

They seem to fascinate him intellectually. He studies their physical, mental, and emotional traits, their joys and sorrows, and the ways in which they deal with their fate. Almost in scientific fashion, he records these observations in his *Farm Book* and in his *Notes on the State of Virginia*, first drafted in 1781 and completed in 1785.

Throughout his life he also reflects on the institution of slavery, and on his personal relationship to it.

In a telling 1805 note to William Burwell, his private secretary, he describes a range of attitudes toward slavery he has encountered among owners:

> *There are many virtuous men who would make any sacrifices to effect it. Many equally virtuous who persuade themselves either that the thing is not wrong, or that it cannot be remedied. And very many, with whom interest is morality.*

Over time, he seems to see himself belonging in the first class—ready to make "any sacrifices" to end the practice. This is clear in a 1788 letter to Jacques Brissot, a leading proponent of abolition in France.

> *You know that nobody wishes more ardently to see an abolition not only of the trade but of the condition of slavery: and certainly nobody will be more willing to encounter every sacrifice for that object.*

He reiterates this, using similar words, a quarter of a century later in an 1814 letter to his friend, the academician Thomas Cooper.

> *There is nothing I would not sacrifice to a practicable plan of abolishing every vestige of this moral and political depravity.*

Like Hamlet, Jefferson asserts that he is ready to act to correct that which is morally wrong to him—if only he can arrive at a proper remedy. And therein lies the rub.

His contact with African people has convinced him that they probably have descended from a different species, and are biologically inferior to white men. Given this, he tells Edward Bancroft in 1789 that releasing the enslaved people would be tantamount to "abandoning children."

> *As far as I can judge from the experiments which have been made, to give liberty to, or rather, to abandon persons whose habits have been formed in slavery is like abandoning children.*

Other barriers to abolition materialize over time.

If freed, African people could never be assimilated. His *Notes* lay out the reasons why.

> *It will probably be asked, Why not retain and incorporate the blacks into the state? Deep rooted prejudices entertained by the whites; ten thousand recollections, by the blacks, of the injuries they have sustained; new provocations; the real distinctions which nature has made; and many other circumstances, will divide us into parties, and produce convulsions which will probably never end but in the extermination of the one or the other race.*

In 1803, a letter to James Monroe cites the events surrounding Toussaint's rebellion in Saint-Domingue (Haiti) as evidence of the inevitable violence between the two races, if freedom is granted.

> *I become daily more & more convinced that all the West India islands will remain in the hands of the people of colour, & a total expulsion of the whites sooner or later take place.*

What is left then is recolonization, the solution he references in an 1814 letter to his Virginian neighbor and anti-slavery advocate, Edward Coles.

> *I have seen no proposition so expedient on the whole, as that of emancipation of those born after a given day, and of their education and expatriation at a proper age.*

So Jefferson appears to come full circle, back to his *Notes*. His intellect tells him that no matter the biological inferiority of African people, taking away their freedom and enslaving them is morally corrupt and an affront to God's justice.

> *The whole commerce between master and slave is a perpetual exercise of the most boisterous passions, the most unremitting despotism on the one part, and degrading submissions on the other. Our children see this, and learn to imitate it... The parent storms, the child looks on, catches the lineaments of wrath, puts on the same airs in the circle of smaller slaves, gives a loose to his worst passions, and thus nursed, educated and daily exercised in tyranny, cannot but be stamped by it with odious peculiarities.*

> *If a slave can have a country in this world, it must be any other in preference to that in which he is to be born to live and labor for another ... or entail his own miserable condition on the endless generations proceeding from him.*

> *Indeed, I tremble for my country when I reflect that God is just: that his justice cannot sleep forever.*

He "trembles" again for his country during the 1820 Missouri crisis—"a fire bell in the night"—and once more, as seer, in an 1821 autobiographical reflection.

> *Nothing is more certainly written in the book of fate than that these people are to be free. Nor is it less certain that the two races, equally free, cannot live in the same government.*

Taken together, Jefferson's rhetoric is of the virtuous man who recognizes the evils of slavery, is ready to make any sacrifice to end it, but simply sees no viable way out of the dilemma.

All that's left for him is to do the best he can in the inevitable presence of slavery—a Herculean task, as he points out in his *Notes*:

> *The man must be a prodigy who can retain his manners and morals undepraved by such circumstances.*

One suspects that Jefferson sees himself in this observation—the rare "prodigy" able to rise above the coarsening realities of slavery that surround him.

But is this truly the case? How well do Jefferson's words match up with his actions as a slave owner?

The record here seems mixed.

There is no evidence to support the notion that he was personally harsh in dealing with enslaved people. However, he did expect reasonable levels of "industry" from them and hired overseers such as William Page and Gabriel Lilly, both known for resorting to the whip to enforce discipline.

More troubling is his assignment of young children to handle some particularly onerous tasks. Because of their short stature, some spend days at a time on hands and knees in the dirt plucking and killing tobacco worms. Others end up in the "nailery," crowded around a flaming forge in the summer heat, converting iron nail rods into various sizes of finished nails. Jefferson is particularly proud of this factory operation, oversees it himself, and remarks on its profitability.

> *I now employ a dozen little boys from 10. to 16. years of age, overlooking all the details of their business myself and drawing from it a profit.*

It is precisely this tendency to prioritize personal profits over the well-being of enslaved people that counts most in calling Jefferson's moral sense into question. On one hand he will insist that they are part of "his family;" on the other, he will sell them off whenever economic necessity calls.

For a man with great sensitivity to language, his words about "breeding women" in his *Farm Book* are both cold and calculating.

The loss of 5 little ones in 4 years induces me to fear that the overseers do not permit the women to devote as much time as is necessary to the care of their children; that they view their labor as the 1ˢᵗ object and the raising their child but as secondary.

I consider the labor of a breeding woman as no object, and a child raised every 2. years is of more profit then the crop of the best laboring man. In this, as in all other cases, providence has made our duties and our interests coincide perfectly.... With respect therefore to our women & their children

I must pray you to inculcate upon the overseers that it is not their labor, but their increase which is the first consideration with us.

Likewise his "investment advice" to friends.

Invest every (spare) farthing in land and negroes, which besides a present support bring a silent profit of from 5 to 10 per cent in this country, by the increase in their value.

Here indeed enslaved people are reduced from "family" to "property," to be bred, fed, and sold at auction. And sell them he does. Never as a "commercial trader" like his father-in-law, rather out of expediency, to buy the many things he wants for Monticello and to pay off debts.

In the decade from 1784 to 1794, records show that he disposes of some 161 enslaved people. More sales would follow, always accompanied by a stated wish to "keep families together"...

To indulge connections seriously formed by those people, where it can be done reasonably.

Always accompanied by...

Scruples about selling negroes but for delinquency, or on their own request.

Reservations aside, the commitment to "silent profit" also extends to Jefferson's last will and testament. Unlike Washington, he refuses to free his slaves upon his death, with the exception of some eight members of the Hemings family.

Words and deeds. Weighed in the balance, the record is mixed. Jefferson is by no means the callous or uncaring slave master, but neither is he the "prodigy" he refers to in his 1805 note to Burwell.

At moments of economic necessity, self-interest too often trumps morality.

## 31

JAMES MADISON'S FIRST TERM

TIME: AUTUMN OF 1808

RUN-UP TO THE ELECTION OF 1808

As the 1808 presidential election approaches, the path to the nomination is open for James Madison despite the negative economic effects of the Embargo Act.

At 57 years old, Madison is eight years younger than Jefferson, who has named him secretary of state and groomed him for the top job. He has been at the center of American politics since the 1787 Constitutional Convention, and is widely credited with being the principle author of the final agreement.

Along with Jefferson, he has guided the Democratic-Republicans to national dominance. Within the party, only the strictest Anti-Federalists retain any reservations about his credentials. This faction is led by John Randolph of Roanoke, George Clinton, Patrick Henry, and James Monroe, states'-rights conservatives who feel that Jefferson and Madison have allowed too much power to rest in federal hands.

Clinton is Jefferson's sitting vice president and a dominant force in New York politics, having served as governor for 21 years before joining Jefferson's cabinet. He has run twice before for the presidency, in 1788 and in 1792, where he records 50 electoral votes against Washington. But he is now 69 years old and his time has passed.

Monroe has also criticized Madison for initially arguing against including a Bill of Rights in the Constitution, rejecting term limits, and supporting a standing army. But he has already lost two races against him for a seat in the House.

When the various state caucuses convene and vote, Madison is nominated 83–3, with Clinton selected once again for vice president.

Meanwhile, the Federalist Party is still in near total disarray. After Washington's death in 1799, Adams's defeat in 1800, and Hamilton's fatal wounding in 1804, no one has been able to step in and mount a national campaign. The result is a party now largely confined to its original roots in New England.

The hub lies in Boston, led by George Cabot, Harrison Otis, and Timothy Pickering, Adams's intensely pro-British secretary of state. Pickering describes the extent of the Federalist disorder as follows:

The Federalists here are in point of numbers so utterly impotent, and the (Republicans) govern in nearly all the states with such an overwhelming majority; nothing would be more remote from their contemplation than to set up candidates of their own for President and Vice-President.

In search of an election plan, Federalists from eight states gather in New York in August 1808 for what is often considered the first attempt at a national political convention. Attendance is sparse and the meetings are held in secret. They consider backing the Democratic-Republican George Clinton, but the majority feel this would further erode "party identity."

Instead they fall back to the same ticket so soundly defeated by Jefferson in 1804—former Revolutionary War general Charles C. Pinckney of South Carolina and Rufus King of New York.

TIME: NOVEMBER–DECEMBER 1808

MADISON WINS THE PRESIDENCY

Voting takes place between November 4 and December 7, 1808, with the Federalists hoping public sentiment against the year-old Embargo Act will swing the outcome their way.

But Madison beats them 2 to 1 in the popular vote and by a comfortable margin in the Electoral College. Six electors from New York honor their "favorite son," Clinton, by writing him in on their presidential ballots despite his lack of public support.

RESULTS OF THE 1808 PRESIDENTIAL ELECTION

CANDIDATES	STATE	PARTY	POP. VOTE	TOTAL EV	SOUTH	BORDER	NORTH	WEST
James Madison	VA	Dem-Rep	124,732	122	56	16	47	3
Charles C. Pinckney	SC	Federalist	62,431	47	3	5	39	
George Clinton	NY	Dem-Rep	---	6			6	
James Monroe	VA	Dem-Rep	4,848	0				
Unpledged			680	0				
Total			192,691	175	59	21	92	3
Needed to win				88				

Note: South (VA, NC, SC, GA), Border (DE, MD, KY), North (NH, MA, NY, NJ, PA, RI, CT, VT), West (OH)

Still the Federalist do make some inroads. Madison's electoral count is 40 votes shy of Jefferson's total in 1804.

CHANGE IN ELECTORAL VOTES: 1808 VS. 1804

YEAR	CANDIDATES	PARTY	ELECTORAL VOTES
1804	Thomas Jefferson	Democratic-Republican	162
1808	James Madison	Democratic-Republican	122

And three New England states—Massachusetts, New Hampshire, and Rhode Island—are carried by General Pinckney.

PARTY POWER BY STATE

SOUTH	1804	1808	PICK UPS
Virginia	Dem-Rep	Dem-Rep	
North Carolina	Dem-Rep	Split	
South Carolina	Dem-Rep	Dem-Rep	
Georgia	Dem-Rep	Dem-Rep	
Tennessee	Dem-Rep	Dem-Rep	
BORDER			
Delaware	Federalist	Federalist	
Maryland	Dem-Rep	Split	
Kentucky	Dem-Rep	Dem-Rep	
NORTH			
New Hampshire	Dem-Rep	Federalist	Federalist
Vermont	Dem-Rep	Dem-Rep	
Massachusetts	Dem-Rep	Federalist	Federalist
Rhode Island	Dem-Rep	Federalist	Federalist
Connecticut	Federalist	Federalist	
New York	Dem-Rep	Split	
New Jersey	Dem-Rep	Dem-Rep	
Pennsylvania	Dem-Rep	Dem-Rep	
WEST			
Ohio	Dem-Rep	Dem-Rep	

In the vice presidential race, George Clinton beats King handily, and will now serve under Madison as he has under Jefferson.

1808 ELECTORAL COLLEGE VOTE FOR VP

CANDIDATE	PARTY	VOTES
George Clinton	Dem-Rep	113
Rufus King	Federalist	47
John Langdon	Dem-Rep	9
James Madison	Dem-Rep	3
James Monroe	Dem-Rep	3
Total		175

TIME: 1808

THE FEDERALISTS MAKE SOME GAINS IN CONGRESS

In the House, the Federalists pick up 23 seats while still trailing well behind the Democratic-Republicans.

ELECTION TRENDS: HOUSE OF REPRESENTATIVES

PARTY	1801	1803	1805	1807	1809	CHANGE
Democratic-Republicans	68	102	114	116	93	(23)
Federalist	38	40	28	26	49	+23
Congress #	7th	8th	9th	10th	11th	
President	TJ	TJ	TJ	TJ	JM	

Most of the Federalist gains are in the North, again reflecting anger over the effects of the embargo on the shipping industry.

HOUSE TRENDS BY REGION

DEMOCRATIC-REPUBLICAN	TOTAL	SOUTH	BORDER	NORTH	WEST
1801	68	30	7	31	
1803	102	42	13	46	1
1805	114	48	13	52	1
1807	116	47	12	56	1
1809	93	41	12	39	1
Change from 1807	(23)	(6)	NC	(17)	NC
FEDERALISTS					
1801	38	8	4	26	
1803	40	7	3	30	
1805	28	1	3	24	
1807	26	2	4	20	
1809	49	8	4	37	
Change from 1807	+23	+6	NC	+17	

The makeup of the Senate is largely unchanged from the prior three session.

ELECTION TRENDS: SENATE

PARTY	1801	1803	1805	1807	1809	CHANGE
Democratic-Republicans	17	25	27	28	27	(1)
Federalist	15	9	7	6	7	+1
Congress #	7th	8th	9th	10th	11th	
President	TJ	TJ	TJ	TJ	JM	

SENATE TRENDS BY REGION

DEMOCRATIC-REPUBLICAN	TOTAL	SOUTH	BORDER	NORTH	WEST
1801	17	10	3	4	
1803	25	10	4	9	2
1805	27	10	4	11	2
1807	28	10	4	12	2
1809	27	10	4	11	2
Change from 1807	(1)	N/A	N/A	(1)	N/A
FEDERALISTS					
1801	15	0	3	12	
1803	9	0	2	7	
1805	7	0	2	5	
1807	6	0	2	4	
1809	7	0	2	5	
Change from 1807	1	N/A	N/A	1	

TIME: 1751–1836

PRESIDENT JAMES MADISON: PERSONAL PROFILE

None other than Thomas Jefferson will refer to James Madison as "the greatest man in the world." The two will know each other over a fifty-year span and will combine their remarkable intellects and prose-writing skills to capture the spirit and structures of America's new government.

James Madison, Jr. is born on March 16, 1751, the first of his parents' twelve children.

Like Jefferson, he grows up amidst privilege on the 4,500-acre Mount Pleasant plantation, some 30 miles northeast of Monticello. The land is located in the Piedmont (or "foothills") region of Virginia, just east of the Appalachians. Madison will later rename the plantation Montpelier, "mount of the pilgrims," after a famous French resort.

"Young Jemmy" is slight of stature and drawn to the life of the mind early on. His curiosity is fed by a series of outstanding tutors who

James Madison (1751–1836)

emphasize a combination of classical studies and the Scottish Presbyterian values of Calvinism.

Between the ages of eleven and sixteen he resides at the Robertson School, an institution set up to provide the children of elite families a European-style education. The headmaster of the school is Donald Robertson, a University of Edinburgh graduate who recognizes and nurtures Madison's intellectual capacities. Many years later, Madison will say of him:

All that I have been in life I owe largely to that man.

After returning home in 1767 he studies under Reverend Thomas Martin, who encourages him to attend his alma mater, the College of New Jersey, also a Calvinist dominated institution. Madison completes a four-year curriculum there in two years, overseen throughout by Reverend Thomas Witherspoon, president of the college. Witherspoon's track record for turning out government leaders is remarkable, including ten cabinet officers, three Supreme Court justices, 28 Senators, and 49 House members, in addition to Madison and Aaron Burr.

Upon graduation in 1771, Madison is able to read six languages, including Greek, Latin, and Hebrew; has engaged in political debate as a member of the Whig Society; and is left pondering a career either in law or the clergy. Despite his obvious talents, Madison tends to be shy and bookish by nature, and it is his friends who push him forward at this early stage of life.

He is back home in Virginia when conflict heats up between the colonists and the crown. At 5'4" tall and weighing under 100 pounds, he is too physically frail to join the military, so he signs on to the Orange County Committee for Safety and begins to draft a constitution for the state. He is also too young and unknown to attend the Declaration of Independence congress of 1776, but engages heavily in Virginia state politics.

His lifelong linkage to Thomas Jefferson develops at this time, when he helps draft the landmark *Virginia Statute for Religious Freedom* in 1777:

Be it enacted by General Assembly that no man shall be compelled to frequent or support any religious worship, place, or ministry whatsoever, nor shall be enforced, restrained, molested, or burthened in his body or goods, nor shall otherwise suffer on account of his religious opinions or belief, but that all men shall be free to profess, and by argument to maintain, their opinions in matters of Religion, and that the same shall in no wise diminish, enlarge or affect their civil capacities.

In 1780, with the outcome of the Revolutionary War still in doubt, he becomes visible at the national level as the youngest delegate to the Second Continental Congress.

He is 36 years old in the summer of 1787 as the Constitutional Convention assembles in Philadelphia. His role here proves pivotal to founding the Union.

As unofficial secretary he sits at the front of the hall and is accountable for listening to and capturing the key issues, and working behind the scenes to iron them out. The "Virginia Plan" he has drafted for Governor Randolph introduces the basic "three branches of government" structure that will prevail in the end. He engages in many of the floor debates, and pushes the delegation to closure, despite strong Anti-Federalist sentiments, often centered in his own Virginia delegation. Then, he overcomes his personal opposition to including a Bill of Rights and drafts the initial twelve Amendments along with 26 of the Federalist Papers that lead to ratification.

The Constitution captures Madison's most lasting and profound insights about the minds and behaviors of men in relation to civil power.

It reflects his roots as a Presbyterian Calvinist—left to their natural instincts (or "passions"), the capacity for self-interest or even evildoing among men is great. Thus a "pure democracy" is doomed to failure. The best alternative is a republic, comprising men most capable of placing the common interest above their own. But even this will prove insufficient, according to Madison. For a "government of the people" to work, power given any one man or body must be kept in check by offsetting power in the hands of others. Only by ensuring that there is consensus between the legislative, executive, and judiciary branches will the people be well-served.

Madison's achievements at the 1787 Convention are obvious to all attendees. From this time on he is widely seen as having the right stuff to someday be president. The College of New Jersey recognizes his work with a Doctor of Laws honoris causa, and with Witherspoon citing him to all alumnae as:

> One of their own sons who had done them so much honor by his public service.

In 1794, Madison is 43 years old and in the third of his four terms in the House of Representatives when he marries Dolley Todd, a 26-year-old widow introduced to him by Aaron Burr. Her outgoing nature complements his reserve, and she will manage social affairs in Washington for both the bachelor Jefferson and her husband.

Philosophically, Madison exhibits a host of Federalist-leaning tendencies early on. He favors a republic over a pure democracy, federal laws trumping state laws, a strong executive with veto powers and no term limits, creation of a standing army, initial opposition to a Bill of Rights, and a national government with sufficient power to unify all factions as needed.

But his center of gravity shifts as he observes the Federalists in action. He concludes that Alexander Hamilton, his colleague in writing *The Federalist Papers*, has co-opted Washington's government and is running it akin to a British monarchy. He becomes so obsessed by Hamilton's activity that he secretly drafts a resolution which he encourages Virginia's William Giles to introduce in the House:

Resolved: That the Secretary of the Treasury has been guilty of maladministration in the duties of his Office, and should, in the opinion of Congress, be removed from his office by the President.

Madison continues to see Hamilton's evil hand manipulating John Adams' term in measures like the Alien and Sedition Acts of 1798, at which point he throws himself into building the Democratic-Republican Party. His goal remains a "national government," but one that won't run roughshod over those standing in opposition to the will of the executive branch. Jefferson later comments on his dedication to this cause:

I do not know in the world a man of purer integrity, more dispassionate, disinterested, and devoted to genuine Republicanism; nor could I in the whole scope of America and Europe point out an abler head.

After Jefferson's victory in 1800, he becomes secretary of state for eight years, despite the fact that he never travels abroad in his lifetime. His time is spent in the middle of the conflict between Napoleon and the British, as both nations interfere with American shipping and commerce on the high seas.

Like Jefferson, Madison tilts toward the French. When offered "honorary citizenship" in France after its revolution, he accepts, unlike Washington and Hamilton. He participates in the 1803 Louisiana Purchase and convinces Jefferson that the 1807 Embargo Act will utilize American commerce to help end Europe's war.

In 1808 he is seen by all as the logical choice to succeed Jefferson, who endorses him enthusiastically. However, Madison is more the exceptional legislator than the decisive executive.

Aside from Albert Gallatin, his cabinet is weak. At times he is easily deceived diplomatically both by Britain and by Napoleon, and he fails to prepare the nation militarily for what his critics call "Mr. Madison's War of 1812." But while being forced to watch the British occupy the capital of Washington, he finally rallies the resistance and emerges with a victory in 1815.

One year later he departs the capital, never to visit again. He still has two decades to live, and focuses this time on Montpelier and on a series of final causes.

Financial difficulties plague this period, mainly related to members of Dolley's family who pile up crippling debts, then look to her to bail them out. The main villain in this group is her son, Payne Todd, whom Madison has adopted. The ex-president hopes to turn operations of his tobacco plantation over to Todd, but the young man proves to be a lifelong ne'er-do-well, drinking, gambling, fighting, and being sentenced to debtor's prison.

Madison hopes that the sale of his notes from the 1787 Convention will provide a windfall profit, and he and Dolley work together to organize them. She will eventually sell them to Congress in 1837 for $30,000 and they will be published in 1840.

Aside from the work on his papers, the aging Madison helps Jefferson found the University of Virginia, and serves as its second president from 1826 to 1836. He also helps rewrite Virginia's state constitution in 1829.

Like Jefferson, he is troubled by the concept of slavery while still regarding Black people as inferior to white people, denying their freedom, utilizing their labor to run his tobacco plantation, and, as he says, "selling off another Negro" as need be. He wishes that slavery would end in America, but cannot conceive of social assimilation. As he tells Lafayette in 1826:

> *The two races cannot co-exist, both being free & equal. The great sine qua non therefore is some external asylum for the colored race.*

The only answer lies in buying their freedom and returning them to Africa. With this outcome in mind, he lends his support to the American Colonization Society in 1817.

Over the years, Madison owns some 300 enslaved people, around 100 at any time. In 1834 and 1835 he sells roughly a quarter of them to cover mounting debts. He ponders freeing the rest at his death, but decides that Dolley's financial well-being prohibits manumission.

The "father of the US Constitution" dies at age 85 on June 28, 1836; just six days shy of the 60th anniversary of the Declaration of Independence.

Dolley Madison is forced to sell Montpelier in 1844 to relieve family debts and moves back to Washington. In 1844 she is honored with a permanent visitor's seat on the floor of the House of Representatives, before her death in 1849.

## 32

THE WAR OF 1812 BEGINS

TIME: MARCH 1809 TO SEPTEMBER 1811

BRITAIN AND FRANCE FRUSTRATE MADISON'S ATTEMPTS TO STAY OUT OF WAR

Madison comes into office still believing that access to trade with America will be enough of a bargaining chip to avoid war and stop British and French interference with US ships and sailors.

The Non-Intercourse Act he inherits bans trade with both combatants, but also opens the door to resumption should either nation declare its intent to end future aggression.

Over the next year, both will manipulate Madison and his diplomats into believing they are complying with America's wishes.

The British take this tack immediately. On April 19, 1809, the British minister, David Erskine, tells Secretary of State Robert Smith that the crown will no longer interfere with American ships at sea. Madison takes this at face value, and reopens American trade with Britain.

On August 9, however, he learns that Erskine's assurance to Smith was not "official" British policy, and so he reinstates the Non-Intercourse ban.

Ten months later, Napoleon steps up the heat on America in his March 23, 1810 Rambouillet Decree, saying that France will seize and sell all American ships it encounters.

A British soldier

The next move belongs to Madison. On May 1, 1810, he seeks reconciliation with both nations in passage of the so-called "Macon's Number 2 Bill," named after its sponsor, Nathaniel Macon, a House member from North Carolina.

This bill seeks a return to normalcy, re-opening trade with both France and Britain.

But with one caveat. Madison still wants public confirmation that interference with American ships has been "officially prohibited" and he offers a "carrot" aimed at getting his way. Should either Britain or France openly announce a favorable change in policy, America will resume the trade embargo on its opponent.

Now it is Napoleon's turn to manipulate Madison. On August 5, 1810, he instructs his foreign minister to tell the Americans that he will renounce future interference with shipping, if they will cut off trade with Britain. At the same time, he secretly orders the seizure of all American ships currently in French harbors.

Madison naively takes Napoleon at his word, and, when three months pass without a corresponding message from Britain, he declares on November 2 that shipping to England will end, effective on March 2, 1811.

This enrages the British, who announce plans to step up their impressment activities and even blockade the port of New York.

TIME: MAY 1−16, 1811

NAVAL BATTLES AMPLIFY WAR FEVER

Two back-to-back naval clashes now increase tensions with Britain.

The first occurs in New York Bay, south of lower Manhattan. On May 1, 1811, the frigate HMS *Guerrière*, with its 38 cannons and crew of 350 men, comes upon the USS *Spitfire*, a sloop sporting three guns and some twenty sailors, off Sandy Hook, New Jersey. The *Spitfire* is stopped and boarded, and an American-born seaman, sailing master John Diggio, is impressed.

An American warship

The second incident, on May 16, involves bloodshed. The American navy now has its guard up as the frigate USS *President* encounters what it erroneously believes to be HMS *Guerrière* off the coast of North Carolina. An exchange of fire follows, with the two sides disagreeing on who shot first. The British ship—which turns out to be the eighteen-gun sloop, HMS *Little Belt*—suffers eleven killed and 21 wounded in the battle.

Relations with Britain will never recover from these incidents. Both occur at a time when Ambassador William Pinkney has already departed for a visit home, leaving a void in diplomatic relations in London.

At the same time, Napoleon continues to have his diplomats reassure the new US ambassador to France, Joel Barlow, about his peaceful intentions toward America.

TIME: NOVEMBER 7, 1811

BRITISH-BACKED SHAWNEE TRIBE DEFEATED AT THE BATTLE OF TIPPECANOE

In addition to the confrontations at sea, suspicions grow that British Canadians are building alliances with Native tribes along the northern border to impede westward settlements.

Going all the way back to 1794, the burden for handling Indian affairs in the Northwest Territory has fallen on the shoulders of William Henry Harrison, son of the former Virginia governor, Benjamin Harrison V. His army career includes numerous battles on the frontier and involvement in a series of negotiations often leading to the forced cession of tribal lands to the United States.

In 1799, at age 26, he is elected to represent the Northwest Territory in the 7th US Congress. His friend, Sec-

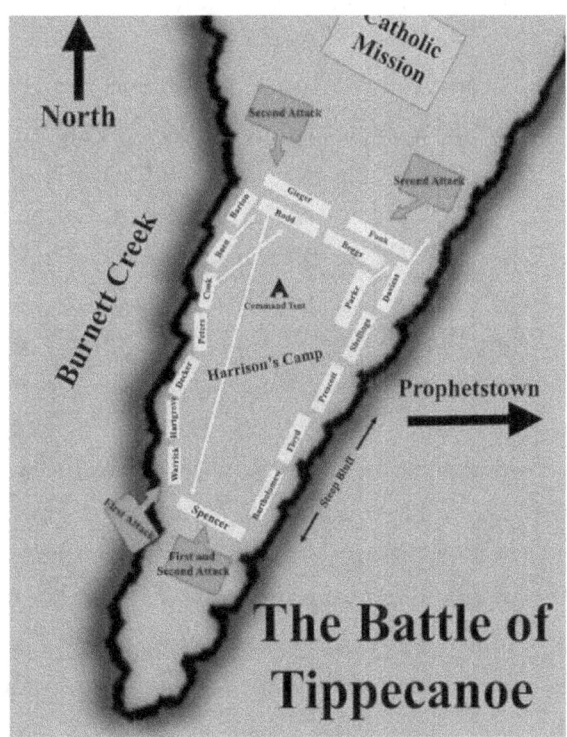

The attack on Harrison's camp
west of Prophetstown

retary of War Thomas Pickering, encourages John Adams to name him governor of the Indiana territory in 1801. Jefferson keeps him on because he seems willing to help the tribes learn agriculture and to become assimilated peacefully. Over time his land negotiations lead to adding millions of acres from Ohio to Wisconsin.

SOME OF THE INDIAN LAND CESSIONS NEGOTIATED BY WILLIAM HENRY HARRISON

YEAR	TREATY OF:	MAIN TRIBES	LAND CEDED TO US
1795	Greenville	Ten tribes together	16.9 million acres, Ohio + strip west to Chicago
1804	Vincennes	Miami and Shawnee	1.6 million acres in central Indiana
	St. Louis	Fox and Sauk	5.0 million acres in Wisconsin
1809	Ft Wayne	Delaware and Miami	3.0 million in eastern and western Indiana

Of course the very notion of "owning land" remains foreign to the Indians, and resistance to these cessions builds as white settlers begin their occupation. In the Great Lakes region, it is the Shawnee tribe that fights back most aggressively. They are led by the charismatic shaman Tenskwatawa, called "The Prophet," and his older brother, Tecumseh.

Tecumseh realizes that promises of support for Native peoples from "the Great Father" in Washington, DC always vanish when the time comes to deliver. In July 1811, he begins to organize a confederation of tribes intent on driving the settlers out and restoring the Indian traditions and way of life. In turn, they tell Harrison that the Ft. Wayne cession is invalid and that they intend to fight for the land. They also signal that their cause is being supported by British allies in Canada.

To prepare for battle, Tecumseh gathers some 5,000 warriors on Miami land in Indiana, near the confluence of the Tippecanoe ("buffalo fish") and Wabash Rivers. This site is called "Prophetstown" by Harrison, and he sets out with a force of 1,000 troops to conquer it in September 1811.

On November 6, 1811, he encounters a tribal delegation near Prophetstown under a flag of truce. At the time, Tecumseh is in the southwest, attempting to recruit more support from the Cherokees. The two sides agree to meet again the next day.

Instead, at 4 a.m. on November 7, the Indians initiate a surprise attack behind The Prophet on Harrison's camp, huddled just east of Burnett Creek. The battle rages for two hours, with the Americans falling back initially and suffering heavy casualties. But unlike Tecumseh, Tenskwatawa is more a religious leader than a warrior. So Harrison rallies his troops, breaks out of his initial trap, and eventually burns Prophetstown to the ground.

This victory at Tippecanoe will insure national fame for William Henry Harrison as a frontiersman who has successfully defeated both the hostile tribes and their British allies.

The truth is much more modest than the legend. Actual losses for each side total only 100 fighters, and the outcome does little to divert Tecumseh and his band from continuing to attack white settlers in the region.

Another two years will pass before Tecumseh's confederation is finally subdued for good at the Battle of the Thames, Harrison's true landmark victory.

TIME: 1811–1813

THREE POLITICAL GIANTS ENTER
THE HOUSE OF REPRESENTATIVES

The buildup to, and outbreak of, the War of 1812 witnesses the emergence of three politicians who will shape US foreign and domestic policy over the next four decades.

Calhoun, Webster, and Clay

Henry Clay and John C. Calhoun enter politics as Democratic-Republicans, before later founding their own political parties in opposition to President Andrew Jackson. Calhoun starts up the "Nullifier" Party in 1828 and Clay begins his Whig Party in 1834.

Daniel Webster is a rock-ribbed Federalist who eventually joins the Whigs while moving back and forth between public office and his lucrative law practice.

Each man will become the leading spokesman for his region of the country—Webster for the Northeastern states, Calhoun for the South, and Clay for the new West. All three play critical roles during the War of 1812 and later on as regional differences over slavery threaten to tear the Union apart, with Clay and Webster trying to hold it together and Calhoun eager to have his South secede.

Along the way they will also battle back and forth for the presidency, Clay running on five occasions, Webster three times, and Calhoun twice. But each man's long and often controversial track record in public office invariably leads to defeat.

Together they will earn their reputation as "the Great Triumvirate."

TIME: JUNE 4, 1812

CONGRESS DECLARES WAR ON BRITAIN

Tensions with Britain continue to build after the two naval encounters in May and the Tippecanoe battle in November, 1811. At this point, Madison is being carried along by calls for war with Britain emanating from the public, the politicians, and his generals.

His new secretary of state, James Monroe—appointed on April 2, 1811 after Robert Smith is ousted—is a former frontline officer in the Revolutionary War and ready to take on the British again.

He is joined by two new members of the House, Henry Clay and John C. Calhoun, who together rally a faction in Congress known as the "War Hawks."

If Britain is not only threatening US shipping, but also encouraging Indian resistance, then America surely needs to respond with force.

As always, when conflict with Britain arises, special attention is focused on Canada.

Many see the continued presence of the British along the northern border as "unfinished business" from the Revolutionary War. They inhibit the growth of America's fur trading industry, provoke tribal resistance on the frontier, and present an invasion threat by garrisoning troops across forts along the border.

This threat becomes even more real throughout the winter and spring of 1812 by importation of British regulars and increased recruiting of local militia across Canada.

On April 10, 1812, Congress gives Madison authority to call up to 100,000 troops from state militias, should the need arise.

American and British diplomats attempt to search for peaceful ways out, but the sticking issue always comes back to impressments. Britain says that it must continue to retrieve its nationals serving on American ships in order to win its naval battles with the French. As much as Madison wants to believe that American commerce is worth more than impressed sailors, this is never the case with the British.

By now, public opinion has swung almost entirely away from the one policy espoused by every president from Washington through Madison—that of maintaining "neutrality in foreign conflicts" and avoiding what Jefferson called the non-productive costs associated with war.

War (is) but a suspension of useful works, and a return to a state of peace, a return to the progress of improvement

The only remaining opposition to war lies with the New England merchants, who regard the prospect as even more fatal to their business prospects than the Jefferson-Madison embargoes.

Finally, the time for compromise runs out. On June 1, 1812, acting in accord with the Constitution, Madison goes to Congress and asks them to declare war against Britain. His principal reasons why include ongoing impressment of seamen, blockades against American shipping, confiscation of ships, and incitement of the Indian tribes in the Northwest territories.

The actual voting, however, is hardly unanimous. The House supports the war measure by 78–45; the Senate is much closer, with passage by only 18–13. The outcome is determined on June 4 along party lines—with no Federalists supporting the president.

Conjecture remains about exactly why the Democratic-Republicans—viscerally anti-war by nature—come to be in favor of taking on the powerful British once again. Perhaps the most likely explanation lies in the lingering wish to remove Britain from Canada once and for all. This, and a belief that an inland war could be won easily and quickly, while America's navy was now strong enough to hold its own against the British fleet in battles close to home.

With passage of the bill, the War of 1812 is about to begin.

TIME: JULY 4, 1812

THE FEDERALIST DANIEL WEBSTER ATTACKS MADISON'S DECISION AND PREPAREDNESS

New England looks for a powerful spokesperson against the war, and they find one in the Federalist, Daniel Webster, a 30-year-old lawyer from New Hampshire who is on his way to becoming a major political figure in Washington, D.C. over the next four decades.

On July 4, 1812, in a speech to the Washington Benevolent Society, Webster assails the president for leaping blindly into a very dangerous war the nation is ill-prepared to fight.

In what will become his usual dramatic fashion, the speech begins by citing the seriousness of the hour, the wisdom of Washington in regard to avoiding warfare, and the woeful lack of preparation for battle.

Daniel Webster

In an hour big with events of no ordinary impact we meet. We come to take counsel of the dead… to listen to the dictates of departed wisdom.

We are in open war with the greatest maritime power on earth. This is a condition not to be trifled with.

Washington embraced competent measures of defence, yet it was his purpose to avoid war. Would to God that the spirit of his administration might actuate this government.

With respect to the war, resistance and insurrection can form no part of our creed. The disciples of Washington are neither tyrants in power, nor rebels without. We are yet at liberty to lament the commencement of the present contest.

We believe that the war is premature and inexpedient. Our shores are unprotected; our towns exposed. It exceeds belief that a nation thus circumstanced should be plunged into sudden war.

He cites the damage to the US economy likely to follow from the conflict.

The voice of the whole mercantile interest is united against the war. We believe that it will endanger our rights, prejudice our best interests.

He also states that, in opposing Britain, America would be strengthening Napoleon's forces, which might soon be redirected against America.

Nor can we shut our eyes to the prospect of a French alliance. That we should make common cause and assist her to subdue her adversary and to extend her chains and despotism over the civilized world seems to be a dreadful departure from true wisdom and honest politics. French brotherhood is an idea big with horror and abomination. What people hath come within the grasp of her power and not been ground to powder?

He closes by calling upon the sons of New England to stand up against the war.

But if it be in the righteous counsel of heaven to bury New England, her religion, her governments, and her laws under the tyranny of foreign despotism, there are those among her sons who will never see that moment.

They cannot perish better than standing between their country and the embrace of a ferocious tyranny. At the appointed hour, they shall, for the last time, behold the light of the sun not with the eyes of slaves or as subjects of an imperious despotism.

Indeed, time will show that while Madison believes an easy victory will follow, he has woefully failed to prepare a military force sufficient to carry the day.

The US Army numbers only 12,000 regulars. Therefore, much of the fighting will often depend on poorly-trained state militias. The US has the largest "neutral" fleet in the world, but it will be no match for the Royal Navy. And since Congress has shut down the US Bank, Madison's access to funding the war is constrained.

Fortunately for Madison, the British are similarly ill-equipped to fight.

In June 1812 the bulk of their ground forces are attacking the French in Spain, under the future Duke of Wellington. Only 6,000 redcoats have been left behind in North America to defend various Canadian forts. Likewise, the British navy has its hands full trying to enforce the blockade of cargoes flowing into France.

TIME: JULY 12 – AUGUST 16, 1812

THE WAR IN WESTERN CANADA BEGINS BADLY

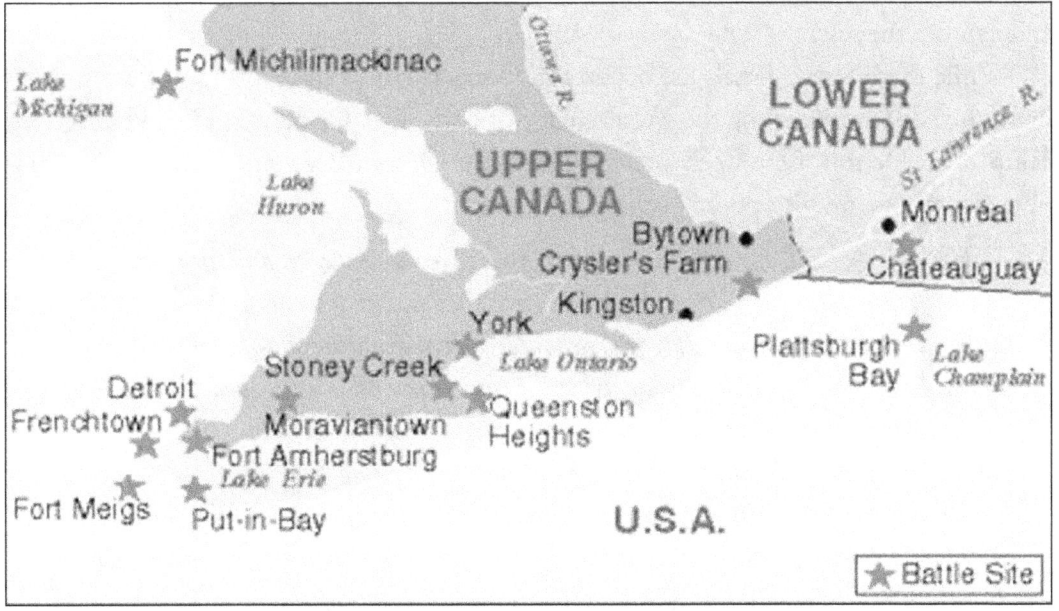

The War of 1812 begins along the Canadian border

As in the war with Britain in 1775, America assumes that a quick strike into Canada will succeed, and perhaps even cause the British to back away from further fighting. As Jefferson says:

The acquisition of Canada this year will be a mere matter of marching.

So the battle begins, with the opening gambits along the western edge of Lake Erie and north into Lake Huron.

Things immediately go badly for the US forces.

On July 17 a contingent of 200–300 British and Indian warriors land on Mackinac Island and surprise Lt. Porter Hanks and the American troops garrisoned at Ft. Michilimackinac, who surrender posthaste on the belief that they are badly outnumbered. Soon after two US sloops are also taken when they come into port believing that the fort is still in friendly hands. Porter is subsequently court-martialed for cowardice, but is killed by a British shell while still under arrest.

Command of the "Army of the Northwest" lies with Brigadier General William Hull, a Revolutionary War veteran praised by Washington, and presently governor of the Michigan territory. But Hull is 59 years old and has tried, unsuccessfully, to avoid the "offer" from Secretary of War Eustis to return to combat.

When Hull learns of the Mackinac Island debacle, he fears that Ft. Dearborn in Chicago may also be attacked and overrun. He orders the immediate evacuation of the fort. On August 15, some 66 soldiers and 27 women and children evacuate under a flag of truce, only to be set upon by Potawatomi warriors who kill over half of the Americans and capture the rest.

While these two reversals are occurring, General Hull and 2,500 troops are preparing to invade Canada along the western edge of Lake Erie. On July 5, 1812 Hull sets up camp at Ft. Detroit. One week later he crosses the Detroit River and issues a proclamation meant to scare his opponents into submission:

> *INHABITANTS OF CANADA: After thirty years of peace and prosperity, the United States have been driven to arms. The injuries and aggressions, the insults and indignities of Great Britain have once more left no alternative but manly resistance or unconditional submission. The army under my command has invaded your country. The standard of the union now waves over the territory of Canada. To the peaceful and unoffending inhabitants it brings neither danger nor difficulty. I come to find enemies, not to make them; I come to protect not to injure you... I have a force which will break down all opposition, and that force is but the vanguard of a much greater. If, contrary to your own interest, and the just expectations of my country, you should take part in the approaching contest, you will be considered and treated as enemies, and the horrors and calamities of war will stalk you.*

Once on Canadian soil, Hull sends out various probes that encounter resistance from a mixture of British regulars, local militia, and various tribesmen, notably Tecumseh.

By August 9, the setbacks convince Hull that he cannot advance into Canada without more troops and cannons, and he retreats over the river to Ft. Detroit.

By now, however, the British are ready to go on the offensive and chase him. They assemble a force of some 300 regulars, 400 militia, and 600 Indians at the Canadian town of Amherstburg, then head out after Hull and his remaining 2,200 men at Detroit.

The redcoat commander, Major General Isaac Brock, decides to bluff Hull into believing he is surrounded by overwhelming opposition. His dispatch to Hull also raises the specter of uncontrollable slaughter waged by his tribal bands:

The force at my disposal authorizes me to require of you the immediate surrender of Fort Detroit. It is far from my intention to join in a war of extermination, but you must be aware, that the numerous bodies of Indians, who have attached themselves to my troops, will be beyond control the moment the contest commences...

On August 15 Brock fires on the fort, using the few cannons at his disposal along with support from two Royal Navy sloops on the nearby river. One day later he follows up with demonstrations led by Indian war whoops intended to spook the Americans.

These succeed immediately. Hull has his daughter and grandchild in the fort, and fears repeat of the slaughter at Ft. Dearborn. He asks Brock for three days to arrange for surrender; Brock gives him three hours.

When news of the capitulation at Detroit reaches Washington, DC, Hull is arrested and his command is handed to William Henry Harrison. A subsequent court-martial sentences Hull to death, but his sentence is commuted by Madison, in light of his long service during the Revolution and his advanced age.

All of these setbacks—Mackinac, Ft. Dearborn, and Detroit—occur as the two parties pick their candidates for the election of 1812.

TIME: 1806-1852

SIDEBAR: PROFILES OF THE "GREAT TRIUMVIRATE"
HENRY CLAY OF KENTUCKY (1777-1852)

After serving two brief stints in the Senate, Henry Clay decides that the House, with its "power over the purse," is where he belongs. In 1811, he is elected to the lower chamber at age 33. On his first day there, March 4, 1811, he is chosen as Speaker of the House by a 75–38 margin, a signal recognition of his intellect and his ability to find middle ground between his Democratic-Republicans and the Federalist opposition. He will serve his country in Washington, DC over a 46-year span, until his death.

Clay is born on April 12, 1777, in eastern Virginia, where his family has lived for 150 years. His first home is a modest-sized plantation with

25 enslaved people, situated in Hanover County near a swampy area known as "the Slashes." When Henry is fourteen years old, his family moves west to Kentucky, leaving him behind to find his way in the world. He moves to Richmond, where he first works in an emporium and then lands a job clerking at the state's high court chancery.

Clay's formal education is minimal, but he is intensely curious about the world, naturally gregarious, and meticulous, especially when it comes to his handwriting. This latter trait recommends him to Judge George Wythe, who suffers from a crippled hand and is looking for a private secretary. Clay lands the job and stays with the judge over a four year period.

Wythe has signed the Declaration of Independence, and become a classical scholar at the College of William & Mary, where he mentors a host of political leaders, including Thomas Jefferson and James Monroe. He transforms Clay intellectually, socially, and inspirationally during their four years together, and prepares him for a career in law. He also advises Clay on slavery, touting the idea that education must accompany freedom if the problem is to be solved. Clay's posture on the dilemma tends to mirror Jefferson's. On one hand he decries it as an evil practice all his life:

> *Can any humane man be happy and contented when he sees nearly thirty thousand of his fellow beings around him, deprived of all rights which make life desirable, transferred like cattle from the possession of one to another… when he hears the piercing cries of husbands separated from wives and children and parents. The answer is no…*

But he too will continue to buy and own enslaved people up to his death, when he finally embraces Wythe's solution: granting emancipation and supporting education and employment for those freed.

In 1797 Clay passes the bar, heads west to visit his family, and settles down in the well-established town of Lexington. Once there, both his civil and his criminal law practice take off. So begins his lasting reputation as Shakespeare's "Prince Hal;" a good fellow, well met, ready to drink, gamble on cards and horses, and share his opinions with all comers. In 1799 he marries Lucretia Hart, adding both wealth and enslaved people in the process. He joins the law faculty at Transylvania College and enters politics in 1803, winning a seat in the Kentucky State Assembly that he will hold for six more years.

In 1806 his national notoriety grows by successfully defending Aaron Burr against charges of treason filed by the Kentucky district attorney.

Ill will over this support for Burr partially accounts for the first of two non-fatal duels Clay will instigate during his career. On January 19, 1809 he exchanges three shots with another legislator, Humphrey Marshall, leaving both men with slight wounds.

Within Democratic-Republican circles, he is known as the "Rising Star of the West."

As a leader of the "War Hawk" faction, he supports Madison's call to war with Britain in 1812.

JOHN C. CALHOUN OF SOUTH CAROLINA (1782–1850)

If Clay brings a western perspective to Congress, John C. Calhoun will become a leading spokesperson for the more conservative partisans of the South across his four decades in office.

He is born on March 18, 1782 in Abbeville, South Carolina, a frontier settlement in the northwest corner of the state abutting Georgia. His ancestors are Scots-Irish immigrants who put down roots in Long Cane, some thirteen miles to the south, before being driven out by hostile Cherokees. His father, Patrick Calhoun, Jr., a survivor of the Cherokee's Long Cane massacre of 1760, builds a cotton plantation worked by his family and 30 enslaved people. Patrick is also active in the state legislature and known for strong Anti-Federalist positions.

John C. Calhoun is raised as a Presbyterian, with its Calvinistic emphasis on hard work, personal discipline, stern demeanor, and a rather bleak view of human nature. He is frail as a youth and drawn early on to academics rather than farming. At first his formal education is limited, but his parents recognize his bent and enroll him at Yale University in the autumn of 1802. While there, his Calvinist traditions come up against early strains of Unitarianism, with its emphasis on beliefs born of rational, independent thought.

He graduates from Yale in 1804 and soon moves on to Litchfield Law School in Connecticut, run by its founder, Tapping Read, whose students include both Calhoun and Aaron Burr. Ironically, Read is an outspoken supporter of a strong national government, something his two famous graduates come to question.

In 1807, Calhoun is back in South Carolina and practicing law when the British frigate HMS *Leopard* attacks the USS *Chesapeake* off the Virginia coast and impresses four of her sailors. Calhoun organizes a protest meeting held at the Abbeville courthouse and delivers a stirring speech in favor of an embargo against Britain and preparations for war. This entry into the political arena leads to two terms of service in the South Carolina state legislature.

At this time he is also falling in love with his first cousin once removed, Floride Bonneau Colhoun, later famous for her outspoken moral rectitude in the 1830 "Petticoat Affair." The strait-laced suitor is uncharacteristically affective in his pursuit of Floride:

> *My dearest one, may our love strengthen with each returning day, may it ripen and mellow with our years, and may it end in immortal joys. … May God preserve you. Adieu my love; my heart's delight, I am your true lover.*

The two marry and move into her 1,100-acre Fort Hill Plantation in the foothills of the Blue Ridge Mountains as Calhoun is about to become a political fixture in Washington. He arrives there soon after the Twelfth Congress convenes on November 4, 1811. Like most congressmen of the time, he resides at a boardinghouse. His is named "the War Mess" and shared with his new colleague and ally, Henry Clay of Kentucky.

His administrative skills are immediately apparent to all, as is his willpower. He is appointed to the House's Foreign Affairs Committee and soon becomes its chair. On June 3, 1812 he sums up the feelings of his fellow committee members toward the recent British aggression:

> *The mad ambition, the lust of power, and commercial avarice of Great Britain, arrogating to herself the complete dominion of the Ocean, and exercising over it an unbounded and lawless tyranny, have left to Neutral Nations—an alternative only, between the base surrender of their rights, and a manly vindication of them… (The committee) feels no hesitation in advising resistance by force—In which the Americans of the present day will prove to the enemy and to the World, that we have not only inherited that liberty which our Fathers gave, us, but also the will & power to maintain it.*

DANIEL WEBSTER OF MASSACHUSETTS (1782–1852)

The third member of the triumvirate who assume political leadership from 1810 to 1850 is Daniel Webster, whose famous oratory captures the sentiments of the elite Federalist establishment in New England.

Webster's antecedents emigrate from Scotland to New Hampshire in 1637. His father, Ebenezer, fights in the French & Indian War and in 1761 carves out a 225-acre farm on the western frontier in the town of Salisbury. In 1775 he organizes the Salisbury Militia and leads it throughout the Revolutionary War. Back home, Eben serves in the New Hampshire state legislature and as an elder in the Congregational Church.

Daniel Webster is born on January 18, 1782, Eben's fourth child. The boy adores his father, who tells him tales of the patriotic war, reads to him from the Bible, and encourages his penchant for learning. Unlike his father, young Webster is frail, more prone to books than farming. In 1796 he is admitted to Phillips Exeter Academy, being placed at the bottom of his class for want of Latin. One year later he has risen to the top rank before being called back to Salisbury to begin working as a teacher.

He escapes this fate with the help of a local minister, Thomas Thompson in nearby Boscawen, who agrees to tutor him for one dollar a week. In 1797 he enrolls at Dartmouth College. Once there, Webster comes fully into his own. His self-confidence grows—some would say into arrogance—and he uses his powerful memory and love of words to become a dominant public speaker and debater. Classmates label him their "ablest man."

After graduating, he is prodded into pursuing a legal career by his father. Webster himself sees the profession as filled with cunning and hypocrisy and says "I pray to God to fortify me against its temptations."

But his feelings change in 1804 when he goes to work in Boston for Christopher Gore, ex-attorney general of Massachusetts, who has made a fortune in financial speculation around Revolutionary War bonds and in representing dispossessed Loyalists in property disputes. Webster regards Gore as a genuine legal scholar to be emulated, and Gore encourages the youth to stick with the law and aim high in his career.

In 1805 Webster passes the bar and opens a law practice in Boscawen. His talents as a trial lawyer are soon evident to all, and his annual income soars to over $2,000 a year.

The courtroom becomes his stage, a place to show off both forensic logic and a love of language, accumulated over years of reading and memorizing doses of the Bible, Shakespeare, and John Milton. One of his legal adversaries admires his innate theatrical talents:

> There never was such an actor lost to the stage as he would have made, had he turned his talent in that direction.

Webster's legal successes and oratorical skills soon draw him into the political arena, despite his warning in an 1809 Phi Beta Kappa address at Dartmouth:

> The main impediments to moral improvements are love of gold and pursuit of politics.

His father's stories of the revolution make him first and foremost a Union man—and his emotionally charged pleadings to preserve the "great experiment of 1776" will form his lasting legacy.

But politically he is a staunch Federalist. His faith lies in the Constitution, in a strong national government and in visionary leaders like George Washington. In an 1812 convention held by New Hampshire Federalists in Rockingham county, he assails Jeffersonian democracy.

> The path to despotism leads through the mire and dirt of uncontrolled democracy.

He also, prophetically, announces another potential path to doom, this time related to secession.

> If a separation of the states shall ever take place, it will be, on some occasion, when one portion of the country undertakes to control, to regulate, and to sacrifice the interest of another.

It is finally the impending war with Britain that draws Webster onto the political stage. He is elected in 1812, at age thirty, to represent New Hampshire in the House.

Once in Washington, he boards with two influential senators: his former mentor, Christopher Gore, and Rufus King of New York.

Unlike Clay and Calhoun, Daniel Webster will be a sharp critic of Madison's preparations for and management of the War of 1812.

## 33

NAPOLEON REACHES HIS ZENITH BEFORE A CRUSHING LOSS IN RUSSIA

TIME: 1806–1811

NAPOLEON CONTROLS ALL OF EUROPE BY 1811

"Mr. Madison's War" results directly from the existential threats posed to Britain by Emperor Napoleon of France. This leads Britain to interfere with American ships and "impress" American sailors in order to man the Royal Navy, to stop a French invasion.

The British have every reason to fear since, between 1806 and 1811, the French empire expands unabated.

By 1807 it controls all of central Europe, after Napoleon and his Spanish ally capture Lisbon on December 1 and the royal family of Portugal transfer their regency to the colony of Brazil.

Further intrigue follows in February 1808, as Napoleon makes a move he has long avoided: he turns against Spain. The betrayal catches the Spanish army by surprise and it quickly gives way. However, bloody public uprisings occur in many cities, including Madrid, and lead to the reprisal executions later immortalized by the artist Francisco Goya. It is not until May 5, 1808 that Napoleon is able to name his older brother, Joseph-Napoléon, king of Spain.

While the local Spanish population refuses to bend to the French will and guerrilla ("little war") actions supported by British expeditionary forces persist over time, Joseph is able to remain on the throne until the tide turns against the French in 1812–1813.

To the east, the Austrian monarch Francis II, loser at Austerlitz, decides to challenge Napoleon once again. He does so in 1809 at Wagram, six miles northeast of Vienna, in a fierce artillery-dominated battle that covers July 5–6, involves

300,000 men, and counts 80,000 casualties—with the French once again emerging victorious.

By 1811, Napoleon's power is at a zenith.

He has effectively isolated Britain from its three potential "coalition partners" on the continent—Austria, Prussia and Russia—by thrashing their armies and by signing peace accords with each.

The only things limiting France's horizons are the presence and superiority of the British navy—and the small chance that Napoleon will eventually make a strategic blunder.

NAPOLEON'S TRIUMPHS IN 1807 TO 1811

1807
Battle of Friedland—Napoleon beats Russia
Peninsular campaign—Napoleon beats Portugal
1808
Napoleon turns on ally Spain, Joseph-Napoléon Bonaparte on throne
1809
Fifth Coalition versus Austria and Britain
Battle of Wagram   Napoleon beats Austria, occupies Vienna
Napoleon divorces Josephine, marries Marie-Louisa of Austria seeking heir
1811
Napoleon and France rule the European continentTime: June 1812 to December 1812

SIDEBAR: FRANCE SUFFERS A CRUSHING DEFEAT IN RUSSIA

In June 1812 Napoleon makes the strategic mistake that will cost him his empire.

When Russia, encouraged by Britain, withdraws from Napoleon's continental blockade of English goods, the emperor decides to invade. He assembles a huge army of over 400,000 men (half French, half foreign conscripts), and begins to march east on June 24, 1812. The Russians retreat at first, under a scorched earth strategy led by Michael Andreas Barclay de Tolly, Russia's minister of war. When troop morale deteriorates, command passes to the 67-year-old veteran, General Mikhail Kutuzov.

Kutuzov has suffered two horrible head wounds in battle, which leave his right eye misshapen and cause him constant pain. He has also fought Napoleon before, losing at Austerlitz, which leads Alexander I to doubt his talents. But Kutuzov is a native Russian, much beloved by the troops, and he is charged with resisting the French approach to Moscow.

By the time Napoleon is ready to attack, the strength of the central army wing under his direct command has already dwindled sharply from a combination of battles, winter cold, dysentery, and typhus.

At 5:30 a.m. on September 7, 1812, his remaining 130,000 men attack Kutuzov's 120,000 troops just west of Borodino, some 65 miles from Moscow. Both generals blunder during the day— Kutuzov's troop deployment is flawed and Napoleon refuses to send in his Old Guard to finish off the battle. It turns into a bloodbath, with French losses at 30,000 and Russian losses at 44,000.

After Kutuzov retreats, Napoleon continues his march to Moscow, reaching the city on September 14. But by that

Napoleon (1769–1821)

time only 15,000 of the city's population of 270,000 have stayed behind, the mayor has put the torch to most of the buildings, and both food and shelter are in short supply.

Napoleon is now some 1,500 miles from Paris and 600 miles from his starting point for the invasion, the Niemen River in Poland. What was the Grande Armée 400,000-strong in July has been reduced to 95,000 tired and starving men eight weeks later.

When Alexander I refuses to discuss a treaty to end the conflict, an exhausted Napoleon decides to exit Moscow on October 19. The road back west is tortuous and marked by death from ambushes, starvation, and disease. While various commanders cite the winter weather as a sizable factor in the defeat, the first snowfall is not recorded until November 5 and temperatures tend to hold in the 15–20 degree Fahrenheit range until early December.

On December 14, 1812, the survivors of the Russian campaign recross the Niemen. Most estimates peg this number at around 30,000 men.

In less than five months Napoleon has suffered over a quarter million dead and wounded and another 100,000 captured. He has lost Russia. And he has forever lost his mantle of invincibility.

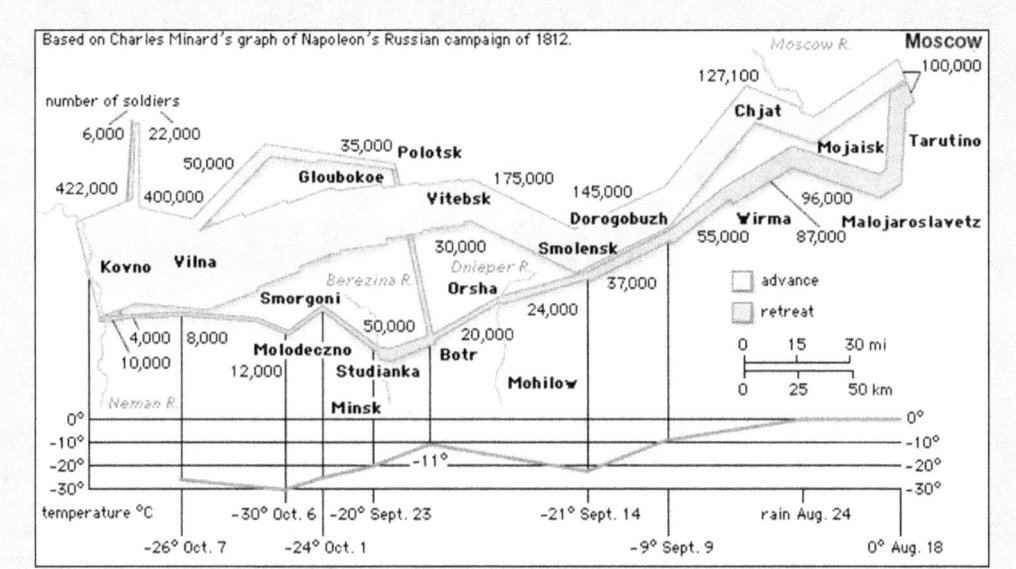

A statistical map of the Russian campaign

## 34

AMERICA WINS
THE WAR OF 1812

TIME: 1812

MADISON IS REELECTED BY A NARROW MARGIN

With things going badly on the battlefield, Madison faces the prospects of a close race for reelection.

Before it takes place, the voting landscape is again altered based on the 1810 Census and the addition of Louisiana to the Union. The data show that the nation's population grows to 7.24 million in 1810, up 36% from 1800.

US POPULATION (MILLIONS)

YEAR	TOTAL	WHITE	FREE BLACK	ENSLAVED BLACK
1800	5.308	4.306	0.108	0.894
1810	7.24	5.863	0.186	1.191
% Change	+36%	+36%	+43%	+33%

With the admission of Louisiana in April 1812, America has a total of eighteen states, nine where slave ownership is permitted and nine where it is banned.

AMERICA'S EIGHTEEN STATES AS OF 1812

Region	Slavery	States
South	Yes	Virginia, North Carolina, South Carolina, Georgia, Tennessee, Louisiana
Border	Yes	Maryland, Delaware, Kentucky
North	No	New Hampshire, Massachusetts, New York, New Jersey, Pennsylvania, Rhode Island, Connecticut, Vermont
West	No	Ohio

With each state allotted two senators, the upper chamber totals 36 members.

SENATE SEATS AFTER CENSUS REAPPORTIONMENT AND NEW STATES

YEAR	TOTAL	SOUTH	BORDER	NORTH	WEST
1790	26	8	4	14	0
1800	32	10 (TN)	6 (KY)	16 (VT)	0
1810	34	10	6	16	2 (OH)
1812	36	12 (LA)	6	16	2

The House allocations are more complicated. As people move from east to west, population shifts from state to state, affecting reapportionment. In the House, a total of seven new seats are added between 1810 (prior to the Census update) and 1812 (after it). The North picks up five seats, the South loses seven, and the migration of settlers into Kentucky almost doubles Border state representation.

HOUSE SEATS AFTER CENSUS REAPPORTIONMENT AND NEW STATES

YEAR	TOTAL	SOUTH	BORDER	NORTH	WEST
1790	65	23	7	35	0
1800	106	38	11	57	0
1810	175	65	11	92	7
1812	182	58	21	97	6

In turn, the sum of senate seats (36) and house seats (182) yields a total of 218 votes in the Electoral College for the 1812 presidential race, assuming all delegates cast ballots. The nine non-slavery states account for 121 votes or 56% of the total.

APPORTIONMENT OF ELECTORAL COLLEGE VOTES AS OF THE 1812 ELECTION

YEAR	TOTAL	SOUTH	BORDER	NORTH	WEST
1812	218	70	27	113	8

The Federalists have high hopes of making a political comeback by throwing Madison out of office.

This possibility has been gaining credibility as cracks appear in the Democratic-Republican party over the failure to resolve tensions with France and Britain. When the initial congressional caucus meets in May, 1812, only 86 of the party's 134 House and Senate members participate, although they do nominate Madison. The question then turns to choosing a vice presidential candidate to replace George Clinton, who has recently died in office. Many favor his nephew, DeWitt Clinton, currently serving his third term as mayor of New York City. But Clinton fails to jump at the chance, and they end up choosing Elbridge

The Presidents of the United States.

Gerry, former governor of Massachusetts, recently famous for redrawing district voting boundaries in his state ("gerrymandering").

Soon enough it becomes clear why DeWitt Clinton has passed up the Democratic-Republican nomination; the Federalists are slating him at the top of their ticket!

He is 43 years old, a former US Senator, and master of New York politics. In 1812 he has already begun to lobby for a project that will forever be associated with his name—construction of the 325-mile Erie Canal, linking inland Albany with the port at Buffalo.

As expected, the campaign revolves around the embargoes and the war, with the Democratic-Republicans defending their record and the Federalists attacking. In the North, Clinton focuses on the economic damage caused by Madison's trade policies; in the South, he assails the president for mishandling the war effort.

After General Hull's embarrassing losses in the West, it is only a few successes by the US Navy in autumn that restores some public faith in Madison prior to the election.

The Federalists' strategy almost succeeds. Clinton wins 49% of the popular vote, along with 89 of the total 217 electoral ballots cast. Madison dominates the South and gets a crucial win up North in Pennsylvania to ensure a second term.

RESULTS OF THE 1812 PRESIDENTIAL ELECTION

1812	PARTY	POP. VOTE	ELECTORS	SOUTH	BORDER	NORTH	WEST
James Madison	Dem-Rep	140,431	128	70	18	33	7
DeWitt Clinton	Federalist	132,781	89	0	9	80	0
Rufus King	Federalist	5,574	0	0	0	0	0
		278,786	217	70	27	113	7
Needed to Win			109				

Note: South (VA, NC, SC, GA, TN, LA), Border (DE, MD, KY), North (NH, MA, NY, NJ, PA, RI, CT, VT), West (OH) Total # electors = 217; must get more than half to win = 109.

Control over both chambers of Congress remain with the president, although Federalists dramatically strengthen their hand in the House.

CONGRESSIONAL ELECTION OF 1812

HOUSE	1811	1813	CHANGE
Democratic-Republicans	107	114	7
Federalist	36	68	32
SENATE			
Democratic-Republicans	30	28	(2)
Federalist	6	8	2
President	Madison	Madison	
Congress #	12th	13th	

Meanwhile, in Congress, the elections of 1810 and 1812 mark a profound changing of the political guard at the national level, with Henry Clay, John C. Calhoun, and Daniel Webster rising to leadership positions.

Madison's second term will be dominated by the war with Britain and some adjusted thinking about the virtues of a standing army and a federal bank.

KEY EVENTS: MADISON'S SECOND TERM (MARCH 4, 1813 TO MARCH 4, 1817)

1813	
March 11	Tsar Alexander offers to negotiate peace, but Britain rejects the overture
April 27	Americans capture and burn Canadian capital of York on Lake Ontario
August 30	Opening of Creek War provokes Andrew Jackson to call up Tennessee militia
September 10	Captain Oliver Hazard Perry wins major naval battle at Ft. Erie
September 18	British evacuate Ft. Detroit after Perry controls Lake Erie
October 5	Harrison defeats fleeing British at Battle of Thames; Tecumseh killed
November 4	British Prime Minister Castlereagh suggests negotiations; Madison picks John Quincy Adams and Clay to lead
November 16	Blockade of American ports along Atlantic coast extended and intensified
December 18	Ft. Niagara falls to British forces
1814	
January 27	Congress agrees to calling up a 62,000-man army after Madison asks for 100,000.
February 9	Treasury secretary steps down to travel to England for peace negotiations
March 27	General Andrew Jackson ends Creek War with victory at Horseshoe Bend
March 31	Madison recommends repeal of the Embargo and Non-Importation Acts
April 6	Napoleon is overthrown in France, freeing British forces to fight in America
July 3	General Jacob Brown's forces move north to take Ft. Erie from the British
July 5	An American victory at Chippewa slows the British advance south to retake Ft. Erie
July 22	Harrison's Treaty of Grenville ends war with Tecumseh's confederation
July 25	Britain's move toward Ft. Erie is delayed in the war's bloodiest battle at Lundy's Lane
August 8	Direct peace negotiations begin in northern Belgium at Ghent
August 24	In the east, American forces are routed at the Battle of Bladensburg
August 25	The British occupy Washington, DC and burn parts in return for the earlier destruction of York
August 27	Madison names James Monroe as interim war secretary replacing Armstrong

September 14	Baltimore withstands attacks by land and sea; Key writes Star Spangled Banner poem
September 17	British abandon siege of Ft. Erie, ending war activities in the Canadian theater
December 15	Federalists issue secession threat at the Hartford Convention
December 24	The Treaty of Ghent officially ends the War of 1812
Year	Francis Lowell opens first US textile mills in Massachusetts
1815	
January 8	After the war is officially over, Andrew Jackson whips the British at New Orleans
February 7	Secretary of navy position in the cabinet is created
March 3	Congress restores open trade with all nations
June 18	Napoleon is defeated at Waterloo
August 5	Captain Stephen Decatur negotiates peace treaty with Tunis to end naval conflicts
December 5	Madison urges congress to support a second US Bank, a strong army, infrastructure work
1816	
January 8	Clay and Calhoun now support US Bank while Webster opposes it
March 14	Congress approves Second Bank of US to open January 1, 1817
March 16	Democratic caucus nominate James Monroe over William Crawford for president
April 11	Black people in Philadelphia open African Methodist Church, first church independent of white control
April 27	Tariff Act passed to protect American manufacturing, with Clay and Calhoun supporting it
October 27	William Crawford named secretary of the Treasury
December 4	James Monroe is elected president
December 11	Indiana is admitted to the Union (#19)
December 28	American Colonization Society founded to send African people to Liberia
1817	
January 1	Second Bank of the US opens in Philadelphia
March 3	Madison vetoes a bill to spend federal funds on infrastructure, calls it unconstitutional

TIME: JUNE 4, 1812 – JANUARY 15, 1815

THE THREE THEATERS OF WAR

America's War of 1812—or "Mr. Madison's War," as it is called by the Federalists—will drag on for two and a half years before a truce is signed.

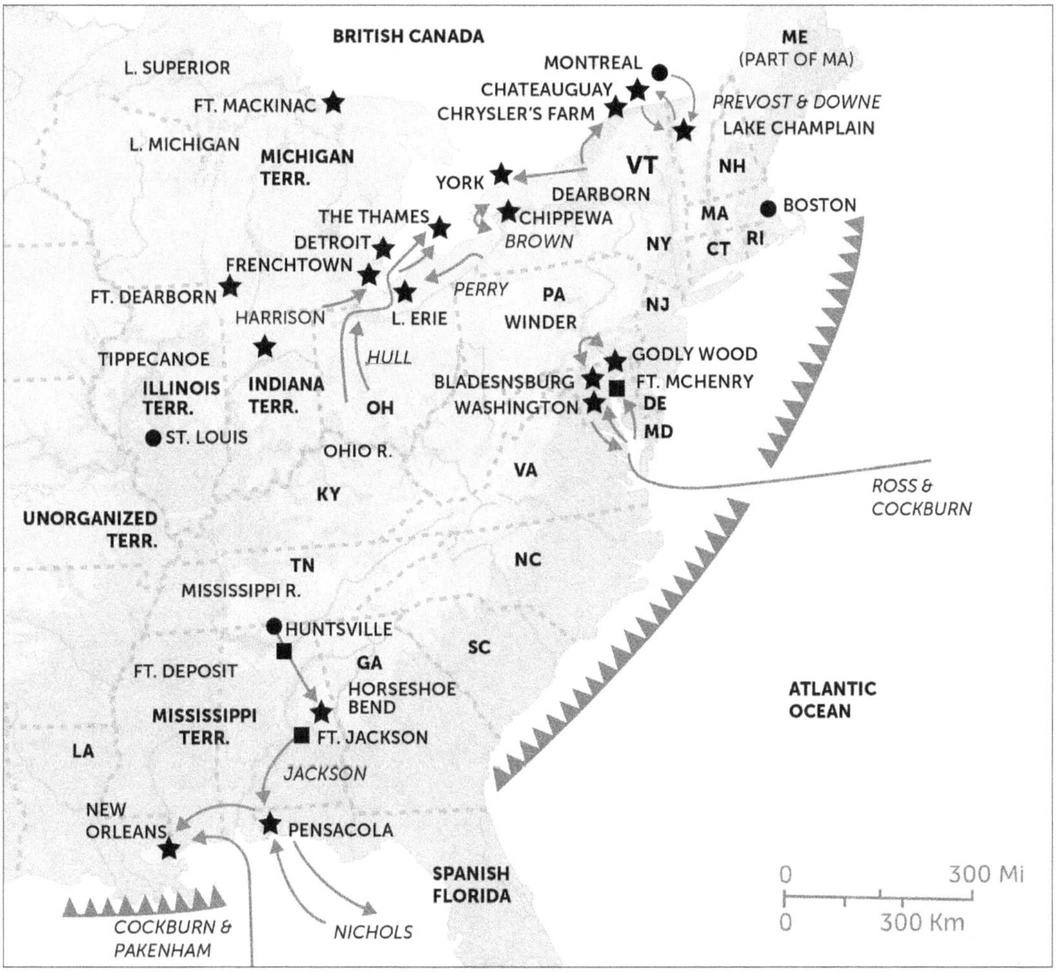

The three theaters in the War of 1812

It is fought on land and water in three separate theaters and phases:

- Along the Canadian border—with the US trying to invade north, and Britain, with certain tribal allies, threatening territories from Ohio to Michigan.
- On the Atlantic coast—featuring the British naval blockade and eventually leading to the short-lived thrusts against Washington, DC and Baltimore.
- In the deep South—culminating in a landmark battle around New Orleans.

It will end when both sides recognize that the costs of continuing to fight outweigh the realistic gains left to be had.

An 1812 war survivor named Lenaux

TIME: AUTUMN TO WINTER 1812

THE WAR ALONG THE BORDER IS STALEMATED

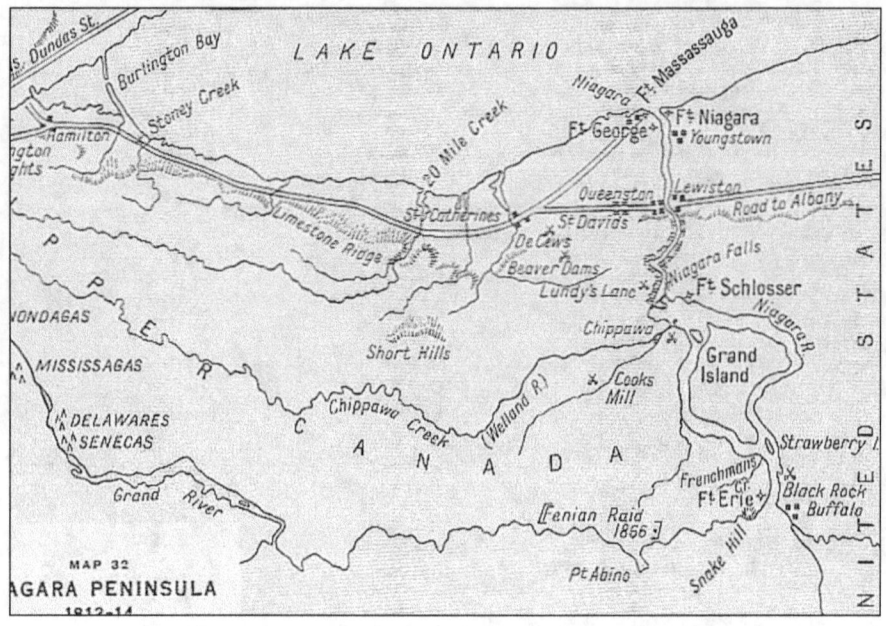

Battle sites from Ft. Niagara (Lake Ontario) to Ft. Erie (Lake Erie)

What Madison and Secretary of War Eustis expect to be easy victories along the western edge of Lake Erie around Ft. Detroit have turned into a string of humiliating defeats capped by the August 16 surrender of the garrison and the firing of General William Hull.

The next American attack takes place on October 13, 1812, some 200 miles to the east of Detroit at Queenston Heights, just north of Niagara Falls. It pits a new US commander, General Stephen Van Rensselaer, and his 3,500 troops against some 1,300 British regulars and Mohawk warriors under Major General Isaac Brock, who had thrashed Hull eight weeks earlier.

Van Rensselaer is a political appointee with limited training in warfare. His attack is a poorly planned attempt to move from the east via Lewistown across the Niagara River and up a 300-foot incline to the entrenched British defenders. As the Americans cross over by boat, they come under withering fire from the British. Van Rensselaer fights heroically while being hit six times by musket balls. But only a fraction of his forces cross the river, the bulk cowering safely on the other side. Finally, those who crossed are forced to surrender.

The Americans suffer 270 killed or wounded and another 800 captured; British losses are around 100 men, most notably General Brock, who dies leading a charge. Van Rensselaer survives his wounds but resigns his command.

These reversals drive increased criticism of Adams' secretary of war, William Eustis. Madison wishes to replace him with Secretary of State James Monroe, a Revolutionary War combat veteran, but Monroe declines. So instead, on January 13, 1813, Madison chooses John Armstrong, former Revolutionary War fighter, senator from New York, and ambassador to France. But Armstrong is also a controversial figure. The Senate confirms him by a narrow 18–13 margin, and he will be replaced eighteen months later for failing to defend Washington.

TIME: SPRING TO AUTUMN 1813

AMERICA SCORES VICTORIES AT YORK, THE NIAGARA FORTS, AND DETROIT

It is not until the spring of 1813 that fortunes begin to turn for the Americans in the Canadian theater. The strategy belongs to Armstrong, and it involves gaining control of Lake Ontario.

On April 27, 1813, General Zebulon Pike, the western explorer, sails from Sackett's Harbor along with 1,700 troops to capture the provincial capital town of York (Toronto), situated on the northwest edge of the lake. The disorganized British defenders are quickly overwhelmed, although Pike is killed when they blow up their own magazine to keep it out of American hands. Over the next two days the US forces plunder and set fire to private homes and to the Legislative Assembly—a favor the British will return sixteen months later in Washington.

Once York is secured, the American forces turn south to the two key British forts along the Niagara River, Ft. George on the southern shore of Lake Ontario and Ft. Erie some 25 miles below it on Lake Erie.

The defenders of Ft. George expect the Americans to bombard and attack from their base at Ft. Niagara on the east side of the river. But instead they come in landing craft on Lake Ontario, led by Lt. Colonel Winfield Scott, whose gallantry in the battle earns him lasting fame.

On May 27 the British commander, fearing encirclement, abandons Ft. George and retreats south past Niagara Falls and toward Ft. Erie.

Ft. Erie is the oldest British bastion in Ontario, and it is supported by Royal Navy vessels under Commander Robert Barclay. On the morning of September 10, 1813, he steers his six-ship flotilla into a line of battle engagement with nine smaller US ships under Admiral Oliver Hazard Perry. By 3 p.m., the Americans have won the day, and Perry sends off a message to General William Henry Harrison, leading ground troops against the fort itself:

> *General. We have met the enemy and they are ours. Two ships, two brigs, one schooner and one sloop. Yours. Perry*

The Battle of Lake Erie is modest in size, but strategically important. It signals America's growing naval strength and it inhibits potential British and tribal incursion into Ohio, Pennsylvania, and western New York.

Next comes an equally important victory, back west toward Detroit, in the Battle of the Thames.

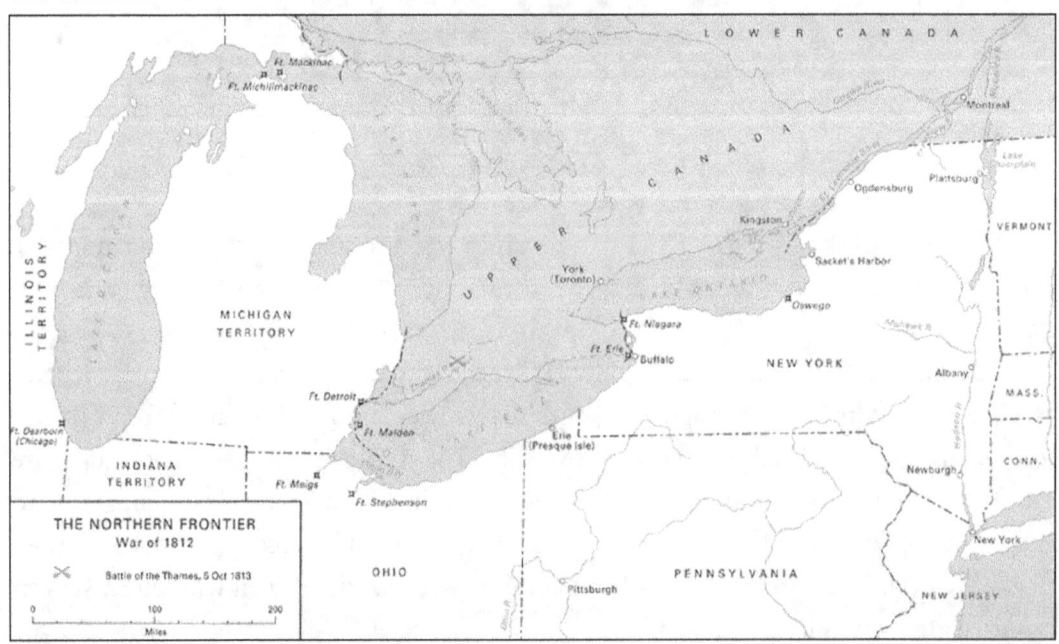

With Perry and the American fleet now in control of Lake Erie, the British garrison at Detroit is immediately vulnerable. The commander, Major General Henry Proctor, moves his 800 regulars inland, to the east along the Thames River. He is accompanied by a contingent of some 500 mostly Shawnee warriors led by Tecumseh.

Harrison's forces number 3,700 men, and he comes onto the retreating British on October 5, 1813 in a swampy area some 65 miles upriver near the town of Thamesville.

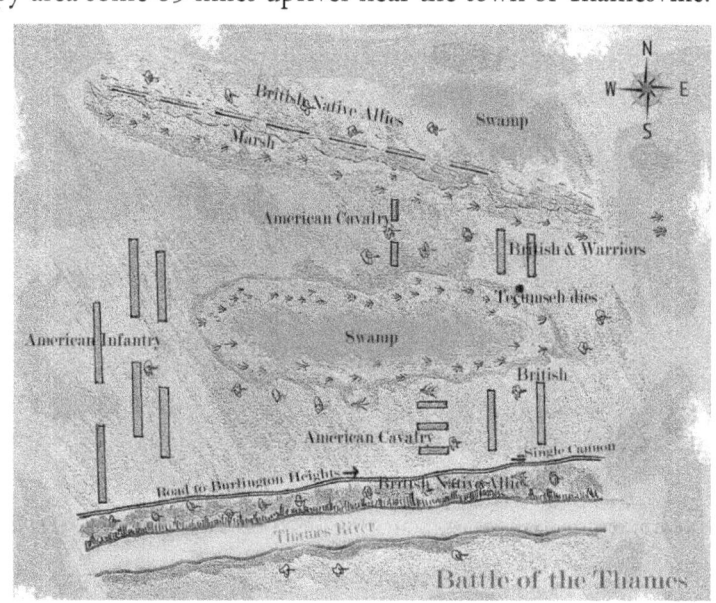

The redcoats are half-starved, fire off a few desultory rounds, and then surrender. Not so for the Shawnees.

They put up stiff resistance led by Tecumseh, who dies in battle. His death ends the threat of coordinated tribal and British action against the northwestern territories. And it propels the victorious "Tippecanoe" Harrison even further into the national spotlight.

After Thames, the Americans are happy to let the border war with Canada stabilize.

TIME: WINTER 1813 TO SUMMER 1814

A DRAWN BATTLE AT LUNDY'S LANE ENDS FIGHTING ON THE BORDER

But now the British refuse to cooperate.

By December 1813, they have retaken control of Ft. George along with America's Ft. Niagara, and begin to consolidate their forces for a drive south down the Niagara River toward Ft. Erie.

By July 5 they are some sixteen miles north of the fort when their progress is halted by American forces under General Winfield Scott at the Battle of Chippewa. Both sides suffer over 300 casualties before the redcoats withdraw from the field.

Three weeks later, on July 25, 1814, the fighting resumes, this time at Lundy's Lane in the bloodiest single battle of the war. The site of the clash is in Canada, roughly two miles west of Niagara Falls, the border line between New York to the east and Ontario to the west.

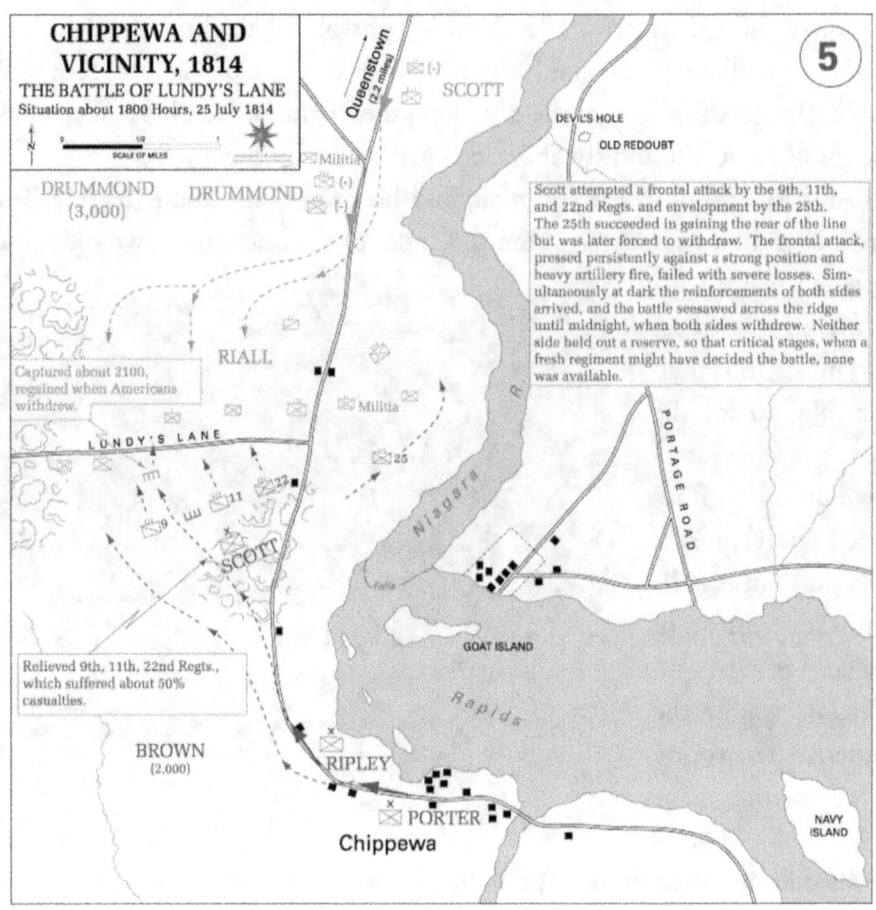

The battle at Lundy's Lane (Ontario) some two miles west of Niagara Falls

This engagement pits 3,500 British troops under Generals Drummond and Riall against 2,500 American troops under General Jacob Brown who come out to meet them.

This battle lasts from morning to midnight, ending in a standoff. Casualties approach 875 men on each side. Among those severely wounded is Winfield Scott, whose military drilling and leadership have earned him the lasting moniker of "Old Fuss and Feathers."

While both generals claim victory at Lundy's Lane, the British continue their march south and begin a siege of Ft. Erie, occupied since July 13 by the US troops under General Edmund Gaines. The siege lasts for a month before the British lift it on September 17, 1814.

At this point the conflict along the Canadian border is essentially over.

The easy victories that Madison expected in 1812 have never materialized. However, the Americans have proven again that they can hold their own with Great Britain, even in modest naval actions like the Battle of Lake Erie.

And, with the death of Tecumseh, they have diminished the threat of a tribal coalition backed by the British impeding westward expansion from Ohio to the Mississippi.

WAR OF 1812: KEY EVENTS ALONG THE CANADIAN BORDER

1812	
July 12	Americans under Hull cross Detroit River into Canada
July 17	British capture Ft. Mackinac in Hull's rear
August 16	Hull surrenders Ft. Detroit without a shot fired
October 13	British win Battle of Queensland Heights, near Niagara Falls
1813	
January 13	Secretary of War Eustis resigns
January 18–23	Battle of Raisin River (Monroe, MI), US prisoners massacred
April 27	US captures York (Toronto) and plunders the town
May 27	Americans capture Ft. George on Lake Ontario
September 10	US Admiral Perry wins Battle of Lake Erie
October 5	William Henry Harrison wins at Thames, killing Tecumseh
December 19	British fight back, taking Ft. George and Ft. Niagara
1814	
July 13	Americans occupy Ft. Erie
July 25	Bloody battle at Lundy's Lane, a standoff
August 14	British begin siege of Ft. Erie
September 17	British retreat from siege

TIME: SUMMER 1812 TO SUMMER 1813

BRITAIN ROUTES AMERICAN FORCES ON THE ATLANTIC COAST

Britain's Royal Navy dominates the second theater of war—on the seas off the Atlantic coast—with a blockade that essentially shuts down America's international commerce, and leads to a secession threat by the New England states.

When hostilities break out, the British have 85 warships already patrolling American waters to enforce their ban on cargoes headed toward France.

The United States, on the other hand, begins with a fleet of 21 ships, comprised of eight frigates and thirteen smaller escort ships. The frigates are light, fast, three-masted vessels each with one deck of 28–44 guns, while the escort ships—war sloops, brigs, and schooners—have 12–18 guns apiece. But no "ships-of-the-line," the three-masted, multi-decked 74-gunners built for broadside attacks.

A British redcoat

With this limited force, all the Americans can hope to do is occasionally break out of their ports and go after an isolated foe.

And one such opportunity arises early in the war, on August 19, 1812, when the frigate USS *Constitution*—44 guns and 456 sailors under Captain Isaac Hull—wins an intense five-hour battle with the 38-gunned HMS *Guerriere* off the coast of Halifax. This victory, the first of five that the *Constitution* will record over British warships, earns the frigate its lasting sobriquet, "Old Ironsides."

But this British defeat proves an anomaly, and the Royal Navy gradually expands its stranglehold on the east coast sea lanes. By the end of 1812 they have shut down American shipping from the Chesapeake Bay, marking the Virginia coast through South Carolina. In April 1814 they extend their tight blockade north into New England, which further stirs opposition to Madison's conduct of the war in Massachusetts and Connecticut.

Both states have refused to place their militia under the federal War Department, and, in turn, Madison has denied them federal funding support for their own defense.

This further prompts the question: Is the government effectively protecting the nation?

In August 1814, the entire nation is reminded of the mortal danger posed by the powerful British navy.

By this time, the war against France has turned and Britain is able to free up more land troops to fight the Americans. One of these is the Dublin-born Major General Robert Ross, who has fought valiantly alongside Wellington and now commands all army troops.

Along with his naval counterpart, three-star Vice Admiral George Cockburn, Ross plans a two-pronged assault aimed at his opponent's heart, the capital city of Washington.

The plan involves a naval flotilla consisting of four ships-of-the-line and twenty more frigates and war sloops under Admiral Alexander Cochrane, along with transport boats to carry Ross and his 4,400 men, mostly veteran royal marines, to land.

On August 19, Ross disembarks at Benedict, Maryland and begins marching northwest toward the town of Bladensburg, about ten miles above Washington on the east branch of the Potomac River. Once there they encounter an American force consisting of 6,500 Maryland militia and 400 US regulars under Brigadier General William Winder.

The Battle of Bladensburg on August 24, 1813 proves to be one of the greatest routs in American military history. Winder has aligned his troops poorly and they are decisively thrashed by Ross. Lacking a planned line of retreat, the US forces turn tail and make a dash for Washington, DC ten miles to the southwest. This flight, which includes both President Madison and Secretary of State Monroe, is immortalized as "the Bladensburg Races" in a satiric British poem in 1816.

Away went Madison, away Monroe went at his heels,
And all the while his laboring back, a merry thumping feels.

TIME: SUMMER 1813 TO AUTUMN 1813

BRITISH SACK WASHINGTON BUT ARE TURNED BACK AT BALTIMORE

But the worst is yet to come on this day. At Washington, DC.

Secretary of War Armstrong is certain that the British will never reach the capital, and has made no preparations to defend it.

Ross' troops arrive in the capital by evening on the August 24 and are shot at when they approach under a truce flag. This leads to a 26-hour rampage in which the Capitol, the White House, and the US Treasury are all pillaged and burned—in return, the British claim, for similar destruction of their provincial capital of York in April, 1813.

With the US government stunned and momentarily homeless, Ross and his troops exit Washington to rejoin Admiral Cochrane's flotilla on August 26 and take aim at their second objective, capturing the critical port city of Baltimore.

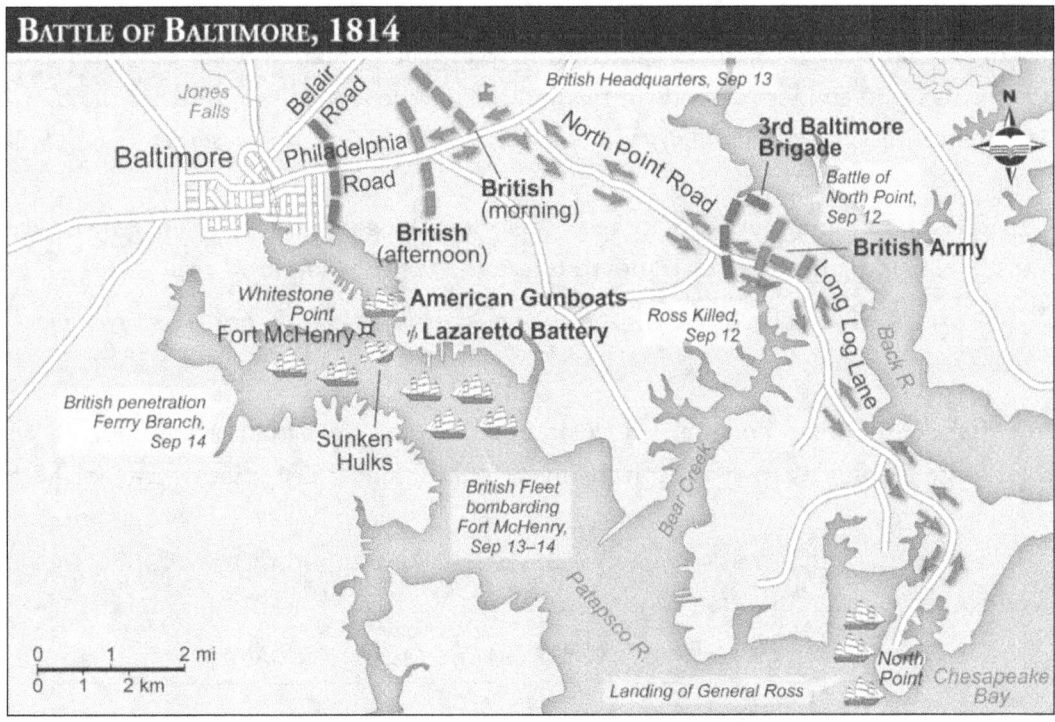

The British attack on Ft. Henry and Baltimore

On September 12, Ross disembarks at the town of North Port on Chesapeake Bay, twelve miles southeast of Baltimore. But now the Americans are ready for him.

General John Stricker has laid out a strong defensive position between North Port and redoubts around the city, marked by tidal swamps and creeks that force the British to funnel through a narrow strip of land, where his 3,200 Maryland militiamen wait.

While the battle ends after two hours with the Americans withdrawing, the British suffer a crucial loss when General Ross is mortally wounded by a musket round that strikes him in his right side.

On September 13, the Battle of Baltimore hangs in the balance.

The now 5,000-strong British ground troops under Colonel Arthur Brooke encounter very stiff resistance at Hampstead Hill from what has grown to be 11,000 militiamen, led by Generals Stricker and William Winder. At 3 a.m., Brooke concludes that the initiative is lost and begins to withdraw his men.

Meanwhile, the Royal Navy is encountering similar opposition on the water.

Admiral Cochrane sails his nineteen-ship flotilla into Baltimore Harbor, briefly exchanges cannon fire with the American defenders in Ft. McHenry, and then anchors just beyond the range of the fort's guns.

He then proceeds to bombard the Americans for almost 25 straight hours, until daylight on September 14 when the Americans send aloft an oversized flag signaling their ongoing presence within the fort.

In the harbor, a 35-year-old American lawyer named Francis Scott Key, on board a British ship to conduct a goodwill mission for President Madison, watches the bombardment through the rainy night and wonders what the morning of September 14 will bring.

At dawn, Key glimpses the Stars and Stripes still flying over the ramparts. The Americans have held Baltimore. Key is moved to capture the moment in words.

Oh say does that star spangled banner yet wave o'er the land of the free and the home of the brave?

After the stalemate along the Canadian border and in the harbor at Baltimore, both nations are growing weary of the now two-year-old conflict. The war in the two northern theaters is over.

But one more great battle remains to be fought in the third theater of the war, the deep South, at New Orleans.

WAR OF 1812: KEY EVENTS ON THE ATLANTIC COAST

1812	
August 19	USS *Constitution* defeats HMS *Guerriere*
November	English ships blockade South Carolina coast
December	Blockade extended to Chesapeake and Delaware Bays

1813	
March	Blockade reaches Long Island and Mississippi
1814	
April	Blockade extended to New England
August 24	British invade and burn Washington
September 13–14	US stops British at Ft. McHenry and Baltimore

TIME: SPRING 1814 TO JANUARY 8, 1815

AMERICAN TRIUMPHS ACROSS THE SOUTH END THE WAR

One figure dominates events in the deep South during the War of 1812: Andrew Jackson, Major General of the Tennessee militia.

Jackson is 45 years old when the second conflict with Britain begins. He has been in the militia since fighting in the Revolutionary War at age thirteen and has lived on the western frontier since 1787. He is a natural leader and the right man to lead American forces in the interior.

General Andrew Jackson, the hero of New Orleans

He does so in the two important battles that take place in the deep South—one at Horseshoe Bend in what will become Alabama, the other at the port of New Orleans.

The war is nearing the two-year mark on March 27, 1814, when Jackson approaches an Indian camp nestled in a bend in the Tallapoosa River. The general is accompanied by a force of 2,700 militia and another 600 Cherokee and Choctaw tribesmen.

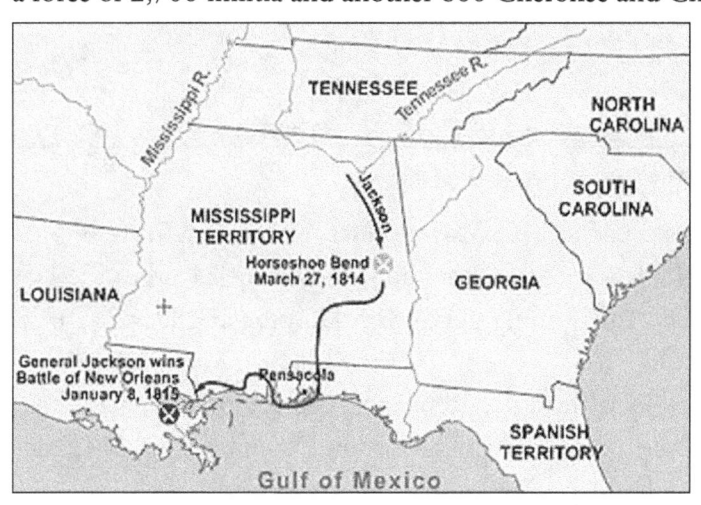

The southern theater in the War of 1812

The encampment they encounter consists of some 700 "Red Stick" Creeks, the tribe that Tecumseh previously recruited to fight alongside his Shawnees and the British.

While the Creeks feel safe surrounded by the river, the fact is that they are trapped in a cul-de-sac, with only one narrow pathway in and out over open ground. When the Red Sticks throw up breastworks to defend this camp entrance, Jackson attacks it repeatedly with artillery and charges. He also sends probes across the river into their rear. After some five hours of battle, the Creeks disintegrate, with over 80% of them being killed, wounded, or captured.

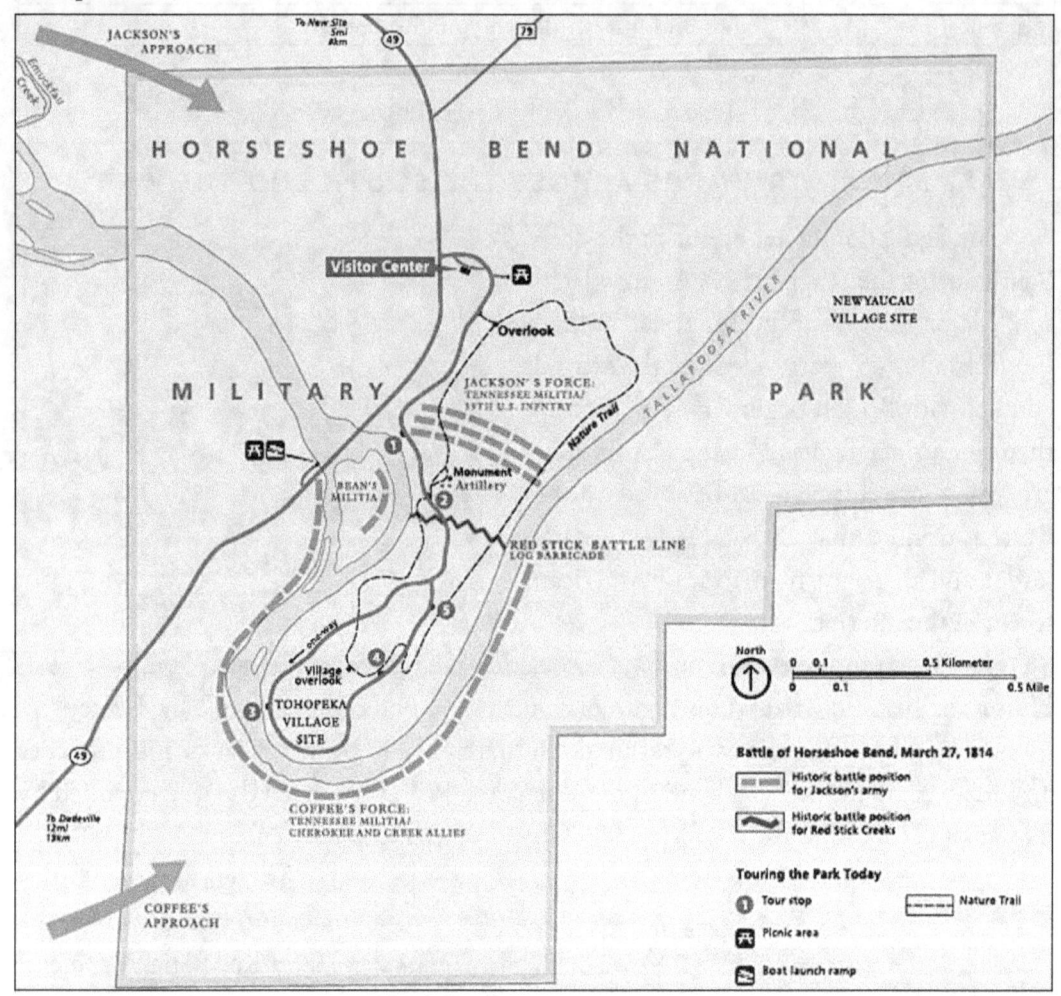

The Battle of Horseshoe Bend

The Battle of Horseshoe Bend ends the Creek resistance, and at the Treaty of Fort Jackson on August 9, the Creek Nation cedes 23 million acres of their land to the US. In addition to Jackson, two other American fighters—Sam Houston and Davey Crockett—win fame from this fight.

Ironically, the other memorable battle in the deep South occurs after diplomats from Britain and the US have signed the peace Treaty of Ghent on December 24, 1814, ending the war.

But the word does not reach America before the British attack is under way.

In late November, General Edward Pakenham, a veteran of the Napoleonic wars and brother-in-law of Wellington, sails from Jamaica with 18,000 crack troops to join the American campaign; his objective being to capture and then govern the city of New Orleans.

But Pakenham and Admiral Alexander Cochrane first need to choose how best to approach the city. One path is to send British ships north some 100 twisting miles up the Mississippi, past Ft. Saint Philip and other outposts, and attack from the south.

The other, which Cochrane chooses, is to locate the fleet in the Gulf of Mexico, just below and to the east of Lake Pontchartrain, and attack overland for some fifteen miles from the east.

On December 12, Cochrane anchors on Lake Borgne at Fisherman's Village and Pakenham disembarks.

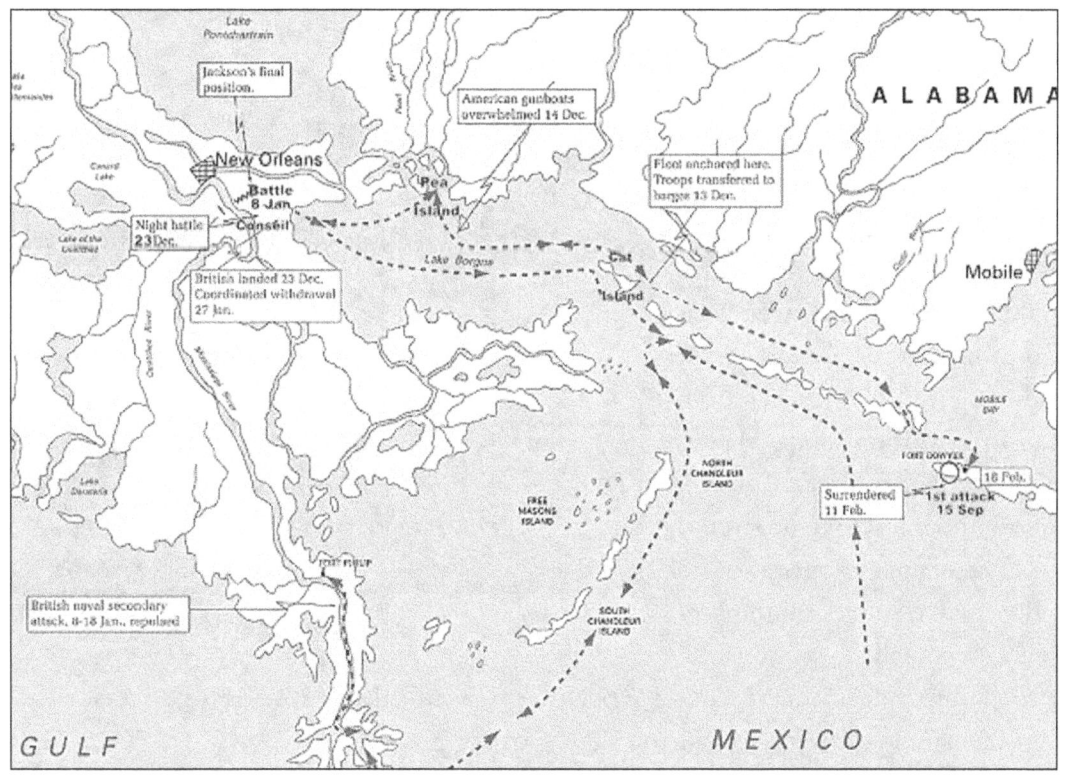

The British and American armies reach the battlefield, seven miles south of New Orleans

However, Pakenham does not race directly toward the prize, instead choosing to proceed at a leisurely pace to set up a base camp and prepare his eventual assault.

This delay gives General Jackson, who doesn't arrive in New Orleans until November 30, the time he needs to organize his opposition.

When he hears on December 23 that Pakenham's advance guard of 1,800 troops under General John Keane have reached the Mississippi at Lacoste's Plantation some seven miles downriver from the city, he sets in motion a three-pronged attack against the encamped British.

His rallying cry at the moment is pure Jackson, the leader of men into battle: "By the Eternal, they shall not sleep on our soil."

The battle on the 23rd proves a standoff, but it slows down the British move north to New Orleans again and gives Jackson even more time to build defensive positions.

On December 28, Pakenham sends out probing attacks to assess the challenge which lies ahead for him.

It is not until January 8, 1815—with all 8,000 troops on hand—that he advances from south to north against the "Jackson Line" set up at Chalmette Plantation five miles below New Orleans.

Jackson's main position is flanked on his right by the Mississippi River and on the left by swampland. He has arrayed his 4,000 militia and sixteen cannons behind breastworks that run roughly 1,000 yards in from the river to the swamp. He has also stationed a force to protect his right flank across the river.

Pakenham's strategy is to drive two separate columns of redcoats straight at Jackson while

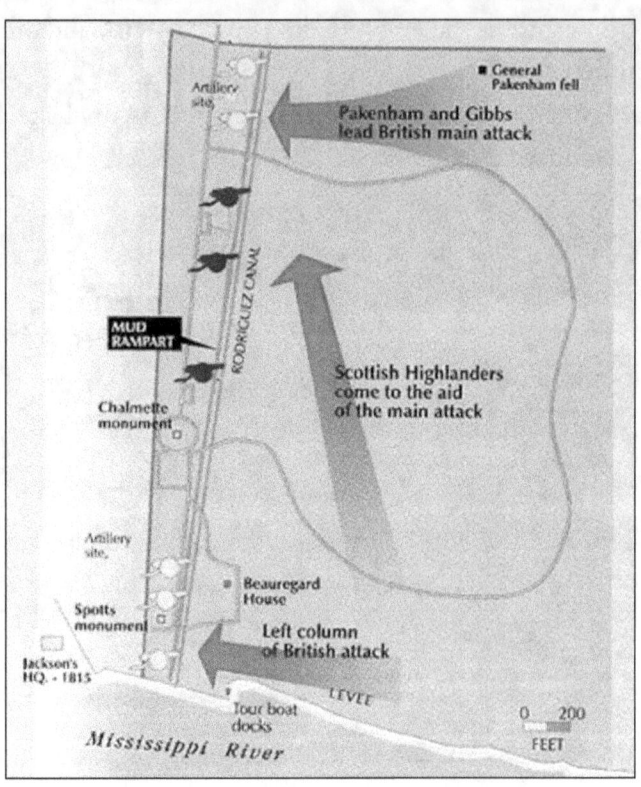

The British assault on Jackson's line of defense

also sending a detachment across the river to try to enfilade the Americans on their right. But the later maneuver develops too slowly for the general.

So he sends his lines forward as the overnight fog lifts on the field, leading to the US positions. First it is General Gibbs with 3,000 men on the British right, who try to force Jackson, but are turned back well short of the ramparts.

Seeing this repulse, Pakenham himself leads Keane's left-side column of 900 highlanders in an oblique march across the face of the American guns to join Gibbs in a second charge. But chaos accompanies this assault as the British command is cut down one by one.

Pakenham is wounded by gunfire in the left knee, then the right arm, and finally is hit by a shell that severs an artery in his leg, bleeding him out in minutes. Gibbs receives a mortal wound in the neck and Keane is also wounded and carried from the field.

Still, the British make a third and final assault on their right, led by a major, the highest-ranking officer left. This time they penetrate all the way into Jackson's lines before being turned back, effectively ending the battle.

Jackson has triumphed and saved New Orleans!

And the casualty figures prove the size of the victory. The defensive-minded Americans suffer 101 killed, wounded, and captured to 2,037 for the attacking British.

After the battle, Andrew Jackson is hailed as a national hero, and begins his trail toward the presidency. Edward Pakenham, a hero of the day in his own right, has his body packed into a preserving cask of rum and shipped home to Ireland for burial.

TIME: DECEMBER 24, 1814

THE TREATY OF GHENT BRINGS PEACE

Henry Clay (1777–1852)   John Quincy Adams (1767–1848)

On December 24, 1814, two American emissaries—John Quincy Adams, serving as ambassador to Russia, and Speaker of the House Henry Clay—sign the Treaty of Ghent with British counterparts, thus ending the War of 1812.

The toll on both sides has been high. Britain has suffered 1,600 killed, 3,700 wounded, and another 3,300 lost to disease; American losses are even higher at 2,260 killed, 4,500 wounded, and 8,000 dead from illnesses. The bill is roughly $100 million for each side.

ESTIMATED CASUALTIES OF AMERICA'S TWO WARS WITH BRITAIN

	YEARS	KILLED	WOUNDED	DISEASE	TOTAL
REVOLUTIONARY WAR	1775–1783				
America		8,000	25,000	17,000	50,000
Britain		4,000	12,000	8,000	24,000
Germans		1,800	3,700	1,700	7,500
WAR OF 1812	1812–1815				
America		2,260	4,505	12,740	20,000
Britain		1,500	3,700	3,300	8,500

And to what end, the costly War of 1812?

Neither side has won new territory from the other, and a major cause of the war—the British practice of seizing American sailors—has ceased after Napoleon's defeat in Russia in 1812.

Still, the United States has some positive things to show for the 30-month conflict:

- The threat to western settlers from Tecumseh's confederated Indian tribes affiliated with Britain has been diminished.
- A series of future national leaders have emerged from the events: Harrison, Scott, and Jackson on the military side and Henry Clay in particular on the political front.
- Of greatest importance, America has once again demonstrated to itself, and to the world, that it has the might and will to hold its own against the powerful British lion.

TIME: DECEMBER 15, 1814 – JANUARY 5, 1815

THE SPECTER OF SECESSION ARISES AT THE HARTFORD CONVENTION

One more fallout from the war is the specter of secession, in this case pitting the Northeast states against the South.

From the opening debate in congress onward, the old-time Federalists of New England have stood in firm opposition to "Madison's War"—a war which has cost their region dearly in terms of lost manufacturing and shipping revenues, and left them feeling vulnerable at any moment to a Royal Navy invasion.

The sack of Washington and the threat to Baltimore over the summer of 1814 heighten their fear and anger.

A powerful trio of Massachusetts' men are outspoken critics of Madison's conduct of the war and its effect on the economy. They include Timothy Pickering, former secretary of state in Washington's cabinet; the Boston lawyer John Lowell, Jr.; and Josiah Quincy, later president of Harvard University.

Others join them in the call for New England to band together and challenge federal operations ad policies.

These ideas are aired at the "Hartford Convention," which is gaveled to order in the Connecticut capital on December 15, 1814.

The convention is chaired by George Cabot, a well-known seaman, merchant, and ex-senator from Massachusetts.

Samuel Hall, a War of 1812 veteran

A total of 26 delegates attend, representing five states—Connecticut, New Hampshire, Rhode Island, Vermont, and Massachusetts. The meetings are held in private over a three-week period and result in a report to be delivered to Congress.

At first glance this final document will appear fairly moderate. It suggests that five Amendments be added to the US Constitution:

1. Prohibit trade embargoes lasting over 60 days.
2. Require a $2/3^{rd}$ vote majority to declare war, impair foreign trade, or admit new states.
3. Limit future presidents to one term.
4. Ensure that future presidents are from different states than the incumbent.
5. End the unfair voting advantage the South has in the House owing to the $3/5^{th}$ slave count.

It is the fifth amendment that quickly stirs regional tensions.

It does so by reopening an old wound—the controversy at the 1787 Constitutional Convention whereby the South was "allowed to count their slaves as semi-citizens" (i.e. the Three-Fifths Enumeration Clause).

The North never quite lets go of this concession, and at Hartford it resurfaces as the source of an "unfair voting advantage" enabling the South to wield more than its fair share of power in Washington.

The result being two more Virginia presidents in a row—Jefferson and Madison—who have imposed trade embargoes and brought on a war that has been ruinous to New England's well-being.

In the face of these "unconstitutional infringements" on the region's wishes, the only recourse left would seem to be breaking with the union or refusing to obey self-destructive laws.

Ironically, this latter option is exactly what John Calhoun and the South will echo down the road, first over the tariff and then over slavery. The states have the "right" to nullify federal statutes detrimental to their well-being.

However, by the time the Hartford Convention report reaches Washington, the outlook for New England's shipping economy is looking up. The war with Britain has ended, and what's left of the French army is straggling back from Moscow. Prospects are suddenly hopeful for a natural return to free and secure trade on the high seas.

Still, the proposed amendments from Hartford will have a residual political effect when the Democratic-Republicans cite them as evidence of Federalist antipathy toward the South and possible disloyalty toward the Union.

## 35

THE END OF THE NAPOLEONIC WARS

TIME: WINTER 1813

JOSEPH-NAPOLÉON IS DRIVEN OUT OF SPAIN

While the military tide in 1812 is turning against Napoleon in the east, it is likewise threatening his brother Joseph's rule in Spain.

The main source of the western threat is none other than the Irishman Arthur Wellesley, destined for future fame as the Duke of Wellington. Wellesley is born into wealth in 1869, educated at Eton, and travels to France to learn horsemanship and to speak French. He wishes to pursue his love of music, but his mother pushes him into the military. He serves multiple tours of duty with the British army in Europe and India, is knighted, and is elected to Parliament. In 1808 he begins a six-year campaign to dislodge France from Portugal and Spain.

Arthur Wellesley, Duke of Wellington (1769–1852)

His efforts bear fruit on July 22, 1812—two days before Napoleon begins his ill-fated march into Russia—when his 52,000-strong coalition army (Britain, Portugal, Spain) defeats the French at the ancient city of Salamanca, 120 miles west of Madrid. The victory makes Wellesley a national hero in Britain, and lays the groundwork for a final drive against the French in Spain.

This culminates on June 21, 1813 at the Battle of Vitoria, in the northwest Basque region of the country.

While Napoleon has been plundering his army in Spain to support the invasion of Russia, General Wellesley has gathered and trained 110,000 troops (52,000 British, the rest from Portugal and Spain).

His attack at Vitoria overwhelms the much smaller French army (60,000 men) under Joseph, and hurls them across the Pyrenees into southwestern France.

All hopes for a French resurgence in Spain disappear in October when Napoleon suffers another major setback in the east, at the Battle of Leipzig.

After Joseph hears of this loss, he officially abdicates the throne of Spain on December 11, 1813.

He will live for another thirty years, first in America from 1817 to 1832 (where he reportedly sells the crown jewels of Spain) and then in Italy where he dies in 1868 and is buried in the Hôtel des Invalides in Paris, along with his younger brothers, Napoleon and Jerome.

TIME: SPRING 1813

SIDEBAR: THE SIXTH COALITION OCCUPIES PARIS

Napoleon's defeat in Russia emboldens the conquered nations of Europe to once again seek their liberation from France.

Prussia makes the first move here, ending its alliance on December 30, 1812, then declaring war on March 16, 1813.

In response, Napoleon assembles a large invasion force and moves east, defeating a combined Prussian and Russian army under General Peter Wittgenstein, first at Lützen on May 2 and then at Bautzen on May 20. Both sides lose roughly 40,000 in these battles.

With the momentum on his side, Napoleon inexplicably agrees to a truce (he calls it "the greatest mistake of my life") which commences on June 4. This gives the allies a chance to regroup and for Austria to join the coalition, tipping the manpower edge against France.

Despite this, Napoleon almost encircles the allied army under Karl Philip, Fürst zu Schwarzenberg of Austria, just outside Dresden on August 26–27. The allies lose almost 40,000 men here to only 10,000 for the French, and were it not for Napoleon's sudden illness, the rout could have been even more devastating.

Six weeks pass before the largest ground battle prior to World War I is fought over a four-day span, October 16–19, 1813, at the Saxon town of Leipzig.

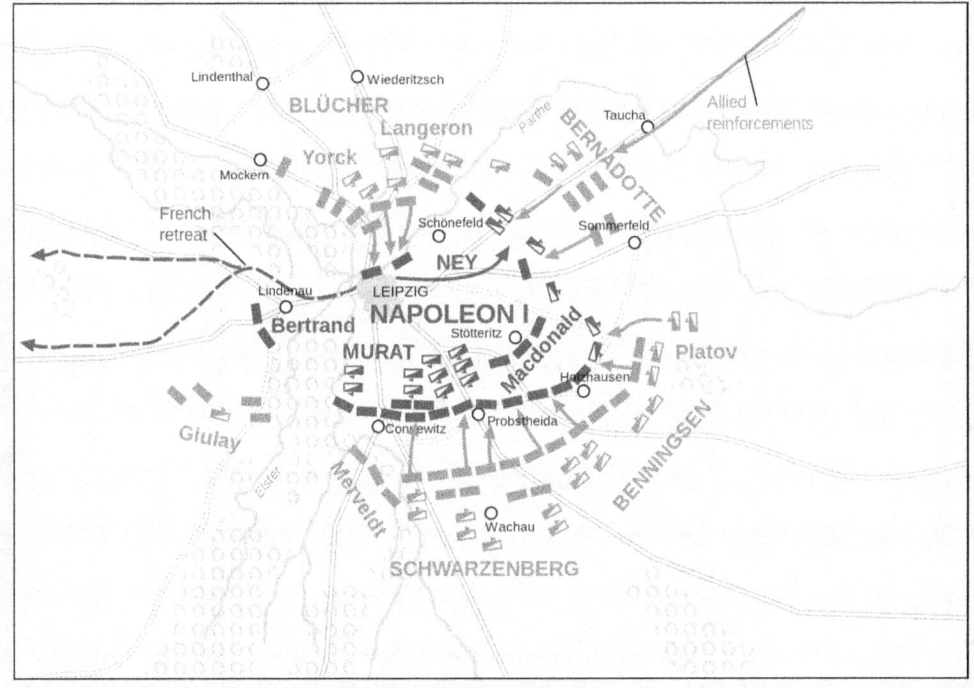

Napoleon is surrounded and retreats at Leipzig

Napoleon fields 195,000 troops, Frenchmen and alliance forces from Italy, Poland, and the German confederation. Together they are led by a host of famous field marshals—Michel Ney, Joachim Murat, Étienne Macdonald, and Józef Poniatowski.

But Napoleon is vastly outnumbered by the 365,000-man coalition army, comprising Russia, under Alexander I; the Austrians, commanded by Schwarzenberg; von Blücher's Prussians; and the Swedes, under Crown Prince Charles John.

The Battle of Leipzig—also known as the Battle of Nations—seals Napoleon's fate.

Over four days the two massive armies fight it out in towns north and south of the central French command in Leipzig. On the morning of October 18 the coalition launches a coordinated attack on all sides that endures for nine hours. By day's end, Napoleon knows that the battle is lost, and he begins a successful retreat westward that continues into the 19th.

The French have suffered 38,000 killed or wounded and another 15,000 taken prisoner; coalition losses are put at 52,000.

Napoleon is now in headlong retreat back across the Rhine toward Paris, with the vastly superior coalition army on his tail.

He has one last moment of brilliance left, in the Six Days' Campaign, from February 10 to February 15, 1814.

The allies have three massive armies coming after him, which means that his only chance lies in beating them in detail. His first move, pitting his 30,000 men against von Blücher's 110,000 some 50 miles northwest of Paris, leads to four consecutive victories.

The allied wave coming his way is now overwhelming. But the coalition is not all together on the endgame it seeks.

Francis I of Austria and his foreign minister, Metternich, hope to conclude a treaty with Napoleon that would cost the French territorial gains but leave the nation strong enough to avoid any chances of an English invasion of Europe.

But Alexander I of Russia wants revenge, with Paris taken, Napoleon both deposed and humiliated, and the French army neutered. In the end, the coalition supports Alexander and marches on Paris. Their cause is helped by assurances to the war-weary population that the goal is to remove Napoleon, not harm the civilians.

After the rear guard resistance is overcome, the allies occupy Paris on March 30, 1814 — the first time it has fallen in nearly 400 years.

TIME: MAY 1814 – MARCH 1815

SIDEBAR: NAPOLEON IS BANISHED TO ALBA BEFORE RETURNING

On April 14, 1814 the French minister, Tall-eyrand, suggests that Louis XVIII, a Bourbon, be chosen to replace Napoleon and to rule under a charter restoring pre-Revolutionary conditions. All sides agree on this option.

This leads to the Treaty of Paris, signed on May 30, 1814, restoring France's 1792 borders and exiling Napoleon to the Isle of Alba, just off the southern coast of France near Corsica, where he was born.

He spends 300 days on Alba before deciding to

King Louis XVIII

return to Paris, in response to rumors of popular uprisings against the monarchy, and fears that his country and army will be victimized by the Congress of Vienna dictates.

On March 1, 1815, he lands with 600 troops near the southern coastal town of Antibes and is back in Paris on March 19, with supporters flocking to his banner and with Louis XVIII in flight.

He quickly holds a plebiscite, showing the world that the French people back him.

His next step will be to restore France to its former preeminence in Europe.

TIME: JUNE 15, 1815

SIDEBAR: THE FRENCH AND COALITION FORCES ARRIVE IN BELGIUM

Despite Napoleon's wishes, the Seventh Coalition countries—mainly Britain, Prussia, Austria, and Russia—will have none of this. They brand him an outlaw and reassemble a huge army to oust him.

True to form when threatened, Napoleon goes on the offensive with his Armée du Nord, 130,000-strong and filled with veterans of his prior victories. He intends to take on the Coalition and attack it in detail, before it is able to concentrate the mass needed to overwhelm him.

He sets his sights on the heavily French-oriented city of Brussels, 160 miles to the northeast of Paris, where he expects to encounter second-tier British troops under Wellesley (soon to be Wellington) and worn-out Prussians under von Blücher.

Field generals at Waterloo

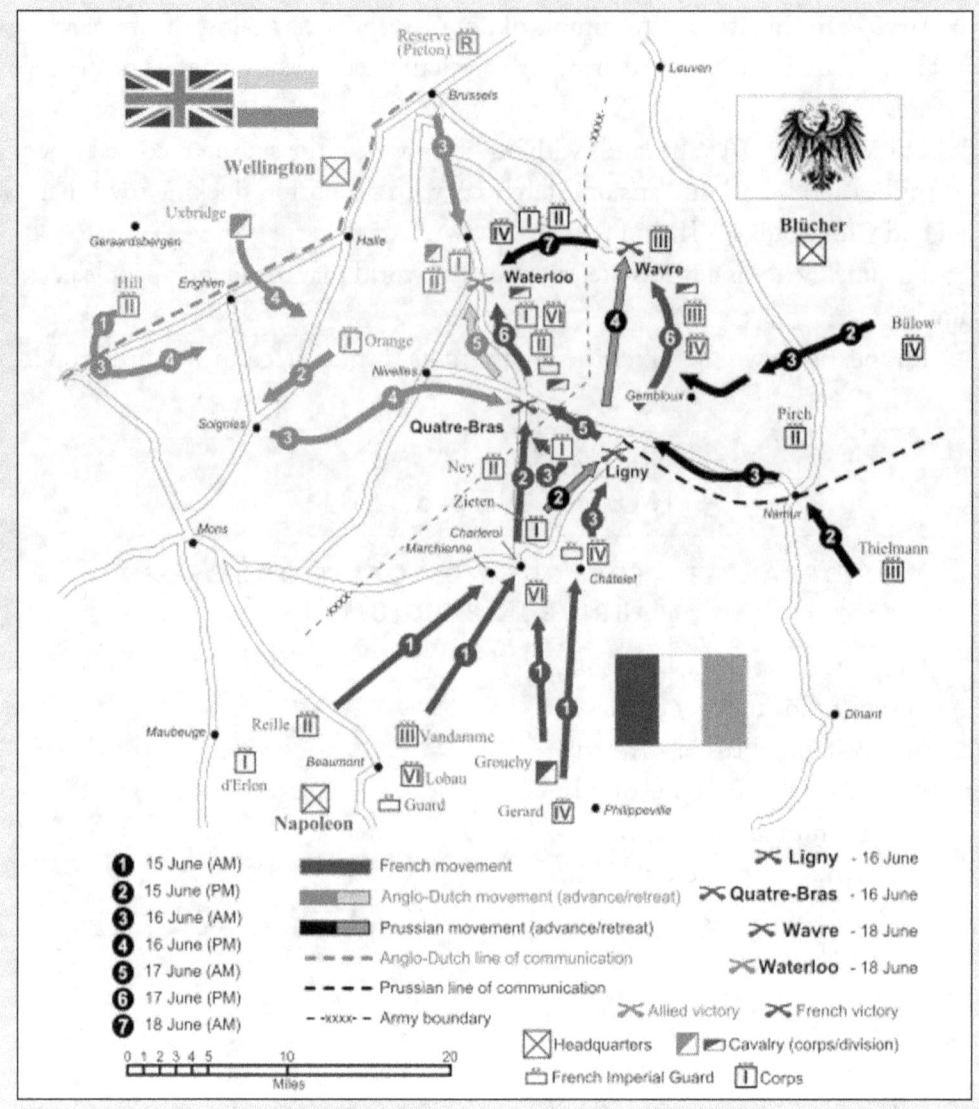

The combatants arrive in the vicinity of Waterloo

As Napoleon draws near, the allies anticipate that he will sweep north in an attempt at encirclement, but instead he dives straight between them—crossing the River Sambre on June 15 and dividing his force in two. At Quatre Bras, he places 70,000 troops under General Ney to block the English on his left, while he moves eastward with 60,000 men to attack von Blücher's force of 83,000 around the town of Ligny.

Ligny will be Napoleon's final victory.

The Battle of Ligny opens at 2:30 p.m. on June 16 and remains in the balance until Bonaparte sends in the Old Guard around 7:45 and drives the Prussians off the field to the west. During the fight, the 72-year-old von

Blücher leads a charge, but is knocked unconscious when his horse is shot and falls on him.

But Napoleon knows that the Prussians have only been bruised at Ligny, not routed, and he worries that they will try to reunite with the British.

He needs to attack again before that can occur.

TIME: JUNE 18, 1815 — 2 A.M. TO 4:30 P.M.

SIDEBAR: THE DECISIVE BATTLE OF WATERLOO BEGINS

Château d'Hougoumont destroyed at the Battle of Waterloo

When Duke Wellington hears the outcome at Ligny, he retreats north from Quatre Bras to a high ground position he has staked out on a 2.5-mile ridge running east and west in front of the town of Mont St. Jean. A country road runs along the ridge and intersects on the east with the main route toward Brussels some eight miles north.

The British general is a long-standing proponent of defensive warfare, and he deploys his forces in a way that will enable him to grind down any frontal assault on his center.

He does this by fortifying three sets of farmhouses and out-buildings: on his right flank, the Château d'Hougoumont, a half mile down from the ridge; on his near left La Haye Sainte; and on his far left Papelotte Farm, along the road west toward the Prussians. Each site is manned and ready to send enfilading fire into all French troops trying to ascend the ridge.

Wellington has one other trick up his sleeve, and that is the ability to have his troops along the ridge lie down along the back slope while enemy artillery charges fly over their heads.

At 2 a.m. on June 18, Wellington, headquartered further north in Waterloo, hears that von Blücher will provide one Prussian corps to support him, if the battle occurs later in the day. This convinces him to make his stand on his current ground.

As the dawn arrives, the two sides each assemble roughly 70,000 men to do battle in a confined space of roughly 2.5 miles by 2.5 miles.

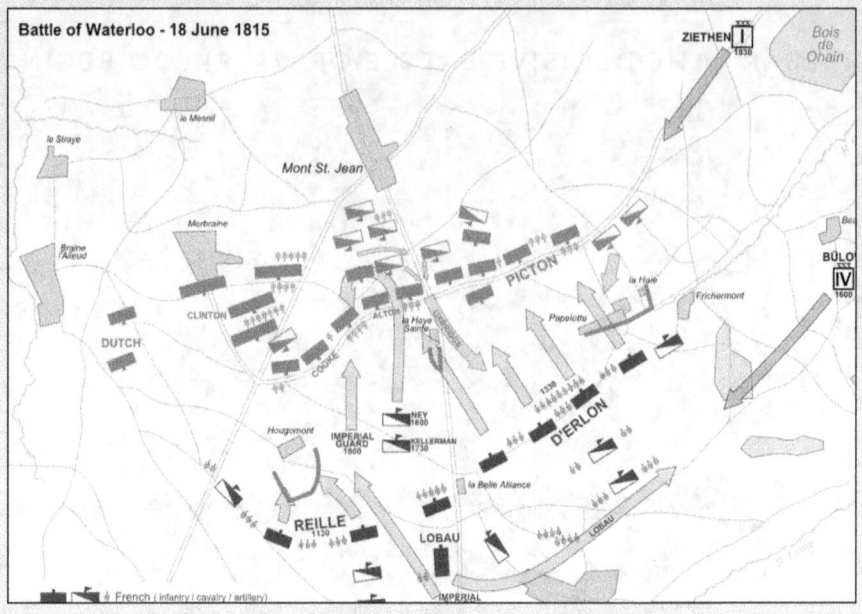

The French forces attack Wellington's high ground position

Napoleon makes his headquarters at La Belle Alliance, south of La Haye Sainte.

He rises at 8 a.m., takes breakfast, and rides north to review his troop alignments: his light infantry chasseurs in bright green; the light cavalry hussars; mounted cavalry dragoons and carabineers with long guns strapped to saddles; cuirassiers wearing metal breastplates; the towering

grenadiers chosen to lead assaults, in their blue and scarlet uniforms and bearskin headgear designed to add to their natural height; the cavalry lancers with their ten-foot wooden staffs tipped by a sharp steel blade; and the artillerymen, "his most beautiful daughters," whose mastery and courage have won him many a victory.

The French emperor is eager to conquer the British in his front and march into Brussels for his evening meal. While he has never met Wellington before, he remains typically confident. And his troops cheer and call out his name as he passes in front of them.

Meanwhile on the ridge, the duke's troops are lined up shoulder to shoulder according to the traditional 21-inch spacing proclaimed in the manuals. Nobody cheers his presence when he passes, because he has forbidden all such shows from within the ranks.

Napoleon is in no rush to attack. It has rained all night on the 17th, and the field of rye across which the French will make their assault is muddy and slippery. So he waits until 11:30 a.m., at which time he makes his first move of the day, against the crucial fortifications on his left at Hougoumont.

If Hougoumont falls, his cannoneers can ascend the ridge on the left, send enfilading fire down the entire British line, and claim a certain victory.

Artillery fire announces the French move, and it is quickly returned in kind: 4–12 pound solid iron balls bouncing along the ground and gouging body parts, sometimes 15–20 soldiers at a time, before being spent. Next comes the infantry, marching in order up the slope to Hougoumont. The hand-to-hand fight there lasts for 90 minutes, the only action on the field.

The north gate at Hougoumont where the British hold

When Hougoumont holds out, Napoleon next tries the British right with a heavy artillery barrage followed by massed infantry 24 columns deep, coming up east of the Brussels road and past the fortified buildings of La Haye Sainte. Again, the defenders drive the French back, led by a heroic cavalry charge behind Sir Thomas Picton, who is mortally wounded.

It is now 3 p.m. and a pause leads many to think the battle is over. While the duke is constantly visible along the ridge, Napoleon remains slouched in a field chair 1.5 miles back from the action, sending few orders and trusting Marshal Ney to manage the tactics. Amazingly, the two do not meet face-to-face from 9 a.m. until 7 p.m.

Around 4 p.m., Ney, evidently on his own, decides to test the British center. He does so in highly irregular fashion, using cavalry alone, unsupported by infantry.

Wellington responds by "forming squares," the traditional defense against cavalry. The goal here is first to discourage the horses via planted pikes, and then to shoot them, leaving their armor-clad riders stumbling on the field.

And this strategy succeeds. Some 12,000 French cavalrymen ascend the slope in magnificent order, only to be broken up into mingling clusters by the square's concentrated firepower. By some estimates they re-form on twelve occasions to charge again and be rebuffed.

By 4:30 p.m., Wellington, stationed openly in one of the squares, tells an aide:

> *The battle is mine, and if the Prussians arrive soon, there will be an end to the war.*

But when the French finally take La Haye Sainte, his confidence lessens and the outcome again hangs in the balance. Wellington has shot his bolt, his troops are exhausted, and his hope for victory rests on the appearance of von Blücher's Prussians to plug his gaps.

TIME: JUNE 18, 1815 – EVENING

SIDEBAR: NAPOLEON LOSES AT WATERLOO AND IS DEPOSED FOR GOOD

By 7 p.m. the emperor now knows that the Prussians, under von Blücher and Bulow, are attacking his right flank through Papelotte and further south at Plancenoit.

His options are running out. He has held fourteen regiments of his best troops, the Garde Impériale, in reserve to the south. Does he use his reserves to hold off the Prussians or fling them up toward the British on the ridge? At 7:30 p.m. he chooses the latter course.

He mounts his horse and leads five regiments of his Garde Impériale north to the battle.

The Garde, also called the "Immortals," are famed for their courage—"the Garde dies, it does not retreat."

Many expect Napoleon himself to ride at the front of his troops, but he turns them over to Ney who has already had five horses shot from under him and is near collapse. Instead

Key battle sites on the field at Waterloo

of taking the Brussels road up to the ridge, Ney veers left across the same ground as his prior cavalry charge. This adds 1,000 yards to the task, with the remains of the British artillery firing away.

As the Garde reaches the apparently accessible ridge, some 1,000 British infantrymen under the command of Major General Peregrine Maitland rise as if from nowhere and shoot them down. The Garde turns and flees back down the slope.

At this moment, the French have lost the battle.

Wellington waves forward his troops, just as the Prussians break through from the east.

Napoleon rallies the remnants of the Garde Impériale south at La Belle Alliance along the Brussels road and enables his troops to exit the field toward the south and west.

Around 9:30 p.m. Wellington and von Blücher meet up on the southern part of the field to seal their victory. The duke has lost 15,000 killed and wounded, von Blücher another 7,000.

Napoleon has lost 15,000 men and his empire.

As the Coalition army closes again on Paris on June 24, Napoleon abdicates. He surrenders personally on July 22 to the British, seeking "hospitality and the full protection of their laws."

According to the traditions of the age, Napoleon again suffers banishment rather than execution. This time he is sent to the Island of St. Helena, one of the most isolated in the world, off southwestern Africa. He lives there until his death in 1821, presumably of stomach cancer. In 1840 his remains are shipped back to Paris, where he lies in the Hôtel des Invalides.

Le jour de gloire has come and gone—for Napoleon and for revolutionary France.

"Le jour de gloire s'en est allé"—the day of glory has vanished

TIME: 1814-1914

THE WORLD RESHAPED AFTER WATERLOO

After the turmoil of the French Revolution and the Napoleonic Wars, the monarchs of Europe are eager to restore their authority and permanence by creating a stable balance of power between their nations.

They use the 1814 Congress of Vienna and the 1815 Paris Peace Conference to attempt to achieve these ends.

At the center of the diplomacy lies ongoing fear of France and a wish to contain any further thoughts of expansion on its part.

Within France itself, a "constitutional monarchy" is created under the Bourbon King Louis XVIII, Napoleon and his heirs are banned for life, reparations of 700 million francs are demanded, and foreign troops remain on French soil until 1818.

Napoleon's tomb at
the Hôtel des Invalides in Paris

In addition, steps are taken to surround France with more formidable border states:

- To the southwest, along the Pyrenees, the Bourbon King Ferdinand VII is returned to the throne of Spain.
- Its southeastern border with Italy is controlled by the Kingdom of Sardinia/Piedmont, backed by Austria, which gains control of Milan and Tuscany.
- Directly east of central France lie a jumble of states sharing both French and German roots, including what will become Switzerland, Alsace-Lorraine, and Luxembourg.
- But to the northeast lie two sizable forces—the first being the new United Netherlands with its seven provinces, including the two Hollands, under King William I of Orange.
- The second of these sizable forces is Prussia, which has traded off some of its claims to Poland to acquire a toehold along both banks of the Rhine River in the incredibly resource-rich Ruhr Valley.

When the Prussian minister Bismarck finally patches together a united Germany in 1867, France will have found a powerful foe all along its eastern border.

What of Britain, Napoleon's original nemesis from the time he came to power?

Their prize is absolute control of the seas with the Royal Navy and of their colonial empire stretching around the globe.

In the end, the French Revolution and the Napoleonic Wars have shaken the monarchical pillars of Europe from Lisbon to Moscow. But by and large the work done in 1815 at the Congress of Vienna and the Treaty of Paris restore their crowns and deliver relative stability over the next one hundred years.

THE NAPOLEONIC EMPIRE: KEY EVENTS 1812–1815

1812	
July 22	French loss at Battle of Salamanca; Wellesley hero in Spain
July 24	Napoleon crosses into Russia
September 7	The French are defeated at Borodino
October 19	Napoleon leaves Moscow and begins retreat
December 14	Napoleon recrosses the River Niemen into France
December 30	Prussia withdraws from French alliance
1813	
March 16	Prussia declares war on France
April 13	France initiates campaign west

1813	
May 2	Napoleon wins at Lutzen
May 20–21	Napoleon gains another victory at Bautzen
June 4	Temporary armistice until August 13
August	Allies regroup and Austria joins coalition
August 26–27	Napoleon's victory at Dresden
June 21	Battle of Vitoria begins, driving the French out of Spain
October 16–19	Napoleon defeated by the allies at Leipzig in the largest battle prior to WWI
December 11	Joseph-Napoléon Bonaparte abdicates throne of Spain
1814	
February 10–14	Six Days' Campaign west of Paris—a brilliant Napoleon victory, but proves futile
March 30	Sixth Coalition occupies Paris
April 14	Louis XVIII placed on French throne
May 30	The Treaty of Paris ends the war; Napoleon exiled to Alba
1815	
March 1	Napoleon escapes Elba and returns to France
March 1–June 18	Napoleon's "Hundred Days" campaign to restore French power and his own.
March 25	The Seventh Coalition is formed to defeat the French
June 18	Waterloo ends the Napoleonic Wars

MADISON CONCLUDES HIS SECOND TERM

TIME: APRIL 13, 1816

THE WAR OF 1812 ADJUSTS MADISON'S VIEWS ON THE ARMY AND THE BANK OF THE UNITED STATES

With the War of 1812 over, President Madison adjusts his thinking about two policy matters—namely, his historical opposition to a standing army and to a federal Bank of the United States (BUS).

As a lifelong Anti-Federalist, Madison has always regarded a standing army as a weapon an aspiring king or dictator can use to muffle popular political dissent.

However, the nation's military vulnerability evident in the destruction of Washington convinces him of the need to strengthen America's defense posture.

On March 3, 1815 he calls for a "standing army" of 20,000 troops, a move that is still anathema to many Democratic-Republicans. He also sees the impact that the Humphrey class frigates, built by the Federalists from 1794 to 1800, have had on battling the British fleet, and supports more upgrades of the navy.

James Madison

The war also causes Madison to change his mind about the value and role of a federal Bank of the United States.

With Jefferson he has previously viewed a federal bank as creating an unelected plutocracy of private financiers who will corrupt the political system by using their "insider knowledge" about upcoming government initiatives to line their own pockets.

A private central bank issuing the public currency is a greater menace to the liberties of the people than a standing army. (Quote attributed to Jefferson.)

In making loans to fund federal projects, the BUS officers will be tipped off in advance of upcoming projects—for example, building a road, canal, railroad, or bridge that crosses state lines. The logical result of this early, private knowledge is almost certain to be "speculative actions" by the insiders. Following this infrastructure example, it would result in a rush to buy up land required for the projects at low prices and then selling the land back to the government at high prices.

Assuming these projects play out as planned, the BUS officials end up with windfall profits, thus unfairly increasing their private wealth and power. The Democratic-Republicans believe that such a bank could threaten the democracy itself.

If the shape of these projects were to change along the way—say a new route is chosen for a road across different land—the BUS's investment losses could prove staggering not only to the bank owners but also to the general public. It could lead to a collapse of the nation's financial system, as follows:

- The BUS sinks public funds into buying land that is suddenly worth less than what it paid.
- Its cash on hand to pay back principal and interest owed to its depositors begins to run out.
- It tries to replenish its cash by selling the original land, but every sale results in a sizable loss.
- Eventually, the cash crisis reaches a point where the BUS is unable to make the payments due.
- News of the shortfalls spread, the public loses confidence in all banks, tries to retrieve deposits.
- Panic runs on all banks break out and bring the entire credit system to a halt.

Fear about this kind of corruption and collapse is why Jefferson had opposed Hamilton's plans for "multiplying capital" (soft money notes backed by hard gold or silver) and for the federal bank. It is also why, on January 15, 1815, Madison vetoes a bill to charter the Second Bank of the United States.

But as 1815 plays out, Madison experiences firsthand the devastating post-war effects of currency instability and inflation on the economy, and a nation again teetering on the brink of bankruptcy. His new secretary of the Treasury, George Dallas of Pennsylvania, a close friend of Albert Gallatin, convinces him to change his mind about the BUS. On April 3, 1816, Congress votes in favor of chartering the Second Bank of the United States and Madison signs the bill.

TIME: APRIL 27, 1816

"DALLAS TARIFF"

The new BUS gives the president a way to issue Treasury bonds as one source of added revenue. But Dallas tells him that far more revenue is needed to cover debts related to the war.

His solution becomes known as the "Dallas Tariff," a tax to be levied on select goods imported from abroad.

Over time, the tariff will become a central issue dividing the South from the rest of the country. But when first proposed under Madison, it easily passes the House on April 27, 1816 by an 88–59 margin.

While Dallas favors a fairly complex framework—varying the duty tax on whether or not US manufacturers could meet the internal demand for a given good—the final plan is simple: a 25% tax

George Dallas (1792–1864)

on all cotton and woolen imports; and a 30% tax on iron, hats, furniture, and fine paper.

This tariff would not only add more revenue to the federal government coffers, but also restore goodwill among New Englanders by "protecting" their emerging manufacturers.

Both Calhoun and Clay support the tariff, regarding it as a way to lessen regional tensions without much threat to their own local interests. The Southern view is that its economy—fueled by cotton and slave sales—is progressing at the moment, the Democratic-Republicans are firmly in control politically, and the tariff is viewed as a temporary measure anyway.

But Madison is not about to bend on one principle—what the Constitution says about the powers vested in the states versus the federal government.

Thus, when Congress allocates funds to build a national road using federal funds from the BUS, the president's last act in office is to veto it based on the Tenth Amendment. Infrastructure projects belong with the states, not in Washington.

TIME: MARCH 4, 1817

MADISON'S TERM ENDS AND A WAR-INDUCED ECONOMIC RECESSION BEGINS

Madison's eight years in the White House are now up. They have been consumed by the threat and reality of war and its impact on the economy. As the data on US exports show, he has twice had to resuscitate American trade, first in 1809 after Jefferson's Embargo Act, and then in 1815 after the end of his own war with Britain. In both instances he has been more successful than not.

VALUE OF US EXPORTS BEFORE AND AFTER EMBARGO ACT OF 1807 AND WAR OF 1812

	1807	1808	1809	1810	1811	1812	1813	1814	1815	1816
$ (000)	108.3	22.4	52.2	66.8	61.3	38.5	28.0	6.9	52.6	81.9
% Change		(79)	133	28	(9)	(37)	(27)	(75)	+++	56

The nation's GDP also experiences a string of dislocations. Domestic activity spikes in 1813 and 1814 in response to fighting the war, then cools off alarmingly in 1814 and 1815 with the peace. It will soon turn into America's first great depression.

CHANGES IN GDP DURING MADISON'S TERMS

	1809	1810	1811	1812	1813	1814	1815	1816
$ Thousands	687	706	767	786	969	1,078	925	819
% Change	6%	3%	9%	2%	23%	11%	(14%)	(11%)
Per Capita	98	98	103	103	123	133	111	96

After leaving Washington, Madison will live another seventeen years until his death at 82 years old, in 1836—the last of the "founding fathers" to pass.

His tobacco plantation at Montpelier has suffered severe financial losses owing to the embargoes, and as his health declines he obsesses over defining and defending his role in in the founding of the republic.

But here he needn't worry. The nation he helped create is now on the brink of achieving the greatness he imagined in 1787 as the acknowledged "father of the Constitution."

## 37

WESTWARD EXPANSION REOPENS CONFLICT OVER THE DESTINY OF AMERICA'S BLACK POPULATION

TIME: 1787 AND ONWARD

NEW STATES MUST WRITE CONSTITUTIONS FOR ADMITTANCE TO THE UNION

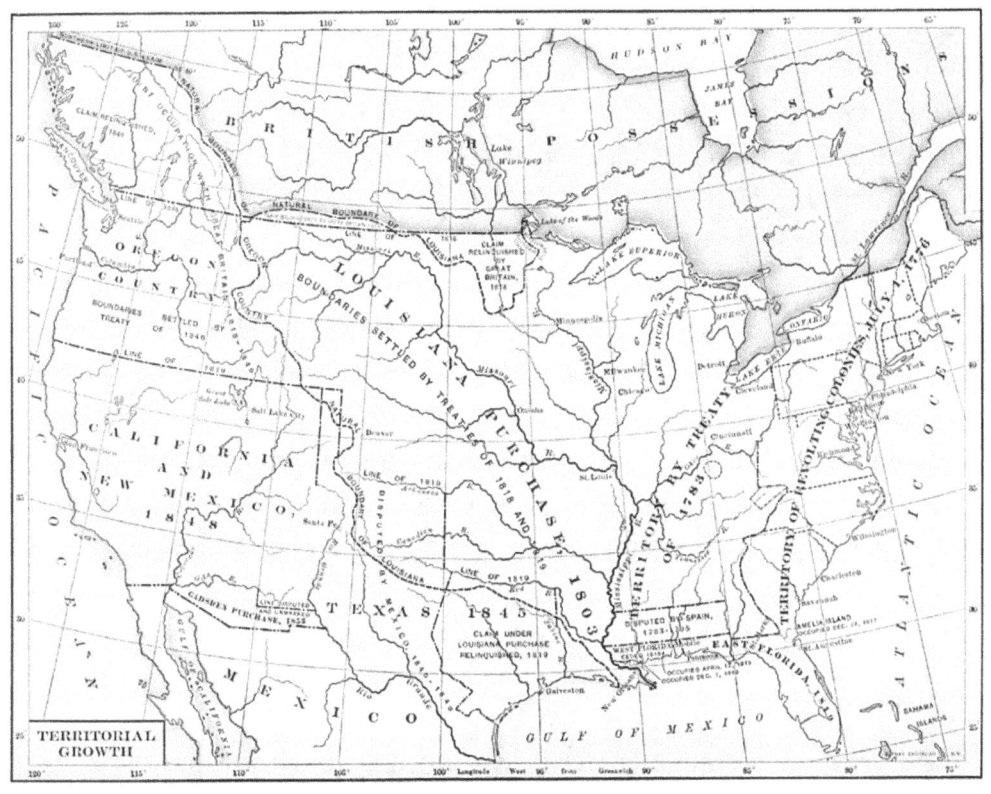

Map of US territories and westward expansion

By the time Napoleon's attempt to conquer Europe ends, America's attempt to expand westward is already well underway.

In 1775 Daniel Boone crosses the Cumberland Gap into Kentucky to create a fourteenth colony he calls Transylvania. He is followed by many other western explorers.

The rugged Meriwether Lewis and his aristocratic partner William Clark voyage down the Ohio River, up the Missouri River, across the Rocky Mountains and the Columbia River, and to the Pacific Ocean in their 1804–1806 expedition.

In 1805 General Zebulon Pike heads north along the Mississippi River to discover its headwaters in Minnesota, followed by his 1806–1807 expedition southwest into New Mexico and Colorado.

To the north, the fur trader John Jacob Astor traverses the Canadian border from east to west, establishing an outpost in 1811 called Ft. Astoria on the Pacific coast in Oregon.

By 1815, American settlers are primed to pack up their families and possessions and move en masse to the western territories.

This migration brings with it a host of issues for federal officials, beyond surveying, pricing and recording sales of the new lands. The most challenging relates to the process by which a new territory will achieve statehood and, in turn, be admitted to the Union.

As of Madison's first term, a total of four new states have been admitted west of the Appalachians—Kentucky (1792), Tennessee (1796), Ohio (1803), and Louisiana (1812). Each has reached a threshold population level within its borders, held a convention to draft a constitution, had it approved by a local vote, and applied for acceptance to the federal Congress.

On the surface this process appears clear and simple.

But in practice, the task of arriving at a state constitution forces the settlers in each state to deal with the same thorny issue that almost sabotaged the founding father's efforts in 1787—namely, how to deal with Black people within their borders, be they enslaved or free.

Resolution is, of course, easy in the South. About-to-be states like Mississippi (1817) and Alabama (1819) will build their economies around the need for enslaved Black people to work their existing plantations and to be bred for sale to those hoping to start new plantations.

In the North, where slavery is already banned, the issue becomes one of how the dominant white settlers intend to deal with freed Black people who hope to settle in the new states.

The answer will quickly become evident in language written into the initial state constitutions for Ohio (1804), Illinois (1816), and Indiana (1818).

TIME: 1804

OHIO TAKES THE LEAD IN TRYING TO "CLEANSE" ITSELF OF BLACK PEOPLE

Ohio is the first western state to express its views regarding the presence of Black people within its borders.

Under the 1787 Northwest Ordinance, slavery is banned in Ohio, although masters are still allowed to come and go with "their property." But it is the body of freed men who might wish to take up permanent residence in the state that most troubles the white settlers.

To deal with this perceived threat, Ohio passes a series of "Black Codes" aimed at "cleansing" the state of its freed men. The centerpiece of an 1804 bill sets up two hard-to-meet requirements for all Black people seeking permanent residence: they must produce court papers proving they are free rather than enslaved, and they must post a $500 bond

Two veteran chimney sweeps

backed by two people to guarantee their "good behavior."

Beyond these hurdles and humiliations, free Black people in Ohio experience the same daily deprivations heaped upon their brethren back east—segregation, poor housing, the lowliest jobs, and little to no education.

The message here from white Ohioans is obvious: "Black people keep out."

It is overlaid by the threat of physical violence, most evident along the banks of the Ohio River, where Black refugees from Kentucky—enslaved or freed—hope to cross to a semblance of freedom.

As one self-defined guardian of the border puts it:

The banks of the Ohio…are lined with men with muskets to keep off emancipated slaves.

TIME: 1813

BLACK ABOLITIONIST JAMES FORTEN PLEADS FOR ASSIMILATION

In the face of these cleansing efforts, James Forten becomes one of the first Black people to issue an emotional plea to white people to look into their hearts and put an end to their prejudices.

Forten's amazing life stands as a symbol of free Black people capable of making their own way in a white-dominated society.

He is born to free Black parents in Philadelphia on September 2, 1766. By age eight he is attending a Quaker school while working alongside his father in a sail-making business. In 1780 he volunteers to serve in the Revolutionary War and ends up on a privateer, which is captured at sea by the British. After refusing to pledge allegiance to the crown, he spends eight months on a prison ship before being exchanged.

After the war, Forten works briefly in London's shipyards before returning home to capitalize on his experience as a sail-maker. He rejoins his old firm in Philadelphia, moves from one job to the next, and when the owner retires in 1798 he is asked to stay on and oversee the operation.

When Forten devises a new sail that facilitates greater speed and maneuverability, customers begin to flock to his loft. In 1801, at age 35, he becomes its owner. His business employs some 30 workers, both white and Black, who are expected to comply with his rigid standards, including punctuality and dedication at work along with abstinence and regular church attendance.

During the War of 1812, he again exhibits his patriotism by recruiting some 2,500 Black people to defend Philadelphia against a possible invasion by the Royal Navy. They construct defensive fortifications along the Schuylkill River and prepare for militia duty.

By the end of the war, the demand for his unique sails makes Forten a wealthy man.

Once in possession of capital, Forten follows Alexander Hamilton's admonitions by leveraging it. In his case this involves investing the money he has made from sail-making in Philadelphia real estate and railroad startups, with both rapidly appreciating in value.

Forten is remarkable not only for his business acumen, but also for his commitment to Black freedom and citizenship. After many discussions about repatriation with Paul Cuffee, another Black abolitionist, he decides that America, not Sierra Leone or Liberia, should be the proper home for future generations of Black people. With that goal in mind, he begins to act on behalf of needed reforms in America.

Like his fellow Philadelphian the Reverend Absalom Jones, Forten recognizes that influencing the political process will be crucial to bettering the lives of both free and enslaved people.

In 1813 he learns that the Pennsylvania senate is considering a bill mimicking efforts in Ohio and Indiana to "cleanse" the state of its free Black population. This would be accomplished through an outright ban on allowing any new free Black people from settling in Pennsylvania. Forten decides to speak out against this act, and he does so by publishing his *Letters From a Man of Colour on a Late Bill Before the Senate of Pennsylvania.*

The five letters stand as a plea to white people of integrity to abandon their unholy abuses of Black people and to grant them the liberty and rights they are due as Americans. In many ways Forten's sentiments and tonality foreshadow a comparable appeal, sixteen years hence, by the Bostonian freedman David Walker.

Forten rejects the popular notion that Black people are somehow a different species from white people.

> *Are we not sustained by the same power, supported by the same food, hurt by the same wounds, pleased with the same delights, and propagated by the same means. And should we not then enjoy the same liberty, and be protected by the same laws.—*

He finds slavery "incredible" in a nation founded on liberty and fair treatment.

> *It seems almost incredible that the advocates of liberty, should conceive the idea of selling a fellow creature to slavery…O miserable race, born to the same hopes, created with the same feeling, and destined for the same goal, you are reduced by your fellow creatures below the brute. The dog is protected and pampered at the board of his master, while the poor African and his descendant, where a Saint or a felon, is branded with infamy, registered as a slave, and we may expect shortly to find a law to prevent their increase, by taxing them according to numbers, and authorizing the Constables to seize and confine everyone who dare to walk the streets without a collar on his neck—what have the people of colour been guilty of, that they more than others, should be compelled to register their houses, lands, servants and children.*

He hopes that the legislature will be guided by humanity and mercy to correct the suffering of all Black people.

> *It is to be hoped that in our legislature there is a patriotism, humanity, and mercy sufficient to crush this attempt upon the civil liberty of freemen, and to prove that the enlightened body who have hitherto guarded their fellow creatures, without regard to the colour of the skin, will stretch forth the wings of protection to that race, whose persons have been the scorn, and whose calamities have been the jest of the world for ages. We trust the time is at hand when this obnoxious bill will receive its death warrant, and freedom still remain to cheer the bosom of a man of colour.*

Passing the exclusion bill before Congress will only increase the degradation that already exists.

Are not men of colour sufficiently degraded? Why then increase their degradation…
If men, though they know that the law protects all, will dare, in defiance of law, to
execute their hatred upon the defenseless black, will they not by the passage of this bill,
believe him still more a mark for their venom and spleen—Will they not believe him
completely deserted by authority, and subject to every outrage brutality can inflict —
too surely they will, and the poor wretch will turn his eyes around to look in vain for
protection.

For the sake of humanity, he entreats the white rulers to become advocates for Black
people rather than add to their despair.

Pause, ye rulers of a free people, before you give us over to despair and violation—we
implore you, for the sake of humanity, to snatch us from the pinnacle of ruin, from
that gulf, which will swallow our rights, as fellow creatures; our privileges, as citizens;
and our liberties, as men!

I have done. My feelings are acute, and I have ventured to express them without
intending either accusation or insult to anyone. An appeal to the heart is my
intention, and if I have failed, it is my great misfortune, not to have laid a power of
eloquence sufficient to convince. But I trust the eloquence of nature will succeed, and
the law-givers of this happy Commonwealth will yet remain the Black's friend, and
the advocates of Freemen, is the sincere wish of every freeman.

James Forten continues his efforts to prove that Black people can thrive in white
society if only given a fair chance. He joins ministers Jones and Allen in supporting
the Free African Society and spends a large share of his fortune paying owners to free
their slaves. Before his death in 1842, he also helps the white abolitionist William
Lloyd Garrison publish his *Liberator* newspaper, and participates in the underground
railroad movement to transport escaping enslaved people to Canada.

In 1833 his wife Charlotte helps found a Female Anti-Slavery Society chapter
in Philadelphia, and his legacy as a Black abolitionist is carried on by his three
daughters.

TIME: 1816

INDIANA'S BLACK CODES FOLLOW OHIO'S PRECEDENT

When the time comes for Indiana's application for admittance, it follows a long history of attempting to allow slavery within its borders.

The territory is officially organized on July 4, 1800 with frontier fighter William
Henry Harrison serving as first governor from 1800 to 1812. Harrison grows up on

Berkeley Plantation in Virginia surrounded by enslaved people. Despite early brushes with Dr. Benjamin Rush and Quaker abolitionists, he concludes that Indiana would be more economically attractive to settlers if slavery were allowed.

In turn, from 1803 onward, he attempts to skirt the sanctions imposed by the 1787 Northwest Ordinance—and white settlers from the South begin to filter into Indiana with enslaved people in tow.

Harrison touts this fait accompli to federal politicians, including Jefferson (who opposes it), but still fails to change the 1787 law. His next ploy is to recast all of the Indiana enslaved people as "indentured servants, serving terms of 90+ years."

What follows is an open battle between white factions in the state that will be replicated over the next 60 years as America moves west. On one side are southern slave owners who insist on the "right" to bring their "property" with them as they settle. On the other are northern white people, unlike Harrison, who want absolutely nothing to do with any Black people—enslaved or free—within their state.

The level of anti-Black vitriol among the latter group is evident in "petitions" they address to the provisional state legislature at the time:

Your Petitioners also humbly pray that if your hournable boddy think propper to allow a donation of land to Setlers, People of Color and Slaveholder may be debarred from the lands so appropriated.

We are opposed to the introduction of slaves or free Negroes in any shape...Our corn houses, kitchens,' smoke houses...may no doubt be robbed and our wives, children and daughters may and no doubt will be insulted and abused by those Africans. We do not wish to be saddled with them in any way.

As usual, Black people are caught in the middle between those white people who wish to treat them as cattle and those who hope they will disappear completely.

By 1810 the population of the Indiana Territory is approaching "admission to statehood" levels, with 23,890 white people counted and 630 Black people—237 recorded as enslaved and 393 as freed.

This leads to a battle over writing a constitution that includes a direct reference to the "Black issues."

With William Henry Harrison off to fight the War of 1812, the thought of converting Indiana into a slavery-welcoming state vanishes, and popular interest shifts to a "cleansing" solution.

In the end, Indiana follows suit with Ohio in its 1816 Black Codes. These require that all Black people must be able to "show their papers" on demand. For example:

I, Andre Lewis, clerk of the Gibson Circuit Court, hereby certify that Lilly Ann Perry, a negro age 28 years, with light complexion, born in the state of North Carolina, resides now in Gibson, Indiana..

They also include posting of the $500 bond to guarantee "good behavior."

But then Indiana goes even further, piling other constraints on its free Black population by barring rights to schooling, to testifying in court, to serving in the militia, and to voting.

TIME: DECEMBER 10, 1815

THE BLACK ABOLITIONIST PAUL CUFFEE EXPLORES THE OPTION OF REPATRIATION

From the inception of slavery in America, heroic Black activists have sought ways to put an end to it.

One of the first is Paul Cuffee.

Cuffee is born in 1759 on Cuttyhunk Island off the coast of Massachusetts. His mother is Native American and his father is African, the latter granted freedom by his Quaker owner. Their values and industriousness shape Cuffee and prepare him to achieve two lifetime goals: starting up a successful shipping business and reuniting Black enslaved people with their African roots.

His life at sea begins as deckhand on a whaler, shifts to running a cargo boat around Nantucket, and builds over time to ownership of several international merchant ships that make him a rich man living on the waterfront in Westport, Massachusetts.

With his newfound wealth, he turns toward restoring freedom and dignity to America's enslaved people.

His travels abroad connect him with freed men in Britain attempting to transport Black people to a new home in Sierra Leone. This crown colony on the west coast of Africa is first established by the "Committee for the Relief of the Black Poor" in 1787.

In 1810 Cuffee sails to Freetown, the capital of Sierra Leone, to assess progress among the early settlers. He then returns to the US to gather financial support for his own initial transport.

On December 10, 1815, he sets off for a return trip with 38 freed people in tow.

With proof of early successes in hand, Cuffee petitions Congress in 1816 for funds to greatly expand the Sierra Leone project, but is turned down.

He continues to search for financial support into 1817, when his health deteriorates and he dies, leaving behind an estate valued at $20,000 (roughly $4 million today).

What refuses to die with Cuffee are two things: Black people's interest in finding their freedom and roots in Africa and white people's interest in repatriation as a solution to the issue of slavery.

TIME: DECEMBER 21, 1816

WHITE PEOPLE PROPOSE A "COLONIZATION" ANSWER

On December 21, 1816, a group of prominent white people on the east coast gather in Washington to form "the Society for the Colonization of Free People of Color of America." The founders include:

- Reverend Robert Finley, a renowned educator and Presbyterian minister who initiates the idea.
- Speaker of the House Henry Clay of Kentucky.
- John Randolph, a Virginia planter and member of the House.
- Richard Lee, Virginia planter, brother of General Harry Lee (whose son is Robert E. Lee).
- Charles Mercer, a Federalist lawyer and member of the Virginia Assembly.

Motivations behind this "American Colonization Society" vary widely.

Some appear to be well-intentioned, viewing repatriation as the best hope for gradually ending slavery and giving those freed a decent life "back home."

But most are driven by fear and prejudice. An address to the opening session of the Society sums this up as follows:

We say in the Declaration of Independence that "all men are created equal and have certain unalienable rights." Yet it is considered impossible, consistent with the safety of the State, and it is certainly impossible with the present feeling towards these people, that they can ever be placed upon this equality…while they remain mixed with us. Some persons may call it prejudice. No matter! Prejudice is as powerful a motive, and will certainly exclude them, as the soundest reason.

This latter faction see colonization as a way for Northerners to achieve the kind of racial "cleansing" being pursued in Ohio and Indiana, and for Southern plantation owners to remove "uppity" enslaved people who might cause uprisings.

The Society first explores a site in the Sierra Leone area already opened up by repatriation proponents in England—but it concludes that conditions there aren't viable.

Instead it sends a ship in 1821 to a potential site at Cape Mesurado, just south of Sierra Leone. Once there the voyagers "buy" land from local tribesmen in exchange for trinkets and set up an outpost.

They name the outpost Liberia and the capital Monrovia, in honor of James Monroe, a member of the Society.

TIME: JANUARY 15, 1817

REV. ALLEN AND AFRICAN METHODIST EPISCOPAL CHURCH OPPOSE COLONIZATION

On January 15, 1817, some three thousand free Black people pack into the Reverend Richard Allen's African Methodist Episcopal Church in Philadelphia to debate and vote on the American Colonization Society's repatriation plans.

Their decision provides a remarkable statement about what the assembly regards as justice for their race.

It begins by citing the vital role that enslaved labor played in building America and the injustice of denying Black people the right to enjoy the fruits of this labor through repatriation.

> *Whereas our ancestors (not of choice) were the first culttors of the wilds of America, we their descendents feel ourselves entitled to participate in the blessings of her luxuriant soil, which their blood and sweat manured; and that any measure…having a tendency to banish us from her bosom would not only be cruel, but in direct violation of those principles, which has been the boast of the republic.*

It then resolves to remain in America, to keep faith with other Black people who are still enslaved, and to support efforts to gain their freedom.

> *It is resolved that we never will separate ourselves voluntarily from the slave population in this country; they are our brethren by the ties of consanguinity, of suffering, and of wrongs; and we feel that there is more virtue in suffering privations with them, than fancied advantages for a season.*

This outcome represents one more turning point on behalf of Black emancipation and assimilation.

Despite this, the American Colonization Society will go forward with its plans. Over the course of the nineteenth century, the Society will transport some 16,000 Black people to the colony of Liberia and in 1847 it will be declared an independent republic.

But the scheme sputters as white proponents find that costs are prohibitive—first to purchase the enslaved people from their owners and then to transport them across the ocean.

Opposition from free Black people like James Forten, Richard Allen, and their followers also eliminates the possibility of using colonization to "cleanse" their cities and frontiers of all people of color.

What remains then for Northern white people who want nothing to do with Black people is to pass ever more burdensome local statutes to discourage new Black residents and to segregate and punish those already in their midst.

## 38

JAMES MONROE'S FIRST TERM

TIME: 1815–1816

RUN-UP TO THE ELECTION OF 1816

As the presidential race of 1816 begins, the popular momentum enjoyed by the Federalist Party during the early struggles of the War of 1812 has dissipated, and their desperate ploy in selecting DeWitt Clinton to run against Madison has left them without a viable candidate going forward.

Largely by default, they put forward Senator Rufus King of New York, who has already been defeated twice, in 1804 and 1808, for the vice presidency.

King's credentials are actually quite credible. He is a graduate of Harvard College, had a brief militia stint during the first war with Britain, was a member of the Committee on Style that drafted the Constitution, a first-rate orator, an outspoken opponent of slavery, and a close ally of that essential Federalist, Alexander Hamilton.

In 1796 Washington offers him the secretary of state post, which he turns down in favor of the ambassadorship to Britain. Remarkably when Jefferson becomes president in 1800, he retains King in that critical assignment until 1803.

Along with the 61-year-old King, some Federalists put forward 64-year-old John Howard of Maryland as a vice presidential candidate. Howard is a Revolutionary War hero, owns a large slave-holding plantation, has served as a US senator in 1803, and appears to have little in common with King.

By contrast, a genuine race for the presidential nomination develops among the Democratic-Republicans.

Jefferson and Madison's hand-picked candidate is their fellow Virginian, James Monroe, currently serving as secretary of state and secretary of war.

However, the long-term anti-Jefferson faction of the party decides to contest the top slot. This wing is led by John Randolph of Roanoke, who argues that Madison's policies have become no more than:

Old Federalism, vamped up into something bearing the superficial appearance of Republicanism.

Their alternative to Monroe is the formidable Georgian William Crawford, who has served under Madison as minister to France and secretary of war.

Crawford is the first of several politicians from his state who will emerge on the national stage with a reputation for arriving at independent positions and promoting them aggressively.

He is a self-made man, growing up in Appling, Georgia along the eastern border with South Carolina. As a young man he is a farmer and teacher before receiving a classical education at Carmel Academy under the tutelage of the well-known Presbyterian minister, Moses Waddel. He is an excellent student and briefly joins Carmel's staff before leaving to teach at Richland Academy, where he also studies law and passes the bar in 1799, at 27 years old. His scholarship on Georgia law and his outgoing personal style carry him readily into politics.

Crawford is physically and verbally a brawny man, and he engages in two bloody duels early in his career, both times involving political rivals backing future governor John Clark. In 1802 he kills a Clark supporter named Peter Van Allen, and in 1806 is wounded in another duel by Clark himself.

Later that year he is off to Washington, where he serves as US senator for six years, and is a popular choice as president *pro tem* in 1812. Madison appoints him minister to France in 1813 and then secretary of war in 1815.

Unlike the "War Hawks" Clay and Calhoun, Crawford is initially opposed to fighting another battle with Britain, but his considerable influence in the Senate fails to carry the day. In 1813 he declines Madison's offer to become the new secretary of war and instead takes a posting as minister to France. After the conflict ends, he accepts the secretary of war slot, and serves from 1815 to 1816, after which he becomes Madison's secretary of the Treasury, a position he will continue to hold over a nine-year stretch until 1825.

Crawford has just begun his new duties when various supporters put him forward as an option to Monroe for the 1816 nomination.

They tend to see in him a commanding presence, inclined to favor "old school" domestic virtues: power to the states over the national government, concerns about a centralized bank, free trade rather than debilitating embargoes, limited taxation and Bill of Rights guarantees on freedom, and a laissez-faire attitude toward slavery.

Others simply see him as an end to the monopoly that Virginians seem to have on the presidency.

Over time, Crawford's flexibility on many issues will fail to conform to the assumed preferences of his backers—but in the 1816 caucus they put up a good fight. In the final balloting for the nomination, he comes up just short, garnering 54 votes against 65 for Monroe.

1816 PRESIDENTIAL NOMINATION

CANDIDATES	VOTES
James Monroe	65
William Crawford	54

As has become the norm by 1816, selection of a running mate for Monroe is more about geographically balancing the party ticket than about lining up a successor for the presidency. If anything, that path for the Democratic-Republicans now runs through tenure as secretary of state.

THE POLITICAL FATE OF EARLY VICE PRESIDENTS VS. SECRETARIES OF STATE

YEAR	PRESIDENT	VICE-PRESIDENT	SECRETARY OF STATE	PRESIDENTIAL NOMINEE
1788	Washington	Adams	Jay, Jefferson	
1792	Washington	Adams	Jefferson, Randolph, Pickering	Adams in 1796
1796	Adams	Jefferson	Pickering, Lee, Marshall	Jefferson in 1800
1800	Jefferson	Burr	Lincoln, Madison	Jefferson in 1804
1804	Jefferson	Clinton	Madison	Madison in 1808
1808	Madison	Clinton/Vacant	Smith/Monroe	Madison in 1812
1812	Madison	Gerry/Vacant	Monroe	Monroe in 1816

In the end, the party settles on Daniel Tompkins, the sitting governor of New York, as its nominee. Tompkins' fame rests on his personal efforts to strengthen the state militia during the War of 1812. Unfortunately this has involved sizable loans to purchase equipment, which he backs against his personal wealth. In the end these bankrupt him and drive him to drink, resulting in an early death only three months after his term as vice president begins.

TIME: NOVEMBER TO DECEMBER 1816

MONROE WINS IN A LANDSLIDE

Actual voting in the election of 1816 is completed between November 1 and December 4. The popular turnout is down dramatically from the 1812 race which featured intense controversy over both the trade embargoes and the war with Britain.

POPULAR VOTING FOR PRESIDENT AND NUMBER OF STATES
WHERE ELECTORS CHOSEN BY THEIR VOTES

1788	1792	1796	1800	1804	1808	1812	1816
43,782	28,579	66,841	67,282	143,110	192,691	278,786	112,370
7 of 12	6 of 15	9 of 16	6 of 16	11 of 17	10 of 17	9 of 18	10 of 19

As expected, Monroe wins in a landslide, carrying sixteen states, losing only in traditionally Federalist strongholds: Connecticut, Rhode Island, and Massachusetts.

RESULTS OF THE 1816 PRESIDENTIAL ELECTION

CANDIDATES	STATE	PARTY	POP. VOTE	TOTAL EV	SOUTH	BORDER	NORTH	WEST
James Monroe	VA	Dem-Rep	76,592	183	70	20	82	11
Rufus King	NY	Federalist	34,740	34	0	3	31	0
Unpledged			1,038					
Total			112,370	217	70	23	113	11
Needed to Win				109				

Note: South (Virginia, NC, SC, GA, TN, LA), Border (DE, MD, KY), North (NH, MA, NY, NJ, PA, RI, CT, VT), West (OH, IN) Total # electors voting = 217; must get more than half to win = 109.

His margin of victory in the Electoral College is well ahead of what Madison accomplished before him, and almost comparable to Jefferson's victory in 1804.

WINNING MARGIN IN ELECTORAL VOTES ACTUALLY CAST

YEAR	CANDIDATES	PARTY	ELECTORAL VOTES
1804	Thomas Jefferson	Democratic-Republican	162 of 176/92%
1808	James Madison	Democratic-Republican	122 of 175/70%
1812	James Madison	Democratic-Republican	128 of 217/59%
1816	James Monroe	Democratic-Republican	183 of 217/84%

TIME: NOVEMBER TO DECEMBER 1816

THE DEMOCRATIC-REPUBLICANS STRENGTHEN THEIR CONTROL OVER THE HOUSE

Two new states—Indiana and Mississippi—participate in the election of the 15th Congress. Both end up in the Democratic-Republican column, sending one House representative and two Senators to Washington.

FIRST TIME VOTING AMONG NEW STATES

YEAR	SOUTH	BORDER	NORTH	WEST
1791			Vermont	
1792		Kentucky		
1796	Tennessee			
1803				Ohio
1812	Louisiana			
1816				Indiana
1817	Mississippi			

Overall the election represents the beginning of the death spiral for the Federalist Party in the House. They give back all of the gains they recorded in 1812 and 1814, and end up with only 40 of the 185 total seats.

ELECTION TRENDS: HOUSE OF REPRESENTATIVES

PARTY	1801	1803	1805	1807	1809	1811	1813	1815	1817
Democratic-Republicans	68	102	114	116	93	107	114	119	145
Federalist	38	40	28	26	49	36	68	64	40
Congress #	7th	8th	9th	10th	11th	12th	13th	14th	15th
President	TJ	TJ	TJ	TJ	JM	JM	JM	JM	JM

Democratic-Republican dominance extends across all geographic regions. They continue to own the South, losing only a few seats in Virginia and North Carolina. In the North, they win the big states of Pennsylvania (23 seats) and New York (27) by wide margins, and even take nine out of twenty races in Massachusetts.

HOUSE TRENDS BY REGION

DEMOCRATIC-REPUBLICAN	TOTAL	SOUTH	BORDER	NORTH	WEST
1801	68	30	7	31	
1803	102	42	13	46	1
1805	114	48	13	52	1
1807	116	47	12	56	1
1809	93	41	12	39	1
1811	107	43	12	51	1
1813	114	49	16	43	6
1815	119	51	14	47	7
1817	145	54	16	68	7
FEDERALISTS					
1801	38	8	4	26	
1803	40	7	3	30	
1805	28	1	3	24	
1807	26	2	4	20	
1809	49	8	4	37	
1811	36	7	4	25	
1813	75	9	9	57	
1815	64	7	7	50	
1817	40	5	5	29	1

The Federalists hold their own in the Senate. Three states—Connecticut, Delaware, and Maryland—remain in their control, and they strengthen their hand near term in Massachusetts, New Hampshire, and Rhode Island.

ELECTION TRENDS: SENATE

PARTY	1801	1803	1805	1807	1809	1811	1813	1815	1817
Dem-Reps	17	25	27	28	27	30	28	26	29
Federalists	15	9	7	6	7	6	8	12	13
Congress #	7th	8th	9th	10th	11th	12th	13th	14th	15th
President	TJ	TJ	TJ	TJ	JM	JM	JM	JM	JM

But the Democratic-Republicans continue to shut them out across the South and the West.

SENATE TRENDS BY REGION

DEMOCRATIC-REPUBLICAN	TOTAL	SOUTH	BORDER	NORTH	WEST
1801	17	10	3	4	
1803	25	10	4	9	2
1805	27	10	4	11	2
1807	28	10	4	12	2
1809	27	10	4	11	2
1811	30	12	4	12	2
1813	28	12	3	11	2
1815	26	12	2	8	4
1817	29	14	2	7	6
FEDERALISTS					
1801	15	0	3	12	
1803	9	0	2	7	
1805	7	0	2	5	
1807	6	0	2	4	
1809	7	0	2	5	
1811	6	0	2	4	
1813	8	0	3	5	
1815	12	0	4	8	
1817	13	0	4	9	

TIME: 1758–1831

PRESIDENT JAMES MONROE: PERSONAL PROFILE

James Monroe is born on April 28, 1758 in Westmoreland County, Virginia, also the

birthplace of George Washington and Robert
E. Lee. His roots are considerably more humble than the three other presidents who precede
him in the so-called "Virginia dynasty."

His father, Spence Monroe, inherits some
500 acres of land and builds a four-room
wooden cabin on it, which measures a mere
58 by 20 feet. He and his wife have five children and own several enslaved people who
help him raise tobacco, corn, barley, and livestock. The family is considered well-off, but
by no means aristocratic.

James Monroe works the farm while attending Campbelltown Academy, where he is
tutored by the Scottish Reverend Archibald
Campbell of the Church of England, along
with his friend John Marshall. In 1774, his
father dies and, as the oldest son, he inherits
the plantation.

James Monroe (1758–1831)

At this point he also comes under the ongo-
ing influence of an uncle on his mother's side, Judge Joseph Jones. Jones has served on
the Virginia courts, as a member of the House of Burgesses, and later as representative to
the Continental Congress. His friendships include Washington, Jefferson, and Madison.
Jones steers Monroe to enroll at the College of William & Mary.

But his education is interrupted after one year by the war with Britain. His father had
been outspoken in his criticism of abuses in colonial taxation, and now Monroe is eager
to take up arms as conflict begins. He joins the 3rd Virginia Militia and, within two weeks
of the Concord battle, he participates in a raid on the arsenal at the governor's palace in
Williamsburg. He is seventeen years old at this time.

Monroe's military career will extend over five years. His regiment is with Washington in August, 1776, when British Generals Clinton and Howe almost trap it in Manhattan. He then joins in the long retreat north, and from there across the Hudson and
back south to New Jersey. On Christmas Day, 1776, he crosses the Delaware along with
Washington and attacks the Hessians at the Battle of Trenton, where he almost loses his
life. A musket ball severs an artery in his shoulder during a heroic assault, and he nearly
bleeds out before a doctor saves him. Monroe's combat role ends with Trenton, although
he does continue to serve in the militia almost until the end of the war.

Monroe's early experiences in life will mirror Washington more so than Jefferson or Madison. His perspectives on America are formed on the battlefield rather than in the library, and they endow him with a bias toward independent thought, leadership, and action.

After the war he returns to Virginia and attends to his personal finances, something that will plague him throughout his life. He picks up the study of law, not out of particular interest, but as a proven path to required income. His connections result in two distinguished tutors, Jefferson and his former teacher, George Wythe, who has also apprenticed John Marshall, Edmund Randolph, and Henry Clay in the law.

In 1783 he sells his inherited farm, passes the bar, and opens a practice in Fredericksburg. But his interest in politics continues. He serves in the state assembly and then as a delegate to the fourth session of the Congress of the Confederation. He is now on the national stage, and focused already on issues of national security and westward expansion that will mark his political future.

> *There are before us some questions of the utmost consequence…whether we are to have standing troops to protect our frontiers or leave them unguarded…whether we will expose ourselves to the…loss of the country westward…and the intrusion on settlers by European powers who border us.*

While in New York at the Congress, he falls in love with Elizabeth Kortright, whose family is prominent in local society. Their marriage in 1786 will span 44 years and produce a son, who dies in infancy, and two daughters.

When time comes for the 1787 Constitutional Convention, Monroe is still outranked by other Virginians and, to his annoyance, is left out of the delegation. His stated views exhibit a streak of political independence. Like the Federalists, he favors a strong central government, and supports its authority to nationalize the militia in times of crisis. But he stands with the Anti-Federalists in demanding the inclusion of a personal Bill of Rights.

Monroe steps up to challenge James Madison, who is eight years his senior, for a House seat in America's first election in 1788. He loses, but is soon selected as a US Senator in 1790. In Philadelphia, he boards with Madison and Jefferson, and aligns with the Democratic-Republican Party. After four years, his old war commander, George Washington, entrusts him with his first ministerial assignment to a Paris dominated by Napoleon.

His thankless task involves coddling France while his counterpart in London, John Jay, negotiates his Amity Treaty of 1794 with the British. Jay keeps him in the dark from start to finish, and Monroe ends up being humiliated when the French learn of the treaty in the press. The fiercely pro-French Monroe lashes out publicly against Jay, and

Alexander Hamilton convinces Washington to recall him. This wound is not forgotten, and Monroe is involved in exposing the Reynolds adultery affair which forces Hamilton to resign in 1795.

He returns home to resume his law career and set up his new plantation called Highland, situated on 1,000 acres immediately adjacent to Jefferson's Monticello. However, his true calling is politics, and in 1799 he is elected governor of Virginia. Then Jefferson becomes president in 1801 and grooms both Madison and Monroe as likely successors. As special envoy to France, Monroe helps negotiate the Louisiana Purchase. He serves as minister to Britain from 1803 to 1808, and rejects attempts by an anti-Jefferson wing of the Democratic-Republican Party to have him run against Madison in the 1808 election. Madison rewards his loyalty by naming him secretary of state, an office he holds from 1811 to 1817. After the British burn Washington on August 24, 1814, he also assumes the post of secretary of war until the fighting is over.

In 1816 he is a natural candidate to succeed Madison, and he goes on to complete two terms (1817–1825) during a period that becomes known as the "Era of Good Feelings"—despite the nation's first tremor around the issue of slavery, leading to the 1820 Missouri Compromise. His own recorded thoughts about slavery mirror Jefferson, and he is an early sponsor of the American Colonization Society. Monrovia, the capital city of Liberia, is named after him.

TIME: 1809

SIDEBAR: FOR SALE — MONROE'S PLANTATION, INCLUDING A STOCK OF CATTLE AND SLAVES

LOUDOUN LAND FOR SALE

For sale on Thursday, the 21st of December next on the premisies, the tract of LAND on which the late Judge Jones resided in Loudoun County with about 25 slaves, and the stock of Horses, Cattle, and Hogs, on the estate. The tract contains nearly 2000 acres [8 km²], and possesses many advantages which entitle it to the attention of those who may wish to reside, in that highly improved part of our country. Two merchant mills are in the neighbourhood, one on the adjoining estate, and the other within two miles [3 km]. It is 10 miles [16 km] from Leesburg, 35 [56 km] from Alexandria and 40 [64 km] from Georgetown. The new, Turn-pike from Alexandria crosses a corner of the land, and terminates at the nearest merchant mill. The whole tract is remarkably well watered, Little river passing through the middle of it, and many small streams on each side emptying into that river. About 50 or 60 acres [200,000 or 240,000 m²] are already well set with timothy, and at leats 300 acres (1.2 km²) are capable of being made excellent meadow. It will be divided into tracts of different dimensions to suit the convenience of purchasers. A credit of one, two and three years will be allowed. Bonds with approved security, and a trust on the land will be required. The negroes are supposed to be very valuable, some of them being good house servants, and the others, principally, young men and women. For them the same terms of credit will be allowed, and that of a year for every other article.

N.B. The above lands, being yet unsold, notice is given that they will be disposed of, by private sale, upon terms which will be made known on application to Israel Lacy Esq. of Goshen, Col. Armstead T. Mason, near Leesburg, Maj. Charles Fenton Mercer of Leesburg, or to the subscriber, near Milton in Albemarle county.

JAMES MONROE.
December, 23d 1809.

TIME: MARCH 4, 1817

MONROE'S FIRST INAUGURAL ADDRESS

The Capitol is still being rebuilt after the 1815 fire when James Monroe is inaugurated on March 4, 1817. The ceremony takes place in the temporary quarters of the House, known as the Brick Capitol. He is sworn in by his childhood friend, Chief Justice John Marshall, and then sets a precedent by stepping outside to deliver his address to a gathered crowd.

His speech begins by reflecting on the current state of the nation, which he finds flourishing under the government institutions in place since the Revolution.

I should be destitute of feeling if I was not deeply affected by the strong proof which my fellow-citizens have given me of their confidence in calling me to the high office whose functions I am about to assume....From the commencement of our Revolution to the present day almost forty years have elapsed...During a period fraught with difficulties and marked by very extraordinary events the United States have flourished beyond example. Their citizens individually have been happy and the nation prosperous.

He then outlines several of his proposed priorities: strengthening the national defense, developing infrastructure and manufacturing to expand the domestic economy and export trade abroad, managing public finances, and achieving harmony between western settlers and the Indian tribes.

James Monroe (1758–1831)

In commencing the duties of the chief executive office it has been the practice of the distinguished men who have gone before me to explain the principles which would govern them in their respective Administrations.

National honor is national property of the highest value… To secure us against dangers our coast and inland frontiers should be fortified, our Army and Navy, regulated upon just principles as to the force of each, be kept in perfect order, and our militia be placed on the best practicable footing.

Other interests of high importance will claim attention, among which the improvement of our country by roads and canals, proceeding always with a constitutional sanction, holds a distinguished place.

Our manufacturers will likewise require the systematic and fostering care of the Government

Equally important is it to provide at home a market for our raw materials, as by extending the competition it will enhance the price and protect the cultivator against the casualties incident to foreign markets.

With the Indian tribes it is our duty to cultivate friendly relations and to act with kindness and liberality Equally proper is it to persevere in our efforts to extend to them the advantages of civilization.

The great amount of our revenue and the flourishing state of the Treasury are a full proof of the competency of the national resources for any emergency, as they are of the willingness of our fellow-citizens to bear the burdens which the public necessities require.

It is particularly gratifying to me to enter on the discharge of these duties at a time when the United States are blessed with peace. It is a state most consistent with their prosperity and happiness. It will be my sincere desire to preserve it...

Monroe concludes with comments on the favorable state of the nation, and a wish for help from both citizens and the Almighty in the job that lies ahead.

Equally gratifying is it to witness the increased harmony of opinion which pervades our Union. Discord does not belong to our system.

Never did a government commence under auspices so favorable, nor ever was success so complete.

Relying on the aid to be derived from the other departments of the Government, I enter on the trust to which I have been called by the suffrages of my fellow-citizens with my fervent prayers to the Almighty that He will be pleased to continue to us that protection which He has already so conspicuously displayed in our favor.

TIME: MARCH 4, 1817 TO MARCH 3, 1821

OVERVIEW OF MONROE'S FIRST TERM

In assembling his cabinet, Monroe begins with a heady move by naming John Quincy Adams as his choice for secretary of state. Adams' foreign experience begins at age eleven when he accompanies his father to his post in Britain. From there he serves as a US senator, then as minister to the Netherlands, Prussia, Russia, and from 1814 to 1817 in England, where he first establishes a level of respect and trust with then Secretary of State Monroe that endures. Politically, Adams has grown up a Federalist, but he is forced out of the party in 1807 when he helps to draft the 1807 Embargo Bill and caucuses with the Democratic-Republican side in choosing Madison as their 1808 nominee. The partnership between Monroe and John Quincy Adams will compare with that between Jefferson and Madison.

The new president retains Crawford in his Treasury post, and reaches out to Congressman John Calhoun, an outspoken supporter of the 1812 conflict. These two, along with Adams, will contend to succeed Monroe when the 1824 presidential race begins.

JAMES MONROE CABINET IN 1817

POSITION	NAME	HOME STATE
Vice President	Daniel Tompkins	New York
Secretary of State	John Quincy Adams	Massachusetts
Secretary of Treasury	William Crawford	Georgia
Secretary of War	John C. Calhoun	South Carolina
Secretary of the Navy	Benjamin Crowninshield	Massachusetts
Attorney General	Richard Rush	Pennsylvania

Adams, like Monroe, believes that America is poised in 1817 to put aside its external concerns about safety and concentrate on its many opportunities for internal development.

Every serious difficulty which seemed alarming to the people of the Union in 1800 had been removed or sunk from notice in 1816. With the disappearance of immediate peril, foreign or domestic, society could devote all its energies…to its favorite objects.

This outlook is so pervasive that, in July 1817, the *Columbia Sentinel* newspaper declares that the nation has entered an "era of good feelings." Symbolic of this view is the start of work on an audacious engineering project that will last for eight years—construction of the Erie Canal, which will ultimately create a water route for commerce from Lake Erie to New York harbor.

Unfortunately, the rosy outlook predicted up front fails to materialize.

First off, Monroe finds that the War of 1812 had serious residual effects on the American economy, and these lead to the so-called "Panic of 1819."

Then events in 1820 multiply the challenges.

In South America, the famous liberator Simón Bolívar is busily overthrowing Spain's colonies, with the effects reaching all the way up to America's southern neighbor, Mexico. Concerns mount about incursions from Spain or surrogates into the Western Hemisphere. Troubles in Spanish Florida around rebel Seminole Indians increase these worries.

Then comes another shock, this time from a Pennsylvania congressman, James Tallmadge Jr., who offers up an amendment to a bill involving statehood for Missouri that sets off a firestorm around the long-suppressed topic of slavery. It will prove to be the opening thrust in a 40-year conflict between the South and the North that ends in civil war.

The good news is that by the close of his first term Monroe has navigated many of these setbacks quite well.

KEY EVENTS: MONROE'S FIRST TERM (1817–1821)

1817	
March 4	Monroe inaugurated
July 4	Construction begins in Rome, NY on DeWitt Clinton's Erie Canal project
July 12	*Columbia Sentinel* newspaper dubs the period "the era of good feelings" in America
Sept 27	Ohio Indians cede 4 million acres of land to state of Ohio
Oct 8	John C. Calhoun named secretary of war
November	First Seminole War begins
Dec 2	Monroe asserts that federal funds can be used for infrastructure projects
1818	
Jan 8	Sharp post-war declines in manufacturing output are recorded
Feb 28	New York passes bill requiring debts be paid with specie or US banknotes
May 24	General Andrew Jackson takes Spanish outpost at Pensacola, Florida
June 20	Connecticut becomes the first eastern state to drop property requirement for suffrage
July 1	Second US Bank tightens money supply by requiring states to pay off debts in gold
Aug 23	First steamship trip goes across Lake Erie to Detroit
Oct 19	Chickasaw Indians cede lands between Mississippi and Tennessee Rivers
Oct 20	US and Britain sign Convention of 1818 on Canadian borders, except for Oregon region
Nov 20	Bank of Kentucky suspends operations, causing public panic
Nov 28	John Quincy Adams informs Spain that it must either control Seminoles or cede Florida to US
Dec 3	Illinois admitted as 21st state
1819	
January	Beginning of widespread bank failures, foreclosure and financial collapse
Jan 12	Clay bill to condemn Andrew Jackson's unilateral actions in Florida fails to pass
Feb 2	In *Dartmouth v. Woodward*, Supreme Court says corporate charters are valid contracts
Feb 13	James Tallmadge Jr. seeks to amend Missouri statehood bill by ending slavery there
Feb 22	In Adams-Onís Treaty, Spain cedes East Florida to US for $5 million and US agrees to boundary limits around Texas
Feb 27	After Tallmadge Amendment passes in House on Feb 17, the Senate votes it down
Mar 6	In *McCulloch v. Maryland*, Supreme Court says the US Bank is legal and that states cannot tax it
May 5	Sermon by William Ellery Channing announces Unitarian schism with Christian churches
June 20	Steamship *Savannah* completes transatlantic journey to Liverpool
Dec 14	Alabama admitted as 22nd state

1820	
Jan 23	The House votes to admit Maine as 23rd state, but the senate holds this up
Jan 26	The House supports the Taylor Amendment allowing Missouri to enter as a slave state
Feb 6	Ship carrying 86 free Black people sets sail from New York headed to Sierra Leone
Feb 17	The Thomas Amendment in the Senate adds the 36'30" free/slave dividing line in LA land
Mar 3	Missouri Compromise admits Maine as a free state, Missouri as a slave state, and 36'30" as redline
Mar 15	Maine is admitted as 23rd state, making twelve free and eleven slave at the moment
April 24	Public Land Act passes: price per acre down from $2 to $1.25; minimum plot from 160 acres to 80 acres
May 15	To stop smuggling of foreign enslaved people into US, Congress deems this piracy punishable by death
July 19	Initial Missouri constitution bars free Black people and mulattos from entering the state
Dec 6	Monroe wins second term in a landslide
December	Kentucky Relief Party set up to relieve debtors, opposed by Clay, supported by Jackson
1821	
	Benjamin Lundy begins publishing *Genius of Universal Emancipation* newspaper
Jan 17	Spain allows Moses and son Stephen Austin to settle 300 Americans in San Antonio
Feb 24	Mexico declares independence from Spain
Mar 2	Congresses agrees to admit Missouri, if it drops unconstitutional ban against free Black people

## 39

AMERICA EXPERIENCES A POSTWAR ECONOMIC DEPRESSION

TIME: 1812–1814

THE WAR OF 1812 PROMPTS A "BOOM CYCLE" IN AMERICA'S ECONOMY

From his first day in office, James Monroe is plagued by the economic troubles he inherits from his predecessor.

A $50 banknote

These materialize out of the "boom-bust cycle" that begins in 1812 as America gears up to fight the war with Britain.

A continental army needs to be formed and equipped, housed and fed, transported and resupplied, all in a short time frame and with no clear end in sight. Additionally, the British blockade of American ports greatly increased the need for domestically-produced goods.

"BOOM CYCLE" DURING WAR OF 1812

GDP	1812	1813	1814
$	786,000	969,000	1,078,000
% Change	2%	23%	11%
Per Capita	103	123	133

Taken together, this increased "demand" represented a windfall opportunity for a host of suppliers—who turn to local bankers to borrow the money needed to invest in added capacity.

The banks are only too happy to comply with this increased demand for more loans, often at higher than usual rates of interest.

But many face a problem: a lack of sufficient cash on hand to complete the loans.

They solve this problem by resorting to a time-honored tactic—simply printing and issuing more soft money banknotes, while ignoring the rules about properly backing them with reserves of gold or silver.

The result is a sharp increase in the money supply in circulation, followed by inflation.

The price of goods across the economy goes up in response to a decline in the true value/buying power of each dollar in the system.

And, in 1812, there is no longer a federal Bank of the United States in place to curtail the printing of soft money unrelated to specie on hand. That's because Jefferson views the BUS as another of Hamilton's monarchistic devices to centralize governmental power— and he allows its charter to expire in 1811.

By 1813 then the American economy is enjoying a "boom cycle."

Those who have taken out loans for investment are reaping large gains in profit, and are able to pay off their debts to the banks in full and on time. In turn, bankers are able to meet their payments to depositors, while also increasing their own private profits.

TIME: 1815–1816

A "BUST CYCLE" FOLLOWS WHEN THE WAR ENDS

The increased prosperity continues until the war with Britain comes to a close in 1815.

At which time the ramped-up demand for goods suddenly drops, and suppliers find themselves with excess inventory they can't sell, along with excess operating costs they need to shed.

The more conservative investors are able to work their way back to a sustainable equilibrium, but others are left with crippling financial losses.

When their banks demand pay back on their loans taken, they are left in default. This signals the shift from "boom cycle" to "bust cycle." The rapid economic growth evident in 1813 and 1814 disappears, and down years take over.

"BUST CYCLE" BEGINS AT END OF WAR

GDP	1814	1815	1816
$	1,078,000	925,000	819,000
% Change	11%	(14%)	(11%)
Per Capita	133	111	96

The early losses materialize in 1815 and 1816, while Madison is still in office. Aggregate demand for goods drops along with production. Prices increase as the excess money supply leads on to inflation.

As alarm sets in, Treasury Secretary Gallatin finally persuades Madison to reverse his opposition to Hamilton's financial model, and the Second Bank of the United States is approved in 1816.

Its role is twofold:

- To restore credibility to the nation's supply of soft money and thereby tamp down inflation; and
- To expand the revenue available to the federal government through the issuance of treasury bonds.

In 1817 the burden falls on Monroe and Crawford to successfully execute this strategy.

TIME: 1817–1818

AMERICA'S FIRST PROLONGED DEPRESSION SETS IN

However, nothing they do can solve the problems facing the banking system—which will culminate in the "Panic of 1819."

Because once the bankers are out on a limb, wantonly printing money to chase windfall profits, there are no easy fixes if the loans they've made cannot be paid back.

By 1818 that outcome is all too often the norm. Widespread defaults on loans rapidly upset the delicate cash flow balance that keeps banks viable. Incoming cash from interest on their loans falls short of outgoing cash needed to pay interest to depositors. The banks are now in a spiraling "money squeeze" of their own.

In an often desperate search for more cash, the banks "foreclose" on customers whose loans are in default. But these foreclosures often leave them with assets (e.g. homes, farms, goods) they don't want to hold and can only sell at rock bottom prices.

Public protests call for "stay laws" to delay loan repayments and foreclosures, as general hostility toward banks spreads. Ohio Congressman William Henry Harrison captures this anger, when he says:

I hate all banks!

As the "squeeze" on local banks continues, the Second Bank of the United States launches a new policy that will make things even more difficult in the short run.

It requires that state banks complete future transactions with the BUS using gold or silver specie rather than paper currency. (Andrew Jackson will repeat this same tactic some seventeen years hence.)

On the surface, the rationale for this move is sound. The federal government itself still needs to pay off sizable loans made by foreign investors during the War of 1812, and the demand here is for gold or silver coins rather than soft money. In addition, transactions in specie are intended to reassert the need for adequate bank reserves, reduce over-printing of soft currency, and reduce inflation. All worthy goals.

But many local banks who wish to borrow money from the BUS to offset their cash flow problems now find that "window" closed to them because their inventory of specie is too limited.

All that's left for them at this point is to refuse payments of interest to their depositors—and when this happens, panic sets in among their customers. "Runs on banks" pop up around the country as depositors line up to withdraw their life's savings before whatever cash left on hand runs out. This simply accelerates the downward cycle until the target banks are forced to close their doors.

In 1818 the Bank of Kentucky suspends all operations—a fate shared by roughly 30% of the nation's 420 state banks over the course of the panic.

TIME: 1819 – 1820

TIME ALONE ENDS THE DOWNTURN

As 1819 plays out, all that can go wrong with America's capitalist system has gone wrong.

The allure of windfall profits has upped the demand for speculative loans. Banks respond by wantonly printing paper money not backed by gold or silver reserves. Uncontrolled expansion of the money supply erodes the true value of cash and leads to damaging price inflation. The anticipated profits dry up due to a sudden change in external conditions (in this case, the end of the war). When loans come due, borrowers are unable to pay them off. Defaults upset the banks' cash flow balance and they lack the money needed to pay interest due on deposits. Panic sets in among all depositors leading to "runs" on banks who are then forced to shut down.

Unfortunately, history will show this pattern of economic boom and bust repeating itself in America every two decades or so—thus the panics of 1837, 1857, 1873, 1893, 1907, 1929, and so forth.

Many lives are damaged by its effects.

In Pennsylvania, land values plummet from $150 per acre in 1815 to $35 in 1819. Over 50,000 men are unemployed in Philadelphia, and some 1,800 are sent to debtors' prison. Beggars appear on city streets, along with soup kitchens and homeless shelters.

Senator John Calhoun sums up conditions in 1820:

There has been within these two years an immense revolution of fortunes in every part of the Union; enormous numbers of persons utterly ruined; multitudes in deep distress.

In the end, the depression extends over six years, roughly from 1815 to 1820—although GDP per capita remains depressed until many years later.

GDP TRENDS DURING THE DEPRESSION FOLLOWING THE WAR OF 1812

	1814	1815	1816	1817	1818	1819	1820	1821	1822	1823	1824	1825
$000	1,078	925	819	769	737	726	710	735	805	759	754	822
% Ch	11%	(14%)	(11%)	(6%)	(4%)	(2%)	(2%)	3%	9%	(6%)	(1%)	9%
Per Capita	133	111	96	87	81	78	74	74	79	72	70	74

Government policies do not escape criticism during the downturn—and ominously some of the anger takes on a sectional tone.

When first passed in April 1816, the "Dallas Tariff" on imported goods is almost universally approved. But three years later, as the depression drags on with Monroe in office, it begins to come under attack.

The South wants the tariff lowered so that prices on finished goods (e.g. clothing) from Europe will fall, domestic sales will grow, and the export market for raw cotton will spike up along with planters' profits.

New Englanders want exactly the opposite. Aside from raising federal revenue, the tariff was adopted to "protect" American manufacturing of finished goods by keeping the prices of domestically produced goods below their European competition.

This North-South tension over the tariff is soon to be further fueled in 1820 by controversies surrounding admission of Missouri as the 23rd state in the Union.

AMERICA ACQUIRES THE TWO FLORIDAS FROM SPAIN

TIME: 1513–1818

THE COMPLEX HISTORY OF LA FLORIDA

Before adding Missouri, the landmass of the United States expands again with the acquisition of "the two Floridas" from Spain.

The history of Florida is mired in the complexities of European colonization and warfare.

The Spanish explorer Ponce de León arrives there on Easter Sunday in 1513, and christens it "La Florida" ("flowering Easter") in tribute to the traditional feast day celebration. In the 1520s and 1530s Hernando de Soto and Álvar Núñez Cabeza de Vaca consolidate Spain's claim to the land, and Jesuit missions begin to spring up from St. Augustine on the east coast to Pensacola 400 miles to the west. But the actual number of settlers remains low over time, in part due to hostility from local Creek and Seminole tribes.

Ownership of La Florida comes into play in 1763, after Britain's victory in the first global

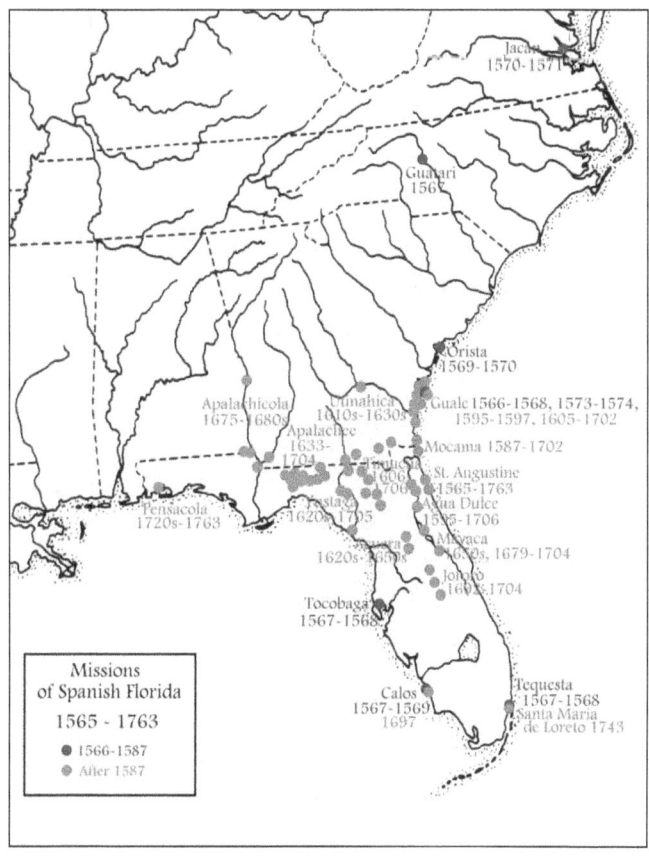

Map of Spanish missions in Florida

conflict known as the Seven Years' War. Spain, on the losing side alongside France, surrenders its control over Cuba when the port city of Havana falls to the Royal Navy. To regain this, it trades La Florida to Britain in exchange for Cuba, as part of the Treaty of Paris.

The British immediately divide the territory into two colonies, east and west of the Apalachicola River. West Florida, comprising some 380,000 acres, has its capital in Pensacola; the much larger East Florida, 2.8 million acres, is anchored in St. Augustine. Both are headed by a governor and administered along the same lines as Britain's original thirteen colonies.

A proclamation issued in 1763 tries to force migration of British citizens into the new Florida colony rather than to the north across the Appalachian range. To sweeten the deal, pioneers are promised generous land grants, and slavery is permitted to draw Southern settlers and crops, especially cotton and indigo.

But British control over the two Floridas is only twelve years old when America's Revolutionary War erupts.

The early settlers side unequivocally with the crown, and local militias are called out for defense. When the conflict shifts to the southern theater in 1780, the Floridians are comforted by early victories at Charleston and Savannah. Then comes the stunning defeat at Yorktown in 1781, followed by the 1783 Treaty of Ghent, where America's negotiators take what they can get: formal recognition of their independence and British land from west of the Appalachians to the Mississippi.

Canada remains in British hands and La Florida is returned to France's ally, Spain.

In regaining the two Floridas, Spain controls almost all of the critical southern port cities along the Gulf of Mexico, save for New Orleans, which America wins in the 1803 Louisiana Purchase. Almost inevitably a string of border disputes erupt between Spain and the US, starting in the west.

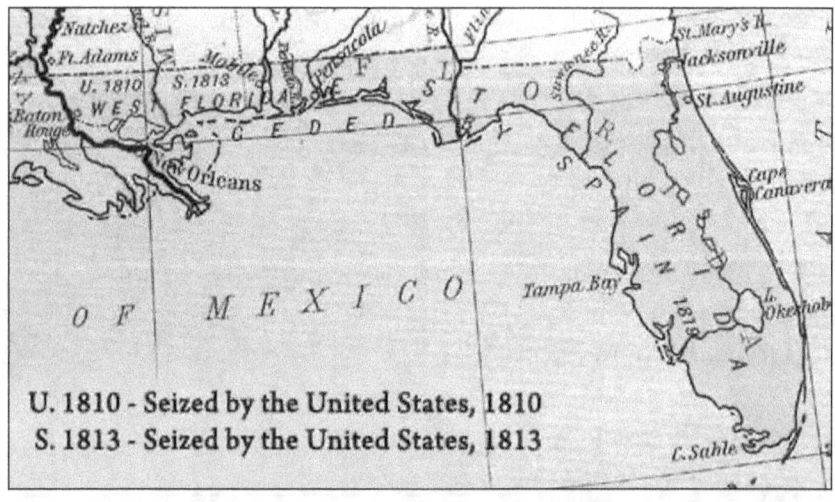

U. 1810 - Seized by the United States, 1810
S. 1813 - Seized by the United States, 1813

American seizures of the two Floridas

Jefferson argues that West Florida is actually a part of its 1803 acquisition from France, and Madison supports the 1810 takeover of Baton Rouge. He then orders American troops to secure control over all of West Florida in 1813.

Under Madison, the focus shifts to East Florida, with tensions centering on its status as a haven for escaping enslaved people from Georgia and South Carolina and ongoing raids by Seminole tribes north of the border. These raids are initially suppressed in 1816 by General Andrew Jackson in the First Seminole War. In 1818, Secretary of War John C. Calhoun again calls upon Jackson to march into Spanish Florida.

TIME: 1818

GENERAL ANDREW JACKSON RAMPAGES ACROSS FLORIDA

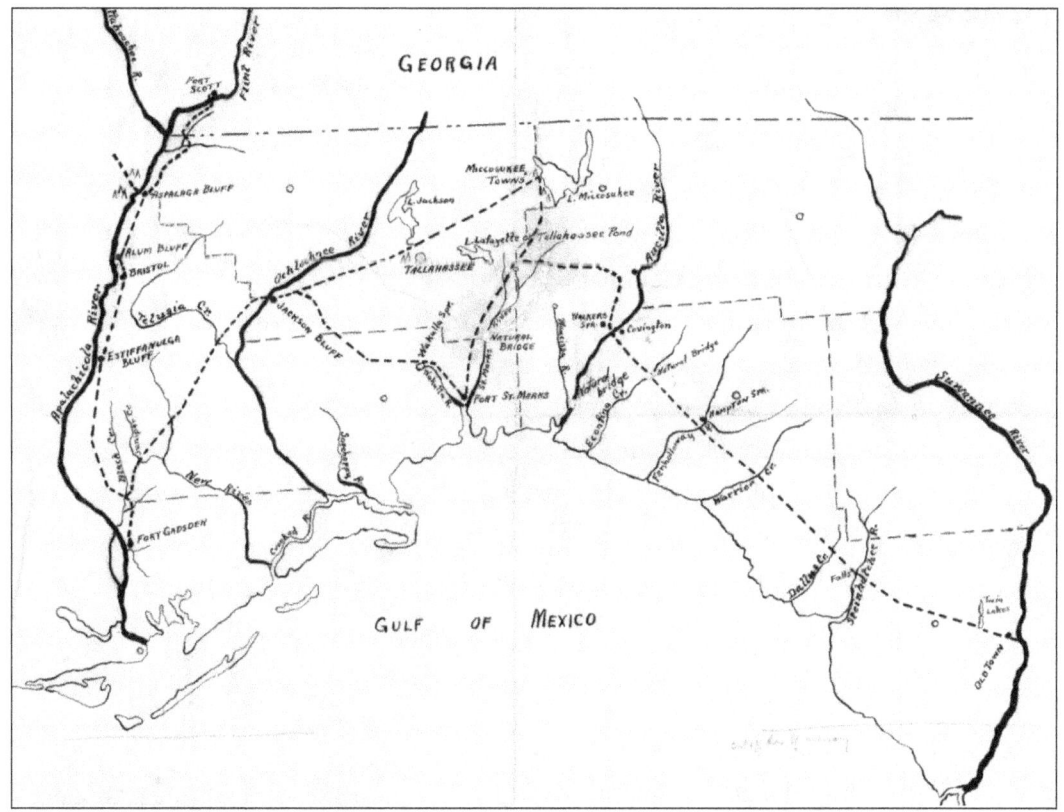

Map of General Andrew Jackson's Florida incursion in 1818
from the Apalachicola River (left) to the Suwannee River (right)

General Jackson of course has won national fame during the War of 1812 with his landmark victories at Horseshoe Bend and New Orleans, so he is well accustomed to leading troops into action.

On March 15, 1818, Jackson sets out against East Florida from Ft. Scott (upper left) with a mixed force of some 4,200 regulars, militia, and friendly Creek Indians. Moving south down the Apalachicola River, he pauses to construct a new stronghold, Ft. Gadsden (lower left), and garrisons some his troops there.

He then swings back up north and east, assaulting and burning an Indian village at Tallahassee on March 31 and taking the town of Miccosukee the following day.

The general continues south to San Marcos de Apalache—a port city on the Gulf of Mexico, home to the Spanish fort of St. Marks—where he finds two British nationals, Robert Ambrister and Alexander Arbuthnot, who are rumored to be selling guns to the Indians. Jackson sets up a court martial to try both men, who are found guilty. On April 29 Ambrister is executed by firing squad and Arbuthnot is hanged.

After a sweep further east along the Suwannee River, Jackson feels he has accomplished his mission and heads back west, first to Ft. Gadsden and then into West Florida, were he reduces the Spanish Ft. Barrancas at Pensacola on May 28.

Andrew Jackson (1767–1845)

This ends Jackson's ten-week rampage across northern Florida.

It is followed by a barrage of criticism back in Washington that will forever make adversaries of Jackson and Speaker of the House Henry Clay, and some twelve years later divide President Jackson and Vice President Calhoun.

Clay regards Jackson's executions at St. Marks and his seizure of Pensacola as "acts of war" carried out in rogue fashion by the general without authorization from Congress, as required in the Constitution.

When Clay's complaint is discussed within Monroe's cabinet, Calhoun attempts to dodge responsibility, saying that Jackson exceeded his orders and should be arrested—a political maneuver that Jackson learns of more than a decade later.

Jackson's successes are again applauded by the public and he defends himself, arguing that he was acting under direct orders to carry out his patriotic duty.

Henry Clay (1777–1852)

But Clay is undeterred. He calls congressional hearings to review the Ambrister and Arbuthnot cases and presses to officially censure Jackson.

At this point, Secretary of State John Quincy Adams steps in and argues that his colleagues should back off from their attacks on Jackson.

My principle is that everything he did was defensive; that as such it was neither war against Spain nor violation of the Constitution.

This works, but the general will neither forget nor forgive Clay, and the Speaker will henceforth refer to Jackson as "King Andrew," ever ready to act above the law.

Their very personal feud will continue until Jackson's death in 1845.

TIME: FEBRUARY 22, 1819

SPAIN CEDES FLORIDA TO AMERICA IN THE ADAMS-ONÍS TREATY

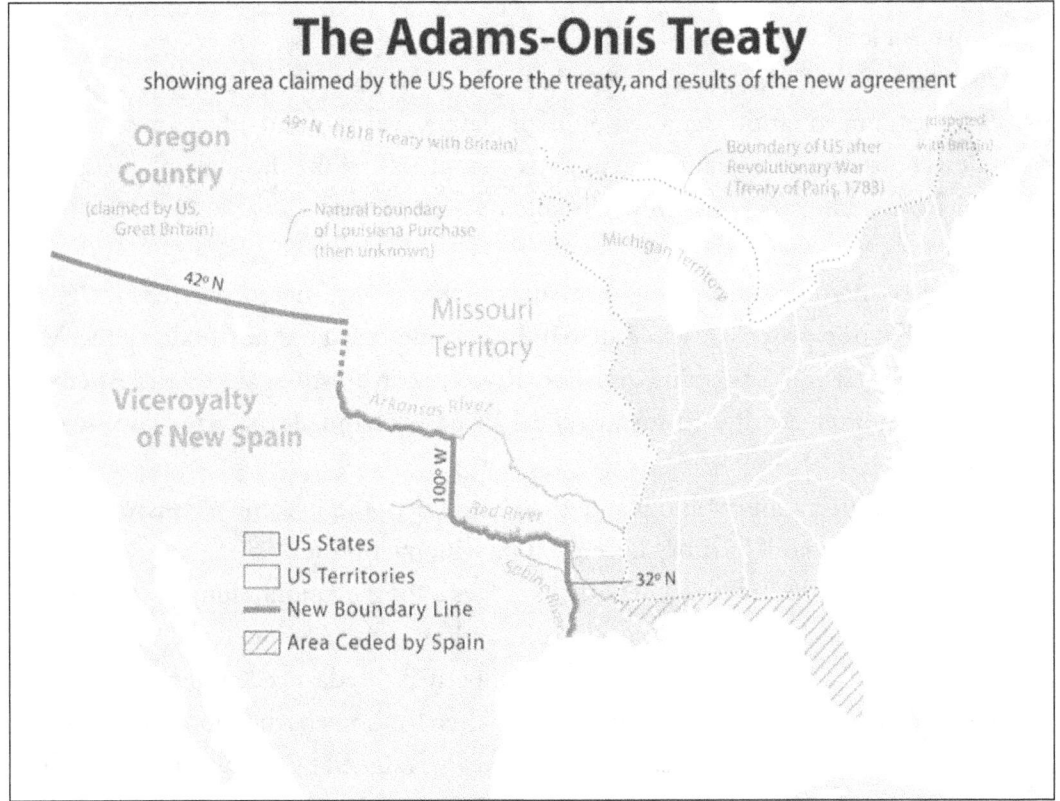

Final boundary settlement

As Jackson is on the march, Adams is continuing to negotiate with Luis de Onís, Spain's ambassador to the United States, to acquire Florida. Onís is a clever adversary according to Adams:

A finished scholar in the Spanish procrastinating school of diplomacy.

The minister has long tried to deflect inquiries about surrendering any of Spain's land holdings in America, be they related to La Florida or to the vast territory west of the Louisiana Territory.

But by 1818 Spain's colonial empire in the western hemisphere is crumbling. One attempt at independence has already been made and turned back in Mexico, and the liberator Simón Bolívar is well on his way to ending Spanish rule in South America.

So when Secretary of State Adams approaches Onís again about Florida, the door is opened to resolution.

Onís recognizes that Spain's military forces in Florida are incapable of controlling the border—either to stop further Seminole incursions into Georgia or to drive out American occupiers. Thus trying to hold on to Florida strikes him as a lost cause.

Instead, his focus turns to protecting Spain's much more important boundaries in the west—from Texas and Mexico all the way across the southwest to the Pacific coast. The key to this lies in defining exactly where America's Louisiana Purchase land ends and where Spanish land begins.

Disputes on this have surfaced repeatedly since Napoleon's 1803 sale, and Adams and Onís begin negotiations far apart on their claims. Adams argues that American land should extend to the Rio Grande River, thus encompassing the province of Tejas. Onís counters by asserting that the proper boundary should be far east, at the Mississippi River.

After this difference stalls progress, Adams takes a hard-nosed stance. He "gives" on the Rio Grande proposal, while demanding a line that goes north along the Mississippi, then west on the Sabine and Red Rivers, then north again to the Arkansas, followed by another northward turn to the 42nd parallel and all the way from there to the west coast.

If accepted, such a line would insure that America would become a transcontinental nation, with the Oregon Territory becoming its window on the Pacific.

To further provoke a settlement, Adams writes a long memorandum to the Spanish government in Madrid asserting that Jackson's actions were in self-defense, and that the "derelict province" of Florida must either be properly policed or ceded immediately.

Spain finally capitulates some nine months after Jackson's occupation. On February 22, 1819, the Adams-Onís (Transcontinental) Treaty is signed by the two diplomats. The key provisions include:

- Spain cedes West and East Florida to the United States for $5,000;
- The western border of the Louisiana Purchase is resolved;
- Spain gives up its claims north of the 42nd parallel (Oregon); and
- The US formally gives up its claims to the Texas territory.

Henry Clay feels that the treaty gives up too much, especially as it relates to Texas, which many have viewed as part of the Louisiana Purchase.

But the Senate passes the Treaty on February 24, 1819 and it goes into effect two years later.

The ever self-critical Adams will later reflect on his work in uncharacteristically effusive terms:

The Florida Treaty was the most important incident in my life, and the most successful negotiation ever consummated by the Government of this nation.

41

THE MARSHALL COURT ISSUES THREE LANDMARK LEGAL RULINGS

TIME: MARCH 16, 1810

IN *FLETCHER V. PECK* THE SUPREME COURT OVERTURNS A STATE LAW AS UNCONSTITUTIONAL

Between 1801 and 1835 President Monroe's childhood friend, John Marshall, will lead the Supreme Court to a series of rulings that define and enforce the laws of the land.

In 1803 his ruling in the famous case of *Marbury v. Madison* establishes the Supreme Court as final arbiter over the meaning of the articles and clauses in the Constitution.

In 1810 the *Fletcher v. Peck* dispute from Georgia finds the Supreme Court further asserting its authority—overturning a bill passed by a state legislature on the grounds that it violates the US Constitution.

The focus here is on "contract law," with the facts of the case as follows.

After the Revolutionary War, the state of Georgia claims ownership of territory to its west, known as the Yazoo lands. This vast expanse, some 35 million acres in total, will ultimately encompass the states of Alabama and Mississippi.

In 1795 land speculators hand over bribes to members of the Georgia state legislature to sell them the Yazoo lands for less than two cents an acre. When word of the bribery slips out, voters elect a new set of representatives in 1796, who pass a statute voiding the prior sale. Widespread confusion about ownership follows, and many lawsuits are filed.

One of these suits involves a parcel of 15,000 acres, sold by John Peck to Robert Fletcher, before the 1796 bill went into effect. Fletcher still wants the land, but wishes to make sure that it is unencumbered by the 1796 statute. So he files a suit against Peck in 1803 to find out for sure.

After many back and forth rulings in lower courts, the suit finally reaches Marshall in February 1810—with the question focused on whether the 1796 state legislature acted legally in overturning the corrupt 1795 land sale.

The opinion is delivered on March 16, 1810, with Marshall summing up a unanimous 5–0 decision.

Despite the corruption surrounding the contract signed in 1795, the Marshall Court decides that the attempt by the 1796 legislature to overturn it violates Article I, Section 10, Clause 1 of the US Constitution.

No State shall pass any Bill of Attainder, ex post facto Law, or Law impairing the Obligation of Contracts.

This decision, favoring Peck's claim of ownership, is the first time the Supreme Court declares that a state law must be voided because it is unconstitutional. It will not be the last time that Marshall limits the power of the states.

TIME: FEBRUARY 2, 1819

DARTMOUTH COLLEGE V. WOODWARD DECISION DEFINES RIGHTS FOR AMERICAN CORPORATIONS

During Monroe's presidency, several other high court decisions will prove particularly impactful.

The first, in 1819, involves an attempt by the state of New Hampshire to take control over Dartmouth College, a private institution, by replacing its existing trustees with a slate of their own.

Dartmouth is founded by a Congregationalist minister, Eleazar Wheelock, as a school for missionaries and Native Americans. A corporate charter, approved by the royal governor of New Hampshire colony in 1769, sets up two boards of trustees—one English and one American—to oversee college finances.

Wheelock dies in 1779 and is succeeded by his son John, who encounters financial difficulties that threaten the viability and assets of the college. This prompts several board members—now all American—to demand his resignation. When he refuses, they turn to Anti-Federalist members of the state legislature, who pass a bill converting Dartmouth from a private to a public school and naming a new set of trustees.

But others on the board oppose the change, arguing that according to Article I, Section 10 of

Daniel Webster (1782–1852)

the Constitution, the government has no right to interfere with the operations of a private corporation.

In February 1817 they file a lawsuit against William H. Woodward, one of the original trustee dissidents, now serving as secretary-treasurer on the replacement state-sponsored board. The suit demands that the college be returned to private status, and that Woodward be compelled to return all records and seals, while also paying a $50,000 fine.

The Supreme Court of New Hampshire rules in favor of Woodward on the grounds that the school's corporate charter was null and void after the Revolutionary War and independence from the crown. This ruling is sufficiently important and controversial that the Marshall Court decides to review it.

The plaintiff's case is argued by Daniel Webster, already regarded as the leading constitutional lawyer in America at 37 years old, and a former two-term member of the House of Representatives from New Hampshire (1813–1817).

Over time, Webster will argue some 223 cases before the Supreme Court, winning roughly half of them. In this instance, the matter is very personal to him, since he is an 1801 Phi Beta Kappa graduate of Dartmouth.

"Black Dan" Webster is forever an imposing figure in the courtroom and the halls of Congress, and his pleas ring with an emotional fervor that seldom fails to touch the minds and the hearts of his audiences. This is again the case in his summation to the chief justice about Dartmouth:

> *This, sir, is my case. It is the case not merely of that humble institution, it is the case of every college in our land... Sir, you may destroy this little institution; it is weak; it is in your hands! I know it is one of the lesser lights in the literary horizon of our country. You may put it out. But if you do so you must carry through your work! You must extinguish, one after another, all those greater lights of science which for more than a century have thrown their radiance over our land. It is, sir, as I have said, a small college. And yet there are those who love it!*

By a 5–1 majority, the Supreme Court comes down in favor of Webster and the inviolability of Dartmouth's corporate charter, albeit originally signed with King George III.

This ruling will have a profound effect on the evolution of private corporations in America.

It establishes the principle that private corporations are allowed to operate in their own self-interest rather than on behalf of the state. They cannot act in violation of state or federal laws. But they have the right to pursue their own ends—for example, adding to the wealth of their shareholders—without arbitrary or frivolous interference from government.

In 1825 the court will revisit the rights of corporations in: *The Society for the Propagation of the Gospel in Foreign Parts v. Town of Pawlet.* Here the state of Vermont tries to revoke land grants held by an English corporation dedicated to Christian missionary work in America.

Again the Marshall court sides with the corporation against the state.

Writing for the majority, Justice Joseph Story concludes that corporations enjoy the same rights to their property as those enjoyed by everyday citizens. Over time, Story's analogy between the rights of individual people and corporations—literally a "body of people"—catches hold as a precedent in common law.

In 1832, Marshall picks up on Story's analogy in defining another characteristic of corporations, namely their right to exist beyond the lifetimes of their original founders.

The great object of an incorporation is to bestow the character and properties of individuality on a collective and changing body of men.

The principle that corporations have the right to establish their own charters, to possess property, and to endure across generations becomes a driving force in the development of private businesses and economic growth in America.

Backed by a 5–1 majority, Marshall argues that a corporate charter is a contract and, as such, it cannot be arbitrarily breached by the state.

TIME: MARCH 16, 1819

MCCULLOCH V. MARYLAND DECISION DECLARES THAT FEDERAL LAWS TRUMP STATE LAWS

On March 16, 1819, six weeks after the Dartmouth College decision the Marshall court again reins in the power of individual state legislatures.

This time the state in question is Maryland, and its adversary is none other than the federal government itself.

The dispute arises when the Second Bank of the United States decides to operate a branch in the city of Baltimore, and the Maryland legislature passes a bill to collect a state tax on transactions done by the bank.

The head of the US Bank, James McCulloch, refuses to pay the tax and goes to court to affirm the legality of his refusal. But the Maryland Court of Appeals not only rules against McCulloch, it also declares that the federal government had no right under the Constitution to even charter a Bank of the United States in the first place.

According to Maryland, the Constitution says nothing about the federal government's role in establishing bank charters, and therefore, under the Tenth Amendment, it is the "state's right" to act as it sees fit.

Here indeed is a constitutional question around defining federal versus state powers that is worthy of the Supreme Court's closest scrutiny.

In the final ruling, backed by a 7–0 majority, Marshall opens the door to a broad interpretation of the powers the founders intended to place in the hands of the federal government.

He first observes that no single document could be expected to provide a list of enumerated powers sufficiently detailed and comprehensive enough to cover all issues coming before the courts.

From there he zeroes in on Article I, Section 8, Clause 18 of the Constitution and the notion that the federal legislature has the power to pass whatever laws it deems "necessary and proper" to fulfill its duty to the citizens.

The Congress shall have power to make all Laws which shall be necessary and proper for carrying into execution…the powers vested by this Constitution in the government of the United States.

But what is "necessary and proper" when it comes to banking?

For the Marshall court, it is whatever the voice of the people deem it to be when the issues are debated and voted upon by their representatives in Congress.

Thus, the fact that the first session of Congress found it "necessary and proper" to charter the First Bank of the United States provides a sound precedent for the legitimacy of a Second US Bank.

Finally, the decision to charter the US Bank was reached at the national level, by majority rule, after all sides had a chance to make their arguments pro or con. Surely the voice of the people operating together as a unified nation deserves to trump the voice of any one dissident state.

So Marshall and his colleagues side unanimously with McCulloch over Maryland.

For the Jeffersonians, this decision threatens their wish to limit federal powers via the Tenth Amendment.

The powers not delegated to the United States by the Constitution, nor prohibited by it to the States, are reserved to the States respectively, or to the people.

If the Congress in DC gets to decide what is "necessary and proper" when it comes to setting up bank charters, what else might follow from this precedent?

For many Southerners, the focus turns immediately to the future of slavery.

Yes, the right to own slaves within the 1787 boundaries of the United States is expressly stated. But does that right extend automatically to new land, such as the Louisiana Territory, acquired after the original contract between the states?

Or, based on this Marshall Court principle, will the federal legislature claim that it is "necessary and proper" for this decision to rest on their shoulders?

If so, many Southerners begin to see the federal legislature as a clear and present danger to their economic prosperity. What would happen to future demand for their cotton and their slaves if the US Congress decided to contain slavery within its original boundaries rather than allow it to spread across the Mississippi River?

In 1820 that question will move from idle speculation among wealthy planters to center stage on the floor of Congress.

## 42

A CRISIS OVER SLAVERY IS AVERTED BY THE MISSOURI COMPROMISE

TIME: FEBRUARY 13, 1819

MISSOURI APPLIES TO BECOME THE NEXT AMERICAN STATE

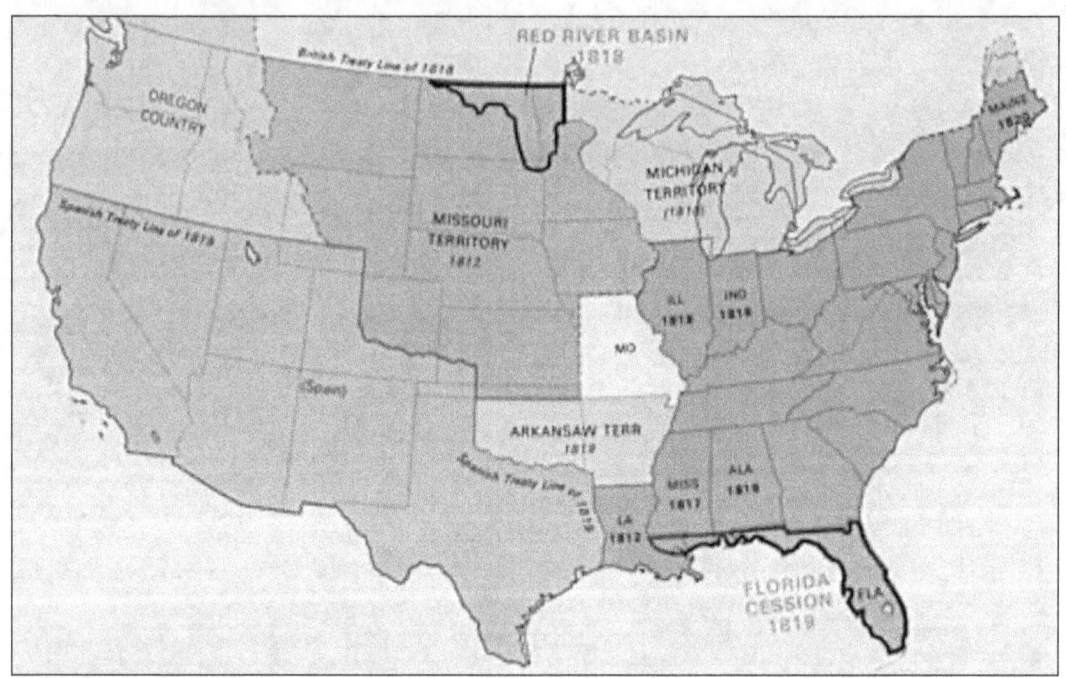

The proposed state of Missouri (yellow), bordering Illinois, in 1819

On February 13, 1819, a bill is laid before the House of Representatives to authorize the settlers in the Missouri territory to form a state constitution and apply for admission to the Union.

Missouri has grown up around the boom town of St. Louis, which the French settled in 1673. By 1818 St. Louis is a key port for the new steamboat trade along the Mississippi, and it offers its 9,500 inhabitants a post office, three banks, a flour mill, several distilleries, and a brewery, along with roughly 40 retail storefronts.

As soon as the territory population hits the 60,000 threshold, Missouri is eager to become America's 23rd state.

At first glance, this seems simple enough. The process required is laid out in the Enabling Act of 1802, and it has been used successfully to admit five new western states from Ohio in 1804 to Illinois in 1818.

But Missouri comes with a difference. It will be the first state west of the Mississippi River, situated on new land acquired in the Louisiana Purchase.

It will also be the first state where the presence or absence of slavery is not determined according to the Ohio River line of demarcation, as laid out in the Northwest Ordinance of 1787.

As such, it ignites a fresh debate about what "slavery policy" should apply on this new soil.

An outcome in favor of extending slavery across the river is crucial to the South for two reasons. The first is eco-

Rochester, Smith, Minn.

A western settler

nomic. The old South has bet its future wealth on opening new plantations in the west to buy its excess slaves and to grow cotton. Missouri is a prime prospect for this scenario, but only if slavery is allowed. The second reason relates to political power. If slavery is allowed, the South would gain a 24–22 edge versus the North in Senate seats and greater leverage over all forms of future federal legislation.

The Southern case is also bolstered by the fact that over 10,000 enslaved people, about one in six of all settlers, already reside in Missouri by 1819.

Surely, the argument goes, the federal government has no right to deprive owners of migrating with their existing "property in slaves" into whatever territory they choose.

TIME: 1607 AND ONWARD

NORTHERNERS FEAR EXPANSION OF THE BLACK POPULATION

However, Northern legislators are not ready to go along with the southern plan.

Their publicly-stated rationales vary widely. Some point to a map showing that 90% of the Missouri landmass lies due west of Illinois, a "free state" under the 1787 Northwest Ordinance line of demarcation traced by the Ohio River. Others argue that making Missouri a "slave state" would set a precedent for its western neighbor, the Nebraska territory, drawing plantation owners onto land already set aside for the "relocation" of the eastern Indian tribes. A few rail against the South for trying to use Missouri to gain a voting edge in the Senate.

But behind these rationales lies a simpler truth: recognition by Northern politicians that their white populations hope to cleanse all Black people, enlaved or free, from living in their midst.

Attempts to do so are already well established by 1819. "Black codes" discouraging freed men from living in Ohio, Indiana, and Illinois are already in place, and "modifications" to state constitutions begin to materialize. Thus the apparently high-minded first clause opposing slavery in the states...

Neither slavery not involuntary servitude shall be hereafter introduced in this state.

Is followed by a subsequent clause which bans free Black people from taking up residency within state borders:

No free negro or mulatto not residing in this state at the time of the adoption of this constitution, shall come, reside or be within this state

The message here is clear: all Black people, enslaved or free, stay out! They are viewed as a menace to white society, and it is up to the South to deal with "their problem," not spread it to the North.

On February 3, 1819, a New York congressman delivers this same blunt message to his colleagues in an amendment to the Missouri admission bill.

TIMELINE: FEBRUARY 13, 1819

THE TALLMADGE AMENDMENT SPARKS A FIRESTORM IN CONGRESS OVER SLAVERY

The congressman is James Tallmadge Jr., a 41-year-old graduate of Brown University, a lawyer, and an ex-soldier in the War of 1812. When the Missouri bill arrives on the floor, he is about to end his one and only term in Congress, and is away from DC mourning the recent loss of an infant son.

He returns with a proposal forever known as the Tallmadge Amendment, which seeks to attach the following rider to the bill granting statehood for Missouri:

Provided, that the further introduction of slavery...be prohibited...and that all children born within the said State after the admission thereof into the Union shall be free, but may be held to service until the age of twenty-five years.

In a flash, the floor debate shifts from admitting Missouri to banning the spread of slavery!

For two days, Tallmadge is attacked by Southerners in the House, before he rises on February 16 to defend his proposal, with arguments that will echo all the way to 1861.

He reassures the audience by acknowledging that slavery was thrust upon America by the British rather than initiated here.

Slavery is an evil brought upon us without our own fault, before the formation of our government, and as one of the sins of that nation from which we have revolted.

He also points out that his amendment does not call for abolition in existing states.

When I had the honor to submit to this House the amendment now under consideration I accompanied it with a declaration…that I would in no manner intermeddle with the slaveholding states.

While we deprecate and mourn over the evil of slavery, humanity and good morals require us to wish its abolition, under circumstances consistent with the safety of the white population.

I admitted all that had been said of the danger of having free blacks visible to slaves, and therefore did not hesitate to pledge myself that I would neither advise nor attempt coercive manumission.

Instead, his focus is on opposing the spread of "the evil" into the new territories.

But, sir, all these reasons cease when we cross the banks of the Mississippi, a newly acquired territory never contemplated in the formation of our government, not included within the compromise or mutual pledge in the adoption of our Constitution — a territory acquired by our common fund, and ought justly to be subject to our common legislation.

He expresses shock over the intemperate responses he has experienced.

When I submitted the amendment now under consideration…I did expect that gentlemen would meet me with moderation. But…expressions of much intemperance followed. Mr. Cobb of Georgia said that "if we persist the Union will he dissolved; and, with a fixed look on me, he told us, "we have kindled a fire, which all the waters of the ocean cannot put out; which seas of blood can only extinguish!"

Sir, has it already come to this — that, in the legislative councils of Republican America, the subject of slavery has become a subject of so much feeling — of so much delicacy — of such danger, that it cannot safely be discussed?

But is unwilling to back down, even if it were to mean civil war.

Language of this sort has no effect on me; my purpose is fixed; it is interwoven with my existence; its durability is limited with my life; it is a great and glorious cause, setting bounds to a slavery, the most cruel and debasing the world has ever witnessed; it is the freedom of man; it is the cause of unredeemed and unregenerated human beings.

If civil war, which gentlemen so much threaten, must come, I can only say, let it come!

1 know the will of my constituents, and, regardless of consequences, I will avow it as their representative, I will proclaim their hatred of slavery, in every shape.

During the debate, the horrors of slavery have passed by the very windows of the Capitol.

A slave driver, a trafficker in human flesh, has passed the door of your Capitol, on his way to the West, driving before him about fifteen of these wretched victims of his power, torn from every relation, and from every tie which the human heart can hold dear.

The males, who might raise the arm of vengeance and retaliate for their wrongs, were hand-cuffed, and chained to each other, while the females and children were marched in their rear, under the guidance of the driver's whip! Yes, sir, such has been the scene witnessed from the windows of Congress Hall, and viewed by members who compose the legislative councils of Republican America.

Enslaved people are both the greatest cause of individual danger and of national weakness.

Extend slavery, this bane of man, this abomination of heaven, over your extended empire, and you prepare its dissolution.

By your own procurement, you have placed amidst your families, and in the bosom of your country, a population producing, at once, the greatest cause of individual danger and of national weakness.

Some enslaved people may be contented, but others might seek revenge if given the chance.

When honorable gentlemen inform us, we overrate the cruelty and the dangers of slavery, and tell us that their slaves are happy and contented... they do not tell us, that the slaves of some depraved and cruel wretch, in their neighborhood, may be stimulated to revenge, and thus involve the country in ruin.

Spreading their presence only threatens the white population and order in our society.

It has been urged... that we should spread the slaves now in our country, and thus diminish the dangers from them.. (But) it is our business so to legislate, as never to encourage, but always to control this evil; and, while we strive to eradicate it, we ought to fix its limits, and render it subordinate to the safety of the white population, and the good order of civil society.

Finally, banning slavery in the new territory in no way violates the 1787 Constitution.

We have been told by those who advocate the extension of slavery into the Missouri, that any attempt to control this subject by legislation, is a violation of that faith and mutual confidence, upon which our Union was formed, and our Constitution adopted.

This argument might be considered plausible, if the restriction was attempted to be enforced against any of the slave-holding states, which had been a party in the adoption of the Constitution. But it can have no reference or application to a new district of country, recently acquired, and never contemplated in the formation of government.

Tallmadge closes his rebuttal with a call for House support of his amendment.

Sir, I shall bow in silence to the will of the majority, on whichever side it shall be expressed; yet I confidently hope that majority will be found on the side of an amendment, so replete with moral consequences, so pregnant with important political results.

In one fell swoop, this February 16, 1819 rebuttal to the South by Tallmadge picks the scab off the sectional wounds that threatened the development of a national Constitution and Union in 1787.

The heated exchanges remind many present of those at Philadelphia between Gouverneur Morris, the ardently anti-slavery delegate from Pennsylvania, and his pro-slavery antagonist James Rutledge of South Carolina.

Tallmadge has let the slavery genie out of the bottle and for the next four decades future members of Congress will be left to struggle with this fact.

Two founding fathers weigh in on the debate. In a letter to his wife, John Adams comments:

Negro Slavery is an evil of Colossal magnitude and I am utterly averse to the admission of Slavery into the Missouri Territories.

Meanwhile, from his peaceful mountaintop in Monticello, the 76-year-old Thomas Jefferson recognizes the import of the Tallmadge Amendment:

*This momentous question, like a **fire bell in the night**, awakened and filled me with terror. I considered it at once as the knell of the Union.*

TIMELINE: FEBRUARY 17, 1819

HOUSE PASSAGE OF THE TALLMADGE AMENDMENT SHOCKS THE SOUTH

On February 17, 1819, the Tallmadge Amendment passes the House with support from Northern and Western congressmen outweighing Southern opposition.

The margin of victory is 87-76 on the clause "prohibiting further introduction" of new enslaved people and 82-78 on the clause "freeing any born after admission at age 25 years."

This loss shocks the South.

Its assumption has been that since some 10,000 enslaved people are already present in the Missouri territory, Congress would have to approve the practice as a fait accompli.

Instead they are faced with several alarming new realities.

First and foremost, that white people outside the South are ready to resist the introduction of Black people within their state boundaries for a variety of reasons. Racism is one reason: the conviction that Black people are an inferior species, only $3/5^{th}$ of a human. Outright fear is another: the belief that Black people will try to kill white people if given the chance. A third centers on western settlers who do not want to compete with rich planters in buying farmland. Then there is a feeling among some that the intrinsic value and dignity of white people's labor is diminished by "sub-human" Black people performing similar tasks under a whip and for no pay.

A second reality is that the House of Representatives will henceforth become a forum for voicing opposition to the further spread of slavery. The topic will no longer be off-limits as has been the case for three decades.

And a third, unavoidable reality that the makeup of the House is going against the South, as the membership tilts North and West in response to shifts in population density.

SHIFT IN HOUSE OF REPRESENTATIVE MEMBERSHIP: 1790–1820

	TOTAL	NORTH	SOUTH	BORDER	WEST
1792	132	72	45	15	0
1820	205	98	58	22	27
Change	+73	+26	+13	+7	+27

TIME: FEBRUARY 21 TO MARCH 2, 1819

THE SENATE REJECTS THE CONTROVERSIAL AMENDMENT

To defend itself, the South looks to the Senate where voting power remains evenly split between the eleven slave states and the eleven free states.

The House bill is brought to the floor on February 21 by Senator Charles Tait of Georgia, who is serving his final year in Congress before appointment as a federal judge.

Vigorous debates follow off and on over the next nine days.

The result, however, is a victory for the South.

The first clause in the Tallmadge Amendment—prohibiting slavery in Missouri—is defeated by a wide margin of 31–7. The second clause—favoring gradual emancipation—is much closer, although still voted down by 22–16. In turn, the original Missouri admission bill minus the Tallmadge Amendment is returned to the House.

But the House is not about to be ram-rodded by the Senate's action.

A serious threat to the entire statehood process is barely avoided when the House refuses a motion to indefinitely suspend consideration of Missouri's application. Instead, the lower chamber votes again in favor of the original Tallmadge Amendment bill and returns it to the Senate.

The process is now stalemated, and the 15th Congress adjourns on March 4, 1819 without a final decision.

TIME: DECEMBER 6, 1819

SPEAKER OF THE HOUSE HENRY CLAY STEPS INTO THE FRAY

Ten months pass before the 16th Congress convenes on December 6, 1819, and the Missouri question is again taken up in the House. During the hiatus, the issue has been debated across the North, South, and West in local legislatures and assemblies.

The expansion of slavery and the Black population across the Mississippi has become front and center, much to the chagrin of the South.

After Henry Clay is again chosen as the Speaker, he takes the lead in searching for a way to move forward on the Missouri admission.

Clay is in his tenth consecutive year of wielding the gavel, and he remains forever suspicious of Monroe's capacity as president.

After the 1816 election, Clay hopes to be named secretary of state—the path to the White House—but Monroe chooses John Quincy Adams instead. In turn, Clay refuses to attend Monroe's inauguration, a sign of the vanity that will both fuel and ultimately inhibit his ambitions. From that point on, Clay will be at loggerheads with Monroe on one issue after another.

But with Missouri, the battle is within his own domain, the House, and he intends to solve it.

Clay's personal positions on slavery are very much akin to Jefferson's. He owns some 25 enslaved people while intellectually regarding the practice as "inhumane." He is con-

Henry Clay (1777–1852)

vinced that Africans are an inferior race who will never be assimilated into white society. The best that could be done for them would be to pay owners for their freedom, then ship them home to Africa, a plan he backs in 1816 as a co-founder of the American Colonization Society. But like so many conflicted slave owners, he opposes all federal mandate that would end the practice.

In the initial floor debate over the Tallmadge Amendment, Clay had been anything but temperate in his response. In fact, he not only says that the proposal violates the Constitution, but also argues that Black people are treated better as slaves in the South than freedmen in the North. Down the road, this initial stance will come back to haunt him in future national campaigns.

However, as he hears the rhetoric in the House heating up on the issue, including a threat of secession from Thomas Cobb of Georgia, Clay recognizes the need for a peaceful compromise.

What he faces is a sectional—rather than party—schism. In fact, the original Federalist Party is so weak and disorganized by 1819–1820 as to be almost irrelevant to the debate, even though many believe that the Federalist leader, Rufus King, has engineered the entire controversy using Tallmadge as a surrogate.

Personal philosophy aside, Clay begins to search for an immediate and practical compromise on Missouri. The solution needs to be one that satisfies both the South and

North, while not jeopardizing his own presidential aspirations vis-à-vis John Quincy Adams, Calhoun, Crawford, and Andrew Jackson.

Monroe himself remains distant from the political fray, in fairly characteristic fashion. His only interest lies in reaching a peaceful solution that doesn't violate the Constitution.

TIME: MARCH 2, 1820

AGREEMENT IS REACHED ON A 36'36" DEMARCATION LINE

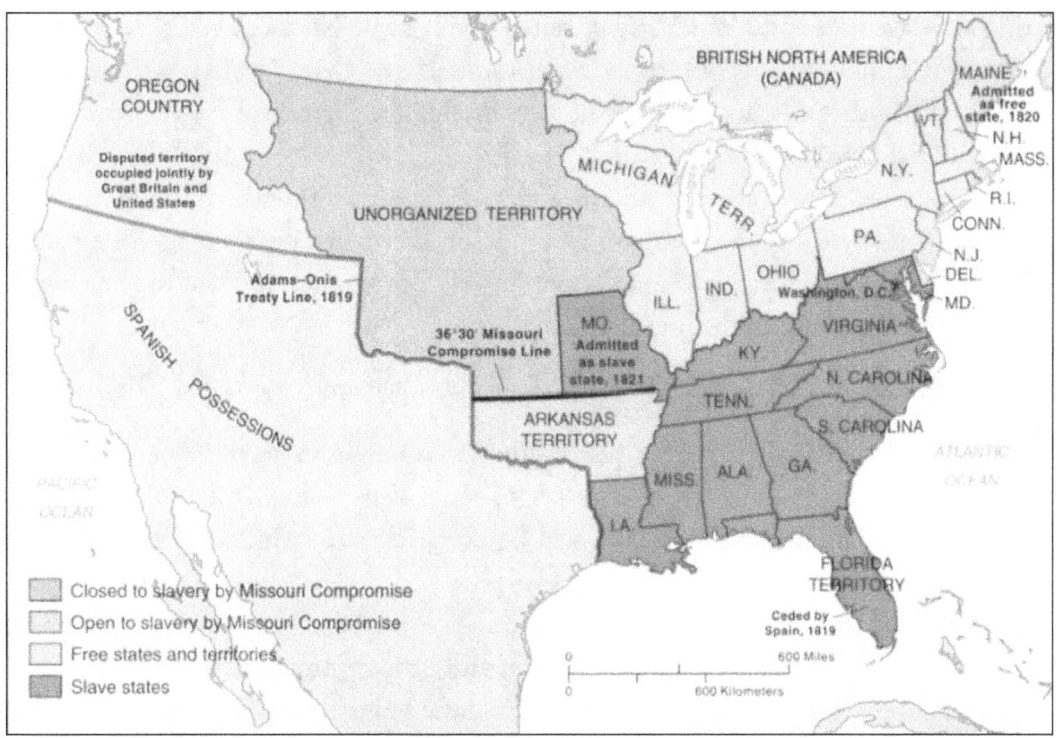

The 36'36" line of demarcation that resolves slavery in the remaining Louisiana territory

Clay recognizes the intemperance he displayed in his initial address to the House, and concentrates now on defusing the anger present in the chamber. A speech from later in his career reveals his down-home approach to tempering the political rhetoric:

We are too much in the habit of speaking of divorces, separation, disunion. In private life, if a wife pouts, and frets, and scolds, what would be thought of the good sense… of a husband who should threaten her with separation? Who should use those terrible words upon every petty disagreement in domestic life? No man …would employ such idle menaces. He would approach with…kind and conciliatory language…which never fail to restore domestic harmony.

But rhetoric alone will not restore harmony in this case. The South sees the North's effort to contain slavery as an existential threat to its economic survival. They believe that slavery will either be allowed to expand geographically, or it will wither and eventually disappear.

Solving the impasse will prove complex and involve two key breakthroughs.

Credit for the first belongs to Clay himself. He recognizes that part of the Northern resistance to allowing Missouri's entry as a slave state is that this would tip the voting power in the Senate in favor of the South. But what if the ongoing efforts to break Massachusetts into two states could be resolved now? Might a quid pro quo—Missouri entering as a slave state and Maine as a free state—swing some Northern votes? This "trade" becomes an important part of the final compromise.

However, the real lightning rod issue remains. Will Congress vote to "contain" slavery east of the Mississippi River or not?

The eventual answer comes from the Senate, where Jesse Thomas of Illinois proposes a Solomon-like solution: simply draw a line on the map west from the Mississippi through the Louisiana territory and declare that all future states north of the line are to be free states and south of the line to be slave states.

Thomas argues that a hard line worked in the 1787 Northwest Ordinance and it should work again with the new territories.

To sweeten the pot here for the North, Thomas proposes to draw the new line from the southern, not the northern, border of Missouri, at latitude 36'30". Thus roughly 80% of the remaining Louisiana land will be declared "free" while only the Arkansas territory will be open to slavery.

On February 17, 1820, a full year after Tallmadge offered his amendment, the Senate passes the Thomas proposal, a watershed moment in the controversy.

Still the Senate version needs confirmation in the House. On March 2, 1820, members agree to allow slavery in Missouri by a very close 90–87 margin, which includes support from fourteen free state representatives.

The final decision now rests with President Monroe.

He recognizes the volatility of the issues, and has largely stayed on the sidelines as his own 1820 reelection campaign plays out. At the same time, as a southerner and a slave owner, he is troubled by the fact that Congress has weighed into the debate at all. The 1787 Constitution has sanctioned slavery and its presence in Missouri has already been established. But the conflict needs resolution, so he signs the bill into law on March 6.

In the end, the Missouri Compromise legislation appears to settle the slavery question by resorting to the same "hard line on a map" solution of the founding fathers.

The South emerges with a tactical victory—Missouri is admitted to the Union as a slave state.

Stability is maintained in the North-South 12:12 state balance of voting power in the Senate.

BALANCE OF POWER IN THE SENATE AFTER THE MISSOURI COMPROMISE

FREE STATES	DATE	# SLAVES	SLAVE STATES	DATE	# SLAVES
Pennsylvania	1787	200	Delaware	1787	4,500
New Jersey	1787	7,500	Georgia	1788	149,000
Connecticut	1788	100	Maryland	1788	107,400
Massachusetts	1788	0	South Carolina	1788	251,800
New Hampshire	1788	0	Virginia	1788	425,200
New York	1788	10,100	North Carolina	1789	205,000
Rhode Island	1790	50	Kentucky	1792	126,700
Vermont	1791	0	Tennessee	1796	80,100
Ohio	1803	0	Louisiana	1812	69,100
Indiana	1816	200	Mississippi	1817	32,814
Illinois	1818	900	Alabama	1819	47,400
Maine	1820	0	Missouri	1821	10,200

Meanwhile the North's wins will prove to be more strategic in nature.

They have given ground on their wish to contain all Black people in the old South, but their long-term leverage on the issue has been greatly strengthened in two ways.

First, to the chagrin of the South, the precedent is now established that Congress has the power to make calls about where slavery will or will not be permitted in all new US territory.

Second, the 36'30" demarcation line set for the Louisiana Purchase land all but guarantees eventual dominance by the Northern free states in the Senate. In fact, the Louisiana land split will yield nine free states versus only three slave states.

Some Southern leaders like the astute John C. Calhoun see this ominous writing on the wall and try to rally opposition. But most are glad with the Missouri state outcome.

TIME: AUGUST 10, 1821

A SECOND COMPROMISE IS NEEDED TO FINALLY ADMIT MISSOURI

The Missouri debate appears to be over until the new state legislature submits a final constitution prior to the seating of its congressional members. This document adds one more ominous coda to the entire debate by seeking to ban all free Black people from taking up residence in the state. In this way, slave owners hope to make sure that freedmen do not stir up trouble and rebellions.

The House, however, balks once again.

Clay resorts to quoting Article IV, Section 2 of the US Constitution in search of closure.

The Citizens of each State shall be entitled to all Privileges and Immunities of Citizens in the several States.

Southerners fire back, this time arguing that free Black people are not "citizens" according to the true meaning of the word in the Constitution.

When this debate threatens to further divide the South and North, Clay again works his way out by offering each side a partial victory. The clause banning free Black people will stay in the Missouri Constitution, but the state will never pass a law to actually enforce it.

After a final flurry, both sides back off, and Missouri officially joins the Union on August 10, 1821.

The outcome on Missouri, however, is no more satisfying for the men of the 15th and 16th Congresses than it was for delegates to the 1787 Convention. Once again sectional divisions around slavery have sounded like Jefferson's "fire bell in the night," and, instead of resolution, another momentary truce prevails.

The North signals its racist resistance to Black people and its intent to try to pen them up in the South, below politically agreed lines of demarcation.

In turn, the South realizes that protecting the future of its plantation economy will rest not on language in the Constitution, but on winning political battles that expand slavery into new territory west of the Mississippi.

This battle is joined by the Tallmadge Amendment and the Missouri Compromise of 1820.

In effect the Missouri debate marks the moment in time when, for many northerners, the South is transformed into the "Slave Power."

THE AMERICAN LANDSCAPE IN 1820

THE TOTAL POPULATION CONTINUES TO GROW AT A RAPID PACE

In the thirty years between 1790 and 1820, America's population has grown explosively, from 3.9 million to 9.6 million, an increase of over 10% per year, tracing to birth rates, not immigration.

TOTAL US POPULATION (000)

1790	1800	1810	1820
3,929	5,237	7,240	9,638
	+38%	+33%	+34%

Compared to the three global powers of Europe, the US is already closing in on both Spain and its former parent, England.

EUROPEAN POPULATION (MM) IN 1820

YEAR	FRANCE	ENGLAND	SPAIN
1820	30.3	11.9*	11.0

* Excludes Scotland and Ireland

Three additions to America's growing population

All three "segments" of the US population have expanded over the decades—white people, free Black people, and enslaved Africans.

US POPULATION GROWTH BY SEGMENT

	1790	1800	1810	1820	1820/1790
Total	3929	3308	7240	9638	+145%
Whites	3172	4306	5863	7867	+148
Free Blacks	59	108	186	233	+295
Slaves	698	894	1191	1538	+120

TIME: 1820

POPULATION GROWTH VARIES SIGNIFICANTLY BY REGION

A dramatic shift, however, has occurred in how Americans are distributed across the geographical landscape—and the effect is not what Southern delegates to the 1787 convention expected.

POPULATION GROWTH BY REGION

	1790	1820	GROWTH
Northeast	1,968	4,360	122%
Northwest	---	793	++
Border	488	1,467	301
Old South	1,473	2,558	74
Southwest	---	460	++
Total	3929	9,638	245

At that time, Southerners were convinced that their region's more favorable year-round climate for farming would cause Northerners to migrate their way, thus expanding their "share" of the total US population and, in turn, their share of votes in the House of Representatives.

But this migration fails to materialize, and instead the South's population share actually drops.

The old South—Virginia, North and South Carolina, and Georgia—declines from 38% of the total population in 1790 to only 24% by 1820. The border South—Delaware, Maryland, and Kentucky—is off slightly from 12% to 11%.

Meanwhile the eight Northeastern states—New Hampshire, Vermont, Massachusetts, Connecticut, Rhode Island, New York, New Jersey, and Pennsylvania—remain stable at a dominant 48% share. This seems to be explained by the growing appeal of Northern cities, with more people being drawn to their diverse and vibrant economic opportunities, easy access to goods and services, and the allure of contemporary culture and society.

The big gains in the population shift occur in the "new West"—the three new Northwest territory states of Ohio, Indiana, and Illinois, and the four Southwest states of Tennessee, Louisiana, Mississippi, and Alabama.

DISTRIBUTION OF US POPULATION

	1790	1820	CHANGE
Northeast	50%	45%	(5)
Northwest	--	8	8
Border	12	15	3

	1790	1820	CHANGE
Old South	38	27	(11)
Southwest	--	5	5
Total	100%	100%	

SETTLERS CONTINUE TO MOVE WEST ACROSS THE APPALACHIAN RANGE

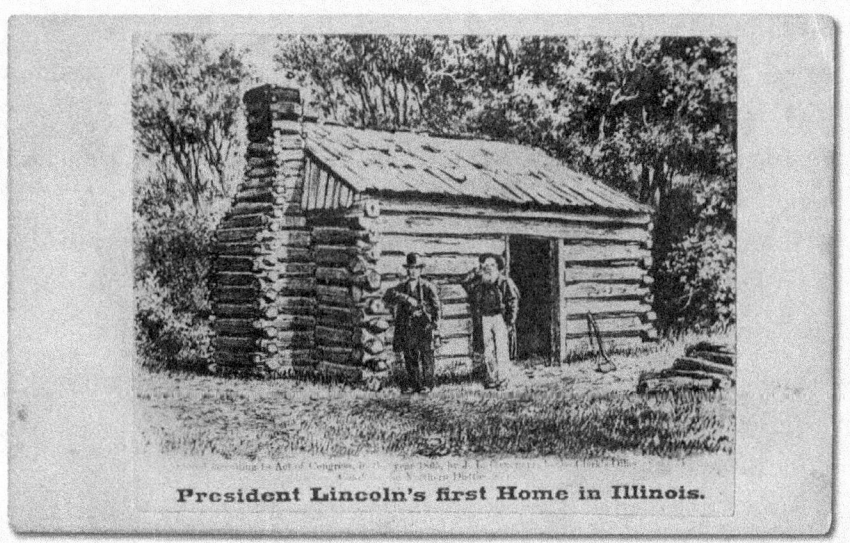

President Lincoln's first Home in Illinois.

A typical log cabin residence in the early 1800s

A remarkable migration west has already taken place between 1790 and 1820. It begins in Kentucky and then filters in all directions—expanding the total number of people living across the Appalachians from 386,000 to over 1.6 million, fully one sixth of the total population.

One by one pioneers have driven through mountain gaps, along primitive trails, into possible danger from Native tribes, facing the uncertainties of building log cabins, planting crops, founding towns, and starting their lives over from scratch on the frontier.

Their motivation is as old as the republic itself—the chance to realize the American Dream, to advance one's wealth and station in life by as much as individual daring and initiative permit. This constant drive for upward mobility is one reward of freedom, and an intrinsic part of the American character. For those moving west, the dream comes in the form of new farmland, more of it, and better than what one had "back East."

AMPLE LAND EXISTS FOR EXPANSION

The land sought extends from the Appalachians, across the Mississippi River and into Louisiana. It has been "extracted," first from Britain by warfare, then France by treaty, and finally from the Indian tribes, largely through force and deception.

By 1820 much of the land is "in the public domain," owned by the federal government and divided into territories. Their boundaries are mostly defined by the meanderings of major rivers and negotiations with the original thirteen states to settle disputed claims.

Terms for the sale of this land vary over the years—the latest established by the Land Act of 1820.

- The minimum size of a tract sold will be 80 acres (reduced from 320 in 1800).
- The price is set at $1.25 per acre (down from $1.65, before the Panic of 1819).
- A minimum down payment of $100 is required of all buyers.

The rest is simple. Frontiersmen are told to find the site that strikes their fancy, have a surveyor define its span, make payment to the government, write and record the deed, and the land is theirs.

As always, speculators flock to acquire the new acreage and parcel it out into smaller lots for resale and quick profits. Despite these maneuvers, data from North Carolina sales indicate that the average settler probably starts their new life with roughly the 80 acres originally intended.

SIZE OF FARMS IN NORTH CAROLINA (1860)

ACRE SIZE	3−9	10−19	20−49	50−99	100−499	500−999	1,000+
% Total	3%	7%	31%	28%	29%	2%	0.5%

THE PROMISE OF FUTURE STATEHOOD IS ALSO APPEALING

Along with the new land comes the opportunity to form new states and be admitted to the Union.

The path to statehood requires that a given territory achieve a threshold population of at least 60,000 residents, establish a local legislative body in some city or town, pass a state constitution, and apply to the federal government for admission.

Between 1790 and 1820, an additional eight western states have already joined the union—with a ninth, Missouri, about to follow suit.

WESTERN STATES' ADMISSION TO THE UNION

#	YEAR	STATE	SLAVERY
15	1792	Kentucky	Yes
16	1796	Tennessee	Yes
17	1803	Ohio	No
18	1812	Louisiana	Yes
19	1816	Indiana	No
20	1817	Mississippi	Yes
21	1818	Illinois	No
22	1819	Alabama	Yes

SIDEBAR: CHANGES APPEAR IN THE AMERICAN LANDSCAPE IN 1820

MOST AMERICANS STILL LIVE ON FARMS

A prosperous rural setting in Connecticut

In 1820, the vast majority of Americans—over nine in ten—still live in the country, on farms.

WHERE AMERICANS LIVE

YEAR	RURAL	URBAN
1820	93%	7%

They are proudly independent and self-reliant, but also neighborly by nature and drawn to establishing communities, for commerce and for the common good.

Gradually their farms are connected to one another by cart paths and dirt roads, some bordered by wooden fences to contain livestock.

At the intersection of these roads, small towns form.

SMALL TOWNS AND "MAIN STREETS" TAKE HOLD

The towns are typically built along a main street lined by storefronts on both sides. Most are simple wooden structures with signs announcing their wares.

The center of activity in town tends to be the general store, a place for people to gather, to socialize, and to buy everyday necessities.

A small town in America circa 1820.

RANGE OF GOODS SOLD IN GENERAL STORES

Soft Goods	Cloth bolts, silk, thread, pins and needles, buttons, underwear, hats, shoes, leather, dungarees, dresses.
Hard Goods	Firearms, ammunition, lanterns, lamps, rope, crockery, tableware, cooking utensils, tools, farm equipment.
Consumables	Coffee beans, tea, flour, sugar, spices, baking powder, crackers, molasses, tobacco, candy, select foods.
Apothecary	Patent medicines, remedies, soaps and toiletries.

As towns expand, other venues open up—a saloon, an inn, stables, possibly a jail, and eventually a post office.

America's first general stores

SIDEBAR: PHYSICAL INFRASTRUCTURE IS UPGRADED

MAJOR ROADS AND TURNPIKES EVOLVE

From the beginning America's "on the make" society searches for ways to rapidly transport both people and produce from here to there.

The first answer lies in roads.

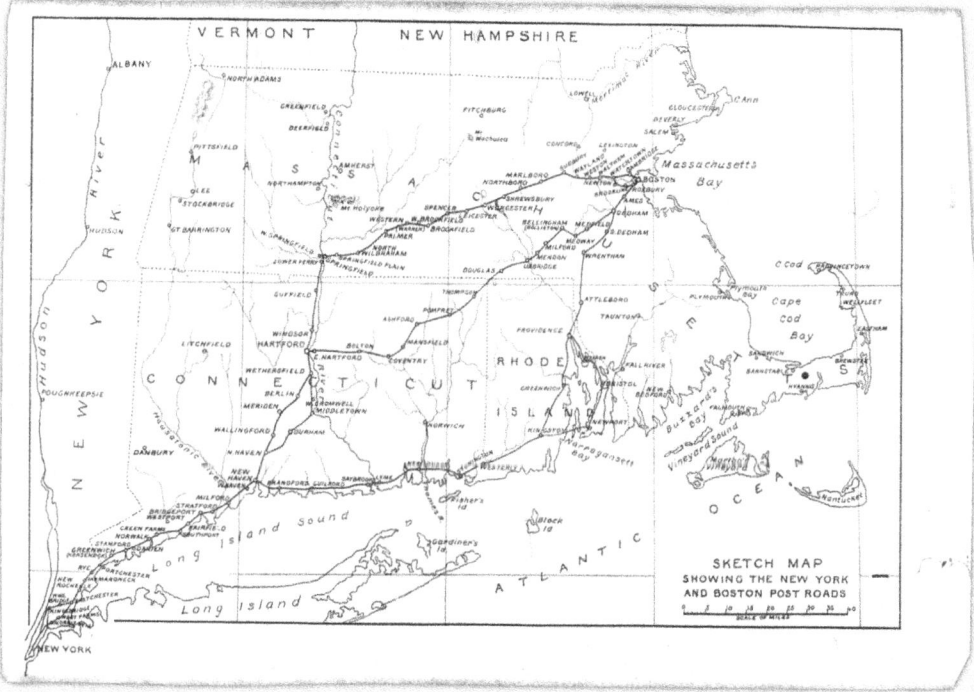

America's first major highway: the Boston Post Road (Boston to New York City)

Many of these originate as Indian trails, and are gradually upgraded to handle increased traffic, including the mail (or "postal letters").

During the colonial period, most roads run roughly north and south, linking the colonies along the Atlantic coast.

The first true thoroughfare is known as the Boston Post Road, from Massachusetts through various "upper and lower" routes in Connecticut, all the way to New York City. Its name derives from the role it plays in delivering mail across the region.

The Great Wagon Road (also known as the Valley Pike) opens the way for settlers and commerce moving into the southern states. It originates at the port of Philadelphia, heads west to Chambersburg and then swoops south through the Shenandoah Valley of Virginia to the Roanoke River and into North Carolina.

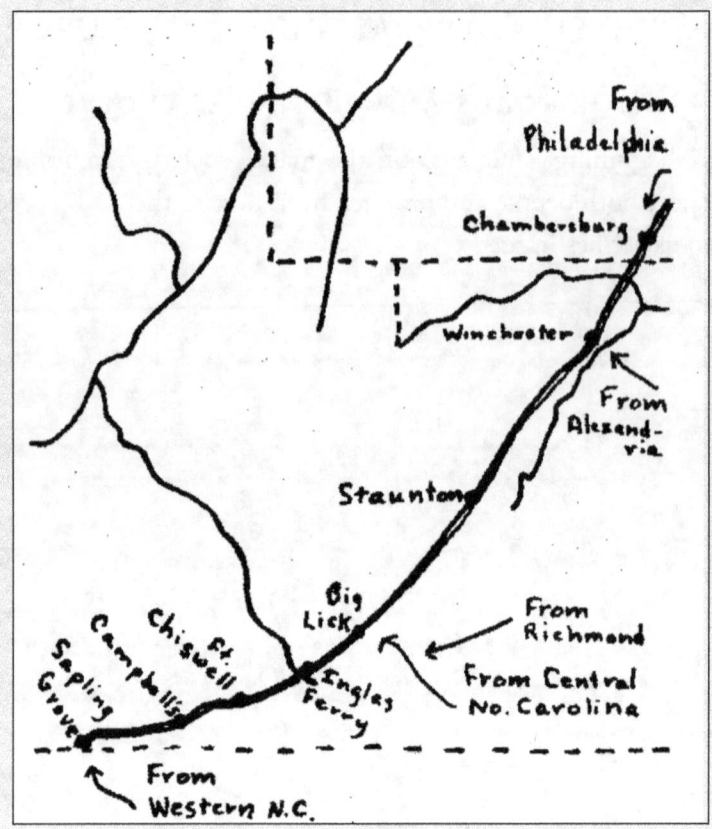

The Great Valley Road from Philadelphia to Lexington, VA

Note: Map by Beverly Whitaker

Other important north-south roads include the original King's Highway, which reaches Charleston, South Carolina, and the Fall Line Road linking Fredericksburg, Virginia and Augusta, Georgia.

IMPORTANT NORTH-SOUTH TRAILS AND ROADS IN THE EAST

NAME	OPENS	FROM	TO	DISTANCE
Lower Post Road	1678	Boston, MA	Greenwich, CT	180
Upper Post Road	1673	Boston, MA	New Haven, CT	135
Boston Post Road	1772	Boston, MA	New York City, NY	215
King's Highway	1650	Boston, MA	Charleston, SC	975
Albany Post Road	1703	New York City, NY	Albany, NY	150
Great Wagon/Valley Road	1744	Philadelphia, PA	Lexington, VA	330
Fall Line Road	1735	Fredericksburg, VA	Augusta, GA	500

Opening up new land across the Appalachian Mountain barrier hinges on development of east to west roads.

IMPORTANT EAST-WEST TRAILS AND ROADS

NAME	OPENS	FROM	TO	DISTANCE
Mohawk Trail	1664	Albany, NY	Buffalo, NY	288
Allegheny Path	1755	Philadelphia, PA	Pittsburgh, PA	305
Pennsylvania Road	1775	Harrisburg, PA	Pittsburgh, PA	200
Braddock's Road	1755	Cumberland, MD	Braddock, PA	95
National Road	1811	Cumberland, MD	Vandalia, IL	615
Federal Road	1806	Washington, DC	New Orleans, LA	1,085
Wilderness Road	1775	Bristol, VA	Frankfort, KY	255
Zane's Trace	1796	Wheeling, VA	Maysville, KY	230

The state of New York is transversed by the Mohawk Trail, from Albany to Buffalo. Travelers move west from Philadelphia to Pittsburgh along the Allegheny Path and the Pennsylvania Road.

The most famous east-west thoroughfare of the time, the National Road, is about halfway

Pennsylvania Road:
Philadelphia to Pittsburgh

finished in 1820, extending west from Cumberland, Maryland—at the "gap" in the Appalachians—to Wheeling in western Virginia. Eventually it will run 611 miles all the way west to Vandalia, Illinois.

The Federal Road will become another critical east-west juncture, eventually linking Washington, DC to New Orleans, over 1,000 miles to the southwest. It comprises a series of roads, dropping down from the capital through the Piedmont region of Virginia and the western Carolinas to Augusta, Georgia, where it swings across Alabama and Mississippi to Louisiana.

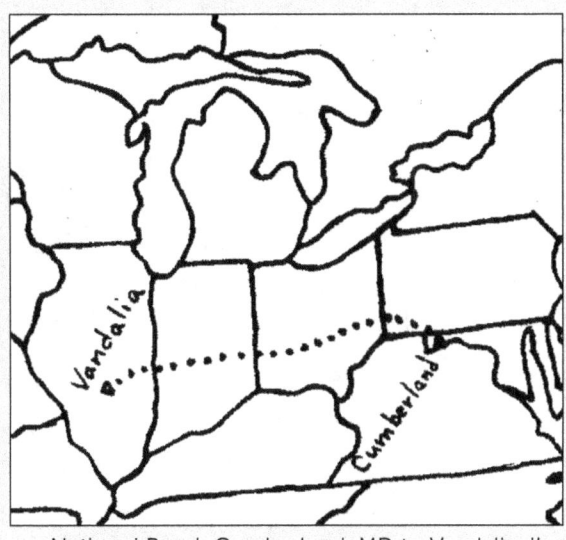

National Road: Cumberland, MD to Vandalia, IL

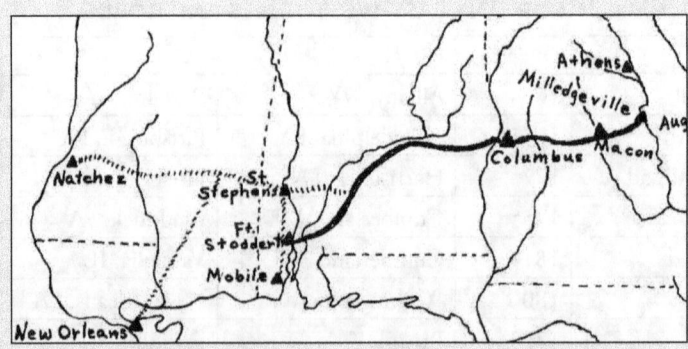

The Federal Road: extension from Augusta to New Orleans

ROAD QUALITY IS TRANSFORMED

The condition of these major roads varies widely in the 1820s.

Most remain dirt paths, albeit smoothed and widened by decades of use.

But some are already being "macadamized," according to construction guidelines developed by the Scotsman John McAdam around 1815 in England. McAdam's idea is a simple one that involves laying a bed of finely crushed stones over a carefully leveled dirt path, slightly bowed in the center to facilitate the draining of rain and snow.

The use of stones enables macadamized roads to avoid the bane of travel along dirt paths, which easily turn into mud in the presence of rain.

The benefits of these improved stone roads are so obvious to users that some become "turnpikes" built by entrepreneurs who line them with "tollbooths" to collect fees and turn a profit.

Bridges, too, facilitate transportation, with those crossing sizable rivers often built by corporations with the intent to reap profits from user fees.

President Monroe proudly reports progress in the construction of "post roads" in his December 2, 1821 address to the Congress:

A bridge under construction

There is established by law 88,600 miles of post roads, on which the mail is now transported 85,700 miles, and contracts have been made for its transportation on all the established routes, with one or 2 exceptions. There are 5,240 post offices in the Union, and as many post masters.

THE WATERWAYS BECOME LONG-DISTANCE HIGHWAYS

America is also able to leverage its rich abundance of waterways to cover long distances. First come triple-masted sailing ships crammed with cargo headed toward European ports.

Then come simpler canoes, boats, and barges heading up and down inland rivers. These rivers cross-hatch the old and new states, and help bind them together around trade. Many flow for hundreds of miles, are easily navigated, and cut across state lines.

MAJOR NORTH-SOUTH RIVERS EAST OF THE MISSISSIPPI

RIVER	MILES	STATES
Kennebec	170	Maine
Connecticut	419	Connecticut, Vermont, New Hampshire
Hudson	315	New York, New Jersey
Susquehanna	464	Maryland, Pennsylvania, New York
Scioto	231	Ohio
Wabash	503	Indiana, Illinois, Ohio
Pee Dee	232	South Carolina, North Carolina
Savannah	301	South Carolina, Georgia
St Johns	310	Florida
Alabama	318	Alabama, Georgia
Oconee	220	Georgia

Others flow east and west, and play a crucial role in opening up the new states west of the Appalachian Mountain range. The Ohio River is the longest eastern river and it becomes the official line of demarcation in 1787 between the free states of the North and the slave-holding states of the South.

MAJOR EAST-WEST RIVERS EAST OF THE MISSISSIPPI

RIVER	MILES	STATES
Ohio	981	Pennsylvania, Ohio, western Virginia, Kentucky, Indiana, Illinois
Cumberland	688	Kentucky, Tennessee
Tennessee	652	Tennessee, Alabama, Mississippi, Kentucky
James	348	Virginia

To the north, across eastern Canada, the linkage of the St. Lawrence River and the Great Lakes runs 2,340 miles from the Atlantic coast to the tip of Lake Superior. This route will prove very important to the fur trade, which is already booming in 1820.

THE ST. LAWRENCE TO GREAT LAKES SYSTEM

COUNTRY	MILES	SPAN
Canada	2,340	Atlantic Ocean to Lake Superior

MAN-MADE CANALS ALSO APPEAR

The notion of taming the natural twists and turns and ups and downs of rivers by digging adjacent man-made canals goes back to ancient times.

By the 1770s, an Englishman named James Brindley pioneers new engineering methods for canal-building that revolutionize the economics of transporting coal from mines to nearby cities.

Both George Washington and Gouverneur Morris learn of the European canals and interest grows in the colonies.

But it takes the construction of the Erie Canal in New York to capture the imagination of the public and the business entrepreneurs alike. The grand vision for the project involves two initiatives:

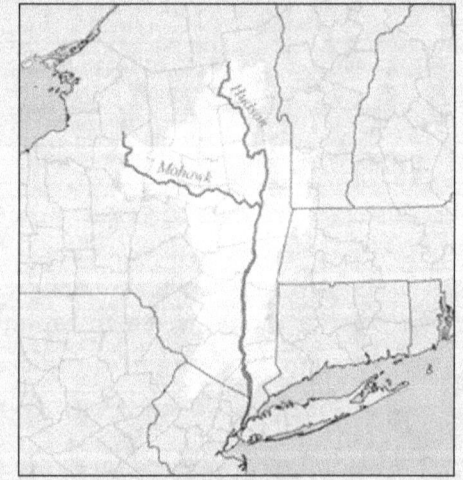

- First, "taming" the Mohawk River, which flows 149 miles east and west through the Appalachian range, between the Adirondacks to the north and the Catskills to the south.
- Then extending the flow another 214 miles west to the city of Buffalo on Lake Erie.

One key to canal building success lies in constructing "navigational locks" that work. Their role is to enable barges or boats to pass through sharp rises or

Junction of the Mohawk and Hudson
Rivers into Manhattan

es or boats to pass through sharp rises or drops in land and river elevations (e.g. waterfalls or rapids) without damage. They do this by "locking" the barge in a contained tank of water, which is then flooded or drained to allow it to rise or fall to a desired height, before an exit door opens to pass it along.

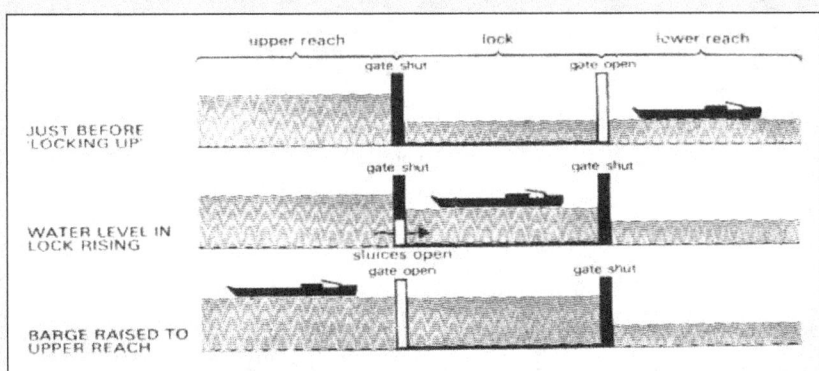

Locking System Schematic

When President Jefferson hears of the Erie Canal scheme in 1808 he calls it "little short of madness."

His conclusion is prompted by the fact that land elevation drops some 600 feet between Buffalo to the west and Albany to the east. With each individual "lock" unable to accommodate more than a twelve-foot change in water height, this means the canal will require construction of over 50 such individual stations at a total cost deemed unaffordable by all who assess it.

That is, all except for one Jesse Hawley, a flour merchant in Geneva, New York who begins to calculate the cost savings the canal could deliver, especially to grain merchants in the Ohio valley. Hawley shares his estimates with Joseph Ellicott, whose Holland Land Company owns land in central and western New York, and hopes the canal will boost its value.

Together these two take their plan to the power-ful politician DeWitt Clinton, who serves as mayor of New York City between 1803 and 1815, and bare-ly loses to Madison in the 1812 presidential election.

Clinton sets up the Erie Canal Commis-sion in 1810 and becomes a fierce and tireless supporter of the venture. His assessment of the proj-ect's effects on the city will prove prescient.

DeWitt Clinton (1769–1828)

The city will, in the course of time, become the granary of the world, the emporium of commerce, the seat of manufactures, the focus of great moneyed operations…and before the revolution of a century, the whole island of Manhattan, covered with inhabitants and replenished with a dense population, will constitute one vast city.

But opposition to the effort—soon labeled "Clinton's Folly"—remains staunch. He perseveres, getting some 100,000 New Yorkers to sign a petition supporting the canal and securing $7 million to fund construction.

Work begins on July 4, 1817 in Rome, New York, heading east some fifteen miles toward Utica. Completion of this phase alone requires two years, which again raises concerns about feasibility. But the early construction lessons prove the hardest, and the building pace picks up sharply.

The canal specifications call for a breadth of 40 feet and a depth of 4 feet. Tow paths are laid out along both sides of the canal, enabling cattle or manpower to tug the barges forward.

The work is backbreaking in many ways. Trees need to be felled and their stumps pulled out. Primitive bulldozer-like plows scrape the soil. Clay and limestone linings form the channel. And complex aqueducts are required to steer the water. The effort continues through the intense summer heat and the frigid winters.

In the end, almost eight years and 57 locks are required to complete the project, one of the engineering marvels of the nineteenth century. Clinton celebrates with a ten-day voyage over the canal, from Buffalo to New York City—ending with a ceremonial "wedding of the waters," pouring a vial from Lake Erie into Manhattan harbor.

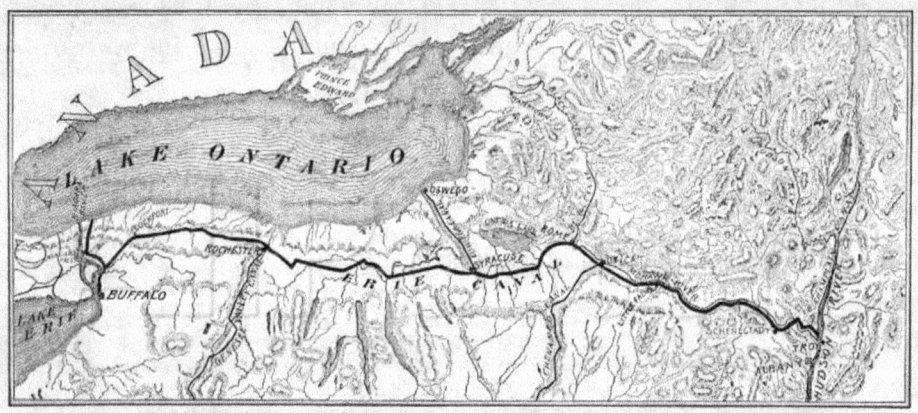

The Erie Canal stretching 363 miles from Albany to Buffalo, New York

The Erie Canal immediately transforms economic prosperity throughout the state. Wheat transport on the waterway jumps from around 3,500 bushels in 1820 to over a million bushels in 1830, with costs per bushel cut by 90%.

Tolls collected for use of the canal pay off the $7 million cost during that same time—and New York becomes the busiest port in America, surpassing Philadelphia, Boston, Baltimore, and New Orleans.

Unfortunately, DeWitt Clinton dies suddenly of heart failure in 1828 and, despite his public prominence, lacks the personal funds even to be properly buried, much less care for his surviving family. Despite this, his famous canal will be forever immortalized in American folklore and song, such as *Low Bridge* by Thomas S. Allen:

I've got a mule, her name is Sal
Fifteen years on the Erie Canal
She's a good old worker and a good old pal
Fifteen years on the Erie Canal
We've hauled some barges in our day
Filled with lumber, coal, and hay
And we know every inch of the way
From Albany to Buffalo

Chorus:
Low bridge, everybody down
Low bridge cause we're coming to a town
And you'll always know your neighbor
And you'll always know your pal
If you've ever navigated on the Erie Canal

An early canal in Bethlehem, Pennsylvania

INFRASTRUCTURE GAINS SUPPORT GROWING URBAN CENTERS

While towns that are inland and "off the beaten path" tend to grow at a slow pace, full-fledged cities are appearing by 1820. Their size is determined by several factors.

One is their proximity to a sizable body of water—the Atlantic Ocean or an inland river or lake—together with a port that accommodates shipping.

Infrastructural supports are also crucial, most notably access to one or more high-traffic roads or, eventually, access to canals and railroad tracks.

When several of these factors overlap, a city's growth can be exponential.

Traffic along Main Street in an emerging city

In the North, for example, Boston, Philadelphia, and Baltimore all double or triple in population between 1790 and 1820—and New York's count reaches 123,706, a fourfold jump.

Two Southern port cities—Charleston and New Orleans—reach the 20,000 mark in total residents.

And the nation's capital, Washington, DC, also joins the top ten list in terms of population.

TOP TEN MOST POPULATED CITIES IN AMERICA

1790	POP	1820	POP
New York	33,131	New York	123,706
Philadelphia	28,522	Philadelphia	63,802
Boston	18,320	Baltimore	62,738
Charleston	16,345	Boston	43,298
Baltimore	13,503	New Orleans	21,176
North Philadelphia	9,913	Charleston	24,780
Salem	7,921	North Philadelphia	19,678
Newport	6,716	South Philadelphia	14,713
Providence	6,380	Washington, DC	13,247
Marblehead	5,661	Salem	12,731
AVERAGE	14,641	**AVERAGE**	39,987

SIDEBAR: THE OVERALL US ECONOMY IN 1820

AMERICA FORMS A VIABLE DOMESTIC MARKETPLACE

A farmer bringing his crop to market

The advent of towns and cities goes hand in glove with the development of a viable domestic marketplace.

At first it has simply been "the farmer's market." On given days and times, families pile their surplus crops into wagons, haul them into towns, and exchange them for cash or barter.

This exchange symbolizes America's free market in action: sellers offering goods or services to buyers with needs or wants in exchange for cash or barter.

Demand for things meets the supply of things, and both buyers and sellers profit from the transactions. One man's bushels of beans are sold for pennies used to buy a much-needed cloth shirt. Once this demand/supply ritual takes hold in rural towns, the domestic economy booms. The engine running the US economy kicks into gear.

Arriving in town to
conduct business

THE MACRO ECONOMY TAKES OFF

As of 1820, one third of all Americans (3.1 million) are participating in the labor force.

This percent is much higher among enslaved people (62%)—where men, women, and older children are forced workers—than among the free population (28%), where non-domestic labor is dominated by men.

LABOR FORCE PARTICIPATION IN 1820

	TOTAL POPULATION	IN LABOR FORCE	% IN LABOR
Free	7,830,000	2,185,000	28%
Enslaved	1,538,000	950,000	62%
TOTAL	9,368,000	3,135,000	33%

Despite some intermittent shocks, growth in the gross domestic product (GDP) is robust, up from $190 million in 1790 to $700 million in 1820.

OVERVIEW OF US ECONOMY: CURRENT DOLLARS (MILLIONS)

	TOTAL GDP	% CHANGE	GDP PER CAPITA	SHOCKS
1790	$190		$48	
1800	$480		$90	
1805	$560	17%	$90	
1810	$700	25%	$97	1807 Embargo Act
1815	$920	31%	$110	1812–1815 War
1820	$700	(24%)	$73	1819 Bank Panic

America's exports follow the same pattern, with rapid growth registered until Jefferson's 1807 embargo on trade and the dampening influences of the War of 1812 against England. But as of 1820, total exports stand at $70 million, up from $20 million in 1790.

VALUE OF US EXPORTS (MILLIONS)

YEAR	TOTAL	% CH
1790	$20	
1805	$96	++%
1810	$67	(30%)
1815	$53	(21%)
1820	$70	33%

Despite some volatility, America's long-term economic outlook looks positive.

THE SHAPE OF THE ECONOMY VARIES SHARPLY BY REGION

While farming and fishing remain dominant in the North, Hamilton's vision of a diverse economy—including manufacturing, distributing, and selling goods—is already materializing.

Roughly 11% of America's total work force are engaged in the manufacturing sector in 1820, with 70% of them located in the North.

PEOPLE WORKING IN MANUFACTURING JOBS IN 1820

REGION	# OF PEOPLE (000)	% OF TOTAL
North	241.2	69%
Border	41.1	12%
South	64.5	19%
Total	346.8	100%

Meanwhile the Southern economy remains steadfastly committed to Jefferson's agricultural model.

SIDEBAR: THE SOUTHERN ECONOMY IN 1820

THE SOUTH BETS ITS FUTURE ON AGRICULTURE

An agent selling Russell Mills Cotton Duck (canvas)

During the colonial period, plantations spring up across the South, with crops varying by terrain and weather. In the upper South—Maryland, Virginia, and North Carolina—tobacco is dominant. The low country states of South Carolina and Georgia, with greater access to irrigation, turn to the generally more profitable production of rice. But the economic die is cast for all Southern states in 1792 once Whitney's seed-removal "gin" transforms the economics associated with growing and harvesting short fiber cotton.

From that moment on, every farmer and plantation owner in the South that can get into cotton does so. And production soars, reaching almost 142 million pounds by 1820.

Prices for the crop vary from year to year in response to shifts in supply and demand, with the latter affected by tariffs levied on finished cotton goods from abroad.

But in 1820, the value reaches $235 million—fully one third of the country's total GDP for the year!

VALUE OF COTTON

YEAR	COTTON LBS (MILLIONS)	AVG. PRICE/LB	$ VALUE (MILLIONS)
1790	0.1	14.44	2
1805	59.9	22.59	135
1810	68.9	14.20	98
1815	81.9	25.90	216
1820	141.5	16.58	235

As cotton profits soar, so too does interest in opening new plantations, particularly to the west of the Appalachian range in the newer states of Alabama, Mississippi, and Louisiana.

To do so, however, requires not only available land, but also available enslaved people.

THE SOUTH ALSO BETS ON "BREEDING" AND SELLING ENSLAVED PEOPLE

By 1820 prosperity in the South rests as much on the domestic sale of enslaved people ("black gold") as on sales of its raw cotton ("white gold") to worldwide textile mills.

Since 1807 the ban on "importation" agreed to in the Constitution has been in effect, hence the only place new plantation owners in the west can get the unpaid labor they need is to buy excess enslaved people being "bred" on plantations in the east.

And "breeding" enslaved people becomes a major industry, especially in the state of Virginia.

This shocking "breeding" practice is described by Maggie Stenhouse, a former slave:

Durin' slave'y there was stockmen. They was weighed and tested. They didn't let 'hem work in the field and they kept them fed up good. A man would rent the stockman and put him in a room with some young women he wanted to raise children from.

Once bred, these "excess" people are shipped to cities like Louisville, Kentucky and New Orleans, where daily slave auctions are advertised in newspapers and held in various locations around town.

The combination of growing demand and limited supply leads to high prices for enslaved people, especially for "prime field hands" and "breeding women." In 1820 the average price for an enslaved person has risen to $393.

This means that the total economic value of the 1.5 million

A typical newspaper ad for upcoming slave sales

enslaved people in the US has reached the staggering level of $600 million, at a time when the annual value of all goods and services (GDP) is $700 million.

THE "ECONOMIC VALUE" OF BRED ENSLAVED PEOPLE

YEAR	# SLAVES (MILLIONS)	PRICE/PERSON	TOTAL MARKET VALUE (MILLIONS)
1805	1.032	$222	$229
1810	1.191	$277	$330
1815	1.354	$272	$368
1820	1.538	$393	$604

Shrewd plantation owners throughout the South will focus on sustaining this economic growth engine.

To do so, they will constantly support the expansion of slavery into new territory west of the Mississippi.

They will also pay careful attention to breeding enslaved people for sale in these new territories.

One such shrewd owner has been Thomas Jefferson, master of Monticello, whose *Farm Book* observations record concerns about his "breeding women" and their offspring:

> *The loss of 5 little ones in 4 years induces me to fear that the overseers do not permit the women to devote as much time as is necessary to the care of their children; that they view their labor as the 1st object and the raising their child but as secondary.*

> *I consider the labor of a breeding woman as no object, and a child raised every 2 years is of more profit then the crop of the best laboring man. In this, as in all other cases, providence has made our duties and our interest coincide perfectly.... With respect therefore to our women & their children I must pray you to inculcate upon the overseers that it is not their labor, but their increase which is the first consideration with us.*

Jefferson's correspondence also encourages his friends to…

> *Invest every (spare) farthing in land and negroes, which besides a present support bring a silent profit of from 5 to 10 per cent in this country, by the increase in their value.*

A MISSED ECONOMIC OPPORTUNITY FOR THE SOUTH

The South's nearsighted focus on agriculture finds it overlooking the economic opportunity to be had in processing cotton into thread, weaving it into whole cloth, and finishing it into the clothes and household goods that Americans need.

Had the South acted on this opportunity to "vertically integrate" its cotton operations—i.e., win all of the profit to be had from raw cotton, spun thread and yarn, woven cloth, and completed wares—its wealth could have increased dramatically.

While the South makes a few attempts to mimic the textile mills in New England, their success is limited. The question is, "Why?"

Several factors seem to explain this missed economic opportunity by the South:

- Planters are probably satisfied making money hand over fist simply by growing raw cotton, and feel no urgent need to tackle the complexities of further processing it.

- The knowledge required to set up and run a textile mill is closely guarded at the time and requires engineering and machine-making skills that the South lacked.
- Smaller cities in the South meant that a local factory would not enjoy the benefits of a nearby, concentrated consumer marketplace for its finished goods.
- Finally, the prospect of hiring white women (like the "Lowell mill girls") to work in textile factories for wages is culturally anathema in the South.

Whatever the causes, the result is that the Northern textile mills reap the profits of whole cloth and finished goods made from the South's raw cotton, an outcome that will cause tensions and rancor between the two regions going forward in time.

SIDEBAR: THE NORTHERN ECONOMY

INDUSTRIALIZATION BEGINS TO TAKE HOLD IN THE NORTH

Workers gathered in front of Brown's Factory in Boston

While the southern economy is narrowly focused, the North is beginning to realize the benefits that Alexander Hamilton envisioned in capitalism and industrialization.

His ambition is to have America lead the world in "manufactures," soon referred to as "manufacturing."

Manufacturing is where supply meets demand for desired goods, especially those things that the typical farm household of the time is unable to make readily on their own. Fine clothing, furniture, glassware, carriages, firearms, timepieces, books, tools, and so forth.

According to Hamilton, manufacturing will be driven by individual entrepreneurs who:

- Spot the emerging needs and wants of consumers
- Design a workshop/factory to produce the desired goods
- Secure needed capital through bank loans, stock offerings, or their own cash
- Locate the space, machines, workers, etc. to start up their operation
- Make and deliver high quality products at affordable prices
- Achieve sufficient profitability to pay back investors for risking their capital

Clearing all these hurdles will prove challenging, and many will fail. But some entrepreneurs will persevere and succeed.

"Specialization" will be one key determinant.

Making bolts of cloth, for example, will require first de-constructing the overall process into discrete steps, and then optimizing methods used at each step. Critical know-how accrues from trial and error—the more bolts of cloth produced, the more efficient and effective the manufacturer becomes.

If high demand and profitability continue over time, opportunities to automate some of their processes may arise. A new machine may be invented to spin cotton into thread or weave it into yarn that produces higher quality cloth at lower costs than was possible using hand labor.

Furthermore, they may be the only manufacturer around with enough "scale" (i.e. demand for their cloth) to be able to invest in the new machine and enjoy its cost economies. This endows them with competitive advantages that can become monopoly-like.

Finally, enough buyers of cloth may decide that one manufacturer consistently delivers better value for their money (high quality at fair prices) than its competitors, and become loyal to that supplier's "brand."

Those few companies that achieve "brand loyalty" can long endure.

EARLIEST MANUFACTURER BRANDS IN THE US

YEAR	BRAND NAME	INDUSTRY
1795	Dixon Ticonderoga	Pencils
1796	Jim Beam	Distillery
1798	Pratt-Read	Tools
1801	Crane & Co.	Papermaking
1802	DuPont	Chemicals
1806	Colgate	Consumer goods
1807	Sterling Sugars	Sugar
1811	Pfaltzgraff	Ceramics
1812	Waterbury Button	Buttons
1815	Loane Brothers	Tents
1816	Remington	Firearms
1818	Brooks Brothers	Clothing

The growth of manufacturing in America is also hastened by events such as the 1807 embargo, the War of 1812, and the Dallas Tariff of 1816, each of which limit foreign imports.

One entrepreneur who takes advantage of these events is Francis Cabot Lowell, who founds the Boston Manufacturing Company in 1814.

Lowell's textile mill in Massachusetts

FRANCIS LOWELL'S PURLOINED TEXTILE MILL STARTS UP

Francis Lowell is born in Newburyport, Massachusetts in 1775 to wealthy and influential parents. After graduating from Harvard in 1793, he starts up a sizable business in Boston that imports textiles made in China and India and sells them from a retail storefront on the city wharf.

The interruption of Lowell's trade owing to Jefferson's Embargo Act of 1807 sparks his interest in manufacturing his own textiles domestically. But he initially lacks the know-how required to start up such a complicated operation.

He solves this on a two-year trip to England and Scotland, where he visits various textile mills and literally memorizes the details of their manufacturing processes in the grand capitalist tradition of "know the world and steal the best."

Upon his return to Boston, he transfers the blueprints he has carried home in his head to paper, sets up a corporation—the Boston Manufacturing Company—and begins the search for the cash needed to build his own factory.

He quickly raises the money by selling $1,000 shares of stock in his corporation to a string of wealthy investors who have enough faith in his venture to risk their own money to back it.

Lowell's first mill, completed in late 1814, is located in Waltham, Massachusetts, with its spinning and weaving machines powered by water turbines driven by the currents of the Charles River. (Steam powered machines will not appear until the 1840s.)

It becomes the first US mill that completes all of the steps required to convert raw cotton into finished cloth under one roof.

Raw cotton → cleaning → carding → spinning to thread/yarn → weaving → whole cloth

As such it delivers on all of the promises of efficient production that Hamilton foresaw and is hugely successful from the beginning.

Unfortunately, Lowell suffers from a condition known as tic douloureux, an excruciatingly painful nerve disease of the face that hastens his death in 1817, at age 42.

But by then a second mill is up and running, and in 1822 several more north on the Merrimack River have been built by Lowell's corporate partners and successors. To honor him, they name their new industrial town Lowell, Massachusetts.

NORTHERN INDUSTRIALIZATION FOSTERS A NEW WORKFORCE

Francis Lowell's textile mill is symbolic of how America's industrial economy opens up new ways to make a living, apart from agriculture. By 1820, about one in five have embraced these other options.

HOW PEOPLE MAKE THEIR LIVING

YEAR	AGRICULTURE	OTHER OPTIONS
1820	79%	21%

"Town workies" is the name many are given, and they have traded a strictly pastoral life on the farm for the more crowded and complex urban setting. The economic path they choose is also very different from that of Jefferson's entirely self-sufficient farmer.

Their city jobs are wide ranging in content and pay.

At one end of the spectrum are the "unskilled workers," such as day laborers, longshoremen, draymen, and factory workers, who live off of muscle power and are hired on or laid off at the whim of their employers. They form

Three town "workies"

the lowest rung of the economic ladder, with jobs that are always threatened, especially by immigrants who may be willing to work for lower wages.

ESTIMATED ANNUAL INCOME: UNSKILLED LABORERS

1790	1800	1805	1810	1815	1820
$37	$60	$62	$88	$92	$67

At the other end are "professionals," such as doctors, engineers, lawyers, teachers, and financiers, who tend to acquire unique skills through higher education, then sell this know-how on a pay for service basis to clients in need of their help. Because of their knowledge, people in these "white collar" jobs retain a high level of independence, often working for themselves as entrepreneurs. In turn both their incomes and prestige tend to be higher than all but the elite "owner classes."

Between the "unskilled" laborers and the professionals are the emerging "urban middle class," some working independently, others as part of a business. Some work with their hands, as artisans who make goods functional or decorative in nature, from clothing to furniture, household items to jewelry, and tools to machinery. Others rely more on their minds, running small businesses, writing for newspapers, and acting as clerks.

The breadth of jobs available varies by the size and geographic location of any given town or city. But in major cities like New York or Philadelphia, the list of occupations is quite amazing.

NON-FARMING OCCUPATIONS: 1820S AMERICA

Raw Materials	Clothing/Appearance	Professionals
Shanty/Lumberman	Seamstress	Clergy
Miner/Sapper	Hatter	Educator
Trapper	Leather dresser	Doctor
Fisherman	Weaver	Attorney
	Tanner	Politician
Transportation/Goods	Tailor/Sartor	Magistrate
Cooper/Barrel maker	Shoemaker/Cobbler	Judge
Riverman	Tonsor/Barber	Surveyor
Sailor		Military
Teamster	Personal Transport	Undertaker
Drayman	Stabler	
	Blacksmith/Farrier	Journalist
Converters	Saddler	Printer
Textile	Carriage maker	Bookbinder
Smelter		
Ironworker		
Plowwright	Food & Drink	Financier
Gunsmith	Baker	
Clower/Nail maker	Butcher	Entrepreneur
Cutlery maker	Packer	Ship owner
Soap maker	Brewer/Maltster	Factory owner
Candle maker	Distiller	Plantation owner
Rope maker		Other capitalists
Watchmaker		
Gold/Silversmith	Merchants	Lower Skill Workers
	Dry goods	Factory labor
Housing	Apothecary	Clerk

Housewright	Haberdasher	Servant
Carpenter	Saloonkeeper	Longshoreman
Mason	Innkeeper/Ostler	Rag picker
Joiner		Peddler
Glazier	Middlemen	Tinker
Cabinetmaker	Warehouser	Chimneysweep
Locksmith	Factor/Broker	Waiter

WOMEN ENTER THE INDUSTRIAL LABOR FORCE

Lowell's textile mills also open the door for women to enter the industrial labor force.

Lowell, Massachusetts soon becomes a boom town, with over 30 textile mills being operated by some 8,000 workers. The majority of these are young women, who become known as "the Lowell girls."

While Charles Dickens found working conditions in the Lowell factories far superior to their counterparts in London, the labor was strenuous. A typical shift for "Lowell girls" ran from 5 a.m. to 7 p.m. on a production line consisting of 80 workers, two male overseers, and the non-stop racket of spinning and weaving machines and air filled with cotton and cloth detritus.

"Lowell girls" work about 70 hours a week on average and are paid about 6 cents per hour or around $4 per week—a generous wage at the time.

"Lowell girls"

The girls live and eat together in company boarding houses, obey a 10 p.m. curfew, and are expected to attend church on the Sabbath and exhibit upright behavior at all times. Time off is granted for short vacations, trips to the city, and exposure to various cultural events.

Despite the offer of steady work, shelter, and pay, the average job tenure for a "Lowell girl" is roughly four years.

JOHN JACOB ASTOR: AN AMERICAN TYCOON

The vast majority of men who travel east to west by 1820 are content to stake out their farm and make enough of a living to raise their family.

But a few are driven by the allure of building vast new businesses that span the continent and offer almost limitless wealth.

These men will become America's first industrial age tycoons. One of them is John Jacob Astor.

John Jacob Astor is generally regarded as the fifth richest man in American history, with assets valued at $116 billion in current dollars. He is also the very symbol of the "rags to riches" dream that has remained in the country's culture from its inception.

John Jacob Astor (1763–1848)

Astor is born in Waldorf, Germany in 1763 and goes to work at age fourteen in his father's butcher shop. Like his brothers before him, he soon flees from home; first to London, where he learns English, and then to New York City in 1784.

On the trans-Atlantic crossing he meets a German passenger whose stories about fur-trading opportunities in America fascinate him.

In 1785 he marries one Sarah Todd, daughter of a prominent Dutch family, who brings with her a sizable $300 dowry and a keen eye for quality fur products. Together they open a shop in the city which she manages in 1786, when he goes off to Canada in search of a steady supply of beaver, otter, ermine, and other pelts.

At the time, the North American fur trade resides in outposts scattered around the great saltwater lake known as Hudson Bay, north of Ontario and bordering on Quebec. These outposts are controlled by the Hudson Bay Company, chartered in 1670 by Britain's Charles II. They trade blankets, tools, and other goods to local Indian tribes for pelts, which are exported abroad and converted into felt hats, coats, and blankets.

Astor ventures off into this wilderness on his own, exhibiting great physical courage along with the business acumen needed to survive and prosper among the Native trappers and cutthroat traders. His instincts for "the right deal" are remarkable. He knows which furs will appeal to the public and how to assess supplies against prices.

As his reputation grows, he connects with leaders of another preeminent firm in Montreal, the North West Company, who help him become the dominant importer of pelts from eastern Canada.

He then leaps to the insight that maximum profit lies not in converting the pelts into clothing, but rather in trading them for other goods available in Europe and China. He studies international shipping, and in 1800 sends a cargo ship loaded with seal skins, beaver skins, and other pelts to Canton in exchange for scarce supplies of silk, satin, porcelain, nutmeg, and lapsang souchong tea.

The China trade makes Astor incredibly wealthy, and he spends $27,000 to buy the Rufus King mansion at 233 Broadway in New York City to house his family of six.

He founds his American Fur Company in 1808 and sets his sights next to cornering the fur trade in western Canada and the Rocky Mountains. He sends an expedition to open the Columbia River port town of Astoria, Oregon, with the intent being to ship pelts from there west to China and back east to New York City. The War of 1812 temporarily dashes his plan, but he perseveres and later dominates the western fur trade.

At no point does Astor relent when it comes to extending his wealth by leveraging his capital.

When Madison desperately needs funds to fight the war, he makes another killing by purchasing high yield bonds. This support, along with his political contacts in the New York City Masonic Lodge, earn him one of the five director's slots on the Second US Bank when it is formed in 1816.

He is also one step ahead of others in understanding market demand.

He sells his American Fur Company in 1834 when he senses a shift from beaver to silk hats.

The profits go into a continuing quest to buy up all available real estate on and around the island of Manhattan. He purchases Greenwich Village. He pays $25,000 to the sugar importer, James Roosevelt (great grandfather of FDR), for 120 city blocks north from 10th Street to 125th and east from 5th Avenue to the East River. After the Bank Panic of 1837, he adds more plots north of the city at bargain prices.

His strategy is to lease his properties rather than build, and by the time of his death in 1848, Astor is known as the "Landlord of New York City" and the richest man in America.

He goes down in history as the first entirely self-made tycoon in the nation's history.

SIDEBAR: GENDER ROLES IN 1820

AMERICA REMAINS A PATRIARCHAL SOCIETY

True to its Protestant roots and its English traditions, America remains a patriarchal society in 1820.

Men are cast as the head of their households and of public affairs in general; women are expected to conform to the subservient roles they are assigned by their fathers and husbands.

Religious beliefs and practices contribute heavily to contemporary views of women, especially the Garden of Eden tale of Eve luring Adam into original sin. For the dominant Calvinist sects such as the Puritans, this forever casts doubt on the moral rectitude of all females. Eternal salvation is in the balance daily, and the prayer "lead us not into temptation" is often focused on women and sins of the flesh. (In 1850, author Nathaniel Hawthorne will capture these Puritan tensions in his novel, *The Scarlet Letter.*)

But women's subservience at this time extends beyond religious doctrine and into the realm of law.

According to English Common Law, carried over to America, women's legal rights are established under the principle of "coverture."

Which means that, once a woman is married (or "covered"), she forfeits her legal rights as an independent person. Thus, she is no longer allowed to own property, to sign contracts, or to participate in any business ventures. As the soon-to-be suffragette, Lucy Stone (1818–1893), will point out:

Coverture gives the custody of the wife's person to her husband.

A host of orthodoxies regarding both men and women follow from these religious and legal precedents.

Men are expected to be in charge of their household, to work hard to support their own family's well-being, and to participate in public affairs, from service in the militia to involvement in politics and government. In all critical decisions facing the family, their word is final.

Women too had clearly defined roles in 1820. Since their futures in society were so directly determined by marriage, girls were tutored early on to find a worthy husband. "Proper behavior" was deemed essential here, including the virtues of outward piety, modesty, appropriate dress, and manners. Marriages were seldom "arranged," and those failing to attract a husband were reduced to "spinsterhood" and probable poverty, left to live at home with their parents.

Once married, women were expected to have children, especially male heirs. Additional implicit duties included raising them properly and contributing to their education. Women also had to carry out a multitude of chores associated with maintaining a household and often had to help out with farm duties, all while supporting and obeying their husbands. While labeled "the weaker sex," the physical demands on farm women were often extreme, doubly so since multiple pregnancies and minimal healthcare were commonplace.

These generalized gender roles were the norm across all regions of the country, although the stereotypes tended to be amplified across segments within the South.

This was particularly true among the elite planter class in Virginia and the

Carolinas, where the culture was prone to mimicking the old-world French traditions of chivalry and elegance over the more down-to-earth mindsets of the English Puritan "Yankees" of New England.

Fragile "Southern belles" placed on pedestals by dashing cavaliers were extant in 1820, but they were few and far between. The vast majority of females, Southern and Northern, were farm women who labored hard from dawn to dusk to care for their homes and families.

ONLY A FEW WOMEN DARE TO MAKE THEIR VOICES HEARD IN 1820

Relatively few women in 1820 deviated much from their subservient roles. But some do.

They are helped along as early as 1742, by the opening of the Bethlehem Female Seminary in Germantown, Pennsylvania. Its charter argues on behalf of a revolutionary idea: "when you educate a woman, you educate an entire family." Its curriculum covers a range of cultural and intellectual topics, spiritual exploration, vocational training, and physical exercises. It encourages women's participation in a range of fields, including education, the ministry, and nursing. It endures today as Moravian College.

Mercy Otis Warren (1728–1814) soon picks up the banner. She is a member of the prominent Otis family of Massachusetts and writes political propaganda surrounding the war with Britain. She also corresponds regularly with America's first three presidents, publishes novels, and befriends another outspoken woman of her time, Abigail Adams.

Adams, of course, becomes the early symbol of a strong and independent woman, demanding to have her say in the "affairs of men." In addition to her role as First Lady during her husband's presidency, she engages many of the founding fathers, especially Thomas Jefferson, on public policy. Her written admonition to her husband, John, sets the stage for things to come during the second great awakening of the 1830s:

> *Remember the Ladies, and be more generous and favorable to them than your ancestors. Do not put such unlimited power into the hands of the Husbands, Remember all Men would be tyrants if they could. If particular care and attention is not paid to the Ladies we are determined to foment a rebellion, and will not hold ourselves bound by any Laws in which we have not voice, or Representation.*

SIDEBAR: OUR EDUCATIONAL SYSTEMS IN 1820

FORMAL EDUCATION REMAINS A HIT OR MISS PROPOSITION

While education is seen as important to most Americans, little progress occurs between 1790 and 1820 in making it broadly available to all children.

Those lucky enough to be born into well-off families across all regions still benefit from personal tutors, prep schools, and the higher-ed universities.

For others, formal education is not always accessible.

The bastion of childhood education is New England, based on its staunchly Puritan heritage. It becomes the model for "grammar schools," open to the public albeit with optional attendance. These facilities are all privately owned until 1821, when the first government-run "public school" appears in Boston.

University graduate in formal garb

The odds of accessing formal education also go up for children clustered in towns and cities, where one-room schoolhouses become more commonplace.

However, in 1820 the majority of America's children still reside on farms outside of New England and lack the family wealth required to hire tutors or go off to school full time.

For them and their parents, learning is probably an aspiration, although hard to come by and relegated to second place behind farm duties and household chores.

Despite all this, the trend lines on literacy and general education are tilting upward by 1820, with more children getting more years of formal education on average.

This traces in part to the greater availability of teachers, as university attendance and graduation rates grow. While the vast majority of graduates are men, the teaching career is already beginning to attract women in search of options to traditional housewifery.

Literacy is also advanced by the fact that reading materials are becoming more prevalent, including children's "readers and spellers," which facilitate in-home schooling.

Parents too are more likely than ever to be reading, with local newspapers growing in popularity.

NEWSPAPERS ADVANCE LITERACY AND POLITICAL AWARENESS

Between 1800 and 1820, the number of local newspapers in circulation more than doubles, from around 200 to over 500. They exist across all states, with New York alone offering roughly 75 different publications.

Their content includes coverage of current events, especially the political arena, public announcements, and advertising for local merchants.

But the vast majority of these newspapers survive for only a few years. Some build a reliable base of paid subscribers, but most cannot generate enough to cover their costs. Their revenue is also hurt by the fact that, once bought, papers are passed around for free.

The ones that do manage to

Time-out to absorb the daily news

survive typically supplement their income by other printing work done for businesses or state governments. To secure the latter, newspapers often align with political parties, who return the favor in the form of patronage.

SOME EARLY NEWSPAPERS

DATE	TITLE	LOCATION
1704	*The Boston News-Letter*	Boston, MA
1721	*The New England Courant*	Boston, MA
1756	*The New Hampshire Gazette*	Portsmouth, NH
1764	*The Hartford Courant*	Hartford, CT
1767	The Boston Chronicle	Boston, MA
1785	*The Augusta Chronicle*	Augusta, GA
1785	*The Poughkeepsie Journal*	Poughkeepsie, NY
1786	*Daily Hampshire Gazette*	Northampton, MA
1786	*Pittsburgh Gazette*	Pittsburgh, PA
1789	*The Western Star*	Stockbridge, MA
1792	*The Recorder*	Greenfield, MA
1794	*The Rutland Herald*	Rutland, VT
1796	*Norwich Bulletin*	Norwich, CT
1801	*New York Post*	New York City, NY
1803	*The Courier*	Charleston, SC

## 43

THE BLACK EXPERIENCE
IN 1820

TIME: 1820

THE ENSLAVED POPULATION IS CONCENTRATED
IN THE SOUTH AND WEST

As of 1820, there are a total of 1.77 million Black people in America, or 18.4% of the entire population. Almost nine out of ten of them are enslaved.

TOTAL US POPULATION IN 1820 BY RACE

	MILLIONS	% TOTAL
Total US Population	9,638	100.0%
Total White	7,867	81.6
Total Black	1,771	18.4
Enslaved	1,538	16.0
Free	233	2.4

But only 117,000 Black people—or 6.6% of the 1.77 million—now reside in the North.

The eight original Northern states account for just under 110,000 Black people, with some 90,000 classified as freedmen and only 18,000 as enslaved. Almost all of them are located in New York and New Jersey, where emancipation progresses at a gradual pace.

THE BLACK POPULATION IN THE ORIGINAL NORTHEASTERN STATES IN 1820

	NY	PA	NJ	CT	MA	RI	VT	NH	TOTAL
Enslaved	10,088	211	7,557	97	0	48	0	0	18,001
Free	29,275	30,202	12,460	7,870	6,740	3,554	903	786	91,790
TOTAL	39,363	30,413	20,017	7,967	6,740	3,602	903	786	109,791
TOTAL POP.	1,372,812	1,049,458	277,575	275,248	523,287	83,059	235,981	244,161	4,061,581

The three new states to the west—Ohio, Indiana, and Illinois—have all written constitutions and local "codes" to keep Black people out. These tactics succeed, and in 1820 their total Black population is only 7,500, or less than 1% of all residents.

BLACK POPULATION IN THREE NEW NORTHWESTERN STATES IN 1820

	OH	IN	IL	TOTAL
Enslaved	0	190	917	1,107
Free	4,723	1,230	457	6,410
TOTAL	4,723	1,420	1,374	7,517
TOTAL POP.	581,434	147,178	55,211	783,823

Meanwhile, 93.4% of all Black people are living in the South and making up sizable percentages of total state populations.

In the original six states below the Mason-Dixon Line, just over four out of every ten people are enslaved, on average. In South Carolina, Virginia, and Georgia, white people and Black people are about equal in numbers. In the two Border states of Maryland and Delaware, the ratio of Black people to white people is about one to four.

THE BLACK POPULATION IN THE SOUTHERN AND BORDER STATES IN 1820

	VA	SC	NC	GA	MD	DE	TOTAL
Enslaved	425,153	251,783	205,017	149,656	107,398	4,509	1,143,516
Free	23,493	13,518	14,612	1,763	3,681	12,958	70,025
TOTAL	448,646	265,301	219,629	151,419	111,079	17,467	1,213,541
TOTAL POP.	938,261	502,741	638,829	340,989	407,350	72,749	2,909,919

But what is most striking about the enslaved population in the South is an accelerated migration to the new states west of the Appalachians.

The driving force here is the economy, with new western plantations starting up and increasing the demand for more slave labor. In turn, this "market" is being met by eastern owners who discover the windfall profits available in "breeding" and selling their inventory of enslaved people.

By 1820, just over 500,000 enslaved people have appeared in states from Kentucky to Louisiana, and this will prove to be only the start of the "rush."

ENSLAVED POPULATION IN WESTERN STATES (000)

STATE	1790	1820	GROWTH
Kentucky	12.4	126.7	10x
Tennessee	0	80.0	++
Georgia	29.3	149.7	5x
Alabama	0	47.4	++
Mississippi	0	32.8	++
Louisiana	0	69.1	++
TOTAL	41.7	505.7	12x

In the five western states below the Ohio River, nearly three in every ten residents are enslaved.

THE BLACK POPULATION IN THE BORDER AND NEW SOUTHERN STATES IN 1820

	KY	TN	LA	AL	MS	TOTAL
Enslaved	126,732	80,107	69,064	41,449	32,814	350,166
Free	2,759	2,737	10,476	1,001	458	17,431
TOTAL	129,491	82,844	79,540	42,450	33,272	367,597
TOTAL POP.	564,317	422,823	153,407	127,901	75,448	1,343,896

TIME: 1619 AND ONWARD

ALL BLACK PEOPLE REMAIN DENIGRATED AND FEARED

The upbeat vision of America in 1820 is not shared by the Black population, be they enslaved or living as freed men and women.

Ever since their arrival in chains they have been dismissed as outcasts. Everything about them—from their skin color to their geographic origins, language, manners, and customs—sets them apart from the largely homogeneous white Anglo-Saxons who first settle the land.

As such, they are regarded as "the other," a different tribe and likely a hostile one, to be subjugated and feared, not embraced.

Beyond that, by arriving in shackles they prick the consciences of those who have traveled to the New World in search of personal freedom and the moral teachings of their Christian faith.

Is their treatment as enslaved people consistent with the tenets of the Bible or not? And, if not, is one in jeopardy of losing eternal salvation by participating in the abuses inherent in their captivity?

From these uncomfortable starting points, the human tendency to accept the status quo—especially when it is self-serving—outweighs the reservations at least for the vast majority of white people focused on their own survival in a new land.

As with all forms of human atrocities, those

An example of anti-Black racial stereotyping

in power come to rationalize their complicity. One in particular comes to symbolize this trait. He is President Thomas Jefferson, who appears particularly conflicted by his own thoughts and behavior toward "his" enslaved people, especially during the early years at Monticello.

This most complex man clearly recognizes the sin of slavery he is engaged in, but proceeds down the path anyway. He does so in the end by deciding that, indeed, Black people are "the other," a different and lesser species, somewhere above his cattle—perhaps the 3/5th of a man agreed to in the US Constitution—and certainly incapable of ever rising to equality with his own white race.

Jefferson of course is joined in this rationalization by seven of America's first twelve presidents—Washington, Madison, Monroe, Jackson, Tyler, Polk, and Taylor—who, like him, will own slaves while in office.

By 1820, slavery has been in place for over two centuries and has achieved institutional status in the nation.

TIME: 1820

THE DAILY LIVES OF THOSE ENSLAVED IN THE SOUTH

The daily life of those enslaved differs dramatically depending upon their assigned role on the farm or plantation. Some serve as field hands, others as domestics. While both exist without precious freedom or respect, their fates are unequal.

Field hands harvesting cotton

Domestics—especially those directly serving the master and mistress—escape from the back-breaking physical labor endured by the field hands. The women are assigned cleaning, cooking, sewing, and gardening chores, along with tending to child care as "mammies." The men may act as butlers or footmen, tackle household repairs, and care for horses and carriages. Both genders are often housed under their owner's roof, have access to better clothing, diet, and medical care, and are exposed to the trappings of up-scale white society and manners.

Since the grooming and behavior of house servants can also be a reflection on the master's wealth and magnanimity, they often become a chip in impressing visitors. Obedient and properly trained house servants signal a properly gentrified lifestyle.

On the other hand, the field hands are out of sight and often the province of hired overseers. Their measure of worth lies not in niceties, but in daily production of cotton.

A cotton crop planted around April 1 is ready to be harvested and sent to the ginning mill in July. An average field hand, bent over or crawling in the hot sun, might pick about 100 pounds of cotton bolls a day, enough to fill up two twelve-foot-long "drag-along" sacks. After about fifteen days of labor, the field hand would have filled a standard 1,500-pound wagon, which would then be shipped to the ginning mill. After ginning, this wagon load would yield 500 pounds of cotton fiber—or one finished "bale"—and 1,000 pounds of seed for replanting or disposal. At a typical price of 20 cents a pound for fiber, the 500-pound bale picked by the field hand would sell for about $100 on the market.

Thomas Jones, an enslaved man from North Carolina, captures the round-the-clock labor imposed seven days a week during the peak seasons.

> *During the planting and harvest season, we had to work early and late. The men and women were called at three o'clock 'n the morning, and were worked on the plantation till it was dark at night. After that they must prepare their food for supper and for the breakfast of the next day, and attend to other duties of their own dear homes. Parents would often have to work for their children at home, after each day's protracted toil, till the middle of the night, and then snatch a few hours' sleep to get strength for the heavy burdens of the next day.*

No one is spared from this toil. Pregnant women work the fields. Older children are formed into groups of weed pickers while younger children tote water from wells to workers.

During breaks, "slave food" is carried in pails to the fields. The typical diet is loaded with starch, in the form of cornmeal and fatback from salted pork. Access to vegetables and fruit goes to those lucky enough to maintain their own small garden plots.

Any perceived lapses in the daily toil are met by the wide range of punishments open to the abuser over the defenseless. On one end is the lash, administered with a whip, tearing and scarring naked backs. On the other, the more subtle indignations, from cutbacks on rations to banning the smallest traces of freedom and dignity, like church gatherings.

Field hands live in dirt floor log cabins held together by clay-based mortar and vulnerable to rain in the summer and cold in the winter. Their dress is derived from flimsy "Negro cloth," worn until disintegration. Many go shoeless while others wear "Negro brogans."

Taken together, the living conditions for enslaved people leave them vulnerable to a host of killing diseases, including malaria, cholera, dysentery, tuberculosis, and pneumonia. Mortality statistics bear this out— the death rate for enslaved babies and

Slave quarters in South Carolina

children up to age fourteen being twice as high as for their white counterparts.

Thus, while plantation owners always wish to expand their "crop" of enslaved people, the daily treatment they afford them backfires, and across the antebellum period, life expectancy for enslaved people is only 21 years as opposed to the 42 years averaged by white people.

TIME: 1790s AND ONWARD

FREED BLACK PEOPLE INCH TOWARD RESPECT

In 1820 there are roughly 233,000 free Black people in America, with some 98,000 in the North and 135,000 in the South.

Freedom has come to them in a host of ways: military service in the War of 1812, buy-outs, manumission, "passing for white," and Northern laws abolishing slavery now or for new births.

Roughly two-thirds of free Black people are females, often left to fend for themselves, frequently with children in tow fathered by men who remain in slavery.

While theoretically free, local "black codes" circumscribe their daily lives.

Failure to produce papers proving their freedom can return them directly to bondage. In the South, their homes often abut plantations, and some continue to live in slave quarters. In the North, they typically find themselves in cities, segregated into all-Black neighborhoods, labeled by names like "Darktown" or "Shantytown."

The first challenge facing these free Black people lies in simple economic survival. Many of them, especially the women, transition from slavery into domestic servitude. Others, especially men, try to scratch out a living as day laborers, draymen, porters, and the like.

A few begin to the move up the economic ladder by acquiring special knowhow and skills always in demand.

A free Black woman

Self-taught skills such as barbering, hairstyling, sewing, and tailoring become popular occupations among free Black people. Some wrangle apprenticeships and find work as blacksmiths, saddlers, carpenters, masons, butchers, or shoemakers. However, access to professional or white-collar jobs is sharply limited by historical prohibitions against teaching them to read, write, or master numbers.

Despite all of these hurdles, Black people who have escaped enslavement begin to inch their way into the white-dominated social structure. Men like Prince Hall, Paul

Cuffee, and James Forten demonstrate the talent and tenaciousness to achieve economic success and work on behalf of others in the Black community.

Black churches in particular provide a refuge from daily oppressions and a place to advance survival skills.

Indeed, the gradual movement toward "colored citizenship" will be shaped inside Thomas Paul's Boston church, the 1819 African Methodist Episcopal Church founded in Philadelphia by Reverend Richard Allen, Samuel Cornish's First Colored Presbyterian Church of New York (1821), the African-American Church of Charleston (1822), the First Black Baptist Church of New Orleans (1826), and others.

TIME: 1820

THE ROLL CALL OF BLACK ABOLITIONISTS IN 1820

Among the early Black fighters for freedom and citizenship, three notables—Prince Hall, Paul Cuffee, and Absalom Jones—have passed from the scene by 1820.

A FEW EARLY BLACK ABOLITIONISTS WHO HAVE PASSED BY 1820

	DEATH	AT AGE
Prince Hall	December 4, 1807	72
Paul Cuffee	September 9, 1817	58
Reverend Absalom Jones	February 13, 1818	72

But James Forten remains, as does the Reverend Thomas Paul, and they are about to be joined by a next generation of reformers who will advance the cause in the decades ahead.

EARLY BLACK ABOLITIONISTS STILL ALIVE IN 1820

	AGE IN 1820
James Forten	56
Reverend Thomas Paul	47
Austin Steward	27
Thomas Dalton	26
Reverend Samuel Cornish	25
Reverend Theodor Wright	23
Sojourner Truth	23
David Walker	22

TIME: 1820

SIDEBAR: OLD FANNY, UNCLE ABRAHAM, AND THE LOTT FAMILY OF BROOKLYN

"Old Fanny" and her mistress, "Uncle Abraham" Aunt Lizzie (Mrs. Nicholls)

One destiny for freed people in the North lay in ongoing servitude to their former owners, and such was the case with "Old Fanny" and "Uncle Abraham" of the Lott household in Brooklyn.

The Lott family migrates from Holland to New York around 1630. At the time, slave ownership is widespread among the Dutch, with Black people originally comprising about 20% of the state's population. In New York City over half of all residents own at least one enslaved person, and the Lott family owns twelve, according to the 1790 census records.

In 1800 Hendrick I. Lott (1760–1840) builds a 22-room home on 245 acres of farmland in the Flatlands (Brooklyn) and moves in with his wife, Mary Brownjohn, daughter of a prominent family also from New York City. Their son Johannes marries

Gashe Bergen in 1817, and fathers seven children. One is Henry DeWitt Lott (born 1820) and another is Eliza Lott (born 1828).

At some point, Henry Lott comes to own the enslaved man named Abraham, while Eliza owns Fanny.

Eventually, Abraham weds Fanny and they have at least one child, a daughter named Fannie Lew, who is owned by Elsie (Ray) Lott.

When slavery finally withers away around 1830 in New York, Abraham and Fanny transition from enslavement to "colored servants" of Henry and Eliza.

A trip into New York City by Eliza probably prompts the photograph above, taken by Fredericks & O'Neill of 5ᵗʰ Avenue of an aging "Old Fanny" standing beside the seated "Lizzie." By the time it is taken, "Uncle Abraham," whose photo originates at Isley's Studio in Jersey City, has presumably passed away.

The Lott property remains a New York City landmark to this day, and restoration work shows that the slave quarters were well-hidden within the building through a trap door in the kitchen. Artifacts found in this space include candle drippings, a mortared-over oven, a cloth pouch, oyster shells, and corncobs, the latter arranged in a starburst pattern suggesting that they were used as part of West African religious rituals.

Conjecture also has it that a secret six by twelve-foot room concealed behind a closet on the second floor of the Lott house may have been used in the 1840s by escaping enslaved people moving north along the Underground Railroad.

Over 150 years have passed since Aunt Lizzie and "Old Fanny" posed for the camera on their visit to New York City. But there they are, captured in time, forever symbolizing a limbo-like moment where some Black people in America were no longer enslaved, but not nearly all the way free and equal.

## 44

A WHITE ABOLITIONIST MOVEMENT GETS UNDERWAY

TIME: 1619 AND ONWARD

MORAL OPPOSITION TO SLAVERY IS MUTED UNTIL THE 1800S

The institution of chattel slavery goes largely unchallenged on moral grounds until the early 1800s.

Indeed there are some exceptions, but these are few and far between.

SOME EARLY ANTI-SLAVERY PROTESTS

DATE	ACTION
1688	*The Germantown Quaker Petition Against Slavery*
1743	Quaker John Woolman's anti-slavery pamphlets and reform tours
1773	Dr. Benjamin Rush's assertion that Black people are not intellectually inferior to white people
1774	Methodist John Wesley's missions to end slavery
1775	Ben Franklin's "Pennsylvania Society for Relief of Negroes Unlawfully Held in Bondage"
1787	Attacks by Gouverneur Morris and Luther Martin at the Constitutional Convention
1785	Rush and Franklin found the New York Manumission Society

Once Northerners find that the international slave trade is no longer profitable, the vast majority focus on segregating and controlling the few Black people left in their own neighborhoods and ensuring that those enslaved in the South stay there.

Southerners by then have discovered that their "peculiar institution" is the basis for their ongoing economic prosperity, and are ready to defend it to the death.

So the only opposition to slavery seems to come from those who would oppose its future geographical spread based on prejudice and greed, not from any drive to end the practice entirely based on moral grounds.

TIME: 1815

THREE QUAKERS FOUND A SMALL-SCALE ABOLITIONIST MOVEMENT

The notion of emancipating all slaves in America has its roots in three New England Quakers, Elias Hicks, Benjamin Lundy, and Lucretia Mott.

Hicks is a New Yorker born in 1748 who becomes a carpenter and farmer by trade. He joins the Assembly of Friends at age 21 and is quickly recognized by his congregation for the spiritual insights he voices during prayer meetings. As such he is chosen as a "recording minister" and becomes an itinerant preacher.

From the beginning he converts his beliefs into action. He frees his family's enslaved people in 1778, sets up a Charity Society for Africans in 1794, and by 1811 advocates an economic boycott of all goods—especially cotton and sugar—produced by enslaved labor. By his words and deeds, Hicks influences not only Ben Lundy but also Lucretia Mott.

"Eminent Opponents of the Slave Power,"
including Ben Lundy (lower right)

Lundy is born in 1789 and raised on a farm in New Jersey. At nineteen years old he moves to Wheeling in western Virginia in order to apprentice as a saddler. While learning the craft, he is exposed to, and horrified by, the slavery that is active in the town. Like many other converts to abolition, he is particularly bothered by the sight of chained "coffles" of enslaved people in pens, awaiting shipment south. He later reflects on this experience:

It grieved my heart, and the iron (to oppose it) entered my soul.

Lundy's saddling business leads to economic success, and in 1815 he moves west to Mt. Pleasant, Ohio where he sets up shop, marries, begins a family, and commences on a quiet and prosperous life.

But his Quaker conscience convinces him that his purpose in life lies in a personal crusade against the evils of slavery he witnessed years ago. So he sells his business and sets out on his mission.

In 1815, with help from other Friends, Lundy founds the Union Humane Society— the first such group in his time to publicly speak up on behalf of emancipation.

He begins to tour the countryside and deliver public lectures attacking the evils of slavery. He also writes articles for a Friends newspaper, and when the owner dies in 1821, he becomes the hands-on publisher. He names the paper *The Genius of Universal Emancipation.*

Over the next eighteen years, Benjamin Lundy will devote all of his resources and strength to eradicating slavery in America, and enlisting important new converts in his cause.

In 1825 he escorts freed people to Haiti, then returns home to learn that his wife has died and his five children have been placed in a foster home. He decides to leave them there and free himself totally to carry on his quest, earning this tribute from the poet John Greenleaf Whittier on his death in 1839:

> *It was (Lundy's) lot to struggle, for years almost alone, a solitary voice crying in the wilderness, and, amidst all, faithful to his one great purpose, the emancipation of the slaves.*

Lundy will also be remembered for one of his final acts in 1829, when he strikes up a conversation in Boston with a 23-year-old named Lloyd Garrison—an iron-willed Baptist and neophyte reformer—whom Lundy encourages to join the crusade. Soon enough Garrison will become the face of the abolitionist movement across the nation.

The third founding member of the early abolitionist movement is the charismatic Lucretia Mott.

She is born Lucretia Coffin in 1793 in Nantucket, Massachusetts. At age thirteen her parents send her off to Nine Partners Quaker Boarding School, where she is educated and where she begins her career as a teacher alongside her future husband, James Mott.

She marries, becomes a teacher, then a biblical scholar, and finally a lay minister in 1821, at the age of 28.

Like her counterparts, she rebels against the rote traditions of her church and calls for:

> *Practical godliness over ceremonial religion.*

The search for "truth," according to Mott, begins by looking inside oneself and connecting with the potential perfection, "the inner light," that lies within.

Then comes action. The duty of the awakened is to go forth and reform the world's ills—something she will pursue all the way to her death in 1880.

By 1815, Mott, along with Lundy, will influence the Quaker General Assembly to speak out on behalf of abolition, declaring that the practice of buying and selling slaves is "inconsistent with the Gospels."

"Mother Mott" will later take Garrison under her wing as his chief spiritual advisor.

Lucretia Mott (1793–1880)

TIME: 1818

A VIRGINIAN ATTACKS SLAVERY

While public criticism of slavery is almost unheard of in the South, one exception is George Bourne, a Presbyterian minister in Virginia.

He begins a lifelong abolitionist crusade in 1818 by issuing his screed, *The Book and Slavery Irreconcilable*, in which he declares that the Bible cites "man-stealing" as a sin.

His sermons against slavery are soon met by a firestorm of resistance, and he is cast off from the ministry, first by his local congregation and then by the General Assembly.

Like all of the outspoken abolitionists of the era, Bourne risks his safety on a daily basis, and he soon abandons his home in Virginia to move north.

He lives until 1845, becoming a newspaper editor in New York City and a leading national voice for immediate abolition.

George Bourne's nominal heirs in this regard will include the martyred editor Elijah Lovejoy and his friends, Lloyd Garrison and the philanthropist Lewis Tappan.

ANOTHER BLOODY SLAVE UPRISING OCCURS

TIME: 1800/1805/1811

GABRIEL, CHATHAM, DESLONDES

The vast majority of enslaved Black people in 1820 have little hope of freedom, either through manumission in America or "re-colonization" to Liberia.

For a few, daily despair leads them to seek revenge on their white masters.

Some aspire to grand schemes along the lines of Toussaint Louverture's successful rebellion across all of Haiti in 1791. Others are smaller in scale, aimed solely at murdering their immediate tormentors.

All will be readily put down by local authorities and avenged with ruthless punishment to deter repetition.

Even so, they play a part in the long road to Black freedom.

One early uprising in 1800 ends with James Monroe himself, then governor of Virginia, calling out the

The stern look of an overseer

state militia for support. An enslaved blacksmith named Gabriel and his brother Martin, a preacher, plan to gather their forces, march on Richmond under the Patrick Henry banner ("Liberty or Death"), kill as many white people as possible, and then sail to Haiti. But word of their plot slips out in advance, and on August 30 Gabriel and others scatter in hopes of escape. Monroe's militia quickly tracks them down and a total of 26 Black people are subsequently hanged, including Gabriel and Martin.

Five years later, in January 1805, spontaneous resistance breaks out at Chatham Manor, the prestigious plantation owned by Washington's friend William Fitzhugh. The enslaved people there overpower and whip their overseer and four other white people. In response one Black person is executed, two die trying to escape, and two others are sold and sent away.

A much broader rebellion takes place in Louisiana in January 1811. It is led by an enslaved mulatto man named Charles Deslondes who hopes to repeat Toussaint Louverture's successful revolution in Haiti. His targets are the cane field plantations along Louisiana's "German Coast" (so named for its original European settlers) and the city of New Orleans some twenty miles to the south.

Deslondes plans well and recruits an initial band of 25 enslaved people to join his attack. It begins on the night of January 8, 1811 on the 1,900-acre Manual Andry Plantation, where 24-year-old Gilbert Andry is hacked to death while his parents barely escape the scene in a canoe. Armed with the Andry's militia gear, the rebels begin their march south along the River Road on January 9, destroying the Reine, Laclaverie, Meuillon, and Fortier plantations and adding upwards of 200 enslaved people to their force.

Upon learning of the raids William C.C. Claiborne, Louisiana's territorial governor, responds quickly. He calls out the local militia and troops under Major General Wade Hampton, seals off the roads and bridges into New Orleans, and imposes a 6 p.m. curfew on all Black males in the city.

Around 8 a.m. on January 10, Deslondes' men are confronted in the Fortier fields by Hampton's troops and some 80 planters, led by Manual Andry himself. A pitched battle ensues until the rebels run out of ammunition and surrender. Roughly twenty Black people are killed in action, 50 are captured, and the rest attempt to escape into the nearby swamps with Deslondes among them. But tracking dogs run him down on January 11, after which reports say "(m)ilitiamen chop off his hands, break his thighbones, shoot him dead and roast his corpse."

On January 13 a five-man tribunal convenes, with many of the rebels tried and hanged or shot before their severed heads are displayed on poles along the River Road entrance to New Orleans.

MAY 30, 1822

DENMARK VESEY'S INSURRECTION

In 1822 the banner is again picked up, this time in South Carolina by an enslaved man named Denmark Vesey.

After spending his youth in Haiti and witnessing the Toussaint revolt, he is brought to America as a house slave by his owner, Joseph Vesey. But luck shines on him when he wins $1,500 in a Charleston city lottery. He uses some of the cash to buy his freedom, then makes his living as a carpenter. He is also instrumental in founding the African Methodist Episcopal Church in Charleston in 1817.

Vesey is well-spoken and involved with the slavery debate. He cites both the Bible and the Declaration of Independence in arguing for abolition. But his hopes are evidently dashed when city authorities shut down his church, and Washington, DC politicians compromise over Missouri.

In response he puts together a plan that mirrors Gabriel's revolt in 1800. This plan, which filters out to many enslaved people in the area, calls for enslaved and free Black people to band together, murder the plantation owners, then rampage through Charleston before sailing off to liberty in Haiti.

All of this is to occur symbolically on July 14, 1822, the 33rd anniversary of Bastille Day in Paris.

But like Gabriel's plan, authorities learn of the attack and arrest a host of possible co-conspirators in advance. As usual they are tried summarily and 67 of them are hanged, including Denmark Vesey. In the tradition of the Roman legions of old, many of their heads are then cut off and displayed on pikes in public places, as a warning.

In hindsight, none of these early uprisings, from Gabriel to Vesey, represent an existential threat to white Southerners' control over the enslaved population. Nevertheless, each one, in its own way, strikes terror in the minds of white people.

The vision of an "African savage" approaching with a pitchfork or scythe in hand becomes every bit as imaginable as that of an Indian tribesman brandishing a war club.

And this is true both for Southerners who live in the midst of Black people and Northerners who progressively conclude that they do not want to.

## 46

JAMES MONROE'S SECOND TERM

TIME: NOVEMBER TO DECEMBER 1820

MONROE WINS REELECTION UNOPPOSED

The economic depression that continues to plague the country in 1820 would seem to offer the Federalists an opportunity to revive their political fortunes, but it is beyond saving for multiple reasons.

Perhaps foremost is the absence of a strong and well-known leader in the mold of Washington, Hamilton, and John Adams. DeWitt Clinton, who ran well against Madison in 1812, has returned to his roots as a Democratic-Republican, and is serving as governor of New York. Senator Rufus King has lost the last two races by large margins and is now 65 years old. Meanwhile, the most logical Federalist contender, 53-year-old John Quincy Adams, has been drummed out of the party for his support of Jefferson's 1807 embargo and is serving as Monroe's secretary of state.

In addition to lacking a credible presidential candidate, the Federalists are without a platform that resonates at the national level. Most people regard them as the party of wealthy New Englanders, touting the narrow wishes of the shipping and mercantile industries, out of touch with the rest of the country. Still others have never forgiven them for their "treasonous threat" at the 1814 Hartford Convention to secede from the Union.

The result is that Monroe in 1820, like Washington in 1792, runs essentially unopposed in the election. The voter turnout is only 107,000, about the same as in 1816. The president wins every state in the Union, and all but one electoral vote. The lone holdout is an elector from New Hampshire who regards Monroe as a failure, and casts his vote for John Quincy Adams.

RESULTS OF THE 1820 PRESIDENTIAL ELECTION

CANDIDATES	STATE	PARTY	POP. VOTE	TOTAL EV	SOUTH	BORDER	NORTH	WEST
James Monroe	VA	Dem-Rep	87,343	229	75	27	107	20
Anti-Monroe (Federalist ballot)	--	Federalist	17,465	0				

CANDIDATES	STATE	PARTY	POP. VOTE	TOTAL EV	SOUTH	BORDER	NORTH	WEST
DeWitt Clinton	NY	Dem-Rep	1,893	0				
John Quincy Adams	MA	Dem-Rep	---	1			1	
Total			106,701	230	75	27	108	20
Needed to Win				116				

Note: South (VA, NC, SC, GA, TN, AL, MS, LA), Border (DE, MD, KY), North (NH, MA, NY, NJ, PA, RI, CT, VT, ME), West (OH, IN, IL) Total # electors voting = 230; must get more than half to win = 116.

The Federalists do continue to slate candidates for Congress, but their influence outside of New England remains trivial.

RESULTS OF CONGRESSIONAL ELECTIONS

HOUSE	1817	1819	1821
Democratic-Republican	146	160	155
Federalist	39	26	32
SENATE			
Democratic-Republican	25	37	37
Federalist	13	9	9
Vacant			2
Congress #	15th	16th	17th
President	Madison	Monroe	Monroe

TIME: MARCH 5, 1821

MONROE'S SECOND INAUGURAL ADDRESS

Since March 4, 1821 falls on the Sabbath, Monroe delays his inauguration until the next day. His speech is lengthy and mixes praise for the nation's progress since independence along with his priorities for his second term.

He begins with foreign policy, recalling the second war with Britain and the nation's need for a strong military to avoid similar costly conflicts in the future.

Just before the commencement of the last term the United States had concluded a war with a very powerful nation…Provision was (then) made for the construction of fortifications at proper points through the whole extent of our coast and…augmentation of our naval force…It need scarcely be remarked that these measures have not been resorted to in a spirit of hostility to other powers. They have been dictated by a love of peace, of economy, and an earnest desire to save the lives of our fellow-citizens from that destruction and our country from that devastation which are inseparable from war when it finds us unprepared for it. It is believed, and experience has shown, that such a preparation is the best expedient that can be resorted to prevent war.

The conduct of the Government in what relates to foreign powers is always an object of the highest importance to the nation. Its agriculture, commerce, manufactures, fisheries, revenue, in short, its peace, may all be affected by it. Attention is therefore due to this subject.

Relations with Spain seem to be progressing well. For the moment, the United States will remain neutral in regard to Spain's ongoing wars with its South American colonies. The recent acquisition of Florida was important to America's future and signals the opportunity for ongoing friendly relations.

The war between Spain and the colonies in South America, which had commenced many years before, was then the only conflict that remained unsettled. Our attitude has therefore been that of neutrality between them, which has been maintained by the Government with the strictest impartiality. Should the war be continued, the United States, regarding its occurrences, will always have it in their power to adopt such measures respecting it as their honor and interest may require. Great confidence is entertained that the late treaty with Spain, which has been ratified by both the parties, and the ratifications whereof have been exchanged, has placed the relations of the two countries on a basis of permanent friendship.

But to the acquisition of Florida too much importance cannot be attached. It secures to the United States a territory…whose importance is…of the highest interests of the Union. It opens to several of the neighboring States a free passage to the ocean…by several rivers…It secures us against all future annoyance from powerful Indian tribes. It gives us several excellent harbors in the Gulf of Mexico for ships of war of the largest size. It covers the Mississippi and other great waters within our extended limits, and thereby enables the United States to afford complete protection to the vast and very valuable productions of our whole Western country…

The outlook for commercial relations with Britain and France are also favorable.

By a treaty…on the 20th of October, 1818, the convention regulating the commerce between the United States and Great Britain…was revived and continued for the term of ten years from the time of its expiration. The negotiation with France for the regulation of the commercial relations…will be pursued on the part of the United States…with an earnest desire that it may terminate in an arrangement satisfactory to both parties.

On the budgetary front, the message is mixed. Some progress has been made on paying down the public debt, without overburdening taxes – but government revenues have fallen and more bonds have been issued to cover expenditures.

> *The situation of the United States in regard to…resources…revenue, and the facility with which it is raised affords a most gratifying spectacle. The payment of nearly $67,000,000 of the public debt, with the great progress made in measures of defense and in other improvements of various kinds since the late war, are conclusive proofs of this extraordinary prosperity, especially when…these expenditures have been defrayed without a…direct tax and…in a manner not to be felt.*

> *Under the present depression of prices, affecting all the productions of the country… revenue has considerably diminished, the effect of which has been to compel Congress… to resort to loans or internal taxes to supply the deficiency. On the presumption that this depression and the deficiency in the revenue arising from it would be temporary, loans were authorized for the demands of the last and present year.*

> *I am satisfied that internal duties and excises, with corresponding imposts on foreign articles of the same kind, would, without imposing any serious burdens on the people, enhance the price of produce, promote our manufactures, and augment the revenue, at the same time that they made it more secure and permanent.*

After turning once again to fair treatment of the Indian tribes, and expressing concerns about renewed conflicts in Europe, he zeroes in on his optimism around America's future.

> *If we turn our attention, fellow-citizens…to our country…we have every reason to anticipate the happiest results In this great nation there is but one order, that of the people. By steadily pursuing this course in this spirit there is every reason to believe that our system will soon attain…such a degree of order and harmony as to command the admiration and respect of the civilized world.*

> *Twenty-five years ago the river Mississippi was shut up and our Western brethren had no outlet for their commerce. The United States now enjoy the complete and uninterrupted sovereignty over the whole territory from St. Croix to the Sabine. New States, settled from among ourselves in this and in other parts, have been admitted into our Union in equal participation in the national sovereignty with the original States. We now, fellow-citizens, comprise within our limits the dimensions and faculties of a great power under a Government possessing all the energies of any government ever known to the Old World, with an utter incapacity to oppress the people.*

> *With full confidence and with a firm reliance on the protection of Almighty God, I shall forthwith commence the duties of the high trust to which you have called me.*

TIME: MARCH 4, 1821 TO MARCH 4, 1825

OVERVIEW OF MONROE'S SECOND TERM

All cabinet members in place at the end of Monroe's first term remain in place through the second, except for one turnover in the Navy post.

JAMES MONROE CABINET IN 1821

POSITION	NAME	HOME STATE
Vice President	Daniel Tompkins	New York
Secretary of State	John Quincy Adams	Massachusetts
Secretary of Treasury	William Crawford	Georgia
Secretary of War	John C. Calhoun	South Carolina
Secretary of the Navy	Smith Thompson	New York
Attorney General	William Wirt	Virginia

The focus of the second term turns out to be foreign policy.

The stage for this is set early in 1821 when Alexander I of Russia asserts a claim to vast acreage in the Pacific northwest, including what becomes the Oregon Territory. Then comes pressure from King Ferdinand VII of Spain, demanding that the United States refrain from recognizing new governments in his breakaway colonies across South America.

Monroe eventually sees both these acts as affronts to America's growing power in the world and in need of a firm response. Secretary of State John Quincy Adams promotes this stance and completes careful diplomacy with Britain and France to head off any thoughts they might have of aligning with either Spain or Russia.

The final word on foreign intrusions comes in Monroe's annual speech to Congress on December 2, 1823. As a lifelong military man, the president places national

B. M BRADY,   WASHINGTON, D. C.

James Monroe (1758–1831)

security ahead of all other duties and decides that the time has come to end further attempts by foreigners to impose their wills within the hemisphere.

In years ahead, this "hands-off" policy becomes known as the "Monroe Doctrine," and it sets the stage for America to achieve hegemony over North America.

As the president's second term plays out, intense jockeying is underway to find his successor in office. Three men in particular—John Quincy Adams, William Crawford, and Andrew Jackson—will vie for the office in an election that will, for the second time, end up decided in the House of Representatives.

James Monroe is 66 years old when he retires to his Highland plantation, which has expanded to some 3,500 acres and is worked by 30–40 enslaved people. But his final six years will not be happy ones. Like Jefferson and Madison, his personal finances are in a shambles, only he lacks their inherited wealth to fend off ruin. He repeatedly petitions government officials for "reimbursement" of expenses incurred during his public service, but to no avail.

He is forced to sell Highland in 1825 and move 125 miles north to the Oak Hill plantation, inherited from his uncle Judge Jones. His wife dies in September of 1830, another terrible blow.

Monroe's final tomb:
Hollywood Cemetery, Richmond

After having lived with the partner of your youth, in so many vicissitudes of life, so long together, and afforded each other comforts which no other person on earth could do… to have her snatched from us, is an affliction which none but those who feel it, can justly estimate.

Monroe lives but ten months after his wife's passing. He is forced to sell Oak Hill and is taken in, virtually destitute, by his younger daughter in New York City. He dies there of heart failure on July 4, 1831.

KEY EVENTS: MONROE'S SECOND TERM

1821	
June 21	Waterford Academy for Young Ladies opens in Waterford, NY

Aug 10	Missouri admitted to the Union as 24th state
Sept 4	Czar Alexander I of Russia claims all of North America north of 51st parallel
	Republic of Liberia opened by American Colonization Society
1822	
Mar 30	East and West Florida joined, with Andrew Jackson as territorial governor
May 30	Enslaved rebellion plot of Denmark Vesey foiled; 35 Black people hanged.
June 19	US recognizes Bolívar's Republic of Gran Columbia
July 20	Tennessee state legislature declares support for Andrew Jackson for 1824 presidential race
July 24	US protests Russian claims to Oregon territory region
Oct 27	270 mile stretch of Erie Canal opened
Nov 18	Kentucky state legislature says it will support Henry Clay for the 1824 nomination
Dec 12	The US recognizes Mexican independence from Spain under emperor Agustín de Iturbide
1823	
Jan 27	The US recognizes Chile and Argentina as independent nations
Feb 18	Iturbide confirms land grant from Mexico to Moses and Stephen Austin in Tejas province
July 17	John Quincy Adams informs Russia that the US will resist any further foreign colonization in the Americas
Aug 20	Britain supports US resistance to Russian claims in the Oregon Territory region
Oct 9	France declares it will not support Spanish efforts to regain colonies in South America
Dec 2	The "Monroe Doctrine" announced in the president's annual speech to Congress
1824	
Feb 14	66 House members nominate Treasury Secretary William Crawford for the 1824 nomination
Feb 15	Boston politicians advance the candidacy of John Quincy Adams for the nomination
Feb	Explorer Jed Smith opens "South Pass" (Wyoming) through Rocky Mountains
Mar 2	In *Gibbons v. Ogden,* Supreme Court says federal government trumps states on interstate commerce issues
Mar 31	Speaker Henry Clay supports protectionist tariff of 1824 and need for infrastructure upgrades
April 17	Russia signs treaty with US renouncing claims south of 54'40", including the Oregon Territory
May 22	Congress supports Clay's tariff of 1824 bill
May 26	The US recognizes Brazil's independence
Jun 17	The Bureau of Indian Affairs is established
Oct 5	The Rensselaer School of Theoretical and Practical Science opens
Dec 1	The 1824 presidential election ends with no candidate getting an electoral college majority
--	Benjamin Lundy moves publishing of *Genius of Universal Emancipation* newspaper to Baltimore

1825	
Jan 3	The utopian New Harmony community opens in Indiana
Feb 9	John Quincy Adams is elected president when Clay supports him over Jackson in a House vote

## 47

MONROE ISSUES HIS "HANDS OFF THE AMERICAS" DOCTRINE

TIME: 1819–1821

SPAIN PRESSURES MONROE OVER DIPLOMATIC POLICIES RELATED TO LATIN AMERICA

With the domestic conflicts over the admission of Missouri palliated, President Monroe and Secretary of State John Quincy Adams turn their attention to diplomatic concerns provoked by King Ferdinand VII of Spain.

Ferdinand has been kicked off his throne in 1808 and imprisoned in France for five years while Napoleon's brother, Joseph-Napoléon Bonaparte, rules the nation. He returns in 1813, after the French army is beaten back from Moscow, only to find that his once far-reaching colonial empire had diminished in his absence.

Ferdinand is particularly distraught over lost revenues from his colonies in Latin America, where various "liberators" are at work, with the effects reaching all the way up to America's southern neighbor, Mexico.

Spain hopes to preserve its colonies in Central and South America

The Mexican independence movement begins in 1810 with the renegade priest Miguel Hidalgo, whose peasant army wins several battles before being defeated in July 1811. After Hidalgo's execution, leadership of the army falls on José María Morelos, who continues the fight and holds a conference declaring independence, but is ultimately defeated and killed in 1815.

Ferdinand is able to hold onto Mexico for seven more years before independence is finally achieved—ironically under the leadership of Colonel Agustín de Iturbide. This caudillo initially opposes the rebels, but then seizes on populist anger with the Spanish throne to declare himself emperor of Mexico.

Further south, the picture is no better for Ferdinand.

There the uprisings against Spanish rule are led by Simón Bolívar, who descends from a long line of Basque aristocrats in Spain and grows up in Caracas, Venezuela. He masters warfare at the military academy there and goes on to assume command of a series of armies which, in 1820, proclaim a new nation called Gran Colombia.

This nation, which will endure for a decade under Bolívar's rule, extends from what is today Panama, south through the top quarter of South America, including Ecuador, northern Peru, Colombia, Venezuela, and northwest Brazil.

By 1820, the Spanish hold over Paraguay, Chile, and Argentina has also collapsed.

King Ferdinand VII hopes to reverse these losses and restore his rule across South America, perhaps with military help from other European monarchists bent on destroying secular governments wherever they are found, including the United States.

Ferdinand uses the Adams-Onís Treaty of 1819 to try to leverage Monroe into tacitly supporting his vision. This diplomatic quid pro quo appalls many American politicians—most notably Henry Clay, who accuses Monroe of siding with an absolutist king over oppressed people seeking freedom and self-rule. Clay's speeches to this effect make him a hero throughout Latin America, and eventually force Monroe and Adams to exhibit a stronger hand with the Spanish monarch.

It is within this context that a new threat of foreign intrusion materializes in the form of Tsar Alexander I, ruler of Russia and member of the powerful Holy Alliance with Austria and Prussia, who issues a decree that further rattles the administration.

In the Ukase (decree) of 1821 the tsar proclaims Russian sovereignty over a large swath of North America, running from Alaska in the north and west all the way down to the 45'50" parallel within the Oregon Country.

TIME: 1741–1821

RUSSIA ENTERS NORTH AMERICA THROUGH ALASKA

Like Britain and America, Russia is originally drawn to the Pacific Northwest by the fur trade.

The tsar's interest here begins in Alaska, or "mainland," in the language of the native Aleutian Islanders who inhabit the region.

In 1741, a Russian expedition led by the Dane Vitus Bering first explores Alaska. It finds a vast expanse, with latitudes ranging from 70 degrees in the north to 55 degrees

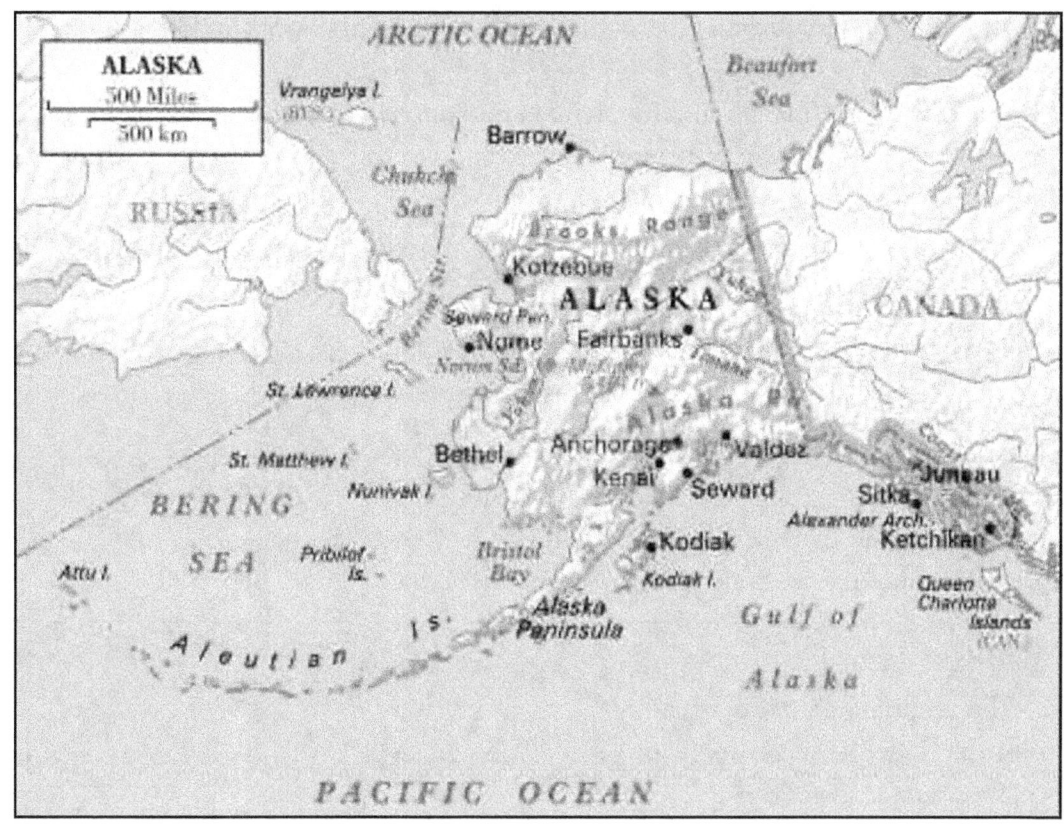

Russia Eyes a Move into Alaska and the Pacific Northwest

in the south, and sub-freezing temperatures lasting upwards of seven months each year in the arctic zone. It also encounters almost endless herds of fur bearing mammals (seals, otters, bears, hares, fox, and ermine) there for the taking.

Russian trappers follow, with settlements springing up mainly along the southern coast. In 1784 one Grigory Shelikhov and 200 settlers found the Three Saints Bay colony on Kodiak Island. In 1799 Tsar Paul I issues an ukase claiming ownership of land south to the 55th parallel and chartering Russia's first joint-stock corporation, the Russian-American Company. It will be led by Aleksandr Baranov, a crafty fur trader and businessman, from 1799 to 1818. He drives along the southern coast, wins a major victory over the native Aleut tribes at the Battle of Sitka in 1804, and begins a push down into the Oregon Country.

Baranov establishes Russian settlements almost to San Francisco after finding that Spain has failed to occupy land in northern California. His operation there is anchored at Fort Ross, a name whose roots tie to the word Russia in his native tongue. The fort thrives from 1812 onward, with inhabitants including Russians and other Slavic people, along with Aleut Indians.

At this point, Russia is operating well south of its recognized territory in Alaska—

and intruding on the Oregon Country land coveted not only by Spain, but also Britain and America.

Along with Ferdinand's ambitions in Latin America, Alexander's Ukase of 1821 serves to reignite American fears over another round of foreign invasions into the western hemisphere.

TIME: SEPTEMBER 4, 1821

RUSSIA ASSERTS A CLAIM TO LAND IN THE OREGON COUNTRY

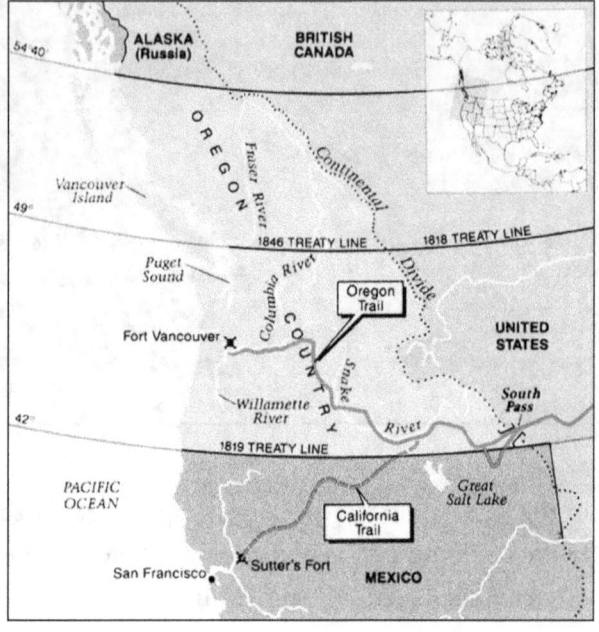

Territorial disputes to the south of Alaska over the Oregon Country are long-standing.

They begin in the late 16th century when ships from both Spain and England sail along the Pacific coast.

The Spanish are first to actually claim the land, after expeditions by explorers such as Juan Pérez in 1774 and Bruno de Heceta and Juan Francisco de la Bodega y Quadra in 1775.

The British christen the territory "Ouragon" in 1765, and Captain James Cook makes land there in 1788 at the 43rd parallel, before proceeding north and mapping all the way over to the Bering Strait.

Then come the Americans, with Captain Robert Gray in his ship *Columbia*, also exploring the region in 1788. Gray is first to enter the mouth of the geographically critical 1,200-mile-long river he names the Columbia in 1792. From Oregon, Gray heads west with a shipload of furs to trade in China, and becomes the first American to circumnavigate the globe. His published journals spur others to pursue trapping and trade around Oregon.

In 1792 British Captain George Vancouver sails up the Columbia River, setting the stage for operations by the Hudson Bay Company in their attempt to dominate the worldwide fur industry. Three decades later, in 1824, Hudson will open Fort Vancouver, inland headquarters of their Columbia District.

The American explorers Lewis and Clark arrive overland in the Oregon Country in 1806. They are followed in 1811 by the tycoon John Jacob Astor, whose American Fur

Company will compete tooth and nail against Hudson Bay over the next two decades from his post at Ft. Astoria.

Spain renounces its claims to Oregon in the Adams-Onís Treaty of 1819, apparently leaving Britain and America as the only two contenders for the land rights.

But then Alexander's Ukase of 1821 adds further complications.

After much cabinet-level discussion, Monroe and Adams decide it's time for America to resolve the borders in the Oregon Country and assert a foreign policy decree of its own.

TIME: DECEMBER 2, 1823

THE MONROE DOCTRINE SPELLS OUT
AMERICA'S FOREIGN POLICY ACROSS THE HEMISPHERE

The policy is quite remarkable, and it signals the rest of the world that American democracy is now on equal footing with the monarchies of Europe and Asia.

This is Monroe at his finest, the last of the Revolutionary War presidents, determined to ensure the nation's political integrity and borders from any and all foreign threats.

Which first means the answer will be "no" to Spain's demand to withhold recognition of the newly independent nations of Latin America, and "no" to Russia's assertion of control over the Oregon Country.

The former comes in June of 1822, when America opens diplomatic ties with Bolívar's Gran Columbia and in December of the same year when an independent Mexico is officially recognized.

James Monroe (1758–1831)

The Russian claims are dealt with soon thereafter in what will become known as the Monroe Doctrine.

The president announces this doctrine in his annual address to Congress of December 2, 1823. The speech is lengthy, but its essence is captured in four paragraphs.

These begin with an olive branch, signaling peaceful intentions into the future, unless America's national interests are menaced.

The citizens of the United States cherish sentiments the most friendly in favor of the liberty and happiness of their fellow men on that side of the Atlantic. In the wars of the European powers in matters relating to themselves we have never taken any part, nor does it comport with our policy so to do.

It is only when our rights are invaded or seriously menaced that we resent injuries or make preparation for our defense. With the movements in this hemisphere we are of necessity more immediately connected, and by causes which must be obvious to all enlightened and impartial observers.

Then comes an obvious but crucial declaration—namely that America's "political system" is fundamentally different from the norm in the rest of the world. It stands for "enlightened citizens" choosing their own governments, and in opposition to the principle of government imposed on people by unelected dictators.

The political system of the allied powers is essentially different in this respect from that of America. This difference proceeds from that which exists in their respective Governments; and to the defense of our own, which has been achieved by the loss of so much blood and treasure, and matured by the wisdom of their most enlightened citizens, and under which we have enjoyed unexampled felicity, this whole nation is devoted.

This is followed by a policy statement informing the heads of state around the world that America will no longer tolerate new attempts at colonization anywhere in the western hemisphere.

We owe it, therefore, to candor and to the amicable relations existing between the United States and those powers to declare that we should consider any attempt on their part to extend their system to any portion of this hemisphere as dangerous to our peace and safety. With the existing colonies or dependencies of any European power we have not interfered and shall not interfere, but with the Governments who have declared their independence and maintained it, and whose independence we have, on great consideration and on just principles, acknowledged, we could not view any interposition for the purpose of oppressing them, or control ling in any other manner their destiny, by any European power in any other light than as the manifestation of an unfriendly disposition toward the United States.

This "Monroe Doctrine" will forever draw a line in the sand against any foreign power wishing to flex its military might in the Americas. It also announces to the world that the grand experiment of 1787—a nation of free men forming their own political system—is both prosperous and viable.

However, it does not resolve all the territorial disputes in Oregon overnight. These take time. Alexander will try to enforce his decree by seizing the American ship *Pearl*, but it is released with compensation paid, after the US government protests. Russia's west coast colonies will linger until the 1840s when they prove unprofitable. Two decades later another tsar, Alexander II, will sell Alaska and all other North American claims to the United States, in what critics will call "Seward's Folly."

Despite the delayed effects, the December 2, 1823 declaration is generally regarded as the defining moment in James Monroe's two terms as president.

48

POLITICAL FAULT LINES RELATED TO GEOGRAPHY AND SLAVERY ARE AMPLIFIED IN THE 1824 PRESIDENTIAL RACE

TIME: 1822

THE DEMOCRATIC-REPUBLICANS SPLIT INTO THREE FACTIONS IN THE 1822 CONGRESSIONAL ELECTION

By the mid-terms of 1822, it's clear that the "Virginia Dynasty" of Jefferson, Madison, and Monroe will come to an end in the upcoming presidential race. So too will the smooth political harmony enjoyed by the Democratic-Republicans over the last 24 years.

Three factions within the party emerge at once: one backing Secretary of State John Quincy Adams, a second favoring Treasury Secretary William Crawford, and a third committed to General Andrew Jackson.

The midterm election in 1822 tests the relative strengths of the presidential contenders.

The results in both the House and the Senate demonstrate that, as of December 1822, no one man enjoys the majority position needed to win the prize.

1822 HOUSE ELECTION

WINNERS WHO SUPPORT	TOTAL	SOUTH	BORDER	NORTH	WEST
John Quincy Adams	87	4	14	58	11
Andrew Jackson	71	26	7	33	5
William Crawford	55	37	2	14	2
	213	67	23	105	18

TIME: SPRING 1824

FIVE CANDIDATES VIE FOR THE PRESIDENCY IN 1824

By 1824, the absence of a clear front-runner expands the list to five contenders.

The most obvious successor to Monroe is John Quincy Adams, 55 years old, son of an ex-president, serving in government for over three decades, and supremely qualified after working alongside Monroe for eight years as secretary of state.

The problem with Adams is his personality, or lack thereof.

He is in the mold of the old-time Puritans, hard working to an extreme, prone to signaling superior moral rectitude, stern, and mostly humorless. All admire his talents and accomplishments; few count him a close friend. His political strength is centered in New England, especially his home state of Massachusetts.

Monroe's treasury secretary, William Crawford of Georgia, enjoys support from two critical centers of electoral gravity: the Virginian trio of Jefferson, Madison, and Monroe, and the so-called "Albany Regency" in New York. The latter is controlled by Martin Van Buren, a political mover and shaker from age seventeen onward, and serving in the US Senate since 1821. His "city hall machine" is built on patronage and can be counted on to deliver the bulk of New York's electors. Van Buren lines these up behind Crawford.

Adams and Crawford are joined in the race by two other powerful Washington men: Secretary of War John C. Calhoun and House Speaker Henry Clay.

Calhoun is respected for his brilliant intellect, but, along with Adams, is seldom well-liked at the personal level. Many regard his demeanor as unpleasantly messianic, as if he alone were capable of discerning what is right for the country while being held back by lesser men around him. His overt ambitiousness leads to questions about his motivations and trustworthiness, and Northerners suspect that his agenda is skewed toward Southern rather than national interests.

Unlike Calhoun and Adams, Henry Clay is a comfortable figure, ever ready to drink, gamble, and party with his fellow politicians. He is flexible about meeting them halfway on most contentious issues. He also comes with a "platform" of sorts, in the form of what he calls his "American System" of government, focused on accelerating economic growth through federally funded infrastructure initiatives, a protective tariff, and a strong central bank. According to his supporters, Clay is a symbol of America's future—born in the east

(Virginia), venturing to the west (Kentucky), and linking the old with the new in search of a strong, enduring Union.

The fifth contender for president, Andrew Jackson, differs from the others. He is a military man rather than a politician—but also a national hero, first for his stunning defeat of the British in 1815 at New Orleans, and more recently for various victories over Indian tribes in Georgia and Florida. As an outsider to Washington, he is initially dismissed as a serious candidate until astute handlers in Tennessee get the state legislature to officially nominate him for the presidency in 1822 and then elect him to the Senate in 1823. From that point forward he bursts on the scene as the frontrunner, and the common target to be stopped by his four competitors.

TIME: AUTUMN 1824

JOHN QUINCY ADAMS AND ANDREW JACKSON EMERGE AS FAVORITES

Jackson's sustained popularity convinces the party leaders that no candidate will be capable of securing an electoral vote majority in December 1824, and that it will ultimately be up to the House to choose Monroe's successor.

According to established rules, the top three vote-getters in the general election will be eligible for a runoff. This sends each candidate in search of locking in states they hope to win in the first round and then individual House members who might tip the balance in the follow-up.

Amidst this scramble, the electoral math shifts dramatically in September of 1823, when William Crawford, favored by the Virginians and Van Buren, becomes ill and is given an overdose of digitalis, a powerful drug that leads to a massive stroke. He is left partially paralyzed, nearly blind, and unable to speak, with none knowing if the condition is temporary or permanent. On the hope that he will recover, his condition is kept largely secret throughout the campaign.

Despite his health, Van Buren tries to force the issue in Crawford's favor through a traditional nominating caucus of congressional members held on February 24, 1824. But only 66 of the 216 members show up, sharply reducing the impact of the Crawford-Gallatin ticket chosen.

Meanwhile, Calhoun's chances vanish when his one hope for northern support, Pennsylvania, declares in favor of Jackson, and Clay is attacked for leading a libertine lifestyle and for promoting programs that sound more like the Federalists than like Jefferson.

Characteristically, John Quincy Adams, who very much wants the presidency, finds it beneath his sense of dignity to campaign for it in any fashion.

TIME: 1824 AND ONWARD

SECTIONAL ISSUES BEGIN TO RESHAPE THE POLITICAL LANDSCAPE

The election of 1824 also amplifies two emerging political factors.

One relates to geography. Over two million Americans, one in every four, already reside west of the Appalachian Mountains, and their number is growing rapidly. The daily lives of these frontier families differ from those in the "settled East," as do some of their wishes and expectations for the national government. The 1824 race represents a chance for their voices to be boosted.

The second factor beginning to divide the electorate involves tension over the long-term fate of the Black population.

As demonstrated by the conflict surrounding the 1819 Tallmadge Amendment,

Southerners are committed to expanding slavery into the western territories, while Northerners want to banish all Black people, enslaved or free.

Taken together, the one nation harmony of 1820 is challenged in 1824 along two regional fault lines: East versus West and North versus South.

POLITICAL FAULT LINES EMERGING IN 1824

GEOGRAPHY	SLAVERY ALLOWED (12)	SLAVERY BANNED (12)
Old Established East Coast States (15)	MD, DE, VA, NC, SC, GA	MA, ME, NH, VT, CT, PA, RI, NY, NJ
Emerging States West of Appalachia (9)	KY, TN, AL, MS, LA, MO	OH, IN, IL

Voting power within these four cells differs dramatically, and is a key determinant in choosing a president. The lion's share (106 in total) of the electoral votes remains in the northeastern states, with Pennsylvania (29) and New York (28) particularly important. States where slavery is banned, and Black people are unwelcome, also enjoy a 129–113 edge.

VOTING POWER IN 1824: # OF SEATS IN CONGRESS

	SLAVERY ALLOWED (12)	SLAVERY BANNED (12)	TOTAL
Old East Coast States (15)	73	106	179
Emerging Western States (9)	40	23	63
Total	113	129	242

Once Calhoun drops out in favor of seeking the vice presidency, four contenders remain.

John Quincy Adams, as the lone representative of the northeast, begins with a solid base, despite his shift in 1808 from his father's Federalist Party to the Democratic-Republican side.

Crawford's original strength in the old South and in New York (via Van Buren), is formidable but weakening as word of his uncertain health spreads. (Miraculously, he eventually recovers some of his faculties and lives until 1834.)

Then come the two "men of the West" who already detest each other: Clay, the Washington political infighter for over a decade, and Jackson, the military man and outsider.

A TROUBLING HOUSE VOTE HANDS THE PRESIDENCY TO JOHN QUINCY ADAMS

TIME: OCTOBER TO DECEMBER 1824

THE GENERAL ELECTION ENDS WITHOUT A WINNER

Voting in 1824 takes place between October 26 and December 2. Turnout surpasses all prior contests, as three in every four states now choose electors based on the popular votes, and real competition draws public interest.

POPULAR VOTING FOR PRESIDENT & NUMBER OF STATES WHERE ELECTORS CHOSEN BY THEIR VOTES

1788	1792	1796	1800	1804	1808	1812	1816	1820	1824
43,782	28,579	66,841	67,282	143,110	192,691	278,786	112,370	106,701	365,833
7 of 12	6 of 15	9 of 16	6 of 16	11 of 17	10 of 17	9 of 18	10 of 19	15 of 24	18 of 24*

* State legislators in Delaware, Vermont, New York, South Carolina, Georgia, and Louisiana still choose electors in 1824

As expected, none of the four candidates reach the 131 electoral votes needed to become president in the traditional fashion. Andrew Jackson comes closest at 99 votes, with Adams a close second. Crawford edges Clay for third place, even though he remains physically incapable of serving.

RESULTS OF THE 1824 PRESIDENTIAL ELECTION

CANDIDATES	STATE	PARTY	POP. VOTE	TOTAL EV
Andrew Jackson	TN	Dem-Rep	151,271	99
John Quincy Adams	MA	Dem-Rep	113,122	84
William Crawford	GA	Dem-Rep	40,856	41
Henry Clay	KY	Dem-Rep	47,531	37
Unpledged			6,616	0
TOTAL			365,833	261
NEEDED TO WIN				131

Jackson alone demonstrates national appeal, garnering significant votes in all four regions of the country. Adams' support is almost exclusively in the northeast. Crawford splits the old South with Jackson, and Clay wins his home state of Kentucky and its northern neighbor, Ohio.

SHIFTING STATE ALIGNMENTS: OLD/NEW AND SLAVERY/FREE

	SLAVERY ALLOWED (12)	SLAVERY BANNED (12)
Old Established East Coast States (15)	36 Crawford 33 Jackson 4 Adams 0 Clay 73 Total	77 Adams 37 Jackson 5 Crawford 4 Clay 103 Total
Emerging States West of Appalachian Range (9)	22 Jackson 17 Clay 2 Adams 0 Crawford 41 Total	16 Clay 7 Jackson 1 Adams 0 Crawford 24 Total

Note: East Coast slavery states (MD, DE, VA, NC, SC, GA); east coast free (ME, MA, NH, VT, CT, PA, RI, NY, NJ); west slavery (KY, TN, AL, MS, LA, MO); west free (OH, IN, IL)

TIME: WINTER 1824

SIDEBAR: DETAILED TABLES FROM THE ELECTION OF 1824

ELECTORAL VOTES CAST: TOTAL US

	TOTAL	JACKSON	ADAMS	CRAWFORD	CLAY
East	196	70	81	41	4
West	65	29	3	0	33
Slave	114	55	6	36	17
Free	147	44	78	5	20

OLD ESTABLISHED EAST COAST STATES: WITH SLAVERY

	TOTAL	JACKSON	ADAMS	CRAWFORD	CLAY
Maryland	11	7	3	1	
Delaware	3	2		1	
Virginia	24			24	
North Carolina	15	15			
South Carolina	11	11			
Georgia	9			9	
TOTAL	73	35	3	35	

OLD ESTABLISHED EAST COAST STATES: NO SLAVERY

	TOTAL	JACKSON	ADAMS	CRAWFORD	CLAY
Massachusetts	15		15		
Maine	9	1	8		
New Hampshire	8		8		
Vermont	7		7		
Connecticut	8		8		
Pennsylvania	29	3	26		
Rhode Island	4		4		
New York	28	28			
New Jersey	17	8		5	4
TOTAL	125	40	76	5	4

EMERGING WESTERN STATES: WITH SLAVERY

	TOTAL	JACKSON	ADAMS	CRAWFORD	CLAY
Kentucky	14				14
Tennessee	11	11			
Alabama	5	5			
Mississippi	3	3			
Louisiana	5	3	2		
Missouri	3				3
TOTAL	41	21	2		17

EMERGING WESTERN STATES: NO SLAVERY

	TOTAL	JACKSON	ADAMS	CRAWFORD	CLAY
Ohio	16				16
Indiana	5	5			
Illinois	2	2			
TOTAL	23	7			16

TIME: FEBRUARY 9, 1825

CLAY MANEUVERS TO ENSURE THAT THE HOUSE ELECTS ADAMS

According to the 12th Amendment rules, the choice of president now falls to the House of Representatives, which meets on February 9, 1825 to decide the outcome. Each state will cast one vote for the winner within their caucus. Since there are 24 states in total, a candidate must take at least 13 to be elected.

In the general election, Jackson led the pack by winning twelve states, with Adams as runner-up with seven.

STATES WON IN GENERAL ELECTION

CANDIDATES	#
Andrew Jackson	12
John Quincy Adams	7
Henry Clay	3
William Crawford	2

However, Jackson's lead quickly slips away in the House. He loses Delaware and North Carolina to Crawford, and then Louisiana to Adams. At the last moment, New York also slips away after Daniel Webster and Henry Clay convince the Dutch patroon Stephen Van Rensselaer to break his promise to Van Buren and cast a deciding vote in the caucus for Adams.

The rest of Jackson's losses also trace directly to the Speaker. From the beginning, Clay dismisses Jackson's readiness to be president in no uncertain terms:

> *I cannot believe that killing 2500 Englishmen at N. Orleans qualifies for the various, difficult and complicated duties of the Chief Magistry.*

He is joined in this conclusion by Jefferson and others who regard the general's temperament as too rash for the office, as demonstrated by his recent rampages in Florida.

But Clay now must choose between Adams and Crawford, and he meets with the former before the House vote. Two very different views of this meeting emerge in hindsight. One is that Adams convinces Clay that he will support the Speaker's "American System" initiatives if elected. The other is that Adams secures Clay's support by promising to name him secretary of state.

Whatever the reason, Clay decides to steer three key states he won in the general election—Kentucky, Missouri, and Ohio—over to Adam's column on the first ballot. This gives him the thirteen states needed for victory.

HOUSE RUN-OFF FOR PRESIDENT: 1ST BALLOT (13 NEEDED TO WIN)

OLD EAST – WITH SLAVERY	GENERAL	JACKSON	ADAMS	CRAWFORD
Maryland	AJ		X	
Delaware	AJ			X
Virginia	WC			X
North Carolina	AJ			X
South Carolina	AJ	X		
Georgia	WC			X
Total		1	1	4

OLD EAST – NO SLAVERY				
Maine	JQA		X	
Massachusetts	JQA		X	
New Hampshire	JQA		X	
Vermont	JQA		X	
Connecticut	JQA		X	
Pennsylvania	JQA	X		
Rhode Island	JQA		X	
New York	AJ		X	
New Jersey	AJ	X		
Total		2	7	0
NEW WEST – WITH SLAVERY				
Kentucky	HC		X	
Tennessee	AJ	X		
Alabama	AJ	X		
Mississippi	AJ	X		
Louisiana	AJ		X	
Missouri	HC		X	
Total		3	3	0
NEW WEST – NO SLAVERY				
Ohio	HC		X	
Indiana	AJ	X		
Illinois	AJ		X	
Total		1	2	0
Grand Total		7	13	4

TIME: APRIL 25, 1825

CLAY FIGHTS YET ANOTHER DUEL TO DEFEND THE ELECTION

When Adams names Clay as his secretary of state, Jackson is convinced that a "corrupt bargain" trumped the will of the American people and cost him an election that was his. He quickly vents his spleen:

Clay voted for Adams and made him President and Adams made Clay Secretary of State. Is this not proof as strong as holy writ of the understanding and corrupt coalition between them? So, the Judas of the West has closed the contract and will receive the thirty pieces of silver. His end will be the same. Was there ever witnessed such a bare faced corruption in any country before.

With that, the 56-year-old general resigns from the Senate and rides back home to Tennessee, with the firm commitment to defeat Adams in 1828 election and oppose Clay at every future step of the way.

Adams attempts to move past the fractious election, but many Jackson supporters are in no mood to either forgive or forget. This soon leads to another episode of violence involving high government officials.

The impetus in this case is a speech made by the ever-volatile Senator John Randolph of Roanoke. In a six-hour harangue on the floor, he accuses the administration of violating America's long-standing policy of "avoiding foreign entanglements" by wishing to participate in Bolívar's upcoming Panama conference.

As his rhetoric becomes increasingly inflammatory, John C. Calhoun, serving as *pro tem* of the Senate, allows him to rail on—a fact which Adams properly interprets as treachery from his own vice president.

Randolph ends with a personal attack on both Adams and Clay, whom he refers to as...

The Puritan and the Blackleg.

The Puritan, of course, is Adams the stern Massachusetts man, and the Blackleg—a vicious disease which kills livestock, not to mention slang for a card-cheat—is Clay.

Randolph is well-known to Clay. He is Thomas Jefferson's cousin, and his career in Congress dates back to 1799. Along with Clay, he is a co-founder of the American Colonization Society in 1816 who will free all of his slaves in his final will.

His political values are those of the extreme "states' rights" wing of the party, including a belief that federal laws can be "nullified" by a vote of local legislators. His fame rests on his general flamboyance, his powerful oratory, his capacity for consuming alcohol, and his shooting prowess.

The latter is no deterrent to Clay, who challenges him to a duel for his remarks on the floor. Attempts by the secretary's friends to avoid the obvious risks are met with characteristic resistance.

No public station, no, not even life, is worth holding, if coupled with dishonor.

Randolph is astonished to receive the challenge, saying that it violates a senator's right to protected speech within the chamber. He informs his aides, but not Clay, that he has no intention of firing to harm should the duel actually take place.

But Clay plunges ahead, much as he had back in 1809 when called a "liar" in the Kentucky State House by Representative Humphrey Marshall. This affair ended with a total of four shots exchanged and both men wounded, Clay to the extent that further rounds were called off.

On April 25, 1825, rowboats carry the combatants across the Potomac to their native Virginia, and the two men—a 51-year-old United States senator and the 49-year-old secretary of state—square off with pistols.

Randolph appears in a vast morning gown, which makes the outline of his body difficult to discern.

Tensions are high, and the hair-trigger on the senator's gun causes a misfire, which Clay forgives.

Both men then let off their first shots, with neither hit. On the second round, Clay's shot nicks Randolph's outer garment, while Randolph fires aimlessly in the air—signaling to the secretary that the event is over.

In accord with tradition, the two men shake hands and exchange cards. Clay purportedly says that he is thankful not to have injured Randolph, and Randolph retorts that Clay now owes him a new coat. With that, the two sail back across the river with at least minimal courtesy restored.

## 50

JOHN QUINCY ADAMS' TERM

TIME: 1767–1848

PRESIDENT JOHN QUINCY ADAMS: PERSONAL PROFILE

While John Quincy Adams' track record of public service qualifies him to become a superb president, his temperament proves ill-suited to the executive role. His lasting fame will rest on his remarkable service both before his term as secretary of state and after, when he returns to the House of Representatives as the first political crusader against the institution of slavery.

JQA, as he calls himself, is born in Braintree, Massachusetts on July 11, 1767, the second child and first son of John and Abigail Adams. His father is a fifth generation American, a farmer and lawyer, and already caught up in the politics surrounding resistance to the British Stamp Act of 1765. His mother is a stern Puritan through and through, who micromanages every aspect of the boy's life into adulthood, sparking a resentment that ends with his failure to attend her sickbed and funeral in 1818.

In the Calvinist tradition, Abigail teaches him that personal discipline is essential to salvation, and that each day must be parceled out in rigid fashion to meet that end: up before dawn, exercise, reading the Bible, duties until evening, diary entries to record achievements and failings, and no more than four or five hours of sleep. Both parents also burden the youth with elevated expectations around public service, his father demanding that he:

Become a guardian of the laws, liberty and religion of your country.

Predictably, Adams suffers early on from a sense of guilt and failure. At age seven, he writes to his parents:

I hope...you will have no occasion to be ashamed of me.

Unlike his two brothers, Charles and Thomas, who wilt under parental pressure into dissolution and alcohol, Adams is blessed with enough fortitude to bear up. This includes enormous intellectual capacity, which by age ten has him mastering Greek and Latin, on his way to fluency in six other languages besides English. By fifteen he devours the historical classics (Hume, Macaulay, Gibbons, Caesar's *Commentaries*, and Cicero's *Oratories* in Latin), masters Adam Smith's economic tome *Wealth of Nations,* and allows himself to indulge in literature from Shakespeare to the English poets. He loves school and is settling into life as a student in 1778.

His plans evaporate, however, when his father is sent by George Washington to join Ben Franklin in Paris as joint ministers seeking French support in the Revolutionary War.

John and Abigail decide that their son's worldview will be broadened if goes along with his father. At age twelve he boards a ship for what will be the first in a long series of back-and-forth stints in Europe. These will propel him into adulthood before his time, make him America's leading diplomat, and set the stage for his presidency.

At fifteen he is an aide in St. Petersburg translating the court language (French) for Ambassador Francis Dana and befriending the future tsar, Alexander I. Three years later he is back home, enrolling at Harvard, then graduating in 1787, opening a law practice, and falling in love, only to be vetoed by his mother, who says he is not financially prepared to support a wife.

In 1794, with backing from his father, then vice president, Adams is named minister to the Netherlands. He is 27 years old at the time, but already a recognized figure in Europe. On a visit to Britain, he meets English-born Louisa Johnson, who becomes his wife in 1797. Abigail calls her "the Siren," and the two remain forever at odds.

As president, his father names him minister to Prussia, and he serves there from 1797 to 1801. With Jefferson now in office, Adams returns to Boston to resume his law practice, but that is again short-lived. Federalist friends convince him to run for state senator and then for the House of Representatives in 1802. He loses this election but is chosen by the state legislature in 1803 to serve as US senator.

During his term, he commits political suicide within the Federalist Party by backing two of Jefferson's controversial acts: the 1803 Louisiana Purchase and the 1807 Trade Embargo on British imports. When he caucuses with the Democratic-Republicans in selecting Madison to run in 1808, the Federalists disown him for good and he resigns his seat in 1808. He continues to teach logic at Harvard University until 1809, when Madison chooses him to be America's first minister to Russia. He remains there for five years before heading to London in 1814 to join Speaker Henry Clay and Treasury Secretary Gallatin in negotiating the Treaty of Ghent, which ends the War of 1812. He stays there until 1817 when Monroe appoints him secretary of state.

Adams is finally back home after eight straight years abroad. He and Louisa have had four children, a daughter who dies in infancy in Russia and three sons, two who descend into alcoholism and one (Charles Francis) who will become an accomplished public servant. Monroe exhibits great confidence in his chief diplomat, and Adams responds in kind. His many achievements include the Adams-Onís/Transcontinental Treaty of 1818 and the framework known as the Monroe Doctrine, announcing America's diplomatic stance as a world power.

Throughout the years Adams retains the steely discipline imposed on him as a child. He works from morning to night, allowing himself only infrequent breaks for a swim in the Potomac, a game of billiards, and the occasional cultural event.

Adams's ascent to the presidency at age 58 is in many ways a fulfillment of the awesome expectations placed upon him by his mother and father. He arrives prepared with vast experience as a diplomat, high moral principles, and a commitment to advancing the welfare of the nation.

However, as a presidential politician he will prove even more inept than his father.

His term in office leaves him vastly disappointed with his achievements, and this is followed by a decisive loss to Jackson in 1828. At this point, most men would simply fade away from the public stage. But not John Quincy Adams.

In 1831, neighbors convince him to run again for the House, and he will serve there for almost seventeen years until his death from a cerebral hemorrhage suffered in the chamber in 1848. This "second act" for the former president far outshines what he was able to accomplish in the White House.

Most notably he emerges as the outright champion of freeing all enslaved people and finding ways to assimilate them into American society. His commitment to this cause brings the taboo subject of slavery into the House and sets the stage for all future political efforts to end it through legislation. In this quest he is every inch the Puritan son seeking the "holiest rights of humanity" for all Americans.

> *They look down upon the simplicity of a Yankee's manners, because he has no habits of overbearing like theirs and cannot treat negroes like dogs. It is among the evils of slavery that it taints the very sources of moral principle. It establishes false estimates of virtue and vice: for what can be more false and heartless than this doctrine which makes the first and holiest rights of humanity to depend upon the color of the skin?*

TIME: 1776–1861

THE SCOPE OF DE TOCQUEVILLE'S TRAVELS SENSITIZESORPS

John Quincy Adams' years as a US diplomat during the nation's earliest and often most hazardous period put him in the company of other important figures who served in London and Paris up through the Civil War.

Included here were five others who became president (John Adams, Thomas Jefferson, James Monroe, Martin Van Buren, and James Buchanan), two vice presidents (William King and George Dallas), and a host of other cabinet officers and congressional leaders.

US AMBASSADORS TO GREAT BRITAIN

YEARS	NAME	APPOINTED BY	PARTY	HIGHEST POLITICAL OFFICE
1785–1788	John Adams	Washington	Federalist	President (1797–1801)
1789–1791	Vacant			
1792–1796	Thomas Pinckney	Washington	Federalist	Governor of SC/Presidential Nominee
1796–1803	Rufus King	Washington	Federalist	US Senator from NY/ Presidential Nominee
1803–1807	James Monroe	Jefferson	Dem-Rep	President (1817–1825)
1808–1811	William Pinkney	Jefferson	Dem-Rep	US Senator from MD
1812–1813	Vacant			
1814–1817	John Quincy Adams	Madison	Dem-Rep	President (1825–1829)
1818–1825	Richard Rush	Monroe	Dem-Rep	Secretary of the Treasury
1825–1826	Rufus King	John Quincy Adams	Federalist	US Senator from NY/ Presidential Nominee
1826–1827	Albert Gallatin	John Quincy Adams	Dem-Rep	Secretary of the Treasury
1828–1829	James Barbour	John Quincy Adams	Dem-Rep	Secretary of War
1829–1831	Louis McLane	Jackson	Democrat	Secretary of State
1831–1832	Martin Van Buren	Jackson	Democrat	President (1837–1841)
1836–1841	Andrew Stevenson	Jackson	Democrat	Speaker of the House
1841–1845	Edward Everett	Van Buren	Democrat	Secretary of State
1845–1846	Louis McLane	Polk	Democrat	Secretary of War
1846–1849	George Bancroft	Polk	Democrat	Secretary of the Navy
1849–1852	Abbott Lawrence	Taylor	Whig	US House Representative from MA
1852–1853	Joseph R. Ingersoll	Fillmore	Whig	US House Representative from PA
1853–1856	James Buchanan	Pierce	Democrat	President (1857–1861)
1856–1861	George Dallas	Pierce	Democrat	Vice President (1845–1849)
1861–1868	Charles Francis Adams	Lincoln	Republican	US House Representative from MA

US AMBASSADORS TO FRANCE

YEARS	NAME	APPOINTED BY	PARTY	HIGHEST POLITICAL OFFICE
1776–1785	Benjamin Franklin	Washington	Independent	Postmaster General
1785–1789	Thomas Jefferson	Washington	Dem-Rep	President (1801–1809)
1790–1792	William Short	Washington	Federalist	None
1792–1794	Gouverneur Morris	Washington	Federalist	US Senator from NY
1794–1796	James Monroe	Washington	Dem-Rep	President (1817–1825)
1796–1797	Charles C. Pinckney	Washington	Federalist	Presidential Nominee
1801–1804	Robert Livingston	Jefferson	Dem-Rep	None
1804–1810	John Armstrong	Jefferson	Dem-Rep	Secretary of War
1811–1812	Joel Barlow	Madison	Dem-Rep	None
1813–1815	William Crawford	Madison	Dem-Rep	Secretary of the Treasury/ Presidential Nominee
1816–1823	Albert Gallatin	Madison	Dem-Rep	Secretary of the Treasury
1824–1829	James Brown	Monroe	Dem-Rep	US Senator from LA
1829–1833	William Rives	Jackson	Democrat	US Senator from VA
1833	Levett Harris	Jackson	Democrat	None
1833–1836	Edward Livingston	Jackson	Democrat	Secretary of State
1836–1842	Lewis Cass	Jackson	Democrat	Secretary of State/Presidential Nominee
1844–1846	William King	Tyler	Democrat	Vice President (1853)
1847–1849	Richard Rush	Polk	Democrat	Secretary of the Treasury
1849–1853	William Rives	Taylor	Whig	US Senator from VA
1853–1859	John Mason	Pierce	Democrat	US Attorney General
1860–1861	Charles Faulkner	Buchanan	Democrat	US House Representative from WV
1861–1865	John Bigelow	Lincoln	Republican	None

TIME: MARCH 4, 1825

ADAMS'S INAUGURAL ADDRESS ANNOUNCES
HIS VISION FOR AMERICA

Chief Justice John Marshall administers the oath of office to Adams in the House chamber. His hand is on a law book at the time, and he is the first president who substitutes modern trousers for the knee-high breeches favored in colonial times. His inaugural speech is 2,915 words long, slightly briefer than Monroe's and more than twice the length of Madison's.

In traditional fashion, Adams begins the speech by recognizing his solemn duties and his commitment to the Constitution while offering praise for America's stellar progress over its first half century.

... I appear, my fellow-citizens, in your presence...to bind myself by the solemnities of religious obligation to faithful performance of the duties allotted to me in the station to which I have been called....In unfolding to my countrymen the principles by which I shall be governed in the fulfillment of those duties my first resort will be to that Constitution which I shall swear to the best of my ability to preserve, protect, and defend.

It has promoted the lasting welfare of that country so dear to us all...Liberty and law have marched hand in hand. All the purposes of human association have been accomplished...at a cost little exceeding in a whole generation the expenditure of other nations in a single year...Such is the unexaggerated picture of our condition under a Constitution founded upon the republican principle of equal rights.

He then turns to partisan politics, likely prompted by the divisive election. He argues that while the emergence of "two great political parties" has at times "shaken the Union to its center," the cause of the "strife" has been laid to rest with the end of the European wars. (This will quickly prove to be a naive wish on his part!)

...From the experience of the past we derive instructive lessons for the future. Of the two great political parties which have divided the opinions and feelings of our country, the candid and the just will now admit that both have contributed splendid talents, spotless integrity, ardent patriotism, and disinterested sacrifices to the formation and administration of this Government, and that both have required a liberal indulgence for a portion of human infirmity and error.

The revolutionary wars of Europe... excited a collision of sentiments and of sympathies which kindled all the passions and embittered the conflict of parties till the nation was involved in war and the Union was shaken to its center...With the catastrophe in which the wars of the French Revolution terminated, and our own subsequent peace with Great Britain, this baneful weed of party strife was uprooted.

From that time no difference of principle, connected either with the theory of government or with our intercourse with foreign nations, has existed or been called forth in force sufficient to sustain a continued combination of parties or to give more than wholesome animation to public sentiment or legislative debate.

Next comes a litany of principles he intends to embrace during his presidency.

Our political creed is that the will of the people is the source…of all legitimate government upon earth; that the best…guaranty against the abuse of power consists in.. the frequency of popular elections; that the General Government of the Union and the separate governments of the States are all sovereignties of limited powers…; that the firmest security of peace is the preparation during peace of the defenses of war; that a rigorous economy and accountability of public expenditures should guard against… the burden of taxation; that the military should be kept in strict subordination to the civil power; that the freedom of the press and of religious opinion should be inviolate; that the policy of our country is peace.…

These principles will continue to work for the nation if only the remnants of party rancor can be laid aside.

There still remains one effort of magnanimity, one sacrifice of prejudice and passion, to be made by the individuals throughout the nation who have heretofore followed the standards of political party. It is that of discarding every remnant of rancor against each other, of embracing as countrymen and friends, and of yielding to talents and virtue alone that confidence which in times of contention for principle was bestowed only upon those who bore the badge of party communion.

As a lifelong astute diplomat, Adams is well aware of the sources of rancor, even if he is overly optimistic about overcoming them. He properly identifies "geographical divisions" as one "dangerous" concern.

The collisions of party spirit which originate in speculative opinions or in different views of administrative policy are in their nature transitory. Those which are founded on geographical divisions, adverse interests of soil, climate, and modes of domestic life are more permanent, and therefore, perhaps, more dangerous.

In turn, he senses renewed tensions around the balance of power between the federal and state governments, and articulates his view of the guidelines laid out in the Constitution.

It holds out to us a perpetual admonition to preserve alike and with equal anxiety the rights of each individual State in its own government and the rights of the whole nation in that of the Union. Whatsoever is of domestic concernment, unconnected with the other members of the Union or with foreign lands, belongs exclusively to the administration of the State governments. Whatsoever directly involves the rights and interests of the federative fraternity or of foreign powers is of the resort of this General Government. The duties of both are obvious in the general principle, though sometimes perplexed with difficulties in the detail. To respect the rights of the State governments is the inviolable duty of that of the Union; the government of every State will feel its own obligation to respect and preserve the rights of the whole.

Adams has served for the past eight years under Monroe and his aspiration is to continue in his footsteps.

I (now) turn to the Administration of my immediate predecessor....In his career of eight years the internal taxes have been repealed; sixty millions of the public debt have been discharged; provision has been made for the comfort and relief of the aged and indigent among the surviving warriors of the Revolution; the regular armed force has been reduced and its constitution revised and perfected; the accountability for the expenditure of public moneys has been made more effective; the Floridas have been peaceably acquired, and our boundary has been extended to the Pacific Ocean; the independence of the southern nations of this hemisphere has been recognized, and recommended by example and by counsel to the potentates of Europe; progress has been made in the defense of the country by fortifications and the increase of the Navy, toward the effectual suppression of the African traffic in slaves; in alluring the aboriginal hunters of our land to the cultivation of the soil and of the mind, in exploring the interior regions of the Union, and in preparing by scientific researches and surveys for the further application of our national resources to the internal improvement of our country.

With foreign threats largely contained, the new president plans to focus on "internal improvements" aimed at the common good, one example being renewed work on "national roads." This emphasis on strengthening domestic infrastructures is essential to what Henry Clay is already calling his "American System."

...improvement in our common condition...will embrace the whole sphere of my obligations. The roads and aqueducts of Rome have been the admiration of all after ages....But nearly twenty years have passed since the construction of the first national road was commenced. The authority for its construction was then unquestioned. To how many thousands of our countrymen has it proved a benefit? To what individual has it ever proved an injury?

Here again he hopes that party differences can be resolved around the federal government's authority to pursue these important upgrades.

I can not but hope that by the...process of friendly, patient, and persevering deliberation...the extent and limitation of the powers of the General Government in relation to this transcendently important interest will be settled and acknowledged to the common satisfaction of all, and every speculative scruple will be solved....

As Adams nears the end of his lengthy address, he acknowledges the "peculiar circumstances" of his election, and asks openly for the trust and support he will need to advance "the welfare of the country."

Fellow-citizens, you are acquainted with the peculiar circumstances of the recent election, which have resulted in affording me the opportunity of addressing you at this time... You have heard the exposition of the principles which will direct me in the fulfillment of the high and solemn trust imposed upon me in this station.

Less possessed of your confidence in advance than any of my predecessors, I am deeply conscious of the prospect that I shall stand more and oftener in need of your indulgence. Intentions upright and pure, a heart devoted to the welfare of our country, and the unceasing application of all the faculties allotted to me to her service are all the pledges that I can give for the faithful performance of the arduous duties I am to undertake.

I shall look for whatever success may attend my public service; and knowing that "except the Lord keep the city the watchman waketh but in vain," with fervent supplications for His favor, to His overruling providence I commit with humble but fearless confidence my own fate and the future destinies of my country.

TIME: MARCH 4, 1825 TO MARCH 4, 1829

OVERVIEW OF JOHN QUINCY ADAMS' TERM

Unlike Monroe, Adams can no longer count on a Congress ready to advance his agenda. In 1825, he still enjoys a slim margin in both houses of Congress—perhaps a signal that the will of the people, not a "corrupt bargain," favored Adams in the recent election. But already congressional members are openly labeled as Pro- versus Anti-Adams.

CONGRESSIONAL MAKEUP IN 1825

	HOUSE	SENATE
Pro-Adams	105	26
Anti-Adams	97	20
	202	46

Unfortunately, Adams squanders whatever slight political edge he has in setting up his administration.

His high moral tone is uncomfortable around using "patronage" to reward loyalty, and his cabinet appointments include turncoats who will actively work on behalf of his opposition. The first is Postmaster General John McLean of Ohio, who backs Jackson throughout his tenure, and is later rewarded by the general with a Supreme Court appointment.

The ever-slippery Calhoun serves as vice president, but soon swings over to Jackson's side while still maneuvering for the top job himself.

The Senate does confirm Henry Clay as secretary of state, but not without embarrassing him with 14 of 41 voting against his appointment.

JOHN QUINCY ADAMS' CABINET IN 1825

POSITION	NAME	HOME STATE
Vice President	John C. Calhoun	South Carolina
Secretary of State	Henry Clay	Kentucky
Secretary of the Treasury	Richard Rush	Pennsylvania
Secretary of War	James Barbour	Virginia
Secretary of the Navy	Samuel Southard	New Jersey
Attorney General	William Wirt	Virginia
Postmaster General	John McLean	Ohio

The decision to name Clay the secretary of state also removes from the House the one man whose legislative mastery would give the American System initiatives their best chance for approval.

Instead, the victories in this regard are few and far between. Congress approves an extension of the National Road through Ohio, the Erie Canal becomes fully operational, and America's first genuine railroad company, the Baltimore and Ohio Rail Road Company, is chartered in Maryland.

But then come a steady stream of setbacks, ironically involving diplomatic issues, Adams' supposed forte.

- Attempts to engage America in building bridges to Latin America are sidelined in Congress.
- Mexico rejects a sizable cash offer aimed at acquiring Texas.
- A border dispute between Maine and New Brunswick turns into violent confrontations.
- Trade with the British West Indies is shut down after negotiations over terms end in failure.
- Efforts to move the Creek tribes out of Georgia provoke a serious federal versus state conflict.

With each misstep, the Pro-Jackson faction in Congress grows more vocal in their attacks on the president.

In the midterm election of 1826, the Anti-Adams/Pro-Jackson forces gain control over both the House (113–100) and the Senate (26 to 21). Of particular note here are gains by Jackson in the Northeast, largely the result of backing from Senator Martin Van Buren of New York.

RESULTS OF HOUSE ELECTIONS IN 1826

	SLAVERY ALLOWED (12)	SLAVERY BANNED (12)
Old Established East Coast States (15)	Pro-Adams – 17 Anti-Adams – 44	Pro-Adams – 61 Anti-Adams – 44
Emerging States West of Appalachian Range (9)	Pro-Adams – 8 Anti-Adams – 21	Pro-Adams – 14 Anti-Adams – 4

Note: East Coast slavery states (MD, DE, VA, NC, SC, GA); east coast free (ME, MA, NH, VT, CT, PA, RI, NY, NJ); west slavery (KY, TN, AL, MS, LA, MO); west free (OH, IN, IL).

RESULTS OF SENATE ELECTIONS IN 1826

	SLAVERY ALLOWED (12)	SLAVERY BANNED (12)
Old Established East Coast States (15)	Pro-Adams – 1 Anti-Adams – 11	Pro-Adams – 12 Anti-Adams – 5
Emerging States West of Appalachian Range (9)	Pro-Adams – 3 Anti-Adams – 9	Pro-Adams – 5 Anti-Adams – 1

While Adams is beset by one political problem after another, he oversees a domestic economy which recovers nicely from the doldrums of the Monroe era.

ECONOMIC OVERVIEW DURING ADAMS' PRESIDENCY

	1824	1825	1826	1827	1828
Total GDP ($MM)	$750	$822	$866	$916	$897
% Change		10%	5%	6%	(2%)
Per Capita GDP	$69	$74	$76	$78	$74

The final years of Adams's term are given over to the lowest forms of political skullduggery on record to date, as the opposing parties attempt to blacken the names of Adams and Jackson before the 1828 election.

One particularly cynical legislative effort by the Jackson forces involves the tariff of 1828 to shift support away from Adams in western "swing states." The bill does this by imposing higher duties on foreign imports of raw wool, rum, and other staples produced by farmers from Pennsylvania to the frontier while adding features almost certain to irritate New England and the old South. Sponsors assume that Adams will veto it in the end, thus costing him western support.

Instead, he actually signs the bill, which is soon labelled the "Tariff of Abominations." Ironically, antagonism toward the bill centered in South Carolina will come back to haunt the Jackson men in the years ahead.

KEY EVENTS: JOHN QUINCY ADAMS' TERM

1825	
Mar 8	John Poinsett approved as first minister to Mexico
Mar 24	Mexican province of Tejas declared open to American settlers
July 25	Approval given to extend the Cumberland Road west from Wheeling through Ohio
Oct	Tennessee legislature nominates Jackson for the 1828 presidential election
Oct 26	Erie Canal is completed
Dec 6	Adams' message to Congress sparks controversy
Dec 26	Congress approves sending two "observers" to Bolívar's Panama Conference
1826	
Jan 6	Anti-Adams newspaper *United States' Telegraph* starts up in Washington, DC
Feb 13	American Temperance Society founded in Boston
April 8	Secretary of State Henry Clay and Senator John Randolph fight a bloodless duel called by Clay
May 2	The US recognizes Peru
July 4	John Adams and Thomas Jefferson both die on 50th anniversary of signing the Declaration of Independence
Sept 12	Former Freemason William Morgan disappears, provoking Anti-Mason Party founding
Oct 7	First US rail tracks laid in Quincy, MA; three miles long and for horse drawn wagons
Nov	Anti-Administration/Pro-Jackson politicians win majority in Congress
1827	
Jan 10	Bill to increase tariff (above 1824) on woolens passes in the House but loses in the Senate on Calhoun's vote
Feb 28	The B&O Rail Road Company chartered by the state of Maryland
July 2	President of South Carolina College, Thomas Cooper, says that the tariff favors North at expense of South
July 30	Delegates from thirteen states meet in Harrisburg to support call for higher tariffs
Aug 6	US and Britain renew 1818 treaty to "share" Oregon Country for another ten years
Nov 15	Creek Indians sign treaty ceding all remaining land in Georgia to US
Dec 24	Congress rejects Harrisburg proposal to raise protective tariff
1828	
Jan 12	US and Mexico agree on Sabine River boundary line in southwest
Jan 31	Jackson forces in Congress to pass cynical tariff hike aimed at embarrassing Adams

April 21	Noah Webster publishes his American Dictionary of the American Language
May 13	Tariff hike passes the House 105–94 and the Senate 26–21
May 19	"Tariff of Abominations" signed into law by Adams
Oct 16	Delaware and Hudson Canal opens
Dec 3	Jackson is elected president
Dec 19	South Carolina legislature "nullifies" the tariff of 1828 according to Calhoun assertions
1829	
Mar 4	Jackson inaugurated

51

PROSPECTS GROW FOR A "SECOND POLITICAL PARTY SYSTEM"

TIME: MARCH 1825 AND ONWARD

THE POLITICAL LANDSCAPE SHIFTS IN 1824

Ever since Washington's exit in 1797, the division in American politics has pitted Federalists such as John Adams against Anti-Federalists such as Thomas Jefferson. This split is known among scholars as the "First Party System."

When the Federalists stagnate, the Jeffersonians enjoy 24 years of essentially one-party rule as Democratic-Republicans during the Virginia Dynasty.

Then something changes in 1824.

Jefferson himself looks at the outcome and concludes that John Quincy Adams and Henry Clay are simply Federalists in disguise, intent on replacing states' rights with federal government mandates.

> *The (party) amalgamation is of name only, not of principle. Their aim is now therefore to break down the rights reserved by the constitution to the states as a bulwark against that consolidation, the fear of which produced the whole of the opposition to the constitution at its birth.*

But a closer examination suggests several other factors at work.

One is the impact of America's shifting population. The North with its large cities is adding voters far in excess of the South. The West is booming and both Clay and Jackson are "men of the West" who will give voice to that region.

A second factor is slavery and the future of the institution, especially as it relates to its expansion into the new territories across the Mississippi River. The Tallmadge Amendment surfaces this issue and, while the 1820 Missouri Compromise tamps it down, the North-South divide remains profound.

Finally, the gap continues to grow between those who favor an agrarian economy and those who support diversification and industrialization.

As much as the Jeffersonians long for the continuation of unchallenged Democratic-Republican rule, the signs are pointing toward a "Second Party System."

For the moment, it will be Adams' "National Republicans" against the Jackson "Democrats."

TIME: 1825–1829

THE ANTI-ADAMS FORCES STYMIE HIS AGENDA

In his inaugural address, Adams lays out a very ambitious agenda built around Clay's American System initiatives designed to insure America's place as a first-rate global power.

His internal plan includes upgrades in physical infrastructure (roads, bridges, and canals), basic knowledge (a national university, a naval academy, and an observatory), science (standardized weights and measures), and exploration (a new Department of the Interior). A protective tariff will help finance these along with any needed measures taken by a strong US Bank.

Diplomatic proposals center on participation in the Pan-American Conference hosted by Simón Bolívar (a "good neighbors" gesture) and continued efforts aimed at expanding the borders across the entire continent.

Accomplishing these goals will require an active federal government, which Adams announces in no uncertain terms.

> *The spirit of improvement is abroad upon the earth…Let us not be unmindful that liberty is power. While foreign nations…are advancing with gigantic strides…were we to slumber in indolence or…proclaim to the world that we are palsied by the will of our constituents, would it not doom ourselves to inferiority?*

The president's cabinet warns him in advance that his proposals will be met with resistance, and they are quickly proven right.

Traditional Democratic-Republicans, in the Jefferson mold, accuse Adams of grabbing power for the national government that has been reserved for the states in the 10th Amendment. In their eyes, Clay's American System is no more than a warmed-over version of what Alexander Hamilton proposed a quarter century earlier.

Andrew Jackson weighs in, latching onto one unfortunate phrase in the speech, which seems to call upon Congress to override the will of their constituents.

> *When I view…the government, embraced in the recommendation of the late message, with the powers enumerated…together with the declaration that it would be criminal for the agents…to be palsied by the will of their constituents, I shudder for the consequence—if not checked by the voice of the people, it must end in consolidation & then in despotism.*

From this moment forward, congressional resistance to both Adams and Clay gains momentum. The result will be a three-year stymie of almost all of the president's programs.

## 52

PRESSURE CONTINUES ON THE EASTERN TRIBES TO ABANDON THEIR HOMELANDS

TIME: MARCH 1825

ADAMS WISHES FOR FAIR TREATMENT OF THE NATIVE AMERICAN TRIBES

Like all presidents before him, John Quincy Adams struggles over how best to deal with America's native tribes.

He clearly agrees with conventional wisdom that Indians are a "lesser race" than their European counterparts, and recognizes the intense pressure from frontiersmen to grab their land and turn it over to white settlers.

Yet, also like his predecessors in office, he is hesitant to act.

Moral qualms play a role here. After all, the tribes have occupied the continent for generations before the settlers arrived, and uprooting them by force smacks of injustice.

But Adams' hesitance seems to run deeper than that.

The answer may lie in the Enlightenment writing of the Frenchman Henri Rousseau, familiar fare for many early presidents. Rousseau touts the vision of

James Fenimore Cooper

what he calls the "noble savage," uncorrupted by the greed and ruthlessness of modern society. These are truly free men, not enslaved, living independently off the land, governed by the communal will of their tribe—all virtues that resonate with the American spirit.

Nothing is so gentle as man in his primitive state, when placed by nature at an equal distance from the stupidity of brutes and the fatal enlightenment of civil man.

This stereotype of the "noble savage" is also reinforced at the time by the author James Fenimore Cooper, who stands alongside Washington Irving as the nation's first popular storyteller. While Irving's tales poke fun at the Dutch knickerbockers of New York, Cooper's fame rests on the adventures of the frontiersman Natty Bumppo and his loyal Mohican companions, Chingachgook and Uncas.

These two are neither fully "civilized" nor Christian, but they do exhibit intelligence, courage, and intense loyalty for their American friend—all traits that suggest a "capacity for growth" almost never accorded the fully beaten-down Africans.

In turn, this seems to prompt the early presidents not to enslave the Indians, but to reform them—to help them realize their potential under the guiding wing of a benevolent "Great White Father."

Monroe's 1817 inaugural address captures the obligations he feels America owes its first inhabitants:

With the Indian tribes it is our duty to cultivate friendly relations and to act with kindness and liberality...

Equally proper is it to persevere in our efforts to extend to them the advantages of civilization.

Adams' 1825 speech reinforces the same theme in his wish to...

Extend equal protection to all the great interests of the nation (and) promote the civilization of the Indian tribes.

But it will not take long for the new president to discover that all the high-minded talk of "civilizing the noble savages" counts for little against the growing demands of speculators and settlers intent on driving the Indians off their homelands.

TIME: 1825–1827

GEORGIA FORCES ADAMS' HAND IN SUPPORT OF "INDIAN REMOVAL"

The day before Adams takes office, the Treaty of Indian Springs is approved by the Senate. The terms have supposedly been worked out between chiefs of the Creek and

Cherokee tribes in Georgia and two US commissioners, with the Indians ceding their lands in Georgia and Alabama in exchange for equal acreage in the West and a cash bonus of $400,000. September 1, 1826 is set as the deadline for the tribes to move west.

But the deal is fraudulent top to bottom, the work of only one Creek leader, John McIntosh, and Georgian officials eager to line their own pockets. When McIntosh is murdered by rival chiefs for his betrayals, the matter comes to Adams' attention.

The president's response is indecisive.

Even though he has signed the treaty, he is troubled by the reports of fraud, and orders a halt to state land surveys scheduled to start sixteen months hence. This triggers a violent response from Governor George Troup of Georgia, who threatens to defy the president and begin the survey at once. At this point General Edmund Gaines is dispatched to investigate further. He sides with the Indians and reports that Troup is a "madman." In turn, Adams signals Troup that US military forces are to be used against any attempt by the state to enter the lands.

After Troup backs off, Adams tells the Creeks that Congress is unlikely to deny the original treaty unless it can be replaced with a new one involving a land trade. The tribes meet and offer an option, but Adams tells them their proposed boundaries are unacceptable. Adams turns to his cabinet in search of a solution.

Secretary of War Barbour argues for gradual diffusion of the Indians rather than any mass exodus, in hopes of seeing them assimilated into white civilization. Clay finds this impractical, saying that the Indians, like the Africans, are an inferior race and will never be successfully integrated.

Senator Howell Cobb of Georgia, a rising Southern spokesperson, tells Adams that his delegation will be forced to side with Jackson unless he acts immediately to enforce the original treaty. In characteristic fashion, Adams fires back at Cobb:

We could not do so without gross injustice. As to Georgia being driven to support General Jackson, I feel little care or concern for that.

After more pressure from Adams, the Creeks agree to the Treaty of Washington on January 24, 1826, which fails its critics on two counts. First, it cedes more, but not all of their Georgia lands; second, it sets a precedent whereby the US officially recognizes the Indian tribes as "sovereign nations."

Adams forwards the new treaty to the Senate, but Governor Troup says that he plans to start surveying the land immediately, on the grounds that…

Georgia is sovereign on her own soil.

Clay urges Adams to send federal troops in to force Troup's hand, but the president opts to push the Creeks once again to surrender more territory. And they do. On November 13, 1827 they cede their remaining land in Georgia in exchange for another $42,000 and a promise that the government will protect them as they move west—a promise ignored when the time comes.

Not only has Adams alienated Georgians and looked weak throughout the negotiations, he also concludes in hindsight that he has violated his own ethical standards along the way.

> *These (treaties) are crying sins for which we are answerable, and before a higher jurisdiction.*

While unknowable, it may be that his sense of failure over treatment of the Indians will lead to his often-heroic stances later in life on behalf of the enslaved Africans.

## 53

A SECOND GREAT RELIGIOUS AWAKENING SWEEPS ACROSS AMERICA

TIME: 1820–1840

A SECURE NATION LOOKS INWARD FOR GUIDANCE

The Monroe and Adams presidencies mark the first time in American history where the nation feels genuinely secure about its ability to withstand threats of war and invasion from abroad. The British have been twice beaten, and the specter of Napoleon is also gone. At long last, the fortress of America is safe.

What follows is a remarkable period of reflection which takes hold of the public consciousness between 1820 and 1840. It resurrects the deeply religious climate of the early colonial period, causing common people to step back from their daily toil and examine the progress made toward their ancestors' visions; namely the creation of a virtuous society, the "shining city on a hill," and their own personal efforts to achieve personal salvation.

The result is a "moral reawakening" that harkens back to the colonists' original flight from England. This eventually leads to an Evangelical movement that will reform the contemporary social fabric.

The seventeenth century voyagers to America were mostly Protestant religious zealots, "puritans" of one form or another. They sought to escape the "corruptions" they associated with the established Anglican Church and find their own path to righteousness and eternal life.

In the First Great Awakening of the 1730s, their quest leads to the formation of a wide range of new sects—Congregationalists, Presbyterians, and Methodists—joining the established Puritan, Anglican, Quaker, and Baptist churches. During the Enlightenment period, non-traditional Deists ("a religion of reason") appear, along with small pockets of Catholic and Jewish immigrants.

But still America remains as congenitally restless over its churches as it is over its government.

Much of the ongoing religious inquiry originates within the walls of America's early universities and seminaries, whose prospective ministers engage in lively theological debates.

AMERICAN UNIVERSITIES FOUNDED BY CHURCHES

NAME	YEAR	CHURCH AFFILIATION
Harvard	1636	Congregationalist
William & Mary	1693	Church of England
Yale	1701	Congregationalist
Princeton	1746	Presbyterian
Columbia	1754	Church of England
Penn	1757	Anglican/Methodists
Brown	1764	Baptist
Rutgers	1766	Dutch Reformed
Dartmouth	1769	Congregationalist

Some of these debates relate to matters of liturgy and doctrine. Others question the authority of a clerical hierarchy to set rules for their laymen. And more seek to fundamentally alter the ways in which preachers interact with their congregations in the search for redemption and salvation.

Taken together they lead to a Second Great Awakening which sweeps across America between 1820 and 1840.

TIME: 1820–1840

AN EVANGELICAL SPIRIT TAKES ROOT

The Second Great Awakening mirrors the fervency brought to bear by the great Puritan preacher Jonathan Edwards. It sounds an Evangelical message that will henceforth become a part of America's religious landscape:

The good news promise of eternal salvation for sinners who adopt Jesus Christ as their savior.

This awakening is much "gentler" than its predecessor. It shifts away from the harsh determinism of Calvinism, where each man is "elected by God" at birth to be saved or damned, and nothing they can do will alter their destiny. Instead it embraces the "Arminian" conviction—proposed by the sixteenth

The Lord's Prayer and other religious admonitions

century Dutch Reformed theologian Jacob Arminius—that every man can be saved by exercising his own free will to live in accord with the virtues set out by Jesus Christ.

This new message is delivered less from the elevated pulpit in solemn church services than in open air tent meetings where Evangelical ministers can wander among the masses and lay their hands on those coming forth to join the crusade.

The word to be shared at these "revivalist events" comes directly from "the good book"—the King James Bible—which is to be read by each person and interpreted into a personal agenda that will lead to salvation.

These individual agendas become "causes" and, as such, they take on great meaning for those making their commitments. As in the biblical book John 12:27:

> *But for this cause, came I, unto this hour.*

The central unifying cause within the Second Great Awakening lies in creating a more virtuous society for the benefit of all citizens.

In helping to save others, the Evangelicals believe they are saving themselves.

TIME: 1825 AND ONWARD

THE AWAKENING IS LED BY REVEREND CHARLES GRANDISON FINNEY

Of all the clergymen who propel the Second Great Awakening none has greater influence than the Reverend Charles Grandison Finney.

Finney is born into a farming family in Warren, Connecticut in 1792, the youngest of fifteen children. As a youth he dabbles in various academic interests before deciding to apprentice as a lawyer. In 1821, he happens to attend a religious revival meeting in the town of Adams, New York and undergoes a spiritual transformation.

> *The Holy Spirit descended upon me in a manner that seemed to go through me, body and soul. I could feel the impression, like a wave of electricity, going through and through me. Indeed it seemed to come in waves of liquid love, for I could not express it in any other way. It seemed like the very breath of God. I can*

Reverend Charles Finney (1792–1875)

remember distinctly that it seemed to fan me, like immense wings. No words can express the wonderful love that was spread abroad in my heart.

Finney has found his calling, and he signs on as an apprentice to George Gale, a Presbyterian minister who tries, unsuccessfully, to have him enroll in a theological seminary. Despite resistance to formal training, he is finally ordained in 1824 and sets off to spread the word of God, beginning in the Oneida county region of central New York.

What distinguishes Finney from other clergymen is his preaching style.

At 6'3" tall and with piercing eyes, he stands in front of his audience and speaks to them in plain terms.

He is not interested in expounding on the intellectual intricacies of church doctrine. Instead, he seeks immediate converts to Christianity among those in his presence. He does so by offering them a choice.

On one hand, they may continue living as sinners in the "City of Man," and face the eternal fire-and-brimstone punishments decreed by the traditional Calvinists. On the other, he invites them to cross over to the "Kingdom of God" to partake in a future of virtuous behavior, eternal salvation, and joy.

Furthermore, he assures them that the power to choose lies entirely in their hands.

"Election" is not predetermined. It is open to all who embrace the "indwelling spirit" of Christ that lives inside each of them. All they need to do is step forward right now to make their commitment to be saved.

After several days of near continuous preaching, a groundswell of emotion—often marked by apparent trances, swoons, and convulsions—dominates these revival meetings. All leading to the denouement, the moment of conversion, with Finney calling out attendees by name and asking them to come forward to declare their rebirth in Christ.

In another break with precedent, his call extends to women, whose role in church and social matters has been one of silence and conformity. Finney asks women to speak up, to share their beliefs and feelings, to become full participants in the cause. Over time, the voices of women he encourages will play a vital role in a host of social reforms in America.

As the legions of Finney's converts grows, both his theological tenets and his preaching style are questioned by the orthodox Protestant clergy of New England, most notably Lyman Beecher, the Yale-educated minister who favors the traditional Calvinist brand of Presbyterianism.

But Finney survives the criticism and expands his reach eastward into Wilmington, New York City, Philadelphia, and Rochester—where his revival meetings would shut down the entire town. Even Beecher is amazed. He concludes that the summer meetings of 1831 in Rochester are:

The greatest work of God, and the greatest revival of religion, that the world has ever seen in so short a time.

Other clergymen liken Finney's effects to a religious prairie fire, and after he departs the towns of western New York, they are forever known as the "burnt over district," signaling no souls left to be saved.

In 1835 Finney moves his home base to the recently founded Oberlin Collegiate Institute in Ohio, where, over the next 40 years, he builds the school into a beacon of light in support of "perfecting" man and society. During his first year, he convinces Oberlin to become the first college in the US to admit Black students. He serves as president of the college from 1851 to 1866 and remains active there until his death in 1875.

Oberlin College, Ohio, where the Reverend Finney served from 1835 to 1866

However, Finney's legacy goes far beyond revival meetings and Oberlin College. The reform work carried out by his converts will shape the nation for years to come. As was the case with the Methodists Wesley and Whitehurst in the 1730s, Finney's intent is to encourage those reborn in Christ to undertake personal missions in support of temperance, caring for the poor, prison reforms, child labor laws, equal treatment for women, and ending slavery in America.

TIME: 1820 AND ONWARD

UNITARIANS JOIN THE CALL FOR SOCIAL REFORM

Others catch the revivalist spirit, spawning a host of uniquely American religious movements, some founded by clerics and others by laypeople.

One that flourishes over time is the Unitarian Church. It traces its roots to various Enlightenment thinkers in mid-sixteenth century England and eastern Europe who dissent from fundamental tenets of both the Catholic and the Protestant churches.

Their most dramatic dissent focuses on the very "nature of God"—arguing that He is "one indivisible entity" rather than the three-person construct of the trinity. In turn, Jesus Christ becomes a symbol for them of a life of perfect virtue to which all men should aspire, but not of "divinity itself," as taught in traditional Christianity. This belief in the unity of God gives the church its name.

The epicenter of the Unitarian movement in America becomes King's Chapel Church in Boston where, in 1785, the Episcopalian minister James Freeman begins to preach some of its core beliefs, which he adopted during his study at Harvard Divinity School.

It is not until 1819 that another Harvard graduate, William Ellery Channing, fully codifies the Unitarian canon.

It rejects the Calvinist notions of original sin and predetermination in favor of an Arminian-like insistence on free will, and the potential for salvation of all who lead a life of virtue like Christ. (Although one branch, the Universalists, posit that an infinitely merciful deity will forgive and save all in the end.)

Channing's formulations also insist that, despite any differences, all men are creatures of God and deserve to be treated in a fair and equal fashion, marked by a sense of dignity and compassion.

The Unitarians' message is met with mixed reactions. Traditional Christians regard the view of Jesus as a prophet rather than a divine aspect as heretical. But others, more drawn to Enlightenment and Deist thought, embrace its

William Ellery Channing (1780–1842)

emphasis on free will and the idea that doing good opens a path to salvation for every man.

One early convert to Unitarianism is none other than John Quincy Adams, who joins the church in 1826 after growing up within the stern tenets of Calvinism and embraces his mission to end slavery in America.

TIME: 1820 AND ONWARD

THE TRANSCENDENTALISTS PREACH SIMPLIFICATION

Transcendentalism is another movement that springs up at Harvard Divinity School during the 1820s and 1830s in conjunction with debates surrounding Unitarianism.

The two philosophies share the conviction that humans are inherently good and capable of attaining salvation through exercising reason and free will on behalf of social progress.

But Transcendentalists emphasize two other beliefs.

One is that the natural world serves as a powerful symbol of God's hand in the universe, and as an inspiration to man to return to the simplicity and purity it offers.

If the Unitarians rely mainly on intellect to guide their followers, the Transcendentalists find inspiration in the beauty, tranquility, and lessons found in the great outdoors. For them, nature "transcends" the limited works of man,

Ralph Waldo Emerson (1803–1882)

especially in the often-debased realms of politics and organized religion, and also in the trend toward materialism and greed.

The other Transcendentalist theme focuses on the unlimited potential of individuals to reshape their lives and society.

These messages will be developed over time by two leaders of the Transcendentalist movement, Ralph Waldo Emerson and Henry David Thoreau.

Emerson is the intellectual, at home in the social milieu of Harvard and Cambridge, eager to debate and lobby for his views. Thoreau is the rebel, inclined to lengthy retreats into the woods at Walden Pond to gain perspective on life, and always ready for personal acts of "passive defiance" against government actions that violate his sense of justice.

Thoreau's consistent mantra—"simplify, simplify"—argues that salvation lies in a return to the enduring values found in nature: beauty, balance, and tranquility, away from the vexations and distractions inherent in modern society.

Emerson's message is twofold. First, he rails against what he sees as America's growing focus on securing possessions ("things") in this world rather than eternal salvation in the next.

Things are in the saddle and ride mankind.

Henry David Thoreau (1817–1862)

Second, he challenges every man to live up to the amazing potential that lies within.

We will walk on our own feet; we will work with our own hands; we will speak our own minds... A nation of men will for the first time exist, because each believes himself inspired by the Divine Soul which also inspires all men. So shall we come to look at the world with new eyes. It shall answer the endless inquiry of the intellect, — What is truth? and of the affections, — What is good? by yielding itself passive to the educated... Will. ...Build, therefore, your own world. As fast as you conform your life to the pure idea in your mind, that will unfold its great proportions. A correspondent revolution in things will attend the influx of the spirit.

54

THE AWAKENING PROMPTS NEW RELIGIOUS MOVEMENTS

TIME: 1820s AND ONWARD

THE CHURCH OF JESUS CHRIST OF LATTER-DAY SAINTS (MORMONISM) IS FOUNDED

Mormonism is founded by Joseph Smith Jr., who grows up in family of Christian mystics in western New York, the epicenter of revivalism.

As a young man, Smith is caught up in the religious fervor surrounding him. He experiences a vision of his personal salvation and begins to share his story with others in his community. He tells of being visited by an angel named Moroni in 1823, who revealed the location of a sacred book comprised of gold plates compiled by the prophet Mormon. He then describes his use of a "seer stone" to translate the engravings on the plates. The result is the Book of Mormon, a history of a long-vanished Christian community living in America from roughly 500 BCE to 500 CE. Some 5,000 copies of the book are printed and distributed around Smith's hometown of Palmyra, New York, in 1830.

Brigham Young (1801–1877) and 21 of his wives

The outcome of Smith's book and his testimonies to others is a quest to locate the land where these aboriginal Christians lived and, once there, to build a new American Jerusalem.

The quest for this New Jerusalem takes Smith and his followers on a sixteen-year journey west, which eventually ends in the Utah Territory. Along the way are many tragic stops involving opposition from those who view the Mormons as heretics.

In 1831, the first stop is in Kirkland, Ohio, where the new "Church of Christ" opens. But Smith's sights for the new Zion are further west—in Jackson County, Missouri—and his missionaries flock there to lay the groundwork. This leads to the First Mormon War of 1838 with the original Missouri settlers, backed by the state's governor, driving the unwelcome band east into Illinois, where they settle in the town of Nauvoo.

In Nauvoo, Smith codifies the underlying beliefs and organizational structure of his church, as well as writing a description of his original heavenly visitation. The doctrines of exultation ("unity with Christ" achieved by living a virtuous life) and "plural marriage" (polygamy) are formulated here.

On June 27, 1844, the long-term viability of the Nauvoo settlement ends when both Joseph Smith and his brother Hyrum are killed by a hostile mob in nearby Carthage, Illinois.

After a crisis over "church succession," Smith's close ally, Brigham Young, emerges as the new leader of the congregation. Young recognizes the need to resume the search for a new, sustainable site, and by 1847 he settles on land beyond current civilization: the "Mormon Corridor" in what will become the state of Utah. There, in the desert region, he begins to build his New Jerusalem.

And it burgeons, driven from a cooperative economic approach, aggressive missionary work (home and abroad), and plural marriage, which supports rapid population growth. At long last the Mormons have found their lasting home.

They face only one more threat, and it turns out to be relatively minor. In 1857, President Buchanan sends a military force to Utah to assert federal authority over the land. This will become known as the Second Mormon War, but it is essentially a bloodless affair, and ends in 1858 when Brigham Young transfers his title as governor over to a non-Mormon resident.

TIME: 1820S AND ONWARD

THE MILLERITES APPEAR AND MORPH INTO THE SEVENTH-DAY CHURCHES

Another purely American sect—the Millerites—also springs up in New York during the awakening period.

Its founder is William Miller, who is born in 1782 in Massachusetts and grows up in Hampton, New York.

Miller becomes a well-respected member of his rural community, a successful farmer, a justice of the peace, and a member of his local militia.

Like others of his era, his limited formal education is no impediment to his determination to study the Bible and interpret it on his own. This process leads him from his religious origins as a Baptist to the Deist view of a God who created the world but is removed from its daily outcomes.

But his convictions change based on his combat experiences during the War of 1812, as a captain in the US Regulars. After a bloody Battle at Plattsburg, Miller decides that God's hand must have saved his unit.

A pastor spreading the word of salvation

> *It seemed to me that the Supreme Being must have watched over the interests of this country in an especial manner, and delivered us from the hands of our enemies... So surprising a result, against such odds, did seem to me like the work of a mightier power than man.*

After the war he returns to his farm and his Bible studies, focusing now on the inevitability of death and prospects for an afterlife. He gradually returns to the Baptist Church in town, becomes a reader, and is "born again" into faith in a savior both compassionate and engaged in the affairs of men.

When his Deist friends challenge his conversion, Miller intensifies his reading of Bible verses, and comes to focus on Daniel 8:14, which he regards as a prophecy about the timing of "the second coming of Christ."

> *Unto two thousand and three hundred days; then shall the sanctuary be cleansed.*

Through further agonizingly detailed scriptural analysis he tries to pinpoint the event on the calendar. In 1822 he declares that the "2,300 days" will be up on or before the year 1843:

> *I believe that the second coming of Jesus Christ is near, even within twenty-one years, on or before 1843.*

In 1832, amidst the awakening fervor, a Baptist newspaper, *The Vermont Telegraph*, publishes a series of articles proclaiming Miller's prediction. This transforms one man's inquiry into a movement; first regional, then national, with thousands of believers known as "Millerites" ordering their lives for the second coming.

Miller finally zeroes in on a time between March 21, 1843 and March 21, 1844 as the day of reckoning. When both dates come and go, a wave of disappointment strikes the movement's followers. A stricken and contrite Miller issues a public apology, while continuing to believe up to his death in 1849 that his miscalculation was a minor one.

Most Millerites now disband—but not all.

One contingent that lives on is drawn more to Miller's intricate textural analyses than the precision of his dates for the reappearance of Christ. It reexamines the ancient scriptures and concludes that the Daniel verse actually foretells an "ascension" into the "Most Holy Place" in heaven rather than a return to earth.

It also sets out to reestablish the practice of observing the Sabbath, not on Sunday—which they regard as a corruption of the Catholic Church—but from sundown Friday through sundown Saturday. This leads to a host of "Seventh-day" Churches, with the Seventh-day Adventists eventually achieving the largest following.

TIME: 1820s AND ONWARD

UTOPIAN MOVEMENTS DOT THE LANDSCAPE

While some movements seek to reform society, others decide to opt out of it.

Their motivations tend to be religious in character, driven from a shared belief that American values have gone astray, with communal well-being and personal salvation sacrificed to materialism and the chase after upward mobility.

For the Amish, Mennonites, Shakers, and others, the way out of this moral trap lies in escape, in accord with the Biblical admonition:

Keep thyself unspotted from the world.

They accomplish this by setting up communities of fellow believers in rural settings, removed from the temptations and distractions they associate with modern society.

Living the contemplative ideal

Their daily lives are marked by a return to nature, asceticism, and contemplation.

They farm the land, dress simply, and reject personal adornments and class distinctions. Some sects attempt to redefine gender roles, others even challenge conventional marital and sexual practices.

Their theology is typically Christian, albeit tilted toward Old Testament dictates.

Outsiders characterize these sects as Utopian, named after a fictional island nation from a book written in 1516 by St. Thomas More, the English lawyer, Lord Chancellor, and Catholic saint, executed for opposing Henry VIII's claim to head the Church of England. More's vision is of an ideal community where:

> *Nobody owns anything but everyone is rich—for what greater wealth can there be than cheerfulness, peace of mind, and freedom from anxiety?*

Thus, the Utopian sects and experiments attempt to flee from the materialistic values they see shaping American society and escape toward a classless alternative based on virtue rather than wealth. More sees simple justice in this transformation into Utopia:

> *For what justice is there in this: that a nobleman, a goldsmith, a banker, or any other man, that either does nothing at all, or, at best, is employed in things that are of no use to the public, should live in great luxury and splendour upon what is so ill acquired, and a mean man, a carter, a smith, or a ploughman, that works harder even than the beasts themselves, and is employed in labours so necessary, that no commonwealth could hold out a year without them, can only earn so poor a livelihood and must lead so miserable a life, that the condition of the beasts is much better than theirs?*

The themes played out in these isolated communities—be they Amish, Mennonite, Shaker, or others that follow—become an integral part of the Second Great Awakening.

TIME: 1820s AND ONWARD

THE LASTING IMPACT OF THE SECOND AWAKENING

The Evangelical fervor that crisscrosses the landscape in the 1820s will prove to be a turning point in antebellum American history.

The constant threat of foreign invasion has waned, and the people step back to reflect on how far the new nation has come in its first 50 years of existence—and what it needs to do next to live up to its original vision.

In characteristic American fashion, the "revival meetings" place the burden for corrective action on each person who steps forward to be saved.

If society needs changing, it is up to individuals to act. And act they will.

A few will seek a better life by retreating to isolated communes; most will pursue remedies for everyday ills they encounter close to home, in their towns and on their streets.

Their "causes" will vary.

A temperance movement gains widespread public support. Calls arise to reform child labor laws. Food kitchens and welfare sites appear to help the impoverished. Efforts are underway to improve prison conditions and to spare debtors from harsh sentencing. Women begin to band together to have their voices heard in the affairs of men.

But one cause will alter the nation's destiny. It is the effort to wash away the stain of slavery that has blemished America's soul since 1607.

## 55

POLITICAL PARTY RESTRUCTURING PRECEDES THE 1828 ELECTION

TIME: 1828 AND ONWARD

THE OLD DEMOCRATIC-REPUBLICANS MORPH INTO "JACKSON DEMOCRATS" AND OPPOSITION "WHIGS"

As the 1828 election approaches, the fault lines within the Democratic-Republican Party are being resolved in the creation of the "Second Party System."

John Quincy Adams still operates under the "National Republican" banner, but he adopts Clay's "American System" platform which will soon become the basis for the "Whig Party." Meanwhile the "anti-Adams" voters eagerly sign up as "Jackson Democrats."

The two candidates in 1828 are never in doubt.

Jackson remains hell-bent on revenging his prior loss—and with help from Martin Van Buren, he has already taken firm control over the internal workings of the party.

Meanwhile, Adams is still the determined child of his domineering parents, and decides to seek a second term despite the frustrations he suffered in the first. His most committed supporter in the race will be Henry Clay, who is dead set on becoming his successor.

As a wizened political strategist, Clay immediately recognizes that Adams is vulnerable—and that he must create an Anti-Jackson Party to win.

In time, this becomes the Whig Party—named after the English movement that began to oppose the absolute monarchy in the late seventeenth century.

The roots of this new party trace to Washington, Hamilton, and the Federalists with their core belief that a strong national government is needed to harmonize the often-competing interests of individual states or regions and to realize America's potential as a global power.

Foreign policy differences between Adams/Clay and Jackson prove relatively minor.

Both support enough military force to defend the nation, should the need arise again. Both hope to eventually expand America's borders across the entire continent.

Both wish to avoid foreign entanglements, although Adams and Clay are more inclined to build diplomatic bridges into Latin America.

Therefore, it is domestic policy which sets the two camps apart. Jackson is a states' rights believer to the core, while Adams calls for:

- A strong national government dedicated to advancing interests common to all citizens;
- More infrastructure projects—roads, bridges, canals, and railroads—to support the domestic economy;
- Educational upgrades (more universities) and "cultural and scientific advancement;"
- Continued exploration and acquisition of land west of the Mississippi;
- A 50%+ tariff on certain foreign imports to support domestic manufacturers and fund spending;
- A powerful central US Bank, to ensure available credit and a stable currency;
- And caution around issues related to Indian affairs and the future of slavery.

Sitting Vice President John C. Calhoun abandons Adams to run with Jackson, while Treasury Secretary Richard Rush joins the president.

Despite residual tensions from the 1820 Missouri Compromise and a smattering of early reform rhetoric from the Second Awakening, the issue of slavery is largely ignored in the 1828 campaign.

TIME: 1828

THE RACE IS MARRED BY MUDSLINGING WITH DIRE CONSEQUENCES

Predictably, the race quickly erodes from policy debates to vicious personal attacks.

Jackson's campaign is run by Senator Martin Van Buren of New York, an organizational genius who, between 1826 and 1828, turns the Democratic Party, initially called "The Democracy," into the well-oiled election machine it becomes. In backing Jackson, Van Buren lays the groundwork for succeeding him down the road.

Van Buren's strategy is clever. The goal lies in linking the old Virginia political junta with the upcoming New Yorkers to form a South-North base that will be unbeatable—especially when the Westerner Jackson is added to the mix.

His tactics are raucous in character and efficient in execution.

Democratic Party newspapers paint Adams as part of an elite eastern clique, out of touch with the common man and intent on lining their own pockets. His straitlaced moral character is then called into question: first for wasting taxpayer money on "gambling devices" for the White House—a charge which boils down to Adams' purchase of a chess set and a billiards table—then for "procuring" an American woman for Tsar Alexander I to secure his friendship while serving in Moscow.

Van Buren also makes widespread promises of federal patronage jobs, mirroring his successful patronage tactics in New York.

Needless to say, the staid Adams is no match for the garrulous Van Buren and Jackson. Adams continues to view public campaigning as beneath the dignity of candidates for high office.

Nonetheless, his surrogates are eager to assail Jackson, and they do so with no holds barred. Their goal is to paint him as temperamentally and morally unfit to be president. His long record of violent behavior is cited:

- In 1806 he kills James Dickinson in a duel over a horse racing wager and attempts to stab his former business partner on the street in Nashville in the same year.
- In 1813 he is wounded in a saloon shoot-out with Jesse and Thomas Hart Benton.
- In 1814 he is accused of murdering Indian non-combatants at Battle of Horseshoe Bend.
- In 1815 he approves execution of six American militiamen for stealing food.
- In 1818 he executes two British nationals in Florida accused of selling guns to local tribes.

Several of these incidents are disseminated by Philadelphia journalist John Binns in what become known as "Coffin Handbills"—poster boards headed by hand-drawn caskets meant to represent the General's murdered victims.

The attacks turn even uglier from there. Jackson is first pictured as a wanton slave-trader, and then as an adulterer.

The latter charge stems from his marriage in 1791 to Rachel Donelson Robards, after she had applied for a divorce from her first husband. When court records show that the decree was not officially granted

John Quincy Adams

until 1793, Jackson and Rachel are labeled adulterers. Again, it is a journalist, Charles Hammond of the *Cincinnati Gazette*, who publicizes the story with his own editorial take:

Ought a convicted adulteress and her paramour husband be placed in the highest offices of this free and Christian land?

Jackson responds publicly to the slander, but Rachel feels that her reputation is lost for good and her health deteriorates. She dies of a heart attack on December 22, 1828, before her husband is inaugurated.

By that time civil discourse between the two parties has given way to outright mud-slinging.

## 56

ANDREW JACKSON'S FIRST TERM

TIME: 1828 AND ONWARD

THE POPULAR VOTE COUNT DETERMINES ELECTABILITY

The election of 1828 is often regarded as the first truly "democratic" exercise in the nation's history.

It takes place between October 26 and December 2, 1828, and witnesses a profound jump in turnout, the result of fewer restrictions on voting rights.

According to the Constitution, decisions about voter qualifications are left up to individual state legislatures—and the answer since 1788 has been "white men who own property and are 21 years of age or older." But in 1828, many states drop the requirement to own property.

The result is a fourfold increase in turnout to 1,148,018, from only 365,833 in 1824.

**POPULAR VOTING FOR PRESIDENT & NUMBER OF STATES
WHERE ELECTORS CHOSEN BY THEIR VOTES**

1800	1804	1808	1812	1816	1820	1824	1828
67,282	143,110	192,691	278,786	112,370	106,701	365,833	1,148,018
6 of 16	11 of 17	10 of 17	9 of 18	10 of 19	15 of 24	18 of 24	22 of 24*

* State legislators in Delaware and South Carolina still choose electors in 1828.

From this point on it becomes clear that future presidents will no longer be chosen exclusively by a small group of wealthy men, but instead by appealing to the mass of common citizens.

SIDEBAR: SUFFRAGE MILESTONES IN AMERICA

By 1842 all states will have dropped the "property test"—meaning that all white males over 21 years old are qualified to cast ballots.

This won't change until after the Civil War when black men are given the right to vote through three "Reconstruction Amendments": the Thirteenth

Amendment outlawing slavery, the Fourteenth Amendment granting citizenship to non-white people, and the Fifteenth Amendment granting eligibility to vote to all men regardless of race.

By 1870, three states (Wyoming, Colorado, and Montana) take the lead in extending suffrage to include women.

From there, however, the tide reverses for some fifty years.

In 1876, several state legislatures maneuver around the Fifteenth Amendment by adding new "qualifications" aimed at excluding Black people and Native people.

The 1882 Chinese Exclusion Act bans all further immigration from Asia and prohibits those already in the United States from becoming naturalized citizens.

It is not until 1920, after "suffragette" battles and the Nineteenth Amendment, that women are given the right to vote.

In 1924 Native people are included via the Indian Citizenship Act, although the state of Utah refuses to enforce this law until 1956.

For both Black Americans and Asian Americans, the wait will extend all the way to the 1965 Voting Rights Act, which finally enfranchises both groups.

TIME: OCTOBER – DECEMBER 1828

JACKSON BEATS JOHN QUINCY ADAMS IN CONVINCING FASHION

In this first more "open" election, it is Jackson, the "common man of the West," who prevails over Adams, the patrician eastern intellectual, by a comfortable margin.

RESULTS OF THE 1828 PRESIDENTIAL ELECTION

CANDIDATES	STATE	PARTY	POP VOTE	% TOT
Andrew Jackson	TN	Democrat	642,553	56%
John Quincy Adams	MA	National Republican	500,897	44%
Unpledged			4,568	0%
TOTAL			1,148,018	100%

In the Electoral College, the general wins 178–83, sweeping the emerging Western states by a 65–0 margin and taking the slave-holding states by 105–9, while losing only in Delaware and splitting Maryland.

He also cuts into Adams' hold on the Northeast, winning Pennsylvania 28–0 and, with Van Buren's help, taking New York by 20–16.

SHIFTING STATE ALIGNMENTS: OLD/NEW AND SLAVERY/FREE

	SLAVERY ALLOWED (12)	SLAVERY BANNED (12)
Old Established East Coast States (15)	64 Jackson 9 Adams 73 Total	74 Adams 49 Jackson 123 Total
Emerging States West of Appalachian Range (9)	41 Jackson 0 Adams 41 Total	24 Jackson 0 Adams 24 Total

Note: East coast slavery states (MD, DE, VA, NC, SC, GA); East coast free states (ME, MA, NH, VT, CT, PA, RI, NY, NJ); Western slavery states (KY, TN, AL, MS, LA, MO); Western free states (OH, IN, IL)

Jackson shifts five states—Virginia, Georgia, Kentucky, Ohio, and Missouri—into the Democratic Party column.

PARTY POWER BY STATE

SOUTH	1824	1828	PICK UPS
Virginia	Dem-Rep (Cr)	Democrat	Democrat
North Carolina	Democrat	Democrat	
South Carolina	Democrat	Democrat	
Georgia	Dem-Rep (Cr)	Democrat	Democrat
Alabama	Democrat	Democrat	
Mississippi	Democrat	Democrat	
Louisiana	Democrat	Democrat	
Tennessee	Democrat	Democrat	
BORDER			
Delaware	Democrat	Nat-Rep	Nat-Rep
Maryland	Democrat	Nat-Rep	Nat-Rep
Kentucky	Dem-Rep (Cl)	Democrat	Democrat
Missouri	Dem-Rep (Cl)	Democrat	Democrat
NORTH			
New Hampshire	Dem-Rep (Ad)	Nat-Rep	
Vermont	Dem-Rep (Ad)	Nat-Rep	
Massachusetts	Dem-Rep (Ad)	Nat-Rep	
Rhode Island	Dem-Rep (Ad)	Nat-Rep	
Connecticut	Dem-Rep (Ad)	Nat-Rep	
New York	Democrat	Democrat	
New Jersey	Democrat	Nat-Rep	Nat-Rep
Pennsylvania	Democrat	Democrat	
WEST			
Ohio	Dem-Rep (Cl)	Democrat	Democrat
Indiana	Democrat	Democrat	
Illinois	Democrat	Democrat	

(**Notes:** Cr = Crawford, Cl = Clay; Ad = John Quincy Adams; NA = National Republicans/Adams)

Jackson's coattails are strong in 1828, with the Democrats solidifying control over both chambers of Congress by 2–1 margins, thus assuring his capacity to start dismantling many of what he regards as Adam's Federalist policies.

CONGRESSIONAL ELECTION TRENDS

US HOUSE	1825	1827	1829
Pro-Jackson	49%	53%	64%
Pro-Adams	51%	47%	36%
US SENATE			
Pro-Jackson	49%	53%	64%
Pro-Adams	51%	47%	34%
Other			2%
PRESIDENT	JQA	JQA	AJ

The loser, John Quincy Adams, is dismayed over what he regards as his failure in office followed by his humiliating defeat at the hands of the lesser man, Andrew Jackson. As he writes:

No one knows, and few conceive, the agony of mind that I have suffered from the time that I was made by circumstances, and not by my volition, a candidate for the Presidency till I was dismissed from that station by the failure of my election.

He leaves Washington without attending Jackson's inauguration and heads back home, not realizing that a remarkable political future lies ahead after his return to the House of Representatives in 1831.

TIME: 1767–1845

PRESIDENT ANDREW JACKSON: PERSONAL PROFILE

Andrew Jackson's narrative is familiar in American political history—the military hero turned president and commander-in-chief.

His roots are "log cabin humble" and in western soil, unlike the refined eastern elites who have run the country up to his time.

Born in 1767, Jackson and his widowed mother are taken in by relatives in Waxhaw, South Carolina, where, at age fourteen, he is wounded and imprisoned by the British General Tarleton during the Revolutionary War.

Andrew Jackson (1767–1845)

At age 21 he moves to Nashville, Tennessee, and in 1790 marries into the renowned Donelson family. With their backing, Jackson's career takes off.

He becomes a successful lawyer and is later elected to the House of Representatives in 1796, followed by a year in the Senate before returning to Tennessee as a state Supreme Court justice. There he invests his wealth in purchasing slaves for The Hermitage, a cotton plantation whose enslaved population rises from nine in 1804 to about 160 by 1820.

From the beginning of his adult life, Jackson is clear and outspoken in his beliefs about the inferiority of Black people and Native people, and white men's need to forcefully suppress both.

Like George Washington before him, Jackson's business and political careers run parallel to his military career. By 1801 he is a colonel in the Tennessee militia, and a supporter of using force to secure the "sacred union" and its borders. The War of 1812 thrusts him into active combat against a host of foes: the British army, the Creek tribe, and the Seminoles.

Having witnessed Indian attacks on settlers, Jackson is ruthless in retribution. In 1814 he defeats the Red Stick Creeks—who are allied with the British—at the Battle of Horseshoe Bend in central Alabama, with support from Lieutenant Sam Houston. After the 1814 Treaty of Fort Jackson which ends the Creek War, the Creeks cede 23 million acres of land in Alabama and Georgia to the US government.

However, Jackson's destiny is sealed on January 8, 1815.

On that day he becomes a national hero by leading his 5,000 troops to victory over a force of 7,500 British regulars at New Orleans, ending the War of 1812 and earning a special "Thanks of Congress" award for this action.

From then on, he is "Old Hickory," with his supporters touting him for the presidency.

TIME: MARCH 4, 1829

JACKSON'S INAUGURATION LAYS OUT HIS PRIORITIES

Jackson's inauguration is unlike anything ever seen before in DC. A crowd of some 20,000 people—"a rabble, a mob, of boys, negroes, women, scrambling, fighting, romping"—flocks into the capital.

After John Marshall administers the oath of office on the East Portico of the Capitol, Jackson delivers a relatively brief but very precise address regarding his views and plans.

He first expresses his gratitude for the honor of being chosen, and then declares his intent to act as "the instrument of the Federal Constitution."

As the instrument of the Federal Constitution it will devolve on me for a stated period to execute the laws of the United States, to superintend their foreign and their confederate relations, to manage their revenue, to command their forces, and, by communications to the Legislature, to watch over and to promote their interests generally.

In carrying out his duties he promises not to overstep the authority given the federal government in relation to that of the individual states. In this regard he echoes the boundaries of the Tenth Amendment.

In administering the laws of Congress I shall keep steadily in view the limitations as well as the extent of the Executive power trusting thereby to discharge the functions of my office without transcending its authority…In such measures as I may be called on to pursue in regard to the rights of the separate States. I hope to be animated by a proper respect for those sovereign members of our Union, taking care not to confound the powers they have reserved to themselves with those they have granted to the Confederacy.

After mentioning his intent to act fairly and equally with all foreign powers, he turns to the importance of carefully controlling national finances, extinguishing the debt, and counteracting the profligate spending of money by the government.

The management of the public revenue…will, of course, demand no inconsiderable share of my official solicitude…Advantage must result from the observance of a strict and faithful economy.…I shall aim at the extinguishment of the national debt, the unnecessary duration of which is incompatible with real independence, and because it will counteract that tendency to public and private profligacy which a profuse expenditure of money by the Government is but too apt to engender.

In gathering revenue, his goal will be equal treatment of agriculture, commerce, and manufacturing. Only certain essential products may expect protection in tariffs.

With regard to…revenue, it would seem to me that the spirit of equity, caution and compromise in which the Constitution was formed requires that the great interests of agriculture, commerce, and manufactures should be equally favored, and that perhaps the only exception to this rule should consist in the peculiar encouragement of any products of either of them that may be found essential to our national independence

He supports internal improvements and education.

Internal improvement and the diffusion of knowledge, so far as they can be promoted by the constitutional acts of the Federal Government, are of high importance.

His fear of a standing army harkens back to the 1787 Convention, and he is convinced that a million-man militia is fully capable of defending against any foreign threat.

Considering standing armies as dangerous to free governments in time of peace, I shall not seek to enlarge our present establishment, nor disregard that salutary lesson of political experience which teaches that the military should be held subordinate to the civil power....But the bulwark of our defense is the national militia... (and) a million of armed freemen, possessed of the means of war, can never be conquered by a foreign foe.

Despite his military record, he says that future treatment of the Indians will be humane and considerate—while caveating the promise in such a way as to negate it entirely in the end.

It will be my sincere and constant desire to observe toward the Indian tribes within our limits a just and liberal policy, and to give that humane and considerate attention to their rights and their wants which is consistent with the habits of our Government and the feelings of our people.

He vows to reform patronage practices which threaten free elections and protect incompetency.

The recent demonstration of public sentiment inscribes on the list of Executive duties...the correction of those abuses that have brought the patronage of the Federal Government into conflict with the freedom of elections... and have placed or continued power in unfaithful or incompetent hands.

He will hire subordinates who are diligent and talented in public service, and look to wise precedents from those who came before him in office.

I shall endeavor to select men whose diligence and talents will insure...the public service... (and) look with reverence to the examples of public virtue left by my illustrious predecessors...

And he closes by pledging cooperation with the other branches of government, and hoping for divine guidance from "that Power" who has protected the nation since its infancy.

The same diffidence induces me to hope for instruction and aid from the coordinate branches of the Government, and for the indulgence and support of my fellow-citizens generally. And a firm reliance on the goodness of that Power whose providence mercifully protected our national infancy...encourages me to offer up my ardent supplications that He will continue to make our beloved country the object of His divine care and gracious benediction.

After the official ceremony, the White House is thrown open to all comers, with bands playing, hard liquor flowing, and food aplenty, including 1,400 lbs. of cheese sent by an admirer. Jackson is swarmed by supporters and finally has to depart to a nearby hotel for his own safety.

The entire demeanor of the event sends shivers through his opponents, who view it as the beginning of his "Mobocracy."

TIME: MARCH 4, 1829 – MARCH 3, 1833

OVERVIEW OF JACKSON'S FIRST TERM

Jackson is about to be 62 years old when he becomes president, and he tells friends that his intent is to achieve his goals in one term.

The cabinet he assembles includes two men, both 46, who very much hope to succeed him: Vice President John C. Calhoun of South Carolina and Secretary of State Martin Van Buren of New York, chosen after serving as Jackson's campaign manager.

Jackson names Samuel Ingham, a paper mill owner and House member from Pennsylvania, to the Treasury slot. His close personal friend and biographer from Tennessee, Senator John Eaton, is tapped for secretary of war; John Branch, Senator from North Carolina, heads the Navy; and the Kentucky jurist, William Barry, becomes postmaster general. For attorney general, Jackson calls on Senator John Berrien of Georgia, a strong proponent of both states' rights and slavery.

Andrew Jackson (1767–1845)

This group will prove troublesome for Jackson, and he will dissolve it in early 1831.

ANDREW JACKSON'S CABINET IN 1829

POSITION	NAME	HOME STATE
Vice President	John C. Calhoun	South Carolina
Secretary of State	Martin Van Buren	New York
Secretary of Treasury	Samuel Ingham	Pennsylvania
Secretary of War	John Eaton	Tennessee
Secretary of the Navy	John Branch	North Carolina
Attorney General	John Berrien	Georgia
Postmaster General	William Barry	Kentucky

As he begins, Jackson has a clear five-point action agenda in mind for the country:
- Above all else, secure the borders and preserve the sacred Union.
- Relocate Indian tribes west, so that white settlers can occupy the southeast.
- Shut down the US Bank, ending its spendthrift eastern elite-focused manipulations.
- Restore tight fiscal constraints, avoid inflation, and pay off the national debt.
- Protect the well-being of the many from the avarice of the few.

His first term is a period when many of the great themes that shape and ultimately undermine America's future are set in motion.

It begins with a threat to the sanctity of the Union, when an emerging Southern coalition, headed by South Carolinians, challenges the national government's authority to impose laws which "sovereign states" find damaging to their own interest.

This leads to a "nullification crisis" over the 1828 tariff and a famous debate in the Senate between Robert Hayne and Daniel Webster over states' rights regarding federal regulation of land sales in the West. It also results in a final breach between Jackson and Calhoun.

The president then turns to a particularly disturbing part of his legacy: the forced removal of Native tribes from their homelands in the East to new settlements west of the Mississippi River. Despite his restrained rhetoric in the inaugural address, Jackson is intent on handing the Indian lands over to white settlers, using whatever means are required. Wars with the Blackhawks and Seminoles signal his determination.

Halfway through the term, a bizarre incident occurs within Jackson's cabinet. Calhoun's wife, Floride, initiates a campaign to discredit and label "as an adulteress" Peggy Eaton, who is married to Jackson's close friend, Secretary of War John Eaton. When other cabinet members fail to support the Eatons, an irate Jackson forces all except Postmaster General Barry to resign—replacing them with what becomes known as his "kitchen cabinet" of long-time insiders.

While seemingly trivial at the moment, the "Petticoat Affair" ends with Calhoun discarding party unity and launching his firebrand role as defender of Southern interests and a leading proponent of secession.

The tinderbox issue of slavery also assumes center stage during Jackson's first term.

A hard core of white Northern abolitionists, influenced by the Second Great Awakening, rally around journalist William Lloyd Garrison in his call for the immediate emancipation of all enslaved people. Garrison's newspaper, *The Liberator*, quickly becomes a lightning rod across the South and the North; the former intent on keeping enslaved people in check, the latter intent on cleansing all Black people from their borders.

Adding to Southern tensions are inflammatory words published by David Walker, a free Black man who pleads for justice while warning of retribution—and inflammatory action in Virginia taken by Nat Turner and a group of enslaved people who slaughter their masters and are slaughtered themselves in return.

As the election of 1832 nears, Jackson concludes that a large part of his agenda—especially closing down the Second US Bank and paying off the national debt—is still undone, and that a second term will be needed.

KEY EVENTS: ANDREW JACKSON'S FIRST TERM

1828	
December	Calhoun attacks the 1828 tariff in his "South Carolina Exposition and Protest" plea
1829	
March 4	Jackson and Calhoun are inaugurated
March 23	Creek tribe ordered to either obey Alabama laws or move across the Mississippi River
August 25	Mexico rejects Jackson's offer to buy Texas
September	David Walker's *Appeal* for emancipation is published
December 8	Jackson's annual message questions the constitutionality of the Bank of the United States
December 29	Connecticut Senator Samuel Foot's bill to temporarily restrict land sales in the West
1830	
January 18	Benton criticizes Foot's bill as an attack by New England on the prosperity of the West
January 19	Robert Hayne of South Carolina backs Benton, calls for states' rights, questions the value of the Union
Jan 20-27	Hayne and Webster square off on states' rights versus national unity
April 6	Mexico moves to block further immigration of white American immigrants and enslaved people
April 6	Joseph Smith founds the Church of Jesus Christ of Latter-day Saints in New York
April 13	Jackson and Calhoun clash at the annual Thomas Jefferson memorial dinner
May 20	Tariff reduced on tea, coffee, molasses, and salt
May 21	Foot's land bill voted down
May 27	Jackson vetoes Kentucky Road bill as not a federal project
May 28	Jackson signs the Indian Removal Bill
May 29	Preemption Act protects western squatters from speculators and allows them to buy 160 acres at $1.25
August 28	Peter Cooper's Tom Thumb train makes first run on B&O
September	National Republicans meet in Hartford and nominate Henry Clay for 1832 presidential election

October 5	Martin Van Buren settles a treaty re-opening trade with British West Indies
December 6	Jackson again attacks the US Bank, federal debt, and using federal funds for infrastructure
1831	
January 1	Garrison publishes first edition of *The Liberator*
January 15	First passenger train opens in Charleston, South Carolina
February 15	Calhoun publishes letters critical of Jackson's actions in Seminole War
February 15	Jackson picks Van Buren as his running mate in 1832
March 18	In *Cherokee v. Georgia* the Supreme Court rules that tribes are not independent nations, but rather "domestic dependents" and therefore cannot sue the state
April 5	Commerce Treaty with Mexico signed
April 7	John Eaton resigns amidst the "Petticoat Affair"
April 26	New York declares that poverty is not a crime and ends prison sentencing
June 30	Chief Black Hawk agrees to move west across the Mississippi River
August 8	Jackson forces all cabinet members, except one, to resign over the Petticoat Affair
August 9	A dissident group meeting in New York City nominates Calhoun for president in 1832
August 21	Nat Turner Rebellion occurs in Virginia
September 26	The Anti-Mason Party meets and nominates William Wirt for president
December 5	John Quincy Adams takes seat in House and begins to file anti-slavery petitions
December 12	National Republicans meet in Baltimore and nominate Henry Clay for president
1832	
January 9	The Second US Bank files for early re-chartering fearing Jackson opposition
January 9	Clay introduces a party plank to abolish the tariff on non-competitive imports
January 21	Virginia Assembly debates an old Jefferson bill for gradual emancipation, but it loses as opponents cite pro-slavery arguments
May 3	In *Worchester v. Georgia*, John Marshall's majority opinion says the federal government has jurisdiction over the state on Indian affairs; Jackson responds, "Let him enforce it"
April 6	Black Hawk War begins; both Abraham Lincoln and Jefferson Davis participate
May 1	First wagon trains head west on the Oregon Trail
May 9	Seminoles sign treaty to exit Florida
May 21–22	First national Democratic Party convention nominates Jackson for a second term
July 10	Jackson vetoes a congressional bill passed to re-charter the Second US Bank
July 14	Tariff of 1832 lowers rates, but the South remains upset
August 2	The Battle of Bad Axe ends the Black Hawk War
September 21	The Sauks agree to move west
November 19–24	The South Carolina legislature votes to nullify the 1828 and 1832 tariffs
December 5	Jackson re-elected easily
December 28	John C. Calhoun resigns as vice president to become senator from South Carolina

The national economy rebounds from Adams' last year in office, and grows nicely throughout Jackson's first term.

KEY ECONOMIC OVERVIEW – JACKSON'S FIRST TERM

	1828	1829	1830	1831	1832
Total GDP ($000)	897	930	1022	1052	1129
% Change	(2%)	4%	10%	3%	7%
Per Capita GDP	74	74	79	79	83

## 57

JOHN CALHOUN TRIES TO "NULLIFY" FEDERAL AUTHORITY

TIME: 1828

JACKSON'S MACHIAVELLIAN VP SPARKS THE NULLIFICATION CRISIS

Andrew Jackson's running mate, John C. Calhoun, believes that his destiny is to become president of the United States.

He sees himself as the natural successor to the "Virginian line," and, in chameleon-like fashion, executes a series of maneuvers aimed at bringing down various rivals in his path.

He begins with Adams, playing the sinister Iago against the president's ever-naïve Othello. He secretly torpedoes Adam's (and Clay's) internal improvement programs from within the cabinet. When he sees that he cannot win the 1828 nomination, he abandons Adams and backs the opposition candidacy of Jackson.

Like Adams, Jackson is at first taken in by Calhoun, and chooses him as vice president, making him only the second man ever to serve in that position under different presidents (joining founding father George Clinton).

But Calhoun always views Jackson as a crass "mobocrat," lacking both executive capacity and grace. If Jackson lives up to his promise of "one term only," Calhoun has every intent of becoming his successor. To do so, however, requires an issue that captures public attention and a solution that he can champion.

The issue he settles on goes all the way back to the 1787 controversies over the sovereignty of the states vis-à-vis the authority of the central government. Calhoun decides that it's time to play the Anti-Federalist card once again.

Within this broad context, he zeros in on one manifestation of the debate sure to draw fire—the power of the federal government to impose potentially onerous taxes on the states.

From the Boston Tea Party to the Whiskey Rebellion, no topic arouses American's passions like taxation.

In December 1828, even before Jackson is inaugurated, Calhoun decides to stir this pot. He does so in his usual anonymous fashion by penning a document called the "South Carolina Exposition and Protest" attacking the 1828 tariff he himself advanced in cynical fashion to undermine Adams.

His basic "exposition" is that the tariff of 1828 was constitutionally flawed, not because it raised revenue, but because the increases were amplified to protect manufacturing industries in the Northeast at the expense of the cotton growers across the South.

From there he argues that when the federal authorities overstep their bounds, it is the right of the sovereign states to decide and act upon a "proper remedy."

If it be conceded, as it must be by every one who is the least conversant with our institutions, that the sovereign powers delegated are divided between the General and State Governments, and that the latter hold their portion by the same tenure as the former, it would seem impossible to deny to the States the right of deciding on the infractions of their powers, and the proper remedy to be applied for their correction.

Of course, this is essentially the same argument that the Supreme Court ruled on as recently as 1819 in the *McColluch v. Maryland* case—citing the "necessary and proper" clause in the Constitution to favor federal laws over state laws.

The Congress shall have power to make all Laws which shall be necessary and proper for carrying Into execution…the powers vested by this Constitution in the government of the United States.

Calhoun recognizes that if this decision achieves "stare decisis" (settled law) status, it would open the door to future federal efforts to limit or even abolish slavery, an outcome which would go far beyond taxation in its negative impact on the Southern economy.

In 1828 he decides to make Anti-Federalism his signature stance, still hoping for another try at the presidency.

TIME: 1790–1830

HISTORY OF TARIFFS LEADING UP TO THE 1828 BILL

The type of tariffs Calhoun attacks have been used since Washington's time by various Treasury secretaries to fund government spending.

They entail a duty or tax levied on imported goods, collected at ports of entry by customs agents before cargo ships can be unloaded. They are enforced by an infant coast guard on hand to curb any attempts at smuggling.

In 1790 the average tariff rate across goods is 10% and it generates $10.8 million, or 83.7% of total federal income. The rate remains fairly stable over time, and it actually decreases in 1815.

TARIFF RATES AND REVENUE GENERATED: 1800–1815

YEAR	TARIFF RATE	TARIFF $ (MM)	TOTAL BUDGET (MM)	% TOTAL FEDERAL INCOME
1800	10.0%	$10.8	$12.9	83.7%
1805	10.7%	$13.6	$14.3	95.4%
1810	10.1%	$9.4	$10.3	91.5%
1815	6.5%	$15.7	$33.8	46.4%

That trend reverses itself when debts associated with the War of 1812 force Madison's Treasury head, Alexander Dallas, to propose sharp increases on a range of imports in 1816.

Cotton and wool duties jump to 25% for three years; iron bar, leather, writing paper, hats, and cabinetwork go to 30%; and each pound of sugar is charged 3 cents. The fact that Britain is hit the hardest by these changes sparks some patriotic overtones, and the Dallas Tariff passes the House 88–54.

But that will prove to be the last smooth sail for tariff bills in Congress.

As Monroe's second term winds down, support widens for a tariff designed to encourage the public to buy goods manufactured in America by raising the duty, hence the price, on foreign imports.

The 1824 tariff is focused on four commodities—iron, lead, hemp, and cotton bagging—that are particularly important to Rhode Island and Connecticut, along with the Northwestern states from Ohio through Illinois, and the South. All four candidates in the 1824 presidential race support the bill, but both cotton and shipping factions are concerned about its economic impact on their interests.

After serious floor battles, the bill squeaks by on a 107–102 vote in the House. By 1825 the average tariff rate has jumped to 22.3% and the revenue generated accounts for nearly 98% of the total federal budget.

Same problem here. See fixes:

TARIFF RATES AND REVENUE GENERATED: 1820–25

YEAR	TARIFF RATE	TARIFF REVENUE (MM)	TOTAL BUDGET (MM)	% TOTAL FEDERAL INCOME
1820	20.2%	$17.9	$21.3	83.9%
1825	22.3%	$20.5	$20.9	97.9%

In 1825, cotton production continues to soar, but the South begins to see some slippage in the price/pound the commodity commands.

PRODUCTION AND VALUE OF COTTON

YEAR	LBS. (MM)	PRICE/LB.	VALUE (MM)	GROWTH	TARIFF
1810	68.9	$.1420	$9.8	--	10.1%
1815	81.9	.2590	21.6	220%	6.5%
1820	141.5	.1658	23.5	9%	20.2%
1825	228.7	.1436	30.9	31%	22.3%

While this decrease in price might be a response to the spike in supply, the South associates it with the increased tariffs imposed in 1824.

Then comes the so-called "Tariff of Abominations" in 1828—driving up the tax on imports of finished goods, often made from cotton, to "protect" domestic manufacturing in the northeast.

The response here will be a sharp reduction in prices for cotton and the "Nullification Crisis of 1832," led by the state of South Carolina and John C. Calhoun.

## 58

BLACK ABOLITIONIST DAVID WALKER CRIES OUT FOR JUSTICE

TIME: 1796–1830

DAVID WALKER PROFILE

While the South is contesting the 1828 tariff, it receives another tangible threat to its slave-based economy from one David Walker, a free Black man living in Boston.

Walker is born in 1796 in Wilmington, Delaware, the son of an enslaved father who dies before his birth and a white mother, whose "free status" is conferred upon him.

During his early years he becomes literate and moves to Charleston, where he joins the African Episcopal Methodist Church. He eventually moves to Boston, where he marries, has a daughter, and opens a clothing resale shop in the wharf district.

In 1825 he joins the African Grand Lodge #459, now headed by the Black abolitionist John T. Hilton. In 1826 he cofounds the Massachusetts General Colored Association, along with Hilton and Wil-

A free Black man

liam Guion Nell whose son will later lead the movement to integrate the Boston public schools.

At this point, Walker is a member of Boston's Black elites, all pushing for freedom, assimilation, and full citizenship for Black Americans.

In 1829 he does something extraordinary for the times.

He writes and then self-publishes a 76-page pamphlet that inflames the passions of both Black people and white people toward slavery:

David Walker's Appeal to the Colored Citizens of the World, But in Particular to Those of the United States of America.

The title itself announces Walker's aspiration to ensure that Black people achieve "colored citizen" status in America and around the world.

His arguments extend beyond the more restrained efforts made by Boston's Black churches and Prince Hall's Freemason lodges.

They are riveting, both logical and emotional, ranging from despair to hope, from helplessness to mounting fury and bloody resolve.

If white people refuse to accept the olive branch he offers, they will experience the sword.

TIME: SEPTEMBER 1829

APPEAL TO THE COLORED CITIZENS OF THE WORLD

Walker begins his *Appeal* by trying to make white men aware of what he calls the daily "wretchedness" of those living as slaves.

We colored people are the most degraded, wretched, and abject set of beings that ever lived... We are destined to dig (the white man's) mines and work their farms, and thus go on enriching them from one generation to another with our blood and our tears!!!!

An observer may see there, a son take his mother, who bore almost the pains of death to give him birth, and by the command of a tyrant, strip her as naked as she came into the world, and apply the cow-hide to her, until she falls a victim to death in the road! He may see a husband take his dear wife, not infrequently in a pregnant state, and perhaps far advanced, and beat her for an unmerciful wretch, until his infant falls a lifeless lump at her feet! Can the Americans escape God Almighty? If they do, can he be to us a God of Justice? I would suffer my life to be taken before I would submit.

Oh! my God, I appeal to every man of feeling—is not this insupportable? Oh pity us, we pray thee, Lord Jesus.

The cause of the Black man's suffering is the white man's greed and unmerciful quest for power.

The whites have always been an unjust, jealous, unmerciful, avaricious and blood-thirsty set of beings, always seeking after power and authority. Ever since we have been among them, they have tried to keep us ignorant, and make us believe that God made us and our children to be slaves to them and theirs. Oh! my God, have mercy on Christian Americans!!!

White people have justified their behavior by declaring that Black people are an inherently inferior species.

They have reduced us to the deplorable condition of slaves under their feet, held us up as descending from ribes of Monkeys or Orang-Outangs.

Mr. Jefferson's rema'ks respecting us—that the blacks, whether originally a distinct race, or made distinct by time and circumstances, are inferior to the whites in the endowments both of body and mind"—have sunk deep into the hearts of millions of whites, and never will be removed this side of eternity.

They have blocked all attempts to provide Black people access to a basic education.

It is lamentable, that many of our children go to school, from four until they are eight or ten, and sometimes fifteen years of age, and leave school knowing but a little more about the grammar of their language than a horse does about handling a musket.

The school committee say "e" forbid the coloured children learnin' grammar—they "uld" not allow any but the white children "to stuy" it.

Even the white churches and clergy have stood silent and allowed these abuses to continue.

The preachers and people of the United States form societies against Free Masonry and Intemperance, and write against Sabbath breaking, Sabbath mails, Infidelity, &c. &c. But the fountain head (slavery and oppression) compared with which, all those other evils are comparatively nothing, is hardly noticed by the Americans.

Our divine Lord and Master said, "all things whatsoever ye would that men should do unto you, do ye even o unto them." But a American minister, with the Bible in is hand, holds us and our children the most abject slavery and wretchedness. Now I ask them, would they like for us to hold them and their children in abject slavery and wretchedness?

What kind!! Oh! what kind!!! Of Christianity can be found this day in all the earth!!!!!!

Instead of trying to elevate Black people into American citizenship, the proposal is to ship them back to Africa.

Will we adhere to Mr. Clay and his colonizing plan? Will any of us leave our homes and go to Africa? I hope not. The greatest riches in all America have arisen from our blood and tears—and will they drive us from our property and homes, which we have earned with our blood?

Because they argue that Black people are incapable of caring for themselves.

They tell us that we the (blacks) are an inferior race of beings! Incapable of self-government!!—We would be injurious to society and ourselves, if tyrants should lose their unjust hold on us!!! That if we were free we would not work, but would live on plunder or theft!!!! That we are the meanest and laziest set of beings in the world!!!!! That they are obliged to keep us in bondage to do us good!!!!!! That are satisfied to rest in slavery to them and their children!!!!!! That ought not to be set free in America, but ought to be sent away to Africa!!!!!!!!

This land which we have watered with our tears and our blood, is now our mother country, and we are well satisfied to stay where wisdom abounds and the gospel is free.

Black people must and shall be free in the end, the only question is how this will be achieved.

Now let us reason—I mean you of the United States, whom I believe God designs to save from destruction, if you will hear. I speak Americans for your good.

We must and shall be free I say, in spite of you. You may do your best to keep us in wretchedness and misery, to enrich you and your children, but God will deliver us from under you. And wo, wo, will be to you if we have to obtain our freedom by fighting.

Throw away your fears and prejudices then, and enlighten us and treat us like men, and we will like you more than we do now hate you; you are not astonished at my saying we hate you, for if we are men we cannot but hate you, while you are treating us like dogs.

And tell us now no more about colonization, for America is as much our country, as it is yours.

Abandon slavery, treat Black people with dignity, and peace and happiness will follow.

Treat us like men, and there is no danger but we will all live in peace and happiness together. For we are not like you, hard hearted, unmerciful, and unforgiving; what a happy country this will be, if the whites will listen.

But Americans, I declare to you, while you keep us and our children in bondage, and treat us like brutes, to make us support you and your families, we cannot be your friends. You do not look for it, do you? Treat us then like men, and we will be your friends. And there is not a doubt in my mind, but that the whole of the past will be sunk into oblivion, and we yet, under God, will become a united and happy people. The whites may say it is impossible, but remember that nothing is impossible with God.

But fail to change and America will be destroyed.

I tell you Americans! That unless you speedily alter your course, you and your Country are gone!!!!!! For God Almighty will tear up the very face of the earth!!!

I call God, I call Angels, I call men to witness, that the destruction of the Americans is at hand, and will be speedily consummated unless they repent.

The time for action is now and it depends on Black men standing up against white injustices.

Are we men! I ask you, O my brethren! Are we men? Did our Creator make us to be slaves to dust and ashes like ourselves?

The man who would not fight under our Lord and Master Jesus Christ, in the glorious and heavenly cause of freedom and of God ought to be kept with all of his children or family, in slavery, or in chains, to be butchered by his cruel enemies.

You have to prove to the Americans and the world, that we are MEN, and not brutes, as we have been represented, and by millions treated.

Once armed with conviction and courage, the black man will be a ferocious fighter in battle.

If you can only get courage into the blacks, I do declare it, that one good black man can put to death six white men; and I give it as a fact, let twelve black men get well armed for battle, and they will kill and put to flight fifty whites. The reason is, the blacks, once you get them started, they glory in death.

The whites have had us under them for more than three centuries, murdering, and treating us like brutes; and, as Mr. Jefferson wisely said, they have never found us out—they do not know, indeed, that there is an unconquerable disposition in the breasts of the blacks, which, when it is fully awakened and put in motion, will be subdued, only with the destruction of the animal existence.

If white people must be put to death to secure Black freedom, then so be it.

(The time has come) to take it away from them, and put everything before us to death, in order to gain our freedom which God has given us. The whites want slaves, and want us for their slaves, but some of them will curse the day they ever saw us. As true as the sun ever shown in its meridian splendor, my colour will root some of them out of the very face of the earth.

He ends in sadness with a question: "what is the use of living, when in fact I (as a slave) am dead?"

If any are anxious to ascertain who I am, know the world, that I am one of the oppressed, degraded and wretched sons of Africa, rendered so by the avaricious and unmerciful, among the whites.

If any wish to plunge me into the wretched incapacity of a slave, or murder me for the truth, know ye, that I am in the hand of God, and at your disposal. I count my life not dear unto me, but I am ready to be offered at any moment. For what is the use of living, when in fact I am dead.

TIME: 1829 AND ONWARD

THE *APPEAL* STRIKES RECOGNITION
AND FEAR AMONG WHITE READERS

Once published, Walker's *Appeal* represents a watershed moment in the relationship of free Black people to white people in America.

The dismissal of all Black people as ignorant and inferior evaporates in the presence of his powerful logic and prose. Here stands a full man, making his case against the injustices of slavery in a nation predicated on freedom and pleading "let right be done."

But what really registers among white people, especially in the South, is Walker's move beyond mere pleading to "demanding" and outright "threatening." On one hand he offers peace: abandon slavery, treat us fairly as "colored citizens" of America, and we will live together in tranquility and happiness. On the other, he issues fatalistic warnings: to root out white enemies, to put them to death, and to rain down destruction on the nation.

When Walker's pamphlets appear in Georgia, the state offers a $10,000 reward for anyone who hands him over alive or $1,000 to anyone who murders him. Other slave-holding states follow suit, confiscating copies of the *Appeal* when found and often arresting those who possess them.

Just as the turmoil surrounding him mounts, David Walker dies.

On June 28, 1830—nine months to the day after his pamphlet is published—he falls victim to tuberculosis, which also kills his daughter.

But Walker has lit a torch that will not be extinguished, the torch of Black freedom and citizenship. It is a torch that will soon be picked up by others, including white people who will risk their lives for his cause.

## 59

THE WHITE ABOLITIONIST MOVEMENT FINDS ITS ONGOING LEADERS

TIME: LATE 1820s

THE "SECOND GREAT AWAKENING" SPARKS THE ABOLITIONIST MOVEMENT IN NEW YORK

As the "Second Great Awakening" spirit of Reverend Charles Grandison Finney builds momentum, it captures three converts in upstate New York who commit to reversing the horrors of slavery—Theodore Dwight Weld and the brothers Lewis and Arthur Tappan.

Weld is the son of a congregational minister who falls under Finney's spell in 1825 when his aunt convinces him to accompany her to one of his services in Utica, New York. He soon discontinues his studies at Hamilton College and enrolls at Oneida Institute—a theological school founded in 1827 and dedicated to the notion that engaging in manual labor is a key element in spiritual development.

Oneida Colony Presbyterian Church

Oneida is situated on 114 acres of farmland owned by the Presbyterian Church which is run by Finney's mentor, Reverend George Gale, and supported by Lewis and Arthur Tappan.

The Tappan brothers grow up in Northampton, Massachusetts, become wealthy running a dry goods business in Portland, Maine, and expand their fortune after moving to New York City in 1826 as importers of silk cloth. While raised as traditional Calvinists, the brothers are influenced in part by Finney—who resides in Arthur Tappan's house for some time—to devote their lives to philanthropy. The Unitarian minister William Ellery Channing also plays a role as Lewis Tappan's pastor, and further influences Tappan's interest in abolition.

Lewis meets Theodore Weld on his visits to Oneida and is so impressed with Weld's preaching that he decides to enlist him in one of the brother's causes. Weld has already earned a reputation as a powerful preacher on behalf of the dignity of manual labor and the damning effects of drunkenness. But the Tappans have another focus in mind for him— the "sacred cause of Negro emancipation." He is also encouraged along this path by a lifetime friend, Charles Smart, who becomes involved with anti-slavery efforts in Britain.

Weld's report to the Tappans about British progress toward emancipation sparks early talk of setting up an American Anti-Slavery Society, but the consensus is that this would be premature.

Nevertheless, the Tappans hire Weld to head their Manual Labor Society and he works tirelessly on this until he moves to Cincinnati in 1833 to found the Lane Theological Seminary. In 1834 he leads a student debate on slavery that lasts over 18 days and ends with a declaration in support of abolition.

When the Lane Board of Directors, headed by President Lyman Beecher, squash the declaration, the majority of students leave the school with many headed to nearby Oberlin.

Weld decides at that time to rejoin the Tappans, who have been busy in their opposition to slavery.

Brother Lewis donates $10,000 to get Oberlin College up and running by 1833. Arthur, meanwhile, supports an all-Black college in New Haven in 1831 and has his house stoned by local citizens in return.

Soon thereafter, the Tappans encounter another abolitionist, William Lloyd Garrison, and they agree to join forces in fighting slavery. Together they form the two great wings of the white abolitionist movement in America:

- The New York wing, comprising Theodore Weld and the Tappan brothers, later joined by Gerrit Smith and James Birney.
- The Boston wing, comprising William Lloyd Garrison, Benjamin Lundy, Lucretia Mott, and a host of their other supporters, including Black figures such as Frederick Douglass and Sojourner Truth.

Over the next thirty years, these abolitionists will risk their welfare and their very lives on behalf of ending slavery in America.

TIME: LATE 1820s

WILLIAM LLOYD GARRISON EMERGES AS
THE NATION'S LEADING ANTI-SLAVERY SPOKESPERSON

In 1828, a chance meeting at a Boston boardinghouse between two fiery journalists and moralists changes the trajectory of the abolitionist movement.

One participant is the 39-year-old Quaker Benjamin Lundy, whose newspaper, *The Genius of Universal Emancipation*, has railed against slavery for the past seven years. The other is the 23-year-old Baptist William Lloyd Garrison, a budding journalist since thirteen, and eager to find the right cause for his own paper.

Lundy convinces Garrison to attack slavery as a worthwhile calling, and from then on, over the next three decades, Garrison will emerge as the acknowledged leader of the abolitionist movement in America.

Three things will set Garrison apart from all but a handful of others in the cause:

William Lloyd Garrison (1805–1879)

- His demand that emancipation be "immediate" rather than gradual;
- His support for keeping freed Black people in America, not sending them to Africa; and
- His unique and unequivocal commitment to assimilation of Black people as full and equal citizens.

In effect, his appeals as a white man mirror those of the contemporary Black reformer, David Walker.

Garrison is shaped for his mission as a child by his mother, Fanny Garrison, whose alcoholic husband abandons his family in Newburyport, Massachusetts when William is only three.

From then on, Fannie struggles to provide for her children and herself, working odd jobs and often needing to place the boys in foster homes around town. Despite her difficulties, she is forever buoyed by her Baptist faith and is known to her congregation as "Sister" Garrison. Nothing matters more to Fanny than passing on her revivalist fervor to her children. Together they attend church services three times every Sunday, and young William takes to humming a line from a favorite psalm, "my heart grows warm with holy fire."

By 1818 the family's financial straits grow even more desperate, and Garrison, age thirteen, begins a job as a "printer's devil" for the *Newburyport Herald*. This job changes his life. He is smitten by all the intricacies of the newspaper trade, and masters them so quickly that he is soon an indispensable part of the operation as shop foreman. The owner of the paper, Ephraim Allen, also opens his personal library to Garrison—and he schools himself in Shakespeare and Milton and the adventure tales of Scott and Byron. His imagination carries him to the possibility of his own form of heroic action on behalf of a cause that his mother would applaud.

In 1822 Garrison recognizes the power of the newspaper to express and disseminate his thoughts to the public. He begins to write his own articles and sees that the early poems of his friend, John Greenleaf Whittier, get published.

Then tragedy strikes, as both his mother and younger sister pass away due to illness in 1823. Sister Garrison's final message to her son marks his future.

> *Dear Lloyd – Lose not the favor of God, have an eye single to His glory and you will not lose your reward.*

Now on his own at age 21, Garrison ends his apprenticeship and launches his own newspaper, *The Free Press*, then shuts it down when his former employer is upset by the new competition.

Garrison makes his way to Boston in 1826, a major city of 60,000 people teeming with enterprise, universities, and churches. Here he finds the common man and the intellectual class, a small enclave of free Black people, and a heavy dose of revivalism. Garrison renews his religious ties and is touched by both Reverend Lyman Beecher—"the way to get good is to do good"—and the Unitarian William Ellery Channing with his gentle admonition to save yourself by acting morally.

Garrison now commits himself to helping humanity through a life of philanthropy.

He first chooses temperance as his cause. Both his father and his older brother ruined their lives through drink, and perhaps he can persuade others to escape their fate. His vehicle for this task will be a newspaper, and in January 1828 the first issue of *The National Philanthropist* appears. While the editorial content focuses on the perils of alcohol and the saving grace of temperance, Garrison also begins to dabble in Federalist politics.

However, he concludes that traditional politics are self-serving and power hungry, and that his focus should remain on "moral politics."

At this point in his life comes his chance encounter with Friend Benjamin Lundy and along with it, his calling: the eradication of slavery. After hearing Lundy's pleas, his response is immediate:

My soul was set on fire then.

TIME: JANUARY 1, 1831 – DECEMBER 29, 1865

GARRISON PUBLISHES HIS ABOLITIONIST PAPER
THE LIBERATOR

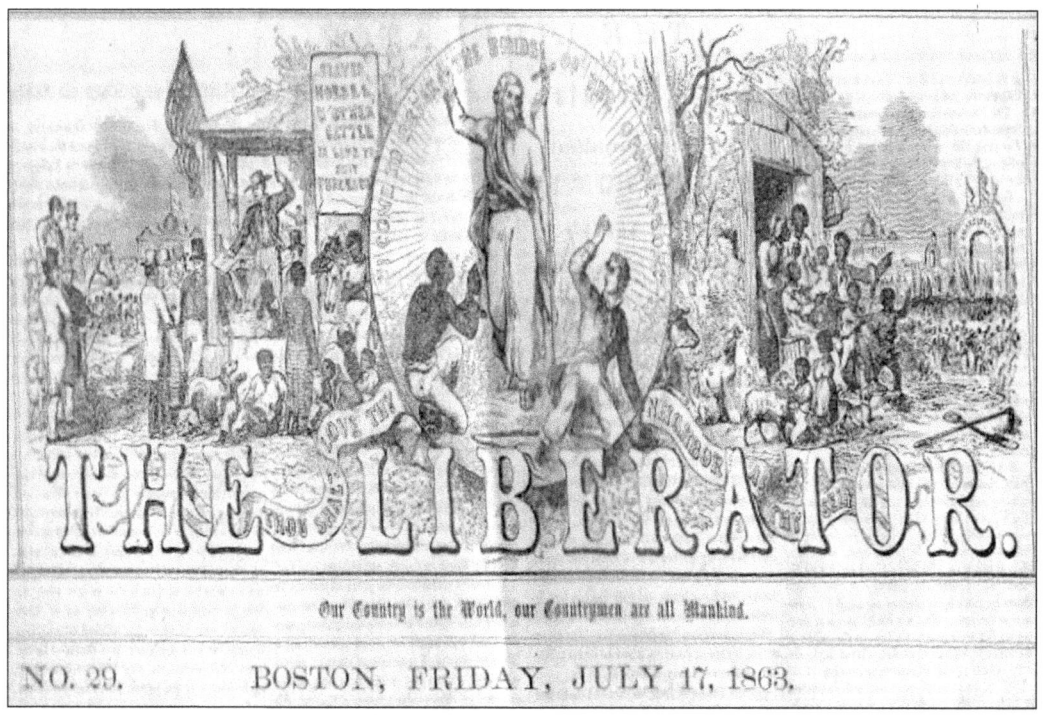

Masthead of Garrison's paper *The Liberator*

Garrison begins his personal crusade by trying to set up an Anti-Slavery Society in Boston, but is rebuffed by locals arguing that it's a Southern problem, not theirs. This resistance angers Garrison and steels him to his task.

He abandons the city briefly for a job in Burlington, Vermont on a pro-Adams newspaper. There he foments political outrage by writing that Andrew Jackson "should be manacled with the chains he has forged for others" as a slave owner.

What he learns from this stint is the power of inflammatory language to gain attention to his cause.

Upon returning to Boston, he takes this lesson into an 1829 public speaking appearance before 1,500 attendees at the Park Street Church, in celebration of the Fourth of July. Here he is transformed into the Puritan zealot, exhorting his audience with what will become familiar themes:

- *Slavery is a national sin—let us be up and doing to stop it.*
- *We have a common interest in demanding abolition.*
- *Would we stand still if slaves were suddenly to become white?*
- *I tremble for the Republic while slavery exists.*

Pushing even farther, he points to Haiti as evidence of Black people's capacity for "equal citizenship."

His conviction about integrating Black people into white society grows from there, as he mixes with Black people living in the enclave on Beacon Hill. This experience tells him that abolition should take place immediately, not gradually, and that he should speak out against re-colonization.

Even those sympathetic to his cause begin to express discomfort with the call for "Immediatism." Thus, the Unitarian minister, Ellery Channing, writes to Daniel Webster: "watch out for rashness of enthusiasts."

But nothing slows Garrison. In the summer of 1829 he moves to Baltimore, reuniting with Lundy and agreeing to co-publish his newspaper, *The Genius of Universal Emancipation.* The two split the editorial tasks—Lundy backing a more moderate path and re-colonization, and Garrison heightening his attacks on the status quo. He calls slave holders "man-stealers," says that "our politics are rotten," and offers a column called "The Black List: Horrible News of the Day."

A turning point for The Genius comes when Garrison convinces Lundy to publish Walker's *Appeal to the Colored Citizens of the World.*

Suddenly the paper's white audience is confronted by the face of slavery as seen through the eyes of those who have endured "wretched lives" under the lash. That much is shocking to readers.

But along with Walker's appeal to free the enslaved people now and live alongside them peacefully in America was equals, comes a threat—if white people fail to act, Black people will take up arms and kill them for freedom.

When copies of the paper containing Walker's *Appeal* reach Southern cities, the cry goes up for Garrison's head for inciting Black people to flee and to murder their masters.

Still, he persists. On April 17, 1830 he is found guilty of libel for accusing a man in Baltimore of slave trading. When sentenced to six months in prison or a $70 fine, he embraces his martyrdom:

A few white men must be sacrificed to open the eyes of this nation and to show the tyranny of our laws.

He remains in jail for 49 days until Arthur Tappan hears of his plight and sends him $100 to get out.

Upon his release, Lundy urges "moderation," as does the Congregationalist preacher, Henry Ward Beecher, who tells him: "if you give up your fanatical notions, and be guided by us, we will make you the Wilberforce of America"—Wilberforce being the lead proponent of abolition in Britain at the time.

Garrison will have none of this, and concludes that the time has come for him to publish his own newspaper, which he starts up in Boston on January 1, 1831. He names the paper *The Liberator,* and will continue to write, print, and distribute it weekly for the next 35 years, until the Thirteenth Amendment, freeing all enslaved people, is finally passed in Congress.

His manifesto is crystal clear from the start: the national sin of slavery must end immediately, and all Black people must be assimilated into American society as full and equal citizens. His tonality is also clear:

"I am in earnest – I will not equivocate – I will not excuse – I will not retreat a single inch –

AND I WILL BE HEARD!"

## 60

A FAMOUS "VALUE OF THE UNION" SENATE DEBATE TOUCHES ON THE STATES' RIGHTS TO SLAVERY

JANUARY 18–19, 1830

A BILL ON FEDERAL SALES OF WESTERN LANDS INITIATES A DEBATE ON STATES' RIGHTS

The sectional flare-up over "nullifying" the tariff re-opens the debate in Congress over the power of the federal government vis-à-vis the "sovereign" states.

This expands just after Christmas of 1829, when Connecticut senator Samuel Foot introduces a bill calling for Congress to suspend land sales in the western territories, as a means of slowing speculation.

On January 18, 1830, Senator Thomas Hart Benton of Missouri accuses Foot of "sectionalism," impeding the growth of the western states on behalf of the interests of New England.

At this point Robert Hayne of South Carolina joins the fray. He is an ally of John C. Calhoun, a bitter critic of the 1828 tariff, and an outspoken supporter of the states' rights to defy burdensome laws proposed by the federal government.

As Hayne launches into his classical attacks, Massachusetts senator Daniel Webster, a rock-ribbed Federalist, is drawn into the ring.

What follows is a twelve-day-long punch and counterpunch exchange between the two men that goes down as perhaps the greatest floor debate on any topic in the history of the upper chamber.

Webster stands with men like Washington and Hamilton, who argued for a strong national government focused on the "common good" of all citizens as the best way to ensure a lasting Union. For the contract to work, individual states must be ready to surrender their parochial interests on behalf of the whole. Or, as the Pennsylvania delegate James Wilson, put it:

> *If no state will part with any of its sovereignty, it is in vain to talk of a national government.*

Hayne's position is staunchly Anti-Federalist, a throwback to men like Patrick Henry, Sam Adams, Elbridge Gerry, George Clinton, and Thomas Jefferson. Together they feared that surrendering the state's power to a central government would lead to an American version of the British monarchy. Their opposition led to passage of the Bill of Rights, especially the Tenth Amendment:

> *The powers not delegated to the United States by the Constitution, nor prohibited by it to the States, are reserved to the States respectively, or to the people.*

What makes the Hayne-Webster debate so important is that it surfaces, with great intensity, the growing fear in the South that Northern control of the national government will ultimately lead to regulations on slavery, or even the demand to abolish it entirely.

Such an outcome would undermine the very basis of the South's economy—its single-minded capacity to grow and sell more cotton and enslaved people.

In January of 1830 Hayne rises as the spokesperson for Southerners who will stand ready to abandon the Union on behalf of their sovereign interests in slavery.

JANUARY 19–20, 1830

SENATORS HAYNE AND WEBSTER TRADE INITIAL JABS OVER THE IMPLICATIONS OF FOOT'S BILL

Hayne begins the debate with Webster by arguing over the land covered in Foot's bill, saying that the soil rightfully belongs to the states, not the federal government, and that money derived from the sales should not be handed to Washington.

> *Every scheme or contrivance by which rulers are able to procure the command of money by means unknown to, unseen or unfelt by, the people, destroys (their) security.*

> *I distrust, therefore, sir, the policy of creating a great permanent national treasury, whether to be derived from public lands or from any other source. It would enable Congress and the Executive to exercise a control over States, as well as over great interests in the country, nay, even over corporations and individuals—utterly destructive of the purity, and fatal to the duration of our institutions.*

But he quickly shifts to the larger issue—the evils which follow when a "consolidated" national government is able to run roughshod over the will of independent states.

PRELUDE TO CIVIL WAR

Sir, I am one of those who believe that the very life of our system is the independence of the States, and that there is no evil more to be deprecated than the consolidation of this Government.

It is only by a strict adherence to the limitations imposed by the constitution on the Federal Government, that this system works well, and... I am opposed, therefore, in any shape, to all unnecessary extension of the powers, or the influence of the Legislature or Executive of the Union over the States, or the people of the States; and, most of all, I am opposed to those partial distributions of favors, whether by legislation or appropriation, which has a direct and powerful tendency to spread corruption through the land; to create an abject spirit of dependence; to sow the seeds of dissolution; to produce jealousy among the different portions of the Union, and finally to sap the very foundations of the Government itself. ...

It is now Daniel Webster's turn to respond to both Benton's narrow criticism of Foot's bill and Hayne's broader attack on the "consolidated government." He begins by asserting that the framers simply saw "consolidation" as the best way to serve the greatest number of citizens, with each state being asked to give a little on behalf of the common good and the Union.

Sir, when gentlemen speak of the effects of a common fund, belonging to all the States, as having a tendency to consolidation, what do they mean? The framers tell that, "in all our deliberations on this subject, we kept steadily in our view that which appears to us the greatest interest of every true American—the consolidation of our Union... This important consideration...led each State in the Convention to be less rigid, on points of inferior magnitude, than might have been otherwise expected.

But from there he decides to jab Hayne and others from "his part of the country" for diminishing the value of the Union, by focusing constantly on its failures and evils. The founders felt the Union was essential to prosperity and safety for all; why does the South now feel differently?

I know that there are some persons in the part of the country from which the honorable member comes, who habitually speak of the Union in terms of indifference... They significantly declare, that it is time to calculate the value of the Union; and their aim seems to be to enumerate...all the evils...which the Government under the Union produces.

I deem far otherwise of the Union of the States; and so did the framers of the constitution themselves. What they said I believe; fully and sincerely believe, that the Union of the States is essential to the prosperity and safety of the States.

Webster then returns to Benton with an impassioned reminder of New England's role from the revolution onward.

I maintain that, from the day of the cession of the territories by the States to Congress, no portion of the country has acted, either with more liberality or more intelligence, on the subject of the Western lands on the new States, than New England.

JANUARY 25, 1830

HAYNE FIRES BACK, EXPANDING THE DEBATE INTO SLAVERY AND NULLIFICATION

At this point the focus of the debate shifts ominously—away from land sales and toward slavery.

Hayne's fires back against Webster's criticism of "his part of the country"—which he interprets as criticism of the South for failing to do away with slavery. His response begins by reminding Webster of the North's complicity in fostering slavery in America, then follows with a vigorous defense of the institution.

Enslaved teens on bales of cotton

The honorable gentleman from Massachusetts...; instead of making up his issue with the gentleman from Missouri, on the charges which he had preferred... goes on to assail the institutions and policy of the South, and calls in question the principles and conduct of the State which I have the honor to represent.

Was the significant hint of the weakness of slave-holding States, when contrasted with the superior strength of free States—like the glare of the weapon half drawn from its scabbard—intended to enforce the lessons of prudence and of patriotism, which the gentleman had resolved, out of his abundant generosity, gratuitously to bestow upon us?

We are ready to meet the question promptly and fearlessly... We are ready to make up the issue with the gentleman, as to the influence of slavery on individual and national character—on the prosperity and greatness, either of the United States, or of particular States.

Hayne contends, like Jefferson and others, that Black people are "of an inferior race."

> *Sir, when arraigned before the bar of public opinion, on this charge of slavery, we can stand up with conscious rectitude, plead not guilty, and put ourselves upon God and our country. Sir, we will not stop to inquire whether the black man, as some philosophers have contended, is of an inferior race, nor whether his color and condition are the effects of a curse inflicted for the offences of his ancestors.*

He correctly asserts that the Northern states played a dominant role in bringing enslaved people to America in the first place, reaping profits along the way.

> *We will not look back to inquire whether our fathers were guiltless in introducing slaves into this country. f an inquiry should ever be instituted in these matters, however, it will be found that the profits of the slave trade were not confined to the South. Southern ships and Southern sailors were not the instruments of bringing slaves to the shores of America, nor did our merchants reap the profits of that "accursed traffic."*

Once the enslaved people were here, Hayne says the South has done its best to care for them.

> *Finding our lot cast among a people, whom God had manifestly committed to our care, we did not sit down to speculate on abstract questions of theoretical liberty. We met it as a practical question of obligation and duty. We resolved to make the best of the situation in which Providence had placed us, and to fulfil the high trust which had developed upon us as the owners of slaves*

He then claims that Black people enslaved in the South are far better off than those that are free, living in wretched conditions in the slums of Philadelphia, Boston, and New York.

> *What a commentary on the wisdom, justice, and humanity, of the Southern slave owner is presented by the example of certain benevolent associations and charitable individuals elsewhere.... Thousands of these deluded victims of fanaticism were seduced into the enjoyment of freedom in our Northern cities. And what has been the consequence? Go to these cities now, and ask the question.*

> *Sir, there does not exist, on the face of the whole earth, a population so poor, so wretched, so vile, so loathsome, so utterly destitute of all the comforts, conveniences, and decencies of life, as the unfortunate blacks of Philadelphia, and New York, and Boston.*

This narrative is followed by a plea often to be heard in the years to come—the North should simply let the South alone to deal with the future of slavery.

On this subject, as in all others, we ask nothing of our Northern brethren but to "let us alone;" leave us to the undisturbed management of our domestic concerns, and the direction of our own industry, and we will ask no more.

But Hayne is not yet done with Webster. He returns to the 1787 Convention and argues that the founders were intent on "consolidating the Union" not on "consolidating the government."

In the course of my former remarks, I took occasion to deprecate, as one of the greatest of evils, the consolidation of this Government....The object of the framers of the constitution, as disclosed in that address, was not the consolidation of the Government, but "the consolidation of the Union." It was not to draw power from the States, in order to transfer it to a great National Government, but, in the language of the constitution itself, "to form a more perfect union;" and by what means? By "establishing justice," "promoting domestic tranquility," and "securing the blessings of liberty to ourselves and our posterity." This is the true reading of the constitution.

His language turns personal, assuring Webster that he will not get away with "casting the first stone" against the South around the threat of disunion.

The honorable gentleman from Massachusetts [Mr. Webster] while he exonerates me personally from the charge, intimates that there is a party in the country who are looking to disunion.... [T]hat gentleman has thought proper, for purposes best known to himself, to strike the South through me... Sir, when the gentleman provokes me to such a conflict, I meet him at the threshold.

The "true friend of the Union," he claims, are those who would deny the boundaries set out by the founders and try to transfer the powers reserved for the states to the consolidated national government.

Who, then, Mr. President, are the true friends of the Union? Those who would confine the federal government strictly within the limits prescribed by the constitution—who would preserve to the States and the people all powers not expressly delegated—who would make this a federal and not a national Union—and who, administering the government in a spirit of equal justice, would make it a blessing and not a curse. And who are its enemies? Those who are in favor of consolidation; who are constantly stealing power from the States and adding strength to the federal government; who, assuming an unwarrantable jurisdiction over the States and the people, undertake to regulate the whole industry and capital of the country.

Hayne now arrives at his central contention—belief that the Constitution gives a state the right to "nullify" any federal actions it deems threatening to its well-being. He says that, despite Webster's readiness to mock this belief as the "Carolina doctrine," it is indeed the only path by which the Union can actually be preserved.

The Senator from Massachusetts, in denouncing what he is pleased to call the Carolina doctrine, has attempted to throw ridicule upon the idea that a State has any constitutional remedy by the exercise of its sovereign authority against "a gross, palpable, and deliberate violation of the Constitution." He called it "an idle" or "a ridiculous notion," or something to that effect; and added, that it would make the Union "a mere rope of sand."

Sir, as to the doctrine that the Federal Government is the exclusive judge of the extent as well as the limitations of its powers, it seems to be utterly subversive of the sovereignty and independence of the States.

I have but one word more to add. In all the efforts that have been made by South Carolina to resist the unconstitutional laws which Congress has extended over them, she has kept steadily in view the preservation of the Union, by the only means by which she believes it can be long preserved—a firm, manly, and steady resistance against usurpation. The measures of the Federal Government have, it is true, prostrated her interests, and will soon involve the whole South in irretrievable ruin.

Both the content and the tone of Hayne's speech riles Webster.

He is right in calling nullification the "Carolina doctrine." It is the work of none other than Jackson's vice president, Calhoun, who will spend the final two decades of his life trying to convince the South of the peril it faces from Northern control in Washington. Webster decides that nullification must be met head on, and he calls upon all of his fine legal reasoning to respond to Hayne over the next two days.

JANUARY 26–27, 1830

WEBSTER'S SECOND REPLY TO HAYNE ADDRESSES THE MEANING AND VALUE OF THE UNION

Webster's second response to Hayne is generally regarded as one of the greatest speeches ever delivered in the Senate. It reviews in detail the principles that created the Union in the first place, shows why the notion of "nullification" violates the intent of the founders, and ends with an emotional and stirring call on behalf of preserving both liberty and the Union.

The address begins calmly, with an attempt to exclude personal animus from the dialogue.

When the honorable member rose, in his first speech, I paid him the respect of attentive listening; and when he sat down…nothing was farther from my intention than to commence any personal warfare.

It shifts to Hayne's defense of slavery, with Webster declaring that while he finds the practice to be morally and politically evil, the people of the North have never sought to interfere with it.

I spoke, sir, of the ordinance of 1787, which prohibited slavery, in all future times, northwest of the Ohio, as a measure of great wisdom and foresight… But, the simple expression of this sentiment has led the gentleman, not only into a labored defence of slavery, in the abstract, and on principle, but, also, into a warm accusation against me, as having attacked the system of domestic slavery, now existing in the

Daniel Webster.

Daniel Webster (1782–1852)

Southern States. For all this, there was not the slightest foundation, in anything said or intimated by me. I did not utter a single word, which any ingenuity could torture into an attack on the slavery of the South.

I know, full well, that it is, and has been, the settled policy of some persons in the South, for years, to represent the people of the North as disposed to interfere with them, in their own exclusive and peculiar concerns… But the feeling is without all adequate cause, and the suspicion which exists wholly groundless. There is not, and never has been, a disposition in the North to interfere with these interests of the South.

The gentleman, indeed, argues that slavery, in the abstract, is no evil. Most assuredly, I need not say I differ with him, altogether and most widely, on that point. I regard domestic slavery as one of the greatest of evils, both moral and political.

[But] the domestic slavery of the Southern States I leave where I find it—in the hands of their own governments. It is their affair, not mine.

The central issue according to Webster is not about slavery, but about Hayne's questioning the value of the Union. Sarcasm marks his tone, as he compares New England's interest in the "good of the whole" against South Carolina's disregard for anything but its own well-being.

This leads, sir, to the real and wide difference, in political opinion, between the honorable gentleman and myself…. "What interest," asks he, "has South Carolina in a canal in Ohio?"

Sir, we narrow-minded people of New England do not reason thus. Our notion of things is entirely different. We look upon the States, not as separated, but as united…. In our contemplation, Carolina and Ohio are parts of the same country; States, united under the same General Government, having interests, common, associated, intermingled.

We who come here, as agents and representatives of these narrow-minded and selfish men of New England, consider ourselves as bound to regard, with equal eye, the good of the whole.

He then directly faces Hayne's assertion that individual states have the right to "nullify" any federal laws they deem harmful to their self-interest.

I understand the honorable gentleman from South Carolina to maintain, that it is a right of the State Legislatures to interfere, whenever, in their judgment, this Government transcends its constitutional limits, and to arrest the operation of its laws.

I understand him to insist, that if the exigency of the case, in the opinion of any State Government, require it, such State Government may, by its own sovereign authority, annul an act of the General Government, which it deems plainly and palpably unconstitutional…. This is the sum of what I understand from him, to be the South Carolina doctrine.

Webster says that the Constitution, the supreme law of the land, was set up to make government accountable to the people as a whole, not to the individual whims of any one state.

This leads us to inquire into the origin of this Government, and the source of its power. Whose agent is it?… This absurdity (for it seems no less) arises from a misconception as to the origin of this Government and its true character. It is, sir, the People's Constitution, the People's Government; made for the People; made by the People; and answerable to the People.

The people of the United States have declared that the Constitution shall be the supreme law. We must either admit the proposition, or dispute their authority. The States are, unquestionably, sovereign, so far as their sovereignty is not affected by this supreme law. But the State legislatures, as political bodies, however sovereign, are yet not sovereign over the people. So far as the people have given the power to the general government, so far the grant is unquestionably good, and the government holds of the people, and not of the State governments. We are all agents of the same supreme power, the people."

Hayne's proposal is nothing more than a throwback to the government that existed under the Articles of Confederation—with State interests able to override the common will of the people. This approach failed before and it would fail again, despite protests to the contrary.

Sir, the very chief end, the main design, for which the whole Constitution was framed and adopted, was to establish a Government that should not be obliged to act through State agency, or depend on State opinion and State discretion. The People had had quite enough of that kind of Government, under the Confederacy.

Finally, sir, the honorable gentleman says, that the States will only interfere, by their power, to preserve the Constitution. They will not destroy it, they will not impair it — they will only save, they will only preserve, they will only strengthen it! Ah! Sir, this is but the old story. All regulated Governments, all free Governments, have been broken up by similar disinterested and well disposed interference! It is the common pretence. But I take leave of the subject.

After holding the floor for several hours over a two-day period, Webster returns to his main theme—his belief that the Union represents America's best chance to simultaneously serve the interests of the people and those of the states. That was the insight the founders came to at the Constitutional Convention of 1787 and it must be preserved. To make the point, he dwells momentarily on a prophetic option—bloody disunion.

I have not accustomed myself to hang over the precipice of disunion to see whether, with my short sight, I can fathom the depth of the abyss below; nor could I regard him as a safe counselor in the affairs of this Government, whose thoughts should be mainly bent on considering not how the Union should be best preserved, but how tolerable might be the condition of the people when it shall be broken up and destroyed.

While the Union lasts we have high, exciting, gratifying prospects spread out before us, for us and our children. Beyond that I seek not to penetrate the veil. God grant that in my day, at least, that curtain may not rise. God grant that, on my vision, never may be opened what lies behind. When my eyes shall be turned to behold, for the last time, the sun in heaven, may I not see him shining on the broken and dishonored fragments of a once glorious Union; on States dissevered, discordant, belligerent; on a land rent with civil feuds, or drenched, it may be, in fraternal blood!

He then closes with the soaring line—"Liberty and Union, now and forever, one and inseparable"—for which the address is forever remembered.

Let their last feeble and lingering glance rather behold the gorgeous ensign of the republic, now known and honored throughout the earth, still full high advanced, its arms and trophies streaming in their original luster, not a stripe erased or polluted, nor a single star obscured, bearing for its motto no such miserable interrogatory as, "What is it all worth?" or those other words of delusion and folly, "Liberty first and union afterwards"; but " everywhere spread all over in characters of living light, blazing on all its ample folds, as they float over the sea and over land, and in every wind under the whole heavens, that other sentiment, dear to every true American heart—Liberty and Union, now and forever, one and inseparable!"

JANUARY 27, 1830

HAYNE OFFERS A FINAL REJOINDER

The fact that Hayne pushes back one last time against Webster signals that the states' rights advocates of the South are not about to surrender. What Webster calls the "Carolina doctrine" is no more than an assertion of the guarantees in the Tenth Amendment of the 1787 Constitution.

Here it will be necessary to go back to the origin of the Federal Government. It cannot be doubted, and is not denied, that before the formation of the constitution, each State was an independent sovereignty, possessing all the rights and powers appertaining to independent nations; nor can it be denied that, after the constitution was formed, they remained equally sovereign and independent, as to all powers, not expressly delegated to the Federal Government. This would have been the case even if no positive provision to that effect had been inserted in that instrument. But to remove all doubt it is expressly declared, by the 10th article of the amendment of the constitution, "that the powers not delegated to the States, by the constitution, nor prohibited by it to the States, are reserved to the States respectively, or to the people."…

No doubt can exist, that, before the States entered into the compact, they possessed the right to the fullest extent, of determining the limits of their own powers—it is incident to all sovereignty. Now, have they given away that right, or agreed to limit or restrict it in any respect? Assuredly not. They have agreed, that certain specific powers shall be exercised by the Federal Government; but the moment that Government steps beyond the limits of its charter, the right of the States "to interpose for arresting the progress of the evil, and for maintaining within their respective limits the authorities, rights, and liberties, appertaining to them," is as full and complete as it was before the Constitution was formed.

He says the issue has never been about "love of the Union."

A State will be restrained by a sincere love of the Union. The People of the United States cherish a devotion to the Union, so pure, so ardent, that nothing short of intolerable oppression, can ever tempt them to do anything that may possibly endanger it. The gentleman has made an eloquent appeal to our hearts in favor of union. Sir, I cordially respond to that appeal. I will yield to no gentleman here in sincere attachment to the Union.

Instead, it has been about embracing a Union that lives up to the rules laid out in the Constitution, which honor the rights of the states versus the "consolidated government."

But it is a Union founded on the Constitution, and not such a Union as that gentleman would give us, that is dear to my heart. If this is to become one great "consolidated government," swallowing up the rights of the States, and the liberties of the citizen, "riding and ruling over the plundered ploughman, and beggared yeomanry," the Union will not be worth preserving. Sir it is because South Carolina loves the Union, and would preserve it forever, that she is opposing now, while there is hope, those usurpations of the Federal Government, which, once established, will, sooner or later, tear this Union into fragments. ...

The exchanges between the two great orators are riveting for all who witness them in the Senate—but the implications extend far beyond mere theater.

Hayne announces the South's growing fear that the federal government may try to impede the future growth of slavery—along with a warning that any such action will be met with resistance that could "tear the Union into fragments."

Webster makes it clear that all attempts by the South to "nullify" federal laws will fail.

Here is an impasse, and ten weeks later it spills over to a sharp exchange within the executive branch.

## 61

JACKSON SPLITS WITH CALHOUN AND SACKS HIS ENTIRE CABINET

APRIL 13, 1829

JACKSON AND CALHOUN OFFER CONFLICTING DINNER TOASTS

Little by little it dawns on Andrew Jackson that his vice president, John C. Calhoun, is not to be trusted.

The president has yet to learn about the attacks on his conduct during the Seminole War made back in 1818 by then Secretary of War Calhoun. At that time, Monroe asks his cabinet if Jackson should be arrested for his actions—with Calhoun saying yes and, ironically, only Secretary of State John Quincy Adams disagreeing.

But Jackson is well aware that Calhoun worked from within against Adams throughout his term, and senses this same pattern developing—this time around the call from South Carolina surrogates like Hayne to "nullify" the 1828 tariff.

The old general is not one to brook insubordination within his ranks for long.

His anger at Calhoun surfaces on April 13, 1829 at the Indian Queen Hotel in

Andrew Jackson (1767–1845)

Washington during the annual celebration dinner honoring the memory of Thomas Jefferson.

When the time for after dinner toasts rolls around, all eyes turn to Jackson, whose words echo like a battlefield command:

Our Union – it must be preserved!

The vice president recognizes that these words are meant for him and his fellow nullifiers. But instead of the usual "hear, hear" support, Calhoun reacts defensively by asserting liberty as the higher calling.

Our Union, next to our liberty, most dear! May we always remember that it can only be preserved by distributing equally the benefits and the burdens of the Union."

The toast is widely regarded as a form of defiance by Calhoun—his attempt to correct the president's misguided commitment to the Union at any price.

The ever-wily Martin Van Buren now offers a third toast, apparently playing the peacemaker but also registering for posterity the growing rivalry between Jackson and his vice president.

Mutual forbearance and reciprocal concessions. Through their agency our Union was founded. The patriotic spirit from which they emanated will forever sustain it.

Both the Hayne-Webster debates and the Jackson-Calhoun toasts set the stage for what lies ahead for America—an ever more crucial search for "mutual forbearance and reciprocal concessions" between the North and the South over the future of slavery.

TIME: 1829–31

THE POLITICAL INFIGHTING IS INTENSIFIED BY THE "PETTICOAT AFFAIR"

Midway into his first term, the short fuse on Jackson's temper is ignited by turmoil within his cabinet.

The root cause is a developing rivalry between factions aligned with Vice President Calhoun and those backing the president and Martin Van Buren.

But the trigger for Jackson is a sustained backbiting campaign to shun Peggy Eaton, the wife of his secretary of war, on grounds of questionable moral standards.

The charge particularly grates on the president because he and his wife, Rachel, suffered comparable smears throughout the mudslinging campaign of 1828. In fact, Jackson remains convinced that Rachel's fatal heart attack just prior to his inauguration resulted from being publicly labeled as an adulteress.

Rumblings about Peggy Eaton go back to her youthful days, working the bar at her father's Franklin House inn near the Capitol. After several courtships, she is married at age seventeen to a 39-year-old Navy man, John Timberlake. Among the couple's friends is John Eaton, a senator from Tennessee, close friend of Jackson, and an early widower.

When Timberlake's personal finances collapse and he turns to alcohol, John Eaton helps out, both with funds and by securing a naval post for him in the Mediterranean fleet. With her husband away, Peggy returns to her job at the Franklin House, which now caters almost exclusively to congressional members and their wives.

Gossip follows quickly—how can a married woman be considered respectable while working for a wage, and in a bar no less? This accelerates when Timberlake dies at sea in April 1828, and a rumor spreads that he killed himself after hearing that Peggy and John Eaton had become lovers. The rumor is supported eight months later when the two are wed—after receiving a blessing from none other than John's mentor, Andrew Jackson.

Despite the couple's connections in Washington, many in the social elite choose to boycott the wedding on the grounds that, in violating the traditional year-long mourning period, Peggy's conduct is unseemly.

When Jackson names Eaton as his secretary of war, the social knives are borne among other cabinet wives—the most notable and vocal being the aristocratic Floride Calhoun, who initiates a series of slights aimed at humiliating the new couple. She asserts that Peggy is "a promiscuous woman" and convinces her allies to refuse to attend social events, especially at the White House, where the Eatons are present.

After enduring almost two years of this, Jackson decides he has had enough of the foolishness. Surely the wives of his cabinet cannot be allowed to undermine Eaton's role as war secretary, and surely it is time for him to step in and protect Peggy's honor. As he says at the time:

> I would rather have live vermin on my back than the tongue of one of these Washington women on my reputation.

Early in 1831 he decides to act.

TIME: AUGUST 31, 1831

JACKSON BREAKS WITH CALHOUN AND SACKS HIS CABINET

The venom he feels is directed particularly at John Calhoun.

He knows that the vice president has been plotting behind his back to nullify the 1828 tariff, and that Floride Calhoun is the ringleader hoping to defame Peggy Eaton. But he also learns in February 1831 that Calhoun is behind the public disclosure of letters critical of Jackson's actions in Florida in 1818 during the Seminole War.

In response he makes it clear that he intends to support Van Buren for vice president in 1832.

This message reaches Calhoun, who recognizes that his chances of ever winning the presidency have all but vanished. Instead, he will henceforth dedicate his political career to convincing the South to face the existential threat he says is building in the North.

Van Buren, who has backed the Eatons all along, sees the so-called "Petticoat Affair" as another attempt by the "Calhounites" in the cabinet—Ingham, Berrien, and Branch—to undermine both Jackson's administration and his own future political aspirations. After he convinces Eaton to resign, the president goes further, requesting that all his appointees step aside.

Francis P. Blair (1791–1876), member of Jackson's new kitchen cabinet

Which they do by August 31, 1831, the only exception being Postmaster Barry, who stays on at Jackson's request. Van Buren quickly assumes the post of ambassador to Great Britain.

In turn, Jackson names a new cabinet, including several members who will play prominent public roles for years to come. Attorney General Roger Taney will succeed John Marshall as chief justice of the Supreme Court and preside for 28 years. Lewis Cass, who fought in the War of 1812 and opened the Michigan territory as governor, will go on to run for president in 1848 and lead the "popular sovereignty" wing of the Democratic Party from then on. Levi Woodbury will eventually become secretary of the Treasury and then associate justice on the Supreme Court. Louis McLane becomes both secretary of the Treasury and secretary of state, then president of the Baltimore & Ohio Railroad Company.

ANDREW JACKSON'S CABINET IN SEPTEMBER 1832

POSITION	NAME	HOME STATE
Vice President	John C. Calhoun	South Carolina
Secretary of State	Edward Livingston	New York
Secretary of Treasury	Louis McLane	Delaware
Secretary of War	Lewis Cass	Michigan
Secretary of the Navy	Levi Woodbury	New Hampshire
Attorney General	Roger Taney	Maryland
Postmaster General	William Barry	Kentucky

As impressive as this replacement cabinet is, Jackson, like many future presidents, decides to rely on a tight circle of long-time trusted advisors to decide on policy and political matters.

Van Buren and Taney are part of this informal "kitchen cabinet." So too is Jackson's nephew and "adopted son," Andrew Jackson Donelson. The rest tend to be long-time friends from Nashville or newspapermen who have helped shape and disseminate his agenda and messages.

JACKSON'S "KITCHEN CABINET" OF INFORMAL ADVISORS

MEMBERS	CONNECTIONS
Martin Van Buren	Campaign manager, protégé, chosen successor
Amos Kendall	Speech/policy writer for Jackson, editor of Kentucky *Argus* paper
Roger B. Taney	Early Jackson backer and legal advisor
Francis P. Blair	Editor of pro-Jackson *Washington Globe*, main party organ
Andrew Jackson Donelson	Nephew and adopted son of Jackson, Hermitage roots, private secretary
John Overton	Nashville pal, Jackson dueling "second," judge, planter, business partner
Isaac Hill	Editor of *New Hampshire Patriot*, politician, early Jackson backer
William B. Lewis	Nashville pal, army quartermaster for Jackson

62

THE FRENCH VISITOR ALEXIS DE TOCQUEVILLE ANALYZES THE AMERICAN SPIRIT AND THE REGIONAL TENSIONS AROUND SLAVERY

TIME: 1831–1832

DE TOCQUEVILLE COMPLETES A TOUR OF AMERICA

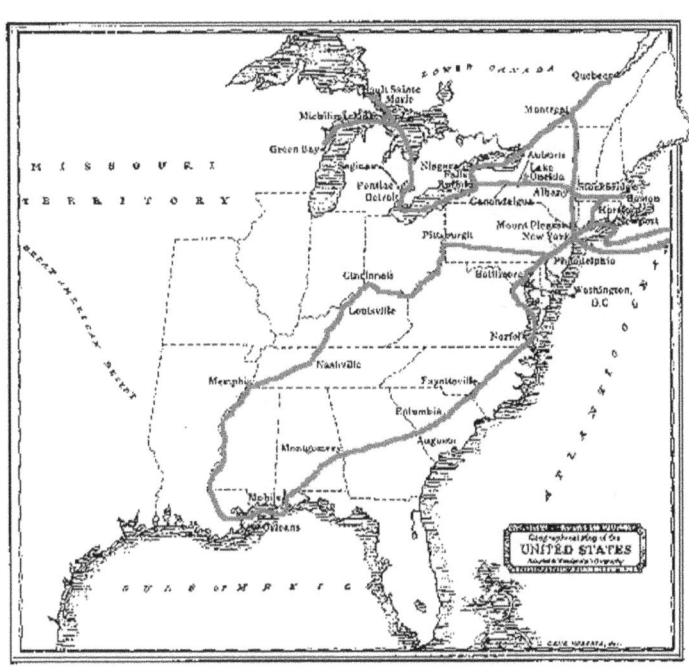

Map showing de Tocqueville's tour of North America in 1831–1832

On May 9, 1831, two young men involved with the French judicial system arrive in Newport, Rhode Island, after a 37-day-long Atlantic crossing. One is Gustave de

Beaumont, a 29-year-old "King's Prosecutor" in Paris. The other is his 25-year-old friend, Alexis de Tocqueville, currently serving as a court-appointed judge.

Their intent is to study North America's prison system in hopes of finding reform ideas they can apply in France.

To do so, they set off on a nine-month journey, utilizing ships, steamboats, stagecoaches, and footpaths to cut a wide swath across the eastern half of the continent.

DE TOCQUEVILLE'S ITINERARY IN NORTH AMERICA

DATES	LOCATION
May 9, 1831	Arrive in Newport, Rhode Island
May 29	Visit Ossining (Sing Sing) Prison
June 7	New York City
July 9	Visit Auburn Prison in New York
July 1	Arrive in Detroit
August 9	At Green Bay (Michigan Territory)
August 19	Back toward east, at Niagara Falls
August 23	Montreal
September 9	Boston
October 12	Interviewing prisoners at Cherry Hill
November 22	Pittsburg
December 1	Cincinnati
December 17	Memphis
January 1	New Orleans
January 3	Mobile
January 15	Norfolk, Virginia
January 17	Washington, DC
February 3	Philadelphia
February 20	Depart from New York to France

Along the way, de Tocqueville records his detailed observations about America in a diary, which he analyzes upon his return home. Together with de Beaumont he publishes *Du systeme penitentiaire aux Etats-Unis et de son application en France*, to fulfill the purpose of the trip.

But de Tocqueville remains fascinated with what he has seen and learned on his whirlwind tour, and decides to publish a second book. He titles it *Democracy in America*, with the first volume published in August 1834, and the second in 1840. The book captures de Tocqueville's experiences and conclusions about a broad range of topics.

PARTIAL TABLE OF CONTENTS: *DEMOCRACY IN AMERICA*

VOLUME 1 (1834)
The Author's Preface
The Exterior Form of North America
Origins of the Anglo-Americans
Social Conditions of the Anglo-Americans
The Principle of the Sovereignty of the People
The Necessity of Examining the States Before the Union at Large
Judicial Power in the US and its Influence on Political Society
The Federal Constitution
How It Can Be Strictly Said That the People Govern in the US
Liberty of the Press in the US
Political Associations in the US
Government of the Democracy in the US
What Advantages American Society Derives from Democracy
Unlimited Power of the Majority and Its Consequences
Causes Which Mitigate the Tyranny of the Majority
Principle Causes Which Serve to Maintain a Democratic Republic
The Present and Probably Future Condition of the Three Races That Inhabit the Territory of the United States

Overall, what de Tocqueville seems to find most profoundly intriguing about America is the "philosophical approach" adopted by its citizens in relation to whatever topics or issues they encounter.

Gone are the old answers to all things, imposed from above by kings or clergymen—replaced by every man using his own common sense and experience to arrive at his own beliefs.

De Tocqueville describes this as follows:

I THINK that in no country in the civilized world is less attention paid to philosophy than in the United States. The Americans have no philosophical school of their own, and they care but little for all the schools into which Europe is divided, the very names of which are scarcely known to them.

Yet it is easy to perceive that almost all the inhabitants of the United States use their minds in the same manner, and direct them according to the same rules; that is to say, without ever having taken the trouble to define the rules, they have a philosophical method common to the whole people.

I discover that in most of the operations of the mind each American appeals only to the individual effort of his own understanding.

To evade the bondage of system and habit…class opinions…of national prejudices; to accept tradition only as a means of information, and existing facts only as a lesson to be used in doing otherwise and doing better; to seek the reason of things for oneself, and in oneself alone; to tend to results without being bound to means, and to strike through the form to the substance--such are the principal characteristics of what I shall call the philosophical method of the Americans

From this uniquely American way of thinking comes a genuine experiment in democracy, which for the Frenchman explains the "social conditions" of the new nation. He summarizes this in bold type as follows:

THE STRIKING CHARACTERISTIC OF THE SOCIAL CONDITION OF THE ANGLO-AMERICANS IS ITS ESSENTIAL DEMOCRACY.

In turn, he pens the line for which he will be most memorialized in the United States:

America is great because she is good, and if America ever ceases to be good, she will cease to be great.

TIME: 1831–1832

THE FRENCHMAN COMMENTS ON REGIONAL DIFFERENCES IN AMERICA

While de Tocqueville sees philosophical similarities across all Anglo-Americans, he distinguishes between the societal milieus he finds in the North versus the South.

His view is that the South has been shaped by the dominance of slavery which has "benumbed" the entire region and left it diminished by "ignorance and pride."

Virginia received the first English colony…in 1607…. The colony was scarcely established when slavery was introduced; this was the capital fact which was to exercise an immense influence on the character, the laws, and the whole future of the South.

Slavery, as I shall afterwards show, dishonors labor; it introduces idleness into society, and with idleness, ignorance and pride, luxury and distress. It enervates the powers of the mind and benumbs the activity of man. The influence of slavery…explains the manners and the social condition of the Southern states.

By contrast, de Tocqueville sees the North rooted in the Puritanism of the New England states, with values shining "like a beacon lit upon a hill." Theirs was never a mad search for wealth and title, but rather the "triumph of an idea"—to create a society where they could "worship God in freedom" and translate religious principles into a political reality for the common good.

In the English colonies of the North…the two or three main ideas that now constitute the basis of the social theory of the United States were first combined… The civilization of New England has been like a beacon lit upon a hill, which, after it has diffused its warmth immediately around it, also tinges the distant horizon with its glow.…

The settlers who established themselves on the shores of New England all belonged to the more independent classes of their native country… a society containing neither lords nor common people, and we may almost say neither rich nor poor. These men possessed, in proportion to their number, a greater mass of intelligence than is to be found in any European nation of our own time.

Nor did they cross the Atlantic to improve their situation or to increase their wealth; it was a purely intellectual craving that called them from the comforts of their former homes; and in facing the inevitable sufferings of exile their object was the triumph of an idea.… the Puritans went forth to seek some rude and unfrequented part of the world where they could live according to their own opinions and worship God in freedom.… Puritanism …was almost as much a political theory as a religious doctrine.

TIME: 1831–1832

VIEWS ON THE PLIGHT OF BLACK PEOPLE LIVING IN AMERICA

The scope of de Tocqueville's travels sensitizes him to the fact that three distinct races are attempting to live in proximity to each other on the continent.

Three races are discoverable among them at the first glance although they are mixed, they do not amalgamate, and each race fulfills its destiny apart.

As a white man himself, he identifies the Anglo-Americans as superior in intelligence, and using this capacity to subjugate both Black people and the Native tribes.

Among these widely differing families of men, the first that attracts attention, the superior in intelligence, in power, and in enjoyment, is the white…below him appear the Negro and the Indian…Both of them occupy an equally inferior position in the country they inhabit; both suffer from tyranny; and if their wrongs are not the same, they originate from the same authors.

If we reason from what passes in the world, we should almost say that the European is to the other races of mankind what man himself is to the lower animals: he makes them subservient to his use, and when he cannot subdue he destroys them.

While both minorities suffer in the relationship, it is the enslaved Black people who are "deprived of almost all the privileges of humanity."

> *Oppression has, at one stroke, deprived the descendants of the Africans of almost all the privileges of humanity.*

> *The Negro of the United States has lost even the remembrance of his country; the language which his forefathers spoke is never heard around him; he abjured their religion and forgot their customs when he ceased to belong to Africa, without acquiring any claim to European privileges. But he remains half-way between the two communities, isolated between two races; sold by the one, repulsed by the other; finding not a spot in the universe to call by the name of country, except the faint image of a home which the shelter of his master's roof affords. The Negro has no family… The Negro enters upon slavery as soon as he is born…Equally devoid of wants and of enjoyment, and useless to himself, he learns, with his first notions of existence, that he is the property of another.*

As de Tocqueville sees it, the response to slavery among Black Americans is every bit as devastating as the condition itself—for intimidation destroys the innate sense of self-worth and identity and replaces it with an instinct to imitate the traits of white masters for the sake of survival.

Once one is officially declared to be three-fifths of a full person, the road back to full equality becomes steep. And it explains why, when the time comes, the roll call of Black abolitionists will all rally around a common battle cry—"I am a man" or "I am a woman."

> *The Negro makes a thousand fruitless efforts to insinuate himself among men who repulse him; he conforms to the tastes of his oppressors, adopts their opinions, and hopes by imitating them to form a part of their community. Having been told from infancy that his race is naturally inferior to that of the whites, he assents to the proposition and is ashamed of his own nature. In each of his features he discovers a trace of slavery, and if it were in his power, he would willingly rid himself of everything that makes him what he is.*

Like the Anglo-Americans of his time, de Tocqueville is not sanguine about emancipation as the path to reversing the damage done by slavery.

> *If he becomes free, independence is often felt by him to be a heavier burden than slavery…In short, he is sunk to such a depth of wretchedness that while servitude brutalizes, liberty destroys him.*

TIME: 1831–1832

VIEWS ON NATIVE TRIBES

De Tocqueville's beliefs about the Indians he encounters are somewhat more nuanced than his views on Black people.

Again, as a white man, he regards them as intellectually inferior, and even "savage" in terms of their natural inclinations. At the same time, he clearly senses something "noble" in their presence, and, citing the Cherokees, concludes that they "are capable of civilization."

Prior to the European invasion, Native people existed in a pure state of nature and liberty.

Before the arrival of white men in the New World, the inhabitants of North America lived quietly in their woods, enduring the vicissitudes and practicing the virtues and vices common to savage nations.

The Indian lies on the uttermost verge of liberty; To be free, with him, signifies to escape from all the shackles of society. As he delights in this barbarous independence and would rather perish than sacrifice the least part of it, civilization has little hold over him.

That freedom is disappearing as the eastern tribes are being driven out of their homelands to suit the wishes of white settlers. The result is "inexpressible sufferings."

The Europeans having dispersed the Indian tribes and driven them into the deserts, condemned them to a wandering life, full of inexpressible sufferings.

The Frenchman also argues that displacement has only served to make the tribes more "disorderly and barbarous" than they once were.

Oppression has been no less fatal to the Indian than to the Negro race, but its effects are different. Savage nations are only controlled by opinion and custom. When the North American Indians had lost the sentiment of attachment to their country; when their families were dispersed, their traditions obscured, and the chain of their recollections broken; when all their habits were changed, and their wants increased beyond measure, European tyranny rendered them more disorderly and less civilized than they were before. The moral and physical condition of these tribes continually grew worse, and they became more barbarous as they became more wretched.

Still, de Tocqueville seems to hold out some hope of ultimate "civilization" for the tribes—achieved "by degrees and by their own efforts."

Nevertheless, the Europeans have not been able to change the character of the Indians; and though they have had power to destroy, they have never been able to subdue and civilize them.

The success of the Cherokees proves that the Indians are capable of civilization, but it does not prove that they will succeed in it. This difficulty that the Indians find in submitting to civilization proceeds from a general cause, the influence of which it is almost impossible for them to escape. An attentive survey of history demonstrates that, in general, barbarous nations have raised themselves to civilization by degrees and by their own efforts.

TIME: 1831–1832

HIS PRESCIENT OBSERVATIONS ABOUT FUTURE REGIONAL CONFLICT

While amazed by the American experiment in democracy, de Tocqueville is not oblivious to the underlying conflicts that could bring the nation down.

He picks this up particularly around the nullification crisis that is swirling around during his visit—something he attributes in part to the envy of declining Southern states versus those on the rise in the North.

The states that increase less rapidly than the others look upon those that are more favored by fortune with envy and suspicion. Hence, arise the deep-seated uneasiness and ill-defined agitation which are observable in the South and which form so striking a contrast to the confidence and prosperity which are common to other parts of the Union.

I am inclined to think that the hostile attitude taken by the South recently [in the Nullification Crisis] is attributable to no other cause. The inhabitants of the Southern states are, of all the Americans, those who are most interested in the maintenance of the Union; they would assuredly suffer most from being left to themselves; and yet they are the only ones who threaten to break the tie of confederation.

In addition, the South is losing its control over government decisions at the federal level.

It is easy to perceive that the South, which has given four Presidents to the Union, which perceives that it is losing its federal influence and that the number of its representatives in Congress is diminishing from year to year, while those of the Northern and Western states are increasing, the South, which is peopled with ardent and irascible men, is becoming more and more irritated and alarmed. Its inhabitants reflect upon their

present position and remember their past influence, with the melancholy uneasiness of
men who suspect oppression.

Thus, the South tries to fight back by arguing that tariff laws, especially on raw cotton, are biased against it, and unless these laws are reversed, its only recourse will be to "quit the association."

If they discover a law of the Union that is not unequivocally favorable to their
interests, they protest against it as an abuse of force; and if their ardent remonstrances
are not listened to, they threaten to quit an association hat loads them with burdens
while it deprives them of the profits. "The Tariff," said the inhabitants of Carolina in
1832, "enriches the North and ruins the South; for, if this were not the case, to what
can we attribute the continually increasing power and wealth of the North, with its
inclement skies and arid soil; while the South, which may be styled the garden of
America, is rapidly declining."

De Tocqueville concludes by arguing that what he sees as Southern envy of the North does the region no good. Its potential to "increase more rapidly than any kingdom in Europe" remains. In applying itself against its "true interests" rather than placing blame on the North, the prospect of future war can be averted.

…It must not be imagined, however, that the states that lose their preponderance also
lose their population or their riches; no stop is put to their prosperity, and they even go
on to increase more rapidly than any kingdom in Europe. But they believe themselves
to be impoverished because their wealth does not augment as rapidly as that of their
neighbors; and they think that their power is lost because they suddenly come in
contact with a power greater than their own. Thus they are more hurt in their feelings
and their passions than in their interests.

But this is amply sufficient to endanger the maintenance of the Union. If kings and
peoples had only had their true interests in view ever since the beginning of the world,
war would scarcely be known among mankind.

## 63

NAT TURNER'S SLAVE REBELLION TERRORIZES THE SOUTH AND PROMPTS SAVAGE RETRIBUTION

TIME: AUGUST 21, 1831

NAT TURNER'S REBELLION

On Sunday, August 21, 1831 the apocalyptic vision laid out in David Walker's *Appeal*—of enslaved people murdering their masters to win freedom—becomes reality on Joseph Travis' farm near Jerusalem, Virginia, in the southeast corner of the state.

That night, seven enslaved people use axes to murder Travis, his wife, Sally, and their two children (one a newborn infant) in their beds.

The leader of this band is 30-year-old Nat Turner, an enslaved man whose first master encourages him to read the Bible, which he does over and over until he is able to quote long passages from the Old Testament and begins to preach on the Turner plantation. However, his status changes when his old master dies and his son angers Turner by treating him as an ordinary field hand. When the son also dies, Turner and his wife are sold to different masters. After protesting this separation, his new master whips him savagely, a punishment that further fosters Turner's rage against his fate. Finally, he ends up on the Travis farm, where he acts more passively in order to receive kinder treatment.

But kind treatment no longer transfers into forgiveness for Turner. Since 1828, his lengthy periods of fasting, prayer, and communion with the spirits have convinced him that his destiny lies in "fighting the Serpent" and putting to death those who have stolen the lives of enslaved people.

In February 1831 he interprets a solar eclipse as a signal that the time for retribution is near. Six months later, after secretly spreading the word to other enslaved people in the neighborhood, he strikes at Travis' farm.

Once steeped in the Travis' blood, he and his growing band rampage from one farm to the next.

Back at his original plantation, he kills the cowering Mrs. Turner with his ax and then joins another enslaved person in dispatching a woman visitor.

As he moves on, his force grows. At another farm, some fifteen enslaved people kill Catherine Whitehead, her grown son, three of her daughters, and a grandchild. Nat later confesses to bludgeoning Margaret Whitehead to death with a fence post.

Now 40 strong, Turner and his avengers head toward the town of Jerusalem, where church bells are already sounding the alarm of the insurrection. At the Waller homestead, they pause to decapitate ten children and murder their mother. As they depart, their strength reaches its zenith of 60–70 enslaved people. Some are drunk, others poorly armed, but all are eager to push onward.

The have sacked fifteen homesteads and killed about 60 white people by the time they encounter a series of town posses who break their momentum and force them to retreat. From there the operation turns against the rebels. They try to regroup and add new recruits, but this fails. Most are captured or killed on the spot. Nat Turner escapes and hides for almost two months in the vicinity of the Travis farm, before he too is caught and jailed. At his trial he is nothing but defiant:

> *"I am not guilty, because I do not feel so...I'm not sorry for killing all those white people. I alone conceived the idea of insurrection, which has been evolving in my mind for several years. And, no I didn't fail. Our names are not written in blood across the map of this county, nor will we be the last."*

TIME: 1831 AND ONWARD

ANTIBLACK RACISM IS HEIGHTENED BY TURNER'S RAMPAGE

News of the Turner rampage shocks white people in the North as well as the South, and sets off predictable ripple effects.

Since the entire plantation system in the South hinges on enslaved people's strict obedience to the will of their masters, the Turner incident becomes a moment to reinforce discipline. The vehicle is swift punishment meted out to any enslaved people known or suspected to be troublemakers. Across the South, 55 enslaved people are "officially hanged" and many others are publicly whipped or lynched.

Nat Turner himself is flayed, beheaded, quartered, and ultimately skinned to make "memento purses," which show up years later in estate sales.

State governments across the South also react with laws prohibiting all Black people from being taught how to read or write, and banning religious meetings unless conducted with a white minister present.

In the North, the reactions are different, but no less devastating to the aspirations of the small band of free Black people seeking equality.

Here the lurid details of Turner's assault serve to reinforce the stereotypes of all Black people as subhuman savages, who, if uncontrolled, will slaughter even defenseless women and children.

White fear of Black people is amplified, even among those who feel that slavery is morally wrong. Hearts are hardened and race-baiters become more vocal in their attacks. In Boston, officials tighten their oversight of free Black people. White abolitionists face angry neighbors, for it is one thing to feel empathy for enslaved people, but quite another to advocate to set them free to roam the American landscape at will.

The whipped slave, Gordon

Surely the atrocity in Jerusalem, Virginia must cause these abolitionists to back off from their call for emancipation. Or so the vast majority of white Americans think.

TIME: ANTEBELLUM PERIOD

ADMINISTERING LASHES TO DISOBEDIENT SLAVES

August 2nd 1852—Maryld 33& 1/3rd wrnt 12& ½—returnable
before P. G. Love, sealed under oath. Judgment that the defendant receive

15 lashes. Sum R. Mattingly 5 cents—attend 33 ½—inflicting
Stripes 50—swearing & witnesses 25. Judge 12 ½.

Cost $2.12 ½

Issue Copy
Test
A.B. Holmes (seal)

Throughout the antebellum period, enslaved people charged with violating whatever behavioral norms were imposed on them by state "codes" are subject to punishment.

The document above represents one such event involving the State of Maryland v. Jno Tracy, an enslaved man owned by H.G. Hayden.

It is dated August 2, 1852, and is cast in the form of an "invoice," presumably directed to Hayden by a state judge named P.G. Love and attested to by a notary, A.B. Holmes.

It requires Hayden to pay the state a total of $2.12 and ½ cent in return for formal whipping of Jno Tracy, his slave, evidently administered by one R. Mattingly and resulting in fifteen "stripes."

The invoice itemizes the total cost as follows:

- 5 cents to Mattingly for his presence
- 170 cents to Mattingly for delivering fifteen "stripes"
- 25 cents in administrative costs for swearing and witnesses
- 12 ½ cents to the judge

## 64

MORE TRIBAL LAND EVICTIONS TRIGGERS THE BLACKHAWK WAR

TIME: MARCH 18, 1831

THE MARSHALL COURT DENIES CHEROKEE PLEAS TO KEEP THEIR LAND

Cherokee villages dot the eastern landscape before removal begins

Ever since the end of the Revolutionary War, settlers crossing the Appalachians into land forfeited by Britain have encountered resistance from Native American tribes defending their homelands.

Between 1791 and 1794, US troops are deployed to Ohio and Indiana to defeat the Shawnees.

Then hostility increases during the War of 1812 as the Shawnee, Miami, and other tribes band with the British, hoping to end the US intrusions. Several landmark battles follow, along with growing public animosity toward the tribes. In 1811 General William Henry Harrison defeats a tribal confederation in Indiana at Tippecanoe, and in 1813 Chief Tecumseh is killed along the Canadian border.

General Andrew Jackson then crushes the Red Stick Creeks in 1814 at Horseshoe Bend, Alabama, and in 1818 attempts to drive the Seminoles out of Florida with mixed results.

Various one-sided treaties follow the major tribal defeats with sizable chunks of territory ceded to the US victors. Thus, by the time Jackson becomes president, the wheels have already been set in motion to allow white settlers to usurp the homelands of eastern Indian tribes. Momentum picks up here on December 28, 1828, when the Georgia legislature passes a law transferring ownership of all Cherokee territory to the state.

In May 1830, the Indian Removal Act barely passes the US Congress, with the North opposing it and the South vigorously in support. This Act calls for the forced transfer of the so-called "civilized tribes" from the southeast to their new reservations west of the Mississippi in the Oklahoma territory. The contrived rationale is that relocation will give the Indians a better chance to master agriculture and "become modernized" in their ways. Also, it is claimed that reimbursements in land or cash will be offered to those displaced.

In June 1830, Chief John Ross, backed by Henry Clay and Daniel Webster, seeks an injunction in federal court to stop "the annihilation of the Cherokee tribe as a political society." His argument is based on the notion that the Cherokees are a "foreign nation"—and, as such, not subject to Georgia's jurisdiction or laws.

On March 18, 1831, the Marshall court hands down its ruling in *Cherokee Nation v. Georgia*. It totally ignores the central issue regarding the "fairness" of the Georgia state legislature's action against the Cherokees. Instead, by a 4–2 vote, it denies Ross' "foreign nation" claim and his right to even petition the court for a ruling on the merits of his case.

An Indian tribe or nation within the United States is not a foreign state in the sense of the constitution, and cannot maintain an action in the (federal) courts of the United States.

Therefore, the Indians—like the Africans—are denied citizenship in the United States. Their political identity also disappears in the process, and their status, as Marshall puts it, becomes that of "a ward to its guardian." In this case, the "guardian" will prove forever unsympathetic to their cause.

TIME: APRIL 6 TO AUGUST 2, 1832

SAUK TRIBES FIGHT BACK IN THE BLACK HAWK WAR

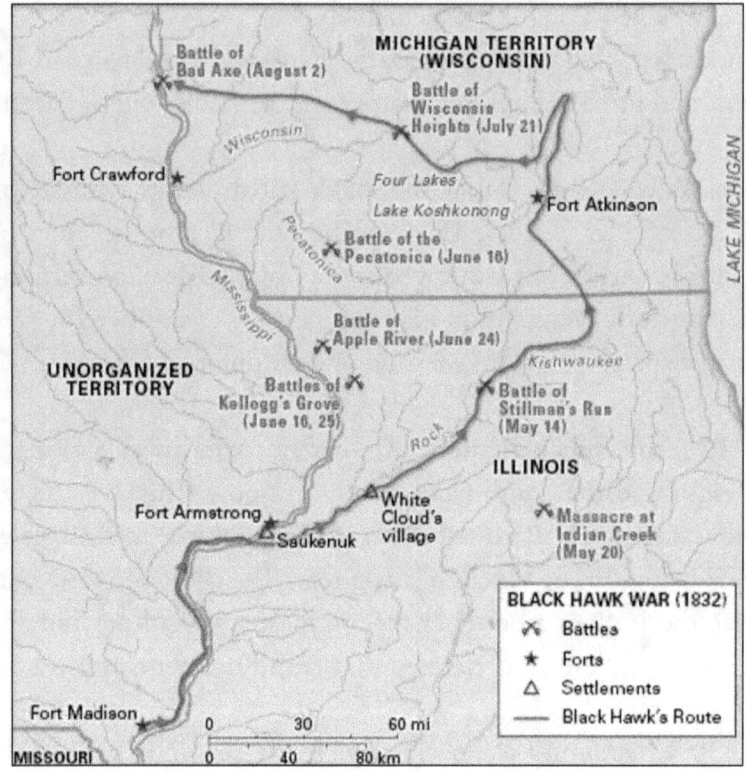

Map of key battles in the Black Hawk War

With the law on his side, Andrew Jackson begins to act against the Native Americans.

In 1831 he orders General Winfield Scott to begin the "removal" process, using regular US Army troops and local militia where needed.

A few tribes decide to resist. One such rebellion breaks out in northwestern Illinois in April 1832.

It is led by the Sauk chief, Black Hawk, who hopes to build a confederation of resisters similar to what the Shawnee Chief Tecumseh achieved in 1811 in the Indiana Territory.

Black Hawk is 65 years old at the time. Since his youth he has fought against the 1804 Treaty of St. Louis which surrendered some five million acres of his homeland, mostly in the southern Wisconsin/Michigan Territory.

During the War of 1812, the British name him a brevet brigadier general, and his Sauks fight alongside the crown to stem the tide of white settlers.

But by June 1831, it seems apparent that his battle is lost, and Black Hawk leads his people west across the Mississippi into the "unorganized territory."

Ten months later he changes his mind. He convinces his Sauk tribesmen to recross the river and reclaim their ancestral lands. To assemble a credible fighting force, he seeks support from a variety of other local nations, including the Kickapoo, Meskwaki, Fox, Ho-Chunk, and Potawatomi nations. Together they hope to form what will be known as the "British Band," given their historic link to the redcoats.

On April 6, 1832, the British Band of roughly 1,000 warriors and their families crosses the Mississippi and heads northeast along the Rock River toward the southern border of Wisconsin.

By May 14 they have traveled 90 miles and reached Old Man's Creek without being joined by any of the allies they anticipated. At this point, with elements of the Illinois militia in his front, Chief Black Hawk is ready to abandon his quest. He sends emissaries to notify the militia of this intent, but they are fired upon.

A melee ensues, with Black Hawk's warriors routing woefully disorganized troops under Major Isiah Stillman. This event is remembered as the Battle of Stillman's Run, ending in humiliation for the Illinois militia leading the governor to call up a force capable of pursuing the Indians.

Over the next ten weeks, Black Hawk fights a series of skirmishes while swinging through southern Wisconsin and eventually retreating toward the Mississippi River. On July 21, the Battle of Wisconsin Heights is fought in Dane County, with remnants of the British Band slipping away to the west. Twelve days later the Black Hawk War ends at the Battle of Bad Axe, where US troops under General Henry Atkinson and Major Henry Dodge wipe out the remaining rebels.

Chief Black Hawk himself is captured and sent to Washington, DC, where he meets with the president before being sent to jail for a short time. There he tells his life story to a reporter who turns it into a biography, making him a celebrity until his death in 1838.

The war which bears his name is also remembered for two famous participants who play cameo roles.

One is 23-year-old Abraham Lincoln, living in New Salem, Illinois and working as a clerk in a village store when he enlists in the Illinois militia. He serves for roughly twelve weeks, mainly as captain of a rifle company in the 31st Regiment out of Sangamon County. Lincoln sees no combat during the war, and later jokes that his greatest challenge was fighting mosquitoes.

The other is 24-year-old Jefferson Davis, graduate of West Point in 1828 and in the Regular Army as a second lieutenant, stationed at Ft. Crawford in Prairie du Chien, Wisconsin. Davis is in Mississippi on furlough during the conflict but is later assigned to escort Chief Black Hawk to Jefferson Barracks near St. Louis.

JACKSON BEGINS HIS ASSAULT ON THE BANKING AND MONETARY SYSTEMS

TIME: 1829–1837

THE PRESIDENT SETS HIS AGENDA FOR FINANCIAL REFORMS

From the time he enters office, Andrew Jackson is determined to put America's financial house back in order.

His instincts in this regard mirror those of Thomas Jefferson, who forty years earlier fought a losing battle to oppose Hamilton's "new American economy" based on capitalism, expanding the "soft money" supply, spending to support industrialization (not just agriculture), and creating the Bank of the United States.

In Jackson's mind, this combination has exposed threats to the nation's financial health.

Too many banknotes (not backed by gold or silver) are now in circulation, leading to wild speculation, inflation, and uncertainty about the true value of the dollar.

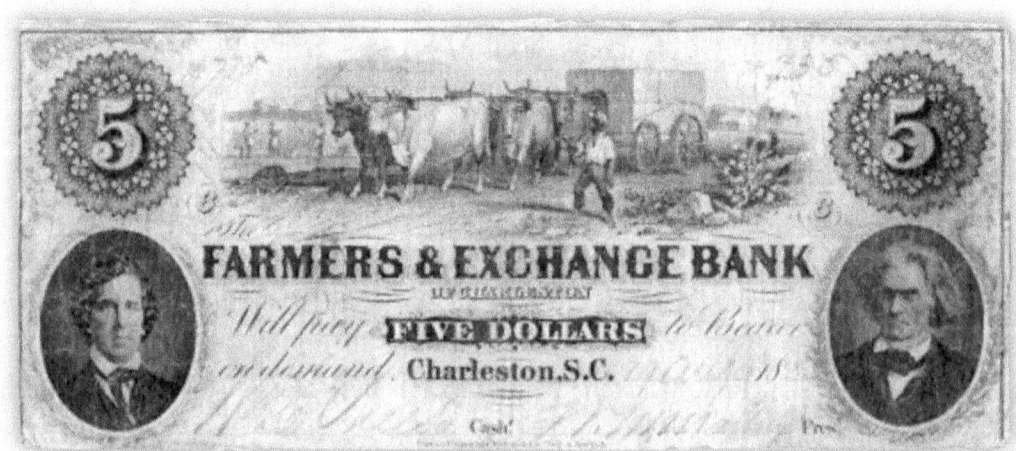

A banknote showing John C. Calhoun

Too much control over the fate of the national economy now rests with a few wealthy men who own the corporation known as the Bank of the United States.

Too much federal spending has now resulted in an alarming amount of federal debt.

In response to these beliefs, Jackson's financial remedies will be threefold:

1. Tighten control over government spending to eliminate the accumulated federal debt.

2. Close the Bank of the United States and deposit all federal revenues it collected into state banks.

3. Ensure the "true value" of the dollar by demanding that banknotes be properly "backed" by gold or silver.

During his tenure, the president will take decisive action on all three fronts.

TIME: 1829–1833

THE FEDERAL DEBT SHRINKS DRAMATICALLY DURING JACKSON'S FIRST TERM

As early as 1824, Jackson calls government debt a "national curse."

Like Jefferson, he arrives at the position that the government is beholden to whichever entities hold the debt and must be reimbursed—a fact which diminishes its freedom to always act on the best interests of the people.

The magnitude of the constraint is in direct proportion to the size of the debt and the political interests of those who actually possess the IOUs.

The worst case here would be a high level of indebtedness to a foreign nation intent on manipulating policies involving America's security. But danger could also lurk in the form of a domestic oligarchy, with government officials influenced by a small cabal who control the debt and use it as a lever to sway their decisions.

Either way, Jackson views the federal debt as hazardous to the nation's well-being.

In 1829, at the beginning of Jackson's first term, the debt level stands at $58.4 million. To begin to drive it down, Jackson ruthlessly cuts government spending while raising revenue through increasing the tariff on imported goods and accelerating sales of federal land.

By 1833, this strategy has reduced the debt by over 90%, down to about $7 million.

HISTORY OF FEDERAL DEBT

YEAR	$ (000)	PRESIDENT
1790	$71,060	Washington
1795	$80,748	Washington
1800	$82,976	Adams
1805	$82,312	Jefferson

YEAR	$ (000)	PRESIDENT
1810	$53,173	Jefferson
1815	$99,834	Madison
1820	$91,016	Madison
1825	$83,788	JQ Adams
1826	$81,054	JQ Adams
1827	$73,987	JQ Adams
1828	$67,475	JQ Adams
1829	$58,421	Jackson
1830	$48,565	Jackson
1831	$39,123	Jackson
1832	$24,322	Jackson
1833	$7,002	Jackson

TIME: DECEMBER 8, 1829

THE PRESIDENT TURNS HIS SIGHTS ON THE BANK OF THE UNITED STATES

With the debt already decreasing, Jackson pivots to dealing with the threat he senses in the Second Bank of the United States.

Again, like Jefferson, Jackson distrusts the BUS because it appears not only to line the pockets of its corporate owners but also give them sway over government spending decisions via their "lending actions."

This concentration of power in the hands of a few private individuals is anathema to the president, and he vows to do away with it in order to:

Prevent a monied aristocracy from growing up around our administration that must bend to its views, and ultimately destroy the liberty of our country.

Jackson launches his attack on the BUS in his first annual message to congress on December 8, 1829. He questions whether the existence of such a bank is valid under the Constitution—despite the affirmation handed down by the Supreme Court in the March 1819 case of *McCulloch v. Maryland*.

At the same time, he announces his growing concerns about the "soft money" supply and his intent to spread future deposits of the government's surplus revenue across both the BUS and various state banks.

The owners of the federal bank view the speech as a warning that Jackson might refuse to renew their corporate charter if he remains president in 1836 when it comes up for renewal.

TIME: 1791–1836

SIDEBAR: HISTORY OF THE FEDERAL BANKS OF THE UNITED STATES (BUS)

Both the First and Second Banks of the United States are corporations chartered by the federal government but privately owned by individual stockholders.

The First Bank of the United States is proposed by Hamilton, backed by Washington, and chartered for twenty years by Congress on February 25, 1791. It is located in Philadelphia, the temporary capital city from 1790 to 1800, while Washington, DC is being built.

After the charter expires in 1811, Madison refuses to renew it. All outstanding shares are purchased by Steven Girard, a former mariner who starts a successful shipbuilding and trading business, and later becomes involved in banking, which makes him fabulously wealthy. Henceforth the Philadelphia establishment becomes known as "Girard's Bank."

As the War of 1812 progresses, Madison faces a critical shortage of cash and offers some $16 million in federal bonds to private investors.

Girard and two other tycoons—John Jacob Astor and David Parrish—purchase most of these securities to fund the war.

When the war ends, these three convince Madison to charter a Second Bank of the United States, with a sizable portion of the shares going to them in exchange for their war bonds. On April 10, 1816, Madison authorizes this Second BUS. He faces opposition from many Jeffersonians, but gains support from Henry Clay and John C. Calhoun.

Aside from its lending role, the Second BUS is also expected to carry out a regulatory duty—ensuring the value and integrity of the nation's paper money supply being printed by state banks.

These state notes flow into the Second BUS on a regular basis to cover payment of federal duties and tariffs. In return for accepting them, the Second BUS requires that each state bank be willing to convert their paper money into gold or silver at any time upon demand.

While this requirement seems foolproof in theory, it quickly falls apart in practice.

As the Napoleonic Wars end, speculators are convinced that demand for American agricultural exports will jump sharply across Europe. What is needed to meet this demand and make a killing along the way is western land, with its surplus of fertile soil. The result is a bidding war for land, with borrowers lining up to secure state banknotes and lenders eager to make loans.

Soon enough, the guidelines on the ratio of state banknotes to gold and silver reserves are breeched; while the target was a 5:1 ratio, it becomes 10:1 in practice.

Instead of enforcing its convertibility mandate, the Second BUS tries to support the state banks by selling off its own supply of gold and silver to them in exchange for their shaky notes.

This artificially props up the state banks until it becomes clear that the forecasted jump in Europe's demand for American agriculture is not materializing. When Britain also begins to import some of its cotton needs from India, the expected boom cycle turns into a bust.

From there, all the dominoes begin to fall.

In August 1818, stockholders in the Second BUS attempt to protect their assets by requiring the state banks to prove they have sufficient gold and silver specie on hand to support the dollar values on their soft money.

In turn, state banks call in loans made to the general public in search of the hard money now being required by the Second BUS. But neither the land speculators nor the average farmer or business owner are able to pay up so precipitously.

Foreclosures and bankruptcies follow, as does unemployment, homelessness, and bank failures. The Panic of 1819 becomes America's first major non-war-related recession.

A mere two years after re-chartering, public trust in the Second BUS plummets.

More bad news follows when fraud is discovered among Second BUS officers in Baltimore, forcing the bank's president, former Secretary of the Navy William Jones, to resign. This is no surprise to the "real financial experts" at the BUS— Girard and Astor—both of whom have questioned Jones' competency from the start.

For the tried-and-true Jeffersonians, the Panic of 1819 is simply more evidence that Hamilton's plan for the US economy is fatally flawed, including his Bank of the United States.

In Andrew Jackson they find just the man to once again shut the BUS down.

## 66

JACKSON ENDS THE NULLIFICATION THREAT FROM SOUTH CAROLINA

TIME: NOVEMBER 18–24, 1832

THE SOUTH CAROLINA LEGISLATURE DECLARES THE FEDERAL TARIFFS NULL AND VOID

As the election of 1832 is playing out nationally, political leaders in South Carolina are beating the drums on behalf of nullifying the 1828 "Tariff of Abominations." One man in particular—28-year-old Congressman Robert Barnwell Rhett—calls the tariff a challenge to Southern "honor," imposed by "insatiable oppressors" in the North, and demanding a courageous response.

Robert Rhett (1800-1876)

But if you are doubtful of yourselves— if you are not prepared to follow up your principles wherever they may lead, to their very last consequence—if you love life better than honor—prefer ease to perilous liberty and glory; awake not! Stir not! Impotent resistance will add vengeance to your ruin. Live in smiling peace with your insatiable Oppressors, and die with the noble consolation that your submissive patience will survive triumphant your beggary and despair.

In turn, South Carolina decides to hold a special convention, running November 19–24, 1832, to address the effects of the 1828 tariff on the cotton industry.

The facts show that the tariff rate indeed jumps from 22.3% in 1825 to 35% by 1830.

US TARIFF RATES

YEAR	1820	1825	1830
Rate	20.2%	22.3%	35.0%
% Change		+10%	+57%

The increases have little obvious effect on the South's production of cotton, which reaches an all-time high of 306.8 million pounds in 1830, a five-fold increase over 1805.

COTTON PRODUCTION

YEAR	1820	1825	1830
LBS. (MM)	141.5	228.7	306.8
% CHANGE		+62%	+34%

But they do depress the prices the South is able to charge for their output.

COTTON PRICES REALIZED

YEAR	1820	1825	1830
CENTS/LB.	16.58	14.36	9.68
% CHANGE		(13%)	(33%)

And they do bring growth in the total value of the cotton crop to a halt as of 1830.

VALUE OF THE COTTON CROP (MILLIONS)

YEAR	1820	1825	1830
VALUE	$235	$309	$297
% CHANGE		+31%	(4%)

As of 1830, the value of the cotton crop—$297 million—is a little over half of the value placed on the South's enslaved population.

VALUE OF ENSLAVED PEOPLE

YEAR	# ENSLAVED (000)	AUCTION PRICE PER PERSON	TOTAL "VALUE" OF SOUTH'S SLAVES
1805	1,032	$222	$229 million
1810	1,191	277	330
1815	1,354	272	368
1820	1,538	393	604
1825	1,758	277	487
1830	2,009	273	548

The convention is dominated by what will become known as the "fire-eaters" and it passes a bill stating that the state will no longer comply with the federal tariff as of February 1, 1833.

We, therefore, the people of the State of South Carolina, in convention assembled, do declare and ordain … that the several acts and parts of acts of the Congress of the United States, purporting to be laws for the imposing of duties and imposts on the importation of foreign commodities… especially, an act…approved on the nineteenth day of May, one thousand eight hundred and twenty-eight and also an act…approved on the fourteenth day of July, one thousand eight hundred and thirty-two, are unauthorized by the constitution of the United States, and violate the true meaning and intent thereof and…shall be held utterly null and void.

TIME: DECEMBER 13, 1832

GOVERNOR ROBERT HAYNE RAISES THE NULLIFICATION STAKES IN HIS INAUGURAL ADDRESS

Since his much-publicized senate debate in January 1830 with Daniel Webster on the "value of the Union," Robert Hayne is elected governor of South Carolina in 1832.

His inaugural address takes place on December 13, with the state legislature's "nullification bill" just three weeks old. He decides to use the occasion to justify the action to Washington and to try to rally other Southern states to join the cause.

His begins with the same broad argument in his Senate speech—that the Constitution guarantees the right of sovereign states to protect their well-being against federal actions that cause them harm.

In the great struggle in which we engaged, for the preservation of our rights and liberties, it is my fixed determination to assert and uphold the SOVEREIGN AUTHORITY OF THE STATE, and to enforce by all the means that may be entrusted to my hands, her SOVEREIGN WILL.

After ten years of unavailing petitions and remonstrances… against a system of measures on the part of the Federal Government fatal to the prosperity of her people… (South Carolina) has made the solemn declaration that this system shall no longer be enforced within her limits.

He challenges "sister states" in the South to decide whether they will stand with South Carolina.

…it is for her sister States, now, to determine, what is to be done in this emergency.

His words then grow more ominous. South Carolina wants peace with the other states, not separation from them. But that will be possible only if limits are placed on the power of the central government.

South Carolina is anxiously desirous of living at peace with her brethren; she has not the remotest wish to dissolve the political bonds which have connected her with the great American family of Confederated States. With Thomas Jefferson, "she would regard the dissolution of our Union with them, as one of the greatest of evils—but not the greatest—there is one greater: SUBMISSION TO A GOVERNMENT WITHOUT LIMITATION OF POWERS;"

A confederacy of sovereign states, formed by the free consent of all, cannot possibly be held together, by any other tie than mutual sympathies and common interest.

If need be, Hayne declares that the state will defend its sovereign rights by force of arms.

The spirit of our free institutions, the very temper of the age, would seem to forbid the thought of an appeal to force, for the settlement of a constitutional controversy. If, however, we should be prepared to meet danger, and repel invasion, come from what quarter it may....

If that fails, the entire South will pay the price along with South Carolina.

If after making those efforts due to her own honor and the greatness of the cause, she is destined utterly to fail, the bitter fruits of that failure, [will fall] not to herself alone, but to the entire South.

To back up his rhetoric, Hayne will go on to assemble a state infantry unit comprising some 25,000 men who will stand at the ready in case of a military response from Washington. This is now a matter of honor, and Hayne is certain that every man will do his duty if called upon.

If the sacred soil of Carolina should be polluted by the footsteps of an invader, or be stained with the blood of her citizens, shed in defense, I trust in Almighty God that… there will not be found, in the wider limits of the state, one recreant son who will not fly to the rescue, and be ready to lay down his life in her defense.

TIME: JANUARY 16 – MARCH 2, 1833

ANDREW JACKSON RESPONDS WITH HIS "FORCE BILL"

In the presence of a threat, especially in the realm of "honor," Andrew Jackson hardly pauses before picking up the challenge from South Carolina.

He may be a fellow plantation owner and slave owner, but first and foremost he is president of the United States, sworn to preserve, protect, and defend the Union.

And he does not mince his words in response to South Carolina's threats.

If a single drop of blood shall be shed there in opposition to the laws of the United States, I will hang the first man I can lay my hands on engaged in such treasonable conduct on the first tree I can find.

To demonstrate his resolve, he sends a message to Congress on January 16, 1833, urging it to pass a bill to slap down any attempts by South Carolina to ignore federal law.

The legislation becomes known as the "Force Bill" for language authorizing Jackson to send US troops into any state that fails to collect the proper tariff on inbound cargo.

In addition, Jackson warns Governor John Floyd of Virginia—who headed the "Nullifier" ticket in 1932—that he will be arrested should he try to impede federal troops marching through his state to South Carolina.

The "Force Bill" becomes law on March 2, 1833, some 28 years before the guns sound at Ft. Sumter.

TIME: MARCH 2, 1833

THE COMPROMISE TARIFF OF 1833 ENDS THE NULLIFICATION CRISIS

On the same day that Jackson signs the "Force Bill" he also signs the "Compromise Tariff of 1833" that resolves the nullification crisis for the moment.

As usual, it is Henry Clay, now in the Senate, who steps forward to craft a solution to the brinksmanship going on between South Carolina and the president.

Clay's position in the controversy is a delicate one. On one hand he wants a sizable tariff to fund his economic development plan for the country, which he calls the "American System." On the other, he learns that Jackson is willing to cut the tariff substantially as long as he doesn't appear to be caving in to a secession threat.

So, how can he find a compromise that maintains reasonably high funding for his plan while resolving the threat of secession and a military response?

Clay's solution is the Compromise Tariff of 1833, in which South Carolina backs off from its nullification threat in exchange for a gradual reduction in the tariff to 20%, phased over a 10-year period.

This compromise passes in the House by a 149–47 margin, is signed by Jackson, and ends the immediate crisis. But the entire episode remains deeply troubling to those intent on maintaining the Union. It signals profound division and animosity between the South and the North.

For astute politicians, it also portends a much more threatening crisis to come—not over taxation, but over slavery. Jackson's instincts in this regard are prescient. Nullification of the tariff was only the pretext for the South's real issue—the "negro question" and secession.

The tariff was only the pretext, and disunion and southern confederacy the real object.
The next pretext will be the negro or slavery question.

Both regions are now digging in once more, much as they did in 1820 around the Missouri statehood crisis.

The South, feeling economically threatened by a federal government no longer in the hands of its Virginia planters, begins to openly discuss breaking with the Union.

The North, wanting nothing to do with the "negro question," begins to assert its growing majority in Congress to bring the "Slave Power" to heel.

In hindsight, the Nullification Crisis of 1832–1833 will prove to be one more dress rehearsal for the Secession Crisis of 1860–1861.

SIDEBAR: HISTORY AND IMPORTANCE OF TARIFFS IN THE US

TARIFF RATES AND NET GOVERNMENT REVENUE GENERATED

YEAR	TARIFF RATE	REVENUE ($MM)	TOTAL US SPENDING	% FROM TARIFF
1800	10.0%	$10.8	$10.8	83.7%
1805	10.7%	$13.6	$13.6	95.4%
1810	10.1%	$9.4	$9.4	91.5%
1815	6.5%	$15.7	$15.7	46.4%
1820	20.2%	$17.9	$17.9	83.9%
1825	22.3%	$20.5	$20.5	97.9%
1830	35.0%	$24.8	$24.8	88.2%
1835	14.2%	$35.8	$35.8	54.1%
1840	12.7%	$19.5	$19.5	64.2%
1845	24.3%	$30.0	$30.0	91.9%
1850	22.9%	$43.6	$43.6	91.0%
1855	20.6%	$65.4	$65.4	81.2%
1860	15.0%	$56.1	$56.1	94.9%

## 67

FOUR PARTIES VIE FOR THE PRESIDENCY IN 1832

TIME: JANUARY 1831

JACKSON ANNOUNCES HIS RUN FOR A SECOND TERM

Despite his promise to serve for one term only, Jackson changes his mind, and in January 1831 the *Washington Globe*—his official newspaper organ edited by Francis Preston Blair—announces that he will run again in 1832.

His opponents have already nicknamed him "King Andrew," for what they regard as his autocratic approach to running the federal government. Their intent is to dislodge him in any way they can.

Three different men from three different political parties will lead the charge against Jackson. Two are very familiar figures on the national stage—Henry Clay and John C. Calhoun.

The third—Thurlow Weed—will achieve fame in the decades ahead, not as a candidate for office, but as a political strategist intent on creating a new Anti-Democrat party capable of winning the White House.

TIME: 1832

HENRY CLAY BECOMES THE FIRST "WHIG PARTY" CANDIDATE

Jackson's principal opponent in 1832 will be his mortal enemy, Henry Clay, who is back in Congress as of November 1831 as a senator from Kentucky.

Clay remains appalled by Jackson's personal comportment, his lack of presidential gravitas, and his willingness to see the executive branch run roughshod over the legislature, which he believes the founders regarded as the dominant branch of government.

Since Adams' defeat in 1828, Clay has established his new "Whig Party" based on the principles laid out in his "American System." But Clay knows that "King Andrew's mobocracy" will be hard to beat in 1832.

Jackson's Democratic Party base centers around the common man struggling to make his way in America: small farmers, western settlers, city laborers, and Irish Catholic immigrants. Its policies call for cheap land prices, opposition to all forms of privilege, and great fiscal restraint to avoid burdening the people with excessive federal spending and taxation.

Clay decides to fight it out with Jackson over management of the economy. He argues that prosperity for all depends on a federal government that invests more money, not less, to support growth.

He says that Jackson is wrong in his *laissez-faire* reliance on individual states to make investments that help America as a whole. Instead, this duty belongs with the federal government.

> *To apply the aggregate industry of our nation...to produce the largest sum of national wealth.*

Rather than relying on exports to maximize wealth, Clay wants to focus on developing a vibrant "home market" for goods.

> *The greatest want of civilized society is a market for the sale and exchange of the surplus of the produce of the labor of its members....The creation of a home market is not only necessary to procure for our agriculture a just reward of its labors, but it is indispensable to obtain a supply of our necessary wants.*

Future economic success also hinges on recognition of the growing power of machinery to complement traditional manual labor.

> *Labor is the source of all wealth; but it is not natural labor only. And the fundamental error of the gentleman from Virginia...consists in their not sufficiently weighing the importance of the power of machinery. In former times, when but little comparative use was made of machinery, manual labor and the price of wages were circumstances of the greatest consideration. But it is far otherwise in these latter times.*

Clay, like Hamilton before him, is in favor of nourishing the manufacturing sector as a necessary path to national wealth.

> *The unprotected manufactures of a country are exposed to the danger of being crushed in their infancy, either by the design or from the necessities of foreign manufacturers.*

Clay's blueprint calls for transforming the nation into an international economic powerhouse by:

- Investing in infrastructure (roads, highways, canals, and schools)
- Supporting a national banking system to distribute capital
- Funding the government through sensible taxation policies

Unfortunately for Clay, his ideas come at a time when most Americans are pleased with the economic results under Jackson.

TIME: 1831–1832

CALHOUN DEDICATES HIS FUTURE TO PROMOTING SOUTHERN STATES' RIGHTS

Once Jackson names Martin Van Buren as his running mate for 1832 and designated heir apparent, John C. Calhoun sets a new political course for himself as the leading national defender of Southern states' rights and the institution of slavery.

His initial launching pad for this new role is the "Nullifier Party," the brainchild of the planter elites in South Carolina who will subsequently be called "fire eaters" for their fierce Anti-Federalist and pro-slavery activities.

Of all the original Southern states, South Carolina is most dependent on slavery for its wealth, and therefore most protective of any federal threats to the institution.

Its values are established at the 1787 Convention by founder John Rutledge, known as "the Dictator," who chairs the

John Floyd (1783–1837)

"Committee of Detail" charged with defining the exact powers of the legislature. Along the way, he makes it crystal clear that South Carolina will resist any federal intrusions related to slavery.

> *I would never agree to give a power by which the articles relating to slaves might be altered by the States not interested in that property and prejudiced against it.*

The state itself prospers throughout the colonial and post-Revolutionary War period, forming large plantations and relying on enslaved labor to bring in a range of crops, initially rice and then cotton. The shape of its population is also unique in that enslaved people make up about 53% of the total residents—a fact that constantly causes fear of rebellion among the white masters.

By the 1820s, however, economic conditions in South Carolina have taken a turn for the worse. The state is hit hard by the 1819 depression and increased competition from plantations in the West operating on more fertile, higher-yielding soil.

Thus, the tariff of 1828 represents one more blow to South Carolina's future prosperity—both for its short-term effect on cotton prices and its potential long-term threat of federal dictates on slavery.

For some leading politicians, John C. Calhoun's "South Carolina Exposition and Protest" of 1828 represents the proper response to any federal laws that are clearly damaging to an individual state: simply pass a state bill "nullifying" them.

Out of this principle, the Nullifier Party is born.

It does not spring from immediate, unanimous agreement in South Carolina. In fact, after Calhoun's document is circulated, roughly half of the state's politicians argue that ignoring federal laws has already been proven to be unconstitutional.

But the "Unionist" faction finally gives way to the prominent South Carolinians who form the core of the Nullifier Party—Calhoun, Robert Hayne, James Henry Hammond, William Preston, George McDuffie, Henry Pinckney, Francis Pickens, and Franklin Elmore.

In 1830, Calhoun declares outright that the South's "peculiar domestick [sic] institution" puts it permanently at odds with the majority of the Union, and that unless it exercises its rights under the Constitution to resist unfair taxation and appropriations, the end will be either civil war or wretchedness.

I consider the tariff act as the occasion, rather than the real cause of the present unhappy state of things. The truth can no longer be disguised, that the peculiar domestick [sic] institution of the Southern States and the consequent direction which that and her soil have given to her industry, has placed them in regard to taxation and appropriations in opposite relation to the majority of the Union, against the danger of which, if there be no protective power in the reserved rights of the states they must in the end be forced to rebel, or, submit to have their paramount interests sacrificed, their domestic institutions subordinated by Colonization and other schemes, and themselves and children reduced to wretchedness.

With the 1832 election looming, the "Nullifiers" must settle on a presidential candidate.

Jackson has already made it clear that he opposes any attempts by individual states to disobey federal laws. Meanwhile, Henry Clay is still associated with John Quincy Adams and is touting his new Whig Party which includes Federalist-like spending on infrastructure that the Nullifiers oppose. This leaves Calhoun as the most likely candidate, but he is too wily a politician to cast his lot with what looks like a fringe faction within the Democrat Party.

In the end, the party nominates 47-year-old John Floyd, a former medical doctor and sitting governor of Virginia. Floyd is an ally of Calhoun, although much less outspoken on slavery than on Jackson, whom he regards as a "tyrant usurper" risking domestic war by denying the sovereign power of the states.

TIME: SEPTEMBER 1830

THURLOW WEED FOUNDS THE ANTI-MASONIC PARTY

Another figure intent on bringing Jackson and the Democrats down is the New Yorker, Thurlow Weed.

Weed is the proverbial self-made man. He grows up on his father's struggling farm in Cairo, New York, which leaves his family "always poor, sometimes very poor." At age eight he works for a blacksmith for 6 cents a day. At ten he earns his "first shilling" as a cabin boy on a Hudson River sloop, with repeat visits to New York City. At twelve, he becomes a printer's apprentice in the village of Catskill. At sixteen he is the quartermaster sergeant of the 40th New York State Militia during the War of 1812. And at eighteen he gets a job as a journeyman printer for the *Albany Register* for $16 a week.

Soon thereafter he begins to write editorials favoring Federalists, particularly New York City mayor DeWitt Clinton. He slides into politics as a member of the New York State Assembly and helps John Quincy Adams achieve victory of Andrew Jackson in the "corrupt bargain" election of 1824.

Thurlow Weed (1797–1882)

During this period, Weed also meets William Seward and forms a lifelong bond that links them politically over the next half century. Both men strongly oppose slavery while shying away from abolitionist zeal.

When "King Andrew" wins in 1828, Weed searches for issues that might attract enough public support to mount a credible attack on the dominance of the Democrats.

His first attempt springs from a mysterious 1826 incident in the western New York town of Batavia that quickly captures the public imagination.

A man named George Morgan is denied membership in a local Free Mason Lodge, and threatens to publish a book revealing its inner workings and secret protocols. He is then evidently kidnapped, and a body, arguably his, washes up on the shore of Lake Ontario.

When Morgan's book, *Illustrations of Masonry*, comes out, it paints a picture of a secret society that appears philanthropic while actually being controlled by "Jesuits and Illuminati who worship Lucifer." It becomes a bestseller and advances a storyline whereby Morgan becomes an American martyr whose right to free speech is denied by a Masonic order bent on undermining Christian religious values.

In 1828, Weed seizes upon the "Morgan affair" and translates it into a political attack on any and all Masons serving in government.

Washington in Masonic garb   Brother Andrew Jackson in the front row

He ignores the fact that George Washington was a renowned Mason, because his true target is "Brother" Andrew Jackson—proud member of St. Tammany Lodge #1 in Nashville, Tennessee since 1800, and an eventual Master of Masons.

To vilify Jackson, Weed launches a newspaper, *The Rochester Anti-Masonic Enquirer*, and forms a new political movement he names the Anti-Masonic Party. Its intent is to exploit two themes that will endure over time with a sizable segment of American voters:

- Fear that everyday citizens may be losing control of their government to secret cabals manipulating policies to satisfy their own separate agendas.

- Growing resentment against Southern slaveholder dominance in national politics, symbolized at the moment by Andrew Jackson of Tennessee.

It argues that all Free Masons must be expelled from public office because their goals and loyalties lie with a secret society whose values conflict with American democracy.

NEW MASONIC TEMPLE, BOSTON.

On September 11, 1830—the anniversary of Morgan's abduction—Thurlow Weed convenes America's first full-fledged "nominating convention" to build a party platform and discuss a potential slate of candidates.

At a second gathering a year later, delegates settle on William Wirt as their presidential candidate. Wirt is a lawyer who gained fame for prosecuting Aaron Burr for treason in 1807 and then for serving as attorney general under Monroe and Adams from 1817 to 1829.

But Wirt is also a deeply flawed choice—he is a former Mason himself, a Southerner from Virginia, and a reluctant candidate who tries repeatedly to back out of the nomination.

Other political figures drawn to Weed's movement include Henry Seward, Thad Stevens, and John McLean.

## 68

ANDREW JACKSON'S SECOND TERM

TIME: NOVEMBER – DECEMBER 1832

JACKSON WINS THE ELECTION OF 1832

Based on the 1830 census, the electoral college map shows sizable gains for the Western states and for those where slavery is banned.

The election is held from November to December 1832 and the voter turnout is up 12% over 1828, rising to nearly 1.3 million voters.

SHIFTING ELECTORAL POWER: OLD/NEW AND SLAVERY/FREE

GEOGRAPHY	1828	1832	CHANGE
Old Established East	196	199	+3
Emerging States West	65	85	+20
Free	147	165	+18
Slavery	114	119	+5

Despite the turmoil surrounding the "Nullification Crisis" and the concerted efforts of the three opposing political parties to bring him down, nothing puts a dent in Jackson's popularity with the public. He wins in a landslide, with 55% of the popular vote and a 223–67 electoral margin.

Clay's National Republicans take only six states. The Nullifier Party wins in one state—South Carolina—where the legislature (not the public) picks the electors. The Anti-Masons garner 8% of the popular vote but also carry only one state, Vermont.

Jackson's victory also bodes well for his secretary of state and long-time confidant, Martin Van Buren of New York, who emerges as a likely successor in 1836.

RESULTS OF THE 1832 PRESIDENTIAL ELECTION

CANDIDATES	PARTY	POPULAR VOTE	ELECTORS	SOUTH	BORDER	NORTH	WEST
Andrew Jackson	Democrat	701,780	223	80	7	97	39
Henry Clay	National Republican	484,205	49	0	23	26	0
John Floyd	Nullifier	0	11	11			

CANDIDATES	PARTY	POPULAR VOTE	ELECTORS	SOUTH	BORDER	NORTH	WEST
William Wirt	Anti-Mason	100,715	7			7	
Total		1,286,700	290	91	30	130	39
Needed to win			146				

The magnitude of Jackson's win is evident in its breadth. He dominates in the North and the East, as well as the South and the West. He is favored in both free states and slavery states.

1832 RESULTS BY REGIONS OF THE US*

	SLAVERY ALLOWED (12)	SLAVERY BANNED (12)	AJ TOTAL
Established Eastern States (15)	52 Jackson 6 Clay 11 Floyd 69 Total	97 Jackson 26 Clay 7 Wirt 130 Total	149 (75%)
Emerging Western States (9)	35 Jackson 15 Clay 50 Total	35 Jackson 0 Clay 35 Total	70 (82%)
AJ Total	87 (73%)	152 (92%)	219 (77%)

*Excluding territorial votes (4)

TIME: 1832

THE DEMOCRATS DOMINATE BOTH HOUSES OF CONGRESS

As was the case in 1828, Jackson's popularity translates into wins for Democrats in Congress.

The tight margin that prevailed during John Quincy Adams' presidency has now widened comfortably in the Democrats' favor.

SEATS IN BOTH HOUSES OF CONGRESS

US HOUSE	1823–25	1825–27	1827–29	1829–31	1831–33	1833–35
TOTAL SEATS	213	213	213	213	213	240
DEMOCRATS	89%	49%	53%	64%	59%	60%
OPPOSITION	11%	51%	47%	36%	41%	40%
US SENATE						
TOTAL SEATS	48	48	48	48	48	48
DEMOCRATS	90%	49%	53%	64%	59%	60%
OPPOSITION	10%	51%	47%	36%	41%	40%
PRESIDENT	Monroe	Adams	Adams	Jackson	Jackson	Jackson

The message here is that the new contenders—be they from Clay, Calhoun, or Weed—will need to find stronger arguments in the future if they hope to unseat the Democrats.

TIME: MARCH 4, 1833

JACKSON'S SECOND INAUGURAL ADDRESS

Jackson is sworn in on March 4, 1833, by Chief Justice John Marshall, who administers the oath in the House chamber of the Capitol.

While the turmoil surrounding South Carolina's tariff nullification threat has been dampened by Jackson's threat of force and a rate compromise, that topic along with the future of the Union are on the president's mind as he delivers his inaugural address.

As usual, the former general is a man of relatively few, but always precise, words.

He begins by expressing his gratitude for the honor of serving again.

Andrew Jackson (1767–1845)

Fellow-Citizens: The will of the American people...calls me before you to...take upon myself the duties of President of the United States for another term. For their approbation of my public conduct through a period which has not been without its difficulties...I am at a loss for terms adequate to the expression of my gratitude. It shall be displayed to the extent of my humble abilities in continued efforts so to administer the Government as to preserve their liberty and promote their happiness.

In regard to foreign policy, he says the nation is at peace and facing "few causes of controversy."

The foreign policy adopted by our Government...has been crowned with almost complete success, and has elevated our character among the nations of the earth. To do justice to all and to submit to wrong from none has been during my Administration its governing maxim, and so happy have been its results that we are not only at peace with all the world, but have few causes of controversy, and those of minor importance, remaining unadjusted.

His focus shifts to the home front, reaffirming his commitment to preserving both the states' rights and the integrity of the Union.

In the domestic policy of this Government there are two objects which especially deserve the attention of the people and their representatives, and which have been and will continue to be the subjects of my increasing solicitude. They are the preservation of the rights of the several States and the integrity of the Union.

A first principle in balancing the two lies in the willingness of the states to obey all laws passed by the federal government. "Nullification" is not an option.

These great objects are necessarily connected, and can only be attained by an enlightened exercise of the powers of each within its appropriate sphere in conformity with the public will constitutionally expressed. To this end it becomes the duty of all to yield a ready and patriotic submission to the laws constitutionally enacted and thereby promote and strengthen a proper confidence in those institutions of the several States and of the United States which the people themselves have ordained for their own government.

At the same time, it is important that the federal government not encroach upon the rights of the states.

My experience…confirm(s)…that the destruction of our State governments or the annihilation of their control over the local concerns of the people would lead directly to revolution and anarchy, and finally to despotism and military domination.… therefore…my countrymen will ever find me…arresting measures which may directly or indirectly encroach upon the rights of the States or tend to consolidate all political power in the General Government.

But what is of "incalculable importance" is ensuring the sacred Union, without which liberty would never have been achieved or could not be maintained.

But of incalculable, importance is the union of these States, and the sacred duty of all to contribute to its preservation by a liberal support of the General Government in the exercise of its just powers. You have been wisely admonished to…indignantly frown upon the first dawning of any attempt to alienate any portion of our country from the rest or to enfeeble the sacred ties which now link together the various parts." Without union our independence and liberty would never have been achieved; without union they never can be maintained.

He turns to his growing concern about "dissolution," arguing that it would lead to the loss of freedom and the end of good government, peace, plenty, and happiness.

Divided into twenty-four, or even a smaller number, of separate communities, we shall see our internal trade burdened with numberless restraints and exactions; communication between distant points and sections obstructed or cut off; our sons made soldiers to deluge with blood the fields they now till in peace; the mass of our people borne down and impoverished by taxes to support armies and navies, and military leaders at the head of their victorious legions becoming our lawgivers and judges. The loss of liberty, of all good government, of peace, plenty, and happiness, must inevitably follow a dissolution of the Union.

He says that the eyes of the world are on America's "existing crisis"—the threat of "nullification"—which must be resolved through a proper mix of "forbearance and firmness" to escape the current dangers.

The time at which I stand before you is full of interest. The eyes of all nations are fixed on our Republic. The event of the existing crisis will be decisive in the opinion of mankind of the practicability of our federal system of government.... Let us exercise forbearance and firmness. Let us extricate our country from the dangers which surround it and learn wisdom from the lessons they inculcate.

He reiterates his ongoing commitment to financial integrity, controlling federal spending and limiting taxation.

At the same time, it will be my aim to inculcate...those powers only that are clearly delegated; to encourage simplicity and economy in the expenditures of the Government; to raise no more money from the people than may be requisite for these objects, and in a manner that will best promote the interests of all classes of the community and of all portions of the Union.

Sensing the growing regional discord, he wishes for compromise and reconciliation "with our brethren in all parts of the country"—with partial sacrifices made by each to preserve the greater good of the whole.

Constantly bearing in mind that in entering into society "individuals must give up a share of liberty to preserve the rest," it will be my desire so to discharge my duties as to foster with our brethren in all parts of the country a spirit of liberal concession and compromise, and, by reconciling our fellow-citizens to those partial sacrifices which they must unavoidably make for the preservation of a greater good, to recommend our invaluable Government and Union to the confidence and affections of the American people.

He ends with a prayer to the Almighty Being on behalf of the nation's continued well-being.

Finally, it is my most fervent prayer to that Almighty Being before whom I now stand, and who has kept us in His hands from the infancy of our Republic to the present day, that He will so overrule all my intentions and actions and inspire the hearts of my fellow-citizens that we may be preserved from dangers of all kinds and continue forever a united and happy people.

TIME: 1789–1861

SIDEBAR: WORD COUNTS FOR THE FIRST SIXTEEN PRESIDENTS' INAUGURAL ADDRESSES

PRESIDENT	DATE	WORDS
George Washington	April 30, 1789 March 4, 1793	1,431 135
John Adams	March 4, 1797	2,321
Thomas Jefferson	March 4, 1801 March 4, 1985	1,730 2,166
James Madison	March 4, 1809 March 4, 1813	1,177 1,211
James Monroe	March 4, 1817 March 4, 1821	3,375 4,472
John Quincy Adams	March 4, 1825	2,915
Andrew Jackson	March 4, 1829 March 4, 1833	1,128 1,176
Martin Van Buren	March 4, 1837	3,843
William Henry Harrison	March 4, 1841	8,460
John Tyler	*Succeeded following Harrison's death*	
James K. Polk	March 4, 1845	4,809
Zachary Taylor	March 5, 1849	1,090
Millard Fillmore	*Succeeded following Taylor's death*	
Franklin Pierce	March 4, 1853	3,336
James Buchanan	March 4, 1857	2,831
Abraham Lincoln	March 4, 1861 March 4, 1865	3,637 700

TIME: MARCH 4, 1833
TO MARCH 3, 1837

OVERVIEW OF JACKSON'S
SECOND TERM

Jackson's second term is largely devoted to finishing up on the goals he set for himself in the first.

He is particularly drawn to initiatives aimed at securing the financial well-being of the nation. These include eliminating the national debt—and in 1835 he becomes the last president in US history who will pay it off entirely.

But, like Jefferson, nothing troubles him more than the monetary and banking systems established by Alexander Hamilton, the perpetual archvillain of the Anti-Federalists. Jackson intuitively fears that simple greed will drive state banks to print an oversupply of soft money unbacked by gold/silver to make speculative loans. He worries that this will result in ruinous inflation and the collapse of America's financial system.

He also believes that the Second Bank of the United States, a corporate entity, concentrates too much power in the hands of a few wealthy capitalists who will prioritize their own interests over the good of the country.

During his second term, Jackson will act on both concerns, first shutting down the Second Bank and then issuing his "Specie Circular" to reestablish the gold standard and the value of the American dollar. The short-run effect of these two moves will be a bank panic that begins in 1837.

The next four years will also see a sharp acceleration in the cession of Native American homelands and the relocation of the eastern tribes to new "reservations" west of the Mississippi. The moves themselves, memorialized as the "Trail of Tears," will forever be associated with Jackson's name.

The issue of US expansion into Mexican territory heats up when American settlers are killed in sieges at the Alamo and Goliad. After responding with a resounding military victory under Sam Houston at the Battle of San Jacinto, the Republic of Texas is founded in 1836. While Congress is eager to recognize and annex Texas, Jackson stalls for wont of starting a war.

Finally, the growth of the abolitionist movement produces social tensions and violent reactions across all regions of the country. By the end of Jackson's second term, the American Anti-Slavery Society will have opened over 500 chapters in the North, the South will attempt to gag the reformers, and Jackson's "sacred Union" will once again be in jeopardy.

KEY EVENTS: ANDREW JACKSON'S SECOND TERM

1833	
March 2	Jackson signs the "Force Bill" and a "Compromise Tariff" to resolve nullification
March 4	Jackson and Van Buren are inaugurated
August 28	Great Britain abolishes slavery in its colonies
September 23	Jackson says government will no longer put federal deposits in the Second BUS
September 26	Roger Taney is named Treasury secretary after predecessor opposes AJ on BUS
December 6	Abolitionists Lewis Tappan and Dwight Weld found the American Anti-Slavery Society
December 26	Clay introduces censure bills against Jackson and Taney for BUS actions
December	Lucretia Mott helps organize the Female Anti-Slavery Society in Philadelphia
All year	Supply of banknotes, unbacked by gold/silver, expands to support west land speculation
1834	
January 3	Stephen Austin arrested after presenting resolution in Mexico to annex Texas
March 28	The Senate supports Clay's bills of censure against Jackson and Taney
April 14	Henry Clay's new political party is christened "Whigs" after Britain's opposition group
April 15	Jackson protests censure bills and vows to defend himself
July 4	An Anti-Slavery meeting in NYC sets off an eight-day anti-Black rampage
October 28	Seminoles ordered to leave Florida as agreed in Treaty of Payne's Landing
November 1	Train from Philadelphia to Trenton starts up
1835	
January 30	Jackson unhurt after assassin's gun misfires as he leaves the House chamber
January	The Whig Party decides to run several regional candidates for president in 1836
May 20	The Democrats nominate Martin Van Buren for 1836
July 6	Supreme Court Chief Justice John Marshall dies; Roger Taney named to succeed him
July 6	Charleston mob burns abolitionist literature and urges a post office ban on it
August 10	An anti-Black mob burns Noyes Academy in Canaan, NY, for admitting Black people
September 13	James Birney and Gerrit Smith strengthen their commitment to emancipation
October 21	Mob parades Lloyd Garrison with rope around his neck after Boston abolition meeting
October 29	A Democrat faction called "Loco Focos" lobbies for urban workingmen's issues
November	A Second Seminole War begins as the Seminole tribe refuses to abandon its lands
December 16	The new Anti-Mason Party nominates William Henry Harrison for 1836 President
December 29	Cherokees sign the Treaty of New Echota to move west in exchange for $5 million

1836	
January 11	Abolitionists present petitions to Congress to end slavery in the District of Columbia
January 27	France finally makes reparation payments to the US for war damages
January	James Birney launches his anti-slavery newspaper, *The Philanthropist*
February 23	The Alamo garrison is overwhelmed by Mexican forces led by Santa Anna (167 die)
March 17	Despite Mexico's ban on slavery, American settlers announce their support for it
March 27	Santa Anna massacres another 300 Americans at Goliad
April 20	Congress splits off the Wisconsin Territory from the old Michigan Territory
April 21	Sam Houston and his Texans defeat and capture Santa Anna at Battle of San Jacinto
May 25	John Quincy Adams delivers House speech opposing Texas annexation for fear of war with Mexico
May 26	Southerners pass "Gag Order" to end reading of anti-slavery petitions in the House
June 15	Arkansas joins the Union as the 25th state
July 1	Congress votes to recognize the Republic of Texas, but Jackson delays fearing war
July 11	Jackson issues the Specie Circular requiring gold/silver to buy federal land to slow inflation
July 12	Mob attacks James Birney's *Philanthropist* office
October 22	Sam Houston sworn in as Texas Republic president
December 7	Martin Van Buren elected president; House election needed to choose Richard Mentor Johnson as vice president
All year	Anti-Slavery Society chapters spread rapidly across the North
1837	
January 26	Michigan is admitted as the 26th state, restoring a 13:13 slavery to free balance in Senate
February 12	Flour warehouse in NYC stormed by mob protesting high cost of housing and food
February 14	Supreme Court affirms community over corporate interest in *Charles River Bridge* case
March 1	Jackson pocket vetoes congressional bill to repeal the Species Circular policy
March 3	Jackson finally recognizes the Republic of Texas on last day in power
March	Cotton prices collapse as concerns about the value of the dollar register globally

The US economy continues to grow nicely throughout Jackson's time in office, including a sharp upswing in 1835 and 1836. But underneath this boom period lies rampant speculation and monetary inflation which is about to usher in a crippling bust cycle to plague Jackson's successor.

KEY ECONOMIC OVERVIEW – JACKSON'S TERMS IN OFFICE

	1829	1830	1831	1832	1833	1834	1835	1836
Total GDP ($000)	930	1022	1052	1129	1158	1219	1340	1479
% Change	4%	10%	3%	7%	3%	5%	10%	10%
Per Capita GDP	74	79	79	83	82	84	90	96

## 69

JACKSON "KILLS" THE SECOND BANK AND PAYS OFF THE FEDERAL DEBT

TIME: SEPTEMBER 23, 1833

JACKSON CRIPPLES THE SECOND BANK BY WITHDRAWING FEDERAL FUNDS

With the "Nullification Crisis" in check, Jackson returns to unfinished financial business from his first term.

Like Jefferson, he is every inch a fiscal conservative—opposed to the burdens and compromises of debt; troubled by "soft money" with its potential for speculation, inflation and unstable dollar values;" and forever suspicious of the Second Bank of the United States.

The Second Bank is established on April 10, 1816 by then President James Madison. It is a private corporation, with 20% of its stock owned by the federal government and the rest largely held by a small group of very wealthy investors. The banks charter calls for it to deposit all funds collected by the federal government and to pay all of its outstanding bills. In addition, it is charged with "regulating the value of dollars in circulation across the US."

This regulatory duty is supposed to be accomplished by making loans of federal money to cash strapped state banks—who can prove they have the proper amount of gold/silver in their vaults to deserve the loans.

Unfortunately the Second Bank, under its initial president, William Jones, proves to be a miserable failure when it comes to protecting the dollar. In pursuit of profits for its own private investors, it prints and loans out a flood of banknotes not properly backed by gold/silver—to support the forecasted boom cycle following the end of the Napoleonic War. When the boom fails to materialize, the regulatory failures of the Second Bank lead on to the financial panic of 1819.

By 1823, savvy Second Bank investors like John Jacob Astor and Stephen Girard, convince Monroe to put Nicholas Biddle in charge, and a major turn-around in operations and results materializes by the time Jackson is first elected. Biddle makes many attempts to convince the President to look favorably upon the revitalized bank.

But Jackson will have none of this.

He is convinced that the bankers use the "monopoly status granted by the public" to enrich themselves and, possibly, even "foreign interests." Also that this great wealth in the hands of a very wealthy few will translate into the power to corrupt the democratic process—in effect, to buy congressmen and votes. And, given the Second Bank's roots in the East, he is forever certain that it operates on behalf of New England over the southern and western states.

He repeatedly refers to the Second Bank of the United States as "The Monster" and sets his sights on "killing it before it kills me."

In his December 1829 address to congress he questions whether, in spite of the 1819 *McCulloch v Maryland* Supreme Court ruling, whether it is really constitutional for the federal government to charter a federal bank. As the hard-core state's rights Virginian Senator John Taylor said a generation earlier:

If Congress could incorporate a bank, it might emancipate a slave.

Congressional supporters of the Second Bank, notably Henry Clay and Daniel Webster, make its fate into an issue in the 1832 race for the presidency – and even pass a bill to immediately renew its corporate charter, four years before it is set to expire. Jackson vetoes this attempt, while asking contemptuously:

Is there no danger to our liberty and independence in a Bank that in its nature has so little to bind it to our country?

With the election won, closing the Second Bank almost becomes an obsession with the President.

To administer the coup de gras he decides to announce that federal funds will no longer be deposited with the Second Bank, but instead be distributed across various state banks.

He asks his own Treasury Secretary, William Duane, to make the announcement, but Duane refuses to comply.

After waiting four months, Jackson fires Duane, replaces him with Roger Taney, and issues the executive order himself, on September 23, 1833.

The order ends all prospects for a re-charter and sends Biddle on a crash mission to protect investors in the Second Bank. Cash on hand at the bank is cut in half within a few months, and to replenish the losses, Biddle "calls in" many outstanding loans, prompting a panic among borrowers, and an effective freeze on making new loans across the country.

TIME: MARCH 28, 1834

CLAY'S CENSURE OF JACKSON IS EFFECTIVELY DEFLECTED

Jackson's critics are apoplectic in the face of his unilateral executive action against the Second Bank.

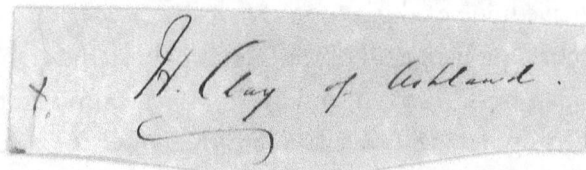

Signature of Henry Clay of Ashland

For Henry Clay, the federal bank is a necessary element in his "American System" plan to fund infrastructure projects, especially roads and canals that cut across state lines.

He argues that, in refusing to sign the bill to re-charter the bank, Jackson has ignored the will of the people and placed the Executive branch above the Legislature.

Clay persuades the Senate on March 28, 1834 to pass a bill of censure against Jackson for "assuming upon himself authority and power not conferred by the Constitution and laws, but in derogation of both."

But once again Jackson outmaneuvers Clay. He lobbies for support in the House, and on April 4 wins approval for all of his actions in closing the Second Bank.

After the Democrats win the 1836 election, the new congress also expunges Clay's censure—closing the chapter on the political controversy.

"King Andrew" has successfully killed the Second Bank for good.

The United States will not see another central bank materialize until 1913, with passage of the Federal Reserve Act, in response to the panic of 1907.

TIME: 1835

JACKSON PAYS OFF THE FEDERAL DEBT

With the Second Bank defeated, the ex-military General serving as President continues his assault on conquering the federal debt.

As in all things, he proves relentless—and in 1835 and 1836 he reaches his goal.

History will show that it is a record event, never to be matched again by any future President or Congress!

HISTORY OF FEDERAL DEBT

YEAR	$ (000)	PRESIDENT
1825	83,788	JQ Adams
1829	58,421	Jackson
1830	48,565	Jackson
1831	39,123	Jackson
1832	24,322	Jackson
1833	7,002	Jackson

YEAR	$ (000)	PRESIDENT
1834	4,760	Jackson
1835	34	Jackson
1836	38	Jackson
1837	337	Van Buren

TIME: 1790–1865

SIDEBAR: LONG-TERM TRENDS ON THE FEDERAL DEBT

Once Jackson exits, the march of the federal debt resumes – reaching heretofore unimaginable levels by the end of the Civil War, despite Abraham Lincoln's imposition of the first personal income tax in August 1861.

HISTORY OF FEDERAL DEBT

YEAR	$ (000)	PRESIDENT
1790	$71,060	Washington
1795	80,748	Washington
1800	82,976	Adams
1805	82,312	Jefferson
1810	53,173	Jefferson
1815	99,834	Madison
1820	91,016	Madison
1825	83,788	JQ Adams
1830	48,565	Jackson
1835	34	Jackson
1840	3,573	Van Buren
1845	15,925	Tyler
1850	63,453	Taylor
1855	35,587	Pierce
1860	64,842	Buchanan
1865	2,680,648	Lincoln

## 70

BRITAIN ABOLISHES SLAVERY

TIME: 1772–1791

OPPOSITION TO SLAVERY GRADUALLY MOUNTS IN BRITAIN

Britain's move away from slavery spans a roughly 60-year period—beginning in 1772 with a King's Bench ruling in *Somerset v. Stewart* that "chattel slavery was unsupported in English Common Law," at least in England and Wales.

From there the abolitionist cause is taken up by William Wilberforce, born the son of a wealthy merchant in 1759, who parties his way through Cambridge University before beginning a 45-year career in Parliament in 1780.

Wilberforce is a typical "hail-fellow-well-met" man in his youth, but then undergoes a spiritual conversion around 1785 while touring Europe with a friend. He starts reading the Bible on a daily basis, reflects on the excesses of his life to date, and seeks spiritual guidance from John Newton, an Evangelical minister in the Anglican Church. Newton counsels him to remain in Parliament but devote himself to promoting Christian causes.

In 1787 Wilberforce bands together with Thomas Clarkson, who has studied for the Anglican ministry and written essays opposing slavery before becoming a founder of the "Society for Effecting the Abolition of the Slave Trade."

Wilberforce and Clarkson, together with Congregationalist minister Dr. Thomas Binney, bring their first anti-slavery bills to Parliament in 1791, and these lead to the end of slave trading in 1807.

But the move to full emancipation takes 30 more years, as opponents argue that Black people are sub-human and actually benefit from their bondage—a view reflected in antebellum America.

TIME: JULY 26, 1833

THE "SLAVERY ABOLITION ACT" PASSES IN PARLIAMENT

After the fall of Wellington's Tory government in 1830, the Whigs take power and resume the push for emancipation. Leading the cause are Prime Minister Charles Grey and Lord Chancellor Henry Brougham.

Acceptance of the final 1833 Act comes after a petition with 187,000 names is submitted by the Ladies' Anti-Slavery Society. This influence of women's groups on abolition (and its first cousin, suffrage) will be repeated in the US.

Consistent with British practice, the bill becomes law after the third reading on the floor of Parliament, which occurs on July 26, 1833—two days after the death of William Wilberforce.

The 1833 Act ends slavery in all British territories with the exception of Ceylon, the island of St. Helena, and provinces controlled by the East India Company (mainly the Indian sub-continent).

Former enslavers are compensated for the emancipation through a special fund of 20 million pounds sterling, an amount that represents almost 40% of the crown's annual budget. The actual amount paid out per freed person varies widely, but the average may have been around 50 pounds, the equivalent of about $250. Records show that many of the elite families of England are recipients of these payouts.

Britain's abolition of slavery comes on the heels of Canada (1804), Spain (1811), and Mexico (1829). France will follow suit in 1848.

Passage of the 1833 Act becomes a message of hope for the still nascent abolitionist movement in America.

PM Charles Grey (1797–1874)   Rev. Thomas Binney (1764–1845)   William Wilberforce (1759–1833)   Henry Brougham (1788–1878)

## 71

THE AMERICAN ANTI-SLAVERY SOCIETY IS FOUNDED

TIME: DECEMBER 6, 1833

THE TWO ABOLITIONIST WINGS JOIN FORCES

In the early 1830s, the two heretofore separate wings of the white abolitionist movements—one in Boston led by Garrison and the other in New York led by Weld and the Tappan brothers—link up to provide more scale and better coordination for the cause.

By December 1833 this pays off in a seminal event—the founding of the American Anti-Slavery Society. The organization takes shape at a meeting held in Philadelphia on December 6, 1833, and is attended by 62 delegates, including 21 Quakers, who are all committed to emancipating the enslaved people.

Garrison drafts a Declaration of Sentiments that lays out the Society's guiding principles. These call for:

- Immediate emancipation of all enslaved people
- Refusal to pay compensation to any "man-stealers"
- Opposition to re-colonization plans
- Efforts to assimilate Black people into white society
- Commitment to achieving these ends peacefully

Arthur Tappan becomes the first president of the Society, and its membership comprises many of the early abolitionist leaders—Theodore Weld, Lucretia Mott, Wendell Phillips, Lucy Stone, Arthur Tappan, Abby Foster, and others.

The Society provides the centralized organizational infrastructure the abolitionists need to accomplish three things:

- Proliferate local anti-slavery chapters from New England to the western territories
- Align the mission and agendas of these chapters with the national priorities
- Coordinate local and national initiatives to maximize public and political attention

Chapters hold regular meetings to hear the latest news from national headquarters and to plan their local campaigns.

The word is spread in a variety of ways.

Public speaking tours feature the Society's leading advocates addressing crowds gathered in local town halls and at Independence Day picnics. These events eventually include moving testimonials from formerly enslaved people and often have a revivalist flair, in search of new converts.

Local newspapers touting abolition rhetoric also begin to spring up, much to the chagrin of citizens who regard the editors as dangerous radicals. While many of these papers are fleeting, a sizable and stable body of writers and publishers backing emancipation will grow over time.

Once up and running, the Society sends out agents to recruit local supporters. By 1840, this number will reach 2,000 chapters with roughly 200,000 members.

TIME: 1835 AND ONWARD

A COURAGEOUS SOUTHERN WOMAN SPEAKS OUT AGAINST SLAVERY

Among the few Southern white people willing to speak out against slavery is Angelina Grimke.

Angelina and her sister, Sarah, are born in Charleston, South Carolina, daughters of a wealthy judge and plantation owner. In a world dominated by men and convention, "Nina" Grimke forms and expresses her own opinions, beginning in childhood.

She is drawn to religious study, converts from her Episcopalian roots to the Presbyterian Church, and teaches Sunday school to enslaved children. The more she reads her Bible, the more convinced she becomes that the slavery she witnesses around her conflicts with Christian moral tenets.

In 1829, at 24 years of age, she stands in front of fellow church members and asks them to end their practice of slavery. When they refuse, her outspoken persistence leads to expulsion, first from the church and then from Charleston society. From this point forward she is an outsider in the South.

True to her character, this outcast status only drives her further into the anti-slavery camp. She and Sarah both adopt Quaker tenets and flee to Philadelphia in 1827. Once there, Angelina becomes a founding member of the radical abolitionist movement, connecting with Garrison and joining the Philadelphia Female Anti-Slavery Society in 1835. Her destiny is now set.

She writes a letter to Garrison in 1835 which he publishes in *The Liberator* as "An Appeal to the Christian Women of the South." The letter includes a carefully crafted review of the history of slavery as outlined in the Bible and its linkage to the American Declaration of Independence.

Its message to the women of the South is clear: those who believe in the teachings of Christ must abandon their support for slavery.

Angelina next trains as an official lecturer for the abolitionist movement and goes on a speaking tour. In 1838 she marries her fellow advocate, Theodore Dwight Weld, and delivers a remarkable testimonial address in Philadelphia as a hostile mob assaults the hall with stones and catcalls.

> As a Southerner I feel that it is my duty to stand up here to-night and bear testimony against slavery. I have seen it—I have seen it. I know it **has horrors that can never be described.** I was brought up under its wing: I witnessed for many years its demoralizing influences, and its destructiveness to human happiness.

> Many times have I wept in the land of my birth, over the system of slavery. I knew of none who sympathized in my feelings—I was unaware that any efforts were made to deliver the oppressed—no voice in the wilderness was heard calling on the people to repent and do works meant for repentance—and my heart sickened within me. Oh, how should I have rejoiced to know that such efforts as these were being made. I only wonder that I had such feelings. I wonder when I reflect under what influence I was brought up, that my heart is not harder than the nether millstone. But in the midst of temptation I was preserved, and my sympathy grew warmer, and my hatred of slavery more inveterate, until at last I have exiled myself from my native land because I could no longer endure to hear the wailing of the slave.

> Many persons go to the South for a season, and are hospitably entertained in the parlor and at the table of the slave-holder. They never enter the huts of the slaves; they know nothing of the dark side of the picture, and they return home with praises on their lips of the generous character of those with whom they had tarried.

> Nothing but the corrupting influence of slavery on the hearts of the Northern people

can induce them to apologize for it; and much will have been done for the destruction of Southern slavery when we have so reformed the North that no one here will be willing to risk his reputation by advocating or even excusing the holding of men as property. The South knows it, and acknowledge that as fast as our principles prevail, the hold of the master must be relaxed.

What if the mob (outside) should now burst in upon us, break up our meeting and commit violence upon our persons—would this be anything compared with what the slaves endure? No, no: and we do not remember them…if we shrink in the time of peril, or feel unwilling to sacrifice ourselves, if need be, for their sake.…There is nothing to be feared from those who would stop our mouths, but they themselves should fear and tremble. The current is even now setting fast against them.

We may talk of occupying neutral ground, but on this subject… there is no such thing as neutral ground. He that is not for us is against us. If you are on what you suppose to be neutral ground, the South look upon you as on the side of the oppressor.

We often hear the question asked, "What shall we do?" Women of Philadelphia! Allow me as a Southern woman with much attachment to the land of my birth, to entreat you to come up to this work. Especially let me urge you to petition. Men may settle this and other questions at the ballot-box, but you have no such right; it is only through petitions that you can reach the Legislature

Men who hold the rod over slaves, rule in the councils of the nation: and they deny our right to petition and to remonstrate against abuses of our sex and of our kind. We have these rights, however, from our God. Only let us exercise them.

Angelina Grimke's heroic break with her pro-slavery upbringing in Charleston serves as inspiration for others, especially women, to join the Abolitionist chorus. She herself will live on to 1879 and witness the rewards of her crusade.

.

## 72

ABOLITIONISTS ARE MET BY ATTACKS IN THE NORTH AND SOUTH

TIME: AS OF 1830

THE VAST MAJORITY OF NORTHERNERS OPPOSE FREEING THE SLAVES

The general public in the North is drawn into the slavery issue by a series of events that touch their lives in one way or another: the 1820 controversy over the admission of Missouri; the week-long revivalist meetings held in their towns; news of the Nat Turner rebellion in Virginia; and the infrequent but vocal calls to end slavery appearing in abolitionist newspapers and town hall meetings.

The vast majority have already made up their minds, based on generations of prejudices.

Those least sympathetic to those enslaved regard Black people as inferior species, incapable of advancement and ready to seek violent revenge against white people if given the chance.

A second, much smaller group exhibits a mixture of guilt and empathy toward enslaved people. They feel it was wrong to bring the Africans to America in the first place and that, while they are by no means "equal" to white people, their continued enslavement is inconsistent with the nation's commitment to freedom for all.

Even so they cannot imagine simply freeing them. The result they predict would be a mass exodus to the North followed not by assimilation, but by increases in poverty, crime, and violence, as well as lower wages for white workers, inter-marriages, and "racial pollution."

Both groups demand "containment"—segregating and controlling Black people in the North and opposing any actions that would allow them to spread beyond the South. In addition, they share a growing resentment toward the Southern "slavocracy" for failing to resolve an issue that is dividing the nation.

Finally, a third group of Northern white people, even more limited in number, convert their empathy with the enslaved people into a willingness to voice their opposition. Some join an anti-slavery chapter, while others become "radical abolitionists."

Like Garrison, they will devote their lives to fighting for immediate emancipation, free migration for Black people, assimilation into white society, and full citizenship.

For their efforts they will be met by public hostility and threats to their lives.

TIME: 1831–1834

RACE RIOTS BREAK OUT IN THE NORTH

The level of antagonism toward Black people and abolitionists in the North is such that even a minor perceived offense can turn into violence.

This is the case in October 1824 in Providence, Rhode Island, when a Black man fails to exhibit proper subservience by not moving off a sidewalk in the presence of oncoming white people. This sparks a race riot, with gangs of incensed white people roaming the segregated Hardscrabble neighborhood, assaulting Black people and destroying upwards of twenty homes.

A similar incident is repeated there in 1831, this time requiring the local militia to stop the attacks.

Then comes the Chatham Street race riot in New York City in the summer of 1834. It springs from an incident involving Lewis Tappan and the Reverend Samuel Cox.

Reverend Samuel Cox (1826–1893)

The impetus is a simple act of kindness on Sunday, June 12, at the Laight Street Presbyterian Church in the notorious "Five Points" district of New York City. When Tappan arrives at the service he encounters a Black minister, Reverend Samuel Cornish, and invites him to sit alongside him in his pew. This causes an immediate stir among other white parishioners, which is then compounded by words from the pulpit.

Reverend Samuel Cox observes the visible hostility toward both Cornish and Tappan and delivers a sermon on the need for goodwill, especially between different races. After all, he intones, it is well-known that the people of the Holy Land—including Jesus himself—were typically dark-skinned.

A hostile press immediately seizes upon Cox's words to fan the flames of antiblack prejudice. Unless radicals like Tappan and Cox can be silenced, white people can expect to have Black people invading their places of worship and ministers asserting that "Jesus was Black." Tensions build from there.

Attempts to hold an abolitionist meeting at the Chatham Street Chapel two blocks south of the Five Points intersection are broken up by angry white mobs on three occasions around the 4th of July.

On July 10 they damage the homes of both Tappan and Cox, and then on the 11th hundreds of white people systematically go about razing the homes, churches, businesses, and welfare centers across the entire Black enclave.

The message here is clear: there is no place in New York City for either abolition or assimilation.

TIME: JULY 6, 1835

THE SOUTH TRIES TO BAN ALL ABOLITIONIST LITERATURE

White Southerners are even more distressed by the abolitionist movement than those in the North.

Of particular concern in the 1830s is the growing number of anti-slavery publications that are filtering into Southern cities through the mail. They are regarded as propaganda efforts by the North, meant to stir up enslaved people and prompt further violence akin to Nat Turner's rampage in Virginia in 1831.

On July 6, 1835, a white mob decides to put an end to this threat. They do so by burning abolitionist tracts outside the Charleston post office and demanding that Charles Huger, the local postmaster, refuse to accept any more anti-slavery materials when they are delivered.

This incident represents the first attempt by the South to officially "gag" the anti-slavery opposition.

Huger contacts Postmaster General Amos Kendall, a Dartmouth graduate close friend of President Jackson, about ordering an end to disseminating anti-slavery materials. Kendall responds by saying he has no legal authority to do so, although he agrees to encourage local offices to do just that, saying:

We owe an obligation to the laws, but a higher one to the communities in which we live.

For many Southerners this is not good enough.

Georgia passes a law in 1835 to impose the death penalty on anyone who publishes material that could provoke an enslaved uprising.

Governor George McDuffie, one of the early secessionist "fire-eaters" from South Carolina, proclaims that:

The laws of every community should punish this species of interference by death without benefit of clergy.

The intensity of these reactions will soon carry the suppression attempts into the political arena in Washington.

TIME: OCTOBER 21, 1835

A WHITE MOB THREATENS TO LYNCH GARRISON

With the American Anti-Slavery Society up and running, Garrison turns his inflammatory rhetoric against what he considers another form of antiblack racism.

On June 1, 1832, he publishes his only book, *Thoughts of African Colonization,* a direct assault on those white people who wish to free the enslaved, but only if they are then put on ships and sent to Liberia.

Colonization, according to Garrison, is nothing more than a ploy by which certain white leaders can appear to embrace anti-slavery idealism, while still holding on to their racist beliefs.

It is one thing to wish to abolish slavery; quite another to support assimilation and Black citizenship. And that is exactly what Garrison demands:

William Lloyd Garrison (1805–1879)

All God's creatures can live in harmony together, of this I am sure.

In May of 1833, a 27-year-old Garrison sails to England to meet William Wilberforce and other abolition leaders and update them on progress in America. On July 12, in an address to a large British crowd at Exeter Hall, he lashes out against his homeland:

America falsifies every profession of its creed in its support for slavery.

When the American Colonization Society reports on Garrison's speech, opponents quickly brand him a traitor to his country, and violent mobs greet him dockside in New York City when he returns home on October 2.

Resistance to abolition also builds in Boston. On September 10, 1835, a burning cross signed by "Judge Lynch" appears on Garrison's front lawn. Six weeks later, on October 21, he is kidnapped by a mob in the city on his way to a lecture event and a hangman's noose is put around his neck. Only a last second rescue by the mayor of Boston saves his life.

The Tappan brothers, Lucretia Mott, and other visible leaders are also attacked.

Even the gentle Unitarian minister William Ellery Channing chides the abolitionists in December 1835 for their "showy, noisy societies" that run the risk of fomenting enslaved rebellions and jeopardizing peace with the Southern states. Characteristically, Garrison responds by calling Channing an "equivocator."

Ironically these attacks draw new supporters to the cause, including James G. Birney and Gerrit Smith, who will eventually steer many abolitionists to search for a political solution.

TIME: JULY 1836

JAMES BIRNEY JOINS THE CAUSE
AND IS ATTACKED IN CINCINNATI

For many years the city of Cincinnati has been a hotbed of racial tension. When James Birney releases his anti-slavery newspaper, *The Philanthropist*, in January 1836, it is greeted with open hostility.

Going all the way back to 1804, one year after Ohio's admission to the Union, the state legislature passes a series of "Black codes" making it clear that Black people are not welcome within the state's border. They are not banned outright—as will be the case with most other new states to the west—but they are required to post an onerous $500 bond to ensure their residence and "proper behavior." Despite the stricture, many enslaved people, especially from Kentucky, flock across the Ohio River seeking relative freedom in towns like Cincinnati.

Birney's new paper is regarded as an invitation for even more Black people to take up residence.

In April 1836, Irish mobs terrorize Black neighborhoods in the city, apparently over competition for low wage jobs. The governor resorts to martial law to end the uproar. But not for long.

The entire month of July is marked by white mob violence against Black people and against Birney himself. On July 12 and again on the 30th, Birney's office is ransacked, his presses broken up and thrown into the river.

Posters offering a $100 bounty for the "fugitive from justice, James Birney"—who they claim is a Black man masquerading in white skin—appear across Cincinnati, and the city council tries to ban further issues of *The Philanthropist.*

However, some white people see these attempts to gag vocal opponents of slavery as an infringement on freedom of speech and decide to speak out in support of Birney.

TIME: 1836

HARRIET BEECHER STOWE AND SALMON CHASE COMMIT

Harriet Beecher Stowe (1811–1896)   Salmon Chase (1808–1873)

The 1836 race riot in particular appalls two prominent residents of Cincinnati.

One is Harriet Beecher Stowe, daughter of the influential Presbyterian minister, Lyman Beecher, who records her fright at seeing "negroes being hunted like wild beasts" during the riots.

The other, Salmon P. Chase, a highly regarded city lawyer, witnesses his sister fleeing to her house for safety and commits himself to reestablishing civil order.

Both will play pivotal roles over the next 25 years in the abolitionist movement.

## 73

THE SOUTHEASTERN TRIBES ARE EVICTED ALONG THE "TRAIL OF TEARS"

TIME: MARCH 1832

THE SUPREME COURT RULES THAT INDIAN TRIBES ARE SOVEREIGN NATIONS

With his campaign against the Second BUS successfully concluded, Andrew Jackson charges after his next priority: forcing the remaining eastern Indigenous tribes to new "reservations" west of the Mississippi River, so that white people can settle on the tribes' land.

This race to occupy Georgia is also accelerated in 1829 by the discovery of gold in the northeastern mountains around Lumpkin County.

The original legal basis for the transfer of land traces to the Indian Removal Act passed in Congress on May 28, 1830.

This, however, is immediately challenged in court by injunctions brought by Henry Clay and Daniel Webster, and the matter ends up with the US Supreme Court. It follows with two contradictory rulings issued a year apart from each other.

The first case, in March 31, is *Cherokee Nation v. Georgia* which denies the claim that Indigenous tribes are "foreign nations." Therefore, they must comply with the congressional act.

But in March 1832, in *Worcester v. Georgia*, the court reverses course, ruling in favor of the tribes by saying that settlers may not occupy Cherokee lands without tribal consent.

Associate Justice Joseph Story expresses relief at the time that justice has finally been served:

Thanks be to God, the Court can wash their hands clean of the iniquity of oppressing the Indians and disregarding their rights.

Former General Jackson is said to have had a very different reaction, and one that will prevail:

John Marshall has made his decision; now let him enforce it!

TIME: DECEMBER 29, 1835

GEORGIA IGNORES THE RULING AND ACQUIRES CHEROKEE LAND IN THE TREATY OF NEW ECHOTA

The state of Georgia simply ignores the federal laws—another act of "nullification"—and supports the land grabs by white settlers.

The president is sufficiently alarmed by the lawlessness to meet with John Ridge, son of a Cherokee chief and educated at the Foreign Mission School in Connecticut, who is acting as counsel for the tribe in Washington, DC.

Jackson assures Ridge that he does not intend to use military force in Georgia, but encourages him to work out a formal treaty to resolve the issue.

Ridge and a subset of Native elders proceed to negotiate the Treaty of New Echota, which legally transfers the Cherokee land. It is signed into law on December 29, 1835, despite opposition from Principal Chief John Ross.

This treaty sounds the death knell for the Southeastern tribes in their efforts to preserve their traditional homelands.

It will also result in the 1839 assassination of John Ridge and his father by the pro-Ross backers who accuse them of betraying their Cherokee heritage.

TIME: 1836 AND ONWARD

THE REMOVAL OF THE EASTERN TRIBES MOVES AHEAD

What happens next is the forced removal of the Cherokees in what becomes known as "the trail where they cried"—later translated into "the Trail of Tears."

In 1836, General Winfield Scott proceeds to drive the remaining Creek resisters in Alabama off their lands. In 1837, he turns to the Choctaws in Mississippi, and in 1838 he leads a force of 7,000 troops against the remaining Cherokees in North Carolina. By 1842, after an expense of nearly $20 million, the wars against the Seminoles are concluded.

**KEY EVENTS RELATED TO THE "INDIAN REMOVAL"
FROM THEIR EASTERN HOMELANDS**

NATIONS	ANCESTRAL HOME	"TRAIL OF TEARS"
Choctaw	Mississippi	About 17,000 moved in 1831, with 3,000–6,000 killed along the way. About 5,500 stay in Mississippi and agree to follow the law, but the white settlers constantly harass them.
Creeks	Alabama	Most moved in 1834, with Scott completing the job in the Creek War of 1836.
Chickasaw	Mississippi	They are concentrated in Memphis in 1837 then driven west and forced to join the Choctaw Nation, until later regaining independent status.
Cherokee	North Carolina	In 1838 Van Buren sends Scott to round up all Cherokees in concentration sites in Cleveland, then drives them west. The Cherokees survive well and their population grows over time.
Seminoles	Florida	The Seminole Wars run from 1817 to 1842, at high cost and with renegade bands finally taking refuge in the Everglades.

A total of around 120,000 people from the so-called "five civilized tribes" are forced to leave their ancestral homes for the new "Indian Territory"—land "reserved" for them in what will eventually become the eastern half of Oklahoma.

Up North, another roughly 90,000 Native people are herded into concentration sites from Memphis to Cleveland, and then transported by wagons and flatboats across the Mississippi to their new reservations.

Of those forced to leave, an estimated 15–25% die from hardship or disease during the exodus.

As America's borders shift into the Louisiana Territory and beyond, local tribes will again be forced to move from their reservations to accommodate the white settlers, often backed by the US Army.

TIME: 1835 AND ONWARD

THE "TRAIL OF TEARS" REPRESENTS THE UNJUST FATE OF AMERICA'S INDIGENOUS TRIBES

In the end, the fate of America's Native peoples is not all that much different from that of the Africans.

Most have greeted the white settlers in peace, helped them navigate the land, and sought favorable relations.

In return, they've gotten empty promises of fair treatment in one inaugural address after another, from Washington through Jackson, each president reneging time and again. High-minded rhetoric quickly gives way to self-interest: the wish to occupy their tribal homelands, the power to make this happen, and justification based on the inherent superiority of the white race.

Some tribes fight back: Tecumseh and the Shawnees in 1813, the Red Stick Creeks in 1814, Blackhawk and the Sauks in 1832, Osceola Seminoles in 1832, and out west, the Comanches and the Sioux. All to little avail beyond the lasting personal honors of counting coup.

As the Africans are enslaved, so too is America's Native population—not in chains, but on reservations.

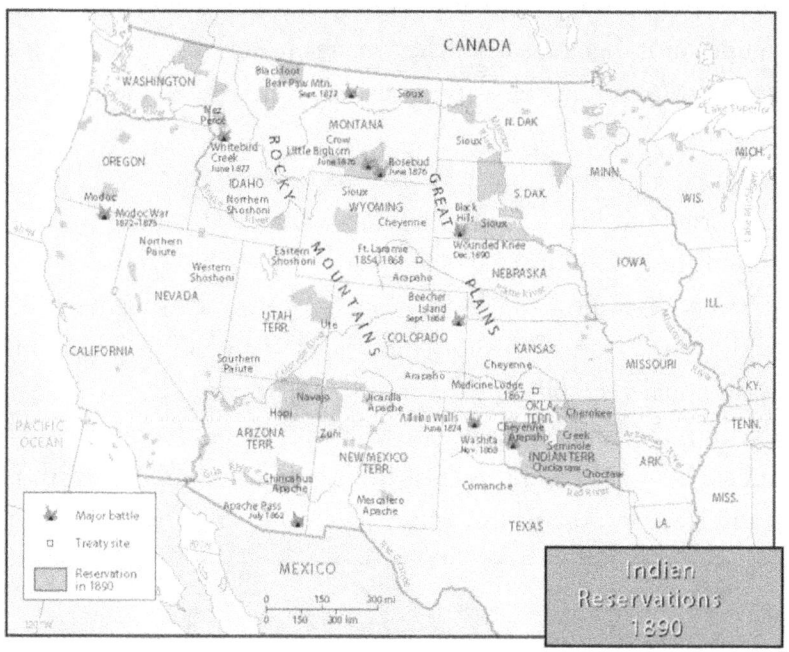

Map of tribal reservations in the West, circa 1890

TIME: JUNE 25, 1876

SIDEBAR: THE TRIBES COUNT COUP ONE LAST TIME AT THE LITTLE BIG HORN

Any residual empathy in the North for the plight of the Indigenous tribes is eroded by events during America's Civil War.

When the conflict breaks out, several tribes who own enslaved people align with the South. Some actually form brigades and engage in the fighting as Confederates—most notably at the 1862 Battle of Pea Ridge in Arkansas. There, both Cherokee and Choctaw warriors fight under the leadership of Albert Pike and

Stand Watie, who is Choctaw himself. Watie grows up in Georgia, is educated, becomes Christian, owns slaves, and eventually is named a Brigadier General in the Confederate Army. As such, he is one of only two Native people of that rank, the other being Ely Parker of the Union Army.

After the Union wins the war, the notion of "Indian independence" vanishes, and the US government is unabashed about coercing all tribes to obey the will of "their great white father" in Washington.

When reservation land is needed to build railroads, DC simply takes it. When gold is found on Indigenous land, they are again "relocated." When tribes, such as the western Cheyenne, need to be moved, other tribes "donate" the needed space.

The Navajo end up in northern Arizona; the Shoshone and Nez Perce in Idaho; the Crow and Blackfeet in Montana; the Sioux in South Dakota; and the Modoc in northern California.

The "treaty revisions" and "relocations" go on until roughly 1889, culminating with white "sooners" rushing into the western half of the original Indian Territory and finally establishing the state of Oklahoma.

In the end, the land "set aside" in 1830 has shrunk by more than half, and it is occupied by a patchwork quilt of Indigenous nations, each with their own cultures and laws, and often with a history of prior conflicts.

George Armstrong Custer (1839–1876)   Chief Sitting Bull (1830–1891)

On June 25, 1876, some Native tribes—this time the Lakota Sioux and the Cheyenne—express their defiance against the white intruders by thrashing General George Armstrong Custer and the Seventh Cavalry at the Little Bighorn River in Montana. After that, the Indigenous nations are forced to retreat to their reservations once again, even as Black enslaved people are being emancipated.

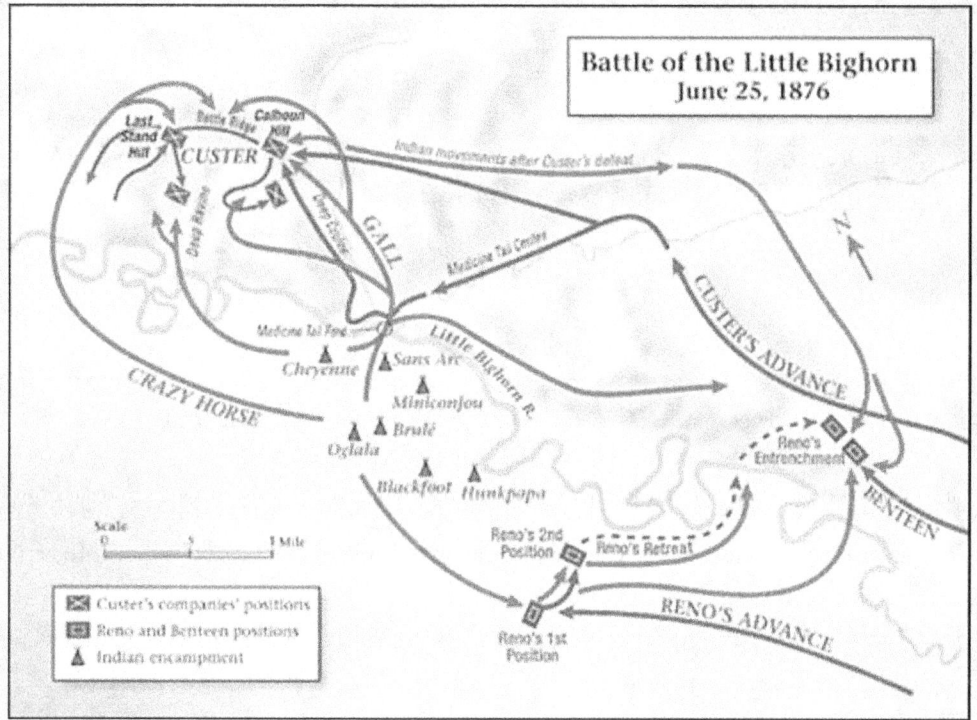

Blunders by an overconfident Custer leads to the loss of 211 men at the Little Big Horn

## 74

JOHN QUINCY ADAMS REFUSES TO COMPLY WITH A HOUSE "GAG RULE" TO SILENCE ANTI-SLAVERY PETITIONS

TIME: MARCH 4, 1831

JOHN QUINCY ADAMS ENTERS THE HOUSE AS AN ANTI-SLAVERY ADVOCATE

After losing to Jackson in 1828, John Quincy Adams retires to his family's "Peace field" mansion in Quincy, Massachusetts. But once there, he grows bored and his friends encourage him to return to Washington.

In 1830, Adams runs for the House of Representatives on the Anti-Masonic ticket and wins the election. He is seated in the House on March 4, 1831, at age 64.

This will be the beginning of a remarkable second chapter in his political life that lasts for almost seventeen years, and where his achievements outshine his time in the presidency.

His return coincides with the rise of organized movements to abolish slavery coming out of the Second Great Awakening. There are two main groups of anti-slavery advocates, each with their own strategy. In Boston, Garrison's approach relies on "moral suasion," with his newspaper and touring lecturers expected to attract more public converts. In New York, the Tappan brothers, Theodore Weld, and James Birney are convinced that political support in Congress will be needed for success.

Together their efforts begin to show up in the form of citizen petitions against slavery which, according to the long-standing rules of the House, are to be read out loud on the floor and then assigned to a standing committee for follow-up responses.

Historically, these petitions related to abolition have trickled into the House one at a time, typically from Quakers. But soon enough, the trickle turns into a flood.

In the name of comity, Northern members hesitate to read the petitions. But not

Adams. Soon enough he is reading these abolitionist pleas in batches of ten or more. All while his Southern colleagues bristle at every word.

TIME: DECEMBER 18, 1835

ADAMS IGNORES A HOUSE "GAG RULE" TO SILENCE THE PETITIONS

Finally, on December 18, 1835, the procedure is challenged on the floor.

The impetus is a petition generated by a local abolitionist society calling on Congress to repeal slavery in the District of Columbia, a territory where the federal government has unilateral control over legal statutes.

As one more appeal from Massachusetts is about to be read on December 18, James Hammond of South Carolina rises to object.

Why, he asks, should the House waste its time on these petitions, since the Constitution specifically guarantees the continuation of slavery? Instead of officially receiving these petitions, shouldn't the rules be changed to ignore them entirely?

Hammond's challenge sets off a fiery debate with Adams. It concludes with a decision to hand the controversy over to the rules committee headed by Henry L. Pinckney, another South Carolina man who supported Calhoun in his nullification challenge.

On May 26, 1836 the Pinckney Committee Resolution is presented:

Whereas it is extremely important and desirable that the agitation on this subject should be finally arrested for the purpose of restoring tranquility to the public mind... resolved that all petitions, memorials, propositions or papers relating in any way... to the subject of slavery or the abolition of slavery, shall, without being printed or referred, be laid on the table and that no further action shall be had thereon.

Adams is outraged by the proposal:

I hold the resolution to be a violation of the Constitution of the US, the rules of this House and the rights of my constituents.

But the proposal passes by a comfortable margin of 117 yea to 68 nay.

Those in opposition henceforth refer to this as the "gag rule" and its actual effect will prove to be very different from the intent of its backers.

Instead of ceasing to send in petitions, the gag rule only serves to spur the abolitionists on—and when received, Adams and others will continue to attempt to bring them up despite the ban.

As time passes, Northerners will come to regard the gag rule as another example of the South trying to unilaterally impose its will on Washington politics.

## 75

AMERICANS LED BY SAM HOUSTON ANNEX TEXAS

TIME: MARCH 1836

A BAND OF SETTLERS FOUND THE REPUBLIC OF TEXAS

Settlers cross the eastern Sabine River border and colonize along the western San Antonio River

Just as Northerners are attempting to "contain" the Black population, Southerners make a bold move on behalf of expansion.

Their target in this case is the Mexican province of Tejas, in roughly the same territory that Aaron Burr tried to invade in 1805 before being arrested for treason. (In later years, as the state of Texas, it will become the nation's number one producer of cotton.)

Controversy over ownership of this land dates back to Jefferson's Louisiana Purchase from France in 1803. America claims that the western boundary of the purchase extends to the Rio Grande River while Spain draws the line much farther east.

The dispute seems settled for good in 1819 with the Adams-Onís Treaty, which acquires Florida from the Spanish and agrees that American territory ends at the Sabine River.

But now Spain makes a tactical error. Because it has been slow to challenge the Comanche and Apache tribes and build settlements in Tejas, it negotiates a deal with an American named Miles Austin. This involves granting Austin some land in Tejas in return for beginning the settlement process. The door is now open a crack to American pioneers.

In 1821 Mexico finally wins independence from Spain, and soon thereafter examines conditions in Tejas.

The result is shock and dismay. Austin's settlers—called Texians—have penetrated all the way from San Jacinto in the east to Goliad and San Antonio de Bexar in the west.

After the Americans try on several occasions to purchase the province from the Mexican government, the Mexicans finally decide to ban further immigration in 1830. But this proves futile and some 38,000 Americans settle in Tejas by 1835, including 5,000 enslaved people, even though slavery has been outlawed across Mexico since 1821.

On March 2, 1836, a convention of settlers declares their independence as a new nation, the Republic of Texas, and elect early settler and political leader David Burnet as their interim president.

TIME: MARCH 5–27, 1836

MEXICO STRIKES BACK AT THE ALAMO AND GOLIAD

Mexico is already trying to regain their land well before the Texians declare their sovereignty.

Initial fighting breaks out in October 1835 with the Mexicans intent on driving the invaders back to the US border at the Sabine River.

In early 1836, their focus is on taking back two fortified garrisons, one at the Alamo in San Antonio de Bexar, the other at Goliad, some 87 miles to the southeast.

Leading the charge against the Alamo is General Antonio López de Santa Anna, a 41-year-old commander who has spent the last fifteen years in the military and in politics, emerging essentially as dictator of the nation.

Santa Anna sets out toward the Alamo in late December and crosses the Rio Grande on February 12, 1836. Eleven days later he is within sight of the Alamo.

A Mexican warrior

The mission is in poor shape to defend itself. Structurally it is designed to hold off small groups of attackers, not an army of 1,800 troops armed with cannon. Conditions are so bad that, in mid-January, Sam Houston sends Sam Bowie to retrieve all artillery and abandon the site. But lacking the needed draft animals for transport, Bowie and Lt. Colonel William Travis decide to try to hold out. They request reinforcements and a few arrive, including former Congressman Davey Crockett. These bring his total troop count to roughly 285 men.

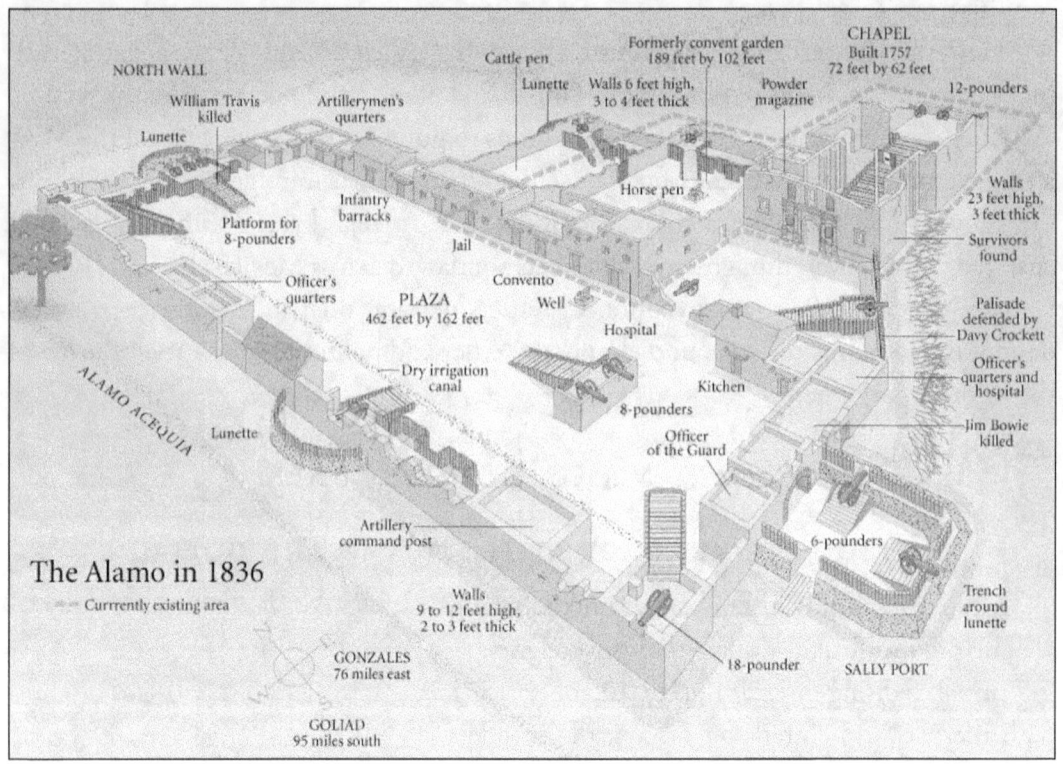

The interior of the Alamo mission defended by the Texians in 1836

Santa Anna surrounds the mission and hauls up a red flag signaling that he intends to take no prisoners.

After a brief siege, Santa Anna attacks the Alamo at 5:30 a.m. on March 5, 1836. The battle lasts for roughly one hour, with the Texians falling back from their outer walls into final defensive positions around the central barracks and church. But they are desperately outnumbered and finally succumb. The entire Texian force is wiped out and their bodies are stacked and burned by the Mexicans.

While Santa Anna is moving overland from the west against the Alamo, a separate Mexican army under General José de Urrea is advancing to the southeast from the Gulf of Mexico. It moves up the San Antonio River and toward the town of Goliad, where Colonel William Fannin commands another small outpost he names Ft. Defiance.

Before Urrea arrives, Fannin is ordered to abandon the fort and retreat west 26 miles to the town of Victoria. But on March 19, Fannin and his army of is surrounded by Urrea's troops on the open prairie. The Texians form a classical Napoleonic square, which holds off the Mexican attacks until nightfall.

Still their situation is hopeless and Fannin surrenders on the morning of March 20—with some 300 survivors marched back to Goliad as prisoners.

What follows becomes known as the Goliad Massacre.

General Urrea pleads with Santa Anna on behalf of fair treatment for the Texian prisoners, but he is rebuffed. On the morning of March 27, 1836, all are shot by Mexican firing squads in the town square.

Santa Anna's ruthlessness here will not be forgotten as the Texians prepare to strike back.

The Alamo mission circa 1901 during a celebration of the Battle of San Jacinto

TIME: APRIL 21, 1836

SAM HOUSTON WINS INDEPENDENCE FOR TEXAS

After the losses at the Alamo and Goliad, the dashing Sam Houston steps in to lead the Texians.

Houston's life has veered in and out of control over the years. He is born in Virginia in 1793, moves to Tennessee at age fourteen, runs away from home to live briefly among the Cherokee and returns to fight in the War of 1812 alongside Andrew Jackson, who becomes his lifelong friend.

After studying law and opening a practice in Tennessee, he is elected to the US Congress from 1823–27, and then becomes governor from 1827–29. He appears ready to follow in Jackson's footsteps when his new marriage suddenly dissolves and he is overtaken by alcoholism. He retreats to live alongside the Cherokee again and marries Tiana Rogers, a Cherokee woman.

Houston regains his bearings and begins the next chapter of his life by moving to Tejas in 1833. Once there he parlays his skills as a lawyer, politician, and military man into a leadership role in the drive for independence. As violence threatens, he is named a major general in the Texas Army and then its commander-in-chief in 1836.

Sam Houston (1793–1863)

After the far western outpost at the Alamo falls, Houston rallies his small army and attacks Santa Anna's forces on April 21, 1836, at the Battle of San Jacinto. The battle is a twenty-minute rout. Houston suffers another of his many war wounds, but Santa Anna is captured and signs a unilateral peace treaty granting Texas its independence.

Houston, henceforth known as "Old San Jacinto," becomes first president of the Republic of Texas on October 22, 1836.

However, the treaty Santa Anna signed to gain his freedom is rejected in Mexico City, leading to ongoing tension and the threat of more conflict.

The Texans turn to hopes for annexation by the United States as a solution to their legitimacy.

TIME: SUMMER 1836

JACKSON SENDS AN EMISSARY TO TEXAS TO ASSESS CONDITIONS

The conflict in Texas and the request for annexation provokes Jackson to send an emissary there in the summer of 1836 to assess the "civil, military, and political conditions" and recommend what action the US should consider taking.

The man chosen for the visit is Henry Mason Morfit, 43 years old, who is born in Norfolk and becomes a practicing attorney before joining the US State Department. Once situated in Texas, Morfit writes a series of ten letters to Jackson over five weeks which describe his findings and "urge against" offering statehood. Two reasons drive Morfit's opinion.

First, he believes the Mexican army is about to gather in force in the spring of 1837 and that it will be able to overwhelm the Texans. Morfit tells Jackson that a commitment to Texas means a commitment to sending US troops into a war against Mexico.

Henry Mason Morfit and granddaughter

> *The old colonists would not by themselves be able to sustain an invasion and, at the same time, supply the means for the war.*

Second, the emissary expresses reservations about the motives underlying the entreaty to Washington.

> *Finally, (there are) suggestions and arguments that this whole enterprise of independence is a mere speculative scheme, concocted and encouraged for the aggrandizement of a few.*

Morfit's main suspicion about the entire Texas "enterprise" is that the Republic is broke and needs federal money to survive.

TIME: SUMMER 1836

JACKSON MAKES A CRUCIAL DECISION AGAINST ANNEXING TEXAS

With the input from Morfit, President Jackson faces one of the most consequential decisions of his entire presidency.

He recognizes that the future of slavery is at the heart of matter, with the South desperately hoping for the annexation and eventual admission to the Union of another pro-slavery state.

But he also knows that such a move would be regarded by those in the North as a surrender to Southerners and would most likely trigger a repeat of the 1820 conflict surrounding Missouri's statehood.

He wisely sees this as a potentially serious threat to the Union he is sworn to pre-
serve, and in turn he rejects Texas' plea for statehood. (Ironically, his protégé and fellow
Tennessean, James Knox Polk, will go ahead and annex Texas in 1845 which leads to the
Mexican War and exactly the kind of North-South schism that Jackson feared.)

## 76

JACKSON'S "SPECIE CIRCULAR" ORDER A MONETARY CRISIS

TIME: JULY 11, 1836

JACKSON ATTEMPTS TO ENSURE THE "TRUE VALUE" OF THE US DOLLAR

From the day he enters office in 1829, Andrew Jackson wars against what he regards as corrupt financial management practices. By 1835 he has recorded two victories: shutting down the Second Bank of the United States and paying off the entire federal debt.

In 1836 he sets his sights on a third objective: protecting the integrity and value of the US dollar against threats he sees from the proliferation of local banks, each allowed to print and issue their own "soft money."

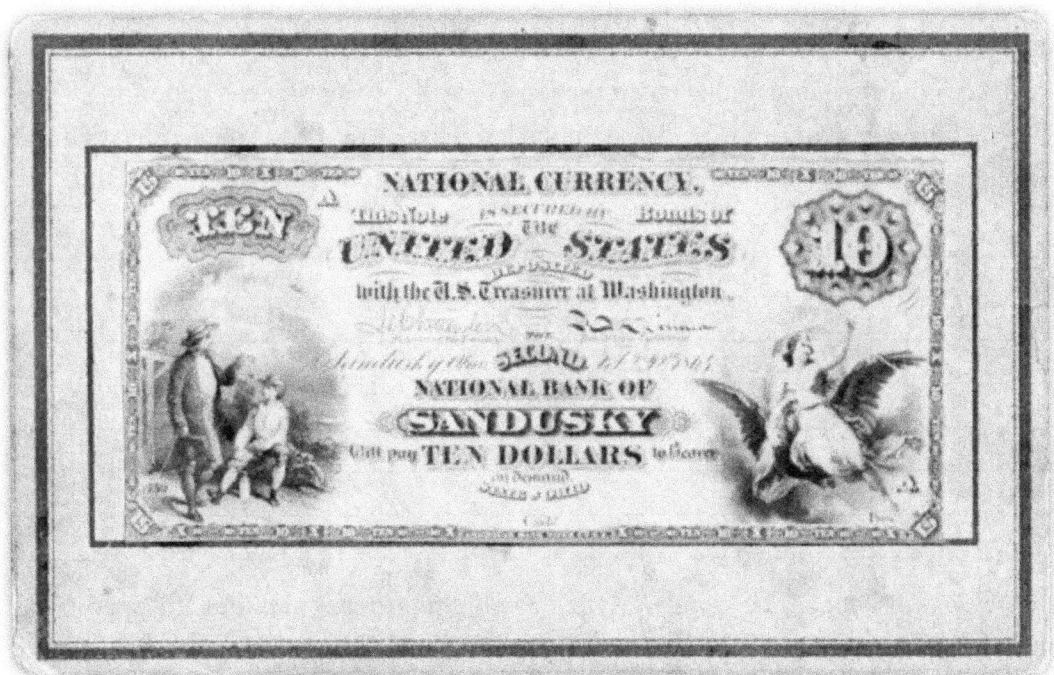

A ten-dollar bill from the Bank of Sandusky, Ohio

Between 1820 and 1835, the number of registered banks in America has more than doubled, and the level of loans outstanding has expanded sevenfold.

ACCELERATED GROWTH IN US BANKING

YEAR	# BANKS	LOANS ($MM)
1820	327	$55.1
1825	330	$88.7
1830	381	$115.3
1835	704	$365.1

The spike in loans signals a spike in personal debt, which is anathema to the fiscally conservative Jackson.

It leads him to reflect again on Hamilton's scheme to fuel capitalism by increasing the nation's money supply. This has been achieved by allowing banks to print a large amount of soft money notes to make loans or investments, with only a small amount of hard gold or silver in their vaults to be "redeemed on demand."

This whole system seems fundamentally flawed to Jackson.

What can the "true value" of the US dollar be if banks no longer have the capacity to redeem each dollar with the "promised amount of hard specie" (minted gold or silver coins)? Beyond that, won't bankers simply print whatever quantities of soft money they deem profitable at any moment in time? And won't this lead to ruinous speculation and debt, not only for the average person—who is often saddled with personal IOUs and inclined to borrow more money than they can repay—but also for the nation?

As a prime example of this, Jackson points to what he regards as the reckless gambles being made in 1835 and 1836 by individuals and bankers on the value of US land.

ACCELERATED SPECULATION IN US LAND

YEAR	$ SALES (000)	% CHANGE
1831	$3,200	
1832	$2,600	(19%)
1833	$3,900	50
1834	$4,800	23
1835	$14,750	307
1836	$24,870	69

What will happen, he wonders, when the bidding frenzy subsides and speculators find that the true value of the land they bought is much less than they thought? And if many of the big speculators are the bank owners themselves, will their debt bring down the financial integrity of the entire country?

One thing Jackson knows for certain is his lifelong distrust of, and disdain toward, bankers in general.

Gentlemen, I have had men watching you for a long time and I am convinced that you have used the funds of the bank to speculate in the breadstuffs of the country. When you won, you divided the profits amongst you, and when you lost, you charged it to the bank. You are a den of vipers and thieves.

He is equally certain that his duty lies in acting before it is too late. He will not leave behind a shaky financial outlook as a legacy when his term is up.

To solve the problem, he must find a way to curtail the rogue printing of banknotes, which fuel speculation, depreciate the real value of the dollar, and result in debt.

He does so by issuing an Executive Order (known as the "Specie Circular") on July 11, 1836 requiring that future purchases of US land by anyone other than actual settlers be paid off in gold or silver, not in banknotes.

Jackson's order rocks the foundation of the financial system in place since Alexander Hamilton's time.

TIME: 1837–1843

THE "SPECIE CIRCULAR" ACTION INITIATES A FINANCIAL PANIC

The "Specie Circular" is widely regarded as a signal that the federal government itself is uncertain about the intrinsic value of the banknotes already in circulation across the economy.

Why else would the president suddenly be asking land investors to pay off their purchases in hard currency rather than soft banknotes?

As this doubt sinks in, the entire economy begins to witness a flight from dollars back into gold and silver—and a contraction of the nation's money supply. The result is a sudden reversal of Hamilton's entire system of "credit" to support capitalism.

A nation accustomed to borrowing money today—to buy property, to run a farm, or to invest in a business—and paying it back with interest later on, now finds that the banks will no longer make these loans. Worse yet, some banks are even demanding that outstanding loans be repaid immediately to protect the assets of their private owners.

What follows is fear, then bankruptcies and foreclosures.

The old general's last campaign has attacked the vulnerabilities of the "fractional" banking system and slowed the tide of both public and federal debt. But not without a cost.

The result will be the second extended depression in US history, one that will continue for almost seven years and have a devastating effect on Jackson's successor, Martin Van Buren.

## 77

ROGER TANEY BECOMES CHIEF JUSTICE OF THE SUPREME COURT

TIME: MARCH 15, 1836

JOHN MARSHALL DIES AND JACKSON NAMES TANEY AS HIS SUCCESSOR

Jackson's second term includes one other legacy that will affect the course of history over the next 28 years: his selection of Roger B. Taney as chief justice of the Supreme Court.

Taney replaces the former chief justice, John C. Marshall, who serves for 34 years and establishes the Supreme Court's status as a co-equal branch of the federal government.

Marshall also proves to be a thorn in the side of Anti-Federalists like his cousin, Thomas Jefferson, and others who follow in the Democratic-Republican Party. He does so by consistently affirming the supremacy of federal laws over state laws, and by extending the scope of cases and issues brought before the court.

Marshall dies on July 6, 1835, and Jackson turns to his longtime friend to fill the vacancy.

Roger Taney (1777–1864)

Roger Taney (pronounced Tawney) is born in 1777, the second son of a wealthy tobacco planter in Maryland. He is a frail youth devoted to his Catholic faith and to his studies. Since his older brother Michael is destined to inherit, their father enrolls Roger at Dickinson College at fifteen, and he graduates from there in 1796.

After further training in the law, he passes the bar in 1799 and opens his own practice in the town of Frederick. His family reputation opens the door to politics for him, and he is elected to the Maryland House of Delegates. He is a staunch Federalist until his support for the War of 1812 accompanies a conversion to the Democratic-Republican camp.

In 1819, his personal circumstances change when Michael Taney stabs a neighbor to death in a fight and then transfers 800 acres of land and thirteen enslaved people to Roger and another sibling in order to protect the family inheritance. A year later, upon his father's death, he frees all of his slaves, and expresses his personal view on the institution:

Slavery is a blot on our national character, and every real lover of freedom confidently hopes that it will be effectually, though it must be gradually, wiped away.

Soon thereafter, Taney becomes an avid supporter of Andrew Jackson and campaigns for him in the "stolen election" of 1824. He then serves as attorney general of Maryland from 1827 to 1831.

His move into national politics comes suddenly in 1831, when President Jackson overhauls his entire cabinet in response to the "petticoat affair" and names Taney his acting secretary of war, a position he holds for ten months. He next serves as US attorney general before Jackson nominates him to become the acting Treasury secretary in 1833, where he seals the fate of the Second BUS. Then, Jackson nominates him for the high court.

The move is met with resistance by those who oppose Jackson at every turn. In January 1835, Clay's Whig supporters deny Taney's nomination to serve as an associate justice on the court.

When the president sends his nomination up again on December 28, 1835, it is still met by stiff opposition from Clay, Calhoun, and Webster. But even that potent combination cannot prevail over a Senate full of Jackson supporters, and Taney is finally confirmed on March 15, 1836.

Taney will go on to become the second-longest-serving chief justice in history, serving for a total of 28 years. His record will place him alongside Marshall and Joseph Story as one of the three greatest justices on the high court. All this despite the criticism registered on the *Dred Scott* ruling in 1857.

TIME: FEBRUARY 14, 1837

COMMUNITY INTERESTS PREVAIL
IN *CHARLES RIVER BRIDGE V. WARREN BRIDGE*

As a justice, Taney is a strict "letter of the law" adherent to the Constitution, and, like Jackson, favors states' rights over federal intrusion.

While he only serves one year out of Jackson's final term, one ruling stands out in particular—that being *Charles River Bridge v. Warren Bridge.*

Here the state of Massachusetts has contracted with the Charles River Bridge Company (CRBC) in 1785 to build a 1,503-foot span connecting Boston to Charleston and saving travelers from an 8-mile roundabout trek. In payment for the bridge, the company is granted rights to collect tolls for a 70-year period, at which time the bridge would become state property.

The bridge proves to be an overnight success, and the original owners eventually reap huge profits by selling their shares to later investors. As the population of Boston grows, so too do the company's profits and the public's complaints about the toll rates being charged. When the new owners refuse to adjust the charges, the state decides to build what will become the nearby Warren Bridge, to be free to travelers after an estimated six-year toll period to pay off the construction costs.

Owners of the Charles River Bridge Company see that this "free" Warren Bridge will end their ability to charge a toll and hence, their source of profits. They view this as a violation of their 70-year contract by the state. They respond with a lawsuit asking the court to prohibit construction of the Warren Bridge.

The case eventually reaches the US Supreme Court in 1831, and it appears that John Marshall and his "pro-business" colleagues are about to side with the company over the state. But administrative matters delay the ruling, and then turnover in the justices, culminating in Marshall's passing, forces the case to be reargued in 1837 with Taney now presiding.

In the interim, the Warren Bridge has actually been built, has achieved a no toll status, and has indeed dried up traffic across the Charles River Bridge.

Despite this outcome, the Taney court votes 5–2 in favor of the state over the CRBC plaintiff.

Taney concludes that the original contract did not overtly grant "exclusivity" to CRBC and that the new Warren Bridge is simply an example of the state doing its job by acting in the best interest of its citizens.

While the rights of private property are sacredly guarded, we must not forget that the community also have rights, and that the happiness and well-being of every citizen depends on their faithful preservation

In regard to the company's lost toll profits, he argues that such outcomes are built into the evolving nature of commerce—canals cut into toll road profits and perhaps the new trains will impact canals in the same fashion. One cannot prioritize company profits over public progress.

Finally, Taney decides that the will of the Massachusetts state legislature should trump any federal issues related to Article I, Section 10: "no state shall pass any…ex-post facto law impairing the obligation of contracts."

A vigorous dissent from Taney is registered by veteran justice Joseph Story. He cites the risks taken by the CRBC investors in building what in 1785 was…

The very first bridge ever constructed, in New England, over navigable tide-waters so near the sea one that many believed would scarcely stand a single severe winter.

And he warns that if the rewards of risking capital are threatened by the state, improving public lives will suffer in return. Massachusetts had a good faith contract with the CRBC and ex-post facto they reneged on it.

I stand upon the old law…and can conceive of no surer plan to arrest all public improvements, founded on private capital and enterprise, than to make the outlay of that capital uncertain and questionable, both as to security and as to productiveness

In 1857 Chief Justice Taney will be involved in another case, *Dred Scott v. Sanford*, that will involve protection of another form of "property"—enslaved people. His decisions here will again prove controversial.

TIME: 1801–1835

SIDEBAR: LEGACY OF THE MARSHALL COURT

SOME OF THE MAJOR DECISIONS MADE BY THE MARSHALL COURT

YEAR	CASE	IMPACT
1803	*Marbury v. Madison*	Judicial review of congressional laws
1807	*Ex Parte Bollman*	Supreme Court power to issue writs/commands to circuit courts
1810	*Fletcher v. Peck*	First overturn of state law, protects property rights contract
1819	*McCulloch v. Maryland*	Implied power of Congress to make necessary and proper laws
1819	*Dartmouth v. Woodward*	Private corporations protected from state interference
1823	*Johnson v. M'Intosh*	Inability of Native tribes to own lands
1823	*Propagation of Faith v. Town of Pawlet, VT*	Corporations are a "group of individuals in perpetuity," with protected rights as such
1824	*Gibbons v. Ogden*	Ends state power to regulate interstate commerce
1825	*The Antelope*	Confirms that enslaved people aboard a ship are legitimate property
1831	*Cherokee Nation v. Georgia*	Indigenous nations as foreign states
1832	*Worcester v. Georgia*	Sanctioning removal of Indigenous tribes
1833	*Barron v. Baltimore*	Bill of Rights cases limited to federal, not state, challenges
1834	*Wheaton v. Peters*	Copyright perpetuity

ANDREW JACKSON'S ENDURING LEGACY

TIME: 1828 AND ONWARD

THE AGE OF JACKSON

Andrew Jackson is remembered as one of America's most ambitious, controversial, and effective presidents. He sets out his grand agenda in his first inaugural address and then proceeds to accomplish nearly every goal he identifies over his two terms.

In hindsight, several of these goals will be judged harshly, especially his cruel uprooting of Eastern Native tribes, his abrupt moves in regard to the Second BUS, and the tightening of the money supply.

His critics will also charge him with expanding the powers of the executive branch far beyond the guidelines laid out in the Constitution. For these men he will forever be cast as "King Andrew."

But what no one can question is his devotion to always doing what he feels is necessary to preserve and protect the sacred Union. Thus, his famous dinner toast in 1829 challenging Calhoun and the "nullifiers:"

Andrew Jackson (1767–1845)

Our Federal union: it must and shall be preserved.

His presidency is truly transformative. It is marked by a series of firsts that forever change the national political scene in America.

- He is the first president elected by the "common man" rather than by land owners only—a change in voting rights that boosts the popular vote from 353,000 in 1824 to 1,287,000 in 1832.

- He is the first "outsider" president, having served only briefly in Congress (1796–98) and never as either vice president or secretary of state. Instead, he sweeps into DC as the "hero of New Orleans" and unabashedly opens his inaugural party at the White House to the public.

- He is the first "western" president, and his election signals the population shift away from the original thirteen east coast states and toward the "new" thirteen inland states.

- He is the first truly "populist president," who sees himself as the protector of the average American against the special interests—especially the "money men" in banking and industry—that he feels are rigging the system in their self-interest.

- He is the first president to accomplish what his predecessors have all called for: elimination of the national debt.

- He is the first president to face a serious threat of Southern secession, stating that the Union is inseparable, and threatening to use force against South Carolina if it violates the federal tariff.

He is also president at a time when the Second Great Awakening is prompting many Americans to face inward in search of social reforms consistent with the founders' vision of a "shining city on a hill." Among these reforms is the abolition of slavery, and during Jackson's tenure the wheels are set in motion by which emancipation will occur and his sacred Union will dissolve.

As a lifelong planter and unrepentant enslaver, he is quick to recognize this threat during the furor over the 1828 tariff. As he says at the time:

The tariff was only the pretext, and disunion and southern confederacy the real object.

The next pretext will be the negro or slavery question.

Like his predecessors, Jackson lacks the know-how to end the sectional tensions he sees developing, with the South needing to carry its enslaved people west of the Mississippi for economic reasons, and the North dead set against allowing any more Black people, enslaved or free, to take up residence in "white men's territory."

But he does have the foresight (despite his personal beliefs) to resist a mad rush to annex Texas, an act certain to reignite the sectional conflict which accompanied the admission of Missouri as a pro-slavery state.

Jackson will also remain true to his role as the voice of the average white citizen, trying his best to protect the well-being of the many from the avarice of the few. As such, his popularity with the "majority" remains untarnished throughout his eight-year term.

TIME: MARCH 4, 1837

HIS FAREWELL ADDRESS WARNS OF DANGERS AHEAD

Like Washington before him, Andrew Jackson feels compelled to summarize his thoughts on the state of the Union in a farewell address which is published on March 4, 1837, the day he leaves office.

The address is lengthy for him, and, while praising the nation's progress to date, he focuses mainly on the dangers that lie ahead.

The president begins by thanking the people for their support, and indicating that America is no longer a "doubtful experiment" but a proven success, "respected by every nation of the world."

FELLOW-CITIZENS: Being about to retire finally from public life, I beg leave to offer you my grateful thanks for the many proofs of kindness and confidence which I have received at your hands...At the moment when I surrender my last public trust I leave this great people prosperous and happy, in the full enjoyment of liberty and peace, and honored and respected by every nation of the world.

We have now lived almost fifty years under the Constitution framed by the sages and patriots of the Revolution. We have had our seasons of peace and of war, with all the evils which precede or follow a state of hostility with powerful nations Our Constitution is no longer a doubtful experiment, and at the end of nearly half a century we find that it has preserved unimpaired the liberties of the people, secured the rights of property, and that our country has improved and is flourishing beyond any former example in the history of nations.

He references early on to the Indian Removal Act as one major advance domestically.

In our domestic concerns there is everything to encourage us, and if you are true to yourselves nothing can impede your march to the highest point of national prosperity. The States which had so long been retarded in their improvement by the Indian tribes residing in the midst of them are at length relieved from the evil, and this unhappy race—the original dwellers in our land—are now placed in a situation where we may well hope that they will share in the blessings of civilization.

In foreign affairs, he says that America is presently enjoying good relations around the world.

If we turn to our relations with foreign powers, we find our condition equally gratifying.

Still, he warns, it is important to recall Washington's admonitions in his farewell, most notably the potential for party politics and sectional disputes to erode the Union.

> *The necessity of watching with jealous anxiety for the preservation of the Union was earnestly pressed upon his fellow-citizens by the Father of his Country in his Farewell Address… and he has cautioned us in the strongest terms against the formation of parties on geographical discriminations, as one of the means which might disturb our Union and to which designing men would be likely to resort.*

Jackson sees these same dangers growing at the moment, dangers which "excite the South against the North and the North against the South." The source of these is a "delicate topic" which stirs "strong emotion." While left unsaid, the president knows that topic to be the institution of slavery.

> *But amid this general prosperity and splendid success the dangers of which he warned us are becoming every day more evident, and the signs of evil are sufficiently apparent to awaken the deepest anxiety in the bosom of the patriot. We behold systematic efforts publicly made to sow the seeds of discord between different parts of the United States and to place party divisions directly upon geographical distinctions; to excite the South against the North and the North against the South , and to force into the controversy the most delicate and exciting topics—topics upon which it is impossible that a large portion of the Union can ever speak without strong emotion.*

The sectional tension over slavery is already infecting the process of choosing the next president and leading to talk of disunion.

> *Appeals, too, are constantly made to sectional interests in order to influence the election of the Chief Magistrate, as if it were desired that he should favor a particular quarter of the country instead of fulfilling the duties of his station with impartial justice to all; and the possible dissolution of the Union has at length become an ordinary and familiar subject of discussion.*

Jackson here elaborates on the many disasters that all Americans would suffer were the Union to come apart.

> *It is impossible to look on the consequences that would inevitably follow the destruction of this Government and not feel indignant when we hear cold calculations about the value of the Union and have so constantly before us a line of conduct so well calculated to weaken its ties.*

The president admits that Congress sometimes passes laws that are unpopular in one region or another, but any attempt to "forcibly resist their execution"—as with the "nullifiers"—must be opposed.

But until the law shall be declared void by the courts or repealed by Congress no individual or combination of individuals can be justified in forcibly resisting its execution. It is impossible that any government can continue to exist upon any other principles. It would cease to be a government and be unworthy of the name if it had not the power to enforce the execution of its own laws within its own sphere of action.

At the same time, he admits that states' rights are to be protected against overreach by the federal government.

It is well known that there have always been those amongst us who wish to enlarge the powers of the. General Government, and experience would seem to indicate that there is a tendency on the part of this Government to overstep the boundaries marked out for it by the Constitution Every attempt to exercise power beyond these limits should be promptly and firmly opposed, for one evil example will lead to other measures still more mischievous.

One example of federal overreach lies in taxation.

There is, perhaps, no one of the powers conferred on the Federal Government so liable to abuse as the taxing power. Congress has no right under the Constitution to take money from the people unless it is required to execute some one of the specific powers intrusted to the Government; and if they raise more than is necessary for such purposes, it is an abuse of the power of taxation, and unjust and oppressive.

The villains behind abuses such as exorbitant tariffs are the "corporations and wealthy individuals" acting in their own self-interest at the expense of the common citizens, along with corrupt politicians who do their bidding.

The corporations and wealthy individuals who are engaged in large manufacturing establishments desire a high tariff to increase their gains. Designing politicians will support it to conciliate their favor and to obtain the means of profuse expenditure for the purpose of purchasing influence in other quarters; and since the people have decided that the Federal Government can not be permitted to employ its income in internal improvements, efforts will be made to seduce and mislead the citizens of the several States by holding out to them the deceitful prospect of benefits to be derived from a surplus revenue collected…

Jackson then talks about the threats he sees lurking in relying on a paper money supply rather than gold and silver coinage, and in the banking industry in general.

The Constitution of the United States unquestionably intended to secure to the people a circulating medium of gold and silver. But the establishment of a national bank by Congress, with the privilege of issuing paper money receivable in the payment of the public dues, and the unfortunate course of legislation in the several States upon the same subject, drove from general circulation the constitutional currency and substituted one of paper in its place.

The evils perpetrated by soft money and unscrupulous bankers fall most heavily on the lower classes.

Some of the evils which arise from this system of paper press with peculiar hardship upon the class of society least able to bear it… the laboring classes of society…whose daily wages are necessary for their subsistence. It is the duty of every government so to regulate its currency as to protect this numerous class, as far as practicable, from the impositions of avarice and fraud.

For Jackson, of course, the leading symbol of this "avarice and fraud" is the Bank of the United States.

But when the charter for the Bank of the United States was obtained from Congress it perfected the schemes of the paper system and gave to its advocates the position they have struggled to obtain from the commencement of the Federal Government to the present hour… The distress and sufferings inflicted on the people by the bank are some of the fruits of that system of policy which is continually striving to enlarge the authority of the Federal Government beyond the limits fixed by the Constitution. The severe lessons of experience will, I doubt not, be sufficient to prevent Congress from again chartering such a monopoly, even if the Constitution did not present an insuperable objection to it.

The common person, the backbone of all that is good in the nation, is forever in danger of losing his liberty and his prosperity to the wealthy and privileged few who control the nation's corporations.

The mischief springs from the power which the moneyed interest derives from a paper currency which they are able to control, from the multitude of corporations with exclusive privileges which they have succeeded in obtaining in the different States… The paper-money system and its natural associations—monopoly and exclusive privileges—have already struck their roots too deep in the soil, and it will require all your efforts to check its further growth and to eradicate the evil…Unless you become more watchful…and check this spirit of monopoly and thirst for exclusive privileges you will in the end find that the most important powers of Government have been given…away, and the control over your dearest interests has passed into the hands of these corporations.

He closes by returning to America's remarkable progress so far, and the duty of those who follow to "preserve it for the benefit of the human race."

The progress of the United States under our free and happy institutions has surpassed the most sanguine hopes of the founders of the Republic. Our growth has been rapid beyond all former example in numbers, in wealth, in knowledge, and all the useful arts which contribute to the comforts and convenience of man, and from the earliest ages of history to the present day there never have been thirteen millions of people associated in one political body who enjoyed so much freedom and happiness as the people of these United States. You have no longer any cause to fear danger from abroad.

Providence has showered on this favored land blessings without number, and has chosen you as the guardians of freedom, to preserve it for the benefit of the human race. May He who holds in His hands the destinies of nations make you worthy of the favors He has bestowed and enable you, with pure hearts and pure hands and sleepless vigilance, to guard and defend to the end of time the great charge He has committed to your keeping.

My own race is nearly run; advanced age and failing health warn me that before long I must pass beyond the reach of human events and cease to feel the vicissitudes of human affairs. I thank God that my life has been spent in a land of liberty and that He has given me a heart to love my country with the affection of a son. And filled with gratitude for your constant and unwavering kindness, I bid you a last and affectionate farewell.

TIME: 1837–1845

THE OLD GENERAL'S FINAL YEARS

Jackson is eleven days shy of his 70th birthday when he leaves the White House.

He has been sickly for years, suffering from assorted ailments. He carries a bullet so near to his heart from his 1806 duel with John Dickinson that surgeons are fearful of removing it. The wound never heals fully, and causes an abscess in his lung leading on to fever, chills, and spitting up blood. In 1813 his left upper arm has been shattered, again by a bullet, this time fired after a tavern brawl incited by the brother of Senator Thomas Hart Benton. During the War of 1812 he suffers a severe bout of dysentery, which becomes chronic in nature. He loses sight in his right eye in 1837 and is frequently racked by stomach cramps and a hacking cough.

Despite these afflictions, he soldiers on, returning to his Hermitage Plantation soon after leaving Washington. His time there is spent organizing his presidential papers and restoring his long-neglected property.

In 1840 he ventures out on his last extended trip, this time to New Orleans to celebrate the 25th anniversary of his victory over the British that brought him national fame.

His heart begins to give out and he is unable to walk by 1844. However, he is still mentally sharp, and begins to work on behalf of James Knox Polk, a fellow Tennessean, in the 1844 race for the Democratic nomination for the presidency.

By May 1845 he is bedridden and fighting constant shortness of breath and swelling from head to toe. The end comes on June 8, 1845, two days after he sends a final note to Polk with his comments on the Oregon crisis.

The president is 78 years old when he passes. He is buried with little fanfare next to his long- deceased wife, Rachel, in the tomb he has designed at the Hermitage.

He is eulogized soon after his death by one Jefferson Davis, who is on the verge of running for Congress at the time.

THE WHIGS PREPARE TO CHALLENGE VAN BUREN IN 1836

TIME: AUTUMN 1836

THE WHIG AND DEMOCRAT PARTY PLATFORMS DIFFER SHARPLY

With Martin Van Buren set to run on the Democrat ticket in 1836, his opponents scramble to organize a credible challenge to his election.

Two of the parties created in 1832 to defeat Jackson—the Anti-Masons and the Nullifiers—have exhibited only limited regional appeal. This means that the race will come down to Henry Clay's Whig Party versus the Jacksonian Democrats.

The platform differences between the two are substantial.

DIFFERENCES BETWEEN DEMOCRAT AND WHIG POLICIES IN 1836

ISSUES	JACKSON'S DEMOCRATS	CLAY'S WHIGS
Political Roots	Jefferson	Hamilton
Political Philosophy	Democracy/common man	Republic/leader class
Core Constituency	Small farmers	Farmers + city wage earners
Core Geography	South + West	Border + Northeast
Labor	Manual power	Manual + machines
Government Power	De-centralized/states' rights	Washington/federal control
Federal spending	Limited/balance budget	Invest in infrastructure
Tariff	Lower and on fewer goods	Higher to protect manufacturers
Land prices	Lower	Higher to fund investments
Money	Hard/specie	Soft/paper
US Bank	Opposed/corporate privilege	Supportive/control currency
Capitalism	Suspicious/elites/corruption	Fundamental to growth

Clay also hopes to broaden the base of the Whig Party by uniting all forces who have opposed the Jackson Democrats, including remnants of the old Federalist and National Republican parties, the New York Anti-Masons, various southerners in the mold of John C. Calhoun, and the pro-business and pro-banking powers across regions.

TIME: AUTUMN 1836

THE WHIGS NOMINATE FOUR REGIONAL CANDIDATES TO SEND THE ELECTION TO THE HOUSE

Having been soundly defeated in 1832, Clay is astute enough to recognize that 1836 is not the time for his name to appear at the top of the ballot.

Instead, he opts for a unique strategy with a Whig ticket built around four candidates, all tied to at least some of the party's core principles, and all possessing regional popularity.

The four Whigs on the ballot are:

- Senator Daniel Webster of Massachusetts, the acknowledged leader of the New England region.
- William Henry Harrison, frontiersman, ex-governor of the Northwest and Indiana Territories, military victor in tribal battles, congressman, diplomat, and currently living on his farm in Ohio. His role in Clay's plan will be to win the far West now that Jackson is off the Democrat ticket.
- Senator Hugh White of Tennessee, a former longtime Jackson supporter who falls out over his belief that the president has failed in the interest of states' rights. White is expected to succeed in the deep South.
- Senator Willie P. Mangum of North Carolina, a momentary Democrat who backs Clay's "American System" objectives and will be asked to campaign in the coastal states of the South.

Clay's hope is that this four-man contingent will deny Van Buren the electoral votes he needs to win outright, and instead throw the final call into the House where a compromise candidate might be chosen—perhaps even himself.

MARTIN VAN BUREN'S TERM

TIME: NOVEMBER – DECEMBER 1836

THE ELECTION OF 1836

Clay's unusual election strategy almost works, but not quite.

Ballots are cast as usual between November 3 and December 7, 1836, with the turnout at 1.5 million voters, up from 1.3 million in 1832.

The winner turns out to be Martin Van Buren, whose margin of victory is only 51% to 49%, a sure sign that Clay's Whig coalition is growing.

1836 PRESIDENTIAL ELECTION RESULTS

CANDIDATES	PARTY	POP. VOTE	ELECTORS	SOUTH	BORDER	NORTH	WEST
Martin Van Buren	Democrat	764,176	170	57	4	101	8
William H. Harrison	Whig	550,816	73	0	28	15	30
Hugh White	Whig	146,107	26	26			
Daniel Webster	Whig	41,201	14			14	
Willie Mangum	Whig	--	11	11			
Total		1,502,300	294	94	32	130	38
Needed To Win			148				

The Democrats carry fourteen states in total, with four pickups from 1832: Rhode Island, Connecticut, Michigan, and Arkansas, the latter two voting for the first time.

The Whigs capture twelve states, with seven additions brought in by the regional favorites: Mangum (South Carolina), White (Georgia and Tennessee), and Harrison (Vermont, New Jersey, Ohio, and Indiana). Meanwhile Webster keeps Massachusetts in the Anti-Jackson column.

The fact that ex-military hero Harrison takes seven states overall and dominates in the West is not lost on Whig Party leaders looking ahead to the 1840 race.

PARTY POWER BY STATE

SOUTH	1832	1836	PICK-UP	EC VOTES
Virginia	Democrat	Democrat		23
North Carolina	Democrat	Democrat		15
South Carolina	Nullifier	Whig (Mangum)	Whig	11
Georgia	Democrat	Whig (White)	Whig	11
Alabama	Democrat	Democrat		7
Mississippi	Democrat	Democrat		4
Louisiana	Democrat	Democrat		5
Tennessee	Democrat	Whig (White)	Whig	15
Arkansas	---	Democrat	Democrat	3
BORDER				
Delaware	Nat-Rep	Whig (Harrison)		3
Maryland	Nat-Rep	Whig (Harrison)		10
Kentucky	Nat-Rep	Whig (Harrison)		15
Missouri	Democrat	Democrat		4
NORTH				
New Hampshire	Democrat	Democrat		7
Vermont	Anti-Mason	Whig (Harrison)	Whig	7
Massachusetts	Nat-Rep	Whig (Webster)		14
Rhode Island	Nat-Rep	Democrat	Democrat	4
Connecticut	Nat-Rep	Democrat	Democrat	8
New York	Democrat	Democrat		42
New Jersey	Democrat	Whig (Harrison)	Whig	8
Pennsylvania	Democrat	Democrat		30
Ohio	Democrat	Whig (Harrison)	Whig	21
Maine	Democrat	Democrat		10
Indiana	Democrat	Whig (Harrison)	Whig	9
Illinois	Democrat	Democrat		5
Michigan	---	Democrat	Democrat	3

A regional analysis shows that Van Buren's win traces to support in Northeast states with high populations and electoral vote counts, most notably New York (42) and Pennsylvania (30).

1836 SHIFTING STATE ALIGNMENTS: OLD/NEW AND SLAVERY/FREE ELECTORAL VOTES

	SLAVERY ALLOWED (13)	SLAVERY BANNED (13)
Old Established East Coast States (15)	Democrats – 38 Whigs – 35	Democrats – 101 Whigs – 29
Emerging States West of Appalachian Range (11)	Democrats – 23 Whigs – 30	Democrats – 8 Whigs – 30

The four larger states west of the Appalachians go for the Whigs—Ohio (21), Kentucky (15), Tennessee (15), and Indiana (9)—while the other seven fall to the Democrats. The thirteen "slavery states" tilt by a slight 7–6 margin in favor of Van Buren.

1836 SHIFTING STATE ALIGNMENTS: OLD/NEW AND SLAVERY/FREE

GEOGRAPHY	DEMOCRATS	WHIGS
Old East Coast States (15)	8 states – 139 votes	7 states – 64 votes
Emerging West States (11)	7 states – 31 votes	4 states – 60 votes
SLAVERY		
Allowed (13)	7 states – 61 votes	6 states – 65 votes
Banned (13)	8 states – 109 votes	5 states – 59 votes

The Democrats are able to retain control over both chambers of Congress in 1836—despite losing a total of sixteen seats in the House.

CONGRESSIONAL ELECTION OF 1836

HOUSE	1834	1836	CHANGE
Democrats	143	127	(16)
Whig	76	102	26
Anti-Masonic	16	7	(9)
Nullifier	7	6	(1)
SENATE			
Democrats	26	35	9
Whigs	24	17	(7)
Nullifier	2	0	(2)

However, the election holds one further surprise, when all 23 of Virginia's electors refuse to cast their votes for Van Buren's designated running mate, Richard Mentor Johnson. The Kentucky congressman has become notorious in parts of the South for declaring that Julia Chinn, an "octoroon" enslaved woman, is his common-law wife.

Virginia's action leaves Johnson short of the 148 votes needed for a majority in the Electoral College, and he assumes the vice presidency only after an affirmative vote in the Senate.

TIME: 1782–1862

PRESIDENT MARTIN VAN BUREN: PERSONAL PROFILE

Martin Van Buren is America's first non-Anglo-Saxon president, the first from New York, and the last Northern president to have grown up in the daily presence of enslaved people.

He is born in 1782 in the Dutch village of Kinderhook, New York, located on the

Hudson River in an area dominated by "patroons"—powerful families—such as the Van Rensselaers and the Livingstons, whose 250,000-acre estates trace to early 17th-century grants. His roots are positively humbling by comparison.

His father owns a small farm along with six enslaved people, and runs a tavern in town. Dutch is spoken at home, and the Van Buren learns it before mastering English. He is a precocious child, but money runs out for schooling and at age thirteen he is apprenticed to a local lawyer.

In 1801 he moves to Manhattan to continue his study and soon comes under the magnetic influence of Aaron Burr, a mentor who will transform his destiny. Burr is already at the peak of his fame, serving as Jefferson's vice president after founding the Tammany Society to ensure his position as godfather of New York politics. While the

Martin Van Buren (1782–1862)

fatal July 1804 duel with Hamilton caps his future, Burr maintains an almost father-son relationship with Van Buren and teaches him the merits of Jeffersonian policies along with the ins and outs of organizing men with diverse interests behind a common cause.

In 1807 Van Buren returns to the Hudson Valley as a new man. He marries, begins to raise a family, and is quickly earning an astonishing $10,000 a year as a lawyer—largely by winning land disputes for small farmers against the powerful patroons who "ran such things" before he joined the scene.

The theme of his law practice—the common man standing up against the power and privilege of the rich—will play out through his career and link him inexorably to both Jefferson and Jackson.

In 1812, at age 29, he enters politics as a state senator by defeating the patrician Edward Livingston.

In Burr-like fashion, he organizes the "Albany Regency," a cadre of like-minded young men who quickly dominate politics in the capital. He reaches a truce with the powerful DeWitt Clinton by backing his Erie Canal project, and in 1821 wins a close election to the US Senate.

Once in Washington, Van Buren sets his sights on transforming the aging Demo-

cratic-Republican apparatus into a modern political machine which he calls "the Democracy." Rather than a loose collection of regional fiefdoms, he envisions a unified
Democratic Party holding national conventions to pick nominees and agree on a platform. Publicity for the candidates would involve a network of supportive journalists and
newspapers. Those who deliver the hard detailed work during a campaign are rewarded
through patronage jobs; "to the victors belong the spoils."

From the beginning, the "sly fox" Van Buren is an excellent vote counter and political strategist. To win the White House and control the national agenda, the Democrats must do two things. First, they have to lock in electoral votes across the entire
South by promising never to interfere with its economically vital practice of slavery.
Second, they must continue to proliferate the Jeffersonian virtues of a small, fiscally
sound federal government dedicated to advancing the interests of yeoman farmers
across the North and West.

Early on, Van Buren recognizes the shift of political power from South to North,
from Virginia to New York, and from slavery states to free states. And he identifies the
associated economic fears felt across Dixieland. What if a Northern-dominated Washington was to suddenly turn against slavery?

New York Congressman James Tallmadge has already signaled this possibility in his
famous anti-slavery amendment during the 1820 debate over the admission of Missouri.
Southerners wonder how this threat, especially from the powerful New Yorkers, can be
kept under control. Who better than the titular head of the Albany Regency?

Starting with his 1824 visit to Jefferson at Monticello, Van Buren tours the South on
behalf of his Democratic Party vision. Ironically, he tries to nominate William Crawford
rather than Andrew Jackson in the 1824 presidential race. But he recovers from this gaffe
and sets his sights on 1828, which lines up perfectly; Jackson completes a New York-Vir-
ginia-Tennessee axis for the Democrats and is up against the dour and vulnerable John
Quincy Adams.

When Jackson wins, he brings Van Buren, his campaign manager, into his cabinet
as secretary of state. Two years later he is in London as US ambassador, and then runs
alongside Jackson as vice president in 1832. The two men become fast friends along the
way, and Van Buren is nominated unanimously at the 1835 Baltimore convention.

TIME: MARCH 4, 1837

VAN BUREN ADDRESSES SLAVERY IN HIS INAUGURAL SPEECH

While Van Buren's inaugural speech is long and tedious, it is remembered for one
startling moment when he openly addresses the highly charged topic of "domestic
slavery."

In doing so, he acknowledges that future political debate in America will be played out within a sectional framework, with the South intent on protecting and expanding slavery and the North seeking to contain it.

He begins by referring to slavery as a "prominent source of discord" and one which the founders treated with "delicacy and forbearance."

Martin Van Buren (1782–1862)

In justly balancing the powers of the Federal and State authorities, difficulties…arose at the outset, and subsequent collisions were deemed inevitable. Amid these it was scarcely believed possible that a scheme of government so complex in construction could remain uninjured.

The last, perhaps the greatest, of the prominent sources of discord and disaster supposed to lurk in our political condition was the institution of domestic slavery. Our forefathers were deeply impressed with the delicacy of this subject, and they treated it with forbearance so evidently wise that in spite of every sinister foreboding it never until the present period disturbed the tranquility of our common country.

But he now feels that the current "violence of excited passions" evident in Congress—presumably the angry floor debates on abolishing slavery in the federal District of Columbia—must now be addressed.

Recent events (have) made it obvious… that the least deviation from this spirit of forbearance is injurious to every interest, that of humanity included. Amidst the violence of excited passions this generous and fraternal feeling has been sometimes disregarded; and I can not refrain from anxiously invoking my fellow-citizens never to be deaf to its dictates.

Perceiving before my election the deep interest this subject was beginning to excite,

I believed it a solemn duty fully to make known my sentiments in regard to it, and now, when every motive for misrepresentation has passed away, I trust that they will be candidly weighed and understood.

At this point, Van Buren announces his stance on slavery. He calls himself an "uncompromising opponent of every effort to abolish slavery in DC" and has decided to "resist the slightest interference with it in the states where it exists."

All of this of course is music to the ears of his Southern constituency.

I must go into the Presidential chair the inflexible and uncompromising opponent of every attempt on the part of Congress to abolish slavery in the District of Columbia against the wishes of the slaveholding States, and also with a determination equally decided to resist the slightest interference with it in the States where it exists.

The (election) result authorizes me to believe that (this view) has been approved by a majority of the people of the United States, including those whom they most immediately affect. It now only remains to add that no bill conflicting with these views can ever receive my constitutional sanction. These opinions have been adopted in the firm belief that they are in accordance with the spirit that actuated the venerated fathers of the Republic, and that succeeding experience has proved them to be humane, patriotic, expedient, honorable, and just.

From there he expresses his confidence that the recent agitation around slavery has failed to threaten "the stability our institutions" or of the government itself.

If the agitation of this subject was intended to reach the stability of our institutions, enough has occurred to show that it has signally failed, and that in this as in every other instance the apprehensions of the timid and the hopes of the wicked for the destruction of our Government are again destined to be disappointed.

After all, he says, slavery is simply one more obstacle of the many America has already overcome on the road to prosperity secured by the Constitution.

We look back on obstacles avoided and dangers overcome, on expectations more than realized and prosperity perfectly secured.

But has prosperity been perfectly secured?

Within thirteen days of Van Buren's optimistic address, a New York financier named Philip Hone writes, "The great (financial) crisis is near at hand, if it has not already arrived."

Much to the new president's chagrin, an economic depression is about to smother his high hopes for a successful administration.

TIME: MARCH 4, 1837 – MARCH 4, 1841

VAN BUREN'S TERM IN OFFICE

Martin Van Buren surely lives up to his nickname as the "Little Magician" when it comes to maneuvering his way into the White House, but his stay there will prove anything but magical from start to finish.

Jackson's "Specie Circular" order, which Van Buren supports, sets off a financial crisis that sweeps across the country and turns the population against the president and the party he has so carefully crafted. A special session of Congress—the first ever assembled for a non-military threat—meets in September 1837, but fails to arrive at a solution to stabilize the currency and restore access to bank loans, the necessary fuel of capitalism. Once again, the proper balance between wild speculation and prudent investment is elusive in an increasingly complex American economy.

On top of the banking woes, the public conscience is soon shocked by the murder of an abolitionist newspaperman, Elijah Lovejoy, by a white mob in Alton, Illinois in November 1837. This event galvanizes anti-slavery advocates across the North, and in hindsight makes Lovejoy "the first casualty of the Civil War" to follow.

Two men in particular regard Lovejoy's murder as a call to action. One is John Brown, owner of a struggling tannery business in Ohio and future abolitionist martyr. The other is Abraham Lincoln, a 28-year-old lawyer in southern Illinois, distressed by the breakdown he sees in law and order.

Lovejoy's death and the lack of punishment for his killers also prompts a renewed flood of Anti-Slavery Society petitions to congress, which John Quincy Adams reads in defiance of the "gag rule" of 1836. Southern politicians rally behind John C. Calhoun's assertion that "slavery is a positive good" and in need of a fresh bill affirming its legal legitimacy for all times.

The growing hostility on the floor turns into open violence again when the Kentucky Whig William Graves challenges and kills Maine Democrat Jonathan Cilley in a duel over an alleged slight of honor.

To deal with the economic meltdown, Van Buren makes repeated attempts to create a new financial institution called an "Independent Treasury" to manage federal funds and stabilize the value of the dollar. He argues that this "Treasury" would eliminate the conflicts of interest inherent in privately held bank corporations, and would print and circulate a new supply of "properly backed" paper money to jumpstart the loan-making process. The Senate backs this initiative, but the House tables it until June 1840, fearing the move would place too much power in the hands of the president.

Conflict and frustrations bleed into Van Buren's final years in the White House.

A Spanish enslaver ship, the *Amistad*, lands in a Connecticut port in August of 1839, piloted by Black abductees who have killed the white crew to secure their freedom. Over the next eighteen months battles will be fought in newspapers and in the courts about whether to return the prisoners to Spain as "slave property" or grant them liberty. Once again, Adams is in the middle of the dispute, arguing for and eventually winning their freedom before the Supreme Court.

Van Buren's final burden centers on what to do about the Republic of Texas. Despite his fervent wish to expand to the west, Andrew Jackson has walked away from annexation in 1836 for fear of war with Mexico and the prospect of a congressional battle over admitting Texas as another pro-slavery state. But the matter doesn't die there. The Texans again seek annexation; the South supports it, and so does Jackson, now from the safety of his retirement at the Hermitage.

Pressure mounts when both France and Britain recognize Texas as an independent nation, hardly the outcome favored by the public. Still Van Buren comes down on the side of restraint, resisting annexation for the same reasons Jackson had four years earlier.

KEY EVENTS: MARTIN VAN BUREN'S TERM

1837	
February 6	(Pre-inauguration) Calhoun delivers his "slavery is a positive good" speech in Congress
March 4	Jackson and Johnson are inaugurated
April	Uncertainty grows about the value of the dollar and access to loans across the country
May 10	Banks in New York stop redeeming dollars for gold/silver and other cities follow
August 4	Texas petitions to be annexed by the US and be admitted as a state
August 31	Ralph Waldo Emerson's speech "The American Scholar" proclaims US intellectual honors
September 5	Special session of Congress discusses "Specie Circular" policy and bank failures
September 14	Bill to create an "Independent Treasury" passes the Senate, but is tabled in the House
October 2	Bank failures lead to omission of fourth installment deposits under the Surplus Revenue Act
October 12	Congress authorizes printing and distribution of $10 million "backed" banknotes
November 7	Abolitionist Elijah Lovejoy is murdered by an angry white mob in Alton, Illinois
November	John Brown "consecrates his life to ending slavery" at memorial service for Lovejoy
December 8	Wendell Phillips responds to Lovejoy's death with his first abolitionist speech
December 19	"Gag rule" renewed, with South seeking affirmation that "slavery must be protected"
Year	Massachusetts Board of Education head Horace Mann reforms teaching systems
1838	
January 10	Calhoun speaks to the Senate about "the importance of domestic slavery"
January 27	Abraham Lincoln addresses Springfield Lyceum about Lovejoy's murder & lawlessness
January 3–12	Senate affirms Calhoun resolution positively "affirming slavery as a legal institution"
February 15	John Quincy Adams defies gag rule by introducing 350 anti-slavery petitions on the House floor

February 16	Kentucky legislature grants suffrage to women who are widows with school-age children
February 24	Kentucky Whig William Graves kills Maine Democrat Jonathan Cilley in a rifle duel.
March 26	House opposes Van Buren's wish to create an "Independent Treasury" not tied to banks
May 17	White mob burns the Pennsylvania Hall in Philadelphia after an anti-slavery meeting
May 21	Jackson's Specie Circular Order is repealed in a joint resolution of congress
June 12	The House finally passes the Independent Treasury Bill by seventeen votes
August 13	New York banks resume payouts of dollars in gold/silver, but crisis not over
August 18	Charles Wilkes sets out on expedition to explore the Pacific and Antarctic
October 12	Texas withdraws annexation request and new President Mirabeau B. Lamar proposes a new nation
1838	
October	Remaining Cherokees removed from their eastern lands
November	Van Buren suffers congressional losses in the midterm election
November 7	Henry Seward is elected governor of New York
December 3	The abolitionist Joshua Giddings is elected to the House
Year	Underground Railroad is formed to help escaping enslaved people
1839	
February 7	Henry Clay attacks abolitionists for risking civil war during Senate debate
February 12	Maine and New Brunswick dispute lumber rights along the Aroostook River
February 20	Congress outlaws dueling in the District of Columbia
August	Enslaved people aboard the *Amistad* overthrow and kill the white crew and land on Long Island
September 25	France recognizes Texas as a new nation
November 13	The Liberty Party is founded by Gerrit Smith and James G. Birney, producing schism with Garrison
December 4	Whig convention nominates William Henry Harrison after Clay drops out for harmony
1840	
January 19	Wilkes Expedition sights Antarctica
March 31	Van Buren signs bill mandating a ten-hour workday for public employees
April 1	The abolitionist Liberty Party convention nominates James Birney for president
May 5	Democrats nominate Van Buren on platform that supports Southern slavery
June 12-23	Anti-Slavery Convention in London denies women delegates prompting backlash
June 30	The House finally passes the Independent Treasury Act
July 4	The Independent Treasury begins to house federal funds and stabilize the money supply
November 13	Britain recognizes the nation of Texas
December 2	The Whig William Henry Harrison is elected president
1841	
March 4	Harrison inaugurated

While he suffers many political losses, Van Buren does record some small victories. The "Wilkes Expedition" explores and maps the Pacific Ocean and Antarctica. A border dispute between Maine and New Brunswick over lumber rights along the Aroostook River is resolved without warfare. And "progress" continues on the ejection of the eastern tribes across the Mississippi.

By 1840 per capita GDP drops sharply as a result of the financial stress caused by Jackson's "Specie Circular" attempt to constrain land speculation and stabilize the value of the dollar. It will not be until 1847, during the Mexican War, when the American public enjoys another sizable jump in personal wealth.

ECONOMIC OVERVIEW: MARTIN VAN BUREN'S PRESIDENCY

	1837	1838	1839	1840
Total GDP ($000)	1,554	1,598	1,661	1,574
% Change	5%	3%	4%	(5%)
Per Capita GDP	98	98	100	92

Martin Van Buren will live on for 21 years after exiting the presidency, first enjoying the life of a "country squire" back in Kinderhook before returning to the political arena, hoping to regain his magical touch within the Democrat Party. But it is not meant to be.

He is actually favored to win the 1844 nomination, but again refuses to back the annexation of Texas. This costs him support from Southerners and Andrew Jackson, and hands the top spot to James K. Polk.

By 1848 he feels betrayed by the Democrats and agrees to head the ticket of the new "Free Soil Party."

During a losing campaign, Van Buren asserts that Congress has the power to limit the spread of slavery to the west—an argument that costs the Democrats a sizable number of Northern white voters and sets the stage for the rise of the Republican Party in 1856.

Toward the end of his life, Van Buren does his best to support those trying to hold the Union together. He lives into the second year of the war, finally passing away on July 24, 1862. Lincoln, who befriends Van Buren in 1842, honors his death by declaring a public day of mourning and ordering all flags to fly at half-mast.

## 81

AMERICA SUFFERS AN ECONOMIC DEPRESSION

TIME: APRIL 1837

BANKS PANIC AS WESTERN LAND PRICES INFLATE

The financial collapse that begins in April 1837 strikes a blow to the American economy that will be unmatched until the Great Depression of 1929. It will also crush Van Buren's hopes for his presidency and threaten the entire Democratic Party he has so cleverly assembled.

The collapse originates with speculative greed on the part of bankers.

In this case, their scheme focuses on buying up new public land west of the Appalachians from the government at low prices, and then re-selling it to settlers at much higher prices.

When Andrew Jackson spots this "get rich quick" move in 1835, it strikes him as one more instance where the few privileged bankers profit mightily at the expense of the many common citizens—and he will have none of that.

Jackson senses that the banks are paying for the public land by printing many more soft money notes than they can "back" through the gold and silver in their vaults. To bring this practice, and the accompanying speculation, to a fast halt, Jackson's 1835 Specie Circular Order requires that all new public land purchased by "non-settlers" be paid for in gold or silver, not banknotes. This executive order triggers two outcomes:

- Recognition among the bankers that the "real value" of the western land they purchased "to make a killing" is artificially inflated, and that settlers will refuse to pay the higher prices they had expected. What previously looked to the bankers like a parcel of land capable of commanding a $100 price and yielding a $25 profit now looks like a $50 price and a $25 loss.
- As western land prices plummet—which was Jackson's intent—the bankers calculate the extent of their looming losses and enter panic mode by trying to build enough cash on hand to stay solvent. To accomplish this, they start selling off the western land at ever decreasing prices ("something is better than nothing") and also "calling in existing loans" made to businesses and the general public.

At this point, the situation begins to spin out of control.

TIME: MAY 10, 1837

PANIC SPREADS TO THE GENERAL PUBLIC

What begins as a panic among bankers now threatens America's entire financial system—premised on a stable value for the dollar and an orderly system whereby everyday citizens can make deposits and loans with confidence.

This confidence begins to disappear early in 1837.

The small farmer who borrowed $100 to plant his crops, expecting to pay back the loan in six months after growing and selling them, is suddenly required by his banker to repay the loan now or lose his land. City merchants and manufacturers suffer a similar fate.

Foreclosures follow for those who cannot comply. But these often fail to solve the bankers' dilemma. They need cash to cover immediate operating expenses, not long-term assets like farms or shops which they can neither run nor sell.

Too young to understand the hard times

As conditions spiral downward, pressures from abroad add to the crisis, with fellow bankers in England and Ireland demanding repayment of their prior US loans.

The Specie Circular Order also causes many citizens to conclude that the banknotes in their wallets or in deposited savings may not be worth the paper it is printed on. To be safe, they head to their local bank to exchange their soft dollars for the gold or silver that the certificates promise them.

Those who arrive early may leave with minted coins. But the principle of "fractional banking" means that covering all demands for hard money will be impossible, if they arrive all at once.

When the Bank of New York announces on May 10, 1837 that it will no longer convert soft money into the promised gold or silver, depositors across the country begin to close out their accounts. As reported:

Distrust (of banks) seized upon the public mind like fires in the great prairies.

The dreaded "run on the banks" is under way.

TIME: 1837–1843

AN ECONOMIC DEPRESSION ENSUES

Once their deposits are withdrawn, the banks themselves go under.

Out of around 850 banks operating across the country in 1837, 343 are forced to close entirely and another 62 are classified as partially failed.

With amazing suddenness, Hamilton's American economy—built on easy access to capital to support profitable investments—is left devoid of available capital. What money there is has been locked up tight in the reserves of the surviving banks, many of whom fueled the crisis in the first place.

In turn, the expansion of America's economy reverses.

Without the bank loans they need to operate, even more farmers are thrown off their land and more businesses shut their doors. Unemployment also spikes, with more than 20,000 out of work in New York city alone. As the supply of goods and services decreases, prices inflate, further strapping the citizenry.

Public confidence is lost as quickly as it was once found.

Instead of the "prosperity perfectly secured" envisioned by Van Buren in his March inaugural address, the nation slips into a severe depression.

TIME: SEPTEMBER 5, 1837

VAN BUREN PROPOSES THE CREATION OF AN INDEPENDENT US TREASURY

Advice on what to do about the dilemma flows into the White House from all sides—with Van Buren's own party divided on the issue.

The Jacksonians want him to bring the supply of banknotes back in line with the supply of gold and silver. Others argue that the banks have been sufficiently punished, that Jackson's order should be repealed, and that Van Buren needs to restore confidence in the system. The public must regain trust in the value of the dollar and in the banks so they are willing to make deposits. The banks must feel secure enough about their own assets to resume making the loans needed to revitalize the economy.

Van Buren is sufficiently alarmed to call for a special session of Congress, an action originally reserved for times of war. The session meets on September 5, 1837, and it hears the president's proposals. Characteristically he attempts to play it down the middle, with something for all sides.

He is not about to exhibit confidence in the motives or the disciplines of private bankers. He says the time has come to stop funneling surplus federal money into state banks that are liable to misuse it. Instead, he proposes the creation of a US Treasury, functioning apart from the private banking system.

The US Treasury would exist to meet the needs of the federal government rather than those of corporate stockholders. It would deposit federal revenue collected from taxes, land sales, and other sources, and disburse the money to pay off federal expenses. It would also make loans to various state banks after first verifying they have the proper gold/silver reserves to back the value of the dollar.

Independent US Treasury funds loaned to these reliable banks could then be used for more loans to farmers, manufacturers, and other businesses, thus revitalizing the capitalist economy. To back up this approach, Van Buren proposes to place $10 million in an Independent US Treasury money into the state banks.

The Senate approves this approach, but the House stalls, fearing that an Independent US Treasury would put too much power in the hands of the president.

This stalemate continues until June 1840 when a third attempt to win House support succeeds by a seventeen-vote majority.

Over time, this Independent US Treasury will help stabilize the value of the dollar and tamp down the speculative expansion of credit. But its effects are imperfect, especially during boom or bust periods where plugging the right amount of money into circulation becomes especially important.

On July 4, 1840, Van Buren finally signs his Independent Treasury into law. He hopes that it will turn the economy around and win him a second term in office. But neither wish will come to pass.

What the Bank Panic of 1837 reveals is a profound change in America's financial systems and economy. The much simpler and more transparent agricultural vision espoused by Jefferson has morphed into Hamilton's multi-faceted industrial economy, dependent on capitalism and corporations whose interests may not always correspond with the good of the commonwealth.

82

THE SOUTH INTENSIFIES ITS DEFENSE OF SLAVERY

TIME: 1820–1836

ANXIETY MOUNTS OVER THE NORTH'S ANTI-SLAVERY INTRUSIONS

Ever since the 1820 controversy over admitting Missouri as a pro-slavery state, Southerners have feared that the North will act against the "peculiar institution" that serves as the basis for their regional prosperity.

The threat level increases during the Second Great Awakening of the 1820s when calls to action by Reverend Charles Finney produce a host of white abolitionists such as William Lloyd Garrison, Theodore Weld, Arthur and Lewis Tappan, Lucretia Mott, Angelina Grimke, Gerrit Smith, and James Birney.

Garrison's 1831 *Liberator* newspaper provides early publicity for the movement, gives voice to pleas for freedom from Black people like David Walker, and attempts to shame the public and the politicians into amending the broken 1787 Constitution. As Garrison proclaims:

That which is not just is not law.

Nat Turner's 1831 rebellion demonstrates what can happen when enslaved people take the law into their own hands and seek retribution against their white oppressors. But this fails to slow down the reformers.

Even the presidency of lifelong planter and slaveholder Andrew Jackson fails to produce the kind of affirmative support for the "interests of the South" that was anticipated. When South Carolina signals its intent, as a sovereign state, to nullify the so-called "tariff of abominations," Jackson signals his intent to send US troops in to enforce federal law.

Then, in 1832, he dumps the leading Southern advocate, John C. Calhoun, off his ticket in favor of a Northern man, Martin Van Buren.

In 1833 the American Anti-Slavery Society organizes chapters across the North who gather abolitionist petitions and send them to Congress to be read on the floor of the House.

When this form of agitation becomes visible in Washington, Southern politicians react by passing the 1836 "gag rule" to try to shut down public debate. But former president John Quincy Adams refuses to comply and the result is even more heated rhetoric.

The Northern congressmen by no means favor abolition, but they also do not appreciate being maneuvered by Southerners—especially now that the population count in "their region" gives them majority voting power in the House.

And then in 1837, the new president from New York feels called upon to openly mention the heretofore taboo subject of slavery in his inaugural address to the nation.

All this adds up to a fear that has endured across the South since the founders met in Philadelphia: at some moment, the North will turn the power of the federal government against the institution of slavery, the fragile foundation of the region's wealth.

TIME: FEBRUARY 6, 1837

JOHN CALHOUN ARGUES THAT "SLAVERY IS A POSITIVE GOOD"

Of course, John C. Calhoun consistently tries to alert the South to the imminent dangers of the federal government intruding on the business of slavery.

On February 6, 1837, with his tenure as vice president and his prospects for the White House over, he rises on the Senate floor to deliver what will become known as his "slavery is a positive good" speech. For the sake of drama, he begins by reading two anti-slavery petitions to his colleagues, then proceeds to counter with his own analyses.

John C. Calhoun (1782–1850)

I hold that in the present state of civilization, where two races of different origin, and distinguished by color, and other physical differences, as well as intellectual, are brought together, the relation now existing in the slaveholding States between the two, is, instead of an evil, a good—a positive good.

Instead of abusing Black people, slavery has actually enlightened and elevated them.

I appeal to facts. Never before has the black race of Central Africa, from the dawn of history to the present day, attained a condition so civilized and so improved, not only physically, but morally and intellectually.

How much better off is the Southern enslaved person than the pauper classes of society at large.

I may say with truth, that in few countries so much is left to the share of the laborer, and so little exacted from him, or where there is more kind attention paid to him in sickness or infirmities of age. Compare his condition with the tenants of the poor houses in the more civilized portions of Europe—look at the sick, and the old and infirm slave, on one hand, in the midst of his family and friends, under the kind superintending care of his master and mistress, and compare it with the forlorn and wretched condition of the pauper in the poorhouse.

Furthermore, the practice of slavery has always been part and parcel of sustaining a prosperous society.

I hold then, that there never has yet existed a wealthy and civilized society in which one portion of the community did not, in point of fact, live on the labor of the other.

The lion's share of all wealth has always gone to those who have risen above the producing classes.

Broad and general as is this assertion, it is fully borne out by history. This is not the proper occasion, but, if it were, it would not be difficult to trace the various devices by which the wealth of all civilized communities has been so unequally divided, and to show by what means so small a share has been allotted to those by whose labor it was produced, and so large a share given to the non-producing classes.

The South has relied on a simple patriarchal approach to extract wealth from its slave class.

The devices (to extract wealth) are almost innumerable, from the brute force and gross superstition of ancient times, to the subtle and artful fiscal contrivances of modern. I might well challenge a comparison between them and the more direct, simple, and patriarchal mode by which the labor of the African race is, among us, commanded by the European.

Because of slavery, the South actually avoids the conflict between labor and capital seen in the North.

There is and always has been in an advanced stage of wealth and civilization, a conflict between labor and capital. The condition of society in the South exempts us from the disorders and dangers resulting from this conflict; and which explains why it is that the political condition of the slaveholding States has been so much more stable and quiet than that of the North.

Preserving slavery is the best path for America to sustain stable political institutions.

I turn to the political; and here I fearlessly assert that the existing relation between the two races in the South, against which these blind fanatics are waging war, forms the most solid and durable foundation on which to rear free and stable political institutions.

Attempts to abolish slavery will end the union between the South and the North.

Abolition and the Union cannot coexist. As the friend of the Union I openly proclaim it. We of the South will not, cannot, surrender our institutions. Maintain(ing) the existing relations between the two races is indispensable to the peace and happiness of both. It cannot be subverted.

The South has the means to defend itself, but only if it awakens to the threats in time.

Surrounded as the slaveholding States are with such imminent perils, I rejoice to think that our means of defense are ample, if we shall prove to have the intelligence and spirit to see and apply them before it is too late. (But) I fear it is beyond the power of mortal voice to awaken it in time from the fatal security into which it has fallen.

Thankfully the dangers can still be avoided if political concert can be achieved.

All we want is concert, to lay aside all party differences and unite with zeal and energy in repelling approaching dangers. Let there be concert of action, and we shall find ample means of security without resorting to secession or disunion. I speak with full knowledge and a thorough examination of the subject, and for one see my way clearly.

This 1837 address by Calhoun will stand the test of time as the clearest declaration of how the plantation aristocrats of the South view the institution of slavery and rationalize it to themselves.

Civilization has always been run and advanced by the superior few, operating off the daily labor of the producing masses—be they better-off enslaved in Southern cotton fields or worse-off in Northern factories. This is the way it is, and the way it must remain. So says the Senator from South Carolina on behalf of his colleagues.

## 83

ABOLITIONIST EDITOR ELIJAH LOVEJOY IS MURDERED BY A MOB IN ALTON, ILLINOIS

TIME: 1833

ORDAINED MINISTER ELIJAH LOVEJOY BECOMES AN ABOLITIONIST IN ST. LOUIS

While Calhoun is correct in warning the South about growing Northern animosity, the basis relates to economic and cultural difference rather than a drive to abolish slavery.

Proof of this lies in the consistent pattern of violent resistance toward local abolitionists evident across the region.

This pattern is repeated during the autumn of 1837 in the southern Illinois town of Alton, across the Mississippi from St. Louis. The victim in this case is the abolitionist Elijah Lovejoy.

Elijah Lovejoy grows up in Maine, the pious son of a Congregationalist minister. He graduates first in his class from Waterville College (later Colby), then heads west to Missouri where he hopes to serve God by using his skills as a teacher to improve society. He finds a home in St. Louis, and starts up a private high school. By 1830, however, he is ready for a new career and becomes co-owner and editor of *The St. Louis Times*.

This lasts until 1832, when he attends a series of revivalist meetings led by the Reverend David Nelson that prompt him toward the ministry. He heads back east to the Theological Seminary at Princeton, and is ordained as a Presbyterian minister on April 18, 1833.

Church friends support Lovejoy's subsequent move back to St. Louis, where he combines preaching in his own church with editing a religious newspaper, *The St. Louis Observer*. While his followers applaud him, others find him increasingly moralistic and outspoken. His criticisms of the Roman Catholic Church become intense and unyielding—which is controversial in such a heavily Catholic city—and his vocal support for abolition is out of step in the pro-slavery state of Missouri.

Hostility toward Lovejoy erupts into open violence in April 1836. A free Black man, one Francis McIntosh, kills a deputy sheriff and wounds another while trying to flee from a crime. He is momentarily jailed, until a mob breaks in and seizes him. Retribution is swift and savage, as McIntosh is tied to a tree and burned alive. When those involved are subsequently tried and acquitted, Lovejoy writes one editorial after another criticizing the outcome.

We must stand by the laws and the Constitution, or all is gone.

But legalities count little when it comes to a Black man killing a white sheriff—and to drive home this point, another mob storms Lovejoy's office and destroys his printing press.

TIME: 1835

LOVEJOY MOVES TO ALTON, ILLINOIS
AFTER BEING ATTACKED BY WHITE MOBS

He responds by moving across the river to the booming city of Alton, in the free state of Illinois. At the time he promises local leaders that he will refrain from trying to turn the town into a center for abolitionist agitation.

However, his actions belie his words. He becomes a Garrison backer, opens a branch of the American Anti-Slavery Society, and on September 27, 1837 convenes a meeting of abolitionists in town. Then comes an editorial in his paper, *The Alton Observer*, calling for the immediate emancipation of all enslaved people.

Many citizens are outraged by Lovejoy's action and they respond much like the mob in St. Louis: they swarm into his newspaper office and throw his presses into the Mississippi River not once, but on three occasions.

When civic leaders warn him to leave the city for his own safety, he comes before them on November 3, still hoping for some kind of compromise. His speech captures both the religious fervor and personal fears so common to those who risk it all for the cause of abolition.

Mr. Chairman—it is not true, as has been charged upon me, that I hold in contempt the feelings and sentiments of this community, in reference to the question which is now agitating it. I respect and appreciate the feelings and opinions of my fellow-citizens.

But, sir, while I value the good opinion of my fellow-citizens, as highly as any one, I may be permitted to say, that I am governed by higher considerations than either the favour or the fear of man. I am impelled to the course I have taken, because I fear God. As I shall answer it to my God in the great day,

I have asked for nothing but to be protected in my rights as a citizen—rights which God has given me, and which are guaranteed me by the constitution of my country.

The question to be decided is, whether I shall be protected in the exercise …of those rights; whether my property shall be protected, whether I shall be suffered to go home to my family at night without being assailed, and threatened with tar and feathers, and assassination; whether my afflicted wife, whose life has been in jeopardy, from continued alarm and excitement, shall night after night be driven from a sick bed into the garret to save her life from the brickbats and violence of the mobs; that sir, is the question.

I know, sir, that you can hang me up, or put me into the Mississippi, without the least difficulty. But what then? Where shall I go? I have been made to feel that if I am not safe at Alton, I shall not be safe anywhere. I recently visited St. Charles to bring home my family, and was torn from their frantic embrace by a mob. And now if I leave here and go elsewhere, violence may overtake me in my retreat, and I have no more claim upon the protection of any other community than I have upon this.

I have concluded, after consultation with my friends, and earnestly seeking counsel of god, to remain at Alton and here to insist on protection in the exercise of my rights. If the civil authorities refuse to protect me, I must look to God; and if I die, I have determined to make my grave in Alton.

TIME: NOVEMBER 7, 1837

LOVEJOY IS KILLED IN AN ARMED BATTLE AT HIS OFFICE

Four days later, Lovejoy's fears are realized.

In a move that will dismay the passive Garrison, Lovejoy decides to arm himself against any further aggression.

He gathers some 20 supporters together at his warehouse to protect a new printing press. At nightfall on November 7 another mob attack begins. *The Alton Observer* reprises what happens next:

As the crowd grew outside, excitement and tension mounted. Soon the pro-slavery mob began hurling rocks at the warehouse windows. The defenders retaliated by bombarding the crowd with a supply of earthenware pots found in the warehouse. Then came an exchange of gunfire. Alton's mayor tried in vain to persuade the defenders inside to abandon the press. They stood fast.

One of the mob climbed a ladder to try to set fire to the roof of the building. Lovejoy and one of his supporters darted into the darkness to over-turn the ladder, for they knew they would be doomed if a fire was set. But again a volunteer mounted the ladder to try to ignite the roof with a smoking pot of pitch.

As Lovejoy assisted in putting out the fire on the roof of the building, he received a blast from a double-barreled shotgun. Five of the bullets fatally struck Lovejoy. He died in the arms of his friend Thaddeus Hurlbut. The mob cheered and said all in the building should die. Amos Roff tried to calm the mob and was shot in the ankle.

Defenders of the press then laid down their weapons and were allowed to leave. The mob rushed the building, found the press, and threw it out a window to the riverbank, broke it into pieces and dumped the broken parts into the river, The body of Lovejoy was left undisturbed, remaining there until morning, guarded by friends who finally carried him home. He was buried on his 35th birthday, November 9, 1837.

Lovejoy's death in Illinois joins the attempted lynching of Garrison in Boston in demonstrating the widespread resistance to abolition among white people in the North.

At the same time, it draws two figures into the public arena: a charismatic Ohio man named John Brown and a young lawyer in Illinois named Abraham Lincoln.

## 84

LOVEJOY'S MURDER BEGETS A FATAL VOW FROM JOHN BROWN

TIME: EARLY 1830s

JOHN BROWN INHERITS HIS FATHER'S ABOLITIONIST FERVOR

No figure in the abolitionist movement will rival John Brown in his willingness to rely on violence to end the practice of slavery.

And likewise, no other abolitionist will quite match his record of living and working closely with Black people on a daily basis. As he befriended them, he became convinced of their capacity to be assimilated into American society.

Brown's early life has been hard, beginning with the death of his mother when he is only eight years old. From then his youth is spent under the iron fist of his father in Hudson, Ohio.

Owen Brown is a strict Calvinist of the old school, dedicated to studying his Bible and trying to achieve daily piety and self-perfection. He is also a lifelong opponent of slavery, who subscribes to Garrison's *Liberator*, becomes a trustee of the Evangelist Charles Finney's progressive Oberlin College, and eventually supports those escaping via the Underground Railroad network.

Owen Brown will pass along his abolitionist fervor to his son John.

John Brown

TIME: NOVEMBER 1837

JOHN BROWN VOWS TO END SLAVERY IN AMERICA

When not praying as a youth, John is working long hours at his father's tannery—a particularly noxious occupation using human waste and chemicals to convert slaughtered animal hides into leather for shoes, belts, jackets, and saddles. Young John Brown will soon master this trade, which he will practice the rest of his life.

At age sixteen, he begins religious studies at the local Congregational Church after publicly repenting and accepting Jesus Christ as his savior. He travels to Litchfield, Connecticut, and enrolls at the Morris Academy, pondering the ministry until both health and financial difficulties chase him back to Hudson within a year.

In 1820 he marries his first wife, whom he describes as "a neat industrious & economical girl, of excellent character, earnest piety & good practical common sense." He opens his own tannery, which he runs until 1825, when he buys a 200-acre farm in northwestern Pennsylvania. His plan is ambitious and involves raising and slaughtering the cattle he will use to make and sell finished leather goods.

His dreams, however, fade by 1832, after two life-shattering events. First, his wife dies following an "instrument-aided" delivery of a stillborn son, her seventh child over a ten-year period. Then Brown himself suffers a prolonged illness that curtails his work and leads to stifling debt.

In 1833, he marries his second wife, the sixteen-year-old Mary Day who will eventually bear thirteen more children. Their days together will include a daily morning gathering where Brown requires each member of the family to read Bible verses, followed by delivering his own religious admonitions.

As a dedicated Calvinist, Brown is forever searching after God's plan for his life, and he eventually believes that ending slavery is the answer.

In his autobiography, Brown writes that his antipathy to slavery begins when he is twelve years old and witnesses a young Black boy being "beaten with iron shovels." As early as 1834, Brown tells his brother Frederick that he is "trying to do something in a practical way for my fellow men that are in bondage." His initial thoughts turn toward bringing a Black youth into his family, educating him and "teaching him the fear of God."

His business debts mount, and in 1836 he moves his family from Pennsylvania to a 92-acre farm in Franklin Mills, Ohio, where he starts up another tannery, largely with borrowed money. But this venture struggles during the Bank Panic of 1837, and he ends up with even more debt to show for his many talents and hard work.

By this time his abolitionist activities are picking up. He organizes a petition to protest Ohio's "black codes," hires freed men to work on his farm, and insists that they be treated respectfully within his local church, much to the dismay of the congregation.

When word reaches him of the Lovejoy assassination, he gathers his family together and reveals his intent to go to wage the "holy war" against slavery that will occupy the final two decades of his life.

His oldest son, John Jr., age thirteen at the time, recalls this event years later:

He asked who of us were willing to make common cause with him in doing all in our power to "break the jaws of the wicked and pluck the spoil out of his teeth. Are you Mary (his second wife), John, Jason and Owen?" As each family member assented, Brown knelt in prayer and administered an oath pledging them to slavery's defeat.

John Brown and his father attend a prayer meeting at the First Congregational Church of Hudson, Ohio to honor Lovejoy's memory. Toward the end of the service, Brown stands, raises his right hand, and makes a pledge:

Here, before God, in the presence of these witnesses, from this time, I consecrate my life to the destruction of slavery!

TIME: 1824–1845

AMERICA STRUGGLES WITH CONFLICTS BETWEEN SPIRITUALITY AND MATERIALISM

John Brown's journey from the search for moral perfection of his Calvinist youth to the murderous acts of his adulthood is in many ways symbolic of an underlying struggle between spirituality and materialism that is playing out at the time.

On one hand, the Second Great Awakening movement tries to return the nation to its religious heritage, the wish for moral perfection represented by the vision of a "shining city upon the hill," the hope for eternal salvation.

On the other, a new generation is being drawn ever more intently toward another familiar but potentially conflicting vision—the "American Dream." It is focused not on eternity, but on the here and now, the chance to settle on your own land, to work hard and get ahead, to accumulate wealth, and achieve a lifestyle previously reserved for the aristocracy, not the common man. As the Transcendentalist Emerson puts it, by 1835 the daily emphasis is now on "things:"

Things are in the saddle and ride mankind.

The period of reflection marking John Brown's early adulthood—1830 to 1840—is therefore in many ways the resumption of a long-term fundamental struggle for the "soul of America."

The striving for immediate material gains associated with the growing economic successes of capitalism versus the echoing voices of the original Puritans focused on eternal salvation.

Like Emerson, the astute de Tocqueville spots this struggle in his observation: "America must remain good to remain great." To fulfill its promise, it must hold true to its original high-minded religious principles, not retreat into Europe's corrupting materialism.

In swearing to "destroy slavery," John Brown asserts the primacy of Calvinist moral righteousness over the injustices of those who would profit economically from human bondage. Surely God's plan for America cannot tolerate this abomination any longer.

He also goes on to embrace a traditional but contentious path to righting wrongs—taking the law in his own hands. So it has been when the witches of Salem are summarily burned at the stake; the sitting vice president kills the secretary of the Treasury in a duel; enslaved people are beaten and lynched as a matter of course; and a minister like Lovejoy is murdered by a mob of neighbors.

His murderous rampages through Kansas in 1856 and Virginia in 1859 will prove to be another test for those who believe that profound social change, such as abolishing slavery, can be achieved solely through legal means, rather than monomania and violence.

TIME: 1835–1860

SIDEBAR: MONOMANIA IN NINETEENTH CENTURY AMERICAN LITERATURE

The literature of the era is drawn repeatedly to all of these uniquely American themes, especially in the 1835–1855 timeframe.

The Salem-born, Bowdoin-educated Nathaniel Hawthorne probes the full range of evils lurking just beneath the surface of the Puritan communities and characters he creates. The Reverend Arthur Dimmesdale is by no means among God's "elect" few, despite appearances to the contrary.

For the Richmond-raised Edgar Allan Poe, the focus lies on individual lives ruined by "fixations" that turn into madness and murder. For some the rage traces to an insult from a prior friend. Others are transformed by a fiancé's

Edgar Allan Poe (1809–1849)

teeth, a pet cat, the fear of impending illness, or an elderly man's "vulture eye." For Poe, the path to insane behavior begins with obsession.

But of course, no figure in antebellum American literature will mirror John Brown's pathology better than Herman Melville's Captain Ahab from his 1851 novel, *Moby Dick*.

Like John Brown, Ahab decides that his fate lies in personally ridding the world of evil, which, in his case, is manifested in the form of the great white whale. In striking off Ahab's leg in a first encounter at sea, Moby Dick becomes for him…

All that most maddens and torments; all that stirs up the lees of things; all truth with malice in it; all that cracks the sinews and cakes the brain; all the subtle demonisms of life and thought; all evil, to crazy Ahab, were visibly personified, and made practically assailable in Moby-Dick. He piled upon the whale's white hump the sum of all the general rage and hate felt by his whole race from Adam down; and then, as if his chest had been a mortar, he burst his hot heart's shell upon it.

Like John Brown, Ahab is seen by his crew as a messianic figure, an avenger out of the Old Testament, the seventh king of Israel, slaughtering the Assyrians at the Battle of Qarqar.

He's a queer man, Captain Ahab—so some think—but a good one. Oh, thou'lt like him well enough; no fear, no fear. He's a grand, ungodly, god-like man, Captain Ahab; doesn't speak much; but, when he does speak, then you may well listen. Mark ye, be forewarned; Ahab's above the common; Ahab's been in colleges, as well as 'mong the cannibals; been used to deeper wonders than the waves; fixed his fiery lance in mightier, stranger foes than whales.

For John Brown, slavery will become his version of Ahab's great white whale. Infinite evil which must be stamped out, no matter what—and the ends justify the means.

From Elijah Lovejoy's murder in 1837 to his 1858 raid on Harper's Ferry, John Brown will be on iron rails headed toward his destiny on a scaffold in Richmond. "A grand ungodly, god-like man." A man obsessed.

## 85

THE MOB BEHAVIOR IN ALTON ALSO DRAWS A PUBLIC RESPONSE FROM ABRAHAM LINCOLN

TIME: 1809–1830

ABRAHAM LINCOLN BECOMES A LAWYER AFTER AN UNPREDICTABLE YOUTH

At the time of Lovejoy's murder, Abraham Lincoln is 28 years old, still a bachelor, living in Springfield, Illinois, and just beginning to practice law under John Stuart after passing the bar in 1836.

His life journey so far has been quite remarkable, given his roots.

He is born in Hardin County, Kentucky, to Thomas Lincoln, an embittered farmer who has lost much of his wealth over disputed land titles, and Nancy Hanks Lincoln, who teaches him "his letters" and shapes his early character. In 1816 Thomas moves his family across the Ohio River into Spencer County, Indiana, where young Abe lives from 9 to 21 years of age. His mother dies soon after the move, and he is subsequently raised by his older sister and then by his stepmother Sarah, who cherishes him.

While his formal education is close to nil,

Abraham Lincon (1809–1865)

Lincoln is innately very smart, intensely curious, and eager to make his way in the world around him. He masters language through repeated readings of the *Bible, Aesop's Fables*,

Pilgrim's Progress, and Shakespeare's plays, and then writing his thoughts on an easel. He masters daily life by throwing himself into it. His physical presence sets him off from others. He is 6'3" tall, remarkably strong from wielding an ax to split lumber, and noted for outwrestling all comers in town. He is also gregarious, loves to debate, and is a natural raconteur. People gather around him to hear his thoughts and share laughter.

Here indeed, at an early age, are the makings of the lawyer and politician he will become.

Throughout these early years, slavery is simply an accepted part of his world.

In Kentucky he sees coffles of enslaved people marching along the road to Nashville near his home. In December 1828, at age nineteen, and again in April 1831, he is hired to crew flatboats carrying cargo on the Mississippi down to New Orleans—with its omnipresent slave pens and auctions and its unmistakeable messages about the innate inferiority of all Black people.

Lincoln's initial response to slavery appears to be simple empathy for its victims, and a visceral sense that it is evil. Looking back in April 1864, he will write:

If slavery is not wrong, nothing is wrong. I cannot remember when I did not so think and feel.

But as a young man, growing up where he does, his response is a very familiar passive one.

TIME: 1831–1837

LINCOLN MOVES TO ILLINOIS AND DABBLES IN POLITICS

In 1831 Lincoln heads out on his own, canoeing down the Sangamon River to the village of New Salem, Illinois.

Once there he embarks on a string of potential careers: running a general store, serving as postmaster, and acting as land surveyor, before deciding to become a lawyer. He begins this final quest, as usual, on his own, repeatedly reading Blackstone's Commentaries.

During his five-year stay in New Salem, two other experiences will influence his future. The first provides him with a brief taste of military life.

When Chief Blackhawk and his Sauks attempt to occupy land along Illinois' northwestern border, Lincoln enlists in the militia on April 21, 1832, and is elected captain of the 31st Regiment. His ten weeks of duty are largely spent marching and camping, although some believe he participates in a burial detail after the Battle of Stillman's Run.

After mustering out on July 10, Lincoln returns to New Salem and decides at age 23 to enter politics, seeking a seat in the Illinois General Assembly.

He runs as a Whig, given his lifelong admiration for Henry Clay, but finishes eigth in a field of sixteen contenders. Despite this initial setback, he runs again and wins the seat in 1834 and again in 1836.

In 1837 Lincoln is called upon to take a stand on slavery, when the Assembly is asked to vote on a resolution asserting that "the right of property in slaves is sacred…the General Government cannot abolish slavery in the District of Columbia…the formation of abolition societies is highly disapproved."

The resolution passes 77–6, with Lincoln being one of the six to vote against it. Several weeks later, he and Representative Dan Stone file a protest to its passage, a rarely-used device to register strong disagreement.

TIME: JANUARY 27, 1838

ABRAHAM LINCOLN SPEAKS OUT AGAINST CIVIL DISOBEDIENCE

In April of 1837, Lincoln moves to Springfield, ready to convert his 1836 law license into a live practice.

Once there, he is drawn to the Young Men's Lyceum, an educational forum attracting local intellectuals and up-and-coming professionals.

Speaking to this group is natural for aspiring politicians like Lincoln, and he addresses it on January 27, 1838. The title of his speech is "The Perpetuation of Our Political Institutions," and he delivers it some ten weeks after the murder of Elijah Lovejoy in nearby Alton.

Many regard this as Lincoln's his first important public address. It is not about slavery, or even about Lovejoy per se. Rather it warns of two risks facing America's democracy.

One involves the threat of dictators, like Caesar or Napoleon, substituting their will for that of the people. The other lies in "savage mobs" imposing their wills on any whom they oppose, as in Alton.

Lincoln declares that any government that tolerates such behavior cannot last.

Whenever the vicious portion of [our] population shall be permitted to gather in bands of hundreds and thousands, and burn churches, ravage and rob provision stores, throw printing presses into rivers, shoot editors, and hang and burn obnoxious persons at pleasure and with impunity, depend upon it, this government cannot last.

A nation has but one path to escape these threats, and that lies in disciplined obedience to the law.

Let every man remember that to violate the law, is to trample on the blood of his father, and to tear the charter of his own, and his children's liberty…Let reverence for the laws be breathed by every American mother…in short let it become the political religion of the nation….

A continued disregard for law signals that "something of ill-omen is amongst us."

I hope I am over wary; but if I am not, there is, even now, something of ill-omen, amongst us. I mean the increasing disregard for law which pervades the country; the growing disposition to substitute the wild and furious passions, in lieu of the sober judgment of Courts; and the worse than savage mobs, for the executive ministers of justice.

Like the wizened Southerner John C. Calhoun, a young Abraham Lincoln is already sensing a fundamental breakdown in the social fabric holding America together in 1838.

However, at this point, he has yet to fully plumb the depths of the disorder.

His brief experience in Illinois state government has taught him that it has to do with conflict over "the right of property in slaves." He also knows that he opposes the notion of slavery on moral grounds.

But how to resolve the matter will absorb him for the remainder of his life.

Unlike John C. Calhoun and John Brown, the Lyceum speech shows that his answer will not lie in "wild and furious passions." Instead, Lincoln the lawyer will seek solutions in following the laws, not breaking them.

## 86

CALHOUN TRIES AGAIN TO RALLY THE SOUTH AGAINST REGIONAL THREATS

TIME: 1830s

SOURCES OF GROWING CONCERN IN THE SOUTH

During the 1830s the consistent Northern hostility toward activists like Lovejoy and Garrison shows that the South has no reason to fear a formal move to abolish slavery where it currently exists.

But still, astute men like Calhoun see dangers for the future of slavery on the horizon—especially as they relate to the South's goal of expanding slavery into new territories. These signals of Northern resistance include:

- The constitutions of new states from Ohio through Illinois opposing Black residency;
- Segregation, race riots, and attempts to rid cities of their Black populations;
- House passage of the 1819 Tallmadge Amendment to ban slavery in Missouri;
- Moral concerns about slavery arising from the Second Great Awakening;
- The appearance of Garrison's inflammatory newspaper *The Liberator*;
- Formation of the American Anti-Slavery Society;
- John Quincy Adams' refusal to discontinue reading anti-slavery petitions in Congress;
- Attacks on slavery in state legislature (Giddings in Ohio and Stevens in Pennsylvania).

Then there are the Census results which show the population—and hence the apportionment of seats in the US House—consistently shifting to the North and the anti-slavery states. What if the House succeeds again in trying to block expansion? What if this can't be overturned in the Senate or by a pro-Southern president?

On top of this, Calhoun senses an almost visceral animosity building between the two regions.

They are constantly at odds over economic policies affecting the South's agriculture needs versus the North's industrialization. The tariff nullification attempt is one example, and it has left many feeling that the South is ready to trample on federal law in order to have their own way. In turn, more Southerners are expressing out loud that the North is intentionally out to damage their economy out of spite toward their "more refined, almost aristocratic" culture and lifestyles.

Calhoun is frustrated that so many of the South's political leaders do not share his sense of urgency over acting on the dangers.

Roughly a year after his "slavery is a positive good" speech, he again rises in the Senate to rally the opposition.

TIME: JANUARY 10, 1838

CALHOUN WARNS AGAINST THE "DELUDED MADMEN" ABOLITIONISTS

He begins with a refrain of his prior message that time and events have shown that instead of being a "moral and political evil," slavery has served the nation and the Black population well.

Many in the South once believed that it was a moral and political evil; that folly and delusion are gone; we see it now in its true light, and regard it as the most safe and stable basis for free institutions in the world.

The "two races, from different parts of the globe" were united in the South in nearly equal numbers by "a mysterious Providence" and the result has been to the benefit of both.

Experience has shown that the existing relation between them secured the peace and happiness of both. Each has improved; the inferior greatly; so much so, that it has attained a degree of civilization never before attained by the black race in any age or country. Under no other relation (than slavery) could they coexist together.

He goes on to paint an idyllic picture of plantations as "little communities" living in balance and harmony, under the hand of a beneficent master.

Every plantation is a little community, with the master at its head, who concentrates in himself the united interests; of capital and labor, of which he is the common representative. These small communities aggregated make the State in all, whose action, labor, and capital is equally represented and perfectly harmonized.

This is unlike the North, where the equilibrium between capital and labor has been disturbed by constant aggression.

In this tendency to conflict in the North between labor and capital, which is constantly on the increase, the weight of the South has and will ever be found on the Conservative side; against the aggression of one or the other side, which ever may tend to disturb the equilibrium of our political system.

The institution of slavery has served both races well, and it has served the South and the entire Union well. It should be left undisturbed.

This is our natural position, the salutary influence of which has thus far preserved, and will long continue to preserve, our free institutions, if we should be left undisturbed.

"Deluded madmen" must not be allowed to tear it down.

Such are the institutions which these deluded madmen are stirring heaven and earth to destroy, and which we are called on to defend by the highest and most solemn obligations that can be imposed on us as men and patriots.

POLITICIANS ONCE AGAIN TURN TO VIOLENCE TO RESOLVE THEIR DIFFERENCES

TIME: WINTER 1838

A CHALLENGE TO DUEL IS ISSUED

Even as Lincoln is calling for civil restraint, America's penchant for settling political disputes through violence is once again materializing in the halls of Congress.

This time it involves a duel between two sitting members of the US House: Jonathan Cilley, a first-term Whig from Maine, and William Graves, a Democrat from Kentucky.

The conflict arises after a speech by Cilley on the floor questioning editorials written by James Watson Webb, owner of the *The New York Courier and Enquirer*. These include vicious attacks on Cilley's fellow abolitionist Lewis Tappan and his praise for rechartering the Second US Bank. When Cilley suggests that Tappan's support for the bank is in return for a $52,000 loan he received, Webb demands an apology.

Webb selects Congressman Graves to deliver the demand, but when he tries, Cilley refuses to accept the note. He tells Graves that his rejection is to avoid any further unpleasantness with Webb.

Graves is initially willing to walk away until several friends, including Kentuckian and repeat duelist Henry Clay, urge him to reject the apology.

So, Graves challenges Cilley to a duel, even though the two have had no prior contact whatsoever.

TIME: FEBRUARY 24, 1838

CONGRESSMAN GRAVES KILLS CONGRESSMAN CILLEY

Cilley accepts and, hearing of Grave's reputation as skilled with handguns, settles on rifles as his weapon of choice.

The two men and their seconds meet on February 24, 1838 at the Bladensburg Dueling Grounds in Maryland.

They are placed 80 yards apart from each other and given the order to fire. When neither man is hit, the seconds attempt to end the matter, especially since both combatants claim no "personal animosity" toward the other.

But a truce is not to be, and another round is fired, again with misses from both men.

However, in the third round, Graves scores a hit, striking Cilley in the upper thigh and puncturing his femoral artery. Cilley falls to the ground and bleeds to death in two to three minutes, absent a tourniquet.

He is 35 years old when killed, and leaves behind a wife, three children, and a sterling reputation.

His close friend and fellow Bowdoin College classmate, Nathaniel Hawthorne, commemorates him in a eulogy at the funeral.

Alas that over the grave of a dear friend my sorrow for the bereavement must be mingled with another grief, —that he threw away such a life in so miserable a cause! Why, as he was true to the Northern character in all things else, did he swerve from his Northern principles in this final scene?

A challenge was never given on a more shadowy pretext; a duel was never pressed to a fatal close in the face of such open kindness as was expressed by Mr. Cilley; and the conclusion is inevitable, that Mr. Graves and his principal second, Mr. Wise, have gone further than their own dreadful code will warrant them, and overstepped

Nathaniel Hawthorne (1804–1864) eulogizes Congressman Jonathan Cilley (1802–1838)

the imaginary distinction, which, on their own principles, separates manslaughter from murder.

But his error was a generous one, since he fought for what he deemed the honor of New England; and, now that death has paid the forfeit, the most rigid may forgive him. If that dark pitfall—that bloody grave—had not lain in the midst of his path, whither, whither might it not have led him! It has ended there: yet o strong was my conception of his energies, so like destiny did it appear that he should achieve everything at which he aimed, that even now my fancy will not dwell upon his grave, but pictures him still amid the struggles and triumphs of the present and the future.

## 88

SOUTHERN FEARS MOUNT FURTHER AS THE SUPREME COURT FREES SLAVES IN THE AMISTAD AFFAIR

TIME: JULY 1839 TO MARCH 9, 1841

ENSLAVED PEOPLE BOUND FOR SPANISH CUBA END UP IN A CONNECTICUT COURTROOM

Everywhere Van Buren looks, he is beset by thorny problems, related either to the economic depression or to political turmoil over slavery.

One slavery incident plays out between July of 1839 and the end of his term in office—and it results in a clear judicial victory for the abolitionists.

The case involves 53 Nigerians who are snatched from their homeland and shipped to Cuba, in violation of bans on international slave trading passed by many nations, including the US and Spain.

Once in Cuba, the enslaved people are sold to two buyers, who give them Spanish names so they appear "homegrown" and can be marketed legally to owners of a sugar plantation on the island. When the deal is done, they are loaded onto a Spanish schooner, *La Amistad* (ironically "friendship" in English), for transport to the plantation.

Then things go awry.

On July 1, 1839, the enslaved people, led by a man known later as Joseph Cinque, break free from their chains, kill the ship's captain and a cook, and demand that the remaining crew sail them back home. But their navigation knowledge is flawed, and the crew eventually lands the ship on Long Island, New York, where they are arrested by US officials on charges of murder and sent to New Haven, Connecticut for trial.

Although the murder charges are eventually dropped, some 36 enslaved people remain in jail, as both the plantation owners and the government of Spain, which rules Cuba, claim them as "property."

When the Spanish ambassador gets involved, President Van Buren is ready to simply ship the enslaved people back to Cuba, to appease the avaricious regents surrounding Queen Isabella II and tamp down any further debates over slavery in America.

However, by the time he is ready to act, the abolitionist Lewis Tappan has taken up the case and sees that a court trial is scheduled. After hearing the evidence, the district court judge Smith Thompson rules that the enslaved people were indeed Nigerians, not Cubans, and as such, they were entitled to their freedom and should be sent back to their homeland.

I find, then, as a matter of fact, that in the month of June, 1839, the law of Spain did prohibit, under severe penalty, the importation into Cuba of negroes from Africa. These negroes were imported in violation of that law, and be it remembered that, by the same law of Spain, such imported negroes are declared to be free in Spain. … If, by their own laws, they cannot enslave them, then it follows, of necessity, they cannot be demanded. When these facts are known by the Spanish minister, he cannot but discover that the subjects of his queen have acquired no rights in these men. They are not the property of Spain. His demand must be withdrawn.

Queen Isabella II of Spain (1830–1904)

This verdict upsets Van Buren and he orders his lawyers to appeal the decision in the Supreme Court.

TIME: FEBRUARY 23 TO MARCH 9, 1841

A SUPREME COURT RULING FREES THE NIGERIANS AND ALARMS THE SOUTH

Arguments before Chief Justice Taney and the high court begin on February 23, 1841.

Making the case for the abducted Nigerians is none other than former president John Quincy Adams. Among the lawyers representing the Spanish crown is Ralph Ingersoll, former US congressman from Connecticut, who had earlier helped the town of New Haven defeat a proposal to open a "negro college."

The oral arguments extend from February 23 to March 2.

Adams wraps up in an appeal that extends over seven hours. He says that American laws, not those of any foreign power, must determine the Nigerians' fates, and that our laws have banned international slave trading since 1808. Hence, they are free men who have been kidnapped illegally.

> *Now the unfortunate Africans, whose case is the subject of the present representation, have been thrown by accidental circumstances into the hands of the authorities of the United States; and it may probably depend upon the action of the United States Government, whether these persons shall recover the freedom to which they are entitled, or whether they shall be reduced to slavery, in violation of the known laws and contracts publicly passed, prohibiting the continuance of the African slave trade by Spanish subjects.*

Under America's *habeas corpus* statutes, no president has the right to seize free men and turn them over to a foreign power at his own discretion.

> *There had been reports in circulation, which is by no means surprising, that the President intended to remove these people to Cuba, by force, gubernativamente, by virtue of his Executive authority—that inherent power which I suppose has been discovered, by which the President, at his discretion, can seize men, and imprison them, and send them beyond seas for trial or punishment by a foreign power*

> *Is there a law of Habeas Corpus in the land? Has the 4ᵗʰ of July become a day of ignominy and reproach. Remember the indignation raised against a former President of the United States for causing to be delivered up…a British sailor, for murder on board of a British frigate on the high seas? And is it for this court to sanction such monstrous usurpation and Executive tyranny as this at the demand of a Spanish minister?*

> *Had the precedent once been set and submitted to, of a nameless mass of judicial prisoners and witnesses, snatched by Executive grasp from the protective guardianship of the Supreme Judges of the land, at the dictate of a foreign minister, would it not have disabled forever the effective power of the Habeas Corpus?*

As free men, the Nigerians belong to no one but themselves; they are not property, and they deserve the right to liberty and justice under both the Constitution and the Declaration of Independence.

The Constitution nowhere recognizes them as property. The words slave and slavery are studiously excluded from the Constitution. Circumlocutions are the fig-leaves under which these parts of the body politic are decently concealed. Slaves, therefore, in the Constitution of the United States are recognized only as persons, enjoying rights and held to the performance of duties.

The moment you come, to the Declaration of Independence, that every man has a right to life and liberty, an inalienable right, this case is decided. I ask nothing more in behalf of these unfortunate men, than this Declaration.

Adams' arguments prevail and the Court decides by a 7–1 majority to uphold the ruling in Connecticut. In releasing Cinque and the others, Senior Justice Joseph Story's opinion states:

The Africans on board the Amistad were free individuals. Kidnapped and transported illegally, they had never been slaves.

After the verdict is in, authorities refuse to authorize a US ship to take Cinque and the others back to their homeland. But once again Lewis Tappan steps in and all 36 survivors of the ordeal arrive in Africa early in 1842.

While the *Amistad* decision has more to do with admiralty law rather than constitutional law, the mere fact of the US Supreme Court deciding to free the Nigerians is troubling to the South.

On hearing the decision, John C. Calhoun says, "This could take us all one step closer to civil war."

Fortunately for Martin Van Buren, the verdict is not handed down until March 9, 1841, five days after he has left office. It serves as a fitting coda for what has been a painful term for both the president and the nation.

## 89

THE SECTIONAL DIVIDE GROWS AS THE ELECTION OF 1840 LOOMS

TIME: 1776 AND ONWARD

THE SOUTH SHAPES A NARRATIVE TO SUPPORT ITS SLAVERY AND CULTURE

As tensions grow between the North and South by 1840, both regions resort to their own narratives to explain why their culture and lifestyles are superior.

The Southern narrative begins with its rationales related to slavery:

- The practice of slavery does not originate in America but is imported here by the British.
- Most of the nation's enslaved people enter the country through ports in the North, not the South.
- Over time, the North manages to cleanse itself of its enslaved population.
- Black people are an inherently inferior and potentially violent species, incapable of being assimilated.
- Then the "burden" of caring for—and controlling—enslaved people falls entirely on the South.
- In return for managing this burden, the South uses enslaved people to support their agrarian economy.
- Enslaved people are also given the chance to embrace Christianity and achieve salvation.
- The best interests of the nation are served by supporting the South's practices and needs related to slavery.
- That kind of regional cooperation was exactly what the founding fathers sanctioned in the 1787 Constitution.
- The Union is being threatened by stealing power from the states and handing it to the federal government.
- The South will leave the Union if the federal power is turned against its interests in slavery.

The institution has endured in the South out of "obligation and duty" to the nation. Black people are "so poor, so wretched, and so vile…as to be totally disqualified from exercising freedom." Instead of criticizing and meddling in slavery, the North should be thankful to the South for "fulfilling the high trust which has devolved on us as owners of slaves."

TIME: 1840

SOUTHERNERS CONDEMN THE NORTH'S ECONOMY AND WAY OF LIFE

Accompanying the South's defense of its "planter society" comes a scathing indictment of the many woes it sees in the North's shift away from Jefferson's agricultural vision and toward Hamilton's capitalism and industrialization.

- The basic freedoms and values Americans hold dear are now threatened across the North.
- No longer is it a place where independent farmers are working their own land, enjoying comparable wealth and influence, avoiding debt, solving their own domestic issues at the local level, and electing a small, fiscally frugal national government whose main role lies in managing foreign affairs.
- Instead wealth and power have been concentrated in the hands of a few at the expense of the many.
- The villains here are capitalism and corporations which place private profits above public good.
- Together they encourage personal greed and "get rich quick" speculation.
- They end all too often with personal debt and corruption.
- A corrupt corporate banking system provides the fuel for these schemes by printing and distributing soft money "unbacked" by gold and silver, thus eroding the "real value" of the dollar for all Americans.
- Corrupt politicians, co-opted by the wealthy few into supporting their profit-making programs, threaten the very notion of a government for the people.
- Corrupt businessmen convert Northern workers into "wage slaves," whose daily lives in factories or offices often leave them worse-off than a Southern field hand picking cotton.
- The credo of industrial capitalism across the North lies in maximizing profits for its stockholders over doing what is in the best interests of the country and the common man.

Most critically, the South argues that personal freedom has been eroded across the

North. Jefferson's yeoman farmer is, above all else a free (white) man, indebted to no one but himself. He is not a wage earner, dependent on a capitalistic owner/boss for his economic well-being. Nor is he a borrower, in hock to a capitalistic banker.

Being free economically, he can be free politically. Government is there to serve him, not vice versa.

TIME: 1840

THE NORTHERN NARRATIVE IS UPBEAT AND ENERGIZED

As Hamilton's diversified, modern economy takes hold, the vast majority of Northerners are delighted by the personal benefits that accrue from it.

The emergence of urban centers greatly facilitates commerce and makes the necessities and luxuries of life more easily available than ever before.

Many trade in their backbreaking labor on the family farm for earning a living based on their wits and acquired skills. And these new jobs often result in increased income and wealth.

While still small, a growing and on-the-make "middle class" begins to assert itself in the North.

Rather than being a blight on the landscape, large cities become a source of pride that America finally belongs as a global power.

Would the average Northerner trade places with their Southern counterparts in 1840? The answer is no way.

TIME: 1840

ANIMOSITY TOWARD THE SOUTHERN "SLAVOCRACY" DEEPENS

By 1840 many Northerners are also developing a negative impression of the South. The basis for this is definitely not moral qualms related to the institution of slavery.

Indeed, the vast majority of white people across the North and West have already signaled in state Constitutions and "black codes" that they want nothing to do with Black people, be they enslaved or free.

Instead, the antipathy seems to center on the privileged Southern planter class, with their vast farms, aristocratic lifestyles, and leisurely indulgences, all built off the backs of enslaved laborers.

That whole system seems like an insult to the hard work recorded daily by the white people of the North, be it on farms or in cities. Northern politicians will later leverage these feelings by labeling the South as a "slavocracy" and an affront "to the dignity of free white labor."

The sense of Southern privilege also seems to be operating within the federal government. The fact that four of the first five US presidents are Virginians is not lost on the Northern politicians in Washington. Nor is the sense that the makeup of the Senate is rigged to ensure that the Southern states retain equal control over the passage of legislation, despite the fact that Census counts show a widening majority of citizens living up North.

Animosity of this sort also grows around actions like the 1836 "gag rule," the South's attempt to shut down debate on abolitionist petitions. It is not that the North supports these petitions—rather, a certain amount of heavy-handed Southern arrogance seems at work in their demands.

As the Northern economy takes off along with city life, the South also begins to appear backwards, as if it has been left behind. In its attempts to block congressional programs to build needed roads, canals, and other infrastructure needs of the country, it appears out of touch and self-serving.

The sum total of these impulses across the North and West is to push back on the South, to "put it in its place," especially when its planter class seems intent on exercising its privilege.

At times in almost perverse fashion, the North will discover that nothing rattles the South like goading it over the institution of slavery.

TIME: 1840

TWO ROADS DIVERGING IN 1840

As a disappointed Van Buren exits the White House, sectional differences that almost prevented the formation of the Union in 1787 are intensifying.

The South is frozen in its agrarian tradition, betting its entire future on crops of cotton and slaves, and grows suspicious that the North will stand in the way of its future success.

The North is impatient to move on to the promises of capitalism and industrialization, and senses a backwards South asserting unwarranted privilege and blocking progress.

The threat of dis-union in the air.

All with echoes of George Washington's 1796 farewell address ringing in the background:

Lady Liberty with slaves

The unity of government which constitutes you one people is …now dear to you.

Discountenance… even a suspicion that it can in any event be abandoned…frown upon…every attempt to alienate any portion of our country from the rest, or to enfeeble the sacred ties which now link together the various parts.

With slight shades of difference, you have the same religion, manners, habits and political principles. You Have in a Common cause fought and triumphed together; the independence and liberty you possess are the work of joint counsels…common sufferings and successes.

The most commanding motives (exist) for carefully guarding and preserving the union of the whole… Protected by the equal laws of a common government…the North…the South…the East…the West…secure enjoyment of …outlets for their own production…across agriculture and manufacturing.

(Beware) of the danger of Parties in the State, with particular reference to the founding of them on geographical discriminations…The alternate domination of one faction over another, shaped by the spirit of revenge, natural to party dissension…

The name of American, which belongs to you… must always exalt the just pride of patriotism.

TIME: 1840

SIDEBAR: THOSE EXITING AND ENTERING THE PUBLIC STAGE IN 1840

EXITING	DEATH	AGE AT DEATH
Charles Pinckney	October 29, 1824	67
Charles C. Pinckney	August 16, 1825	79
William Eustis	February 6, 1825	71
John Adams	July 4, 1826	90
Thomas Jefferson	July 4, 1826	83
Luther Martin	July 10, 1826	78
Rufus King	April 29, 1827	72
John Jay	May 17, 1829	83
David Walker	August 10, 1830	33
James Monroe	July 4, 1831	73
Reverend Thomas Paul	April 13, 1831	58
John Marshall	July 6, 1835	79

EXITING	DEATH	AGE AT DEATH
James Madison	June 28, 1836	85
Aaron Burr	September 14, 1836	80
Elijah Lovejoy	November 7, 1837	34
Tecumseh	October 3, 1838	71
Benjamin Lundy	August 22, 1839	50
Robert Hayne	September 24, 1839	47
Aging	Born	Age in 1840
Albert Gallatin	Jan 29, 1761	79
James Forten	September 2, 1766	74
John Quincy Adams	July 11, 1767	73
Andrew Jackson	March 15, 1767	73
William H. Harrison	Feb 8, 1773	67
Roger Taney	March 17, 1777	63
Henry Clay	April 12, 1777	63
James Tallmadge, Jr.	January 28, 1778	62
Richard M. Johnson	October 17, 1780	60
Daniel Webster	January 18, 1782	58
Thomas Hart Benton	March 14, 1782	58
John C. Calhoun	March 18, 1782	58
Lewis Cass	October 9, 1782	58
Martin Van Buren	Dec 5, 1782	58
Zachary Taylor	Nov 24, 1784	56
Arthur Tappan	May 22, 1786	54
Winfield Scott	June 13, 1786	54
Theo Frelinghuysen	March 28, 1787	53
John J. Crittenden	September 10, 1787	53
Lewis Tappan	May 23, 1788	52
John Tyler	Mar 29, 1790	50
George McDuffie	August 10, 1790	50
Francis P. Blair	April 12, 1791	49
James Buchanan	April 23, 1791	49
James Birney	February 4, 1792	48
Thaddeus Stevens	April 4, 1792	48
Willie P. Mangum	May 10, 1792	48
George Dallas	July 10, 1792	48
Rev. Charles Finney	August 29, 1792	48
Lucretia Mott	January 3, 1793	47
Sam Houston	March 2, 1793	47
Austin Steward	(Date unknown) 1793	47
Thomas Dalton	October 17, 1794	46

EMERGING	BORN	AGE IN 1840
Silas Wright	May 24, 1795	45
Joshua Giddings	October 6, 1795	45
James Polk	Nov 2, 1795	45
Reverend Samuel Cornish	(Date unknown) 1795	45
John Bell	February 18, 1796	44
Andrew Butler	November 18, 1796	44
Gerrit Smith	March 6, 1797	43
Thurlow Weed	November 15, 1797	43
Sojourner Truth	(Date unknown) 1797	43
Reverend Theodore Wright	(Date unknown) 1797	43
Millard Fillmore	January 7, 1800	40
Caleb Cushing	January 17, 1800	40
Daniel Dickinson	September 11, 1800	40
Robert B. Rhett	December 21, 1800	40
Henry Seward	May 16, 1801	39
Brigham Young	June 1, 1801	39
Ralph Waldo Emerson	May 25, 1803	37
Theodore Weld	November 23, 1803	37
Henry Foote	February 28, 1804	36
Nathaniel Hawthorne	July 4, 1804	36
Franklin Pierce	November 23, 1804	36
Angelina Grimke	February 20, 1805	35
William Lloyd Garrison	December 12, 1805	35
John Hale	March 31, 1806	34
Henry Wise	December 3, 1806	34
Preston King	October 14, 1806	34
Robert E. Lee	January 19, 1807	33
David Atchison	August 11, 1807	33
Salmon Chase	January 13, 1808	32
Jefferson Davis	June 3, 1808	32
Edgar Allan Poe	January 9, 1809	31
Abraham Lincoln	February 12, 1809	31
Robert M.T. Hunter	April 21, 1809	31
Hannibal Hamlin	August 27, 1809	31
Charles Lenox Raymond	February 1, 1810	30
David Ruggles	March 15, 1810	30
Robert Toombs	July 2, 1810	30
Robert Purvis	August 4, 1810	30
Charles Sumner	January 6, 1811	29
Owen Lovejoy	January 6, 1811	29

EMERGING	BORN	AGE IN 1840
Horace Greeley	February 3, 1811	29
Harriet Beecher Stowe	June 14, 1811	29
Lewis Hayden	December 2, 1811	29
John McClernand	May 12, 1812	28
Alexander Stephens	February 11, 1812	28
John Fremont	January 21, 1813	27
Stephen A. Douglas	April 23, 1813	27
William Yancey	August 10, 1814	26
Howell Cobb	September 7, 1815	25
Nathaniel Banks	January 30, 1816	24
Henry David Thoreau	July 12, 1817	23
Frederick Douglass	February 1818	22
Herman Melville	August 1, 1819	21
David Wilmot	January 14, 1820	20
John C. Breckinridge	January 16, 1821	19
Ulysses S. Grant	April 27, 1822	18

## 90

THE SOUTH'S FIRST CASH CROPS: TOBACCO, RICE, COTTON, AND SUGAR

The South's three dominant agricultural crops in the eighteenth century are tobacco, rice, and sugar, and together they provide the foundation behind most of the aristocratic planter families of colonial America. In the nineteenth century they will be joined by "King Cotton."

TOBACCO

Early on, tobacco production is concentrated in Virginia and parts of North Carolina, with Kentucky and Tennessee coming later. But growing tobacco is a complex and labor-intensive undertaking, from transplanting seedlings into the soil to proper fertilization and harvesting. The tobacco leaves are heavy and dirty, and after cutting into "hands" (packets), they must be hung over five-foot long poles to properly dry and cure. Getting all of this right is not easy.

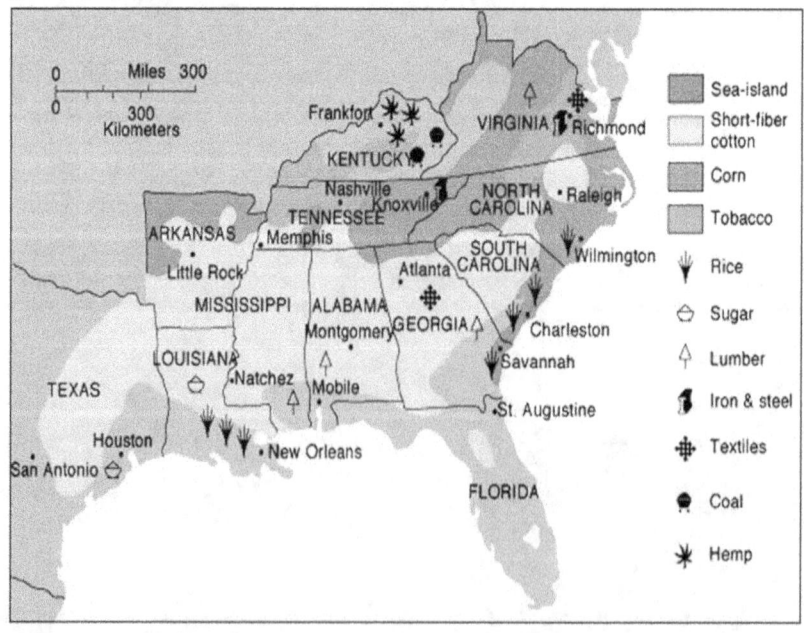

Map of the "agricultural belts" across the South

Tobacco is also an "exploitive" plant, sucking nitrogen out of the soil and depleting its capacity to replenish needed nutrients year after year. The early growers are also either ignorant of the need for crop rotations or are too eager for short-term profits to care. Thus by 1840 much of the tobacco land is worn out, and the Virginia planters in particular are searching for new options to protect their fortunes. One ominous answer will lie in "breeding" enslaved people for sale.

SOME OF VIRGINIA'S ELITE TOBACCO FAMILIES

NAMES	DATES
Richard Lee	1617–1664
Robert "King" Carter	1663–1732
Benjamin Harrison III	1673–1710
William Byrd II	1674–1744
William Fairfax	1691–1757
William Beverly	1696–1756
Mann Page II	1716–1780
William Fitzhugh	1741–1809

RICE

Further south, along the coast of South Carolina and Georgia, the gentry is built on the production of rice, ironically using methods taught to them by the Africans they enslaved. Success is predicated on the presence of swampland, fed by non-saline freshwater rivers and lakes, and temperatures that are reliably warm during the 5–6 month growing season. Preparing and managing a rice field is an arduous task: first to drain and level the swamp, then to plant seedlings in the mud, and finally to add water needed to support growth and fight off weeds. Between April and September, stalks will reach about eighteen inches tall, at which time they are cut down, left to dry in the sun for two weeks, "flailed" to capture pods, and then milled to arrive at the desired rice kernels.

The entire process is fraught with risks. Inland swamps are subject to flooding after heavy rains, while coastal swamps are forever threatened by the ocean's saltwater. Losing a crop to water damage is not uncommon and severe financial losses can follow. Swampland is also the breeding ground for mosquitos and the two main killing diseases they transmit, malaria and yellow fever. Still, the mega-rice planters like Joshua Ward at "Brookgreen" and William Aiken, Jr. on Jehossee Island thrive in 1840 while searching for swampland in Louisiana in order to expand.

SOME OF SOUTH CAROLINA'S ELITE RICE FAMILIES

NAMES	DATES
Joseph Blake	1663–1700
Arthur Middleton	1742–1787
Nathaniel Heyward	1766–1851
Joseph Alston	1779–1816
William Aiken, Sr.	1779–1831
Joshua Ward	1800–1853

SUGAR

The third great Southern crop—sugar—takes off in Louisiana in the 1790s, as a replacement for lagging sales of indigo dye. Advanced know-how in raising sugarcane arrives along with immigrants from plantations in Santo Domingo. It is a form of grass that develops into bamboo-like stalks which grow ten to fourteen feet tall. Planting of seedling stalks occurs in autumn, with fresh shoots appearing the following spring, leading to summer growth and autumn harvesting. Then begins the elaborate process by which the stalks are crushed to give up their sugar juice, which is concentrated by repeated boiling into "cane syrup" (or blackstrap molasses). Once cooled and further purified the syrup is converted into crystalized granules, first as brown sugar and, after more processing, as white sugar.

Credit goes to one Étienne de Boré (1741–1820), a Creole living on a plantation above New Orleans, and Haitian émigrés Antoine Morin and Antonio Menendez, for creating the first profitable operation to produce granulated sugar around 1795. From there, Louisiana becomes the home of American sugar production and of some of the wealthiest planter families. The one main threat to success lies in the Louisiana weather where, unlike the Caribbean clime, a sudden frost can wipe out both a current sugarcane crop and future seedlings.

SOME OF LOUISIANA'S ELITE SUGAR FAMILIES

NAMES	DATES
Steven Minor	1760–1815
James Brown	1766–1835
Lewis Stirling	1786–1858
Michel Bringier	1789–1847
Wade Hampton II	1791–1858
John Burnside	1810–1881
Meredith Calhoun	1805–1869

COTTON

Cotton of course becomes the South's dominant agricultural crop in the nineteenth century. It originates along the east coast from Virginia to Florida, as "sea island cotton," noted for its remarkably long strands of fiber. It then moves inland after Eli Whitney invents his "(en)gin" in 1794, which efficiently sorts seeds from bolls and opens the door to growing "short strand/staple cotton." Seeds are planted in the spring; three-foot high shrubs bearing flower buds ("bolls") appear during the summer; and the back-breaking task of harvesting occurs in autumn.

The crop tends to be hearty as long as droughts are avoided, weeding is completed, and the two key pests (bollworms and boll weevils) are contained. Once plantations open up from Alabama to Texas, cotton becomes the dominant source of wealth across the South.

SOME OF THE SOUTH'S ELITE COTTON FAMILIES

NAME	STATE	DATES
Dr. Stephen Duncan	MS	1787–1867
John Manning	LA	1815–1889
Joseph Acklen	LA	1816–1863
John Robinson	MS	1811 1870?
Jeremiah Brown	AL	1800–1863
Elisha Worthington	AR	1808–1873
Dr. John C. Jenkins	MS	1809–1855

Each of these four crops requires a minimum of 600 acres (1 square mile) of land and over twenty enslaved laborers to prosper. Then come the mega-plantations with over 100 enslaved laborers, which vary widely in acreage. Jefferson's Monticello property spans 5,000 acres or 8 square miles. Washington's Mount Vernon is larger, at 7,600 acres. One of Joshua Ward's rice plantations, "Brookgreen," extends over 9,000 acres, while William Aiken, Jr.'s Jehossee Island is 33,000 acres, or an almost unimaginable 55 square miles.

But there is one thing they all have in common: success rests on owning enough enslaved people and working them to near exhaustion, especially during the critical planting and harvesting seasons.

## 91

THE BREADTH
OF SLAVE OWNERSHIP
IN THE SOUTH

DISTRIBUTION OF ENSLAVED PEOPLE

It's estimated that 30% of all white families across the early Southern states enslaved people—with the incidence ranging from a high of 70% in Georgia to a low of 18% in Maryland.

PERCENT OF FAMILIES OWNING SLAVES

STATE/REGION	%
"Old South"	30
Maryland/DC	18
Virginia	33
North Carolina	27
South Carolina	48
Georgia	70
Kentucky	29
Tennessee	26

From 1840 US Census

Starting with a white population of 4.8 million in 1840 and assuming an average of six people per household, there are just over 800,000 families in total across the South.

Thirty percent of that number yields some 240,000 families who are owners of the 2.5 million enslaved Black people. The distribution of these enslaved people is sharply skewed.

Thus about 70% of all enslavers run small to mid-sized farms with under ten enslaved laborers, while only 12% have the twenty or more required to operate actual plantations.

But the real tycoon elites of the South comprise only about 8,000 families who enslave roughly 600,000 people.

ESTIMATED DISTRIBUTION OF ENSLAVED PEOPLE IN 1840

# SLAVES OWNED	# FAMILIES	% OF ALL FAMILIES	% OF ALL OWNERS	# SLAVES	% OF ALL SLAVES	WORKING LAND OWNED
0	560,000	70	--	--	--	
1	40,000	5	17	40,000	2	Small farm
2–4	72,000	9	30	195,000	8	Small farm
5–9	56,000	7	24	332,000	15	Mid-sized farm
10–19	40,000	5	17	540,000	23	Larger farm
20–49	24,000	3	9	800,000	29	Small plantation
50–99	5,300	0.66	2	350,000	14	Large plantation
100+	2,700	0.33	1	243,000	9	Mega-plantation
Total	800,000	100	100	2,500,000	100	

While enslavers are overwhelmingly white people, a small number are free Black people. In South Carolina, for example, data from 1840 show 402 free Black people owning 2,002 slaves, or an average of five per family. The highest ownership among free Black people traces to three sugar plantations in Louisiana, with 215 enslaved people belonging to Nicholas Metoyer and his family, 152 to widow Ciprien Richards and her son, and another 70 to Antoine Dubuclet and his wife, Claire.

Planter James Marshman

THE SOUTHERN PLANTER TYCOONS

TWENTY LARGEST SLAVE OWNERS ACROSS THE SOUTH

# ENSLAVED PEOPLE	NAME	LOCATION	CROP	PROFILE
2,340	Nathaniel Heyward (1766–1851)	Colleton, SC	Rice	"The Bluff." A shrewd businessman who acquires nineteen plantations over time. Dabbles in politics and signs "nullification" doc. Nearly $1 million estate at his death in 1851.
1,130	Joshua J. Ward (1800–1853)	Georgetown, SC	Rice	"Brookgreen." Known as "king of the rice planters." Born on plantation, leads development of premium "Carolina gold long rice," becomes SC Lt. governor 1850–52.

# ENSLAVED PEOPLE	NAME	LOCATION	CROP	PROFILE
858	Dr. Stephen Duncan (1787–1867)	Issaquena, MS	Cotton	"Saragossa." Born in PA, MD degree, goes to Natchez, participates in efforts to re-colonize Africans, later becomes anti-secession.
753	John Burnside (1810–1881)	Ascension, LA	Sugar	"Houmas House." Belfast, Ireland native, buys from Wade Hampton for $1 million.
709	Meredith Calhoun (1805–1869)	Rapides, LA	Sugar	"Calhoun's Landing." From PA to Red River estate, editor of *National Democrat*.
700	William Aiken, Jr. (1806–1887)	Colleton, SC	Rice	"Jehossee Island." Other businesses are canals and railroads, SC governor 1844–46 then US House 1851–57.
670	John Manning (1816–1889)	Ascension, LA	Cotton	"Millford." SC governor's son, Princeton, marries Hampton daughter, enters politics, SC governor 1852–54, moderate secessionist, Beauregard staff in war, refuses oath to secure Senate seat.
659	Joseph Acklen (1816–1863)	W. Feliciana, LA	Cotton	"Angola." Lawyer, marries plantation heiress and widow of major slave trader Isaac Franklin, lawyer, link to Texas Republic, and triples value of his estate.
631	R.F.W. Allston (1801–1864)	Georgetown, SC	Rice	"Chicora Wood." West Point grad, marries into elite J.L. Petigru family, scientific work on rice, SC governor 1856–58, opposes secession.
575	Joseph Blake (???)	Beaufort, SC	Rice	"Bonnie Hall." One of three Blakes, all heirs of colonial era governor of Carolina, owns slaves in England also. Little known.
550	John Robinson (1811–1870s)	Madison, MS	Cotton	"Annandale." Aristocratic life with little interest in farming operations.
540	Jeremiah Brown (1800–1863)	Sumter, AL	Cotton	"Lowden." Son of wealthy Baptist minister, SC College, law degree, large donations to Howard College (later Samford), equips Confederacy troops.
538	Arthur Blake (???)	Charleston, SC	Rice	"Blake's Plantation." Related to Joseph and Daniel. Little known.
530	John I. Middleton (1800–1877)	Beaufort, SC	Rice	"Middleton Place." Family from Barbados, father was SC governor and ambassador to Russia. He supports re-opening global slave trade and secession.
529	Elisha Worthington (1808–1873)	Chicot, AR	Cotton	"Sunnyside." Little known beyond reported romance with enslaved woman. Resulting children attended the anti-slavery institution, Oberlin College.

# ENSLAVED PEOPLE	NAME	LOCATION	CROP	PROFILE
527	Daniel Blake (???)	Colleton, SC	Rice	"Board House." Related to Joseph and Arthur Blake. Little known.
523	Dr. John C. Jenkins (1809–1855)	Wilkinson, MS	Cotton	"Elgin." Father a wealthy PA iron manufacturer, MD from Dickinson, inherits plantation from uncle. Performs scientific experiments. Dies along with wife and many enslaved people in yellow fever outbreak.
511	J. Harleston Read (1815–1866)	Georgetown, SC	Rice	"Rice Hope." Born on plantation and inherits from his MD father. Little known.
505	John Mease Butler (1808–1863)	McIntosh, GA	Rice and Cotton	"Butler Plantation." Inherits via mother, Sarah Meese, who is daughter of Revolutionary War veteran and founder Pierce Butler. He changes his name to Butler, deplorable conditions, and his brother (Pierce) was an even worse master.
491	Charles Heyward (1802–1866)	Colleton, SC	Rice	"Rose Hill." Grandfather signs Declaration of Independence, attends Princeton, keeps extensive illustrated diary about property.

## 92

THE SOUTH'S SECOND CASH CROP: BREEDING AND SELLING ENSLAVED PEOPLE

THE PRACTICE OF BREEDING

From early on, astute planters understand that "breeding" more enslaved people is both a necessity and a crucial opportunity for financial growth.

With the 1787 Constitution banning further importation of Africans as of 1808, owners must rely on their current enslaved population to reproduce sufficiently to offset workers lost to aging or death. Beyond that, they also recognize that any "excess" sold will bring handsome profits in the auction market.

Two enslaved women

Thomas Jefferson, who sells 110 enslaved people in his lifetime, announces the cold calculations associated with "breeding" in his *Farm Book* entries:

I consider a woman who brings a child every two years as more profitable than the best man of the farm…What she produces is an addition to the capital, while his labors disappear in mere consumption.

The numbers are stark and revealing:

- Twenty-six child-bearing years per woman, ages 18–44;
- A minimum of thirteen potential pregnancies, with early weaning to restart ovulation;
- Perhaps 8–10 children each, given the 66% survival rate at birth;
- At an average sale price of $300, these offspring add $2,500–$3,000 in capital;
- All from the womb of one enslaved woman, before even counting her daughters.

Despite these forecasted "returns," the harsh conditions of enslaved life—between hard work, physical punishment, and unhealthy housing and diets—seldom lead to 8–10 surviving children per enslaved woman.

Jefferson, for example, only records one instance (Minerva Granger and her husband, Bagwell) of nine maturing children among his 175 slaves at Monticello.

By 1840, the former president's economic insights are becoming apparent to more and more plantation owners, especially as growth from the tobacco and rice crops along the Atlantic coast tapers off, and cotton sales begin to boom to the West. Production of "white gold" jumps four-fold between 1820 and 1840, and the dollar value more than doubles, even at lower unit prices.

VALUE OF COTTON

YEAR	COTTON LBS.	PRICE/LB.	TOTAL $	% CH.
1820	142 MM	$.1658	$235 MM	
1840	587	.0900	526	+224%

Like clockwork, the demand for more cotton triggers the demand to "breed" more enslaved people, as attested to later recollections of freed Black people and enslavers alike.

TESTIMONIALS OF ENSLAVED PEOPLE AND MASTERS ABOUT "BREEDING"

Recollections of "slave breeding" abound in letters and diaries from the prewar period, collected from both victims and perpetrators.

William Ward, a formerly enslaved man from Georgia, compares the practice to breeding livestock:

Durin' slavery if one marster had a big boy en 'nuther had a big gal, de marsters made dem libe tergedder. Ef'n de woman didn't hab any chilluns, she wuz put on de block en sold en 'nuther woman bought. You see dey raised de chilluns ter mek money on jes lak we raise pigs ter sell.

Chris Franklin, from Louisiana, reports on the humiliating process owners used to select enslaved people for "mating" and to then ensure that impregnation has occurred:

On this plantation were more than 100 slaves who were mated indiscriminately and without any regard for family unions. If their master thought that a certain man and woman might have strong, healthy offspring, he forced them to have sexual relations even though they were married to other slaves. If there seemed to be any slight reluctance on the part of either of the unfortunate ones, "Big Jim" would make them consummate the relationship in his presence. He used the same procedure if he thought a certain couple was not producing children fast enough. He enjoyed these orgies.

Hilliard Yellerday of North Carolina tells of her futile attempts to avoid bearing children she didn't want:

I goes to de missy and tells her what Rufus wants and missy say dat am de massa's wishes. She say, "Yous am de portly gal and Rufus am de portly man. De massa wants you-uns for to bring forth portly chillen." I's thinkin bout what de missy say, but say to mysef, "I's not gwine live with dat Rufus." Dat night when him come in de cabin, I grabs de poker and sits on de bench and says, "Git 'way from me, nigger, 'fore I busts yous brains out and stomp on dem." He say nothin' and git out. De nex' day de massa call me and tell me, "Woman, I's pay big money for you and I's done dat for de cause I wants yous to raise me chillens. I's put yous to live with Rufus for dat purpose. Now, if you doesn't want whippin' at de stake, yous do what I wants." I thinks 'bout massa buyin' me offen de [auction] block and savin' me from bein' sep'rated from my folks and 'bout bein' whipped at de stake. Dere it am. What am I's to do? So I 'cides to do as de massa wish and so I yields.

Owners also add their perspectives on breeding.

One observation belongs to Francis "Fannie" Kemble, a British actress married for a decade to the infamous planter, Pierce Mease Butler. She writes that the enslaved women exhibited a…

Distinct and perfect knowledge of their value to their owners as property…by bringing new slaves into the world…(declaring) "look missis, little niggets for you and massa, plenty little niggits for you."

Failure to meet an owner's demands for more children is met with harsh retribution. Thus, Davison McDowell, master of "Exchange Plantation" in South Carolina notes in his diary on September 16, 1830:

Sibby miscarried, believe she did so on purpose. Stop her Christmas (gift) and lock her up.

Another South Carolinian, one David Gavin, reveals his own astonishing lack of compassion by reacting to the death of "Celia's slave child" with the same self-centered irritation expressed over the loss of his horses.

Celia's child, about four months old, died Saturday the 12th. That is two Negroes and three horses I have lost this year.

A good summing up comes from the testimonial of John Cole, a formerly enslaved man from Georgia, who ends by wondering aloud how "Christian men" could allow this "breeding" to exist:

A slave girl was expected to have children as soon as she became a woman. Some of them had children at the age of twelve and thirteen years old.... Mother said there were cases where these young girls loved someone else and would have to receive the attentions of men of the master's choice. This was a general custom.... The masters called themselves Christians, went to church worship regularly and yet allowed this condition to exist.

The explanation, of course, lies in the allure of personal greed which can trump all feelings of human empathy. Thus, the utter sickness of slavery, with innocent children diminished to "additions to capital."

And, by 1840, the value of total "slave capital" is already estimated to be $938 million—with demand for excess laborers taking off as aspiring plantation owners cross into the cotton-rich lands from Alabama to Texas.

VALUE OF ENSLAVED PEOPLE

YEAR	# SLAVES	$/SLAVE	TOTAL $	% CH.
1820	1,538 M	$393	$604 MM	
1840	2,487	377	938	+155%

THE INCREASE IN ENSLAVED PREGNANCIES

In response to growing demand for enslaved people, total pregnancies among Black women are exceeding their white counterparts by 1840.

The first indication lies in the relative "fertility rate"—the number of children alive between the ages of 0–4 per 1,000 women aged 18–44 years old. This rate is 6% higher among Black women.

CHILDREN AGED 0–4 PER 1,000 WOMEN 18–44

RACE	IN 1840
Black	1,154
White	1,085
Ratio (Black/White)	106%

While data on death rates in the 0–4 age range are not available, there is good reason to believe that more Black children are lost early, given their subpar birth weights (5.5 lbs. on average), the fact that they are quickly weaned off their mother's milk, and that their replacement diets are starch-laden and lacking in the necessary nutrients to sustain health.

Finally, there are stillborn rates, which show that Black infants are 57% more likely than white infants to die at birth.

STILLBORN RATES

RACE	DEATHS PER 1,000 BIRTHS
White	217
Black	340
Ratio (Black/White)	157%

Taken together, the evidence shows that by 1840 Southern owners are already increasing the rate of Black pregnancies to build their "inventories of excess slaves."

## 93

SELLING ENSLAVED PEOPLE

SHIPMENT OF ENSLAVED PEOPLE TO THE WEST

The ultimate destinations for "excess" enslaved people are the new cotton plantations opening up west of the Appalachian range.

Thus, the staggering growth in the enslaved population occurring between 1820 and 1840 in states such as Mississippi (+595%), Missouri (+582%), and Alabama (+535%), along with the more than doubled population recorded in Louisiana (+144%) and Tennessee (+128%), with Georgia (+88%) just behind.

The leading "supplier state" for these western enslaved people is Virginia, with its very large Black population (over 425,000 in 1820) and its need to address lagging profits on its tobacco plantations.

Other "supplier states" include North Carolina (also suffering erosion in its principal tobacco crops), South Carolina (the "rice kingdom," but with most suitable lowlands already owned), and the two border states, Delaware (where only 2,600 enslaved people remain) and Maryland.

CHANGES IN ENSLAVED POPULATIONS BY STATE

OLD SOUTH	STATEHOOD	1820	1840	CHANGE	% CH.
South Carolina	1788	251,800	327,000	75,200	30
Georgia	1788	149,000	280,900	131,900	88
Virginia	1788	425,200	449,100	23,900	6
North Carolina	1789	205,000	245,800	40,800	20
Border States					
Delaware	1787	4,500	2,600	(1,900)	(42)
Maryland	1788	107,400	89,700	(17,700)	(16)
Kentucky	1792	126,700	182,200	55,500	44
Missouri	1821	10,000	58,200	48,200	582
EXPANDED SOUTH					
Tennessee	1796	80,100	183,100	103,000	128
Louisiana	1812	69,100	168,400	99,300	144
Mississippi	1817	32,800	195,200	162,400	595
Alabama	1819	47,400	253,500	206,100	535
Arkansas	1836	0	19,900	19,900	+++

THE ARMFIELD COFFLE OF 1834

Map of domestic slave trading routes opened by 1840

The task of rounding up excess enslaved people in Virginia and other eastern states and transporting them west and south for sale belongs to a small group of firms which accumulate vast wealth from their efforts.

One pioneer slave trading firm is Franklin & Armfield, headquartered as of 1828 in Alexandria, Virginia. Residing there is John Armfield, who is born in 1797 in North Carolina. His uncle and business partner is Isaac Franklin, born in 1789 to a Tennessee planter, veteran of the War of 1812, astute investor, and owner of plantations in Tennessee and Louisiana. Over time the two develop a transportation route for moving "herds" of enslaved people overland for some 650 miles from Alexandria to Nashville, then from there to river barges for another 500–700-mile journey toward auction houses in Natchez, Mississippi, and New Orleans.

One such transport—known as the "Armfield Coffle of 1834"—sets out with 300 enslaved people in August. A witness describes the sight as follows:

> *Armfield sat on his horse in front of the procession, armed with a gun and a whip. Other white men, similarly armed were arrayed behind him. They were guarding 200 men and boys lined up in twos, their wrists hand-cuffed together, a chain running*

the length of their hands. Behind the men another 100 women and children were tied with rope. Then came six or seven big wagons carrying food, infants, and suits of clothing reserved to display the negroes at auction.

A list of six children who made this particular journey survives:

SOME ENSLAVED CHILDREN IN THE 1834 COFFLE

NAME	GENDER	AGE	HEIGHT
Bill Keeling	Male	11	4'5"
Elizabeth	Female	10	4'1"
Monroe	Male	12	4'7"
Lovey	Female	10	3'10"
Robert	Male	12	4'4"
Mary Fitchett	Female	11	4'11"

The coffle moves at about three miles an hour and 20 miles a day in the sweltering summer heat. It travels from Alexandria along a variety of trails beginning with the Great Wagon Road through the Shenandoah Valley. On September 6, it makes a risky 125-yard crossing of the New River south of Roanoke to avoid a ferry toll. From there it moves west toward Knoxville and then to Gallatin, Tennessee, some 30 miles northeast of Nashville.

Once there, Armfield turns the coffle over to Isaac Franklin's nephew, James, to complete the final leg of the trip. While records end at this point, the enslaved people are likely put on flatboats for a three-day ride down the Cumberland River to the Ohio, and then one more day to connect with the Mississippi. After another two-week voyage south, they will likely dock at Natchez for sale. A contemporary visitor to that city claims that...

There is no branch of trade in this part of the country more brisk and profitable than that of buying and selling negroes.

The terminal for the Armfield Coffle of 1834 is probably Isaac Franklin's auction house located at Forks of the Road, near the end of the Natchez Trace. It has moved to this remote site after Franklin is caught burying enslaved people who have died of cholera in 1833, causing panic and reprisals by city officials.

Sales at the Forks site follow a ritual, with enslaved people dressed up in finery and paraded *en masse* in front of potential bidders.

The men dressed in navy blue suits with shiny brass buttons...as they marched singly and by twos and threes in a circle... The women wore calico dresses and white aprons, with pink ribbons in their hair.

After this showing, they are grouped by age and size within gender categories. Sales are determined by haggling, not by an auctioneer. Thus, a prospective buyer will point to an enslaved person, who will follow them to a more private site for closer inspection. This typically involves the enslaved person undressing and standing naked while the buyer examines their teeth and back (the latter in search of prior whip marks, signaling defiance). The enslaved person may also be asked to speak, sing, or dance, and to describe what work and skills they possess.

The entire process is one of abject humiliation.

Some of the Armfield Coffle may have ended up in New Orleans, the biggest "slave market" in the country, with over fifty dealers in business. A white visitor expresses his discomfort at the wide-open nature of the city:

> You have to squeeze through a countless multitude of men, women and children of all ages, tongues and colors of the earth until you get into the city proper. (The people) are made of the worst portion of the human race. No wonder that there should be robberies and assassinations in such a population.

The actual auctions are often seen as social events, with gawkers outnumbering bidders. Advertisements in local papers boast of "Virginia-bred" enslaved people (meaning compliant) and "fancy girls" (sex slaves) who often go for top dollar. A diary records one such sale of a woman named Hermina:

> On the block was one of the most beautiful women I ever saw…She was sold for $1250 to one of the most lecherous looking old brutes I ever set eyes on.

The Armfield Coffle of 1834 is, of course, only one incident in an "industry" that thrives as prospective plantation owners move west. In total, it's estimated that over half a million American-born enslaved persons are sold over the years in New Orleans. Among the results are shattered families and heart-rending "seeking notices" that follow after the end of the Civil War. Here is one example from a Mary Haynes, living in Texas:

> I wish to inquire after my relatives whom I left in Virginia about twenty-five years ago. My mother's name was Matilda. My name was Mary. I was nine years old when I was sold to a trader named Walker, who carried us to North Carolina. My younger sister Bettie was sold to a man named Reed, and I was sold and carried to New Orleans and from there to Texas. I had a brother, Sam, and a sister, Annie, who were left with mother. If they are alive, I will be glad to hear from them.

## 94

FREE BLACK PEOPLE ARE MAKING PROGRESS

DATE: 1840

THE STATUS OF FREE BLACK PEOPLE IN 1840

In 1840 roughly 13% of all Black people in the US are living free—with slightly over half residing in pro-slavery states. Some are manumitted by their owners, some buy their way out, others are runaways. A relative few are born free, as determined by their mother, whose "status" they inherit.

GROWTH OF THE FREE BLACK POPULATION

	1790	1820	1840
NORTHEAST	26,800	91,790	141,560
NORTHWEST	---	6,410	30,524
OLD SOUTH	18,327	53,386	162,610
BORDER +SW	12,056	34,070	44,604
TOTAL	57,183	185,656	379,298

Regardless of their path to freedom, the latitude they enjoy is sharply constrained. This is especially the case in the South, where white people fear that the presence of free Black people will spark uprisings among those left in slavery. In the North, they are typically living in cities within segregated neighborhoods and subject to written or informal "black codes" which leave them uneducated, poorly housed, unemployed, beyond the protection of basic legal rights, regarded as inferior, and often feared and unwelcome.

Still they persevere, rallying around their own institutions—Black churches, freemason halls, barber shops, and small storefronts—and around community leaders who have mastered the ways of white society and are determined to advance their cause.

Freedwoman Flora Stewart
(age 117)

DATE: 1840

A NEXT GENERATION OF BLACK LEADERS
FIGHT FOR RECOGNITION

By 1840, many of the early leaders have passed—men like Prince Hall, Paul Cuffee, Thomas Paul, Richard Allen, and Absalom Jones. The youthful abolitionist David Walker dies suddenly in 1831. The successful businessman and crusader, James Forten, is 74 and only two years from death.

But a next generation of successors is already beginning to make its mark.

Thomas Dalton works his way up from bootblack and tailoring jobs in Boston to owning a successful clothing store. In 1834 he marries his wife, Lucy Lew, who is educated in an integrated school, and together they embark on a series of efforts to strengthen their community. Dalton becomes a trustee in the AMEZ church, Grand Master of the Prince Hall Lodge, president of the Massachusetts General Colored Association, and co-founding the New England Anti-Slavery Society alongside William Lloyd Garrison.

Reverend Samuel Cornish graduates from the Free African School in Philadelphia, is ordained a minister in 1822, opens the first Black Presbyterian Church in Manhattan, and then co-founds the first

Freedman named T. Hepworth

Black newspaper in America, *Freedom's Journal*. The initial editorial declares its mission:

> *Too long have others spoken for us. Too long have the public been deceived…We wish to plead our own cause.*

Reverend Theodore Wright, the first Black graduate of the Princeton Theological Seminary in 1829, follows Cornish in the Manhattan church pulpit and becomes a founding member of the American Anti-Slavery Society in 1833, which unites white and Black abolitionists and records some 250,000 recruits by 1838. His home becomes a "station" on the Underground Railroad and he eventually supports radical action by Black people to end slavery.

Charles Lenox Remond benefits from his parents' successful catering and barbering businesses and becomes a traveling lecturer and agent for Garrison's *Liberator* newspaper in 1832. He becomes a powerful speaker, addressing the 1840 World Anti-Slavery Convention in London, and later delivering the first speech by a Black man to the Massachusetts state legislature. Remond's younger sister, Sarah, will follow in his footsteps as an abolitionist before moving to Italy and becoming a medical doctor.

Robert Purvis is born in Charleston to a white father, a wealthy cotton merchant who had emigrated from England, and a formerly enslaved mother. After graduating from Amherst College, his father dies, and he is left with a sizable fortune that he uses on behalf of supporting other Black people. He sets up the Library Company of Colored People in Philadelphia, helps Garrison found the American Anti-Slavery Society in 1833, drafts a constitutional amendment on voting rights, and heads Vigilance Committees to prevent Black kidnappings.

David Ruggles attends church school in Connecticut before moving to New York City at age sixteen, where he works as a seaman and operates a grocery store before becoming an agent for the *Liberator*. He then opens a bookstore and edits *The Mirror of Liberty* journal. Like Purvis, he is intently concerned about protecting the freedom of those who have escaped slavery, including Frederick Douglass. He is briefly imprisoned in 1838 for assisting an enslaved man, Thomas Hughes, who escapes after being brought to New York by his Virginia master, John Darg. For his visible work on behalf of escaping enslaved people, he is assaulted and his bookstore is burned down.

While his father is enslaved, Martin Delaney is born free because his mother has previously been manumitted. The youth learns to read from a primer given to him by a peddler, then becomes interested in medicine. After being accepted at Harvard Medical School but denied enrollment, he moves to Pittsburg where he completes his apprenticeship. He attends the 1835 National Negro Convention and later joins the anti-slavery movement. Delaney records remarkable achievements over the next fifty years: helping Frederick Douglass in launch his *North Star* newspaper, authoring articles and novels on the horrors of slavery, and eventually receiving the rank of Major in the Union Army, after meeting with Abraham Lincoln and leading the effort to recruit Black troops.

Born enslaved in Maryland, Henry Highland Garnett escapes at age nine, and gains a high school education in New York city, before graduating from the Oneida Institute in 1839. From there he becomes a church pastor and embarks on a forty-year crusade to end slavery. This includes his call for Black people to start an armed rebellion to win their own freedom, which he delivers at the National Negro Convention of 1843.

William Cooper Nell's father is a freedman in Boston who helps found the Massachusetts General Colored Association in the 1820s. As a young man, he studies law but refuses to swear allegiance to the Constitution, which he calls a racist document, and is never admitted to the bar. By 1840 he is a member of Garrison's inner circle of Boston abolitionists, and works for the rest of his remarkable life on ending slavery, aiding those escaping slavery, and integrating schools and organizations (including those which are Black-only). He joins Frederick Douglass on the *North Star* paper, until it begins to criticize Garrison.

Sojourner Truth (1797–1873)

In 1840 two women who will leave their mark on the abolitionist movement remain in the wings. One is 43-year-old Isabella Baumfree, who escapes from enslavement in New York. Three years later she "hears the spirit" and rechristens herself Sojourner Truth, beginning a series of speaking tours on behalf of abolition. The other is Harriet Tubman, later "general" of the Underground Railroad, but only eighteen at the time, and still suffering great physical abuse while enslaved in Maryland.

Then, of course, there is Frederick Douglass, who will go on to lead the Black citizenship movement over the next three decades. In 1840, he is 22 years old and living in Bedford, Massachusetts with his wife, after escaping slavery in Maryland. He has already become a licensed preacher and avid reader of the *Liberator*, but is yet to achieve the prominence that will follow his landmark August 1841 address to the Massachusetts Anti-Slavery Society on Nantucket Island.

THE NEXT GENERATION OF BLACK LEADERS IN 1840

NAME	AGE	BORN
Thomas Dalton	46	Free
Reverend Samuel Cornish	45	Free
Reverend Theodore Wright	43	Free
Isabella Baumfree/Sojourner Truth	43	Enslaved
Charles Lenox Remond	30	Free
Robert Purvis	30	Free
David Ruggles	30	Free
Martin Delaney	28	Free
Henry Highland Garnet	25	Enslaved
William Cooper Nell	24	Free
Frederick Douglass	22	Enslaved

THE POLITICAL SCENE IN 1840

DATE: 1840

THE SOUTH FACES A MORE THREATENING ELECTORAL TERRAIN

Heading into the 1840 presidential campaign it's clear that the plantation scions of the South have reasons to fear that their control over the federal government may be slipping away.

Their linchpin for over 50 years has been the strength of the Democratic Party, flowing from Jefferson through Andrew Jackson, always attentive to tamping down any anti-slavery rumblings across the North.

But dissatisfaction with Jackson's hand-picked presidential successor, Martin Van Buren, has intensified as the economic recession following the Panic of 1837 persists. It is evident in the 1838 mid-term election, where Henry Clay's Whig Party acquires seats in both chambers of Congress.

ELECTORAL TRENDS IN US CONGRESS

	1834	1836	1838
HOUSE			
Total # of Seats	240	240	240
Whigs (%)	37%	41%	45%
Democratic (%)	59	53	52
Other (%)	4	6	3
SENATE			
Total # of Seats	52	52	52
Whigs (%)	31%	33%	42%
Democratic (%)	59	67	58
Other (%)	10	0	0
President	AJ	MVB	MVB

Even more ominous to the Southerners are the population shifts reported in the 1840 Census.

From the beginning, the South anticipated that its warmer, agriculturally friendly climate would translate into a growing share of the total US population, and hence increase its power in the US House. Instead, it is the North that expands in response to the trend away from rural farming and toward a more diverse economy and big cities.

By 1840, 57% of all Americans are living in the "free states" of the North, while only 43% reside in the "slavery states" of the South—and movement to the West only adds to this disparity.

DISTRIBUTION OF US POPULATION

	1790	1820	1840
TOTAL FREE STATE POP.	50%	53%	57%
Northeast	50	45	40
Northwest	---	8	17
TOTAL SLAVERY STATE POP.	50%	47%	43%
Border	12	15	13
Old South	38	27	19
Southwest	---	5	11
GRAND TOTAL	100%	100%	100%

Since total seats in the House are allocated according to shares of the total population, this 57%–43% split in 1840 is very troubling to the South.

It is accompanied by another worrisome signal, a sense that those with anti-slavery sentiments in the North may come together in an organized fashion for the first time.

While outspoken abolitionists like Garrison are still viewed as "radicals," the American Anti-Slavery Society founded in 1833 has some 1,300 local chapters and a quarter of a million members enrolled by 1838.

If this movement continues to grow, the South fears that pressure will build in Congress to stop the future expansion of slavery.

As control of the US House slips away, the South must rely on two other sources of political power to protect its interest. The first is the Senate, which stands evenly split in 1840 between anti-slavery versus pro-slavery states, based on a series of "gentlemen's agreement" compromises to date.

SENATE MAKEUP IN 1840

SOUTH – "SLAVERY"	BORDER – "SLAVERY"	NORTHEAST – "FREE"	NORTHWEST – "FREE"
1788 South Carolina	1787 Delaware	1787 Pennsylvania	1803 Ohio
1788 Georgia	1788 Maryland	1787 New Jersey	1816 Indiana
1788 Virginia	1792 Kentucky	1788 Connecticut	1818 Illinois
1789 North Carolina	1821 Missouri	1788 Massachusetts	1837 Michigan
1796 Tennessee		1788 New Hampshire	

SOUTH – "SLAVERY"	BORDER – "SLAVERY"	NORTHEAST – "FREE"	NORTHWEST – "FREE"
1812 Louisiana		1788 New York	
1817 Mississippi		1790 Rhode Island	
1819 Alabama		1791 Vermont	
1836 Arkansas		1821 Maine	

The second Southern defense lies in trying to elect a president who will defend, not threaten, slavery.

DATE: FEBRUARY 7, 1839

CLAY'S "I'D RATHER BE RIGHT THAN BE PRESIDENT" SPEECH WILL PROVE PROPHETIC

The Whig Party founder, Henry Clay, is convinced the time has come for him to save the country from the "tyrannies" of King Andrew Jackson and his successor. As he says, we will finally "see the Goths expelled from the Capitol." And his confidence is high:

If we do not beat him (Van Buren), we deserve to be gibbeted.

For three decades, since becoming Speaker of the House in 1811, Clay has been the most dominant force in Congress; he leads the debate on foreign policy, holds the nation together through political compromises, and seeks to strengthen its economy and infrastructure. His fierce belief in the centricity of the legislative branch has placed him in conflict with the imperial presidency of Andrew Jackson, and his Whig Party is dedicated to ending Democratic Party dominance.

Clay feels that the 1840 election will be his time to reach all of his lifelong goals.

While he has advanced the Whig Party cause by touting the economic promises of his "American System," he has historically shied away from speaking directly about the issue of slavery—although it is well known that he enslaves 48 people who toil away on his Ashland plantation.

On February 7, 1839, he decides to remedy this in a landmark speech to the Senate, titled "Petitions for the Abolition of Slavery." As usual, his analysis is pristine and prescient, with main points as follows:

- Slavery has been a long-standing moral stain on the nation.
- It is understandable that abolitionists wish to put an end to it.
- However, this wish is both impractical and dangerous.
- Abolition would devastate the South's cotton economy.
- It would threaten social control and the safety of the white population.
- In turn abolition would encourage a fearful South to secede from the Union.

Before the speech, Clay reviews the remarks with a Southern friend, Senator William Preston of South Carolina, who warns him that it will lead to attacks from those on both sides of the issue. Clay's response to Preston defines the speech for all time:

I trust the sentiments and opinions, and I'd rather be right than be president.

Preston's assessment will prove right.

Much to Clay's chagrin, the arch pro-slavery Democrat, Calhoun, immediately praises the speech on the Senate floor! This only reinforces the belief among Northern "Conscience Whigs" that Clay has simply offered another lousy slaveholder's defense of the status quo.

At the same time, many Southern Whigs are offended by his labeling slavery a "moral stain" and by the notion that he "understands the abolitionists' cause."

TIME: MAY 5–6, 1839

THE DEMOCRATS RENOMINATE VAN BUREN

Sensing an uphill battle, the Democrats hold an early convention on May 5–6, 1839, in Baltimore.

Once there, Van Buren demonstrates that he remains in firm control of the party apparatus by winning the nomination on the first ballot.

However, the delegates signal a small slavery-related mutiny by refusing to support Van Buren's current vice president, Richard Mentor Johnson.

Southerners oppose him for having maintained an open liaison with Julia Chinn, a woman he enslaved (now deceased). Some Northern opponents object to having any slaveholder on their ticket.

When the two sides fail to agree on an alternative, Van Buren is left to run by himself.

DATE: DECEMBER 4–7, 1839

THE WHIGS NOMINATE WILLIAM HENRY HARRISON

On December 4, 1839, the Democratic Whig National Convention opens in Harrisburg, Pennsylvania. By this time, the race is down to three men after Daniel Webster, hated broadly, drops out. All three have won early national fame going way back to their roles in the War of 1812:

- Clay, whose war hawk stance prompted the conflict, and who negotiated the peace treaty ending it;
- General Winfield Scott, whose gallantry in battle helps secure Ft. George in 1813; and

- General William Henry Harrison, victor at Tippecanoe in 1811 and over Tecumseh in 1813.

Ten months after Clay's controversial speech on slavery, several elements within his party join hands to oppose his candidacy.

The Anti-Masonic wing, notably Thurlow Weed of New York and Thad Stevens of Pennsylvania, attack Clay, first for refusing to renounce his Grand Master status in the Kentucky Lodge, then as a two-timing loser. As the acerbic Stevens says:

Clay is a Mason and a loser.

They are joined by a cadre of New Englanders who still hold a grudge against Clay for failing to aggressively support Daniel Webster's nomination in 1836.

Clay's campaign managers also underestimate Harrison's strength among the various factions in the Whig coalition. Veterans of the Indian wars remain loyal to "Old Tip." He is no Freemason. His record of winning seven states in the 1836 election proves his popular potential. And his geographical reach extends from his birthplace in Virginia to his time spent as governor of the Indiana Territory, and to his adopted state of Ohio.

After the first ballot is cast, Clay holds a slim lead when his opponents pounce.

New Yorkers such as Weed and Henry Seward believe that Clay will lose to Van Buren, and on the second ballot, they peel away their support of Clay in Connecticut and Michigan in favor of Scott, their temporary "blocking candidate." Then Stevens spreads a false rumor among Southern delegations that Scott supports abolition, and they swing to Harrison, putting him over the top on the third ballot.

1839 WHIG NOMINATION VOTING

BALLOT	CLAY	HARRISON	SCOTT
1	103	91	57
2	95	91	68
3	90	148	16

Harrison is not chosen until midnight on December 6, at which time the weary crowd begins to search for a way to console their deeply disappointed party founder, and to ensure unity going forward.

They explore naming one of Clay's supporters to the ticket as vice president, but all three men—John Clayton, Benjamin Leigh, and Reverdy Johnson—decline.

On the following day, the delegates settle on their "general plus a Southerner" strategy by selecting the Virginian John Tyler to run with Harrison. This is Tyler's second official appearance on a Whig ticket, having previously run for vice president with two of the Whigs' four regional candidates in 1836.

His choice, apparently a trivial afterthought, will soon boomerang on the Whigs in a profound way.

## 96

ABOLITIONISTS ENTER POLITICS AFTER AN INTERNAL SCHISM

TIME: 1839

GARRISON ALIENATES SOME SUPPORTERS BY FURTHER RADICALIZING HIS AGENDA

While the Whigs and Democrats are forming up their plans for the 1840 elections, the issue of "political action" is dividing what was heretofore a united abolitionist front.

From the beginning, the Boston-based abolitionists—Lundy, Garrison, Phillips, Mott, Whittier, and Douglass—have refused to turn their cause into a political movement, which they fear would lead to compromising and softening their attacks on slavery.

However, by 1839, this perspective is being challenged by leaders like James Birney, Theodor Weld, the Tappan brothers, and Gerrit Smith, who represent the New York and Ohio wings of the movement.

This division is exposed at a January 1839 meeting of the Massachusetts Anti-Slavery Society.

Lloyd Garrison (1805–1879)

Garrison is at his shrillest over a full range of American social norms and institutions.

He moves beyond calls for immediate emancipation and Black assimilation to open support for racial intermarriage, gender equality, women's suffrage, and passive resistance to laws he rejects. He castigates the clergy and all political parties, and urges others to join him in no longer voting in elections.

Much of this is beyond the pale for the more moderate New York and Ohio faction. Instead of drawing additional mainstream Americans into their cause, they see Garrison's increasingly radical messages as driving people away and destroying the one practical path to their end—gathering enough popular support to pass abolition laws in Washington.

From 1839 onward, the abolitionists will find themselves split into two wings.

Garrison's Boston-based followers will try to stay out of politics, and rely strictly on what he terms "moral suasion" to free the enslaved—his *Liberator*, other written material, the itinerant public lecturers, and various public societies.

The New York and Ohio-based wing will jump into the political arena, first by forming their own abolitionist party, and later by backing anti-slavery Whigs and Democrats. Later on, a few will also support violent means to achieve their ends.

DATE: 1839 ONWARD

JAMES BIRNEY AND GERRIT SMITH EMBRACE A POLITICAL PATH TO ABOLITION

Two men in particular will lead the abolitionists into the political arena—James Birney, a former enslaver living in Ohio, and Gerrit Smith, the philanthropic reformer from upstate New York.

Birney grows up in Danville, Kentucky, where slavery is taken for granted. His father is a slaveholder, and Birney is given several enslaved people as a wedding present when he marries the aristocratic Agatha McDowell. His education at the College of New Jersey (Princeton) leads to a very successful legal practice in Danville. He is a powerful debater, and enters the political arena in 1816 when elected to the state legislature.

In 1819 he moves to Alabama to try his hand at running a cotton plantation that includes some 43 enslaved workers. Once there he helps write the constitution that leads to statehood in 1819, and eventually serves in

Gerrit Smith (1797-1784)

the state's first legislature. His political stance is staunchly pro-Clay and anti-Andrew Jackson.

On the surface, Birney's future as a Southern planter and politician seems fixed by age 28, in 1820.

But then his world comes apart. He suffers crop failures which, combined with gambling debts and lavish spending, lead to financial ruin. He loses a child and becomes an alcoholic. Finally, he decides to sell off most of his enslaved workers to pay debts, and moves to Huntsville to try to pick up the pieces as a lawyer.

This works. Birney joins the Presbyterian Church in 1826, which restores his bearings. He serves as a state attorney, and then is elected mayor of the city in 1829. But much of his energy focuses on a personal quest—exploring his past involvement with slavery. His final conclusion shocks fellow Southerners:

> Slavery is a sin before God. Men have no more right to enact slavery than they have to enact murder.

Birney now follows through on his new convictions. He frees and pays off the remaining people he had enslaved, actively works on behalf of the American Colonization Society, and formally connects with the abolitionist movement through Theodore Weld.

After moving back to Danville in 1835 Birney leaps into the center of the controversy by publishing an abolitionist paper, *The Philanthropist*. When local mobs threaten his safety, he moves north to the free state of Ohio, only to see his paper become a precipitating cause of the race riots that disrupt Cincinnati in 1836. The attacks on Birney and the riots bring another prominent Ohio figure, Salmon P. Chase, into the abolitionist cause.

These two will soon be joined by Gerrit Smith, a figure well-known for supporting experiments in social reengineering.

Smith is born in Utica, New York into fabulous wealth accumulated by his father, Peter, who is a long-term partner in John Jacob Astor's fur trading empire. After graduating from Hamilton College, he takes over management of the estate and grows it handsomely.

Like many other reformers of his era, Smith's life is reshaped by the Reverend Charles Finney. In 1835 he attends revivalist services led by Finney in Utica, New York. From then on, he becomes a lifelong supporter of the preacher and a major financial contributor to his Oberlin College.

Under Finney's influence, Smith defines his agenda as a philanthropist. He begins with temperance, then branches out into abolition, land and prison reform, women's suffrage, and even vegetarianism and Irish independence.

In 1839, Smith's focus lies on working with Birney and Chase to move the abolition cause into the political arena where rhetoric can be translated into laws and action.

DATE: NOVEMBER 13, 1839

ABOLITIONISTS FOUND THE LIBERTY PARTY

On November 13, 1839, a coalition including Birney, Chase, Smith, Arthur Tappan, and New York Judge William Jay, meet in Warsaw, New York, and agree on a charter for the "Liberty Party."

Arthur Tappan (1786–1865)

Resolved, That, in our judgment, every consideration of duty and expediency which ought to control the action of Christian freemen requires of the Abolitionists of the United States to organize a distinct and independent political party, embracing all the necessary means for nominating candidates for office and sustaining them by public suffrage.

The new party holds its first convention at City Hall in Albany, New York on November 13, 1839, with 121 delegates from six states present. James Birney is nominated to run for president, with Thomas Earle, a notable lawyer and journalist from Pennsylvania, joining the ticket as vice president.

## 97

WILLIAM HENRY HARRISON'S ONE-MONTH PRESIDENTIAL TERM

TIME: AUTUMN 1841

HARRISON BECOMES AMERICA'S NINTH PRESIDENT

The election of 1840 is marked by another dramatic upswing in the number of popular votes cast, probably the result of growing public unrest with the economy and the excitement surrounding Harrison's candidacy.

POPULAR VOTES CAST FOR PRESIDENT

YEAR	NUMBER	% VS Y-A
1832	1,286,700	+12.1%
1836	1,502,300	+16.8
1840	2,411,808	+60.5

The race itself marks a turning point in the character of political campaigning. Instead of focusing on "issues"—where Harrison's positions are typically vague—the Whigs focus on selling his "personal story" vis-à-vis Van Buren.

Despite patrician roots in Virginia, Harrison is cast as "Old Tip," a "log cabin and hard cider" common man of the West, and a military hero in wars against the Indians and the British. Meanwhile, the Whigs paint Van Buren as "Van Ruin," a New York snob detached from the economic suffering of the people caused by the inept policies of his administration.

Harrison actively pursues the high office by touring the country, making speeches, and handing out log cabin-shaped bottles of whiskey. Van Buren

William Henry Harrison (1773–1841)

follows tradition, staying in the White House and allowing surrogates to reach out on his behalf.

Voting runs from October 30 to December 2 with 80% of all eligible voters taking part. The Whigs win nineteen of 26 states, sending the Democrats and Martin Van Buren to an eye-opening defeat. The popular count—53% to 47%—turns out closer than many expect. But in the Electoral College, Harrison runs away from Van Buren by a margin of 234 to 60.

The abolitionists' new Liberty Party records fewer than 7,000 votes in total.

RESULTS OF THE 1840 PRESIDENTIAL ELECTION

CANDIDATE	PARTY	POP. VOTES	ELECT. VOTES	SOUTH	BORDER	NORTH	WEST
Harrison	Whig	1,275,390	234	50	28	123	33
Van Buren	Democrat	1,128,854	60	44	4	7	5
Birney	Liberty	6,797	0	0	0	0	0
Other		767					
		2,411,808	294	94	32	130	38

State by state returns show the North turning against Van Buren, including his home state of New York, along with a pronounced weakening of the Democrats' hold on the "solid South."

PARTY POWER BY STATE

SOUTH	1836	1840	GAIN
Virginia	Democrat	Democrat	
North Carolina	Democrat	Whig	Whig
South Carolina	Whig (Mangum)	Democrat	Democrat
Georgia	Whig (White)	Whig	
Alabama	Democrat	Democrat	
Mississippi	Democrat	Whig	Whig
Louisiana	Democrat	Whig	Whig
Tennessee	Whig (White)	Whig	
Arkansas	Democrat	Democrat	
Border			
Delaware	Whig (Harrison)	Whig	
Maryland	Whig (Harrison)	Whig	
Kentucky	Whig (Harrison)	Whig	

NORTH	1836	1850	GAIN
New Hampshire	Democrat	Democrat	
Vermont	Whig (Harrison)	Whig	
Massachusetts	Whig (Webster)	Whig	
Rhode Island	Democrat	Whig	Whig
Connecticut	Democrat	Whig	Whig
New York	Democrat	Whig	Whig
New Jersey	Whig (Harrison)	Whig	
Pennsylvania	Democrat	Whig	Whig
Ohio	Whig (Harrison)	Whig	
Maine	Democrat	Whig	Whig
Indiana	Whig (Harrison)	Whig	
Illinois	Democrat	Democrat	
Iowa	Democrat	Democrat	
Michigan	Democrat	Whig	Whig

The Whigs also sweep to victory in both houses of Congress.

CONGRESSIONAL ELECTION OF 1840

HOUSE	1838	1840	CHANGE
Democrats	126	98	(28)
Whigs	108	144	36
Anti-Masonic	6	--	(6)
Conservative	2	--	(2)
Other			
SENATE			
Democrats	29	22	(7)
Whigs	23	29	6
PRESIDENT	Van Buren	Harrison	

For the first time since John Quincy Adams' victory in the 1824 election, the Democratic Party's stranglehold on political control has been broken!

TIME: 1773–1841

PRESIDENT WILLIAM HENRY HARRISON: PERSONAL PROFILE

Harrison's career mirrors Andrew Jackson's in many ways. He is born a British citizen in the old South, although in his case to a wealthy father who signed the Declaration of Independence, served as governor of Virginia, and is master of the Berkeley Plantation. After studying medicine at Penn College, he joins the army and in 1794 serves under Mad Anthony Wayne in his fight against Indigenous tribes in the North-west Territory.

Harrison's future now lies in the West, much like Jackson. He marries an Ohio woman, resigns from the army to enter politics, and in 1799 wins a seat in the US House. In 1800 he pushes the Harrison Land Act through Congress, winning lasting approval from settlers by lowering the per acre price for new homesteads. John Adams names him the first governor of the vast Indiana Territory (what will become Indiana, Michigan, Illinois, Wisconsin, and part of Minnesota), and he serves from 1801 to 1812.

During that period, he tries hard to allow slavery into the territory even though it is officially banned.

On November 6, 1811 he defeats a confederation of tribes (Shawnee, Pottawatomie, Miami, and others) near Prophetstown, Indiana, at the Battle of Tippecanoe. In 1812 he wins the Battle of Thames in upper Ontario, killing Chief Tecumseh, who had sided with Britain in the war and is the acknowledged leader of the uprisings.

Like Jackson, these victories on the battlefield mark him forever as a national hero.

After serving in the House and Senate from Ohio between 1816 and 1828, Harrison retires to his farm to breed horses and open a distillery. But in 1836 he is back in politics as the newly formed Whig Party convinces him to run for president. While losing to Van Buren, he records over 550,000 votes.

As the slavery issue heats up, Harrison's views prove sufficiently ambiguous to not alienate any Whig factions.

Southerners are comforted by the fact that he has grown up on a Virginia plantation, and that as territorial governor he supported bringing slavery into Indiana.

Meanwhile, anti-slavery elements find reassurance in an 1833 speech, where he declares:

> I am accused of being friendly to slavery. From my earliest youth to the present moment, I have been the ardent friend of Human Liberty. At the age of eighteen, I became a member of an Abolition Society established at Richmond, Virginia; the object of which was to ameliorate the condition of slaves and procure their freedom by every legal means... I have been the means of liberating many slaves, but never placed one in bondage... I was the first person to introduce into congress the proposition that all the country above (North of) Missouri... should never have slavery admitted into it.

By 1840, Harrison's enslaved laborers have been "converted" into indentured servants, and he publicly adopts what will become the "centrist position" on the issue—concern about the morality of the institution, a hope that it will wither away over time, combined with a promise to not have the federal government interfere in the states' rights of the South.

TIME: MARCH 4, 1841

INAUGURAL ADDRESS

Harrison is 68 years old when he steps to the podium on March 4, 1841, to take the oath of office from Chief Justice Taney. The temperature is 48 degrees, but a brisk wind chills the onlookers. As the oldest president elect at that time, Harrison is intent on demonstrating his personal vitality, so he refuses to wear an overcoat, hat, or gloves. He also delivers the longest inaugural address in history, lasting for one hour and 45 minutes.

His opening line sounds a particularly ironic note given his fate—the old warrior called out of retirement to spend the "residue of (his) life" as chief executive:

Called from a retirement which I had supposed was to continue for the residue of my life to fill the chief executive office of this great and free nation, I appear before you, fellow-citizens, to take the oaths which the Constitution prescribes as a necessary qualification for the performance of its duties; and…to present to you a summary of the principles which will govern me in the discharge of the duties which I shall be called upon to perform.

In a thinly disguised slam at Jackson and Van Buren, he reassures the nation that his administration will reject any notions of "divine right" when it comes to wielding executive power:

We admit of no government by divine right…the Constitution… contains declarations of power granted and of power withheld.

From there he launches into a lengthy and thoughtful analysis of the 1787 Constitution, citing issues facing the founders, precedents from the Romans and Greeks, and his interpretation of the core principles and how he intends to treat them while in office.

He dwells on the veto and promises to use it, but only sparingly. He cites the founders' early fears about the federal government drowning out the voice of the individual states—but concludes that this hasn't happened.

The great dread (was that) the States would be absorbed by those of the Federal Government and a consolidated power established, leaving to the States the shadow only of that independent action for which they had so zealously contended and on the preservation of which they relied as the last hope of liberty…(But) the General Government has seized upon none of the reserved rights of the States.

He attacks the patronage system as a force for corrupting government, and the "unhallowed union" which has developed between the Treasury and the executive branch.

(Regarding) the divorce, as it is called, of the Treasury from the banking institutions.

It is not the divorce which is complained of, but the unhallowed union of the Treasury with the executive department, which has created such extensive alarm.... I have determined never to remove a Secretary of the Treasury without communicating all the circumstances attending such removal to both Houses of Congress.

He admonishes politicians for staying too long in office, and promises that he will exit after one term:

I give my aid to it by renewing the pledge heretofore given that under no circumstances will I consent to serve a second term.

He insists that all revenue generating schemes originate with the legislature, not the executive branch, and that those wishing to abolish paper currency are dead wrong.

An exclusively metallic currency...appears to me to be fraught with more fatal consequences than any other scheme having no relation to the personal rights of the citizens that has ever been devised

He promises to protect the absolute freedom of the press and the shared rights of all living in the District of Columbia. Avoiding conflicts between states or sections is paramount to the overriding goal of preserving the sacred Union.

Of all the great interests which appertain to our country, that of union—cordial, confiding, fraternal union—is by far the most important, since it is the only true and sure guaranty of all others... The spirit of liberty is the sovereign balm for every injury which our institutions may receive.

Foreign policy is touched on briefly, with the usual assurances about maintaining friendly relations with all.

I should give some indications to my fellow-citizens of my proposed course of conduct in the management of our foreign relations. I assure them, therefore, that it is my intention to use every means in my power to preserve the friendly intercourse which now so happily subsists with every foreign nation

Like many of his predecessors, he turns to the threat to both liberty and the Union that he sees in partisan politics.

Before concluding, fellow-citizens, I must say something to you on the subject of the parties at this time existing in our country... The true spirit of liberty...is mild and tolerant and scrupulous as to the means it employs, whilst the spirit of party, assuming to be that of liberty, is harsh, vindictive, and intolerant...

If parties in a republic are necessary to secure a degree of vigilance sufficient to keep the public functionaries within the bounds of law and duty, at that point their usefulness ends. Beyond that they become destructive of public virtue...It was the beautiful remark of a distinguished English writer that "in the Roman senate Octavius had a party and Anthony a party, but the Commonwealth had none."

Always the friend of my countrymen, never their flatterer, it becomes my duty to say to them from this high place to which their partiality has exalted me that there exists in the land a spirit hostile to their best interests—hostile to liberty itself. It is a spirit contracted in its views, selfish in its objects. It looks to the aggrandizement of a few even to the destruction of the interests of the whole. The entire remedy is with the people…It is union that we want, not of a party for the sake of that party, but a union of the whole country for the sake of the whole country…All the influence that I possess shall be exerted to prevent the formation at least of an Executive party in the halls of the legislative body. I wish for the support of no member of that body to any measure of mine that does not satisfy his judgment and his sense of duty to those from whom he holds his appointment…

By now cold to the bone, he takes his leave—a leave that will last only 31 days.

I deem the present occasion sufficiently important and solemn to justify me in expressing to my fellow-citizens a profound reverence for the Christian religion and a thorough conviction that sound morals, religious liberty, and a just sense of religious responsibility are essentially connected with all true and lasting happiness…

Fellow-citizens, being fully invested with that high office to which the partiality of my countrymen has called me, I now take an affectionate leave of you.

TIME: APRIL 4, 1841

HARRISON DIES AFTER ONE MONTH IN OFFICE

Harrison begins his term by visiting and studiously evaluating all six departments of government, and then naming his cabinet. It includes men who will be marked by their dedication to preserving the Union, including, to Clay's chagrin, Daniel Webster as secretary of state.

WILLIAM HENRY HARRISON'S CABINET

POSITION	NAME	HOME STATE
Secretary of State	Daniel Webster	Massachusetts
Secretary of the Treasury	Thomas Ewing	Ohio
Secretary of War	John Bell	Tennessee
Attorney General	John Crittenden	Kentucky
Secretary of the Navy	George Badger	North Carolina
Postmaster General	Francis Granger	New York

Other administrative duties descend swiftly on Harrison.

Despite criticism of the patronage or "spoils" system established by Jackson and Van Buren, he is immediately besieged at the White House by those seeking favors. To escape, he takes to walking unaccompanied around the capital.

One such stroll ends with a downpour, from which he develops what appears to be a severe cold.

On March 26, when his condition worsens, Harrison calls upon his doctor, Thomas Miller, complaining of fatigue and "derangement of the stomach and bowels." Miller is 35 years old at the time, an 1829 graduate of the University of Pennsylvania medical school, and a highly regarded professor and surgeon.

Miller proceeds to "purge" Harrison's intestinal system through doses of laxatives, opium, and a series of enemas, administered over the next eight days. Nothing works, and the president suffers increased intestinal pain and bouts of delirium.

At 3 p.m. on April 3, he is hit by "profuse diarrhea," with his extremities turning blue and his pulse fading. He dies at 12:30 a.m. on April 4.

Miller attributes the death to pneumonia, but admits to uncertainty about his diagnosis. Modern analysis suspects typhoid fever, attributable to the same polluted drinking water in Washington that later sickens President Polk and perhaps kills President Taylor. If in fact Harrison suffered from salmonella pathogens in his intestines, Miller's "treatment" probably hastened his end, since opium inhibits natural expulsion of the infection and enemas only spread its effects.

Dr. Thomas Miller (1806–1863)

The death leaves the country without a sitting president for the first time in its history.

Its initial response lies in providing a proper funeral for Harrison. The White House is draped in black crepe and the Episcopalian ceremony, by invitation only, is held in the East Room. Six white horses carry the former president's body on a two-mile journey, filled with well over 10,000 onlookers, to a public vault where it is stored until a later trip home to North Bend, Ohio for final burial. May 14 is declared as a day of national mourning.

The recorded cost of the funeral is $3,088, including $90 for a walnut coffin. Harrison's wife is later awarded $25,000, the one-year salary allotted the chief executive.

## 98

JOHN TYLER COMPLETES THE PRESIDENTIAL TERM

TIME: APRIL 6, 1839

VICE PRESIDENT TYLER
CLAIMS THE OVAL OFFICE

While the burial ceremonies proceed, Daniel Webster's son, Fletcher, rides to Williamsburg, Virginia to inform John Tyler of Harrison's death. The vice president is there because he has no responsibilities in Washington until the Senate reconvenes in June. But Tyler has received reports of Harrison's illness and is poised to assert his claim to successor status. He makes a hasty journey to DC, arriving on April 6 to meet with the cabinet and assume command.

At this point, a legal debate ensues, with opponents of Tyler arguing that he is merely the "acting president," serving until another election can be called to choose a permanent successor. They try to make their case around wording in the 1804 Twelfth Amendment which says the vice president shall "act as president" not "become" president.

If the House shall not choose a President...then the Vice-President shall act as President, as in the case of the death or other constitutional disability of the President.

Tyler simply ignores the issue and takes the oath of office, and at 51 years old becomes the youngest man so far to serve as president.

Critics of Tyler like John Quincy Adams are immediately alarmed:

Tyler is a political sectarian, of the slave-driving, Virginian, Jeffersonian school, principled against all improvement, with all the interests and passions and vices of slavery rooted in his moral and political constitution—with talents not above mediocrity, and a spirit incapable of expansion to the dimensions of the station upon which he has been cast by the hand of Providence, unseen through the apparent agency of chance. No one ever thought of his being placed in the executive chair.

Henceforth opponents will refer to him with the snickering epithet "His Accidency."

TIME: 1790–1862

PRESIDENT JOHN TYLER: PERSONAL PROFILE

John Tyler grows up on the "Greenway" plantation, a 1,200-acre estate on the James River that relies on enslaved labor to grow tobacco.

His father, "Judge" John Tyler Sr., serves in the Continental Army but opposes the Constitution on grounds that it limits states' rights and disadvantages the South. As governor of Virginia (1808–1811) he remains a staunch anti-Federalist. He is also a friend of Thomas Jefferson, who often dines at Greenway with the Judge and his son.

Young Tyler is a precocious student, graduating from the College of William & Mary at seventeen years old and passing the bar at nineteen. By 1811 he has built his own reputation as a criminal defense attorney and through his connections is elected to Virginia's House of Delegates. He joins the militia during the War of 1812, but sees no action. In 1813

John Tyler (1790–1862)

Tyler inherits Greenway upon the death of his father, then marries the beautiful but reclusive Letitia Christian, who also brings her own wealth to the union.

He is elected to the US House at age 26, and remains there from 1816 to 1821, consistently voting against Henry Clay's attempts to build the nation's infrastructure, pass protective tariffs, and establish a strong central bank. His views on slavery are those of the aristocratic planters—a stated moral discomfort with the practice, followed by rationalization of its necessity, additions to his personal ownership, and some vague wish to see it wither away over time. In line with these views, he votes against the Missouri Compromise of 1820 for imposing what he considers an illegal constraint on the spread of slavery into the West.

By no stretch of the imagination do his thoughts or votes to this point peg him as a future Whig supporter!

Tyler abandons Congress in 1821, frustrated by what he considers the constant erosion of states' rights. He returns home to Virginia, but is soon bored by farming and jumps back into politics, serving as governor from 1825 to 1827. After that, he returns to DC and the US Senate in 1827, replacing the unhinged John Randolph and proclaiming himself a Jackson Democrat.

But he turns against Jackson in 1833 during the Nullification Crisis. He views the

"Force Bill," aimed at blocking South Carolina secession, as one more overreach by the federal government against the sovereign wishes of the states. He is the only Southern Democrat that doesn't vote in the Senate on the measure.

A year later, he has flipped his support over to Henry Clay, almost as a "lesser evil" than Jackson. When he sides with Clay to "censure" Jackson for removing funds from the US Bank, the legislature in Virginia orders him to reverse his course. This leads him to resign his seat in 1836.

At this point, Clay and the Whigs begin to view Tyler as a handy political pawn in their scheme to defeat the Democrats.

He plays along with this in the 1836 election, running as a vice presidential candidate on two of the four Whig "regional tickets" designed to deny Van Buren an outright victory and throw the final choice into the House. His role is to attract Southern votes, based on his status as a Virginian, an enslaver, and an opponent of a "too powerful" executive.

While Van Buren wins in 1836, Tyler is henceforth viewed as an affable "go-along" politician, one who could pass as a Southern Whig despite his early ties to the opposition.

It is this shallow assessment which causes the weary Whig delegates at the December convention to select Tyler to run as vice president, after three "Clay men" have turned the offer down.

At that moment, none recognize that the "Tippecanoe and Tyler Too" union will backfire when Harrison dies and a true "closet Democrat" replaces him in the White House.

TIME: APRIL 9, 1841

TYLER'S MESSAGE TO THE NATION

On April 9, Tyler issues a brief message outlining some thoughts about his presidency. He begins by acknowledging the unique circumstances leading to his position, and the potential for attacks based on the "spirit of faction."

> *For the first time in our history the person elected to the Vice-Presidency of the United States, by the happening of a contingency provided for in the Constitution, has had devolved upon him the Presidential office. The spirit of faction, which is directly opposed to the spirit of a lofty patriotism, may find in this occasion for assaults upon my Administration.*

Instead of a full inaugural address he says he will offer...

> *A brief exposition of the principles which will govern me in the general course of my administration of public affairs (which) would seem to be due as well to myself as to you.*

He begins with foreign affairs, possibly anticipating tensions between Mexico and the Republic of Texas.

In regard to foreign nations, the groundwork of my policy will be justice on our part to all, submitting to injustice from none. While I shall sedulously cultivate the relations of peace and amity with one and all, it will be my most imperative duty to see that the honor of the country shall sustain no blemish.

He then expresses concerns over the "spoils system" (i.e., patronage) that so troubled him about both the Jackson and Van Buren administrations. His reference to "removals from office" may portend future changes he has in mind for the cabinet inherited from Harrison.

The patronage incident to the Presidential office, already great, is constantly increasing…I will at a proper time invoke the action of Congress upon this subject, and shall readily acquiesce in the adoption of all proper measures which are calculated to arrest these evils, so full of danger in their tendency. I will remove no incumbent from office who has faithfully and honestly acquitted himself of the duties of his office, except in such cases where such officer has been guilty of an active partisanship or by secret means… I have dwelt the longer upon this subject because removals from office are likely often to arise, and I would have my countrymen to understand the principle of the Executive action.

He shifts to financial management, promising to avoid public debt in time of peace and to end the "war between the Government and the currency"—an evident reference to Jackson's distrust of soft money.

In all public expenditures the most rigid economy should be resorted to, and, as one of its results, a public debt in time of peace be sedulously avoided. A strict responsibility on the part of all the agents of the Government should be maintained and peculation or defalcation visited with immediate expulsion from office and the most condign punishment. The public interest also demands that if any war has existed between the Government and the currency it shall cease… I shall promptly give my sanction to any constitutional measure which, originating in Congress, shall have for its object the restoration of a sound circulating medium, so essentially necessary to give confidence in all the transactions of life…

In regard to familiar tensions between state and federal sovereignty, he will be the strict constructionist, "abstain(ing) from all attempts to enlarge the range of powers… granted…the Government," since to do otherwise would "break asunder the bond of union…or end in a bloody scepter and iron crown."

Those who are charged with its administration should carefully abstain from all attempts to enlarge the range of powers thus granted to the several departments of the Government other than by an appeal to the people for additional grants, lest by so doing they disturb that balance which the patriots and statesmen who framed the Constitution designed to establish between the Federal Government and the States composing the Union.

The observance of these rules is enjoined upon us by that feeling of reverence and affection which finds a place in the heart of every patriot for the preservation of union and the blessings of union....An opposite course could not fail to generate factions intent upon the gratification of their selfish ends, to give birth to local and sectional jealousies, and to ultimate either in breaking asunder the bonds of union or in building up a central system which would inevitably end in a bloody scepter and an iron crown.

With those vague and wandering guidelines on the record, Tyler begins his controversial four-year term.

TIME: 1841–1845

OVERVIEW OF TYLER'S TERM

Tyler's term will prove both controversial and consequential regarding America's destiny.

After being sworn in, the assumption throughout the capital is that the "accidental president" will bend his will to the hierarchy within the Whig Party. As Preston Blair, editor of the Democrat newspaper *The Washington Globe*, puts it: Tyler will be "Clay's pliant tool" in the White House.

But Clay is not the only one seeking control, as Tyler finds out when his inherited cabinet tells him of Harrison's intent to count their votes as equal to his with regard to policy decisions. His response sets the tone for what is soon to follow:

I am very glad to have in my cabinet such able statesmen...and I shall be pleased to avail myself of your counsel and advice. But I can never consent to being dictated to. I am the President and I shall be responsible for my administration.

From then on, Tyler shows his true political colors as a states' rights Democrat and a slaveholder.

He immediately frustrates Clay's attempt to create another federal bank to fund the Whigs' infrastructure projects. In response, they gather and officially oust him from the party, then follow by hurling rocks at the White House terrifying his stroke-ridden wife and leading to a police patrol to guard the property.

From there they do their best to thwart every move he makes. On three occasions, the Senate refuses to confirm Caleb Cushing—a Whig who stays loyal to Tyler—as secretary of the Treasury. They also turn away all four of his Supreme Court nominees.

Still Tyler's term witnesses a series of events that will dramatically heighten the sectional tensions over slavery and eventually set the stage for war.

First is an increase in the number of Northerners who are at least "troubled" by the notion of human bondage. This feeling is sparked during the "religious awakening" phase, with its calls for moral perfection and social reform. It is broadened by agitation from abolitionists like Garrison and his formation of organized anti-slavery societies. Then it's carried into the political arena by the likes of John Quincy Adams and Joshua Giddings in Congress, and philanthropists Gerrit Smith and the Tappan brothers with their Liberty Party.

This draws a response from the South with clergyman James Henley Thornwell arguing that slavery is "ordained by the Bible"—a claim that provokes heated disputes within the three main Protestant churches and ends with ominous North–South doctrinal schisms.

Tyler also encounters more ongoing challenges to the Fugitive Slave Act. One involves a mutiny aboard the American ship *Creole*, which ends with some 135 enslaved people being freed in Nassau by a British court. This act, along with other sea and border disputes, threatens warfare until resolved by the Ashburton-Webster Treaty of 1842. A second controversy involves an enslaved woman who ends up living in Pennsylvania and sues for her release under the theory of "once free, forever free." Much to the dismay of the abolitionists, this notion is dismissed by the US Supreme Court in the landmark *Prigg v. Pennsylvania* decision.

Finally, it is during Tyler's term that Americans become enamored with the notion of "Manifest Destiny," the idea that its borders should extend all the way to the Pacific Ocean, across territory currently owned by Mexico. This leads to a series of exploratory expeditions by the Army Corps of Engineers and Lt. John C. Fremont to produce accurate maps of the Oregon Trail and the coast of California. His lyrical descriptions of these journeys are an overnight sensation and heighten public support for westward expansion, beginning with the annexation of Texas—a fateful move that Tyler supports, and that eventually leads to the Mexican War and reopens the toxic debate over slavery.

On the economic front, the economic depression Tyler inherits from Van Buren continues to plague the nation up to 1844, when some signs of recovery appear.

ECONOMIC OVERVIEW: JOHN TYLER'S TERM

GDP	1840	1841	1842	1843	1844
TOTAL ($MM)	$1,574	$1,652	$1,618	$1,550	$1,690
% CHANGE	(5%)	5%	(2%)	(4%)	9%
PER CAP.	$92	$94	$89	$83	$88

John Tyler is 54 years old when his term ends. He reflects on his "accidental presidency" in brief remarks on his last day in the White House:

In 1840 I was called from my farm to undertake the administration of affairs, and I foresaw that I was called to a bed of thorns…I rely on future history, and on the candid and impartial judgment of my fellow citizens, to award me the meed due to honest and conscientious purposes to serve my country.

The former president will live on for another fifteen years, mostly at his Virginia plantation, "Sherwood Forest." One of his remaining joys will be his youthful new bride, Julia, whom he marries in June 1844 after losing his first wife in September 1842. Together they will have seven children to go along with the eight Tyler fathered before.

As the threat of war reaches a boiling point in April 1861, Tyler returns to Washington to sponsor the Virginia Peace Conference, which fails to find a compromise. At that point, he goes with his home state, Virginia, and is elected to the CSA House. But he dies on January 18, 1862, before its opening session.

KEY EVENTS: TYLER'S TERM

1841	
April 4	President Harrison dies after 31 days; Tyler is first to succeed as vice president
April 10	Horace Greeley begins to publish his pro-Whig and anti-slavery *New York Tribune*
August 6	Congress passes Whigs' Fiscal Bank Bill (similar to Bank of US)
August 11	Frederick Douglass addresses an anti-slavery meeting in Nantucket
August 13	Congress repeals Van Buren's Independent Treasury Act
August 16	Tyler vetoes Whigs' Fiscal Bank Bill as unconstitutional
September 2–3	Another race riot breaks out in Cincinnati
September 3	Congress passes revised Fiscal Bank Bill to address Tyler's concerns
September 9	Tyler vetoes the new bill and attempt to override veto voted down in Senate
September 11	Tyler's cabinet resigns *en masse*, all except for Secretary of State Daniel Webster
November 7–9	Enslaved people on *Creole*, going from Virginia to New Orleans, kill crew and are freed in Nassau
Year	George Ripley starts up his Brook Farm utopian community
1842	
January 24	John Quincy Adams presents Haverill, Massachusetts petition or peaceful dissolution of the Union
March 1	Supreme Court in *Prigg v. Commonwealth of Pennsylvania* says that the state cannot forbid seizure of escaping enslaved people—but says enforcement is left up to the state, not federal government

March 21–23	Abolitionist Joshua Giddings censured in House for supporting escape of *Creole* occupants and opposing all shipping of enslaved people in US waters; he resigns his seat on March 23
March 30	Highly protective Tariff of 1842 passes Whig-controlled Congress
March 31	Henry Clay resigns from Senate to prepare run for White House; Martin Van Buren also sees opportunity to succeed Tyler
March	Massachusetts Chief Justice Lemuel Shaw rules that a union is a legal organization and may strike
April	Alexander Baring, 1st Baron Ashburton arrives to negotiate US–UK issues
May	John C. Fremont embarks on first expedition to the Rocky Mountains
June 10	Lt. Charles Wilkes returns from four-year, 90,000-mile voyage across Pacific coast
August 9	Webster, Tyler, and Ashburton agree on a US–UK Treaty
August 29	The Senate approves the Webster-Ashburton Treaty
September 10	First Lady Leticia Tyler dies at the White House
September 11	Mexican soldiers invade Republic of Texas and capture San Antonio
October 20	George Latimer, escaping enslaved man from Virginia, arrested in Boston
Autumn	Fremont returns from his successful mapping expedition to the South Pass and Whigs suffer massive losses in Congress during mid-term elections
1843	
May 8	Daniel Wester resigns as secretary of state
May 22	Large band of settlers head from Missouri to Oregon territory
May	Fremont leaves Missouri on expedition to Columbia River and California
July 24	Abel P. Upshur confirmed as secretary of state
August 14	Second Seminole War ends in Florida
August 23	Mexican President Santa Anna warns US that annexation of Texas would lead to war
August 30-31	Abolitionist Liberty Party nominates James Birney for president
Year	Vermont state assembly votes to ignore Fugitive Slave Act
1844	
March 6	John C. Calhoun becomes secretary of state after Abel P. Upshur killed in ship explosion
March	Fremont expedition arrives in Sacramento
April 4	Fourierist socialist organization elects George Ripley (Brook Farm) as president
April 12	Tyler signs Texas Annexation Treaty negotiated by Calhoun and submits to Senate
April 27	Both Clay and Van Buren publicly oppose Texas Annexation Treaty

May 1	Whigs nominate ticket of Henry Clay and Theodore Frelinghuysen
May 6–8	Violent clash between Catholics and Protestants in Philadelphia, with twenty killed
May 27–29	Democrats reject Van Buren and nominate dark horse James Polk, backed by Jackson
June 8	Senate rejects Texas Annexation Treaty
June 27	Mormon leader Joseph Smith murdered in Nauvoo, Illinois
December 3	House repeals 1836 gag rule in response to John Quincy Adams' calls
December 4	Polk defeats Clay for presidency
Year	Baptist Church splits North vs. South over members' slave ownership
1845	
February 28	Congress "resolution" (not a 2/3rds majority treaty) annexes Texas
March 3	Florida admitted to Union as 27th state
March 4	Polk is inaugurated

## 99

TYLER TURNS AGAINST THE WHIGS AND THEY TURN AGAINST HIM

TIME: AUGUST 6, 1841

THE WHIGS PASS A FISCAL BANK BILL

A bank and custom house in Savannah

The Whigs' victory in 1841 is driven in large part by public anger over the uncertain currency and sluggish economy that has plagued the country since Jackson's "Specie Circular" order and the subsequent Panic of 1837.

A year earlier, on July 4, 1840, Van Buren finally gets congressional support to create his Independent US Treasury, where all federal revenues received are held in a "public entity" (the Treasury Department) rather than being distributed to "private state banking corporations," whose motives are forever distrusted by the Democrats.

While this approach does help stabilize the currency, it is also bureaucratic in nature, slowing down the circulation of capital to private entrepreneurs willing to take the risks to grow their own wealth and that of the total economy.

Men like Henry Clay, who are intent on aggressively boosting investment in roads, bridges, canals, trains, and other "infrastructure enablers," argue that the US will lag behind as long as risk-averse government investors are in charge of the capital.

Their solution lies in chartering the Third Bank of the United States, after the closure of the first in 1811 by Jefferson, and the second by Jackson in 1833.

Starting in May 1841, Clay pleads with Tyler to support this bank. When Tyler says he needs more time to consider the matter, Clay says that his answer is unacceptable. Tyler's comeback signals the end of all hope for comity between the two:

Then, sir, I wish you to understand this—that you and I were born in the same district; that we have fed upon the same food, and have breathed the same natal air. Go you now then, Mr. Clay, to your end of the avenue, where stands the Capitol, and there perform your duty to the country as you shall think proper. So help me God, I shall do mine at this end of it as I shall think proper

Clay proceeds to repeal Van Buren's Independent Treasury Act and then comes forward with his replacement, camouflaged as the "Fiscal Bank," which Congress approves on August 6, 1841.

The language in the act is intended to force Tyler's hand, since it "mandates" that each state create a branch, whether or not their legislature supports it. Were the president to approve this wording, it would alienate the states' rights Democrats and bring Tyler to heel as a Whig; on the other hand, a veto would reveal his true colors as a Jeffersonian.

Tyler recognizes the trap, saying to friends:

My back is to the wall, and while I deplore the assaults, I shall…beat back the assailants…Those who all along have opposed me will still call out for further trials, and thus leave me impotent and powerless.

TIME: AUGUST 15 – SEPTEMBER 9, 1841

TYLER ISSUES TWO VETOES

On August 15 Tyler vetoes the "Fiscal Bank" bill as unconstitutional. Democrats salute the veto, while Whigs are appalled:

Poor Tippecanoe! It was an evil hour that "Tyler too" was added to make out the line. There was rhyme, but no reason to it.

Clay launches into a 90-minute diatribe in the Senate against Tyler on August 18, suggesting that he resign. He is joined in the House by John Minor Botts, a Virginian previously friendly with Tyler who now accuses the president of lying to him all along about his support for the new bank.

In the early morning of August 19, a drunken mob pelts the White House with rocks and fires off guns, frightening Tyler's frail and reclusive wife, Leticia, and further upsetting the president. He asks that a police force be approved to guard the mansion.

Clay is anything but the "great compromiser" at this moment, and returns to Congress with a slightly revised bill featuring a name change. What was the "Fiscal Bank" is now cast as the "Fiscal Corporation."

This passes Congress on September 3.

Tyler picks up the gauntlet and vetoes it on September 9, accompanied by another message to the people:

> *I distinctly declared that my own opinion had been uniformly proclaimed to be against the exercise "of the power of Congress to create a national bank to operate per se over the Union"…*

> *…It is with great pain that I now feel compelled to differ from Congress a second time in the same session…It has been my good fortune and pleasure to concur with them in all measures except this. And why should our difference on this alone be pushed to extremes? It is my anxious desire that it should not be. I too have been burdened with extraordinary labors of late, and I sincerely desire time for deep and deliberate reflection on this the greatest difficulty of my Administration. May we not now pause until a more favorable time, when, with the most anxious hope that the Executive and Congress may cordially unite, some measure of finance may be deliberately adopted promotive of the good of our common country?*

TIME: SEPTEMBER 11–13, 1841

TYLER'S CABINET RESIGNS
AND HE IS DRUMMED OUT OF THE PARTY

Events now move quickly and dramatically.

Tyler has sensed all along that his cabinet is against him.

> *(I am) surrounded by Clay men, Webster men, Anti-Masons, original Harrisons, old Whigs and new Whigs…. (and) not a single sincere friend…*

He is proven right just two days after his second veto, on September 11, when every member—except for Secretary of State Daniel Webster—turns in their resignation.

Clay believes, or at least hopes, that Tyler will also resign and that, as Senate president pro tempore, he will be elevated to the office he deserves.

However, Tyler is bolstered by Webster's decision to stay on and, in so doing, to oppose Clay. He is also ready to name a replacement cabinet and does so promptly. They are regionally balanced and all are professed Whigs, except for Hugh Legaré, a "Unionist Democrat" who opposed John C. Calhoun's call for nullification.

JOHN TYLER'S "REPLACEMENT" CABINET

POSITION	NAME	HOME STATE
Secretary of State	Daniel Webster	Massachusetts
Secretary of the Treasury	Walter Forward	Pennsylvania
Secretary of War	John C. Spencer	New York
Attorney General	Hugh Legaré	South Carolina
Secretary of the Navy	Abel Upshaw	Virginia
Postmaster General	Charles Wickliffe	Kentucky

The fact that Tyler is able to recruit these Whigs gives him hope and confirms the presence of an anti-Clay wing of the party that helped Harrison win the 1840 nomination in the first place.

On September 13 some 50–80 "Clay men" in Congress gather at Capitol Square and formally expel Tyler from the Whig Party. The president records his own thoughts on this and on his plan for the future, which will have a distinctly Democratic cast to it.

I shall act upon the principles which I have all along espoused…derived from the teachings of Jefferson and Madison.

Meanwhile, in sticking with Tyler, Webster dooms his chances of becoming president. He will try twice for the Whig nomination, losing both in 1848 and 1852.

## 100

FREDERICK DOUGLASS MAKES HIS FIRST GREAT SPEECH AGAINST SLAVERY

TIME: AUGUST 11, 1841

DOUGLASS TELLS HIS STORY
TO THE NANTUCKET ANTI-SLAVERY CONVENTION

Just as John Tyler alters the course of the Whigs' first presidency, the future course of the abolition movement in America is being re-shaped off the southern tip of Massachusetts.

On August 11, 1841, the Quaker abolition-ist David Joy is hosting an Anti-Slavery Convention at Atheneum Hall on Nantucket Island. This is a rare mixed-race event, with speakers including Garrison and Charles Ray, the Black editor of *The Coloured American* newspaper.

After the formal speeches are concluded, a free Black man named Frederick Douglass is in-vited to say a few words to the crowd about his life as an enslaved man. As Garrison recalls in a letter written five years later, his demeanor and narration prove captivating to his audience.

FRED. DOUGLASS.

Frederick Douglass (1818–1896)

A beloved friend from New Bedford prevailed on Mr. DOUGLASS to address the convention: He came forward to the platform with a hesitancy and embarrassment, necessarily the attendants of a sensitive mind in such a novel position. After apologizing for his ignorance, and reminding the audience that slavery was a poor school for the human intellect and heart, he proceeded to narrate some of the facts in his own history.

His story begins with his mixed-race birth into slavery, in 1818 in Talbot County, Maryland, as Frederick Augustus Washington Bailey. He lives at the Great House Farm on a large plantation owned by Colonel Edward Lloyd, with over 300 enslaved workers growing tobacco, wheat, and corn.

In his autobiographical *Narrative*, published by Garrison in 1845, Douglass recalls his first home:

> *There are certain secluded and out-of-the-way places, even in the state of Maryland, seldom visited by a single ray of healthy public sentiment—where slavery, wrapt in its own congenial, midnight darkness, can, and does, develop all its malign and shocking characteristics; where it can be indecent without shame, cruel without shuddering, and murderous without apprehension or fear of exposure.*

His master is an overseer named Aaron Anthony, a vicious man who terrifies the small boy by humiliating and whipping his Aunt Hester in his presence.

Anthony soon passes ownership of Douglass on to his daughter, Lucretia, who is married to Thomas Auld, also employed on Lloyd's plantation. From there, at age seven, he is sent to Baltimore to live with Thomas Auld's brother, Hugh, and his wife, Sophia. Douglass views this "escape" from plantation to city life as the beginning of his search for eventual freedom.

At first, Sophia Auld, who has never owned slaves, treats the boy with kindness, even agreeing to teach him the alphabet when Douglass shows curiosity about words. However, her warmth vanishes after Hugh warns her that educating enslaved people makes them rebellious and is strictly forbidden. But Sophia's slip has opened the door to literacy for Douglass and he is on his way to becoming a voracious, albeit clandestine, reader.

Douglass says that his time with Sophia Auld teaches him two things: the necessity of education to set Black people free and the moral damage that institutionalized slavery can do, even to well-intentioned white people like Mrs. Auld.

He remains in Baltimore for roughly seven years, working in a shipyard and experiencing the urban world around him. The local newspapers inform him about John Quincy Adams and the early calls for abolition. He buys and devours a popular anthology called *The Colombian Orator*, which includes essays and speeches arguing for and against slavery. With help from dockworkers, he begins to learn how to form letters and to write words and sentences. Like Lincoln as a boy, he is educating himself.

In 1833 Hugh Auld has a falling out with his brother, Thomas, who in turn reclaims Douglass and makes him a kitchen servant in his house. When Thomas senses his independent spirit, he rents him out to a farmer named Edward Covey, known locally as a "slave breaker." He is a thoroughly despicable man, who goes so far as to invite neighbors to sleep with enslaved women for "breeding" purposes.

Covey converts Douglass into a "field hand" for the first time, and vows to "tame" his sixteen-year-old charge. After six months of being starved and beaten, Douglass almost gives up.

My natural elasticity was crushed, my intellect languished, the disposition to read departed, the cheerful spark that lingered about my eye died; the dark night of slavery closed in upon me; and behold a man transformed into a brute!

But when Covey comes again to beat him, Douglass meets violence with violence and fights him off. While he risks execution in raising a hand to his master, Covey does not want the word of this resistance to leak out, so he backs off and never tries to whip Douglass again. In his autobiography he refers to this fight as the "turning point in my life."

You have seen how a man was made a slave; now you see how a slave was made a man.

He also comes to regard Covey and the Aulds—all ardent churchgoers—as symbols of the failure of the white Christian ministry to speak out against the evil of slavery.

In 1835, Douglass is rented out to another farmer, the more lenient William Freeland, who is rebuffed by locals for allowing Douglass to teach enslaved people to read at Sunday school services. At this point, Douglass ponders an escape, but his plans are foiled. He returns to Baltimore where Hugh Auld puts him to work as a caulker in a shipyard.

Again, Douglass makes the most of his chances here in a broader external world. He joins the East Baltimore Mental Improvement Society, where free Black people hold debates. Through the society he meets and falls in love with Anna Murray, a housekeeper. He is now nineteen years old and on the brink of his escape to freedom.

His break occurs on September 3, 1838. With help from Anna, Douglass dons a red shirt, tarpaulin hat, and black scarf, posing as a free Black sailor and moves by boat and train from Maryland to Delaware to Philadelphia and finally to New York City, where he is housed by the Black abolitionist, David Ruggles. Anna Murray follows him there and they are married two weeks later. He is given a new last name by a friend, Nathan Johnson, to help conceal his runaway status. The name is Douglass, after a hero in Sir Walter Scott's epic poem, *Lady of the Lake*.

Douglass and Anna settle down in New Bedford, Massachusetts, where he takes on a series of menial jobs while searching for his new identity in free society. He joins the local African Methodist Episcopalian Zion Church. He subscribes to Garrison's paper, *The Liberator*, and begins to sense his calling. In April 1839 he hears Garrison lecture in New Bedford, and decides to attend a convention of the Massachusetts Anti-Slavery Society, held on Nantucket Island.

This event will change the arc of his future.

TIME: AUGUST 1841

GARRISON REACTS TO DOUGLASS' TALK

Those listening to Douglass on Nantucket are both moved by his narrative and surprised by the eloquence of his delivery. Garrison writes:

> *I shall never forget his first speech at the convention—the extraordinary emotion it excited in my own mind—the powerful impression it created upon a crowded auditory, completely taken by surprise—the applause which followed from the beginning to the end of his felicitous remarks.*

Garrison sees in Douglass a confirmation of his belief that Black people possess all the natural capacities of white people, if only given support and a small amount of cultivation.

> *I think I never hated slavery so intensely as at that moment; certainly, my perception of the enormous outrage which is inflicted by it, on the godlike nature of its victims, was rendered far more clear than ever. There stood one, in physical proportion and stature commanding and exact—in intellect richly endowed—in natural eloquence a prodigy—in soul manifestly "created but a little lower than the angels"—yet a slave, ay, a fugitive slave, trembling for his safety, hardly daring to believe that on the American soil, a single white person could be found who would befriend him at all hazards, for the love of God and humanity! Capable of high attainments as an intellectual and moral being—needing nothing but a comparatively small amount of cultivation to make him an ornament to society and a blessing to his race—by the law of the land, by the voice of the people, by the terms of the slave code, he was only a piece of property, a beast of burden, a chattel personal, nevertheless!*

Garrison compares Douglass' pleas for liberty and justice to those announced by Patrick Henry.

> *As soon as he had taken his seat, filled with hope and admiration, I rose, and declared that PATRICK HENRY, of revolutionary fame, never made a speech more eloquent in the cause of liberty, than the one we had just listened to from the lips of that hunted fugitive. So I believed at that time—such is my belief now.*

SIDEBAR: THOMAS RICE AND THE LEGACY OF "JIM CROW"

While the abolitionist attendees at Nantucket are hearing the articulate Frederick Douglass recount his history as an enslaved man, other white audiences are watching the actor Thomas Rice reinforce their antiblack racial prejudices in America's theaters.

Rice's fame rests on a single blackface routine featuring his character, "Jim Crow," whose stereotypical behaviors are intended to draw mocking derision and laughter. The highlight of Rice's performance is a soft shoe dance titled "Jump Jim Crow," accompanied by nonsense lyrics delivered in a broken drawl. Throughout the 1840s, Rice plays before packed houses throughout the US and in London.

"Jump Jim Crow" T.D. Rice (1808–1860)

## 101

ANOTHER RACE RIOT BREAKS OUT IN CINCINNATI

TIME: SUMMER 1841

ANTI-SLAVERY ACTIVISTS INCREASE RACIAL TENSIONS IN THE CITY

Five years have passed since the border town of Cincinnati was last torn apart by racial violence.

At that time white mobs pillaged Black neighborhoods following the publication of inflammatory newspaper articles by the abolitionist James Birney.

Why the so-called "Queen City of the West" fosters such racial animosity may be explained in a telling observation from the French historian, Alexis de Tocqueville, who visits America in 1831:

> *Race prejudice seems stronger in those states that have abolished slavery than in those where it still exists, and nowhere is it more intolerant than in those states where slavery was never known.*

Ohio is one such state that has never known slavery since entering the Union in 1803.

A free Black man standing tall

However, by 1840 the 95% white population in Cincinnati is living alongside 2,240 free Black people, many of whom have earned enough money to purchase their freedom. They have built their own community in the "Bottoms" neighborhood around the Bethel

AME and Union Baptist Churches, opened three schools run by the Coloured Education Society, and hold upwards of 90 skilled labor jobs, from barbering to mechanics.

Still, the majority of mainstream white citizens want nothing to do with Black people.

Not only do they regard Black people as a lesser species—the traditional 3/5th of a full man in the Constitution—but also as a danger to both their physical safety and their economic future. Cincinnati lies directly across the Ohio River from the pro-slavery state of Kentucky, where its commercial transactions depend heavily on a willingness to oppose both talk of abolition and support for those escaping enslavement.

The presence of Lane Theological Seminary in Cincinnati further complicates the matter.

Lane opens in 1829 to train Presbyterian ministers in the West. In 1834 it is the site of fierce debates over slavery, which divides its president, Lyman Beecher, who favors gradual emancipation and colonization, from students led by Theodore Weld, a Finney disciple who calls for freedom now and assimilation. While Weld's faction transfers to Oberlin College some 220 miles to the North, abolitionist fervor still lingers in Cincinnati.

One proponent of abolition, the lawyer Salmon P. Chase, arouses the ire of local merchants in May 1841 when he wins a court case on behalf of Mary Towns, a runaway enslaved woman from Kentucky. This prompts the pro-slavery *Cincinnati Enquirer* newspaper to initiate a campaign against "trouble-makers" riling up the Black population.

TIME: SEPTEMBER 3–4, 1841

FREE BLACK PEOPLE FIGHT BACK
AGAINST RAMPAGING WHITE MOBS

As summer rolls on, the city is hit by a prolonged heat wave and drought, which causes the river to fall, along with jobs on boats and wharves. Tensions increase daily and random fights break out.

It's unclear exactly what sparks the riot, but it begins at a candy store on Fifth Street owned by an abolitionist named Cornelius Burnett. Along with his sons, Burnett has recently fought local police who were demanding that he turn over a runaway enslaved person. The incident is not forgotten and a white mob begins their rampage by demolishing Burnett's store before heading into a Black enclave, "Bucktown." Once there they begin to pillage Black homes and businesses.

But rather than repeating their passive stance during the 1836 riots, Black citizens fight back, with some 50 organized and armed fighters led by 28-year-old named Major James Wilkerson, grandson of a Revolutionary War soldier and elder in the AME church.

After Wilkerson's band initially drives them back on the night of September 3, white forces return with a six-pound cannon and resume their reign of terror.

The violence ends when local militiamen step in to enforce martial law. But the order restored is anything but fair for the free Black population. The city authorities arrest 300 Black people and no white people; they allow Kentuckians to visit jail cells in search of people escaping slavery; they reinstitute the 1807 requirement that Black citizens post $500 personal bonds; and they seize all weapons held by Black people.

## 102

PRIGG V. PENNSYLVANIA ADDS TO MOUNTING TENSIONS OVER "FUGITIVE SLAVES"

TIME: MARCH 1, 1842

THE SUPREME COURT UPHOLDS THE FUGITIVE SLAVE ACT

Cincinnati is only one of many cities where issues arise over people escaping slavery. In 1842 the spotlight shifts to York County, Pennsylvania and a Black woman named Margaret Morgan.

Margaret's parents were enslaved by a mill owner named John Ashmore in Hartford County, Maryland, who declares in 1820 that he has set them free. While Ashmore never signs formal manumission papers, Margaret believes she is free and marries a free Black man, Jerry Morgan.

They start a family and live for several years in Maryland before deciding to move to York County, Pennsylvania in 1832. Ashmore makes no protest regarding the move.

But then, five years later in 1837, John Ashmore dies and a female heir, his niece Margaret Beamis, claims that both Morgan and her children are now her property.

She hires a neighbor, Edward Prigg, to capture and return the "runaways." While Prigg has a warrant, the constable in York County refuses to act on it, so Prigg forcibly abducts Morgan and her two children, and sells them to a slave dealer who plans to ship them South.

A grand jury in Pennsylvania indicts Prigg and his three accomplices for violating the state's 1826 Personal Liberty statute, and asks Maryland to arrest and extradite him. Maryland's government agrees to do so with the understanding that, if convicted, Prigg will not be jailed until the US Supreme Court rules on the case.

Prigg is tried in Pennsylvania and found guilty of kidnapping under the state law in question:

If any person...after the passing of this act, by force and violence, take and carry

away...any negro or mulatto, from any part or parts of this commonwealth...with
a design and intention of selling and disposing of...such negro or mulatto, as a slave
or servant for life...his or their aiders or abettors, shall on conviction thereof...be
deemed guilty of a felony...

This decision alarms the pro-slavery states, especially Maryland, which appeals the
decision in May 1840 on behalf of Prigg. It argues that the 1826 Pennsylvania law violates the euphemistic "Fugitives from Labor Clause" in Article IV of the Constitution,
and the subsequent 1793 Fugitive Slave Act:

No person held to service or labor in one state, under the laws thereof, escaping into
another, shall, in consequence of any law or regulation therein, be discharged from
such service or labor; but shall be delivered up, on claim of the party to whom such
service or labor may be due.

While clear about intent, neither law spells out whether enforcement belongs at the
state or federal level.

On appeal, the Prigg case finally reaches the Supreme Court, where arguments are
heard by Roger Taney and his associates during February 8–10, and a judgment is rendered on March 1, 1842.

Justice Joseph Story issues the overall opinion of the court which, by an 8–1 majority,
strikes down the Pennsylvania law and rules in favor of Maryland and Prigg.

TIME: MARCH 1, 1842

A LOOPHOLE IN THE *PRIGG* DECISION
LEAVES ENFORCEMENT IN DOUBT

However, that apparent unanimity is diminished when seven of the justices feel compelled to publish their own individual interpretations.

One such clarification belongs to Chief Justice Taney, ever a states' rights advocate
and a stickler for detail. He agrees that it is the right of the master to arrest a runaway in
any state where found, but objects to the notion that local laws to support the effort have
no bearing *vis-à-vis* federal statutes.

I concur in the opinion pronounced by the Court that the law of Pennsylvania, under
which the plaintiff in error was indicted, is unconstitutional and void, and that the
judgment against him must be reversed. But...I do not assent to all the principles
contained in the opinion...(and) I agree entirely in all that is said in relation to the
right of the master, by virtue of the third clause of the second section of the Fourth
Article of the Constitution of the United States, to arrest his fugitive slave in any

State wherein he may find him… But, as I understand the opinion of the Court, it goes further, and decides that the power to provide a remedy for this right is vested exclusively in Congress, and that all laws upon the subject passed by a State since the adoption of the Constitution of the United States are null and void…

A second opinion comes from the lone dissenter in the case, the formidable John McLean of Ohio. McLean is nominated to the high court in 1829 by Andrew Jackson and serves for 32 years while repeatedly being offered various cabinet posts, and is even considered as a presidential candidate.

He is nicknamed the "Politician on the Supreme Court" and is outspoken in his lifelong opposition to slavery. His dissent in the *Prigg* decision is one that will be heard in many future runaway cases under the rubric of "once free, forever free."

Thus, McLean contends that Margaret Morgan was de facto a free woman, having lived as such for five years without objection from Ashford in the state of Pennsylvania. he was no longer enslaved and the plaintiff had no right to abduct her in the first place.

This basic logic will be embraced by abolitionists and repeated over time. McLean himself will rely on it in his 1857 dissent from Taney in the landmark *Dred Scott* case.

None of the ongoing legal debates help either Margaret Morgan or her children. With the verdict in, they are returned to captivity in Maryland, and no records exist as to their subsequent fates.

But ironically the 8–1 decision in *Prigg* is not an entire loss for anti-slavery forces. A close reading of Story's majority opinion opens a loophole around enforcing the law. It says that local magistrates will not be bound to cooperate with slave catchers if "prohibited by state legislation" from doing so.

This caveat leads to passage of just such "non-cooperation" statutes across the North which serve to infuriate Southern slaveholders.

SIDEBAR: THE SHIFTING SIZE AND MAKEUP OF THE SUPREME COURT

While *Prigg* is decided by a total of nine justices in 1842, that number varies over time. The US Constitution establishes the Supreme Court, but leaves it up to the first Congress to settle on its size. In 1789 that number is set at six. Adams tries to reduce it to five in 1801, but Jefferson bumps it back up to six in his first term and then seven in his second. It stays there until Jackson's final day in office, when it moves up to nine.

NUMBER OF SCOTUS JUSTICES

DATE	LEGISLATION	# JUSTICES	PRESIDENT
Summer 1787	US Constitution	TBD	----
Sept 24, 1789	Judiciary Act of 1789	6	Washington
March 2, 1801	Judiciary Act of 1801	5	Adams cuts by one
April 29, 1802	Judiciary Act of 1802	6	Jefferson adds back
Feb 24, 1807	7th Circuit Act	7	Jefferson
March 3, 1837	8th and 9th Circuit Acts	9	Jackson

From the beginning, presidents attempt to "stack the court" judges who share their political views. Federalist-minded judges dominate until Jefferson moves toward Democratic-Republicans in 1804, aided by the expansion to seven seats. Van Buren completes Jackson's shift toward Democrats achieving a 9–0 majority by 1841. This configuration holds until Fillmore names a Whig in 1851. Lincoln names four Republicans and one Democrat during his tenure. It is not until 1870, under Grant, that the Republicans control the court.

POLITICAL MAKEUP OF THE JUSTICES

PRESIDENT	TERM END	# NAMED	SPLIT AT START	SPLIT AT END
Washington	1797	11	6 Federalists	6 Federalists
J. Adams	1801	3	6 Federalists	6 Federalists
Jefferson	1809	3	6 Federalists	4 Fed – 3 Dem-Rep
Madison	1817	2	4 Fed – 3 Dem-Rep	2 Fed – 5 Dem-Rep
Monroe	1825	1	2 Fed – 5 Dem-Rep	2 Fed – 5 Dem-Rep
JQ Adams	1829	1	2 Fed – 5 Dem-Rep	2 Fed – 5 Dem-Rep
Jackson	1837	5	2 Fed – 5 Dem-Rep	2 Dem-Rep – 5 Dem
Van Buren	1841	3	2 Dem-Rep – 7 Dem	9 Dem
Harrison	1841	0	9 Dem	9 Dem
Tyler	1845	1	9 Dem	9 Dem
Polk	1849	2	9 Dem	9 Dem
Taylor	1850	0	9 Dem	9 Dem
Fillmore	1853	1	9 Dem	8 Dem – 1 Whig
Pierce	1857	1	8 Dem – 1 Whig	8 Dem – 1 Whig
Buchanan	1861	1	8 Dem – 1 Whig	9 Dem
Lincoln	1865	5	9 Dem	5 Dem – 4 Republicans

Over this period, six men serve as Chief Justice, with two of them—John Marshall and Roger Taney—dominating their contemporaries in terms of influence on the cases taken and the final rulings.

CHIEF JUSTICES OF THE COURT

NAME	TENURE	NOMINATED BY	PARTY
John Jay	1789–1795	Washington	Federalist
John Rutledge	1795	Washington	Federalist
Oliver Ellsworth	1796–1800	Washington	Federalist
John Marshall	1801–1835	Adams	Federalist
Roger Taney	1836–1864	Jackson	Democrat
Salmon Chase	1865–1873	Lincoln	Republican

## 103

THE PRIGG DECISION PROMPTS GARRISON TO CALL FOR DISUNION

TIME: MARCH 1842

GARRISON TELLS ENSLAVED PEOPLE TO FREE THEMSELVES BY RUNNING AWAY

Abolitionists are shocked by the high court's ruling in the *Prigg* case and none more so than Garrison, who characterizes the decision as follows:

> *The slaveholding power (may now) roam without molestation through the Northern states seeking whomever it may devour.*

In typical fashion, Garrison uses the adverse news to notch up his inflammatory rhetoric in *The Liberator*.

His first barrage calls upon enslaved people to continue to free themselves by running away from their masters.

His inner circle—including Lucretia Mott—support this plea, but others feel that inciting enslaved people to escape will only lead to greater hardships and repression. Garrison is unbowed. The timid may embrace caution, but he will not.

William Lloyd Garrison (1805–1879)

TIME: 1842

HE THEN CALLS FOR AN END TO THE NORTH–SOUTH UNION

Thus comes his second salvo—an outright call for disunion.

Ever the investigative journalist, Garrison has now read Madison's "secretarial notes" on the closed-door debates from the 1787 Convention, finally published in 1840, three years after the ex-president's death. He is appalled by the litany of immoral compromises made on slavery to achieve the union.

This was a Union at the expense of our coloured population.

In turn, he throws his outrage directly into the faces of the Boston Brahmins who are ever ready to defend the wisdom and courage of the founding fathers.

The Constitution, he writes, is "the Devil's pact" and he declares the time has come to break the bond.

The repeal of the Union between Northern liberty and Southern slavery is essential.

In 1842, Garrison is virtually alone in his call for disunion.

Mainstream Americans, both Southern and Northern, dismiss him as a radical troublemaker, and those within the emerging "political wing" of the abolitionist movement see one more reason to distance themselves from him.

Yet his core supporters, mostly members of the New England Anti-Slavery Society he founded in 1831, remain loyal. On May 31, 1844, this regional group votes 250–24 in favor of disunion.

## 104

THE CREOLE REBELLION LEADS TO DIPLOMATIC AND CONGRESSIONAL CONFLICTS

TIME: NOVEMBER 7, 1841 – APRIL 16, 1842

BRITAIN FREES MUTINOUS ENSLAVED AMERICANS FROM THE *CREOLE* BRIG

Three weeks after the *Prigg* decision, another slavery-related controversy is played out in the US House.

This one is reminiscent of the 1839 *Amistad* affair, again involving a bloody revolt aboard a slave ship.

In this case the vessel is the *Creole*, a brig owned by a Richmond firm, and transporting 135 enslaved people from Virginia to the auction market in New Orleans.

On November 7, 1841, an open hatch allows a band of nineteen captives to come on deck and overpower the ten-man crew. They severely wound the captain, Robert Ensor, and murder a slave dealer, John Hewell. During the melee, several others are hurt, including an enslaved person who subsequently dies.

The leader of the rebels is 25-year-old Madison Washington, a former runaway to

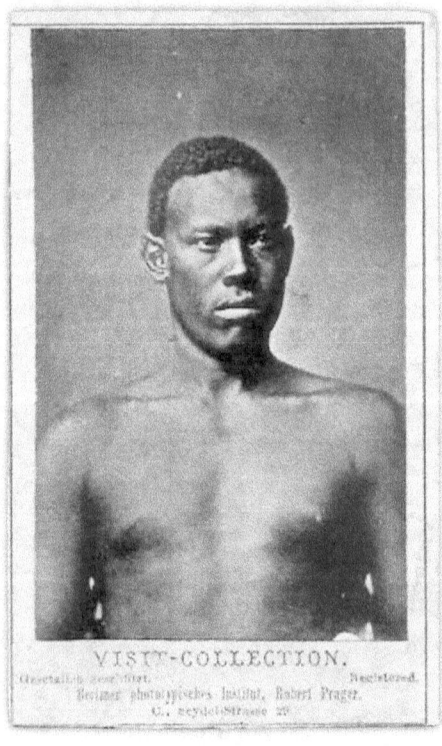

An African man

Canada, who had been recaptured in Virginia after coming back to retrieve his wife. Once in control of *Creole,* he orders the helmsman to sail east toward the free colony of Liberia, but alters course because the ship lacks the necessary provisions. Instead he turns south and, on November 9, arrives at Nassau, a British-owned island in the Bahamas, where slavery has been banned since 1834.

When the American counsel to the Bahamas, John Bacon, learns of the incident, he assembles a contingent of sailors to board the ship and return it to a US port. The British Governor General Sir Francis Coburn, who fought in the War of 1812, learns of Bacon's plan and responds by sending local boats to surround the *Creole* in port.

Two days later, on November 14, Coburn finishes an investigation of the rebellion and announces his verdict. Nineteen of the enslaved people are to be held for possible trial as "pirates," while the remaining 116 are immediately free to depart.

As a further snub to American slavery laws, British authorities subsequently conclude that they have no right to try Americans in their courts, and that there are no "extradition treaties" in place to send Madison Washington and the other rebels to the US. On April 16, 1842, the charges of "piracy" are dropped and all are officially released from custody.

Madison Washington vanishes from history at that moment, only to be remembered and romanticized in the 1852 novella, *The Heroic Slave,* written by Frederick Douglass.

The *Creole* outcome sets off a diplomatic firestorm between the United States and British diplomats, as well as between Southerners and the small band of vocal anti-slavery advocates in Congress.

A British veteran of the War of 1812

TIME: MARCH 23, 1842

ABOLITIONIST JOSHUA GIDDINGS IS CENSURED BY THE HOUSE

The congressional conflict is sparked by the 75-year-old former president John Quincy Adams, the first and still foremost abolitionist in Washington since rejoining the House in 1833.

Ten weeks have passed since the initial release of the *Creole* captives in Nassau, and Adams is on the House floor reading a series of "petitions" from his local constituents, again in clear violation of the 1836 gag rule. These range from a demand to dissolve the Union in light of the *Prigg* fugitive slave decision, to censuring John Bacon, the American counsel to the Bahamas, for trying to interfere in the *Creole* incident.

On January 25, 1842, when Adams refuses to relinquish the floor, Representative Henry Wise of Virginia moves to censure him for "plotting with Britain to end slavery in America." After cooler heads prevail on behalf of the former president, Southerners turn their fire on an easier target, Joshua Giddings, who also weighs in on the *Creole* case.

Joshua Giddings (1795–1864)

On March 21 the Ohio abolitionist presents a nine-part argument which asserts that the minute the *Creole* captives left jurisdictional waters off Virginia, their status was no longer determined by state law.

> *When a ship belonging to the citizens of a state leaves the waters of that state, and enters upon the high seas, the persons on board cease to be subject to the slave laws of that state and are governed by the law of the United States.*

This interpretation mirrors the "once free, forever free" view argued by Associate Justice John McLean in the *Prigg* ruling.

But Giddings goes further, saying that slavery violates "natural law" which supersedes municipal law.

> *Slavery is an abridgement of the natural rights of man (which) can exist only by force of positive municipal law.*

Giddings' argument is much more threatening to the South than Adams' was in the *Amistad* case one year earlier. There, the enslaved people were owned by foreigners and found to be from Africa, a clear violation of the 1808 ban on international trading. Here, the *Creole* captives are born in America and owned by American citizens.

The Southerners immediately pounce on Giddings.

The only laws that govern the *Creole*, they say, are the Constitution and the Fugitive

Slave Act—both declaring that owners are free to transport their human "property" into "free states" without changing their enslaved status.

They pursue a formal "motion to censure"—first for "introducing an anti-slavery resolution deemed to be incendiary," and second for "upsetting delicate treaty negotiations" between the US and Britain focused on settling the Maine–Canada border disputes.

Giddings is given no chance to defend himself and becomes only the second member in House history to be condemned to this degree. After the vote he responds by rising from his chair, walking to Adams' desk to shake his hand, and resigning.

However, this flexing of Southern power is short-lived. Six weeks after exiting the House, a special election in Ohio returns Giddings to the chamber by a vote of 7,469 to 383.

## 105

THE WEBSTER-ASHBURTON TREATY RESOLVES A SERIES OF DISPUTES WITH BRITAIN

TIME:1837–1842

THREATS OF ANOTHER WAR WITH BRITAIN MATERIALIZE

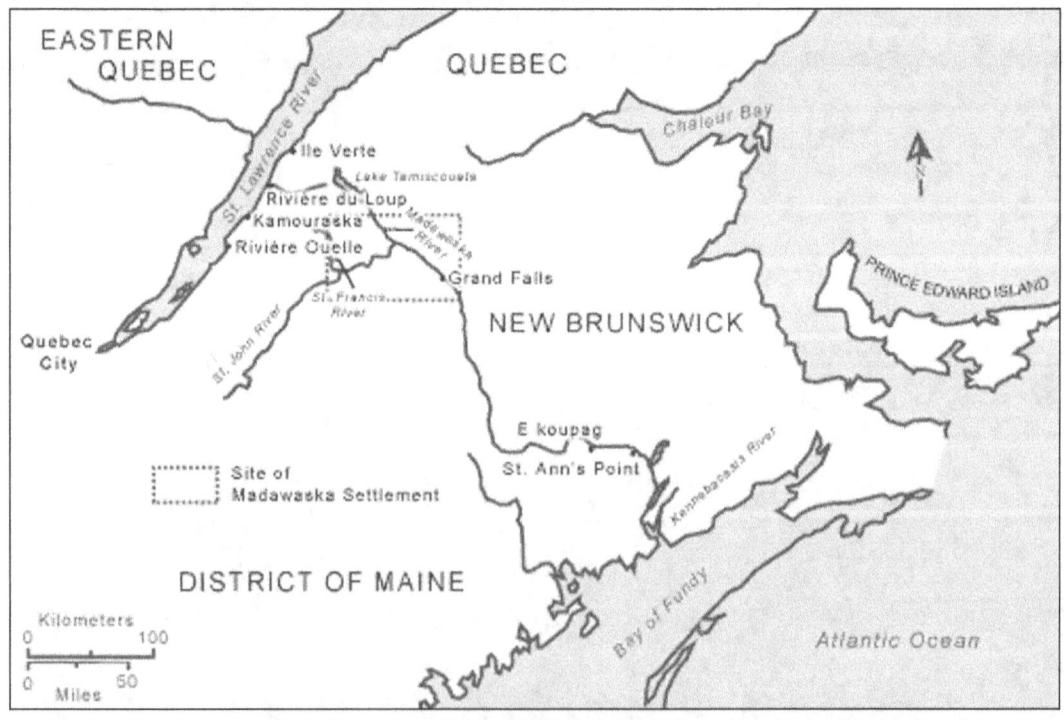

Map showing the area around Maine and New Brunswick

While the *Creole* incident plays out, negotiations are already underway toward resolving a series of other long-standing disputes between Britain and the United States.

The War of 1812 is a quarter century in the past, but violent confrontations continue to break out, especially along the Canadian border.

In 1837 anti-British protests by farmers in Ontario province lead to a "Republic of Canada" insurgency, which wins support from some Americans living on the Michigan and Ohio borders. In the process of suppressing the rebels, Britain finds that the American steamship *Caroline* has been carrying arms to the enemy. On December 29, 1837, they assault the ship in port, kill a sailor, torch it, and set it adrift on Lake Niagara heading toward the falls.

The drama of its dying plunge over Niagara Falls is captured in newspaper headlines and lithographs which anger the American public and embed "Remember the *Caroline*" in the national lexicon. When formal protests to London from Van Buren are ignored, a retaliatory blow is struck in May 1838 as the British steamship *Sir Robert Peel* is boarded and burned in American waters.

A thornier and more long-standing conflict exists on the east coast.

Its roots go back to the Revolutionary War and the 1783 Treaty of Paris, which fails to spell out the border between Maine and the maritime province of New Brunswick. The disputed land is rich in timber, and many violent episodes over cutting rights tend to erupt. But for Britain the issue goes beyond commerce to military security, with northern Maine viewed as a roadblock in their direct route from the Atlantic to the crucial citadel at Quebec City.

Tensions rise in 1838 when the British build an east–west road extending across the Aroostook Valley on land claimed by Maine. This leads to a series of clashes between lumberjacks, which escalate into national saber rattling. In 1839, Congress authorizes a $10 million expense for Van Buren to enlist 50,000 volunteers to drive out the intruders, and Britain declares its intent to fight back as needed. But actual fighting is avoided when Van Buren realizes that American financial problems are already severe enough without adding a costly war. So ends the so-called "Aroostook War," with a whimper, not a bang.

In 1840 the two sides are back at it over a postscript to the *Caroline* affair. Alexander McLeod, a Canadian sheriff who brags about his role in the event, is arrested in New York and charged with "murdering the sailor" during the raid. When the British learn of the arrest, they threaten war unless McLeod is released, up to the time the trial ends in an acquittal.

Between the *Creole* decision in Nassau, the *Caroline* incident, the Aroostook "war," and the McLeod arrest, it becomes clear to the leaders of both nations that the time has come for peace talks.

DATE: AUGUST 9, 1842

THE WEBSTER-ASHBURTON TREATY RESOLVES THE CONFLICTS

The search for resolution is apparently initiated by Sir Robert Peel, a Tory who begins his second stint as prime minister in August 1841, in the fourth year of Queen Victoria's 63-year reign.

Peel selects the formidable Alexander Baring, 1st Baron Ashburton, to negotiate with the Americans. He is the 67-year-old retired chairman of Baring Brothers & Co., the international merchant banking firm founded by his father in 1762. The firm's relations with the United States go way back in time, including a central role in closing the 1803 Louisiana Purchase deal. Ashburton's wife is from Philadelphia, and he owns roughly one million acres (1,500 square miles) of land in the contested region of Maine, so he is personally motivated to find a border resolution.

Robert Peel (1788–1850)

Ashburton is also a long-term associate of Secretary of State Daniel Webster, having hired him to handle various legal matters for Baring Brothers in US courts. In turn, Webster is a lifetime Anglophile, who has been a guest of Ashburton's on visits to London.

Daniel Webster (1782–1852)

Ashburton arrives in April 1842 and meets with Webster and Tyler, the latter whom he regards as "conceited and weak" until the president wins him over with his hospitality. The two Americans need the negotiations to work out every bit as much as their guest, given their politically embattled status with the Clay-dominated Congress.

The talks focus on the central bone of contention, the border between Maine and New Brunswick. Maps and records from the 1783 Treaty of Paris are resurrected in advance by Harvard historian Jared Sparks, who concludes that the boundary proposed by the British is probably correct. Still Webster intends to rely on his negotiating talents and relationship with Ashburton to achieve a more attractive outcome.

However, the British are not the only ones who need to be won over. Fierce resistance to any compromise exists in northern Maine, and a secret government "contingency fund" is spent on a propaganda campaign to gin up state support. Some consider this expenditure an impeachable offense, but a later inquiry turns this aside.

The two parties remain at an impasse until Tyler meets personally with Ashburton, pleading that "if you cannot settle (the dispute), what man in England can?" This appeal leads to a final agreement reached on August 9, 1842.

The deal addresses four issues.

First and foremost is the creation of a new compromise map for the Maine–New Brunswick border. In the deal, British Canada ends up with 5,000 square miles to the north, which satisfies their wish for a more direct passageway in the 650-mile trek from Halifax to Quebec. In return the US gets 7,000 square miles below the British line in Maine, along with 6,500 square miles of land out west in northern Minnesota—the "Mesabi Range" where vast deposits of iron ore are discovered in 1866.

Those Easterners who dismiss the value of the British concession out west are soothed by $125,000 payments made by Washington to the states of Maine and Massachusetts (the latter at one time having included all of Maine in its boundary).

When Webster raises the *Creole* affair, Ashburton initially dodges, saying that he lacks authority on the matter since the Nassau rulings transpired while he was in route to the US. But when pushed, he reaffirms the British position that any enslaved person reaching UK commonwealth soil will automatically be declared free. This principle—an enslaved person reaching free territory is freed—is precisely what the South fears most, if applied domestically. So, Webster persists, earning two concessions in the end: British officials in the West Indies will be instructed to avoid such incidents in the future when possible, and a commission will be set up to discuss compensation (which is later granted to the tune of $100,000) for owners of the *Creole* captives.

Ashburton is even less sympathetic when the torching of the *Caroline* is discussed. The message to America is to stay out of future internal affairs in Canada, or else. For general face-saving purposes the word "regrets" is floated out to the public.

Finally, Tyler proposes and Ashburton accepts a revised plan whereby US and UK ships at sea would avoid future boardings in search of international enslaved cargoes.

With the four frictions apparently resolved, the negotiators shake hands on August 9.

Webster anticipates resistance to several aspects of the treaty within the Senate, and two Democrats in particular—Thomas Hart Benson of Missouri and James Buchanan of Pennsylvania—attack it. But John C. Calhoun supports the deal as does Tyler's nemesis in Virginia politics, William Rives, chairman of the Foreign Relations Committee.

On August 20, 1842 the Senate approves the treaty by a vote of 39–9, marking the one significant accomplishment that Tyler will achieve in foreign policy during his tenure.

## 106

AMERICA'S DRIVE TO EXPLORE THE WEST GAINS MOMENTUM

TIME: 1769 AND ONWARD

WESTERN EXPLORATION MILESTONES PRIOR TO 1840

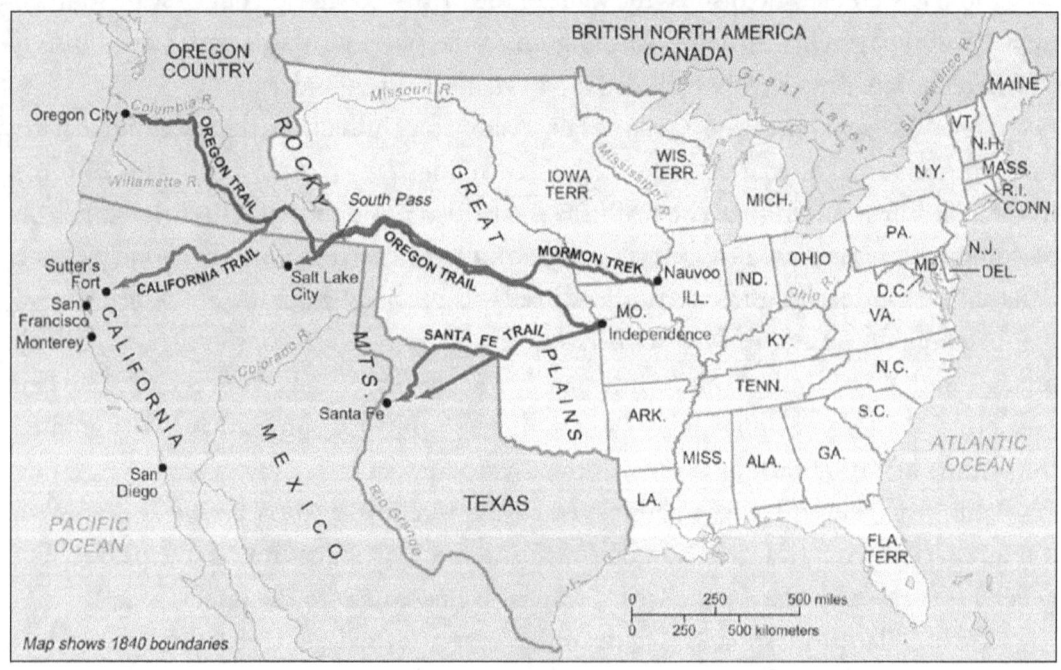

Map of the great trails heading west as of 1840

While Webster and Ashburton are resolving border disputes centered on the Atlantic coast, America continues to turn its attention toward the West, the vast frontier land across the Mississippi still claimed by Spain.

By 1800 overland routes through the Appalachian range have taken early settlers like Daniel Boone through Kentucky into Missouri. The Scottish fur trader, Alexander Mackenzie, has completed two expeditions across Canada, from Montreal to the Pacific

Ocean. Captain Robert Gray of Rhode Island has sailed from Boston around the tip of South America at Cape Horn, and on to what he names the Columbia River in Oregon.

By 1820 Thomas Jefferson's dream of exploring land routes to the west coast has been realized in expeditions led by Meriwether Lewis, William Clark, and Zebulon Pike. The allure of great wealth to be had in the fur trade has drawn the likes of John Jacob Astor to establish a commercially viable outpost on the Oregon coast.

Trail blazing follows across east to west pathways founded by America's Native tribes. The Oregon Trail to the Pacific Northwest; the California Trail branch leading south to Sacramento; the Santa Fe Trail through New Mexico, then connecting with the Old Spanish Trail to Los Angeles. Along with these trails come settlers, commerce, and the prospect of new states to join the Union. Arkansas becomes the second addition west of the Mississippi in 1836, the same year that a brash band of ranchers lays claim to the Republic of Texas.

With the east now tamed, the message to the venturesome is to go west. The timing and origin of this advice remains in some dispute, but according to the native Vermonter and later Iowa Congressman Josiah Grinnell, the phrase belongs to Horace Greeley, who tells him in 1833:

> *Go West, young man, go West. There is health in the country, and room away from our crowds of idlers and imbeciles.*

AMERICANS EXPLORING THE WEST

DATE	
1769	Daniel Boone's expedition crosses the Cumberland Pass
1778	George Rogers Clark travels down the Ohio river to Vincennes, Indiana
1792	Captain Robert Gray of Rhode Island sails to the Pacific northwest, names a river "Columbia" after his ship and goes twelve miles inland on it.
1793	Scotsman Alexander Mackenzie crosses Canada to the Pacific for the North West Company
1796	Thomas Jefferson expresses a wish to map the western lands
1799	Boone opens a settlement on Spanish territory in Missouri
1803	Jefferson asks Congress to fund a Northwest Passage exploration
1804	Lewis and Clark set out from Missouri to the Pacific in Oregon
1806	Lewis and Clark arrive back home with maps and other records
1806	Zebulon Pike begins to explore the Arkansas River
1807	Fur trader John Colter discovers geysers at Yellowstone in Wyoming
1808	John Jacob Astor founds his American Fur Company
1811	The Fort Astoria fur trading outpost is established in northwest Oregon
1821	Missouri trader William Becknell blazes the southwest Santa Fe Trail

1822	Jim Bridger leads first trapping expedition into the Rocky Mountains
1822	Jedediah Smith reaches Fort Henry on the Yellowstone River
1823	Stephen Austin opens the first American settlement in Tejas province
1824	Jed Smith is the first to cross the "South Pass" in the Rockies; Jim Bridger reaches Great Salt Lake in Utah
1825	The Erie Canal links the Hudson River to Lake Erie
1826	Jed Smith reaches San Diego, California
1828	Jed Smith travels up the west coast from California to Oregon
1830	Jed Smith crosses the South Pass again and continues to Oregon
1832	Native land declared sovereign in *Worcester v. State of Georgia* ruling
1833	Bonneville expedition to Idaho, Nevada, and the California Trail
1834	Fort Laramie trading post opens on the North Platte River in Wyoming
1836	Arkansas admitted to the Union; Republic of Texas starts up
1837	Michigan admitted to the Union

TIME: 1824

JEDEDIAH SMITH LOCATES THE "SOUTH PASS" AND CIRCUMNAVIGATES THE WEST COAST

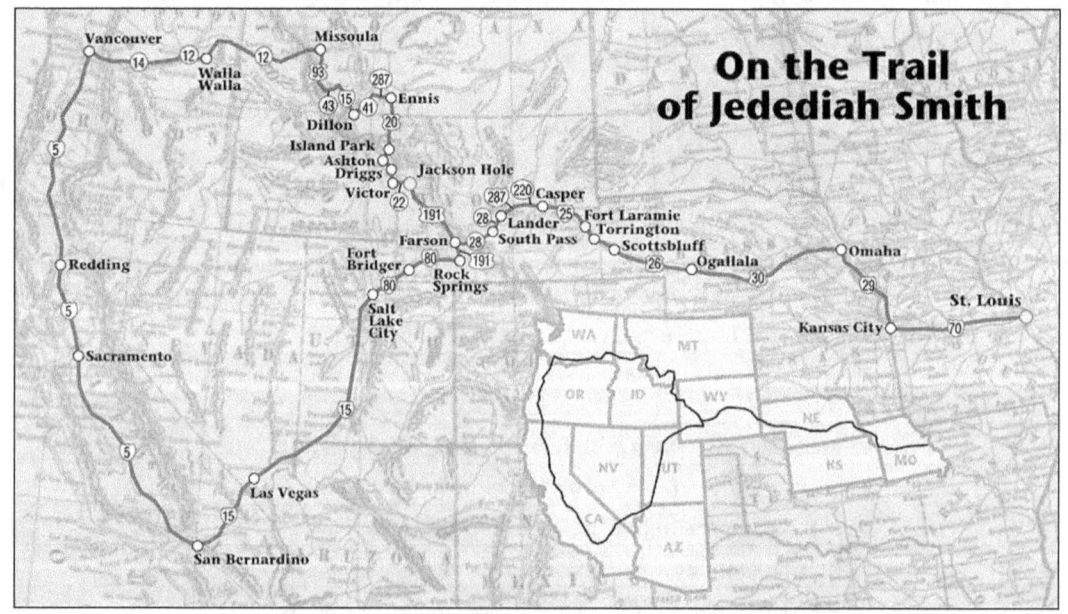

Westward loop explored by Jedediah Smith (1799–1831)

The legendary mountain man, Jedediah Smith, is born in New York in 1799 and explores the West between 1822 and his untimely death in 1831.

Smith's destiny is fixed as a youth by poring over a copy of Lewis and Clark's journals and landing a job on a Lake Erie boat, where he first encounters the fur trade. This lures him west to St. Louis in 1822, where he signs on as a member of the Rocky Mountain Fur Company.

The company is owned by General William Ashley and Major Andrew Henry, both veterans of the War of 1812. The men they recruit become famous as "Ashley's Hundred," known for their exploratory daring and their success with fur trapping and trading.

Two of Ashley's men become famous throughout the region—one is Jim Bridger (1804–1881), the other is Jedediah Smith.

Both men travel up the Missouri River in 1822 to the mouth of the Yellowstone River in North Dakota. After a winter of trapping in the area, twelve members of the party are killed by members of the Arikara tribe while traveling back down the river. Both Smith and Bridger survive, and later mount a reprisal attack alongside their Lakota Sioux allies. The sobriquet "Captain Smith" is granted to Jedediah for his bravery, something further attested to by a reported life-and-death struggle he survives with a grizzly bear.

Smith's greatest contribution as an explorer occurs in 1824 when, with guidance from local Crows, he becomes the first white man to cross the Rocky Mountains at the "South Pass," which subsequently serves as the principal pathway to Idaho, Nevada, and California.

Smith's prowess as a trapper leads to business partnerships, first with Ashley and later with William Sublette, who goes on to found Fort Laramie, the resupply depot for future travelers along the Oregon Trail.

Between 1824 and 1830, Jedediah Smith executes a vast circumference of the west, from the South Pass down through Utah and Nevada to San Bernadino, California, then up the entire coast to Vancouver, and back west via Montana and Wyoming to the Rockies crossing.

This journey also marks him as the first white man to cross Nevada and the Sierra Range, and to transverse the coast.

He departs St. Louis on April 10, 1831 with a party of 74 men carrying goods to trade in Santa Fe. They proceed some 670 miles west to Wagon Bed Springs, Kansas. At a camp there, Smith breaks off from the group to scout for water, and is never seen again.

Several months later, some of his personal belongings show up in Santa Fe in the hands of a local *Comanchero*, a Mexican who trades with the Comanches. This leads to speculation that Smith was probably killed by the Comanches.

TIME: 1833–1834

THE BONNEVILLE EXPEDITION OPENS
A NEW PATH INTO CALIFORNIA

Benjamin Louis Eulalie de Bonneville is a Parisian by birth who arrives in America in

1803 at age seven, courtesy of an Atlantic crossing paid for by his godfather, the patriot pamphleteer Thomas Paine. He graduates from West Point in two years and serves at several frontier outposts— Ft. Smith (Arkansas), Ft. Gibson (Oklahoma), and the Jefferson Barracks (Missouri).

Like Jed Smith, he is bitten by the exploration bug, and asks for a two-year leave of absence from the army to join an expedition to the "Oregon Country," sponsored by the tycoon John Jacob Astor and his American Fur Company. The time is 1832.

Oregon is still hotly disputed between Britain and the United States. Bonneville's leave is granted on the condition that he reports back to his commanders on the situation he finds out west.

He assembles a party of 110 men and departs from Missouri in May 1832. He heads across Missouri to the Platte River and follows it through

General Benjamin Louis Eulalie de Bonneville (1796–1876)

Nebraska and into Wyoming, where he builds a fur trading post along the Green River dubbed Fort Bonneville, and remains there through the winter of 1832–33.

In the spring of 1833, Bonneville continues west to Idaho, following the Snake River route.

With Utah and the Great Salt Lake sitting south of his route, he makes what will prove to be a crucial decision by splitting his party in two. His personal charge is to continue west to the "Oregon Country," but he either senses, or has been encouraged by the army, to also find a route into California.

Whatever the cause, on July 27, 1833 he breaks off a contingent of fifty—led by his right-hand man, Joe Walker—to explore the Great Salt Lake region and search for a path to Alta California.

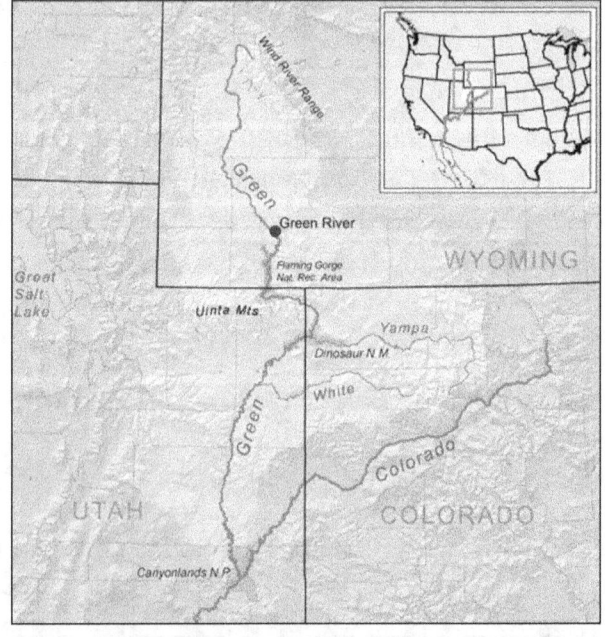

Ft. Bonneville (black dot) on the Green River in Wyoming

Walker's journey pays off. He drifts southwest through Utah and finally picks up the Humboldt River which runs horizontally through Nevada to the base of the Sierra Mountains. Once there, his band ascends the Virginia Creek to the Virginia Lakes, followed by a final 1,700-foot climb to the summit at Mono Pass, some 10,600 feet above sea level. The journal kept by one Zenas Leonard says they cross the snow-covered pass in mid-October 1833.

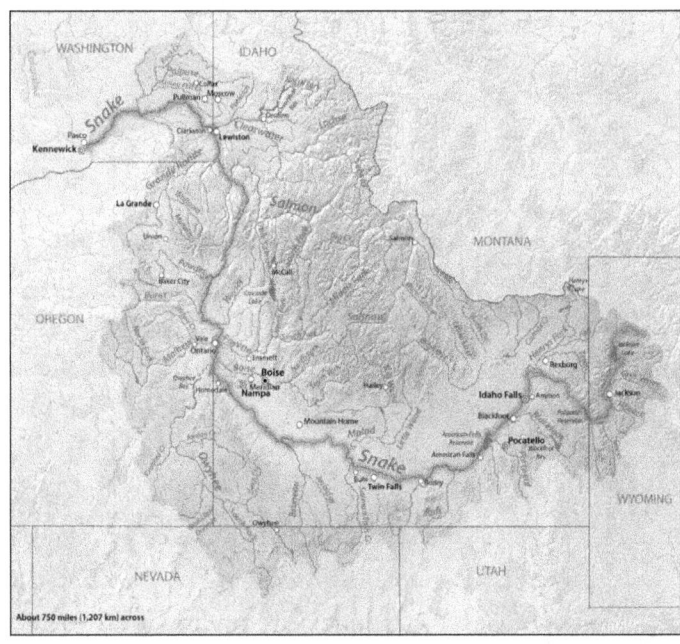

The Snake River route across Idaho

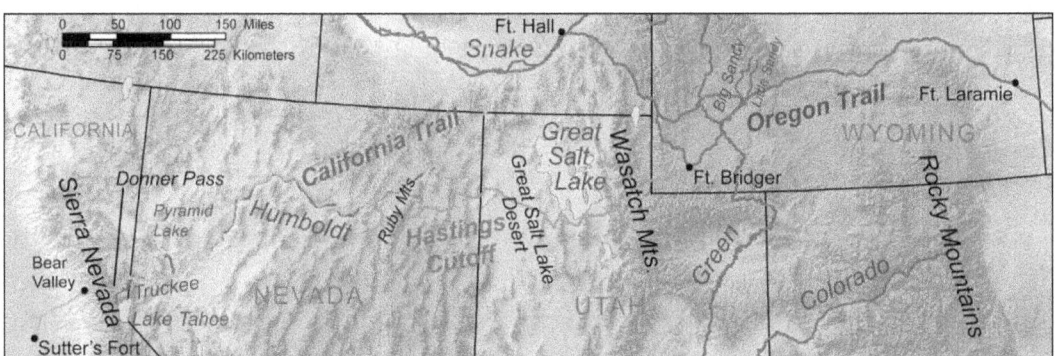

Bonneville heads west along the Snake River while Walker cuts south toward the Humboldt

The descent down the western slope of the Sierra range is treacherous and they are soon slaughtering their own horses for food. As Leonard records:

Twenty-four of our horses died since we reached the top of the mountain, seventeen which we eat the best parts....We searched for a place that was a smooth and gradual in the descent as possible...and by fastening ropes around (our horses) let them down one at a time without doing them any harm.

Each day is spent searching for a path through the remaining, albeit smaller, mountains. They encounter great sequoia (redwood) trees along the way, and finally follow an Indigenous path to the Stanislaus River, which takes them into the Great California Valley some 75 miles south of Sacramento. The Spanish town of Monterrey is their final destination and they remain there until February 14, 1834, when they head back home.

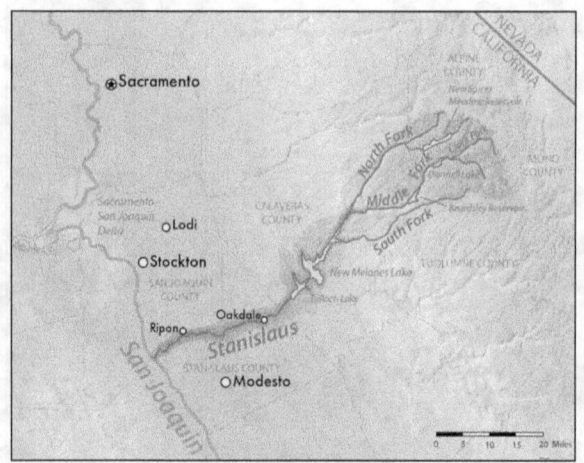

In locating the Humboldt River path and weaving through the Sierras, Walker contributes to what becomes known as the California Trail, traveled by thousands of Americans after gold is discovered there in 1848. Walker lives until 1876, leading John C. Fremont's third expedition west in 1845, and then mounting a successful search for gold around Prescott, Arizona.

Meanwhile, Bonneville's main party backtracks into Wyoming to conduct fur trading with the Shoshone tribe, and ends up at the fort he constructed on the way out. He stays there until January 1834, when he resumes his trek west across the Snake River and into Oregon, stopping in March 1834 in tribal territory at Ft. Nez Perce, owned by the rival Hudson Bay Company.

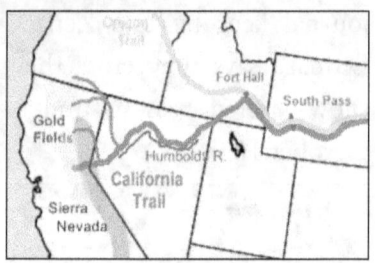

The California Trail discovered by Joe Walker

He will make two separate attempts to trade with the Hudson firm at the fort, but is turned away both times. The British simply want nothing to do with their longtime rival, John Jacob Astor. This same rejection repeats itself when he heads further west toward Ft. Vancouver—discouraged, he turns back east, staying the rest of the winter in upper Utah, again trading with the Shoshones. In April 1835, Bonneville heads home, arriving at Independence, Missouri in August.

Once there he finds that his army commission has been revoked after overstaying his two-year leave by almost fifteen months. However, he is well-connected and makes his appeal to John Jacob Astor and Secretary of War Lewis Cass, who reinstates him. After service at various western forts, he fights in the Mexican War at Veracruz, is promoted to colonel, and given command over the Department of New Mexico. At the start of the Civil War, he is breveted as brigadier general and helps recruit troops in Missouri. He dies there in 1871, at age 82.

## 107

JOHN FREMONT'S FIRST EXPEDITION REACHES THE SOUTH PASS

TIME: MAY 22, 1842

THE 1842 FREMONT EXPEDITION TO THE SOUTH PASS IS ORGANIZED

Between 1842 and 1854, frontiersman, topographical engineer, and future presidential candidate John C. Fremont will complete five separate expeditions to the West.

By the time Congress sets aside $30,000 to fund his first trip west, the main routes he will follow along the Oregon and Santa Fe Trails have been thoroughly "blazed" by a host of Indigenous people and trappers alike.

However, as of 1842, none of them have produced reliable maps or detailed descriptions of the trails. Fremont lays out the scientific process required.

There was a mass of astronomical and other observations to be calculated and discussed before a beginning on [a map] could be made. Indeed, the making of such a map is an interesting process. It must be exact. First, the foundations must be laid

John C. Fremont (1813–1890)

in observations made in the field; then the [mathematical] reductions of these
observations to latitude and longitude; afterward the projection of the map, and the
laying down of positions fixed by the observation; then the tracings from the sketch-
books of the lines of the rivers, the forms of the lakes, the contours of the hills. Specially,
it is interesting to those who have laid in the field these foundations, to see them all
brought into final shape—fixing on a small sheet the results of laborious travel over
waste regions, and giving to them an enduring place on the world's surface.

The tasks will fall to Fremont and his companions.

The initial 1842 expedition is led by three men, each uniquely qualified for the
journey.

In overall command is 2nd Lt. John Fremont, who joins the United States Army Corps
of Topographical Engineers in 1838. His background is anything but conventional.

His mother, Anne, is the daughter of a wealthy Virginia planter whose estate is
dissipated, leaving her to fend for herself. She marries an elderly Richmond man, then
carries on an affair with a French expatriate, Charles Fremon, who had fought for the
monarchy. Together they have an out-of-wedlock son, John Fremon, in 1813. After
two years at the College of Charleston, Fremon embarks on a military career, teaching
mathematics aboard a naval sloop. His interests
shift to topographical engineering and in 1838
he begins to survey land west of St. Louis, where
the Missouri River, flowing eastward from the
Rockies, empties into the Mississippi River.

In 1840, Fremont (who has added a "t" to
his name) is in Washington, DC to report on
his survey, where he meets Jessie Benton, the
fifteen-year-old daughter of Senator Thomas
Hart Benton. Jessie has been reared like a son
by her powerful father, Missouri's first senator
since 1821, a fierce Jackson man, and a leading
advocate of US territorial expansion. Much to
his chagrin, the ever-willful Jessie elopes with
Fremont in 1841.

Reconciliation follows banishment, and in
1842 Senator Benton secures a commission for
Fremont to begin mapping the West, a journey
that will eventually lead to his sobriquet as "the
Pathfinder" and to future fame.

Kit Carson (1809–1868)

As his designated expedition "guide," Fremont selects Christopher "Kit" Carson, who grows up in Franklin, Missouri along the Santa Fe Trail, on land his father purchases from Daniel Boone. He is a restless youth, and in 1826, at age 17, sets out West with a band of trappers. Over the next fifteen years, he becomes a well-known mountain man, hunting and trading up and down the Rocky Mountains, while often living among various Indigenous tribes. Like Fremont, his mapping expeditions will secure him lasting fame.

The third key figure is Charles Preuss, who is born in Germany in 1803, studies geodesy (the science associated with measuring the earth), and becomes a surveyor and mapmaker for the government of Prussia. He immigrates to America in 1834 and is hired by Fremont for his expertise—to accurately measure longitudes, latitudes, temperatures, and barometric pressures—and for his artistic talent to create visually attractive maps.

Fremont rounds out his band with 21 others, mostly experienced French trappers who are familiar with the routes and are known by various Native tribes and outpost proprietors along the way. Foraging for game will be crucial, so he hires an Illinois hunter named Maxwell. He also adds Randolph Benton, the twelve-year-old son of his powerful father-in-law senator, "for development of mind and body which such an expedition would give."

Together they set out from St. Louis on May 22, 1842, heading west 240 miles by steamboat along the bend of the Missouri River to Independence, where America's two great early highways converge—the Santa Fe Trail drifting southward to New Mexico and the Oregon Trail headed to Oregon in the north.

TIME: JULY 1842

THE PARTY REACHES THE PLATTE RIVER IN EARLY JULY

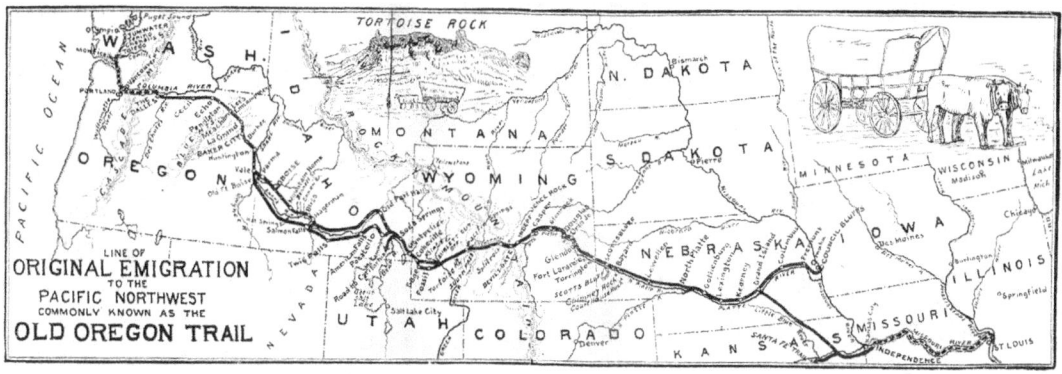

Map of the old Oregon Trail leading all the way back to St. Louis, Missouri

Once at Independence, Fremont further outfits the expedition with wagons, livestock, provisions, and scientific gear for the overland trip ahead.

The goal for their trip is fairly modest in scope—to reach the South Pass break in the Rocky Mountains in Wyoming and then come home with detailed maps and descriptions in hand.

They will follow the Oregon Trail, originally traveled by predecessors including Native American tribes; Lewis, Clark, and Colter; Jim Bridger; Jedediah Smith; and de Bonneville.

On June 10, they pick up the trail heading due west alongside the Kansas River. They arrive at the approximate future site of Lawrence, Kansas on June 12, and Topeka on June 14. From there they turn north toward the Nebraska Territory, on a route that parallels the Big Blue River. On June 17, they mingle with a local Indigenous tribe. Fremont, who speaks French fluently, observes this moment in time:

> *A number of Kanzas Indians visited us today…(and) I found one sitting on the ground among the men, gravely and fluently speaking French…as any of my party, nearly all of French origin.*

They move up the Big Blue into the Nebraska Territory to the Platte River, making roughly twenty miles on an average day, and again shift west to the head of the Little Blue River, which they reach on June 22. Fremont captures their daily routine:

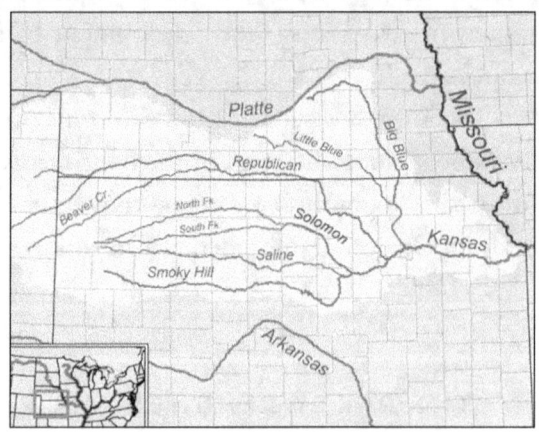

Map of the Kansas and Big Blue Rivers heading to the Platte

> *During the day…making astronomical observations…to lay down the country…(and) keep up our map regularly in the field.*

Along with basic survey work comes detailed descriptions from the realm of earth sciences—plants, soil content, geologic formations, types of timber, grasslands, and species of animals.

The landscapes opening up before their eyes are breathtaking. On June 30, in language that will later capture the imagination of the American public, Fremont describes his initial sighting of the Great Plains' buffalo herds:

> *June 30th. First view of buffalo. The air was keen the next morning at sunrise, the thermometer standing at 44 degrees and it was sufficiently cold to make overcoats very comfortable. A few miles brought us into the midst of the buffalo swarming*

in immense numbers over the plains, where they had left scarcely a blade of grass standing. Mr. Preuss, who was sketching at a little distance in the rear, had at first noted them as large groves of timber.

In the sight of such a mass of life, the traveler feels a strange emotion of grandeur. We had heard from a distance a dull and confused murmuring, and when we came in view of their dark masses, there was not one among us who did not feel his heart beat quicker. It was the early part of the day when the herds are feeding, and everywhere they were in motion. Here and there a huge old bull was rolling in the grass and clouds of dust rose in the air from various parts of the bands, each the scene of some obstinate fight. Indians and buffalo make the poetry and life of the prairie and our camp was full of their exhilaration.

On July 1, Fremont further captures the spirit of adventure around a hunt for cow meat:

*My horse was a trained hunter, famous in the West, under the name of Proveau…in a few minutes he brought me alongside the cow, and rising in my stirrups, I fired at a distance of a yard, the bullet entering at the termination of the long hair **and** passing near the heart…felling her.*

July 2 brings the party to the branch of the Platte River, with the north branch some 2,250 feet wide and the south branch a mere 450 feet. The main party heads up the northern artery, their destination being the fur trading outpost at Laramie in the Wyoming Territory.

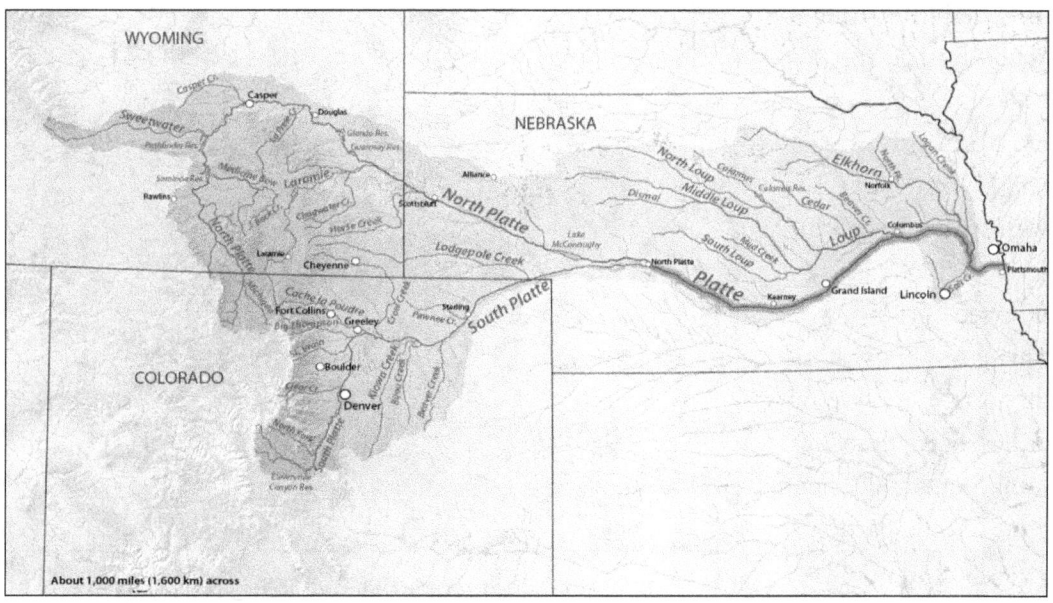

The Platte River branching north along the Oregon Trail and south along the Santa Fe Trail

TIME: AUGUST 1842

THEY REACH THEIR SOUTH PASS DESTINATION

On July 9, excitement builds as their final destination finally comes into view.

This morning we caught the first faint glimpse of the Rocky Mountains, about sixty miles distant.

But their exuberance is tempered by dwindling supplies, especially foodstuffs, where their diaries bemoan a lack of coffee, salt, sugar, bread, macaroni, and cow meat in particular.

Preuss, the taciturn mapmaker, emerges as the chief grumbler among the crew, often critical of Fremont's leadership, especially as it relates to what he considers foolish gambles.

It is ridiculous (of him) to risk lives to find the elevations of every mountain range.

At 4 p.m. on July 13 the weary travelers arrive at the fur trading outpost at Laramie. The site is first developed in 1815 by a French trapper, Jacques La Ramee. It is converted into a fort in 1834 by the Kentucky native William Sublette, who names it Fort William in his own honor. In 1841 John Jacob Astor's firm buys the land and rechristens it Fort John. But all along it is referred to as the fort at the Laramie River, and thus it becomes Fort Laramie in 1849 after the US Army buys it for $4,000 to support and protect settlers heading toward the gold fields of California.

By 1842, the structure itself has been modified from a modest 80 by 100 feet log enclosure to a much more expansive quadrangle made of clay, with walls reaching 15 feet high and reinforced inside by a square tower with rifle ports. On occasion it has been tested by local Sioux and Cheyenne raiding parties.

Their stay at Fort Laramie lasts for eight

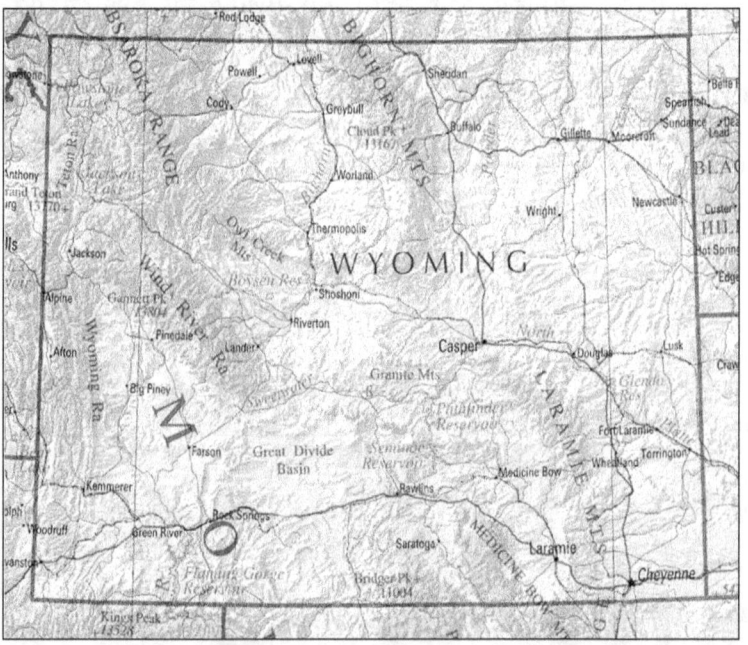

Map showing Fremont's Fort John (Laramie)–Platte–Sweetwater–South Pass route

days, from July 13 to July 20. They use this time to rest up and refit their caravan for the winding 320-mile uphill climb toward the Rockies.

On July 21 they begin their ascent across the High Plains of Wyoming, heading northwest along the Platte, then swinging back southwest along the Sweetwater River toward the summit of the South Pass.

By July 28 they are one week into their trudge and encountering the effects of a severe drought. The ground is now covered daily by swarms of grasshoppers and other insects, which devour the grass needed for grazing. This depletes the buffalo herds, threatens the Plains' Indigenous tribes with starvation, and raises the specter of hostile raiding parties. Some argue in favor of turning back, but Fremont brushes them aside and plunges onward.

On August 7 they reach the mouth of the Sweetwater River and on August 8 they are at their destination, the summit of the South Pass, where they are greeted by a severe storm of hail.

Map of the South Pass

When Fremont arrives there, the South Pass is less well-known than its northern counterpart, the Lemhi Pass, which Lewis and Clark followed in their 1805 "water route" sortie to the Pacific coast.

Both passes are roughly 7,400 feet above sea level, or half the height of the Rocky Mountain range.

The South Pass is 35 miles wide. Those previously crossing it include the Astorian trapper Robert Stuart in 1811, the fur merchant W.H. Ashley in 1824, and the colorful army captain Benjamin Louis de Bonneville in 1832.

Once at his planned destination, Fremont is amazed by the grandeur that surrounds him at daybreak.

The scenery becomes hourly more scenic and grand…the sun has just shot above the wall, and makes a magical change. The whole valley is growing and bright, and all the mountain peaks are gleaming like silver…the pines on the mountain seem to give it much additional beauty.

While he reckons that the party has come 950 miles from the Kansas River, once Fremont views the Wind River Mountains to his north, he can't resist the temptation to conquer them.

I left the valley a few miles from our encampment intending to penetrate the mountains as far as possible.

TIME: AUGUST 15 – OCTOBER 17, 1842

FREMONT PLANTS HIS AMERICAN FLAG ON WIND RIVER MOUNTAIN PEAK

The Wind River Mountain slashes some 100 miles in a northwesterly fashion from the entrance to the South Pass.

The range is split down the middle by its portion of the Great Continental Divide, the series of mountains running the length of North and South America from the Bering Strait to the Strait of Magellan—with rivers to the west running to the Pacific Ocean and those to the east seeking the Atlantic.

On his ascent, Fremont encounters an idyllic lake.

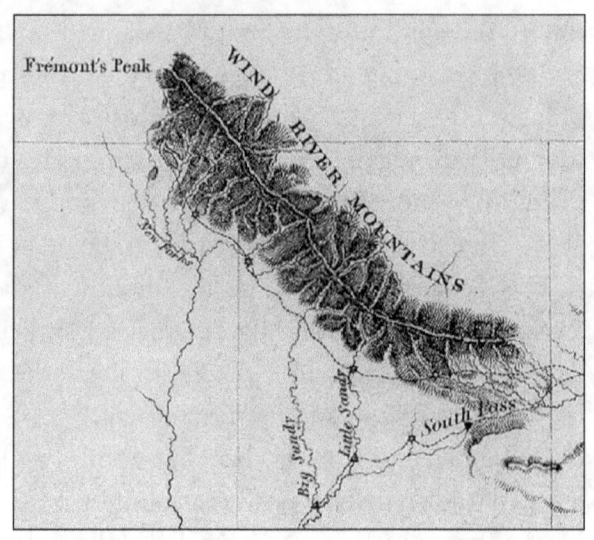

The Wind River Mountains with Fremont's Peak
(actually about 80% up the spine)

Winding our way up a long ravine, we came unexpectedly in view of a most beautiful lake, set like a gem in the mountains. I have called it the Mountain Lake.

The natural beauty of the place draws him onward. On August 12 he writes:

Of all the strange places on…our long journey none left so vivid an impression on my mind as this place.

On August 13, he reflects on the "savage sublimity of the naked rock" all around him, and compares its "wildness" to the unbound, pioneering character of the American people.

It is not by the splendor of far off views, which have lent such a glory to the Alps, that these impress the mind; but by a gigantic disorder of enormous masses, and a savage sublimity of naked rock, in wonderful contrast with innumerable green spots of a rich floral beauty, shut up in their stern recesses. Their wildness seems well suited to the character of the people who inhabit the country.

His band finally settles on scaling a high promontory point they spot, about three-quarters of the way up the spine of the ridge. On August 15, 1842 they reach their objective and celebrate by planting a flag.

I sprang upon the summit, and another step would have precipitated me into an immense snow field 500 feet below. (Once there) we fixed a ramrod in a crevice (and) unfurled the national flag to wave in the breeze where never a flag waved before.

Thereafter this site will become known as Fremont's Peak.

Having more than accomplished their duties, the band begins their two-month journey back home. Fremont arrives in St. Louis on October 17, where he learns of a new challenge coming his way.

## 108

FREMONT'S SECOND EXPEDITION EXPLORES THE WEST COAST

TIME: MAY 29, 1843 – AUGUST 1844

A SECOND FREMONT JOURNEY EXTENDS SOUTH ALONG THE CALIFORNIA COAST

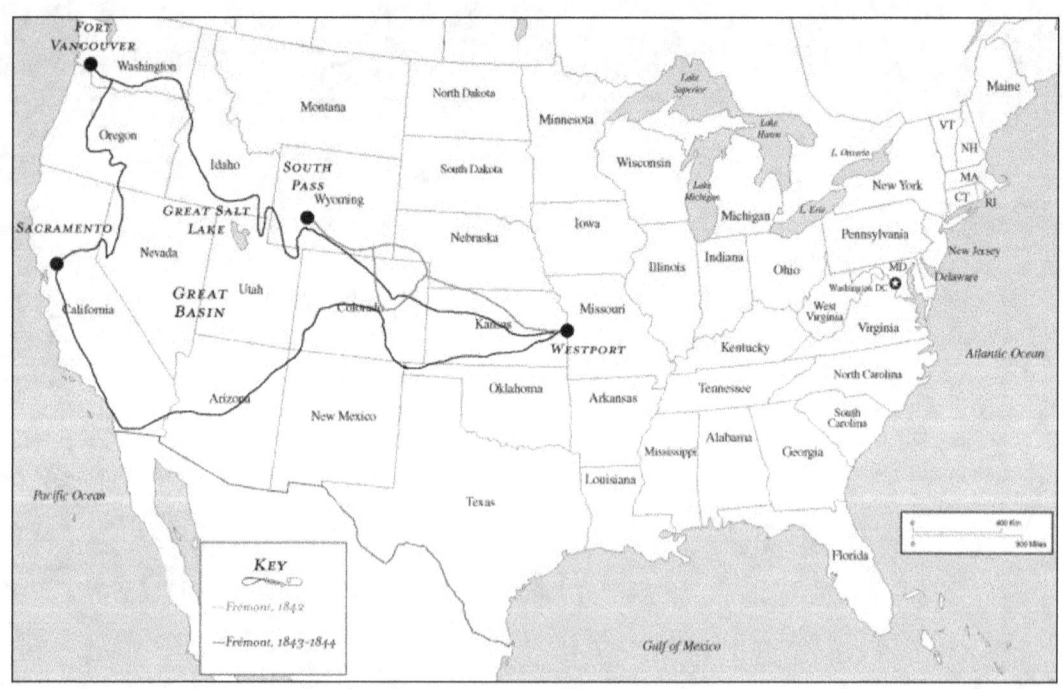

Map of Fremont's second expedition

No sooner does Fremont return from his first journey than preparations begin for a second.

His assignment this time is to finish up mapping the entire Oregon Trail route, pushing beyond the South Pass and heading northwest all the way to Fort Vancouver.

Fremont reassembles his 27-man crew, again including both Kit Carson and Charles

Preuss, and sets out from St. Louis on May 29, 1843.

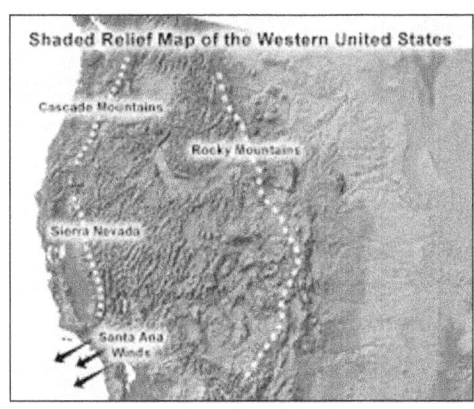

Map of the Sierra Nevada range
heading south

The outward trip is relatively uneventful, with the party reaching the Great Salt Lake on September 6 and Fort Vancouver in early November. At this point Fremont's orders are to turn around and return home by the same route he has just completed. Instead he ignores tribal warnings about the winter ahead, and decides to swing south, heading along the eastern face of the Sierra Nevada range toward Sacramento, California. It is a decision which almost proves fatal.

By January 27, 1844, the expedition—some 27 men, 67 horses and mules, and a wheeled cannon—is strung out and stymied in the mountains. Charles Preuss captures the moment.

We are now completely snowed in. The snowstorm is on top of us. The wind obliterates all tracks which, with incredible effort, we make for our horses. The horses are about twenty miles behind and are expected to arrive tonight, or rather, they are now no longer expected. How could they get through? At the moment no one can tell what will really happen. It is certain we shall have to eat horse meat.

Indeed, they do end up eating their horses before being saved by Kit Carson who finally finds a pass to the west slope of the Sierras and safety. The guide carves his initials into a tree marking the location, henceforth known as Carson's Pass.

Another two-week struggle finally ends on March 6, 1844, as they limp into Fort Sutter, east of Sacramento and soon to be famous for the nearby discovery of gold. A three-week rest there prepares them for the trip home, which takes them through the San Joaquin Valley to the Old Spanish Trail through the Rockies in Utah.

Their fourteen-month journey ends in August, when they arrive back in St. Louis.

Upon his return, Fremont is breveted to the rank of captain by the army, receives national publicity from the press, and is transformed into the "Great Pathfinder" by an adoring public. He is 31 years old, with a future ahead that will find him repeatedly in America's spotlight over the next four decades.

TIME: 1842–1844

IMPACT OF FREMONT'S FIRST TWO EXPEDITIONS TO THE WEST

In reality, casting Fremont as the "Great Pathfinder" is more the product of publicity than performance, since almost all of the trails he takes have been traveled by many others before him.

Still his impact on America's drive to "open the West" is profound.

For the first time, thanks to Fremont's band, those eager to move across the continent have access to accurate maps to guide their way. These will prove invaluable in a few short years, first for the army during west coast conflicts with Mexico and Britain, and later when a flood of "forty-niners" head to the gold fields of California.

But beyond the sheer utility of the maps lies the magic of Fremont's often poetic descriptions of the natural beauty he encounters from one camp to the next. How much of this prose springs from his pen versus that of his wife and co-author, Jessie, remains unknown. However, its effect on the imagination of the American public is undeniable.

For the first time those living east of the Mississippi can sense the vastness of the Great Plains, the majesty of the Rocky Mountains, the fertile California vineyards, the mighty roar of buffalo herds, rushing rapids, and the Pacific Ocean.

Any early stirrings about expansion that the politicians and public might have felt since the Louisiana Purchase are suddenly amplified by Fremont's first two expeditions. In that sense, he becomes an important pathfinder of America's commitment to manifest destiny.

SIDEBAR: BIRTHS AND DEATHS OF FRONTIERSMEN

It is not surprising that Americans who abandoned hearth and home on their own precarious journey across the Atlantic would form a love affair with the frontiersmen who ventured overland to the Pacific.

Daniel Boone heads through the Cumberland Gap into Kaintucky. John Jacob Astor chases fur pelts across Canada to the west coast. George Clark and Meriwether Lewis blaze the Oregon Trail. Zebulon Pike finds his 14,000-foot peak in the southern Rockies. Tennessee Congressman Davy Crockett and Jim Bowie lose their lives on behalf of the Republic of Texas. The Missouri trader, William Becknell, is the first to walk the Santa Fe Trail. The mountain men Jedediah Smith, William

Mountain man Seth Kinman
(1815–1888)

Ashley, Jim Bridger, and William Sublette make their living in the Rockies, cross the Mojave Desert, and reach southern California. Ceran St. Vrain and William Bent build their trading post near Taos, New Mexico. John Sutter's sawmill in Coloma, California will spark the 1849 gold rush. John Fremont, Kit Carson, and Charles Preuss draw maps that will prove invaluable to all who follow. And there is a host of largely unknown Indigenous people who were there first, and who often guided the way for the settlers.

These are America's very own explorers, their names on towns and monuments, their deeds forever memorialized in literature and songs, their spirit embedded in the psyches of those about to realize the vision of "manifest destiny" in the latter half of the 19th century.

NAME	BIRTH	DEATH
Daniel Boone	Oct. 22, 1734	Sept. 26, 1820
George Rogers Clark	Nov. 19, 1752	Feb. 13, 1818
Robert Gray	May 10, 1755	July 1806
John Jacob Astor	July 17, 1763	Mar. 29, 1848
Alexander Mackenzie	1764	Mar. 12, 1820
Toussaint Charbonneau	1767	1843
William Ashley	1770	Mar. 26, 1838
Meriwether Lewis	Aug. 18, 1774	Oct. 11, 1809
John Colter	1774	Nov. 22, 1813
Zebulon Pike	Jan. 5, 1779	Apr. 27, 1813
Davy Crockett	1786	1836
William Becknell	1788	Apr. 30, 1865
Sacagawea	1788	1812
Stephen Austin	Nov. 3, 1793	Dec. 27, 1836
Benjamin Bonneville	Apr. 14, 1796	June 12, 1878
James Bowie	1796	Mar. 6, 1836
Charles Wilkes	Apr. 3, 1798	Feb. 8, 1877
William Sublette	Sept. 21, 1798	July 23, 1845
Joseph Walker	Dec. 13, 1798	Oct. 27, 1876
Jedediah Smith	Jan. 16, 1799	May 27, 1831
Ceran St. Vrain	May 5, 1802	Oct. 28, 1870
John Sutter	Feb. 20, 1803	June 18, 1880
Charles Preuss	1803	1854
Jim Bridger	Mar. 17, 1804	July 17, 1881
Kit Carson	Dec. 24, 1809	May 23, 1868
William Bent	May 23, 1809	May 19, 1869

NAME	BIRTH	DEATH
John Grizzly Adams	1812	1860
John C. Fremont	Jan. 21, 1813	July 13, 1890
Seth Kinman	Sept. 29, 1815	Feb. 24, 1888
Jim Baker	1818	1898

## 109

THE WILKES EXPEDITION ADDS LUSTER TO AMERICA'S GLOBAL REPUTATION

TIME: 1838–1842

LT. CHARLES WILKES' "EXPLORATORY EXPEDITION" SAILS AROUND THE WORLD

On June 10, 1842, just as Fremont is starting his journey west in Kansas, another adventurer, naval commander Lt. Charles Wilkes, sails into New York harbor after completing a four-year trip to navigate the globe.

The eventual "Wilkes Expedition" has been a long time in the making. President John Quincy Adams initiated the idea in 1828, but failed to convince Congress for the funding needed. Andrew Jackson picks up the cause and gains approval in 1836. Still, two more years are needed to organize the six-ship flotilla and outfit it properly with 342 sailors and scientists and necessary provisions. It is officially named the US Exploratory Expedition, abbreviated as the "Ex Ex."

Overall command belongs with 40-year-old Lt. Charles Wilkes, whose surveys of the Narragansett Bay lead to his position as head of the Navy's Department of Charts and Instruments.

Charles Wilkes (1798–1877)

Wilkes' main objective lies in exploring and mapping the Pacific Ocean, and collecting various earth science data and artifacts at stops along the way. He is aided by all the modern tools available to a mariner of his time to plot exact positions across the ocean.

For millennia, sailors had been relying on celestial navigation—sighting on stars above them at night—to approximate their locations in open water. Around 1730 the first crude sextant is invented to more accurately record the position of the stars at the time of measurement. This enables a ship to determine its latitude, or how far north or south it lies relative to Earth's equator. In 1764, the Englishman John Hadley solves the other half of the ship location puzzle by building the first chronometer, a precise marine clock. It enables an accurate measure of longitude, or how far east or west they sit relative to the prime meridian, the line leading from the North Pole through the city of London and on to the South Pole. Together these two devices enable the expedition to deliver on their mapping mission.

Wilkes' crew totals 346 men, including nine scientists ranging from naturalists to plant biologists, mineralogists, a taxidermist, and an expert in languages. Naval personnel are assigned the tasks associated with collecting positional data and converting it into accurate maps.

On August 19, 1838, the fleet heads out to the open seas from Hampton Roads, Virginia. Since the entire flotilla consists of sailing ships, their course will be determined by the winds they encounter. Thus, while their first destination is Rio de Janeiro, Brazil, they are blown directly east to the Madeira Islands before they can tack south. What was to be a six-week first leg turns into a frustrating 95-day detour.

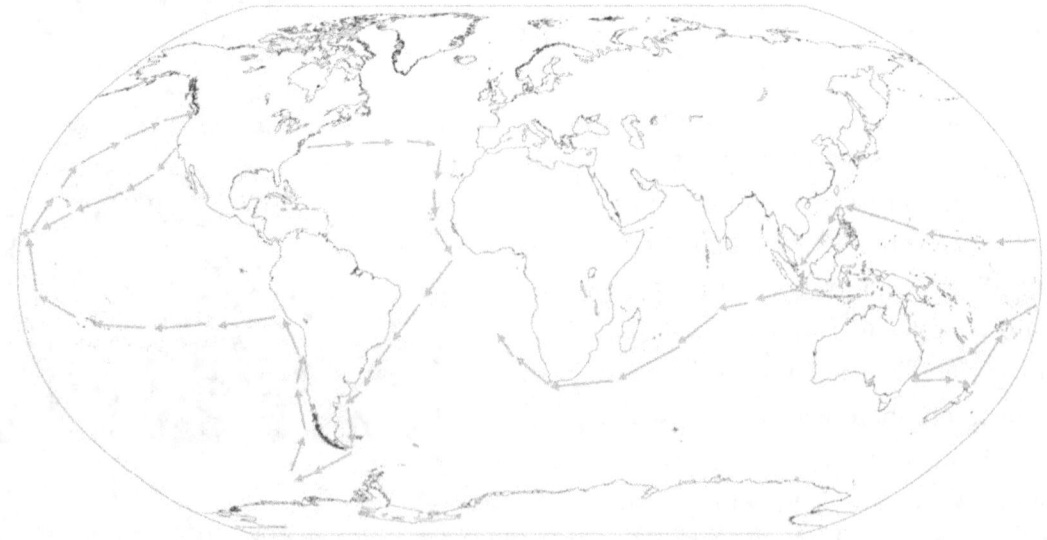

Map of the Wilkes expedition's four-year route around the world

Over the next four years the Exploratory Expedition will zigzag its way around the globe, creating detailed maps that will support navigation of future naval vessels and merchant ships alike. It will also spark additional interest in America's west coast, which Wilkes explores briefly in the summer of 1841.

ROUTE TAKEN BY THE WILKES EXPEDITION

1838	LOCATIONS
September 16	Blown east cross Atlantic to Madeira Islands
November 23	Back along South American coast to Rio de Janeiro
1839	
Early	Around Cape Horn and north to Chile and Peru
Later	Across Pacific to Sydney, Australia
1840	
January 25	Fleet reaches "ice island" of Antartica
July	Fiji Islands where two crew members are killed in conflict with Fijians
1841	
April	Head north to the Gilbert Islands then east toward US
July	In Oregon and head south along the coast to San Francisco Bay
Later	Back west to Pacific Ocean and Wake Island
1842	
Early	Further west into Philippines, Singapore, Polynesia
Later	Past the Cape of Good Hope in southern Africa
June 10	Arrive back home in New York harbor

The scientists aboard are also busy at every stop doing experiments and collecting artifacts that will describe what they see on the journey. The breadth of the specimens is remarkable.

SCIENTIFIC AND CULTURAL SPECIMENS CATALOGUED AND BROUGHT HOME

ROLE	NAME	SPECIMEN
Naturalists, Horticulturalists	Charles Pickering, Titian Peale, William Brackenridge, William Rich	10,000 species of pressed plants, 1,000 live plants, 648 seeds, 2,150 stuffed birds, 134 mammals, 588 species of fish, and 5,300 species of insects
Geologist	James Dana	300 fossils, 400 coral, 1,000 crustaceans
Linguistics, Ethnographist	Horatio Hale	4,000 pieces, from Fijian war clubs to feathered baskets, carved rattles, fishhooks, artworks, etc.
Artists	Alfred Agate, James Drayton	Tracings of collections using new "camera lucida" to project images onto paper

Of the 342 voyagers who set out in 1838, a total of 223 return either on the expedition ships or other American vessels. Fifteen have died along the way, 62 have been discharged for cause, and another 42 have deserted.

For Wilkes the homecoming sadly brings additional trials. First, his claim to being the first seaman to reach Antarctica is challenged by both English and French explorers who are in the same region in January 1840. Then complaints about his authoritarian rule throughout the voyage lead to the Naval Court of Inquiry. In July 1842, he is acquitted of all charges save one, for administering more than the maximum twelve lashes to six sailors accused of stealing liquor.

Despite these setbacks, Wilkes finishes up his written record of the voyage, which spans five volumes and is finally published by Congress in 1845. It is a tedious rendition and fails to earn the fame that Fremont enjoys from the journals he publishes (perhaps with some ghostwriting help from his talented wife, Jessie).

Meanwhile the collections from the trip are hailed by its sponsors and by the scientific community, both eager to demonstrate America's capacity to rival Europe in the arena of research and the pursuit of new knowledge.

As the vast amount of cargo is being off-loaded, the question arises as to where it will be housed. The answer will eventually be America's first national museum, the Smithsonian Institution.

SIDEBAR: THE SMITHSONIAN INSTITUTION HOUSES THE "EX EX" TREASURES

Original Smithsonian Institution sitting alone on the future mall

The challenge of housing artifacts brought back from the Exploratory Expedition provokes an end to the back and forth political haggling about how best to utilize a monetary windfall arriving in America in 1835.

The windfall is 104,960 gold sovereigns, packed in sacks and valued at $500,000, willed to the US Treasury by a British citizen named James Smithson, who dies at age 64 in 1829.

Smithson's life has been filled with adventure. He is the illegitimate son of an English duke and a widowed royal mother who leaves him a sizable inheritance. He uses part of the money to study chemistry and mineralogy at Oxford, where he becomes friends with noted scientists of his era, including Henry Cavendish, famed for his discovery of hydrogen. He travels broadly and is known to have published some 27 scholarly papers, focusing especially on the chemical properties of a zinc ore known as calamine. His work earns him admission to the prestigious Royal Society in London.

When the initial heir to his estate dies without offspring, a clause in Smithson's will directs the money across the Atlantic to the American government.

I then bequeath the whole of my property, . . . to the United States of America, to found at Washington, under the name of the Smithsonian Institution, an Establishment for the increase & diffusion of knowledge among men.

The motivation behind Smithson's gift remains a mystery. While books in his library include references to the US, he has never traveled there, nor does it appear he even met anyone from America. Speculation tends to focus on possible "wounds" in Britain related to his illegitimacy and a sense that the impact of his gift might be greater in a vigorous new nation just beginning to assert its role in science.

Whatever the cause, America is delighted to receive the bounty which arrives in 1838, only to be lost when an investment in Arkansas bonds goes bust. This injustice is finally righted by John Quincy Adams who persuades his House colleagues to restore the fund and spend it according to Smithson's directive.

On August 10, 1846, Tyler's successor, President James Polk, signs legislation to establish the Smithsonian Institution as a perpetual government trust.

While collections from the Ex Ex eventually end up at the Smithsonian, they are initially stored at the new Patent Office, secured by physician and former Secretary of War Joel Poinsett, an early proponent of America's scientific development.

Unfortunately, the first curator at the Patent Office totally mishandles the coding of the material before being fired for incompetence. Order is eventually restored by his initial replacement, Charles Pickering (the lead naturalist on the Ex Ex), and then by Commander Wilkes himself who christens the Great Hall with a sign in gold letters reading "Collection of the Exploring Expedition."

The original Smithsonian building—known as the Castle—is finally completed in 1855 on an isolated site about 1.3 miles west of the Capitol, before becoming anchored to the mall as America's first national museum.

## 110

TWO POWERFUL BLACK ABOLITIONISTS MAKE THEIR VOICES HEARD

TIME: SUMMER 1843

FREDERICK DOUGLASS BECOMES A NATIONAL SPOKESMAN FOR THE ABOLITIONIST MOVEMENT

On Nantucket in August 1841, the leader of the abolitionist cause, William Lloyd Garrison, recognizes the powerful effect that Frederick Douglass could have on breaking through to white audiences about the evils of slavery.

Frederick Douglass 1818–1895

It was at once deeply impressed upon my mind, that, if Mr. DOUGLASS could be persuaded to consecrate his time and talents to the promotion of the anti-slavery enterprise, a powerful impetus would be given to it, and a stunning blow at the same time inflicted on northern prejudice against a colored complexion.

He invites Douglass to formally join the movement and Douglass accepts, immediately throwing himself into his destined mission.

In 1843, at age 25, he joins the "One Hundred Conventions" tour as a lecturer. This is a grueling affair which takes him from upstate New York through Pennsylvania, Ohio, and Indiana. Danger accompanies him at all stops. In Pendleton, Indiana he is beaten by a white mob and ends up with a broken right hand that is never again fully functional.

Speaking mostly to white audiences, he recounts his own life experiences to establish his main themes:

- Black people who are given a fair chance in America will, like himself, succeed and become good citizens.
- But slavery shuts off that opportunity by reducing humans to the status of "brutes."
- In the process of debasing Black people, white people commit atrocities that tarnish their immortal souls.
- They are often reinforced by white churches that fail to live up to Christ's teachings.
- The "slavery problem" can be solved if Black people are taught to read and write, and given their freedom.
- Douglass himself is living proof of what is possible for America's enslaved population.

The South quickly views the eloquent Frederick Douglass as a threat to their narrative about Black people as a separate species from white people, universally and irretrievably inferior, potentially violent, and best kept in captivity.

Douglass violates those stereotypes, as do other free Black people now intent on making themselves heard.

TIME: AUGUST 1843

BLACK PREACHER HENRY HIGHLAND GARNET URGES ENSLAVED PEOPLE TO RESIST THEIR OPPRESSORS

In 1843, while Frederick Douglass is intent on using moral persuasion to convince white masters to end slavery, the Black preacher Henry Highland Garnet is calling for physical resistance as the only option left.

Like Douglass, Garnet escaped slavery, smuggled out of Maryland at nine years old by his parents, George and Henrietta Trusty, who settle in New Hope, Pennsylvania before moving to New York City in 1824. Once there, the family name is changed from Trusty to Garnet in order to throw off possible pursuers.

George finds work as a shoemaker and is able to enroll Henry in the African Free School when he is eleven. He soon falls in with a handful of other youths who will become leaders in the abolitionist movement: the future Episcopal minister Alexander Crummel; college professor Charles Reason; and the Dr. James McCune Smith. Together they found the Garrison Literary and Benevolent Society, in honor of the white reformer.

In 1829 slave-catchers in New York temporarily scatter Garnet's family, and he ends up working on a Long Island farm. He suffers a severe leg injury there while playing sports which leaves him on crutches and eventually ends with amputation. The disability turns him more inward, and soon both his studies and his faith pick up. In 1835 he joins the First Colored Presbyterian Church and falls under the sway of the renowned Reverend Theodore Wright, co-founder of the American Anti-Slavery Society.

Later that year, Garnet attends an academy in New Hampshire run by the controversial utopian "perfectionist," John Humphrey Noyes. After protestors destroy the schoolhouse, he moves to graduate from the Oneida Institute.

In 1840 he moves to Troy, New York, where he completes his education under the direction of Reverend Nathan Beman, one of Charles Finney's "New School" converts. A year later he marries a Boston schoolteacher, begins preaching at Liberty Street Presbyterian Church, and edits *The National Watchman,* a Black newspaper.

Garnet's fame as a preacher spreads, and in August, 1843 he is asked to address the National Negro Convention in Buffalo, an annual gathering of Black leaders searching for ways to free their enslaved brethren. The speech he delivers sounds the same moral outrage and call to arms as David Walker's 1829 "Appeal to Colored Citizens."

He opens by declaring that prior attempts to end slavery have been in vain.

Brethren and Fellow Citizens:—Your brethren of the North, East, and West have been accustomed to meet together in National Conventions, to sympathize with each other, and to weep over your unhappy condition. …But, we have hoped in vain. Years have rolled on, and tens of thousands have been borne on streams of blood and tears, to the shores of eternity.

In particular the Christian Churches have stood idly by and watched.

…Two hundred and twenty-seven years ago, the first of our injured race were brought to the shores of America.…The first dealings they had with men calling themselves Christians, exhibited to them the worst features of corrupt and sordid hearts; and convinced them that no cruelty is too great, no villainy and no robbery too abhorrent for even enlightened men to perform, when influenced by avarice and lust.

The bleeding captive plead his innocence, and pointed to Christianity who stood weeping at the cross.…But all was in vain. Slavery had stretched its dark wings of death over the land, the Church stood silently by, the priests prophesied falsely, and the people loved to have it so…The colonists tried to blame slavery on Britain, but then embraced it on their own.

The colonists threw the blame upon England.…But time soon tested their sincerity. In a few years the colonists grew strong, and severed themselves from the British

Government…did they emancipate the slaves? No; they rather added new links to our chains.…

The time has come to recognize that God views it as sinful to continue submitting to this oppression.

…He who brings his fellow down so low, as to make him contented with a condition of slavery, commits the highest crime against God and man. Brethren, your oppressors aim to do this. They endeavor to make you as much like brutes as possible. …TO SUCH DEGREDATION IT IS SINFUL IN THE EXTREME FOR YOU TO MAKE VOLUNTARY SUBMISSION.…Your condition does not absolve you from your moral obligation. The diabolical injustice by which your liberties are cloven down, NEITHER GOD, NOR ANGELS, OR JUST MEN, COMMAND YOU TO SUFFER FOR A SINGLE MOMENT. THEREFORE IT IS YOUR SOLEMN AND IMPERATIVE DUTY TO USE EVERY MEANS, BOTH MORAL, INTELLECTUAL, AND PHYSICAL THAT PROMISES SUCCESS.

Brethren, it is as wrong for your lordly oppressors to keep you in slavery, as it was for the man thief to steal our ancestors from the coast of Africa. You should therefore now use the same manner of resistance, as would have been just in our ancestors when the bloody foot prints of the first remorseless soul thief was placed upon the shores of our fatherland.…

In turn, the time has come for the slaves to "strike the blow" for themselves!

Brethren, the time has come when you must act for yourselves. It is an old and true saying that, "if hereditary bondmen would be free, they must themselves strike the blow." You can plead your own cause, and do the work of emancipation better than any others.

…The combined powers of Europe have placed their broad seal of disapprobation upon the African slave trade. But in the slaveholding parts of the United States, the trade is as brisk as ever. They buy and sell you as though you were brute beasts.…Look around you, and behold the bosoms of your loving wives heaving with untold agonies! Hear the cries of your poor children! Remember the stripes your fathers bore. Think of the torture and disgrace of your noble mothers. Think of your wretched sisters, loving virtue and purity, as they are driven into concubinage and are exposed to the unbridled lusts of incarnate devils.

It is better to "die freemen than live to be slaves."

…Then go to your lordly enslavers and tell them plainly, that you are determined to be free. Appeal to their sense of justice, and tell them that they have no more right to oppress you, than you have to enslave them… If they then commence the work of death, they, and not you, will be responsible for the consequences. You had better all die immediately, than live slaves and entail your wretchedness upon your posterity. If you would be free in this generation, here is your only hope. However much you and all of us may desire it, there is not much hope of redemption without the shedding of blood. If you must bleed, let it all come at once—rather die freemen, than live to be slaves.

Escape is impossible, with Garnet presciently citing free Mexico as an expansionist target for the South.

> It is impossible like the children of Israel, to make a grand exodus from the land of bondage. The Pharaohs are on both sides of the blood red waters! You cannot move en masse, to the dominions of the British Queen—nor can you pass through Florida and overrun Texas, and at last find peace in Mexico. The propagators of American slavery are spending their blood and treasure, that they may plant the black flag in the heart of Mexico and riot in the halls of the Montezumas.

> Fellow men! Patient sufferers! behold your dearest rights crushed to the earth! See your sons murdered, and your wives, mothers and sisters doomed to prostitution. In the name of the merciful God, and by all that life is worth, let it no longer be a debatable question whether it is better to choose Liberty or death.

Then comes a litany of heroes of freedom—Vesey, Turner, Cinque, and Washington.

> In 1822, Denmark Veazie [Vesey], of South Carolina, formed a plan for the liberation of his fellow men. In the whole history of human efforts to overthrow slavery, a more complicated and tremendous plan was never formed. …That tremendous movement shook the whole empire of slavery. The guilty soul thieves were overwhelmed with fear. It is a matter of fact, that at that time, and in consequence of the threatened revolution, the slave States talked strongly of emancipation. But they blew but one blast of the trumpet of freedom and then laid it aside.

> The patriotic Nathaniel Turner followed Denmark Veazie [Vesey]…, and future generations will remember him among the noble and brave…Next arose the immortal Joseph Cinque, the hero of the Amistad…Next arose Madison Washington that bright star of freedom, and took his station in the constellation of true heroism. He was a slave on board the brig Creole…

> Noble men! Those who have fallen in freedom's conflict, their memories will be

cherished by the true hearted and the God fearing in all future generations; those who are living, their names are surrounded by a halo of glory.

Like David Walker fourteen years earlier, Garnet ends with plea to the four million to "strike for your lives and liberties" against those "defiling your wives and daughters."

Brethren, arise, arise! Strike for your lives and liberties. Now is the day and the hour. Let every slave throughout the land do this, and the days of slavery are numbered. You cannot be more oppressed than you have been—you cannot suffer greater cruelties than you have already. Rather die free men than live to be slaves. Remember that you are FOUR MILLIONS!

It is in your power so to torment the God cursed slaveholders that they will be glad to let you go free.... But you are a patient people. You act as though, you were made for the special use of these devils. You act as though your daughters were born to pamper the lusts of your masters and overseers. And worse than all, you tamely submit while your lords tear your wives from your embraces and defile them before your eyes. In the name of God, we ask, are you men? Where is the blood of your fathers? Has it all run out of your veins? Awake, awake; millions of voices are calling you! Your dead fathers speak to you from their graves. Heaven, as with a voice of thunder, calls on you to arise from the dust.

Let your motto be resistance! resistance! RESISTANCE! No oppressed people have ever secured their liberty without resistance. What kind of resistance you had better make, you must decide by the circumstances that surround you, and according to the suggestion of expediency. Brethren, adieu! Trust in the living God. Labor for the peace of the human race, and remember that you are FOUR MILLIONS.

Everything about Garnet's speech is anathema to the South. It recalls decades-old memories of the Vesey and Turner attacks, and the more recent adverse legal decisions in the *Amistad* and *Creole* cases. It calls out politicians who would expand slavery into Texas and Mexico, along with Christian clergymen who would defend it where it already exists.

It reminds owners of the blood already on their hands and invokes the image of blood to be spilled by four million Black people seeking revenge.

As such, it will soon provoke a backlash across the South, led in part by the clergy.

PUBLIC ATTITUDES TOWARD SLAVERY BEGIN TO SHIFT IN THE NORTH

TIME: 1840S

Lucretia Mott (1793–1880) co-founder of the American Anti-Slavery Society

In the early 1840s public opinion in the North about slavery begins to shift.

The shift is not about discarding convictions that Black people are an inferior and dangerous race or supporting the abolitionists' demand that all enslaved people be immediately freed.

Instead, it is a growing sense that chattel slavery is inconsistent with the vision and values laid out by the founders. How can a nation based on freedom for all keep some four million Black people in captivity?

This question surfaces out of most people's own religious reflections associated with the Second Great Awakening. It is then reinforced by a variety of perfectionist movements and high-profile events.

The 1833 founding of the American Anti-Slavery Society attracts many members who would shy away from the "too radical" abolitionists. Public testimonials by Black spokesmen like Frederick Douglass heighten awareness of, and empathy toward, the plight of enslaved people. Newspaper accounts of race riots and the breakdown of law and order are frightening—and resistance hardens against bounty hunters searching private homes for those escaping slavery.

So, more and more Northerners are becoming convinced that slavery is a moral stain on the nation and that something must be done about it. But what?

Soon enough the search for answers turns to America's churches who prove once again that they are not up to the task.

THE ISSUE OF SLAVERY CAUSES A SCHISM WITHIN THE PROTESTANT CHURCHES

TIME: 1607 FORWARD

CHRISTIAN CHURCHES HAVE BEEN A UNIFYING FORCE IN AMERICA'S HISTORY

Savanah Church

The notion of looking to religion and the clergy for moral guidance goes back to the colonial period.

The French visitor Alexis DeTocqueville observes this phenomenon in his journals:

America is…the place in the world where the Christian religion has most preserved genuine powers over souls; and the country where (Christianity) exercises its greatest empire is at the same time the most enlightened and most free.

Almost all Americans are active in their churches, either as formal members or as regular attendees at Sunday worship services.

For many, these gatherings are the centerpiece of their moral, intellectual, and social lives.

Attendance cuts across a vast variety of denominations. Methodists, Baptists, and Presbyterians are the most dominant in the early nineteenth century.-

NUMBER OF CHURCHES IN AMERICA

	1790	1860
Methodist Episcopalian	700	20,000
Baptist	900	12,000
Presbyterian	700	6,000
Roman Catholic	NA	2,500
Jewish Synagogues	NA	77

The clergymen who oversee these churches are likely trained at one of the nation's sixty universities, almost all founded and run by the clergy.

AMERICAN UNIVERSITIES FOUNDED BY CHURCHES

NAME	YEAR	CHURCH AFFILIATION
Harvard	1636	Congregationalist
William & Mary	1693	Church of England
Yale	1701	Congregationalist
Princeton	1746	Presbyterian
Columbia	1754	Church of England
Penn	1757	Anglican/Methodists
Brown	1764	Baptist
Rutgers	1766	Dutch Reformed
Dartmouth	1769	Congregationalist

Each denomination develops its own doctrines, governing hierarchies, and liturgies – and each is focused on solidifying and expanding its membership rolls.

Despite doctrinal differences, most church-goers hear a fairly common message from the pulpit. Read "the good book;" live according to the Golden Rule; band together to make America into St. Augustine's "shining city on a hill," a beacon of God's light for the rest of the world to see and to emulate.

America's churches, divinity schools, and clergymen are there to insure, as De Tocqueville says, that the "soul" of the country remains enlightened and dedicated to "essential goodness."

They are also there to preserve the Union. The old world has been torn apart by religious conflicts, but America has always found in its churches a powerful source of national unity.

TIME: 1825 – 1840

THE SECOND AWAKENING BEGINS TO FRAY CHURCH BONDS

This church unity, however, begins to fray in response to the religious revivals of the 1825-1840 period known as the Second Great Awakening.

At first the turmoil centers on religious doctrine, mainly within the Presbyterian denomination. It pits the so-called "Old School" minsters such as Charles Hodge and Lyman Beecher, often associated with the Princeton Theological Seminary, against the "revivalist" preachers of the "New School," such as Charles Finney and the Unitarians.

At stake, according to the "Old Schoolers," is the very essence of Calvinism, which shuns the notion of individual men interpreting the Bible on their own, "reforming their own way" to salvation, or mixing religious and secular affairs.

DOCTRINAL DEBATE AMONG THE PRESBYTERIANS

	"OLD SCHOOL"	"NEW SCHOOL"
Salvation open to:	The Elect	Everyman
Based upon:	Predestination	Free Will
Bible interpretation:	Literal	Figurative
Final authority:	Church Hierarchy	Each Individual
Preaching style:	From The Pulpit	In The Crowd
Symbols:	Charles Hodge	Charles Finney
	Lyman Beecher	The Unitarians

As "New School" revival meetings win more converts, it becomes clear that differences here are irreconcilable.

At their 1837 general assembly, the Old School faction carries a vote to oust the four main New School synods, thus effectively dividing the Presbyterians for good.

But the effects of the Second Awakening extend far beyond internal debates over

Instead, they foster a new generation who believe that every man is capable of achieving eternal salvation by striving for Christ-like "moral perfection" – reforming both themselves and their society as a whole.

Soon enough these "reformers" band into organized movements. Some promote temperance; others try to strike down abuses directed at child labor, the indigent or the incarcerated; a few seek greater rights for women, especially related to suffrage.

But one "cause" soon takes center stage – putting an end to slavery in America.

In large part this results from the work of one man in particular, the Presbyterian New School preacher Charles Grandison Finney – who directly touches the hearts and minds of many of the most important white abolitionists of the time, including William Lloyd Garrison, Theodor Dwight Weld, Arthur and Lewis Tappan, Gerritt Smith, and James Birney.

Together these and other reformers begin to pressure the Protestant churches to take a stand on slavery.

TIME: 1830s - FORWARD

LAYMEN CRITICS BLAST CHURCH SILENCE OVER THE ISSUE OF SLAVERY

The only on-going church opposition to slavery has come from the Quakers and from black clergymen.

The others have simply chosen to look the other way.

This evasion is now challenged by white reformers like Lloyd Garrison who call on the churches to play a decisive role in ending slavery.

Nothing but extensive revivals of pure religion can save our country. Emancipation has to be from Christianity.

By 1836, however, Garrison concludes that the institutional church has substituted "legal righteousness and ritual observance" for the true meaning of the Gospel. His wrath is particularly directed at the passivity of churchmen like his fellow Bostonian, Old School Pastor Lyman Beecher, who he says…

Sides only with the rich and powerful, goes with the South, lulls conscience-ness, aligns with traffickers in souls.

Garrison is not alone in his castigation of the white churches. Another very visible critic is the fiery Stephen Symonds Foster.

Foster grows up in New Hampshire, in a family which speaks out against slavery. He decides to do missionary work and attends Dartmouth College, where he invites the abolitionist Angelina Grimke to speak to the Young Men's Anti-Slavery Society. After graduation, he enrolls at Union Theological Seminary, but leaves when the administration tries to silence his dissent. Henceforth he will embrace the label of a "come outer," after the biblical admonition "come out from among them...and touch not the unclean thing, and I will receive you."

In 1839 Foster becomes an itinerant lecturer for the New Hampshire Anti-Slavery Society, and is nearly beaten to death three years later by a mob in Portland, Maine, intent upon silencing his demand for emancipation.

In his 1843 book, *The Brotherhood of Thieves: A True Picture of the American Church and Clergy*, Foster skewers the church clergy.

> *Taken together they are apologists and supporters of the most atrocious system of oppression beneath which humanity has ever groaned – while Southerners perpetuate slavery for the sole purpose of supplying themselves concubines from among the hapless victims.*

Foster is also famous for delivering his attacks by standing up during Sunday services and aiming his opinion directly at the minister in the pulpit, a practice which gets him ousted from his own Congregational church.

Later in life, Foster marries the reformer, Abby Kelley, and together the two crusade on for abolitions and for female equality and suffrage.

TIME: 1840 FORWARD

THE ANTI-SLAVERY SOCIETIES ALSO CALL FOR CHURCH ACTION

Pressure on the churches also comes from the American Anti-Slavery Societies at both the local and national level.

By 1836, in three short years since its founding, the Society has grown to over 500 chapters through the combined efforts of Lewis Tappan, William Lloyd Garrison, and their inner circles.

Chapter resolutions related to church positions on slavery multiply quickly.

A New England convention in 1836 asks whether opposition to slavery should become a necessary sign of "the true and real church of God." A year later this same group adopts a call to "urge the necessity of ex-communication for slave owners."

The 1839 national convention passes a proposal to "push the slave question in churches, to abolitionize them if possible, and if not, to secede from them."

In 1840, The Massachusetts Society, holds that "a man who apologizes for slavery, or neglects to use his influence against it, has no claim to be regarded as Christ's minister, and churches who do not take a stand against slavery should not be supported."

Both the national and local groups continue to call for the hierarchy within all churches to take a formal stand in favor of abolition and to cleanse their ministries of all slave-owners.

The effects of these efforts will soon be felt in America's two largest churches.

TIME: JUNE 1844

THE METHODIST EPISCOPAL CHURCH BREAKS APART OVER SLAVERY

In the summer of 1844, the Methodist Church breaks apart over a challenge to clergymen owning slaves.

As early as 1774, the church founder, John Wesley, speaks out against slavery. While his followers tend to agree, they conclude that the issue is too divisive to pursue at that time.

This official passivity continues for six decades until three New England ministers fire up the internal debate.

One is the Vermonter, Reverend Orange Scott, who is ordained at twenty-two, and rises steadily in the church hierarchy. Scott is dedicated to reinfusing the spirit of John Wesley by founding in 1843 the Wesleyan Methodist New Connexion, "an anti-slavery, anti-intemperance, anti-every-thing wrong, church organization." His words echo Garrison and Foster in offering a ringing indictment of those who would compromise in the presence of slavery.

…Though public opinion commanded Mr. Wesley to desist through the medium of mobs, still he stood it out! Shame on his compromising sons! The Methodists in all parts of the United States have braved, and, finally, to a considerable extent, changed public opinion. Every man's hand has been against us, and yet we have stood firm.

But now comes up the new doctrine of compromise! Let it be banished from the breast of every patriot, philanthropist, and Christian…Shall we turn our backs upon the cause of suffering humanity, because public opinion frowns upon us? No! Never!!

…The principle of slavery—-the principle which justifies holding and treating the human species as property, is morally wrong—-or, in other words, that it is a sin. The principle, aside from all circumstances, is evil, ONLY EVIL, and that CONTINUALLY! …no hand could sanctify it—-no circumstances could change it from bad to good. It was a reprobate—-too bad to be converted—-not subject to the law of God, neither indeed could be…Circumstances might palliate, and circumstances might aggravate, but no circumstances could justify the principle." "He who has made of one blood, all nations of men to dwell on the earth' [Acts 17:26] must look with disapprobation upon such a system of complicated wrongs, as American slavery…

In 1842, Scott officially withdraws from the Methodist Episcopal Church, to protest what he considers a refusal by the bishops to even allow open discussions of slavery at annual gatherings. He is joined at that time by two other vocal anti-slavery ministers, La Roy Sunderland and Jotham Horton.

The debate over slavery comes to a head at the quadrennial General Conference of church leaders which convenes in New York City on May 1, 1844. Three weeks into the meeting, regional tensions flare when two northern elders offer a resolution "affectionately asking" that Bishop James Andrew of Georgia either divest his slaves or resign from the church.

This places Andrew in the awkward positioning of defending himself in public. He says that he never bought nor sold a slave on his own. Instead his first slave was inherited, while another four have come his way through two marriages. While Georgia law prohibits manumission, he claims that all have been told to "live wherever they so choose."

After making his plea, a vote goes against Andrew—and he volunteers to resign to quell the firestorm.

The Conference spends the next twelve days trying to find a compromise solution. Some argue that a judicial trial is needed to remove a bishop. Others propose that a final decision be delayed until the next meeting in 1848.

Along the way, however, attendees also learn that Andrew's case is not unique, that another 1200 or so Methodist clergymen are current slave owners.

At this point the conflict ratchets up, with southern bishops digging their heels in to support Andrew, citing the now familiar arguments that slavery is sanctioned in the Bible and is a "positive good" for society.

This tactic finally pushes the northern contingent over the edge. On June 8, they offer a "Plan of Separation" which passes, splitting the church into two wings.

Henceforth there will be the Wesleyan Methodist Church of the North and the Methodist Episcopal Church of the South.

It will be ninety-four years before this breach is finally healed for the Methodists.

TIME: MAY 1845

THE BAPTIST CHURCH ALSO DIVIDES

Within a year of the Methodist schism, the Baptist Church also suffers a schism over a similar slavery-related issue.

In 1638, the Church is founded with a strong missionary tradition that sees it expanding rapidly beyond its original home base in Rhode Island. By the 1830s its membership ranks second in the nation, trailing only the Methodists.

The sect becomes especially strong across the South and on plantations – where some owners regard slave baptisms as proof of their virtue in bringing salvation to their black charges.

Because of this membership tilt toward the South, the Baptists are especially inclined to avoid controversy over slavery for as long as possible. But this strategy breaks down, as various northern ministers begin to attack the institution.

One of them is Abel Brown, an intensely religious youth, who becomes a Baptist minister after studying at Hamilton College. His first cause is intemperance, and his approach to stamp out "demon drink" is to cite the names of known offenders in a public forum. For this he is attacked by a mob and run out of town in Auburn, New York. In 1838, he turns his attention to slavery, speaking against it from the pulpit, and carrying through to action by helping run-aways escape across the Ohio River near his home in Pennsylvania. He characterizes his efforts in military terms:

> *I have been in close action with the enemy. Friday, Saturday, and Sunday, was one continued row. A mob drove me from the house on Friday night. Saturday night I could not get to the house unless through showers of stones, and Sunday, the house was found nailed up.*

Brown eventually becomes a leading figure in operating the Underground Railroad, joins the Liberty Party in 1840, and serves as an itinerant lecturer on behalf of abolition before his premature death in 1844 at thirty-four.

A second Baptist opponent of slavery is Reverend Elon Galusha, whose father and uncle have both served as Governors of Vermont. Galusha takes up the ministry after studying law, and serves his first sixteen years in Oneida County, New York, the hotbed of early revivalism and abolitionism. In 1839, he becomes the first president of the Baptist Anti-Slavery Society, whose constitution calls for the church to repent for its participation in sin:

> *Slavery is utterly at variance with the gospel of Jesus Christ….(It) is a sin in which the churches have largely and criminally participated, we feel it our duty to do all we can to induce repentance and by kind, prudent, prayerful, and persevering measures endeavor to exert a purifying influence upon the churches with which we are associated.*

In 1840 the Society turns up its rhetoric:

> *As Christians we can have no fellowship with those who, after being duly enlightened on the subject, still advocate and practice its abominations and thus defile the church of God.*

In response, Southern Baptist ministers fire back.

Our brethren at the South with great unanimity deprecate the discussion as unwarranted, the measures pursued as fatal to their safety and complain of the language occasionally employed as cruel and slanderous.

The Baptist Church delays an immediate crisis by the fact that governance of the Baptist Church is far less centralized than in other denominations. Each church is free to operate as it chooses, as long as the principle of "baptism of professed believers through total immersion" is maintained.

The closest thing to a forum on national policy is a triennial "General Convention of the Baptist Denomination in the United States." It is formed to seek consensus on which missions – both domestic and foreign – the membership wishes to fund in the next three-year period.

In 1841, the anti-slavery contingent treis to force the Triennial body to ban slave holders from holding missionary positions. But their pleas are brushed aside as too inflammatory. In 1843, a Northern Baptist Missionary Society is formed to continue to agitate for change.

As the 1844 cycle rolls around, Southern members decide to "test" the will of the Triennial board. They do so in April of that year through a Georgia Convention recommendation to appoint Elder George Reeves to a Home Missions position. The application states that Reeves is a current slave-owner.

The Alabama Convention follows by demanding a Triennial policy making slave-owners eligible for any missions being funded in part or whole by Southern members.

The Home Missions council is now forced to make a decision – and they choose to ignore the Reeves nomination on the basis that their policy is to remain neutral on any and all controversies over slavery.

This deflection hardly satisfies the Southern contingent.

In May 1845, they gather in Augusta, Georgia, and vote to abandon the Triennial Convention for good. Gentler souls depart in sadness:

With no sharpness of contention, with no bitterness of spirit, . . . we part asunder and open two lines of service to the heathen and the destitute.

Others depart in anger:

We are no longer willing to work in societies where slave holders are called sinners and reviled as thiefs.

Further efforts to repair the breech fail and future governance of the church is split between The Southern Baptist Convention and the North's Triennial Convention.

TIME: 1845

THE CHURCH SCHISMS PREVIEW THE GROWING NORTH-SOUTH DIVIDE

By 1845, all the dominant Protestant denominations have divided over slavery.

While the Methodists and the Baptists are most visibly split along north-south lines, similar tensions also strike the Presbyterians and the Congregationalists.

Even families and friends diverge.

The conservative "Old School" Presbyterian icon, Lyman Beecher, witnesses his son and daughter swing sharply to the abolitionist cause. The Unitarians are aligned in their opposition to slavery, but not on the remedy. The abolitionists are "too showy, too noisy" for Ellery Channing and "they would jeopardize peace with the South." Meanwhile younger hardliners such as Theodore Parker and Thomas Higginson begin to line up alongside those calling for effective, even violent, action over mere intellectual hand-wringing.

All of the church schisms have been played out in a relatively short time, largely between the 1833 founding of the American Anti-Slavery Society and the national convocations of 1844 and appear to be over relatively minor policy matters.

Harriet Beecher Stowe, Lyman Beecher, and Henry Beecher

It is not as if the northern churchmen are demanding that the South free its slaves.

Nor does it signal any wish in the North to invite freed slaves into their midst, to embrace them and make them citizens. The schisms are not about abolition and assimilation. They are not about abandoning the anti-black stereotypes entrenched in American culture since Jamestown.

Instead, they are more about appearance than substance. Perhaps the churches should not seem to be condoning ownership of slaves by its officials. So, say the Northerners.

This is a subtle shift, but still sufficient in the climate of 1844 to blow apart the bonds of good will that have held the three major churches together.

As such, the church break-up presages the eventual collapse of the political Union. Both Henry Clay and John Calhoun sense this outcome.

Clay says at the time:

The sundering of the religious ties which have hitherto bound our people together, I consider the greatest source of danger to our country.

Calhoun's observation is even more ominous:

Now nothing will be left to hold the states together except force.

Twenty years later, Abraham Lincoln wonders how the war has come when…

Both sides read the same Bible and pray to the same God.

If the churches cannot hold, the political center cannot. It is just a matter of time.

## 113

JAMES THORNWELL & OTHER CLERGYMEN OFFER A BIBLICAL DEFENSE OF SLAVERY

TIME: 1843-1850

REVEREND JAMES HENLEY THORNWELL EMERGES AS A SOUTHERN SPOKESPERSON

Perhaps the leading defender of slavery among the Southern clergy is Presbyterian minister, James Henley Thornwell.

Thornwell is born to modest means in 1812 in the Pee Dee River region of Marlborough County, SC. His father dies when he is 8 years old, and his mother is too poor to support his education. But his intellectual prowess is apparent to a lawyer named William Robbins, who becomes his benefactor. Thornwell attends Charaw Academy, exhibits remarkable scholarship, and at sixteen abandons a legal career to become a preacher.

Reverend James Henley Thornwell (1812-1862)

A chosen vessel of the Lord, to bear His name before the Gentiles and kings, and the children of Israel;" to assert eternal Providence and justify the ways of God to men.

In 1829, he enrolls at South Carolina College described as follows by a fellow classmate:

In personal appearance he was, perhaps, the most unpromising specimen of humanity that ever entered such an institution. Very short in stature, very lean in flesh, his manners were unpolished, but his air was self-reliant. He was evidently conscious of the mental power within him, which would- make him more than a match for most men, and would throw into the shade his physical defects.

He is initially drawn to Calvinism and to the Presbyterian church when he happens to read the Westminster "Confessions of Faith."

I felt that I had met with a system which held together with the strictest logical connection; granting its premises, the conclusions were bound to follow.

In December 1831, after graduating at the top of his class, he wanders for eighteen months between scholarly studies and writing essays. This uncertainty ends on May 13, 1832, when he joins the Concord Presbyterian Church, a life-changing moment he recalls as follows:

O God! I have to-day made a public profession of my faith in the blessed Redeemer, and taken upon me the solemn covenant of the Church.' I would not impute to myself any merit on this account, as I have only done, and that, too, after a long delay, what was expressly enjoined on me in Thy holy Word. But, O God! I feel myself a weak, fallen, depraved, and helpless creature, and utterly unable to do one righteous deed without Thy gracious assistance. Wilt Thou, therefore, send upon me Thy cheering Spirit, to illumine for me the path of duty; and to uphold me, when I grow weary; to refresh me, when I faint; to support me against the violence of temptation and the blandishments of vice. Let me, I beseech Thee, please Thee in thought, word and deed. Enable me to go on to perfection, support me in death, and finally save me in Thy kingdom; and to the glorious Three-in-one be ascribed all the praise. Amen. "

In 1832, at 22 years old, he is ordained as a pastor, and heads off first to Andover and then to Harvard Divinity School to continue his studies. There he aligns himself with the "Old School" Presbyterians against the "New School" Cambridge Unitarians who embrace "free will" over "determinism."

It is an open defiance of all the established laws of exegesis; and the doctrines, which need such miserable subterfuges to support them, cannot come from God. No, my friend, we are never safe in departing from the simple declarations of the Bible. The Unitarian will tell you that experimental religion is all an idle dream; but, my friend, believe not the tale. It is no such thing.

Like John Calvin in 1540, Thornwell's belief system springs from his literal reading of the Bible.

It tells him a hard and unswerving truth – that all men are depraved sinners who are assigned their places in life according to God's providential plan, and are granted or denied salvation by grace alone.

Thornwell soon returns to South Carolina, where his fame as a preacher and scholar quickly spreads.

In 1835, he marries Nancy Witherspoon, a member of one of the oldest and most prestigious families in South Carolina. Her father is Colonel James Witherspoon, ex-Lieutenant Governor of the state, and master of "Thorntree" Plantation, a 300-acre estate using slave labor to grow indigo. In giving his daughter away, the Colonel overlooks Thornwell's meager finances in favor of his growing reputation as the "John C. Calhoun of the Pulpit."

Through the marriage, Thornwell acquires, for the first time, both wealth and slaves of his own.

TIME: 1840s FORWARD

THORNWELL ASSERTS THAT SLAVERY IS PART OF GOD'S PLAN FOR MANKIND

Thornwell's life now revolves around his plantation, his speaking engagements, and his continued scholarship at South Carolina College, where he serves as Chaplin and as Professor of Sacred Literature and Evidence of Christianity.

His sermons become famous for their pristine logic and their emotional impact. Later in his career, none other than Daniel Webster, the senate spellbinder, will call him "the greatest pulpit orator I ever heard."

As northern reformers increase their attacks on slavery, Thornwell focuses his analytical mind on formulating a foolproof defense, one that the South will employ over the decades ahead.

Slavery, he asserts, is part of God's plan for mankind.

He arrives there by "reasoning his way" from Calvinist religious principles to a belief that the institution is sanctioned by the Bible and therefore morally proper.

He argues that the unknowable will of God shapes man's destiny and that, from time immemorial, the practice of slavery has been a part of this destiny. The Old Testament verifies slavery, from Genesis 9:25 ("Cursed be Canaan, a servant of servants shall he be unto his brethren") to the enslavement of the patriarch, Joseph, the concubine Hagar, and the entire people of Israel. The fact that Christ, living amidst Roman slavery, failed to condemn it in his preaching, further proves its historical legitimacy.

He theorizes that slavery may have originally come into the world as a punishment, perpetual in nature, with the children of slaves becoming enslaved themselves. But it has always been a reality in God's plan.

Then comes a remarkable departure by Thornwell from the conventional Southern narrative.

In no way does slavery reflect on the enslaved person's ultimate worth. Thornwell absolutely rejects the notion that Africans are biologically or morally inferior to whites. They are like everyman, searching equally for salvation. They have simply been handed their place in the social order, under a biblically approved system. Their duty is to render obedience and service to their master in exchange for needed provisions and fair treatment.

Slavery is also essential, he says, to the progress of civilization and of industry. The notion that all men play an equal role in advancing society is patently false. Some are meant to lead by the power of their minds; others to follow, lending the sweat of their brows to completion of their assigned tasks.

Slavery is a needful stimulus to industry; all enterprise would stagnate without it.

Furthermore, the duty of slave-owners is to be just. Any abuses of the enslaved, reflect negatively on the masters and not on the system itself. Among the highest duties of the master is to facilitate religious enlightenment – and this, Thornwell says, is one of the great blessings, the positive good, of slavery in America:

Slavery is the state in which the African is most effectually trained to the moral end of his being.

Thus, Thornwell admonishes masters to construct places of worship for the enslaved, so they can learn about salvation and commit their life to seeking it. Lacking freedom of the body in no ways inhibits the quest for freedom of the soul. Each man's fate is in the hands of God.

TIME: 1840s

SOUTHERN CLERICS ALIGN BEHIND THE "BIBLICAL DEFENSE" OF SLAVERY

Other Southern clergy also rally behind the Biblical defense of slavery.

The Presbyterian preacher, Robert Dabney, sums up the matter as follows:

We must go before the nation with the Bible as the text, and "thus sayeth the Lord" as the answer. We know that on the Bible argument the abolition party will be driven to unveil their true infidel tendencies. The Bible being bound to stand on our side, they have to come out and array themselves against the Bible.

Stephen Elliott, the Harvard trained Episcopalian Bishop of Georgia, asserts that "slavery is ordained by God."

Baptist pastor and slave-owner, Dr. Richard Furman, of South Carolina, also cites scripture:

...the right of holding slaves is clearly established in the Holy Scriptures, both by precept and example... Had the holding of slaves been a moral evil, it cannot be supposed that the inspired Apostles ... would have tolerated it for a moment in the Christian Church. In proving this subject justifiable by Scriptural authority [Luke 12:47], its morality is also proved; for the Divine Law never sanctions immoral actions.

Methodist pastor Samuel Dunwoody finds textual support for the notion that "some of the most eminent of the Old Testament saints were slave holders," including Abraham, Jacob, Isaac, and Job. Given this it cannot be evil.

Thus, God, as he is infinitely wise, just and holy, never could authorize the practice of a moral evil. But God has authorized the practice of slavery, not only by the bare permission of his Providence, but the express provision of his word. Therefore, slavery is not a moral evil.

Thornwell sums it up by asserting that there is no room for religious debate over slavery. God sanctioned the practice in the Bible, and those who question it stand on the side of evil.

He says the parties in the conflict are not merely abolitionists versus slaveholders—they are atheists, socialists, communists, red republicans, Jacobins, on one side, and the friends of order and regulated freedom on the other. The world is the battleground—Christianity and Atheism the combatants; and the progress of humanity at stake.

Opponents, he says, are the same "New School" ministers - like the Unitarians and Charles Finney's Evangelicals - who risk the salvation of their flocks by straying beyond the literal words of the Bible into their own speculations.

If the spirit of speculation on theological subjects should once become propagated among them, there is no telling where the evil would stop."

Likewise, they distort the message of the New Testament by failing to understand that Jesus Christ was not sent here to make social reforms, but to help mankind atone for its total depravity.

Thus, the message from the Southern pulpit to Northern reformers becomes loud and clear:

Leave (slavery) where God has left it, and deal with it as God has dealt with it.

114

THE QUESTION OF TEXAS ANNEXATION AGAIN ASSUMES CENTER STAGE

TIME: 1836-1843

TEXAS ANNEXATION STALLS BETWEEN 1836 AND 1843

In 1844, as John Tyler nears the end of his "accidental" term as President, he makes a decision that will eventually lead to the dissolution of the Union.

It involves the lingering question of whether or not to annex the Republic of Texas.

Eight years earlier, in 1836-37, Presidents Andrew Jackson and Martin Van Buren, both committed expansionists, decide against this move, after Henry Morfit, emissary to the Texas leader Sam Houston, warns that annexation will result in war with Mexico and renewed national controversy over slavery.

The courtship, however, carries on. By March 1837, the Texans have solidified their territorial hold when the United States officially recognizes them as an independent nation. In January 1838, South Carolina Senator William Preston introduces a bill to negotiate an annexation treaty with Mexico and Texas, but John Quincy Adam vigorously opposes him in the House, citing his opposition to warfare and to slavery.

In early January 1839, Texas finally breaks off unification talks and decides to go it alone as an independent Republic.

The reaction in Mexico is one of growing hostility toward the American intruders. On September 11, 1842, the Texas town of San Antonio is attacked and occupied. A year later, on August 23, 1843, President Antonio Lopez de Santa Anna openly warns the U.S. that annexation would be regarded as a declaration of war.

This warning fails to deter Tyler, who continues to add Texas as another accomplishment in his legacy. He is swept along in this regard by a rising tide of public interest in opening the west.

Among southern slave owners, such a move is an economic necessity, enabling them to grow more cotton and sell more slaves.

For others, the expansionary fervor seems to build off publicity surrounding the Fremont expeditions and cheerleading from journalists such as Horace Greeley and John L. O'Sullivan.

TIME: 1839

JOHN O'SULLIVAN "MANIFEST DESTINY" VISION RESONATES WITH THE PUBLIC

The cheerleader for westward expansion is John L. O'Sullivan is an Irish immigrant who arrives in the States in 1813 as an infant. He graduates at age eighteen from Columbia University and takes up law before settling on a career in journalism. In 1837, he founds the *United States Magazine* and *Democratic Review*, based in Washington.

The paper unabashedly supports Andrew Jackson and O'Sullivan first

HORACE GREELEY

Horace Greeley (1811-1872)

articulates his own views on the subject in an 1839 article titled, "The Great Nation of Futurity."

He begins by asserting that the United States represents a fundamental break with the past – the beginning of a new history for mankind in the realm of moral, political and national life.

> *The American people having derived their origin… on the great principle of human equality…have, in reality, but little connection with the past history of any (other nations)…. On the contrary, our national birth was the beginning of a new history… which separates us from the past and connects us with the future only; and so far as regards the entire development of the natural rights of man, in moral, political, and national life, we may confidently assume that our country is destined to be the great nation of futurity.*

Unlike prior societies where humanity was oppressed, America's core values make it "destined for better deeds."

> *What friend of human liberty, civilization, and refinement, can cast his view over*

the past history of the monarchies and aristocracies of antiquity, and not deplore that they ever existed?

America is destined for better deeds. It is our unparalleled glory that we have no reminiscences of battle fields, but in defence of humanity, of the oppressed of all nations, of the rights of conscience, the rights of personal enfranchisement.

Its "destiny" lies in "manifesting to mankind the excellence of divine principles."

The far-reaching, the boundless future will be the era of American greatness. In its magnificent domain of space and time, the nation of many nations is destined to manifest to mankind the excellence of divine principles; to establish on earth the noblest temple ever dedicated to the worship of the Most High—the Sacred and the True.

Given this calling, America will become the "great nation of futurity."

For this blessed mission to the nations of the world, which are shut out from the life-giving light of truth, has America been chosen…. Who, then, can doubt that our country is destined to be the great nation of futurity?

O'Sullivan's themes mirror those of the Puritan preacher, Jonathan Edward, one hundred years earlier.

He goes on to amplify his vision through-out the 1840s – most notably six years later in a second more famous article titled "Annexation." The article steps into the realm of foreign policy with an argument that becomes known as Manifest Destiny – the notion that to realize its full potential, America must extend its national borders all the way to the Pacific.

It is by the right of our manifest destiny to overspread and to possess the whole of the continent which Providence has given us for the development of the great experiment of liberty and federated self-government entrusted to us.

O'Sullivan's call, however, is not for warfare – rather an expectation that other nations, like Mexico, will recognize the exceptional character of America's democracy and choose to unify peacefully.

TIME: APRIL – JUNE 1844

BENTON MOMENTARILY FOILS TYLER'S ATTEMPT TO ANNEX TEXAS

By 1844, Tyler is convinced that annexation of Texas will be popular with the public, and pave the way for his independent party candidacy in the upcoming election.

He orders his Secretary of State, Abel Upshur, a Virginia Whig dedicated to the cause of expanding slavery to the west, to open a new round of treaty negotiations with Sam Houston, President of the Texas Republic.

Houston's primary aim is to avoid conquest by a militarily superior Mexico.

After the 1836 Alamo defeat, he looks to the US as a savior, and certainly the average Texan always favors that solution. But other political leaders disagree. One is the powerful Miramar Lamar, a Georgian by birth, who wants to rid Texas of Comanches and Mexicans alike and make it a new and independent nation with borders extending to the Pacific. Over time, Houston is also tempted by this vision, which includes a potentially explosive component—an alliance between Texas and Britain.

Negotiations are well along when a navel gun explodes during a celebratory outing on the USS Princeton, suddenly killing Upshur.

Calhoun quickly closes on a proposed treaty, with several key terms, applauded across the South:

- Texas would enter the Union as a state, and not a territory;
- It would be allowed to retain slavery;
- The U.S. would assume its national debts, in exchange for its public lands; and
- The U.S. would be obligated to defend Texas against any attacks by Mexico.

On April 22, 1844, Tyler submits the treaty to the U.S. Senate for approval, arguing that it is essential to keeping Texas out of the hands of the British. Opponents counter by downplaying this threat, especially in relation to the near certainty that annexation would provoke a costly war with Mexico.

The President now bumbles forward, alienating various constituencies. When he offers to placate Mexico by forgiving $6 million in debt, he undermines the Texas's standing as an independent republic. From there he plays up the benefits of acquiring new territory for slavery and voting power for the South, immediately alienating northern congressmen. Calhoun secretly pushes the point even further, suggesting that the matter comes down to "Texas or Disunion."

Thomas Hart Benton (1782-1858)

When the treaty debate begins in May, Missouri Senator, Thomas Hart Benton, leads the opposition.

Benton, a Southerner, a loyal Democrat, Jackson man and ardent expansionist is also a slave-holder beginning to shift away from support for the institution. Still, he cannot stomach what seems like outright theft of land rightfully belonging to Mexico.

> *The treaty, in all that relates to the boundary of the Rio Grande, is an act of unparalleled outrage on Mexico. It is the seizure of 2,000 miles of her territory without a word of explanation with her, and by virtue of a treaty with Texas, to which she is no party.*

The vote on the treaty occurs on June 8, 1844, and it provides the Whigs, who dominate the Senate, with one more chance to humiliate Tyler. Needing a two-thirds majority for passage, the treaty garners only 16 ayes against 35 nays, with all but one of the 29 Whigs in opposition.

At this point, Texas annexation again feels like a dead issue.

But that is about to change as the election of 1844 nears.

SIDEBAR: THOMAS HART BENTON

Thomas Hart Benton will make his presence known in American politics across nearly four decades – forever on the side of protecting the Union against all external and internal threats.

In 1782, he is born on a plantation in North Carolina. As a young man he moves to Tennessee to oversee his family's 40,000-acre estate, studies law, and passes the bar in 1805.

When the War of 1812 breaks out, he volunteers and serves as an aide on the staff of General Andrew Jackson.

Both men share volatile tempers, and Benton is quick to blame Jackson for apparently provoking a duel involving his brother, Jesse. The time for vengeance arrives on September 4, 1813 when Jackson, bullwhip in hand, calls out the two brothers in a Nashville bar. Both draw their guns and fire at Jackson, shattering his left shoulder and almost causing him to bleed to death.

Remarkable as it seems, the two strong-willed combatants will subsequently make up and become loyal friends for life.

Benton soon moves to St. Louis, where he builds his legal reputation and becomes editor of the *Missouri Enquirer* newspaper. In 1817 his short-fuse again leads to violence, and he kills Charles Lucas, an opposing attorney, in a duel.

Still his popularity continues to grow across Missouri, and in 1821, when the state is admitted to the Union, he becomes its first senator.

From then on, he is a leading force in Congress, intent on passing Democratic Party legislation, especially in opposition to a federal bank and in favor of hard money. These traits earn him the nickname "Old Bullion," and explain this reminiscence about his one-time foe:

> *General Jackson was a very great man. I shot him, sir. Afterward he was of great use to me, sir, in my battle with the United States Bank.*

His sharp mind will be matched by an equally sharp tongue and a willingness to push his rivals over the edge—as evidenced by a Mississippi colleague who points a pistol at him on the floor of the senate.

Despite his many controversies, Thomas Hart Benton will also be remembered as a principled man, prone to question his own moral compass, especially later on around the propriety of the Mexican War and the practice of slavery. His opposition to expanding slavery into the new west will end his senate career in 1851.

## 115

THREE PARTIES NOMINATE CANDIDATES FOR THE PIVOTAL 1844 ELECTION

TIME: FALL 1842

THE WHIGS SUFFER BIG SET-BACKS IN THE MID-YEAR ELECTIONS

Whig Party anxiety mounts as the 1844 election approaches, and for good reason.

With President William Henry Harrison dead after only one month in office, and the apostate John Tyler in charge since then, almost none of Henry Clay's American System policies have escaped the veto pen. In turn, the economic recovery promised by the Whigs in 1840 has failed to materialize – with GDP trends falling back into negative territory by 1842.

SHORT-RUN ECONOMIC TRENDS

GDP	1840	1841	1842
Total ($000)	1574	1652	1618
% Change	(5%)	5%	(2%)
Per Cap	92	94	89

Vetoes notwithstanding, the country signals its displeasure with the Whigs by returning overwhelming control of the House to the Democrats in the 1842 mid-term election.

OFF YEAR CONGRESSIONAL ELECTION OF 1842

HOUSE	1840	1842	CHG
Democrats	98	148	50

HOUSE	1840	1842	CHG
Whigs	144	73	(71)
Anti-Masonic			
Conservative			
Other		2	2
Senate			
Democrats	22	23	1
Whigs	29	29	NC
Anti-Masonic			
Conservative			
Other			
PRESIDENT	Harrison	Tyler	

TIME: APRIL 1, 1844

THE LIBERTY PARTY AGAIN NOMINATES ABOLITIONIST JAMES BIRNEY

The anti-slavery Liberty Party is first to hold a nominating convention in 1844, meeting in the western New York town of Arcade.

Its delegates are drawn from the New York and Ohio wings of the abolitionist movement, as distinct from the Boston-based supporters of William Lloyd Garrison.

Both groups seek an end to slavery, but they differ fundamentally on the means required. Garrison remains committed to writing and speaking out against the slave-holders, the churches, and the federal government—most recently calling the Constitution "an agreement with hell" and urging people not to vote. The Liberty Party men view Garrison as naïve, and argue that only through political action will their end be achieved.

The party's first foray into politics occurs in 1840 and is a fiasco, with nominee James Birney

Salmon Chase (1808-1873)

winning less than 7,000 votes nationwide in the election. This time, they intend to do better.

In 1837, after Birney is attacked in Cincinnati by anti-abolitionist mobs, Ohioan Salmon P. Chase joins the cause. For the next seven years, Chase attempts to build the Liberty Party into a national force.

A highly skilled lawyer, Chase recognizes that the Constitution and the Northwest Ordinance affirm the lasting presence of slavery in the southern states east of the Mississippi. But, he argues, that principle does not extend to other new states admitted to the Union. Stopping its spread is not the full answer sought by the Garrison forces, but Chase regards it as a solid starting place to bring politics and law to bear on the South.

Over time this strategy—stopping the future expansion of slavery – will fuel the Republican Party and lead to Southern secession and civil war.

But in 1844, the Liberty Party still lacks a political candidate capable of competing on the national stage. It again is left with James Birney to head the ticket, along with Tom Morris, ex-Senator from Ohio, as his running mate.

Together they will garner a paltry 2% of the popular vote in the upcoming election – although many will later argue that their showing in New York actually costs Henry Clay a victory.

TIME: MAY 1, 1844

THE WHIGS AGAIN CALL ON HENRY CLAY

Despite the mid-term losses, the Whigs continue to believe the public, both North and South, will again support their platform for building the country's infrastructure.

They are heartened by party solidarity against the annexation of Texas in the Senate—even though over half of all Whigs in the chamber are from slave-holding states.

Likewise in the House, where one of their emerging spokesmen, Alexander Stephens of Georgia, dismisses the Tyler-Calhoun treaty proposal as a "humbug," designed simply to weaken Whig unity.

Instead of promoting costly and dangerous military schemes to expand America, the Whigs want to consolidate and improve the capacities of states already in the Union. As Clay says:

> *I think it is far more wise an important to compose and harmonize the present confederacy, as it now exists, than to introduce a new element of discord and distraction (i.e. Texas) into it.*

This has been the Whig's message since their origin in 1828.

America's greatness will follow from its ability to create an economic juggernaut, advantaged over the rest of the world. Successful international trade is one aspect of this, but vital "home markets" are its essence. The efficient production and distribution of goods from the East coast to the Mississippi will guarantee the "American dream" for all citizens.

It will result from the Whig's "American System" of investments in infrastructure and education, a sound currency and reliable banks, and sensible regulations and tariffs.

And no one speaks for this system better than its founder, Henry Clay.

Though thoroughly beaten by Jackson in 1832 and rejected in favor of the war hero, Harrison, in 1840, Clay is certain his time has come to succeed Tyler in the White House.

The Whigs signal their confidence in him through a brief, mostly perfunctory, national convention in Baltimore on May 1, 1844, where he is nominated by acclaim, and ex-New Jersey Senator Theodore Frelinghuysen is chosen as his running mate.

TIME: 1840s

THE "YOUNG AMERICA" MOVEMENT RE-SHAPES THE DEMOCRAT PARTY

For the Democrats, the 1840 loss to Harrison serves as a wake-up call to transition from the Jackson-Van Buren era to a new generation of national leaders.

The path they choose is the "Young America Movement," patterned after similar "young" initiatives materializing across Europe. The author Cornelius Matthews describes it in a speech he delivers on June 30, 1845:

Whatever that past generation of statesmen, law-givers and writers was capable of, we know. What they attained, what they failed to attain, we also know. Our duty and our destiny is another from theirs. Liking not at all its borrowed sound, we are yet (there is no better way to name it,) the Young America of the people: a new generation; *and it is for us now to inquire, what we may have it in our power to accomplish, and on what objects the world may reasonably ask that we should fix our regards.*

In the hands of the politicians, the message is one of "American Exceptionalism."

It is marked by a rugged assurance that the nation is destined by history to lead the world in everything, government to commerce, intellectual to cultural advances.

It embraces free trade across the globe, certain that it will profit most by opening new markets.

It welcomes wide open borders with immigrants from all over given a chance to share in life, liberty, and the pursuit of happiness – while also joining the Democratic Party.

It breaks beyond the constraints of the agrarian-centric economy and supports industrialization, infrastructure upgrades, even modest tariffs to support domestic manufacturing.

And it is absolutely committed to expanding the nation's borders to the west coast, and even into the Caribbean and Central America.

TIME: 1840s

STEPHEN A. DOUGLAS SYMBOLIZES THE YOUNG AMERICANS MOVEMENT

In 1843, a new figure leaps onto center stage in Congress, representing the Young America Movement and dedicated to restoring Democratic Party control in Washington. That figure is Stephen A. Douglas, of Illinois.

Stephen Douglass (he later drops the second "s") is born in Brandon, Vermont, in 1813 to a sixth generation New England family. His father is a physician dies suddenly at thirty-two when Douglass is only two months old. He is raised by his mother and her bachelor brother (his uncle) on their combined family farms. He is also influenced as a youth by his grandfather, Benajah Douglass, an outspoken five term member of the Vermont General Assembly.

His early formal education is very limited, only 3-4 months of schooling whenever his duties on the farm allow. At fifteen, he becomes fed up with his situation and decides to move out on his own, 14 miles away to the town of Middlebury, where he apprentices as a carpenter. He is there for eight months during the 1828 presidential campaign, a moment where he first becomes enthralled with politics and aligns himself with the Democratic Party principles of Andrew Jackson.

Douglas remains in Brandon for two more years, working as a carpenter and attending grade school. In 1830, his mother marries a man from Canandaigua, New York. He accompanies her there in December and enrolls in the Canandaigua Academy. He is known as a diligent student who actively engages in in the debate club and is seen as a future politician by his peers.

Upon graduating, Douglas sets his sights on becoming a lawyer, but recognizes that the standards for passing the bar in New York State require four more years of study. This prompts his decision to head west where no such academic rigor is demanded. In June,1833, he begins a six- month journey with brief stops in Cleveland and St. Louis before he finally settles down in Winchester, Illinois. There, he runs a grade school for 40 students, while adding enough bits and pieces of legal know-how to pass a brief oral exam and secure a law certificate.

In 1834, Douglas opens a practice in Winchester, but quickly finds that his true calling lies in the political arena. He dedicates himself to organizing a vibrant Democratic Party in Morgan County, 36 miles west of Springfield, which becomes the state capital in 1839. He attends sessions of the Illinois General Assembly as a lobbyist, and persuades legislators to pass a bill whereby states attorneys in Illinois are chosen by the people rather than appointed. In turn, he is elected to his first official office on February 10, 1835, as States Attorney for the First District, riding the circuit across eight counties, meeting voters, initiating his moniker as "Judge Douglas."

In August, 1836, as his career gains momentum, he is elected to represent Morgan County in Illinois's Tenth General Assembly, which includes Abraham Lincoln, James Shields, Edward Baker, James Semple, and other future political leaders.

In March 1837, his campaign work on behalf of John Van Buren's presidential election lands him a patronage job paying $3,000 a year as Registrar of the Springfield Land Office. In November, his Democratic Party nominates him to run for the U.S. House – but he loses in 1838 by 36 votes (out of 36,495 cast) to John Stuart, a Whig and law partner of Abraham Lincoln.

On March 2, 1839 he resigns as Registrar and devotes himself to strengthening his party and re-electing Van Buren in his race vs. Benjamin Harrison. This leads to the first series of public debates against his local rival, Abraham Lincoln, to be repeated nearly twenty years later when both vie for a U.S. Senate seat. A topic where they already disagree is over a bill to ban abolition societies in Illinois. The bill passes 77-6 with Douglas supporting it and Lincoln in the minority.

All in all, Douglas makes 207 speeches around the state on behalf of the Democrats and Van Buren, who carries Illinois while losing nationally.

In November 1840, Douglas's political efforts are again rewarded when the Democratic controlled legislature appoints him as Illinois Secretary of State. In 1841, the legislature appoints him Associate Justice of the state Supreme Court. Despite the fact that he is only twenty-eight years old, he has already argued fifteen cases before the high court, winning twelve and losing three. During his two-year stint on the court, he comes down hard against an abolitionist for harboring a run-away slave, while supporting Joseph Smith and the Mormons, earning their lasting praise.

In 1842, he loses his second political race, this time for a U.S. Senate seat, which goes to another more senior Democrat, Sidney Breese. He undaunted by the set-back and on August 7, 1843 he wins a race for the U.S. House. When the 28th Congress convenes on December 4, Douglas joins an impressive freshman class which includes the Georgia Whigs, Cobb and Stephens; anti-slavery men, Hale and Hamlin; states' rights southerners, Slidell and Clingman.

But none will come to representing the diverse factions within the Democratic Party better than Stephen Douglas, over the next fifteen years. He is a northern man by birth;

an expansionist westerner by choice; a full-fledged protégé of Andrew Jackson; a believer in the sacred Union, the Constitution, the will of the people; and, by 1848, an owner through marriage of a Mississippi plantation and over one hundred slaves.

He also brings an aggressive style to the floor of congress that justifies his nickname as "the Little Giant." He is 5'4" tall, with a large head and a barrel chest mounted on short stubbly legs, and a stentorian voice firing short assertions seldom lacking in certainty.

With President Andrew Jackson's death on June 8, 1845, and Van Buren on the ropes after his difficult term, Stephen Douglas at age thirty intends to revitalize the Democratic Party and ride it into a White House win for himself.

THE AMAZING RISE OF STEPHEN A. DOUGLAS TO NATIONAL PROMINENCE

DATE	MILESTONES
April 23, 1813	Douglas born in Brandon, Vermont
June 1813	Father dies and mother and her brother merge farms
1820-1827	Works on farm and attends 3-4 months of grade school per year
Spring 1828	Moves to Middlebury, apprentice carpenter, interest in politics
Winter 1828	Back in Brandon, rejects farming, carpentry, Andrew Jackson backer
December 1830	Mother remarries and he moves with her to Canandaigua, New York
1831-1833	Finishes grade school, begins to read law with well-known attorneys
June 24, 1833	Departs for west since New York bar standards requires 4 more years of study
Summer 1833	Stays briefly in Cleveland
Fall 1833	Another brief stop-over in St Louis before off to Jacksonville, Illinois
November 1833	Out of funds and walks to Winchester, IL to settle down
December 1833	Opens grade school for 40 children for support while studying law
March 1834	Closes school after 4 months and obtains a law certificate despite "gaps"
Spring 1834	Opens practice and decides to organize Democratic Party in his county
December 1834	Attends Illinois legislative session in capital of Vandalia to build Party
January 30, 1835	As lobbyist, writes successful bill to enable residents to choose States Attorneys
February 10, 1835	He is elected States Attorney for 1st District riding circuit for 8 counties
1835	Law practice sputters and he settles on politics as his true calling
April 1835	Arranges first Democratic Party convention in Morgan County, IL
August 1836	Wins election to represent Morgan City in 10th Illinois General Assembly
March 9, 1837	Resigns Leg seat & named by MVB Registrar of Springfield Land Office
November 1837	Nominated by Democrats to run for US House vs. John Stuart, AL law partner
Fall 1838	Douglas loses to Whig Stuart by 36 votes out of 36,495 cast

DATE	MILESTONES
March 2, 1839	Resigns Land Registrar job to focus on building Democratic party and himself
November 1839	He and Lincoln begin series of debates over us bank, Martin Van Buren administration
March 1840	Over 1,000 in Jacksonville hear a Douglas-Lincoln debate
Summer 1840	Douglas delivers 207 political speeches across Illinois
November 30, 1840	Democrat-controlled Illinois State Senate names him Secretary of State
By end 1840	Has argued 15 cases before Illinois Supreme Court with 12-3 record
1841	Resigns as Secretary of State and named (at 28) to Illinois Supreme Court
June 1841	Judge Douglas orders Mormon leader Joseph Smith to be freed from jail
1842	Van Buren visits during election season and Democrats win in August elections
December 16, 1842	Douglas loses US Senate nom to Sidney Breese on 19th conv ballot by 56-51
April 1843	Decides against abolitionist Richard Eells for harboring run-aways
June 5, 1843	Douglas wins nomination for US House vs. Whig Orville Browning
June 28, 1843	He resigns from Supreme Court after 2 years
August 7, 1843	He is elected to House at age 30
December 4, 1843	Opening session of 28th congress/news

TIME: MAY 27, 1844

THE DEMOCRATS CHOOSE A "DARK HORSE" IN JAMES POLK

Based on the collapse of the Whig agenda after Harrison's death, and their strong showing in the 1842 off-year elections in the House, the Democrats are confident they can retake the presidency in 1844.

The only thing standing in their way is agreement on the right presidential candidate.

On May 27, the party's nominating convention convenes in Baltimore, four weeks after the Whigs have selected Clay. It plays out in the context of the fiery debate in the Senate over whether or not to annex Texas. So far, the opponents   have been prevailing, led on the Democratic side by Thomas Benton of Missouri.

George Bancroft (1800-1891) who nominates Polk

In April, Martin Van Buren is drawn into the controversy and, like Clay, he publicly argues against a Texas deal, fearing war.

What he fails to realize at the time is that his mentor, Andrew Jackson, has switched positions, now favoring the annexation, and still wielding enough political power within the party to get his way.

When the opening gavel sounds, Van Buren remains the clear-cut favorite to win the nomination for a third straight time, despite his loss to Harrison in 1840. His main challenger is a 61-year-old Lewis Cass, whose credentials include graduation from Exeter Academy, freemason, General in the War of 1812, first Governor of the Michigan Territory, Jackson's Secretary of War, Ambassador to France, and supporter of adding Texas to the Union.

Alarm bells sound immediately in Van Buren's camp when his opponents—who refer to him as "Van Ruin"—pass a rule requiring the nominee to win by a two-thirds majority, a near impossibility now for the ex-president.

Van Buren leads after the first ballot, but then falls steadily until the fifth round when Cass overtakes him.

FIRST FIVE BALLOTS IN 1844 RACE (174 TO WIN)

CANDIDATE	1	2	3	4	5
Van Buren-NY	146	127	121	111	103
Lewis Cass-Mich	83	94	92	105	107
Rich Johnson-Ky	24	33	38	32	29
Calhoun-SC	6	1	2	0	0
Buchanan-Pa	4	9	11	17	26

Cass adds a few more delegates in the next two ballots reaching the 123 level, still well short of the 174 votes needed to win. By the eighth ballot, it's clear that neither man can win, and the search is on for a "dark horse" or compromise candidate.

Andrew Jackson has had one in mind all along, his fellow Tennessean, James Knox Polk.

Polk arrives at the convention with almost no standing. He plans to support Van Buren and, if the New Yorker wins, hopes to be considered as Vice-President. But the odds are against him, until the convention is stalemated.

At that point, Polk's mentor Jackson seizes the initiative. Three supporters, Gideon Pillow, his ex-law partner, advisor Cave Johnson, and George Bancroft of Massachusetts join forces and offer his name on the eighth ballot, before either James Buchanan or Richard Johnson can try to fill the void. A quickly convened ninth ballot becomes a stampede in favor of Polk. Pennsylvania Governor, George Dallas, is chosen as Vice-President – and the Democrats have their ticket for 1844.

FULL VOTING RESULTS AT THE 1844 DEMOCRATIC CONVENTION (174 TO WIN)

CANDIDATE	1	2	3	4	5	6	7	8	9
VAN BUREN-NY	146	127	121	111	103	101	99	104	0
LEWIS CASS-MICH	83	94	92	105	107	116	123	114	29
RICH JOHNSON-KY	24	33	38	32	29	23	21	0	0
CALHOUN-SC	6	1	2	0	0	0	0	0	0
BUCHANAN-PA	4	9	11	17	26	25	22	0	0
POLK-TENN								44	231

The candidate is "Little Hickory"—Southerner, successful lawyer, militia man, slave-holder, pro-states' rights, anti-US Bank, friend of Andrew Jackson and Sam Houston, and ardent supporter of "manifest destiny."

But Polk's surprising win will come at the expense of unity within the Democratic Party – especially among the powerful New York block who feel that Van Buren has been robbed by Southerners in Baltimore. In the years ahead they will seek revenge, earning the nickname as party "Barnburners."

TIME: 1844

THE NATIVIST AMERICAN PARTY MAKE ITS FIRST APPEARANCE

One other nascent political party also makes its first appearance during the 1844 election cycle. It is referred to early on as the American Republican Association, before morphing into the Native American Party and finally, the "Know Nothings."

It originates with South Carolinian, Lewis Charles Levin, son of Jewish parents, who graduates from the state university and tries his hand at the law and teaching before becoming a Methodist preacher. His temperament, however, is anything but pastoral, and he is known for engaging in fistfights and gun duels. After one such incident he is forced to leave Mississippi, and lands in Philadelphia.

Once there, he throws himself into a crusade against alcohol, carried out in his newspaper, the *Temperance Advocate*, and in elaborate public events dubbed "bonfires of booze," aimed at shutting down taverns. This cause, however, soon gives way to another, his obsessive attacks against Catholic immigrants.

Since the early 1830's, immigration to America is on the rise, with Roman Catholics fleeing Ireland and Germany comprising most of the immigrant population.

IMMIGRATION TRENDS BY COUNTRY

5 YEARS	TOTAL	IRISH	GERMAN	ALL OTHER
1820-4	74.8	11.7	1.9	25.1
1825-9	130.3	40.0	3.8	46.0

5 YEARS	TOTAL	IRISH	GERMAN	ALL OTHER
1830-4	326.5	54.1	39.3	137.1
1835-9	389.8	116.6	85.5	105.8
1840-4	481.2	181.7	100.5	117.8

Levin regards the Catholics as untrustworthy and dangerous for reasons mirroring the Anti-Masonic fervor in upstate New York in 1828. Theirs is a secret society, he says, whose allegiance is to the Pope in Rome, not to the government in Washington. Its corrupt religious practices and authoritarian rule are what drove settlers to America in the first place. What sense does it make to open the nation's borders to a proven enemy?

Latching on to these themes, in 1844, Levin organizes the American Republican Association in Philadelphia and publishes another newspaper, *The Daily Sun*, devoted to attacking Catholic immigrants.

A flashpoint comes when Francis Kenrick, the Bishop of Philadelphia, asks the local School Controllers to excuse Catholic students from participating in the traditional practice of reading from the Protestant Bible at the start of each day. When the request is granted, Levin's backers claim that the real intent is to eliminate all traces of the Protestant religion from the school curriculum.

What follows in Philadelphia in the spring and early summer of 1844 is a recreation of European-style religious battles between Protestant and Catholic. The first outbreak takes place on May 3, 1844, when Irish protestors break up an attempt by Lewis Levin to speak in the Catholic neighborhood of Kensington. Levin returns with 3,000 supporters and fighting continues through May 8 when local police are outmanned and unable to quell the mobs. The toll includes fourteen deaths, another fifty injured, and two hundred left homeless. The Sisters of Charity Seminary is attacked, along with the Hibernia fire station. Two Catholic churches—St. Michaels and St. Augustine's—are burned to the ground, and the rioting ends only after the state militia under General George Cadwallader is called into action.

A second outbreak occurs in July, centered on St. Philip Neri's Catholic Church. Fearing a nativist attack during the July 4 celebrations, the church pastor asks Pennsylvania Governor David Porter for support from the militia. On the evening of July 6, a sizable defensive force, again under Cadwallader, confronts a rock-throwing mob of several thousand, resulting in a stand-off. This truce breaks down a day later and open warfare —including cannon fire from both sides in the streets – leaves another fifteen killed and many others wounded. This time a military force of 5,000 troops ends the carnage.

Newspapers across the country report on the alarming level of violence in Philadelphia, and the difficulty faced by officials in stopping it. The Catholic Church sues the city for failing to adequately protect its property, winning a $45,000 payment, and begins opening its own schools to teach the faith. Meanwhile the city fathers pass bills requiring that one policeman be hired for every 150 residents, and designating a full infantry regiment, along with artillery and cavalry support, for call-up in case of any more disturbances.

While not yet sufficiently organized to impact national voting in 1844, it elect six U.S. House members.

One of them is Levin himself, joined by one other Pennsylvania congressman and four from neighboring New York.

Together they begin the campaign to halt further immigration and secure America for "real Americans," not foreigners.

## 116

JAMES KNOX POLK TERM

TIME: 1844

THE 1844 PRESIDENTIAL CAMPAIGN TURNS NASTY

The Democrats are energized by the thought of James Polk — "another Jackson" — leading the party back to its historical dominance in Washington.

To ensure this outcome, they go on the offensive, first to discredit Henry Clay's character with attacks on his well-known reputation for drinking, gambling, blasphemy, womanizing, and dueling.

Next, they then turn to undermining him across the South, focusing on three issues.

They claim his "American System" prioritizes federal authority over states' rights, and results in high tariffs on cotton goods and increases in the national debt. Next comes the assertion that he opposes slavery, has referred to it as a "moral stain," and may even be in league with the abolitionists. Finally, they zero in on his public statements opposing the annexation of Texas.

Theodore Frelinghuysen (1787-1862)

Failure to expand into Texas would represent a critical blow to the Southern economy, which by 1844 depends on opening more cotton plantations and selling more bred slaves into the west. Clay's stance also draws fire from his old nemesis, Andrew Jackson, who says that it demonstrates his military naiveté and threatens the national defense.

In an 1844 letter to John Mason, Secretary of the Navy, the old General raises the specter of an alliance between the Republic of Texas and Great Britain to conquer the entire western half of the continent.

Texas ought to have been & now must be (added), or the safety of the south & west is jeopardized, New Orleans insecure, and our revenue destroyed, by smuggling, & in a war with England, her & Texas united, a British force might in ten days from the Sabine make a lodgment on the Mississippi...possess herself of the command of the navigation of Red River, raise a servile war, capture New Orleans, excite our Indians placed on our western borders to hostilities against us - with these [ancillaries], and her armies from Canada uniting on our west, how much blood & treasure would it take to regain New Orleans, put down the servile & Indian War thus created and supported by Great Britain. There is not an American heart & eye, that should not now be opened to the great security Texas will give to the United States & it ought to be seized with the greatest promptitude.

Discrediting Clay in the North is more challenging, but it too eventually succeeds.

The "Texas question" again plays the leading role in the strategy, with Clay being painted as "unpatriotic" for standing against America's aspiration to control the entire continent. Those who oppose slavery or its spread to the west are also reminded that Clay, like Polk, is a slave owner. This fact cuts into his support among the "Conscience Whigs."

For good measure, the Democrats decide to smear Clay's running mate, Theodore Frelinghuysen. While in the Senate, he earns the nickname of "the Christian statesman," based on his intense Bible study and support for various Dutch Reformed missions. But he earns Jackson's wrath for a six-hour speech on the floor in 1830 in opposition to the Indian Removal Act. For this transgression, he is tarred during the campaign as an anti-Catholic bigot, and opponent of the separation of church and state.

The Whigs respond in kind.

They characterize Polk as a weak puppet of Jackson, and one who would involve America in an illegitimate and costly war to steal land from Mexico for the purpose of extending slavery into the west.

They also engage in character assassination through political pamphlets which accuse Polk of branding his initials onto the shoulders of forty of his slaves, a total fabrication, and resurrect a rumor that his grandfather, Ezekiel, was a British sympathizer during the Revolutionary War.

As the race plays out, both candidates are actively engaged.

To the surprise of many, Polk proves to be a crafty politician. He reassures Pennsylvania leaders that his tariff will protect their industries, while downplaying the duties in the South. He convinces Jackson to nudge Tyler out of running as an independent. He announces that he will serve only one term, encouraging future contenders like Cass, Buchanan and Calhoun to get out the Democratic vote.

Clay meanwhile senses the easy victory he anticipated slipping away. He finally realizes that his position on Texas is on the wrong side of emerging public sentiment, but several attempts to walk back his prior opposition fall flat. For many the "Great Compromiser" looks like he is abandoning his principles to win the White House.

TIME: NOVEMBER-DECEMBER 1844

JAMES K. POLK AND THE DEMOCRATS EMERGE VICTORIOUS

James Knox Polk (1795-1849)

Ballots are cast in the 15th quadrennial election for president between November 1 and December 4, 1844. The total popular vote count exceeds the hotly contested 1840 race and reaches 2.7 million, with just under 80% of all age-eligible citizens participating

POPULAR VOTES CAST FOR PRESIDENT

YEAR	NUMBER	% VS Y-A
1832	1,286,700	+12.1%
1836	1,502,300	+16.8
1840	2,411,808	+60.5
1844	2,701,552	+12.0

When the results are in, the "dark horse" James Polk has won a razor thin victory, with 49.6% of the popular vote to 48.1% for Henry Clay.

1844 PRESIDENTIAL ELECTION RESULTS

1844	PARTY	POP VOTE	ELECT TOT	SOUTH	BORDER	NORTH	WEST
Polk	Democrat	1,339,494	170	60	7	77	26
Clay	Whig	1,300,004	105	24	23	35	33
Birney	Liberty	62,054	0				
		2,701,552	275	84	30	112	59

Polk loses in both his birth state of North Carolina and his home state of Tennessee, but carries most of the South, along with the Northern states of New York, Pennsylvania, New Hampshire and Maine.

PARTY POWER BY STATE

SOUTH	1840	1844	PICK-UP
VIRGINIA	Democrat	Democrat	
NORTH CAROLINA	Whig	Whig	

SOUTH	1840	1844	PICK-UP
SOUTH CAROLINA	Democrat	Democrat	
GEORGIA	Whig	Democrat	Democrat
ALABAMA	Democrat	Democrat	
MISSISSIPPI	Whig	Democrat	Democrat
LOUISIANA	Whig	Democrat	Democrat
TENNESSEE	Whig	Whig	
ARKANSAS	Democrat	Democrat	
BORDER			
DELAWARE	Whig	Whig	
MARYLAND	Whig	Democrat	Democrat
KENTUCKY	Whig	Whig	
NORTH			
NEW HAMPSHIRE	Democrat	Whig	Whig
VERMONT	Whig	Whig	
MASSACHUSETTS	Whig	Whig	
RHODE ISLAND	Whig	Whig	
CONNECTICUT	Whig	Whig	
NEW YORK	Whig	Democrat	Democrat
NEW JERSEY	Whig	Whig	
	Whig	Democrat	Democrat
	Whig	Democrat	Democrat
	Whig	Democrat	Democrat
	Whig	Whig	
	Democrat	Democrat	
	Democrat	Democrat	
	Whig	Democrat	Democrat

Clay's hopes are shattered when he loses New York State by only 5,106 votes. The difference here may have traced to the 15,812 ballots won by James Birney of the abolitionist Liberty Party, a former supporter of Clay. Had the state's 36 electoral votes shifted to Clay, he would have won the presidency in the Electoral College by a margin of 141-134, rather than losing 105-170.

1844 RESULTS IN NEW YORK STATE

1844	PARTY	POP VOTE	ELECT TOT
POLK	Democrat	237,588	36
CLAY	Whig	232,482	0
BIRNEY	Liberty	15,812	0

The Democrats retain the firm control over the House they've held since the Whig collapse in 1842.

U.S. HOUSE ELECTIONS

PARTY	1840	1842	1844
DEMOCRATS	98	148	142
WHIGS	144	73	79
NATIVE AMERICAN			6
OTHER		2	2

They also regain control in the Senate.

U.S. SENATE ELECTIONS

PARTY	1840	1842	1844
DEMOCRATS	22	23	27
WHIGS	29	29	24
OTHER			1

TIME: 1795-1845

PRESIDENT JAMES KNOX POLK: PERSONAL PROFILE

James Polk is born in 1795 in Mecklenburg County, North Carolina, named after Charlotte, wife of King George III, and famous for being first to publicly declare independence from Great Britain in 1775. His mother descends from the Scottish Presbyterian minister, John Knox, and his father is a lifelong Deist, who refuses to "affirm his faith" at a planned christening event, leaving James unbaptized until his deathbed 53 years later.

Both father and grandfather are outspoken Jefferson men who inculcate states' rights and anti-Federalist principles early on. Sam Polk is also a savvy businessman, a successful farmer and slave owner, who decides in 1806 to move his family from the eastern piedmont range in NC across the Appalachians and into Tennessee.

Son James is a sickly youth, suffering from stomach ailments and, at age seventeen, a severe case of urinary stones, leading to life-threatening and primitive surgery and leaving him impotent for life. He is home schooled at first, until enrolling at the University of North Carolina in 1816, where he shines as a student and commencement speaker.

After graduation his future is shaped by studying law in Nashville with Felix Grundy, the top criminal lawyer in the state and future US Senator and Attorney General from 1838-40 in Van Buren's cabinet. Grundy prepares him to pass the bar in 1820 and introduces him to the inner workings of the state legislature and the political arena that quickly captures his imagination.

His law practice flourishes and his income soars. He rounds out his credentials by joining the state militia and becoming a freemason. He wins a seat in the US House in 1825 as a strong supporter of Andrew Jackson, a friend of his father and grandfather alike, and his future political mentor.

Polk remains in the US House for seven consecutive terms, fighting for Jacksonian principles and for his legislative agenda as President, including his controversial war with the U.S. Bank. In his last four years he is elected Speaker of the House, and at age forty-three is widely regarded as a future presidential candidate.

In 1838 he decides to run for Governor of Tennessee against Newton Cannon, a Whig and fierce opponent of Jackson, seeking his third consecutive term in the office. Polk wins a very narrow 51-49% victory and is sitting in the Governor's chair when the fall-out from the Bank Panic of 1837 rocks the nation and his home state.

After a frustrating first term, Polk runs again in 1840, at the same time the electorate decides to oust his party leader, Martin Van Buren, in favor of the first Whig President, Harrison. Polk loses 53-47%. In 1842, he tries again, and loses again by the same margin.

What appeared to Polk in 1840 to have been a soaring political future has fallen flat in 1844 as he heads off to the Democratic Party nominating convention in Baltimore.

There, after eight stalemated ballots, lightning strikes him as "the dark-horse nominee."

TIME: MARCH 5, 1845

POLK SUPPORTS THE TEXAS ANNEXATION IN HIS INAUGURAL SPEECH

Polk is sworn in as President by Chief Justice Roger Taney on March 5, 1845, a rain-filled day in DC. At 49 years of age, he is the youngest man yet to hold the office. His inaugural address to a crowd gathered on the east side of the Capitol opens with obligatory appreciation for his election victory.

Fellow-Citizens: Without solicitation on my part, I have been chosen by the free and voluntary suffrages of my countrymen to the most honorable and most responsible office on earth...I am deeply impressed with gratitude for the confidence reposed in me. Honored with this distinguished consideration at an earlier period of life than any of my predecessors.

It segues to the principles Polk intends to follow in office, beginning with a classical restatement of Jefferson's Tenth Amendment call for limitations on the power of the Federal government over the States, to avoid "unfortunate collisions" which could threaten the Union.

It will be my first care to administer the Government in the true spirit of (the

Constitution), and to assume no powers not expressly granted or clearly implied in its terms…(to avoid) those unfortunate collisions between the Federal and State authorities which have occasionally so much disturbed the harmony of our system and even threatened the perpetuity of our glorious Union… "To the States, respectively, or to the people" have been reserved "the powers not delegated to the United States by the Constitution nor prohibited by it to the States." Each State is a complete sovereignty within the sphere of its reserved powers.

While the Constitution calls for "majority rules," it also protects the rights of the minorities against acts of oppression.

By the theory of our Government majorities rule, but this right is not an arbitrary or unlimited one It is a right to be exercised in subordination to the Constitution and in conformity to it. One great object of the Constitution was to restrain majorities from oppressing minorities or encroaching upon their just rights. Minorities have a right to appeal to the Constitution as a shield against such oppression. The inestimable value of our Federal Union is felt and acknowledged by all.

An example he cites is the Tariff, where he will oppose high "protective" rates benefiting some businesses or regions at the expense of others.

One of the difficulties which we have had to encounter in the practical administration of the Government consists in the adjustment of our revenue laws and the levy of the taxes necessary for the support of Government. In the general proposition that no more money shall be collected than the necessities of an economical administration shall require all parties seem to acquiesce. Nor does there seem to be any material difference of opinion as to the absence of right in the Government to tax one section of country, or one class of citizens, or one occupation, for the mere profit of another.

I have also declared… that I was "opposed to a tariff for protection merely, and not for revenue." … To reverse this principle and make protection the object and revenue the incident would be to inflict manifest injustice upon all other than the protected interests.

Polk promises to run a frugal administration and avoid federal debt.

A national debt has become almost an institution of European monarchies…. Such a system is incompatible with the ends for which our republican Government was instituted… Ours was intended to be a plain and frugal government, and I shall regard it to be my duty to recommend to Congress and, as far as the Executive is concerned, to enforce by all the means within my power the strictest economy in the expenditure of the public money which may be compatible with the public interests.

True to Democratic Party doctrine, he will oppose a private national bank.

We need no national banks or other extraneous institutions planted around the Government to control or strengthen it in opposition to the will of its authors. Experience has taught us how unnecessary they are as auxiliaries of the public authorities—how impotent for good and how powerful for mischief.

He addresses growing "agitation" over slavery, never overtly mentioning the word as had Van Buren in 1836, but instead citing calls by one section for "the destruction of domestic institutions existing in other sections…which were recognized and protected in the Constitution."

It is a source of deep regret that in some sections of our country misguided persons have occasionally indulged in schemes and agitations whose object is the destruction of domestic institutions existing in other sections--institutions which existed at the adoption of the Constitution and were recognized and protected by it. All must see that if it were possible for them to be successful in attaining their object the dissolution of the Union and the consequent destruction of our happy form of government must speedily follow.

His policy will be to tamp down such "sectional jealousies and heartburnings" which could lead to disunion. The "patriotic sentiment" he quotes is from Andrew Jackson's famous toast vs. John Calhoun in 1832.

…Sectional jealousies and heartburnings must be discountenanced, and all should remember that they are members of the same political family, having a common destiny… Every lover of his country must shudder at the thought of the possibility of its dissolution, and will be ready to adopt the patriotic sentiment, "Our Federal Union—it must be preserved."

When it comes to foreign affairs, they are the province of the national government.

To the Government of the United States has been intrusted the exclusive management of our foreign affairs…In the management of our foreign relations it will be my aim to observe a careful respect for the rights of other nations, while our own will be the subject of constant watchfulness

And here he focuses on the annexation of Texas, which will lead to the war with Mexico and become the overarching focus of his administration. He begins by asserting that Texas was a part of the Louisiana Purchase, then "unwisely ceded" in the 1819 Adams-Onis Treaty to Spain, and now is simply wishing to rejoin the United States.

The Republic of Texas has made known her desire to come into our Union, to form a part of our Confederacy and enjoy with us the blessings of liberty secured and guaranteed by our Constitution. Texas was once a part of our country--was unwisely ceded away to a foreign power—is now independent, and possesses an undoubted right to dispose of a part or the whole of her territory and to merge her sovereignty as a separate and independent state in ours. I congratulate my country that by an act of the late Congress of the United States the assent of this Government has been given to the reunion, and it only remains for the two countries to agree upon the terms to consummate an object so important to both.

As an independent Republic, it also has the perfect right to take this action. The annexation is not a conquest, simply a matter of free choice by the residents.

I regard the question of annexation as belonging exclusively to the United States and Texas. They are independent powers competent to contract, and foreign nations have no right to interfere with them or to take exceptions to their reunion.... Foreign powers should therefore look on the annexation of Texas to the United States not as the conquest of a nation seeking to extend her dominions by arms and violence, but as the peaceful acquisition of a territory once her own, by adding another member to our confederation, with the consent of that member, thereby diminishing the chances of war and opening to them new and ever-increasing markets for their products.

To cement his argument, he raises Jackson's specter of a "foreign nation more powerful than Texas" taking control of the Republic and of the entire Southwest.

None can one fail to see the danger to our safety and future peace if Texas remains an independent state or becomes an ally or dependency of some foreign nation more powerful than herself. Is there one among our citizens who would not prefer perpetual peace with Texas to occasional wars, which so often occur between bordering independent nations?

Bringing Texas into the Union will be an immediate priority.

To Texas the reunion is important, because the strong protecting arm of our Government would be extended over her, and the vast resources of her fertile soil and genial climate would be speedily developed, while the safety of New Orleans and of our whole southwestern frontier against hostile aggression, as well as the interests of the whole Union, would be promoted by it....I shall on the broad principle which formed the basis and produced the adoption of our Constitution, and not in any narrow spirit of sectional policy, endeavor by all Constitutional, honorable, and appropriate means to consummate the expressed will of the people and Government of the United States by the re-annexation of Texas to our Union at the earliest practicable period.

With regard to contested territory further west, he asserts that America has "clear and unquestionable" rights to the entire Oregon country land, already occupied by our settlers.

Nor will it become in a less degree my duty to assert and maintain by all Constitutional means the right of the United States to that portion of our territory which lies beyond the Rocky Mountains. Our title to the country of the Oregon is "clear and unquestionable," and already are our people preparing to perfect that title by occupying it with their wives and children.

In neither the case of Texas nor of Oregon does he threaten warfare against Mexico or Britain – but both nations are implicitly put on notice by his contentions.

Polk ends his speech with the standard invocation of the Divine Being to watch over the United States.

Confidently relying upon the aid and assistance of the coordinate departments of the Government in conducting our public affairs, I enter upon the discharge of the high duties which have been assigned me by the people, again humbly supplicating that Divine Being who has watched over and protected our beloved country from its infancy to the present hour to continue His gracious benedictions upon us, that we may continue to be a prosperous and happy people.

What comes next is one of the most consequential presidential terms in American history.

TIME: MARCH 1845

POLK NAMES HIS CABINET

Shortly after his election victory, Polk meets with Andrew Jackson. Among the topics discussed is the formation of his cabinet, where he hopes to avoid the many pitfalls the old General experienced with connivers like John C. Calhoun, the sitting Secretary of State under Tyler. Polk eventually offers Calhoun the job of Ambassador to Britain, but he turns it down to return to the Senate, as self-styled "defender of the South."

In the end Polk names six men, all lawyers, save for Bancroft, his choice for the Navy post.

While he fully intends to oversee foreign affairs on his own, he chooses the Senator from Pennsylvania, James Buchanan, a twenty year veteran of Congress, as his Secretary of State. Buchanan soon proves troublesome, and Polk offers to appoint him to the Supreme Court when Justice Henry Baldwin dies, but Buchanan declines, wanting to stay put and try to succeed Polk after his promised single term is up.

For Treasury he picks Senator Robert J. Walker of Mississippi, whose early adulthood is in Pennsylvania, before moving South to build a successful business career speculating in land, cotton and slaves. Walker is a passionate defender of slavery and a straight Jacksonian, including aversion to any talk of dissolving the Union.

Secretary of War, William Marcy, at age fifty-eight, is the oldest member of the cabinet. His military credentials trace to combat experience in Canada as a militia captain early in the War of 1812. He then becomes the consummate New York politician, a member of the Albany Regency, Van Buren's patronage machine, and coiner of the phrase, "to the victors belong the spoils." He wins three elections at New York Governor before losing in 1838 to Henry Seward and falling out with Van Buren, who warns Polk not to name him, and is offended when his advice is ignored.

Tyler's Secretary of the Navy, John Mason of Virginia, is retained by Polk, but in the position of Attorney General. His legal training traces to the famed Tapping Reed School, and his public service includes three years as a district court judge. His political history includes three terms in the U.S House. He is a Southern planter and a life-long backer of Jackson and Van Buren.

The only non-lawyer in the cabinet is George Bancroft, a Massachusetts' man who earns a PhD in history from the University of Gottingen, and teaches Greek at Harvard College. He ventures into the political realm in 1837 when Van Buren appoints him Customs Collector for the port of Boston. He loses a run for Massachusetts' Governor in 1844, collecting only 41% of the vote, and is an opponent of slavery. But he favors the Texas Annexation and is a Northern Democrat who eventually comes out for Polk at the critical moment in the 1844 nominating convention.

Lastly Polk names his long-term Tennessee friend and advisor, Cave Johnson, as the new Postmaster General. He is a four-time member of the U.S House, Polk's campaign manager during his run for the White House, and the "fixer" of problems throughout the term.

JAMES KNOX POLK'S CABINET

POSITION	NAME	HOME STATE
Secretary of State	James Buchanan	Pennsylvania
Secretary of Treasury	Robert Walker	Mississippi
Secretary of War	William Marcy	New York
Attorney General	John Mason	Virginia
Secretary of Navy	George Bancroft	Massachusetts
Postmaster General	Cave Johnson	Tennessee

Four of his six appointees will serve all four years. Mason will switch back to his old position as Secretary of the Navy when Bancroft departs. His Attorney General post will go to Nathan Clifford and then Isaac Toucey.

## 117

THE REPUBLIC OF TEXAS IS ANNEXED

TIME: DECEMBER 1844 – FEBRUARY 1845

THE LAME DUCK CONGRESS AGAIN DEBATES THE TEXAS QUESTION

Polk's aggressive stance on the annexation of Texas has much to do with his election victory – and he hopes that Congress will authorize its go-ahead by the time he is sworn in.

But complexities abound, not the least of which is to clarify the exact territorial boundaries being claimed by the Texans. At one extreme, "Imperial Texas" encompasses a swath of land from the Rio Grande River in the South to a northern tip in later day Wyoming, and extending west into later day New Mexico.

Meanwhile there is the much smaller land mass occupied by the Republic, sandwiched between two rivers, on the north and east, the Arkansas; on the south and west, the Rio Grande.

Both "claims" regarding the actual Texas boundaries are hotly disputed by the Government of Mexico.

The debate over annexation is taken up by the 28th Congress in its lame duck session, which opens in December 1844, with Tyler still in the White House and Calhoun as Secretary of State.

While their Annexation Treaty was rejected six months earlier, both are convinced by the election results that public opinion now favors approval. To make passage easier this time, they

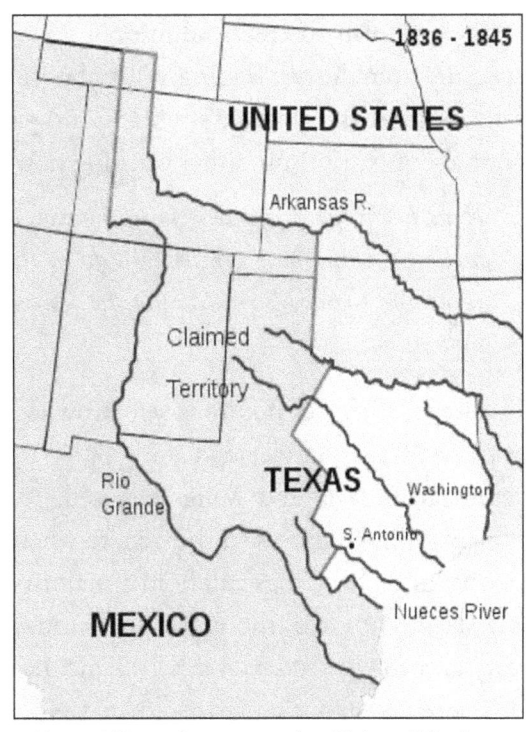

Map of Texas Proper vs. the Claimed Territory

abandon the prior attempt to approve a "treaty" with Mexico—needing a two-thirds majority in the Senate—and instead go for a standard legislative bill, requiring only a simple majority.

In the House, however, efforts to shape a final bill are stalled over a host of issues, including: final "boundary definitions;" whether Texas will become a territory or a state; its "status" regarding slavery; and how its accumulated debts will be handled.

On January 13, 1845, a proposed solution is offered by Milton Brown, a Tennessee Whig, who studies law under Polk's mentor, Felix Grundy, before becoming a leader among Southern Whigs, and a consistent thorn in the side of the Democrats. Brown argues in favor of immediately annexing the generally accepted, "narrow borders" of the Texas Republic, and holding over the broader land claims until Polk is in office.

His proposal involves four points:

1. Act now to annex the existing Republic of Texas land, and immediately grant it status as a slave state.
2. Assign all acreage to the state along with responsibility for any outstanding debts.
3. Delay resolution over the "claimed land" until further U.S. treaty negotiations with Mexico can occur.
4. Divide up any additional land acquired in the treaty negotiations into four new states.

Brown's plan to create additional slave states around Texas draws immediate fire, especially from the two leading Whig abolitionists in the House, John Quincy Adams and Joshua Giddings. Giddings's remarks are particularly scathing. He says the annexation is not about patriotism; rather opening new slave markets to increase Southern wealth.

Texas is engaged in a war with Mexico and wants us to fight her battles…and a portion of this House say, we will do it, if, by that means, we can keep up slavery in Texas and thereby furnish a market for our slave-breeding states to sell their surplus population.

After further debate, however, Brown's bill carries the House on January 25, 1845 by a 120-98 margin, decided along party, not regional, lines—with the vast majority of Democrats in favor and Whigs opposed.

The bill now moves to the Senate where it faces an even greater challenge, for two reasons: first, the Whigs still hold a majority during the lame duck session; and second, only six months ago, the powerful Thomas Hart Benton of Missouri, opposed Tyler's treaty and convinced seven other Democrats to also vote no.

Benton is sixty-two years old in 1845, a volatile figure who permanently shatters Andrew Jackson's left arm in an 1813 duel, before reconciling with him. From then on, he becomes a leading force in Congress for passing the General's legislation, especially around banking and hard money—where he earns the nickname, "Old Bullion." Although a fierce "expansionist"—and father-in-law of the western explorer, John Fremont—his moral compass remains uncomfortable with any open-ended land grab from Mexico. Likewise, his beliefs about slavery are evolving, especially around the wisdom of spreading it further into new states. This hesitancy will eventually cause Missouri voters to oust him in 1851.

But with Polk about to be in the White House, Benton changes his mind on Texas and decides to support the annexation. He calls for the existing Texas land ("narrow borders") to be admitted immediately as a state, while any added land to become a territory, with "boundary and slavery issues" to be decided later by a five man commission set up by Polk. He feels that by delaying final calls on "slave vs. free" status for any other new states, more Northern Democrats will support the annexation.

Meanwhile Calhoun and his hardcore faction in the Senate are lobbying for the broadest Texas borders, with all other land acquired becoming open to slavery right away.

TIME: FEBRUARY 28, 1845

THE TEXAS ANNEXATION BILL IS FINALLY APPROVED

At this point, Polk is frustrated by the lack of decisive action in the Senate. A possible solution comes from his soon-to-be Treasury Secretary, Senator Robert Walker of Mississippi, who proposes a combination of Brown's plan to immediately annex existing Texas ("narrow borders") along with Benton's plan to delay closure on the broader "claimed lands" until later.

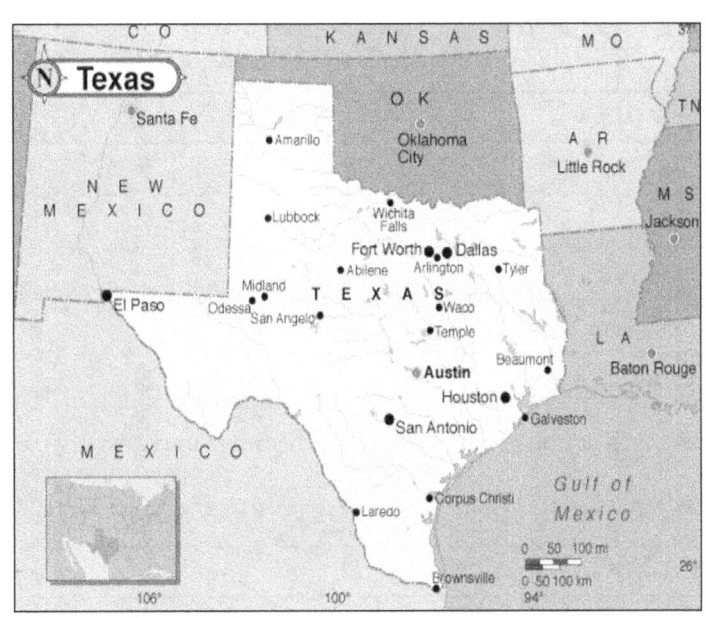

Map of the Eventual State of Texas Bordered
by the Rio Grande River

Benton signs on, believing, incorrectly, that Polk will be cautious in dealing with Mexico over "claimed land" conflicts, and on slavery-related issues. In turn, he whips all 25 Democrats into supporting the bill.

The Whigs, with 27 votes to cast, still threaten to defeat the annexation until two defectors from slave-holding states—the Maryland Senator, William Merrick, and the Louisiana man, Henry Johnson—swing the balance in favor of passage—27 ayes vs. 25 nays.

SENATE VOTE ON TEXAS ANNEXATION BILL: FEBRUARY 28, 1845

REGION	DEMS-YES	DEMS-NO	WHIGS-YES	WHIGS-NO
Northeast	8	0	0	10
Northwest	5	0	0	2
Border	3	0	1	5
Southeast	4	0	0	4
Southwest	5	0	1	4
Total	25	0	2	25

Note: Northwest = Ohio, Indiana, Mich, IL; Southwest = TN, Ala, Miss, La, Ark

Aside from giving Polk the go-ahead to secure Texas, the annexation votes also shows that, on some issues, the Congress remains split along party lines – Democrats vs. Whigs – rather than along sectional/slavery lines – South vs. North.

ANALYSIS OF TEXAS ANNEXATION VOTE

STATUS	YES	NO
Democrats	25	0
Whigs	2	25
South States	14	13
North States	17	17

Surprisingly in supporting the annexation, the North also goes along with handing the South a momentary two state advantage in the balance of voting power in the Senate.

POST-TEXAS ADMISSION

STATUS	COUNT
South/Slave States	17
North/Free States	15

On March 1, 1845, President Tyler signs the final Annexation bill into law.
The next step for Texas now belongs to a response from the Mexican government.

DATE: MARCH 1, 1845

SIDEBAR: FINAL TEXAS ANNEXATION BILL CALLING FOR POPULAR SOVEREIGNTY OVER SLAVERY

28th Congress Second Session. Joint Resolution for annexing Texas to the United States.

Resolved by the Senate and House of Representatives of the United States of America in Congress assembled, That Congress doth consent that the territory properly included within, and rightfully belonging to the Republic of Texas, may be erected into a new state, to be called the state of Texas, with a republican form of government, to be adopted by the people of said republic, by deputies in Convention assembled, with the consent of the existing government, in order that the same may be admitted as one of the states of this Union.

And be it further resolved, That the foregoing consent of Congress is given upon the following conditions, and with the following guarantees, to wit:

First-said state to be formed, subject to the adjustment by this government of all questions of boundary that may arise with other governments; and the constitution thereof, with the proper evidence of its adoption by the people of said republic of Texas, shall be transmitted to the President of the United States, to be laid before Congress for its final action, on or before the first day of January, one thousand eight hundred and forty-six.

Second-said state, when admitted into the Union, after ceding to the United States all public edifices, fortifications, barracks, ports and harbors, navy and navy-yards, docks, magazines, arms, armaments, and all other property and means pertaining to the public defence belonging to said republic of Texas, shall retain all the public funds, debts, taxes, and dues of every kind which may belong to or be due and owing said republic; and shall also retain all the vacant and unappropriated lands lying within its limits, to be applied to the payment of the debts and liabilities of said republic of Texas; and the residue of said lands, after discharging said debts and liabilities, to be disposed of as said state may direct; but in no event are said debts and liabilities to become a charge upon the government of the United States.

Third- New states, of convenient size, not exceeding four in number, in addition to said state of Texas, and having sufficient population, may hereafter, by the consent of said state, be formed out of the territory thereof, which shall be entitled to admission under the provisions of the federal constitution. And such states as may be formed out of that portion of said territory lying south of thirty-six degrees thirty minutes north latitude, commonly known as the Missouri compromise line, shall be admitted into the Union with or without slavery, as the people of each state asking admission may desire. And in such state or states as shall be formed out of said territory north of said Missouri compromise line, slavery, or involuntary servitude, (except for crime,) shall be prohibited.

And be it further resolved, That if the President of the United States shall in his judgment and discretion deem it most advisable, instead of proceeding to submit the foregoing resolution to the Republic of Texas, as an overture on the part of the United States for admission, to negotiate with that Republic; then, Be it resolved, that a state, to be formed out of the present Republic of Texas, with suitable extent and boundaries, and with two representatives in Congress, until the next apportionment of representation, shall be admitted into the Union, by virtue of this act, on an equal footing with the existing states, as soon as the terms and conditions of such admission, and the cession of the remaining Texan territory to the United States shall be agreed upon by the governments of Texas and the United States: And that the sum of one hundred thousand dollars be, and the same is hereby, appropriated to defray the expenses of missions and negotiations, to agree upon the terms of said admission and cession, either by treaty to be submitted to the Senate, or by articles to be submitted to the two Houses of Congress, as the President may direct.

J W JONES
Speaker of the House of Representatives.
WILLIE P. MANGUM
President, pro tempore, of the Senate.
Approv'd March 1. 1845
JOHN TYLER

Note: The Texas legislature previously approves the annexation and a constitution on Oct 13, 1845.

TIME: MAY 1845

A SMALL MINORITY RESISTS THE ANNEXATION AS IMPERIALISTIC

Despite the public popularity behind adding Texas, some Americans are troubled by what they see as Polk's imperialistic actions.

The abolitionist William Lloyd Garrison calls the Texas annexation "the greatest crime of our age."

The New England transcendentalist, Henry David Thoreau, refuses to pay his $1 Massachusetts's poll tax in protest, and spends a night in jail. While released the next day, this experience leads to his 1849 treatise on "Civil Disobedience," where he poses questions of conscience that resonate with time.

Henry David Thoreau (1817-1862)

Can there not be a government in which majorities do not virtually decide right and wrong, but conscience? Must the citizen ever for a moment, or in the least degree, resign his conscience to the legislator?

How does it become a man to behave toward this American government to-day? I answer, that he cannot without disgrace be associated with it. I cannot for an instant recognize that political organization as my government which is the slave's government also.

It is not a man's duty, as a matter of course, to devote himself to the eradication of any, even the most enormous wrong?

Ohio congressman Joshua Giddings expresses his conscientious objections in no uncertain terms:

War, with all its horrors and its devastation of public morals, is infinitely preferable to a supine, inactive submission to the slaveholding power that is to control this nation if left in its present situation.

But these are the predictable abolitionist voices of protest – hardly enough to derail the momentum on Polk's side.

## 118

WAR BREAKS OUT WITH MEXICO

TIME: MARCH 6, 1845 – NOVEMBER 10, 1845

AN ANGRY MEXICO BREAKS RELATIONS AND OPENS THE DOOR TO NEGOTIATIONS

The Mexican government is predictably outraged by U.S. passage of the Annexation bill on March 1, 1845, and doubly so because it involves not only Texas proper (north and west of the Nueces River), but also another huge area of "claimed land" south to the Rio Grande.

They signal their anger on March 6, 1845, two days after Polk's inauguration, by recalling their minister and severing diplomatic relations with Washington.

Anticipating possible hostilities, the President in May 1845 sends General Zachary Taylor and 2,400 troops to the Nueces River border of Texas "for defensive purposes."

When Polk's long-time mentor, Andrew Jackson, dies on June 8, 1845 at 78, in Nashville, "Young Hickory" is left to stand on his own amidst the controversies.

John Slidell (1793-1871)

Animosity toward Mexico builds into the summer. Public sentiment in favor of expansion further is spurred by the journalist John L. O'Sullivan whose *Democratic Review* continues to assert that America's "manifest destiny (is) to overspread the continent:"

It is now time for the opposition to the Annexation of Texas to cease, (for) our manifest destiny (is) to overspread the continent for the free development of our yearly multiplying millions.

The strained relations continue until October, when Mexican President Jose Herrera, who hopes to avoid war, signals that he is willing to engage in talks about border issues, by which he means the original seizure of the Texas Republic. Polk seizes upon this apparent "opening" to not only resolve the "claimed land" borders to the Rio Grande, but also to explore Mexico's willingness to part with additional territory west to California.

Louisiana Senator John Slidell is chosen by Polk as Minister to Mexico on November 10, and is sent on a mission to negotiate a trade of land for money – the Rio Grande border in exchange for forgiving a $3.5 million Mexican debt owed to the U.S., the New Mexico territory for $5 million, and the ports of San Francisco and Monterrey for another $20 million.

He is also directed to inform Herrera that the U.S. would intervene in any move by Mexico to sell this land to a foreign power such as Britain or France.

TIME: NOVEMBER 29, 1845 – APRIL 24, 1846

TREATY TALKS STALL AND SHOTS ARE FIRED ALONG THE BORDER

On November 29, 1845, Slidell arrives at the gulf port of Veracruz, ready to engage Herrera in Mexico City.

But Herrera's tenure in office is about to end, as the hawkish General Mariano Paredes, who had previously ousted Santa Anna, marches on the capitol and takes power on December 30.

Slidell is now left in a holding pattern, waiting to learn Paredes's stance on the border issues.

Polk, however, is not in a waiting mood.

On January 12, 1846, when news of Paredes' stalling tactics reach him, Polk orders Taylor's forces to advance further southwest from the Nueces line and across disputed land to the east bank of the Rio Grande.

Paredes fires back by refusing to accept

President of Mexico Mariano Paredes
(1797-1849)

Slidell's credentials as a diplomat. After standing idly by for over three months, the treaty mission officially ends in March 1846.

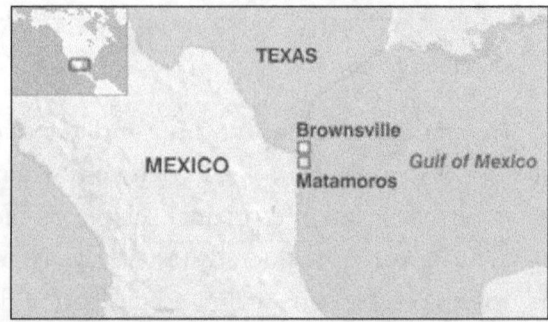

Map Showing Matamoros
just south of the Rio Grande

Meanwhile Taylor's troops, now 3,500 men strong, are strung out along the north bank of the Rio Grande opposite the town of Matamoros, on the eastern side of the river.

On April 24, 1846, they are attacked by Mexican forces, with sixteen Americans killed in action.

TIME: MAY 13, 1846

CONGRESS DECLARES WAR ON MEXICO

On May 8, Slidell is back in Washington briefing Polk and his cabinet on his failed mission to Mexico City.

The President finds "ample cause for war" in Parades' treatment of Slidell, and is in the process of drafting a message to Congress, when word reaches him that fighting has already broken out.

Polk responds by sending up a declaration of war to Congress on May 13, confident that any hold-outs will now be ready to act.

His assessment proves right, and his request quickly passes the Senate by 40-2 and the House by 174-14.

The only declared opponents at that moment are a small cluster of House Whigs led by John Quincy Adams, Hannibal Hamlin of Maine, and Jacob Brinkerhoff of Ohio who join the avowed abolitionist Joshua Giddings in labeling the conflict an "aggressive, unholy, unjust war."

TIME: MAY 1846

POLK ORGANIZES HIS FORCES AS THE CONFLICT BEGINS

When war is declared against Mexico, America's army is weak. Despite its actual and often anticipated conflicts with Britain, the notion of a large standing army is still seen by many Americans as a potential threat to preserving the nation's democracy. Should war break out, the fighting is to be done by a volunteer militia, led by a small Regular Army corps.

Since 1802, officers for the army corps are trained at the U.S. Military Academy in

West Point, NY. But the academy is modestly funded, with a total of only 59 graduates in the entire renowned class of 1846.

U.S. Military Academy at West Point

Meanwhile the U.S. Naval Academy at Annapolis, Maryland, has just opened its doors on October 10, 1845, as the brainchild of George Bancroft, Polk's Secretary of the Navy.

U.S. Naval Academy

On May 13, 1846, muster for the Regular Army stands at a mere 6,562 men comprising 14 regiments, with eight infantry, four artillery and two dragoons (mounted troops). To bolster this count, Polk asks Congress to fund an additional 50,000 volunteers.

On top of the need for more volunteers, Polk faces another challenge in deciding who should command his expeditionary army.

The obvious choice is Major General Winfield Scott, the ranking officer in the army since his June 1841 promotion. Scott is 59 when war is declared and has served his country since 1809. At 27, he had become a Brigadier General after being severely wounded at Lundy's Lane in the War of 1812. From there, he has been called upon by one president after another to oversee any and all military crises.

Polk's reservations about naming Scott to lead the troops in Mexico are political in nature.

Although the imposing 6 foot 5-inch General grew up on a Virginia plantation, he is an outspoken critic of slavery and a Whig who was considered for the presidency in 1840, before the nomination went to William Henry Harrison. Polk views him more as a political competitor than a military subordinate.

Given this, Polk decides to leave Brigadier General Zachary Taylor in command, since he is already in action on the Rio Grande and, unlike Scott, professes no interest in politics, at least so far.

TIME: MAY 3-8, 1846

THE OPENING BATTLE FOR FORT TEXAS

As the war begins, Taylor's initial strategy is two-fold:

- Meet and defeat the Mexican forces at the southern tip of the Rio Grande, and then move inland to the immediate west; and

- Send troops to occupy the northern provinces of New Mexico and Alta California so these can become U.S. territory when the conflict is over.

The hard fighting is under way for ten days before the official May 13 declaration passes Congress.

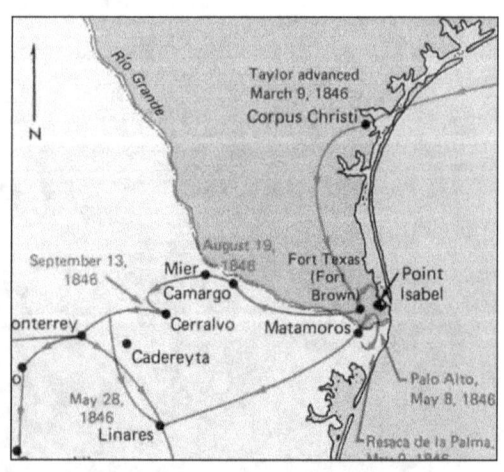

Map Showing Point Isabel, Ft. Texas and Matamoros

The first objective for the Mexicans is a star-shaped earthen defense outpost that Taylor's troops have built on the east side of the Rio Grande. It is christened Ft. Texas, and later re-named Ft. Brown, after the heroic major who falls there. It is occupied by only 500 U.S. troops when General Mariano Avista begins to shell it on May 3 from his side of the river in Matamoros. He then advances across the river, surrounds the fort, and begins an all-out siege.

After five days of steady bombardment, the fort is still holding out, when Taylor, stationed 22 miles away to the east at Fort Isabel, sets out with 2200 men and 150 wagons to relieve the pressure.

General Avista hears of the movement and pivots the troops he has north of Ft. Texas, heading out along the Point Isabel Road to intercept Taylor.

General Mariano Arista
(1802-1855)

TIME: MAY 8-9, 1846

TAYLOR WINS HIS FIRST VICTORIES AT PALO ALTO AND RESACA DE LA PALMA

Taylor is outnumbered by Avista – on the order of two to one – when the armies meet on May 8 on an open plain bordering the high chaparral, or shrub land, known as Palo Alto.

The action is particularly bloody, since neither side entrenches and there are no natural walls or fences to provide protection from artillery fire.

Over a five-hour period, repeated changes by the Mexican infantry and dragoons are repulsed by the American's "flying artillery," lightweight cannon with exploding shells maneuvered by horses to critical areas of the field. Avista finally abandons his at-

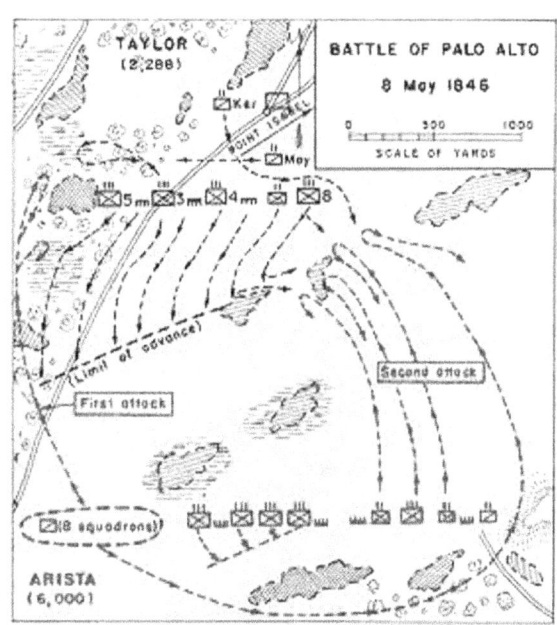

Map of Palo Alto Battlefield North of Ft. Texas

tack, with casualties upwards of 600 killed or wounded vs. Taylor's losses reported at 4 killed and 37 wounded.

On the morning of May 9, the Mexicans fall back in good order some five miles to defensive fortifications they had previously prepared along the Point Isabel road to Fort Texas. Taylor chases after him.

Fronting the Point Isabel road is an ancient run-off channel of the Rio Grande, known locally as Resaca de la Palma, a ravine with waist-deep water surrounded by palm trees and other shrubs. Arista locates his headquarters to the south while arraying his troops (in red on the maps) along the arc of the ravine, both west and east of the road.

His position is a strong one, and Taylor attacks it head on from the northwest. One of his young lieutenants, Ulysses S. Grant, describes his early assault as follows:

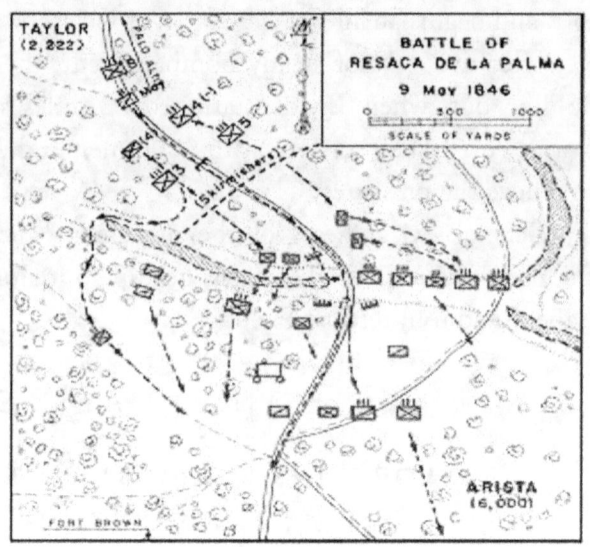

Map of Resaca De La Palma between Palo Alto and Ft. Texas

> I was with the right wing and led my company through the thicket wherever a penetrable place could be found…that would carry me to the enemy. At last I got pretty close up without knowing it. The balls commenced to whistle very thick overhead cutting the limbs of the chaparral left and right.

Another later-to-be-famous warrior, Lt. James Longstreet, offers his memories of the fight:

> After a considerable march the battalion came to the body of a young Mexican woman. This sad spectacle unnerved us a little, but the crush through the thorny bushes brought us back to thoughts of heavy work…All of the enemy's artillery opened, and soon his musketry. The lines closed in to short work, even to bayonet work at places…A pause was made to dip our cups for water, which gave a moment for other thoughts; mine went back to her whom I had left behind. I drew her daguerreotype from my breast pocket, had a glint of her charming smile, and with quickened spirit mounted the bank (ahead).

The Americans continue this "heavy work" against the Mexican lines throughout the afternoon. They finally break through after a small force under Captain Robert Buchanan flanks the defender's left wing and comes up in the rear of Arista's men. This surprise infiltration collapses the Mexican line, wins the battle. The Mexican army begins a panicked 200-mile retreat due west to their bastion at Monterrey.

During the two days of fighting, the Americans suffer 34 killed and 113 wounded, while the Mexicans lose over 1500 men, killed, wounded or drowned during flight, along with the capture of 7 major artillery pieces.

With these opening victories, the Americans secure the Rio Grande border, demonstrate their tactical superiority on the battlefield, and prepare to drive further west into the interior of Mexico.

Lt. Ulysses S. Grant (1822-1885)　　　　Lt. James Longstreet (1821-1904)

## 119

THE OREGON BOUNDARY DISPUTE WITH BRITAIN IS RESOLVED

TIME: 1800-1840

THE OREGON BOUNDARY LINES REMAIN IN DISPUTE

As the war with Mexico gets under way, Polk acts to resolve another long-standing territorial dispute, this time with Great Britain.

In question is a vast area in the Pacific Northwest, known to the Americans as the Oregon Country and to the British as the Columbia District of the Hudson Bay Trading Company.

Over time this land has played an important role in development of the fur trading industry.

America first enters the region in 1805, when Jeffer-

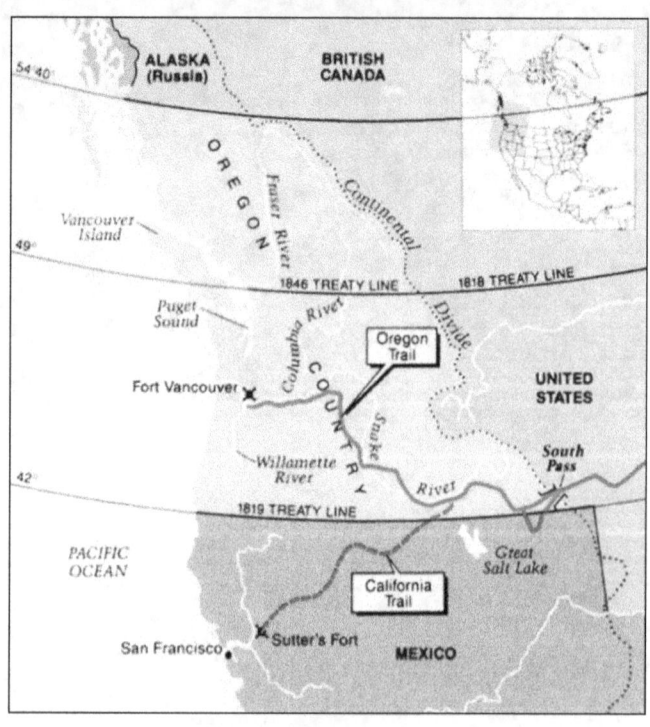

The Disputed Oregon Territory

son's Lewis & Clark expedition reaches the headwater of the Columbia River, where it empties into the Pacific. In 1811 a subsequent mission, funded by the tycoon, John Jacob Astor, arrives there and builds Ft. Astoria, a fur trading station servicing both Astor's Pacific Fur Company and another British competitor known as The North West Company.

The British seize Ft. Astoria during the War of 1812 and rename it Ft. George, until the 1814 Treaty of Ghent returns conditions to the status quo ante.

President James Monroe attempts to settle the Oregon borders with Britain during his first term.

In 1818 he tries to gain acceptance of the 49th parallel as the northern demarcation between Canada and the U.S., but Britain demands a line further south, for direct access to the Columbia River port. These talks end with a ten year "joint occupation" agreement allowing settlers from both countries to live side by side.

Monroe's negotiations with Spain over the southern border are more successful and the 1819 Adams-Onis Treaty sets the 42nd parallel as the boundary between the Oregon and Spanish California. (This is also the same treaty that sets the Texas line along the Nueces River, which Polk bemoans in his inaugural address.)

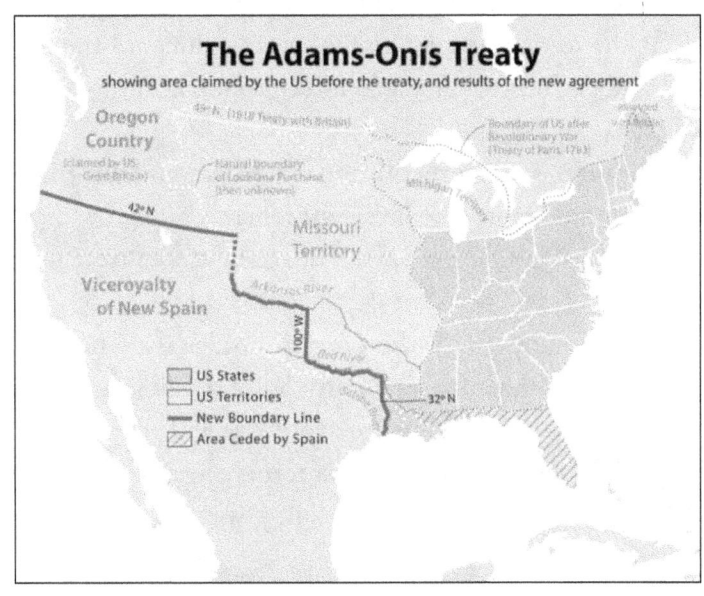

The 1819 Adams-Onis Treaty Borders with Spain

Over the next two decades, Oregon develops gradually, with Ft. Vancouver, 90 miles inland from Ft. Astoria, becoming the hub of the fur trade, and the Hudson Bay Company reasserting its dominance. The 1818 "joint occupation" bargain with Britain is extended in 1827.

But things begin to change in the early 1830s as the Oregon Trail becomes passable for pioneer families. American settlers flock into the region, build homesteads, and outnumber the British. Like the settlers in Texas, the Oregon population now looks to Washington to validate their land claims.

TIME: JUNE 18, 1846

POLK SECURES A FINAL TREATY ON OREGON WITH WHIG SUPPORT

The demands of the Oregon settlers are reflected in the Democratic Convention platform of 1844, and Polk himself reinforces them in his March 4, 1845 inaugural address:

Our title to the country of Oregon is 'clear and unquestionable' and already are our
people preparing to perfect that title by occupying it with their wives and children.

Once that assertion is made public, final resolution with Britain on the exact
northern boundary becomes a necessity.

A few Western hawks in Congress rally behind the slogan "fifty-four forty or fight," a
line that would gouge 300 miles north into British Canada. But Polk and his Southerners
hope to solve the issue without the war that would likely follow.

Early discussions with England go badly. Polk's "blustering announcement" in his
inaugural is booed roundly in the British parliament.

Things worsen with a clumsy July 16 letter from Secretary of State James Buchanan
to Sir Richard Packenham, which first reiterates America's right to the entirety of Oregon,
then backs off to a 49th parallel compromise in the "spirit of moderation." Packenham
rejects the terms outright, refuses even to forward the letter to Prime Minister Robert
Peel, and declines to offer a counter-proposal. In turn, Polk takes his initial proposal off
the table.

Within the cabinet, Polk and Buchanan go head-to-head with the Secretary calling
for accommodation. The President remains intent on staying silent and forcing Britain's
hand. As Young Hickory says, "The only way to treat John Bull is to look him straight
in the eye."

In December 1845, the Oregon border issue heats up in Congress, as westerners
again demand the Fifty-four Forty Solution. Southerners support the 49th parallel, and
Northerners simply wishing to avoid war with Britain. The debate in the House carries
over to the New Year, where a first term congressman from Ohio named John Cummins
articulates a vision for an America in possession of the Oregon country:

(Oregon) is the master key of the economic universe, with flourishing towns and
embryo cities (facing toward the Asian markets.) The commerce of the world would
thus be revolutionized...Britain must lose her commercial supremacy in the Pacific...
and (trading partners) must pay tribute to us.

On February 9, 1846, the House passes a bill calling on Polk to terminate the "joint
occupancy" agreement with Britain inside of one year – while also encouraging a new
border settlement that is amicable. When the bill goes to the Senate, the western wing
of the Democratic Party led by Lewis Cass and the southern wing led by Calhoun
clash, to Polk's dismay. This persists until April 23, when a re-written joint "termination"
directive passes the House 142-46 and the Senate 42-10.

Now the ball is back with the British, and a revised Parliament looks for resolution.
On June 3, a letter from Packenham proposes a 49th parallel solution, as long as British

settlers south of the line retain their lands, and access to the Columbia River is granted British ships. This breaks the stalemate, and on June 18, Polk sends a final treaty proposal to the Senate, which ratifies it by a 41-14 vote.

Remarkably, all 23 Whig senators support Polk's measure – unlike his own Democrats who remain split.

Cass of Michigan is opposed to the compromise border. He is joined by other westerners including Atchison of Missouri, both senators from Illinois (Breese and Semple) and from Indiana (Hannegan and Bright), along with William Allen of Ohio, chairman of the Foreign Relations Committee, who resigns his post in protest.

COMPOSITION OF SENATE VOTES ON THE OREGON BILL

	SUPPORT	OPPOSE
DEMOCRATS	18	14
WHIGS	23	0

By early June 1846, Polk declares victory on his promise to resolve Oregon, a move that adds a full 10% to America's total land mass.

## 120

POLK GETS HIS TARIFF BILL APPROVED

TIME: 1828-1845

TARIFF RATES CONTINUE TO CAUSE NORTH-SOUTH FRICTION

U.S. Treasury Department

For the hard-charging President Polk, the first three months in office have been a whirlwind, although he remains determined to complete all his identified objectives in one term.

On June 18, 1846 he has settles the border dispute over Oregon, and his forays into Texas and Alta California are progressing well. Now, he decides to tackle nagging issues related to tariffs.

In 1828, Polk was a second term member of the U.S. House when the "Tariff of

Abominations" bill – cynically designed to undermine the South's political opponents – backfired on John C. Calhoun, and was signed into law. It doubled the tax on imported goods to an average of 45%.

For the nascent New England manufacturers, this high tariff on imported goods such as cotton, wool and pig iron provides marketplace "protection" by keeping their retail prices in line with what is offered by their competition – the larger and hence more efficiently run factories in Europe.

The West also favors the higher rates, since they stand to benefit disproportionately from increases in the government's infrastructure spending that will follow.

FEDERAL SPENDING ON INTERNAL IMPROVEMENTS (1820-29)

REGION	% SPENDING	% POPULATION
North	49%	47%
South	19	40
West	32	13

Malone (1998)/Douglas Irwin

Meanwhile Southern planters are outraged by the negative effects of the tariff on their cotton industry. This leads to the attempt by South Carolina to "nullify" the law and Jackson's "Force Bill" threating to send in troops to ensure compliance.

Jackson lowers the rates in 1830, only to have the "protectionists" drive them back up in 1832.

The Compromise of 1833 delivers a framework that holds up well until 1842. It focuses on all imported goods currently being taxed at high rates and imposes a formula for gradual yearly reductions to adjust them down to a 20% target by 1842.

But when 1842 arrives, the Whigs have taken control in Congress, and, despite two vetoes by Tyler, Henry Clay's so-called "Black Tariff" drives the levies back up to roughly 40%.

TIME: JULY 28, 1846

CONGRESS PASSES THE "WALKER TARIFF OF 1846"

As a congressman, Polk experiences all of this regional turmoil, and hopes to never see it repeated.

He believes – with good cause – that America's manufacturing sector is now well established, and no longer in need of "protection" from the federal government. At the same time, however, he recognizes that tariff revenues continue to supply upwards of two-thirds of all money coming into DC. These funds will now be needed to carry on the Mexican War, in addition to further infrastructure projects.

Polk charges his Treasury Secretary, Robert Walker, with arriving at a new tariff bill that lowers the tariff while striking a proper balance between the financial needs of the nation and the political needs of his Democrat party.

The "Walker Tariff of 1846" breaks imported goods into five classes, assigning staggered rate to each, from a high of 100% to a low on 0%, reserved for coffee and tea. The historically most fought-over items fall into the "C-Class" (iron, other metals, wood, glass, paper, wool, woolens, leather) taxed at 30%, and the "D-Class" (including cotton) at 25%.

The Bill breezes through the House but ends in a tie 27-yea vs. 27-nay vote in the Senate – and only due to a last-ditch effort by the Governor of Tennessee to convince Whig Senator Spencer Jarnigan to vote "yes."

Responsibility for breaking the tie falls on the shoulders of Polk's Vice-President, George Dallas, of Pennsylvania. Dallas plans to run for President in 1850 and knows that his backing in New England will erode if he supports the lower tariff. Still, as a Democrat, he has no real choice in the matter. He votes "aye" on July 28, 1846, and the Walker Tariff becomes the law of the land. It will survive until 1857 when rates are further reduced to 17% on average.

## 121

AMERICANS OCCUPY CALIFORNIA AND NEW MEXICO

TIME: SUMMER 1846

TENSIONS RISE FOR AMERICAN SETTLERS LIVING IN ALTA CALIFORNIA

Polk is pleased by General Taylor's victories south of the Rio Grande in the Spring of 1846, but his sights remain set on acquiring all of the land identified the year before, in November 1845, when he sent Congressman John Slidell to negotiate with the Mexicans.

He is particularly focused on Alta California, the upper part of the province, sparsely populated by Mexicans and largely ignored by their civil government. Included are the ports of San Francisco and Los Angeles and the surrounding valleys where clusters of American settlers have already put down roots.

"Mountain men" like Joseph Walker, who explores the region in 1832 along with the Paris-born, West Point graduate, Benjamin Bonneville; Isaac Graham, who opens a

John C. Fremont (1813-1890)

distillery in 1836 and tries to form up a Texas-style Republic; and Johan Suter (later John Sutter), a German immigrant, who travels the Oregon Trail to the west coast, takes on Mexican citizenship, and opens a fort bearing his name 90 miles northeast of

San Francisco. By 1845, Ft. Sutter is well-known locally as a resting place for weary pioneers. Two years later it becomes world famous when gold is discovered on the land.

As customary, Polk acts aggressively on his goals – expanding the scope of the war beyond the border of Texas and over to Mexican territory on the west coast.

He sends American warships to blockade the Pacific coast ports and orders Colonel Stephen B. Kearney to march from Kansas toward Alta California. Kearney, 50, began his military career in the War of 1812, has explored the West, and earned fame as the "father of the U.S. Cavalry" for his decades of service protecting settlers across the Great Plains. Kearny rides out of Leavenworth on June 3, with 1700 men and his immediate sights are set on reaching Santa Fe, 750 miles to the west.

Before he gets that far, Polk's quest for control of California is almost resolved through the actions of a band of local settlers around Sacramento, aided by the western adventurer, Captain John C. Fremont.

Together, Kearney and Fremont engineer a military filibuster known thereafter as the Bear Flag Revolt.

TIME: JUNE - JULY 1846

AMERICA SEIZES ALTA CALIFORNIA IN THE "BEAR FLAG REVOLT"

On June 8, 1846, Fremont, Kit Carson and a band of 55 armed troopers encamp at Sutter Butte, in the Sacramento Valley, near Yuba City.

They have arrived after Fremont's third expedition – mapping the route of the Arkansas River – has morphed into a year-long journey into the Oregon Country and then down into Alta California, where he makes contact with American settlers in the region.

The Mexicans regard Fremont as a nuisance and chase him back into Oregon. But as word reaches Fremont of possible hostilities, he re-positions his troops back in the valley.

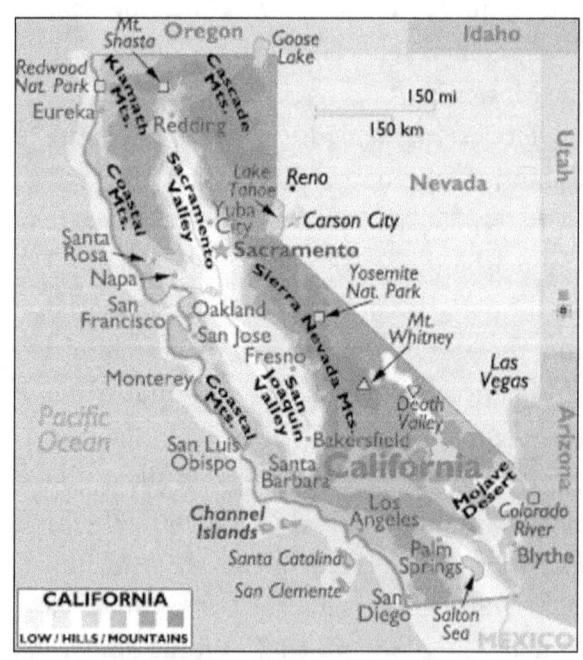

Map Showing the Sacramento Valley, Yuba City And San Francisco

I saw the way opening clear before me. War with Mexico was inevitable; and a grand opportunity presented itself to realize in their fullest extent the far-sighted views of Senator Benton. I resolved to move forward on the opportunity and return forthwith to the Sacramento valley in order to bring to bear all the influence I could command.

Once there, Fremont is approached by a band of local Americans led by William Ide and Ezekiel Merritt, who claim that Mexican troops are about to drive all foreign settlers out of Sacramento. They ask Fremont if he would be willing to support them in establishing a Texas-like republic.

Evidently Fremont encourages them to proceed, but without committing his own troopers to any action.

Ide and Merritt plunge forward, assembling and equipping their own thirty-man posse and head back toward San Francisco to launch a military-style filibuster.

On June 14, 1846, they arrive at the sleepy Mexican outpost in Sonoma, 45 miles north of the port city, and surround the home of General Mariano Vallejo, "Commandante of Northern California." They arrest both Vallejo and his brother, and declare Alta California's new status as an independent nation.

The Commander in Chief of the Troops assembled at the Fortress of Sonoma… declares his object to…defend himself and companions in arms who were invited to this country by a promise of Lands on which to settle themselves and families, and who were also promised a "republican government," (but) when arriving in California were denied even the privilege of buying or renting Lands of their friends… and instead of being allowed to participate in or being protected by a "Republican Government" were oppressed by a "Military Despotism."

A white bedsheet serves as their makeshift flag, painted across the top with the outline of a California grizzly bear and a single red star, mimicking Texas.

On July 1, the "Bear Flag" rebels, now under Fremont's direct leadership, reach San Francisco and occupy the Presidio compound, which is undefended. At first, they raise their banner over the works, but within days it is replaced by the stars and stripes. This ends the brief history of the "Bear Flag Revolt" and begins the de facto seizure of Alta California from the Mexicans.

## 122

THE WILMOT PROVISO IS AN EXISTENTIAL THREAT TO THE SOUTH

TIME: AUGUST 8, 1846

WILMOT'S PROVISO SIGNALS A NEW CRISIS

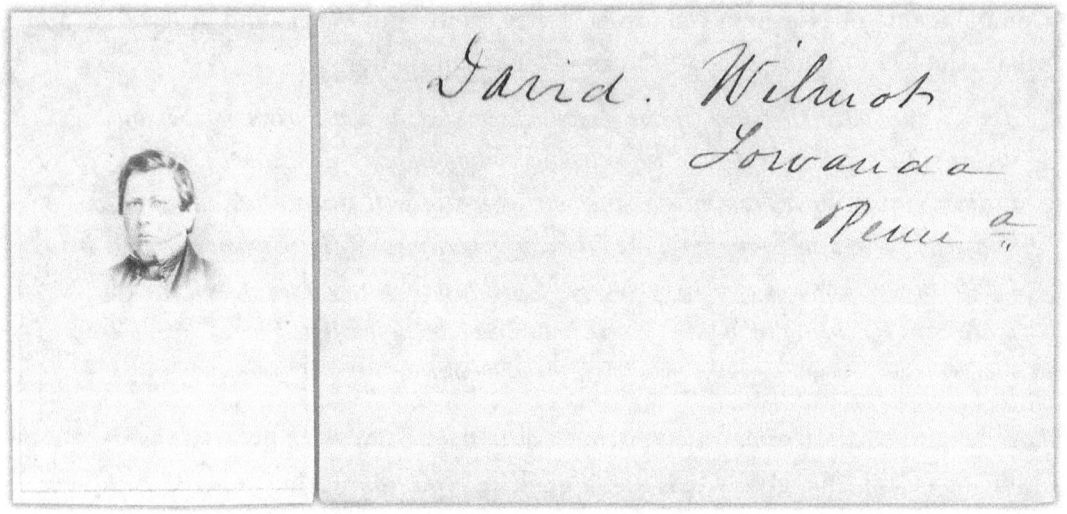

Congressman David Wilmot (1814-1868) and Signature –
whose 1846 "Proviso" Helped Spark The Civil War

Polk is enjoying a remarkable string of victories when everything he has accomplished is suddenly threatened by a crisis in the U.S House.

The impetus here is a straight forward appropriations bill to set aside $2 million to fund the Mexican War, which the President hopes to pass in the final two days before the 29th Congress adjourns for recess.

Polk fully expects the bill to prompt the usual criticism of the war from his Whig opponents, and this occurs when the New Yorker, Hugh White, says the conflict is a Southern plot to "extend the limits of slavery" into the west. He promises to vote against funding the war unless the language in the bill...

Forever precludes the possibility of extending the limits of slavery…and I call upon the other side to propose such an amendment…as evidence of their desire to restrain that institution within it constitutional limits.

The next member to speak is first term Democrat congressman David Wilmot, representing the 12th district of Pennsylvania.

Wilmot is only 32 years old, but imposing in stature, sporting a chaw of tobacco, and ever ready to buck the system on behalf of speaking his mind. After being recognized by the Speaker as a likely-to-be friendly voice in the storm, Wilmot announces that he will support Polk's bill, but only if a "proviso" is added.

Provided, That, as an express and fundamental condition to the acquisition of any territory from the Republic of Mexico by the United States, by virtue of any treaty which may be negotiated between them, and to the use by the Executive of the moneys herein appropriated, neither slavery nor involuntary servitude shall ever exist in any part of said territory, except for crime, whereof the party shall first be duly convicted.

His fellow Democrats are stunned by his declaration!

When asked to explain his amendment, he says that he voted for the Texas annexation, and has no moral qualms over slavery, nor any wish to abolish it. Rather his intent is simply to preserve "free soil" out west in order to "uphold the dignity of white men's labor."

I would preserve for free white labor a fair country, a rich inheritance where the sons of toil of my own race and color, can live without the disgrace which association with negro slavery brings upon free labor….If free territory comes in, God forbid that I should be the means of planting this institution upon it.

In this moment Wilmot offers up a new rationale for opposing slavery.

It is directed at upholding the value of white men's labor, not ending the black man's suffering.

To achieve this end, it flat out prohibits any further spread of slavery.

As such it is the worst nightmare for Polk and the men of the South – and it originates with a Democrat!

TIME: 1844-1846

THE COMPLEX ROOTS OF REBELLION AMONG NORTHERN DEMOCRATS

Once Wilmot's shocking Proviso is out in the open, Polk's supporters scurry to identify its origin and to determine just how much support it has, especially within the Democrat Party.

What they learn is deeply distressing.

Wilmot's dissent is widely shared among Northern Democrats, and aimed at Polk and the Southern wing of the party. Its origins trace all the way back to the 1844 Nominating Convention, where many feel that Van Buren was robbed of his chance for a second term.

Much of it is concentrated in New York, especially among men "Van Buren men" like Senator John Dix and Governor Silas Wright.

They are joined by others, including Preston King of New York, Hannibal Hamlin of Maine and Jacob Brinkerhoff of Ohio, who go beyond sheer political animosity and see a Southern cabal at work, one determined to take over the party and put a pro-slavery man in the White House who will back their regional agenda.

Hannibal Hamlin (1809-1891   Preston King (1806-1865

This opposition group becomes known as the "Barnburner Democrats," accused by other members of being more willing to destroy the party than to back the President. Indeed many will assert that it is actually Brinkerhoff or Preston, rather than Wilmot, who pens the August 8 Proviso in the first place.

Other factors also play into this notion that the "Slave Power" has co-opted the Democrat Party, to the detriment of Northern interests.

Two powerful Democratic senators, Lewis Cass of Michigan and William Allen of Ohio, have led the "Fifty-four forty or fight" cry to occupy all of the Oregon Country. When Polk compromises with Britain on the 49th parallel boundary, the suggestion is that he will fight for slave territory in Texas, but not for free land in Oregon.

Then there is the Walker Tariff, perceived by many Northerners as a reduction in rates to satisfy the planters of the South at the expense of manufacturing in the east and added infrastructure in the west.

Finally comes the widening of the war against Mexico, no longer confined to disputed land within Texas, but now extending across the Southwest and opening the way to a host of new slave states.

Out of these combined grievances a sizable group of Northern Democrats in the House decide that it is time to send a signal to their Southern colleagues that their interests will not be ignored.

And what better way than to threaten the one thing the Southerners want most – the extension of slave plantations west of the Mississippi.

TIME: AUGUST 8, 1846

THE WILMOT PROVISO PASSES IN THE HOUSE

With time nearing on a final vote, House Democrats scramble to find an option to the Wilmot Proviso.

The main attempt comes from the Indiana Democrat William Wick, who offers up an alternative solution for all new land west of the Mississippi.

Wick's proposal is one that will be heard over and over in Congress between 1846 and the collapse of the Union in 1861.

Instead of a universal ban on slavery in the new Territories, why not simply extend the old 36'30" Missouri Compromise line to the Pacific, with states falling south of the line allowing slavery and north of the line prohibiting it. That solved the conflict in 1820 and why shouldn't it work again in 1846.

The answer in the House is a resounding "no." Wick's proposal goes down by an 89-54 margin.

At this point it becomes clear that the usual political calculus has broken down.

The rejection is not a matter of a split along traditional party lines, as in unified Democrats against unified Whigs.

Instead *both parties are split along regional lines* – with Northern members favoring Wilmot's ban on extending slavery and Southerners in opposition.

Once this division is clear, Southern forces in the House try to stall. The floor debate continues into the evening, with procedural votes taken on the wording of the Proviso and then on whether to table consideration of the bill until the House reconvenes in December. Both attempts fail.

At last, Polk's Appropriation Bill with the Wilmot Proviso added comes to a vote. It passes by a narrow margin of 85-80, with only small differences showing up in total between Democrats and Whigs.

HOUSE VOTE ON APPROPRIATION BILL WITH THE WILMOT PROVISO ADDED

REGION	DEMOCRATS YES - NO	WHIGS YES - NO	AMERICAN YES - NO	TOTAL YES – NO
Northeast	37 - 0	24 - 6	5 - 0	66 - 6
Northwest	15 - 4	2 - 2		17 - 6
Border	0 - 9	2 - 9		2 - 18
Southeast	0 - 27	0 - 7		0 - 34
Southwest	0 - 15	0 - 1		0 - 16
Total	52 - 55	28 - 25	5 - 0	85 - 80
Not Voting	(32)	(23)	(1)	(56)

VoteView/Library of Congress Records

But looked at along regional lines, the final vote shows that Northern members support Wilmot by 83-12 while Southerners oppose it 68-2.

NORTH VS. SOUTH SPLIT OVER THE WILMOT PROVISO: AUGUST 8, 1846

REGION	DEMOCRATS YES - NO	WHIGS YES - NO	AMERICAN YES - NO	TOTAL YES - NO
North	52 - 4	26 - 8	5 - 0	83 - 12
South	0 - 51	2 - 17	-- - --	2 - 68
Total	52 - 55	28 - 25	5 - 0	85 - 80

This outcome is NOT about a moral judgment on slavery, NOT about conscience-stricken Northern whites wishing to end the suffering of Southern slaves.

Rather it is a direct shot by Northerners in both parties across the bow of Polk and the South. It expresses their wish to reserve any new territory in the west for the exclusive benefit of white settlers — unencumbered by the prospect of rich planters trying to buy the best acreage, and black slaves who would erode the "dignity" of their labor, threaten the safety of their families, and diminish the social fabric.

As such, the Wilmot Proviso represents an irreversible line in the sand between Southerners and those in the North and West.

TIME: AUGUST 10, 1846

SOUTHERNERS FINALLY STALL THE WILMOT PROVISO IN THE SENATE

After the House passes the Wilmot Proviso, all that's left for the Southern coalition to try to delay a vote in the Senate, until the clock runs out toward recess of the 29th congress on August 10.

This strategy works, despite a filibustering effort by the Massachusetts Senator "Honest John" Davis to force a vote.

On August 10 both chambers adjourn, leaving Polk without approval of his $2million appropriation request to fund the war, and the Northerners without approval of their Wilmot Proviso.

Still, a clear-cut message from the North to the South has been delivered.

The astute Southern leader, John Calhoun, sums it up as follows:

- The North now enjoys a commanding majority of the votes in the House;
- The Wilmot measure shows that the North intends to stop the spread of slavery to the west;
- The South can no longer count on unwavering support for their cause from Northern Democrats;
- Nor does it have a ready-made solution in extending the old 36'20" compromise line.

Unless some new accommodation between the two sections can be found, disunion will be inevitable.

As usual, the South Carolina man accurately foretells the future.

From August 10, 1846 onward, the leaders of congress will begin a 15 year search for a new accommodation capable of holding the nation together.

In the end, they will fail.

TIME: AUGUST 1846 FORWARD

THE PROFOUND IMPLICATIONS OF THE PASSAGE OF THE WILMOT PROVISO

This vote on the Wilmot Proviso will become a watershed moment in the eventual dissolution of the Union.

It expresses a flat "no" to Southern plans to extend slavery west of the Mississippi, even under the 34'30" line set in the 1820 Missouri Compromise.

It also initiates a dramatic shift in the number of whites willing to stand against the further spread of slavery.

Before Wilmot, this is largely confined to a small eastern band of so-called "radical abolitionists."

After Wilmot, one need not be a "radical" to want to pen slavery up in the South.

That's because of a new battle cry – "free soil for free men" – that will soon catch fire in the North and West.

It adds two pragmatic reasons against expanding slavery that go beyond mere anti-black racism and fear.

The first is that land prices for western settlers will go way up if average white farmers have to compete with rich plantation owners in the bidding.

The second is more subtle, but every bit as powerful.

It taps into America's long-standing embrace of the "Protestant work ethic" – the belief that with hard labor comes both dignity and monetary rewards. But, as Wilmot argues, both suffer when blacks are doing the same work as white men, but for free. He calls this a "disgrace" – with white labor diminished to the level of slave labor.

If the value of white labor in America is to be preserved, it must not exist side by side with slave labor.

From this notion new political movements will soon take hold, the Free Soilers, the Know-Nothing Nativists, and eventually the Republican Party. All dedicated to preserving the new western land for white men.

When the South balks at this outcome, it will be branded by more and more Northerners as "the Slavocracy"—forever prioritizing the self-interest of its rich plantation elites over the good of the white settlers.

The savvy abolitionist Lloyd Garrison quickly recognizes the power of this new theme and the Wilmot Proviso votes to serve his own ends, characterizing it as "the beginning of the end of our fight." to.

## 123

THE WAR WITH MEXICO PICKS UP MOMENTUM

TIME: AUGUST 15 - SEPTEMBER 21, 1846

SANTA FE IS CAPTURED AND THE BATTLE FOR MONTERREY BEGINS

While the "Bear Flag" land grab is playing out in California during June-July 1846, further U.S. incursions into Mexico are under way.

On August 15, 1846, General Stephen Kearny captures Sante Fe, the capital of the province of New Mexico, without firing a shot.

At the same time, General Taylor is heading west at a leisurely pace in pursuit of the Mexican army, which he defeated at Resaca de la Palma back in April.

He will find it in September, holed up at Monterrey, an enclave of 10,000 inhabitants, and the capital of Nuevo Leone province.

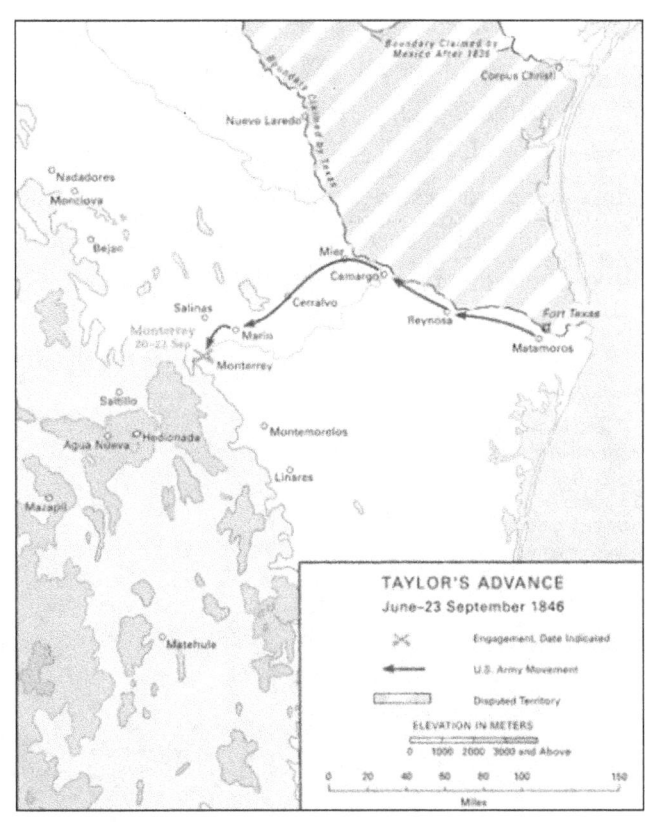

Map of Taylor's Route From Matamoros To Monterrey

The city sits in a valley surrounded on two sides by the 4,000 foot peaks of the Mitre mountains, with the Santa Catarina River running along its eastern and southern flanks. Its location along the main road through the mountains toward Saltillo makes it strategically important to the westward advance of Zachary Taylor's army—and knowing this, General Pedro Ampudia, who has now replaced Avista, decides to defend Monterrey.

In addition to its natural advantages in terrain, Monterrey is also well protected by a series of redoubts and stone buildings that dot the roads in from the northeast. General Ampudia concentrates his 9,000 troops across these fortifications, and confidently awaits the Americans.

Taylor, however, pauses for several weeks after his opening victories, and it is not until June 12 that he sends Ben McCulloch and his Texas Rangers out to scout the whereabouts of the Mexican army. When Taylor learns they are dug in at Monterrey, he sets three divisions and some 6600 troops in motion under Generals William Worth, David Twiggs and John Quitman. They arrive in early September and begin to plan their strategy.

Lacking heavy artillery, Taylor knows that he must assault rather than siege Monterrey. After studying the ground, he settles on a daring two-prong attack. Quitman and Twiggs will send the bulk of the army headlong at the heavily defended fortresses north and east of the city. Worth and 1700 men will swing west 7 miles under cover and arrive in the enemy's rear on the Saltillo road, cutting off the Mexican's supply and escape routes. If practicable, Worth will then launch a surprise attack against the more lightly defended western edge of the city. On September 20, Worth's flanking movement secures the Saltillo road, after a brief cavalry battle. Mexico's northern army is now effectively trapped in Monterrey as Taylor's assault begins on September 21.

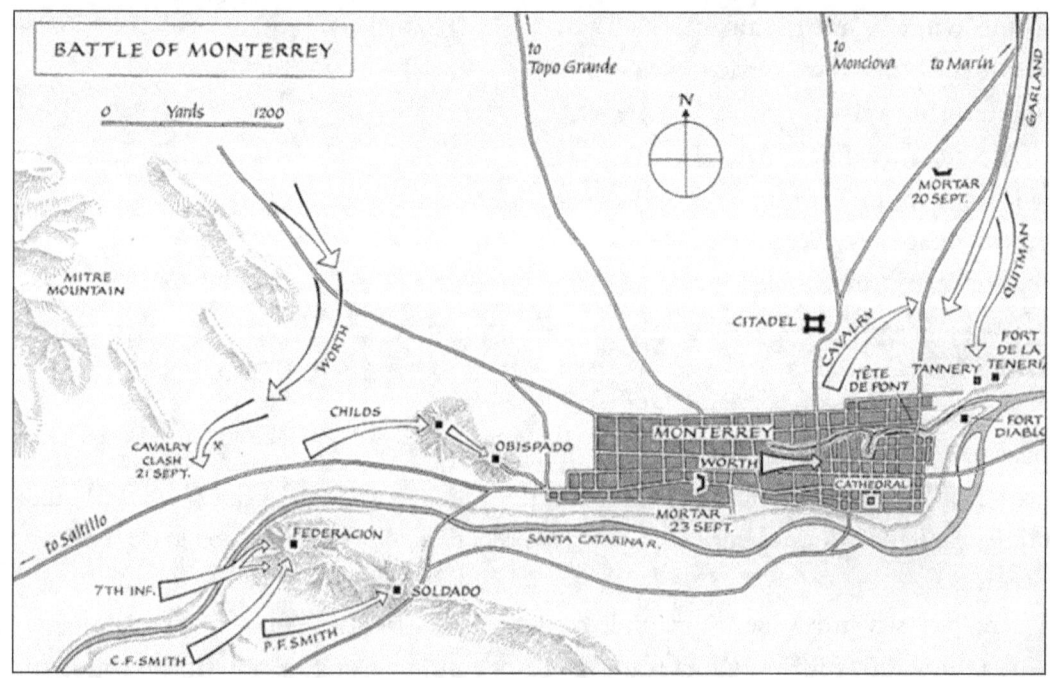

Zachary Taylor's Attack on Monterrey

Colonel John Garland, leading Twigg's division, opens the battle against the eastern fortifications, with support from Mississippi and Tennessee units under Quitman and Colonel Jefferson Davis. They capture Fort de al Teneria and the bridge leading over the river to Ft. Diablo. Ohio troops under General Butler join the attack on Diablo, but it is successfully defended throughout the day by General Ampudia's forces. After ferocious street to street combat the Americans have gained a solid toehold on the eastern side of the city by nightfall.

Progress to the west is even greater, with the hero of the day being Captain Charles F. Smith, who leads his four companies up a spur of Mt. Mitre known as Federacion Hill, drives off the Mexican defenders, and turns decisive artillery fire down on the city. As

Brvt Colonel Charles F. Smith
(1807-1862)

the first day of battle to the west ends, General Worth is poised to invade Monterrey from the west.

TIME: SEPTEMBER 22-24, 1846

MONTERREY FALLS TO TAYLOR

Overnight, General Ampudia decides to consolidate his two wings in the center of the city. He abandons Ft. Diablo, and draws back all his forces to the Cathedral and Central Plaza area, for a last stand.

At daybreak on September 23, General Quitman and a force of Texas Rangers resume their advance on Ft. Diablo and, finding it empty, race past it into the city, with shouts of "Alamo and Goliad" ringing through the streets. Taylor, however, is unaware of their breakthrough, and orders them to hold for the moment.

Meanwhile, General Worth hears the early sounds of battle and sends his troops forward to capture the western end of the city and envelop the remaining Mexicans. They quickly take the Bishop's Palace outpost and begin house to house fighting.

General John Quitman
(1798-1858)

By nightfall Worth has reached to within one block of the Plaza, and is in contact with Quitman and his troops, now nearby. The fates of the Mexican army and of the city of Monterrey are sealed – and General Ampudia knows it. On the night of September 23, he approaches General Worth for "terms of surrender."

The agreement he finally works out with General Taylor is so stunning in its generosity that when word filters back to Washington, Polk wants to relieve Taylor of his command, despite the victory.

In return for ceding all public property in Monterrey to the Americans, Ampudia is allowed to evacuate his army, along with its small arms, within seven days, and any further conflict is suspended for the next six weeks.

While Taylor has lost 500 soldiers in the battle, to over 1,000 for the enemy, he is evidently so convinced that the Mexican army is defeated once and for all that he allows it to walk off the field in another retreat west.

Five months later he will realize that this calculation was not quite right.

SIDEBAR: MILESTONES IN TAYLOR'S INVASION THROUGH TEXAS

TAYLOR'S 190 MILE DRIVE FROM MATAMOROS TO MONTERREY

DATE	EVENTS
April 24, 1846	Taylor attacked along the Rio Grande
May 9	Taylor victory at Resaca de la Palma
May 13	Official declaration of war
May 18	Taylor occupies Matamoros
June – July	California taken in Bear Flag Revolt
August 15	Kearney secures New Mexico
September 24	Taylor victory at Monterrey

TIME: WINTER 1846

POLK'S CABINET DEBATES WAR STRATEGY AND COMMANDERS

Ever since General Zachary Taylor's troops are first attacked along the Rio Grande on April 25, 1846, the conflict with Mexico has all gone the American's way. His northern army, under Kearney, has planted the American flag from Santa Fe through California, and Taylor's central force has driven inland to capture Monterrey.

The only thing lacking so far is a formal capitulation by the Mexican government and a treaty resolving final ownership of the conquered lands. Various emissaries from Mexico hint at this resolution, but so far it remains simply a wish.

So the question becomes one of what it will take to bring the war to closure. This topic is hotly debated within Polk's cabinet. As usual, the President is clear about his preference – to expand the invasion until the enemy gives in.

His cabinet, led by the ever bothersome Secretary of State, James Buchanan, and the War minister, William Marcy, object to his proposal for three reasons:

- A broader invasion will extend the fighting and produce more agitation in Congress;
- They do not believe that General Winfield Scott is up to the task of leading the troops; and
- Both Scott and Taylor are Whigs who might run for president in 1848.

Polk floats out the possibility of promoting Senator Benton of Missouri to Lieutenant General, ranking Scott and taking overall command in the field, but he backs off when others resist. It's now clear that whatever future course the war takes, Scott will remain the lead general.

As the cabinet ponders options to end the war, critics begin to assert that Polk's hidden intent is to conquer all of Mexico, absorb it into the United States, and reinstitute slavery, banned there in 1829.

Polk flatly rejects these charges and insists that all future decisions about slavery in new territory acquired from the war will be left to the will of the settlers, as they write their state constitutions.

But this assurance isn't enough for the skeptics in congress – who again wave the Wilmot proviso in the face of the President and the Southerners.

TIME: WINTER 1846

GENERAL SCOTT ANNOUNCES HIS PLAN

As political controversies over the war swirl about Washington, all eyes look toward the 61 year old General Winfield Scott for his plan to resolve the conflict.

Scott is a Southerner by birth and grows up on a Petersburg, Virginia plantation. He briefly attends the College of William & Mary, studies and practices law, then enlists in the Virginia militia. He comes to fame in the War of 1812, in the back and forth battles around Lake Ontario. He is wounded twice in the fighting, first as a Colonel, while capturing Ft. George, and later as a Brigadier General, near Niagara Falls at the Battle of Lundy's Lane. For his heroism, he is made a Brevet Major General at age 27. But the bullet wound to his left shoulder leaves him with a partially paralyzed arm, and he is unable to resume field duty.

After the 1812 War, Scott studies military strategy in France, writes various military manuals on drilling and tactics, and continues to advance his career. President Jackson calls on him to help put down the Nullification threat in 1832, to fight the Seminoles in 1836, to relocate the Cherokees in 1838. He becomes the ranking officer in the army in 1845, as a full Major General.

Scott is an enormous man, standing 6'5" and weighing over 250 lbs. His manner is imperious; he is a stickler for discipline; and he constantly decks himself out in elaborate uniforms. Hence the nickname, "Old Fuss and Feathers." Polk regards him in 1847 as a man filled with "arrogance and inordinate vanity."

General Winfield Scott
(1786-1866)

Nevertheless, the General finally steps forward with a plan to win the war. He will assemble and personally lead an invasion force of some 14,000 troops, capture the port city of Veracruz, then march overland to overwhelm and occupy the capital of Mexico City.

Polk reluctantly adopts the plan, and orders go out for Taylor to hold his position at Monterrey, while detaching the bulk of his army to join up with Scott's invasion force.

The fate of the President's war now rest in the hands of two Whig Generals, both of whom he distrusts as military commanders and as potential political opponents of his Democratic Party.

## 124

CONGRESS DEBATES THE MORALITY AND IMPLICATIONS OF THE MEXICAN WAR

TIME: DECEMBER 7, 1846

POLK TRIES TO STEM DIVISIVENESS IN HIS ANNUAL ADDRESS TO CONGRESS

Polk's words show that he is clearly alarmed by the House vote on the Wilmot Proviso, which leaves him without funding for the war and with disunity in his own party over the future expansion of slavery.

The slavery question is assuming a fearful and most important aspect.

When the second and final session of the 29th Congress reconvenes on December 7, 1846, his Annual Message first attempts to align all sides behind his war efforts. His address begins with reassurances that the intent of the war is not to annihilate Mexico, and that the wish is end it as soon as the enemy will accept peace terms.

James K. Polk (1795-1849)

In my (last) annual message...I declared that —The war has not been waged with a view to conquest, but, having been commenced by Mexico, it has been carried into the enemy's country and will be vigorously prosecuted there with a view to obtain an honorable peace.... It has never been contemplated by me, as an object of the war, to make a permanent conquest of the Republic of Mexico or to annihilate her separate existence as an independent nation....Whilst our armies have advanced from victory to victory from the commencement of the war, it has always been with the olive branch of peace in their hands, and it has been in the power of Mexico at every step to arrest hostilities by accepting it.

He then turns to the delicate topic of slavery, not mentioning it explicitly, rather choosing to invoke the memory of George Washington and his warnings about geographical divisiveness as a threat to the Union.

(Washington) that greatest and best of men foresaw.. the danger to our Union of "characterizing parties by geographical discriminations--Northern and Southern, Atlantic and Western--whence designing men may endeavor to excite a belief that there is a real difference of local interests and views," and warned his countrymen against it.

So deep and solemn was his conviction of the importance of the Union and of preserving harmony between its different parts, that he declared to his countrymen in that address: It is of infinite moment that you should properly estimate the immense value of your national union to your collective and individual happiness; that you indignantly frown upon the first dawning of every attempt to alienate any portion of our country from the rest or to enfeeble the sacred ties which now link together the various parts.

After the lapse of half a century these admonitions of Washington fall upon us with all the force of truth.

From there he boldly attempts to dismiss the battle over the Wilmot Proviso as nothing more than "differences of opinion upon minor questions of public policy."

It is difficult to estimate the "immense value" of our glorious Union... How unimportant are all our differences of opinion upon minor questions of public policy compared with its preservation, and how scrupulously should we avoid all agitating topics which may tend to distract and divide us into contending parties, separated by geographical lines, whereby it may be weakened or endangered.

Polk's message on December 7, 1846 is one that both he and his immediate successors will wish to believe – that sectional resistance to the presence of Africans, either slave or free, west of the Mississippi is a nothing more than a minor diversion.

Going forward, Congress should simply "avoid (these) agitating topics which may tend to distract and divide" the country.

TIME: JANUARY 16, 1847

THE HOUSE DEBATES LEGAL PRECEDENTS FOR DECLARING OREGON A "FREE STATE"

Despite Polk's plea, the political jockeying over extending slavery into new western territory resumes early in the new session.

The initial focus is not the Southwest, but rather the Oregon Territory.

While all sides agree that Oregon should be declared a "Free State," they argue over the legal basis for the call.

The rationale cannot be the Wilmot Proviso, since Oregon is acquired in the June 1846 treaty with Britain, and does not involve territory associated with the Mexican War.

But why then should Oregon have Free State status?

Southern members, led by Calhoun's man, Armistead Burt of South Carolina assert that the

Hannibal Hamlin (1809-1891)

precedent should be the 1820 Missouri Compromise, simply extending the 34'30" line to the west coast. This is the same proposal offered six months earlier by Indiana's William Wick and supported by Stephen Douglas.

Again it meets resistance. Congressman Hannibal Hamlin of Maine, an outspoken abolitionist, says that the Missouri line "has no more application to the territory of Oregon than it has with the East Indies."

A contrived rationale finally emerges around the 1797 Northwest Ordinance ban on slavery, and it musters enough votes to ram the bill through a still rebellious House, on January 16, 1847.

The bill declaring Oregon a Free State goes on to the Senate, where it is immediately tabled.

TIME: FEBRUARY 11, 1847

TOM CORWIN WARNS OF THE DAMAGE TO FOLLOW FROM THE MEXICAN WAR

The next volley over slavery comes when the Senate turns to a modified request from Polk for funds to prosecute the war with Mexico.

The ante has now risen from $2 million to $3 million, as it becomes clear that a more substantial invasion will be required to force an end to the fighting.

The leading spokesman for the Whigs is the ex-Governor now Senator from Ohio, Tom Corwin.

Corwin addresses his colleagues on February 11, 1847 in an eloquent and balanced speech, intended to challenge Polk's justification of the Mexican War and to warn members that geographical divisions over slavery is destined to lead on to "civil conflict."

Corwin begins by recalling Mexico's recent struggle for freedom from Spain, from Father Hidalgo's "cry" ("El Grito de la Independencia") at the town of Dolores in 1810 to the final Treaty of Cordova in 1821. And now, says Corwin, America comes as a new invader, seeking land the Mexicans bled over.

Senator Thomas Corwin
(1794-1865)

> *What is the territory, Mr. President, which you propose to wrest from Mexico? It is consecrated to the heart of the Mexican by many a well-fought battle with his old Castilian master. His Bunker Hills, and Saratogas, and Yorktowns are there! The Mexican can say, "There I bled for liberty! and shall I surrender that consecrated home of my affections to the Anglo-Saxon invaders? What do they want with it? They have Texas already.*

The Senator then looks directly at the topic that Polk has treated in elliptical fashion – the potential for a war of acquisition to divide the Union over the issue of expanding slavery.

> *There is one topic connected with this subject which I tremble when I approach, and yet I cannot forbear to notice it. I allude to the question of slavery.*

> *Opposition to its further extension, it must be obvious to everyone, is a deeply rooted determination With men of all parties in what we call the nonslaveholding states. New York, Pennsylvania, and Ohio, three of the most powerful, have already sent their legislative instructions here. So it will be, I doubt not, in all the rest.*

> *How is it in the South? Can it be expected that they should expend in common their*

blood and their treasure in the acquisition of immense territory, and then willingly forgo the right to carry thither their slaves, and inhabit the conquered country if they please to do so? Nay, I believe they would even contend to any extremity for the mere right, had they no wish to exert it.

Once divided, Corwin argues, the result will be a civil conflict at home – which means, in turn, that bills calling to continue and fund the war are nothing less than "treason to the Union."

I believe (and I confess I tremble when the conviction presses upon me) that there is equal obstinacy on both sides of this fearful question

This bill would seem to be nothing less than a bill to produce internal commotion. Should we prosecute this war another moment, or expend one dollar in the purchase or conquest of a single acre of Mexican land, the North and the South are brought into collision on a point where neither will yield.

Why should we precipitate this fearful struggle, by continuing a war the result of which must be to force us at once upon a civil conflict? Sir, rightly considered, this is treason, treason to the Union, treason to the dearest interests, the loftiest aspirations, the most cherished hopes of our constituents. It is a crime to risk the possibility of such a contest. It is a crime of such infernal hue that every other in the catalogue of iniquity, when compared with it, whitens into virtue.

The only way out is to abandon the war with Mexico, along with its demands for land beyond Texas. Mexico already knows that it cannot prevail on the battlefield, so peace terms will be readily accepted.

Let us abandon all idea of acquiring further territory and by consequence cease at once to prosecute this war. Let us call home our armies, and bring them at once within our own acknowledged limits. Show Mexico that you are sincere when you say you desire nothing by conquest. She has learned that she cannot encounter you in war, and if she had not, she is too weak to disturb you here. Tender her peace, and, my life on it, she will then accept it.

Once cleansed of Mexican blood, Corwin says, America can escape the prospect of its own civil war and restore "ancient accord and eternal brotherhood" at home.

Let us then close forever the approaches of internal feud, and so return to the ancient concord and the old ways of national prosperity and permanent glory. Let us here, in this temple consecrated to the Union, perform a solemn lustration; let us wash Mexican blood from our hands, and on these altars, and in the presence of that image of the Father of his Country that looks down upon us, swear to preserve honorable peace with all the world and eternal brotherhood with each other.

TIME: FEBRUARY 15, 1847

SENATOR JOHN CALHOUN ISSUES A SOUTHERN WARNING OVER WILMOT

Like Corwin, John Calhoun of South Carolina is another prescient commentator on the consequences of the war and of the Wilmot bill. He sums up his thoughts in a senate speech delivered four days later.

The ever dour Calhoun begins by summing up the situation in congress as he sees it – with non-slaveholding states in both chambers apparently determined to prohibit slavery in the new "public domain" lands to the west.

John Calhoun (1772-1850)

Mr. President, I rise to offer a set of resolutions in reference to the various resolutions from the State legislatures upon the subject of what they call the extension of slavery, and the proviso attached to the House bill...

It was solemnly asserted on this floor...that all parties in the non-slaveholding States had come to a fixed and solemn determination...that there should be no further admission of any States into this Union which permitted, by their constitutions, the existence of slavery; and...that slavery shall not hereafter exist in any of the territories of the United States; the effect of which would be to give to the non-slaveholding States the monopoly of the public domain... At the same time, two resolutions which have been moved to extend the compromise line from the Rocky

Mountains to the Pacific, during the present session, have been rejected by a decided majority... It is a scheme, Mr. President, which aims to monopolize the powers of this Government and to obtain sole possession of its territories.

The slaveholding states, he says, are already in the minority in the House (138-90) and in the Electoral College (168-118).

Sir, already we —I use the word "we" for brevity's sake—are already we are in a minority in the other House, in the electoral college, and I may say, in every department of this Government, except at present in the Senate of the United States—there for the present we have an equality.

There are two hundred and twenty-eight representatives, including Iowa, which is already represented there. Of these, one hundred and thirty-eight are from non-slaveholding States, and ninety are from what are called the slave States—giving a majority, in the aggregate, to the former of forty-eight. In the electoral college there are one hundred and sixty-eight votes belonging to the non-slaveholding States, and one hundred and eighteen to the slaveholding, giving a majority of fifty to the non-slaveholding.

Only in the Senate do the slaveholding states retain enough voting power to block the will of the majority, and this is transitory. The admission of Iowa and Wisconsin will give the Free States a 32-28 edge in Senate seats, and if 12-15 more Free States are added, the South will be further overwhelmed.

We, Mr. President, have at present only one position in the Government, by which we may make any resistance to this aggressive policy which has been declared against the South...And this equality in this body is one of the most transient character. Already Iowa is a State...Already Wisconsin has passed the initiatory stage, and will be here the next session. This will add...four in this body on the side of the non-slaveholding States, who will thus be enabled to sway every branch of this Government at their will and pleasure.

Sir, there is ample space for twelve or fifteen of the largest description of States in the territories belonging to the United States.... How will we then stand? There will be but fourteen on the part of the South—we are to be fixed, limited, and forever—and twenty-eight on the part of the non-slaveholding States! Twenty-eight! Double our number! And with the same disproportion in the House and in the electoral college! The Government, Sir, will be entirely in the hands of the non-slaveholding States—overwhelmingly. ...If this scheme should be carried out...wo! wo! I say, to this Union!

This brings Calhoun to a favorite theme of his, echoed over decades: the need for the majority to avoid trampling on the wishes of the minority. So, he says, if the North denies the rights and the needs of the South on slavery, there will follow revolution, civil war and disaster.

Sir, the day that the balance between the two sections of the country ...is destroyed, is a day that will not be far removed from political revolution, anarchy, civil war, and widespread disaster.

His solution is forever grounded in the literal words and promises of the U.S. Constitution, guaranteeing "perfect equality" for all. It says that each man has the right to transport their "property" (in the form of slaves) into any state or territory they choose. The majority simply cannot deny that guarantee without violating the law.

Now, Sir, I put again the solemn question—Does the constitution afford any remedy?

The whole system is based on justice and equality—perfect equality between the members of this republic. Now, can that be consistent with equality which will make this public domain a monopoly on one side—which, in its consequences, would place the whole power in one section of the Union, to be wielded against the other sections? Is that equality?

And is it consistent with justice—is it consistent with equality, that any portion of the partners, outnumbering another portion, shall oust them of this common property of theirs—shall pass any law which shall proscribe the citizens of other portions of the Union from emigrating with their property to the territories of the United States?

Furthermore, the essence of American democracy lies with the right of the people "to establish what government they may think proper for themselves." It is simply an "outrage against the constitution" to demand that the people in all new territories must ban slavery before being admitted to the Union.

Mr. President… that proposition…which undertakes to say that no State shall be admitted into this Union which shall not prohibit by its constitution the existence of slaves, is equally a great outrage against the constitution of the United States.

Sir, I hold it to be a fundamental principle of our political system that the people have a right to establish what government they may think proper for themselves; that every State about to become a member of this Union has a right to form its government as it pleases; and that, in order to be admitted there is but one qualification, and that is, that the Government shall be republican.

And yet, Sir, there are men of such delicate feeling on the subject of liberty—men who cannot possibly bear what they call slavery in one section of the country—although not so much slavery, as an institution indispensable for the good of both races—men so squeamish on this point, that they are ready to strike down the higher right of a community to govern themselves.

Calhoun turns to extending the 34'30" Missouri line as a possible compromise. Ever the purist, he argues that the line has always been unconstitutional – before saying that he would "acquiesce to it to preserve the peace of the Union."

Mr. President, the resolutions that I intend to offer present, in general terms, these great truths… Overrule these principles, and we are nothing! Preserve them, and we will ever be a respectable portion of the Union.

Sir, here let me say a word as to the compromise line. I have always considered it as a great error—highly injurious to the South, because it surrendered, for mere temporary purposes, those high principles of the constitution upon which I think we ought to stand. I am against any compromise line. Yet I would have been willing to acquiesce in a continuation of the Missouri compromise, in order to preserve, under the present trying circumstances, the peace of the Union…. But it was voted down by a decided majority. It was renewed by a gentleman from a non-slaveholding State, and again voted down by a like majority.

I see my way in the constitution. I cannot in a compromise. A compromise is but an act of Congress. It may be overruled at any time. It gives us no security. But the constitution is stable. It is a rock. On it we can stand…. Let us be done with compromises. Let us go back and stand upon the constitution!

Nearing the end of his speech, the sixty-four year old South Carolina planter reflects on his personal history and his commitment to not surrendering his sense of honor, to "not sinking down into acknowledged inferiority."

But I may speak as an individual member of that section of the Union. Here I drew my first breath; there are all my hopes. There is my family and connections. I am a planter—a cotton-planter. I am a Southern man and a slaveholder—a kind and a merciful one, I trust—and none the worse for being a slaveholder. I say, for one, I would rather meet any extremity upon earth than give up one inch of our equality—one inch of what belongs to us as members of this great republic! What acknowledge inferiority! The surrender of life is nothing to sinking down into acknowledged inferiority!

He closes with his four proposed "resolutions" to protect the rights of the slaveholding states under the constitution.

Resolved, That the territories of the United States belong to the several States composing this Union, and are held by them as their joint and common property.

Resolved, That Congress, as the joint agent and representative of the States of this Union, has no right to make any law, or do any act whatever, that shall directly, or by its effects, make any discrimination between the States of this Union, by which any of them shall be deprived of its full and equal right in any territory of the United States, acquired or to be acquired.

Resolved, That the enactment of any law, which should directly, or by its effects, deprive the citizens of any of the States of this Union from emigrating, with their property, into any of the territories of the United States, will make such discrimination, and would, therefore, be a violation of the constitution and the rights of the States from which such citizens emigrated, and in derogation of that perfect equality which belongs to them as members of this Union—and would tend directly to subvert the Union itself.

Resolved, That it is a fundamental principle in our political creed, that a people, in forming a constitution, have the unconditional right to form and adopt the government which they may think best calculated to secure their liberty, prosperity, and happiness; and that, in conformity thereto, no other condition is imposed by the Federal Constitution on a State, in order to be admitted into this Union, except that its constitution shall be republican; and that the imposition of any other by Congress would not only be in violation of the constitution, but in direct conflict with the principle on which our political system rests."

In February 1847, Calhoun's speech is regarded as radical, just one more attempt on his part to run for the presidency. A decade later, after his death, it will reflect the sentiments of most men across the South.

TIME: FEBRUARY 15, 1847

THE HOUSE PASSES A NEW AND HARSHER PROVISO ON EXPANDING SLAVERY

While the debate continues in the Senate, the House takes up the Three Million Dollar Bill to fund the war.

Once again, the New York "Barnburner," Preston King, proposes an amendment in the form of a revised version of the Wilmot Proviso.

King's version is even more onerous to the South than Wilmot's. It declares that slavery be banned in "any territory on the continent of America which shall hereafter be acquired." This being a direct shot at expansionists who wish to annex all of Mexico and Cuba and perhaps even parts of central America.

Polk calls this a "mischievous and foolish amendment…with (no) connection to making peace with Mexico."

Regardless, the House passes the bill on February 15 by a margin of 115-106 and sends it to the Senate.

## 125

GENERAL ZACHARY TAYLOR WINS LASTING FAME AT BUENA VISTA

TIME: SEPTEMBER – DECEMBER 1846

GENERAL TAYLOR DRIFTS SOUTHWEST FROM HIS VICTORY AT MONTERREY

After scoring his decisive victory at Monterrey on September 23, 1846, General Zachary Taylor allows the Mexican army to leave the field, much to the chagrin of Polk and his cabinet.

His orders from Washington are to consolidate his hold on Monterrey, but instead he continues westward, taking the town of Saltillo on November 16, and ordering General John Wool to move south to Aqua Nuevo, where he arrives on December 21.

As Taylor drifts further into the interior, Mexican General Ampudia is sacked in favor of the familiar figure of Antonio Lopez de Santa Anna.

His is a chequered past, starting with early support of Spanish rule, then flipping sides after independence is won in 1821 and finally defeating Spain's attempt to reconquer Mexico at the 1829

Zachary Taylor (1784-1850)

Battle of Tampico. This victory makes him a national hero and leads to a political career, whereby he is in and out of the presidency on seven occasions, his last term ending in exile to Cuba after a coup.

But in late 1846 he again "offers his services to the country" to put down the American invaders – just as he did in March 1836 defeating the Texans at The Alamo and then in the Goliad Massacre.

With his return comes a guarantee to the government to stay out of politics, and a secret hint to the U.S. that he is ready to sign a peace treaty. He quickly abandons both promises, re-taking political control in 1847 and fighting tooth and nail against the U.S. invaders.

Santa Anna remains a courageous warrior, despite the loss of his left leg to a cannon ball in 1838.

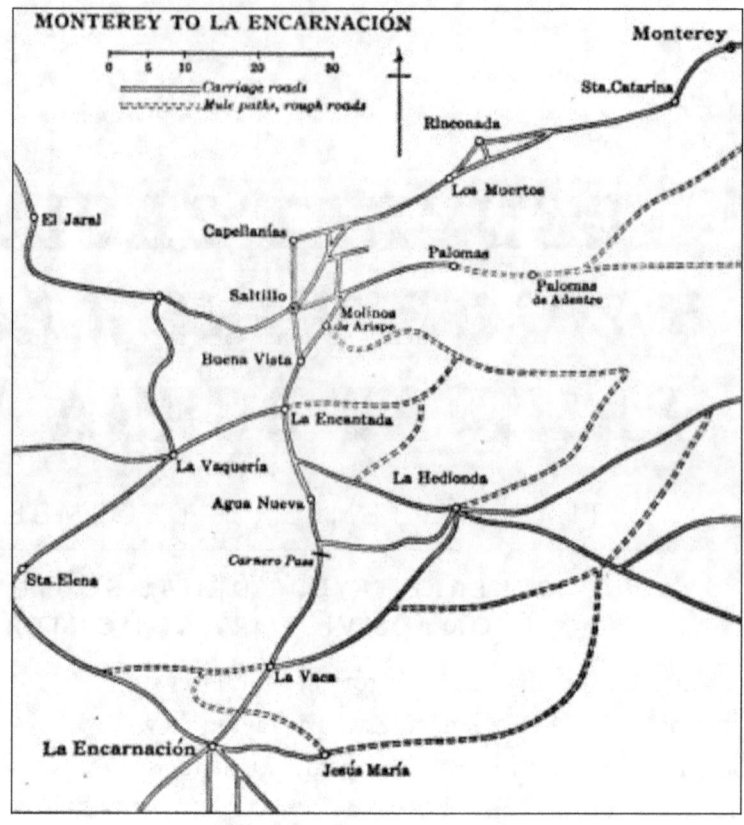

Map Showing Route from Monterrey
to Saltillo and Buena Vista

He is a sound military planner, and also confident of victory – believing that he can first destroy Taylor's depleted forces up north and then sweep down south on any invaders aiming at Mexico City.

His first move will play out just below the town of Saltillo, at Buena Vista.

DATE: FEBRUARY 22-23, 1847

THE BATTLE OF BUENA VISTA ENDS THE CAMPAIGN IN NORTHERN MEXICO

General Taylor appears to play right into Santa Anna's hand on February 22, 1847 when his 5,000 man force, heading toward Aqua Nuevo, suddenly finds Santa Anna's 20,000 man army directly in his front.

Taylor responds quickly by establishing a strong defensive position along the road leading back north to Buena Vista. On the west side of the road are impassable plateaus, while on the east side, where Taylor deploys, are a series of arroyos, or deep gullies, which inhibit massed infantry attacks. Still Santa Anna remains so confident of victory that he sends an emissary to seek immediate surrender – which Taylor promptly declines.

At 8AM on February 23, the Mexicans launch a ferocious two-pronged attack. The main body of their infantry crashes into Taylor's left center which wavers until pivotal artillery support from Lt. George Thomas and Captain Braxton Bragg stiffens the defense. Meanwhile another contingent of roughly 1500 lancers head far east and north to encircle the American's left flank. These lancers break through and pose a serious threat to Taylor's rear – until a courageous rush by Colonel Jefferson Davis and his 7th Mississippi Rifles hurls them back.

Santa Anna still believes by mid-afternoon that the U.S. forces will break under one more concentrated assault. At 5PM he throws everything he has left against the American center and again forces it backwards until Bragg's flying artillery and Davis's infantry are once again able to save the day.

When Santa Anna retreats from Buena Vista the next day, his Mexicans will have come as close to securing a battlefield victory as they will at any time during the entire war.

The butcher's bill for the day of fighting on February 23 is high – with 3700 men killed/wounded/missing on the Mexican side and 750 on the American side.

Two U.S. heroes emerge from the battle.

The first is Zachary Taylor, who, despite disobeying orders and marching into a 4:1 manpower trap, has escaped with another victory to close out his campaign to secure the Rio Grande border for Texas.

The second, ironically, is Taylor's son-in-law, Jefferson Davis, who suffers a severe wound to his foot at Buena Vista, ending his military duty and leaving him on crutches for two years. He returns

Battle of Buena Vista – February 23, 1847

Map Showing Santa Anna Flanking Movement Against Taylor's Left

Jefferson Davis (1808-1889)

as a hero, and is chosen by Governor Brown serve in the U.S. Senate, which is vacant by a death in office.

Davis joins the Senate on August 10, 1847 and immediately becomes a leader in the Democratic Party.

SIDEBAR: DEATH OF HENRY CLAY, JR.

Among those lying dead on the field at Buena Vista is Henry Clay, Jr., age 36, son of a famous father whose presidential ambitions have been derailed by his opposition to the Mexican War.

The younger Clay is the seventh of eleven children in the family, and the one chosen not only to bear his father's given name, but also to follow in his public footsteps.

Unlike his two older brothers, Henry Clay, Jr. exhibits his father's energy and ambition early in life. After graduating from Transylvania College, he goes on to finish second in his class at West Point in 1831. He resigns his commission, studies the law, and marries the 18 year old beauty, Julia Prather, in 1832. A single term in the Kentucky House in 1835-36, is followed by overseeing the Ashland Plantation and caring for two of the four children who have survived infancy.

Then, in 1840, his world changes when Julia dies after delivering another son, who survives. But the younger Clay never fully recovers from this loss. He remains dutiful to his family, but loses some of the "purpose" that marked his youth.

The War with Mexico lends him a new cause, a chance to serve his country, in the tradition set by his father. He helps to form the Second Kentucky Volunteer Infantry unit, assuming the rank of Lt. Colonel. He arrives in Mexico, but doesn't reach Taylor's command until after the victory at Monterrey. At that point, it looks like he will miss all of the fighting.

On February 23, 1847, however, Taylor, and Clay, are confronted by a Mexican army with a 4-1 manpower advantage, at Buena Vista. The 2nd Kentucky is caught in the front ranks as the battle begins, and is soon overrun by Santa Anna's forces.

Lt. Colonel Henry Clay, Jr. falls with a severe wound in the left thigh. His men attempt to move him to the rear, but they fail, and he hands them his pistols and orders them to flee and save their own lives. When the Mexican lancers arrive on the field, they spear the remaining wounded, including Clay, to death.

After Taylor's remarkable victory at Buena Vista, Clay's body is temporarily buried in Saltillo. It rests there until the summer, when the remains of many Kentucky soldiers are re-interred in a cemetery in Frankfort. On July 20, 1847, the Clay family, along with some 20,000 other local citizens attend the final service. It becomes immortalized in a long poem – *The Bivouac of the Dead* – written by a Kentucky trooper named Theodore O'Hara. The opening stanza:

HENRY CLAY and WIFE.

Entered according to Act of Congress, in the year 1861, in the Clerk's Office of the District Court of the United States for the Eastern District of Pennsylvania, by Jas. Cremer, No. 18 South Eighth St. Philadelphia.

Henry Clay (1777-1852) and
Lucretia Hart Clay (1781-1864)

> *The muffled drum's sad roll has beat*
> *The soldier's last tattoo;*
> *No more on life's parade shall meet*
> *The brave and daring few.*
> *On Fame's eternal camping-ground*
> *Their silent tents are spread,*
> *And Glory guards with solemn round*
> *The bivouac of the dead.*

For the seventy year old Henry Clay, and his aging wife, Lucretia, the day is marked by deep sadness, rather than glory. They have just lost the seventh of their eleven children, and here in a war that Clay has already called "calamitous, as well as unjust and unnecessary."

## 126

CONGRESS FINALLY APPROVES A FUNDING BILL WITHOUT A BAN ON SLAVERY

TIME: MARCH 1, 1847

THE SENATE OPPOSES THE HOUSE BILL AGAIN AND PASSES ITS OWN OPTION

With the final session of the 29th Congress set to adjourn on March 3, 1847, both chambers feel a sense of urgency about funding the Mexican War.

The House has already passed a bill, but with the amendment from Preston King prohibiting any future expansion of slavery in the west or in other lands acquired by the United States. This prohibition, even more drastic than that from Wilmot, is considered too divisive in the Senate. On March 1, it goes down to defeat with 21 ayes and 32 nays.

Senator Thomas Hart Benton then proposes a $3 Million Appropriations Bill without the King amendment. It passes 29-23 on March 1, 1847, with Simon Cameron of Pennsylvania, a strong opponent of slavery, the only Democrat voting "no". The only Whig "yes" belongs to Henry Johnson of Louisiana, who cast the earlier decisive vote to annex Texas.

SENATE VOTE ON APPROPRIATION BILL – WITHOUT WILMOT (MARCH 1, 1847)

REGION	DEMOCRATS YES - NO	WHIGS YES – NO	OTHER YES - NO	TOTAL YES – NO
Northeast	6 - 1	0 - 8	0 - 3	6 - 11
Northwest	5 - 0	0 - 2		5 - 2
Border	2 - 0	0 - 5		2 - 5

REGION	DEMOCRATS YES - NO	WHIGS YES – NO	OTHER YES - NO	TOTAL YES – NO
Southeast	3 - 0	0 - 4	1 - 0	4 - 4
Southwest	10 - 0	1 - 1	1 - 0	12 - 1
Total	26 - 0	1 - 20	2 - 3	29 - 23
Not Voting	(2)	(1)		(3)

Vote View/Library of Congress Record

TIME: MARCH 3, 1847

THE HOUSE PASSES THE APPROPRIATION BILL
WITHOUT THE WILMOT PROVISO

With time running out, the Senate bill is back in the House for reconciliation, where those opposing the spread of slavery make one final attempt to add back the King Amendment. It goes down to defeat by a narrow spread of 97 ayes to 102 nays.

This funding battle has lasted since August 8, 1846, a full nine months, and many House members now seem to conclude they have been operating in a dark and dangerous place far too long.

American soldiers are in the field in Mexico; they deserve to be properly funded and supported; the time has come to push on and win the war. Also, one war seems enough for the moment — without adding the visible threats of disunion that have surfaced over the Wilmot and King injunctions. Better to step back from this cliff for now, and possibly return to it later.

Stephen Douglas (1813-1861)

This is the theme promoted by the indefatigable Illinois congressman, Stephen Douglas, who lobbies hard to convince Northern Democrats to delay the battle over the spread of slavery until the various territories have been established, settlers have arrived and debated their state constitutions, and requests for admission are filed with congress.

This line of reasoning mirrors the plea from Calhoun that the people in each new state should determine their own form of government. As a principle it will soon become known as "popular sovereignty," a new option to Wilmot/King and the 34'30" compromise line and one that postpones North-South violence until Kansas applies for statehood in 1856.

The efforts by Douglas and other party leaders pay off when the final bill passes by a comfortable 115-82 margin in the House on March 3, 1847.

HOUSE VOTE AN APPROPRIATION BILL WITHOUT A SLAVERY BAN

REGION	DEMOCRATS YES - NO	WHIGS YES – NO	AMERICAN YES - NO	TOTAL YES – NO
Northeast	31 - 7	0 - 40	1 - 3	32 - 50
Northwest	22 - 3	0 - 10		22 - 13
Border	10 - 0	0 - 8		10 - 8
Southeast	28 - 0	0 - 5		28 - 5
Southwest	22 - 0	1 - 6		23 - 6
TOTAL	113 - 10	1 - 69	1 - 3	115 - 82
NOT VOTING	(20)	(9)	(1)	(30)

Vote View/Library of Congress Records

Analysis of the final outcome on the $3 Million Bill shows a remarkable shift among the Democrats in the seven months since the Wilmot Proviso passed the House on August 8, 1846. At that time, 52 Democrats voted in favor of the bill limiting the spread of slavery; by March 1847, only 10 of them are left. This is an early testament to Stephen Douglas's powers of persuasion.

SHIFT IN DEMOCRAT VOTES FOR THE WAR APPROPRIATIONS BILL

BILL LIMITING SPREAD OF SLAVERY	AUG 8, 1846	MAR 3, 1847	CHANGE
# Democrats Voting Aye	52	10	(42)
# Democrats Voting Nay	55	113	+58

The ten hold-outs are Northern Democrats, led by David Wilmot, and joined by others including Preston King, Jacob Brinkerhoff, and Hannibal Hamlin.

THE TEN HOLD-OUT NORTHERN DEMOCRATS

NAME	STATE
Jacob Brinkerhoff	Ohio
John Campbell	Pa
Martin Grover	New York
Hannibal Hamlin	Maine
Joseph Hoge	Illinois
Preston King	New York
Mace Moulton	New Hampshire

NAME	STATE
John Wentworth	Illinois
Horace Wheaton	New York
David Wilmot	Pennsylvania
Bradford Wood	New York

Meanwhile, the House Whigs remain solidly against the appropriation bill and the war itself.

SIDEBAR: RECAP OF THE KEY VOTES ON THE WILMOT PROVISO

CHAMBER	DATE	FORM OF BILL	YES	NO	(NV)	RESOLUTION
House	August 8, 1846	$2MM + Wilmot	85	80	(56)	Senate Tables
House	February 15, 1847	$3MM + King	115	106	(6)	House Passes
Senate	March 1, 1847	$3MM + King	21	32	(3)	Senate Opposes
Senate	March 1, 1847	$3MM w/o Proviso	29	23	(3)	Senate Passes
House	March 3, 1847	$3MM + Wilmot	97	102	(28)	House Opposes
House	March 3, 1847	$3MM w/o Proviso	115	82	(30)	House Passes

## 127

WHIGS MAKE LARGE GAINS IN THE OFF-YEAR ELECTION OF 1846

TIME: AUGUST 1846 – NOVEMBER 1847

WHIGS TAKE BACK THE HOUSE WHILE DEMOCRATS HOLD THE SENATE

With the war and the Wilmot controversy swirling in the background, the off-year congressional elections drag on for fifteen months, from August 1846 to November 1847. As usual, House members are chosen by popular vote of all white men, with Senators selected by state legislators.

The results in the House are a serious blow to Polk and the Democrats – as the Whigs pick up 37 seats to gain narrow control over the lower chamber.

HOUSE ELECTION RESULTS FOR 1846

PARTIES	1844	1846	CHANGE
Democrats	143	112	-31
Whigs	79	116	+37
Others	6	6	NC

The largest gains for the Whigs – 26 of their new 37 seats – occur in the North. Fourteen of these are in New York State alone, where the Democratic rift between Van Buren men (the "Barnburners") and the Polk backers ("Hunkers") hands the outcome to the Whigs.

But Democrat losses also occur across the board, suggesting unease about extending the war with Mexico beyond the borders of Texas, and about the aftermath, as it relates to national strife over the slavery issue.

WHIG GAINS IN THE HOUSE: 1846 ELECTION

	1844	1846	CHANGE
Northeast	19	40	+21

	1844	1846	CHANGE
New York	9	23	+14
Pennsylvania	10	16	+6
New Hampshire	0	1	+1
Northwest	10	15	+5
Ohio	8	11	+3
Indiana	2	4	+2
Border	9	10	+1
Maryland	2	4	+2
Kentucky	7	6	(1)
Southeast	7	14	+7
Virginia	1	6	+5
North Carolina	3	6	+3
Georgia	3	4	+1
Southwest	1	4	+3
Florida	0	1	+1
Alabama	1	2	+1
Mississippi	0	1	+1
TOTAL WHIG GAINS			+37

In the Senate, with its staggered six year terms, only one-third of the seats are in play, and all votes are cast by state legislators rather than the public.

The results here are much more comforting to Polk than those in the House – with his Democrat Party ending up with a solid 37-21 majority.

COMPOSITION OF THE SENATE: 1846 ELECTION

	DEMOCRAT	WHIG	TOTAL
Free States	16	10	26
Northeast	9	9	18
Northwest*	7	1	8
Slave States	19	11	30
Border	2	6	8
Southeast	5	3	8
Southwest	12	2	14
	35	21	56

* Iowa admitted in 1846, with two vacancies filled by Democrats in 1848.

Wisconsin will be admitted in 1848, restoring free/slave balance to 24/24

TIME: SPRING 1847

IMPORTANT NEW FACES JOIN CONGRESS IN 1847

By the time the 30th Congress convenes on December 6, 1847 for its first session, the South has assembled a roster of outspoken pro-slavery Senators who are determined to defeat the Wilmot Proviso and restore unity to the Democrat Party.

John C. Calhoun returns to the Senate after serving one year as Tyler's Secretary of State. He is joined by his fellow South Carolinian, Andrew C. Butler, another fierce States' Rights advocate.

Virginia also elects two new senators – Robert T.M. Hunter, former Speaker of the House, and Calhoun's close friend, James Mason.

Jefferson Davis graduates from the House to the Senate in August, 1847, after his heroic war duty at Buena Vista.

Abraham Lincoln (1809-1865)

Three other sitting Democrat will complete the inner circle, one a Southerner and the other two, Northern men with strong pro-Southern sympathies. The Southerner is David Rice Atchison of Missouri, who is elected President Pro Temp of the Senate. The two Northerners – both future Presidential nominees – are Lewis Cass of Michigan and Stephen A. Douglas of Illinois.

As of 1847, opponents of the Southern agenda in the Senate lack enough depth and alignment to have their way.

The political turmoil impacting the House Democrats in New York State is muted in the Senate. Daniel Dickinson remains a Polk loyalist, offsetting the Van Buren "Barnburner," John Dix.

On the Whig side, Henry Clay, has left the Senate after losing to Polk in the 1844 election. The equally formidable Daniel Webster continues to serve in the chamber, but his party support has faded after he chooses to remain Secretary of State under the "turn-coat Whig," John Tyler. Two other esteemed Whigs, Senators John Bell of Tennessee and John J. Crittenden of Kentucky, are both from Slave States and uninclined toward any actions that might threaten the Union.

Still the South will need to contend with two aggressive adversaries in the Senate:

the Whig, Tom Corwin of Ohio, and the Democrat-turned-Independent, John P. Hale of New Hampshire.

Hale has been a Democrat throughout his career, and supports the Polk-Dallas ticket in 1844. But he has also been a consistent critic of slavery, joining the Whig JQ Adams in the House in opposing various "Gag Rules." This leads to an attempt by his state adversary, Franklin Pierce, to oust him from the party – a move that ends with a crusade by Hale to turn New Hampshire against slavery and his first election to the Senate in 1846.

While men like Hale and Corwin and Dix will begin to push back against the strong pro-Southern forces in the Senate, they will make little progress until additional support arrives in the election of 1848.

The House of Representatives is another story. It has already passed the Wilmot Proviso and is beginning to latch on to the powerful new notion of "free soil for free men" – and is eager to fight for both.

It is also joined in 1847 by a first term congressman from Illinois, Abraham Lincoln.

Lincoln is the lone Whig in a House delegation dominated by the members of Senator Stephen Douglas' statewide machine. He will serve a single term before returning to his Springfield law practice – and a circuitous path toward the presidency.

## 128

GENERAL SCOTT MOVES INLAND IN MEXICO

TIME: MARCH 9-29, 1847

SCOTT TAKES VERA CRUZ BY SIEGE AND MOVES INLAND

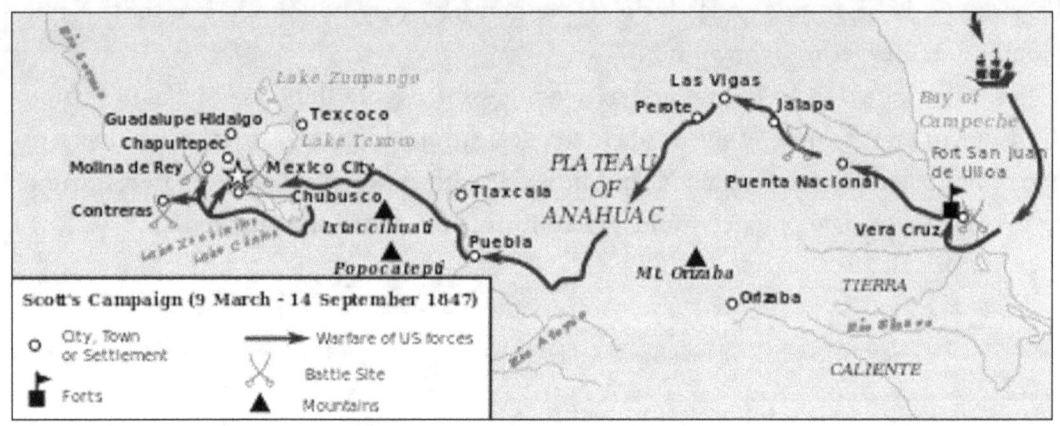

Map of Winfield Scott's Mexican Campaign

Two weeks after Taylor's victory at Buena Vista, Scott executes America's first major amphibious invasion, landing 11,000 American troops on Sacrificios Island, just below the fortress city of Veracruz. The operation involves repeated trips ashore by 65 surf boats, each packed with 100 men and equipment, and lasts for over six hours. Once ashore, the men march north to surround the Veracruz enclave, which includes 5,000 local civilians in addition to 4,400 garrisoned troops, under General Juan Morales.

The terrain leading into Veracruz is marked by the high chaparral and deep arroyos typical of Mexico's landscape. In addition to these natural obstacles, cannons are arrayed along a 15-foot -high stone wall encircling the city. The road in is guarded by the formidable castle of San Juan D'Ulloa, and another 1,000 troops.

Scott immediately decides to siege the city. Colonel Joseph Totten oversees the plan, along with help from a 40-year-old engineer, Captain Robert E. Lee. Lee's placements of three 32-pound naval guns hauled on land will prove critical as the siege develops. Aside from Lee, several other soon to be famous West Pointers experience their first taste of battle at Veracruz, including Thomas Jonathan Jackson and George McClellan.

On March 22, Scott is ready to launch an all-out bombardment from land and sea, but, before beginning, he asks Morales to surrender. When the offer is refused, Scott begins his attack.

Robert E. Lee (1807-1870)

The results are devastating. For three days Veracruz suffers under constant barrages from field artillery and naval guns. Mortars lob solid iron balls weighing upwards of 30 lbs. into the city from the west. In the bay to the east, the U.S. fleet unleashes its Paixhans guns, with 68 lb. shells that whistle in at low trajectories and explode on contact. Some 6700 shot and shell weighing over 450,000 lbs. rain down on the defenders.

Naval officer Sydney Smith Lee, Robert's older brother, observes the action from his frigate:

The battery's fire was terrific. The shells were constant and regular discharges, so beautiful in their flight and so destructive in their fall. It was awful! My heart bled for the inhabitants.

By March 25, the buildings and walls of Veracruz are crumbling. When Morale's finally requests a truce to evacuate civilians, Scott refuses, insisting on a full surrender. After haggling, the final details are worked out on March 29.

Scott's siege has lasted 20 days, and he has sustained a mere 58 casualties.

His gaze now shifts toward Mexico City, 225 miles inland.

Scott knows that this will not be an easy target. His army will be outnumbered along the way, and fall further distant from its supply base as it marches off. His enemy will have superior knowledge of the terrain ahead, and be motivated by fighting on and for its homeland. Still the General is confident of success.

Sidney Lee (1802-1869), Robert's brother, on the left

He also knows from studying French General Napoleon Bonaparte's battles that strict discipline in the ranks will be required to avoid alienating the local population and provoking partisan activity. His General Order 20 outlines harsh penalties for all Americans, soldiers or civilians, involved in robbery, rape, murder, destruction of property, and any acts affecting Catholic churches and worship.

TIME: APRIL 17-18, 1847

THE BATTLE AT CERRO GORDO

Map Showing City of Xalapa Where Battle of Cerro Gordo Occurs

On April, 8, after securing his hold over Veracruz, Scott sends a lead force of 8,500 men out of the city heading northwest along the national road, with General David Twiggs and his 2nd Division in the lead.

Six days later, on the winding road to Xalapa, Santa Anna plans to ambush and kill them.

The Mexican General knows this ground particularly well since it lies on his private estate. His plan is to lure the U.S. troops into a cul du sac formed by the Rio del Plana flowing along his right flank and the 950-foot-high Cerro Gordo ("fat hill") guarding his immediate left.

He arrays the bulk of his 12,000 troops in a classical L-shaped formation, with artillery batteries and infantry scattered across the Jalapa Road and

David Twiggs (1790-1862)

additional units ready to fire down from the Cerro Gordo on his left.

He also stations troops along a plateau to the east of the road, hoping to lure the Americans in or close off their subsequent line of retreat. With their shooting gallery in place, the Mexicans await the U.S. columns.

But Twiggs and his West Point engineers know an ambush when they see one, and they halt on April 14, north of the bend in the road leading down into Santa Anna's position.

After scouting the area, they settle on a plan involving a trap of their own. It hinges on enveloping the Mexicans, by hacking out a new road across the gullies and plateaus north of Santa Anna's left flank, without being discovered. The work requires three full days to complete.

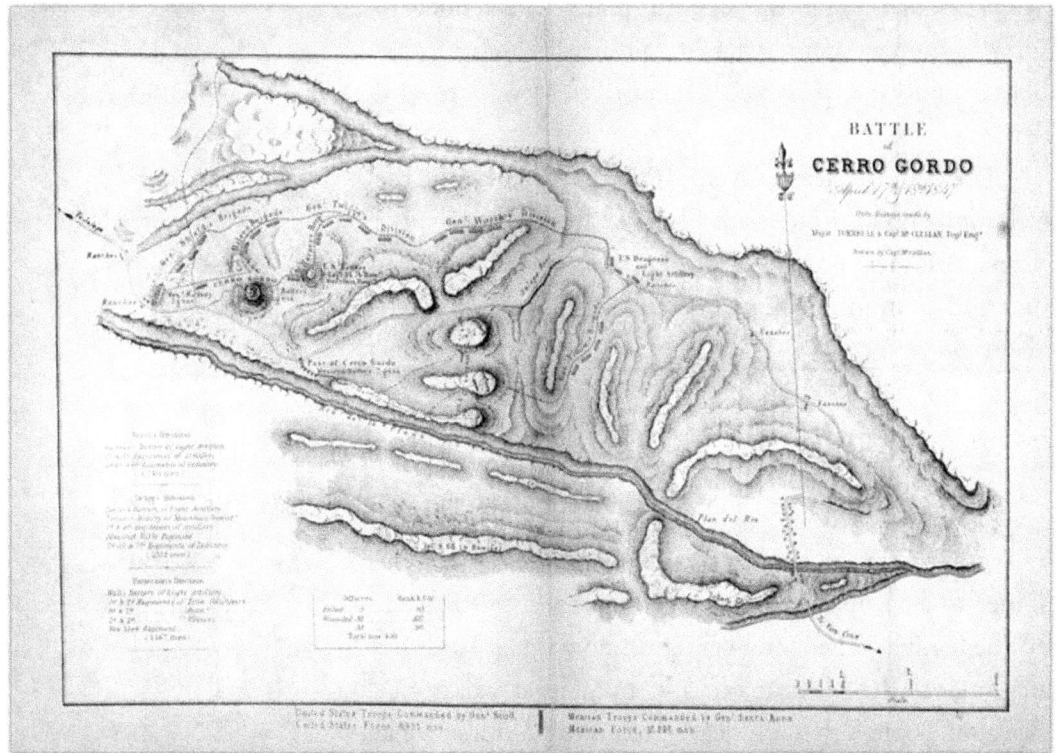

U.S. Troops encircle the Mexican Forces at Cerro Gordo

On April 17 Scott divides his army and advances. His light left wing, under Polk's ex-law partner, General Gideon Pillow, demonstrates against the Mexican forces east of the road, while his main body, comprising Twiggs' and Worth's divisions, swoop down on Santa Anna from behind Cerro Gordo.

Battery placements by Lt. George B. McClellan prove especially galling to the Mexicans, and the Lieutenant is cited for valor during the assault.

By nightfall the surprised Mexicans are desperately trying to organize a credible defensive line.

George B. McClellan
(1826-1885)

On April 18, as daybreak dawns Colonel William Harney and his First Brigade dragoons deprive the Mexicans of all hope – clawing their way to the top of Cerro Gordo and occupying the fortress there known as the Tower.

From this vantage point, American artillery now dominates the entire field below.

Once the American flag appears atop the Tower, Santa Anna knows that his position is hopeless.

Gideon Pillow (1806-1878)

His troops along the eastern plateau surrender to Pillow's command, and Santa Anna himself barely escapes on foot, amidst a panicked general retreat west toward Jalapa.

His losses are steep. Over 1100 Mexicans fall in the battle, and 3000 prisoners are taken, including five general officers. Another substantial depletion in artillery, smaller arms, and ammunition also further weakens their capacity to fight on.

TIME: MAY – JULY, 1847

SCOTT PAUSES TO BALANCE DIPLOMACY AND WARFARE

Scott's successes on the battlefield lead Polk and his cabinet to step up their plans for negotiating a treaty to end the conflict. The issues center on how much land they can convince the Mexicans to give up, and at what price. The cabinet agrees that an ideal outcome would involve all territory west, from where the upper Rio Grande touches New Mexico, to the Pacific – at a price not to exceed $30 million.

Secretary of War Marcy drafts an outline of the plan, to be delivered to Scott by Nicholas Twist, the number two official at the state department under Buchanan. Twist arrives at Veracruz on May 6, on the start of what will be a long and rocky mission.

General Winfield Scott
(1786-1866)

By this time, Scott's army has chased the Mexicans all the way from Cerro Gordo to Puebla, 80 miles east of the capital.

This produces a mood within Mexico City that is a mixture of outrage and panic. After finally driving out the Spaniards to win independence, here comes another foreign invader – and a Protestant-dominated one at that – in search of conquest.

Calls go up in the capital to sack the government, declare martial law, draft all able-bodied men, commence guerrilla warfare.

The last thing Scott wants to hear is talk of a religious war involving guerrilla bands operating outside the boundaries of conventional warfare.

On May 8, 1847, he issues a carefully worded proclamation to the people of Mexico. It asserts that the war is with government leaders, not with the people; that it's about policy, not religion; and that, once ended, the Americans will exit Mexico, not occupy it.

With these reassurances comes a warning. Scott's army is powerful and about to double in size, and it would be wise for the population to stay peacefully in their homes until the fighting is over.

Mexicans! At the head of a powerful army, soon to be doubled-a part of which is advancing upon your capital...I think myself called upon to address you.

Americans are not your enemies, but the enemies, for a time, of those men who, a year ago, misgoverned you, and brought about this unnatural war between two great republics. We are the friends of the peaceful inhabitants of the country we occupy, and the friends of your holy religion, its hierarchy and its priesthood. The same church is found in all parts of our own country, crowded with devout Catholics, and respected by our government, laws and people...

Let all good Mexicans remain at home, or at their peaceful occupation...should Mexicans wisely accept this, war may soon be happily ended, to the honor and advantage of both belligerents. Then Americans, will be happy to take leave of Mexico and return to their own country.

Truth be told, in May, Scott's army is much less prepared to advance on the capital than he lets on.

The inevitable diseases that plague troops in the field have taken their toll, and the enlistment term for several volunteer regiments is about to expire. With his battle-ready forces under 6,000 men, he pauses in place at Puebla for eight weeks awaiting reinforcements.

129

THE MORMONS FIND THEIR HOME AND SUPPORT THE WAR

TIME: JULY 24, 1847

THE MORMONS ARRIVE AT THEIR "NEW JERUSALEM" IN SALT LAKE CITY

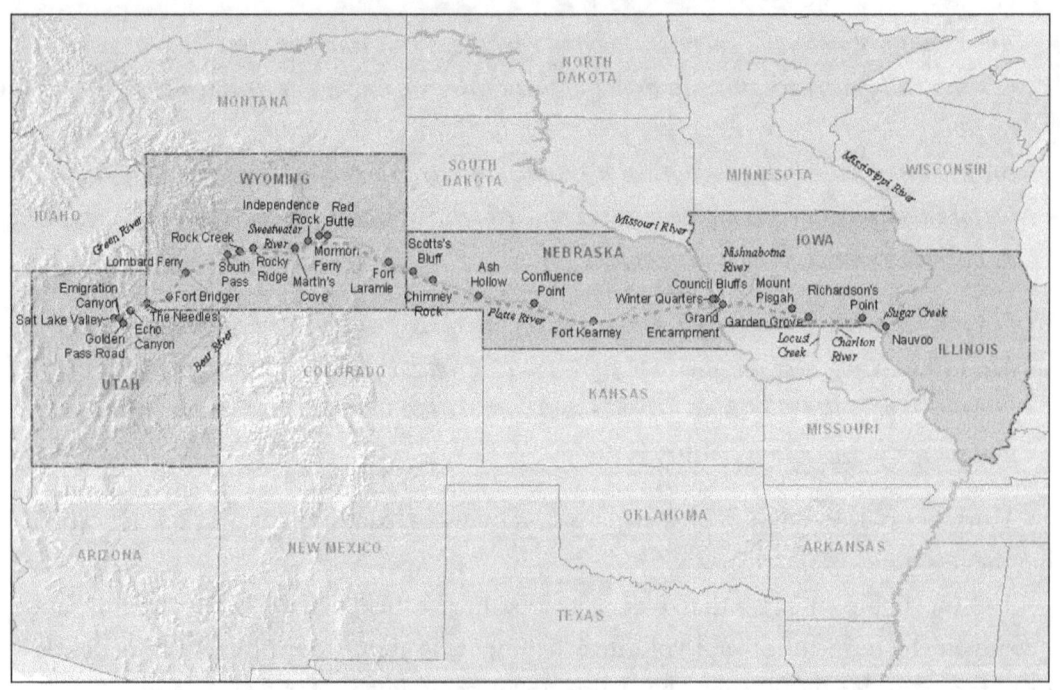

Map of Mormon Trail From Nauvoo, Illinois to Salt Lake City

While the U.S. Army marches toward Mexico City, followers of the Church of Jesus Christ of Latter-day Saints, or Mormons, are on their way toward their "New Jerusalem" home in Salt Lake City.

Their journey has been marked by a long string of setbacks.

In 1839, they are driven out of their home base in Missouri for the practice of polygamy, and settle in Illinois at the city of Nauvoo on the banks of the Mississippi River, roughly 200 miles upstream from St. Louis. Here, too, local attacks on members of the sect soon materialize. On June 27, 1844, their charismatic leader, Joseph Smith, and his brother Hyrum are murdered while under arrest for ordering an attack on an opposition newspaper in town.

Many assume that Smith's death will mark the end of the sect, among them *The New York Herald*, which writes:

The death of the modern mahomet (Mohammed) will seal the fate of Mormonism. They cannot get another Joe Smith. The holy city must tumble into ruins, and the 'latter-day saints' have indeed come to the latter day.

With Smith gone, the Mormons are shaken and deeply divided over the choice of a successor. When the main body settles in 1845 on Brigham Young, one of the Twelve Apostles, several splinter groups depart from Nauvoo and scatter to new sites. Young recognizes the need to abandon the town and looks to the west in search of a permanent home.

In February, 1846, he leads an initial contingent of 4,000 of the faithful out of Nauvoo. They struggle across the frozen Mississippi 300 miles to Council Bluffs, Iowa, where they set up winter quarters.

In spring, 1847, a small group resumes what will become another laborious three month journey. Accompanying Young here are 143 men, three women, and two boys, traveling in 72 wagons. As they set out, they are accompanied by 93 horses, 66 oxen, 52 mules, 19 cows, 17 dogs, and a flock of chickens.

Their path takes them west along the Oregon Trail, the well-known and well-traveled route mapped in 1842 by the John Fremont expedition – whose records Young relies on to guide his way.

The Mormons pass through Ft. Kearney and Ft. Laramie and, after the usual hard uphill climb, they cross the Rockies at the "South Pass," veering south from there to Ft. Bridger and down through Echo Canyon.

On July 22, 1847, an advance contingent emerges from the Wasatch Mountains and gazes upon a valley southwest of the 2,000 square mile Great Salt Lake –the sixth largest lake in America, with salinity levels far in excess of ocean water. They set up camp and await the arrival of Young himself, who lags behind due to illness.

Two days later when Young arrives, several members of the party urge him to continue on to California – but he demurs, saying simply:

It is enough. This is the right place.

Land for the Mormon's Salt Lake Temple and the adjoining Tabernacle is dedicated within days, and the settlers begin to lay out their city grid, build homes, plant crops, and begin their new lives.

They will be soon be joined by thousands of others who hope to finally practice their religion in peace.

In December, 1847, Brigham Young – "prophet, seer, and revelator to the world" – becomes the Second President of the Church (succeeding Joseph

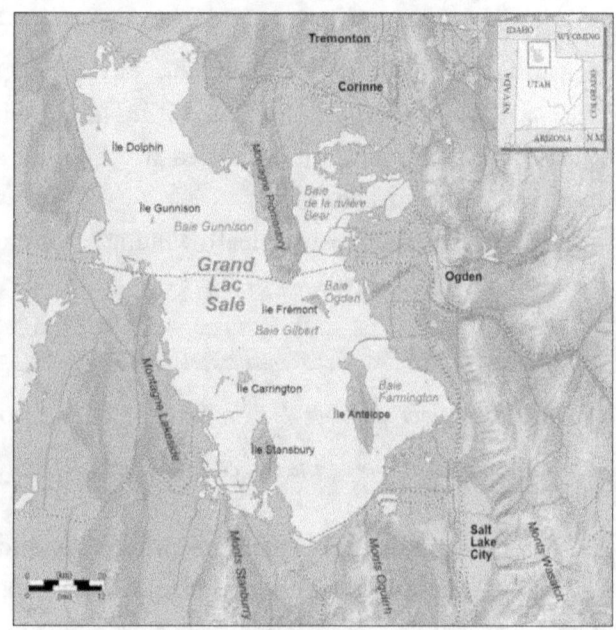

Map of the Great Salt Lake and Vicinity

Smith), an office he will hold until his death in 1877.

At long last, the Church of the Latter-day Saints have found their new leader and their permanent home.

TIME: JULY 1846-47

A MORMON BRIGADE SUPPORTS THE WAR WITH MEXICO

During their stay in Illinois, the Mormons have consistently supported the Democratic Party, including both Stephen Douglas and James Polk.

In 1845, Brigham Young writes to Polk, asking for government protection of his followers. Polk expresses his support for the Mormons, including a small personal donation of $10 to their cause.

From that time on, Young looks for a way to repay the debt, and the opportunity arises as they trek toward Utah during the early days of the War with Mexico.

Polk desperately needs additional troops to prosecute the war, especially in the far west.

In 1846, he asks Young to assemble a 500-man force to

Map of The "Mormon Brigade's" Overland March –
July 1846-47

support the fight, to demonstrate the sect's loyalty to the United States and, in turn, to dampen public opposition to their religious beliefs.

Thus, in July, 1846, the "Mormon Battalion," roughly 550 men strong, is mustered into the U.S. Army and sent on the longest overland military march in history, southwest through Kansas, New Mexico, and Arizona to their destination at Los Angeles.

However, like most troops in the northern theater, the Mormon Battalion sees no actual combat.

After their one year-long enlistment expires; many Mormons stay on in California. In January, 1847, one of them, Henry Bigler lands on a sawmill construction project near Ft. Sutter – where he earns lasting fame, along with Jim Marshall, as the first to discover gold along the American River. Over time, a total of $17,000 will be contributed to the Mormon cause by Brigade members who participate in the subsequent 1849 Gold Rush.

In the end, the Battalion's efforts have served Young's ends, establishing good will with Polk and the public, and also providing funds from the $30,000 total pay the unit receives for its year of service to purchase livestock, wagons, and supplies needed for the Mormon's trek to their new home.

## 130

GENERAL SCOTT CONQUERS MEXICO CITY AND ENDS THE WAR

TIME: AUGUST 20, 1847

FIGHTING RESUMES AT CHURUBUSCO IN THE VALLEY OF MEXICO

General Scott's pause after his victories at Vera Cruz and Cerro Gordo allows time for envoy Nicholas Trist to negotiate for peace, and for Scott to add more men before moving further inland toward his next goal, Mexico City.

The first contingent of 2,000 troops arrives in July, followed soon by another 2,400, under Brigadier General Franklin Pierce. On August 10, 1847, Scott decides that he is ready, and his total force of 10,700 men—half new untested volunteers—heads west.

Soon, they crest the mountains east of the capital where they come upon a dazzling landscape in the valley below. There, at 7250 feet above sea level, lays the city built by the Aztecs in 1325 and ruled by them until Cortez overthrew Montezuma in 1519. The historian, Horatio Ladd, in his 1883 chronicle of the war, describes the sight:

> A few miles beyond Rio Frio they came suddenly upon an enchanting vision of the valley of Mexico. It was a dazzling picture of earthly beauty. The rich spring verdure of the plains dotted with the white walls of villages and haciendas, the silvery lines of mountain streams, the blue surfaces of lakes whose shores, winding about the base of mountains, stretched far into the green valleys and the hills rising to lofty ranges white with snow and glistening beneath the soft blue sky, all presented a scene that made the romance of Spanish conquests in the days of Montezuma appear like the truths of sober history.

Scott now must decide how he plans to conquer the capital city.

By August 16, he has recon-
noitered the direct approach from
the east over the National Road
through El Peñon Viejo, and concluded that it will leave him with
only one line of assault on the
capital. So, he settles instead on
a difficult 27-mile march heading south of Lake Chalcothen
east along the Acapulco Road. He
intends to bypass the Mexican
defenses at San Antonio, march
around the Padregal lava fields to
the town of Contreras, and attack
north from there.

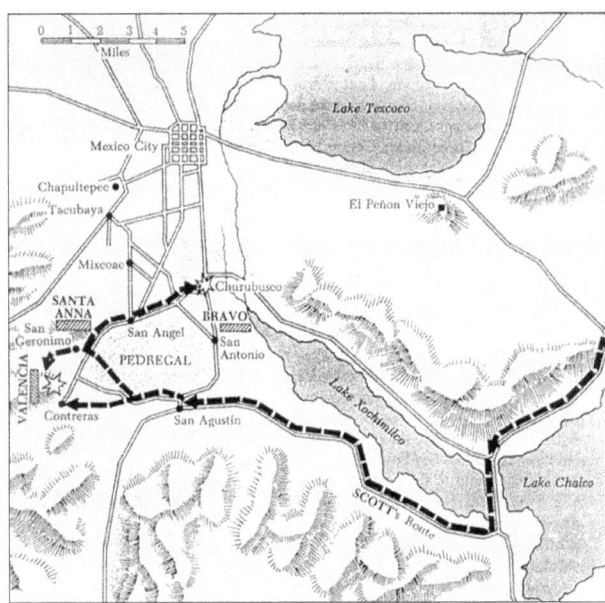

Lake Chalco Where Scott Swings South
to Attack the Capital from Below

Santa Anna, anticipates Scott's
path and intends to attack him along the road from Contreras to Churubusco. He lays
out strong positions over the entire route with General Valencia's 7,000 men on a steep
hill bordering Contreras, his own 11,000 men two miles to the north, General Ruicon
with another 6,000 at Churubusco guarding a river bridge, and General Bravo with
3,000 men above San Antonio.

Once again, as at Cerro Gordo, Santa Anna is confident of victory. His 27,000
soldiers outnumber Scott by 3:1, and they are fighting to protect the capital city of their
nation.

But once again, Scott finds a way to outmaneuver and defeat the Mexicans despite
their courageous efforts.

On August 19, General Persifor Smith's brigade first comes up against Valencia.
They are beaten back and trapped at the foot of the Contreras hill. That night Valencia
celebrates, passing out brevets along with hard liquor to his troops. As the Mexicans
revel, Smith's engineers find a way out of their trap – a passable ravine that circles to
the right of the hill and comes up on Valencia's rear. At 3 a.m., Smith's men race up the
slopes. According to Smith, it has "taken just 17 minutes" to clear the Mexicans off the
hill and send them scurrying toward Churubusco.

Santa Anna tries to stabilize his troops throughout the day, but to no avail. General
William Worth forces his way through San Antonio on the Mexican left and unites
with Twiggs and Pillow at Churubusco. They are slowed briefly by stiff resistance from
a heavily fortified church convent, but soon break through and seize the key bridge over
the Churubusco River.

The first line of defense protecting the capital city has been breached by Scott in his three victories. American casualties for the day total 120 killed and 816 wounded. The Mexicans suffer 3,250 total casualties, along with 2,627 prisoners.

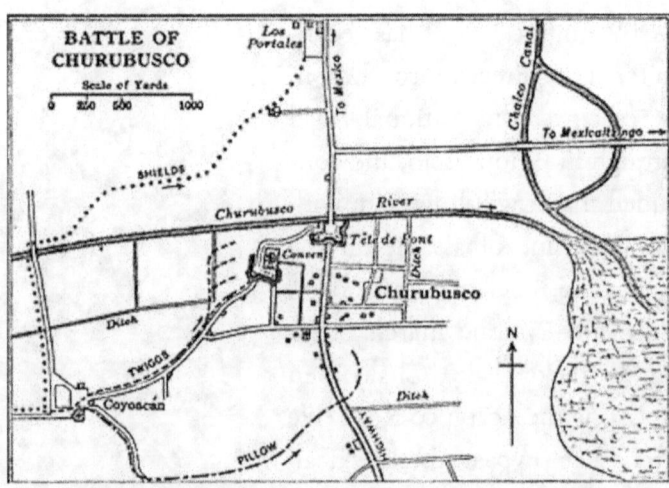

Map Showing Twiggs and Pillow Assaulting Cherubusco

Four and a half months have elapsed since U.S. forces left Veracruz on their audacious mission.

Now all that's left is one final push.

Instead of rushing headlong to the capital, Scott turns momentarily cautious. He fears that his army has been fought out at Churubusco, and wants time for his engineers to plot the best approaches into the city.

When he halts, Santa Anna sends emissaries out under a flag of truce to explore an armistice. Buchanan's man, Twist, joins the talks, and soon the lull in battle reaches two weeks. By then Scott concludes that Santa Anna is simply stalling for time to strengthen his defenses, and he ends the armistice on September 7.

His army is refitted and his strategy laid out. On September 8, 1847, he resumes his advance.

TIME: SEPTEMBER 8, 1847

THE BATTLES OF MOLINO DEL REY AND CASA DE MATA

The ancient city now in front of Scott was originally built on an island just off the western edge of Lake Texcoco. By the late 17th century, the population is expanding and the lake is being drained away to prevent flooding and to provide more living space. Eventually the

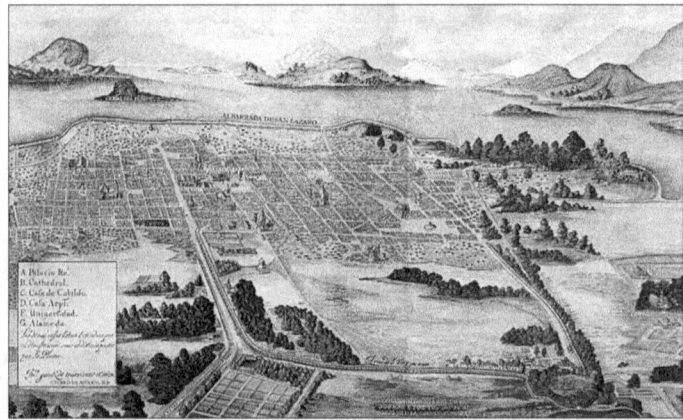

Painting of Mexico City Around 1629

lake vanishes into marshland, with eight elevated causeways built as routes into the city.

To reach the interior, Scott must first overcome three formidable outposts guarding the entrance to the western causeways – the citadel at Casa de Mata, the Molino del Rey mill and foundry, and the daunting Chapultec Castle, regarded by many as the strongest fort on the North American continent.

A bitter dispute over strategy for attacking the Molino erupts between Scott and General William Worth, his right-hand man since the War of 1812. Scott prevails, but Worth never fully forgives him for the carnage that follows.

At dawn on September 8, Lt. John Foster leads the first head-on attempt to storm the Molino. This ends in a hail of musket fire and grapeshot that repulses the Americans and leaves Foster lying with a shattered leg on the field. And there he stays for another two hours of sustained violence in what turns out to be one of the bloodiest battles of the war.

The Americans eventually prevail at both the Molino and the Casa de Mata citadel, but at a cost of 729 casualties, including 58 officers. The Mexican losses top 3,000, with Santa Anna's top two commanders killed outright, General Leon at Molino and General Valderez at de Mata.

John G. Foster (1823-1874)

TIME: SEPTEMBER 16, 1847

ASSAULT ON CHAPULTEPEC CASTLE
AND THE HALLS OF MONTEZUMA

With the Molino secured, Scott decides to storm the capitol from two directions. His main attack will come from the west under General Pillow along the six-foot-high causeway leading to the San Cosme (customs house) Gate. Infantry units will support Pillow under Mississippi General John Quitman, driving from the south against the Belen Gate.

To succeed, Pillow must first pass the Chapultepec Castle, jutting out on a rock ledge 150 feet above the ground, surrounded by walls that are 4 feet thick and 20 feet high. The castle, formerly home to Aztec emperors, is now the site of the Mexican Military Academy, their West Point.

But not even this imposing barrier can hold up under the advanced artillery hardware and engineering tactics that have helped the Americans prevail from one battle to the next.

On September 12, four U.S. batteries, in easy range and well sheltered, begin to reduce the fort's defenses.

On September 13, as the bombardment continues, the Americans storm Chapultepec.

Pillow's troops race through the Molino grounds and into a cypress grove, where the General falls with a severe wound to his ankle. His men, however, move steadily forward and deploy scaling ladders to begin their ascent of the rocky hill leading to the castle itself. One officer who particularly distinguishes himself is Lt. Tom Jackson, who wins another brevet for his artillery work alongside Captain John Magruder.

Chapultepec Castle by Nathaniel Currier, 1847

A post-war photo of the Mexican citadel

Pillow's troops are quickly joined by General Quitman coming up from the other side of the hill. Both contingents encounter fierce resistance, but nothing is about to deny the Americans at this point. By late morning shouts go up across the battlefield as the Stars & Stripes appear on the castle ramparts.

During the assault on the castle, a litany of future civil war military heroes have suffered wounds. Lt. PGT Beauregard is hit twice in the action. Major William Loring loses his left arm. Second Lt. James Longstreet goes down with a bullet to his thigh while carrying a regimental flag he hands off to Lt. George Pickett. Others wounded include Lt. Colonel Joseph Johnston, Captains Silas Casey and John Magruder, Lts. Innis Palmer, Lewis Armistead, Earl Van Dorn, Isaac Stevens, and John Brannan.

Lt. Tom Jackson,
later Stonewall
(1824-1863)

The Mexican troops are both astonished and demoralized by the fall of Chapultepec, and they flee east along the two major causeways toward the central city.

The Americans follow with Worth picking up the lead for Pillow toward the San Cosme Gate. Quitman's forces, under the wounded General James Shields, close in on Belen.

Shields is a hot-headed Irish politician from Springfield, Illinois, who, in 1842, had challenged Abraham Lincoln to duel over a perceived slight. His battle temper is similarly up, and by 1 p.m., he breaks through Belen and into the city proper only to come under heavy fire from the Citadel in the central Plaza. By evening Shields and Quitman hunker down and wait for Scott's next orders.

James Shields (1810-1879)

Worth's drive toward San Cosme proves to be much slower going despite courageous initiatives from men like Second Lieutenant Ulysses S. Grant, who sets up a howitzer in the belfry of a church and scatters defenders in his front. Rearguard skirmishes and sniper fire continue on this causeway throughout the afternoon, and Worth halts his men by 8PM within easy artillery range of his assigned gate.

On September 14, emissaries from the city come out to meet Scott. They inform him that Santa Anna has resigned his presidency and that the main body of the Mexican army has fled overnight out the backdoor

Ulysses S. Grant (1822-1885) and his Horse Cincinnati

exit along the National Road. They also request that control over the population, some 200,000 strong, be assigned to municipal authorities and the church.

Scott has not come this far to leave the capital in Mexican hands, and he immediately orders his troops forward.

The right wing, under Quitman and Shields, already inside the city, proceed toward the Grand Plaza and the National Palace, seat of the Mexican government. Once there, General Quitman is given the honor of raising the American flag in the square.

Clean-up operations against diehards continue over the next day and a half, until the morning of September 16, when control over the entire city has been secured.

On September 16, 1847, Scott names Quitman military governor of Mexico City, a position he will hold until July 20, 1848 when the U.S. occupation ends. At the same time, Scott allows the local city council to continue to function, along with the local police force, and justice system. The Americans fine the city 150,000 pesos to care for wounded soldiers, and ensure payment by controlling the customs gates. Eventually some of the funds collected go toward efforts to rebuild the city.

General John Quitman
(1798-1858)

Since entering the Valley of Mexico on August 10 with 10,700 troops, Scott has suffered 2,703 killed or wounded, including 383 officers. Mexican losses stand at 7,000 total casualties, along with 3,700 prisoners. When asked about "why" his massively outnumbered forces have prevailed in Mexico, Scott points to the superior military training and leadership of his West Point officer corps.

I give it as my fixed opinion, but that but for our graduated cadets the war between the United States and Mexico might, and probably would, have lasted some four or five years, with, in its first half, more defeats than victories falling to our share; whereas in two campaigns we conquered a great country and (won) peace without the loss of a single battle or skirmish.

The 78-year-old Duke of Wellington, victor at Waterloo, attributes the victory to Scott, calling him "the greatest living soldier" and his Mexican expedition "unsurpassed in military annals." On the other hand, General Pillow declares himself the "hero of Chapultepec" and is court marshaled by Scott, along with Worth, for writing after-battle reports considered self-laudatory and unprofessional.

Scott's attention now turns to working toward a peace treaty, in conjunction with Nicholas Twist.

SIDEBAR: MILESTONES IN SCOTT'S DRIVE TO MEXICO CITY

SCOTT'S 275 MILE DRIVE FROM VERA CRUZ TO MEXICO CITY

DATE	EVENTS
March 29, 1847	Amphibious assault at Vera Cruz
April 20	Battle of Xalapa/ Cerro Gordo
Spring	Pause as Trist negotiations proceed
August 27	Win at Cherubusco
September 8	Molina del Rey
September 16	Mexico City

TIME: SEPTEMBER 1847

LAND OCCUPIED IN MEXICO BY THE END OF WAR

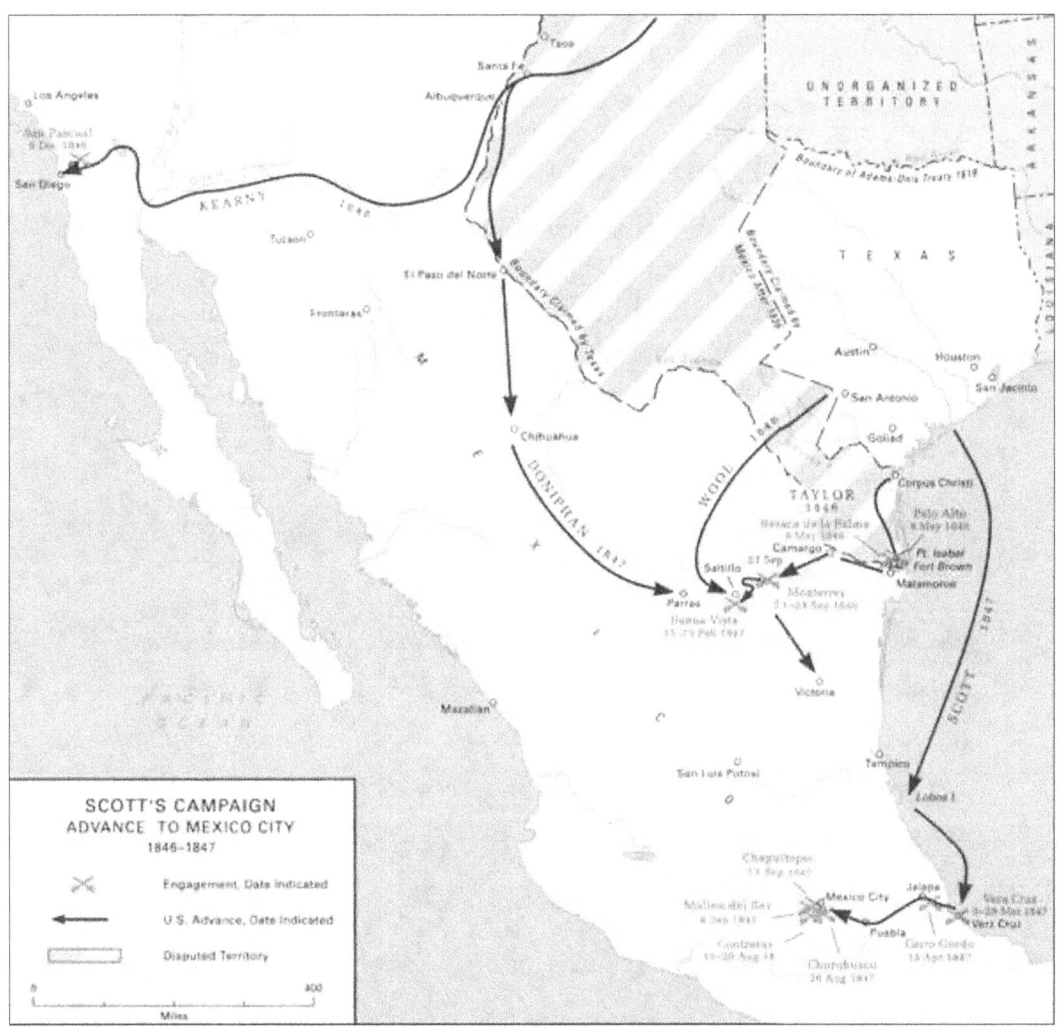

Map of Kearny, Doniphan and Scott Advances through Mexico

Despite sporadic, mostly guerrilla fighting after the capital falls, America is now the de facto ruler of all Mexico, only 26 years after that nation's independence from Spain.

Occupational garrisons are set up across all three theaters of the conflict.

To the north, General Kearny and Commodore Stockton control key cities due west from Amarillo in northern Texas through Santa Fe and Albuquerque to Los Angeles.

In the center, Generals Doniphan and Taylor have gouged out a semicircle of land below the originally disputed Rio Grande border. Doniphan has driven down from Santa Fe to victories at El Paso on December 25, 1846; Chihuahua in February, 1847; to meet Taylor who has secured Palo Alto, Monterrey, and Buena Vista.

To the South, Scott holds a horizontal slash of 300 miles west from Veracruz to Mexico City.

Yet, two questions remain for the conquerors: What land do they want to acquire permanently? And, how can they get the Mexicans to agree on a final peace treaty?

SIDEBAR: OTHER CIVIL WAR GENERALS WHO FIGHT TOGETHER IN THE MEXICAN WAR

The fighting in Mexico will serve as a dress rehearsal for the strategies and tactics employed fifteen years hence in the American Civil War.

It also provides the ground of combat that produces many of that war's senior commanders – 194 Union and 142 Confederate general officers in all.

Before these men are enemies at Bull Run, Antietam, and Gettysburg, they have been brothers at Buena Vista, Monterrey, and Veracruz. Together, their deeds are nothing short of remarkable.

The capture of Mexico City is one of them. As future CSA General William Gardner (West Point class of 1846) says:

The idea of 10,000 men marching through a hostile country upon a capital containing upwards of 200,000 inhabitants, defended by 30,000 troops equipped with 100 pieces of cannon, and fortified by both nature and art! The capture of the city of Mexico under such conditions was a feat of arms to astound the world.

CONFEDERATES/CSA

James Longstreet (1821-1904)   George Pickett (1825-1875)   Joe Johnston (1807-1891)

Ambrose P. Hill
(1825-1865)

P.G.T. Beauregard
(1818-1893)

A. S. Johnston
(1803-1862)

UNION/USA

Samuel French
(1818-1910)

John Gibbon
(1827-189)

Winfield Scott Hancock
(1824-1886)

Joseph Hooker
(1814-1879)

Henry Hunt
(1819-1889)

George Meade
(1815-1872)

## 131

TWO SPLINTER PARTIES NOMINATE THEIR PRESIDENTIAL CANDIDATES

TIME: SEPTEMBER 10-11, 1847

THE NATIVE AMERICAN PARTY SELECTS ZACHARY TAYLOR

THE IRISH "JANTIN" CAR

Derogatory Depiction of Irish Catholic Immigrants in the 1840s

With the Mexican War winding down, Lewis Levin and his anti-immigrant Native American Party try to get a jump on the 1848 election by holding their first national convention.

The party has won six House seats in the 1844 race, but is down to one – Levin himself – after the off-year balloting. Its goal now is to revitalize itself, arrive at a platform, try to strengthen its organization, and broaden its base of voters.

The name of Levin's party will vary over the next decade.

At first, the party is known as the American Republican Association. By 1847, it morphs into the Native American Party, or the American Party for short. An off-shoot, The Order of the Star-Spangled Banner, surfaces in 1849. A skeptical journalist, Horace Greeley, finds members reciting a set response. When asked about the party principles, they reply, "I know nothing."

Greeley responds by handing the group its enduring nickname, the "Know Nothing Party."

The party convention is held on September 10-11 at the Assembly Building in Philadelphia, with roughly one hundred delegates in attendance.

A full party platform won't be fleshed out until 1852, but for now they agree on several things:

- The country should "belong" to American born, white Protestant citizens.
- The sharp rise in overall immigration in the 1840s threatens this outcome.
- The danger is compounded by the fact that many immigrants are Catholics beholden to Rome.

In turn, the solution to "saving the country" lies in a host of actions aimed at the "foreign invaders" from shutting down further immigration to waging "war to the hilt" against Catholics already in the country.

When the time comes for the American Party to nominate their choice for President, they settle on the warrior of the Mexican War, General Zachary Taylor.

For Vice-President, they choose 64-year-old Henry A. S. Dearborn, son of Revolutionary War General Henry Dearborn, and current Mayor of Roxbury, Massachusetts.

TIME: OCTOBER 20, 1847

THE LIBERTY PARTY SPLITS IN TWO

The 1848 race will be the third and final campaign for the abolitionist Liberty Party.

Its roots trace back to 1839 and the schism within the movement between the Boston-based followers of William Lloyd Garrison and the New Yorkers, drawn to the philanthropists Gerritt Smith, brothers, Arthur and Lewis Tappan; and Cincinnati journalist, James Birney.

Both groups share the same ends – immediate emancipation and full citizenship for all who remain enslaved – but differ on the means.

The Garrisonians refuse to be drawn into the political arena, arguing that the Constitution and office holders in D.C. have kept the Africans in chains. Change will occur only through appealing directly to the good will of the public. They point to the steady progress made by their Anti-Slavery Societies and local lecture tours to support their convictions.

In 1846 Garrison labels the Mexican War "the greatest crime of our age" and campaigns against it. He calls the 1846 Wilmot Proviso a "landmark of anti-slavery resistance," and in the fall of 1847, lectures to 20,000 people across fifteen towns, frequently referring to the Union as "a sinful abomination." He also burns the U.S. Constitution as a public protest.

But his inflammatory rhetoric and anti-political posture is gradually costing him some

Salmon P. Chase (1808-1873)

support including that of his long-time protégé, Frederick Douglass. In 1847, Douglas decides to start up his own abolition paper, *The North Star*, without first informing Garrison. From then on, their relationship grows distant.

Others, like the strategist, Salmon Chase, simply conclude that Garrison's strategy is naïve, and that the only realistic path to ending slavery will be to undermine its support in Congress through new legislation. In 1840, the Liberty Party is born out of this belief.

Its election performance, however, proves anemic. In 1840, James Birney tops the ticket and receives only 7,000 votes nationally. In 1844, he is again nominated, garnering 62,000 votes or 2% of the ballots cast.

These results provoke an internal split between the Gerrit Smith faction and the Salmon Chase faction, which surfaces at the party convention held in Buffalo on October 20, 1847.

The politically astute Chase is impressed by the anti-slavery traction evident in the congressional votes cast on the Wilmot Proviso, and argues that the Liberty Party would be better off in the short run by fighting the westward spread of slavery rather than by focusing exclusively on total abolition now.

The majority of the delegates line up behind this tactical shift, and nominate the vocal anti-slavery Senator John P. Hale of New Hampshire over his one competitor, Gerrit Smith, on the first and only ballot.

INITIAL VOTE OF THE LIBERTY PARTY (1847)

CANDIDATE	VOTES
John P. Hale	103
Gerrit Smith	41

When Smith learns of this outcome, he claims that the party has been hijacked by moderates who would forfeit the abolition crusade for a few more political votes.

His response is to hold a convention of his own on June 2, 1848, in Rochester, New York, where his loyalists back him for President, and Presbyterian minister Charles C. Foote of Michigan as Vice-President.

## 132

POLK GETS THE INDEPENDENT TREASURY HE WANTS

TIME: 1800 – 1845

CONTROVERSY OVER A FEDERAL BANK CONTINUES

With the Mexican War essentially won and the Wilmot Proviso threat apparently contained, Polk returns to his search for a satisfactory federal money management plan for the nation.

Going all the way back to Jefferson, Democrats distrust the notion of a privately run bank corporation having control over the government's money and, in turn, the future direction of the economy. From their perspective, this puts too much power in the hands of un-elected officials, offers too many temptations to put selfish interests above the public good, and lacks the transparency needed to avoid corruption.

Polk's mentor, Andrew Jackson, launches a personal crusade against the Second Bank of the United States which he calls "the monster on Chestnut Street." In 1834, he discovers that rampant speculation by banks has driven up land prices for western settlers and undermined the true value of all soft money. In response he

The Presidents of the United States.
JAMES K. POLK—11TH.

James K. Polk (1795-1849)

abruptly shuts down the BUS, provoking the financial panic of 1837.

At that time, Thomas Hart Benton, offers an option to the BUS which he calls the National Exchequer Bank. It would still handle all revenue deposits and sell insurance backing independent transactions, but have nothing whatsoever to do with impacting the course of the economy. Jackson likes this option, but Congress refuses to go along.

After the crash of 1837, Van Buren proposes an Independent Treasury, run by government officials and not private investors. It would receive tax payments in hard money, and operate within a narrow charter – depositing federal revenue, disbursing funds to cover federal spending, and making loans to demonstrably solvent state banks.

Van Buren finally gets congressional approval in 1840, at the end of his term. Jackson applauds the move as does his hard money advisor, William Gough, who cites the utter simplicity of the solution:

So plain would be the accounts that we might choose for the chief bookkeeper...a cordwainer (shoemaker)...who daily threw into the leg of one boot his receipts for the day, and into another...his expenditures.

But the Independent Treasury stands for only one year before Henry Clay and his Whigs repeal the bill – hoping to establish a Third U.S. Bank, to keep more credit in the marketplace, and to back their spending on infrastructure.

When Tyler vetoes this effort, all federal revenues are deposited directly into state banks.

TIME: AUGUST 6, 1848

AN INDEPENDENT TREASURY IS ESTABLISHED WITH HELP FROM BENTON

In 1846, the need to fund the Mexican War forces Polk's hand on the banking system.

He has begun as a strict Jacksonian, inclined to hard money and suspicious of all private banks and bankers. But he grudgingly comes around to seeing the need for banknotes to support daily commerce and for a public agency to handle the government's cash flow and insure the value of the currency.

He decides that Van Buren's Independent Treasury is the best path to meeting these goals – and supports a bill to re-instate it, along with a clause giving Secretary Walker the power to issue short-term notes (bonds) to bolster cash-on-hand, as needed.

The Independent Treasury Act passes Congress on July 29, 1846, with votes cast along straight party lines.

"Old Bullions" Benton applauds it as the final divorce between the State and the Banks.

Henceforth decisions about spending federal money will rest with elected officials and not private corporations.

## 133

GOLD IS DISCOVERED IN CALIFORNIA

TIME: 1841-1843

JOHAN SUTTER DREAMS OF A "NEW SWITZERLAND" COMMUNITY ALONG THE CALIFORNIA TRAIL

In January, 1848, the U.S. conquest of the Mexican province of Alta California takes on new and dramatic importance with the announcement that gold has been discovered 35 miles northeast of Sacramento at a sawmill being constructed near Fort Sutter.

The fort is named for the German immigrant, Johann August Suter, who, in 1834, flees from a debt-ridden past in Switzerland to start a new life in America. He is 31 and anglicizes himself as "Captain John Sutter of the Swiss Guard." He is multilingual and mixes easily in the French, German, and Spanish communities around St. Louis before joining the westward tide, first to Santa, and then to the "Oregon Country."

John Sutter (1803-1880)

There, he learns the fur trapping and trading business, and decides to settle down in northern California.

Since the territory is in the hands of Mexico, he goes through the laborious process of gaining permission to settle on the land although his legal rights to the property will later be contested, much to his misfortune. In August, 1840, he qualifies as a Mexican citizen and in June, 1841, is given title to 49,000 acres along the American River. He christens the site "New Helvetia (Switzerland)" and dreams of establishing an old- world agricultural community capable of thriving economically and fending off threats from both local tribes and the Mexican militia.

Between 1841 and 1843 he constructs his town center, Fort Sutter, comprising roughly six acres of land surrounded by walls that are 2.5 feet thick and fifteen feet high. Inside the compound are housing, a large kitchen and bakery, a smithy, carpentry shop, distillery, jail, a blanket factory, extensive storage facilities, and a supply depot and grocery store for travelers heading up or down the California Trail. Outside the compound are a flour mill, herds of cattle; and farmland capable of providing the food and cash crops needed to sustain both settlers and guests.

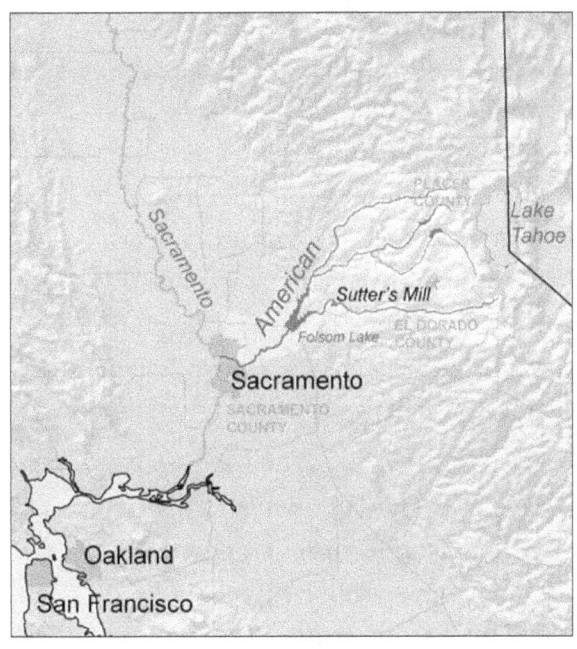

Map showing Fort Sutter and the Surrounding Area

The American River runs along the west side of the fort, with a dock and boats that ferry passengers ninety miles down to San Francisco Bay.

"New Helvetia" thrives, and Sutter is soon in need of additional lumber to keep up with his plans to expand the town. To supply it, he decides to construct his own sawmill at Coloma, 40 miles upstream from the fort. Work on the mill is contracted out to James Marshall, who, in 1845, comes to the fort as a carpenter. He will go on to fight alongside John C. Fremont in the 1846 "Bear Flag Revolt" before rejoining Sutter in 1847.

Sutter and Marshall form a partnership. Marshall is charged with building the sawmill in exchange for wages and a share of the lumber produced. He hires a construction crew composed of local Nisenan tribesmen, and members of the "Mormon Battalion" who have stopped temporarily at the fort after the Mexican War on their way home to Salt Lake City.

Work on the mill gets under way in August 1847.

TIME: JANUARY 24, 1848

GOLD IS DISCOVERED NEARBY AT SUTTER'S SAWMILL

Constructing a nineteenth century water-powered saw mill is a complex endeavor. In January, 1848, when Marshall starts construction, he immediately encounters a problem. The flow of water into and through the wheel which drives the saw blades is not fast enough to generate the rotations per minute needed. Marshall analyzes the flow and concludes that the run-off ditch (or "trace") below the wheel must be deepened and widened. A crew begins digging to widen this trace.

On the morning of January 24, 1848, Marshall is inspecting progress on the new ditch when he spots an unusual mineral formation. One of the Mormon crew members, James S. Brown, later records Marshall's words:

Twelve Western Miners

This is a curious rock, I am afraid that it will give us trouble…I believe that it contains minerals of some kind, and I believe that there is gold in these hills… Well, we will hoist the gates and turn in all the water that we can to-night, and tomorrow morning we will shut it off and come down, and I believe we will find gold or some kind of mineral here.

The drama continues the next day, as recalled by Brown:

Marshall said, Boys, I have got her now. I, being the nearest to him, and having more curiosity than the rest of the men, jumped from the pit and stepped to him, and on looking in his hat discovered say ten or twelve pieces of small scales of what proved to be gold. I picked up the largest piece, worth about fifty cents, and tested it with my teeth, and as it did not give, I held it aloft and exclaimed, "gold, boys, gold!" At that they all dropped their tools and gathered around Mr. Marshall.

The crew agrees to keep the find a secret among themselves while fanning out across the area around the mill for their own discoveries. Over the next few days, more nuggets materialize and the excitement builds.

Marshall decides that he must share the news with Sutter, and he sends a message back to the fort with an Indian courier. Sutter's reactions are predictable. He first tries to contain the news locally, and then to determine whether he has any claims to the land around the mill.

Containment fails owing to a man named Samuel Brannan, a Mormon and an early settler in California, who founds a newspaper in San Francisco and tries to convince Brigham Young to settle there. One of Brannan's duties is to collect tithes for the church, and he learns of the find when several Mormons at the sawmill hand him bits of gold on his visit. His response is immediate. He buys up all of the gold mining equipment he can find – using the church tithes along with his own money – and opens a supply store near Fort Sutter – then walks the streets of San Francisco shouting out the news of "gold found along the American River!"

For his efforts, Brannan becomes one of the first gold rush millionaires, earning expulsion by the Mormon church for fraud.

Sutter also learns that all of the land around his sawmill is considered "in the public domain," and is available to any miner who stakes out a claim to mineral rights on "their plot." In response, he heads to Coloma and tries his hand at mining, but never makes a strike.

The gold rush also proves unkind to Sutter's utopian wish for New Helvetia.

Get-rich-quick explorers from across the globe are soon squatting on his land and siphoning off his crops and livestock. His attempts to regain control are overwhelmed by the hoards, and his debts mount quickly. In 1849, he sells his fort for $7,000, deeds his remaining land to his son, and takes up residence in Yuba City, fifty miles to the north. For the next thirty years, John Sutter attempts to convince the U.S. Congress to reimburse him $50,000 for loss of the land originally granted to him by Mexico, and for his important contribution to colonizing California. In June 18, 1880, he is again ignored, and he dies two days later of heart failure at his latest residence in Lititz, Pennsylvania.

TIME: 1849

THE MINER 49ERS RUSH TO CALIFORNIA TO GET RICH QUICK

At first, the public regards the news of the "find" at John Sutter's sawmill with the usual skepticism, despite an initial report published on August 19, 1848, by James Gordon Bennett's prestigious *New York Herald*.

The response changes on December 5, 1848, when President Polk confirms the discovery of quantities of the precious ore that "would scarcely command belief:"

Recent discoveries render it probable that these mines are more extensive and valuable than was anticipated. The accounts of the abundance of gold in that territory are of such an extraordinary character as would scarcely command belief were they not corroborated by the authentic reports of officers in the public service who have visited the mineral district and derived the facts which they detail from personal observation.

With that, the rush of 1849 is on!

The first challenge for the 49ers lies in getting to California from the east. Primary paths are identified in the press: across the Isthmus of Panama; through Nicaragua; around Cape Horn; overland along the Oregon and California Trails or various southern routes over the former or current Mexican territory. A Cape Horn ship is the safest and fastest (25-30 days) option, but the price quickly skyrockets to $400.

In January 1849, Samuel McNeil, a shoemaker from Lancaster, Ohio, sets out on a journey that will cover over 3300 miles, take five months to complete, and be memorialized in his publication, *McNeil's Travels In 1849 In California.*

He reaches New Orleans by steamboat down the Ohio and Mississippi Rivers on February 20. His intent is to continue west through Nicaragua, but instead he ends up on the overland route across Mexico,

Two Mining Pards off to make their fortunes

reaching the town of Brazos where he buys a mule and rides it for over 1,000 miles arriving at the coast at Mazatlán on May 10. He completes the remaining 1500 miles on May 30, 1849, when the ship he is on arrives at the port of San Francisco – still a tent city, comprising less than one thousand residents.

McNeil is finally ready to try his hand at mining for gold. Armed with a pick and shovel, "cradle" and pan, he has acquired at grossly inflated prices, he is ready to apply whatever knowledge he has gleaned from various "how-to" write-ups already appearing in print. His destination is "Smith's Bar," north of Sacramento at the fork of the Bear and Feather Rivers.

Once there, McNeil makes his claim to mineral rights (but not land ownership) by putting stakes down on the plot. These plots are either along the banks of a river, creek, or mid-stream in the water flow. The searching Site process is done by hand. The miner scoops shovels of black sand and gravel into either a 4-foot long "cradle" or a simple pan, drains off the water, and shakes the container in search of flecks or nuggets of gold.

It is a back-breaking task, but made tolerable by the pay-off for success. While day laborers back east are lucky to earn $1.00 a day in wages, McNeil reports that the average prospector is finding $16 a day in gold, and some fabulous finds yield $9,000 a week.

Such good fortune does not befall McNeil himself. He gives up after several futile weeks and decides to earn his fortune in a different fashion – by opening The Sycamore Tree Establishment," a combination saloon and brothel. While business is brisk, he is soon homesick for Ohio. On September 2, 1849, three months after his arrival in California, he has sold his saloon, clearing a $2,000 profit, and is back on a ship headed home to resume his former life and publish his memoirs.

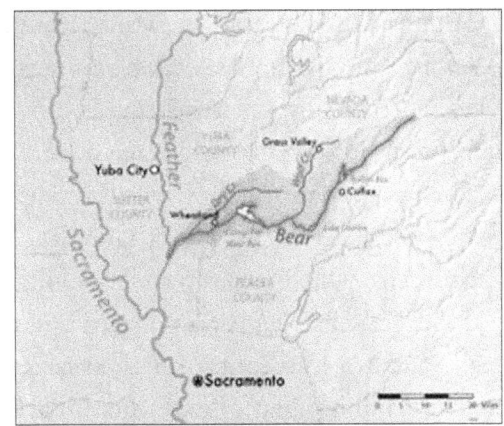

Site of Samuel McNeil's Brief Dig on the Feather & Bear Rivers

As McNeil departs, other more determined 49ers pour into San Francisco.

By 1850, San Francisco is a full-fledged "boom town," with 25,000 settled residents, and 300,000 prospectors passing through over the next decade. Included are thousands of Chinese immigrants, who are mistreated in ways generally reserved for the native tribes. Upwards of 90% of new residents are males, whose lifestyles justify the wild-wild west label they are handed.

The value of the gold they produce is staggering – reaching a high of $81 million in 1852 and tapering off to $45 million prior to the Civil War. The individual prospector, panning by hand in the middle of a river, soon gives way to larger enterprises using industrialized equipment familiar in other mining operations.

GOLD PRODUCED IN CALIFORNIA

YEAR	GOLD OUTPUT (000)
1848	$245.3
1849	$10,151.4
1850	41,273.1
1851	75,938.2
1852	81,294.7
1853	67,613.5
1854	69,433.9
1855	55,485.4
1856	57,509.4
1857	43,628.2
1858	46,095.1
1859	44,095.2

Along with the rapid growth in people and wealth comes a merchant class eager to service every wish of successful miners with gold to spend. Demand for goods and services perpetually outstrips supply, and those capable of meeting immediate needs often profit more than the average miners themselves.

Success stories abound. Two start-up bankers, Henry Wells and William Fargo, provide their customers with a safe place for their daily finds. They also open a stage-coach service which ferries travelers, along with mail, back and forth across the prairie.

John Studebaker makes wheelbarrows just south of the gold-fields when the news breaks, and uses the profits from their sales to become a leader in manufacturing carriages. The German immigrant Levi Strauss arrives in 1850 with plans to make canvas tarps for covered wagons, then shifts to blue denim work pants quickly popularized in dry goods stores. The famous butcher and meatpacker, Philip Armour, builds his business from the $8,000 bankroll he accumulates during the rush period.

Aside from the personal fortunes created and the impact on the national economy, the gold rush of 1849 puts the issue of governance of the territory of California front and center on the agenda for the politicians in Washington.

## 134

POLITICAL BATTLES INTENSIFY OVER A PROPER PEACE TREATY WITH MEXICO

TIME: WINTER-SPRING 1847

DISPUTES EXIST OVER TERMS FOR PEACE

By the winter of 1847, Polk realized that winning the war with Mexico has not ended the political battles surrounding the original annexation of Texas and the Wilmot Proviso ban on slavery in land acquired by the conflict.

Within his own Democratic Party, divisions run deep about what to do with Mexico and its territory.

Polk's Treasury Secretary, Robert Walker, wants to annex the entire country.

James Buchanan, who publicly opposed any land acquisition when the war began, now turns acquisitive, to boost his odds for the presidential nomination. Once again, Polk is enraged by his erratic Secretary of State.

Abraham Lincoln (1809-1865)

Senator John C. Calhoun, whose hawkishness over Texas provoked the war, expresses horror at this thought, which would blemish America's racial purity.

We have never dreamt of incorporating into our Union any but the Caucasian race – the free white race. To incorporate Mexico, would be the very first instance of (including) an Indian race. Ours, sir, is the government of the white man... To erect

these Mexicans into a territorial government and place them on an equality with the
people of the United States is (something) I protest.

Then there is the especially galling New York wing of the party, now being called the
"Wilmot Proviso Democrats," who continue to insist on the slavery ban.

Polk himself opposes a wholesale annexation, but argues that America must
be "indemnified" (i.e. compensated) for the costs of a war Mexico started by "their
invading U.S. soil" along the Rio Grande on April 25, 1846. He decides to "wait out"
the Mexicans, hoping they will offer up attractive peace terms.

He has sent his version of the territorial boundaries he favors to Nicholas Trist of the
State Department, to advance talks toward a treaty.

But gradually he learns that Trist is negotiating on his own terms, with potential
concessions in Texas and Alta (upper) California that Polk opposes. He also hears that
Scott has court marshaled his confidante, Pillow, and joined Trist in working out a
treaty, including a possible $1 million bribe to Santa Anna.

At this point, Polk concludes that the time has come to sack both Trist and Scott, but
he is emotionally so averse to personal confrontations that both men stay on by default.

TIME: FEB 12, 1848

THE WHIG, ABRAHAM LINCOLN, CALLS THE WAR
A "SHEER DECEPTION"

Polk's troubles from his Democrats are now
matched by an increasingly vocal Whig opposition,
with its 116-112 majority in the House.

On November 13, 1847, Henry Clay lays out the
Whig position in a speech in Lexington, Kentucky.
The war was one of "aggression," not defense, initiated
by Polk's false claim that Mexico invaded U.S. land.
The end must not lie in annexing all of Mexico or in
any extension of slavery into new land. Hearing these
words, Polk's supporters label Clay a convert to the
abolitionist movement.

As the second session of the 30th Congress convenes,
Clay's arguments are amplified in two addresses by
the 38-year-old freshman representative from Illinois,
Abraham Lincoln.

Since speaking out after the 1837 murder of the

Abraham Lincoln (1809-1865)

abolitionist Elijah Lovejoy, Lincoln has devoted his energy to building a law practice in Springfield, courting and marrying Mary Todd in 1842, buying a home, and raising his first two sons, Robert and Willie. He has also dabbled in local politics, serving four terms in the Illinois House. In 1846, he is elected to the United States House as the only Whig in a delegation dominated by Douglas and his Democrats.

Lincoln's reputation is that of a "free soil man," opposing those who would seek to extend slavery geographically, while not calling for abolishing it entirely. As such he will vote five times in favor of Wilmot's proviso during his term in office.

His first address to the House, on December 22, 1847, is very brief, but pointed. It becomes known as the "spot speech" for its "respectful request" of the President to inform the members…

> *1st. Whether the spot on which the blood of our citizens was shed, as his messages declared, was or was not within the territory of Spain, at least after the treaty of 1819, until the Mexican revolution.*

> *2d. Whether that spot is or is not within the territory which was wrested from Spain by the revolutionary Government of Mexico.*

> *3d. Whether that spot is or is not within a settlement of people, which has existed ever since long before the Texas revolution, and until its inhabitants fled before the approach of the United States army.*

After eight such constructions, Lincoln has made the case that American was intruding on Mexican land, and not vice versa, when the fighting began.

Lincoln's second speech comes nine days after the House has passed a resolution by a vote of 85-81 saying that the war was "unnecessarily and unconstitutionally begun by the President of the United States." It paints a picture of a President who deceived the nation into starting a war to grab land belonging to Mexico, and is now "bewildered" about how to force the Mexicans into a treaty that makes it all look legal.

> *Mr. Chairman: Some if not all the gentlemen on the other side of the House… have spoken complainingly …of the vote given a week or ten days ago declaring that the war with Mexico was unnecessarily and unconstitutionally commenced by the President…I am one of those who joined in that vote; and I did so under my best impression of the truth of the case*

> *The President, in his first war message of May, 1846, declares that the soil was ours on which hostilities were commenced by Mexico… Now, I propose to try to show that the whole of this issue and evidence is from beginning to end the sheerest deception.*

> *All of this is but naked claim; and what I have already said about claims is strictly*

applicable to this. If I should claim your land by word of mouth, that certainly would not make it mine.

I am now through the whole of the President's evidence… (and) I more than suspect already that he is deeply conscious of being in the wrong.

My way of living leads me to be about the courts of justice; and there I have sometimes seen a good lawyer, struggling for his client's neck in a desperate case, employing every artifice to work round, befog, and cover up with many words some point arising in the case which he dared not admit and yet could not deny and from just such necessity, is the President's struggle in this case.

He insists that the separate national existence of Mexico shall be maintained; but he does not tell us how this can be done, after we shall have taken all her territory… As to the mode of terminating the war and securing peace, the President is equally wandering and indefinite.

As I have before said, he knows not where he is. He is a bewildered, confounded, and miserably perplexed man. God grant he may be able to show there is not something about his conscience more painful than his mental perplexity.

A decade later, Stephen Douglas will cite these speeches as evidence of Lincoln's "lack of patriotism" when the two pair off in a race for a senate seat.

## 135

"POPULAR SOVEREIGNTY" BECOMES THE DEMOCRAT'S ANSWER TO THE WILMOT PROVISO

TIME: WINTER 1847-48

THE DEMOCRATS SEARCH FOR A "SOLUTION" TO THE WILMOT PROVISO

While the Whigs continue to hammer away at Polk over his motives for the war, the Democrats desperately search for a path to secure peace within their own party.

They must arrive at an option to Wilmot's total ban on the expansion of slavery into the west, which is anathema to their entire Southern wing.

The house has repeatedly rejected their first choice—declaring that the 34'30" Missouri Compromise line be the boundary for Slave vs. Free State designation in all newly acquired land.

As a fallback, they turn to a new option, one that will become known as "popular sovereignty."

On the surface the idea is simple and consistent with the original spirit of personal liberty in America—namely, that the people themselves should determine the rules by which they will be governed.

Daniel Dickinson (1800-1866)

John Calhoun's February 15, 1847, address in opposition to the Wilmot Proviso cites this theme in his "fourth resolve:"

Resolved, That it is a fundamental principle in our political creed, that a people,

in forming a constitution, have the unconditional right to form and adopt the
government which they may think best calculated to secure their liberty, prosperity,
and happiness; and that, in conformity thereto, no other condition is imposed by the
Federal Constitution on a State, in order to be admitted into this Union, except that
its constitution shall be republican; and that the imposition of any other by Congress
would not only be in violation of the constitution, but in direct conflict with the
principle on which our political system rests."

This classical argument of the States' Rights Democrats goes back to Jefferson, and is
disputed by the Federalist conviction that local "sovereignty" is trumped by the majority
will of the nation as a whole. Sixty years after the 1787 "constitutional contract" this
fundamental dispute still simmers and, as always, within the context of Southern
demands related to slavery and its economic imperatives.

On December 22, 1847, the notion of a "popular sovereignty" solution is floated on
the floor of the Senate by Senator Daniel Dickinson of New York. He is a member of
the "Hunker" faction in the state, men who seek to smooth tensions with the South, and
who oppose the "Barnburner" wing's attempt to stop the spread of slavery.

THE ENDURING RIFT WITHIN THE NEW YORK DEMOCRATS

FACTIONS	KEY MEMBERS
"Barnburners" (Pro-Wilmot)	Martin Van Buren, John Van Buren, Preston King, Silas Wright, John Dix
"Hunkers" (Anti-Wilmot)	Daniel Dickinson, William Marcy, Horatio Seymour, Edwin Crosswell, Samuel Beardsley

Since New York, with 36 votes, remains the top prize in the Electoral College,
healing the division is critical to the Democrats' chances in the 1848 political race. It
is also considered "in play" in 1848 with the Whig Harrison having carried it in 1840,
and Polk in 1844.

TOP TEN ELECTORAL VOTE STATES IN 1848

NY	PA	OHIO	VA	TENN	MASS	KY	IND	NC	GA	ALL-OTHER	TOTAL US
36	26	23	17	13	12	12	12	11	10	172	290

It will now be up to two powerful Western Democrats – Lewis Cass of Michigan and
Stephen Douglas of Illinois—to make the case for "popular sovereignty" as the road to
alignment and victory in 1848.

With Polk holding true to his promise of one term in office, both men also have
their eyes on the nomination.

TIME: WINTER 1847-48

DEMOCRATIC SENATOR STEPHEN DOUGLAS PROMOTES "POPULAR SOVEREIGNTY"

Stephen A. Douglas, 35, becomes the most visible spokesperson for "pop sov" from the beginning.

From early on, two raw ambitions drive "the Little Giant": power and wealth.

Power has come to Douglas through a meteoric political career. He organized the Democratic Party machine in Illinois, headed to the U.S. House in 1843, and the Senate in 1847.

His idol is Andrew Jackson and, like the ex-President, he is an outright racist, as his harsh rhetoric demonstrates. In March 1847, he also becomes a slave-owner through his marriage to Martha Martin who inherits a large cotton plantation in Mississippi.

This property will provide Douglas with wealth and spare capital, which he uses throughout his career to buy land around Chicago, always with an eye to routing a trans-continental railroad through the city and reaping the profits.

Stephen A. Douglas (1813-1861)

To protect his political image in the North, Douglas manages his Mississippi plantation surreptitiously.

Both his views on Blacks and his personal stake in the future of cotton and slaves make him an ideal ally for his Southern colleagues in the capital. In fact, while in D.C., he shares his living quarters with four leading Southerners, and their slave servants, in what becomes known as the "F-Street mess." Three of his house mates chair important Senate Committees—Finance (Robert T.M. Hunter of Virginia), Foreign Affairs (James Mason of Virginia), and Judiciary (Andrew Butler of South Carolina). The fourth is the outspoken pro-slavery Missouri Senator, David Atchison.

Douglas himself is Chairman of the Committee on Territories, a perfect position from which to shape and promote "popular sovereignty" in the new western lands. He describes the process to statehood as follows:

- Once a sizable number settle in a new Territory, they will hold a State convention.
- At this convention, they will write and debate a State Constitution.
- Included in this document will be a "free state" or "slave state" declaration.

- The Constitution will then be voted on—yes or no—by all citizens of the State.
- Once a Constitution has passed, the Territory will apply to Washington for recognition.

In other words, popular sovereignty becomes…

Simply let the people decide!

Once formulated, Douglas and Lewis Cass attempt to rally the party and the public to their solution.

With this formulation, they are convinced that "popular sovereignty" will thread the political needle between Northerners, uncertain about extending slavery into the west; and Southerners, demanding it. His next step is to try it out among his Southern colleagues.

DATE: FEBRUARY 14-15, 1848

THE SOUTHERN "FIRE-EATERS" RESPOND WITH THE 1848 "ALABAMA PLATFORM"

What Douglas and Cass find when they go to "sell popular sovereignty" is a growing band of Southern Democrats who will become known as the "Fire-eaters"—whose zeal around expanding slavery is every bit as intense as the Northern "Barnburners" wish to contain it.

The Fire-Eaters understand that the economic future of the South rests on raising cotton and selling slaves west of the Mississippi from Texas to California – and they want "guarantees" of this outcome from Washington.

"Popular sovereignty" boosts their odds of success above Wilmot's flat-out ban; but it falls well short of the "certainties" they point to in the U.S. Constitution, and even the 1820 Missouri Compromise. Simply put, the risks of a "pop-sov" vote going against them are too high to bear.

One "Fire-Eater" who joins Calhoun in attempting to unite the South behind a better option is Senator William L. Yancey of Alabama.

Yancey is born in Georgia and educated at Williams College in Massachusetts. His stepfather is a New School Presbyterian minister who supports abolition. Other family members are strongly pro-Union.

After college, he moves to South Carolina, edits a local newspaper, and speaks out against the 1832 "Nullification Bill" proposed by John Calhoun. In 1834, he passes the bar and begins to practice law.

At this point he looks like anything but a future pro-slavery secessionist.

In 1858, his views shift when he marries the daughter of a wealthy Alabama planter and receives a dowry. Near the town of Cahaba he is given extensive cotton-producing land and 35 slaves of his own. Yancey takes up residence and quickly blends into the lifestyle of the southern aristocrat. To give voice to his now outspoken support of slavery, he becomes editor of *The Cahaba Southern Democrat*, and enters politics, first in the state legislature, then, in 1844, as a member of the Alabama delegation to the U.S. House.

In his personal life, Yancey embraces the "code duello," which defines "honorable behavior" for men of the South, a how-to series of rules - how to manage a plantation, treat women and slaves, interact in society, serve one's country, uphold traditions. Also, how to avenge insults or sleights, something Yancey does on two noteworthy occasions: first, when he kills a doctor who offends him, in a brawl, which leads to a jail term; and second, in 1846, when he fights a harmless duel with Thomas Clingman, a Whig congressman, who criticizes his speech on the Texas Annexation.

In 1848, Yancey focuses his ire on the continuing push in Congress to approve the Wilmot Proviso.

Like Calhoun, he believes the time has come for the South to take a united stand against all threats to abolish or limit the expansion of slavery. To create a united front, he orchestrates the development of five principles related to the Mexican Cession lands that become known as the "Alabama Platform:"

1. Mexico's 1821 law abolishing slavery must be revoked for the new US territories.
2. Settlers must be able to bring slaves into any territory once it is opened up.
3. The federal government must protect the rights of slaveholders in the territory.
4. Slavery will be legal until and unless a formal state Convention votes to prohibit it.
5. Alabama delegates will oppose all presidential candidates supporting either Wilmot or a "pop sov" version that prohibits bringing slaves into any new territories.

Yancey's demands are all aimed at "rigging" any popular voting in favor of slavery by making it a fait d'accompli in a new territory well in advance of any state constitution or election.

Yancey believes will accomplish this by first rushing slaves onto farms and plantations in new territories as quickly as possible. Once that is accomplished, he will delay any popular vote until the institution is well established. His premise is simple: Removing slavery once it has taken root will be more difficult than banning it from the start.

Yancey admits that his "fait d'accompli strategy" is not the ironclad guarantee the South would ideally seek, but it does build off the Democrat's "popular sovereignty" platform, while tipping the scales of any live vote in favor of slavery.

The 5-point "Alabama Platform" is approved by his home state legislature on February 14-15, 1848. Yancey then tries to "sell it" across the South. He succeeds in three other states—Virginia, Georgia, and Florida—and, on May 22, will take his case to the Democratic National Convention in Baltimore.

## 136

THE SENECA FALLS CONVENTION COALESCES THE WOMEN'S RIGHTS MOVEMENT

TIME: JULY 19-20, 1848

THE FEMALE DECLARATION OF INDEPENDENCE AT SENECA FALLS

Eight years after Mott and Stanton experience the "seating humiliation" at the 1840 Anti-Slavery Convention in London, the topic of injustices against women comes up at a tea party they attend at Jane Mott's house in Boston. The date is July 9, 1848, but Stanton recalls it decades later:

> *I poured out, that day, the torrent of my long-accumulating discontent, with such vehemence and indignation that I stirred myself, as well as the rest of the party, to do and dare anything.*

Elizabeth Cady Stanton (1815-1902)

What she decides to do mirrors the founding fathers, circa 1776 – hold her own continental congress and announce a Declaration of Independence from an authoritarian rule which governs her life without her consent.

Immediately the wheels are set in motion for an event to be held on July 19-20 at the Wesleyan Methodist Chapel in Seneca Falls, New York, to…

Discuss the social, civil and religious condition and rights of women.

To boost attendance, word goes out that reform luminaries such as Mott, Sarah Grimke, Lydia Marie Child and Frederick Douglass will be present. Next comes an agenda for the session, with Day One reserved for women only and Day Two open to both sexes. The burden of writing and delivering the keynote addresses falls to Stanton. She is assisted by the Quaker reformer, Mary McClintock, and by her attorney husband, who searches for historical precedents to make her arguments.

They decide to document the case using the frameworks laid out by the founders against Britain—beginning with a list of "Sentiments" that capture their grievances and followed by "Resolves" describing the remedies they intend to pursue in response.

TIME: JULY 19, 1848

DAY ONE OF THE SENECA FALLS CONVENTION

The first day of the convention opens with roughly two hundred women filling the chapel. Stanton and Mott begin with keynotes encouraging the attendees to listen with open minds to the ideas presented—especially regarding the "depth of their degradation" at the moment—and to make a personal commitment to changing the status quo.

Excitement builds when Stanton reads her "Declaration of Sentiments," fashioned after the bill of particulars supporting the 1776 break with Britain. In this case, the rupture is cast as "one portion of the family of man…seeking a position different from that which they have hitherto occupied."

> *When, in the course of human events, it becomes necessary for one portion of the family of man to assume among the people of the earth a position different from that which they have hitherto occupied, but one to which the laws of nature and of nature's God entitle them, a decent respect to the opinions of mankind requires that they should declare the causes that impel them to such a course.*

Then come the ringing assertions that "all men and women are created equal," that they share the same "unalienable rights;" that in the face of an "absolute despotism" which violates these rights, it is proper to "throw off" the sources of oppression and "demand the equal station to which they are entitled."

With this foundation established in the preamble, Stanton enumerates the "degradations" which justify the revolution she demands. These are captured in sixteen "repeated injuries and usurpations on the part of man toward women" intended to "establish an absolute tyranny over her."

1. *He has never permitted her to exercise her inalienable right to the elective franchise.*
2. *He has compelled her to submit to laws, in the formation of which she had no voice.*

3. *He has withheld from her rights which are given to the most ignorant and degraded men—both natives and foreigners.*

4. *Having deprived her of this first right of a citizen, the elective franchise, thereby leaving her without representation in the halls of legislation, he has oppressed her on all sides.*

5. *He has made her, if married, in the eye of the law, civilly dead.*

6. *He has taken from her all right in property, even to the wages she earns.*

7. *He has made her, morally, an irresponsible being, as she can commit many crimes with impunity, provided they be done in the presence of her husband. In the covenant of marriage, she is compelled to promise obedience to her husband, he becoming, to all intents and purposes, her master—the law giving him power to deprive her of her liberty, and to administer chastisement.*

8. *He has so framed the laws of divorce, as to what shall be the proper causes of divorce; in case of separation, to whom the guardianship of the children shall be given; as to be wholly regardless of the happiness of women—the law, in all cases, going upon the false supposition of the supremacy of man, and giving all power into his hands.*

9. *After depriving her of all rights as a married woman, if single and the owner of property, he has taxed her to support a government which recognizes her only when her property can be made profitable to it.*

10. *He has monopolized nearly all the profitable employments, and from those she is permitted to follow, she receives but a scanty remuneration.*

11. *He closes against her all the avenues to wealth and distinction, which he considers most honorable to himself. As a teacher of theology, medicine, or law, she is not known.*

12. *He has denied her the facilities for obtaining a thorough education—all colleges being closed against her.*

13. *He allows her in Church as well as State, but a subordinate position, claiming Apostolic authority for her exclusion from the ministry, and, with some exceptions, from any public participation in the affairs of the Church.*

14. *He has created a false public sentiment, by giving to the world a different code of morals for men and women, by which moral delinquencies which exclude women from society, are not only tolerated but deemed of little account in man.*

15. *He has usurped the prerogative of Jehovah himself, claiming it as his right to assign for her a sphere of action, when that belongs to her conscience and her God.*

16. *He has endeavored, in every way that he could to destroy her confidence in her own powers, to lessen her self-respect, and to make her willing to lead a dependent and abject life.*

The call for redress, in the form of full citizenship, follows:

Now, in view of this entire disfranchisement of one-half the people of this country, their social and religious degradation,—in view of the unjust laws above mentioned, and because women do feel themselves aggrieved, oppressed, and fraudulently deprived of their most sacred rights, we insist that they have immediate admission to all the rights and privileges which belong to them as citizens of these United States.

Along with recognition of the likely resistance to be faced and a determination to press on.

In entering upon the great work before us, we anticipate no small amount of misconception, misrepresentation, and ridicule; but we shall use every instrumentality within our power to affect our object. We shall employ agents, circulate tracts, petition the State and national Legislatures, and endeavor to enlist the pulpit and the press in our behalf. We hope this Convention will be followed by a series of Conventions, embracing every part of the country.

Stanton closes with a call to end the "degradation of women" so that America can finally become the "great and virtuous nation" the founders intended.

The world has never yet seen a truly great and virtuous nation, because in the degradation of women the very fountains of life are poisoned at their source.

DATE: JULY 19, 1848

THE DEMAND FOR VOTING RIGHTS STIRS CONTROVERSY

After reading the "Sentiments" through from start to finish, Stanton opens up the floor to discuss them individually.

She finds near unanimous agreement in the hall, with one exception – the issue of women's suffrage.

This is not a surprise to her.

Just four weeks earlier, her cousin Gerritt Smith is roundly criticized when the platform of his Liberty Party calls for universal suffrage.

She is also warned by those who help with the draft that the majority of women would prefer to focus on changes related to the social and religious arenas – and to stay away from politics. This admonition reflects the generally accepted orthodoxy that men's intellectual superiority equips them to engage in the civic arena, while women's innate moral superiority is best focused on home and church.

Even Lucretia Mott tries to convince Stanton to back off from the "voting rights" call:

Why Lizzie, thee will make us ridiculous.

And her almost always supportive husband seconds the caution.

You will turn the proceeding into a farce.

But with Garrison-like certainty, she will have none of this—as evidenced by her decision to launch her list of "degradations" with being deprived of her "inalienable right to the elective franchise," and "submitting to laws" in which she has no voice.

When the Sentiments are read aloud on Day One, the only stumbling block to outright consensus centers on reservations about female suffrage – and Stanton decides to hold this topic over for further discussion.

Garritt Smith (1797-1874)

TIME: JULY 19, 1848

ELEVEN "RESOLUTIONS" ARE THEN PRESENTED

Stanton's Sentiments lay the predicate that women have been ill-treated when it comes to coverture, employment, wage equality, suing for divorce, education, admission to the ministry – even to the erosion of their self-confidence and self-respect. With all of these violations tracing to the "false supposition of the supremacy of man."

In lawyerly fashion, she turns during the afternoon session on July 19 from the list of grievances to a list of proposed solutions. These are presented in the form of eleven "Resolutions:"

1. *Resolved, That such laws as conflict, in any way, with the true and substantial happiness of woman, are contrary to the great precept of nature, and of no validity; for this is "superior in obligation to any other.*

2. *Resolved, That all laws which prevent woman from occupying such a station in society as her conscience shall dictate, or which place her in a position inferior to that of man, are contrary to the great precept of nature, and therefore of no force or authority.*

3. *Resolved, That woman is man's equal—was intended to be so by the Creator, and the highest good of the race demands that she should be recognized as such.*

4. *Resolved, That the women of this country ought to be enlightened in regard to the laws under which they live, that they may no longer publish their degradation, by declaring themselves satisfied with their present position, nor their ignorance, by asserting that they have all the rights they want.*

5. *Resolved, That inasmuch as man, while claiming for himself intellectual superiority, does accord to woman moral superiority, it is pre-eminently his duty to encourage her to speak, and teach, as she has an opportunity, in all religious assemblies.*

6. *Resolved, That the same amount of virtue, delicacy, and refinement of behavior, that is required of woman in the social state, should also be required of man, and the same transgressions should be visited with equal severity on both man and woman.*

7. *Resolved, That the objection of indelicacy and impropriety, which is so often brought against woman when she addresses a public audience, comes with a very ill grace from those who encourage, by their attendance, her appearance on the stage, in the concert, or in the feats of the circus.*

8. *Resolved, That woman has too long rested satisfied in the circumscribed limits which corrupt customs and a perverted application of the Scriptures have marked out for her, and that it is time she should move in the enlarged sphere which her great Creator has assigned her.*

9. *Resolved, That it is the duty of the women of this country to secure to themselves their sacred right to the elective franchise.*

10. *Resolved, That the equality of human rights results necessarily from the fact of the identity of the race in capabilities and responsibilities.*

11. *Resolved, therefore, That, being invested by the Creator with the same capabilities, and the same consciousness of responsibility for their exercise, it is demonstrably the right and duty of woman, equally with man, to promote every righteous cause, by every righteous means; and especially in regard to the great subjects of morals and religion, it is self-evidently her right to participate with her brother in teaching them, both in private and in public, by writing and by speaking, by any instrumentalities proper to be used, and in any assemblies proper to be held; and this being a self-evident truth, growing out of the divinely implanted principles of human nature, any custom or authority adverse to it, whether modern or wearing the hoary sanction of antiquity, is to be regarded as self-evident falsehood, and at war with the interests of mankind.*

After further discussion of each Resolve, the convention adjourns for the day, with these assertions on the table:
- Women and men are created equal;
- Women deserve equal treatment under the law;
- The traditions of coverture must be abandoned;
- All other forms of female degradation must end;
- Their educational opportunities should be expanded;
- The voice of women should be heard in public;

- Their career options should extend beyond teaching and nursing;
- They should receive equal pay for equal work;
- They must be granted the "sacred right to vote."

TIME: JULY 20, 1848

DAY TWO AT SENECA FALLS

The audience on the second day grows, as men are invited to join in and speak up.

Their presence shifts some of the dynamics in the hall—one sign being that a man, James Mott, Lucretia's husband, is asked to chair the meeting, given the "mixed" audience. Despite the revolutionary spirit in the air, traditional gender decorum still prevails at the moment.

The morning session is filled with various speeches, including a hopeful update about a "married women's property act" currently being considered at a New York state constitutional convention. This reinforces the feeling that laws must be changed for the movement to ultimately succeed.

After lunch, Stanton re-reads the "Sentiments" and the "Resolves," which leads to renewed debate about "female suffrage." Ironically it is none other than the ex-slave Frederick Douglass who speaks up on the topic -- arguing that if he as a black man deserves the vote, then justice demands the same right for all women. His endorsement rallies enough support in the room to have the call for suffrage included in the final documents.

The closing session is again chaired by a man, Thomas McClintock, whose wife Mary has helped plan the event. Both speak to the audience. He provides a detailed review of the onerous laws of coverture currently on the books; she follows with a plea to lobby on behalf of their repeal.

With the July temperature hovering in the nineties, the convention heads into the homestretch.

Much awaited talks by the convention's two most famous figures, Frederick Douglas and Lucretia Mott, lead into a call for attendees to step forward and sign the Sentiments and the Resolves.

As with the 1776 Declaration of Independence, the act of affirming a controversial document in writing is not taken lightly, and less than half of those present do so. Still one hundred sign on. The gender split is 68 women and 32 men; their ages range from 14 to 81 years old; 25 are Quakers; Douglass is the lone black; only one of the signers will live to 1920 when the Nineteen Amendment finally grants female suffrage.

The end of the convention brings a sigh of relief to Stanton, Motts and the other organizers, who are generally pleased with the outcomes.

What they cannot realize at the moment is how transformative their hastily assembled event will be in the long march ahead toward equality. It is not a stretch to speak of July 10-20 at Seneca Falls in the same breath as July 4 at Philadelphia. Both put a permanent stake in the ground on behalf of revolutionary change impacting the nation.

TIME: 1848

PUBLICITY ABOUT THE CONVENTION VARIES WIDELY

The Seneca Falls Convention does not go unnoticed in the popular press, first locally and then broadly. The reactions are about evenly split.

Some papers like the St. Louis *Daily Reveille* are content to simply acknowledge the event itself, without taking a stance one way or the other on the issues debated.

Horace Greeley (1811-1872)

> *The flag of independence has been hoisted for the second time on this side of the Atlantic, and a solemn league and covenant has just been entered into by a convention of women at Seneca Falls, New York.*

Others like *The Oneida Whig* go on the attack – while exhibiting in their rhetoric the exact brand of female "degradation" decried at the event.

> *This bolt is the most shocking and unnatural incident ever recorded in the history of womanity. If our ladies will insist on voting and legislating, where, gentleman, will be our dinners and our elbows? Where our domestic firesides and the holes in our stockings?*

The Philadelphia *Public Ledger and Daily Transcript* is similarly clumsy in its ringing affirmation of "the ladies" who remain in their proper place, as wives and mothers, not crusaders.

> *A woman is nobody. A wife is everything... and a mother is, next to God, all powerful....The ladies of Philadelphia, therefore, ...are resolved to maintain their rights as Wives, Belles, Virgins, and Mothers, and not as Women*

The Seneca County Courier finds the convention's assertions startling, and their resolutions radical:

The meeting was novel in its character and the doctrines broached in it are startling to those who are wedded to the present usages and laws of society. The resolutions are of the kind called radical."

Meanwhile, leave it to Horace Greeley, the 37 year old editor of *The New York Tribune*, to support that which so many of his colleagues consider radical. Greeley dabbles in various utopian movements, becomes an outspoken abolitionist, adopts a vegetarian diet – and his staff includes Margaret Fuller, one of the earliest and most articulate advocates for female equality. Greeley's editorial applauds the revolutionary spirit and proposed reforms at Seneca Falls, albeit with some reservations about suffrage:

When a sincere republican is asked to say in sober earnest what adequate reason he can give, for refusing the demand of women to an equal participation with men in political rights, he must answer, None at all…however unwise and mistaken the demand, it is but the assertion of a natural right, and such must be conceded.

TIME: 1848 FORWARD

THE INTREPID FEMALE AGENTS OF CHANGE

And so time will pass.

Some thirty years after the Seneca Falls Convention, Stanton recalls the aftermath in particularly painful terms:

Frances Willard (1839-1898)

So pronounced was the popular voice against us, in the parlor, press, and pulpit that most of the ladies who had attended the convention and signed the declaration, one by one, withdrew their names and influence and joined our persecutors. Our friends gave us the cold shoulder and felt themselves disgraced by the whole proceeding.

For her and others, the battle for gender equality proves every bit as challenging and lengthy as black emancipation.

The sage Lucretia Mott foretells this early on, with a warning to her young colleagues:

Thou wilt have hard work to prove the intellectual equality of women with men – facts being so against such an assumption in the present stage of women's development.

For those in the front lines, the fight for the rights of women follows naturally from their efforts against slavery.

The plight of America's slaves and women is by no means equivalent! But both groups suffer many of the same indignities. Both share a sense of bondage, be it to a master or a husband. Both are systematically deprived of education and of basic legal rights and remedies. Both are often pushed beyond their physical limits, between constant pregnancies and daily labor. It is not by accident that Stanton chooses the word "degradations" to characterize the experience.

But above all else, what nineteenth century American women have in common with slaves is the stigma of being born as a lesser being – the stigma that leads Lucy Stone's mother to apologize to her father for delivering another girl.

Fighting back from this stigma requires courage. As Anthony says:

Cautious, careful people always casting about to preserve their reputation and social standing can never bring about a reform

The litmus test of leadership falls to those brave women who take to the lecture circuit—in front of an audience including men, often appalled at the sight of a short-haired woman, dressed in a jacket and trousers, speaking up and challenging the role they have been assigned in society, by the Bible, the common law, and tradition.

The traveling routine itself is a challenge: lining up venues, often finding either tiny or hostile audiences, flopping into rented rooms, and then moving on to the next site, especially, as Amelia Bloomer reports, in the dead of winter:

My ardor in the cause of women chills at the thought of stage rides in temperatures of twenty-five below zero.

Even that most tenacious lecturer, Lucy Stone, recalls the physical and mental toll of these tours:

I am completely exhausted by long & hard field service, and my back is giving me so much pain, I am going home to rest.

For those who dare, however, the moments of public speaking are quintessentially liberating.

And once the battle is joined at Seneca Falls, the women's rights movement picks up momentum. The lessons learned from the campaign against slavery are soon repeated – more organized conventions, the creation of "societies," petitions to congress, pamphlets and publicity.

Stanton's essays are a constant goad to all opponents, especially those in government. In February 1854, she makes the case to the New York state legislature:

We demand full recognition of our rights as citizens of the Empire State. We are persons; native, free born citizens; property-holders, tax-payers. We support ourselves, and, in part, your schools, churches, poor-houses, prisons, army, navy, the whole machinery of government, and yet we have no voice in your councils. We have every qualification required by age constitution, necessary to the legal other, but the one of sex.

In 1869 the National Women Suffrage Association starts up, with Stanton as president and Anthony alongside

That same year also finds the two of them editing and publishing their own newspaper, *The Revolution*, dedicated to the cause.

As with almost all reform groups, an internal schism occurs, in this case over the 14th and 15th Amendments, which guarantee the rights of blacks, including the vote for men. Stanton and Anthony are outraged by the absence of equal entitlements for women. As Stanton tells congressmen at the time:

You now place the negro, so unjustly degraded by you, in a superior position to your own wives and mothers.

Meanwhile Lucy Stone, along with Paulina Wright Davis and her clerical sister-in-law, Antoinette Brown, are unwilling to try to derail any advances for the former slaves, even if they are disappointed by the outcome. This leads them to found a separate group, the American Women Suffrage Association. Unlike the NWSA, it allows men to participate, and tends to favor the Republican Party.

The NWSA or Stanton-Anthony wing of the movement is also inclined to more confrontational tactics, especially "storming the polls" on election days. In 1872, Stanton herself votes, before being arrested, fined, and released.

These wounds heal by 1890, and the old warriors reunite under the merged banner, National American Women Suffrage Association, with Anthony serving as president. She is seventy years old at the time, with Stanton at seventy-five and Lucy Stone at seventy-two.

Their time on stage is almost up. Stone dies in 1893, Stanton in 1902, Anthony in 1906. So none live to see women granted the vote, either in America in 1920 or in the UK in 1928.

They will, however, remain eternally together, along with Lucretia Mott and others, on the rolls of those who liberated women from bondage, always, as Stanton said, by overcoming fear and speaking the truth.

The moment we begin to fear the opinions of others and hesitate to tell the truth that is in us, and from motives of policy are silent when we should speak, the divine floods of light and life no longer flow into our souls

A next generation of leaders will carry this tradition forward—and, fittingly, it includes both Harriot Stanton Blatch (1856-1940) and Alice Stone Blackwell (1857-1950), every inch their mother's daughters.

## 137

WOMEN REFORMERS BEGIN TO BATTLE FOR GENDER EQUALITY

TIME: 1820-1845

THE SECOND AWAKENING SPARKS DEBATE OVER THE ROLES AND RIGHTS OF WOMEN

While the two major parties are focused on slavery and politics, a movement to reshape the roles and rights of women in society quietly picks up momentum.

From Jamestown forward, women and men operate in different spheres as codified by Blackstone's English common law, biblical admonitions, and social norms.

Men are born to rule, to be masters of their own households, to become the nation's ministers, lawyers, doctors and businessmen, to venture out into the affairs of state, participating in the militia, politics, and the civic arena.

Women's roles are defined by domesticity and subservience, first in relation to their fathers, and then to their husbands.

Those who "fail" to marry become "spinsters," relegated to living at home with their likely-to-be disappointed parents.

A single woman (*feme sole)*, however, retain her personal "right" to own property, run a business, retain wages, write and sign contracts, create a will, and dispose of her own possessions.

Once married, women "surrender" these rights to their husbands under the English law of "coverture"—whereby her wishes are assumed to be "covered," or subjugated, under the will of her husband.

From then on, her charge lies in supporting her husband, first by producing heirs — ten lifetime pregnancies being common—and providing a well-run household. The duties here are nonstop and laborious. Laundry done with well water, cooking over an open fire, mending clothes, gardening, milking cows, helping with crops, raising children, caring for sick family members, attending church, and instilling proper moral values.

The effect is the near total exclusion of women from the civic arena. Speaking out in a public forum, especially with men present, becomes a "radical" act, and voting in elections is considered out of the question. As Thomas Jefferson put it…

The ballot must be reserved for every man who fights and pays.

The notion of separate spheres between the sexes is reinforced in popular publications of the day. A Southern journal sums it up as follows:

His aspirations are for thrones and large dominions; she is queen of the household; her diadem is the social affections; her scepter, love.

Godey's Ladies Book offers a "Code of Instructions for Ladies," with a full litany of "nevers"—never contradict your husband, give advice unless asked, criticize his behavior, respond during arguments, censor his morals, and so forth.

Testimonials to the traditional hierarchy abound, this one from a contented wife in Georgia:

True to my sex, I…love to feel my woman's weakness protected by man's superior strength.

Few challenges to this hierarchy materialize during the Revolutionary era. The rare exceptions originate with women like the anti-British political pamphleteer, Mercy Otis Warren and Abigail Adams, the outspoken wife of the second U.S. President, who warns of a "ladies rebellion."

It is not, however, until the height of the Second Great Awakening between 1820 and 1845 that America begins to seriously rethink "women's roles and rights" – along with other social reforms like temperance, slavery, debtor's prisons, poverty, abuses of child labor, and the physically handicapped.

The spirit is every bit consistent with the nation's revolutionary instinct to challenge all orthodoxies associated with its European heritage.

Under the umbrella of "liberty and power to the individual," Americans rethink the structure of government, churches, financial institutions, and the economy. How natural for women to reconsider the structure within their own households – especially given its overtones of monarchy and serfdom!

TIME: 1830s FORWARD

EDUCATIONAL ADVANCES EXPAND THE HORIZONS FOR WOMEN

The women who initiate the debates on gender tend to benefit from parents who encourage their early intellectual curiosity and provide them with a formal education—often through tutors or attendance at one of the new "female seminaries" that spring up between 1820 and 1840, during the height of the Awakening.

These seminaries are the successors to earlier "dame schools" or "finishing schools," where young girls are taught the four values required to lead a virtuous life: religious piety, submission to a husband's will, sexual faithfulness; and home-making skills, including cooking, sewing, gardening, and child care.

The founders of these new schools are intent on replacing this narrow "domesticity" curriculum with one that mirrors what is offered to males—world literature, languages, mathematics, and science. Since for-men-only colleges refuse to recognize the merits of these subjects for females, the "radicals" who start up these seminaries plow forward on their own—often under the more acceptable guise of training women to become better teachers.

Lurking within the halls of these new "female seminaries," however, are educators like Mary Lyon of Mount Holyoke; and students like Lucy Stone, who are dedicated to using their schools to reshape the ambitions and opportunities for women in American society.

EARLIEST COLLEGES ADMITTING WOMEN IN AMERICA

DATE	NAME	WHERE	CURRICULUM
1742	Bethlehem Female Seminary Moravian College	Germantown, Pa.	Link to Moravian Church, becomes a secondary school for girls 8-15, broad academic curriculum along with moral guidance, vocational training, physical exercise, and social skills.
1772	Single Sister's House Salem Female Academy	Winston-Salem, N.C.	Link to Moravian Church, similar to Bethlehem in structure, among the first to accept Black students.
1792	Litchfield Academy	Litchfield, Connecticut	Founded by Sarah Pierce to provide "Republican Motherhood" vision of women as capable teachers of their own children. Pierce also authors her own history textbooks.
1796	Nine Partners School	South Millbrook, New York	Quaker run co-ed school for ages 7-15 years. Both Lucretia and James Mott attended the school and later taught there.
1803	Bradford Academy Bradford Teachers Seminary	Bradford, Mass.	Three-year college prep school, which shifted to women only in 1836, with focus on preparing teachers. Cost of $4-6 per semester.
1806	Byfield Female Seminary	Byfield, Mass	Run by Congregationalist minister, Joseph Emerson Attendees include Zilpah Grant and Mary Lyon.

DATE	NAME	WHERE	CURRICULUM
1811	Boston Lyceum for Young Women	Boston, Mass	Founded by educator and journalist, John Park and attended by Margaret Fuller.
1818	Elizabeth Female Academy	Washington, Miss.	Methodist Church connections with emphasis on spirituality, In1822, James Audubon taught drawing. Varina Davis was an attendee.
1821	Troy Female Seminary Emma Willard School	Troy, New York	College prep boarding school founded by Emma Willard who, with Beecher and Lyon, created a curriculum matching that taught to boys. Graduates include Elizabeth Cady Stanton.
1823	Hartford Female Academy	Hartford, Connecticut	Founded by educator Catharine Beecher with an emphasis on early childhood education.
1825	Science Hill School	Shelbyville, Ky	Founded by Julia Ann Hieronymous Tevis with focus on teaching science to young women.
1827	Linden Wood School for Girls	St. Charles, Missouri	Presbyterian Church; founded by the teacher, Mary Easton and her explorer husband, George Sibley. Full range of courses for college prep.
1828	Ipswich Female Seminary	Ipswich, Mass.	Founded by Zilpah Grant, colleague of Mary Lyon. Focuses on the joy of learning vs. rote memorization.
1830	Charleston Female Seminary	Charleston, Mass.	Opened by Baptist ministers, followed by educator Martha Whiting. Attendees include Mary Livermore.
1833	Columbia Female Academy	Columbia, Missouri	Baptist link. First mistress was Lucy Wales; college prep.
1833	Friends Select School	Philadelphia, Pa.	Quaker run, Anna Dickinson attended.
1834	Wheaton Female Seminary	Norton, Mass.	Founded by education pioneer, Mary Lyon, with "curriculum mirroring that offered to men." No church ties.
1837	St. Mary's Hall	Burlington, New Jersey	All-girls academic boarding school, founded by Episcopal Bishop, George Doane.
1837	Mount Holyoke Female Academy	South Hadley, Mass.	Educator Mary Lyon's finest legacy; emphasizes science and math, moral purpose, physical fitness; campus work to defray costs, affordable to all; major advances in educating teachers. Sister school to Andover Academy for Boys.
1839	Georgia Female College Wesleyan Female College	Macon, Georgia	Methodist Church links; First president was Rev. George Pierce; college level courses focused on the sciences.

DATE	NAME	WHERE	CURRICULUM
1842	Quaboag Seminary	Warren, Mass.	College prep for both sexes, Lucy Stone attends before going to Oberlin.
1844	St. Mary's College	Notre Dame, Indiana	Sisters of the Holy Cross of France. Catholic college prep boarding school.
1848	Philadelphia School of Design for Women	Philadelphia, Pa.	Founded by Sarah Worthington King to prepare poor women with skills to enter trade; teaches wood carving, lithography, and household design.

Each of the four women who will lead the "Women's Movement" attend one of these progressive schools—Lucretia Mott (Nine Partners), Elizabeth Cady Stanton (Troy), Lucy Stone (Oberlin College), and Susan B. Anthony (Moulson's Female Seminary).

TIME: INTO THE 1840s

ROLL CALL FOR THE WOMEN'S RIGHTS MOVEMENT

Lydia Marie Child (1802-1880)   Mary Livermore (1820-1905)   Louisa May Alcott (1832-1888)

But early education is only one mark of those leaders.

With few exceptions, they are all confirmed, and activist abolitionists.

Several join Lloyd Garrison's inner circle—Lucretia Mott becomes, in effect, his spiritual advisor; Sojourner Truth, the Grimke sisters, Abby Kelley, and Maria Weston Chapman are traveling lecturers and agents; Margaret Fuller, Lydia Marie Child, Anna Dickinson, and others contribute essays to his *Liberator* newspaper.

Religion typically plays a significant role in their upbringing. Several are Quakers;

among them Mott, the Grimkes, and Abby Kelley. Some belong to mainstream Protestant sects or break-aways, such as the Unitarians (Stone, Howe, Chapman, and Alcott) and the Universalists. Others, like Susan B. Anthony, move from one sect to another, only to abandon all formal affiliation out of frustration with the failure of church officials to deal with the "degradations" suffered by Blacks and women.

A few are so-called "Freethinkers" from early on, aware of the formal religious traditions, but inclined to rely on their own reason and instincts to move through life. The utopian socialist Fanny Wright and the precocious Lydia Marie Child belong here, as does the always unconventional Elizabeth Cady Stanton.

With very few exceptions, women in the movement marry—almost always to husbands who are supportive of their full equality. Most also become mothers, although as a group they are much less inclined toward very large families common at the time. Stanton is one exception, giving birth on eight separate occasions.

Even with one or two children, they are left with the challenge of taking care of their families, while simultaneously devoting their remaining time to their causes and personal careers. These careers are fundamental to altering their spheres of influence beyond home and church, and into arenas historically reserved for men.

Many begin in a safe zone by teaching or tutoring. From there, however, they break out in multiple directions.

Some establish and run their own academies: Sarah Pierce, Zilpah Grant, Mary Easton, Emma Willard, Mary Lyon, Catherine Beecher.

Others turn to writing fiction and poetry (Alcott, Child); hard-hitting essays (Warren, Fuller, Stanton, Child, McClintock, Howe); running newspapers (Mary Shad Cary, the Forten sisters, Fuller, Stanton, Anthony, and others).

Lucretia Mott and Antoinette Brown Blackwell are both ordained ministers, the former in the Quaker Church, the latter a Congregationalist. Mary Walker earns an M.D. degree and practices medicine, while others labor as nurses.

Many are responsible for founding and operating major reform organizations. Early on, they include the Female Anti-Slavery Societies, in Philadelphia (Mott, the sisters Grimke, and Forten) and in Boston (Maria Weston Chapman). When the American Anti-Slavery Society finally admits women—in 1839, six years after its founding – the roster includes Mott, the Grimkes, Kelley, Stanton, Stone, Anthony, and others.

Later on, Stanton and Anthony found the National Woman Suffrage Association (1869), Stone and Brown the American Woman Suffrage Association (1869), and Francis Willard the Women's Christian Temperance Union (1873).

Together these courageous leaders will fundamentally change the rights and roles of women during the second half of the nineteenth century.

SOME OF THE LEADING FIGURES IN THE WOMEN'S MOVEMENT
DURING THE 19TH CENTURY

NAME	DATES	EDUCATION	RELIGION	MARRY	ABOLITIONIST
Mercy Otis Warren	1728-1814	Tutored by local minister	Puritan	Y- 5 children	
Abigail Adams	1744-1818	Home schooled by mother	Unitarian	Y- 6	
Sarah Pierce	1767-1852	New York School for Teachers	Presbyterian		
Emma Willard	1787-1870	Public school in Berlin, Connecticut	Christian	Y-1	
Sarah Grimke	1792-1873	Private tutors on plantation	Quaker	Y-0	Y
Lucretia Coffin Mott	1793-1880	Nine Partners School	Quaker	Y-6	Y
Zilpah P. Grant	1794-1874	Byfield Female Seminary	Congregationalist	Y-0	
Fanny Wright	1795-1852	Home school in United Kingdom by aunt	Freethinker	Y-1	Y
Mary Lyon	1797-1849	Byfield Female Seminary	Congregationalist		
Sojourner Truth *	1797-1883	Enslaved, education banned	Methodist	Y-5	Y
Catharine Beecher	1800-1878	Litchfield Academy + self-taught	Presbyterian		
Mary Easton Sibley	1800-1878	Women's boarding school in Kentucky	Presbyterian	Y-0	
Mary Ann McClintock	1800-1884	Westtown School	Quaker	Y-5	Y
Lydia Maria Child	1802-1880	Self-taught	Freethinker	Y-0	Y
Amy Post	1802-1889	Self-taught	Quaker	Y-4	Y
Angelina Grimke Weld	1805-1879	Private tutors on plantation	Quaker	Y-0	Y
William Lloyd Garrison	1805-1879				
Martha Coffin Wright	1806-1875	Quaker schools in Philadelphia	Quaker/left	Y-7	Y
Margaretta Forten*	1806-1875	Private Black academy in Philadelphia	AME		Y

NAME	DATES	EDUCATION	RELIGION	MARRY	ABOLITIONIST
Maria Weston Chapman	1806-1885	Schools in United Kingdom	Unitarian	Y-4	Y
Margaret Fuller	1810-1850	Father tutor, Boston Lyceum	Transcendalist	Y-1	Y
Harriet Forten Purvis *	1810-1875	Private black academy in Phil	AME	Y-8	Y
William Henry Channing	1810-1884				
Ernestine Potovsky Rose	1810-1892	Hebrew school in Poland	Judaism/left	Y-0	Y
Abby Kelley Foster	1811-1887	New England Friends School	Quaker	Y-1	Y
Wendell Phillips	1811-1884				
Jane Hunt	1812-1889	Home school	Quaker	Y-4	Y
Paulina Wright Davis	1813-1876	Public school in New York	Presbyterian	Y-2	Y
Elizabeth Cady Stanton	1815-1902	Troy Female Seminary	Freethinker	Y-8	Y
Lucy Colman	1817-1906	Self-taught	Spiritualist	Y-1	Y
Lucy Stone	1818-1893	Oberlin College	Unitarian	Y-1	Y
Amelia Bloomer	1818-1894	New York public grade school	Episcopal		
Julia Ward Howe	1818-1910	Home schooled by tutors	Unitarian	Y-6	Y
Susan B. Anthony	1820-1906	Moulson's Female Seminary	Q/Uni/left		Y
Mary Livermore	1820-1905	Charleston Female Seminary	Universalist	Y-0	Y
Elizabeth Smith Miller	1822-1911	Philadelphia Friends School	Unknown		Y
Mary Ann Shadd Cary *	1823-1893	Quaker school in Pennsylvania	AME/left	Y-2	Y
Edna Dow Cheney	1824-1905	Private girls' schools	Transcendentalist	Y-2	Y
Antoinette Brown Blackwell	1825-1921	Oberlin College '47	Congregationalist	Y-7	
Thomas Higginson	1828-1911				
Louisa May Alcott	1832-1888	Father + Transcendentalist tutors	Unitarian		Y
Dr. Mary Walker	1832-1919	Syracuse Medical College	Freethinker	Y-0/ Divorce	Y

NAME	DATES	EDUCATION	RELIGION	MARRY	ABOLITIONIST
Victoria Woodhull	1838-1927	Public grade school in Ohio	Spiritualist	Y-2/ Divorce	
Frances Willard	1839-1898	Northwestern Female College	Methodist		
Anna Dickinson	1842-1932	Friends Select School in Pa.	Quaker		Y

* African-Americans   Y=Yes, Blank=No

TIME: 1820 FORWARD

LUCRETIA MOTT EMERGES AS THE ROLE MODEL FOR THE WOMEN'S MOVEMENT

No single figure has greater impact on the women's movement than Lucretia Coffin Mott.

Her remarkable life begins in 1793 on the island of Nantucket, some thirty miles south of Cape Cod, Massachusetts. Her father is a seafarer, captain of a sailing vessel, trading in seal skins, voyaging as far away as South America and China. His often year-long absences place the burden of caring for the family—which includes eight children—and for a small supply store, directly into the hands of her mother. Later in life, Lucretia recalls the skills and independence shown by the women of the Island while their husbands were away.

Lucretia Mott (1793-1880)

I remember how our mothers were employed, while our fathers were at sea. They were obliged to go to Boston… mingle with men, make their trades and with all of this, have very little help in the family, to which they must discharge their duties.

In addition to witnessing and admiring her mother's self-confidence and initiative, she also grows up in a Quaker community that rejects hierarchical privilege, believes in coeducation; and encourages women to think for themselves and to speak up in mixed public forums, even to serve in the official church ministry.

In 1804, the Lucretia Coffin's family moves to Boston so her father can transition from the risky life at sea to more stable pursuits as a tradesman. At thirteen, Lucretia begins her studies at the Nine Partners co-educational school in Poughkeepsie, New York. The venue is a Quaker Meeting House and the superintendent is Adam Mott, who fosters a sense of duty among his students on behalf of abolition. Lucretia is moved by her reading about slavery and by those who speak against it including the Quaker preacher, Elias Hicks.

My sympathy was early enlisted for the poor slave, by the class-books read in our schools, and the pictures of the slave-ship, as published by Clarkson. The ministry of Elias Hicks and others, on the subject of the unrequited labor of slaves, and their example in refusing the products of slave labor, all had their effect in awakening a strong feeling in their behalf.

From Hicks, Lucretia is also persuaded that one's moral compass should be guided by "obedience to the light within" rather than conformity to often misguided institutional norms.

By fifteen, she is hired at Nine Partners as an assistant teacher, and learns a distressing lesson about such norms around the issue of wage difference between women and men.

The unequal condition of women in society also early impressed my mind. Learning, while at school, that when they became teachers, women received but half as much as men for their services, the injustice of this was so apparent, that I early resolved to claim for my sex all that an impartial Creator had bestowed.

One of Lucretia's fellow teachers is James Mott, son of the superintendent, and the man she marries in 1811, after her family moves to Philadelphia. Together they will become activists on behalf of abolition and gender equality over their next 57 years together until his death in 1867.

Putting an end to slavery tops Lucretia's list from the beginning. In 1815, she joins forces with another Quaker, Benjamin Lundy, in trying to convince the Friends General Assembly to publicly support abolition. In 1819, she sees slaves first-hand on a trip into Virginia.

The sight of the poor slaves was indeed affecting: though…we were told their situation was rendered less deplorable by kind treatment from their masters.

While raising her children—eventually numbering six—she masters her Bible studies to the point where, in 1821, age twenty-eight, she is ordained as a Quaker minister. From there she is drawn into leading "a more public life:"

At twenty-five years of age, surrounded with a little family and many cares, I felt called to a more public life of devotion to duty, and engaged in the ministry in our Society, receiving every encouragement from those in authority, until a separation among us…when my convictions led me to adhere to the sufficiency of the light within us, resting on truth as authority, rather than taking authority for truth.

This puts her on-stage in front of large audiences for the first time. It instills the courage she will need to advocate in public for her causes, as well as providing a model for other women to participate in civil discourse.

In 1823, she and James initiate the Philadelphia Free Produce Society, a co-op dedicated to boycotting the use of all products derived from slave labor—from sugar to cotton to tobacco. Conforming to this ban proves challenging to the Mott's financial future, and it comes at a time of pressure from within the Quaker community to denounce their "Hicksite" convictions.

Lucretia moves forward amidst the upheavals, balancing her private and public responsibilities. This trait is repeatedly commented upon by other women…

She is proof that it is possible for a woman to widen her sphere without deserting her home life.

On January 1, 1831, the nascent abolitionist movement is transformed by William Lloyd Garrison, a new arrival, who publishes the first edition of his paper, *The Liberator*. Garrison quickly to mobilizes his forces. In December 1833, 62 delegates (21 Quakers) meet in Philadelphia to found the American Anti-Slavery Society, which, over the next five years will boast a quarter million members, eventually including the four main leaders of the Women's Rights movement, Mott, Stanton, Stone, and Anthony.

At the opening convention, however, a vote is taken and women are denied membership!

Despite this affront, Lucretia is undismayed, and speaks out at the plenary session about the wording of the "pledge of faith." This meeting also marks the beginning what will be her lifelong association with Lloyd Garrison.

Along with Lydia Maria Child and Margaretta Forten, the African-American daughter of the Black abolitionist, James Forten, Mott soon founds the Philadelphia Female Anti-Slavery Society. Its mission includes gathering petitions, collecting money for black schools, writing pamphlets and lecturing to public audiences. In 1835 the fiery southern white abolitionist Angelina Grimke joins Mott as an itinerant lecturer, further emboldening more women to speak their minds on a range of reform issues.

Along with their zeal comes not only verbal abuse but also physical risk. In 1838, a mob breaks up an anti-slavery meeting at the Pennsylvania Hall, then burns it to the ground and threatens the homes of local abolitionists, including Lucretia and James

Mott. Such attacks are not unusual and the gentle "Mother Mott" will continue to face them.

In June 1840, at the first World Anti-Slavery Convention in London, the Women's Rights Movement becomes a cause celèbre. The meeting is called to applaud the English for freeing some 800,000 slaves since their Emancipation Act of 1833, and to encourage other nations, especially the U.S., to follow suit. A total of 300 official delegates are present, including 50 from America. Seven women are invited, among them the now famous Mott and the baroness widow of the English poet, Lord Byron.

At the opening session, the question of seating the female delegates suddenly takes center stage, with a lively debate consuming most of the day. One irate U.S. delegate sums up the situation…

> *What a misnomer to call this a world convention of abolitionists when some of the oldest and most thorough going supporters are denied the right to be represented.*

But a final vote goes against the women by a 90% nay to 10% yea margin, and the females, including Lucretia Mott, are forced to observe the session away from the official floor. This well-publicized "degradation" will energize women intent on changing their status in society.

The 1840 London Convention becomes the first encounter between the 47-year-old icon, Mott, and one of her eventual protégés, Elizabeth Cady Stanton, the 24-year-old newlywed accompanying her husband Henry Stanton, a U.S. delegate. Elizabeth's reaction to Mott is one of awe:

> *It seemed to me like meeting a being from some larger planet, to find a woman who dared question the opinions of Popes, Kings, Synods, Parliaments, with the same freedom that she would criticize an editorial in the London Times, recognizing no higher authority than the judgment of a pure-minded, educated woman.*

Mott is likewise impressed by Stanton's views on changing the standing of women and by her self-assurance. Over the next eight years, the two are in frequent touch, with the culmination being the landmark Seneca Falls Convention of 1848, and Stanton's famous Declaration of Sentiments on behalf of women.

TIME: 1830 FORWARD

ELIZABETH CADY STANTON BECOMES CHIEF STRATEGIST FOR THE WOMEN'S MOVEMENT

Stanton's family lineage is considerably more prestigious than others in the inner circle of the women's movement.

Her maternal roots trace back to Colonel James Livingston, whose service in the Revolutionary War is rewarded with a 3500-acre land grant in New York State. One of his daughters marries Peter Smith, a fabulously wealthy partner of John Jacob Astor and father of the philanthropist reformer, Gerrit Smith. Another daughter, Margaret, weds Daniel Cady, a prosperous attorney, who serves a term in the U.S. House (1815-17), before eventually being named a justice on the New York Supreme Court.

"Judge Cady" and Margaret have eleven children, with Elizabeth, born in 1815, the eighth in line. She is raised in Johnstown, New

Elizabeth Cady Stanton (1815-1902)

York, amidst privileges that include horseback riding, chess lessons, access to her father's extensive library, and a formal education – first in a local grammar school and then at Troy Female Seminary, Emma Willard's college prep boarding school. At 16, Elizabeth enrolls and completes an academic curriculum, from math to science, classical languages, religion, and composition.

Reflecting on her youth, Elizabeth later admits to the pain of her father's "preference for boys," and her desire to win his affection by matching her brother's every accomplishment. Her formula is simple:

I thought that the chief thing to be done in order to equal boys was to be learned and courageous. So, I decided to study Greek and learn to manage a horse.

After graduating from Troy, she connects with her well-to-do cousin, Gerrit Smith, eighteen years her senior, and his circle of friends, who are already engaged in temperance and abolitionist activities. Ironically, Elizabeth has grown up with a slave in her own household. Her father had owned a slave whom he freed in 1827 under New York law.

Gerrit Smith, one of Henry Stanton's acquaintances, begins his career as a journalist. In 1832, Smith enrolls at Lane Theological Seminary where he intends to become a Presbyterian Minister. The Seminary is embroiled in debates over slavery. Stanton leaves before graduation to become a lecturer on behalf of abolition, and to help Smith found the Liberty Party in 1840.

Elizabeth is also drawn into the reform fervor of the 1830s. She finds in the decade older Stanton, a man already making his mark as a public speaker and writer on causes she favors. Despite her father's uncertainties about Henry's future prospects, the two are married in 1840, agreeing that "obey your husband" be omitted in the vows.

Six weeks after the wedding, they are in London attending the World Anti-Slavery Convention, a pivotal moment where she meets Lucretia Mott and witnesses first-hand the refusal to seat female delegates, which she recalls as…

A burning indignation that filled my soul.

Garrison remembers her as "a fearless woman…who goes for woman's rights with all her soul."

One signal of her commitment lies in what she calls her "debut in public" in a speech on temperance. She recounts this in an 1841 letter to her friend, Eliza Neall, saying that one hundred men were present and that the "homeopathic doses of Women's Rights" she infuses brought tears to the eyes of her audience and herself. She also concludes that…

The more I think on the present condition of women, the more am I oppressed with the reality of her degradation. The laws of our country, how unjust are they! Our customs, how vicious! What God has made sinful, both in man and woman, custom has made sinful in woman alone.

From this speaking triumph also comes a life-long lesson:

The best protection any woman can have … is courage.

Eight years will elapse between the 1840 London Convention on slavery and the landmark 1848 Seneca Falls gathering on women's rights. Elizabeth spends much of that time in Boston raising her seven children (one dies at birth), and mingling with activists like Garrison and Douglass, and intellectuals like Emerson and the Alcotts.

While the Mexican War and sectional tensions over slavery dominate public discourse, a small cadre of protesters form on behalf of "the women's issues." In 1845, the Transcendentalist Margaret Fuller publishes her treatise on *Women In The Nineteenth Century*, laying out a litany of denied basic rights and directing a scathing attack against men who exhibit a "tone of feeling toward females as toward slaves."

A smattering of men also lobby for change. Judge Elisha Hurlbut condemns "coverture" as "the law of the male sex gathering unto themselves dominion and power at the sacrifice of the female." Wendell Phillips and Garrison add their support. The Unitarian minister, Samuel May, goes so far as to tell his congregation that justice demands equality for women, including an astonishing plea for their right to vote.

Elizabeth's outward protests remain fairly muted so far. She refuses to be called "Mrs. Stanton," and adopts a new form of less formal dress favored by liberated women.

But in her few spare moments away from housekeeping she pens a series of essays on women's roles and rights that prove forerunners to the legally cast declarations she will offer at the Seneca Falls Convention of 1848, which will change her destiny.

TIME: 1840 FORWARD

LUCY STONE ADDS HER INDOMITABLE WILL ON BEHALF OF GENDER EQUALITY

Lucy stone is a third pioneer in the women's movement.

As a child she lives under the shadow of the words her mother,

Francis Stone, shared with her father when she was born: "Oh dear, I am sorry it is a girl."

In 1818, the year Lucy is born, Francis is hoping for another son to help work his farm in western Massachusetts, not a girl, unlikely to even offset her own consumption with the light labor she can provide. Throughout her youth, Lucy's father rules his domain with an iron hand, while her mother is left to comply on all things.

There was only one will in our family, and that was my father's.

Lucy steels herself against repeating this subservience in her own life. This leads to her

Lucy Stone (1818-1893)

vows to become as educated as a man, to always earn and keep her own wages, and above all to avoid the surrender of her basic rights through marriage.

As a youth, she also hears that Congress refuses to accept anti-slavery petitions written by women. Ministers in her own Congregational Church condemn the abolitionist Sarah Grimke for "assuming the place of a man" by speaking out in public. She learns that a Connecticut anti-slavery meeting refuses to count the vote of the firebrand Abby Kelley who proceeds to defiantly raise her hand.

Lucy's early education in a local school is limited, but still sufficient to land her a teaching position at sixteen. When she asks about her wages, she is told that "women can afford to teach for one half, or even less, the salary which men would ask."

In 1838, Lucy reads newspaper excerpts of Sarah Grimke's *Letters on The Equality of the Sexes and the Condition of Women*, aimed at demolishing biblical justifications for subjugating women and forcing them to operate in different spheres from men.

In 1839, she enrolls at Mount Holyoke, only to discover that open support for abolition and women's rights is frowned upon by school officials. She transfers to Quaboag Seminary to learn enough Latin and Greek to pass college entrance exams. In 1843, she has accumulated enough savings to apply to Oberlin College, which nine years earlier becomes the first university to accept women.

Lucy thrives at Oberlin, mastering its classical curriculum. She works part-time to pay her way, and convinces the administration to adjust her wages upward to equal her male counterparts. She protests faculty resistance to a visiting lecture by abolitionist Kelley, and sets up a clandestine female debating society, where she hones her own speaking skills. In 1847, she graduates with honors, but refuses to write a commencement address after learning that it must be read by a man.

Her years at Oberlin also lead to a lasting friendship with Antoinette Brown, later the first woman ordained to the ministry by the Congregational Church. The two become sisters-in-law six years later, after Lucy changes her mind and decides to marry Henry Blackwell. An Englishman by birth, Blackwell immigrates to America, becomes a successful hardware salesman, and falls in love with Lucy after hearing one of her lectures. The marriage is preceded by an extensive prenuptial agreement, vacating all of the "coverture" rules abhorrent to Lucy since her youth.

In 1848, Abby Kelley convinces her to become a Lecturing Agent for the Massachusetts Anti-Slavery Society, which fully connects her to Lloyd Garrison's supporters, including Lucretia Mott.

Standing in front of a mixed and often openly hostile crowd, sporting a short, almost masculine haircut, and wearing a loose-fitting jacket over "bloomer" trousers, Lucy vigorously makes the case for the cause of equality for women.

Over the coming decade, her prowess and fearlessness as a public speaker will make her famous nationwide.

SIDEBAR: OBERLIN COLLEGE

In 1833, Oberlin College is founded within the context of yet another of the era's "utopian communities," this one imagined by two young religious zealots seeking "moral perfection."

In 1832, Reverend John Shipherd, influenced by revivalist preacher Charles Finney, conducts his own evangelical meetings in Elmyra, Ohio. His friend from prep school, Philo

Stewart, serves as a missionary to the Choctaw tribes in the area. Both are troubled by the lack of religious dedication in the west, and decide to found a colony, whose "sole mission is to save souls and prepare the world for the coming millennium of Christ."

With support from their Congregational church back east, they acquire 550 acres of land thirty miles southeast of Cleveland, and christen their colony Oberlin, after a French educator they admire.

Like other utopian experiments, Oberlin suffers severe financial difficulties, until one of Shipherd's fundraising trips connects him with the philanthropist Lewis Tappan who has just learned that attempts to promote abolition at Lane Theological Seminary have run afoul of its conservative head, Lyman Beecher. Trustee Asa Mahan and 50 students walk out.

Tappan Hall on the Campus of Oberlin College

Shipherd works out a quid pro quo, whereby Tappan will donate $10,000 and 8 professorships to Oberlin if the local college guarantees that students do manual labor to pay operating expenses. In addition to enrolling men, the college will also agree to enroll women and Blacks.

Shipherd willingly accepts the deal on his own. In 1833, the Oberlin Collegiate Institute opens its doors, with Asa Mahan as its first president and a class largely composed of the Lane defectors.

By 1835, the community Trustees have still not lived up to the deal with Tappan. Their resistance demonstrates the disparagement toward females and Blacks that prevails at the time, even among a supposedly idealistic white enclave.

While admitting women has been approved, it comes with the caveat that their curriculum be confined to two departments – "Female" and "Teachers" – and not "Collegiate" and "Theological."

Enrolling Blacks is another matter. The responses are symbolic of the intense racial bias that dominates America's white society, South and North. Opponents argue that enrolling Blacks at Oberlin would be madness, that internal church funding would disappear, and that...

> Hundreds of Negroes would be flooding in...and as soon as the darkies begin to come, the whites will begin to leave...and we will become a Negro school.

At first, Shipherd tries to counter with moral persuasion, while tempering his plea with assurances that hands-off distance can still be maintained between whites and the inferior Blacks.

> *None of you will be compelled to receive them into your families, unless, like Christ, the love of your neighbor compels you to...as Christ ate with publicans and sinners... But this should be passed because it is a right principle and God will bless us in doing right...If we refuse to deliver our Black brethren... I cannot hope that God will smile upon us.*

This too fails, and the Trustees' opposition is strengthened by a student vote of 32-26 vote against admitting Blacks. All that's left for Shipherd is threat. On February 9, 1835, he tells the Trustees that the school will not only lose Tappan's crucial financial support, but he will also leave the community. By a margin of one last vote, cast by the abolitionist minister, John Keep, the motion to admit Blacks carries.

From that moment on, Oberlin College will become a beacon of light shining across America on behalf of educating females and Blacks.

Five years will pass before sixteen-year-old George Vashon becomes the first Black to be enrolled. He is the son of Pennsylvania abolitionist, John Vashon. In 1844, he graduates with honors and goes on to have a distinguished career as a lawyer, professor, and reformer.

Progress happens faster for the Oberlin women. The curriculum for females is expanded to include the full range of "Collegiate" courses. In 1837, three women sign up. In 1841, two go on to become first in the nation to receive a Bachelor of Arts, BA, degree. Twenty-one years later, in 1858, Oberlin will award a BA to Mary Patterson, the first Black woman to receive it.

In 1843, Lucy Stone will enroll at Oberlin and graduate in 1847. Her experiences will reinforce many of the prejudices against women that are the norm in her day, including wage inequities and efforts to stifle her voice at campus debates and commencement. But, her time at Oberlin also proves transformative, as she begins her leadership in the Women's Rights Movement. As she later observes:

> *Whatever the reason, the idea was born that women could and should be educated. It lifted a mountain load from woman. It shattered the idea, everywhere pervasive as the atmosphere, that women were incapable of education, and would be less womanly, less desirable in every way, if they had it.*

And what of Shipherd and Stewart, the two men who fought so hard to create a utopian community and college in the backwoods of Ohio? Shipherd dies of malaria at age forty-two in Michigan where he is in the process of founding Olivet University, his "next Oberlin" in the West. Stewart lives on to seventy and continues to help fund Oberlin through profits from a stove he invents.

TIME: 1840 FORWARD

SUSAN B. ANTHONY BRINGS HER UNIQUE ORGANIZATIONAL TALENTS TO THE CAUSE

Susan Brownell Anthony is the fourth member of the early women's movement.

Born in 1820, she is five years younger than Elizabeth Cady Stanton and two years younger than Lucy Stone.

She grows up on a modest farm situated in the far northwestern edge of Massachusetts. To supplement the family income, her father Daniel operates a small cotton mill, which employs local women, several of whom are housed on the farm. This exposes Susan from to the hard labor demands placed on women in their households and in factories.

Daniel is a "Hicksite Quaker," like Lucretia Mott, who relies on his "inner light" rather than church authority to shape his beliefs. He is not only a freethinker but also a reformer, dedicated especially to temperance, abolition, and equal education for women.

Susan B. Anthony (1820-1906)

In 1826, Daniel and a wealthy friend form a partnership to operate a much larger cotton mill, and the family moves forty miles north to a new home in Battenville, New York. Once settled, he constructs a one room schoolhouse on his new property, and hires a teacher, Mary Perkins, to instruct his own children and those of his mill workers. Susan is an eager student ready to expand her educational horizons.

At seventeen, she is offered the opportunity to attend Deborah Moulson's Female Seminary, a Quaker boarding school in Philadelphia. The curriculum is ideal – math, science, literature, physiology—but she finds the environment stifling, with Moulson an overbearing religious zealot, perpetually criticizing her sunny disposition and her work.

This bittersweet academic interlude ends abruptly a few year later, when the aftershock of Andrew Jackson's Bank Panic of 1835 crushes her father's business and leaves the family in poverty.

In 1838, she returns home, determined to help pay off the family debts.

In 1840, she begins teaching at Eunice Kenyon's Friends Seminary in New Rochelle, New York. While there, she becomes increasingly self-confident and brushes off several marriage proposals to protect her independence. Her anti-slavery instincts are heightened in New Rochelle by the systematic humiliations she sees free Blacks suffering at the hands of "supposedly Christian" whites. She also learns to her dismay that her wage at the Seminary is only one-fourth of her male counterparts.

In 1845, she is back home in a Quaker community near Rochester on a farm which becomes a gathering place for activists, including the famous Unitarian minister, Samuel May, who preaches in nearby Syracuse, and, over time, Frederick Douglass, who will become Susan's lifelong friend. Three "causes" are bubbling up for her – temperance, abolition, and the career and wage constraints placed on women by traditional social norms.

A year later, in 1846, she ventures out again on her own. This time for a position her uncle arranges as headmistress of the "Female" Department at Canajoharie Academy where she teaches for three years and earns a reputation for intelligence and drive. While there, she joins the Daughters of Temperance, and begins to break away from some of her strict Quaker heritage, evident in a more colorful choice of dresses and involvement with theater and dance.

The landmark Seneca Falls Convention on women's rights takes place on July 19-20, 1848, while she is still living and teaching at Canajoharie. But both of her parents and her younger sister, Mary, attend the Rochester Women's Rights Convention which follows on August 2, and sign the Declaration of Sentiments document, which defines the movement.

Susan returns to Rochester in 1849 when Canajoharie closes and takes on responsibility for overseeing her parent's farm, while her father sets up a new insurance business. But she is soon drawn into applying the skills she has acquired on behalf of her causes. Like Lucy Stone, she goes forth as a traveling lecturer.

In May 1851, Amelia Bloomer introduces Anthony to Elizabeth Cady Stanton at a Lloyd Garrison event in Seneca Falls. The Anthony-Stanton partnership will define the Women's Rights Movement over the next fifty years. The two are perfect complements. Stanton is the theoretician; and Anthony, the get-it-done practitioner. In 1902, Anthony who sums up their friendship and partnership in a eulogy:

She forged the thunderbolts and I fired them.

SIDEBAR: THE "LOOK" OF THE LIBERATED WOMAN

While the women's movement enjoys near unanimity on its messages, settling on the "proper look" for its messengers stirs lots of controversy.

Those in one camp, insist that a change in appearance is required to signal a change in station leading them toward shorter haircuts and loose-fitting trousers worn under waist or knee-length jackets. The move away from the traditional whalebone corsets and hoop skirts, some of which weigh up to twelve pounds that most have worn since their teens.

Others feel that these changes will open them up to mockery "for trying to look like men" – and that this in turn will detract attention from the arguments they wish to make.

Dr. Mary Walker (1832-1919)

The leading early proponent of the new look is Amelia Bloomer, a Seneca Falls journalist and advocate for female rights. She claims that women, not men, should determine the dress they prefer, and that the choice should be driven by what they find comfortable and healthy.

> *The costume of women should be suited to her wants and necessities. It should conduce at once to her health, comfort, and usefulness; and, while it should not fail also to conduce to her personal adornment, it should make that end of secondary importance.*

Be they straight legged or puffed out in a Turkish design, the trousers are christened "bloomers" in honor of their sponsor—and the entire ensemble becomes the "Bloomer Costume."

Gone is the static, ornamental, predictable impression of the hoop skirts. Women now carry themselves with a heightened sense of motion, energy, and substance. They are dressed for action, rather than for men.

The stage actress, Fanny Kemble, an abolitionist once married to the scurrilous slave owner, Pierce Meese Butler, causes an early stir by donning the "Turkish dress" at public events. Proponents of physical fitness for women discard their corsets. A group calling themselves the "Lowell Bloomer Institute" declare their intent to abandon...

The whimsical and dictatorial French goddess Fashion (in favor of) the demands and proffers of Nature.

The feminist Elizabeth Smith Miller introduces the new look to her cousin, Stanton, who appreciates the freedom of movement it provides, and begins to debut it at her lectures.

Another Stanton cousin, Gerrit Smith supports a Dress Reform Association along with Amelia Bloomer's efforts to promote the new designs to a mass market.

But, of course, the nay-sayers latch unto "the bloomer look" as one more reason to ridicule the radical women.

The accusations range from tasteless and unladylike to impersonation of men and encouraging promiscuity. A variety of "Bloomer Polkas" add fodder to the put-downs.

In the end, most of the reformers, including Stanton, decide to reverse course. Paulina Wright Davis sums up the entire fashion matter as follows:

If I put on this dress, it would cripple my movements in regard to our work at this time, and crucify me ere my hour had come.

AFTERWORD

This volume covers Part 1 of the events leading to the Civil War, namely the period between 1619 when the first enslaved Africans arrive at Jamestown, and 1848 when the war with Mexico is concluded by the Treaty of Guadalupe Hidalgo.

Mexico will transfer 525,000 square miles of its land to the U.S. from Texas through the New Mexico and Utah territories to Alta California. This cession proves to be a double-edged sword. On one hand it concludes America's "Manifest Destiny" to span the continent. On the other it reopens the sectional conflict over the further expansion of slavery. This is an essential part of the South's economic strategy based on opening new plantations in the west to produce more cotton and to purchase, at auctions, excess slaves bred in the east. (The market value of the slaves will reach $3.1 billion in 1860 versus a national GDP of $4.3 billion.)

The North's intention to contain slavery, evident in the 1819 Tallmadge Amendment, gets replayed in the Wilmot Proviso which demands that the cession territories be preserved for "free white men and the dignity of free labor." This is accompanied by ongoing efforts in Northern state statutes and constitutions to "cleanse" America of all Blacks, enslaved or free.

(Oregon will become the first state to ban Black residency when it is admitted in 1859.)

The 1848 discovery of gold in California, and its plea to join the Union as a Free State, accelerates the sectional crisis over slavery. In passing the 1850 Compromise Bill, Congress escapes a repeat of the South's secession threat during the 1832 Tariff Nullification Crisis. One key element in the bill calls for holding local elections – called Popular Sovereignty (PopSov) – to have settlers choose between a Free State versus Slave State designation. Moderates in the South grudgingly go along with this, at least temporarily, as a better option than a Wilmot style ban.

The highly controversial 1854 Kansas-Nebraska act creates two new western territories on Louisiana Purchase land. Both are located north of the 1820 Missouri Compromise line, which means they should automatically be declared Free States. However, the bill is crafted to assuage the South, and it substitutes PopSov in place of the prior 36'30" longitudinal line.

Several bands of angry Northerners gather to form blueprints for a new Republican Party. Former one-term Congressman, Abraham Lincoln, reenters politics to challenge the bill and prove that the Founders intended that slavery wither away.

The first test of PopSov comes in 1854 in the Kansas Territory, and it proves disastrous for the Union, the Democratic Party, and for its author Stephen Douglas.

When the polls open, Pro-Slavery forces in Missouri led by Senator David Rice Atchison cross the river into Kansas and stuff ballot boxes to win the election. They do so again in March 1855 this time ending up with their "bogus legislature" and a representative in Washington.

Their actions are supported by President Franklin Pierce, ridiculed as a "Doughface" – born up North but ready to do the South's bidding especially on slavery. As such, he pushes throughout his term for admitting Kansas as a slave state.

Gradually the Northern opponents, an unlikely fusion of "Free Soil" racists and abolitionists, gather to craft their Topeka Constitution, which calls for Free State status while also banning Blacks from residing in Kansas. They submit it to Congress where it is accepted in the House, but then blocked in the Senate.

An acceleration of violence in "Bloody Kansas" follows. A band 800 pro-slavery men under Sheriff Samuel Jones raid the town of Lawrence, using cannon fire to level the Free State Hotel after wrecking the local newspaper presses and the town library. Three days later, abolitionist John Brown and four of his sons hack five pro-slavery men to death with broadswords in the Potawatomie Massacre – and more savagery follows.

Angry rhetoric in Congress gives way to violence when strident abolitionist Charles Sumner is almost caned to death on the Senate floor by a South Carolina congressman upset by a five hour long "Crime Against Kansas" speech mocking his cousin. Sumner remains incapacitated for three years; the attacker receives replacement canes from Southerners applauding his act.

Throughout this period, the pleas for freedom and respect voiced earlier by Black clergymen and activists are picked up by leaders such as Frederick Douglas, Sojourner Truth, and Harriet Tubman. They are backed by white abolitionists including William Lloyd Garrison, Lucretia Mott, Gerrit Smith, Salmon Chase, and Harriet Beecher Stowe. Her book, Uncle Tom's Cabin and the American Anti-Slavery Society chapters, begin to build some empathy for those enslaved.

Political pressure also grows as anti-slavery advocates (Giddings, Chase, Stevens, Wade, and others) claim seats in the House and Senate.

The 1856 election of President James Buchanan only adds to the turmoil in Kansas and in Washington. Like Pierce he owes his power to southern support and tries repeatedly to ram the Pro-Slavery Lecompton Constitution through the Senate, despite its multiple losses in PopSov elections.

His hope to solve the slavery debate in one fell swoop ends when the North chooses to ignore the Supreme Court's Dred Scott ruling given vigorous dissents by two justices. From there, warfare in Kansas continues until Pro-Slavers burn the town of Osawatomie. Governor John Geary calls in U.S. troops to end the slaughter, before he too resigns.

In 1858 Lincoln delivers his famous "House Divided" speech and campaigns against Douglas for the latter's U.S. Senate seat. The national spotlight falls on eight debates focused on slavery with Lincoln calling slavery a moral sin and Douglas, a covert slave owner himself, arguing that America belongs to white men, not inferior Blacks. While the Illinois state legislature hands the victory to Douglas, Lincoln merges as a credible national politician.

The failure of PopSov elections to win Slave State status in Kansas emboldens radical southerners to step up their demand for secession. Still powerful moderates like the Georgian's Cobb, Toombs and Stevens resist, while calling for a Congressional act to approve slavery in the west.

In October 1859, all hope for reconciliation ends when John Brown leads his 22-man party (17 whites and 5 Blacks) on a raid at Harper's Ferry, Virginia. It is the South's worst nightmare: a Northern white man leading an army of armed slaves in attacking their plantations. The raid is put down after Brown's initial recruits, fearful of retribution, refuse to pick up the 6-foot-long pikes he offers them. Thirteen of the raiders are killed in action and another seven are subsequently tried and hanged, including Brown.

At first, both sides condemn the raid as the work of a madman. Spurred on by the New England Transcendentalists, Brown's image in the North morphs from madman to martyr in a worthy cause. On the eve of his execution, Emerson writes:

His martyrdom…will make the gallows glorious like the cross.

From then on, the secessionists have the upper hand throughout most of the South, and they show it at the Democratic Convention in April, 1860. While regarding Buchanan as a total failure, they are also displeased with Douglas for publicly opposing the fraudulent Kansas elections and the Lecompton Constitution.

Led by Alabama fire-eater William Yancey, the southern delegates insist on a platform including passage of a Congressional mandate allowing slavery in the west. When this is voted down by 138-165, nine states walk out of the hall. This leaves Douglas left short of the votes needed and he is left scheduling a follow-up convention in June.

In the interim, antagonism grows, and when the delegates reconvene, the party splits in two over a credentials fight. The rump session of Northern Democrats nominates Douglas, while the Southern Democrats meet elsewhere and select sitting Vice-President, John C. Breckinridge, to head their ticket. In tandem, a third party called the Constitutional Unionists forms with John Bell as its nominee.

These divisions lead the way for the Republicans and Lincoln to win in November, which he does. But he achieves only 39.8% of the popular vote, with none recorded in the South. In effect then, he becomes the North's President.

At first, Lincoln refuses to believe that his ban on expanding slavery in the west will cause the South to secede in order to protect their future wealth based on selling cotton and auctioning slaves. But the truth will gradually dawn.

On December 20, 1860 the South Carolina legislature votes 159-0 to leave the Union, and it immediately demands that the federal forts in Charleston Harbor be abandoned. Seven more states follow suit. On February 6, 1861, the Confederate States of America are officially founded, with Jefferson Davis as President.

All of this occurs before March 4 when Lincoln is inaugurated and makes his plea to the "better angels of our nature" to restore unity and good will. His remaining hope is that Virginia will remain loyal and carry the upper South along with them.

Meanwhile, several political efforts are made in search of a compromise. In the House, it is the Committee of Thirty-Three; in the Senate, the Committee of Thirteen followed by the "Old Gentleman's Peace Conference" chaired by ex-President Tyler. The best these groups come up with is the Crittenden Compromise calling for a new boundary line at 36'30" extending across the southwest to the coast. It has already been rejected by both sides and is rejected again.

The powder keg now centers on the Confederate's threat to attack Ft. Sumter should it refuse to surrender peacefully. After a furious debate within Lincoln's cabinet, the President decides to send reinforcements. But before they arrive, the bombardment begins at 4:30 a.m. on April 12.

The Greek tragedy of the American Civil War is about to begin.

On April 15, Lincoln titles the conflict an "insurrection" hoping to avoid recognition of the CSA by Britain and France. He also calls for 75,000 recruits for a 3-month enlistment, anticipating a quick victory. But four more states - Virginia, Arkansas, North Carolina, and Tennessee - join the Confederacy adding to their manpower and geography.

The end will not come in three months but four years and 750,000 deaths later.

NOTE

To those who wish to read Part 1 and 2 of this book online, and learn more about American History circa 1619-1865, please see the author's website at:

ROADTOTHECIVILWAR.ORG

ACKNOWLEDGMENTS

The author wishes to thank the team at Tree of Life Books for believing in the story, and dealing with a first-time author to bring the book to fruition. Editorial praise belongs with Joy Stocke, Vincent Allen, and Raquel Pidal who sharpened themes and exorcized excess words from start to finish. Comparable kudos go to style-master, Tim Ogline, who created the book design, cleverly integrated the text and photographs, and made countless improvements to the explanatory maps.

ABOUT THE AUTHOR

After earning a Master of Arts Degree in Literature from the University of Wisconsin, Madison, Bob Drane embarked on a 35-year corporate career with Quaker Oats and Oscar Mayer. He became a recognized leader in new product development, leading the team that invented the Lunchables® brand. For over a decade, Bob taught innovation and marketing at the University of Wisconsin, Madison, Graduate School of Business. After retiring, his interest turned to studying and writing about early American history. He is an avid collector of original 19th century archival material, maps, and photographs.

www.ingramcontent.com/pod-product-compliance
Lightning Source LLC
Chambersburg PA
CBHW082006140626
46553CB00020B/2424